ENCYCLOPEDIA OF
FILM THEMES, SETTINGS
AND SERIES

ENCYCLOPEDIA OF FILM THEMES, SETTINGS AND SERIES

RICHARD B. ARMSTRONG
MARY WILLEMS ARMSTRONG

McFarland & Company, Inc., Publishers
Jefferson, North Carolina, and London

Library of Congress Cataloguing-in-Publication Data

Armstrong, Richard B., 1956–
    Encyclopedia of film themes, settings and series / Richard B. Armstrong
[and] Mary Willems Armstrong.
       p.   cm.
    Rev. ed. of: The movie list book. 1990.
    ISBN 0-7864-0893-6 (illustrated case binding : 50# alkaline paper) ∞
    1. Motion pictures — Plots, themes, etc. — Encyclopedias.   I. Armstrong,
Mary Willems, 1957–   II. Armstrong, Richard B., 1956– Movie list book.
III. Title.
PN1997.8 .A76   2001
791.43'75'03 — dc21   00-64009

British Library cataloguing data are available

Cover image ©2000 Index Stock

Manufactured in the United States of America

McFarland & Company, Inc., Publishers
  Box 611, Jefferson, North Carolina 28640
    www.mcfarlandpub.com

For Galahad

And pets everywhere

In appreciation of your unquestioning love

and joyous companionship

TABLE OF CONTENTS*

Throughout the work are "see" references not reflected in this table of contents.

INTRODUCTION

This encyclopedia continues our never-ending task of categorizing movies by topics. Whereas many film books tell you about a specific film, this work tells you about a specific topic and then provides a list of the movies that fall under that topic. Therefore, you will not find a capsule review of the 1984 science fiction film *C.H.U.D.* But you will find *C.H.U.D.* mentioned under the entries **Acronyms in Title** and **Cannibalism** and **Sewers**. After all, the title is an acronym (standing for Cannibalistic Humanoid Underground Dwellers), the main characters ate people for dinner, and they resided in sewers.

We have defined over 670 categories, ranging from film themes and series to settings, occupations, animals and happenstances. Each category, or entry, consists of two parts: a narrative description that defines the category and a *representative* list of films in chronological order.

Typically, the narratives present an historic overview of the entry or subcategorize the films within it. For example, the **Television** entry traces its treatment in films from the early 1930s to the present. The **Gangsters (Real-Life)** entry discusses how various individuals have been treated in the movies. At the conclusion of the narrative portion of some entries, we have included "see also" references to other entries. For example, the **Abominable Snowman** entry refers readers to the **Bigfoot** entry. We figure that if you're interested in one type of large, hairy beast, you might want some information on similar creatures.

In addition to the "see also" references, the abbreviations *q.v.* or *qq.v.* may appear in parentheses following one or more subjects mentioned in an entry's narrative. A *q.v.* indicates that the subject in question appears as a separate entry elsewhere in the book. A *qq.v.* following a group of subjects indicates that they all appear as separate entries. For example, the **Plants** entry notes that the Mummy *(q.v.)* was revived with tana leaves in some films. The *(q.v.)* informs readers that there is a separate entry for **The Mummy**.

The films within each entry are listed chronologically, their dates indicating when the films were released theatri-

cally or broadcast in their country of origin. Made-for-television movies are denoted with the abbreviation TVM. If a film played theatrically after its broadcast premiere, we still annotate it as a TV movie. The first title is the film's most widely known U.S. title. Alternative titles, including the original foreign title if part of a series, are shown in parentheses. The size of the film lists varies from three to eighty titles depending on the scope of the entry (i.e., few movies have featured **Gorgons**; many films have taken place on **Trains**).

We have refrained from listing credits and plot summaries for each title. Most of the listed films can be found readily in mainstream reference works like Leonard Maltin's *Movie & Video Guide*, *Halliwell's Film and Video Guide*, and *The Motion Picture Guide*. More obscure films are likely to be found in periodicals such as *Variety* or cult movie volumes such as *The Psychotronic Encyclopedia of Film*.

We have tried to compile an exhaustive list of English-language film series and, in the process, have included information on well-documented characters such as Sherlock Holmes and Tarzan. We have done this for two reasons. First, new movies are continually being made about these popular characters (e.g., Disney's 1999 animated *Tarzan*). Secondly, we felt this book should be a one-stop reference on film series, at least for some users. A film buff trying to find out the name of Charlton Heston's only Sherlock Holmes film (it was the 1991 TV movie *The Crucifer of Blood*) will find this a handy volume. A Holmesian scholar seeking more explicit details would be advised to seek a reference work devoted exclusively to the Baker Street sleuth. We formed some general ground rules to limit the scope of the book to a manageable size:

1. Most of the films listed are English-language pictures released during the sound era. Occasionally, we have included silent or foreign films to give the reader a historical or international perspective of the category. For example, no write-up of **Hood, Robin** would be complete without mentioning the Douglas Fairbanks, Sr., 1922 version.

2. A notable exception to the above rule is the inclusion of popular foreign film series. For example, the Mexican

wrestler Santo appeared in a film series spanning four decades, and many of these pictures have eventually shown up on American television. The Japanese Tora-san films are virtually unknown in the United States, but they comprise the longest running film series with the same star in the world. We have listed foreign series films under their most common English-language titles, although the original foreign titles are shown as well.

3. We defined a series as three or more movies linked by a recurring theme or characters. Thus, we did not include the films of Abbott and Costello, the Marx Brothers, or Laurel and Hardy. Their movies can be found in biographical film reference books. For the same reason, we left out Roy Rogers and Gene Autry — although they do play the same character (themselves) in most of their movies. B-Western fans can rest assured, however, that their favorite genre is well represented by the *Durango Kid*, the *Range Busters*, *Red Ryder*, and others.

4. If a category contains movies that are part of a series, then we listed only the first film in the series and included a "see also" reference to the corresponding film series entry. For example, only the first *Death Wish* film appears under **Vigilantes**; a "see also" reference refers readers to the **Death Wish Series** which lists the other *Death Wish* movies.

5. To avoid redundancy in the lists, we sometimes omitted remakes of movies already included. For example, all the versions of *And Then There Were None* could be listed under **Judges**, but we figured readers would get the idea by just including the original film. Likewise, the **Rabbits** entry includes only the first Hollywood sound version of *Alice in Wonderland* and Disney's animated adaptation — although the white rabbit played a significant role in all the *Alice* movies.

6. We have included many lengthy lists, but the sheer size of others mandated their exclusion. For example, a narrative overview and a representative sampling of Civil War or World War II movies would require a write-up far beyond the scope of this book. On the other hand, there are relatively few films about the Korean War and Vietnam. Hence, we have included entries on them. We expect that our decisions on what to include and exclude will spark some debate. Constructive criticism is most welcomed.

7. We included TV movies only if they were shown originally in no more than two parts or were subsequently edited into a single film. Therefore, miniseries such as *The Thornbirds* and *The Stand* were excluded. The theatrical movie *The Quatermass Conclusion*, which was culled from the British miniseries *Quatermass*, was included.

8. Our cutoff point was movies released or broadcast through August 2000.

We have been delighted with the previous editions' enthusiastic reception by readers and critics. We continue to receive many suggestions for additional entries and titles. To that end, we have added over two hundred new entries to the original edition published (as *The Movie List Book*) in 1990. We have also updated the lists with thousands of new titles. To our entries on film series, we have added the obvious (the **Highlander** movies), the obscure (**Roller Blade Seven**), and the offbeat (**Mr. Vampire**). Other new categories range from **Bowling** to **Clocks and Watches** to **Zorro**. We work hard to double-check our entries, but mistakes can still find their way into a volume of this size. We have corrected all known errata from the earlier editions.

It would be difficult to acknowledge everyone who added a film or two, but there are some who made significant contributions. Readers Michael Will and Jeanna F. Gallo provided many excellent suggestions for the third edition. Likewise, film buff Kent Armstrong of Mitchell, Indiana, offered some useful recommendations. The Wisconsin Center for Film Research in Madison gave us the opportunity to view vintage films from its collection when compiling our original lists. We'd like to thank those people in the publishing business who worked on the various versions of this encyclopedia. Finally, we'd like to express our love and gratitude to our families and friends who have provided steady support and encouragement over the years.

We heartily encourage reader correspondence, whether it be corrections, recommended additions, or comments over exclusions of favorite movies. Please address your letters to us in care of the publisher.

Mary Willems Armstrong
Richard B. Armstrong
Summer 2000

The Abominable Snowman

Also known as the Yeti, the Abominable Snowman is a hairy, manlike creature reportedly inhabiting the Himalayas. His movie appearances have been almost as scarce as Yeti photographs. His film debut was probably 1954's *Snow Creature*, a King Kong–inspired cheapie in which a Yeti is captured and brought back to Los Angeles (where he escapes, of course). *Man Beast* (1955) kept the action in the Himalayas, but didn't live up to its outrageous ad campaign: "See women stalked and captured for breeding by Yeti monsters!" A friendly snowman turned up unexpectedly at the earth's core in the 1993 TV movie *Journey to the Center of the Earth*. However, the only semi-intelligent film on the subject was *The Abominable Snowman of the Himalayas*, scripted by sci-fi/fantasy writer Nigel Kneale. The Yeti in *Shriek of the Mutilated* (1974) turned out to be a man in a costume. See also **Bigfoot**.

Snow Creature (1954); *Half-Human* (1955); *Man Beast* (1955); *The Abominable Snowman of the Himalayas* (aka *Abominable Snowman*) (1957); *The Seven Faces of Dr. Lao* (1964); *Shriek of the Mutilated* (1974); *The Werewolf and the Yeti* (aka *Night of the Howling Beast*) (1976); *Snowbeast* (1977 TVM); *Yeti* (1977); *Journey to the Center of the Earth* (1993 TVM); *To Catch a Yeti* (1995); *Bigfoot: The Unforgettable Encounter* (1995)

Acronyms and Abbreviations in Title

The nondescriptive nature of abbreviations has made them unpopular title choices, especially among theater owners. They have been the ones forced to field complaints from irritated patrons, such as the ones distraught to discover that Sylvester Stallone's *F.I.S.T.* was not a boxing film (but the story of a truckers' union). Still, that has not deterred the occasional use of acronym titles. Studios concerned about pronounceable titles have shown a preference toward acronyms that spelled familiar words, as in the case of *D.A.R.Y.L.* and *M*A*S*H*. In addition to film titles, acronyms have been used extensively in screenplays. For example, in *Our Man Flint* and *In Like Flint*, secret agent Derek Flint (James Coburn) worked for Z.O.W.I.E.—Zonal Organization on World Intelligence Espionage. On TV and in the movies, Robert Vaughn and David McCallum worked for U.N.C.L.E., which stood for United Network Command for Law and Enforcement.

The Bride Came C.O.D. (1941) Cash on Delivery; *O.S.S.* (1946) Office of Strategic Services; *D.O.A.* (1950) Dead on Arrival; *The D.I.* (1957) Drill Instructor; *A Matter of W.H.O.* (aka *A Matter of Who*) (1961) World Health Organization; *The V.I.P.s* (1963) Very Important Persons; *The T.A.M.I. Show* (1964) Teenage Awards Music International; *Agent for H.A.R.M.* (1966) Human Aetiological Relations Machine; *U.M.C.* (aka *Operation Heartbeat*) (1969 TVM) University Medical Center; *M*A*S*H* (1970) Mobile Army Surgical Hospital; *R.P.M.* (1970) Revolutions Per Minute; *F.T.A.* (1972) Free (or F--k) The Army; *Z.P.G.* (1972) Zero Population Growth; *F.I.S.T.* (1978) Federation of Interstate Truckers; *C.H.O.M.P.S.* (1979) Canine Home Protection System; *H.E.A.L.T.H.* (1979) Happiness, Energy and Longevity Through Health; *H.O.T.S.* (1979) Help Out the Seals; *S*H*E* (1980 TVM) Security Hazards Expert; *S.O.B.* (1981) Standard Operating Bullshit; *Looker* (1981) Light Ocular-Oriented Kinetic Emotive Responses; *T.A.G.: The Assassination Game* (1982); *Angel of H.E.A.T.* (1982) Harmony's Elite Attack Team; *M.A.D.D.: Mothers Against Drunk Driving* (1983 TVM); *C.H.U.D.* (1984) Cannibalistic Humanoid Underground Dwellers; *R.S.V.P.* (1984) Répondez S'il Vous Plaît; *D.A.R.Y.L.* (1985) Data Analyzing Robot Youth Lifeform; *C.A.T. Squad* (1986 TVM) Counter Assault Tactical Squad; *R.O.T.O.R.* (1988) Robotic Officer of Tactical Operations Research; *B.O.R.N.* (1989) Body Organ Replacement Network; *Navy SEALS* (1990) Sea Air Land; *Robo-C.H.I.C.* (1990) Computerized Humanoid Intelligence Clone; *Josh and S.A.M.* (1993) Strategically Altered Mutant; *M.A.N.T.I.S.* (1994 TVM) Mechanically Augmented Neuro-Transmitter System.; *P.C.U.* (1994) Port Chester University; *S.F.W.* (1994) So F—g What; *A.P.E.X.* (1994) Advanced Prototype Extermination; *D.R.O.P. Squad* (1994) Deprogramming and Restoration of Pride; *F.T.W.* (1994) Frank T. Wells or F--k the World; *W.E.I.R.D. World* (1995 TVM) Wilson Emery Institute for Research and Development; *Day of the Warrior* (aka *L.E.T.H.A.L. Ladies: Day of the Warrior*) (1996) Legion to Ensure Total Harmony and Law; *Nick Fury: Agent of S.H.I.E.L.D.* (1998 TVM) Supreme Headquarters International Espionage Law-Enforcement Division; *DWM* (1999) Divorced White Male; *Titan A.E.* (2000) After Earth

Ad Lines (Selected)

As a general rule, bad movies have the best ad lines — which makes a lot of sense when you think about it. After all, if the movie stinks, then there must be something else — like a catchy advertising phrase — to lure unsuspecting patrons into the theater. That's why some of the most memorable (and tasteless) ad lines come from bottom-of-the-barrel horror flicks like *The Driller Killer* ("Several pints of blood will spill when teenage girls confront his drill"). Of course, a clever phrase can still accompany a big-budgeted science fiction film (*Alien*: "In space, no one can hear you scream") or a cult classic (*I Walked with a Zombie*: "She's alive … yet dead! She's dead … yet alive!"). Some of the cinema's more memorable ad lines:

"Out of the dark fantastic madness of his science … He created them! Pig-Men … Wolf-Women…Thoughtful Human Apes — and His Masterpiece … The Panther Woman … Throbbing to the hot flush of new found love!" *Island of Lost Souls* (1933); "Jungle love tease! Bob Preston tears the heart out of Preston Foster by making jungle love to exciting Dorothy Lamour under that burning Burma moon!" *Moon Over Burma* (1940); "Bing Bong! Bing Bong! With song and sarong they hit the gong!" *The Road to Singapore* (1940); "Kiss me and I'll claw you to death." *The Cat People* (1942); "How'd you like to tussle with Russell?" *The Outlaw* (1943); "Body of a boy! Mind of a monster! Soul of an unearthly thing!" *I Was a Teenage Frankenstein* (1957); "It crawls! It creeps!" *The Blob* (1958); "You'll be sick, sick, sick from laughing!" *A Bucket of Blood* (1959); "Beware the beat of cloth wrapped feet!" *The Mummy* (1959); "Just ring for doom service!" *Horror Hotel* (aka *The City of the Dead*) (1960); "Beware the eyes that paralyze." *Children of the Damned* (1964); "They're young … they're in love … and they kill people." *Bonnie and Clyde* (1967); "The story of a homosexual who married a nymphomaniac." *The Music Lovers* (1971); "You have nothing to lose but your mind." *Asylum* (1972); "To avoid fainting, keep repeating: It's only a movie … it's only a movie …" *The Last House on the Left* (1972); "They'll love the very lives out of your body!" *Invasion of the Bee Girls* (1973); "If this movie doesn't make you scream and squirm, you'd better see a psychiatrist — quick!" *They Came from Within* (aka *The Parasite Murders*; *Shivers*) (1975); "The only thing more terrifying than the last twelve minutes of this film are the first 80." *Suspiria* (1976); "Just when you thought it was safe to go back into the water." *Jaws 2* (1978); "Roses are red. Violets are blue. 'My Bloody Valentine' is absolute grue." *My Bloody Valentine* (1981); "The story of a man who wanted to keep the world safe for democracy — and meet girls." *Stripes* (1981); "Herbert West has a very good head on his shoulders — and another one in his desk." *Re-Animator* (1985); "So young! So bad! So what?" *Reform School Girls* (1986); "Like father, like son, like hell." *At Close Range* (1986); "Sleep all day, party all night. It's fun to be a vampire." *The Lost Boys* (1987); "There are no limits." *Hellraiser* (1987); "A comedy about sex, murder, and seafood." *A Fish Called Wanda* (1988); "You have the right to remain silent … forever!" *Maniac Cop* (1988); "Trapped in time. Surrounded by evil. Low on gas." *Army of Darkness* (aka *Army of Darkness: Evil Dead 3*) (1993); "All Singing! All Dancing! All Flesh Eating!" *Cannibal! The Musical* (1996); "U-Turn, U-die!" *Trucks* (1997 TVM); "Size does matter!" *Godzilla* (1998); "The sequel with balls!" *Phantasm: Oblivion* (aka *Phantasm IV: Oblivion*; *Phantasm: oblIVion*) (1998)

Addresses in Title

Street addresses have been used infrequently for movie titles, probably since they don't provide much in the way of description. Still, Gary Cooper played a nagging husband who found solace with younger woman Suzy Parker at *Ten North Frederick* (1958). A murder occurred at *10 Rillington Place* (1971), a fact-based account of the Christie-Evans case which ended capital punishment in Britain. On the lighter side, Anthony Hopkins and Anne Bancroft formed a lasting friendship through exchanging letters mailed to *84 Charing Cross Road* (the address of Hopkins' bookstore).

Forty-Second Street (1933); *15 Malden Lane* (1936); *52nd Street* (1937); *13 Rue Madeleine* (1946); *Green Dolphin Street* (1947); *Dulcimer Street* (aka *London Belongs to Me*) (1948); *711 Ocean Drive* (1950); *Sunset Boulevard* (1950); *99 River Street* (1953); *Ten North Frederick* (1958); *13 West Street* (1962); *Madison Avenue* (1962); *10 Rillington Place* (1971); *11 Harrowhouse* (aka *Anything for Love*; *Fast Fortune*) (1974); *Hester Street* (1975); *Hanover Street* (1979); *Cannery Row* (1982); *Half Moon Street* (1986); *84 Charing Cross Road* (1987); *102 Boulevard Haussman* (1990); *29th Street* (1991)

Airplanes

Airplanes have provided the setting or functioned as the focal point for dozens of movies. Early efforts typically revolved around the adventures of World War I dogfight pilots or pioneer air mail carriers. William Wellman's *Wings* (1927), the first film to win a Best Picture Oscar, established the standard for combat flying sequences and sealed Gary Cooper's stardom. Howard Hughes'

Hell's Angels (1930) also featured magnificent dogfight footage, but is best remembered for launching Jean Harlow's career (her famous line: "Do you mind if I slip into something more comfortable?"). Despite their now-dated techniques, these World War I aerial actioners, along with both versions of *The Dawn Patrol*, still surpass similar films made in the 1960s and 1970s (e.g., *The Blue Max*, *Aces High*, *Von Richthofen and Brown*). The plight of air mail flyers proved an equally popular subject in the 1930s, with such memorable efforts as *Air Mail*, *Ceiling Zero*, and *Only Angels Have Wings* (the latter two directed by Howard Hawks). Airplanes played a strictly supporting role in most World War II pictures, although Hawks' *Air Force* and (much later) *Battle of Britain* gave them proper recognition. Interest in aviation had hit a low ceiling when, in 1954, Wellman's *The High and the Mighty* transplanted *Grand Hotel* drama into the clouds and added a generous dose of in-flight disaster. This successful formula was not fully exploited until 16 years later, when Ross Hunter mounted an expensive adaptation of Arthur Hailey's best seller *Airport* (q.v.). This time, a mass of second-class imitators flooded the screens, including three *Airport* sequels and eventually the highly-successful spoof *Airplane!* (1980). Undoubtedly, the most bizarre airplane disaster film was the 1972 TV movie *The Horror at 37,000 Feet*, in which a sacrificial druid stone unleashed evil spirits on screeching passengers. Films about real-life aviators have been scarce, consisting primarily of *The Spirit of St. Louis* (Charles Lindbergh), *The Winds of Kitty Hawk* (the Wright Brothers), *Amelia Earhart*, *Flight for Freedom* (Earhart again), *The Right Stuff* (Chuck Yeager), *Pancho Barnes*, and *The Wings of Eagles* (Frank "Spig" Wead). Jet pilots can also lay claim to being ignored in favor of fictional dogfight specialists. Howard Hughes' *Jet Pilot* sat on the shelf for seven years before its 1957 release. Clint Eastwood's high-tech *Firefox* fared better, but it took 1986's *Top Gun* to give the jet pilot his proper recognition. However, Tom Cruise's cocky hero ("I feel the need — the need for speed!") was a far cry from the serious aviators portrayed in the films of Hawks, Hughes, and Wellman. While the jets in these latter films looked impressive, none of them compared favorably with the Batplane from 1989's *Batman* in terms of sheer aesthetic design. But, alas, the Batplane proved to be just a pretty package when the Joker shot it down with his long-barreled hand gun. Plane crashes have played important roles in several memorable yarns, most notably *Lost Horizon*, *Back from Eternity*, *Fate Is the Hunter*, *Phone Call from a Stranger*, *Fearless*, *The Edge*, *A Simple Plan*, and *The Flight of the Phoenix*. In the latter film, James Stewart and his fellow crash survivors escaped from the desert by building a mini-plane from the wreckage. On a lighter note, *Flying Down to Rio* deserves an honorable mention for its delirious dance number featuring chorines high-stepping on top of an airplane's wings. See also **Airport Series**; **Balloons, Hot Air**; **Dirigibles**; **Helicopters**; **Iron Eagle Series**; **Skydiving**.

Wings (1927); *Hell's Angels* (1930); *The Dawn Patrol* (aka *Flight Commander*) (1930); *Air Mail* (1932); *Christopher Strong* (1933); *Flying Down to Rio* (1933); *Central Airport* (1933); *Ceiling Zero* (1935); *Wings in the Dark* (1935); *China Clipper* (1936); *Non-Stop New York* (1937); *Lost Horizon* (1937); *Sky Giant* (1938); *The Dawn Patrol* (1938); *Men with Wings* (1938); *Five Came Back* (1939); *Only Angels Have Wings* (1939); *Flight Angels* (1940); *Dive Bomber* (1941); *Spitfire* (aka *First of the Few*) (1942); *Flight for Freedom* (1943); *Air Force* (1943); *Gallant Journey* (1946); *Broken Journey* (1948); *Chain*

Lightning (1950); *Breaking the Sound Barrier* (aka *The Sound Barrier*) (1952); *Phone Call from a Stranger* (1952); *The High and the Mighty* (1954); *Escapade* (1955); *Back from Eternity* (1956); *Zero Hour* (1957); *Bombers B-52* (1957); *The Spirit of St. Louis* (1957); *The Wings of Eagles* (1957); *Jet Pilot* (1957); *Wings of Chance* (1961); *Fate Is the Hunter* (1964); *Those Magnificent Men in Their Flying Machines, or How I Flew from London to Paris in 25 Hours 11 Minutes* (aka *Those Magnificent Men in Their Flying Machines*) (1965); *The Doomsday Flight* (1966 TVM); *The Flight of the Phoenix* (1966); *The Blue Max* (1966); *Battle of Britain* (1969); *Airport* (1970); *Von Richthofen and Brown* (aka *The Red Baron*) (1970); *Terror in the Sky* (1971 TVM); *Wild in the Sky* (aka *Black Jack*) (1971); *Only One More Day Left Before Tomorrow* (aka *How to Steal an Airplane*) (1971 TVM); *Skyjacked* (aka *Sky Terror*) (1972); *The Horror at 37,000 Feet* (1972 TVM); *Ace Eli and Rodger of the Skies* (1973); *The Great Waldo Pepper* (1975); *Amelia Earhart* (1976 TVM); *Aces High* (1977); *Flight to Holocaust* (1977 TVM); *Crash* (1978 TVM); *The Winds of Kitty Hawk* (1978 TVM); *Cloud Dancer* (1980); *Airplane!* (1980); *Firefox* (1982); *Airplane 2: The Sequel* (1982); *The Right Stuff* (1983); *Tail of the Tiger* (1984); *The Aviator* (1985); *International Airport* (1985 TVM); *Top Gun* (1986); *Iron Eagle* (1986); *Pancho Barnes* (1988 TVM); *Batman* (1989); *Party Plane* (1989); *Slipstream* (1989); *Die Hard 2* (aka *Die Hard 2: Die Harder*) (1990); *Memphis Belle* (1990); *Miracle Landing* (1990 TVM); *Crash: The Mystery of Flight 1501* (1990 TVM); *The Tragedy of Flight 103: The Inside Story* (1990 TVM); *Hot Shots!* (1991); *Into the Sun* (1992); *Passenger 57* (1992); *Alive* (1993); *Fearless* (1993); *Nurses on the Line: The Crash of Flight 7* (1993 TVM); *Mercy Mission: The Rescue of Flight 771* (1993 TVM); *Final Mission* (1994); *Amelia Earhart: The Final Flight* (1994 TVM); *Terminal Velocity* (1994); *The Tuskegee Airmen* (1995 TVM); *Fly Away Home* (1996); *Angel Flight Down* (1996 TVM); *Executive Decision* (1996); *Hijacked: Flight 285* (1996 TVM); *Pandora's Clock* (1996 TVM); *Alaska* (1996); *Turbulence* (1997); *Con Air* (1997); *The Edge* (1997); *Air Force One* (1997); *Six Days, Seven Nights* (1998); *A Simple Plan* (1998); *A Wing and a Prayer* (1998 TVM); *Pushing Tin* (1999); *Wild Wild West* (1999); *Fly Boy* (1999)

Airport Series

Ross Hunter's glossy adaptation of Arthur Hailey's best-seller has a lot to answer for, although it was little more than a slight variation of William Wellman's *The High and the Mighty* (1954). In addition to begetting three progressively inane sequels, *Airport* refined the all-stars-in-peril formula that kicked off the disaster movie (q.v.) craze of the 1970s. On its own terms, *Airport* was a slick entertainment package that afforded Helen Hayes another opportunity to win an Oscar. Burt Lancaster, as the dependable chief of airport operations, headed a cast that also included Dean Martin as a pilot, Jacqueline Bisset as a stewardess (and Dean's mistress), Van Heflin as a bomber, and sturdy George Kennedy as Burt's right-hand man. Kennedy was the only one who returned for *Airport 1975*, a silly sequel requiring stewardess Karen Black to take over the jet's controls after a midair collision. Charlton Heston gave her support from the sidelines, while the all-star passenger list included Helen Reddy as a singing nun (q.v.) and Linda Blair as a sick kid. *Airport '77* sent a jet crashing into the ocean, while *The Concorde: Airport '79* featured Robert Wagner as a ruthless tycoon out to destroy the jet. George Kennedy stood around in these films as well, just to lend some consistency to the proceedings. Oddly, the films never spawned a TV series, perhaps because the ill-fated 1970-71 *San Francisco International Airport* had already beaten the producers to the punch. See also **Airplanes**; **Disaster Movies**.

Airport (1970); *Airport 1975* (1974); *Airport '77* (1977); *The Concorde: Airport '79* (aka *Airport '79*) (1979)

Aladdin Series

Disney followed up its Oscar-nominated *Beauty and the Beast* with this colorful, tune-filled Arabian Nights tale. Thanks to a clever bit of casting — Robin Williams as a wisecracking genie with a knack for impersonations — *Aladdin* quickly become Disney's most successful animated film. Yet, just two years later, its impressive box-office tallies would be eclipsed by 1994's *The Lion King*. Except for Williams' seemingly ad-libbed scenes, *Aladdin* relies heavily on the animated musical formula originated in *The Little Mermaid* (1989) and perfected in *Beauty and the Beast* (1991). All three films feature young lovers kept apart, cute supporting characters, big production numbers, and a soaring ballad. In *Aladdin*, the lovers are Aladdin and Jasmine (who are both a bit bland). The cute supporting characters include a charismatic magic carpet and a mischievous monkey named Abu. The big production number, courtesy of Williams, is a "A Friend Like Me." And the ballad is the Oscar-winning song "A Whole New World" (which became a hit single for Peabo Bryson and Regina Belle). Despite several impressive sequences, the formula grows tiresome as the film progresses. Even the songs cannot match the two previous Disney animated outings, perhaps because lyricist Howard Ashman died during production (and was replaced by Tim Rice). Some critics suggested that Williams deserved an Oscar nomination for his voice work, but the Academy did not concur. Spurred by huge videotape sales, Disney produced an animated Saturday morning TV series in 1993. It featured Dan Castellaneta (Homer on *The Simpsons*) as the voice of the genie. Several episodes were later edited into a direct-to-video "movie" *The Return of Jafar*. Its success subsequently prompted a second videotape feature, *Aladdin and the King of Thieves*, which marked Robin Williams' return as the genie. See also **Animated Movies (Feature-Length)**; **Genies**.

Aladdin (1992); *The Return of Jafar* (1994); *Aladdin and the King of Thieves* (1996)

Alcoholism

The plight of the problem drinker has been glossed over by most major Hollywood pictures. Even Billy Wilder's landmark portrait of an alcoholic, 1945's *The Lost Weekend*, ended on an upbeat note with Ray Milland's "hero" indicating that he's on the road to recovery. Still, Wilder's film broke new ground with its straightforward treatment — Milland begging for drinks, stealing a woman's purse, experiencing D.T.s, etc. The female side of alcoholism followed three years later, with Susan Hayward giving a mannered performance in *Smash-up, the Story of a Woman*. Bing Crosby, playing against type, gave one of the best performances of his career as a singer battling the bottle in the film version of Clifford Odets' *The Country Girl* (1954). Once again, though, an optimistic ending blunted the film's impact, with Grace Kelly passing up caring William Holden to stay with unreliable husband Crosby. Blake Edwards' *The Days of Wine and Roses* (1962) injected a jolt of realism into its depressing story of married alcoholics. After introducing wife Lee Remick to the "pleasures" of drinking, Jack Lemmon becomes a reformed drinker by joining Alcoholics Anonymous. His wife lacks his strength, however, and her alcoholism keeps them apart. The drawing power of the stars made the film a hit, but few producers in the 1960s were interested in duplicating its downbeat ending. Subsequently, movies about alcoholism moved to television where they flourished during the 1970s and 1980s. Veteran TV nice guys Dick Van Dyke, David Janssen, and Andy Griffith played self-destructive drunks in *The Morning After* (1974*)*, *A Sensitive, Passionate Man* (1977), and *Under the Influence* (1986), respectively. Linda Blair, who battled a demon in *The Exorcist*, fought her own alcoholic demons in 1975's then-topical *Sarah T.—Portrait of a Teenage Alcoholic*. James Woods played the co-founder of Alcoholics Anonymous in the fact-based TV biography *My Name Is Bill W.* (1989). Back on the big screen, Nicolas Cage earned a Best Actor Oscar for playing an incredibly self-destructive alcoholic in *Leaving Las Vegas* (1995). Dozens of movies, not principally about alcoholism, have featured main characters inflicted with the disease. Some of the most memorable performances have come from Albert Finney in *Under the Volcano* (1984), Dudley Moore in *Arthur* (1981), and Errol Flynn as John Barrymore in *Too Much, Too Soon* (1958). See also **Drug Addiction**.

The Lost Weekend (1945); *Smash-up, the Story of a Woman* (aka *A Woman Destroyed*) (1948); *Come Fill the Cup* (1951); *Something to Live For* (1952); *The Country Girl* (1954); *I'll Cry Tomorrow* (1955); *The Bottom of the Bottle* (1956); *The Voice in the Mirror* (1958); *The Days of Wine and Roses* (1962); *The Fire Within* (1963); *The Late Liz* (1971); *The Morning After* (1974 TVM); *Sarah T.—Portrait of a Teenage Alcoholic* (1975 TVM); *A Sensitive, Passionate Man* (1977 TVM); *A Cry for Love* (1980 TVM); *The Boy Who Drank Too Much* (1980 TVM); *Special Treatment* (1980); *Life of the Party: The Story of Beatrice* (1982 TVM); *Under the Influence* (1986 TVM); *Shattered Spirits* (1987 TVM); *The Betty Ford Story* (1987 TVM); *My Name Is Bill W.* (1989 TVM); *Torch Song* (1993 TVM); *When a Man Loves a Woman* (1994); *My Name Is Kate* (1994 TVM); *Leaving Las Vegas* (1995); *Drunks* (1995); *No Laughing Matter* (1998 TVM)

Aldrich, Henry

"Wimmen — they bore me!" proclaimed the ad to *Henry Aldrich Gets Glamour*, thus separating Henry from rival film teen, and renowned girl chaser, Andy Hardy (q.v.). Yet, for the most part, the Henry Aldrich series was Paramount's B-movie answer to MGM's more successful Andy Hardy films. Ezra Stone originated the character in Clifford Goldsmith's 1937 Broadway play *What a Life*. It spawned a popular radio program (also with Stone) and a big screen version, adapted by Billy Wilder and Charles Brackett and starring veteran child actor Jackie Cooper as Henry. Two years later, Cooper and co-star Eddie Bracken (as pal Dizzy) returned to their roles in *Life with Henry* ("You'll get a bang out of Henry and his gang!"). But Paramount sought a fresh face for its third installment and introduced Jimmy Lydon as Henry in 1941's *Henry Aldrich for President*. Lydon, who had made an impact two years earlier in *Tom Brown's Schooldays*, was the ideal choice for the bumbling, likable Henry. He made nine films, supported by Charles Smith as Dizzy, John Litel as his stern father, and Olive Blakeney as his mother. Like the Hardy films, the series ended shortly after World War II. However, in 1949, original author Goldsmith revived his characters in the half-hour TV series *The Aldrich Family*. It ran for four years and starred five different actors as Henry.

What a Life (1939); *Life with Henry* (1941); *Henry Aldrich for President* (1941); *Henry and Dizzy* (1942); *Henry Aldrich, Editor* (1943); *Henry Aldrich Gets Glamour* (1943); *Henry Aldrich Haunts a House* (1943); *Henry Aldrich Swings It* (1943); *Henry Aldrich, Boy Scout* (1944); *Henry Aldrich's Little Secret* (1944); *Henry Aldrich Plays Cupid* (1944)

Alien Series

The four *Alien* films provide hard evidence that stylish thrills can make big audiences overlook repetitive, mundane plotting borrowed from a forgotten 1958 sci-fi feature. That latter film was the low-budget *It! The Terror from Beyond Space*, a tidy programmer about a Martian monster which stows away on a U.S. spaceship and proceeds to dispose of the crew members one by one. Screenwriter Dan O'Bannon served up the same storyline, albeit with a pleasant twist, in 1979's *Alien*. The film's popular success, though, can be attributed to Sigourney Weaver's likable heroine Ripley, director Ridley Scott's old-fashioned dark corridor chills, and the sharp special effects (especially H. R. Giger's terrifying creature). The 1986 sequel was a vast improvement, primarily due to director James Cameron's instinctive feel for the genre (he was coming off 1984's smash *The Terminator*). *Aliens* takes place 57 years after *Alien* and finds Ripley, the original's lone human survivor, in hibernation. It's not long, though, before she returns to the planet where the creature was found — and discovers that it was not an only child! Ripley also finds a little girl and gets to display her maternal instincts in a terrific showdown with the "mother of all aliens." It's the highlight of the series and would have made a fitting conclusion. Unfortunately, Weaver returned for the depressing *Alien³*, which begins and ends with the deaths of the series' most endearing characters. Ripley spends almost the entire film on a prison planet where the disbelieving inmates are being devoured in Agatha Christie–like fashion. Director David Fincher, a music video veteran at the time, created a grimy, murky atmosphere, but displayed no gifts for storytelling or chill-creating. The downbeat climax put an apparent end to the series. However, *Alien Resurrection* (1997) brought back Ripley (well, a clone of her) so scientists could remove an alien baby from her womb. Unfortunately, like *Alien³*, the fourth installment was a box-office disappointment and put an end to the series. Weaver played Ripley in all four films, with Lance Henriksen as the Bishop androids in the second and third chapters.

Alien (1979); *Aliens* (1986); *Alien³* (1992); *Alien Resurrection* (1997)

The Alilenas

These twin six-inch princesses hailed from Infant Island, home of the giant caterpillar Mothra (q.v.). They had the power to summon Mothra, which unfortunately required them to talk (which they did in unison — a very irritating habit). Stars Emi and Yumi Ito recorded songs in Japan as the Peanuts Sisters. In later films, the Infant Island princesses were known by different names and played by different actresses. They were called the Cosmos in *Godzilla vs. Mothra* (1992) and the Aliases in *Mothra* (1996) and *Mothra 2* (1997). See also **Mothra**.

Mothra (aka *Mosura*) (1962); *Godzilla vs. The Thing* (aka *Godzilla vs. Mothra*; *Godzilla tai Mothra*) (1964); *Ghidrah, the Three-Headed Monster* (aka *The Greatest Battle on Earth*; *Sandai*

Kaiju Chikyu Saidai No Kessen) (1965); *Godzilla vs. the Sea Monster* (aka *Ebriah-Terror of the Deep*; *Nankai No Dai Ketto*) (1966); *Godzilla vs. Mothra* (aka *Gojira vs. Mothra*) (1992); *Mothra* (aka *Mosura*) (1996); *Mothra 2* (aka *Mosura 2—Kaitei No Daikessen*; *Mothra 2—Showdown Beneath the Sea*) (1997)

Alligators and Crocodiles

These much-maligned reptiles made their mark in horror films, but are more fondly remembered for their dancing and comedic talents. Dancing gators performed a ballet parody in the "Dance of the Hours" sequence from Disney's *Fantasia*. A pet alligator played cupid for a young British couple in the 1955 romantic comedy *An Alligator Named Daisy*. Daisy proved to be a gifted comic, especially in the scene where she was discovered in an upright piano. Prior to writing and directing intellectual fare like *Matewan* and *Eight Men Out*, John Sayles penned 1980's *Alligator*, a campy horror picture about a giant alligator running amok in Chicago's sewers. Between *The Texas Chainsaw Massacre* and *Poltergeist*, director Tobe Hooper made *Eaten Alive*, a barely-released film about a Louisiana hotel owner who feeds unwelcome guests to his pet crocodile. After creating TV series like *Ally McBeal* and *The Practice*, David E. Kelley wrote the screenplay for *Lake Placid* (1999), a horror-comedy about a 30-foot-long crocodile. Stephen McNally really kept alligators in the moat of *The Black Castle*, while Whit Bissell was dead serious when he threatened to throw victims to the alligators in *I Was a Teenage Frankenstein*. Richard Crane slowly turned into an alligator in 1959's *The Alligator People*, a sobering little horror picture with a most sympathetic monster. *Crocodile Dundee* is the most famous "croc" hunter while Tarzan (q.v.) surely holds the record for most crocodile wrestling matches. James Bond (Roger Moore) disguised himself as a crocodile to infiltrate a secret hideout in 1983's *Octopussy*.

Fantasia (1940); *The Black Castle* (1952); *Peter Pan* (1953); *An Alligator Named Daisy* (1955); *I Was a Teenage Frankenstein* (1957); *Naked Earth* (1958); *The Alligator People* (1959); *The Three Worlds of Gulliver* (1960); *The Happiest Millionaire* (1967); *Live and Let Die* (1973); *99 and 44/100% Dead* (aka *Call Harry Crown*) (1974); *Eaten Alive* (aka *Starlight Slaughter*; *Death Trap*; *Horror Hotel Massacre*; *Legend of the Bayou*) (1976); *The Rescuers* (1977); *Crocodile* (1979); *Alligator* (1980); *The Great Alligator* (1980); *Octopussy* (1983); *Romancing the Stone* (1984); *Crocodile Dundee* (1986); *All Dogs Go to Heaven* (1989); *Howling VI: The Freaks* (1991); *Alligator II: The Mutation* (1991); *Jumanji* (1995); *Happy Gilmore* (1996); *The Legend of Gator Face* (1996); *Eraser* (1996); *Gone Fishin'* (1997); *Wild America* (1997); *Lake Placid* (1999)

American Film Theatre Presentations

Producer Ely Landau created the American Film Theatre (AFT) in 1972 as a vehicle for preserving quality plays on film while concurrently introducing these notable works to large audiences. His project attracted a number of outstanding performers, such as Fredric March (*The Iceman Cometh*), Alan Bates (*Butley*), Katharine Hepburn (*A Delicate Balance*), and Maximilian Schell (Oscar nominated for *The Man in the Glass Booth*). Although Laurence Olivier's *Three Sisters* was released as part of the series in 1974, it was actually made independently and released in Britain in 1970. The AFT films were originally distributed to movie theaters on a subscription basis. Despite critical acclaim, the series folded in 1975.

Three Sisters (1970); *The Iceman Cometh* (1973); *The Homecoming* (1973); *A Delicate Balance* (1973); *Galileo* (1973); *Rhinoceros* (1974); *Butley* (1974); *Luther* (1974); *Lost in the Stars* (1974); *The Man in the Glass Booth* (1975); *In Celebration* (1975)

American Ninja Series

Title tells all in this Cannon Films action series about a U.S. soldier schooled in ninja-style martial arts. Michael Dudikoff played quiet-but-lethal Joe Armstrong in the first two films. Karate expert David Bradley, portraying a different character, took over in 1989's *American Ninja 3: Blood Hunt*. Both Dudikoff and Bradley appeared in the fourth entry, which found Dudikoff coming out of "retirement" to rescue captive Bradley. In *American Ninja 5* (1993), Bradley joins forces with Lee Reyes, a former junior karate champion. Steve James appeared as the hero's two-fisted sidekick in the first three movies. For other martial arts films, see **Best of the Best Series**; **Bloodfist Series**; **The Karate Kid**; **Kickboxer Series**; and **No Retreat, No Surrender Series**.

American Ninja (1985); *American Ninja 2: The Confrontation* (1987); *American Ninja 3: Blood Hunt* (1989); *American Ninja 4: The Annihilation* (1991); *American Ninja 5* (1993)

Amityville Series

In 1979, American International Pictures turned Jay Anson's allegedly nonfiction best seller about a haunted house, *The Amityville Horror*, into its biggest hit. It was a sorry excuse for a horror picture, despite the presence of the once-reliable Rod Steiger as a troubled priest. The 1982 sequel, *Amityville: The Possession*, turned out to be a prequel—but no one really cared either way. The third installment, *Amityville 3-D* (1983), made no attempt to connect itself with the first two films. Its box-office failure (despite the added allure of 3-D) apparently signaled the end of a theatrical series. The series moved briefly to television, with the 1989 Patty Duke–Jane Wyatt movie *Amityville: The Evil Escapes*, before finding its niche with additional direct-to-videotape entries. See also **Ghosts**; **House Series**.

The Amityville Horror (1979); *Amityville: The Possession* (1982); *Amityville 3-D* (aka *Amityville: The Demon*) (1983); *Amityville: The Evil Escapes* (1989 TVM); *The Amityville Curse* (1990); *Amityville 1992: It's About Time* (1992); *Amityville: A New Generation* (1993); *Amityville: Dollhouse* (1996)

Amnesia

A plot device staple, despite its unlikely real-life occurrence, amnesia has shown no favoritism toward any particular genre nor sex. Screen legend Greta Garbo made it fashionable for women to forget their identities in 1932's *As You Desire Me*, thus inspiring other actresses to ponder "Who am I?" A sample roster spans five decades and includes Jennifer Jones (*Love Letters*), Ava Gardner (*Singapore*), Karen Valentine (*Jane Doe*), and Lindsay Wagner (*Stranger in My Bed*). Males have proven to be equally forgetful, especially William Powell and Gregory Peck, both of whom suffered two bouts of amnesia (Powell in *I Love You Again* and *Crossroads*, Peck in *Spellbound* and *Mirage*). Greer Garson, who dealt with Ronald Colman's loss of memory in *Random Harvest* (1942), experienced it herself earlier in *Remember?* (1939). In an unusual plot twist, she and Robert Taylor played a bickering couple who take a potion that causes amnesia and then wind up falling in love again. Amnesia has also separated lovers in high-class soap operas like *Random Harvest, Love Letters*, and *Singapore*. It's hard to remember many amnesiac comedies, although *Desperately Seeking Susan* and *The Road to Hong Kong* spring to mind with little difficulty. The most interesting amnesiac plots have appeared in mysteries and espionage thrillers. Gregory Peck played the new head of an asylum who turns out to be an imposter with amnesia in Hitchcock's *Spellbound* (1945). Warner Baxter's *The Crime Doctor* (q.v.) was a sleuthing psychologist who had been a master criminal before being reformed by amnesia. Unethical psychiatrist Tony Perkins tried to manipulate amnesiac killer Charles Bronson into murdering his wife's lover in the 1971 thriller *Someone Behind the Door*. James Garner, unable to remember his name, saw a Budweiser truck and an airplane and decided to call himself *Mister Buddwing* (1966). It was certainly one of the more commercial films of its time.

As You Desire Me (1932); *Remember?* (1939); *Missing Ten Days* (aka *Spy in the Pantry; Ten Days in Paris*) (1939); *I Love You Again* (1940); *Crossroads* (1942); *Dr. Gillespie's New Assistant* (1942); *Street of Chance* (1942); *Random Harvest* (1942); *The Crime Doctor* (1943); *Two O'Clock Courage* (1945); *Identity Unknown* (1945); *Love Letters* (1945); *Spellbound* (1945); *The Unknown* (1946); *Somewhere in the Night* (1946); *While I Live* (aka *The Dream of Olwen*) (1947); *Singapore* (1947); *High Wall* (1947); *Lost Honeymoon* (1947); *Girl in the Painting* (aka *Portrait from Life*) (1948); *Shadow on the Wall* (1950); *The Woman with No Name* (1950); *A Tale of Five Women* (aka *A Tale of Five Cities*) (1951); *Home at Seven* (aka *Murder on Monday*) (1952); *The Unholy Four* (aka *A Stranger Came Home*) (1953); *Man in the Dark* (1953); *The Long Wait* (1954); *The Constant Husband* (1955); *Istanbul* (1957); *Forger of London* (1961); *Sundays and Cybele* (1962); *The Road to Hong Kong* (1962); *The Double* (1963); *Hysteria* (1964); *Mirage* (1965); *The Third Day* (1965); *Mister Buddwing* (1966); *Project X* (1968); *Jigsaw* (1968); *Run a Crooked Mile* (1969); *Someone Behind the Door* (1971); *Richie Brockelman: The Missing 24 Hours* (1976 TVM); *Beyond the Door 2* (aka *Shock*) (1979); *The Return of the Soldier* (1981); *Jane Doe* (1983 TVM); *Blackout* (1985 TVM); *Desperately Seeking Susan* (1985); *Stranger in My Bed* (1986 TVM); *Lilac Dream* (1987); *The Stranger* (1987); *Overboard* (1987); *Murder by Night* (1989 TVM); *The Lady Forgets* (1989 TVM); *Moving Target* (1990); *Memories of Murder* (1990 TVM); *Total Recall* (1990); *Finding the Way Home* (1991 TVM); *Regarding Henry* (1991); *Dead Again* (1991); *Shattered* (1991); *A Stranger in the Family* (1991 TVM); *With a Vengeance* (1992 TVM); *The Disappearance of Nora* (1993 TVM); *Bloodfist V: Human Target* (1993); *The Blonde* (aka *La Bionda*) (1994); *Snapdragon* (1994); *Amateur* (1994); *Clean Slate* (1994); *See Jane Run* (1995 TVM); *All Men Are Mortal* (1995); *Tough and Deadly* (1995); *Sweet Dreams* (1996 TVM); *The Perfect Daughter* (1996 TVM); *The Long Kiss Goodnight* (1996); *Yesterday's Target* (1996 TVM); *Amnesia* (1996); *Anastasia* (1997); *Dark City* (1998)

Amusement Parks *see* Fairs and Carnivals

Androids and Cyborgs

Much to the dismay of science fiction purists, the cinema has often confused androids and cyborgs. The term "android" refers either to an artificial man made of organic substance or, in a looser sense, to a human-like robot. The most famous artificial man, Mary Shelley's Frankenstein Monster (q.v.), is seldom described as an android, though he certainly fits the first definition. On a larger scale, Vincent Price tried to create a race of "synthetic men" and move them into government positions in 1970's *Scream and*

Scream Again. However, artificial humans such as these remain rare, with most movie androids hailing from the human-like robot school. In Fritz Lang's highly influential *Metropolis* (1925), a mad scientist kidnapped a peace-minded tunnel worker and replaced her with a trouble-making robot lookalike. Androids ran amok in a fantasy resort in Michael Crichton's *Westworld* (1973) and its semi-sequel *Futureworld* (1976). Men replaced their female companions with more easily controlled androids in *The Stepford Wives* (1975) and *Cherry 2000* (1988), although the hero of the latter film ultimately chose Melanie Griffith over his robot lover. Some androids, such as the "replicants" in *Blade Runner* (1982), gradually became so human-like as to question their own identities. Androids far outnumber their relatives, the cyborgs. The term "cyborg," a contraction of "cybernetic organism," describes a hybrid between man and machine. Television's *The Six Million Dollar Man* and *The Bionic Woman* brought fame to cyborgs. Indeed, the pilot movie for *The Six Million Dollar Man* (q.v.) (1973) was originally called *Cyborg*. Technically, former Jedi knight Darth Vader had become a cyborg by the time Luke Skywalker encountered him for the first time in *Star Wars* (1977). Likewise, the Tin Man was one when he and Dorothy met in *The Wizard of Oz* (1939). In futuristic Detroit, a cop left for dead was transformed into the cyborgic crimefighter RoboCop, one of the most popular movie heroes of 1987. *RoboCop*, together with the inexpensive *Cyborg* (1989), inspired a 1990s "mini-genre" of low-budget action films about cyborgs and androids. See also **Computers**; **Cyborg Series**; **Cyborg Cop Series**; **Nemesis Series**; **RoboCop**; **Robots**; **Shadowchaser Series**; **The Six Million Dollar Man Series**; **The Stepford Wives**; **Universal Soldier Series**.

Metropolis (1925); *The Wizard of Oz* (1939); *The Perfect Woman* (1949); *Creation of the Humanoids* (1962); *Dr. Goldfoot and the Bikini Machine* (1965); *The Human Duplicators* (1965); *Cyborg 2087* (1966); *Scream and Scream Again* (1970); *The Six Million Dollar Man* (1973 TVM); *Westworld* (1973); *The Questor Tapes* (1974 TVM); *The Stepford Wives* (1975); *Futureworld* (1976); *Future Cop* (1976 TVM); *The Cops and Robin* (1978 TVM); *Alien* (1979); *Galaxina* (1980); *Android* (1982); *Blade Runner* (1982); *Prototype* (1983 TVM); *The Terminator* (1984); *D.A.R.Y.L.* (1985); *J.O.E. and the Colonel* (1985 TVM); *Condor* (1986); *The Vindicator* (aka *Frankenstein '88*) (1986); *Deadly Friend* (1986); *Eliminators* (1986); *RoboCop* (1987); *Making Mr. Right* (1987); *Not Quite Human* (1987 TVM); *Cherry 2000* (1988); *Cyborg* (1989); *Vice Academy II* (1989); *Slipstream* (1989); *Class of 1999* (1990); *Hardware* (1990); *Robo-C.H.I.C.* (1990); *Syngenor* (1990); *Edward Scissorhands* (1990); *Steel and Lace* (1991); *Eve of Destruction* (1991); *Cybernator* (1991); *Terminator 2: Judgment Day* (1991); *Bill and Ted's Bogus Journey* (1991); *The Running Delilah* (1992 TVM); *Project: Shadowchaser* (1992); *Universal Soldier* (1992); *Toys* (1993); *Nemesis* (1993); *Cyborg Cop* (1993); *Mandroid* (1993); *Cyber Tracker* (1994); *American Cyborg: Steel Warrior* (1994); *The Companion* (1994 TVM); *Star Trek Generations* (1994); *Oblivion* (1994); *Circuitry Man II: Plughead Rewired* (1994); *Cyber Tracker 2* (1995); *The Android Affair* (1995 TVM); *Cyberzone* (1995); *Droid Gunner* (1995); *Screamers* (1995); *Dark Future* (1995); *Solo* (1996); *The Tomorrow Man* (1996 TVM); *Phoenix* (1996); *Precious Find* (1996); *Alien Resurrection* (1997); *Omega Doom* (1997); *Austin Powers: International Man of Mystery* (1997); *Leprechaun 4 in Space* (aka *Leprechaun 4*) (1997)

Angel Series

"High school honor student by day, hooker by night!" proclaimed the ad line to 1984's *Angel*. It's a concise plot summary, actually, except that 15-year-old Angel (Donna Wilkes) gets "rescued" from a life of prostitution by caring cop Cliff Gorman. Viewers lured by the exploitative advertising campaign were probably disappointed by the film's tame content. Nevertheless, this B-picture generated some unexpected box-office noise and New World Pictures rushed out a sequel. Busy B-film actress Betsy Russell took over the title role for 1985's *Avenging Angel*, which found our heroine studying for a legal career. However, when her cop friend is murdered, she cuts her academic endeavors short, reverts to her tough girl persona, and hits the streets again to exact vengeance. Rory Calhoun and Susan Tyrell had supporting roles in these first two films. For a couple of years, it appeared as though Angel had fired her last bullet. Then, in 1988, *Angel III: The Final Chapter* reached the screen with Mitzi Kapture, who would later find fame on the late night TV series *Silk Stalkings*. This installment sent Angel, now an undercover cop, on a mission to rescue her kidnapped sister. After a six-year hiatus, the series resumed with 1994's *Angel 4: Undercover*, which starred Darlene Vogel. Angel, now a police photographer called Molly, infiltrates the world of rock 'n' roll to discover who murdered a former hooker friend.

Angel (1984); *Avenging Angel* (1985); *Angel III: The Final Chapter* (1988); *Angel 4: Undercover* (1994)

Angels

One rather expects to find angels in heavenly fantasies like *Green Pastures* (1936), *Stairway to Heaven* (1946), and *Made in Heaven* (1987). However, earthbound angels outnumber their celestial counterparts on film. They have also made a more lasting impression, perhaps because they appear in smaller numbers, one or two to a film, allowing them to become more personable (and in some cases, more mortal-like). Guardian angels are the most common variety and have been sent to Earth to rescue misguided mortals from suicide, ambition, and lousy baseball playing. Henry Travers played Clarence, an angel trying to earn his wings, in Frank Capra's annual Christmas favorite *It's a Wonderful Life* (1946). He dissuades a distraught family man (James Stewart) from ending his life by showing him how he has affected the lives of others. Cloris Leachman replaced Travers as the angel in the sticky-sweet 1977 TV movie remake *It Happened One Christmas*, while Robert Carradine took his turn in the 1990 TV movie sequel *Clarence*. Another holiday feature, 1985's *One Magic Christmas*, cast Harry Dean Stanton as an unlikely-looking angel who comes to the aid of a confused woman (Mary Steenburgen) who has lost the Christmas spirit. Cary Grant made a charming angel in *The Bishop's Wife* (1947), helping clergyman David Niven realize that his desire to build a cathedral had begun to cut him off from his family and his own love of God. Grant's angel also found himself in the precarious position of falling in love with Niven's wife (Loretta Young). Other angel-mortal love affairs occurred in the Jeanette MacDonald–Nelson Eddy musical *I Married an Angel* (1942), Wim Wenders' lyrical *Wings of Desire* (1987), its American remake *City of Angels* (1998), and the ridiculous comedy *Date with an Angel* (1987). Baseball collided with heavenly forces in *Angels in the Outfield* (1951), in which an angel guides the woebegone Pittsburgh Pirates (not the yet-unformed California Angels) to a winning season. The spirit of baseball great Shoeless Joe Jackson returned to Earth to play on farmer Kevin Costner's baseball

diamond in 1989's *Field of Dreams*. The role call of performers who have played angels is an impressive one: Edmund Gwenn in *Between Two Worlds* and *For Heaven's Sake*, James Mason in *Forever Darling* and *Heaven Can Wait*, Claude Rains in *Here Comes Mr. Jordan*, Sidney Poitier in *The Angel Levine*, and Clifton Webb in *For Heaven's Sake*. See also **Heaven**.

Green Pastures (1936); *Here Comes Mr. Jordan* (1941); *I Married an Angel* (1942); *Cabin in the Sky* (1943); *Between Two Worlds* (1944); *The Horn Blows at Midnight* (1945); *That's the Spirit* (1945); *It's a Wonderful Life* (1946); *Stairway to Heaven* (aka *A Matter of Life and Death*) (1946); *The Bishop's Wife* (1947); *Heaven Only Knows* (aka *Montana Mike*) (1947); *For Heaven's Sake* (1950); *Angels in the Outfield* (aka *Angels and the Pirates*) (1951); *The Angel Who Pawned Her Harp* (1954); *Forever Darling* (1956); *Barbarella* (aka *Barbarella, Queen of the Galaxy*) (1968); *The Angel Levine* (1970); *It Happened One Christmas* (1977 TVM); *Heaven Can Wait* (1978); *Human Feelings* (1978 TVM); *Fear No Evil* (1981); *The Kid with the Broken Halo* (1982 TVM); *Two of a Kind* (1983); *It Came Upon a Midnight Clear* (1984 TVM); *The Heavenly Kid* (1985); *One Magic Christmas* (1985); *Date with an Angel* (1987); *Made in Heaven* (1987); *Wings of Desire* (aka *Der Himmel über Berlin*) (1987); *Field of Dreams* (1989); *Always* (1989); *Soultaker* (1990); *Clarence* (1990 TVM); *Earth Angel* (1991 TVM); *Defending Your Life* (1991); *Hi Honey, I'm Dead* (1991 TVM); *Far Away, So Close!* (1993); *Heart and Souls* (1993); *Angels in the Outfield* (1994); *Dark Angel: The Ascent* (1994); *The Prophecy* (aka *God's Army*) (1995); *Heaven Sent* (1995); *Michael* (1996); *Lover's Knot* (1996); *The Preacher's Wife* (1996); *Angels in the Endzone* (1997 TVM); *A Life Less Ordinary* (1997); *City of Angels* (1998); *Fallen* (1998); *The Prophecy II* (1998); *What Dreams May Come* (1998); *Dying to Live* (1999 TVM); *Dogma* (1999); *The Soul Collector* (1999 TVM); *Angels in the Infield* (2000 TVM)

Animal Instincts Series

Inspired by a sordid real-life case, *Animal Instincts* (1992) chronicled the tale of a police officer (Maxwell Caufield) "turned on" by watching his wife (Shannon Whirry) have sex with other men. The provocative subject matter could have resulted in an incisive examination of voyeurism, exhibitionism, and sexual behavior. However, in the hands of "erotic thriller" director Gregory Hippolyte, *Animal Instincts* never amounted to more than softcore sex. Its only distinction is the launching of Whirry's career as a "video vixen." In addition to *Animal Instincts 2*, Whirry would display her voluptuous body in other erotic thrillers such as *Body of Influence*, *Mirror Images II*, and *Private Obsession*. Much to the dismay of Whirry fans, Wendy Schumacher took over the lead role in *Animal Instincts: The Seductress*. Director Hippolyte, who got his start in adult films, helmed all *Animal Instinct* movies and a bunch of other erotic thrillers. See also **Body Chemistry Series**; **Night Eyes Series**; and **Secret Games Series**.

Animal Instincts (1992); *Animal Instincts 2* (1994); *Animal Instincts: The Seductress* (aka *Animal Instincts III: The Seductress*) (1995)

Animated Movies (Feature-Length)

Not only was Walt Disney the father of feature-length animated films, but his studio completely dominated the field for nearly three decades. The Disney artists produced 13 movies during that span, beginning with 1937's landmark motion picture *Snow White and the Seven Dwarfs*. For the most part, Disney had little competition, chiefly due to the high costs associated with animation.

Nevertheless, Max Fleischer, creator of Betty Boop and Popeye, mounted some rival productions in the early forties. His *Gulliver's Travels* and *Hoppity Goes to Town* earned good reviews for their artwork, but critics complained about weak storytelling. Husband-and-wife team John Halas and Joy Batchelor produced an ambitious adaptation of George Orwell's *Animal Farm* in 1955. It was oriented toward a more sophisticated adult audience — but did not find one. The UPA studio, home of Mr. Magoo, tried unsuccessfully to duplicate the Disney magic with 1959's *1001 Arabian Nights* and 1963's *Gay Purr-ee*, a musical tale about Parisian cats. The latter film signalled the end of an era, as even the Disney product began to exhibit a lowering of standards. Rising costs and Walt Disney's death (in 1966) undoubtedly contributed to the decline. However, in 1972, a 32-year-old animator named Ralph Bakshi revived the feature-length cartoon in grand fashion, with his stylish, controversial X-rated film *Fritz the Cat*. Although Bakshi's subsequent movies made little money, they acquired a strong cult following, principally among college-age viewers raised on Disney cartoons. Sadly, soaring costs prevented Bakshi from completing his *Lord of the Rings* films. His 1978 adaptation ended abruptly, promising a sequel that was never made. Meanwhile, internal problems at the Disney studio resulted in scarce output during the 1970s. Several Disney animators, led by Don Bluth, quit and formed their own studio. Bluth's first independent feature *The Secret of NIMH* (1982) was a colorful, heartwarming return to the Disney formula. It led to a revival of quality feature-length cartoons in the 1980s, culminating with the simultaneous 1988 releases of Disney's *Oliver and Company* and Bluth's *The Land Before Time*. There were even novel experiments like *Starchaser: The Legend of Orin* (1985), the only feature-length 3-D cartoon. However, the genre became glutted with lower quality cartoon features based on best-selling toys such as the Care Bears (q.v.), the Pound Puppies, Rainbow Brite, and My Little Pony. These films, like their Saturday morning counterparts, strove to sell as much as entertain. Animated films needed a renaissance and Disney provided one in 1989. After suffering major disappointments such as *The Black Cauldron*, Disney went back to the drawing board and reinvented the animated feature as a Broadway musical. *The Little Mermaid* (1989) captivated children and adults with its charming characters, splashy production numbers, and catchy songs (including Oscar winner "Under the Sea"). The next Disney film *Beauty and the Beast* improved on the same formula and became the first animated feature to be nominated for a Best Picture Academy Award. Disney animated films continued to achieve blockbuster status, with *The Lion King* (1994) eventually earning over $300 million. Other studios took note of Disney's success and set up their own animation divisions. Between 1997 and 1998, Twentieth Century–Fox produced *Anastasia*, Warner made *Quest for Camelot*, and Dreamworks SKG produced *Prince of Egypt*. The last film, developed by former Disney exceecutive Jeffrey Katzenberg, became the first non–Disney animated film to gross over $100 million. In the interim, Disney pioneered the first feature-length, computer-generated animated film with *Toy Story* (1995). Its box-office success, along with the computer-animated *Antz* and *A Bug's Life*, opened up a new world for feature film animators. See also **Aladdin Series; The Care Bears; Cartoon/Live Action Features; The Land Before Time Series; Peanuts Series; The Swan Princess Series.**

Snow White and the Seven Dwarfs (1937); *Gulliver's Travels* (1939); *Pinocchio* (1940); *Fantasia* (1940); *Dumbo* (1941); *Hoppity Goes to Town* (aka *Mr. Bugs Goes to Town*) (1941); *Bambi* (1942); *Make Mine Music* (1946); *Cinderella* (1950); *Alice in Wonderland* (1951); *Peter Pan* (1952); *Animal Farm* (1955); *Lady and the Tramp* (1955); *Sleeping Beauty* (1959); *1001 Arabian Nights* (1959); *One Hundred and One Dalmations* (1961); *Alakazam the Great* (1961); *The Sword in the Stone* (1963); *Gay Purr-ee* (1963); *Pinocchio in Outer Space* (1964); *Hey There, It's Yogi Bear* (1964); *A Man Called Flintstone* (1966); *Gulliver's Travels Beyond the Moon* (1966); *The Jungle Book* (1967); *Yellow Submarine* (1968); *A Boy Named Charlie Brown* (1969); *The Phantom Tollbooth* (1969); *The Aristocats* (1970); *Shinbone Alley* (1971); *The Point* (1971 TVM); *Fritz the Cat* (1972); *Snoopy, Come Home* (1972); *Charlotte's Web* (1973); *Robin Hood* (1973); *Fantastic Planet* (1973); *Journey Back to Oz* (1974); *The Nine Lives of Fritz the Cat* (1975); *Hugo, the Hippo* (1975); *The Rescuers* (1977); *Wizards* (1977); *The Hobbit* (1977 TVM); *Raggedy Ann and Andy* (1977); *Watership Down* (1978); *The Lord of the Rings* (1978); *Animalympics* (1979); *Grendel, Grendel, Grendel* (1980); *American Pop* (1981); *The Fox and the Hound* (1981); *Heavy Metal* (1981); *Hey, Good Lookin'* (1982); *Heidi's Song* (1982); *The Secret of NIMH* (1982); *The Plague Dogs* (1982); *The Last Unicorn* (1982); *Fire and Ice* (1983); *Twice Upon a Time* (1983); *Rock & Rule* (1983); *Lensman* (1984); *The Smurfs and the Magic Flute* (1984); *The Black Cauldron* (1985); *Vampire Hunter D* (1985); *The Cosmic Eye* (1985); *The Care Bears Movie* (1985); *Here Come the Littles* (1985); *Starchaser: The Legend of Orin* (1985); *Rainbow Brite and the Star Stealers* (1985); *Vampires in Havana* (1985); *The Great Mouse Detective* (aka *The Adventures of the Great Mouse Detective*) (1986); *Heathcliff: The Movie* (1986); *My Little Pony* (1986); *GoBots: Battle of the Rock Lords* (1986); *An American Tail* (1986); *The Chipmunk Adventure* (1987); *The Brave Little Toaster* (1987); *Pinocchio and the Emperor of the Night* (1987); *Pound Puppies and the Legend of Big Paw* (1988); *Oliver and Company* (1988); *The Land Before Time* (1988); *Light Years* (1988); *All Dogs Go to Heaven* (1989); *The Little Mermaid* (1989); *Daffy Duck's Quackbusters* (1989); *Jetsons: The Movie* (1990); *Duck Tales: The Movie — Treasure of the Lost Lamp* (1990); *The Rescuers Down Under* (1990); *The Nutcracker Prince* (1990); *Happily Ever After* (1990); *Rock-a-Doodle* (1991); *The Magic Riddle* (1991); *Beauty and the Beast* (1991); *Rover Dangerfield* (1991); *An American Tale: Fievel Goes West* (1991); *The Tune* (1992); *FernGully … The Last Rainforest* (aka *FernGully*) (1992); *Bebe's Kids* (1992); *Little Nemo: Adventures in Slumberland* (1992); *Freddie as F.R.O.7* (1992); *Tom and Jerry: The Movie* (1992); *Aladdin* (1992); *The Princess and the Goblin* (aka *A Hercegno es a Kobold*) (1992); *Jonny's Golden Quest* (1993 TVM); *Batman: Mask of the Phantasm* (1993); *Once Upon a Forest* (1993); *A Troll in Central Park* (1994); *Hans Christian Andersen's Thumbelina* (1994); *Felidae* (1994); *The Swan Princess* (1994); *The Lion King* (1994); *Jonny Quest vs. the Cyber Insects* (1995 TVM); *Balto* (1995); *A Goofy Movie* (1995); *The Pebble and the Penguin* (1995); *Pocahontas* (1995); *The Wind in the Willows* (1995); *Toy Story* (1995); *The Hunchback of Notre Dame* (1996); *Beavis and Butthead Do America* (1996); *All Dogs Go to Heaven 2* (1996); *Hercules* (1997); *Pippi Longstocking* (1997); *The Princess Mononoke* (1997); *Beauty and the Beast: The Enchanted Christmas* (1997); *Cats Don't Dance* (1997); *Anastasia* (1997); *Aaron's Magic Village* (1997); *Ferngully 2: The Magical Rescue* (1998); *Pocahontas II: Journey to a New World* (1998); *Quest for Camelot* (1998); *Mulan* (1998); *Pokémon: The First Movie* (1998); *Hercules and Xena — The Animated Movie: The Battle for Mount Olympus* (1998); *The Lion King: Simba's Pride* (1998); *The Prince of Egypt* (1998); *The Rugrats Movie* (1998); *The King and I* (1999); *Doug's 1st Movie* (1999); *Tarzan* (1999); *South Park: Bigger, Longer & Uncut* (1999); *The Iron Giant* (1999); *Toy Story 2* (1999); *Fantasia 2000* (1999); *Bartok the Magnificent* (1999); *Pokemon: The Movie 2000* (aka *Pokemon X: Revelation Lugia*) (1999); *The Road to El Dorado* (2000); *The Tigger Movie* (2000); *Dinosaur* (2000); *Titan A.E.* (2000)

Anthologies

Also called "episode films," anthology movies contain two or more separate stories, typically linked by a framing device. The format descended from D.W. Griffith's *Intolerance* (1918), which interwove four stories set in different time periods. One of the first American films to separate its "internal plots" was 1932's *If I Had a Million*. Richard Bennett played a millionaire who gave fortunes to people (e.g., Charles Laughton, Gary Cooper, W.C. Fields) randomly selected from the phone book. In the early 1940s, French immigrant Julien Duvivier directed two highly-acclaimed anthology films, *Tales of Manhattan* and *Flesh and Fantasy*. The former film used a dress tailcoat to link five stories, while Robert Benchley tied the stories together in the latter film. Curiously, the three-part *Flesh and Fantasy* originally included a fourth tale, which was expanded by Reginald LeBorg into 1944's *Destiny*. Britain's initial foray in anthology films resulted in the classic 1945 chiller *Dead of Night*. Ironically, this film is best remembered for its frame, as opposed to the stories. It opens with an architect who visits a country manor and engages in a conversation about dreams with its inhabitants. After the last dream is told and a shocking murder takes place, the architect wakes up — for he has been dreaming all along. That morning, he drives to a client's estate in the country and arrives at the same manor. The recurring, and endless, nightmare has begun again. In the wake of *Dead of Night*, British studios produced three highly successful adaptations of Somerset Maugham short stories: *Quartet*, *Trio*, and *Encore*. These inspired a 1952 U.S. author anthology, *O. Henry's Full House*, featuring John Steinbeck as narrator. Budget-conscious director Roger Corman reacquainted the anthology format with horror tales in his 1962 Edgar Allan Poe collection *Tales of Terror*. Amicus, a small British studio, followed Corman's example with 1964's *Dr. Terror's House of Horrors* and subsequently specialized in producing anthology horror films. It made seven additional anthology movies between 1968's *Torture Garden* and 1974's *From Beyond the Grave*. Throughout the 1960s, episodic films enjoyed great popularity in France and Italy, with distinguished filmmakers such as François Truffaut and Federico Fellini contributing segments to international efforts like *Love at Twenty* and *Spirits of the Dead*. In the 1970s, attempts to adapt the anthology format to U.S. made-for-TV movies met with modest success. Television viewers seemed to prefer the interlocking-story format made popular by the *Love Boat* and *Fantasy Island* TV series.

If I Had a Million (1932); *Tales of Manhattan* (1942); *Flesh and Fantasy* (1943); *Dead of Night* (1945); *On Our Merry Way* (1948); *Bond Street* (1948); *Quartet* (1948); *Trio* (1950); *Actors and Sin* (1952); *Encore* (1952); *O. Henry's Full House* (1952); *Tonight at 8:30* (aka *Meet Me Tonight*) (1952); *It's a Big Country* (1952); *The Story of Three Loves* (1953); *Love in the City* (1953); *Daughters of Destiny* (aka *Love, Soldiers and Women*) (1953); *Letters from My Windmill* (1954); *Three Cases of Murder* (1954); *Invitation to the Dance* (1957); *Of Life and Love* (1957); *Rising of the Moon* (1957); *Love and the Frenchwoman* (1961); *The Devil and the Ten Commandments* (1962); *Tales of Terror* (1962); *Seven Capital Sins* (1962); *Yesterday, Today, and Tomorrow* (1963); *Twice Told Tales* (1963); *Black Sabbath* (1964); *Kwaidan* (1964); *Bambole!* (1965); *Dr. Terror's House of Horrors* (1965); *Let's Talk About Women* (1965); *Woman Times Seven* (1967); *Dr. Terror's Gallery of Horrors* (aka *Return from the Past*; *The Blood Suckers*) (1967); *The Oldest Profession in the World* (aka *The Oldest Profession*) (1967); *The Torture Garden* (1968); *Spirits of the Dead* (1968); *The Illustrated Man* (1969); *Night Gallery* (1969 TVM); *The House That Dripped Blood* (1970); *The Decameron* (1970); *Triple Play* (1971 TVM); *Asylum* (aka *House of Crazies*) (1972); *Everything You Always Wanted to Know About Sex (But Were Afraid to Ask)* (1972); *Tales from the Crypt* (1972); *The Canterbury Tales* (1972); *Tales That Witness Madness* (1973); *Vault of Horror* (aka *Tales from the Crypt 2*) (1973); *From Beyond the Grave* (aka *Creatures from Beyond the Grave*) (1974); *Immoral Tales* (1974); *Arabian Nights* (1974); *Trilogy of Terror* (1975 TVM); *How Funny Can Sex Be?* (1976); *The Uncanny* (1977); *Roseland* (1977); *Movie Movie* (1978); *Tigers in Lipstick* (aka *Wild Beds*) (1979); *Sunday Lovers* (1980); *Heavy Metal* (1981); *Creepshow* (1982); *Nightmares* (1983); *Twilight Zone — The Movie* (1983); *Jealousy* (1984 TVM); *Cat's Eye* (1985); *Creepshow 2* (1987); *New York Stories* (1989); *After Midnight* (1989); *Two Evil Eyes* (aka *Due Occhi Diabolici*) (1990); *Tales from the Darkside: The Movie* (1990); *Grim Prairie Tales* (1990); *Women and Men: Stories of Seduction* (1990 TVM); *Campfire Tales* (1991); *Seduction: Three Tales from the Inner Sanctum* (1992 TVM); *Hotel Room* (1993 TVM); *Two Mikes Don't Make a Wright* (1993); *Bedevil* (1993); *Weird Tales* (aka *Strane Storie*) (1994); *Baltic Love: Three Stories* (1994); *Being Human* (1994); *Four Rooms* (1995); *Tales from the Hood* (1995); *Flirt* (1995); *Necronomicon: Book of the Dead* (1996); *Quicksilver Highway* (1997 TVM); *The Red Violin* (1999)

Apartments

The narrow confines of apartment living have created stress-inducing problems for many tenants, while implicating others romantically. In Roman Polanski's *Repulsion* (1965), a sexually-repressed girl (Catherine Deneuve) spends a weekend alone in her sister's London flat and winds up murdering the lecherous landlord with a dinner knife. Polanski himself played an apartment dweller who became obsessed with his pad's former occupant in 1976's *The Tenant*. The Kowalskis' claustrophobic apartment served to feed the sexual tensions in Elia Kazan's 1951 adaptation of *A Streetcar Named Desire*. Supernatural creatures have displayed a special fondness for apartment living in films like *The Sentinel* (1977), *Poltergeist III*, and *Demons 2* (both 1988). Even the Devil showed up, amid a building full of satanic tenants, in *Rosemary's Baby* (1968). A temporary housing shortage forced Jean Arthur to share her small Washington, D.C., apartment with Joel McCrea and Charles Coburn in the 1943 comedy *The More the Merrier*. Naturally, she and Joel discovered true love. The same plot, with a different setting (Tokyo), surfaced in 1966 as *Walk, Don't Run*. Apartments have also been the site for illicit love affairs. Fred MacMurray paid Shirley MacLaine's rent for *The Apartment* (1960), while Jason Robards visited Jane Fonda on *Any Wednesday* (1966) at his company-paid flat. The close proximity to his neighbors inspired James Stewart to engage in some hazardous window-peeping in Hitchcock's *Rear Window* (1954). Other nosy apartment neighbors proved meddlesome in *Terraces* (1977) and *Through Naked Eyes* (1983). In the 1943 comedy *Johnny Doesn't Live Here Anymore* (1943), Simone Simon discovered that keys to her apartment were distributed freely during the war. *The Key* (1958) was an emotional drama about a woman (Sophia Loren) who passes the key to her apartment to a series of fighting Naval officers. In *The Night We Never Met* (1993), complications naturally ensued when three people time-shared the same apartment on different days of the week. See also **Hotels**.

Bachelor Apartment (1931); *The More the Merrier* (1943); *There Is a Family* (1944); *Johnny Doesn't Live Here Anymore* (aka *And So They Were Married*) (1944); *Apartment for Peggy* (1948); *A Kiss in the Dark* (1949); *A Streetcar Named Desire* (1951); *Love Nest* (1951); *Rear Window* (1954); *The Key* (1958); *The Apartment* (1960); *Why Bother to Knock?* (aka *Don't Bother to Knock*) (1961); *The Notorious Landlady* (1962); *Boys' Night Out* (1962); *Repulsion* (1965); *That Funny Feeling* (1965); *Any Wednesday* (1966); *Walk, Don't Run* (1966); *Wait Until Dark* (1967); *Barefoot in the Park* (1967); *The Penthouse* (1967); *Rosemary's Baby* (1968); *The Odd Couple* (1968); *The Landlord* (1970); *Strangers in 7A* (1972 TVM); *Nightmare* (1974 TVM); *They Came from Within* (aka *Shivers; The Parasite Murders; Frissons*) (1975); *The Tenant* (1976); *Terraces* (1977 TVM); *The Sentinel* (1977); *Through Naked Eyes* (1983 TVM); *The Guardian* (1984 TVM); *The Family* (1987); *Demons 2* (1988); *Poltergeist III* (1988); *Apartment Zero* (1989); *Pacific Heights* (1990); *The Super* (1991); *World Apartment Horror* (1991); *Scissors* (1991); *Single White Female* (1992); *Through the Eyes of a Killer* (1992 TVM); *Sliver* (1993); *Roommates* (1994 TVM); *Shallow Grave* (1994); *House Call* (aka *De Flat*) (1994); *Joe's Apartment* (1996); *Un Divan à New York* (aka *A Couch in New York*) (1996); *Addicted to Love* (1997); *Two Girls and a Guy* (1998); *The Landlady* (1998); *The 4th Floor* (2000)

Apes and Monkeys

Ape and monkey performers have earned a notorious reputation for stealing scenes from their human co-stars. The chimpanzee Bonzo had little trouble upstaging future president Ronald Reagan in *Bedtime for Bonzo*. Clyde, a mugging orangutan, showed far more facial expression than iron-jawed Clint Eastwood in *Every Which Way but Loose*. King Kong towered over Fay Wray and Robert Armstrong in terms of on-screen impact as well as sheer size in his 1933 film debut. Although Kong reigns as the cinema's biggest ape in terms of popularity, his physical dimensions have been equalled by *Mighty Joe Young* (1949), *Konga* (1961), *Goliathon* (1977), and, to a lesser extent, *Son of Kong* (1933). There have been no oversized monkeys, although an equally unusual winged species abducted Dorothy and took her to the Wicked Witch's castle in *The Wizard of Oz* (1939). Ordinary apes have proven to be meddlesome as well, especially in horror/mystery fare such as *Murders in the Rue Morgue* (1932), *The Ape* (1940), and *Gorilla at Large* (1954). Typically, though, a villainous human lurks behind the ape's ghastly deeds — and in some cases, the true murderer turns out to be a man in an ape suit. Rene Russo played a 1920s socialite who raised a gorilla as her son in the fact-based *Buddy* (1997). David Warner longed to be a gorilla — and carry off his estranged wife — in the 1966 satire *Morgan!* Mad scientist Dr. Moreau (Charles Laughton) transformed apes into men with dubious results ("Are we not men?") in 1933's *The Island of Lost Souls*. John Carradine turned a female ape into pretty Acquanetta in the *Captive Wild Woman* series, while Bela Lugosi injected himself with an ape-transforming serum in 1943's *The Ape Man*. Apes and humans became intellectual and sociological equals in *The Planet of the Apes* films (q.v.). For most of that series, the simian society was the dominant one, although it experienced internal conflicts between its chimpanzee scientists, orangutan politicians, and gorilla military leaders. The right to teach the theory that man evolved from apes was hotly debated in *Inherit the Wind* (1960), based on the famous Scopes Monkey Trial. A mysterious monolith brought intelligence to earthly apes in the dramatic opening of Stanley Kubrick's *2001: A Space Odyssey* (1968).

Finally, Marlene Dietrich, in one of her most memorable scenes, sang "Hot Voodoo" while wearing a gorilla suit in 1932's *Blonde Venus*. See also **Dupree, Paula (The Ape Woman); King Kong; Planet of the Apes Series.**

Murders in the Rue Morgue (1932); *The Monster Walks* (1932); *Island of Lost Souls* (1933); *King Kong* (1933); *The Wizard of Oz* (1939); *The Ape* (1940); *The Ape Man* (aka *Lock Your Doors*) (1943); *Captive Wild Woman* (1943); *Nabonga* (aka *Gorilla*) (1944); *Mighty Joe Young* (1949); *Bedtime for Bonzo* (1951); *Road to Bali* (1952); *Bonzo Goes to College* (1952); *Monkey Business* (1952); *Phantom of the Rue Morgue* (1954); *Gorilla at Large* (1954); *The Bride and the Beast* (aka *Queen of the Gorillas*) (1958); *Alakazam the Great* (1961); *Konga* (1961); *The Monkey's Uncle* (1965); *Sands of the Kalahari* (1965); *Morgan!* (*Morgan—A Suitable Case for Treatment*) (1966); *Monkey, Go Home* (1967); *2001: A Space Odyssey* (1968); *Planet of the Apes* (1968); *The Barefoot Executive* (1971); *A Cold Night's Death* (1973); *A*P*E* (1976); *Goliathon* (1977); *Every Which Way but Loose* (1978); *The Mafu Cage* (aka *My Sister, My Love*) (1978); *Bye Bye Monkey* (1978); *The Wild and the Free* (1980); *The Ivory Ape* (1980 TVM); *Any Which Way You Can* (1980); *The Incredible Shrinking Woman* (1981); *Going Ape!* (1981); *Greystoke: The Legend of Tarzan, Lord of the Apes* (1984); *Phenomena* (aka *Creepers*) (1984); *In the Shadow of Kilimanjaro* (1986); *Link* (1986); *Project X* (1987); *Gorillas in the Mist* (1988); *Monkey Shines: An Experiment in Terror* (1988); *Animal Behavior* (1989); *The Fifth Monkey* (1990); *Shakma* (1990); *The Entertainers* (1991 TVM); *Monkey Trouble* (1994); *The Lion King* (1994); *Congo* (1995); *The Barefoot Executive* (1995 TVM); *Born to Be Wild* (1995); *Jumanji* (1995); *Dunston Checks In* (1996); *Ed* (1996); *Buddy* (1997); *George of the Jungle* (1997); *Pippi Longstocking* (1997); *Rocketman* (1997); *Rudyard Kipling's The Second Jungle Book: Mowgli and Baloo* (aka *Jungle Book Two*) (1997); *Mighty Joe Young* (1998); *Summer of the Monkeys* (1998); *Babe: Pig in the City* (1998); *The Rugrats Movie* (1998); *Primal Force* (1999 TVM); *Instinct* (1999); *Being John Malkovich* (1999); *Return to Me* (2000)

Apu Trilogy

Satyajit Ray's simple, powerful films about the son of a Brahmin priest brought international attention to Indian cinema in the 1950s. Ray adapted the first film, 1956's *Pather Panchali*, from Bibhuti Bannerji's acclaimed novel. He bought the book's rights for a modest $1,300, but encountered financial problems early in the production. He pawned his wife's jewelry (a last resort in Indian families) before eventually securing backing from the West Bengal government. The film's story dealt with life in a small village as seen through the eyes of Apu, a young boy. He watches his sister die, his father leave to find work, and finally his family forced to move from their home. This visually stunning, emotional drama soon attracted the attention of international critics. It was voted a special award at the 1956 Cannes Film Festival and was subsequently honored by festivals in Berlin, Tokyo, and Denmark. Ray returned to Apu as both a young boy and an adolescent in 1957's *Aparajito*. In 1959's *Apur Sansar*, Apu marries and becomes isolated from village life by his own education.

Father Panchali (aka *Pather Panchali; Song of the Road*) (1956); *The Unvanquished* (aka *Aparajito*) (1957); *The World of Apu* (aka *Apur Sansar*) (1959)

Arthur, King, and the Knights of the Round Table

The legendary 6th century British king, oddly ignored during Hollywood's swashbuckling days, has gradually evolved into one of the cinema's most durable mythic heroes. He was strictly a supporting character in the film versions of Mark Twain's *A Connecticut Yankee in King Arthur's Court*. British comedian Arthur Askey dreamed he was a knight of the Round Table in 1942's *King Arthur Was a Gentleman*. Then in 1953, MGM followed its blockbuster *Ivanhoe* with the gloss-dripping Arthurian spectacle *Knights of the Round Table*. Mel Ferrer made a noble Arthur, with Ava Gardner (beautiful, but not quite right) as Guinevere and dashing Robert Taylor (a bit old, actually) as Lancelot. Despite its dramatic shortcomings, it remained the most complete recounting of the Arthurian legend for almost three decades. The next version of the legend came from an unlikely source, action star Cornel Wilde. He produced, directed, and starred in *The Sword of Lancelot*, a straightforward well-done drama focusing on the romance between Lancelot (Wilde) and Guinevere (Jean Wallace). Brian Aherne made a low-key Arthur. Novelist T.H. White's *The Once and Future King* provided the basis for Disney's animated feature *The Sword in the Stone* (1963) and the Broadway musical/film *Camelot* (1967). The former was a bland tale of Arthur's youth, while the latter benefited from star turns by Richard Harris and Vanessa Redgrave as Arthur and Guinevere. In the 1970s, French directors Robert Bresson and Eric Rohmer contributed the atmospheric, sometimes esoteric, knightly tales *Lancelot of the Lake* and *Perceval*, respectively. The Monty Python troupe spoofed Arthurian films hilariously in their finest feature, 1975's *Monty Python and the Holy Grail*. Disney added an unnecessary remake of *A Connecticut Yankee* in 1979, dubiously titled *Unidentified Flying Oddball*. Two years later, director John Boorman brought atmosphere, mystery, and sexuality to his epic *Excalibur*. Based on Malory's *Le Morte d'Arthur*, Boorman's picture gave equal time to Merlin (played by Nicol Williamson) while telling Arthur's (Nigel Terry) tale in depth. The 1998 two-part TV movie *Merlin* devoted even more footage to the sorcerer, relegating Arthur to a supporting character. *First Knight* (1995) focused again on the love triangle of Arthur (Sean Connery), Guinevere (Julia Ormond), and Lancelot (Richard Gere) with middling results. Malcolm McDowell made a passable Arthur in the otherwise dreadful 1985 TV movie *Arthur the King*, which co-starred Dyan Cannon as a contemporary lass who falls through a hole in Stonehenge and winds up in Camelot. George Romero's heavyhanded 1981 parable *Knightriders* told the Camelot story in a contemporary setting with Ed Harris as the leader of a troupe of jousting motorcycle riders. In *Seaview Knights* (1994), a bank robber becomes delusional after a head injury and believes he is King Arthur.

A Connecticut Yankee (1931); *King Arthur Was a Gentleman* (1942); *A Connecticut Yankee in King Arthur's Court* (1949); *Knights of the Round Table* (1953); *The Black Knight* (1954); *The Sword of Lancelot* (aka *Lancelot and Guinevere*) (1963); *The Sword in the Stone* (1963); *Siege of the Saxons* (1964); *Camelot* (1967); *Gawain and the Green Knight* (1973); *Lancelot of the Lake* (aka *Lancelot du Lac; Le Graal; The Grail*) (1974); *Monty Python and the Holy Grail* (1975); *King Arthur, the Young Warlord* (1975); *Perceval* (aka *Perceval le Gallois*) (1978); *Unidentified Flying Oddball* (aka *A Spaceman in King Arthur's Court*) (1979); *Excalibur* (1981); *Knightriders* (1981); *The Sword of the Valiant* (1982); *Arthur the King* (1985 TVM); *Waxwork II: Lost in Time* (1991); *Army of Darkness* (aka *Army of Darkness: Evil Dead 3*) (1993); *Seaview Knights* (1994); *First Knight* (1995); *A Kid in King Arthur's Court* (1995); *Merlin* (1998 TVM); *Quest for Camelot* (1998); *A Knight in Camelot* (1998 TVM)

Artists *see* Painters

Assumed Identity

The plot device where one person assumes another's identity has evolved into one of the cinema's most reliable conventions. Frequently, it is paired with related plotlines such as amnesia, disguises, lookalikes (qq.v.), and undercover cops. For example, amnesiac Gregory Peck assumed the identity of asylum director Dr. Edwardes in Hitchcock's *Spellbound*. In *The Great Impostor* (1960), Tony Curtis played real-life master of disguises Ferdinand Demara, who assumed the identities of a prison warden, a naval doctor, a school teacher, and others. Ronald Colman played a dashing gent who substitutes for his lookalike, the king of Ruritania, in an effort to thwart an usurper in 1937's *The Prisoner of Zenda*. Undercover cops and FBI agents with fake identities have been played by Laurence Fishburne (*Deep Cover*) and Johnny Depp (*Donnie Brasco*). Despite the utilities of these plotline pairings, some of the more intriguing films about assumed identities involve neither amnesia, disguises, nor lookalikes. In 1975's *The Passenger*, Jack Nicholson played a man so unhappy with his own life that he assumed the identity of a dead man he knew nothing about. In *The Inspector General* (1949), Danny Kaye was mistaken for the title character, but he readily assumed the role once he realized the power it possessed. Gerard Depardieu was executed for assuming another man's identity in *The Return of Martin Guerre* (1982), even though everyone seemed to prefer him to the real Martin Guerre. Richard Gere experienced a similar fate in the 1993 Americanized version *Sommersby*. Poor Janet Leigh woke up from her wedding night with a stranger in her bed claiming to be her husband in the appropriately-titled *Honeymoon with a Stranger* (1969). Still, that's not as bad as Gloria Talbott, who actually married an alien who had assumed her fiancé's identity in *I Married a Monster from Outer Space* (1958). See also **Amnesia; Disguises; Lookalikes.**

The Masquerader (1933); *Maniac* (1934); *The Great Impersonation* (1935); *The Prisoner of Zenda* (1937); *The Great Impersonation* (1942); *The Impostor* (aka *Strange Confession*) (1944); *Spellbound* (1945); *Detour* (1945); *Hollow Triumph* (aka *The Scar*) (1948); *The Inspector General* (1949); *No Man of Her Own* (1949); *The House on Telegraph Hill* (1951); *Scarlet Angel* (1952); *Arrow in the Dust* (1954); *I Married a Monster from Outer Space* (1958); *Libel* (1959); *The Great Impostor* (1960); *Purple Noon* (aka *Plein Soleil*) (1960); *Honeymoon with a Stranger* (1969 TVM); *One More Time* (1970); *The Passenger* (1975); *Kagemusha* (aka *Kagemusha, the Shadow Warrior*) (1980); *The Ninth Configuration* (aka *Twinkle, Twinkle Killer Kane*) (1980); *The Return of Martin Guerre* (1982); *I Married a Shadow* (1982); *The Impostor* (1984 TVM); *Critical Condition* (1987); *The Killing Time* (1987); *The Couch Trip* (1988); *Caroline?* (1990 TVM); *Paper Mask* (1990); *Taking Care of Business* (1990); *The Stranger Within* (1990 TVM); *Shattered* (1991); *True Identity* (1991); *Chameleon Street* (1991); *White Sands* (1992 TVM); *Deep Cover* (1992); *Body Language* (1992 TVM); *Sommersby* (1993); *Dave* (1993); *Dream Lover* (1994); *The Counterfeit Contessa* (1994 TVM); *Princess Caraboo* (1994); *Houseguest* (1995); *Mrs. Winterbourne* (1996); *The Truth About Cats and Dogs* (1996); *The Associate* (1996); *Donnie Brasco* (1997); *Face/Off* (1997); *Trial and Error* (1997); *The Man Who Knew Too Little* (1997); *The Man in the Iron Mask* (1998); *Mr. Headmistress* (1998 TVM); *There's Something About Mary* (1998); *The Impostors* (1998); *Blue Streak* (1999); *The Talented Mr. Ripley* (1999)

Asteroids, Meteors, and Comets

In 1993, a House of Representatives Committee on Science, Space, and Technology heard congressional testimony on "The Threat of Large Earth-Orbit Crossing Asteroids." Five years later, Hollywood offered not one, but two, big-budget science fiction films that hypothesized what might happen if the Earth collided with an asteroid or comet. Studio insiders fretted that the competing films would cancel each other out at the box-office (which happened the year before with the lava-spewing rivals *Dante's Peak* and *Volcano*). However, moviegoers embraced both *Deep Impact* and *Armageddon*, turning both disaster epics into big hits. Despite the hype and costly special effects that accompanied these films, their premise was far from original. In 1930, Abel Gance (*Napoleon*) produced *End of the World*, a preachy treatise about a comet hurtling toward Earth. In 1951, producer George Pal offered a sobering scenario with *When Worlds Collide*, a thoughtful yarn noted for its then state-of-the-art special effects and for being one of the few films in which Earth is actually destroyed (see **End of the World/Post-Apocalypse**). Other films in which Earth is threatened by an asteroid, comet, or meteor include: *The Day the Sky Exploded* (1958), *War of the Planets* (1965), *A Fire in the Sky* (1978), *Meteor* (1979), *Night of the Comet* (1984), and *Asteroid* (1997). Of course, some meteors and comets have threatened Earthlings in ways other than a massive collision. In *The Invisible Ray* (1936), a meteor emitting "radium X" transformed scientist Boris Karloff into a mad man with a deadly touch. Karloff encountered a similar problem in *Die, Monster, Die!* (1965), in which a radioactive meteorite turned family members into mutants. An unofficial remake, *The Curse* (q.v.) featured a meteorite that turned a family into murderous zombies. Clever aliens have used comets and meteors as modes of transportation. Halley's Comet delivered vampire-like aliens in Tobe Hooper's *Lifeforce* (1985), while meteorites delivered and later activated people-eating alien plants in *The Day of the Triffids* (1963). To make matters worse, the meteorites in *Triffids* blinded most of the Earth's population. Several movies have taken place on asteroids, although the one in *Phantom Planet* (1961) merits special mention for being invisible. See also **Disaster Movies**.

End of the World (1930); *The Invisible Ray* (1936); *The Heavenly Body* (1943); *When Worlds Collide* (1951); *Riders to the Stars* (1954); *The Day the Sky Exploded* (aka *Death from Outer Space*) (1958); *Valley of the Dragons* (1961); *The Phantom Planet* (1961); *The Day of the Triffids* (1963); *War Between the Planets* (aka *Planet on the Prowl*) (1965); *Die, Monster, Die!* (aka *Monster of Terror*) (1965); *A Fire in the Sky* (1978 TVM); *Meteor* (1979); *Night of the Comet* (1984); *The Curse* (aka *The Farm*) (1987); *The Meteor Man* (1993); *Super Mario Bros.* (1993); *August in the Water* (aka *Mizu No Naka No Hachigatsu*) (1995); *Asteroid* (1997 TVM); *Doomsday Rock* (1997 TVM); *Falling Fire* (1998); *Meteorites!* (1998 TVM); *Deep Impact* (1998); *Armageddon* (1998); *Dinosaur* (2000)

Asylums

The line between sanity and madness has frequently been portrayed as a thin one in films with an asylum setting. A common plot device has a sane person feigning insanity in order to be committed to an asylum. Journalist Peter Breck pulled the trick to win a Pulitzer Prize in Samuel Fuller's *Shock Corridor* (1963). He lost his mind as a result. The following year's *Shock Treatment* found Stuart Whitman as an actor who entered an asylum to discover where Roddy McDowell hid a fortune. However, the most famous picture along these lines was the 1975 multiple Oscar winner *One Flew Over the Cuckoo's Nest*. Jack Nicholson's Randle Patrick McMurphy faked temporary insanity because he preferred a mental institution over hard labor at a prison. He discovered that the patients were saner—in their own way—than the medical staff. Alan Bates made a similar observation in 1966's *King of Hearts*, in which a group of inmates escaped into an evacuated town during World War I. Bates learned that these charming lunatics may be "touched," but at least they were not fighting a war to destroy each other. Another oft-filmed plot—sane people who are revealed to be mad—has been featured prominently in *The Cabinet of Dr. Caligari* and *The Ninth Configuration*. A highly influential expressionistic film, *Caligari* (1919) is ultimately the vision of a lunatic, for in its famous closing scene, the narrator is revealed to be a patient recounting the story to the head of an asylum. William Peter Blatty's *The Ninth Configuration* (1980) takes a similar theme one step further—the asylum director (Stacy Keach) turns out to be a mad impostor. Other movies which take place principally within the confines of an asylum include *Bedlam*, *The Snake Pit*, and *Marat/Sade*. Escaped inmates are played for laughs in *Road Show* and horror in *Alone in the Dark*. *Frances*, the true story of actress Frances Farmer, and the James Stewart comedy *Harvey* have memorable closing scenes in mental institutions. See also **Hospitals**; **Psychiatrists**.

The Cabinet of Dr. Caligari (1919); *Road Show* (1941); *Random Harvest* (1942); *Spellbound* (1945); *Bedlam* (1946); *The Snake Pit* (1948); *Behind Locked Doors* (1948); *Harvey* (1950); *Blood of the Vampire* (1958); *Suddenly, Last Summer* (1959); *The Hideout* (1961); *The Cabinet of Dr. Caligari* (1962); *Shock Corridor* (1963); *The Caretakers* (aka *Borderlines*) (1964); *Shock Treatment* (1964); *Signpost to Murder* (1965); *King of Hearts* (1966); *Marat/Sade* (1967); *The Big Cube* (1969); *The Night Visitor* (1970); *Asylum* (aka *House of Crazies*) (1972); *Don't Look in the Basement* (1973); *Frankenstein and the Monster from Hell* (1973); *One Flew Over the Cuckoo's Nest* (1975); *High Anxiety* (1977); *I Never Promised You a Rose Garden* (1977); *Down the Ancient Stairs* (1977); *The Other Side of Hell* (1978 TVM); *Dracula* (1979); *The Ninth Configuration* (aka *Twinkle, Twinkle Killer Kane*) (1980); *Alone in the Dark* (1982); *Frances* (1982); *Hellhole* (1985); *The Dream Team* (1989); *Crazy People* (1990); *Committed* (1990); *Disturbed* (1991); *Against Her Will: An Incident in Baltimore* (1992 TVM); *Without Consent* (1994 TVM); *Asylum* (1997)

Atomic Bombs

The atomic bomb has been the subject of earnest fact-based dramas, escapist science fiction, chilling thrillers, and one wild satire. The fact-based films began with 1947's *The Beginning or the End*, a stilted, but historically interesting, government-approved story of the Manhattan Project. The personal drama behind the bombing of Hiroshima was better explored in 1952's *Above and Beyond* and in the 1980 TV movie *Enola Gay: The Men, the Mission, the Atomic Bomb*. PBS's American Playhouse produced 1986's *Desert Bloom*, a perceptive family drama set in Nevada during the 1950s atomic bomb tests. Another American Playhouse production, 1983's *Testament* (1983), featured a powerful performance by Jane Alexander as a mother coping with her family's survival in the aftermath of an atomic explosion. It easily eclipsed the similar, heavily-hyped 1983 TV-film *The Day After*. Both films owe a minor debt to Ray Milland's 1962 B-movie *Panic in the Year Zero*, a taut tale of a family's struggle to survive in a post-atomic world, and a major debt to Peter Watkins' bleak *The War Game* (1967). Using a pseudo-documentary approach, Watkins showed what an atomic bomb would do to London. It's a brutal, frightening picture — so scary that its sponsor, the British Broadcasting Company, refused to air it on television. Today, it's shown frequently in conjunction with anti-nuclear protests. On a more positive note, scientists have used atomic devices for worthy purposes, such as destroying city-crunching monsters like 1953's *The Beast from 20,000 Fathoms*. Ironically, as in the case of *The Beast*, many of these creatures were also created by atomic bomb testing. Mutant humans worshipped an atomic bomb in *Beneath the Planet of the Apes* (see **Planet of the Apes**) (1970). It was detonated in the film's climax and destroyed the world. At the conclusion of 1964's *Fail Safe*, President Henry Fonda ordered the atomic destruction of New York City (while his family was there) to avoid a nuclear confrontation with the Soviet Union. Other thrillers pale in comparison, although *The Bedford Incident* (1965) served as a potent reminder of just how easily an atomic war can be initiated. Industrious teenagers almost caused nuclear war in *WarGames* (1983) and *The Manhattan Project* (1986). In the latter film, a high school student built an atomic bomb to prove a point — a sobering premise despite an insufficient amount of credibility. The only film to effectively poke fun at atomic bombs and the threat of nuclear war remains Stanley Kubrick's *Dr. Strangelove, or How I Learned to Stop Worrying and Love the Bomb* (1964). Kubrick's black comedy closed with a classic image: Slim Pickens riding a falling bomb bronco-style to the closing strains of "We'll Meet Again." See also **End of the World/Post-Apocalyse**.

The Beginning or the End (1947); *Children of Hiroshima* (1952); *Above and Beyond* (1952); *The Beast from 20,000 Fathoms* (1953); *The 49th Man* (1953); *Split Second* (1953); *Port of Hell* (1954); *The Flight That Disappeared* (1961); *Panic in the Year Zero* (1962); *Dr. Strangelove, or How I Learned to Stop Worrying and Love the Bomb* (1964); *Fail Safe* (1964); *The Bedford Incident* (1965); *Finders Keepers* (1966); *The War Game* (1967); *The Day the Fish Came Out* (1967); *Beneath the Planet of the Apes* (1970); *Enola Gay: The Men, the Mission, the Atomic Bomb* (1980 TVM); *The Atomic Cafe* (1982); *Testament* (1983); *The Day After* (1983 TVM); *WarGames* (1983); *One Night Stand* (1984); *Threads* (1985); *Desert Bloom* (1986); *The Manhattan Project* (1986); *Day One* (1989 TVM); *Fat Man and Little Boy* (1989); *True Lies* (1994); *Hiroshima* (1995 TVM); *Broken Arrow* (1996); *Executive Decision* (1996); *Mulholland Falls* (1996); *The Rock* (1996); *Warhead* (1996); *The Peacemaker* (1997); *The World Is Not Enough* (1999); *Fail Safe* (2000 TVM)

Ator

Shortly after achieving (very) minor celebrity status playing *Tarzan, the Ape Man* (1981) opposite Bo Derek, hunky Miles O'Keeffe landed in this brief Italian sword-and-sorcery (q.v.) series. Aside from poor dubbing and O'Keeffe's inept thesping, these films are notable for their atrocious special effects (e.g., the hilarious giant spider slain by Ator in the original). Incredibly, Sean Connery played O'Keeffe's father in the non–Atorian *Sword of the Valiant* (1982). Meanwhile, Ator's son (Eric Allen Kramer) hit the quest trail to free Margaret Lenzey in 1990's *Quest for the Mighty Sword*, a direct-to-videotape release in the U.S. See also **Sword and Sorcery**.

Ator, the Fighting Eagle (1983); *Blademaster* (aka *Ator, the Invincible*) (1984); *Iron Warrior* (1987); *Quest for the Mighty Sword* (1990)

Auto Racing

The high-velocity thrills of auto racing date back to Howard Hawks's 1932 speedway drama *The Crowd Roars* with James Cagney as a cocky driver. Yet, despite other vintage efforts like *Speed* (1936), *Indianapolis Speedway* (a 1939 remake of *The Crowd Roars*) and *The Big Wheel* (1949), auto racing was virtually ignored by filmmakers until the late 1950s. The sport's grass-roots popularity grew rapidly in the early 1960s and so did the number of big screen racing dramas. Some pictures catered to Southern stock car fans (e.g., 1960's *Thunder in Carolina*), while others offered European locales and sleek formula cars (e.g., 1963's *The Young Racers*). The common denominator in all these films was an inexpensive look supplemented by plenty of stock footage. Then, in 1966, director John Frankenheimer shifted racing films into high gear with his visually spectacular (but emotionally shallow) epic *Grand Prix*. With its trendy split-screen effects and international cast, *Grand Prix* made it fashionable for big stars to get behind the wheel. Paul Newman and Robert Wagner played pit stop rivals in 1969's *Winning* and Steve McQueen took to the track in 1971's *Le Mans*. Other movies substituted real-life stories for big-name stars. Stock car legend Richard Petty played himself in 1972's *Smash-Up Alley*. Jeff Bridges portrayed Junior Jackson in *The Last American Hero* (1973), while his brother Beau played another race car driver in *Heart Like a Wheel* (1983), the biography of drag racing champion Shirley "Cha Cha" Muldowney (Bonnie Bedelia). Beau was also in *Greased Lightning* (1977), the story of Wendell Scott (Richard Pryor), professional racing's first black driver. Of course, not all auto racing films have taken place at racetracks. Cross-country races have made popular film subjects ever since two genteel couples raced their antique roadsters across the English countryside in 1953's *Genevieve*. Blake Edwards's 1965 comedy *The Great Race* added a bevy of stars to the cross-country racing plot — a formula that's been duplicated in numerous films such as *Those Daring Young Men in Their Jaunty Jalopies* (1969), *Cannonball Run* (1981), and *Speed Zone* (1989). College campus cult movie *Death Race 2000* (1975) featured a cross-country race in which drivers earned points for running down pedestrians. See also **Automobiles** (for nonracing films); **Herbie, the Love Bug**.

The Crowd Roars (1932); *Racing Youth* (1932); *Speed* (1936); *Indianapolis Speedway* (1939); *The Big Wheel* (1949); *To Please a Lady* (1950); *Genevieve* (1953); *Race for Life* (1954); *Johnny Dark* (1954); *The Racers* (aka *Such Men Are Dangerous*) (1955); *Checkpoint* (1956); *The Killing* (1956); *The Devil's Hairpin* (1957); *Speed Crazy* (1959); *Thunder in Carolina* (1960); *The Green Helmet* (1961); *The Young Racers* (1963); *The Killers* (1964); *The Lively Set* (1964); *Viva Las Vegas* (aka *Love in Las Vegas*) (1964); *The Great Race* (1965); *Red Line 7000* (1965); *Fireball 500* (1966); *Grand Prix* (1966); *Spinout* (aka *California Holiday*) (1966); *A Man and a Woman* (1966); *Thunder Alley* (1967); *Fireball Jungle* (1968); *Track of Thunder* (1968); *Speed Lovers* (1968); *Speedway* (1968); *The Wild Racers* (1968); *Those Daring Young Men in Their Jaunty Jalopies* (aka *Monte Carlo or Bust*) (1969); *Drive Hard, Drive Fast* (1969 TVM); *The Love Bug* (1969); *Pit Stop* (1969); *Winning* (1969); *The Challengers* (1969 TVM); *Le Mans* (1971); *Corky* (aka *Lookin' Good*) (1971); *Smash-Up Alley* (aka *43: The Petty Story*) (1972); *Baffled*

(1972 TVM); *The Last American Hero* (aka *Hard Driver*) (1973); *Death Race 2000* (1975); *Win, Place or Steal* (1975); *Cannonball* (aka *Carquake*) (1976); *The Gumball Rally* (1976); *Bobby Deerfield* (1977); *Checkered Flag or Crash* (1977); *Greased Lightning* (1977); *Bob Johnson and His Fantastic Speed Circus* (1978 TVM); *The Betsy* (aka *Harold Robbins' The Betsy*) (1978); *Cannonball Run* (1981); *Safari 3000* (1982); *Six Pack* (1982); *Heart Like a Wheel* (1983); *Stroker Ace* (1983); *Cannonball Run II* (1984); *Born to Race* (1988); *Speed Zone* (1989); *Days of Thunder* (1990); *Checkered Flag* (1990)

Autobiographical Films

Many people have played themselves on film, but few have played themselves in film biographies. The reasons are obvious: the scarcity of motion picture biographies of living persons; the fact that "real" people do not necessarily make believable actors; and the image problem — that of having a big ego — created by portraying oneself in a favorable light. Sports players dominated early film autobiographies, tracing the careers of boxer Joe Louis (*Spirit of Youth*), baseball legend Jackie Robinson (*The Jackie Robinson Story*), track star Bob Mathias (*The Bob Mathias Story*), and football players Tom Harmon (*Harmon of Michigan*) and Elroy "Crazylegs" Hirsch (*Crazylegs*). None of these one-time actors went on to pursue an acting career (though Harmon's son Mark eventually did). Boxing great Muhammad Ali once said: "When you're as great as I am, it's hard to be humble." So naturally, he played himself in the modestly-titled biopic *The Greatest* (1977). Actresses Ann Jillian, Sophia Loren, Shirley MacLaine, Patty Duke, and Suzanne Somers all played themselves in made-for-TV biographies. MacLaine's film was adapted from her best-selling autobiography *Out on a Limb*. Ray Charles also appeared as himself in 1964's *Ballad in Blue*. To date, the best autobiographical film remains 1955's *To Hell and Back*, in which Audie Murphy traced his own rise from farm boy to the nation's most decorated soldier in World War II to movie star. Although not autobiographical, Will Rogers, Jr., played his father in *The Will Rogers Story* (1952) and Marie Osmond played her mother in *Side by Side: The True Story of the Osmond Family* (1982). In the following list, the subject's name is included in parentheses unless specified in the title. See also **Film Star Biographies; Pop, Rock, and Country Singer Biographies.**

Spirit of Youth (1937) (Joe Louis); *Harmon of Michigan* (1941) (Tom Harmon); *The Fabulous Dorseys* (1947); *The Jackie Robinson Story* (1950); *Crazylegs* (*Crazylegs, All American*) (1953) (Elroy Hirsch); *The Bob Mathias Story* (aka *The Flaming Torch*) (1954); *To Hell and Back* (1955) (Audie Murphy); *Rock Around the World* (aka *The Tommy Steele Story*) (1957); *Ballad in Blue* (aka *Blues for Lovers*) (1964) (Ray Charles); *Smash-Up Alley* (aka *43: The Petty Story*) (1972) (Richard Petty); *The Greatest* (1977) (Muhammad Ali); *Sophia Loren: Her Own Story* (1980 TVM); *Victims for Victims — The Theresa Saldana Story* (1984 TVM); *Out on a Limb* (1987 TVM) (Shirley MacLaine); *The Ann Jillian Story* (1988 TVM); *Call Me Anna* (1990 TVM) (Patty Duke); *Keeping Secrets* (1991 TVM) (Suzanne Somers); *Miss America: Behind the Crown* (1992 TVM) (Carolyn Sapp); *Tears and Laughter: The Joan and Melissa Rivers Story* (1994 TVM); *Never Say Never: The Deidre Hall Story* (1995 TVM); *Private Parts* (1997) (Howard Stern)

Automobiles

While a number of auto-oriented movies revolve around auto racing (q.v.), they represent but one model in an eclectic line of car pictures. More imaginative auto movies have featured flying vehicles, gimmicky cars, living vehicles, and high-speed car chases. Airborne autos appeared in the TV movie *M.A.N.T.I.S.* (1994) and the children's fantasies *The Absent Minded Professor* (1961), its remake *Flubber* (1997), and *Chitty Chitty Bang Bang* (1968). The latter film was adapted from a book by Ian Fleming, whose secret agent James Bond encountered an AMC Matador-turned-airplane (!) in *The Man with the Golden Gun* (1974). Bond movies are well-known for Q's gimmick-laden cars, the most memorable being the Aston Martin in *Goldfinger* (1964). It boasted radar, machine guns, a smokescreen device, and an ejector seat that shot unwanted passengers out the roof. Its nearest competitor, gimmick-wise, was the Batmobile from 1989's *Batman*. In addition to an impressive battery of Bat-weapons, the Batmobile could be maneuvered at high speed by remote control and cover itself with protective armor in a matter of seconds. The next step up from remote-controlled vehicles are living ones. Alas, most self-functioning vehicles have exhibited a bad streak. *Christine*, a bright-red '58 Plymouth, mowed down quite a few teens after deciding she had been insulted. *The Car* (1977) proved to be equally troublesome, as did other independent-minded vehicles in *Killdozer* (1974), *The Hearse* (1980), *Nightmares* (1983), *Maximum Overdrive* (1986), and *The Wraith* (1986). There have been friendly autos, though, such as Herbie the Love Bug (q.v.), a romance-minded Volkswagen Beetle which starred in four Disney movies. On television, Ann Sothern was reincarnated as a 1928 Porter in the 1965-66 sitcom *My Mother the Car*. In Steven Spielberg's 1971 TV movie *Duel*, the director showed only fleeting shots of the driver of the truck dead-set on running Dennis Weaver off the road. Another 1971 picture, *Vanishing Point*, starred Barry Newman as an obsessed driver who turns a wager (Denver to San Francisco in 15 hours) into a high speed death drive. Consisting mostly of highway car chase footage, *Vanishing Point* attracted an enthusiastic youth audience and set the pattern for similar low-budget outings like *Dirty Mary, Crazy Larry* (1974), *Eat My Dust!* (1976), and *Grand Theft Auto* (1977). However, the most spectacular car chases of the 1970s and 1980s consisted of single extended sequences in cop thrillers, a practice perfected in the classic high-speed pursuit through San Francisco in 1967's *Bullitt*. Some films integrated the chase into the plot (e.g., *The French Connection*), while others hyped the chase scene as the main selling point (e.g., *The Seven-Ups*). Elaborate chase scenes faded in the 1980s, though William Friedkin staged a nail-grinding drive down a wrong-way street in 1985's *To Live and Die in L.A.* The 1988 Dirty Harry picture *The Dead Pool* spoofed the *Bullitt* chase with a scene of Harry being pursued through San Francisco by a remote-controlled toy roadster carrying a bomb. Of related interest, *Free for All*, *The Formula*, and *The Water Engine* dealt with the invention of more cost-efficient gasoline. The cars in 1975's *Idaho Transfer* used people for fuel. See also **Auto Racing; Buses; Chauffeurs; Herbie, the Love Bug; Taxi Drivers; Truck Drivers.**

Excuse My Dust (1951); *Jalopy* (1953); *Inside Detroit* (1955); *Young and Wild* (1958); *The Absent Minded Professor* (1961); *The Yellow Rolls Royce* (1964); *Goldfinger* (1964); *Chitty Chitty Bang Bang* (1968); *The Reivers* (aka *The Yellow Winton Flyer*) (1969); *Traffic* (aka *Trafic*) (1970); *Duel* (1971 TVM); *Vanishing Point* (1971); *Two-Lane Blacktop* (1971); *Killdozer* (1974 TVM); *Dirty Mary, Crazy Larry* (1974); *Cars That Eat People* (aka *The Cars That Ate Paris*) (1974); *Gone in 60 Seconds* (1974); *The Man with the*

Golden Gun (1974); *Idaho Transfer* (1975); *Eat My Dust!* (1976); *The Van* (1976); *Car Wash* (1976); *The Car* (1977); *Double Nickels* (1977); *Grand Theft Auto* (1977); *Corvette Summer* (1978); *Zero to Sixty* (1978); *The Charge of the Model Ts* (1979); *The Hearse* (1980); *Used Cars* (1980); *The Last Chase* (1981); *Christine* (1983); *Nightmares* (1983); *Repo Man* (1984); *Back to the Future* (1985); *Car Trouble* (1985); *Maximum Overdrive* (1986); *Black Moon Rising* (1986); *Gung Ho* (1986); *The Wraith* (1986); *Ford: The Man and the Machine* (1987 TVM); *Tucker: The Man and the Dream* (1988); *Dangerous Curves* (1988); *Batman* (1989); *Coupe De Ville* (1990); *The Ambulance* (1990); *Wheels of Terror* (1990 TVM); *Drive Like Lightning* (1992 TVM); *M.A.N.T.I.S.* (1994 TVM); *The Van* (1996); *Crash* (1997); *Flubber* (1997); *Captured* (1998); *Gone in Sixty Seconds* (aka *Gone in 60 Seconds*) (2000)

Babies

Infants have often exhibited a total disregard for adults, dropping in on unlikely fathers and unwed mothers at the most inconvenient times. *The Three Godfathers*, the story of three tough bandits who "adopt" an orphaned baby, has been filmed at least seven times as: *Bronco Billy and the Baby* (1909), *Three Godfathers* (1916), *Marked Men* (1920), *Hell's Heroes* (1929), *Three Godfathers* (1936), *Three Godfathers* (1948), and *The Godchild* (1974 TVM). John Ford's 1948 version remains the most popular, with John Wayne, Pedro Armendariz, and Harry Carey, Jr., as the improbable parents. *The Baby and the Battleship* (1956) updated the premise and increased the number of dads, but still derived its humor out of showing macho males struggling helplessly to care for a little one. The same sturdy plot surfaced again in the 1985 French comedy *Three Men and a Cradle* and its 1987 American remake *Three Men and a Baby*. However, the most unlikely fathers were the dads-to-be in *Night of the Blood Beast* (1958), *Rabbit Test* (1978), and *Junior* (1994)—unusual films about pregnant *men*. Unexpected infants provided the source of obvious misunderstandings for bachelorettes Ginger Rogers and Debbie Reynolds in the comedy *Bachelor Mother* (1939) and its remake *Bundle of Joy* (1956). Betty Hutton forgot who got her pregnant in Preston Sturges' *Miracle of Morgan's Creek* (1944), but her troubles ended when she gave birth to sextuplets. Tragically, no one believed the young mothers-to-be who claimed to have been blessed with immaculate conceptions in *Agnes of God* and *Hail Mary* (both 1985). A psychotic woman conceived (sans husband) "children of rage" in David Cronenberg's complex chiller *The Brood* (1979). Undesirable babies surprised their mothers in *Rosemary's Baby* (1968), *It's Alive* (1974), *The Stranger Within* (1974), *The Devil Within Her* (1975), and, most disturbingly, David Lynch's *Eraserhead* (1977). *Bobbikins* (1960), a baby who could talk like an adult, was surely a shock to his parents, too. Finally, some movies have dealt with societies which outlawed the birth of babies, as in 1971's *Zero Population Growth* and its TV movie equivalent *The Last Child* (1971). See also **Babysitters; Child Custody Disputes; Having Babies Series; It's Alive Series; Governesses and Nannies; Look Who's Talking Series; Surrogate Motherhood.**

Bronco Billy and the Baby (1909); *Three Godfathers* (1916); *Marked Men* (1920); *The Kid* (1921); *Hell's Heroes* (1929); *A Bedtime Story* (1933); *Three Godfathers* (aka *Miracle in the Sand*) (1936); *Bachelor Mother* (1939); *East Side of Heaven* (1939); *Little Accident* (1939); *Miracle on Main Street* (1939); *Miracle of Morgan's Creek* (1944); *Three Godfathers* (1948); *Father's Little Dividend* (1951); *The Little Kidnappers* (aka *The Kidnappers*) (1953); *The Baby and the Battleship* (1956); *Bundle of Joy* (1956); *Night of the Blood Beast* (aka *Creature from Galaxy 27*) (1958); *Rock-a-Bye Baby* (1958); *Unwed Mother* (1958); *Bobbikins* (1960); *A Global Affair* (1964); *Rosemary's Baby* (1968); *Zero Population Growth* (aka *ZPG*) (1971); *The Last Child* (1971 TVM); *A Brand New Life* (1973 TVM); *The Godchild* (1974 TVM); *It's Alive* (1974); *The Stranger Within* (1974 TVM); *Unwed Father* (1974 TVM); *The Devil Within Her* (aka *I Don't Want to Be Born*) (1975); *Having Babies* (aka *Giving Birth*) (1976 TVM); *Eraserhead* (1977); *Rabbit Test* (1978); *The Brood* (1979); *Possession* (1981); *He's Not Your Son* (1984 TVM); *Agnes of God* (1985); *Hail Mary* (1985); *Three Men and a Cradle* (1985); *Raising Arizona* (1987); *Baby Boom* (1987); *Three Men and a Baby* (1987); *Look Who's Talking* (1989); *The Guardian* (1990); *The Little Kidnappers* (1990 TVM); *Baby on Board* (1991); *Switched at Birth* (1991 TVM); *Baby Snatcher* (1992 TVM); *Born Too Soon* (1993 TVM); *The Baby of Macon* (1993); *Junior* (1994); *The Unborn II* (1994); *Babyfever* (1994); *Heart of a Child* (1994 TVM); *Moment of Truth: Cradle of Conspiracy* (1994 TVM); *Million Dollar Babies* (1994 TVM); *Baby's Day Out* (1994); *Father of the Bride Part II* (1995); *Never Say Never: The Deidre Hall Story* (1995 TVM); *The Bachelor's Baby* (1996 TVM); *Maternal Instincts* (1996 TVM); *A Smile Like Yours* (1997); *A Thousand Men and a Baby* (1997 TVM); *The Baby Dance* (1998 TVM); *Baby Geniuses* (1999); *Half a Dozen Babies* (1999 TVM); *Two Babies: Switched at Birth* (1999 TVM); *Labor Pains* (2000)

Babysitters

Stalked by psychos and harassed by bratty children, it was inevitable that a babysitter or two would turn out bad. It finally happened in the 1980 TV movie *The Babysitter*, with practically-perfect sitter Stephanie Zimbalist first seducing her employer (much to the chagrin of his wife), then taking over the family and plotting murder. Diane Franklin was equally menacing in 1983's *Summer Girl*. However, nasty babysitters have been the exception, of course. More typically, they have been portrayed as helpless victims in low-grade horror fare like *Fright, Trick or Treats*, and *Halloween* (though Jamie Lee Curtis managed to defend herself reasonably well). The favorite plot of babysitter comedies has been entrusting the child care to hapless males. Actually, Clifton Webb's *Mr. Belvedere* (q.v.) turned out to be a very capable babysitter in 1948's *Sitting Pretty*. However, Jerry Lewis played a stereotypically inept male babysitter in *Rock-a-bye Baby*, but then triplets could tax even a veteran sitter. Overall, though, the perils of babysitting were best explored in the hectic 1987 comedy *Adventures in Babysitting*. Teen sitter Elisabeth Shue and her charges somehow transformed a dull night of TV watching into a wild series of connected adventures through the streets of Chicago. Fortunately, they still made it back home before the parents' return, but only by a matter of seconds. Marilyn Monroe made the least likely of all babysitters, portraying a mentally disturbed one contemplating suicide in 1952's *Don't Bother to Knock*. See also **Babies** (for similar films like *Three Men and a Baby*); **Belvedere, Mr. (Lynn); Governesses and Nannies.**

Sitting Pretty (1948); *Don't Bother to Knock* (1952); *Rock-a-Bye Baby* (1958); *The Babysitter* (1969); *Fright* (1971); *The Babysitter* (aka *Wanted: Babysitter*) (1975); *Halloween* (1978); *When a Stranger Calls* (1979); *The Babysitter* (1980 TVM); *Trick or Treats* (1982); *Summer Girl* (1983 TVM); *First Affair* (1983 TVM); *Rita, Sue and Bob, Too* (1986); *Twisted* (aka *Twisted: A Step Beyond Insanity*) (1986); *Adventures in Babysitting* (1987); *Uncle Buck* (1989); *Don't Tell Mom the Babysitter's Dead* (1991); *The Sitter* (1991 TVM); *The Baby-Sitters Club* (1995); *The Babysitter's Seduction* (1996 TVM)

Back to the Future Series

Robert Zemeckis was a University of Southern California film student when he met wunderkind director Steven Spielberg during the 1973 filming of *Sugarland Express*. Spielberg went on to play a crucial role in Zemeckis' Hollywood career, executive producing his first film (1978's *I Wanna Hold Your Hand*) and directing the Zemeckis–Bob Gale script *1941* (1979). Yet, despite Spielberg's support, Zemeckis found few studios interested in a time travel comedy he co-wrote with Gale in 1980. Then, Zemeckis hit the big time with 1984's lighthearted adventure *Romancing the Stone*. With a big hit to his credit, his script for *Back to the Future* became a hot property. Eric Stoltz, best known for his acclaimed performance as Rocky Dennis in 1985's *Mask*, was cast in the lead role of Marty McFly. However, after five weeks of filming, Zemeckis decided that Stoltz was not right for the part. He replaced Stoltz with Michael J. Fox, who was still filming his TV series *Family Ties*. Despite some mixed reviews (which those critics will probably now deny), 1985's *Back to the Future* went on to become a monster hit and transform Fox from a TV personality to a film star. The film's plot sent teenager Marty back in time (via a modified DeLorean sports car) to 1955. He encounters his parents as high schoolers and, in something of an oedipal twist, has to fend off the advances of his mother. Marty's presence in the past gradually threatens his existence in the future — for if his mother doesn't marry his father, the McFly family will cease to exist. Fox, in a very appealing performance, receives excellent support from Christopher Lloyd as Dr. Emmett Brown, and Lea Thompson and Crispin Glover as Marty's parents. The 1989 sequel, *Back to the Future II*, confused most viewers with a complex plot sending Marty and Doc to various points in time. The series' third installment, *Back to the Future III*, was filmed concurrently and released less than six months later. It finds Marty and Doc in the Old West, with Mary Steenburgen on hand as a love interest for Doc Brown. An animated *Back to the Future* TV series ran briefly on Saturday mornings. See also **Time Travel**.

Back to the Future (1985); *Back to the Future II* (1989); *Back to the Future III* (1990)

Backwoods Feuds

The bitter, deadly feud between the Hatfields and the McCoys has served as the basis for two films: 1949's *Roseanna McCoy* with Joan Evans in the title role and the 1975 TV movie *The Hatfields and the McCoys*, with Karen Lamm as Rose Ann McCoy. However, dramatically, both these films probably owe more to *Romeo and Juliet* than to the real-life feuding families. The fictitious *Trail of the Lonesome Pine* (1936) earned a place in cinema history as the first outdoor movie shot completely in Technicolor. It may also be the best feudin' film, with memorable performances by Fred MacMurray and Henry Fonda. Other serious films about backwood feuds include *Lolly Madonna XXX* (1973) and the subdued Kurt Russell–Kelly McGillis vehicle *Winter People* (1989). Feuds have provided a rich source of gags for many comedians, such as Buster Keaton (*Our Hospitality*), Abbott and Costello (*Comin' Round the Mountain*), the Bowery Boys (*Feudin' Fools*), and Donald O'Connor (*Feudin', Fussin' and A-Fightin'*). The latter film also featured Majorie Main and Percy Kilbride, though not officially as Ma and Pa Kettle (q.v.).

Our Hospitality (1923); *Kentucky Kernels* (1934); *In Old Kentucky* (1935); *Trail of the Lonesome Pine* (1936); *Kentucky Moonshine* (1938); *Feudin', Fussin' and A-Fightin'* (1948); *Roseanna McCoy* (1949); *Comin' Round the Mountain* (1951); *Feudin' Fools* (1952); *Lolly Madonna XXX* (aka *The Lolly Madonna War*) (1973); *The Hatfields and the McCoys* (1975 TVM); *Winter People* (1989)

The Bad New Bears

The combination of Walter Matthau as a beer-guzzling coach and Tatum O'Neal as a foul-mouthed, female pitcher turned this little league baseball comedy into a surprise 1976 hit. Neither star appeared in the 1977 follow-up *The Bad News Bears in Breaking Training*, which weighed down the comedy with a large dose of sentiment. William Devane played the team's new coach. But he too was nowhere to be found in 1978's *The Bad News Bears Go to Japan*, a weak outing that ended the series. Young Jackie Earle Haley was the only Bear to star in all three films. A half-hour CBS TV series aired briefly during 1979. See also **Baseball**.

The Bad News Bears (1976); *The Bad News Bears in Breaking Training* (1977); *The Bad News Bears Go to Japan* (1978)

Baines, Scattergood

Guy Kibbee starred as Clarence Budington Kelland's genial country philosopher in this RKO series. Actually, the films were produced by little Pyramid Pictures Corporation, which convinced RKO that a six-film series based on the popular radio program was bound to be profitable. It wasn't — the public never warmed up to Scattergood, not even when RKO tried to hide the fact that a movie was part of the series (the studio changed the title of *Scattergood Swings It* to *Cinderella Swings It*). Nevertheless, the storekeeper of Coldriver stayed busy for three years, helping horseback orphans (*Scattergood Rides High*) and would-be recording stars (*Cinderella Swings It*).

Scattergood Baines (1941); *Scattergood Meets Broadway* (1941); *Scattergood Pulls the Strings* (1941); *Scattergood Rides High* (1942); *Scattergood Survives a Murder* (1942); *Cinderella Swings It* (aka *Scattergood Swings It*) (1943)

Balboa, Rocky *see* Rocky

Ballet/Ballerinas

The challenge of integrating a dynamic theatrical art form into the confines of cinema has proven to be a difficult task. Consequently, it has been undertaken almost exclusively by filmmakers/ballet lovers, whose artistic successes have been mixed equally with unmitigated failures. British filmmakers Michael Powell and Emeric Pressburger produced two outstanding ballet films, with Powell also contributing a third, less memorable solo effort. The first Powell-Pressburger ballet film was 1948's *The Red Shoes*, which starred real-life ballerina Moira Shearer as a young dancer driven to her death by her inability to choose between ballet and a "normal" life. The highlight of this dazzling, colorful film is a 14-minute ballet of Hans Christian Andersen's fairy tale *The Red Shoes*, brilliantly danced and photographed against stylized sets. The elaborate sets returned in 1951's *Tales of Hoffman*, a fusion of drama, singing, and ballet based on Offenbach's opera and featuring ballerina Shearer again. Powell turned to ballet once more, sans Pressburger, in 1959's all-but-forgotten *Honeymoon*, which featured excerpts from the Spanish ballets "Los Amantes de Teruel" and "El Amor Brujo." The most interesting pre–*Red Shoes* ballet picture was *The Specter of the Rose* (1946), an offbeat drama about a young dancer who is slowly losing his mind. It featured a rare screen appearance by drama teacher Michael Chekhov and the potent presence of Dame Judith Anderson. Gene Kelly, after choreographing a modern ballet for a set piece in *An American in Paris* (1951), incorporated ballet into his all-dance 1957 picture *Invitation to the Dance*. Shot in 1952, this three-part anthology boasted energetic dancing and clever direction (including a combination of live action and cartoon), but it crashed at the box-office and almost ended Kelly's career. In contrast, Herbert Ross's *The Turning Point* (1977) was a solid popular and critical favorite. Shirley MacLaine and Anne Bancroft had the starring roles as a pair of former ballerinas, but Mikhail Baryshnikov stole the film every time he took to the dance floor. Ballets filmed in their entirety have been rare, but have nevertheless been captured in *Peter Rabbit and the Tales of Beatrix Potter* (1971), *Nutcracker* (1982), and *Nutcracker: The Motion Picture* (1986). There have been numerous films, not expressly about ballet, which have featured ballerinas as principal characters. The role call of actresses who have played ballerinas is a varied one: Greta Garbo (*Grand Hotel*); Maureen O'Hara (*Dance, Girl, Dance*); Vivien Leigh (*Waterloo Bridge*); Loretta Young (*The Men in Her Life*); Margaret O'Brien (*The Unfinished Dance*); Janet Leigh *(The Red Danube)*; Gene Tierney (*Never Let Me Go*); and Leslie Caron (*Gaby*). Ballet segments have highlighted many mainstream musicals, though the sequences in *An American in Paris, Oklahoma!* and *On Your Toes* stand out.

Grand Hotel (1932); *On Your Toes* (1939); *Dance, Girl, Dance* (1940); *Waterloo Bridge* (1940); *The Men in Her Life* (1941); *The Dancing Masters* (1943); *Specter of the Rose* (1946); *Carnival* (1946); *The Unfinished Dance* (1947); *The Imperfect Lady* (1947); *The Red Shoes* (1948); *The Red Danube* (1949); *Illicit Interlude* (aka *Summer Play; Summer Interlude*) (1950); *An American in Paris* (1951); *Tales of Hoffman* (1951); *Limelight* (1952); *Never Let Me Go* (1953); *Dance Little Lady* (1955); *Oklahoma!* (1955); *Gaby* (1956); *Meet Me in Las Vegas* (aka *Viva Las Vegas*) (1956); *Invitation to the Dance* (1957); *Angel in a Taxi* (1959); *Honeymoon* (1959); *Vampire and the Ballerina* (1962); *Peter Rabbit and the Tales of Beatrix Potter* (aka *The Tales of Beatrix Potter*) (1971); *The Turning Point* (1977); *Slow Dancing in the Big City* (1978); *Nutcracker* (1982); *The Cowboy and the Ballerina* (1984 TVM); *Nutcracker: The Motion Picture* (1986); *Dancers* (1987); *Dancing for Mr. B: Six Balanchine Ballerinas* (1989); *Brain Donors* (1992); *Tender Heart* (aka *Alciz Shurek; Coeur Fragile*) (1994)

Balloons, Hot Air

Phileas Fogg may be the world's most famous balloonist, but *Around the World in Eighty Days* is but one of several balloon movies (indeed, Phileas's balloon flight is relatively short). Red Buttons and Barbara Eden spent *Five Weeks in a Balloon* in Irwin Allen's 1962 adaptation of Jules Verne's adventure tale. Civil War prisoners escaped via a hot air balloon and blew off course onto a *Mysterious Island* (1961) in another Verne-inspired epic. Toto's mad dash from the Wizard's hot air balloon kept Dorothy from returning home in a conventional fashion in *The Wizard of Oz* (1939). Good thing she kept those ruby slippers. Katharine Hepburn helped two children launch a balloon — and nearly land on an orchestra conductor — in *Olly, Olly, Oxen Free* (1978), while a boy and his grandfather made a transcontinental flight in the 1981

TV movie *Charlie and the Great Balloon Chase*. James Bond (Roger Moore) made an unexpected arrival via hot air balloon in *Octopussy* (1983). Jessica Lange took a pleasure ride with Joan Cusack in 1990's *Men Don't Leave*. Baron von Munchausen created a hot air balloon made of ladies' bloomers in 1989's *The Adventures of Baron Munchausen*. Magical balloons grew from the ground like plants in the Disney TV movie *Balloon Farm* (1999). See also **Airplanes**; **Dirigibles**; **Helicopters**.

Queen of the Jungle (1935); *Penrod's Double Trouble* (1938); *The Wizard of Oz* (1939); *Around the World in Eighty Days* (1956); *Flight of the Lost Balloon* (1961); *Mysterious Island* (1961); *Five Weeks in a Balloon* (1962); *Those Magnificent Men in Their Flying Machines, or How I Flew from London to Paris in 25 Hours 11 Minutes* (aka *Those Magnificent Men in Their Flying Machines*) (1965); *The Great Race* (1965); *Chitty Chitty Bang Bang* (1968); *Charlie Bubbles* (1968); *Olly, Olly, Oxen Free* (aka *The Great Balloon Adventure*) (1978); *Charlie and the Great Balloon Chase* (1981 TVM); *Night Crossing* (1981); *The Flight of the Eagle* (1982); *Ingenjör Andrées Luftfärd* (1982); *Octopussy* (1983); *Cloud Waltzing* (1987 TVM); *The Adventures of Baron Munchausen* (1989); *It Nearly Wasn't Christmas* (1989 TVM); *Men Don't Leave* (1990); *Jefferson in Paris* (1995); *The Avengers* (1998); *Balloon Farm* (1999 TVM); *The World Is Not Enough* (1999); *Mermaid* (2000 TVM)

Bancroft, Brass

A promising young star named Ronald Reagan played secret service agent Brass Bancroft in a series of four Warner Bros. programmers, beginning with 1939's *Secret Service of the Air*. The films were inspired by the memoirs of William H. Moran, a former secret service chief. Reagan's heroics, though, were strictly Saturday afternoon kid's stuff. Brass fought smugglers, counterfeiters, and experimental death rays in his brief career. In real life, Reagan fought Warner Bros. to shelve his second Bancroft film, *Code of the Secret Service*, because he felt it was unfit for release. Director Bryan Foy backed Reagan and Warner Bros. compromised (slightly) by not releasing the film in Los Angeles. Eddie Foy, Jr., the director's brother, played Brass's sidekick Gabby Watters.

Secret Service of the Air (1939); *Code of the Secret Service* (1939); *Smashing the Money Ring* (1939); *Murder in the Air* (1940)

Barbers/Hairdressers

On those rare occasions when hairdressers are featured characters in a film, their profession rarely receives much exposure. Murder witness Kim Basinger could have easily been mistaken for a model instead of a hairdresser in *Nadine* (1987). Likewise, the fact that Frances McDormand's character was a beautician in *Mississippi Burning* (1988) had little bearing on the plot. Still, hairdressers have made a major impact in a handful of films. Warren Beatty played an amorous one in his 1975 hit *Shampoo* and Julie Walters received an Oscar nomination for portraying an uneducated hairdresser seeking to better herself intellectually in 1983's *Educating Rita*. *Sweeney Todd, the Demon Barber of Fleet Street* (1936) was about a barber who killed his customers and turned them into "meat pies." Composer Stephen Sondheim transformed the same story into the Broadway musical smash *Sweeney Todd*.

Smart Money (1931); *Diplomaniacs* (1933); *Sweeney Todd, the Demon Barber of Fleet Street* (1936); *Keep Fit* (1937); *The Great Dictator* (1940); *Abbott and Costello in Hollywood* (aka *Bud Abbott and Lou Costello in Hollywood*) (1945); *Monsieur Beaucaire* (1946); *Wait 'Til the Sun Shines, Nellie* (1952); *The Adventures of Hajji Baba* (1954); *Staircase* (1969); *Five on the Back Hand Side* (1973); *Don Quixote* (1973); *Female Trouble* (1974); *Shampoo* (1975); *Outrageous!* (1977); *Educating Rita* (1983); *Old Enough* (1984); *Nadine* (1987); *Conspiracy of Love* (1987 TVM); *Mississippi Burning* (1988); *Getting It Right* (1989); *Steel Magnolias* (1989); *Earth Girls Are Easy* (1989); *Skin Deep* (1989); *Highway 61* (1991); *Stan and George's New Life* (1991); *Victor's Big Score* (1992); *The Crying Game* (1992); *The Hairdresser's Husband* (1992); *Who's the Man?* (1993); *Poetic Justice* (1993); *Wrestling with Ernest Hemingway* (1993); *The Grass Harp* (1995); *The Beautician and the Beast* (1997); *I Want You* (1998); *Summer of Sam* (1999); *Stigmata* (1999); *The Big Tease* (1999)

The Barrytown Trilogy

Author Roddy Doyle's humorous, affectionate novels about a working-class family living in Barrytown, a suburb of Dublin, provided the source for this well-done film trilogy. Doyle's three books traced the exploits of the Rabbitte family: *The Commitments* was about Jimmy Jr.'s attempts to start a blues band; *The Snapper* (Irish slang for "baby") focused on unwed, pregnant daughter Sharon; and *The Van* put the spotlight on father Jimmy Sr. The screen adaptations followed the same plotline, although the family's name and its members change from film to film. For example, although Colm Meaney played the family patriarch in all three movies, his characters' names were Mr. Rabbitte, Dessie Curley, and Larry. Meany played a supporting role in *The Commitments* (1991), a charming tale merging energetic young performances with great music (including a show-stopping rendition of "Try a Little Tenderness"). It's more of an ensemble picture than *The Snapper* (1993) and *The Van* (1996), which devote most of their running times to Meaney's character — as he tries to discover his daughter's lover in the former film and start a restaurant in a broken-down van in the latter film. His performances, especially in *The Snapper*, capture the joys and frustrations of a goodhearted man dealing with independent children, unemployment, and the Irish soccer team in the World Cup.

The Commitments (1991); *The Snapper* (1993); *The Van* (1996)

Barton, Dick

Barton, a British Dick Tracy (q.v.), evolved from a popular 1948 radio series. Don Stannard played him in three low-budget movies with villains that used "germ bombs" and atomic weapons. The series concluded following the actor's death in 1949.

Dick Barton, Detective (aka *Dick Barton, Special Agent*) (1949); *Dick Barton Strikes Back* (1949); *Dick Barton at Bay* (1950)

Baseball

Football may have been played in more movies, but no sport surpasses baseball in providing subjects for inspirational film biographies. Lou Gehrig, Babe Ruth, Ty Cobb, Dizzy Dean, Grover Cleveland Alexander, Jackie Robinson, Jimmy Piersall, Ron LeFlore, Roy Campanella, and Monty Stratton have all had their stories brought to the screen — often with conviction, almost always with sentiment. Baseball fantasies have proven to be popular, too. In *It Happens Every Spring* (1949), college professor Ray Milland became a star pitcher for St. Louis when he accidentally invented a chemical that repelled wood (i.e., baseball bats). The Devil and an angel turned last-place teams into winners in, re-

spectively, *Damn Yankees* (1958) and *Angels in the Outfield* (1951). In 1989's *Field of Dreams*, Kevin Costner built a baseball diamond in lieu of planting crops, so the legendary Shoeless Joe Jackson and other heavenly ball players would have a place to play their beloved game. Most filmmakers have preferred to gloss over the game's darker days, although John Sayles' *Eight Men Out* (1988) presented a factual account of the 1919 "Black Sox" scandal. Corruption was also an issue in 1984's *The Natural*, an unusual morality tale of a highly-gifted player (Robert Redford) confronted by temptation and evil. Baseball comedies have ranged from the hilarious to the ridiculous, with some of the more successful ones incorporating unusual angles. The 1951 *Rhubarb* was about a baseball team owned by a cat. *The Bad News Bears* (1976) were a team of foul-mouthed little leaguers transformed into winners by beer-guzzling coach Walter Matthau. Abbott and Costello recreated their famous vaudeville baseball routine "Who's on First?" in 1945's *The Naughty Nineties*. Films about female baseball/softball players include *Aunt Mary* (1979), *Squeeze Play* (1980), and the 1992 fact-based hit *A League of Their Own*. See also **The Bad News Bears; Major League Series**.

Fireman, Save My Child (1932); *Elmer the Great* (1933); *Death on the Diamond* (1934); *Alibi Ike* (1935); *The Pride of the Yankees* (1942); *Ladies' Day* (1943); *Whistling in Brooklyn* (1943); *The Naughty Nineties* (1945); *The Babe Ruth Story* (1948); *It Happens Every Spring* (1949); *The Kid from Cleveland* (1949); *The Stratton Story* (1949); *Take Me Out to the Ball Game* (1949); *Kill the Umpire* (1950); *The Jackie Robinson Story* (1950); *Angels in the Outfield* (aka *Angels and the Pirates*) (1951); *Rhubarb* (1951); *The Winning Team* (1952); *The Pride of St. Louis* (1952); *The Kid from Left Field* (1953); *The Big Leaguer* (1953); *Roogie's Bump!* (1954); *The Great American Pastime* (1956); *Fear Strikes Out* (1957); *Damn Yankees* (1958); *Moochie of the Little League* (1959); *Safe at Home!* (1962); *Bang the Drum Slowly* (1973); *It's Good to Be Alive* (1974 TVM); *The Bad News Bears* (1976); *The Bingo Long Travelling All-Stars and Motor Kings* (1976); *Murder at the World Series* (1978 TVM); *One in a Million: The Ron LeFlore Story* (1978 TVM); *Here Come the Tigers* (aka *Manny's Orphans*) (1978); *A Love Affair: The Eleanor and Lou Gehrig Story* (1978 TVM); *Goodbye, Franklin High* (1978); *Aunt Mary* (1979 TVM); *The Kid from Left Field* (1979 TVM); *Squeeze Play* (1980); *The Comeback Kid* (1980 TVM); *Don't Look Back: The Story of Leroy "Satchel" Paige* (1981 TVM); *Chasing Dreams* (1982); *Million Dollar Infield* (1982 TVM); *Tiger Town* (1983 TVM); *Blue Skies Again* (1983); *The Natural* (1984); *Brewster's Millions* (1985); *The Slugger's Wife* (1985); *A Winner Never Quits* (1986 TVM); *Long Gone* (1987 TVM); *Amazing Grace and Chuck* (1987); *Bull Durham* (1988); *Eight Men Out* (1988); *Stealing Home* (1988); *Trading Hearts* (1988); *Major League* (1989); *Field of Dreams* (1989); *Night Game* (1989); *The Court-Martial of Jackie Robinson* (1990 TVM); *Blood Games* (1991); *Pastime* (aka *One Cup of Coffee*) (1991) (about the minor leagues); *Talent for the Game* (1991); *A League of Their Own* (1992); *Mr. Baseball* (1992); *The Babe* (1992); *The Comrades of Summer* (1992 TVM); *The Sandlot* (1993); *Rookie of the Year* (1993); *Cooperstown* (1993 TVM); *The Man from Left Field* (1993 TVM); *Angels in the Outfield* (1994); *The Scout* (1994); *Little Big League* (1994); *Cobb* (1994); *Ed* (1996); *The Fan* (1996); *The Big Squeeze* (1996); *Joe Torre: Curveballs Along the Way* (1997 TVM); *BASEketball* (1998) (a combination of baseball and basketball); *For Love of the Game* (1999); *Mean Streak* (1999); *Angels in the Infield* (2000 TVM); *Perfect Game* (2000)

Basket Case Series

Frank Henenlotter's original *Basket Case* (1982) mixed gore and black comedy with enough wit to earn a cult reputation among midnight movie fans and mainstream film critics. The plot centers on Duane and Belial Bradley, Siamese twins severed at birth by quack doctors who tossed the hideously-deformed Belial into the garbage. Belial survives and eventually gets reunited with Duane (Kevin Van Hentenryck), with whom he has formed a telepathic bond. With Belial in a wicker basket, Duane heads to New York City to take revenge on the unsuspecting doctors. Belial, despite being a homicidal monster, earns viewer sympathy for most of the film (until he kills Duane's girlfriend in a tasteless scene). Shot over three years, *Basket Case*'s reputation can be attributed chiefly to Henenlotter's quirky humor and offbeat supporting characters. These same qualities were present, but to much less effect, in Henenlotter's long-awaited sequel, 1990's *Basket Case 2*. It finds Duane (Van Hentenryck again) and Belial taking refuge in the Staten Island home of Granny Ruth (jazz singer Annie Ross), who provides sanctuary to a variety of freaks. Duane and Belial fall in love with Siamese twins Susan and Eve, but a nosy reporter interrupts their bliss and Susan winds up dead. In *Basket Case 3: The Progeny* (1992), Eve becomes pregnant and has a "litter" of little mutant babies. The children are kidnapped by some nasty Southern deputies, who naturally receive their comeuppance in gruesome fashion. The two sequels borrow their basic premise from Tod Browning's 1932 classic *Freaks*: The "normal" people are portrayed as cruel and thoughtless, while the "freaks" are presented as caring individuals who simply want to be left alone. Unfortunately, neither *Basket Case* sequel can match the first film's inventiveness. Henenlotter fared much better with his gory Frankenstein (q.v.) satire *Frankenhooker* (1990). See also **Twins**.

Basket Case (1982); *Basket Case 2* (1990); *Basket Case 3: The Progeny* (1992)

Basketball

While other sports films, particularly those involving baseball and football, have devoted extensive footage to real-life personalities, basketball movies have emphasized fiction over fact. Naturally, there have been a few exceptions. *The Harlem Globetrotters* (1951) and *Go, Man, Go* (1954) employed realistic settings, even though they took dramatic license with their plots. *Hoosiers* (1986) was a fact-based story about a small-town Indiana high school team which staged an amazing series of upsets en route to a state title. Other fact-based basketball movies include *Passing Glory* (1999), the documentary *Hoop Dreams* (1994), and the TV movie biographies *The Pistol* (1990), *Final Shot: The Hank Gathers Story* (1992), and *Michael Jordan: An American Hero* (1999). However, most basketball movies have opted for make-believe tales which climax in dramatic last-minute "buzzer shots," as in 1977's *One on One*. For a change of pace, *The Absent-Minded Professor* and *Teen Wolf* featured some rather bizarre basketball games. In the former film, professor Fred MacMurray ironed "flubber" onto the shoes of his college's team, allowing the players to bounce higher than the backboard. In *Teen Wolf*, mediocre player Michael J. Fox suddenly transformed into a basketball phenomenon after becoming a werewolf. Anthony Perkins (*Tall Story*) and Robby Benson (*One on One*) played more conventional star players. Inspirational coaches have been played by Robert Mitchum (*That Championship Season*), Bruce Dern (*Drive, He Said*), Gabe Kaplan (*Fast Break*), and Cathy Lee Crosby (*Coach*).

And real-life players have appeared in *Cornbread, Earl and Me* (Jamaal Wilkes), *The Fish That Saved Pittsburgh* (Kareem Abdul Jabbar, Meadowlark Lemon, Julius Erving), and *Amazing Grace and Chuck* (Alex English).

Here Come the Coeds (1945); *The Harlem Globetrotters* (1951); *Go, Man, Go* (1954); *Tall Story* (1960); *The Absent-Minded Professor* (1961); *Drive, He Said* (1971); *Shirts/Skins* (1973 TVM); *Maurie* (aka *Big Mo*) (1973); *Mixed Company* (1974); *Cornbread, Earl and Me* (1975); *One on One* (1977); *The Greatest Thing That Almost Happened* (1977 TVM); *Coach* (1978); *Fast Break* (1979); *The Fish That Saved Pittsburgh* (1979); *Inside Moves* (1980); *The Harlem Globetrotters on Gilligan's Island* (1981 TVM); *That Championship Season* (1982); *Teen Wolf* (1985); *Porky's Revenge* (1985); *Hoosiers* (1986); *Amazing Grace and Chuck* (1987); *Laker Girls* (1990 TVM); *The Pistol* (aka *The Pistol: Birth of a Legend*) (1990); *Heaven Is a Playground* (1991); *One Special Victory* (1991 TVM); *Final Shot: The Hank Gathers Story* (1992 TVM); *White Men Can't Jump* (1998); *Above the Rim* (1994); *Hoop Dreams* (1994); *Blue Chips* (1994); *Forget Paris* (1995); *The Basketball Diaries* (1995); *Slam Dunk Ernest* (1995); *Eddie* (1996); *Space Jam* (1996); *Sunset Park* (1996); *Celtic Pride* (1996); *Rebound: The Legend of Earl "The Goat" Manigault* (1996 TVM); *The Sixth Man* (1997); *Air Bud* (1997); *Flubber* (1997); *He Got Game* (1998); *BASEketball* (1998) (a combination of baseball and basketball); *Passing Glory* (1999 TVM); *Michael Jordan: An American Hero* (1999 TVM); *That Championship Season* (1999 TVM); *Love & Basketball* (2000)

Batman

"Criminals are a superstitious, cowardly lot, so my disguise must be able to strike terror into their hearts — I must be a creature of the night, black, terrible ... a ... a ... a bat!" With that announcement, Bruce Wayne transformed himself into the epic comic book superhero Batman. Created by Bob Kane in 1939, Batman first appeared in *Detective Comics* before getting his own comic book a year later. The Batman mythology may be the most extensive in comic book literature, matched only by Superman. Over the years, *Batman* readers saw the Dark Knight acquire sidekicks in Robin, Batgirl, and Ace, the Bat-Hound (who also wore a mask). There have even been more than one Batman (e.g., one for Earth 1, another for Earth 2) and multiple Robins, too. Yet, despite this extensive literary history, Batman's film appearances have been surprisingly few and, for the most part, uninspired. Two routine movie serials appeared in the 1940s: Batman (Lewis Wilson) fought Japanese saboteurs in *Batman* (1943); Robert Lowery took over the role for *Batman and Robin* (1949), which pitted the Caped Crusader against an evil scientist called The Wizard. In 1966, Batman's popularity soared with the debut of Twentieth Century–Fox's campy TV series starring Adam West and Burt Ward as the Dynamic Duo. The series burned out quickly as TV viewers tired of the corny dialogue and broad performances. However, before the series ended, Fox mounted a big screen version featuring super villains The Riddler (Frank Gorshin), The Penguin (Burgess Meredith), The Joker (César Romero), and The Catwoman (Lee Meriwether). Subsequent attempts to bring Batman to the silver screen failed until Frank Miller's brooding graphic novel *The Dark Knight Returns* appeared in 1986. Miller's work revived interest in Batman and created a dark landscape of Gothic proportions. Director Tim Burton and set designer Anton Furst (who won an Oscar) created a similar world of shadows for the 1989 box-office smash *Batman*. Comic book fans howled when they heard that Michael Keaton, best known for comedy roles like *Beetlejuice*, had been cast as Bruce Wayne/Batman. But Keaton, in a grim and determined portrayal, held his own against a flamboyant performance by Jack Nicholson as The Joker. The film's success resulted in a series, although each entry has been less interesting than its predecessor. Burton and Keaton teamed up again for the visually splendid *Batman Returns* (1992), but the film spent too much time focusing on the origins of the grotesque Penguin (Danny DeVito) and the sensuous Catwoman (Michelle Pfeiffer). Keaton bowed out of the series and was replaced by Val Kilmer for *Batman Forever* (1995). New director Joel Schumacher took a different approach than Burton, injecting more action and making the film more colorful. Unfortunately, the result was an entertaining but forgettable entry that introduced Chris O'Donnell as Robin and featured Jim Carrey as The Riddler. Schumacher also helmed *Batman and Robin* (1997), which introduced George Clooney as the least memorable Batman yet. It also starred O'Donnell, Arnold Schwarzenegger as Mr. Freeze, Uma Thurman as Poison Ivy, and a miscast Alicia Silverstone as Batgirl. Although *Batman Forever* made a lot of money, it cost a lot and most industry insiders labeled it a disappointment. On television, there have been several Batman cartoon series, including the popular *Batman: The Animated Series*, which debuted in 1992. It inspired a theatrical animated feature called *Batman: Mask of the Phantasm* (1993), a direct-to-video sequel *Batman & Mr. Freeze: Subzero* (1998), and a TV movie *The Batman/Superman Movie* (1998). In 1999, *Batman: The Animated Series* was revamped as the futuristic *Batman Beyond* animated series. Its premiere episode was released on videotape as *Batman Beyond—The Movie*. Kevin Conroy provided the voice for Batman in both of the aforementioned animated series. See also **Bats**; **Comic Book Characters**.

Batman (1966); *Batman* (1989); *Batman Returns* (1992); *Batman: Mask of the Phantasm* (1993); *Batman Forever* (1995); *Batman and Robin* (1997); *Batman & Mr. Freeze: Subzero* (1998); *The Batman/Superman Movie* (1998 TVM); *Batman Beyond—The Movie* (1999)

Bats

Although bats have been hanging around in movies for years, they have usually been relegated to supporting roles in vampire films. Even then, though, they have stolen their share of scenes. In *Kiss of the Vampire* (1963), a horde of bats circled the vampire's castle and played a critical role in the destruction of an entire vampire cult. On the lighter side, when vampire Leslie Nielsen transformed into a bat in *Dracula: Dead and Loving It* (1995), the creature still retained Nielsen's head. Despite its promising title, *The Vampire Bat* (1933) wasn't about a bloodsucking bat, but rather a mad scientist (Lionel Atwill) in search of a blood substitute. However, Bela Lugosi successfully raised giant killer bats in *The Devil Bat*—at least, that's how it seemed until the sequel *Devil Bat's Daughter* (1946) revealed that the crazed scientist was actually a kindly researcher. David Warner really did hunt bloodsucking vampire bats in New Mexico in 1979's *Nightwing*. Along similar lines, genetically-mutated bats harassed Utah residents in *Bats* (1999). In *Chosen Survivors* (1974), an unexpected colony of vampire bats caused problems for 11 people living in an underground nuclear fallout shelter. In children's movies, Robin Williams battled bats, along with other unforeseen creatures, in

Jumanji (1995), while Hank Azaria provided the voice for Bartok the bat in the animated musical *Anastasia* (1997). A scientist bitten by a bat turned into a homicidal "bat-man" in *The Bat People* (1974). There are no bats in *The Last Man on Earth* (1964), although Vincent Price believes he survived a vampire plague because he was once bitten by one. Likewise, no bats appear in *The Bat* (1926), *The Bat Whispers* (1931), and *The Bat* (1958)—all three films were based on Mary Roberts Rinehart's novel about a master criminal called The Bat. See also **Batman**; **Birds**; **Vampires**.

The Devil Bat (1940); *Kiss of the Vampire* (aka *Kiss of Evil*) (1963); *Chosen Survivors* (1974); *The Bat People* (aka *It Lives by Night*) (1974); *Last Days of Planet Earth* (aka *Catastrophe 1999: The Prophecies of Nostradamus*) (1974); *Nightwing* (1979); *House by the Cemetery* (1981); *Ace Ventura: Pet Detective* (1994); *Jumanji* (1995); *Dracula: Dead and Loving It* (1995); *Anastasia* (1997); *Bats* (1999); *Bartok the Magnificent* (1999)

Beach Party Series

1959's *Gidget* (q.v.) and 1960's *Where the Boys Are* may have been the first mainstream pictures to put teens on the beach, but AIP's *Beach Party* (1963) was the one that spawned six sequels, accounted for countless clones, and made teen stars of Frankie Avalon and Annette Funicello. The formula was simple: Start with swimsuit-clad teens, add a way-out motorcycle gang, some cameos by aging stars (e.g., Buster Keaton, Elsa Lanchester, Boris Karloff), and plenty of surf music (provided by the likes of Dick Dale and the Del-Tones, the Hondells, and Little Stevie Wonder). Frankie and Annette, who had briefly dated earlier in their careers, displayed a natural chemistry on the screen. Many of their supporting cast appeared in four or more Beach Party films. These "regulars" included: Harvey (*Stalag 17*) Lembeck as bike gang leader Eric Von Zipper; singer Donna Loren; dancer Candy Johnson; John Ashley, usually cast as Frankie's good-looking sidekick; Don Rickles; and Jody McCrea (Joel's son) who played dimwitted characters with colorful names like Bonehead, Deadhead, and Big Lunk. *Beach Blanket Bingo* is generally considered the best Beach Party picture. It features Frankie and Annette skydiving, Bonehead falling in love with a lovely mermaid (Marta Kristen from TV's *Lost in Space*), and creepy pool shark South Dakota Slim (Timothy Carey) trying to saw singer Sugar Cane (Linda Evans) in half. Still, some fans prefer *Pajama Party* which boasts a great female supporting cast in beautiful Susan Hart, charming Elsa Lanchester, statuesque Bobbi Shaw, and Teri Garr in one of her first roles. *Pajama Party* also includes the most bizarre musical number in the series, as Annette—wearing a short nightie that looks as if it came from Madonna's wardrobe—sings to stuffed animals about her boy problems. Tommy Kirk and one-time *Gidget* Deborah Walley took over for Frankie and Annette in the final series entry, 1966's *The Ghost in the Invisible Bikini*. Annette played the female lead in the first six films, while Frankie headlined four films and made cameo appearances in two others. The Frankie substitutes were Tommy Kirk (a Martian teen in 1964's *Pajama Party*) and Dwayne Hickman (1965's *How to Stuff a Wild Bikini*). Twenty years after *Beach Party*, Frankie and Annette tried to spoof their old images in *Back to the Beach*, a good-natured but overdone effort. See also **Gidget**.

Beach Party (1963); *Muscle Beach Party* (1964); *Bikini Beach* (1964); *Pajama Party* (1964); *Beach Blanket Bingo* (1965); *How to Stuff a Wild Bikini* (1965); *The Ghost in the Invisible Bikini* (1966); *Back to the Beach* (1987)

The AIP film *Ski Party* (1965) is not considered part of the Beach Party series, but it stars many of the same performers (e.g., Frankie Avalon, Deborah Walley) and the formula remains the same. The AIP Beach Party series also fostered rival mid–1960s sand-and-surf pictures, such as:

Ride the Wild Surf (1964); *For Those Who Think Young* (1964); *The Horror of Party Beach* (aka *Invasion of the Zombies*) (1964); *Surf Party* (1964); *The Girls on the Beach* (1965); *Beach Ball* (1965); *Seaside Swingers* (1965); *It's a Bikini World* (1967); *Catalina Caper* (1967)

Bears

Someone at Walt Disney Productions must have had a soft spot for bears, for the company produced four pictures about the furry forest denizens between 1947 and 1974. The first two were animated bears, Brer Bear in *Song of the South* (1946) and Baloo in *The Jungle Book* (1967). As voiced by Phil Harris, Baloo has the distinction of being the only bear to sing an Oscar-nominated song — "Bare Necessities." The real-life Disney bears proved to be considerably less talented and, as a consequence, *King of the Grizzlies* (1970) and *The Bears and I* (1974) were also less entertaining. *Gentle Giant* (1967), a juvenile tale about a boy with a pet 650-pound black bear, could have passed for a Disney production. Its modest box-office success led to a 1967–69 TV series starring Clint Howard (Ron's brother) and Dennis Weaver. Clint Walker encountered a less sociable bear in the climax of *Night of the Grizzly* (1966), while another wild bear mauled Richard Harris and left him for dead in *Man in the Wilderness* (1971). Christopher George had the worst luck with bears, battling an 18-foot, 2,000-pounder in the 1976 *Jaws* rip-off *Grizzly* and then running into another one in the following year's *Day of the Animals* (actually, this latter bear was nice enough to dispose of troublemaker Leslie Nielsen). The most versatile bear performances were given by Bart the Bear, a 1,470-pound Kodiak who played a reluctant foster father in *The Bear* (1989) and a mauling killer in *The Edge* (1997). The mutant, pollution-made monster in John Frankenheimer's *Prophecy* (1979) looked like a conglomeration of several animals, but it was probably more bear than anything else. In the offbeat 1961 fantasy *The Two Little Bears*, Eddie Albert discovered that his two little children could turn into bear cubs at night. Director-actor Jean Renoir dressed as a bear to attend the climactic country manor costume party in his classic social satire *The Rules of the Game* (1939). Natassja Kinski sported a bear costume as well in John Irving's *The Hotel New Hampshire* (1984). In the 1978 TV movie *B.J. and the Bear*, the "Bear" turned out to be a chimpanzee. Apparently, that was supposed to be funny. See also **The Care Bears.**

Song of the South (1946); *The Two Little Bears* (1961); *Hey There, It's Yogi Bear* (1964); *Night of the Grizzly* (1966); *Jungle Book* (1967); *Gentle Giant* (1967); *King of the Grizzlies* (1970); *Man in the Wilderness* (1971); *The Bears and I* (1974); *Grizzly* (aka *Killer Grizzly*) (1976); *The Life and Times of Grizzly Adams* (1976); *Day of the Animals* (1977); *Prophecy* (1979); *The Bear* (1989); *The Whipping Boy* (1994 TVM); *Jonathan of the Bears* (1994); *Alaska* (1996); *The Edge* (1997); *Wild America* (1997); *Grizzly Falls* (1999)

Beastmaster

Director Don Coscarelli followed up his 1979 cult horror hit *Phantasm* (q.v.) with this sword and sorcery epic about a muscular, revenge-minded lad who can communicate with animals. Marc Singer stars as Dar, a combination of Conan and Dr. Doolittle, who seeks out his rightful place on the throne when his "foster family" is massacred. Rip Torn overacts zealously as the villainous Maax, while Tanya Roberts — a year removed from TV's *Charlie's Angels* — underplays Dar's eventual love interest. Alternately silly and mindlessly engaging, *The Beastmaster* became a cable favorite in the early 1990s and, at one time, ranked with *Gone with the Wind* as one of the TNT cable network's most popular movies. Interestingly, Coscarelli clashed with executive producer Sylvio Tabet over the film's casting. He wanted Klaus Kinski for the Rip Torn role and a then-unknown named Demi Moore in lieu of Tanya Roberts. Tabet took over the directorial reins for the belated 1991 sequel *Beastmaster 2: Through the Portal of Time*, which transported the loin-clothed Dar (Singer) to contemporary L.A. in a plot somewhat reminiscent of *Tarzan's New York Adventure*. Drive-in movie host Joe Bob Briggs described the third installment, *Beastmaster III: The Eye of Braxus,* in succinct fashion: "The Beastmaster has to invade the desert fortress, rescue his weenie beefcake brother, the king, and kill Lord Agon before he uses the amulet to turn into a fire-spitting lizard-headed beast." In 1998, plans for a TV series called *Beastmaster: The Legend Continues* were announced. Tanya Roberts cashed in on her *Beastmaster* fame by playing the jungle heroine in 1984's *Sheena* — only this time, she was the one who could talk with animals. See also **Sword and Sorcery.**

The Beastmaster (1982); *Beastmaster 2: Through the Portal of Time* (1991); *Beastmaster III: The Eye of Braxus* (1995)

Beauty Contests

Behind-the-scene exposés of the beauty pageant business, complete with bickering contestants and deceitful judges, have been the subject of *Contest Girl* (1964), *The Great American Beauty Contest* (1973), *Smile* (1975), *Miss All-American Beauty* (1982), and *Drop Dead Gorgeous* (1999). Ironically, while these films sought to criticize beauty contests, they are best remembered for the exposure they provided attractive young actresses such as Diane Lane, Farrah Fawcett, Melanie Griffith, and Annette O'-Toole. The lighthearted side of beauty contests was on display in 1950's *Peggy*, the story of a Rose Bowl queen, and 1951's *Lady Godiva Rides Again*, which introduced Joan Collins as a young contestant. A nonexistent woman won a beauty contest when Dick Powell submitted a composite photograph in the 1935 comedy *Page Miss Glory*. Carolyn Sapp played herself in 1992's *Miss America: Behind the Crown*, which focused on her relationship with an abusive boyfriend. *The Queen* was a well-received 1968 documentary about a beauty pageant for transvestites.

Case of the Lucky Legs (1935); *Page Miss Glory* (1935); *Waikiki Wedding* (1937); *Fast and Furious* (1939); *The Crystal Ball* (1943); *The Duchess of Idaho* (1950); *Peggy* (1950); *Lady Godiva Rides Again* (1951); *Marry Me Again* (1953); *Hear Me Good* (1957); *Contest Girl* (aka *The Beauty Jungle*) (1964); *The Queen* (1968); *The Great American Beauty Contest* (1973 TVM); *Smile* (1975); *The Night They Took Miss Beautiful* (1977 TVM); *Pick-up Summer* (aka *Pinball Summer; Pinball Pick-up*) (1981); *Miss All-American Beauty* (1982 TVM);

Miss Firecracker (1989); *Miss America: Behind the Crown* (1992 TVM); *I Know What You Did Last Summer* (1997); *Drop Dead Gorgeous* (1999); *Happy, Texas* (1999); *Scary Movie* (2000)

The Becker Family *see* Children of the Bride

Belvedere, Mr. (Lynn)

Clifton Webb created pompous, but likable, genius Lynn Belvedere in 1948's *Sitting Pretty*, in which Robert Young and Maureen O'Hara hired the 59-year-old as a babysitter (q.v.). The film inspired two sequels, sending Belvedere back to college and then to stir things up at a home for the elderly. Webb played a similar character in 1953's *Mister Scoutmaster*. Christopher Hewett played the title character in the 1985–90 TV series *Mr. Belvedere*, which was loosely based on the movies.

Sitting Pretty (1948); *Mr. Belvedere Goes to College* (1949); *Mr. Belvedere Rings the Bell* (1951)

Benji

What do a man-eating shark and a playful pooch have in common? Both were the subject of major hit films in 1975. While *Jaws* garnered waves of free publicity, *Benji*, a 1974 release, built its family-oriented following on word-of-mouth. No one expected Joe Camp's Texas-shot, canine kiddie feature to snowball into a box-office heavyweight. The familiar story thrust a stray little dog into a kidnap plot involving two youngsters. Benji, as played by a canine actor named Higgins, exuded plenty of charm and the low-camera angles playfully conveyed a dog's point-of-view. The 1977 follow-up, *For the Love of Benji*, found the little pooch in Athens, with enemy spies seeking a valuable formula stamped on his paw. This sequel failed to duplicate the success of its predecessor, causing Camp to make a major miscalculation with his third Benji film. *Oh, Heavenly Dog!* starred Chevy Chase as a murder victim who returns to Earth as a dog to find his killer (a plot reversal of 1951's superior *You Never Can Tell*). Chevy as Benji (he voices the dog's thoughts) lacked the charm of Benji as himself. Furthermore, the film's romance elements seemed aimed at adults. After a seven-year hiatus, Camp returned to his original formula with *Benji: The Hunted*, a children's film in which our canine hero "adopts" two orphaned cougar cubs. See also **Dogs**.

Benji (1974); *For the Love of Benji* (1977); *Oh, Heavenly Dog!* (1980); *Benji: The Hunted* (1987)

Bermuda Triangle

In the mid–1970s, Charles Berlitz published two books about this site of several inexplicable disappearances in the Atlantic Ocean. A brief flurry of movie activity followed, beginning with 1974's made-for-TV feature *Satan's Triangle* and the pseudo-documentary *The Devil's Triangle*. Similar subpar films came in quick succession. Berlitz went on to write about Atlantis, Noah's Ark, and how to speak Italian, French, and German.

The Devil's Triangle (1974); *Satan's Triangle* (1974 TVM); *Beyond the Bermuda Triangle* (1975 TVM); *Mysteries from Beyond the Bermuda Triangle* (1977); *The Bermuda Triangle* (1978); *The Bermuda Depths* (1978 TVM); *Lost in the Bermuda Triangle* (1999 TVM)

Best of the Best Series

High-flying Phillip Rhee co-produced and co-wrote the story for 1989's *Best of the Best*, a run-of-the-mill karate film enlivened only by a well-choreographed fight between Rhee and his real-life brother. Rhee starred as one of five martial artists selected to represent the U.S. in a team competition against a tough Korean squad. The U.S. coach, played by James Earl Jones, provides little guidance, preferring to offer clichéd words of wisdom such as: "A team is not a team if you don't give a damn about each other." Of course, the coach gets stuck with a motley group of lads, which include: Tommy Lee (Rhee), who teaches karate to youngsters; Alex (Eric Roberts), a single dad battling an old fighting injury; and Travis (Christopher Penn), an obnoxious hefty dude who sports a cowboy hat. Like the *Rocky* films, the grueling training sessions are set to a pulsing music (Ike Stubblefield tries to make the title rock song sound like Survivor's "Eye of the Tiger"). Despite an unexpected feel-good ending, *Best of the Best* gets all-around low marks for originality. The 1993 sequel reteamed Rhee, Roberts, and Penn in a more violent tale about illegal martial arts bouts in Las Vegas, a plot similar to 1989's *Kickboxer*. Rhee directed, as well as starred in, *Best of the Best 3: No Turning Back* (1996), which also featured Gina Gershon, who attracted far greater attention in the previous year's *Showgirls*. Rhee played Tommy Lee in all the *Best of the Best* films. For other martial arts films, see **American Ninja Series**; **Bloodfist Series**; **The Karate Kid**; **Kickboxer Series**; and **No Retreat, No Surrender Series**.

Best of the Best (1989); *Best of the Best 2* (1993); *Best of the Best 3: No Turning Back* (1996); *Best of the Best IV: Without Warning* (1998)

A Better Tomorrow Series

This violent gangster series smashed box-office records in its native Hong Kong and also scored well in many other Southeast Asian markets. American critics have praised the films, comparing them to the tough, fast-paced Warner Bros. gangster pictures of the 1930s. Produced and co-written by Tsui Hark, 1986's *A Better Tomorrow* focuses primarily on a pair of explosive contemporary gangsters named Ho (Lung Ti) and Cheung Chi-Keung (or Mark in subtitled prints). The film made an action star of actor Chow Yun Fat, but also created a dilemma for writer Hark, who killed off the most popular character in the film's climax. Using a plot device familiar to American TV soap fans, Hark brought back Chow Yun Fat as Mark's revenge-minded twin brother Ken in *A Better Tomorrow II* (1988). However, Chow Yun Fat was back as Mark for *A Better Tomorrow III* (1989), a prequel (q.v.) set in Saigon in 1974. The plot centers on Mark's efforts to secure exit visas for relatives. When a North Vietnamese soldier double-crosses him, Mark rectifies the situation by engaging in a bloody shoot-out. Although the *Better Tomorrow* films received very limited theatrical showings in the U.S., they attracted a cult following on videotape and became largely responsible for the birth of the "Hong King action film" genre. John Woo, who directed the first two series entries, reteamed with Chow Yun Fat on other big Asian hits (*The Killer*, *Hard-Boiled*). In the mid–1990s, Woo made a successful transition to Hollywood with films such as *Hard Target* and *Broken Arrow*, paving the way for Hark's U.S. debut in 1996 (directing *Double Team*) and Chow Yun Fat two years later (starring in *The Replacement Killers*). The 1994 *Return to a Better Tomorrow*, which features none of the original characters, does not appear to be part of the series.

A Better Tomorrow (aka *Gangland Boss*; *Ying Hung Boon Sik*) (1986); *A Better Tomorrow II* (aka *Ying Hung Boon Sik II*) (1988); *A Better Tomorrow III* (aka *Love and Death in Saigon*; *Ying Hung Boon Sik III*) (1989)

Beverly Hills Cop Series

After scoring hits opposite Nick Nolte (*48 HRS.*) and Dan Aykroyd (*Trading Places*), Eddie Murphy took charge of his solo career with the 1984 blockbuster *Beverly Hills Cop*. Ironically, the film was originally written as an action vehicle for Sylvester Stallone (who allegedly integrated some of his *Beverly Hills Cop* ideas into 1986's *Cobra*). The Oscar-nominated screenplay by Daniel Petrie, Jr., and Danilo Bach deftly combined two proven formulas: a fish-out-of-water story and a buddy action film premise. Murphy plays Axel Foley, a Detroit cop who travels to the West Coast to track down the murderer of a friend. To keep the hot-headed Foley out of trouble, Beverly Hills police lieutenant Ronny Cox assigns two straight-and-narrow detectives (Judge Reinhold and John Ashton) to stick with Foley. Surprisingly, Reinhold and Ashton generated a lot of the humor — a point lost in the subsequent sequels. *Beverly Hills Cop* spawned two top five songs: the instrumental "Axel F" by Harold Faltermeyer and "The Heat Is On" by former Eagle Glenn Frey. After appearing in the panned pictures *The Best Defense* (1984) and *The Golden Child* (1986), Murphy reprised his role as Axel Foley for the noisy, over-produced *Beverly Hills Cop II* (1987). This sequel featured a Stallone connection, too, since lead actress Brigitte Nielsen was once married to Sly. Though essentially a remake of the original film, *Beverly Hills Cop II* made over $100 million at the box-office. That turned out to be double the box-office take of the belated third installment, a lame 1994 effort which emphasized comedy over action. Reinhold and Ashton appeared in the first sequel, but only Reinhold came back for *Beverly Hills III*. See also **Buddy Action Films**.

Beverly Hills Cop (1984); *Beverly Hills Cop II* (1987); *Beverly Hills Cop III* (1994)

Bicycles

Vittorio De Sica's touching 1949 Italian classic *The Bicycle Thief* chronicled a poor man's desperate search for the stolen bicycle on which his family's livelihood depended. *Breaking Away* (1979) and *American Flyers* (1985), both written by cycling enthusiast Steve Tesich, dealt with amateur riders and their infatuation with bike racing. Stockbroker Kevin Bacon dropped out of the rat race and became a bicycle messenger in *Quicksilver* (1986). Many movies have featured bicycles in memorable scenes, including *E.T.*, *Butch Cassidy and the Sundance Kid*, and *The Wizard of Oz* (Toto jumping off the back of Miss Gulch's two-wheeler).

Six Day Bike Rider (1934); *A Boy, a Girl, and a Bike* (1947); *The Bicycle Thief* (1949); *Isn't Life Wonderful?* (1952); *Elephant Walk* (1954); *Smiley* (1957); *And Soon the Darkness* (1970); *The Gang That Couldn't Shoot Straight* (1971); *Breaking Away* (1979); *BMX Bandits* (1983); *American Flyers* (1985); *Pee Wee's Big Adventure* (1985); *Quicksilver* (1986); *Rad* (1986); *Tracks of Glory* (1992); *Tread: The Movie* (1994); *Messenger* (1994)

Big Town Series

A CBS radio program provided the inspiration for this short-lived Paramount film series about crusading newspaper editor Steve Wilson (Philip Reed). Hillary Brooke played police reporter Lorelei Kilbourne, Wilson's spunky sidekick.

Big Town (aka *Guilty Assignment*) (1947); *Big Town After Dark* (aka *Underworld After Dark*) (1947); *I Cover Big Town* (aka *I Cover the Underworld*) (1947); *Big Town Scandal* (1948)

Bigamy

It is amazing that so few filmmakers have explored the dramatic possibilities inherent in a serious film about bigamy. It's as if a discouraging cloud of "uncomfortableness" hung over the subject matter. Interestingly, a woman (Ida Lupino) directed one of the first serious films about a bigamous husband, 1953's appropriately titled *The Bigamist*. Although it failed to probe deeply into its protagonist's motivations, it was superior to 1988's *Double Standard* and 1993's *The Man with Three Wives*, two pointless TV movies "inspired by true-life cases." The cinema's inability to deal seriously with bigamy has resulted in a plethora of multiple marriage comedies. William Bendix, an unlikely candidate for bigamy, traveled up and down New York state visiting his two wives in *Don Juan Quilligan* (1945). Alec Guinness played a ferry-boat captain with a wife in every port (well, two ports to be exact) in 1953's hilarious *Captain's Paradise*. Other male bigamists have included Rex Harrison (*The Constant Husband*), Clifton Webb (*The Remarkable Mr. Pennypacker*), and Dudley Moore (*Micki and Maude*). Female bigamists have been rare in the movies, perhaps reflecting a male chauvinistic attitude among filmmakers. Karen Valentine played a stewardess with multiple families in *Coffee, Tea, or Me* (1972). Dyan Cannon's fashion design business allowed her to keep a husband on each coast in *Having It All* (1982). Sally Field lived with two husbands in *Kiss Me Goodbye* (1982), but one of them was a ghost (thus, according to the law, she was not a bigamist). Jean Seberg had two husbands in the gold rush musical *Paint Your Wagon* (1969), but that's only because Lee Marvin and Clint Eastwood bought her wifely services jointly at an auction. The movie bigamist with the most spouses was the one found dead on the floor of a hotel room in the beginning of *15 Wives* (1934). Needless to say, there was no shortage of murder suspects.

15 Wives (1934); *Don Juan Quilligan* (1945); *Monsieur Verdoux* (1947); *Captain's Paradise* (1953); *The Bigamist* (1953); *The Constant Husband* (1955); *Autumn Leaves* (1956); *Witness for the Prosecution* (1958); *The Remarkable Mr. Pennypacker* (1959); *Two Wives at One Wedding* (1960); *Decline and Fall of a Bird Watcher* (aka *Decline and Fall*) (1968); *Paint Your Wagon* (1969); *Coffee, Tea or Me* (1972 TVM); *Handle with Care* (aka *Citizen's Band*) (1977); *Sweet William* (1980); *Child Bride of Short Creek* (1981 TVM); *Having It All* (1982 TVM); *Micki and Maude* (1984); *Double Standard* (1988 TVM); *Near Misses* (aka *Near Mrs.*) (1990); *Deceived* (1991); *The Man with Three Wives* (1993 TVM); *She Led Two Lives* (1994 TVM); *Frequent Flyer* (1996 TVM)

Bigfoot

The Abominable Snowman's North American cousin has been the subject of several bottom-of-the-barrel features, such as *Bigfoot* (1969), *Curse of Bigfoot* (1972), and *Sasquatch* (1978). He was portrayed as a lovable big guy in 1987's *Harry and the Hendersons* and in the same year's made-for-TV feature *Bigfoot*. The pseudo-documentary *The Legend of Boggy Creek* (1973) traced the exploits of a Bigfoot-like creature that roamed around Fouke, Arkansas. John Frankenheimer's *Prophecy* (1979) was about a Bigfoot relative, a gangling mutant monster created by chemical pollution. See also **Abominable Snowman**; **Boggy Creek Series**.

Bigfoot (aka *Big Foot*) (1969); *Curse of Bigfoot* (1972); *Shriek of the Mutilated* (1974); *The Mysterious Monsters* (1976); *Creature from Black Lake* (1976); *Sasquatch* (1978); *Night of the Demon* (1980); *Harry and the Hendersons* (aka *Bigfoot and the Hendersons*) (1987); *Bigfoot* (1987 TVM); *Bigfoot: The Unforgettable Encounter* (1995)

Billy Jack

Tom Laughlin's peace-loving, half-breed, former Green Beret first appeared in the 1967 biker film *Born Losers*, in which he protected the innocent, defied ineffective small-town police, and beat up bad guys. He did basically the same things in Laughlin's 1971 follow-up *Billy Jack*, but this time moviegoers identified with his loner hero and made the picture a low-budget smash. The movie's simplistic politics and thematic inconsistencies (Billy Jack preaches peace, but doesn't hesitate to use violence when necessary) dated it almost immediately. Laughlin's overblown 1974 sequel *The Trial of Billy Jack* focused on government corruption, as did *Billy Jack Goes to Washington* (1977). Allegedly, the latter was a remake of Frank Capra's classic *Mr. Smith Goes to Washington*. Neither of the last two films came close to duplicating *Billy Jack*'s success, so the series mercifully died. Laughlin and wife/co-star Delores Taylor produced, directed, and wrote most of the series (often using the pseudonym T.C. Frank).

Born Losers (1967); *Billy Jack* (1971); *The Trial of Billy Jack* (1974); *Billy Jack Goes to Washington* (1977)

Billy the Kid/Billy Carson

This low-budget PRC studio series had little to do with the real Billy the Kid. Its initial entry, 1940's *Billy the Kid Outlawed*, presented Billy as a wronged hero, a victim of small-town corruption. He even went on to become a lawman in the next film, *Billy the Kid in Texas*. Veteran screen cowboy Bob Steele, one of the Three Mesquiteers (q.v.) in the 1930s, played Billy in the first six films. Steele left after 1941's *Billy the Kid in Santa Fe*, though he continued to appear in Westerns and eventually wound up as Trooper Duffy on TV's *F Troop* (1965–67). Serial star Buster ("Flash Gordon") Crabbe replaced Steele in 1941's *Billy the Kid Wanted* and remained for the rest of the series. Al St. John played Billy's grizzly sidekick Fuzzy Q. Jones, who was at least as popular as Billy (one film was even titled *Fuzzy Settles Down*). Sam Newfield directed all the films using various pseudonyms (e.g., Sherman Scott, Peter Stewart). Newfield's real name was Neufeld and his brother, Sigmund, was the head of PRC. Newfield shot the Billy the Kid films in two or three days, using the same footage for chases and gunfights repeatedly. In the late 1940s, after the series ended, Eagle Lion re-edited (and drastically cut) some of the films and released them with different titles. Thus, the 65-minute *Western Cyclone* became the 39-minute *Frontier Fighters*. See also **Outlaws (Real-Life Western)**.

Billy the Kid Outlawed (1940); *Billy the Kid in Texas* (1940); *Billy the Kid's Gun Justice* (1940); *Billy the Kid's Range War* (1941); *Billy the Kid's Fighting Pals* (1941); *Billy the Kid in Santa Fe* (1941); *Billy the Kid Wanted* (1941); *Billy the Kid's Roundup* (1941); *Billy the Kid Trapped* (1942); *Billy the Kid's Smoking Guns* (1942); *Law and Order* (aka *Billy the Kid's Law and Order*) (1942); *Sheriff of Sage Valley* (aka *Billy the Kid, Sheriff of Sage Valley*) (1942); *The Mysterious Rider* (aka *Panhandle Trail*) (1942); *The Kid Rides Again* (1943); *Fugitive of the Plains* (aka *Raiders of Red Rock*) (1943); *Western Cyclone* (aka *Frontier Fighters*) (1943); *Cattle Stampede* (1943); *The Renegade* (1943); *Devil Riders* (1943); *Frontier Outlaws* (1944); *Thundering Gunslingers* (1944); *Valley of Vengeance* (1944); *The Drifter* (1944); *Fuzzy Settles Down* (1944); *Blazing Frontier* (1944); *Rustler's Hideout* (1944); *Wild Horse Phantom* (1944); *Oath of Vengeance* (1944); *Lightning Raiders* (1945); *His Brother's Ghost* (1945); *Shadows of Death* (1945); *Gangster's Den* (1945); *Stagecoach Outlaws* (1945); *Border Badmen* (1945); *Fighting Bill Carson* (1945); *Prairie Rustlers* (1945); *Gentlemen with Guns* (1946); *Terrors on Horseback* (1946); *Ghost of Hidden Valley* (1946); *Prairie Badmen* (1946); *Overland Riders* (1946); *Outlaw of the Plains* (1946)

Birds

The mere word has a Hitchcockian ring to it now. But long before Hitch turned them into formidable little killers in 1963, birds were making their cinematic presence known. In Britain, a pair of rare birds disrupted a quiet hamlet in the quaint comedy *Tawny Pipit* (1944). Scottish islanders created some rare birds with a little paint in 1957's *Mad Little Island*, reasoning that such a discovery would block the construction of a government missile base. The establishment of bird sanctuaries provided the background for another British picture *Conflict of Wings* (1953) and an American romantic comedy *Something for the Birds* (1952). Shirley Temple went looking for the blue bird of happiness in the colorful 1940 fantasy *The Blue Bird*, her consolation prize for not being loaned to MGM for *The Wizard of Oz*. A toucan spread a "happiness virus" throughout New York City in George (*Miracle on 34th Street*) Seaton's *What's So Bad About Feeling Good?* (1968). In contrast, giant birds of the horrific variety flew across the screen in the Japanese import *Rodan* (1956) and the inept U.S.-lensed *The Giant Claw* (1957). A contemporary witch brought a threatening stone eagle to life and sent it on a murderous mission in the 1962 supernatural gem *Burn, Witch, Burn*. Norman Bates (Anthony Perkins) stuffed birds for a hobby in Hitchcock's *Psycho* (1960), a film overloaded with bird symbolism. Its first murder victim, Marion *Crane*, was first glimpsed in *Phoenix*, Arizona. Hitch's next picture was, naturally, *The Birds* (1963), a vague, but exciting, thriller adapted from Daphne du Maurier's short story. There was nothing horrific or fantastic about 1962's *Birdman of Alcatraz*, an engrossing biography of convict-turned-bird-expert Robert Stroud (Burt Lancaster). However, cruel sorcerer Boris Karloff turned Peter Lorre into a black bird in 1963's amusing *The Raven*. Akim Tamiroff transformed himself into a ridiculous-looking bird/man in *The Vulture* (1967), while fetching Michelle Pfeiffer spent half her days as a hawk in the 1985 sword-and-sorcery fantasy *Ladyhawke*. Roddy McDowall believed himself to be an extinct bird in human form in the oddball satire *Lord Love a Duck* (1966). Army hospital schizophrenic Matthew Modine wanted to become a bird in *Birdy* (1984), while comic book writer Michael Crawford took flight — albeit briefly — as his own creation *Condorman* (1981). Audrey Hepburn played Rima the Bird

Girl in the 1959 adaptation of W.H. Hudson's *Green Mansions*. Hunky warrior Marc Singer communicated with birds (and other animals) in 1982's *The Beastmaster*, yet another sword-and-sorcery picture. A frigid woman could make love only to a man in a bird suit in Roger Vadim's bizarre 1980 film *Night Games*. Finally, Larry Cohen's *Q—The Winged Serpent* (1982) flew and lived in a nest, but was an Aztec god and not a bird at all. See also **Bats**.

The Blue Bird (1940); *Tawny Pipit* (1944); *Champagne for Caesar* (1950); *Something for the Birds* (1952); *Conflict of Wings* (aka *Fuss Over Feathers*) (1953); *Rodan* (1956); *Mad Little Island* (aka *Rockets Galore!*) (1957); *The Giant Claw* (1957); *Green Mansions* (1959); *Psycho* (1960); *Burn, Witch, Burn* (aka *Night of the Eagle*) (1962); *Birdman of Alcatraz* (1962); *The Birds* (1963); *The Raven* (1963); *Those Calloways* (1965); *Lord Love a Duck* (1966); *The Vulture* (1967); *What's So Bad About Feeling Good?* (1968); *Harpy* (1970 TVM); *Jonathan Livingston Seagull* (1973); *The Blue Bird* (1976); *Night Games* (1980); *Condorman* (1981); *Clash of the Titans* (1981); *The Beastmaster* (1982); *Birdy* (1984); *Ladyhawke* (1985); *Sesame Street Presents Follow That Bird* (1985); *Beaks: The Movie* (1987); *Where Pigeons Go to Die* (1990 TVM); *The Dark Half* (1993); *The Crow* (1994); *The Pelican Brief* (1994); *Fly Away Home* (1996); *Paulie* (1998); *Little Voice* (1998); *Chicken Run* (2000); *Ghost Dog: The Way of the Samurai* (2000)

Black Cobra Series

With solid hits like *Black Caesar* and *Hell Up in Harlem* (both 1973), Fred "The Hammer" Williamson ranked as one of the biggest action stars of the "blaxploitation" films (q.v.). Yet, by the middle of the next decade, the 48-year-old Williamson's audience had defected to newer action heroes like Chuck Norris, Sylvester Stallone, and Arnold Schwarzenegger. Unwanted in his homeland, Williamson headed to Europe to make movies like Eastwood and Bronson before him. Unfortunately, Williamson's foreign stint did little for his career — the *Black Cobra* movies were released directly to videotape in the U.S. Lensed in Italy, though set in the U.S., 1986's *Black Cobra* casts Williamson as a big city detective named Robert Malone with a penchant for violence. The title appears to be an attempt to capitalize on Sylvester Stallone's *Cobra*, which was released the same year. *Black Cobra 2* (1989) improved on the original by sending detective Malone on an INTERPOL exchange program to Manila (shades of *Coogan's Bluff*). Once settled in the Phillipines, he teams up with Nicholas Hammond (Spider-Man in the short-lived TV series) to find Hammond's kidnapped daughter. In the following year's *Black Cobra III: The Manila Connection*, INTERPOL calls in Malone when terrorists steal an arsenal of high-tech weapons. *The Black Cobra* films offer nothing to distinguish themselves from any of the other low-budget, foreign-set action film series of the 1980s (e.g., *Bloodfist, Eye of the Eagle*, and *No Retreat, No Surrender*).

Black Cobra (aka *Cobra Nero*) (1986); *Black Cobra 2* (1989); *Black Cobra III: The Manila Connection* (1990)

Blackie, Boston

Jack Boyle's thief-turned-detective has enjoyed a steady screen career, beginning with 1919's *Boston Blackie's Little Pal*. Bert Lytell, Lionel Barrymore, and William Russell played Blackie in silent films. However, Chester Morris kicked off the "official" series with 1941's *Meet Boston Blackie*. Morris made an agreeable hero, always willing to bend the law to crack a case, and the series concluded a profitable run in 1949. Just two years later, Blackie turned up on TV, with Kent Taylor replacing Morris. The Boston Blackie TV series ran for 58 episodes from 1951 to 1953. Morris starred in all of the following film entries.

Meet Boston Blackie (1941); *Confessions of Boston Blackie* (1941); *Alias Boston Blackie* (1942); *Boston Blackie Goes to Hollywood* (1942); *After Midnight with Boston Blackie* (1943); *The Chance of a Lifetime* (1943); *One Mysterious Night* (1944); *Boston Blackie Booked on Suspicion* (1945); *Boston Blackie's Rendezvous* (1945); *A Close Call for Boston Blackie* (1946); *The Phantom Thief* (1946); *Boston Blackie and the Law* (1947); *Trapped by Boston Blackie* (1948); *Boston Blackie's Chinese Venture* (1949)

Blackouts

Films revolving around power blackouts include *The Night the City Screamed* (1980*)*, *The Trigger Effect* (1996), *Where Were You When the Lights Went Out?* (1968), and *Blackout* (1978). The latter two films were inspired by real-life power failures in New York City. The Doris Day vehicle *Where Were You* played the massive 1965 blackout for forced laughs, while *Blackout* went for thrills in its tale of apartment tenants victimized by a gang during the 1977 power failure. The same New York City blackout was depicted in Spike Lee's *Summer of Sam* (1999). In other films: A blackout allowed inmates to escape from an asylum in *Alone in the Dark*; Gregory Peck lost his memory during a blackout in *Mirage*; and the entire world suffered a temporary blackout so Michael Rennie could make a point in *The Day the Earth Stood Still*.

The Day the Earth Stood Still (1951); *Mirage* (1964); *Where Were You When the Lights Went Out?* (1968); *Blackout* (1978); *The Night the City Screamed* (1980 TVM); *Alone in the Dark* (1982); *The Trigger Effect* (1996); *Summer of Sam* (1999)

Blane, Torchy

Short story writer Frederick Nebel's ace reporter Torchy Blane had a knack for getting involved with murder cases, which she did in nine B-movies churned out by Warner Bros. during 1937–39. Glenda Farrell played Torchy in all but two films, getting support from Barton MacLane as her charmless boyfriend, police detective Steve McBride (Steve to Torchy: "You're going to settle down and marry me before I throw you in jail"). The two non–Farrell films starred Lola Lane (*Torchy Blane in Panama*) and 25-year-old Jane Wyman (*Torchy Plays with Dynamite*). The series dates badly and Steve's thoughtless attitude toward Torchy's career, especially in the Farrell films, is almost offensive. Still, the Torchy series contained a few offbeat touches — such as the appropriately-titled Jerome Kern tune "Why Do I Have to Sing a Torch Song?" in *Smart Blonde* and the absence of a Chinatown setting in *Torchy Blane in Chinatown*.

Smart Blonde (1937); *Fly-Away Baby* (1937); *The Adventurous Blonde* (1937); *Blondes at Work* (1938); *Torchy Blane in Panama* (1938); *Torchy Gets Her Man* (1938); *Torchy Blane in Chinatown* (1939); *Torchy Runs for Mayor* (1939); *Torchy Plays with Dynamite* (1939)

Blaxploitation Films

The term "blaxploitation" was coined in the early 1970s to describe a rash of low-budget, action pictures that featured mostly black performers and typically played in black neighborhood theaters. Many critics considered these movies offensive, charging that they portrayed blacks as stereotyped private eyes, drug kingpins, and prostitutes. While that may be true, these films nevertheless kept some talented performers employed (e.g., Richard Pryor in *The Mack*, Godfrey Cambridge in *Cotton Comes to Harlem*). A handful of action stars emerged, such as Tamara Dobson (as *Cleopatra Jones*), karate champion Jim Kelly, and Richard Roundtree (*Shaft*). However, their fame was fleeting and, by 1975, they were relegated to supporting roles in more mainstream films. A few blaxploitation films, such as *Shaft* and *Blacula*, broke the typical mold, gained wider distribution, and evolved into sizable hits. *One Down, Two to Go* (1983) attempted to revive the genre. Yet, despite a formidable cast headed by Jim Brown, it flopped miserably. In 1989, Keenen Ivory Wayans, who would later create TV's *In Living Color*, produced a blaxploitation parody called *I'm Gonna Git You Sucka* starring the likes of Eve Plumb (*The Brady Bunch*) and Clarence Williams III (*The Mod Squad*). See also **Coffin Ed and Grave Digger Jones**; **Shaft, John**; **Superfly**.

Cotton Comes to Harlem (1970); *Shaft* (1971); *Come Black, Charleston Blue* (1972); *Cool Breeze* (1972); *Top of the Heap* (1972); *Melinda* (1972); *Hammer* (1972); *Hit Man* (1972); *Slaughter* (1972); *Shaft's Big Score* (1972); *Blacula* (1972); *Superfly* (1972); *Black Caesar* (1973); *Cleopatra Jones* (1973); *Coffy* (ad line: "Coffy...she'll cream you!") (1973); *Detroit 9000* (1973); *Ganja and Hess* (1973); *Hell Up in Harlem* (1973); *The Mack* (1973); *Scream, Blacula, Scream* (1973); *Shaft in Africa* (1973); *Slaughter's Big Rip-Off* (1973); *Superfly TNT* (1973); *Blackenstein* (aka *Black Frankenstein*) (1973); *Abby* (1974); *Black Eye* (1974); *Black Gunn* (1974); *Foxy Brown* (1974); *Hangup* (aka *Superdude*) (1974); *Three the Hard Way* (1974); *Truck Turner* (1974); *T.N.T. Jackson* (1974); *Bucktown* (1975); *The Black Gestapo* (1975); *Cleopatra Jones and the Casino of Gold* (1975); *Friday Foster* (1975); *Dr. Black, Mr. Hyde* (aka *The Watts Monster*; *Dr. Black and Mr. White*) (1976); *Black Belt Jones* (1976); *Black Fist* (aka *The Black Streetfighter*) (1976); *Hot Potato* (1976); *The Big Score* (1983); *One Down, Two to Go* (1983)

The Blind Dead

A gory Spanish import, the Blind Dead series based its premise on legendary 13th-century Templarios Knights who were blinded and then executed for their ritualistic killings of young women. In 1972's *The Blind Dead*, they were resurrected (as rotting, hooded ghouls) and promptly set about in search of more nubile females. The film proved immensely popular in Europe and earned a small cult following in the U.S., chiefly due to its Bava-style atmosphere. Director Armando De Ossorio directed three additional, similarly-plotted installments.

The Blind Dead (aka *Tombs of the Blind Dead*; *La Noche del Terror Ciego*) (1972); *Return of the Blind Dead* (aka *El Ataque de los Muertos sin Ojos*; *Attack of the Blind Dead*) (1973); *Horror of the Zombies* (aka *El Buque Maldito*; *Ghost Ships of the Blind Dead*) (1974); *Night of the Seagulls* (aka *La Noche de las Gaviotas*; *Night of the Death Cult*) (1975)

Blindness

Although films dealing exclusively with blindness can be narrowed to a select few, there have been a disproportionate number of films featuring blind characters in critical roles. Edward Arnold played a blind detective in *Eyes in the Night* (1942) and *The Hidden Eye* (1945), while sleuths-by-chance have included

writer Van Johnson in *23 Paces to Baker Street* (1956), reporter Karl Malden in *The Cat O'Nine Tails* (1971), and insurance investigator James Franciscus in *Longstreet* (1970). Blind people have been portrayed as musicians of startling talent in *The Enchanted Cottage* (1945), *Night Song* (1947), *Goha* (1957), *Blues for Lovers* (1964), and *If You Could See What I Hear* (1982). The latter two films were partially biographical, with Ray Charles playing himself in *Blues* and Marc Singer as composer Tom Sullivan in *If You Could See*. *Seven in Darkness* (1969) was a tense tale about a plane which crashed en route to a convention for the blind, thus stranding its seven sightless passengers in the wilderness. An alien-directed "meteorite shower" blinded most of the Earth's population in the opening frames of John Wyndham's *Day of the Triffids* (1963). As for serious films about persons adjusting to the sudden loss of their sight, few movies can match the emotional impact of *Bright Victory* (1951). Arthur Kennedy earned an Oscar nomination for his wrenching portrait of a blind ex-soldier who no longer knows his place in society. A labrador retriever seeing-eye dog provided Elizabeth Montgomery with much needed support in the superior TV movie *Second Sight: A Love Story* (1984). A blind couple desperately fought to adopt a child in the fact-based 1987 TV movie *Eye on the Sparrow*. Along more traditional lines, a playboy responsible for a woman's blindness became a surgeon so he could cure her in both versions of Lloyd C. Douglas' tear-jerker *Magnificent Obsession*. Al Pacino won a Best Actor Oscar for his portrayal of a blind retired army colonel in 1992's *Scent of a Woman*.

Orphans of the Storm (1922); *Thunder Below* (1932); *Wings in the Dark* (1935); *Magnificent Obsession* (1935); *Bride of Frankenstein* (1935); *The Dark Angel* (1935); *The Human Monster* (aka *Dark Eyes of London*) (1939); *The Secret of Dr. Kildare* (1939); *The Light That Failed* (1939); *The Four Feathers* (1939); *Eyes in the Night* (1942); *Mr. Skeffington* (1944); *The Enchanted Cottage* (1945); *Pride of the Marines* (aka *Forever in Love*) (1945); *The Hidden Eye* (1945); *Night Song* (1947); *Bright Victory* (aka *Lights Out*) (1951); *Journey into Light* (1951); *On Dangerous Ground* (1951); *The Green Scarf* (1954); *Magnificent Obsession* (1954); *23 Paces to Baker Street* (1956); *No Road Back* (1957); *Goha* (1957); *Witness in the Dark* (1959); *Faces in the Dark* (1960); *The Miracle Worker* (1962); *Day of the Triffids* (1963); *Blues for Lovers* (aka *Ballad in Blue*) (1964); *A Patch of Blue* (1965); *Cauldron of Blood* (aka *Blind Man's Bluff*) (1967); *Wait Until Dark* (1967); *Seven in Darkness* (1969 TVM); *How Awful About Allan* (1970 TVM); *Longstreet* (1970 TVM); *The Cat O'Nine Tails* (1971); *See No Evil* (aka *Blind Terror*) (1971); *In Broad Daylight* (1971 TVM); *Butterflies Are Free* (1972); *Blindman* (1972); *Journey from Darkness* (1975 TVM); *Love's Dark Side* (1978 TVM); *Blind Rage* (1978); *Ice Castles* (1979); *The Miracle Worker* (1979 TVM); *To Race the Wind* (1980 TVM); *If You Could See What I Hear* (1982); *Second Sight: A Love Story* (1984 TVM); *Eye on the Sparrow* (1987 TVM); *See No Evil, Hear No Evil* (1989); *Blind Fury* (1989); *Blind Witness* (1989 TVM); *Blind Fear* (1989); *Wild Hearts Can't Be Broken* (1991); *Afraid of the Dark* (1991); *Proof* (1992); *Jennifer 8* (1992); *Scent of a Woman* (1992); *Blindsided* (1993 TVM); *Blink* (1994); *What Love Sees* (1996 TVM); *Good Luck* (1997); *Touch* (1997); *At First Sight* (1999); *A Song from the Heart* (1999 TVM)

Blondie

Probably more so than any other film series, *Blondie* established the format and style of the television "sitcom"—13 years before *I Love Lucy*. Penny Singleton and Arthur Lake starred as Chic

Young's comic strip couple Blondie and Dagwood Bumstead in an amazing 28 films spanning 12 years. Their supporting cast remained intact for most of the series, too, with Larry Simms as Baby Dumpling, Jonathan Hale as Mr. Dithers, and Marjorie Kent as Cookie. In 1950, long after most film series had expired, Blondie came to an end. Arthur Lake continued as Dagwood (with Pamela Britton as Blondie) in a short-lived 1957 television series. Meanwhile, Penny Singleton provided the voice for Jane during the original 1962-63 run of the TV cartoon series *The Jetsons*. She later became a union activist and then returned to Broadway in the 1970s in *No, No, Nanette*. In 1968, Patricia Harty and Will Hutchins revived the Blondie and Dagwood characters for another TV series. It lasted but a half-season. Ironically, the film series that inspired the TV sitcom genre never made it as a successful sitcom itself. See also **Comic Strip Characters**.

Blondie (1938); *Blondie Brings Up Baby* (1939); *Blondie Meets the Boss* (1939); *Blondie Takes a Vacation* (1939); *Blondie Has Servant Trouble* (1940); *Blondie on a Budget* (1940); *Blondie Plays Cupid* (1940); *Blondie Goes Latin* (1941); *Blondie in Society* (1941); *Blondie's Blessed Event* (1942); *Blondie for Victory* (1942); *Blondie Goes to College* (1942); *Footlight Glamour* (1943); *It's a Great Life* (1943); *Leave It to Blondie* (1945); *Blondie Knows Best* (1946); *Blondie's Lucky Day* (1946); *Life with Blondie* (1946); *Blondie's Anniversary* (1947); *Blondie's Big Moment* (1947); *Blondie's Holiday* (1947); *Blondie in the Dough* (1947); *Blondie's Reward* (1948); *Blondie's Big Deal* (1949); *Blondie Hits the Jackpot* (1949); *Blondie's Secret* (1949); *Beware of Blondie* (1950); *Blondie's Hero* (1950)

Bloodfist Series

Real-life World Karate Association champion Don "The Dragon" Wilson took a shot at "kung fu" stardom in this low-budget action series. Yet, despite fancy footwork, Wilson failed to duplicate the mainstream success of rival martial arts star Jean-Claude Van Damme. In 1989's *Bloodfist*, Wilson's character Jake treks off to Manila when his brother is murdered following a kickboxing match. Wilson returns as Jake in the following year's sequel, *Bloodfist II*, which borrows much of its plot from Bruce Lee's 1973's genre classic *Enter the Dragon*. It sends Jake back to Manila after he accidentally kills a man in a kickboxing bout. After some close encounters in the city, Jake finds himself on an island fortress ruled by a villain named Su. The third film in the series dispenses with Jake altogether — Wilson plays another character named Jimmy Boland who finds himself fighting behind prison bars (a premise similar to Van Damme's 1990 picture *Death Warrant*). The remaining *Bloodfist* films also feature Wilson as different characters who get involved with arms merchants (*Bloodfist IV*), terrorists (*Bloodfist VI*), and kidnappers (*Bloodfist VIII*). For other martial arts films, see **American Ninja Series**; **Best of the Best Series**; **The Karate Kid**; **Kickboxer Series** and **No Retreat, No Surrender Series**.

Bloodfist (1989); *Bloodfist II* (1990); *Bloodfist III: Forced to Fight* (1991); *Bloodfist IV: Die Trying* (1992); *Bloodfist V: Human Target* (1993); *Bloodfist VI: Ground Zero* (1994); *Bloodfist VII* (aka *Manhunt*) (1995); *Bloodfist VIII: Trained to Kill* (1996)

The Blue Demon

This masked Mexican wrestler, known in his homeland as El Demonio Azul, briefly challenged fellow-wrestler Santo (q.v.) for the mid–1960s monster-destroyer crown. Santo proved to be the people's favorite, however, and the Blue Demon eventually joined forces with him to create a potent tag team to battle vampires, werewolves, witches, and other evil creatures in a series of lively, but ludicrous, films. See also **Santo**; **Neutron** (yet another Mexican monster wrestler); **Wrestling**.

The Blue Demon (aka *El Demonio Azul*) (1964); *Blue Demon Against the Satanical Power* (aka *Blue Demon Contra el Poder Satanicon*) (1964); *The Shadow of the Bat* (aka *La Sombra del Murcielago*) (1966); *Blue Demon vs. the Infernal Brains* (aka *Blue Demon Contra Cerebros Infernales*; *Cerebro Infernal*) (1968); *Santo Against Blue Demon in Atlantis* (aka *Santo Contra Blue Demon en la Atlántida*) (1969); *The World of the Dead* (aka *El Mundo de los Muertos*) (1969) (with Santo); *Santo and Blue Demon vs. the Monsters* (aka *Santo y Blue Demon Contra los Monstruós*) (1969); *Blue Demon and the Seductresses* (aka *Blue Demon Contra Las Invasoras*) (1969); *The Mummies of Guanajuato* (aka *Las Momias de Guanajuato*) (1970) (with Santo); *The Beasts of Terror* (aka *Las Bestias del Terror*) (1972) (with Santo); *Santo and Blue Demon vs. Dracula and the Wolf Man* (aka *Santo y Blue Demon Contra Dracula y el Hombre Lobo*) (1972); *Santo and Blue Demon vs. Dr. Frankenstein* (aka *Santo y Blue Demon Contra el Dr. Frankenstein*) (1973); *Mystery in Bermuda* (aka *Misterio en las Bermudas*) (1977) (with Santo)

Boarding Schools

Boarding schools have provided atmospheric settings for a wide variety of films — sentimental tales of dedicated teachers, satanic thrillers, mischievous comedies, and student revolutions. Jean Vigo's 1933 surrealistic classic *Zero for Conduct* blended revolution with comedy in the story of mistreated students who rebel against a regimented boarding school run by a midget principal. British director Lindsay Anderson expanded on the same premise in his 1968 film *If...* (q.v.), in which defiant Malcolm McDowell and fellow students gun down the school's faculty on Speech Day (or is this massacre merely imagined by McDowell's character?). The girls known as *The Belles of St. Trinian's* (q.v.) (1951) were rebellious too, but never mounted a revolt since they pretty much ran the school anyway. Convent and church-run schools have been especially prone to attracting mischief-making students, as evidenced by *The Trouble with Angels* (1966) and *Goodbye, Children* (1988). Dedicated teachers molded mischievous youths into mature students of life in *Goodbye, Mr. Chips* (1939 and 1969) and *Dead Poets Society* (1989). In contrast, schoolmaster David Hemming's students threatened to murder him — like they did his predecessor — in *Unman, Wittering and Zigo* (1981). Clint Eastwood found himself in a worse situation as a virile male hiding out in a girls' school populated by lonely, jealous females in 1971's *The Beguiled*. Pamela Franklin entered a girl's boarding school to investigate her sister's suicide in the 1973 TV movie *Satan's School for Girls*. Despite its title, it turned out to be a nicer place than the demonic school run by a witches coven in Dario Argento's stylish *Suspiria* (1976). Many films such as *Jane Eyre* (1944) and *Oliver Twist* (1948) have been partially set in boarding schools. See also **Military Academies**; **St. Trinian's Series**.

Maedchun in Uniform (1931); *Zero for Conduct* (aka *Zero de Conduite*) (1933); *Girls' Dormitory* (1936); *Housemaster* (1938); *Goodbye, Mr. Chips* (1939); *Tom Brown's School Days* (aka *Adventures at Rugby*) (1940); *The Happy Years* (1950); *The Browning Version* (1951); *Tom Brown's Schooldays* (1951); *Her Twelve Men* (1954); *The Belles of St. Trinians* (1954); *Les Diaboliques* (aka *Diabolique*; *The Fiends*) (1955); *Tea and Sympathy* (1956); *The Ladies' Man* (1961);

13 Frightened Girls (1963); *The Trouble with Angels* (1966); *If...* (1968); *Goodbye, Mr. Chips* (1969); *The House That Screamed* (aka *The Boarding School*) (1969); *Walk a Crooked Path* (1969); *The Beguiled* (1971); *Unman, Wittering and Zigo* (1971); *Child's Play* (1972); *Satan's School for Girls* (1973 TVM); *Our Time* (aka *Death of Her Innocence*) (1974); *Suspiria* (1976); *Boarding School* (aka *The Passion Flower Hotel*) (1977); *Deadly Lessons* (1983 TVM); *Goodbye, Children* (aka *Au Revoir, Les Enfants*) (1988); *Dead Poets Society* (1989); *Courage Mountain* (1989); *Flirting* (1991); *Assault at West Point: The Court-Martial of Johnson Whitaker* (1994 TVM); *A Little Princess* (1995); *Diabolique* (1996)

Body Chemistry Series

A film series about Glenn Close's psycho stalker from *Fatal Attraction*? Surprisingly, that's the basic idea behind *Body Chemistry* (1990), an erotic thriller in which sex therapist Dr. Claire Archer (Lisa Pecsia) develops a fatal attraction for fellow researcher Tom Redding (Marc Singer). As in Close's film, Claire Archer (possibly an in-joke reference to *Fatal Attraction* star Anne Archer) threatens to expose her married lover's adulterous exploits. Indeed, Tom's wife eventually learns about the affair and leaves her husband. An enraged Tom confronts Claire and, after a brief struggle, Claire pulls a gun from her nightstand and shoots him. When the police arrive, Claire claims she was acting in self-defense against a jilted lover who had turned violent. In a nifty switch from *Fatal Attraction*, she gets away with murder. Pecsia reprised her role as Claire for *Body Chemistry II: The Voice of a Stranger* (1992). Now a radio talk show host, Claire gets involved with a former police officer (Gregory Harrison) trying to overcome his violent behavior. Unfortunately, Claire's "therapy" only makes matters worse and the poor guy winds up being shot by some of his cop friends. Shari Shattuck took over for Pescia in *Body Chemistry III: Point of Seduction* (1994), while erotic movie veteran Shannon Tweed played Claire in *Body Chemistry 4: Full Exposure* (1995). Neither of these films improved upon the first two installments, although both featured Andrew Stevens as actor/producer. Stevens forged a profitable career in the erotic thriller genre, having been in front or behind the camera for films such as *Night Eyes* (1990), *Scorned* (1994), and *Victim of Desire* (1995). He also managed to appear in the fourth film after Claire killed him in the third one. Even if it was only a flashback, that's pretty good considering Claire's homicidal track record. See also **Animal Instincts Series**; **Night Eyes Series**; and **Secret Games Series**.

Body Chemistry (1990); *Body Chemistry II: The Voice of a Stranger* (1991); *Body Chemistry III: Point of Seduction* (1994); *Body Chemistry 4: Full Exposure* (1995)

Body Switching

The most overworked premise of 1988 was this one: A young person's soul magically changes places with an older person's, so that the youngster acts like an adult and the adult behaves like a kid. Actually, the plotline dates back to Peter Ustinov's then-original 1947 fantasy *Vice Versa*, in which a magic stone caused stockbroker Roger Livesey and school-aged son Anthony Newley to temporarily switch bodies. Disney updated the plot and changed the gender for 1977's *Freaky Friday*. It starred Barbara Harris and Jodie Foster as the mother and daughter making the switch for a day. A trio of mediocre 1988 releases revived the plotline (al-

though in *18 Again*, George Burns played a body-switching grandfather). The best of the three was *Vice Versa*, a semi-amusing, one-joke affair benefiting from funny performances by Judge Reinhold and Fred Savage. Unfortunately, it was released late in the cycle and faded quickly at the box-office. Even fewer people saw the 1989 body switching comedy *Dream a Little Dream*, despite a potentially interesting cast headed by Jason Robards. Of course, not all films have involved a transfer between parent and child. Actually, the first body-switching comedy, 1940's *Turnabout*, had a more risqué premise, with husband and wife Adolphe Menjou and Carole Landis switching bodies (courtesy of a magic Buddha). The film, based on a story by *Topper* author Thorne Smith, served as the basis for a very short-lived 1979 sitcom. The 1986 Disney TV movie *Hero in the Family* altered the body switching premise slightly, with an astronaut finding himself in a chimpanzee's body. Dr. Frankenstein (Peter Cushing) transferred a dying man's soul into the body of his lover in 1967's *Frankenstein Created Woman*. Technically, that's not body switching since both souls resided in one body — but it's certainly close. See also **Brain Transplants**.

Turnabout (1940); *Vice Versa* (1947); *Freaky Friday* (1977); *Hero in the Family* (1986 TVM); *18 Again* (1988); *Vice Versa* (1988); *Like Father, Like Son* (1988); *Dream a Little Dream* (1989); *Prelude to a Kiss* (1992); *Freaky Friday* (1995 TVM); *Dating the Enemy* (1996); *Naked Souls* (1996); *Wish Upon a Star* (1996); *A Saintly Switch* (1999 TVM); *Dogmatic* (1999 TVM)

Bodybuilding

This mini-genre's sole superstar, Arnold Schwarzenegger, has appeared in only two films about bodybuilding. He played a supporting role in 1976's *Stay Hungry*, a Jeff Bridges–Sally Field vehicle about a rich young man who becomes infatuated with the flavorful characters he meets at a second-rate gym. Arnold's first "starring" role was in the following year's *Pumping Iron*, a popular documentary about bodybuilding competitions which also featured Lou (*The Incredible Hulk*) Ferrigno. A sequel of sorts, 1985's *Pumping Iron II: The Women*, promoted Rachel McLish as the superstar of female bodybuilders. She had already made a brief appearance in the 1984 TV movie *Getting Physical*, in which Alexandra Paul becomes obsessed with pumping iron after being mugged. Like Schwarzenegger, McLish gradually transitioned into mainstream action films like 1992's *Aces: Iron Eagle III*. Another real-life bodybuilder, the late Jayne Mansfield's husband Mickey Hargitay, appeared as himself in 1988's *Mr. Universe*. On a lesser note, Harry Grant — holder of the Mr. Southern California and Mr. Los Angeles titles — directed and starred in *Flex 90*. Finally, Bill Travers played the movies' most charming bodybuilder: the scrawny Scottish lad who sends off for a weightlifting program and becomes an Olympic hammer thrower in *Wee Geordie*.

Wee Geordie (aka *Geordie*) (1956); *Muscle Beach Party* (1964); *Stay Hungry* (1976); *Pumping Iron* (1977); *The Hustler of Muscle Beach* (1980 TVM); *The Rainbow Serpent* (1983); *Getting Physical* (1984 TVM); *Pumping Iron II: The Women* (1985); *Echo Park* (1986); *Mr. Universe* (1988); *Flex 90* (1990); *Léola* (1992)

Bodyguards

There are few films about professional bodyguards who make a living protecting their clients. Still, these tough guys have been played by a diverse group of actors that includes William Bendix (*The Glass Key*), Lawrence Tierney (*Bodyguard*), Edmund O'Brien (*The Web*), and Kevin Costner (*The Bodyguard*). Costner may have had the showiest role as the bodyguard assigned to protect singer Whitney Houston. However, the most intellectual bodyguard was surely the one played by Chazz Palminteri in *Bullets Over Broadway*. When not protecting his mobster boss, he proved adept at writing plays. Secret Service agents have pulled bodyguard duty in a number of films, including *Assassination* (1987), *In the Line of Fire* (1993), and *Guarding Tess* (1994). Police officer Harrison Ford was assigned to protect a little boy who saw a murder in *Witness* (1988), while a female security officer performed similar duties for a deaf man in *His Bodyguard* (1998). A high school student besieged by bullies hired an alleged "killer" classmate to protect him in the charming *My Bodyguard* (1982). On television, Robert Loggia played a cat burglar–turned-bodyguard in the short-lived 1966 series *T.H.E. Cat* (his initials stood for Thomas Hewitt Edward) and Pamela Anderson Lee made a most unlikely bodyguard in the 1998 series *V.I.P.*

The Glass Key (1942); *The Web* (1947); *Bodyguard* (1948); *Assassination* (1987); *Man on Fire* (1987); *Witness* (1988); *The Bodyguard* (1992); *Brain Smasher...A Love Story* (1993); *In the Line of Fire* (1993); *Guarding Tess* (1994); *Bullets Over Broadway* (1994); *His Bodyguard* (aka *Silent Echoes*) (1998 TVM); *Blackjack* (1998)

Boggy Creek Series

A "docudrama" about a Bigfoot-type beast glimpsed roaming around Fouke, Arkansas, 1972's *The Legend of Boggy Creek* peaked enough interest to earn a tidy profit for exploitation producer Charles B. Pierce. Sadly, Pierce's extensive use of "reenactments" has become increasingly popular in television news programs. *Return to Boggy Creek* (1977) was not a sequel, but rather a children's film about a friendly monster helping out some lost kids. It co-starred Dawn Wells, better known as Mary Ann on *Gilligan's Island*. In 1985, Pierce returned to Boggy Creek by casting himself as an anthropology professor in *The Barbaric Beast of Boggy Creek*. See also **Bigfoot**.

The Legend of Boggy Creek (1972); *Return to Boggy Creek* (1977); *The Barbaric Beast of Boggy Creek, Part II* (aka *Boggy Creek II*) (1985)

Bomba, the Jungle Boy

After playing "Boy" for eight years, Johnny Sheffield must have expected to find meatier parts following his farewell Tarzan picture, 1947's *Tarzan and the Huntress*. But no one seemed interested in a 16-year-old star so strongly identified with one role. Then, Monogram producer Walter Mirisch came up with a foolproof series for Sheffield and signed the teen to play Bomba, a junior Tarzan created by Roy Rockwood in the 1920s. *Bomba, the Jungle Boy* (1949) was a low-budget, backlot adventure that relied heavily on stock footage (from a 1930 documentary called *Africa Speaks*). The subsequent Bomba films were pretty routine, though journeyman director Ford Beebe managed to make them tolerable. The series ended in 1955, the 24-year-old Sheffield having outgrown the "jungle boy" look.

Bomba, the Jungle Boy (1949); *Bomba on Panther Island* (1949); *The Lost Volcano* (1950); *Bomba and the Hidden City* (1950); *Bomba and the Elephant Stampede* (aka *Elephant Stampede*) (1951); *The*

Lion Hunters (1951); *African Treasure* (1952); *Bomba and the Jungle Girl* (1952); *Safari Drums* (1953); *The Golden Idol* (1954); *Killer Leopard* (1954); *Lord of the Jungle* (1955)

Bond, James

With the release of 1999's *The World Is Not Enough* Ian Fleming's secret agent celebrated 37 years of silver screen success. Sean Connery debuted as Bond in 1962's *Dr. No* and now — four Bonds and over a dozen movies later — 007 is still going in the person of Pierce Brosnan. Interestingly, Connery was not Fleming's first choice for Bond. The author envisioned an actor closer to Cary Grant. And technically, the first Bond was played by American Barry Nelson in an adaptation of *Casino Royale* that appeared on the TV anthology series *Climax* in the late 1950s. The Bond movies, with the lead actor in parentheses, are listed below in chronological order. *Casino Royale* (1967), a spoof starring David Niven as an elder Bond, is not included since it was not part of the Cubby Broccoli–produced series. *Never Say Never Again* (1983), which was also not part of the "official" series, is included because it starred Connery. As Bond trivia buffs know, *Never* is actually a remake of *Thunderball* and was made only after a long legal dispute. See also **Bond Heroines**; **Bond Villains**.

Dr. No (1962) (Sean Connery); *From Russia with Love* (1963) (Connery); *Goldfinger* (1964) (Connery); *Thunderball* (1965) (Connery); *You Only Live Twice* (1967) (Connery); *On Her Majesty's Secret Service* (1969) (George Lazenby); *Diamonds Are Forever* (1971) (Connery); *Live and Let Die* (1973) (Roger Moore); *The Man with the Golden Gun* (1974) (Moore); *The Spy Who Loved Me* (1977) (Moore); *Moonraker* (1979) (Moore); *For Your Eyes Only* (1981) (Moore); *Octopussy* (1983) (Moore); *Never Say Never Again* (1983) (Connery); *A View to a Kill* (1985) (Moore); *The Living Daylights* (1987) (Timothy Dalton); *License to Kill* (1989) (Dalton); *GoldenEye* (1995) (Pierce Brosnan); *Tomorrow Never Dies* (1997) (Brosnan); *The World Is Not Enough* (1999) (Brosnan)

Bond Heroines

The ladies who play opposite 007 are famous not only for their beauty, but also their outrageous names. Who can forget such memorable monikers as Pussy Galore, Tiffany Case, and Holly Goodhead? Even more interesting, though, is the fascinating trivia surrounding the actresses. For instance, prior to portraying Ms. Galore in 1964's *Goldfinger*, Honor Blackman played Patrick MacNee's sleuthing partner on the TV series *The Avengers*. Her popular *Avengers* replacement was Diana Riggs, who went on to play Tracy (aka Mrs. Bond) in 1969's *On Her Majesty's Secret Service*. That same film featured a supporting performance by Joanna Lumley, who would later play Purdey, MacNee's female sidekick in *The New Avengers* TV series. Maud Adams is the only actress to play in two Bond flicks — she was a supporting villain–turned-good in *The Man with the Golden Gun*, then graduated to the title role in *Octopussy*. Claudine Auger and Kim Basinger played the same character; Claudine played Domino in *Thunderball* and Kim was Domino in *Never Say Never Again*. The Bond movies, the leading ladies, and the characters are as follows:

Dr. No — Ursula Andress (Honeychile Rider); *From Russia with Love* — Daniela Bianchi (Tatiana Romanova); *Goldfinger* — Honor Blackman (Pussy Galore); *Thunderball* — Claudine Auger (Domino Vitali); *You Only Live Twice* — Mie Hama (Kissy Suzuki); *On Her Majesty's Secret Service* — Diana Rigg (Teresa [Tracy], the Countess di Vicenzo); *Diamonds Are Forever*—Jill St. John (Tiffany Case); *Live and Let Die*—Jane Seymour (Solitaire); *The Man with the Golden Gun*—Britt Ekland (Mary Goodnight); *The Spy Who Loved Me*—Barbara Bach (Major Anya Amasova); *Moonraker*—Lois Chiles (Holly Goodhead); *For Your Eyes Only*—Carole Bouquet (Melina Havelock); *Octopussy*—Maud Adams (Octopussy); *Never Say Never Again*—Kim Basinger (Domino); *A View to a Kill*—Tanya Roberts (Stacey Sutton); *The Living Daylights*—Maryam D'Abo (Kara Milovy); *License to Kill*—Carey Lowell (Pam Bouvier); *GoldenEye*—Izabella Scorupco (Natalya Siminova); *Tomorrow Never Dies*—Michelle Yeoh (Wai Lin); *The World Is Not Enough*—Denise Richards (Dr. Christmas Jones)

Bond Villains

Joseph Wiseman established the prototype for Bond villains as Dr. No in the first 007 film. A veteran character actor, Wiseman projected power, confidence, and an overwhelming desire to win at all costs. The best Bond villains fit this mold — and they don't take it lightly when they lose at anything. In *Goldfinger*, the fabulously wealthy Auric Goldfinger (Gert Frobe) cheats at cards and golf. When he "loses" his mistress to Bond, he orders his henchmen to kill her by covering her body with gold paint. Still, these self-assured Bond villains relish a worthy challenge and, of course, 007 always provides one. In *The Man with the Golden Gun*, Scaramanga, a superb pistol marksman, allows himself only one bullet when he stalks an armed Bond in a noisy funhouse. Maximillian Largo challenges Bond to a 3-D video game called Domination in *Never Say Never Again*. The stakes start small — Spain and $9,000 — but escalate until the grand prize is the world. The best known Bond villain is probably Ernest Stavro Blofeld, the head of the international criminal organization S.P.E.C.T.R.E. (Special Executor for Counter-Intelligence, Terrorism, Revenge, and Extortion). Blofeld makes brief appearances, typically with his white cat, in *From Russia with Love*, *Thunderball*, *For Your Eyes Only*, and *Never Say Never Again*. However, he is the featured villain in three consecutive entries: *You Only Live Twice*, *On Her Majesty's Secret Service*, and *Diamonds Are Forever*. Unlike other Bondian bad guys, Blofeld proves to be skillful at escaping when his plans turn sour. His reappearance at the end of *On Her Majesty's Secret Service* proves devastating to 007 when Blofeld murders Bond's bride Tracy. Blofeld, as portrayed by Donald Pleasance in *You Only Live Twice*, served as the inspiration for Mike Myers' Dr. Evil in the *Austin Powers* spy spoofs. In a few Bond films, the villain's chief henchman has almost overshadowed the man in charge. Richard Kiel's physically imposing, steel-mouthed henchman Jaws was so popular in *The Spy Who Loved Me* that he returned for *Moonraker*. Rosa Klebb (Lotte Lenya) made spiked-toe shoes fashionable in *From Russia with Love*. And the silent but deadly Oddjob (Harold Sakata) almost stole *Goldfinger* from Auric Goldfinger. The Bond movies, the actors, and the villainous characters are as follows:

Dr. No—Joseph Wiseman (Dr. No); *From Russia with Love*—Vladek Sheybal (Kronsteen); *Goldfinger*—Gert Frobe (Auric Goldfinger); *Thunderball*—Aolfo Celi (Emilio Largo); *You Only Live Twice*—Donald Pleasance (Ernst Stavro Blofeld); *On Her Majesty's Secret Service*—Telly Savalas (Ernst Stavro Blofield); *Diamonds Are Forever*—Charles Gray (Ernst Stavro Blofeld); *Live and Let Die*—Yaphet Kotto (Dr. Kanaga [aka Mr. Big]); *The Man with the Golden Gun*—Christopher Lee (Francisco Scaramanga); *The Spy Who Loved Me*—Curt Jurgens (Karl Stromberg); *Moonraker*—Michael Lonsdale (Hugo Drax); *For Your Eyes Only*—Julian Glover (Aris Kristatos); *Octopussy*—Louis Jourdan (Kamal Khan); *Never Say Never Again*—Klaus Maria Brandauer (Maximillian Largo); *A View to a Kill*—Christopher Walken (Max Zorin); *The Living Daylights*—Joe Don Baker (Brad Whitaker); *License to Kill*—Robert Davi (Franz Sanchez); *GoldenEye*—Sean Bean (Alec Trevelyan [Agent 006]); *Tomorrow Never Dies*—Jonathan Pryce (Elliot Carver); *The World Is Not Enough*—Robert Carlyle (Renard)

Bounty Hunters

What do disenchanted lawmen do when the system won't let them get their man? They become bounty hunters, of course. Thus, Rutger Hauer played an ex-government agent turned modern-day, high-tech bounty hunter in 1987's *Wanted: Dead or Alive*. Interestingly, Rutger's character was supposed to be the grandson of Josh Randall, the Western bounty hunter made famous by Steve McQueen in the 1958–61 TV series *Wanted: Dead or Alive*. McQueen played real-life bounty men in his last two films, 1979's *Tom Horn* and 1980's *The Hunter* (based on the life of Ralph "Pappy" Thorson). Robert De Niro and Clint Eastwood played skip tracers, contemporary bounty hunters specializing in bail jumpers, in the lighthearted adventures *Midnight Run* (1988) and *Pink Cadillac* (1989). Westerns typically portray bounty hunters in a negative light. *The Reward* (1965), for example, concerned a group of greedy bounty men who kill each other for a larger share of the reward money. Kenny Rogers played a kinder, more gentle, bounty hunter in the Western telefilm *Rio Diablo*. Sybil Danning proved that women could do the job just as well as men in 1989's *L.A. Bounty*.

The Naked Spur (1953); *The Bounty Hunter* (1954); *The Bounty Killer* (1965); *The Reward* (1965); *The Shooting* (1966); *Any Gun Can Play* (aka *For a Few Bullets More*) (1967); *The Bounty Man* (1972 TVM); *Joe Kidd* (1972); *Santee* (1972); *Manhunter* (1974 TVM); *Truck Turner* (1974); *Tom Horn* (1979); *The Hunter* (1980); *Rivkin: Bounty Hunter* (1981 TVM); *Critters* (1986); *Wanted: Dead or Alive* (1987); *The Blue Iguana* (1988); *Midnight Run* (1988); *Pink Cadillac* (1989); *The Bounty Hunter* (1989); *L.A. Bounty* (1989); *Grim Prairie Tales* (1990); *Into the Badlands* (1991 TVM); *Rio Diablo* (1993 TVM); *It's Nothing Personal* (1993 TVM); *Home for Christmas* (aka *Little Miss Millions*) (1993); *Bounty Hunter 2002* (aka *2002: The Rape of Eden*) (1994); *Beverly Hills Cop III* (1994); *The Awakening* (1995 TVM); *The Huntress* (2000 TVM)

The Bowery Boys

The chronology of this popular, low-budget juvenile series spans three decades, from the Dead End Kids in the 1930s to the Little Tough Guys and the East Side Kids in the 1940s to (finally) the Bowery Boys in the 1950s. It all began with 1937's *The Dead End*, an adaptation of the sober 1935 Broadway play about New York slum life. That film introduced teen performers Leo Gorcey and Huntz Hall, an odd couple who would eventually form the comedy core of all these movies. At Warner Bros., the Dead End Kids appeared with major stars like James Cagney (1938's *Angels with Dirty Faces*) and John Garfield (1939's *They Made Me a Criminal*). These efforts, though, did not constitute a series since they featured the Kids in changing roles. Some of the Kids (e.g., Billy Halop, Huntz Hall) defected to Universal in 1938 and made *Little Tough Guy*, a *Dead End* imitation with a downbeat ending (Halop goes to reform school). Additional Little Tough Guy movies followed, although the cast and characters again changed on a regular basis. Jackie Cooper even cropped up as the lead Little Tough Guy in 1938's *Newsboy's Home*. In the early 1940s, enterprising producer Sam Katzman brought some of the boys, including Gorcey and Halop, to Monogram Pictures and redubbed them the East Side Kids. Under Katzman's guidance, the series gradually shifted from juvenile drama to broad comedy. Gorcey and Hall also emerged as the principal stars. With their agent Jan Grippo, they revamped the series in 1946 and launched the Bowery Boys pictures for Monogram. As Terence Alyosius Mahoney (Slip) and Horace Debussey Jones (Sach), Gorcey and Hall mugged their way through 48 Bowery Boy comedies. The humor frequently centered around hapless Sach acquiring some strange power. A throat operation turned him into a great singer in *Blues Busters*. A punch in the nose gave him telepathic powers in *Private Eyes*. He also became clairvoyant (*Master Minds*), acquired great physical strength (*No Holds Barred*), and learned how to smell diamonds (*Jungle Gents*). In the end, though, he always returned to normal, inspiring Slip to slap him with his hat. Other Bowery Boys who appeared with some regularity were: Whitey (Billy Benedict), Chuck (Gorcey's brother David), Gabe (Gabriel Dell), and Bobby (Bobby Jordan). The Boys hung out at Louie's Sweet Shop, which was run by Louie Dumbrowsky (Gorcey's father Bernard), who was always sorry for listening to Slip and company. Bernard Gorcey died in 1955, after completing *Dig That Uranium*. His father's death and his own alcoholism caused Leo Gorcey to leave the series after 1956's *Crashing Las Vegas*. Stanley Clements (Gloria Grahame's ex-husband) took over as Duke, the gang's new leader, in the series' final seven films. Post–Bowery Boy Huntz Hall continued to appear in movies in supporting roles. He and Gorcey had a cameo together in the dismal 1970 satire *The Phynx*.

THE EAST SIDE KIDS: *East Side Kids* (1941); *Boys of the City* (1941); *That Gang of Mine* (1941); *Pride of the Bowery* (1941); *Flying Wild* (1941); *Bowery Blitzkrieg* (1941); *Spooks Run Wild* (1941); *Mr. Wise Guy* (1942); *Let's Get Tough* (1942); *Smart Alecks* (1942); *'Neath Brooklyn Bridge* (1942); *Kid Dynamite* (1943); *Clancy Street Boys* (1943); *Ghosts on the Loose* (1943); *Mr. Muggs Steps Out* (1943); *Million Dollar Kid* (1944); *Follow the Leader* (1944); *Block Busters* (1944); *Bowery Champs* (1944); *Docks of New York* (1945); *Mr. Muggs Rides Again* (1945); *Come Out Fighting* (1945)

THE BOWERY BOYS: *In Fast Company* (1946); *Mr. Hex* (1946); *Spook Busters* (1946); *Bowery Bombshell* (1946); *Live Wires* (1946); *Hard-Boiled Mahoney* (1947); *News Hounds* (1947); *Bowery Buckeroos* (1947); *Angels' Alley* (1947); *Trouble Makers* (1948); *Smuggler's Cove* (1948); *Jinx Money* (1948); *Angels in Disguise* (1949); *Hold That Baby!* (1949); *Fighting Fools* (1949); *Master Minds* (1949); *Blonde Dynamite* (1950); *Blues Busters* (1950); *Lucky Losers* (1950); *Triple Trouble* (1950); *Ghost Chasers* (1951); *Crazy Over Horses* (1951); *Let's Go Navy* (1951); *Bowery Battalion* (1951); *Hold That Line* (1952); *Feudin' Fools* (1952); *Here Come the Marines* (1952); *No Holds Barred* (1952); *Clipped Wings* (1953); *Jalopy* (1953); *Loose in London* (1953); *Private Eyes* (1953); *Paris Playboys* (1954); *Jungle Gents* (1954); *The Bowery Boys Meet the Monsters* (1954); *Bowery to Bagdad* (1955); *High Society* (1955); *Spy Chasers* (1955); *Jail Busters* (1955); *Dig That Uranium* (1956); *Crashing Las Vegas* (1956); *Fighting Trouble* (1956) (first with Clements); *Hot Shots* (1956); *Hold That Hypnotist* (1957); *Spook Chasers* (1957); *Looking for Danger* (1957); *Up in Smoke* (1958); *In the Money* (1958)

Bowling

Professional bowlers have been a screen oddity, although they have been played by the likes of Tim Matheson, Michael J.

Fox, and Bill Murray. Matheson played a sensitive bowler in 1979's *Dreamer*, a pale *Rocky* imitation that left plenty of pins standing. Michael J. Fox portrayed a bowler who quit the tour to pursue a rich uncle's money in *Greedy* (1994). In the outrageous 1996 comedy *Kingpin*, Bill Murray played an unscrupulous sequin-wearing bowler trying to beat Amish rival Randy Quaid and his washed-up mentor Woody Harrelson. The offbeat *Shakes the Clown* (1991) featured Julie Brown as a former bowling champ and girlfriend to Bobcat Goldthwait's title character. Finally, although not a professional bowler, Janeane Garofalo played a would-be super hero called The Bowler in the 1999 comedy *Mystery Men*. In contrast to these few films about bowlers, several movies have employed a bowling alley setting (a rich source of eccentric characters). The wonderfully-titled films—1982's *Dear Mr. Wonderful* and 1993's *Mr. Wonderful*— dealt with, respectively, a bowling alley manager and five blue-collar workers who open their own lanes. Nicolas Cage and Sean Penn worked as pinspotters in a bowling alley circa 1943 in *Racing with the Moon* (1984). Jack Nicholson has one of his best roles in 1970's *Five Easy Pieces*, as a pianist-drifter who has a brief affair with a girl working in a bowling alley. In the Coen Brothers' bizarre 1998 comedy *The Big Lebowski*, the Dude (Jeff Bridges) and his pals spent way too much time at the bowling alley. The action film *Collision Course* (1987) showed that bowling alleys can be used for more than just bowling. Paul Muni's *Scarface* (1932) set the precedent for bowling alley violence when Boris Karloff's rival gangster leader was gunned down during a game of ninepins. On a relatively lighter note, two righteous babes stole a bowling trophy—occupied by an evil imp—in the outlandish 1988 horror-comedy *Sorority Babes in the Slimeball Bowl-O-Rama*.

Scarface (1932); *Five Easy Pieces* (1970); *Dreamer* (1979); *Dear Mr. Wonderful* (1982); *Racing with the Moon* (1984); *Collision Course* (1987); *Sorority Babes in the Slimeball Bowl-O-Rama* (1988); *Shakes the Clown* (1991); *Mr. Wonderful* (1993); *Greedy* (1994); *The Flintstones* (1994); *The Next Karate Kid* (1994); *Kingpin* (1996); *Dream with the Fishes* (1997); *The Big Lebowski* (1998); *Pleasantville* (1998); *Buffalo '66* (1998)

Boxing

Filmmakers have long been fascinated by the sweaty, brutal world of boxing, making it by far the most popular sport in movies. Film biographies have chronicled the careers of John L. Sullivan (*The Great John L.*), Jim Corbett (*Gentleman Jim*), Jack Johnson (*The Great White Hope*), Joe Louis (*The Joe Louis Story*), Rocky Graziano (*Somebody Up There Likes Me*), Jake La Motta (*Raging Bull*), Muhammad Ali (*The Greatest*), Jack Dempsey (*Dempsey*), Rocky Marciano (*Marciano* and *Rocky Marciano*), and Boom Boom Mancini (*Heart of a Champion: The Ray Mancini Story*). Fictitious prizefighters have fared even better, with Rocky Balboa (q.v.), Joe Palooka (q.v.), and Too Sweet (see **Penitentiary**) earning their own film series. Some movie boxers have hailed from other, more unusual professions. John Derek was a young minister who entered the ring to earn money for his congregation in *The Leather Saint* (1956). William Holden played a young man forced to choose between prizefighting and a promising career as a violinist in *Golden Boy* (1939). Almost every male comedy star has included a boxing routine in one of his movies. Danny Kaye made an unlikely boxer in *The Kid from Brooklyn* (1946), but he looked pretty good compared to Donald O'Connor in *Francis in the Navy* (1955), a hypnotized Jimmie Walker in *Let's Do It Again* (1975), Don Knotts in *The Prize Fighter* (1979), and Lou Costello in *Abbott and Costello Meet the Invisible Man* (1951). In the latter film, Costello's boxing prowess was aided considerably — and hilariously — by the presence of an invisible boxing chum. Serious fight films have tended to focus on the corruption within the sport. These include some of the genre's finest films — *The Champ* (1931), *Battling Bellhop* (aka *Kid Galahad*) (1937), *Body and Soul* (1941), *Champion* (1949), *The Set-Up* (1949), and Rod Serling's *Requiem for a Heavyweight* (1962). *The Set-Up* has the added distinction of taking place in real time, as indicated by the clocks shown at the beginning and end of the film. Bare-fisted fighters have been limited to backroom brawls, though Charles Bronson brought one to life memorably in *Hard Times* (1975) and Clint Eastwood had one of his biggest box-office success as slugger Philo Beddoe in *Every Which Way But Loose* (1978). The most bizarre boxer has to be the spunky kangaroo in *Matilda* (1978), though Elvis Presley rates a close second for his pugilist performance in *Kid Galahad* (1962). See also **Penitentiary Series**; **Rocky**; **Wrestling**.

Battling Butler (1926); *Iron Man* (1931); *The Champ* (1931); *Winner Take All* (1932); *The Prizefighter and the Lady* (aka *Every Woman's Man*) (1933) (with real-life boxers Jack Dempsey and Max Baer); *King for a Night* (1933); *The Life of Jimmy Dolan* (aka *The Kid's Last Fight*) (1933); *Cain and Mabel* (1936); *Battling Bellhop* (aka *Kid Galahad*) (1937); *When's Your Birthday?* (1937); *Ex-Champ* (1939); *Golden Boy* (1939); *Invitation to Happiness* (1939); *They Made Me a Criminal* (1939); *Kid Nightingale* (1939); *City for Conquest* (1940); *Body and Soul* (1941); *Here Comes Mr. Jordan* (1941); *Knockout* (1941); *Ringside Maisie* (aka *Cash and Carry*) (1941); *Gentleman Jim* (1942); *The Great John L.* (aka *A Man Called Sullivan*) (1945); *The Kid from Brooklyn* (1946); *Mr. Hex* (1946); *Leather Gloves* (1948); *Whiplash* (1948); *The Big Punch* (1948); *Champion* (1949); *The Set-Up* (1949); *The Golden Gloves Story* (1950); *Right Cross* (1950); *Abbott and Costello Meet the Invisible Man* (1951); *The Fighter* (1951); *Iron Man* (1951); *Flesh and Fury* (1952); *The Ring* (1952); *The Joe Louis Story* (1953); *Champ for a Day* (1953); *Tennessee Champ* (1954); *Francis in the Navy* (1955); *Killer's Kiss* (1955); *The Leather Saint* (1956); *The Harder They Fall* (1956); *Somebody Up There Likes Me* (1956); *World in My Corner* (1956); *Kid Galahad* (1962); *Requiem for a Heavyweight* (1962); *Confessions of Tom Harris* (aka *Childish Things*) (1967); *The Legendary Champions* (1968); *AKA Cassius Clay* (1970); *The Great White Hope* (1970); *Ripped Off* (aka *The Boxer*) (1971); *Jack Johnson* (1971); *Fat City* (1972); *The All-American Boy* (1973); *Hard Times* (1975); *Let's Do It Again* (1975); *Rocky* (1976); *The Greatest* (1977); *Every Which Way But Loose* (1978); *Penitentiary* (1978); *Ring of Passion* (1978 TVM); *Matilda* (1978); *Movie Movie* (the "Dynamite Hands" segment) (1978); *The Main Event* (1979); *Marciano* (1979 TVM); *The Champ* (1979); *The Prize Fighter* (1979); *Any Which Way You Can* (1980); *Raging Bull* (1980); *Body and Soul* (1981); *Honeyboy* (1982 TVM); *Edith and Marcel* (1983); *The Fighter* (1983 TVM); *The Last Fight* (1983); *Dempsey* (1983 TVM); *Heart of a Champion: The Ray Mancini Story* (1985 TVM); *Streets of Gold* (1986); *Heart* (1987); *Spike of Bensonhurst* (1988); *Split Decisions* (1988); *Triumph of the Spirit* (1989); *Champions Forever* (1989); *Blonde Fist* (1991); *Gladiator* (1992); *Far and Away* (1992); *Diggstown* (1992); *Night and the City* (1992); *Percy and Thunder* (1993 TVM); *Pulp Fiction* (1994); *Wind from Wyoming* (aka *Le Vent du Wyoming*) (1994); *The Great White Hype* (1996); *When We Were Kings* (1997); *Don King: Only in America* (1997 TVM); *Twenty Four Seven* (1997);

The Boxer (1997); *Snake Eyes* (1998); *Rocky Marciano* (1999 TVM); *Fight Club* (1999); *Knockout* (1999); *Hurricane* (1999); *Play It to the Bone* (1999); *Girlfight* (2000); *Ali: An American Hero* (2000 TVM); *King of the World* (2000 TVM)

Boy Scouts

Comedy and sentimentality have dominated movies about Boy Scouts. Clifton Webb played a grouchy kid-hater who wound up leading a scout troop — and liking it — in the 1953 comedy *Mister Scoutmaster*. In 1949's *The Great Lover*, scout leader Bob Hope had his hands full aboard a ship filled with his rowdy troupe, a murderer, and luscious Rhonda Fleming. On the sentimental side, Fred MacMurray portrayed a man who devoted his life to his boys in the sticky-sweet Disney picture *Follow Me, Boys!* (1966). *The Wrong Guys* was a 1988 comedy about a Cub Scout reunion, while the 1989 Shelley Long vehicle *Troop Beverly Hills* gave equal time to some Girl Scouts. In the prologue to *Indiana Jones and the Last Crusade* (1989), young Indiana Jones (River Phoenix) showed up in a scout's uniform. Of course, not all scouts and scoutmasters have been portrayed as model citizens. Robert De Niro portrayed a scoutmaster with a drill sergeant attitude in 1993's *This Boy's Life*. Tim Robbins played a terrorist who once led a Junior Discoverer scout troop in the chilling *Arlington Road* (1999). And Rupert Everett battled a persistent group of flesh-eating boy scout ghouls in *Cemetery Man* (1994). There were neither scoutmasters nor den mothers in 1991's *The Last Boy Scout*—only Bruce Willis as a rumpled private detective.

Henry Aldrich, Boy Scout (1944); *The Great Lover* (1949); *Mister Scoutmaster* (1953); *It Happened to Jane* (aka *Twinkle and Shine*) (1959); *Cuckoo Patrol* (1965); *Follow Me, Boys!* (1966); *Scout's Honor* (1980 TVM); *The Wrong Guys* (1988); *Troop Beverly Hills* (1989); *Indiana Jones and the Last Crusade* (1989); *Edge of Honor* (1991); *This Boy's Life* (1993); *Cemetery Man* (aka *Dellamorte Dellamore*; *Of Death and Love*) (1994); *Arlington Road* (1999)

Brain Transplants

Mad scientists have been obsessed with transplanting brains since the days of silent films. Almost all Frankenstein films (q.v.), beginning with Edison's 1910 version, have dealt with brain transplanting of some fashion. In James Whale's 1931 *Frankenstein*, the doctor's assistant Fritz stole a criminal's brain from a medical lab, thus explaining the Monster's homicidal tendencies. Yet, the basic Frankenstein operation — the implant of a spare brain into a nonliving body — is but one kind of brain transplant. More interesting films have involved the transplant of a brain from one living creature to another. *On Time* (1924) was a strange little adventure film with a subplot about some thugs trying to replace the hero's brain with a gorilla's. The reversal of that plot describes 1941's *The Monster and the Girl*, in which the implanted brain of a killer transformed an ape into the "Mangle Murderer." Similarly, John Carradine's brain wound up in the skull of a missing link in 1944's *Return of the Ape Man*. In contrast to such silliness, the 1986 TV movie *Who Is Julia?* was a serious affair about a brain-dead mother (Mare Winningham) who receives new gray cells courtesy of a recently-deceased model. Surprisingly, Terence Fisher's *Frankenstein Must Be Destroyed* (1969) dispensed with the required gruesome monster and opted for a straightforward brain transplant plot. In this ironic tale, Frankenstein (Peter Cushing) "cures" a brain-damaged fellow scientist by transplanting the man's brain into a new body. However, the scientist's gratefulness turns to bitter hate when his wife spurns his new appearance — the face of a stranger. In 1969's *Change of Mind*, a dying white district attorney awakes one day to find his brain in the body of a black man, but, after the initial shock, it all ends happily. The funny side of brain switching has been explored by Abbott and Costello (*A&C Meet Frankenstein*), the Bowery Boys (*Spook Busters* and *Master Minds*), and Steve Martin (*The Man with Two Brains*). Martin's delightful 1983 film cast him as a brain surgeon in love with a body-less brain (although he eventually finds a happy home for it). Although it did not involve brain transplanting, *Hauser's Memory* (1970) deserves special mention for its plot about a man who injected himself with another's brain fluid to learn a valuable secret. See also **Body Switching**.

On Time (1924); Frankenstein (1931); The Man Who Lived Again (aka The Man Who Changed His Mind) (1936); Black Friday (1940); The Monster and the Girl (1941); The Ghost of Frankenstein (1942); Return of the Ape Man (1944); Spook Busters (1946); Abbott and Costello Meet Frankenstein (1948); Master Minds (1949); The Black Sleep (1956); The Revenge of Frankenstein (1958); The Head (1959); Monstrosity (aka The Atomic Brain) (1964); Frankenstein Must Be Destroyed (1969); Change of Mind (1969); Blood of Ghastly Horror (aka The Fiend with the Atomic Brain; Psycho a Go-Go!; The Love Maniac; The Man with the Synthetic Brain; The Fiend with the Electronic Brain) (1972); Brainwaves (1982); The Man with Two Brains (1983); Who Is Julia? (1986 TVM)

Brainwashing

By strict definition, brainwashing is the process by which a person is forcibly induced to forsake political, religious, or social beliefs in favor of contrasting views. *Ticket to Heaven* (1981) and *Split Image* (1982) both explored how susceptible youths were brainwashed by religious cults and then rescued and "deprogrammed." A loathsome punk named Alex (Malcolm McDowell) was brainwashed by Liberals with the "Ludovico technique" in Stanley Kubrick's cult fantasy *A Clockwork Orange* (1971). The fact-based *Patty Hearst* (1988) detailed how the famous heiress was kidnapped and subsequently brainwashed into joining her terrorist captors. The Australian horror picture *Thirst* (1979) offered an intriguing twist, whereby a secret society tried to brainwash a young woman into becoming a vampire. Normal rebellious teens were brainwashed into robotic "perfect" children in the underrated *Disturbing Behavior* (1998). Other movies have altered the definition of "brainwashing" to include plots in which a person is controlled subconsciously (usually by hypnosis) and forced to perform uncharacteristic acts. A Robert Frost poem, delivered over the telephone, triggered nice folks into becoming autonomous saboteurs in the thriller *Telefon*. The spy hero of *The Ipcress File* (Michael Caine) used self-induced pain as a defense against hi-tech brainwashing techniques. However, the most famous film of this type remains John Frankenheimer's controversial classic *The Manchurian Candidate* (1962). Laurence Harvey starred as a patriotic soldier turned into a time-delayed assassin controlled by his own mother (Angela Lansbury). The only brainwashing comedy of note is *Simon*, a decidedly offbeat tale in which a psychology professor (Alan Arkin) is brainwashed into thinking he's an alien from another world. See also **Hypnotists**; **Psychiatrists**.

1984 (1956); Brainwashed (1961); The Manchurian Candidate (1962); Thirty-Six Hours (1964); The Ipcress File (1965); On Her Majesty's Secret Service (1969); A Clockwork Orange (1971); Hunter (1972 TVM); Telefon (1977); Thirst (1979); Simon (1980); Ticket to Heaven (1981); Split Image (1982); Circle of Power (aka Mystique; Brainwash; The Naked Weekend) (1983); 1984 (1984); Patty Hearst (1988); Total Recall (1990); The Sleep Room (1998); Disturbing Behavior (1998); Holy Smoke (1999)

Bullfights *see* Matadors/Bullfights

Buddy Action Films

The "buddy action picture" requires careful definition. These films have existed for years, but were not accorded their own genre until the late 1980s. The prototypical buddy film pairs up two individuals of the same sex — but opposite personalities — and throws them into a situation requiring them to work together. Of course, this formula can be traced back to much earlier films, such as 1958's *The Defiant Ones*. Sidney Poitier and Tony Curtis played the convicts, one black and one white, connected only by a pair of handcuffs and their mutual desire for freedom. In the end, they gained respect for each other, and that's the classical ending for all buddy films. Actually, the buddies do not always have to be the same sex. However, when one's a woman and one's a man, they typically fall in love and the film becomes a romantic adventure. For example, *The 39 Steps* (1935) is a romantic adventure because the relationship between fugitives Robert Donat and Madeleine Carroll eventually blossoms into romance. That's significantly different from the mutual admiration which develops between detective Clint Eastwood and Tyne Daly in 1976's *The Enforcer* (one of the few male-female buddy films). The label "buddy picture" may have been first used to describe 1982's *48 HRS*, the Eddie Murphy–Nick Nolte vehicle whose financial success guaranteed plenty of Hollywood knock-offs. By the end of the decade, moviegoers had encountered a variety of odd couples: black family man/cop Danny Glover and white out-of-control cop Mel Gibson in *Lethal Weapon* (q.v.); Chicago cop James Belushi and Russian cop Arnold Schwarzenegger in *Red Heat*; alien cop Kyle MacLachlan and Earthling cop Michael Nouri in *The Hidden*; slob cop Kurt Russell and neat cop Sylvester Stallone in *Tango & Cash*; and, for a change of pace, down-on-his-luck private eye Bruce Willis and former football quarterback Damon Wayans in *The Last Boy Scout*. Although Susan Sarandon and Geena Davis were friends at the start of *Thelma and Louise* (and hence did not experience the mandatory initial conflict), some critics labeled it a female buddy picture. The genre, and *Lethal Weapon* in particular, were spoofed unevenly in 1993's *National Lampoon's Loaded Weapon 1*. See also **Beverly Hills Cop Series**; **Lethal Weapon Series**.

48 HRS (1982); Renegades (1986); Lethal Weapon (1987); The Hidden (1987); Collision Course (1987); The Wild Pair (1987); Red Heat (1988); Midnight Run (1988); Tango & Cash (1989); The Rookie (1990); Another 48 HRS (1990); Pure Luck (1991); The Last Boy Scout (1991); National Lampoon's Loaded Weapon 1 (1993); Money Train (1995); Bad Boys (1995); Bulletproof (1996); The Glimmer Man (1996); Gridlock'd (1997); Rush Hour (1998); Chill Factor (1999)

Buried Alive

A plot staple in most film adaptations of Edgar Allan Poe, the "buried alive" premise has been best used as a subplot.

Nevertheless, it has been the focus of a few movies. In 1958's *Macabre*, a doctor frantically searches for his little girl, whom some fiend had buried alive. Producer-director William Castle hyped it by offering viewers fright insurance. In *The Screaming Woman* (1972), no one believed recently-released asylum resident Olivia de Havilland when she told them she heard a voice in the ground — but there was someone down there, all right. Kidnappers buried their victim in a tiny underground compartment in *The Longest Night* (1972), a film which should have conveyed a more claustrophobic feeling. In the made-for-cable *Buried Alive*, Tim Matheson portrayed a man poisoned by his wife and buried — only to recover from the nonlethal dose in his coffin. A similar fate befell Ally Sheedy in the sequel *Buried Alive II*.

Isle of the Dead (1945); *Macabre* (1958); *The House of Usher* (aka *The Fall of the House of Usher*) (1960); *The Premature Burial* (1962); *The Oblong Box* (1969); *The Screaming Woman* (1972 TVM); *The Longest Night* (1972 TVM); *Buried Alive* (1990 TVM); *83 Hours 'Til Dawn* (1990 TVM); *Buried Alive* (aka *Edgar Allan Poe's Buried Alive*) (1990); *Haunting Fear* (1991); *Guarding Tess* (1994); *Buried Alive II* (1997); *Oxygen* (1999 TVM)

Buses

The Big Bus (1976) may be the only film which takes place almost exclusively on a bus. A disaster movie spoof, it starred Joseph Bologna, Lynn Redgrave, and Ruth Gordon as some of the passengers aboard the world's first nuclear-powered bus during its maiden journey from New York to Denver. In 1980's *Detour to Terror*, O.J. Simpson played a driver whose tour bus is hijacked en route to Las Vegas by a group of terrorists. In the 1994 box-office smash *Speed*, a bomb aboard a Los Angeles city bus was rigged to explode if the bus's speed dipped below 50 miles per hour. Carl Betz and family set out aboard a restored bus to rediscover the U.S. in the 1971 TV movie *In Search of America*. Despite their blue-collar reputation, buses have boasted their share of pulchritudinous passengers. Joan Collins and Jayne Mansfield took a ride on *The Wayward Bus*, adapted from a John Steinbeck story, while *Bus Stop* featured Marilyn Monroe as a rodeo champ's reluctant girlfriend. Alfred Hitchcock considered the bus explosion in *Sabotage* one of his greatest mistakes, since it cruelly killed the heroine's innocent younger brother. The issue of forced busing to schools was examined in the 1980 TV movie *All God's Children*. Karl Malden portrayed a heroic bus driver in the fact-based 1993 TV movie *They've Taken Our Children: The Chowchilla Kidnapping*. A bus crash that killed 20 school children haunted a Canadian town in Atom Egoyan's *The Sweet Hereafter* (1997). On the lighter side, a ghost drove a bus through the air in *High Spirits* (1988) and John Candy led fellow bus passengers in singing TV songs (much to Steve Martin's dismay) in 1987's *Planes, Trains, and Automobiles*. See also **Automobiles; Truck Drivers.**

Friday the Thirteenth (1933); *Sabotage* (aka *A Woman Alone*) (1936); *Pardon My Sarong* (1942); *Dead of Night* (1945); *Mexican Bus Ride* (aka *Ascent to Heaven; Subida Al Cielo*) (1951); *The Runaway Bus* (1954); *Bus Stop* (aka *The Wrong Kind of Girl*) (1956); *The Wayward Bus* (1957); *Night of the Iguana* (1964); *Where Angels Go, Trouble Follows* (1968); *In Search of America* (1971 TVM); *The Magic Carpet* (1971 TVM); *On the Buses* (1971); *The Laughing Policeman* (1974); *The Big Bus* (1976); *The Gauntlet* (1977); *Long Journey Back* (1978 TVM); *Lady on the Bus* (1978); *Detour to Terror* (1980 TVM); *All God's Children* (1980 TVM); *Bustin' Loose* (1981);

Planes, Trains and Automobiles (1987); *High Spirits* (1988); *Wheels of Terror* (1990 TVM); *Defending Your Life* (1991); *Love Field* (1992); *They've Taken Our Children: The Chowchilla Kidnapping* (1993 TVM); *A Bronx Tale* (1993); *Speed* (1994); *The Adventures of Priscilla, Queen of the Desert* (1994); *Deadly Outbreak* (1996); *Get on the Bus* (1996); *Carla's Song* (1996); *Sudden Terror: The Hijacking of School Bus No. 17* (1996 TVM); *The Sweet Hereafter* (1997); *Just Write* (1997); *The Siege* (1998); *The Cruise* (1998); *Ride* (1998)

Butchers

Thanks to Ernest Borgnine, butchers have avoided cinematic stereotyping as psychotic killers who chop more than meat with their sharp instruments. Borgnine earned a well-deserved Best Actor Oscar for his realistic portrayal of a lonely, likable butcher in 1955's *Marty*. George Dzundza also played a sympathetic butcher — one befuddled by his bride's clairvoyance — in *The Butcher's Wife* (1991). Other butchers, though, have displayed murderous tendencies. In 1989's *Out Cold*, butcher John Lithgow mistakenly believes he has killed his partner when he finds a body in the freezer. Claude Chabrol's psychological thriller *Le Boucher* (1969) mixes murder and love in an unusual tale of a lonely, murderous butcher who finds romance with a quiet schoolteacher. Victor Buono, in a role he'd like to forget, played a more conventional butcher-killer in 1972's Italian-lensed *The Mad Butcher*. The murderer in the 1981 Australian thriller *Road Games* may have been a butcher, but it's hard to say. Rory Calhoun turned people into sausage in 1980's *Motel Hell*, but he was not a butcher by profession. Likewise, the deranged family in *The Texas Chainsaw Massacre* films (q.v.) consisted of former slaughterhouse employees — so they were not technically butchers. On the lighter side, TV's *The Brady Bunch* (1969–74) featured Sam the butcher as Alice the housekeeper's boyfriend.

Rationing (1944); *People Will Talk* (1951); *Marty* (1955); *Le Boucher* (aka *The Butcher*) (1969); *The Mad Butcher* (aka *Meat Is Meat; Strangler of Vienna*) (1972); *The Homecoming* (1973); *Road Games* (1981); *The Cold Room* (aka *The Prisoner*) (1984 TVM); *Big Meat Eater* (1984); *Out Cold* (1989); *The Butcher's Wife* (1991); *So I Married an Axe Murderer* (1993); *A Man of No Importance* (1994); *The Man Who Knew Too Little* (1997)

Butlers

Stereotypically stuffy and very British, butlers have been cast as supporting characters for the most part. Even then, they have managed to upstage the principal stars, as exemplified by John Gielgud's scene-stealing performance in *Arthur* (1981). Arthur Treacher practically made a career of playing butlers, his most famous portrayal being that of P.G. Wodehouse's perfect butler Jeeves in 1936's *Thank You, Jeeves* and its 1937 follow-up *Step Lively, Jeeves*. Irrepressible Eric Blore made a very funny, very cynical valet to Fred Astaire in *Top Hat* (1935) and subsequently specialized in butler roles, too. Although butler leads have been rare, Charles Laughton and William Powell played them in two comedy classics. In 1935's *Ruggles of Red Gap*, Western millionaire Charlie Ruggles won British butler Laughton in a poker game. The cultured butler's clash with American customs provided much of the comedy, but his eventual understanding of American freedom gave the film a surprisingly patriotic ending. Bob Hope reprised the role in the loose 1950 remake *Fancy Pants*. William Powell played a millionaire mistaken by Carole Lombard for a bum in *My Man Godfrey* (1936). She undertakes it as a personal project to transform him into a proper butler. It was also remade in 1957 with David Niven and June Allyson. Niven, who had played opposite Treacher in the first Jeeves film, played a butler again in Disney's *Candleshoe* (1977). Other memorable butlers have been played by Dan Duryea, Ralph Richardson, Dirk Bogarde, and Anthony Hopkins. Duryea's butler pretended to be the master of the house while his employer was on vacation in the 1946 comedy *White Tie and Tails*. In *The Fallen Idol* (1948), a young boy idolized the family butler (Richardson) until murderous suspicions took their toll on the friendship. Bogarde played the screen's creepiest valet in Joseph Losey's *The Servant*, a character study in which a butler becomes master of his employer. Anthony Hopkins earned a Best Actor Oscar nomination as a loyal, unbending head butler in *Remains of the Day* (1993). On television, the future stars of *Dallas* and *Knots Landing*, Larry Hagman and Donna Mills, played an average American couple masquerading as a butler and cook for millionaire David Wayne in the 1971-72 sitcom *The Good Life*. See also **Chauffeurs**; **Maids and Housekeepers**.

The Old Dark House (1932); *Get Off My Foot* (1935); *She Married Her Boss* (1935); *If You Could Only Cook* (1935); *Ruggles of Red Gap* (1935); *My Man Godfrey* (1936); *Thank You, Jeeves* (1936); *Step Lively, Jeeves* (1937); *The Baroness and the Butler* (1938); *Her Man Gilbey* (aka *English Without Tears*) (1944); *Nothing but Trouble* (1944); *White Tie and Tails* (1946); *The Fallen Idol* (1948); *Fancy Pants* (1950); *My Man Godfrey* (1957); *Light Fingers* (1957); *The Admirable Crichton* (aka *Paradise Lagoon*) (1957); *The Servant* (1963); *The Adventures of Bullwhip Griffin* (1967); *Fitzwilly* (aka *Fitzwilly Strikes Back*) (1967); *Blue Blood* (1973); *Candleshoe* (1977); *Arthur* (1981); *Clue* (1985); *The Remains of the Day* (1993); *The Grotesque* (1995); *Three Lives and Only One Death* (1996); *Gentlemen Don't Eat Poets* (1997)

La Cage aux Folles Series

The 1978 film version of Jean Poiret's French stage farce racked up an impressive $8 million in North America, making it the continent's top all-time grossing foreign-language film at that time. Ugo Tognozzi and Michel Serrault played the gay couple who try to "clean up their act" when Tognozzi's son brings his fiancée and her family over to dinner. Tognazzi and Serrault teamed up again for two mild sequels, neither of which approached the original's raging success. However, *La Cage aux Folles* was adapted into a smash Broadway musical headlining Gene Barry. It was also remade as the popular 1996 Robin Williams–Nathan Lane comedy *The Birdcage*.

La Cage aux Folles (1978); *La Cage aux Folles II* (1980); *La Cage aux Folles III: The Wedding* (1985)

Cagney & Lacey

Cast changes, cancellations, Emmys — the first "feminist detective series" traveled a rocky road into television history. Detectives Christine Cagney and Mary Beth Lacey first surfaced in a 1981 TV movie, with Loretta Swit and Tyne Daly in the lead roles. When CBS commissioned a regular series the following year, Swit was unavailable and the Cagney role was recast with Meg Foster. The series drew poor ratings and Cagney was recast again, this time with Sharon Gless whom CBS executives thought would show a softer side to Cagney. The ratings failed to improve, though, and CBS axed the series in 1983. Fans protested loudly, but CBS failed to take action until Emmy nominations were handled out to both Gless and Daly (who won for Outstanding Lead Actress in a Drama Series). CBS renewed the show in 1984 and it enjoyed a successful four-year run, with Daly earning four additional Emmy awards and Gless two. Unlike other buddy-cop TV series like *Starsky and Hutch*, *Cagney & Lacey* focused on the characters' personal lives as well as their detective work. During the series, Lacey had another child and Cagney battled alcoholism. A decade after the show ended, Daly and Gless reunited for the TV movie *Cagney & Lacey: The Return*. It found Lacey in retirement and Cagney married to a wealthy businessman and promoted to lieutenant. When Lacey's husband has a heart attack, she seeks employment and winds up working with Cagney again. This reunion movie scored big ratings and prompted three follow-ups. Sadly, Cagney — who always had a difficult love life — gets divorced and ends up single again. See also **Television Series Reunion Films**.

Cagney & Lacey (1981 TVM); *Cagey & Lacey: The Return* (1994 TVM); *Cagney & Lacey: The View Through the Glass Ceiling* (1995 TVM); *Cagney & Lacey: Together Again* (1995 TVM); *Cagney & Lacey: True Convictions* (1995 TVM)

Callahan, Harry *see* Dirty Harry

Camels

Although steadily employed in desert epics, camels have failed to land many starring roles. Indeed, the looney Western comedy *Hawmps* (1976) and its offbeat inspiration, 1954's *Southwest Passage*, may be the only pictures expressly about camels. *Passage* was a 3-D Western which had Rod Cameron experimenting with using camels to transport settlers across the desert. Interestingly, the Indians refrain from attacking the wagon train because they fear the strange-looking camels. Unfortunately, a camel dies and the Indians get wise. The less-serious *Hawmps!* headlined James Hampton (Dobbs on TV's *F Troop*) as a cavalry officer trying to convince the army to use camels instead of horses. In yet another Western, Disney's *One Little Indian* (1973), James Garner played a cavalryman trudging through the desert with an Indian boy and a trusty camel. Despite its promising title, 1967's *Follow That Camel* was nothing more than a *Carry On* (q.v.) spoof of *Beau Geste*. Two scene-stealing talking camels added some dry commentary to Hope and Crosby's wacky *Road to Morocco* (1942). Another talking camel had a cameo in Yvonne de Carlo's *Slave Girl*, while a blind camel had the best scene in the Dustin Hoffman–Warren Beatty flop *Ishtar* (1987). The Israeli film *The Flying Camela* (1994) was about a statue of a camel with wings. There was nary a camel in the 1931 Charlie Chan mystery *The Black Camel*, the title being derived from Charlie's line: "Death is the black camel that kneels unbidden at every gate."

Road to Morocco (1942); *Slave Girl* (1947); *Southwest Passage* (aka *Camels West*) (1954); *Follow That Camel* (aka *Carry On Follow That Camel*) (1967); *One Little Indian* (1973); *Hawmps!* (1976); *The Camel Boy* (1984); *Ishtar* (1987); *The Flying Camela* (1994); *Arabian Nights* (2000 TVM)

Cannibalism

Cannibalism, prior to the gore-explicit 1970s, was restricted mostly to jungle adventure films such as *Cannibal Attack* (1954). A pleasantly gruesome exception was the 1936 film version of the old school melodrama *Sweeney Todd, the Demon Barber of Fleet Street*. Tod Slaughter, a noted British ham, portrayed the title character, who not only cut hair, but also cut up his customers and sold them in "meat" pies. The story also served as the basis for 1970's *Bloodthirsty Butchers* and Stephen Sondheim's hit Broadway musical *Sweeney Todd*. By the mid–1960s, cannibalism had crept its way into exploitative, drive-in horror films. Often, the cannibalism was somewhat muted by the inclusion of fantastic elements. A man was barbecued and eaten in *Two Thousand Maniacs* (1964), but the "cannibals" turned out to be ghosts. The flesh-eaters in George Romero's cult classic *Night of the Living Dead* (1968) were ghouls (q.v.), not normal humans. However, the demented family in 1964's *Spider Baby* was physically normal. Its cannibalistic tendencies were a result of inbreeding. Three cannibal films were released in 1972. Both *The Folks at Red Wolf Inn* and *Cannibal Girls* played their grisly subject matter for laughs with jokes about spare ribs and lady fingers. The latter film starred SCTV alumni Eugene Levy and Andrea Martin and was directed by Ivan (*Ghostbusters*) Reitman. *Raw Meat* was an offbeat chiller about descendants of people trapped in a London subway tunnel who devour unsuspecting passers-by. Four other cannibal movies of the 1970s and early 1980s blossomed into cult hits. The most notorious was Tobe Hooper's *The Texas Chainsaw Massacre* (1974), a ghastly tale about a family of flesh-eaters. It was condemned by critics for its violence, which was more implied than explicit. Ruggero Deodato's pseudodocumentary *Cannibal Holocaust* (1979) is still considered one of the most gruesome films ever made. Former cowboy star Rory Calhoun played Farmer Vincent, whose popular sausages were made from human meat, in 1980's *Motel Hell* (the "o" in Motel Hello having burned out). Cannibalism played a small but very significant role in Paul Bartel's *Eating Raoul* (1982), a black comedy about a couple who hit upon a way to finance their dream restaurant when they accidentally commit murder. *Survive!* (1976) was a nonhorror, Mexican import about plane crash survivors who resorted to eating dead fellow passengers to stay alive — a story told with better production values in 1993's *Alive*. The tragic, real-life story of the Donner party, who turned to cannibalism to avoid starvation in the harsh West, was whitewashed in the 1978 TV movie *Donner Pass: The Road to Survival*, but recounted accurately in the 1992 documentary *The Donner Party*. Anthony Hopkins won a Best Actor Oscar for his portrayal of Hannibal "The Cannibal" Lecter in Jonathan Demme's 1991 hit *The Silence of the Lambs*. Prior to creating the popular animated TV series *South Park*, Trey Parker and Matt Stone produced the little-seen *Cannibal! The Musical* (1996). See also **Ghouls**; **The Texas Chainsaw Massacre Series**. The following list excludes jungle adventure films with cannibal natives:

Sweeney Todd, the Demon Barber of Fleet Street (aka *The Demon Barber of Fleet Street*) (1936); *Mondo Cane* (aka *It's a Dog's Life*) (1963); *Blood Feast* (1963); *Spider Baby* (aka *Spider Baby, or the Maddest Story Ever Told; The Liver Eaters; Cannibal Orgy*) (1964); *Do You Like Women?* (1964); *The Undertaker and His Pals* (1967); *Bloodthirsty Butchers* (1970); *The Folks at Red Wolf Inn* (aka *Terror at Red Wolf Inn; Terror House*) (1972); *Cannibal Girls* (1972); *Raw Meat* (aka *Deathline*) (1973); *The Texas Chainsaw Massacre* (1974); *Survive!* (1976); *Desperate Living* (1977); *Donner Pass: The Road to Survival* (1978); *The Hills Have Eyes* (1978); *Cannibal Holocaust* (1979); *Motel Hell* (1980); *Eating Raoul* (1982); *Cannibals*

in the Street (aka *Invasion of the Flesh Hunters*) (1982); *Raw Force* (1982); *C.H.U.D.* (1984); *The Texas Chainsaw Massacre 2* (1986); *Eat the Rich* (1987); *Flesh Eating Mothers* (1988); *Lucky Stiff* (1988); *Parents* (1989); *Cannibal Women in the Avocado Jungle of Death* (1989); *C.H.U.D. II: Bud the Chud* (1989); *The Cook, the Thief, His Wife & Her Lover* (1989); *Tales from the Darkside: The Movie* (1990); *Fried Green Tomatoes* (1991); *The Silence of the Lambs* (1991); *Delicatessen* (1991); *The Donner Party* (1992); *Alive* (1993); *Braindead* (aka *Dead/Alive*) (1993); *Iron Horsemen* (1994); *Cannibal! The Musical* (1996); *Ravenous* (1999); *The 13th Warrior* (1999)

Cannon Movie Tales

In the late 1980s, Menahem Golan and Yoram Globus tried to move their Cannon Group into the lucrative children's film market dominated by Disney. They developed a series of live-action movies based on famous fairy tales. While these "Cannon Movie Tales" lacked big budgets, they featured well-known performers such as Morgan Fairchild (*Sleeping Beauty*), Rebecca DeMornay (*Beauty and the Beast*), and Diana Rigg (*Snow White*). Still, the films failed to attract interest in the U.S. where the Cannon "brand" had become a trademark for mediocrity. The first Cannon Movie Tale, *Rumpelstiltskin*, is notable as a family affair for star Amy Irving: It co-starred her mother and stepfather; her brother, David Irving, directed and wrote the screenplay.

Rumpelstiltskin (aka *Cannon Movie Tales: Rumpelstiltskin*) (1987); *Little Red Riding Hood* (aka *Cannon Movie Tales: Little Red Riding Hood*) (1987); *Hansel and Gretel* (aka *Cannon Movie Tales: Hansel and Gretel*) (1987); *The Emperor's New Clothes* (aka *Cannon Movie Tales: The Emperor's New Clothes*) (1987); *Beauty and the Beast* (aka *Cannon Movie Tales: Beauty and the Beast*) (1987); *Snow White* (aka *Cannon Movie Tales: Snow White* (1987); *Sleeping Beauty* (aka *Cannon Movie Tales: Sleeping Beauty*) (1987); *Puss in Boots* (aka *Cannon Movie Tales: Puss in Boots*) (1988); *The Frog Prince* (aka *Cannon Movie Tales: The Frog Prince*) (1988)

The Care Bears

Media-product tie-ins were the rage of the early 1980s, with toy companies eagerly licensing their best-selling items to TV cartoon producers and vice versa. Few products were more popular than the Care Bears, nice little pastel-colored bears with sentimental names like Wish Bear, Bedtime Bear, and Tenderheart Bear. Just for a touch of realism, there was also Grumpy Bear. The Care Bears, along with My Little Pony and He-Man, were big enough to attract the attention of movie producers, too. Indeed, the first Care Bears film, a feature-length animated musical, did surprisingly well at the box-office. However, the law of diminishing returns and the short-lived nature of toy trends limited those nice, little bears to two sequels. See also **Animated Movies (Feature-Length)**; **Bears**.

The Care Bears Movie (1985); *The Care Bears Movie II: A New Generation* (1986); *The Care Bears Adventure in Wonderland* (1987)

Carnosaur Series

"Driven to extinction…back for revenge!" proclaimed the ads for *Carnosaur*, a low-budget dinosaur film released in 1993 to capitalize on the impending release of *Jurassic Park*. Based on Harry Adam Knight's novel, the plot involved genetically-engineered dinosaurs that, contrary to the film's ads, showed no appetite for revenge. They preferred simply to eat people as part of a well-balanced diet. Diane Ladd played Dr. Jane Tipton, the mentally-unbalanced scientist who schemes to destroy mankind with a deadly virus so her dinosaurs can rule the Earth. Although strictly low-brow fare, *Carnosaur* benefits from some unexpected plot turns. Tipton mixes the dinosaur's DNA with humans — in fact, she dies giving birth to a baby dino. And the heroes, a bright night watchman and a pretty ecologist, are killed by federal forces tasked with eliminating all personnel in a quarantined area. Ladd overacts outrageously as Tipton, but her casting is a movie trivia buff's dream since her real-life daughter, Laura Dern, starred in *Jurassic Park*. The two *Carnosaur* sequels owe more to *Alien* than to *Jurassic Park*. In both films, a small group of people is trapped in isolated locales (a uranium mine in the desert, a ship out to sea) where they are devoured, one by one, by the clever, hungry dinos. The humans eventually prevail in both pictures, although one of the mutant dinosaurs survives in *Carnosaur 3*, setting up a potential fourth series entry that never materialized. See also **Dinosaurs**.

Carnosaur (1993); *Carnosaur II* (1995); *Carnosaur 3: Primal Species* (1996)

Carry On Series

This lowbrow British comedy series made an inauspicious debut in 1958 with *Carry On Sergeant*, a silly army farce littered with bad jokes ("Your rank, soldier!" "That's a matter of opinion."). But while the critics scorched it, the public ate it up. Subsequent *Carry On* films were not sequels in a narrative sense, but they featured the same cast members (Kenneth Connor, Charles Hawtrey, Sid James) and the same vaudeville sense of humor. The series highlight was 1959's *Carry On Nurse*, which even earned respectable reviews, although it is chiefly remembered for a scene in which distinguished Wilfred Hyde White gets a daffodil stuck up his rear end. The series got progressively racier during the 1960s (Cleopatra to Caesar: "I have seen your bust." Caesar: "I wish I could say the same.") and finally featured nudity for the first time in 1969's *Carry On Camping*. The films also suffered a sharp decline in quality (what quality there was), although no one seemed to notice since the *Carry On* movies had become a British institution by then. To its credit, the *Carry On* gang considered nothing sacred and spoofed *Cleopatra* (*Carry On Cleo*), *The Third Man* (*Carry On Spying*), *The Scarlet Pimpernel* (*Don't Lose Your Head*), *Beau Geste* (*Follow That Camel*), and *Anne of the Thousand Days* (*Carry On Henry*, which was memorably subtitled *Anne of a Thousand Lays*). The series died in the late 1970s after producing 29 films — only to be revived unexpectedly in 1992 with *Carry On Columbus*, which found the famous explorer encountering streetwise Indians with Brooklyn accents. The cast featured familiar faces from the *Carry On* troupe, such as Jim Dale, Jack Douglas, June Whitfield, and former–Dr. Who Jon Pertwee. The 1977 compilation *That's Carry On!* featured clips from previous films hosted by series regulars Kenneth Williams and Barbara Windsor.

Carry On Sergeant (1958); *Carry On Nurse* (1959); *Carry On Teacher* (1959); *Carry On Constable* (1960); *Carry On Regardless* (1961); *Carry On Cruising* (1962); *Carry On Cabby* (1963); *Carry On Jack* (aka *Carry On Venus*) (1963); *Carry On Cleo* (1964); *Carry On Spying* (1964); *Carry On Cowboy* (1965); *Carry On Screaming* (1966); *Carry On Doctor* (1967); *Don't Lose Your Head* (aka *Carry On Don't Lose Your Head*; *Carry On Pimpernel*) (1967); *Follow That Camel* (*Carry On Follow That Camel*) (1967); *Carry On Up the Khyber* (1968); *Carry On Again Doctor* (1969); *Carry On Camping* (1969); *Carry On Henry* (1970); *Carry On Loving* (aka *One Thing on Top of Another*) (1970); *Carry On Up the Jungle* (aka *Carry On Jungle Boy*) (1970); *Carry On at Your Convenience* (aka *Carry On Round the Bend*) (1971); *Carry On Abroad* (1972); *Carry On Matron* (1972); *Carry On Girls* (1973); *Carry On Dick* (1974) (as in Dick Turpin, famed British outlaw); *Carry On England* (1976); *That's Carry On!* (1977); *Carry On Behind* (1978); *Carry On Emmanuelle* (1978); *Carry On Columbus* (1992)

(Note: 1957's *Carry On Admiral* was not a part of the series.)

Carson, Billy *see* Billy the Kid

Carter, Nick

Ormond C. Smith and John Russell Coryell created this turn-of-the-century detective for New York Weekly. Yet, while Nick Carter seemed a sure bet for a long-running B-movie series, his screen career has been modest at best. Andre Liabel made four French serials in 1909–12, while both Edmund Lowe (a future Philo Vance) and Thomas Corrigan appeared in Nick Carter short features in the 1920s. MGM launched an updated three-film series in 1939 with Walter Pidgeon in the lead. The series was dropped when Pidgeon went on to bigger roles in bigger movies (e.g., 1941's *How Green Was My Valley*). Eddie Constantine, best known as tough detective Lemmy Caution (q.v.), played Carter in France while Robert Conrad revived the character for American audiences in the 1972 TV movie *The Adventures of Nick Carter*. The latter film was the pilot for a television series that never materialized. The detective reappeared unexpectedly in 1978's *Nick Carter in Prague* (aka *Dinner for Adele*), a tongue-in-cheek Czech film that's attracted a minor cult following in the U.S.

Nick Carter, Master Detective (1939) (Walter Pidgeon); *Phantom Raiders* (1940) (Pidgeon); *Sky Murder* (1940) (Pidgeon); *License to Kill* (aka *Nick Carter and the Red Club*; *Nick Carter Va Tout Casser*) (1964) (Eddie Constantine); *The Adventures of Nick Carter* (1972 TVM) (Robert Conrad); *Nick Carter in Prague* (aka *Dinner for Adele*; *Adele Hasn't Had Her Supper Yet*) (1978) (Michael Docolomansky)

Cartoon/Live Action Features

These films fall into two categories: Those which simply intercut "live" footage and animated sequences (e.g., *Allegro Non Troppo*) and those which show live and animated characters in the same frame, interacting together. The latter films are the more interesting, typically relying on an expensive optical trick called a travelling matte. The use of mattes can be traced back to 1925's *The Lost World*, in which special effects wizard Willis (*King Kong*) O'Brien masked out the shape of a dinosaur in a crowd scene and then inserted footage of an animated model into that "optical hole." As one might expect, Walt Disney Productions has produced the most cartoon/live action movies, featuring such memorable sequences as the carousel horse race in *Mary Poppins* and Roger Rabbit's initial transition from cartoon-world to real-world in *Who Framed Roger Rabbit?* MGM, however, rates a close second with *Anchors Aweigh* (Tom and Jerry dancing with Gene Kelly), *Dangerous When Wet* (T & J swimming with Esther

Williams) and *Invitation to the Dance*. At Warner Bros., Bugs Bunny showed up in a dream sequence in Doris Day's *My Dream Is Yours* (1949). One of the most unique uses of animation was in 1968's *The Charge of the Light Brigade*, in which animated line drawings were used to convey Britain's political atmosphere. See also **Animated Features (Feature-Length)**.

Hollywood Party (1934); *Victory Through Air Power* (1943); *The Three Caballeros* (1945); *Anchors Aweigh* (1945); *Song of the South* (1946); *So Dear to My Heart* (1948); *Two Guys from Texas* (1948); *My Dream Is Yours* (1949); *The Four-Poster* (1952); *Dangerous When Wet* (1953); *The Girl Next Door* (1953); *Invitation to the Dance* (1957); *The Snow Queen* (1959); *The Incredible Mr. Limpet* (1964); *Mary Poppins* (1964); *The Daydreamer* (1966); *The Charge of the Light Brigade* (1968); *The Phantom Tollbooth* (1969); *The Picasso Summer* (1969); *Bedknobs and Broomsticks* (1971); *Funnyman* (1971); *Two Hundred Motels* (1971); *Heavy Traffic* (1973); *Monty Python and the Holy Grail* (1975); *Coonskin* (aka *Streetfight*) (1975); *Allegro Non Troppo* (1976); *Pete's Dragon* (1977); *Gulliver's Travels* (1977); *The Water Babies* (1978); *9 to 5* (1980); *Xanadu* (1980); *Pink Floyd — The Wall* (1982); *One Crazy Summer* (1986); *Who Framed Roger Rabbit?* (1988); *Fletch Lives* (1989); *Cool World* (1992); *Stay Tuned* (1992); *The Pagemaster* (1994); *In Search of Dr. Seuss* (1994 TVM); *Space Jam* (1996); *James and the Giant Peach* (1996); *Run Lola Run* (aka *Lola Rennt*) (1998); *The Adventures of Rocky and Bullwinkle* (2000)

Cartoonists

Dean Martin as a cartoonist? Only in a movie in which he steals the ideas for his comic strips from Jerry Lewis' telepathic dreams — which was precisely the plot of 1955's *Artists and Models*. In the Bob Hope comedy *That Certain Feeling*, a "ghost artist" drew a comic strip for a cartoonist who had lost his touch. James Thurbers' drawings and writings inspired 1972's *The War Between Men and Women*, which starred Jack Lemmon as a half-blind cartoonist hassled by his wife's ex-husband. Two years earlier, the same material had provided the basis for the William Windom TV sitcom *My World and Welcome to It*. Michael Crawford played a cartoonist who turned into his own comic book hero in the 1981 Disney misfire *Condorman*.

Piccadilly Jim (1936); *The Girl Next Door* (1953); *Artists and Models* (1955); *That Certain Feeling* (1956); *How to Murder Your Wife* (1965); *The War Between Men and Women* (1972); *Condorman* (1981); *The Hand* (1981); *One Crazy Summer* (1986); *Slamdance* (1987); *Brenda Starr* (1989); *Funny About Love* (1990); *Cool World* (1992); *Chasing Amy* (1997)

Casper

Created by Sy Reit and Joe Oriolo in 1945, Casper made his film debut in the Paramount cartoon "The Friendly Ghost." Each Casper cartoon followed the same formula: Casper, a lonely ghost boy, would try to befriend humans — only to accidentally frighten them until coming to the rescue of a person in trouble. Although Casper got his own comic book in 1949, he never attained the popularity of Warner Bros. characters like Bugs Bunny and Daffy Duck. In 1958, Paramount sold its rights to the Casper character and cartoons to Harvey Publishing. Harvey repackaged the cartoons, which aired first on ABC and then in syndication, where Casper enjoyed his greatest fame. In 1990, Jeffrey Montgomery, a Steven Spielberg associate, bought Harvey Entertainment so he could produce a theatrical Casper movie. With a $50 million

budget and an updated storyline, *Casper* (1995) proved the friendly ghost could still charm audiences by grossing over $250 million worldwide. Though more somber in tone than the cartoons, the film followed the proven Casper formula, with the amiable spirit (computer-generated, but voiced by Malachi Pearson) coming to the aid of teenage, motherless girl (Christina Ricci). A second film, *Casper: A Spirited Beginning* (1997), found the friendly ghost protecting Applegate Mansion from being demolished while befriending a boy neglected by his father. It bypassed movie theaters and made its debut on videotape. Another direct-to-video feature, *Casper Meets Wendy* (1998) introduced Wendy, the "good little witch" who was also a Harvey cartoon character. Hiliary Duff played Wendy and her three bewitching aunts included Teri Garr, Shelley Duvall, and Cathy Moriarty. Jeremy Foley provided the voice of Casper in both direct-to-video features. See also **Ghosts**.

Casper (1995); *Casper: A Spirited Beginning* (1997); *Casper Meets Wendy* (1998)

Cassidy, Hopalong

William Boyd, the undisputed king of B-movie Westerns, made 66 Hopalong Cassidy movies for Paramount and United Artists between 1935 and 1948. Clarence E. Mulford created the character in 1912 in a series of "old school" novels. But no one took an interest in them until veteran Western producer Harry (Pop) Sherman envisioned a profitable low-budget series for Paramount. Many actors were considered for the lead role (including David Niven, according to one source), but Sherman finally settled on Boyd. A popular silent actor, Boyd was a favorite of Cecil B. DeMille's and appeared in such classics as *King of Kings* (1927). A gambling scandal involving another William Boyd contributed to his fading star status in the early 1930s, so he welcomed the opportunity to play Hopalong. *Hop-A-Long Cassidy* (the hyphens were later dropped) was a surprise hit for Paramount in 1935 and no wonder — the Cassidy Westerns cost less than $100,000 and usually grossed twice that amount. Screenwriter Doris Schroeder whitewashed Mulford's original character considerably, so that the movies' Hoppy never smoked nor drank liquor. The first films sometimes ran as long as 88 minutes, but later ones lasted just over an hour, which made for plenty of action. James Ellison played Jimmy Nelson, Hoppy's young sidekick at the Bar 20 ranch, with additional support by Gabby Hayes or Andy Clyde. After producing 41 Hopalong films, Paramount sold the rights to United Artists in 1942, which released 25 more entries. The last 12 UA films were produced by Boyd's own Hopalong Cassidy Productions. Boyd eventually pawned almost everything he owned and bought rights to all the Hopalong Cassidy Westerns. He sold these to television and, when the film series ended in 1948, began making new episodes for his TV program. Edgar Buchanan played Hoppy's TV sidekick during the series' 1949–51 run.

Hop-A-Long Cassidy (1935); *The Eagle's Brood* (1935); *Bar 20 Rides Again* (1935); *Call of the Prairie* (1936); *Three on the Trail* (1936); *Heart of the West* (1936); *Hopalong Cassidy Returns* (1936); *Trail Dust* (1936); *Borderland* (1937); *Hills of Old Wyoming* (1937); *North of the Rio Grande* (1937); *Rustler's Valley* (1937); *Hopalong Rides Again* (1937); *Texas Trail* (1937); *Heart of Arizona* (1938); *Bar 20 Justice* (1938); *Pride of the West* (1938); *In Old Mexico* (1938); *Sunset Trail* (1938); *The Frontiersman* (1938); *Partners of the Plains*

(1938); *Cassidy of Bar 20* (1938); *Range War* (1939); *Law of the Pampas* (1939); *Silver on the Sage* (1939); *The Renegade Trail* (1939); *Santa Fe Marshal* (1940); *The Showdown* (1940); *Hidden Gold* (1940); *Stagecoach War* (1940); *Three Men from Texas* (1940); *Doomed Caravan* (1941); *In Old Colorado* (1941); *Border Vigilantes* (1941); *Pirates on Horseback* (1941); *Wide Open Town* (1941); *Outlaws of the Desert* (1941); *Riders of the Timberline* (1941); *Secret of the Wastelands* (1941); *Stick to Your Guns* (1941); *Twilight on the Trail* (1941); *Undercover Man* (1942); *Lost Canyon* (1942); *Colt Comrades* (1943); *Bar 20* (1943); *Hoppy Serves a Writ* (1943); *Border Patrol* (1943); *The Leather Burners* (1943); *False Colors* (1943); *Riders of the Deadline* (1943); *Mystery Man* (1944); *Forty Thieves* (1944); *Texas Masquerade* (1944); *Lumberjack* (1944); *The Devil's Playground* (1946); *Fool's Gold* (1947); *Hoppy's Holiday* (1947); *Marauders* (1947); *Unexpected Guest* (1947); *Dangerous Venture* (1947); *Sinister Journey* (1948); *Silent Conflict* (1948); *Strange Gamble* (1948); *Borrowed Trouble* (1948); *The Dead Don't Dream* (1948); *False Paradise* (1948)

Cats

As befits their nature, felines have maintained a subtle screen profile. While dogs (q.v.) have panted their way through major film series (see **Lassie** and **Rusty**), cats have been content with a pawful of starring roles and a few choice parts. A frisky ginger cat inherited a wretched baseball team in 1951's *Rhubarb* and turned it into a winner (with a little help from motivational publicist Ray Milland). A female cat narrated Disney's *The Three Lives of Thomasina*, a charming Scottish tale spanning but one-third of her nine lives. Other Disney feline features starred: Siamese cats (*That Darn Cat!* and *Lady and the Tramp*), alien cats (*The Cat from Outer Space*), and animated cats (*The Aristocats* and *Oliver and Company*). *Gay Purr-ee* was a non–Disney feature-length cartoon with the voices of Robert Goulet and Judy Garland. Tom, the animated cat of Tom and Jerry fame, danced with Gene Kelly in *Anchors Aweigh* and swam with Esther Williams in *Dangerous When Wet*. For the best supporting feline performance, the nod goes to Art Carney's co-star in 1974's *Harry and Tonto*. This bittersweet comedy about the travels of an elderly man and his cat earned Carney a Best Actor Oscar. James Bond's archnemesis Blofeld had a white Persian kitty for a pet in some of the 007 films, most notably 1971's *Diamonds Are Forever*. Gale Sondergaard played Shirley Temple's self-centered cat Tylette in the 1940 adaptation of the Oz-like fantasy *The Blue Bird*. Humans have transformed into cats (typically not the domestic variety) in the 1942 and 1982 versions of *The Cat People* and *Cat Girl* (1957). A dead girl's soul possessed a cat in 1946's *The Cat Creeps*, while an Egyptian cat goddess possessed human victims in the 1973 TV movie *The Cat Creature*. The nastiest cats were the ones that unknowingly ate human flesh in *The Corpse Grinders* (1971) and decided they liked the taste. See also **Lions and Tigers**.

Alice in Wonderland (1933); *The Black Cat* (1934); *The Blue Bird* (1940); *The Black Cat* (1941); *Anchors Aweigh* (1945); *The Cat Creeps* (1946); *Alice in Wonderland* (1950); *Alice in Wonderland* (1951); *Rhubarb* (1951); *Dangerous When Wet* (1953); *Lady and the Tramp* (1955); *Bell, Book, and Candle* (1958); *The Shadow of the Cat* (1961); *Gay Purr-ee* (1963); *The Incredible Journey* (1963); *Cassandra Cat* (aka *When the Cat Comes; The Cat*) (1963); *The Three Lives of Thomasina* (1964); *That Darn Cat!* (1965); *Eye of the Cat* (1969); *The Aristocats* (1970); *The Corpse Grinders* (1971); *Alice's Adventures in Wonderland* (1972); *The Cat Creature* (1973 TVM); *Harry and Tonto* (1974); *The Blue Bird* (1976); *The Cat from Outer Space* (1978); *ffolkes* (aka *Assault Force*) (1980); *Cat's Eye* (1985); *The Richest Cat in the World* (1986 TVM); *Puss in Boots* (aka *Cannon Movie Tales: Puss in Boots*) (1988); *Oliver and Company* (1988); *The Adventures of Milo and Otis* (1989); *Two Evil Eyes* (aka *Due Occhi Diabolic*) (1990); *Tales from the Darkside: The Movie* (1990); *Strays* (1991 TVM); *Tom and Jerry: The Movie* (1992); *Homeward Bound: The Incredible Journey* (1993); *Felidae* (1994); *Homeward Bound II: Lost in San Francisco* (1996); *When the Cat's Away* (1996); *Whiskers* (1996 TVM); *That Darn Cat* (1997); *Cats Don't Dance* (1997); *Murder, She Purred* (aka *Murder, She Purred: A Mrs. Murphy Mystery* (1998 TVM); *Alice in Wonderland* (1999 TVM); *Stuart Little* (1999)

Caution, Lemmy

American actor Eddie Constantine played Peter Cheyney's two-fisted pulp detective in a series of modest French mysteries, beginning in the early 1950s and lasting through the mid–1960s. A bit player in American films, Constantine followed his dancer wife to Paris, where he achieved minor popularity as a singer. His first Caution film, 1953's *Gun Moll*, cost a paltry $50,000, but earned impressive grosses. European audiences responded enthusiastically to his man-of-action image, which naturally transcended language barriers. Interestingly, Constantine's overseas stardom foreshadowed the 1960s European successes of other American actors such as Clint Eastwood, Charles Bronson, and Lee Van Cleef. The hard-drinking, womanizing Caution made little impact in the U.S., although later efforts such as *Attack of the Robots* (1962) and *Your Turn, Darling* (1963) eventually wound up on American television. Acclaimed French director Jean-Luc Godard cast Constantine as Lemmy Caution in his baffling, esoteric, futuristic "thriller" *Alphaville* (1965). It's considered the best of the Caution pictures, although it is certainly not representative of the series. In 1991, Godard directed *Germany Year 90 Nine Zero*, an hour-long follow-up with Constantine reprising his role as Lemmy Caution.

Gun Moll (aka *La Mome Vert-de-Gris*) (1953); *This Man Is Dangerous* (aka *Dangerous Agent; Cet Homme Est Dangereaux*) (1953); *Dames Don't Care* (aka *Les Femmes s'en Balancent*) (1954); *You Dig?* (aka *Vous Pigez?*) (1956); *Women Are Like That* (aka *Comment qu'elle Est!*) (1960); *Attack of the Robots* (aka *Cards on the Table; Cartes sur la Table*) (1962); *Lemmy and the Girls* (aka *Ladies' Man; Lemmy Pour Les Dames*) (1962); *Your Turn, Darling* (aka *Lemmy Caution, FBI Agent; You Do It, Cuties; A Toi de Paire, Migonne*) (1963); *Alphaville* (aka *Alphaville, Une Etrange Aventure de Lemmy Caution*) (1965); *Germany Year 90 Nine Zero* (aka *Allemagne Année 90 Neuf Zero*) (1991)

Cave People

Cavewoman to caveman in *When Dinosaurs Ruled the Earth*: "N'dye krasta m'kan neecro tedak." As any film buff with a prehistoric dictionary knows, that translates to: "Come fast. Kill evil flying monster." Those kinds of dialogue limitations have hampered storylines for prehistoric people pictures. The genre's best films have been visually arresting pieces with plots borrowed from silent films and the added excitement of a dinosaur or two (scientific accuracy being a minor concern). Hal Roach's 1940 opus *One Million B.C.* set the standard with its tale of forbidden love between Tumak (Victor Mature) of the violent Rock People and Loana (Carole Landis) of the peaceful Shell People. The dinosaurs were economically created by magnifying living lizards. *Variety* called the picture "corny" at the time of release and, indeed, it inspired no 1940s imitations. In 1950, the low-budget *Prehistoric Women* added a feminist angle and some narration (in addition to character grunts). Roger Corman's *Teenage Caveman* (1958) was obviously targeted toward young adults, which partially explains the rationale for the twist ending of revealing the past to be the future. However, Britain's Hammer Pictures deserves total credit for turning cave people epics into profitably sturdy box-office performers. Its 1966 remake *One Million Years B.C.* brilliantly paired a scantily-clad Raquel Welch with Ray Harryhausen's impressive stop-motion dinosaurs (q.v.), thus appealing to both older and younger male viewers. Hammer followed it with *Prehistoric Women* (1967), *When Dinosaurs Ruled the Earth* (1970), and *Creatures the World Forgot* (1971). *The Tribe* was a 1974 TV movie along the same lines, only minus the nudity and dinosaurs. Ringo Starr and his wife Barbara Bach spoofed caveman epics in the 1981 hit comedy *Caveman*. Another 1981 release, *Quest for Fire* was a big-budgeted "serious" effort, featuring a cave people language devised by novelist Anthony (*A Clockwork Orange*) Burgess. *Clan of the Cave Bear* (1985) was a dismal flop despite its best-seller origins and the presence of then-popular star Daryl Hannah. Of course, not all cave people films have been set in prehistoric times. The contemporary caveman has been around since scientists discovered one roaming about modern-day Africa in the 1927 silent comedy *The Missing Link*. Lightning revived a caveman in *Dinosaurus* (1960), Joan Crawford discovered a missing link hiding in an obscure cave in *Trog* (1970), and scientist Timothy Hutton found a Neanderthal frozen in ice in *Iceman* (1984). The overanxious scientists in *The Neanderthal Man* (1953) and *Monster on the Campus* (1958) actually turned themselves into prehistoric men. In the former film, the serum that turned Robert Shayne into a Neanderthal also transformed his dog into a vicious wolf. See also **Dinosaurs**.

The Missing Link (1927); *One Million B.C.* (aka *Man and His Mate*; *The Cave Dwellers*) (1940); *Prehistoric Women* (1950); *The Neanderthal Man* (1953); *Monster on the Campus* (1958); *Teenage Caveman* (aka *Prehistoric World*) (1958); *Dinosaurus* (1960); *Valley of the Dragons* (1961); *Eegah!* (1962); *One Million Years B.C.* (1966); *The Oldest Profession in the World* (aka *The Oldest Profession*) (1967) ("Prehistoric Era" sketch); *Prehistoric Women* (aka *Slave Girls*) (1967); *Trog* (1970); *When Dinosaurs Ruled the Earth* (1970); *When Women Had Tails* (1970); *Skullduggery* (1970); *Creatures the World Forgot* (1971); *Schlock* (aka *The Banana Monster*) (1971); *The Creeping Flesh* (1973); *The Tribe* (1974 TVM); *The People That Time Forgot* (1977); *Sinbad and the Eye of the Tiger* (1977); *Caveman* (1981); *Quest for Fire* (1981); *History of the World–Part I* (1981); *Iceman* (1984); *Clan of the Cave Bear* (1985); *Cavegirl* (1985); *Link* (1986); *Encino Man* (1992); *Being Human* (1994) (segment); *The Flintstones* (1994); *Encino Woman* (1996 TVM); *Savage* (1996); *The Flintstones in Viva Rock Vegas* (2000)

Centerfolds

Life's been tough for girls posing in the buff. Kim Basinger played a model whose career went into a tailspin after appearing in a girlie magazine in *Katie: Portrait of a Centerfold* (1978). Apparently, the film had little impact on Basinger, who eventually did pose in *Playboy* (but not as the centerfold). The sad real-life story of Dorothy Stratten, a Playmate-turned-actress murdered by her former lover, reached the small screen in 1981 and the big screen

two years later. Jamie Lee Curtis played Stratten in the TV movie *Death of a Centerfold: The Dorothy Stratten Story*, while Mariel Hemingway took the lead in Bob Fosse's *Star 80* (1983). Other fact-based telefilms include 1991's *Posing: Inspired by Three Real Stories* and 1983's *Policewoman Centerfold*, the story of a lady cop who lost her job after posing for a nude layout. In a case of ideal casting, *Playboy* centerfold Erika Eleniak played a centerfold in Steven Seagal's *Under Siege* (1992). Except for rarities like *Man of the Year* (1995), the film industry has failed to exploit the plight of male nude models, once again confirming the industry's chauvinistic tendencies toward women. See also **Fashion Models**; **Strippers**.

The Centerfold Girls (1974); *Katie: Portrait of a Centerfold* (1978 TVM); *Death of a Centerfold: The Dorothy Stratten Story* (1981 TVM); *Star 80* (1983); *Policewoman Centerfold* (1983 TVM); *I Married a Centerfold* (1984 TVM); *Posing: Inspired by Three Real Stories* (aka *I Posed for Playboy*) (1991 TVM); *Under Siege* (1992); *Man of the Year* (1995); *Attack of the 60 Foot Centerfold* (1995); *The People vs. Larry Flynt* (1996); *Hefner Unauthorized* (1999 TVM)

Chainsaws

In addition to bit parts in lumberjack films (q.v.), chainsaws have made memorable appearances in a handful of horror movies — almost expressly for purposes other than cutting wood. The cannibalistic killers in *The Texas Chainsaw Massacre* movies (q.v.) used them to prepare people for dinner. Bruce Campbell discovered that chainsaws were ideal for decapitating demons in the second and third *Evil Dead* movies (q.v.). In fact, after severing his own hand (it was possessed), Campbell attached a chainsaw to his arm. Chainsaw duels were featured prominently in *Motel Hell*, *Phantasm II*, *The Texas Chainsaw Massacre 2*, and the subtly-titled *Hollywood Chainsaw Hookers*. The latter film featured the catchy ad line: "They charge an arm and a leg." It also starred Gunnar Hansen (Leatherface of *Texas Chainsaw Massacre* fame) as the cult leader of the chainsaw-toting prostitutes. See also **The Texas Chainsaw Massacre Series**.

The Texas Chainsaw Massacre (1974); *Motel Hell* (1980); *Evil Dead 2: Dead by Dawn* (aka *Evil Dead 2*) (1987); *The Running Man* (1987); *Hollywood Chainsaw Hookers* (1988); *Phantasm II* (1988); *Army of Darkness* (aka *Army of Darkness: Evil Dead 3*) (1993); *Phantasm III: Lord of the Dead* (aka *Phantasm III*) (1994); *The Monster* (1994); *Leprechaun 3* (1995)

Chan, Charlie

Sherlock Holmes reigns as cinema's busiest sleuth, but Charlie Chan ranks a surprising — and very strong — second, with over forty mysteries to his credit. Although Earl Derr Bigger's novels were popular in the 1920s, his Hawaiian police detective was relegated to a strictly supporting role in his big-screen debut, 1926's *The House Without a Key*. He fared better in subsequent outings, but didn't make an impact until Warner Oland made the part his own in 1931's *Charlie Chan Carries On*. Although Swedish by birth, Oland specialized in Oriental roles and, at one point in his career, was playing detective Chan and villain Fu Manchu (q.v.) simultaneously. Oland brought warmth and deceiving wit to the role, masterfully phrasing words of wisdom such as: "Alibi, like dead fish, cannot stand test of time." Keye Luke usually played Charlie's #1 son, providing youth appeal and comic support, as did other sons Benson Fong and Victor Sen Yung in later entries. The Oland Chan films are considered the best of the series, with *Charlie Chan at the Opera* (co-starring Boris Karloff and a young Ray Milland) as the highlight. When Oland died in 1938, American-born Sidney Toler assumed the role and continued the 20th Century–Fox series in capable fashion until 1942: Toler returned as Chan in 1944 for a series at Monogram. On his death in 1947, he was replaced by Roland Winters, who made the last Monogram entry in 1949. Eight years later, Chan resurfaced in the form of J. Carrol Naish in a syndicated TV series called *The New Adventures of Charlie Chan*. It lasted for only 39 half-hour episodes. Ross Martin, best known as Artemus Gordon on TV's *The Wild Wild West*, made an unlikely Chan in the 1973 TV movie *Happiness Is a Warm Clue* (aka *The Return of Charlie Chan*). Filmed for U.S. television in 1970, this attempt to revive Chan sat on the shelf for three years, showed up on British TV in 1973, and finally made its American debut on the late show in 1979. At least, the 1981 spoof *Charlie Chan and the Curse of the Dragon Queen* received a general release, though to little avail. Critics panned it and audiences proved that they greatly preferred Oland and Toler to a feebly unfunny Peter Ustinov. The Chan character was much better parodied in Neil Simon's *Murder by Death* (1976). Two of the most potentially interesting Chan films were never made. In *The Four Star Murder Case*, Charlie would have teamed up with Philo Vance, Mr. Moto, and Michael Shayne to solve one mighty tough case. *Charlie Chan at College* would have cast the Oriental detective as a visiting professor demonstrating the finer aspects of crime-solving to his students.

The House Without a Key (1926) (George Kuwa); *The Chinese Parrot* (1928) (Sojin); *Behind That Curtain* (1929) (E.L. Park); *Charlie Chan Carries On* (1931) (Warner Oland); *The Black Camel* (1931) (Oland); *Charlie Chan's Chance* (1932) (Oland); *Charlie Chan's Greatest Case* (1932) (Oland); *Charlie Chan's Courage* (1934) (Oland); *Charlie Chan in London* (1934) (Oland); *Charlie Chan in Egypt* (1935) (Oland); *Charlie Chan in Shanghai* (1935) (Oland); *Charlie Chan in Paris* (1935) (Oland); *Charlie Chan at the Circus* (1936) (Oland); *Charlie Chan at the Opera* (1936) (Oland); *Charlie Chan at the Race Track* (1936) (Oland); *Charlie Chan's Secret* (1936) (Oland); *Charlie Chan on Broadway* (1937) (Oland); *Charlie Chan at the Olympics* (1937) (Oland); *Charlie Chan at Monte Carlo* (1938) (Oland); *Charlie Chan in Honolulu* (1938) (Sidney Toler); *Charlie Chan at Treasure Island* (1939) (Toler); *Charlie Chan in Reno* (1939) (Toler); *Charlie Chan in the City of Darkness* (1939) (Toler); *Charlie Chan at the Wax Museum* (1940) (Toler); *Charlie Chan's Murder Cruise* (1940) (Toler); *Murder Over New York* (1940) (Toler); *Charlie Chan in Panama* (1940) (Toler); *Charlie Chan in Rio* (1941) (Toler); *Dead Men Tell* (1941) (Toler); *Castle in the Desert* (1942) (Toler); *Charlie Chan in Black Magic* (aka *Charlie Chan in Meeting at Midnight*; *Charlie Chan at Midnight*; *Black Magic*) (1944) (Toler); *Charlie Chan in the Secret Service* (1944) (Toler); *The Chinese Cat* (1944) (Toler); *The Jade Mask* (1945) (Toler); *The Red Dragon* (1945) (Toler); *The Scarlet Clue* (1945) (Toler); *The Shanghai Cobra* (1945) (Toler); *Charlie Chan in Dangerous Money* (aka *Dangerous Money*) (1946) (Toler); *Dark Alibi* (1946) (Toler); *Shadows Over Chinatown* (1946) (Toler); *The Trap* (1947) (Toler); *The Chinese Ring* (1947) (Roland Winters); *Charlie Chan and the Golden Eye* (aka *The Golden Eye*; *Mystery of the Golden Eye*) (1948) (Winters); *Docks of New Orleans* (1948) (Winters); *The Feathered Serpent* (1948) (Winters); *The Shanghai Chest* (1948) (Winters); *Sky Dragon* (1949) (Winters); *Happiness Is a Warm Clue* (aka *The Return of Charlie Chan*) (1973 TVM) (Ross Martin); *Charlie Chan and the Curse of the Dragon Queen* (1981) (Peter Ustinov)

Chauffeurs

Although they are privy to intimate auto conversations, chauffeurs have never acquired a cinematic stature equal to butlers (q.v.) and ladies-in-waiting. Perhaps it's because they usually live over the garage, thereby missing the essential upstairs and downstairs activities at the main house. Certainly, chauffeurs have fared poorly when it comes to romance. Both Carlo Justini and Robert Shaw mistakenly believe their female employers are interested in them in, respectively, *A Novel Affair* and *The Hireling*. Jean Simmons and chauffeur Robert Mitchum become romantically involved in *Angel Face*, but it's an unhappy affair that ends with a car zooming over a cliff. Even chauffeur's daughter Audrey Hepburn endures romantic entanglements when rich brothers William Holden and Humphrey Bogart clash over her affections in *Sabrina*. Female limo drivers are rare in the movies, although Deborah Foreman played one in 1986's *My Chauffeur*. Jack Lenoir, who once was Ginger Rogers' chauffeur, played her driver in *Once in Paris…* (and earned better notices than Ginger). Morgan Freeman played the cinema's best known chauffeur in 1989's *Driving Miss Daisy*. He earned a Best Actor nomination for his performance as Hoke, Miss Daisy's (Jessica Tandy) loyal driver and steadfast friend. See also **Automobiles**; **Butlers**; **Maids and Housekeepers**; **Taxi Drivers**.

Passion Flower (1930); *Downstairs* (1932); *Merrily We Live* (1938); *Mr. Muggs Steps Out* (1943); *Native Son* (1950); *Angel Face* (1953); *Sabrina* (aka *Sabrina Fair*) (1954); *A Novel Affair* (aka *The Passionate Stranger*) (1957); *Endless Night* (aka *Agatha Christie's Endless Night*) (1971); *The Hireling* (1973); *Law and Disorder* (1974); *Once in Paris…* (1978); *Arthur* (1981); *Sunset Limousine* (1983 TVM); *Native Son* (1986); *My Chauffeur* (1986); *Cookie* (1989); *Driving Miss Daisy* (1989); *This Can't Be Love* (1994 TVM); *Sabrina* (1995); *Strange Days* (1995)

Cheerleaders

When relegated to supporting roles in football (q.v.) movies and campus comedies, cheerleaders have been typically stereotyped as shallow, image-conscious individuals. Thus, one would think that cheerleader movies would tend to paint more positive views of the primary promoters of school spirit. Instead, the post–1970 cheerleader era has consisted primarily of sex comedies, slasher films, and bizarre true stories. The sex "comedies" include such notorious fare as *The Cheerleaders* (originally rated X, but since downgraded to an R) and the infamous XXX-rated *Debbie Does Dallas*. When not removing their clothes, cinematic cheerleaders often find themselves coping with killers in bloody pictures such as *Cheerleaders' Wild Weekend* and *Cheerleader Camp* (which boasts the memorable alternate title *Bloody Pom-Poms*). Even the slasher film spoof *Pandemonium* (1982) was set appropriately in a school for cheerleaders. Made-for-television movies have opted to present "true stories" about cheerleaders. The unexpected popularity of the Dallas Cowboy Cheerleaders was examined in two highly-rated films. However, viewers showed far less interest in the Los Angeles Lakers' cheering squad. And a high school cheerleader's mother plotted murder in *Willing to Kill: The Texas Cheerleader Story*, an exploitative TV drama torn from the headlines. The same fact-based incident served as the basis for HBO's dark comedy *The Positively True Adventures of the Alleged Texas Cheerleader-Murdering Mom*. Finally, Olivia Newton-John played a nice, wholesome cheerleader in *Grease*, but she ditched her pom-poms for black leather in order to keep boyfriend John Travolta. Given the fate of other movie cheerleaders, it was probably a wise decision. See also **Basketball**; **Football**.

The Cheerleaders (1972); *The Pom-Pom Girls* (1976); *Satan's Cheerleaders* (1977); *Debbie Does Dallas* (1978); *Grease* (1978); *Dallas Cowboy Cheerleaders* (1979 TVM); *Dallas Cowboy Cheerleaders II* (1980 TVM); *Pandemonium* (1982); *Cheerleaders' Wild Weekend* (1985); *Cheerleader Camp* (aka *Bloody Pom-Poms*) (1987); *Laker Girls* (1990 TVM); *Willing to Kill: The Texas Cheerleader Story* (1992 TVM); *The Positively True Adventures of the Alleged Texas Cheerleader-Murdering Mom* (1993 TVM); *Flesh Gordon 2: Flesh Gordon Meets the Cosmic Cheerleaders* (1993); *A Friend to Die For* (1994); *Jailbreakers* (1994 TVM); *Pretty Poison* (1996 TVM); *But I'm a Cheerleader* (2000); *Bring It On* (2000)

Chess

The game's intensity has been best captured by *Dangerous Moves*, 1985's Best Foreign Film about how two brilliant players eventually become manipulated by their own obsessions. Christopher Lambert played a chess player who becomes a murder suspect in 1992's *Knight Moves*. *Searching for Bobby Fischer* (1993) recounted the story of seven-year-old chess prodigy Josh Waitzkin. Several movies have featured memorable chess games. Max Von Sydow played chess with Death in Ingmar Bergman's symbolic *The Seventh Seal* (1957). Steve McQueen and Faye Dunaway practically made love over a game board in *The Thomas Crown Affair* (1968), a scene later spoofed in *Austin Powers: The Spy That Shagged Me* (1999). Sherlock Holmes (Basil Rathbone) used people as chess pieces to solve the puzzle of the Musgrave Ritual in 1943's *Sherlock Holmes Faces Death*. Philo Vance (Rathbone again) clashed with a devious murderer who left a chess piece and Mother Goose rhymes as clues in S.S. Van Dine's *The Bishop Murder Case* (1930). Along similar lines, jewel thief Ryan O'Neal played a chess game with the police in 1973's *The Thief Who Came to Dinner*.

The Bishop Murder Case (1930); *Sherlock Holmes Faces Death* (1943); *Scared Stiff* (aka *Treasure of Fear*) (1945); *The Seventh Seal* (1957); *From Russia with Love* (1963); *The Thomas Crown Affair* (1968); *The Thief Who Came to Dinner* (1973); *The Chess Players* (1977); *Dangerous Moves* (1985); *The King of Chess* (aka *Kei Wong*) (1991); *Knight Moves* (aka *Face to Face*) (1992); *Searching for Bobby Fischer* (1993); *The Joy Luck Club* (1993); *Fresh* (1994); *The Chess Game* (aka *La Partie D'Echecs*) (1994); *Angus* (1995); *Austin Powers: The Spy That Shagged Me* (1999)

Child Custody Disputes

The commercial success of 1979's *Kramer vs. Kramer* brought the bitter struggles over child custody into close focus and undoubtedly contributed to public awareness. However, earlier movies periodically visited the same subject, often just as effectively. An obscure 1942 Paramount film, *My Heart Belongs to Daddy*, featured Martha O'Driscoll as a dancer fighting her in-laws, who maintain that her profession is unsuitable for raising her baby. Bing Crosby gave his best non-singing performance as a father fighting desperately to keep his son in 1957's *Man on Fire*. As in *Kramer*, *Man on Fire* painfully depicts a no-win situation, with a young boy caught in the middle. *One Potato, Two Potato* (1964) injected intriguing controversy, with Barbara Barrie as a woman who marries a black man and then clashes with her ex-husband

on custody of her daughter. Another variation cropped up in 1974's *Unwed Father*, in which a young man tries to gain custody of his illegitimate daughter. Post-*Kramer* films include the sensitive Australian import *Careful, He Might Hear You* (1983) and *Ernie Kovacs: Between the Laughter* (1984). The latter real-life story dealt with Kovacs' efforts to retrieve his two daughters, who were kidnapped by their mother after a child custody dispute. The television networks acquired a taste for fact-based child custody cases in the 1990s, broadcasting numerous films such as *Locked Up: A Mother's Rage* (1991), *A Mother's Right: The Elizabeth Morgan Story* (1992), *Because Mommy Works* (1994), and *Two Mothers for Zachary* (1996). Overly-cute Drew Barrymore sued parents Shelley Long and Ryan O'Neal for custody of herself in 1984's *Irreconcilable Differences*. That same plot took on real-life implications in two 1993 telefilms, *Gregory K* and *A Place to Be Loved*, which recounted the actual case of a 12-year-old who sued to terminate his parents' custodial rights.

Bright Eyes (1934); *The Great Man Votes* (1939); *My Heart Belongs to Daddy* (1942); *Trouble Along the Way* (1953); *The Divided Heart* (1954); *Man on Fire* (1957); *One Potato, Two Potato* (1964); *Unwed Father* (1974 TVM); *Kramer vs. Kramer* (1979); *Mark, I Love You* (1980 TVM); *Little Gloria...Happy at Last* (1982 TVM); *Careful, He Might Hear You* (1983); *Irreconcilable Differences* (1984); *Ernie Kovacs: Between the Laughter* (1984 TVM); *This Child Is Mine* (1985 TVM); *A Question of Love* (1987 TVM); *Over the Top* (1987); *After the Promise* (1987 TVM); *The Good Father* (1987); *The Good Mother* (1988); *In the Best Interest of the Child* (1990 TVM); *Locked Up: A Mother's Rage* (1991 TVM); *In the Best Interest of the Children* (1992 TVM); *Jonathan: The Boy Nobody Wanted* (1992 TVM); *A Mother's Right: The Elizabeth Morgan Story* (1992 TVM); *Gregory K* (1993 TVM); *Desperate Rescue: The Cathy Mahone Story* (1993 TVM); *A Place to Be Loved* (1993 TVM); *A Matter of Justice* (1993 TVM); *Moment of Truth: A Child Too Many* (1993 TVM); *Scattered Dreams: The Kathryn Messenger Story* (1993 TVM); *For the Love of Aaron* (1993 TVM); *In the Best of Families: Marriage, Pride and Madness* (1994 TVM); *A Simple Twist of Fate* (1994); *The Yarn Princess* (1994 TVM); *Someone Else's Child* (1994 TVM); *Because Mommy Works* (1994 TVM); *Thicker Than Blood: The Larry McLinden Story* (1994 TVM); *Whose Daughter Is She?* (1995 TVM); *Two Mothers for Zachary* (1996 TVM); *Hollow Reed* (1997); *A Father for Brittany* (1998 TVM); *Two Babies: Switched at Birth* (1999 TVM)

Children of the Bride Series

The saga of the Becker and Hix families proved that television viewers—if not theatrical moviegoers—still had a soft spot for schmaltzy drama in the early 1990s. The focus of this TV movie series is Margaret Becker (Rue McClanahan), a middle-aged divorcee, who falls in love with, and eventually marries, younger man John Hix. In *Children of the Bride* (1990), Margaret's four adult offspring experience difficulties coping with this unexpected development in their mother's life. Naturally, they eventually discover that John is a swell guy. In the 1991 follow-up *Baby of the Bride*, Margaret becomes pregnant unexpectedly and each of her children must cope with their own problems: Mary has to adjust to life as a single parent; Dennis has a fling with his female boss; twice-divorced Anne gets romanced by Nick, a charming policeman); and Andrew "kidnaps" his children from his ex-wife. A tidy conclusion resolves everything and the Beckers and Hixes enjoy two years of non-televised bliss. Then, with 1993's *Mother of the Bride*, Anne and Nick decide to get married, Margaret's ex-husband Richard (Paul Dooley) shows up suddenly, and Mary becomes attracted to a motorcycle-riding construction worker named Ken. Throughout the series, much of the cast remained the same: McClanahan as Margaret, Kristy McNichol as Mary, Anne Bobby as Anne, and Connor O'Farrell as Andrew. Patrick Duffy played John Hix in the first film, with Ted Shackleford replacing him in the two sequels. Interestingly, Duffy and Shackleford played brothers Bobby and Gary Ewing on TV's *Dallas*. Kristy McNichol must have seemed a natural for her role, having spent four seasons on the TV series *Family*.

Children of the Bride (1990 TVM); *Baby of the Bride* (1991 TVM); *Mother of the Bride* (1993 TVM)

Children of the Corn Series

Film adaptations of Stephen King's literary works have ranged from the sublime (*The Dead Zone*) to the mundane (*Pet Sematary*). The original film version of *Children of the Corn* (1984) falls somewhere in between. Linda Hamilton and Peter Horton star as a couple driving cross-country who stop in rural Gatlin, Nebraska, when they run over a boy's dead body. Gatlin is not a typical midwestern town — there are no adults, only children led by a young "prophet" named Isaac who serves a god called He Who Walks Behind the Rows. The stranded couple soon learns that they're next in line to be sacrificed to the mysterious corn-god. With apologies to King, the plot borrows elements from superior fare like *Village of the Damned* (where children rule a town) and *The Wicker Man* (where people are sacrificed to a fertility god). Still, *Children of the Corn* benefits from its likable leads, who were on the verge of minor stardom: Hamilton made a splash in the same year's *The Terminator* and Horton would make his mark in 1987 in the TV series *thirtysomething*. Neither actor appeared in the belated sequels that started with 1993's *Children of the Corn II: The Final Sacrifice*, which picks up the story eight years later with the Gatlin children being placed in foster homes in a nearby town. Not surprisingly, the town's adult residents start to die, often in bizarre ways (e.g., a woman gets crushed under her own house). The rest of the series entries follow the same formula with the children worshippers of He Who Walks Behind the Rows harassing adults and even causing havoc in high schools (*Children of the Corn III*). Incidentally, the original Stephen King short story appeared in his anthology *Night Shift*. See also **Sometimes They Come Back... Series**

Children of the Corn (aka *Stephen King's Children of the Corn*) (1984); *Children of the Corn II: The Final Sacrifice* (1993); *Children of the Corn III* (aka *Children of the Corn III: Urban Harvest*) (1994); *Children of the Corn IV: The Gathering* (1996); *Children of the Corn V: Field of Terror* (1998); *Children of the Corn 666: Isaac's Return* (1999)

Children Raised by Animals

This theme dates back to the Roman myth about twin brothers Romulus and Remus, who were abandoned in the woods as infants and left to die, only to be found and nursed by a she-wolf. Unfortunately, this splendid legend was recounted in perfunctory terms in its only major screen version, the 1961 Italian costume epic *Duel of the Titans*. Wolves were parents again in Rudyard Kipling's *Jungle Book*, in which the young boy Mowgli joined a wolfpack after a vicious tiger separated him from his parents. Alexander Korda produced 1942's *The Jungle Book*, a lavish live action adaptation starring the charismatic child actor Sabu (who made a career of similar roles). The Disney Studios turned Kipling's book into both a 1967 cartoon musical and a handsome 1994 live action feature starring Jason Scott Lee. The life of Edgar Rice Burroughs's Tarzan (q.v.) has been detailed in many films, although his childhood among the apes was best portrayed in 1984's *Greystoke: The Legend of Tarzan, Lord of the Apes*. François Truffaut's *The Wild Child* (1969) was a fact-based story about a boy who raised himself in the woods and the doctor dedicated to "civilizing" him. The 1976 TV movie *Stalk the Wild Child* was a thinly-disguised American version about a boy raised by wolves. It was followed by a second TV movie called *Lucan*, in which a former "wolf child" sets out to find his parents and his own identity. It served as the pilot for the 1977-78 *Lucan* TV series. Howie Mandel played a man raised by wolves in the dismal 1987 comedy *Walk Like a Man*. A parentless youth raised himself and lived in the sewers in another best-forgotten satire, 1987's *Wild Thing*. See also **Tarzan**.

The Jungle Book (1942); *Zamba* (1949); *Duel of the Titans* (1961); *The Jungle Book* (1967); *The Wild Child* (1969); *Stalk the Wild Child* (1976 TVM); *Lucan* (1977 TVM); *Greystoke: The Legend of Tarzan, Lord of the Apes* (1984); *Walk Like a Man* (1987); *The Jungle Book* (1994); *The Flintstones* (1994); *Rudyard Kipling's The Second Jungle Book: Mowgli and Baloo* (aka *Jungle Book Two*) (1997)

Child's Play Series

Director Tom Holland, who fashioned an effective vampire chiller with *Fright Night* (1985), tackled a difficult challenge with 1988's *Child's Play*. Holland burdened himself with a preposterous premise and then set about to make his audience believe it. His film opens with a shootout in which killer Charlie Lee Ray (Brad Dourif) takes refuge in a toy store. A dying Ray grabs an innocent-looking doll and transfers his soul to it. Shortly thereafter, a thoughtful mother (Catherine Hicks) buys the doll for her son Andy (Alex Vincent). Andy quickly realizes that this murderous doll has a life of its own, but, as usual, the adults don't believe him until it's almost too late. To his credit, Holland manufactures some legitimate thrills and almost makes Chucky the doll believable. Since *Child's Play* turned into a sleeper hit, there had to be a sequel (it's the law according to money-minded producers). *Child's Play 2* plucks traumatized Andy into a foster home while his mother recovers in an institution. Naturally, Chucky shows up at Andy's new home, despite being thoroughly mangled at the end of the first film. Alex Vincent reprised his role as Andy and Brad Dourif provided the voice again for Chucky, but John Lafia replaced Holland as director. To prove you can't keep a good villain down, Chucky came back for *Child's Play 3* (1991) and *Bride of Chucky* (1998). The third installment shifted the setting to a military academy (q.v.) and featured Justin Whalin as an older Andy. The more imaginative — and preposterous — *Bride of Chucky* paired Chucky (still voiced by Brad Dourif) with a murderous female doll (voiced by Jennifer Tilly). It boasted the catchy ad line: "Chucky gets lucky." See also **Dolls**.

Child's Play (1988); *Child's Play 2* (1990); *Child's Play 3* (1991); *Bride of Chucky* (1998)

A Chinese Ghost Story Series

This wildly stylish, Hong Kong–lensed supernatural series features such memorable "monsters" as the Tree Devil (with his disgustingly long tongue) and the lumbering Mountain Devil. It also mixes romance, humor, and spectacular special effects for a unique film experience. Indeed, *New York Times* film critic Walter Goodman described 1987's *A Chinese Ghost Story* as "98 minutes of bounding and bouncing, flying and flailing, slashing and slaying." The plot revolves around two travelers who take refuge from a storm in a haunted temple. During the night, they encounter a beautiful, seductive ghost and the aforementioned Tree Devil. The equally imaginative sequel, *A Chinese Ghost Story II* (1990), featured a delirious mix of mistaken identities, reincarnation, and unexpected magic. Leslie Cheung starred in the first two films, which racked up big box-office grosses in Hong Kong. The third installment did not fare quite as well as its predecessors. It featured Tony Leung Chiu-wai as a different lead character and took place a century later — still within the confines of a haunted temple. Cult horror film director Tsui Hark served as executive producer and co-wrote the screenplays. In 1997, Hark remade the original film as an animated feature. See also **Ghosts**.

A Chinese Ghost Story (aka *Qian Nu Youhun*; *Sinnui Yauman*) (1987); *A Chinese Ghost Story II* (aka *Sinnui Yauman II*) (1990); *A Chinese Ghost Story III* (aka *Sinnui Yauman III: Do Do Do*) (1991); *A Chinese Ghost Story: The Tsui Hark Animation* (aka *Xiaoqian*) (1997)

Christian, Dr. (Paul)

Prior to his screen debut as paternal country doctor Paul Christian, Jean Hersholt had already provided the character's radio voice and starred in a similar role in three 20th Century–Fox films. Daryl Zanuck was the man behind Fox's *The Country Doctor* (1936), a family drama based on the birth of the Dionne Quintuplets (and featuring a brief appearance by star-to-be Tyrone Power). Hersholt scored as the family's rural physician and appeared in two sequels: *Reunion* (1936) and *Five of a Kind* (1938). A year later, Hersholt moved to RKO and initiated a new series with *Meet Dr. Christian*. Christian was the Marcus Welby of his era and, in the span of an hour, could cure an epidemic of spinal meningitis and solve a handful of personal crises for his patients. True to character, Hersholt was a great humanitarian himself and received two special Academy Awards for work with the Motion Picture Relief Fund. In 1956, the year of his death, the Academy of Motion Picture Arts and Sciences created an annual humanitarian award to be given in his name. Other Christian series regulars included Dorothy Lovett as the doctor's faithful nurse and Robert Baldwin as her boyfriend, the town druggist. Ring Lardner, Jr., wrote several of the scripts. In 1956, MacDonald Carey played the title role in the syndicated TV series *Dr. Christian*. The Dionne Quintuplets, minus Dr. Christian, were the subjects of the fact-based 1994 TV movie *Million Dollar Babies*.

Meet Dr. Christian (1939); *The Courageous Dr. Christian* (1940); *Dr. Christian Meets the Women* (1940); *Remedy for Riches* (1940); *Melody for Three* (1941); *They Meet Again* (1941)

Christmas

There was a time when the coming of the yuletide season promised that lesser-known holiday favorites, such as *The Cheaters* and the 1951 *A Christmas Carol*, would be pulled from the vaults to air alongside annual classics like *The Bishop's Wife*, *It's a Wonderful Life*, and *Miracle on 34th Street*. But a glut of recently-pro-duced Christmas fare, mostly made-for-TV movies, has diluted the holiday marketplace and sent the "lesser knowns" back into the film vaults. No fewer than 31 Christmas-oriented TV movies were broadcast by the major networks between 1977 and 1992. Nine theatricals were also released during the same period. Ironically, the networks' heaping servings of Christmas sentiment were undoubtedly inspired by the lasting popularity of holiday classics like *It's a Wonderful Life* (which was remade for TV as 1977's *It Happened One Christmas*). As one would expect, Charles Dickens' *A Christmas Carol* has provided the source material for the most yuletide films: *A Christmas Carol* (1938) with Reginald Owen as Scrooge, *A Christmas Carol* (1951) with Alastair Sim, the musical *Scrooge* (1970) with Albert Finney, *An American Christmas Carol* with Henry Winkler (1979 TVM), *A Christmas Carol* with George C. Scott (1984 TVM), the 1988 contemporary take-off *Scrooged* with Bill Murray, *The Muppet Christmas Carol* (1992), and others (not to mention the famous cartoon short "Mr. Magoo's Christmas Carol"). Santa Claus has appeared rather less than one would think, notching appearances in *Babes in Toyland* (1961), *Santa Claus Conquers the Martians* (1964), *The Christmas That Almost Wasn't* (1966), *Santa Claus: The Movie* (1985), *Ernest Saves Christmas* (1988), and *The Santa Clause* (1994). Art Carney played St. Nick in *The Night They Saved Christmas* (1984), a part he knew well as a result of his 1960 appearance in the touching "Night of the Meek" episode of the TV show *The Twilight Zone*. He starred as a drunken department store Santa who loses his job, only to find a magic bag of toys and become the real St. Nick. Of course, not everyone in a Santa suit experiences that kind of magic. Christopher Plummer played an unstable murderer who robbed a bank disguised as Santa in *The Silent Partner* (1978). A psychotic killer sported a Santa suit in the tasteless 1984 slasher film *Silent Night, Deadly Night* (q.v.).

A Christmas Carol (1938); *Beyond Tomorrow* (1940); *Holiday Inn* (1942); *Christmas Holiday* (1944); *The Cheaters* (aka *The Castaway*) (1945); *Christmas in Connecticut* (aka *Indiscretion*) (1945); *It's a Wonderful Life* (1946); *The Bishop's Wife* (1947); *Christmas Eve* (aka *Sinner's Holiday*) (1947); *Miracle on 34th Street* (aka *The Big Heart*) (1947); *Holiday Affair* (1949); *A Christmas Carol* (aka *Scrooge*) (1951); *The Lemon Drop Kid* (1951); *The Holly and the Ivy* (1952); *White Christmas* (1954); *Babes in Toyland* (1961); *Santa Claus Conquers the Martians* (1964); *The Christmas That Almost Wasn't* (1966); *The Christmas Tree* (aka *When Wolves Cry*) (1969); *Scrooge* (1970); *The Homecoming—A Christmas Story* (1971 TVM); *Home for the Holidays* (1972 TVM); *Tales from the Crypt* (1972) (the segment "All Through the House"); *A Dream for Christmas* (1973 TVM); *Miracle on 34th Street* (1973 TVM); *Silent Night, Bloody Night* (1973); *Black Christmas* (aka *Silent Night, Evil Night*; *Stranger in the House*) (1975); *Young Pioneers' Christmas* (1976 TVM); *Sunshine Christmas* (1977 TVM); *Christmas Miracle in Caufield, U.S.A.* (aka *the Christmas Coal Mine Miracle*) (1977 TVM); *The Gathering* (1977 TVM); *It Happened One Christmas* (1977 TVM); *A Christmas to Remember* (1978 TVM); *The Gift of Love* (1978 TVM); *An American Christmas Carol* (1979 TVM); *Christmas Lilies of the Field* (1979 TVM); *The Gathering, Part II* (1979 TVM); *The Man in the Santa Claus Suit* (1979 TVM); *A Christmas Without Snow* (1980 TVM); *You Better Watch Out* (aka *Christmas Evil*; *Terror in Toyland*) (1980); *The Gift of Love: A Christmas Story* (1983 TVM); *A Christmas Story* (1983); *A Christmas Carol* (1984 TVM); *It Came Upon a Midnight Clear* (1984 TVM); *The Night They Saved Christmas* (1984 TVM); *Silent Night, Deadly Night* (1984); *One Magic Christmas* (1985); *Santa Claus: The*

Movie (aka *Santa Claus*) (1985); *Christmas Eve* (1986 TVM); *The Christmas Gift* (1986 TVM); *The Christmas Star* (1986 TVM); *Christmas Comes to Willow Creek* (1987 TVM); *The Christmas Visitor* (aka *Bushfire Moon*) (1987 TVM); *I'll Be Home for Christmas* (1988 TVM); *Ernest Saves Christmas* (1988); *Scrooged* (1988); *A Very Brady Christmas* (1988 TVM); *The Christmas Wife* (1988 TVM); *National Lampoon's Christmas Vacation* (1989); *Prancer* (1989); *Guess Who's Coming for Christmas?* (1990 TVM); *The Kid Who Loved Christmas* (1990 TVM); *Home Alone* (1990); *In the Nick of Time* (1991 TVM); *All I Want for Christmas* (1991); *Yes, Virginia, There Is a Santa Claus* (1991 TVM); *Christmas on Division Street* (1991 TVM); *Miracle in the Wilderness* (1991 TVM); *Christmas in Connecticut* (1992 TVM); *The Man Upstairs* (1992 TVM); *The Muppet Christmas Carol* (1992); *To Grandmother's House We Go* (1992 TVM); *Home Alone 2* (1992); *Tim Burton's The Nightmare Before Christmas* (aka *The Nightmare Before Christmas*) (1993); *Home for Christmas* (aka *Little Miss Millions*) (1993); *Home of Angels* (1994); *Mixed Nuts* (1994); *Miracle on 34th Street* (1994); *The Santa Clause* (1994); *Trapped in Paradise* (1994); *One Christmas* (1994 TVM); *A Christmas Romance* (1994 TVM); *The Christmas Box* (1995 TVM); *Ebbie* (1995 TVM); *Reckless* (1995); *Jingle All the Way* (1996); *The Preacher's Wife* (1996); *Breathing Room* (1996); *Mrs. Santa Claus* (1996 TVM); *A Different Kind of Christmas* (1996 TVM); *I'll Be Home for Christmas* (1997 TVM); *Holiday in Your Heart* (1997 TVM); *On the 2nd Day of Christmas* (1997 TVM); *Borrowed Hearts: A Holiday Romance* (1997 TVM); *Ms. Scrooge* (1997 TVM); *I'll Be Home for Christmas* (1998); *Secret of Giving* (1999 TVM); *Santa and Pete* (1999 TVM); *A Christmas Carol* (1999 TVM); *Reindeer Games* (2000)

Cinerama

Former Paramount special effects technician Fred Waller invented this widescreen process, which produces a 165-degree curved image, in the early 1950s. It evolved from an earlier Waller system called Vitarama, which used eleven synchronized projectors to create an illusion of vastness and motion on a curved theater screen. Vitarama was a big hit at the 1937 World's Fair, but its expense and technical requirements made it impractical for common use. Waller refined it over the next two decades and introduced a new version in 1952 with the travelogue film *This Is Cinerama*. The Cinerama process required a film to be shot with three cameras, one facing straight ahead and the other two slightly to the left and right of the middle camera. Three synchronized projectors then projected all three films on a curved screen simultaneously. Like *This Is Cinerama*, the early films shown in the process focused on spectacular visual effects — breathtaking roller-coaster rides and soaring plane flights over the Grand Canyon. Unlike 3-D, Cinerama survived the 1950s, perhaps because its equipment restrictions limited the number of theaters that could show Cinerama films and elevated the process to special event status. The first nontravelogue was 1962's *How the West Was Won*. Occasional films continued to be made in Cinerama throughout the 1960s. However, technical difficulties, specifically problems with keeping the projectors synchronized, drove the development of a one-projector Cinerama process. The "new" Cinerama amounted to little more than projecting a 70mm image on a curved screen. It was abandoned in the 1970s, though expositions and amusement parks continue to exhibit popular Cinerama-like projection systems. See also **3-D**; **Gimmicks**.

This Is Cinerama (1952); *Cinerama Holiday* (1955); *Seven Wonders of the World* (1956); *Search for Paradise* (1957); *South Seas Adventure* (1958); *How the West Was Won* (1962); *The Wonderful World of the Brothers Grimm* (1962); *It's a Mad, Mad, Mad, Mad World* (1963); *Circus World* (1963); *The Best of Cinerama* (1964); *Battle of the Bulge* (1965); *Grand Prix* (1966); *2001: A Space Odyssey* (1968); *Ice Station Zebra* (1968); *Custer of the West* (1968); *Krakatoa, East of Java* (aka *Volcano*) (1969)

Circuses

The allure of the big top setting faded in the 1970s, but for four decades, it was an ideal place to find high-wire dramatics, ferocious beasts, incognito killers, and perhaps a troupe of vampires. Laughs, too, as evidenced by the number of comedies set against a circus backdrop. W.C. Fields played a ringmaster in *You Can't Cheat an Honest Man* (1939), the Marx Brothers saved a big top from bankruptcy in *At the Circus* (1939), and even Dean Martin and Jerry Lewis got into the act with *Three Ring Circus* (1954). Movie murderers have also exhibited a special fondness for circuses, as evidenced in *Charlie Chan at the Circus* (1936), *Circus of Horrors* (1960), *Psycho Circus* (1967), and *Berserk* (1968). On a classier level, James Stewart played a murder suspect hiding out as a mild-mannered clown in Cecil DeMille's 1952 extravaganza *The Greatest Show on Earth*. This multicharacter melodrama garnered a Best Picture Oscar and tallied record box-office figures for Paramount. The film's successful behind-the-scenes formula was more or less copied in *The Big Circus* (1959), *The Big Show* (1961), and *Circus World* (1964). The life of the world's greatest circus showman was chronicled in 1934's *The Mighty Barnum* and 1986's *Barnum*, with Wallace Beery and Burt Lancaster in the title roles, respectively. Serious European directors have used circuses for symbolic purposes, as in Ingmar Bergman's *Sawdust and Tinsel* (1953), Federico Fellini's *La Strada* (1954), and Wim Wenders' *Wings of Desire* (1987). Four Disney pictures have taken place at least partially under the big top: *Dumbo* (1941), *Toby Tyler* (1960), *A Tiger Walks* (1964), and *The Three Lives of Thomasina* (1964). *Lady in the Dark* (1944) had a musical dream sequence set in a circus, while Rodgers and Hart's *Billy Rose's Jumbo* (1962) revolved around a circus owned by Doris Day. The circus in 1961's *Gorgo* featured a dinosaur as its main attraction. Unfortunately, it turned out to be a baby with a mad mother in hot pursuit. See also **Fairs and Carnivals**.

He Who Gets Slapped (1924); *The Circus* (1928); *Dangerous Curves* (1929); *Freaks* (aka *Nature's Mistakes*) (1932); *Rain or Shine* (1930); *Polly of the Circus* (1932); *The Big Cage* (1933); *The Mighty Barnum* (1934); *Circus Clown* (1934); *Charlie Chan at the Circus* (1936); *At the Circus* (1939); *You Can't Cheat an Honest Man* (1939); *Chad Hanna* (1940); *Dumbo* (1941); *Road Show* (1941); *Sunny* (1941); *The Wagons Roll at Night* (1941); *The Dark Tower* (1943); *Lady in the Dark* (1944) (dream sequence); *Dual Alibi* (1947); *Caged Fury* (1948); *The Fat Man* (1951); *Encore* (1952) (segment); *The Greatest Show on Earth* (1952); *Sawdust and Tinsel* (aka *The Naked Night*) (1953); *Man on a Tightrope* (1953); *Three Ring Circus* (aka *Jerrico, the Wonder Clown*) (1954); *La Strada* (aka *The Road*) (1954); *Carnival Story* (1954); *Ring of Fear* (1954); *Trapeze* (1956); *Invitation to the Dance* (1957); *Merry Andrew* (1958); *The Big Circus* (1959); *The Flying Fontaines* (1959); *Circus of Horrors* (1960); *Toby Tyler, or Ten Weeks with a Circus* (1960); *The Big Show* (1961); *Gorgo* (1961); *Hippodrome* (1961); *Bimbo the Great* (1961); *Billy Rose's Jumbo* (aka *Jumbo*) (1962); *The Main Attraction* (1962); *Circus World* (aka *The Magnificent Showman*) (1964); *A Tiger Walks* (1964); *The Seven Faces of Dr. Lao* (1964); *The Three Lives of Thomasina* (1964); *Rings Around the World* (1967); *Psycho Circus* (aka *Circus of Fear*) (1967); *Berserk* (1968); *Vampire Circus* (1971); *The Clowns* (1971); *Parade* (1974); *Punch and Jody* (1974 TVM); *The Last Circus Show* (aka *The Balloon Vendor*) (1974); *The Great Wallendas* (1978 TVM); *When the Circus Comes to Town* (1981 TVM); *Side Show* (1981 TVM); *Octopussy* (1983); *Barnum* (1986 TVM); *Wings of Desire* (aka *Der Himmel über Berlin*) (1987); *Big Top Pee Wee* (1988); *Shadows and Fog* (1992); *Freaked* (1993); *When Night Is Falling* (1995); *Rudyard Kipling's The Second Jungle Book: Mowgli and Baloo* (aka *Jungle Book Two*) (1997); *P.T. Barnum* (1999 TVM)

Cisco Kid

The origins of the Cisco Kid separate him from his many rival B-movie Western heroes. The Kid's sound debut was 1929's *In Old Arizona*, which had the triple distinction of being based on an O. Henry short story, featuring an Oscar-winning turn by Warner Baxter as Cisco, and introducing the popular song "My Tonia" (recorded by Nic Lucas). The film was a sizable hit for Fox, chiefly due to the expert direction of Western specialist Raoul Walsh. Baxter starred in the 1930 semi-sequel *The Arizona Kid* before officially reprising his Robin Hood–like Mexican outlaw in 1931's *The Cisco Kid*. *In Old Arizona* alumnus Edmund Lowe also returned as the dedicated Texas Ranger bent on capturing Cisco. After this second Cisco film, Baxter strove to avoid typecasting and appeared in musicals (*42nd Street*), biographical dramas (*Prisoner of Shark Island*), and comedies (*Daddy Long Legs*). However, by 1936, his popularity was declining and he appeared in the Cisco-like *Robin Hood of El Dorado*. Three years later, 20th Century–Fox hailed his comeback in *The Return of the Cisco Kid*. Yet, unlike the earlier films in the series, *Return* was a programmer, running just 70 minutes and co-starring young performers like Cesar Romero. In fact, Romero stepped up into the lead role in the follow-up *The Cisco Kid and the Lady* and five subsequent films. Fox dumped the series in 1941, but four years later, Monogram picked it up and installed former *Three Mesquiteers* (q.v.) supporting player Duncan Renaldo as Cisco. Renaldo starred in three films, beginning with 1945's *The Cisco Kid Returns*, before Monogram replaced him with Gilbert Roland, the only Latin actor to portray the Kid. An affable, sturdy performer, Roland made six modestly entertaining Cisco entries before Monogram ended its series. Surprisingly, United Artists revived the series in 1949 and recalled Renaldo to reprise the Mexican bandit hero. Renaldo made five entries, assisted by Leo Carillo as his sidekick Pancho. In late 1950, Renaldo and Carillo transitioned from hour-long theatrical features to a half-hour syndicated TV series. *The Cisco Kid* quickly became the biggest non-network hit of the 1950s. Its 156-episode run concluded in 1956, although it is still shown on television today (since the producers were smart enough to film in color). In 1994, Jimmy Smits and Cheech Marin played Cisco and Pancho in the TV movie *The Cisco Kid*.

In Old Arizona (1929) (Warner Baxter); *The Cisco Kid* (1931) (Baxter); *The Return of the Cisco Kid* (1939) (Baxter); *The Cisco Kid and the Lady* (1939) (Cesar Romero); *The Gay Caballero* (1940) (Romero); *Lucky Cisco Kid* (1940) (Romero); *Viva Cisco Kid* (1940) (Romero); *Romance of the Rio Grande* (1941) (Romero); *Ride On, Vaquero* (1941) (Romero); *The Cisco Kid Returns* (1945) (Duncan Renaldo); *In Old Mexico* (aka *The Cisco Kid in Old Mexico*) (1945) (Renaldo); *South of the Rio Grande* (1945) (Renaldo); *The Gay Cavalier* (1946) (Gilbert Roland); *South of Monterey* (1946) (Roland); *Beauty and the Bandit* (1946) (Roland); *King of the Bandits* (1947)

(Roland); *Riding the California Trail* (1947) (Roland); *Robin Hood of Monterey* (1947) (Roland); *The Valiant Hombre* (1949) (Renaldo); *The Daring Caballero* (1949) (Renaldo); *The Gay Amigo* (1949) (Renaldo); *Satan's Cradle* (1949) (Renaldo); *The Girl from San Lorenzo* (1950) (Renaldo); *The Cisco Kid* (1994 TVM) (Jimmy Smits)

Clairvoyants and Fortunetellers

The ability to predict the future has been a liability as often as a blessing in the movies. Claude Rains played a phony fortune-teller in 1935's *The Clairvoyant* who discovers that his predictions — including one of his death — are coming true. A similar fate befell Akim Tamiroff in *The Great Gambini* (1937) and Edward G. Robinson in *Night Has a Thousand Eyes* (1948). Five years earlier, Robinson played a man fatally obsessed with a palm reader's uncanny predictions in the eeriest tale in Julien Duvivier's anthology *Flesh and Fantasy*. Mr. Big forcibly employed the clairvoyant Solitaire (Jane Seymour) in the 1973 Bond adventure *Live and Let Die*. Alas, 007 put an end to Solitaire's prophetic powers, since they were somehow tied to her virginity. Clairvoyants capable of predicting murders aided the police in *The Eyes of Charles Sand* (1972), *Man on a Swing* (1974) and *Eyes of Laura Mars* (1978). The 1971 TV movie *Sweet, Sweet Rachel* spun off the short-lived 1972 series *The Sixth Sense*, which starred Gary Collins as a psychic private investigator. Traditional gypsy and roadside fortune tellers have had brief, but memorable, scenes in *The Wizard of Oz*, *The Wolf Man*, and *The Leopard Man*. The finest clairvoyant comedy, Rene Clair's *It Happened Tomorrow* (1944), featured Dick Powell as a reporter who gets tomorrow's newspaper delivered a day early. Other lighthearted fortune-telling tales include Eddie Cantor's *Palmy Days* (1932) and Ealing's *The Oracle* (1952). See also **Mediums and Seances**.

The Hole in the Wall (1929); *Palmy Days* (1932); *The Clairvoyant* (aka *The Evil Mind*) (1935); *The Great Gambini* (1937); *The Wizard of Oz* (1939); *The Wolf Man* (1941); *The Crystal Ball* (1943); *Flesh and Fantasy* (1943); *The Leopard Man* (1943); *It Happened Tomorrow* (1944); *Inner Sanctum* (1948); *Night Has a Thousand Eyes* (1948); *The Oracle* (1952); *Dr. Terror's House of Horrors* (1965); *Sweet, Sweet Rachel* (1971 TVM); *The Eyes of Charles Sand* (1972 TVM); *Visions…* (aka *Visions of Death*) (1972 TVM); *Baffled* (1972 TVM); *Live and Let Die* (1973); *Man on a Swing* (1974); *From Beyond the Grave* (aka *Creatures from Beyond the Grave*) (1974); *The Premonition* (1976); *Eyes of Laura Mars* (1978); *Mind Over Murder* (1979 TVM); *The Dead Zone* (1983); *The Clairvoyant* (1985); *Second Sight* (1989); *Black Rainbow* (1989); *The Butcher's Wife* (1991); *Psychic* (1992 TVM); *Nostradamus* (1994); *Dead on Sight* (1994); *Eyes of Terror* (1994 TVM); *The Haunting of Lisa* (1995 TVM); *Yesterday's Target* (1996 TVM); *You Lucky Dog* (1998 TVM)

Class Reunions

Class reunions have reunited former sweethearts and provided a convenient grouping of classmates for revenge-minded killers. Betty Hutton and Dana Andrews played former classmates who discover love again 15 years after college in *Spring Reunion* (1957). In *Class of '63*, a college reunion convinces Cliff Gorman that wife Joan Hackett is still in love with former flame James Brolin. And, in 1980's *Reunion*, Kevin Dobson finds himself attracted to both his former high school sweetheart and her 17-year-old daughter. His predicament, although fraught with complexities, seems minor compared to those facing the potential slasher victims in

Slaughter High (1986) and *Terror Stalks the Class Reunion* (1992). *National Lampoon's Class Reunion* (1982) played the classmate-killer angle for laughs (which were in short supply). John Cusack portrayed a hit man who kills an assailant with a ballpoint pen at his high school reunion in *Grosse Pointe Blank* (1997). In addition to class reunions, there have been a number of films about high school or college friends getting together after several years: *The Return of the Secaucus 7* (1980), *Over Forty* (aka *Beyond Forty*) (1982), *The Big Chill* (1983), *Windy City* (1984), *Peter's Friends* (1993), and *Indian Summer* (1993).

Tales of Manhattan (1942); *Spring Reunion* (1957); *Class of '63* (1973 TVM); *Reunion* (1980 TVM); *National Lampoon's Class Reunion* (1982); *Peggy Sue Got Married* (1986); *Something Wild* (1986); *Slaughter High* (1986); *Terror Stalks the Class Reunion* (1992 TVM); *Parallel Lives* (1994 TVM); *The Favor* (1994); *Grosse Pointe Blank* (1997); *Romy and Michele's High School Reunion* (1997); *Since You've Been Gone* (1998)

Clocks and Watches

The image of Harold Lloyd hanging by the hands of a giant clock in 1923's *Safety Last* ranks as the clock's finest hour. Still, other filmmakers have devised inventive uses for clocks and watches. The murderer in *Laura* (1944) hid his shotgun in his would-be victim's grandfather clock. A fifteenth-century mantel clock caused several murders in *Amityville 1992: It's About Time*. Clocks also played major roles in murder mysteries such as *The Big Clock* (1948) and *Sherlock Holmes Faces Death* (1943). In the Holmes picture, a clock in the tower of the Musgrave mansion sounded 13 ominous chimes just before the death of a family member. Orson Welles's Nazi war criminal met his demise atop a clock tower in 1946's *The Stranger*. The intricate clock tower depicted in *The Hudsucker Proxy* provided the setting for a symbolic fight between good and evil. Ingmar Bergman employed a symbolic clock without hands in 1957's *Wild Strawberries*. And Peter Greenaway used clock faces to depict some of the mysterious numerals "hidden" throughout 1987's *Drowning by Numbers*. On a lighter note, a small clock company caused major problems for an incompetent board of directors in the 1957 Judy Holliday comedy *The Solid Gold Cadillac*. The cinema's only walking, talking (and very courteous) mantel clock was voiced by David Ogden Stiers in Disney's *Beauty and the Beast*. Clocks playing supporting roles in two other Disney animated films. In *Peter Pan* (1953), a ticking clock consumed by an alligator kept Captain Hook apprised of the reptile's whereabouts. Geppetto, the woodcarver, boasted a collection of unique clocks in 1940's *Pinocchio* (as did H.G. Wells's time-traveling hero in 1960's *The Time Machine*). In contrast to stately clocks, most watches have been utilized for their gimmickry. Warren Beatty communicated via a two-way radio wristwatch in 1990's *Dick Tracy*. James Bond (Roger Moore) escaped from the clutches of archvillain Kanaga (Yaphet Kotto) by employing a watch with a super magnet in 1973's *Live and Let Die*. Rival secret agent Derek Flint (James Coburn) used a nifty watch to bring himself out of a deep sleep resembling death in the 1966 spy spoof *Our Man Flint*. An even more fantastical watch — capable of stopping time — provided the premise for both *The Girl, the Gold*

Watch & Everything and its 1981 sequel. Several movies, such as *High Noon* (1952) and *Nick of Time* (1995), have used clocks to emphasize the passing of time. *The Set-Up* (1949) featured opening and closing shots of a clock to remind viewers that the boxing yarn took place over real time. The Wicked Witch of the West flipped over an hourglass to count down the time remaining to Dorothy's demise in *The Wizard of Oz*. That's neither a clock nor watch, but certainly a time-telling device worthy of an honorable mention. See also **Time Travel**.

The Times Are Out of Joint (1910); *Safety Last* (1923); *The Wizard of Oz* (1939); *Pinocchio* (1940); *Sherlock Holmes Faces Death* (1943); *My Learned Friend* (1943); *Laura* (1944); *The Stranger* (1946); *The Big Clock* (1948); *Peter Pan* (1953); *The Solid Gold Cadillac* (1956); *The Green Man* (1956); *Wild Strawberries* (1957); *The Time Machine* (1960); *Our Man Flint* (1966); *The Clockmaker* (aka *L'Horloger de St. Paul*; *The Watchmaker*) (1973); *Live and Let Die* (1973); *The Thirty-Nine Steps* (1978); *The Girl, the Gold Watch & Everything* (1980 TVM); *The Girl, the Gold Watch & Dynamite* (1981 TVM); *Back to the Future* (1985); *Drowning by Numbers* (1987); *Radium City* (1987); *Dick Tracy* (1990); *Golden Braid* (1990); *Timebomb* (1991); *Beauty and the Beast* (1991); *Amityville 1992: It's About Time* (1992); *The Hudsucker Proxy* (1994); *Pulp Fiction* (1994); *The Little Riders* (1996 TVM); *Clockmaker* (1998)

Clones *see* Lookalikes

Coffin Ed Johnson and Grave Digger Jones

"You steal money from white folks — that's your business; you steal money from blacks, that's MY business," warns detective Coffin Ed Johnson as he shakes down a black con artist in 1970's *Cotton Comes to Harlem*. This trend-setting adaptation of Chester Himes' detective novel mixed violence, humor, nudity, and racial satire to predictably mixed results. The humor works best, with most of it being provided by tough, cynical Harlem detectives Coffin Ed Johnson (Raymond St. Jacques) and Grave Digger Jones (Godfrey Cambridge). As they search for a mysterious bale of cotton, Coffin Ed and Grave Digger administer their own type of justice — exposing a crooked black evangelist, dealing with stupid white cops, and finally working out a deal with a Mafia kingpin. But through it all, they maintain their personal ethics (Coffin Ed reminds a violent mob: "We may have broken some heads, but we never broke no promises."). The film has serious flaws, including a mismatched music score and a rambling pace, but its popular success contributed substantially to the beginning of the "blaxploitation" (q.v.) film cycle of the 1970s. St. Jacques and Cambridge reprised their roles for the 1972 follow-up *Come Back, Charleston Blue*. Based on Himes' novel *The Heat's On*, the storyline finds Grave Digger and Coffin Ed involved with a series of gruesome murders, missing razor blades, the Harlem drug trade, and a Mafia chief. This sequel failed to duplicate the first film's success and the series apparently came to a quick conclusion. Then, 19 years later, another Himes novel hit the screens. *A Rage in Harlem* is primarily the tale of a naive undertaker (Forest Whitaker) who falls under the spell of a provocative femme fatale (Robin Givens). She's involved with some heavy-hitting gangsters and a pair of relentless detectives: Coffin Ed Johnson (Stack Pierce) and Grave Digger Jones (George Wallace). Although relegated to supporting roles, Coffin Ed and Grave Digger lend a boost to this entertaining action-comedy. Sadly, *A Rage in Harlem* failed to catch on with either moviegoers or videotape renters. See also **Blaxploitation Films**.

Cotton Comes to Harlem (1970); *Come Back, Charleston Blue* (1972); *A Rage in Harlem* (1991)

The Cohens and the Kellys

The Jewish Cohens and the Irish Kellys were feuding families in a series of seven Universal comedies that spanned the transition from silent to talking pictures. *The Cohens and the Kellys* (1926), was based on Aaron Hoffman's play *Two Blocks Away*, although the obvious similarities to Anne Nichols' Broadway hit *Abie's Irish Rose* resulted in a lawsuit. This first picture established the framework for the series, with the families being drawn together by the romance between the Kellys' son and the Cohens' daughter and the inheritance of a fortune. Jewish shopkeeper Cohen initially inherited the money, only to discover that it actually belonged to Irish cop Kelly. In the end, they became partners, setting the stage for a series of wild adventures in Africa (buying elephant tusks for a piano company), Scotland (entering the tartan business), and even Atlantic City. In most of the films, George Sidney and Vera Gorden played the Cohens with Charlie Murray and Kate Price as the Kellys. *The Cohens and Kellys in Scotland* is considered the best of the series, although *Hollywood* featured guest bits by Tom Mix, Boris Karloff, and Lew Ayres. Almost forty years after the last Cohen-Kelly movie, the premise of feuding Jewish and Irish families popped up again in the TV series *Bridget Loves Bernie*.

The Cohens and the Kellys (1926); *The Cohens and the Kellys in Paris* (1928); *The Cohens and Kellys in Atlantic City* (1929); *The Cohens and Kellys in Scotland* (1930); *The Cohens and Kellys in Africa* (1930); *The Cohens and Kellys in Hollywood* (1933); *The Cohens and Kellys in Trouble* (1933)

Color/B&W Features

The dramatic use of color in black and white films (and vice versa) attracted little interest until 1939's *The Wizard of Oz*, which transported Dorothy from monochrome Kansas into exciting, colorful Oz. The same trick was repeated in *The Blue Bird* (1940), a similar fantasy in which a black and white prologue gave way to a lengthy color dream sequence. The idea of filming reality in black and white and fantasy in color was neatly reversed in 1946's *Stairway to Heaven* (aka *A Matter of Life and Death*). It starred David Niven as a wounded pilot destined to die, but so determined to live that he argues his case in a celestial trial. Because he wants to continue his existence in this world, the earthly segments are shown in color, while the scenes in Heaven are in black and white. Forty-one years later, Heaven reverts to color and reality to B&W in the opening of *Made in Heaven* (later in the movie, the earthly scenes acquire color, too). In *Pleasantville* (1998), two teens magically "entered" the world of a black and white television series and literally colorized it. Less elaborate uses of color are displayed in *Portrait of Jennie*, *The Picture of Dorian Gray*, and *The Moon and Sixpence*, three B&W films in which paintings appear in color. In other films: Judy Holliday drove away in a gold auto in the original B&W print of *The Solid Gold Cadillac*. In William Castle's gimmicky *The Tingler*, there's a brief-but highly effective sequence in which bright red blood splashes out of a B&W bathroom sink faucet. And in George

Romero's *Martin*, a would-be teen vampire has black and white dreams of his earlier life as a bloodsucker.

Dixiana (1930); *Kid Millions* (1934); *Victoria the Great* (1937); *The Wizard of Oz* (1939); *The Blue Bird* (1940); *The Moon and Sixpence* (1942); *Stairway to Heaven* (aka *A Matter of Life and Death*) (1946); *Portrait of Jennie* (1948); *I'll Never Forget You* (1951); *Jack and the Beanstalk* (1952); *The Solid Gold Cadillac* (1956); *The Tingler* (1959); *The Private Lives of Adam and Eve* (1960); *A Man and a Woman* (1966); *If...* (1968); *Putney Swope* (1969); *And Now My Love* (1975); *Martin* (1978); *Movie Movie* (1978); *Stalker* (1979); *Zelig* (1983); *19/19* (1985); *Kiss of the Spider Woman* (1985); *Mishima* (1985); *She's Gotta Have It* (1986); *Night of the Creeps* (1986); *Made in Heaven* (1987); *Radium City* (1987); *Wings of Desire* (aka *Der Himmel über Berlin*) (1987); *D.O.A.* (1988); *The Navigator: A Medieval Odyssey* (aka *The Navigator*) (1988); *Transylvania Twist* (1989); *Truth or Dare* (aka *In Bed with Madonna*; *Truth or Dare: In Bed with Madonna*) (1991); *Dead Again* (1991); *Kafka* (1991); *Eclipse* (1994); *Pleasantville* (1998); *Space Cowboys* (2000)

Columbo, Lieutenant

The trench coat-clad Lieutenant Columbo made his first TV appearance in an episode of the 1960-61 anthology *The Chevy Mystery Show* and was played by Bert Freed. William Link and Richard Levinson, who created the rumpled but sharp police detective, cast Thomas Mitchell as Columbo for their Broadway play *Prescription: Murder*. When Link and Levinson adapted their play as a TV movie, they tried to convince Bing Crosby to take the role. When Crosby refused, Peter Falk was cast in the role that would make him a household name. The 1968 TV movie *Prescription: Murder* costarred Gene Barry as a physician convinced he had committed the perfect murder. The film established what would become the Columbo formula: A murder would be shown in its entirety to the audience, then the seemingly slow-witted Columbo would enter and cleverly trap the murderer. Three years later, Levinson and Link produced a follow-up, *Ransom for a Dead Man*, that served as a pilot for a TV series. Lee Grant played the murderer, giving a performance that earned her an Emmy nomination. That same year, a *Columbo* TV series debuted as the most successful element of the *The NBC Mystery Movie*. Over the next six years, Falk starred in almost forty 90-minute and two-hour *Columbo* TV episodes. When NBC cancelled *The NBC Mystery Movie* in 1977, Falk continued to play Columbo in several 1977 and 1978 TV movies. In 1989, ABC launched its own *Mystery Movie* TV series and added Columbo to the rotating elements. A year later, the series was axed — though Columbo again lived on in periodic made-for-TV films. The most interesting *Columbo* TV movie was probably *Ashes to Ashes*, because it paired Falk with Patrick McGoohan (as a murderer) for the fourth time. McGoohan won Emmys in 1974 and 1990 for his guest appearances on the *Columbo* TV series. For the record, Columbo's first name has never been revealed. The list below includes the TV movies only, not episodes broadcast on the NBC and ABC television series. See also **Television Series Reunion Films**.

Prescription: Murder (aka *Columbo: Prescription Murder* (1968 TVM); *Ransom for a Dead Man* (1971 TVM); *Try and Catch Me* (1977 TVM); *Murder Under Glass* (1978 TVM); *Make Me a Perfect Murder* (1978 TVM); *How to Dial a Murder* (1978 TVM); *The Conspirators* (1978 TVM); *Columbo Goes to the Guillotine* (1978 TVM); *Columbo Goes to College* (1990 TVM); *Death Hits the Jackpot* (1991 TVM); *Caution: Murder Can Be Hazardous to Your*

Health (1991 TVM); *Columbo and the Murder of a Rock Star* (1991 TVM); *No Time to Die* (1992 TVM); *A Bird in the Hand...* (1992 TVM); *It's All in the Game* (1993 TVM); *Butterfly in Shades of Grey* (1994 TVM); *Undercover* (1994 TVM); *Strange Bedfellows* (1995 TVM); *A Trace of Murder* (1997 TVM); *Ashes to Ashes* (1998 TVM); *Murder with Too Many Notes* (1998 TVM)

Coma

The frightening side effects of unusual comas provided the premise for two exceptionally clever films, 1970's *The Mind of Mr. Soames* and 1983's *The Dead Zone*. Both films effectively balanced science fiction, horror, and reality by concentrating on the personal traumas of the coma victims. *The Dead Zone*, adapted from Stephen King's best seller, starred Christopher Walken as an accident victim who emerges from a five-year coma with the ability to foresee the future of those he touches. This apparent gift drives him to commit murder to prevent a disaster. In *The Mind of Mr. Soames*, a scientist revives a man from a 30-year coma — which began with his birth. Thus, he is "born" as an adult with the mind of a baby. More mainstream pictures include 1978's *Coma*, with Genevieve Bujold as a dedicated doctor who discovers that the body parts of comatose patients are being auctioned in an organ blackmarket. *Patrick* (1978) was a telekinetic teen, á la *Carrie*, who wrecked havoc while in a comatose state. *Seizure: The Story of Kathy Morris* (1980) was the real-life story of a singer's struggle to recover from a coma. See also **Suspended Animation**.

The Clay Pigeon (1949); *The Mind of Mr. Soames* (1970); *Coma* (1978); *Patrick* (1978); *Seizure: The Story of Kathy Morris* (1980 TVM); *Brimstone and Treacle* (1982); *The Dead Zone* (1983); *Bad Dreams* (1988); *Silent Night, Deadly Night III: You Better Watch Out!* (1989); *Hard to Kill* (1990); *Awakenings* (1990); *Reversal of Fortune* (1990); *Absolute Strangers* (1991 TVM); *Prom Night IV: Deliver Us from Evil* (1991); *She Woke Up* (1992 TVM); *That Eye, the Sky* (1994); *Past Tense* (1994 TVM); *While You Were Sleeping* (1995); *Savage (1996); Commandments* (1997); *Forever Love* (1998 TVM); *The Cell* (2000)

Comets *see* Asteriods, Comets, and Meteors

Comic Book Characters

With the notable exceptions of Superman and Batman (qq.v.), few comic book characters have encountered significant success in feature films. During the 1940s, they thrived in action-packed serials like Columbia's *Batman* and *Captain America*. A young Robert Wagner brought Prince Valiant to life in a 1954 film, and the briefly popular 1966–68 TV series *Batman* spawned a campy feature-length theatrical film. Both movies were intended for juvenile audiences and no sequels followed. In the mid–1970s, comic book superheroes achieved minor popularity in the form of made-for-TV movies (both *The New Original Wonder Woman* and *The Incredible Hulk* led to TV series). And then in 1978, the big-budgeted *Superman* caught the public's fancy and three progressively less interesting, but still profitable, sequels appeared over the next decade. Meanwhile, a pair of Japanese samurai imports, based on the *Lone Wolf and Cub* comic book series, acquired a cult following in the U.S. The films were *Lightning Swords of Death* and *Shogun Assassin* and they traced the exploits of a hunted warrior who pushes his son around in an armed baby cart. Comic books, as a literature form, acquired a serious adult following in the 1980s, a trend that ultimately led to the 1989 brooding blockbuster version of *Batman* and its sequels. The success of *Batman* ushered in a whole new era of films based on comic books. Producers mounted adaptations of old comic books (*Captain America*), dark comic books (*The Crow*), and cult comic books (*Tank Girl*). See also **Batman; The Incredible Hulk; Lone Wolf and Cub; Lupin III; Superman; Teenage Mutant Ninja Turtles**.

Superman and the Mole Men (1951); *Prince Valiant* (1954); *Batman* (1966); *Danger: Diabolik* (aka *Diabolik*) (1968); *The Adventures of Barry McKenzie* (1972); *Lone Wolf and Cub: Sword of Vengeance* (aka *Kozure Ôkami: Kowakashi udekashi tsukamatsuru; Sword of Vengeance*) (1972); *Barry McKenzie Holds His Own* (1974); *Wonder Woman* (1974 TVM); *Lightning Swords of Death* (1974); *The New Original Wonder Woman* (1975 TVM); *The Incredible Hulk* (1977 TVM); *Spider-Man* (1977 TVM); *Dr. Strange* (1978 TVM); *Superman* (1978); *Captain America* (1979 TVM); *Mandrake* (1979 TVM); *Swamp Thing* (1982); *Howard the Duck* (1986); *The Spirit* (1987 TVM); *Return of the Swamp Thing* (1989); *Batman* (1989); *The Punisher* (1989); *The Dark Avenger* (1990 TVM); *Teenage Mutant Ninja Turtles* (1990); *The Rocketeer* (1991); *The Guyver* (1991); *Dr. Giggles* (1992); *Captain America* (1992); *Cemetery Man* (aka *Dellamorte Dellamore; Of Death and Love*) (1994); *The Crow* (1994); *Richie Rich* (1994); *The Mask* (1994); *Judge Dredd* (1995); *Tank Girl* (1995); *Barb Wire* (1996); *Generation X* (1996 TVM); *The Crow: City of Angels* (1996); *Spawn* (1997); *Steel* (1997); *Men in Black* (1997); *Nick Fury: Agent of S.H.I.E.L.D.* (1998 TVM); *Mystery Men* (1999); *Witchblade* (2000 TVM); *X-Men* (2000)

Comic Book–Style Movies

There have been sporadic attempts to recreate the content and look of the old EC horror comics on the silver screen. Amicus Productions, which specialized in horror anthologies in the late 1960s and early 1970s, produced two comic book–style anthologies: *Tales from the Crypt* (1972) and *Vault of Horror* (1973). The tales mixed horror and dark humor with middling results. For example, the "Midnight Mess" story in *Vault of Horror* had vampires drinking from a tap inserted into an upside-down victim's neck. In 1982, Stephen King teamed with director George Romero on *Creepshow*, a more successful clone of the EC Comics, complete with animated introductions. Unfortunately, the 1987 *Creepshow 2* was an unimpressive bargain basement sequel. In 1989, HBO launched the popular cable TV series *Tales from the Crypt*. Two feature films were produced under the *Tales from the Crypt* banner: *Demon Knight* (1995) and *Bordello of Blood* (1996). Neither of those films were anothologies, although they maintained the tongue-in-cheek approach of the TV series.

Tales from the Crypt (1972); *Vault of Horror* (aka *Tales from the Crypt 2*) (1973); *Creepshow* (1982); *Creepshow 2* (1987)

Comic Strip Characters

Comic strips have provided a rich source of film material, serving as the basis for several popular film series. The most influential was undoubtedly Chic Young's "Blondie" (q.v.) strip, which was adapted into a 27-film series that lasted from 1938 to 1951. No other comic strip favorite has matched that level of success, although Dick Tracy, Jiggs and Maggie, Jungle Jim, Red Ryder, Dick Barton, and the Peanuts Gang (qq.v.) also earned their own film series. *Dick Tracy* and *Dennis the Menace* reached mass audiences as big-budget theatrical films in 1990 and 1993, respectively. However, other famous funnies' characters have floundered on the screen. Even an earlier Dennis the Menace movie debuted as a throwaway 1987 telefilm. A similar fate befell *Brenda Starr* (1976), *Archie: To Riverdale and Back* (1990), and *Buck Rogers in the 25th Century* (1979), although the latter made-for-TV movie actually received a theatrical distribution. The exploits of Li'l Abner and Little Orphan Annie were adapted into splashy, overblown musicals which sadly lost sight of their characters' charms. Film versions of adult comic strips have been scarce, consisting mostly of a couple of sexy heroines (*Barbarella*, *Modesty Blaise*) and sex-obsessed cats (*Fritz the Cat*). See also **Blondie**; **Jiggs and Maggie**; **Jungle Jim**; **Peanuts Series**; **Ryder, Red**; **Tracy, Dick**.

Ella Cinders (1926); *Skippy* (1931); *Sooky* (1931); *Little Orphan Annie* (1932); *Joe Palooka* (aka *Palooka*) (1934); *L'il Abner* (1940); *Reg'lar Fellows* (1941); *Prince Valiant* (1954); *The Sad Sack* (1957); *Li'l Abner* (1959); *Dondi* (1961); *Modesty Blaise* (1966); *Barbarella* (aka *Barbarella, Queen of the Galaxy*) (1968); *Danger: Diabolik* (aka *Diabolik*) (1968); *Fritz the Cat* (1972); *The Nine Lives of Fritz the Cat* (1975); *Friday Foster* (1975); *Brenda Starr* (1976 TVM); *Piedone l'africano* (1977); *Buck Rogers in the 25th Century* (1979); *Flash Gordon* (1980); *Annie* (1982); *The Perils of Gwendoline in the Land of the Yik Yak* (1984); *Dennis the Menace* (1987 TVM); *Brenda Starr* (1989); *Dick Tracy* (1990); *Archie: To Riverdale and Back* (1990 TVM); *Little Nemo: Adventures in Slumberland* (1992); *Dennis the Menace* (1993); *The Phantom* (1996)

Compilation Films (Fictional)

The birth of the "compilation film" can be traced to its widespread use by documentary filmmakers during the two World Wars. Gifted filmmakers such as Frank Capra edited selected newsreel footage to produce historical time capsules and effective propaganda pieces. In the late 1950s, former Pathé News employee Robert Youngson, who had directed the 1950 newsreel compilation *Fifty Years Before Your Eyes*, turned the compilation movie into a tool for preserving—and reviving—fictional films. His 1957 compilation *The Golden Age of Comedy* featured choice clips of silent classics starring Laurel and Hardy, Will Rogers, and Harry Langdon. It revived interest in the great silent comedians, prompting Charlie Chaplin to release *The Chaplin Revue* (1958), which was simply three shorts strung together with some behind-the-scenes footage (actually, earlier Chaplin shorts had been packaged together as far back as 1938). The following year, Youngson returned with another superior silent comedy compilation, *When Comedy Was King*. In the 1960s, he raided the studios' vaults and produced *The Days of Thrills and Laughter* (1961), *Thirty Years of Fun* (1963), *MGM's Big Parade of Comedy* (1964), *Laurel and Hardy's Laughing 20's* (1965), *The Further Perils of Laurel and Hardy* (1967), and *Four Clowns* (1970). Youngson died in 1974, the same year in which Jack Haley, Jr., produced the highly-successful MGM musical compilation *That's Entertainment*. Haley's film was a financial bonanza for MGM, costing next to nothing and providing glamorous publicity for the studio's 50th anniversary. The inevitable sequel *That's Entertainment Part 2* appeared in 1976, this one combining the musical clips with "straight" scenes (e.g., Garbo playing *Camille*). Haley added a belated third installment to his MGM compilation series with 1985's *That's Dancing*. Despite a marvelous selection of dance footage, it failed

to attract the younger audiences which flocked to the contemporary hit *Flashdance* (1983). Although Youngson and Haley's compilations are the most fondly remembered, other filmmakers have utilized the format effectively. Warner Bros. compiled its best Looney Tunes cartoons and released them into the theatres in features such as *Bug Bunny, Superstar* (1975), *The Great American Chase* (1979), and *Daffy Duck's Movie: Fantastic Island* (1983). The funniest segments from Sid Caesar's classic TV series *Your Show of Shows* surfaced in the 1973 compilation *Ten from Your Show of Shows* (1973). A year earlier, skits from British television's *Monty Python's Flying Circus* came stateside as *And Now for Something Completely Different*. Science fiction and horror film retrospectives have reached the screen as *It Came from Hollywood* (1982) and *Terror in the Aisles* (1984). *It's Showtime* (1976) was an enjoyable compilation of animal movie clips, highlighted by a canine rendition of "Singin' in the Rain." See also **That's Entertainment Series**.

Charlie Chaplin Carnival (1938); *Charlie Chaplin Cavalcade* (1938); *Charlie Chaplin Festival* (1938); *The Golden Age of Comedy* (1957); *The Chaplin Revue* (1958); *When Comedy Was King* (1959); *The Days of Thrills and Laughter* (1961); *Harold Lloyd's World of Comedy* (1962); *Harold Lloyd's Funny Side of Life* (1963); *Laugh with Max Linder* (1963); *Thirty Years of Fun* (1963); *The Great Chase* (1963); *Marilyn* (1963); *MGM's Big Parade of Comedy* (1964); *The Love Goddesses* (1965); *The World of Abbott and Costello* (1965); *Laurel and Hardy's Laughing 20's* (1965); *The Further Perils of Laurel and Hardy* (1967); *The Crazy World of Laurel and Hardy* (1967); *Four Clowns* (1970); *And Now for Something Completely Different* (1972); *Ten from Your Show of Shows* (1973); *That's Entertainment* (1974); *Bugs Bunny, Superstar* (1975); *It's Showtime* (1976); *America at the Movies* (1976); *Gizmo* (1976); *The Great American Chase* (aka *The Bugs Bunny/Roadrunner Movie*) (1979); *Bugs Bunny's 3rd Movie: 1001 Rabbit Tales* (1982); *It Came from Hollywood* (1982); *Daffy Duck's Movie: Fantastic Island* (1983); *Terror in the Aisles* (1984); *The Puppetoon Movie* (1987); *Daffy Duck's Quackbusters* (1989)

Composers (Classical)

Hollywood-produced biographies, supplemented by a handful of imports, have glossed over the history of classical music by focusing almost exclusively on a select number of composers. A French director (Julien Duvivier) made Hollywood's first major composer biography of the sound era with 1938's *The Great Waltz*, the story of Johann Strauss (the Younger) and his unforgettable "The Blue Danube." Co-star/soprano Miliza Korjus and lyricist Oscar Hammerstein II turned two Strauss melodies into the popular hits "I'm in Love with Vienna" and "One Day When We Were Young." Despite the film's success, seven years elapsed before the Chopin biography *A Song to Remember* (1945) made a star of Cornel Wilde and inspired a trio of imitations. Stewart Granger played violinist virtuoso/composer Niccolo Paganini in *The Magic Bow* (1947). *Song of Love* (1947) cast Katharine Hepburn and Paul Henried as Clara and Robert Schumann and Robert Walker as their friend Johannes Brahms. Jean-Pierre Aumont played Rimsky-Korsakov in 1947's campy *Song of Scheherezade*, which dealt primarily with the composer's infatuation with a Spanish-Moroccan dancer (Yvonne De Carlo). Occasional films about classical composers continued to appear during the next two decades. However, a new trend did not emerge until Ken Russell introduced his unconventional biographies in the early 1970s. Russell made his mark on British television in the 1960s with critically-acclaimed documentaries and biographies of Wagner, Debussy, and Elgar. His theatrical films have been greeted less enthusiastically due to his penchant for excess (the descriptive publicity line for his 1971 Tchaikovsky biography *The Music Lovers* was: "The story of a homosexual who married a nymphomaniac"). Russell's rollercoaster style has managed to confuse his critics for years. His 1974 biopic *Mahler* earned praise for its intelligence and restraint, but the director's excesses were on display again in the following year's *Lisztomania*, a rock version of Liszt's life starring The Who's Roger Daltrey. In the post-Russell era, Czech director Milos Forman has made the biggest impact with his splendid 1984 Best Picture *Amadeus*. Peter Shaffer adapted the film from his own play about the conflict between Mozart contemporary Salieri and the Master himself.

Beethoven (aka *Un Grand Amour de Beethoven*; *The Life and Loves of Beethoven*) (1936); *The Great Waltz* (1938) (Johann Strauss); *The Great Victor Herbert* (1939); *Melody Master* (1941) (Franz Schubert); *The Great Mr. Handel* (1942); *A Song to Remember* (1945) (Frederic Chopin); *The Magic Bow* (1947) (Niccolo Paganini); *Song of Love* (1947) (Robert and Clara Schumann); *Song of Scheherazade* (1947) (Rimsky-Korsakov); *The Great Gilbert and Sullivan* (aka *The Story of Gilbert and Sullivan*) (1953); *Deep in My Heart* (1954) (Sigmund Romberg); *Magic Fire* (1956) (Richard Wagner); *Song Without End* (1960) (Franz Liszt); *The Magnificent Rebel* (1962) (Ludwig van Beethoven); *The Waltz King* (1963) (Johann Strauss); *Song of Norway* (1970) (Edvard Grieg); *The Music Lovers* (1971) (Peter Tchaikovsky); *The Great Waltz* (1972) (Johann Strauss); *Mahler* (1974); *Lisztomania* (1975) (Liszt); *Wagner* (1983) (Richard Wagner); *Amadeus* (1984) (Wolfgang Amadeus Mozart and Antonio Salieri); *Spring Symphony* (1984) (Clara Schumann); *Testimony* (1988) (Dmitri Shostakovich); *Impromptu* (1991) (Chopin and Liszt); *Tous les Matins de Monde* (1991) (Sainte Columbe and Marin Marais); *Immortal Beloved* (1994) (Beethoven); *Carl, My Childhood Symphony* (aka *Min Fynske Barndom*) (1994) (Carl Nielsen); *Topsy-Turvy* (1999) (W.S. Gilbert and Arthur Sullivan)

Composers (Popular)

Few popular composers have lived long enough (or been famous enough) to see their life stories reach the screen. However, there have been some noteworthy exceptions: Richard Rodgers was in his prime when 1948's *Words and Music* was released and Cole Porter was still composing when Cary Grant played him in *Night and Day* (1945). Jerome Kern died during the filming of *Till the Clouds Roll By* (1946) and George M. Cohan passed away the year that *Yankee Doodle Dandy* was released (1942). Turn-of-the-century songwriters have proven to be popular film subjects, with Twentieth Century–Fox specializing in them in the 1940s. Victor Mature played Gay '90s Broadway composer Paul Dresser in *My Gal Sal* (1942); singer Dick Haymes was songwriter Ernest R. Ball in Damon Runyon's *Irish Eyes Are Smiling*; and Mark Stevens played Joseph E. Howard in *I Wonder Who's Kissing Her Now* (1947). Some fields of music are represented by merely a movie or two, as evidenced by the biographies of folk songwriter Woody Guthrie (*Bound for Glory*), minstrel man Dan Emmett (*Dixie*), and marching band composer John Philip Sousa (*Stars and Stripes Forever*). See also **Pop, Rock, and Country Singer Biographies**.

Swanee River (1939) (Stephen Foster); *My Gal Sal* (1942) (Paul Dresser); *Yankee Doodle Dandy* (1942) (George M. Cohan); *Dixie* (1943) (Dan Emmett); *Irish Eyes Are Smiling* (1944) (Ernest R.

Ball); *Rhapsody in Blue* (1945) (George Gershwin); *Night and Day* (1945) (Cole Porter); *Till the Clouds Roll by* (1946) (Jerome Kern); *I Wonder Who's Kissing Her Now* (1947) (Joe Howard); *Words and Music* (1948) (Rodgers and Hart); *Oh, You Beautiful Doll* (1949) (Fred Fisher); *Three Little Words* (1950) (Bert Kalmar and Harry Ruby); *I Dream of Jeannie* (1952) (Stephen Foster); *I'll See You in My Dreams* (1952) (Gus Kahn); *Stars and Stripes Forever* (1953) (John Philip Sousa); *St. Louis Blues* (1958) (W.C. Handy); *Bound for Glory* (1976) (Woody Guthrie); *Scott Joplin* (1977); *If You Could See What I Hear* (1982) (Tom Sullivan); *Thelonious Monk: Straight, No Chaser* (1989); *Listen Up: The Lives of Quincy Jones* (1991)

Computers

The fact that the HAL 9000 remains the best-remembered character from *2001: A Space Odyssey* is a testament to the dramatic potential of movie computers. Given a speaking voice and a significant role, the computer can effectively dominate its human co-stars in interesting science fiction films like *The Forbin Project* (1970). However, the early film appearances of computers showed little sign of their potential. A nuclear brain called Novac took control of a secret subterranean laboratory in 1954's *Gog*. Unfortunately, the computer's "artificial intelligence" turned out to be enemy agent programming. Humans manipulated the computers in *Desk Set* (1957) and *The Honeymoon Machine* (1961) for comedic purposes. Then in 1965, the computer took a giant step forward with Jean-Luc Godard's dense, futuristic thriller *Alphaville*. Godard presented a bleak world of emotionless people controlled by a super-computer. Stanley Kubrick made HAL more human-like in 1968's *2001*, giving the computer a warm personality and a friendly voice ("Everything's under control, Dave"). But HAL nevertheless took a turn for the worse and sought to eliminate his human colleagues to gain control of a spaceship. The super-computer in *The Forbin Project* displayed larger-scale ambitions, setting its sights on world domination. It achieved that goal, too, by linking up with its Soviet counterpart and thus controlling the defense systems for both the U.S. and the Soviet Union. Proteus IV, the computer in 1977's *Demon Seed*, was more concerned with propagating itself than with controlling the world. To that end, it trapped its creator's wife (Julie Christie) in her house and "raped" her. Another computer, named Edgar, did not go that far, but it too found itself attracted to his owner's love interest in 1984's *Electric Dreams*. Less interesting computers have played small parts in many movies. College students used a computer to create a line of credit for an imaginary man in the 1971 TV movie *Paper Man*. An electrical accident dumped a computer's memory banks into college student Kurt Russell's brain in Disney's *The Computer Wore Tennis Shoes* (1969). George Segal had a small computer surgically implanted into his brain, with horrifying results, in 1974's *The Terminal Man*. Two teens showed the power of the personal computer when they used one to create gorgeous Kelly LeBrock in 1985's *Weird Science*. See also **Androids and Cyborgs; Robots**.

Gog (1954); *Desk Set* (aka *His Other Woman*) (1957); *The Invisible Boy* (1957); *The Honeymoon Machine* (1961); *Alphaville* (aka *Alphaville, Une Etrange Aventure de Lemmy Caution*) (1965); *Billion Dollar Brain* (1967); *2001: A Space Odyssey* (1968); *Hot Millions* (1968); *The Computer Wore Tennis Shoes* (1969); *The Forbin Project* (aka *Colossus: The Forbin Project*) (1970); *Paper Man* (1971 TVM); *The Terminal Man* (1974); *Dark Star* (1975); *Demon Seed* (1977);

Institute for Revenge (1979 TVM); *Alien* (1979); *Tron* (1982); *WarGames* (1983); *Electric Dreams* (1984); *Deadly Impact* (1985); *Weird Science* (1985); *Jumpin' Jack Flash* (1986); *The Rachel Papers* (1989); *The Lawnmower Man* (1992); *Journey to the Center of the Earth* (1993 TVM); *Jackpot* (aka *Cybereden*) (1993); *Ghost in the Machine* (1993); *Hackers* (1995); *Virtuosity* (1995); *Lawnmower Man: Beyond Cyberspace* (1996); *The Net* (1996); *Dream House* (1998 TVM); *Fatal Error* (1999 TVM); *Pirates of Silicon Valley* (1999 TVM); *The Matrix* (1999); *Universal Soldier: The Return* (1999)

Concert Movies

The filmed rock 'n' roll concert came into vogue in the early 1970s, though technically 1969's *Monterey Pop* ushered in the new genre with lively performances by the Mamas and the Papas, Janis Joplin, and others. *Woodstock* and *Gimme Shelter* are the best known concert films, both for their music and social commentary. The Rolling Stones have starred in more movies than any other rock act, with *Gimme Shelter, Let's Spend the Night Together, The T.A.M.I. Show,* and *Ladies & Gentlemen, the Rolling Stones.* Surprisingly, the genre has acquired a certain appeal for well-known, contemporary directors — Martin Scorese directed a documentary about The Band called *The Last Waltz,* while Jonathan Demme helmed the Talking Heads' *Stop Making Sense* (1984). The latter film was one of only a handful made during the 1980s, signalling that young rock fans preferred the free footage provided by MTV. Nevertheless, concert films still appear occasionally, as evidenced by U2 1988's release *Rattle and Hum.* Rob Reiner's *This Is Spinal Tap* tells the history of a fictitious group and is a hilarious parody of rock documentaries and concert films. See also **Pop, Rock, and Country Singer Biographies.**

Jazz on a Summer Day (1959); *The T.A.M.I. Show* (1964); *The Big T.N.T. Show* (1966); *Don't Look Back* (1967); *Monterey Pop* (1969); *Woodstock* (1970); *Gimme Shelter* (1970); *Popcorn* (1970); *Johnny Cash: The Man, His World, His Music* (1970); *Mad Dogs and Englishman* (aka *Joe Cocker: Mad Dogs and Englishman*) (1971); *Medicine Ball Caravan* (1971); *Celebration at Big Sur* (1971); *This Is Elvis!* (1971); *Soul to Soul* (1971); *Fillmore* (1972); *Concert for Bangladesh* (1972); *Let the Good Times Roll* (1973); *Ladies and Gentlemen, the Rolling Stones* (1975); *The Song Remains the Same* (1976) (Led Zeppelin); *The Last Waltz* (1977); *The Punk Rock Movie* (1978); *Rust Never Sleeps* (1979) (Neil Young); *Divine Madness* (1980) (Bette Midler); *Rockshow* (1980) (Paul McCartney); *No Nukes* (aka *The Muse Concert: No Nukes*) (1980); *Heartland Reggae* (1980) (Haile Selassie); *Emerson, Lake and Palmer in Concert* (1981); *D.O.A.* (1981); *Let's Spend the Night Together* (1982); *Gospel* (1982); *Stop Making Sense* (1984) (The Talking Heads); *Bring on the Night* (1985) (Sting); *Home of the Brave* (1986) (Laurie Anderson); *Hail! Hail! Rock 'n' Roll* (aka *Chuck Berry Hail! Hail! Rock 'n' Roll*) (1987); *Rattle and Hum* (1988) (U2); *Big Time* (1988) (Tom Waits); *Depeche Mode 101* (1989); *Year of the Horse* (1997) (Neil Young); *Spice World* (1997) (The Spice Girls); *Wild Man Blues* (1998) (Woody Allen)

Confessions… Series

Only the first of this feeble series of British sex farces was released in the U.S. Reviews were unkind, with the *New York Times* commenting that *Confessions of a Window Cleaner* "reeks of something…once called Swinging London." Still, the movies eventually showed up on pay-cable as "adults-only" features. Actor Robin Askwith was the principal series regular. Sadly, the films also featured faded British stars like Diana Dors (*Confessions of a Driving Instructor*).

Confessions of a Window Cleaner (1973); *Confessions of a Pop Singer* (1975); *Confessions of a Driving Instructor* (1976); *Confessions from a Holiday Camp* (1977)

Corman's Poe Series

In his 1990 autobiography, low-budget auteur Roger Corman wrote: "I felt that Poe and Freud were working in different ways toward a concept of the unconscious mind, so I tried to use Freud's theories to interpret the work of Poe." Such literate aspirations may not come across in the finished films, but Corman's Poe adaptations nonetheless exemplify quality, low-budget filmmaking. The series began with 1960's *House of Usher,* a moody mixture of Poe themes produced in two weeks for a measly $270,000. The film introduced the distinguishing features of most of Corman's Poe movies: a crazed performance by Vincent Price, Daniel Haller's atmospheric period sets, Floyd Crosby's florid color photography, and a well-crafted screenplay. Indeed, all but one script were penned, in part, by either Richard Matheson (*Duel*) or Charles Beaumont, both *Twilight Zone* veterans. The lone exception was the final series entry, 1964's *Tomb of Ligea,* written by Robert Towne (an Oscar winner for *Chinatown*). Corman followed up *Usher* with 1961's *The Pit and the Pendulum,* a clever reworking of Poe themes featuring a lively torture dungeon climax. Ray Milland replaced Vincent Price as the flat lead in 1962's *The Premature Burial,* the series' weakest entry. However, Price was back for good in Corman's follow-up, the 1962 anthology *Tales of Terror,* which also featured veteran stars Peter Lorre and Basil Rathbone. Lorre joined Price and Boris Karloff for *The Raven,* a silly but entertaining comedy bearing no relation to Poe's poem (the plot introduces Lorre as a raven — a victim of warlock Karloff's magic). *The Haunted Palace* includes a fragment of the title poem, but it's really a straightforward adaptation of H.P. Lovecraft's novella *The Case of Charles Dexter Ward.* Corman produced his last two Poe films in 1964, with *The Masque of the Red Death* emerging as a critical favorite. Shot in England with a bigger budget than its predecessors (and using leftover sets from *Beckett*), *Masque* attracted attention chiefly due to Nicholas Roeg's stylish photography. Roeg, who replaced Corman's regular cameraman Crosby, went on to direct *Don't Look Now* (1973) and *The Man Who Fell to Earth* (1976). Corman concluded his Poe series after *Tomb of Ligea* because he felt (rightly so) that the films were becoming repetitive. Nevertheless, his Concorde Films tried to initiate a new Poe series over two decades later with *Masque of the Red Death* (1989) and *The Haunting of Morella* (1990). Corman did not direct these later Poe adaptations.

House of Usher (1960); *The Pit and the Pendulum* (1961); *The Premature Burial* (1962); *Tales of Terror* (1962); *The Raven* (1963); *The Haunted Palace* (1963); *The Masque of the Red Death* (1964); *The Tomb of Ligea* (1964)

Cotton Comes to Harlem *see* Coffin Ed Johnson and Grave Digger Jones

Country Singer Biographies *see* Pop, Rock, and Country Singer Biographies

Courts-Martial

Several fine courtroom dramas have revolved around military courts-martial. Stanley Kubrick's chilling *Paths of Glory* detailed the plight of three French soldiers tried for cowardice during World War I after their doomed mission failed. In terms of emotional power, its only rival is the incisive 1979 Australian picture *Breaker Morant*. This potent drama, set during the Boer War, also concerned three soldiers facing court-martial as scapegoats. Tom Courtenay played court-martial defendants in *Private Potter* (1962) and *King and Country* (1964). In the first film, he portrayed a soldier, accused of cowardice, who claimed to have seen God. In the World War I–set *King and Country*, Dirk Bogarde defended Courtenay of a desertion charge. Richard Basehart and Lee Marvin gave strong performances as soldiers facing courts-martial during the Korean War in *Time Limit* (1957) and *Sergeant Ryker* (1968), respectively. Herman Wouk's Pulitzer Prize–winning novel *The Caine Mutiny* (1954) climaxed in a court-martial, with Van Johnson and Robert Francis as the naval officers who rebelled against Humphrey Bogart's neurotic Captain Queeg. The fact-based *Sergeant Matlovich vs. the U.S. Air Force* (1978) chronicled a homosexual serviceman's struggle to remain in the military. The British officers stationed in India in *Conduct Unbecoming* (1975) conducted their own court-martial when they suspected one of the group of perverse acts. Bryan Brown, who played one of the defendants in *Breaker Morant*, played the prosecuting officer in 1990's *Blood Oath*. Bradford Dillman and Peter Graves starred in a 1966 TV series called *Court-Martial* set during World War II. Although not technically a court-martial, *The Winslow Boy* (1950) offered a fascinating fact-based account of the fight for a young boy's right to a trial after expulsion from a British military academy. See also **Judges**.

The Winslow Boy (1950); *The Caine Mutiny* (1954); *Court Martial* (aka *Carrington, V.C.*) (1954); *The Court-Martial of Billy Mitchell* (1955); *The Rack* (1956); *Paths of Glory* (1957); *Time Limit* (1957); *Sergeant Rutledge* (1960); *The Court-Martial of Major Keller* (1961); *Private Potter* (1962); *Billy Budd* (1962); *King and Country* (1964); *The Man in the Middle* (1964); *Sergeant Ryker* (1968); *Conduct Unbecoming* (1975); *Sergeant Matlovich vs. the U.S. Air Force* (1978 TVM); *Breaker Morant* (1979); *A Rumor of War* (1980 TVM); *The Caine Mutiny Court-Martial* (1988 TVM); *The Court-Martial of Jackie Robinson* (1990 TVM); *Blood Oath* (1990); *Prisoner of Honor* (1991 TVM); *A Few Good Men* (1992); *Assault at West Point: The Court-Martial of Johnson Whitaker* (1994 TVM); *The Winslow Boy* (1999); *Rules of Engagement* (2000)

Crabs and Lobsters

Most movie crabs have probably appeared on dinner plates, but there have been a few exceptions. A giant pink crab, animated by special effects wizard Ray Harryhausen, had a choice scene in 1961's *Mysterious Island*. Yet, even it was killed, boiled, and devoured. The title creatures of *Attack of the Crab Monsters* (1957) ate human heads which enabled them to telepathically lure more human prey for supper entrees. Still another giant crab washed ashore in 1982's *Night of the Claw* (aka *Island Claws*). The shadow of an alien crab-like creature accompanied the title visitors to Earth in 1959's *Teenagers from Outer Space*. Sebastian the Crab sang the Oscar-winning song "Under the Sea" in Disney's *The Little Mermaid*. Edible, normal-sized crabs and lobsters have been the subjects of restaurant business dramas (*King Crab*), lobster fisherman sagas (*High Tide at Noon*), and even a Doris Day comedy (*It Happened to Jane*).

Port Sinister (aka *The Beast of Paradise Island*) (1952); *Attack of the Crab Monsters* (1957); *High Tide at Noon* (1957); *Teenagers from Outer Space* (1959); *It Happened to Jane* (aka *Twinkle and Shine*) (1959); *Mysterious Island* (1961); *The Lost Continent* (1968); *Multiple Maniacs* (1970); *Annie Hall* (1977); *King Crab* (1980 TVM); *Night of the Claw* (aka *Island Claws*) (1982); *Lobster Man from Mars* (1989); *The Little Mermaid* (1989); *Simply Irresistible* (1999)

Crane, Bill

Universal made three Crane mysteries in the late 1930s as part of its "Crime Club" series. The intent was to develop B-movies from popular, but lesser-known, detectives. Author Jonathan Latimer's Bill Crane certainly fit the bill. A private eye with a drinking problem, Crane wandered through a downbeat world layered with cynicism. Such an existence would make Sam Spade and Philip Marlowe genre legends in later movies. The mysteries involved cases such as a missing corpse and a murder in a locked room (a subject explored previously by Philo Vance in 1929's *The Canary Murder Case*). Preston Foster played Crane.

The Westland Case (1937); *The Lady in the Morgue* (*Corpse in the Morgue*; *Case of the Missing Blonde*) (1938); *The Last Warning* (1938)

The Creature from the Black Lagoon

The Gill Man (as he's fondly known) was the brainchild of producer William Alland, who was inspired by a vague South American legend about a prehistoric monster that roamed the swamps. Universal Pictures spared no expense on 1954's *Creature from the Black Lagoon*, shooting the film in 3-D (q.v.) and investing $12,000 in the creature suit. The story, another reworking of "Beauty and the Beast," sends a scientific expedition down the Amazon where it discovers a man/fish creature with a fondness for human women. Like Kong, the Creature was a sympathetic monster, who simply asked to be left alone. But Universal had other ideas. The Gill Man was back in 1955's *The Revenge of the Creature*, in which he's captured and transported to a Florida aquarium before female trouble again causes his demise. The worst was yet to come. He becomes a land mammal — thanks to unwanted surgery — in 1956's *The Creature Walks Among Us*, the final film in the trilogy. In the movie's closing scene, the Gill Man walks into the ocean, apparently aware that he will drown in the water that was once his home. Ricou Browning played the Creature in all three movies, although Ben Chapman handled the land scenes in the first film and Don Megowan was the "transformed" Creature in the last. A puppet version of the Gill Man made an appearance in the children's musical *Mad Monster Party?* (1967). And a generic Creature (looking suspiciously like a Black Lagoon resident) surfaced in 1987's juvenile adventure *The Monster Squad*.

Creature from the Black Lagoon (1954); *The Revenge of the Creature* (1955); *The Creature Walks Among Us* (1956); *Mad Monster Party?* (1967); *The Monster Squad* (1987)

The Crime Doctor

Despite a past clouded by amnesia, Dr. Robert Ordway became a leading criminal psychologist — only to discover that he was once a criminal himself. Armed with "insider knowledge" of how the criminal minds works, Ordway repaid society by bringing villains to justice. Such was the premise for this series of slightly offbeat detective films starring Warner Baxter as Ordway. The series originated from Max Marcin's long-running radio program and resulted in ten films over a six-year period. Baxter, an Oscar winner as the Cisco Kid (q.v.) in 1929's *In Old Arizona*, was the only actor ever to play the Crime Doctor.

The Crime Doctor (1943); *The Crime Doctor's Strangest Case* (1943); *Shadows in the Night* (1944); *The Crime Doctor's Courage* (1945); *The Crime Doctor's Warning* (1945); *The Crime Doctor's Manhunt* (1946); *Just Before Dawn* (1946); *The Millerson Case* (1947); *The Crime Doctor's Gamble* (1948); *The Crime Doctor's Diary* (1949)

Critters Series

If you were a little, furry, fanged alien who had just hijacked a spaceship after escaping from a prison asteroid, where would you go? To Kansas, of course! The sleepy rural town of Grovers Bend, to be exact. That's the premise behind 1986's *Critters*, an easygoing science fiction/comedy which mixed predictable characters with a quirky sense of humor. For example, the bounty hunters who pursue the escaped "Krites" assume Earthling form: One takes on the appearance of a video rock star and the other a dead deputy with fresh wounds — neither one blends very well with the local folks. As for the Krites, they mumble a lot (their dialogue is subtitled) and seem to exist to eat (humans being a favorite food). However, their intelligence level is questionable, since one unwisely eats a stick of explosive with a burning fuse. The residents of Grovers Bend eventually outwit the Critters, only to be harassed by their hatched offspring in the disappointing 1988 follow-up *Critters 2: The Main Course*. A second sequel, 1991's *Critters 3*, found the furry aliens wrecking havoc in a downtown apartment complex. The fourth installment began as an *Aliens* spoof with Charlie the bounty hunter (series regular Don Opper) and the last two Krites leaving behind Kansas and hurdling into space while in suspended animation (q.v.). Years later, a group of space salvagers discover Charlie and the Krites and revive them aboard a space station. The film contains little humor (the "hero" dies and a nice character turns cruel) and the Critters have little screen time. Still, the series must have its fans or the law of diminishing returns would have killed it long before this third sequel.

Critters (1986); *Critters 2: The Main Course* (1988); *Critters 3* (1991); *Critters 4* (aka *Critters 4: They're Invading Your Space*) (1992)

Crusoe, Robinson

Daniel Defoe's classic novel about a man's struggle for survival on an isolated island influenced so many books and films that literary critics created a term for the genre: Robinsonnade. Spanish surrealist director Luis Buñuel made the best screen version, a remarkably straightforward, lyrical 1952 film starring Dan O'Herlihy. Douglas Fairbanks updated the tale as a gent whose island existence was the result of a bet in 1932's *Mr. Robinson Crusoe*. Amanda Blake played the title role in 1954's *Miss Robin Crusoe*, an unexceptional female variation, and Dick Van Dyke updated the story for children in Disney's *Lt. Robin Crusoe, USN* (1966). *Man Friday* (1976) gradually reversed the roles of master Crusoe

(Peter O'Toole) and manservant Friday (Richard Roundtree). Despite its promising premise, the film deteriorated into an unpleasant affair. A more successful twist was displayed in 1964's *Robinson Crusoe on Mars*, a colorful adventure which substituted a barren planet for the typical remote island. It was remade as *Enemy Mine* in 1986 with Dennis Quaid and Lou Gossett, Jr. 1989's *Crusoe* was a return to Defoe's original, though Aidan Quinn's hero was younger than his predecessors. Many films, such as *Swept Away* (1975) and *Castaway* (1987), have borrowed the shipwrecked plot. Indeed, Defoe's original even predated Wyss's *The Swiss Family Robinson* and thus indirectly influenced film and TV variations of that novel — to include *Gilligan's Island*. See also **Islands**.

Mr. Robinson Crusoe (1932); *Adventures of Robinson Crusoe* (aka *Robinson Crusoe*) (1952); *Miss Robin Crusoe* (1954); *Robinson Crusoe on Mars* (1964); *Lt. Robin Crusoe, USN* (1966); *Swept Away … By an Unusual Destiny in the Blue Sea of August* (aka *Swept Away*) (1975); *Man Friday* (1976); *Enemy Mine* (1986); *Castaway* (1987); *Crusoe* (1989)

Curse Series

The four films comprising this "series" are connected in name only. Actor David Keith (*An Officer and a Gentleman*) directed 1987's *The Curse*, a straightforward adaptation of an H.P. Lovecraft tale ("The Colour Out of Space") about a fallen meteorite which causes mutations. In 1989's *Curse II: The Bite*, a man is bitten by a snake, given the wrong antidote, and exposed to radiation. As one would expect, his arm turns into a snake's head. Christopher Lee starred in *Curse III: Blood Sacrifice* (1990), a conventional voodoo film originally titled *Panga*. In *Curse IV: The Ultimate Sacrifice*, a demon is unleashed from the catacombs beneath a church.

The Curse (aka *The Farm*) (1987); *Curse II: The Bite* (1989); *Curse III: Blood Sacrifice* (aka *Panga*) (1990); *Curse IV: The Ultimate Sacrifice* (1993)

Cyborg Cop Series

The first two films in this low-budget action series starred David Bradley as D.E.A. agent Jack Ryan (no relation to Tom Clancy's hero). Ryan is not a cyborg nor technically a cop — but he does work in law enforcement and helps his brother battle a mad scientist who turns humans into cyborgs. Bradley specialized in these types of roles in the 1990s, having previously taken over for Michael Dudikoff in the *American Ninja* films (q.v.). *Cyborg Cop 3* bears no relation to the first two films. It's about a reporter investigating a company called Delta Tech that manufactures cyborgs. See also **Androids and Cyborgs**.

Cyborg Cop (1993); *Cyborg Cop 2* (aka *Cyborg Soldier*) (1994); *Cyborg Cop 3* (aka *Terminal Impact*) (1995)

Cyborg Series

The surprising success of the low-budget *Cyborg* (1989) played a critical role in propelling Jean-Claude Van Damme from B-movies to major studio pictures such as *Universal Soldier* and *Hard Target*. Yet, while Van Damme's star status quickly faded, *Cyborg* gained minor prominence as an influential film. In retrospect, it inspired its own "mini-genre" consisting of similar-themed, low-budget android/cyborg action pictures such as

Robo-C.H.I.C. (1990), *Cybernator* (1991), *Project: Shadowchaser* (1992), *Nemesis* (1993), *Cyborg Cop* (1993), and *Cyber Tracker* (1994). On its own, *Cyborg* is a modestly entertaining film in which Van Damme fights to protect a cyborg programmed with a cure for a post-apocalytic plague. The film's highlights are Van Damme's flashy martial arts moves and an extended chase sequence in a sewer. A belated 1993 sequel, *Cyborg 2*, includes some stock footage of Van Damme, but otherwise bears no relation to the original film. *Cyborg 3: The Recycler* (1995) has nothing to do with the two previous films — except that it's about cyborgs, one of whom mates with a human and has a cyborg baby. See also **Androids and Cyborgs**.

Cyborg (1989); *Cyborg 2* (aka *Cyborg 2: Glass Shadow*) (1993); *Cyborg 3: The Recycler* (1995)

Cyclops

These one-eyed mythological Titans who forged thunderbolts for Zeus have been largely misrepresented in their few film appearances. Kirk Douglas fought one as *Ulysses* (1955) and special effects genius Ray Harryhausen brought one to life with thrilling results in his classic fantasy *The Seventh Voyage of Sinbad* (1958). However, the title creature in Bert I. Gordon's contemporary sci-fi feature *Cyclops* (1957) was just a 50-foot-tall man (Dean Parkins) with a flap of skin covering one eye. Parkins played a similar creature in Gordon's *War of the Colossal Beast* (1958). Just to confuse matters, this latter film bore no relation to *Cyclops* (although the creatures look quite similar), but it was a sequel to Gordon's non–Cyclopean picture *The Amazing Colossal Man* (1957). A gentle Cyclops warrior, considerably shorter (at about eight feet), aided Ken Marshall on a quest to save his beloved princess in *Krull* (1983). Albert Dekker played the devious *Dr. Cyclops* (1940), a mad scientist obsessed with shrinking humans. The film featured nary a Cyclops, its title being simply a reference to the doctor's poor eyesight. See also **Giants**; **Gorgons**; **Unicorns**.

Ulysses (1955); *Cyclops* (1957); *The Seventh Voyage of Sinbad* (1958); *War of the Colossal Beast* (1958); *Atlas Against the Cyclops* (aka *Monster from the Unknown World*; *Maciste nella Terror dei Ciclopi*) (1961); *Santo and Blue Demon vs. the Monsters* (aka *Santo y Blue Demon Contra los Monstruos*) (1969); *Krull* (1983)

Dancer, Joe

Three years after his "Baretta" series went off the air, Robert Blake returned to star as rugged private detective Joe Dancer in the 1981 TV movie *The Big Black Pill*, a pilot for a new show. The movie drew insufficient ratings to warrant a series, but Blake refused to give up. He played Dancer in two additional films. The effort proved fruitless, however, for a regular series still failed to materialize.

The Big Black Pill (aka *Joe Dancer*) (1981 TVM); *The Monkey Mission* (1981 TVM); *Murder 1, Dancer 0* (1983 TVM)

Danger Zone Series

Flesh Gordon alumnus Jason Williams produced, cowrote, and starred in this series about an ex-cop hunting down the nasty biker (appropriately named Grim Reaper) who killed his girlfriend. Mounted aboard his own chopper as he treks across the desert, loner hero Wade Wilson (Williams) looks and acts like he stepped out of a Western revenge picture. Interestingly, the series' third entry even involves a Western subplot, in which Reaper and his gang search for gold hidden by Quantrill's Raiders during the Civil War. The first two films were released directly to video, while *Danger Zone III* received a theatrical distribution. *Danger Zone IV* (1992) combined recycled footage from previous entries with a ludicrous plot about scantily-clad, revenge-minded biker girls.

Danger Zone (1987); *Danger Zone II: Reaper's Revenge* (1988); *Danger Zone III: Steel Horse War* (1990); *Danger Zone IV: Mad Girls, Bad Girls* (aka *Mad Girls, Bad Girls*) (1992)

Daninsky, Waldemar (El Hombre Lobo)

Paul Naschy, Spain's number one film star of the 1970s, created and portrayed the Polish werewolf Waldemar Daninsky — better known in his homeland as El Hombre Lobo. Naschy's films, like the better Mexican horror movies of the 1960s, stressed atmosphere at the expense of logic. Additionally, Naschy believed in the Mexican adage that horror can be multiplied by increasing the number of monsters. El Hombre Lobo encountered vampires in *Mark of the Werewolf*, Jekyll/Hyde in *Dr. Jekyll and the Werewolf*, and aliens, a mummy, the Frankenstein Monster, and Dracula in the monster all-star epic *The Man Who Came from Ummo*. Despite his European popularity, Naschy (real name Jacinto Molina) has found little fame in the U.S. For its American release, 1968's 3-D *Mark of the Werewolf* was typically shown in 2-D under the misleading title *Frankenstein's Bloody Terror* and minus 45 minutes of footage. See also **Werewolves**.

Mark of the Werewolf (aka *La Marca del Hombre Lobo*; *Frankenstein's Bloody Terror*; *Hell's Creatures*) (1968); *Nights of the Werewolf* (aka *Las Noches del Hombre Lobo*) (1969); *The Werewolf's Shadow* (aka *La Noche de Walpurgis*; *The Werewolf vs. the Vampire Women*) (1970); *The Man Who Came from Ummo* (aka *El Hombre Que Vino de Ummo*; *Assignment Terror*; *Los Monstruos Del Terror*; *Dracula vs. Frankenstein*) (1970); *Fury of the Wolfman* (aka *La Furia del Hombre Lobo*) (1970); *Dr. Jekyll and the Werewolf* (aka *Dr. Jekyll y el Hombre Lobo*) (1971); *Curse of the Devil* (aka *El Retorno de la Walpurgis*) (1973); *The Werewolf and the Yeti* (aka *La Maldicion de la Bestia*; *Night of the Howling Beast*) (1976); *Return of the Wolfman* (aka *El Retorno del Hombre Lobo*; *The Craving*) (1980); *The Werewolf and the Samurais* (aka *La Bestia y la Espada Magica*; *La Bestia y Los Samurais*) (1983); *Howl of the Devil* (aka *El Aullido del Diablo*) (1987)

Dark Shadows Series

Producer-director Dan Curtis has milked a lot of mileage out of his 1966–71 supernatural daytime soap *Dark Shadows*, turning it into two theatrical films, a two-part television movie, and a prime-time series revival. The original Gothic TV series owed most of its popularity to Jonathan Frid's compelling portrayal of New England vampire Barnabus Collins. His story formed the basis for *House of Dark Shadows*, a low-budget 1970 feature which also starred TV regulars Joan Bennett (Elizabeth Collins), Grayson Hall (Julia Hoffman), and Kathryn Leigh Scott (Maggie Evans). In the film's bloody climax, Barnabus encountered a fatal stake through the heart fired with a crossbow. His absence in the 1971 sequel *Night of Dark Shadows* shifted the emphasis to witchcraft and hauntings. However, audiences showed little interest in a

Dark Shadow movie sans Barnabus. Thus, the film series — like its TV counterpart — died. Amazingly, the TV series found an afterlife in syndication and on videotape. Meanwhile, Dan Curtis, after directing *The Winds of War* and *War and Remembrance*, mounted a TV movie revival starring Ben Cross (*Chariots of Fire*) as Barnabus. It was followed by a short-lived prime-time series also featuring Jean Simmons and Roy Thinnes. See also **Vampires**.

House of Dark Shadows (1970); *Night of Dark Shadows* (1971); *Dark Shadows* (1991 TVM)

Darkman

Sam Raimi's inventive, stylish ode to comic-book superheroes somehow fell short of both box-office gold and cult movie status. Still, it remains an exciting and even touching tale of a brooding hero unable to recapture the life he lost. Liam Neeson hits all the right notes as scientist Peyton Westlake, who should have died in a laboratory explosion meant for his lawyer girlfriend Julie (Frances McDormand in an understated pre–*Fargo* role). Disfigured by the flames and mentally unbalanced due to experimental pain therapy, Peyton finds temporary salvation in the form of his lab-developed artificial skin. He can use his artificial skin to assume the identity of anyone, but there's a catch — the stuff melts away in 99 minutes. This flaw in his creation causes significant problems as he tries to rekindle his relationship with Julie and wreak his revenge on the criminals responsible for his injuries. While the story lacks originality, Raimi propels it with several breathtaking set pieces (the highlight being a sequence in which Darkman hangs from a speeding helicopter). Neeson and McDormand provide the emotional depth that lifts the film above a series of incredible action scenes. Raimi even includes some unexpected cameos for sharp-eyed film buffs (e.g., John Landis, Bruce Campbell, cult film director William Lustig). After *Darkman* and *Army of Darkness* (see **The Evil Dead**), Raimi graduated to star-driven vehicles like *The Quick and the Dead* (1995). Thus, he turned over the directorial reins to Bradford May for two *Darkman* sequels released directly to videotape in the mid–1990s. May, a cinematographer, does a decent job despite lower budgets and Arnold Vosloo subbing for Liam Neeson. In fact, both *Darkman* sequels are entertaining B-movies, although the villains become more interesting than Peyton Westlake. A scene in *Darkman III*— where a disguised Peyton tries to escape from a surprise birthday party before his face melts — rivals Raimi's best work. It's too bad the *Darkman* did not extend beyond the third installment. See also **Disguises**.

Darkman (1990); *Darkman II: The Return of Durant* (1995); *Darkman III: Die Darkman Die* (1996)

Dates in Title

In addition to the *Friday the 13th* films (q.v.), other "date films" include *Saturday the 14th*, *The Night of January 16th*, and *September 30, 1955*. The latter film dealt with how James Dean's death (on that date) affected a fanatical fan (Richard Thomas). See also **Year in Title**.

The Night of January 16th (1941); *D-Day the Sixth of June* (1956); *September 30, 1955* (aka *9/30/55*; *24 Hours of the Rebel*) (1978); *Friday the 13th* (1980); *Saturday the 14th* (1981); *The 32nd of December* (1988); *Saturday the 14th Strikes Back* (1988); *October 32nd* (1992)

The Daughters of Joshua Cabe Series

When fur trapper Buddy Ebsen suddenly needs a "family" to hold on to his homestead, he hires a prostitute, a thief, and a pickpocket to pose as his daughters. Karen Valentine, Lesley Ann Warren, and Sandra Dee played the original *Daughters of Joshua Cabe* in this unexpectedly popular 1972 "ABC Movie of the Week." Two subpar sequels followed, each featuring entirely different casts.

The Daughters of Joshua Cabe (1972 TVM); *The Daughters of Joshua Cabe Return* (1975 TVM); *New Daughters of Joshua Cabe* (1976 TVM)

The Dead End Kids *see* The Bowery Boys

Deafness

The world of the deaf has received little attention in film. Like blindness (q.v.), it has been misused as a plot gimmick in syrupy romances. Opera star Mario Lanza found love with a deaf girl in the massively sentimental *For the First Time*. Loretta Young played a deaf socialite in love with poor physician Alan Ladd in the 1944 romance *And Now Tomorrow*. Five years earlier, Young had portrayed a deaf person with more conviction in *The Story of Alexander Graham Bell*. *Johnny Belinda* (1948) hinted at the unjust prejudice experienced by deaf people. The 1952 British film *The Crash of Silence* opened new vistas with its touching, semidocumentary look into the world of a deaf girl. Few films about deafness have matched its power. *Silent Victory: The Kitty O'Neil Story* (1979) was an inspirational real-life account of a deaf woman who became a successful stunt person (q.v.). The Emmy Award-winning *Love Is Never Silent* (1985) co-starred Phyllis Frelich and Ed Waterstreet, acclaimed performers from the National Theatre for the Deaf. Deaf actress Marlee Matlin won a Best Actress Oscar for 1986's *Children of a Lesser God*, an unsentimental story of the love between an independent-minded deaf woman and a teacher of the deaf (William Hurt). Despite its exploitative title, 1975's *Deafula* was merely the famous vampire story told in sign language.

The Man Who Played God (aka *The Silent Voice*) (1932); *Beethoven* (aka *Un Grand Amour de Beethoven*; *The Life and Loves of Beethoven*) (1936); *The Story of Alexander Graham Bell* (aka *The Modern Miracle*) (1939); *And Now Tomorrow* (1944); *Johnny Belinda* (1948); *The Crash of Silence* (aka *Mandy*) (1952); *Flesh and Fury* (1952); *Sincerely Yours* (1955); *No Road Back* (1957); *Man of a Thousand Faces* (1957); *For the First Time* (1959); *The Miracle Worker* (1962); *Gigot* (1962); *The Heart Is a Lonely Hunter* (1965); *Psych-Out* (1968); *Deaf Smith and Johnny Ears* (aka *Los Amigos*) (1973); *Deafula* (1975); *Silent Victory: The Kitty O'Neil Story* (1979 TVM); *And Your Name Is Jonah* (1979 TVM); *The Miracle Worker* (1979 TVM); *Voices* (1979); *Dummy* (1979 TVM); *Amy* (aka *Amy on the Lips*) (1981 TVM); *Johnny Belinda* (1982 TVM); *Hear No Evil* (1982 TVM); *Love Is Never Silent* (1985 TVM); *Children of a Lesser God* (1986); *Crazy Moon* (1986); *Bridge to Silence* (1989 TVM); *See No Evil, Hear No Evil* (1989); *Hear No Evil* (1993); *The River Wild* (1994); *Mr. Holland's Opus* (1995); *Dead Silence* (1997 TVM); *His Bodyguard* (1998 TVM); *The Break Up* (1998); *Where the Truth Lies* (aka *Ninety Days at Hollyridge*) (1999 TVM)

Dear Ruth Series

A teenage girl pens passionate love letters to a soldier and encloses her older sister's photograph. When his leave comes due, he decides to pay her a visit. The casting of William Holden (the soldier), Joan Caulfield (the older sister), and Mona Freeman (the younger sister) propelled the routinely-plotted *Dear Ruth* into one of Paramount's biggest hits of 1947. In the belated sequel, *Dear Wife* (1949), newlyweds Caulfield and Holden encounter family problems when troublesome Freeman sets up Holden as a rival Senatorial candidate to the girls' father (Edward Arnold). Freeman had the spotlight to herself in 1951's *Dear Brat*. Holden had gone on to bigger parts (*Sunset Boulevard*) and Caulfield to television briefly (1953's *My Favorite Husband*) and then semiretirement. See also **Letters**.

Dear Ruth (1947); *Dear Wife* (1949); *Dear Brat* (1951)

Death Incarnate

The personification of Death has been portrayed in various ways, as a lonely romantic, a beautiful temptress, and a hideous skeleton-creature greedy for souls. Fredric March played a curious Death anxious to understand why humans cling so desperately to life in *Death Takes a Holiday* (1934). He takes a vacation to investigate the phenomenon and falls in love, while the world suffers during his leave of absence — for dying people can no longer die. That interesting twist is nowhere to be found in the 1998 remake *Meet Joe Black*, which starred Brad Pitt as Death. Feisty Lionel Barrymore proved more than a match for Cedric Hardwicke's Mr. Brink (aka Death), by literally chasing Death up a tree in the 1939 comedy *On Borrowed Time*. In Ingmar Bergman's *The Seventh Seal* (1956), Max Von Sydow played a 14th century knight who matches wits with Death in a game of chess. That scene was parodied in *Bill and Ted's Bogus Journey* (1991), with the two California dudes playing "His Royal Deathness" in Clue, Twister, and Battleship. Death was among the uninvited guests at evil Prince Prospero's (Vincent Price) masquerade ball in Roger Corman's stylish *Masque of the Red Death* (1964). Jessica Lange made an elegant Death in Bob Fosse's *All That Jazz*, while a dreadful decaying Death swarmed anxiously about John Neville whenever he was about to give up on life in *The Adventures of Baron Munchausen*. On television, Robert Redford played Mr. Death in the memorable 1962 "Nothing in the Dark" episode of *The Twilight Zone*.

Death Takes a Holiday (1934); *On Borrowed Time* (1939); *Orpheus* (1949); *The Seventh Seal* (1956); *Masque of the Red Death* (1964); *The Devil's Bride* (aka *The Devil Rides Out*) (1968); *Death Takes a Holiday* (1971 TVM); *All That Jazz* (1979); *Monty Python's The Meaning of Life* (1983); *The Adventures of Baron Munchausen* (1989); *Edgar Allan Poe's Masque of the Red Death* (1989); *Bill and Ted's Bogus Journey* (1991); *The Detective and Death* (aka *El Detective Y La Muerte*) (1994); *Cemetery Man* (aka *Dellamorte Dellamore*; *Of Death and Love*) (1994); *Meet Joe Black* (1998)

Death Wish Series

Charles Bronson's biggest hit cast him as a mild-mannered architect transformed into an emotionless vigilante after a gang of punks attacked his wife and daughter. Some critics condemned the film's questionable ethics, with *New York Times* reviewer Vincent Canby writing: "The movie seems to have been made for no reason except to exploit its audiences' urban paranoia and vestigial fascination with violence for its own sake." Even writer Brian Garfield, who wrote the original novel, attacked the film for advocating vig-

ilantism. He later appealed to CBS to not broadcast the film in prime time (which it did). Despite the controversy, *Death Wish* was a blockbuster and some tabloids even claimed that it briefly lowered the crime rate in New York City. Still, Bronson and director Michael Winner avoided making a sequel for eight years. They should have kept it that way. *Death Wish II* was an embarrassing rehash of the original, transplanted to Los Angeles. The additional Bronson sequels were not much better. See also **Vigilantes**.

Death Wish (1974); *Death Wish II* (1982); *Death Wish III* (1985); *Death Wish IV: The Crackdown* (1987); *Death Wish V: The Face of Death* (1994)

Deathstalker

"Can you imagine what it would be like to change into Barbi Benton in two minutes?" pondered drive-in movie critic Joe Bob Briggs after viewing 1984's *Deathstalker*. Joe Bob was referring to a hilarious scene in this sword-and-sorcery (q.v.) mishmash in which an evil wizard transforms his ugly henchman into buxom Playmate Benton. Unfortunately, this inspired piece of unintentional camp turned out to be the best part of this Argentina-lensed *Conan* rip-off. Still, the combination of muscular men and half-naked women appealed to action-oriented videotape renters. A 1987 sequel starring former *Penthouse* Pet Monique Gabrielle was released directly to video. Its typical genre plot cast Gabrielle as a princess trying to regain her throne with the help of hunky John Terlesky. After a third installment with John Allen Nelson in the lead, Rick Hill — the original Deathstalker — returned for 1991's *Deathstalker IV: Match of the Titans*. Surprisingly, Hill's acting ability apparently improved during his absence from the series. After all, it takes some definite thespian skill to deliver, with a straight face, dialogue like: "I should have known — I'm always getting mixed up with princesses." See also **Sword and Sorcery**.

Deathstalker (1984); *Deathstalker II* (aka *Deathstalker II: Duel of the Titans*) (1987); *Deathstalker and the Warriors from Hell* (1989); *Deathstalker IV: Match of the Titans* (aka *Deathstalker IV*) (1991)

Delta Force Series

After a superior outing in 1985's *Code of Silence*, action star Chuck Norris appeared poised to take his place beside genre stalwarts Eastwood and Bronson. The following year's *Delta Force* was intended as his final stepping stone — it featured an Academy Award–winning co-star, decent production values, and a plot torn from the headlines. Unfortunately, even though it earned a profit and spawned two sequels, *Delta Force* sealed Norris's fate as a performer who had reached his potential and could advance no further. *Delta Force* cast Norris as Colonel Scott McCoy, whose special forces unit receives a mission to rescue a planeload of passengers held captive by Middle East terrorists. Lee Marvin (the aforementioned Oscar winner) plays Norris' special forces sidekick, while the supporting cast includes familiar TV faces such as Joey Bishop, Robert Forster, Susan Strasberg, and Robert Vaughn. Both script and execution were by-the-numbers, making Delta Force a painfully obvious action picture with a stiff lead performance, even by Norris's standards. Still, it's superior to the 1990 follow-up, *Delta Force 2*, which pits Norris against ruthless South American drug lords. Sadly, five people were killed in a helicopter crash during this film's production in the

Phillipines. Chuck bowed out of the third installment, forcing Norris fans to settle for son Mike. The Fred Williamson films *Delta Force Commando* (1987) and *Delta Force Commando Two* (1991) are not a part of the Norris series.

Delta Force (1986); *Delta Force 2* (aka *Delta Force 2: The Colombian Connection*; *Delta Force 2: Stranglehold*; *Delta Force 2: Operation Stranglehold*) (1990); *Delta Force 3: The Killing Game* (1991)

Dentists

The movie dentist has experienced a checkered career since his extravagant 1924 debut in Erich von Stroheim's nine-hour marathon silent movie *Greed*. Gibson Gowland played von Stroheim's lead, an appropriately greedy lower-class dentist with an illegal practice (a fellow dentist is called "Painless" Potter). However, the bad side of dentistry is better represented by murderer Ralph Bellamy in *Footsteps in the Dark*, Nazi torture specialist Laurence Olivier (who drills holes in healthy teeth) in *Marathon Man*, and wacko Corbin Bernsen in *The Dentist*. Sadistic dentists have been played for laughs in both the 1960 and 1986 versions of *The Little Shop of Horrors*. Jack Nicholson was a masochistic patient in the former, while Steve Martin enthusiastically sang "I'm a Dentist" in the latter. Bob Hope played a dentist who accidentally became a gunslinging Western hero in 1948's *The Paleface*. It spawned the Hope sequel *Son of Paleface* (1952) and the Don Knotts remake *The Shakiest Gun in the West* (1968). The murder of a playboy dentist set the mystery into motion in 1985's light-hearted affair *Compromising Positions*. Government agent Peter Falk drafted dentist Alan Arkin into the spy business in *The In-Laws* (1979). Daniel Day-Lewis was a traveling dentist in the offbeat *Eversmile, New Jersey* (1989). And W.C. Fields portrayed cinema's most perverse dentist in his hilarious pre–Hays Code short *The Dentist* (1932). His struggle to pull a tooth results in some very compromising—and funny—positions with a female patient. Raquel Welch played a skydiving dental assistant in *Fathom* (1967), although her occupation had nothing to do with the plot.

Greed (1924); *The Dentist* (1932); *One Sunday Afternoon* (1933); *Silly Billies* (1936); *Hotel Haywire* (1937); *Aren't Men Beasts!* (1937); *Footsteps in the Dark* (1941); *The Strawberry Blonde* (1941); *The Great Moment* (1944); *One Sunday Afternoon* (1948); *The Paleface* (1948); *The Fat Man* (1951); *Son of Paleface* (1952); *Bells Are Ringing* (1960); *Dentist in the Chair* (1960); *Come Dance with Me* (1960); *The Little Shop of Horrors* (1960); *Get on with It* (aka *Dentist on the Job*; *Carry on TV*) (1961); *Fathom* (1967); *The Shakiest Gun in the West* (1968); *Cactus Flower* (1969); *Marathon Man* (1976); *The In-Laws* (1979); *Ten* (1979); *Straight Through the Heart* (1983); *Compromising Positions* (1985); *The Little Shop of Horrors* (1986); *Rocket to the Moon* (1986 TVM); *Fight for Life* (1987 TVM); *Eversmile New Jersey* (1989); *Serial Mom* (1994); *Captives* (1994); *Houseguest* (1995); *Waiting for Guffman* (1997); *The Dentist* (1996); *Jitters* (1997 TVM); *The Dentist II* (aka *The Dentist 2: Brace Yourself*) (1998); *The Whole Nine Yards* (2000)

Desperado Series

NBC sought to revive the TV Western with these cliché-ridden television "movies" revolving around a young loner named McCall (Alex McArthur). Actually, each film played like an unsold TV pilot, complete with reliable guest stars like Pernell Roberts,

Robert Vaughn, and Robert Foxworth. The series' premise was simple enough: After McCall guns down David Warner and a half-dozen other baddies in the first film, understanding marshal Pernell Roberts gives the would-be gunfighter a chance to clear his name. However, Roberts points out that McCall will be a fugitive from justice. So, just like David Jansen, TV's original "Fugitive," McCall travels from town to town, helping out nice folks along the way. Mystery author Elmore Leonard wrote the screenplay for 1987's *Desperado* and, yes, the Eagles' hit song of the same name was featured prominently. Interestingly, although NBC never picked up *Desperado* as a TV series, ABC launched the similar *Young Riders* as an hour series and enjoyed minor success for a couple of seasons. As for star Alex McArthur, he eventually got a TV series, but not as a cowboy. He played a spy with amnesia in the short-lived 1992 NBC series *The Fifth Corner*.

Desperado (1987 TVM); *The Return of Desperado* (1988 TVM); *Desperado: Avalanche at Devil's Ridge* (1988 TVM); *Desperado: Legacy* (1989 TVM); *Desperado: The Outlaw Wars* (1989 TVM)

Deth, Jack *see* Trancers

The Devil

Mr. Scratch, Beelzebub, Mephistopheles, Lucifer, Satan—the Devil has been known by many names throughout history. And on the screen, he has been portrayed in many guises by a diverse group of performers. Walter Huston played a cunning, though admittedly likable, Mr. Scratch in 1941's *All That Money Can Buy*, adapted from Stephen Vincent Benet's 19th century New England variation of Faust. Although ultimately outwitted by lawyer Daniel Webster (Edward Arnold), Scratch displayed a sharp talent for turning the tables. When Webster demanded an American jury for his client, Scratch produced 12 of history's worst criminals and then made the point: "Dastard, liar, traitor, knave…Americans all." Peter Cook's George Spiggot (aka The Devil) proved equally adept at crafty tricks in 1967's *Bedazzled*, an hilarious updating of Faust with Dudley Moore as the woeful short-order cook who sells his soul for seven wishes. At one point, Moore's inability to be specific with his wishes results in his transformation into a nun (i.e., he wishes to be in love with a woman in a place where no men are around). The Devil has been played for comedy in less memorable films as well, by Vincent Price in *The Story of Mankind* (1957), Christopher Lee in *Poor Devil* (1973), Bill Cosby in *The Devil and Max Devlin* (1981), and George Burns (in both title roles) in *Oh God, You Devil!* (1984). The Devil, as the incarnation of evil, has taken a back seat to his disciples in most horror films. Still, Robert De Niro made an eerie villain—one Mr. Lou Cipher—in the moody horror/mystery *Angel Heart* (1987). Soap star Susan Lucci proved that the Devil could easily be a woman in the 1984 TV movie *Invitation to Hell*. Viggo Mortensen's Lucifer turned out to be an unlikely ally of the good guys fighting the dark angel Gabriel in *The Prophecy* (1994). Victor Buono made an unexpected appearance as the Devil beneath a possessed house in 1978's *The Evil*. His scenes were cut from some prints, indicating that the filmmakers were as confused as the audience in regard to his sudden presence in a haunted house movie. Nigel Kneale's intriguing 1967 sci-fi/fantasy *Five Million Years to Earth* (see **Quatermass**) suggested that the Devil's origins were extraterrestrial. The Devil's son — the Antichrist —first gained prominence in 1976's *The Omen* (q.v.). See also **Hell**; **The Omen Series**.

The Sorrows of Satan (1927); *All That Money Can Buy* (aka *The Devil and Daniel Webster*) (1941); *Cabin in the Sky* (1943); *Heaven Can Wait* (1943); *Angel on My Shoulder* (1946); *Alias Nick Beal* (1949); *Meet Mr. Lucifer* (1953); *The Story of Mankind* (1957); *Damn Yankees* (1958); *The Private Lives of Adam and Eve* (1960); *Bedazzled* (1967); *Five Million Years to Earth* (aka *Quatermass and the Pit*) (1967); *Torture Garden* (1967); *The Devil's Bride* (aka *The Devil Rides Out*) (1968); *Doctor Faustus* (1968); *The Devil in Love* (1968); *The Devil's Daughter* (1972 TVM); *Poor Devil* (1973 TVM); *The Sentinel* (1977); *The Evil* (1978); *The Devil and Max Devlin* (1981); *Invitation to Hell* (1984 TVM); *Oh God, You Devil!* (1984); *Crossroads* (1986); *Angel Heart* (1987); *Hunk* (1987); *Prince of Darkness* (1987); *Mr. Frost* (1990); *Girlfriend from Hell* (1990); *Switch* (1991); *Speak of the Devil* (1991); *Needful Things* (1993); *The Prophecy* (aka *God's Army*) (1995); *Devil's Food* (1996 TVM); *Hercules* (1997); *The Devil's Advocate* (1997); *South Park: Bigger, Longer & Uncut* (1999); *End of Days* (1999); *H-E Double Hockey Sticks* (1999 TVM); *Bedazzled* (2000)

ANTICHRIST: *The Omen* (1976); *The Chosen* (aka *Holocaust 2000*) (1978); *The Visitor* (1979); *Fear No Evil* (1981); *Child of Light, Child of Darkness* (1991 TVM); *Servants of Twilight* (1991 TVM)

Dinosaurs

The evolution of the cinematic dinosaur begins and ends with Willis O'Brien. A master of special effects photography, O'Brien perfected the stop-motion animation technique used in nearly all the memorable dinosaur sequences. After stints as a cowboy, prize fighter, and sculptor, O'Brien made his first dinosaur film in 1917, a short called *The Dinosaur and the Missing Link*. He filmed his brontosaurus (a jointed wooden skeleton covered by clay) one frame at a time, moving the model slightly between each picture to create an illusion of motion. O'Brien continued making other shorts (e.g., *The Ghost of Slumber Mountain*) and eventually landed the job of special effects creator for *The Lost World* (1925), an adaptation of Arthur Conan Doyle's novel about a journey into a prehistoric land. O'Brien's brilliant effects shine even today, especially the final sequence in which an escaped brontosaurus wrecks havoc in London. O'Brien went on to create his masterpiece in 1933's *King Kong* (q.v.), which featured a dynamic struggle between Kong and a Tyrannosaurus Rex. In 1949, he finally won an Oscar for *Mighty Joe Young*, another giant ape opus. However, his most cherished projects were never realized. These included two cowboy/dinosaur scripts called *Creation* and *Gwangi*. O'Brien eventually sold the idea for the former film, which sadly made it to the screen as the forgotten, low-budget feature *The Beast of Hollow Mountain* (1956). However, O'Brien protégé Ray Harryhausen created some superb animation sequences for the 1969 dinosaur Western *The Valley of Gwangi*. Harryhausen, who dominated stop-action animation for decades, was also responsible for the dinosaur that trashed the amusement park in *The Beast from 20,000 Fathoms* (1953) and the pterodactyl that snatched Raquel Welch in *One Million Years B.C.* Of Harryhausen's rivals, Jim Danforth and David Allen have received the highest marks for their lifelike creatures in, respectively, *When Dinosaurs Ruled the Earth* (1970) and *Caveman* (1981). The high cost of stop-motion photography has limited its use over the years and filmmak-

ers have resorted to alternate methods for creating dinosaurs. In 1940's *One Million B.C.*, live lizards were photographed on miniature sets. The effect was convincing enough to warrant use of that footage in countless low-budget features. In the 1950s, Japan's special effects wizard Eiji Tsuburaya perfected the man-in-a-monster suit approach with Toho's *Godzilla* films (see separate entries for Japanese monsters **Godzilla**, **Ghidrah**, **Rodan**, **Mothra**, and **Gamera**). Director Steven Spielberg used puppets, models, computer technology, and $65 million to create the impressive prehistoric beasts of 1993's *Jurassic Park*. Finally, animated dinosaurs have appeared in *Fantasia* (the creation of the world segment) and *The Land Before Time*, a children's film about lost baby dinos searching for their parents. See also **Carnosaur Series**; **Cave People**; **Dragons**; **The Land Before Time Series**; **Prehysteria Series**.

The Lost World (1925); *The Savage* (1926); *King Kong* (1933); *One Million B.C.* (1940); *Fantasia* (1940); *Two Lost Worlds* (1950); *Unknown World* (1951); *The Lost Continent* (1951); *The Beast from 20,000 Fathoms* (1953); *King Dinosaur* (1955); *The Animal World* (1956); *The Beast of Hollow Mountain* (1956); *The Giant Behemoth* (1959); *The Lost World* (1960); *Dinosaurus* (1960); *Gorgo* (1961); *Reptilicus* (1962); *One Million Years B.C.* (1966); *When Dinosaurs Ruled the Earth* (1970); *The Valley of Gwangi* (1969); *The Last Dinosaur* (1977 TVM); *The Crater Lake Monster* (1977); *Where Time Began* (aka *Trip to the Centre of the Earth*) (1978); *Caveman* (1981); *Baby…Secret of the Lost Legend* (1985); *My Science Project* (1985); *The Land Before Time* (1988); *Adventures in Dinosaur City* (1991); *Steel Justice* (1992 TVM) (a robotic dinosaur); *The Lost World* (1992); *Return to the Lost World* (1992); *Carnosaur* (1993); *Super Mario Bros.* (1993); *Jurassic Park* (1993); *Prehysteria* (1993); *Dinosaur Island* (1994); *Theodore Rex* (1996); *The Lost World: Jurassic Park* (1997); *Gargantua* (1998 TVM); *Barney's Great Adventure: The Movie* (1998); *Dinosaur* (2000)

The Dionne Quintuplets *see* Christian, Dr. (Paul)

Dirigibles

The motorized gas-filled aircraft known as dirigibles, airships, zeppelins, and blimps have made irregular screen appearances since airplanes replaced them in the 1930s. Howard Hughes' World War I aerial spectacular *Hell's Angels* (1930) confirmed the birth and signalled the death of the movie dirigible. The zeppelin raid over London, although elaborately staged, paled in comparison to the film's classic airplane dogfights. Dirigible crashes occurred at the climaxes of *The Lost Zeppelin* (1929), *Madam Satan* (1930), *Dirigible*, (1931) and *Murder in the Air* (1940). The latter film, which starred Ronald Reagan as secret service agent Brass Bancroft (q.v.), was built around actual footage, obtained by industrious producer Bryan Foy, of a dirigible crashing into the ocean. The airship disaster in *Madame Satan* was preceded by a wild onboard party and followed by a happy ending. Over two decades later, a madman named Robur (Vincent Price) set out to conquer the world from his flying airship fortress, The Albatross, in the 1961 Jules Verne fantasy *Master of the World*. The year 1971 featured two realistic films about dirigibles. *Zeppelin* was a World War I tale of intrigue about an attempt to steal secrets from a German zeppelin factory. The fact-based *The Red Tent* chronicled a disastrous 1928 airship flight over the North

Pole (a plot reminiscent of 1929's *The Lost Zeppelin*). Another fact-based drama, 1975's *The Hindenberg*, was about the 1937 New York dirigible explosion that claimed the lives of almost half the passengers and crew. Its weak narrative lead up to a chilling climax featuring actual newsreel of the Hindenberg. The familiar sight of a blimp hovering over the Super Bowl was played for suspense in 1977's *Black Sunday*, a presidential assassination thriller. James Bond grappled with a villain aboard an airship over the Golden Gate Bridge in *A View to a Kill* (1985), while Indiana Jones and his father hijacked a Nazi airplane attached to an airborne dirigible in *Indiana Jones and the Last Crusade* (1989). See also **Airplanes**; **Balloons, Hot Air**.

Zeppelin Attack on New York (1917); *The Lost Zeppelin* (1929); *Hell's Angels* (1930); *Madame Satan* (1930); *Dirigible* (1931); *Murder in the Air* (1940); *The Fabulous World of Jules Verne* (1958); *The Fabulous Baron Munchausen* (1961); *Master of the World* (1961); *The Stolen Dirigible* (aka *Two Years Holiday*) (1966); *The Assassination Bureau* (1968); *Zeppelin* (1971); *The Red Tent* (1971); *Island at the Top of the World* (1974); *The Hindenberg* (1975); *Black Sunday* (1977); *A View to a Kill* (1985); *Indiana Jones and the Last Crusade* (1989); *The Rocketeer* (1991); *Little Nemo: Adventures in Slumberland* (1992); *The Dirigible* (1994)

The Dirty Dozen

Robert Aldrich's 1967 original was a solid World War II action film about 12 ruthless criminals offered parole in return for participating in a deadly mission behind German lines. Lee Marvin played the tough major who whipped the gang into top-notch soldiers. For the record, the original dozen were played by: John Cassavetes, Jim Brown, Telly Savalas, Donald Sutherland, Charles Bronson, Trini Lopez, Tom Busby, Colin Maitland, Al Mancini, Stuart Cooper, Ben Carruthers, and Clint Walker. Although the film became MGM's number one grosser of the year, a sequel did not appear until 18 years later — and then as a TV movie. Probably inspired by the runaway success of 1985's *Rambo*, NBC telecast *The Dirty Dozen: The Next Mission* later that year. Lee Marvin reprised his role as the Dozen's leader and Ernest Borgnine and Richard Jaeckel returned in their original supporting roles. Telly Savalas starred in two more TV movie sequels before the Fox television network introduced the very short-lived *Dirty Dozen* TV series. Interestingly, although the original *Dirty Dozen* spawned a host of imitators in the late 1960s (e.g., *The Devil's Brigade*, *A Reason to Live, a Reason to Die*), the plot was borrowed from Roger Corman's 1964 quickie *The Secret Invasion*. See also **Television Movie Sequels to Theatrical Films**.

The Dirty Dozen (1967); *The Dirty Dozen: The Next Mission* (1985 TVM); *The Dirty Dozen: The Deadly Mission* (1987 TVM); *The Dirty Dozen: The Fatal Mission* (1988 TVM)

Dirty Harry

Clint Eastwood created San Francisco police inspector Harry Callahan, a ruthless distributor of justice, in Don Siegel's influential 1971 action picture *Dirty Harry*. Armed with his trademark .44 magnum pistol, Eastwood/Callahan became the perfect antihero for the 1970s, reassuring the public that criminals above the law could — and would — be punished. Not surprisingly, the character mellowed as the series progressed, with Harry even teaming up with a female partner (Tyne Daly) in *The Enforcer*. Ironically,

the series' weakest entry, *Sudden Impact*, introduced Harry's infamous quote: "Go ahead…Make my day." Imitators, such as Jack Palance in *One Man Jury* (1978), Sylvester Stallone in 1986's *Cobra* and Steven Seagal in 1988's *Above the Law*, have failed to duplicate Eastwood's success — perhaps because they lack his grimacing humor.

Dirty Harry (1971); *Magnum Force* (1973); *The Enforcer* (1976); *Sudden Impact* (1983); *The Dead Pool* (1988)

Disaster Movies

Films climaxing in disasters date back to the 1930s — with the earthquake that rocked Gable and Tracy in *San Francisco*, the storm sequence in *Hurricane*, and the locusts that stripped the fields in *The Good Earth*. All these were grand spectacles, but mere movie subplots. The disaster film, as a genre, came into vogue in the early 1970s with the releases of *Airport* and *The Poseidon Adventure*. A canny producer named Irwin Allen exploited the latter film, a tale of an upside-down ocean liner, into a box-office smash ("Who will survive?" ads asked) and quickly became known as the King of Disaster Films. He followed it with the fiery all-star opus *The Towering Inferno* and suddenly disaster films were all the rage. Cheap rip-offs and foreign imports filled America's screens with avalanches, volcanic eruptions, and tidal waves. Then Allen's lavish disaster epic about killer bees, 1978's *The Swarm*, crashed at the box-office and the fate of the genre went down with it. Allen's follow-ups, including a *Poseidon* sequel and three made-for-TV films, generated little interest. By the time 1979's *Meteor* came hurling toward Earth, moviegoers treated it like a real disaster — avoiding it like the plague while flocking to the parody *Airplane!* Other disaster movie spoofs include *The Big Bus* (1976), a movie-within-a-movie in *Drive-In*, and the "That's Armaggedon!" segment in *Kentucky Fried Movie* (1977). See also **Airport Series**; **Asteroids, Comets, and Meteors**; **Earthquakes**; **Floods**; **Hurricanes and Tornadoes**; **Volcanoes**.

Airport (1970); *The Poseidon Adventure* (1972); *Earthquake* (1974); *The Towering Inferno* (1974); *The Hindenberg* (1975); *Tidal Wave* (1975); *The Big Bus* (1976); *Irwin Allen's Flood* (aka *Flood!*) (1976 TVM); *Irwin Allen's Fire* (aka *Fire!*) (1977 TVM); *The Cassandra Crossing* (1977); *Avalanche* (1978); *Gray Lady Down* (1978); *The Swarm* (1978); *Beyond the Poseidon Adventure* (1979); *Meteor* (1979); *City on Fire* (1979); *Airplane!* (1980); *When Time Ran Out…* (aka *Earth's Final Fury*) (1980); *Airplane 2: The Sequel* (1982); *The Night the Bridge Fell Down* (1983 TVM)

Disguises

The cinema's most renowned master of disguises was probably the murderer in John Huston's stylish murder mystery *The List of Adrian Messenger*. The film employed an interesting gimmick too, in that the crafty criminal (Kirk Douglas) was flanked by four heavily-disguised, heavyweight performers (Frank Sinatra, Tony Curtis, Robert Mitchum, and Burt Lancaster). Rod Steiger wore all the disguises himself as the psychotic murderer in *No Way to Treat a Lady*, while Tony Curtis played a nice guy — and a real-life disguise specialist — in 1960's *The Great Impostor*. Several performers have disguised themselves as the opposite sex for extended periods. Ginger Rogers tried to pass for a boy to save on train fare in *The Major and the Minor* (1942), while Barbra Streisand did it to get an education in *Yentl* (1983). Her charade ran into several complications when she became engaged to Amy Irving and fell in love with best friend Mandy Patinkin. Liv Ullmann experienced a worse fate, however, when her male disguise was revealed in *Pope Joan* (1972). As for male performers, Jack Lemmon and Tony Curtis (again) donned skirts, wigs, and high heels and joined an all-girls' band to elude gangsters in Billy Wilder's *Some Like It Hot*. Dustin Hoffman played an unemployed actor who became a popular soap opera actress in *Tootsie* (1982). Several performers have disguised themselves as *Charley's Aunt* in the various screen versions of Brandon Thomas' play. In the Jungle Jim movie *Mark of the Gorilla* (1950), Nazis hunting for gold disguised themselves as apes! Movie characters noted for their disguises include Sherlock Holmes (q.v.), Inspector Neilson (John Barrymore) in the Bulldog Drummond films (q.v.), and bumbling Inspector Clouseau (see **Pink Panther** series). It is difficult to single out a best disguise, but Marlene Dietrich was hardly recognizable in a key scene in *Witness for the Prosecution* (1958) and Debra Winger fooled a lot of movie-goers playing a male angel named Emmett in 1987's *Made in Heaven*, going unbilled for her performance. See also **Darkman**; **Plastic Surgery**.

Sylvia Scarlett (1935); *The Phantom Strikes Again* (aka *The Gaunt Stranger*) (1938); *Hold That Co-ed* (aka *Hold That Girl*) (1938); *Charley's Big-Hearted Aunt* (1940); *Charley's Aunt* (aka *Charley's American Aunt*) (1941); *The Major and the Minor* (1942); *I Was a Mail War Bride* (1949); *Mark of the Gorilla* (1950); *The Ringer* (1952); *Where's Charley?* (1952); *Witness for the Prosecution* (1958); *Some Like It Hot* (1959); *The Great Impostor* (1960); *The List of Adrian Messenger* (1963); *No Way to Treat a Lady* (1968); *Pope Joan* (aka *The Devil's Impostor*) (1972); *Sleuth* (1972); *Triple Echo* (1973); *Toma* (1973 TVM); *Tootsie* (1982); *Yentl* (1983); *Her Life as a Man* (1984 TVM); *Just One of the Guys* (1985); *Fletch* (1985); *Dr. Otto and the Riddle of the Gloom Beam* (1986); *Soul Man* (1986); *He's My Girl* (1987); *Too Outrageous!* (1987); *Darkman* (1990); *Little Sister* (1992); *Mrs. Doubtfire* (1993); *All Men Are Liars* (1995); *Twelfth Night: Or What You Will* (1996); *The Saint* (1997); *Mulan* (1998); *Big Momma's House* (2000)

District Attorney, Mr.

Like many film series of the 1940s, this one was adapted from a hit radio show. However, Republic Pictures' movies never matched the popularity of the radio programs, which were based on the career of New York D.A. (and future presidential candidate) Thomas E. Dewey. Dennis O'Keefe played young P. Cadwallader Jones in 1941's *Mr. District Attorney*, which co-starred Peter Lorre. James Ellison replaced O'Keefe in 1941's *The Carter Case* and John Hubbard played the role in 1943's *Secrets of the Underground*. Although the series failed to catch on, O'Keefe revived the role (though the character was now named Steve Bennett) in 1946's *Mr. District Attorney*. Following its failure, radio show creator Edward C. Byron set his sights on television and produced the 1951-52 small-screen series *Mr. District Attorney* starring Jay Jostyn. Following its cancellation, a 1954 syndicated series with David Brian ran for a single season.

Mr. District Attorney (1941); *The Carter Case* (1941); *Secrets of the Underground* (1943); *Mr. District Attorney* (1946)

Doctor in the House Series

This well-done, lightweight 1954 comedy about British medical students featured rising star Dirk Bogarde, lovely Kay Kendall, and ever-dependable Kenneth More. But character actor James Robertson Justice, as the blusterous chief surgeon Sir Lancelot Spratt, stole the show from them all. Bogarde and Justice teamed again in the follow-up, 1955's *Doctor at Sea*, which cast Dirk as a young ship's physician romancing Brigitte Bardot while tolerating the endless tirades of Captain Hogg (Justice). The third film, *Doctor at Large* (1957), gave Justice (as Spratt again) more screen time and set the pattern for the rest of the series. Whether the handsome male lead was Bogarde, Leslie Phillips, or Michael Craig, the real star was always Justice. He consistently made the *Doctor* films diverting entertainment. The 1970 British TV series *Doctor in the House* lasted for three seasons. See also **Hospitals**.

Doctor in the House (1954); *Doctor at Sea* (1955); *Doctor at Large* (1957); *Doctor in Love* (1960); *Doctor in Distress* (1963); *Doctor in Clover* (1966); *Doctor in Trouble* (1970)

Doctor Who *see* Who, Doctor

Dogs

Man's best friend has enjoyed a long and prosperous film career, both as a supporting player and a major star. A German Shepherd named Rin Tin Tin became the first canine box-office attraction in silent films such as *The Clash of the Wolves* (1924) and *A Dog of the Regiment* (1930). He died in 1932, although two of his descendants went on to play the lead in the 1954–59 TV series *The Adventures of Rin Tin Tin*. Lassie (q.v.) eventually replaced Rinty as Hollywood's top dog, but other canines have also starred in their own film series, including Rusty (q.v.) and Benji (q.v.). Nick and Nora Charles's little dog Asta stole her share of scenes in *The Thin Man* (q.v.) films, as did Daisy in the *Blondie* (q.v.) movies. Walt Disney Productions seemed to specialize in dog films in the late 1950s and early 1960s. Animated tales paired two unlikely dog lovers in 1955's *Lady and the Tramp* and let loose the cinema's biggest litter in 1961's *101 Dalmatians* (although technically, the two Dalmatian parents adopted most of those puppies). Mouseketeer Tommy Kirk starred in the sentimental boy-and-dog story *Old Yeller* (1957) and its more upbeat sequel *Savage Sam* (1962). Other Disney dogs include the Irish setter in *Big Red* (1962), the three dogs (two good and one mean) in *The Incredible Journey* (1963), *The Ugly Dachshund* (1966), and the animated sniffer in *The Fox and the Hound* (1981). Some of the screen's most memorable dog pictures were derived from classic canine books like Jack London's *Call of the Wild* (1935), Ouida's *A Dog of Flanders* (1959), Albert Peyton Terhune's *Lad: A Dog* (1962), Richard Adams's *The Plague Dogs* (1982), and, of course, Eric Knight's venerable *Lassie Come Home* (1943). Mongrels easily outnumber any breed as the most popular dogs in the cinema. Still, there have been a lot of German Shepherds — the Rin Tin Tin movies, the *Rusty* series, *The Littlest Hobo*, *Kelly and Me*, *Won Ton Ton*, *K-9*, and *We Think the World of You*. And Doberman pinschers unexpectedly became the trendy dogs of the early 1970s, appearing in movies like *They Only Kill Their Masters* (1972), *The Doberman Gang* (1972), *The Daring Dobermans* (1973), and *The Amazing Dobermans* (1976). Not all dogs have been portrayed as man's best friend. *Cujo* (1983) was about a rabid Saint Bernard dead set on devouring Dee Wallace, while *Dogs* (1976) and *The Pack* (1977) were remarkably similar thrillers about humans being stalked by wild dogs. James Brolin played a man stranded overnight in a department store — and at the mercy of vicious security dogs — in the 1973 TV movie *Trapped*. *Devil Dog: The Hound of Hell* (1978) featured an evil, possessed pooch, while a vampire dog distinguished *Dracula's Dog* (1977). David Warner may have encountered the most frightening of all movie dogs when he threatened the safety of the Antichrist in 1976's *The Omen*. Canine fantasies have opted for a lighter tone. An ancient spell periodically turned Tommy Kirk into a lovable sheepdog in 1959's *The Shaggy Dog*. Dean Jones experienced a similar problem in the 1976 sequel *The Shaggy D.A.* A murdered German Shepard returned to Earth as private eye Rex Shepard (Dick Powell) to find his killer in 1951's hilarious *You Never Can Tell*. *Oh, Heavenly Dog!* (1980) reversed the premise and lost the laughs, despite the presence of Chevy Chase and Benji. A cast of humans portrayed the anxious dogs awaiting either new homes or death in Robert Downey's off-the-wall satire *Pound* (1970). A crafty pup named Blood communicated telepathetically with his dense human companion (Don Johnson) in the post-apocalypse satire *A Boy and His Dog* (1975). And henpecked husband Walter Abel found solace with a talking dog in *The Fabulous Joe* (1947). See also **Benji**; **Lassie**; **Rusty**; **The Shaggy Dog Series**; **Watchers Series**.

The Clash of the Wolves (1924); *A Dog of the Regiment* (1930); *Skippy* (1931); *Lucky Dog* (1933); *The Kennel Murder Case* (1933); *Call of the Wild* (1935); *The Voice of Bugle Ann* (1936); *Storm in a Teacup* (1936); *The Hound of the Baskervilles* (1939); *The Biscuit Eater* (1940); *Lassie Come Home* (1943); *It Shouldn't Happen to a Dog* (1946); *The Tender Years* (1947); *The Fabulous Joe* (1947); *The Emperor's Waltz* (1948); *You Never Can Tell* (1951); *Behave Yourself!* (1951); *Bloodhounds of Broadway* (1952); *Lady and the Tramp* (1955); *It's a Dog's Life* (aka *Bar Sinister*) (1955); *Goodbye My Lady* (1956); *Kelly and Me* (1957); *Old Yeller* (1957); *The Man Who Wagged His Tail* (1957); *The Littlest Hobo* (1958); *A Dog of Flanders* (1959); *The Hound of the Baskervilles* (1959); *The Shaggy Dog* (1959); *The Silent Call* (1961); *Greyfriars Bobby* (1961); *101 Dalmatians* (1961); *Big Red* (1962); *Savage Sam* (1962); *Lad: A Dog* (1962); *Wild and Wonderful* (1963); *The Incredible Journey* (1963); *Git* (1965); *The Ugly Dachshund* (1966); *The Spy with a Cold Nose* (1966); *Alexander* (1968); *Pound* (1970); *The Aristocats* (1970); *They Only Kill Their Masters* (1972); *Call of the Wild* (1972); *Sounder* (1972); *White Fang* (1972); *The Doberman Gang* (1972); *The Daring Dobermans* (1973); *Trapped* (1973 TVM); *Where the Red Fern Grows* (1974); *Digby-The Biggest Dog in the World* (1974); *A Boy and His Dog* (1975); *The Great Adventure* (1975); *Dogpound Shuffle* (aka *Spot*) (1975); *The Omen* (1976); *Call of the Wild* (1976 TVM); *Dogs* (1976); *Won Ton Ton, the Dog Who Saved Hollywood* (1976); *The Amazing Dobermans* (1976); *The Shaggy D.A.* (1976); *The Pack* (aka *The Long Dark Night*) (1977); *Dracula's Dog* (aka *Zoltan, Hound of Hell*) (1977); *Devil Dog: The Hound of Hell* (1978 TVM); *C.H.O.M.P.S.* (1979); *The Black Marble* (1980); *Oh, Heavenly Dog!* (1980); *The Courage of Kavik, the Wolf Dog* (aka *Kavik, the Wolf Dog*) (1980); *The Fox and the Hound* (1981); *Rottweiler* (aka *Dogs of Hell*) (1981); *The Plague Dogs* (1982); *Hear No Evil* (1982 TVM); *Skeezer* (1982 TVM); *White Dog* (1982); *Cujo* (1983); *Second Sight: A Love Story* (1984 TVM); *Love Leads the Way* (1984 TVM); *Hambone and Hillie* (1984); *Gus Brown and Midnight Brewster* (1985 TVM); *A Cry in the Dark* (1988); *Oliver and Company* (1988); *Pound Puppies and the Legend of Big Paw* (1988); *Watchers* (1988); *K-9* (1989); *We Think the World of You* (1989); *Turner and Hooch* (1989); *The Adventures of Milo and Otis* (1989); *All Dogs Go to Heaven* (1989); *Watchers 2* (1990); *Chips, the War Dog* (1990 TVM); *Baxter* (1990); *White Fang* (1991); *Rover Dangerfield* (1991); *Bingo* (1991); *Beethoven* (1992); *Homeward Bound: The Incredible Journey* (1993); *Call of the Wild* (1993 TVM); *To Dance with the White Dog* (1993 TVM); *Look Who's Talking Now* (1993); *Homeward Bound: The Incredible Journey* (1993); *White Fang 2: Myth of the White Wolf* (1994); *Iron Will* (1994); *Clean Slate* (1994); *Eyes of an Angel* (aka *The Tender*) (1994); *Lassie* (1994); *Far from Home: The Adventures of Yellow Dog* (1995); *Babe* (1995); *Balto* (1995); *Fluke* (1995); *Top Dog* (1995); *101 Dalmatians* (1996); *All Dogs Go to Heaven 2* (1996); *Bad Moon* (1996); *The Truth About Cats and Dogs* (1996); *Zeus and Roxanne* (1997); *The Call of the Wild* (1997 TVM); *Shiloh* (1997); *Air Bud* (1997); *Air Bud: Golden Receiver* (1998); *You Lucky Dog* (1998 TVM); *In the Doghouse* (1998 TVM); *Atomic Dog* (1998 TVM); *My Magic Dog* (1998); *Babe: Pig in the City* (1998); *Soccer Dog: The Movie* (1998); *Murder, She Purred* (aka *Murder, She Purred: A Mrs. Murphy Mystery* (1998 TVM); *Lost and Found* (1999); *Bowfinger* (1999); *Dog Park* (1999); *A Dog of Flanders* (1999); *Shiloh 2: Shiloh Season* (1999); *Dogmatic* (1999 TVM); *The Duke* (1999); *My Dog Skip* (1999); *Ghost Dog: The Way of the Samurai* (2000)

Doinel, Antoine

French director François Truffaut introduced his cinematic alter ego as an imaginative, troublemaking adolescent in 1959's *The 400 Blows*. The film also marked Truffaut's feature film debut — an impressive one that earned him a Grand Prix for direction at the Cannes Film Festival and contributed much to the success of the French "New Wave" films of the 1960s. Jean-Pierre Leaud played Antoine, a 14-year-old who steals and lies in defiance of adults, particularly his neglectful parents. He is finally sent to a reform school for his theft of a typewriter, but manages to escape. However, Truffaut and Leaud brought Antoine back and gave him his first girlfriend in the "Antoine and Colette" episode in the 1962 anthology *Love at Twenty*. In 1968's *Stolen Kisses*, Antoine gets kicked out of the Army, becomes a night watchman, gets fired, and joins a detective agency. More importantly, he falls in love with Christine, who rejects him until he becomes interested in an older woman. Their subsequent marriage comes apart, despite the birth of a son, in 1970's *Bed and Board*. They are divorced at the beginning of 1979's *Love on the Run*, a reflective closing episode combining new footage with clips from the four previous films. Leaud was the only actor to portray Antoine Doinel.

The 400 Blows (aka *Les Quatre Cents Coups*) (1959); *Love at Twenty* (aka *L'Amour À Vingt Ans*) (1962); *Stolen Kisses* (aka *Baiser Volés*) (1968); *Bed and Board* (aka *Domicile Conjugal*) (1970); *Love on the Run* (aka *L'Amour En Fuite*) (1979)

Dolls

Horror and fantasy filmmakers have found the most imaginative uses for dolls. A dying killer transferred his soul into a happy-looking "Chucky" doll in Tom Holland's 1988 sleeper hit *Child's Play* (q.v.). Amazingly, the film's characters — and the movie-going public — readily took to the idea of a little doll running around an apartment wielding a knife and shouting profanities. A living doll also harassed Karen Black in the most chilling segment of 1975's *Trilogy of Terror*. Other murder-minded dolls stalked human prey in *Cathy's Curse*, a 1977 *Exorcist* clone about a possessed rag doll, and in cult director Stuart Gordon's *Dolls* (1987). Voodoo dolls have cropped up in several films, though none to better effect than in 1962's *Burn, Witch, Burn*. Teen nerds Anthony Michael Hall and Ilan Mitchell-Smith turned a Barbie doll into fetching Kelly LeBrock in the 1985 comedy *Weird*

Science. The title murderer in *The Psychopath* (1966) left dolls as a calling card at the scene of his crimes. In non-horror films, dolls have been used as unlikely hiding places. Narcotic drugs were hidden in dolls in the movie version of the Broadway play *Wait Until Dark* (1967) and in the 1961 drive-in picture *Wild Youth*. In one of his best performances, Robert Mitchum pursued two children and a doll filled with money in 1955's *The Night of the Hunter*, Charles Laughton's haunting fable of good vs. evil. Despite its title, the dolls in Tod Browning's *The Devil-Doll* (1936) were really shrunken people. The most bizarre doll film was also one of the first, 1907's *The Doll's Revenge*. It was about a little boy who destroys his sister's doll, only to have the parts reassemble themselves. The doll then grew to an "alarming" size, was joined by another doll, and the two of them pulled the wicked boy apart and devoured him. Both *The Incredible Shrinking Man* (1957) and *The Incredible Shrinking Woman* (1981) used doll houses for temporary residences. See also **Child's Play Series; Puppets**.

The Doll's Revenge (1907); *Black Doll* (1938); *Night of the Hunter* (1955); *Wild Youth* (aka *Naked Youth*) (1961); *Burn, Witch, Burn* (aka *Night of the Eagle*) (1962); *Jack the Giant Killer* (1962); *The Doll* (1963); *The Psychopath* (1966); *Wait Until Dark* (1967); *Trilogy of Terror* (1975 TVM); *Cathy's Curse* (aka *Cauchemares*) (1977); *The Dollmaker* (1984 TVM); *Weird Science* (1985); *River's Edge* (1986); *Dolls* (1987); *Child's Play* (1988); *Dolly Dearest* (1991); *The Tommyknockers* (1993 TVM); *The Baby Doll Murders* (1993); *Secrets in the Attic* (1993); *The Inkwell* (1994); *Toy Story* (1995); *Amityville Dollhouse* (1996); *Blood Dolls* (1999); *Toy Story 2* (1999); *Life Size* (2000 TVM)

Dolphins

Flipper, the biggest dolphin star, made the theatrical features *Flipper* (1963) and *Flipper's New Adventure* (1964) before settling into a 1964–68 TV series. Mitzi the Dolphin (who died of a heart attack in 1971 at the age of 22) played Flipper on the big screen. Suzy the Dolphin replaced her in the TV version. A *Flipper* remake surfaced in 1996, no doubt inspired by the success of the previous year's killer whale family film *Free Willy*. It featured Luke Halpin, who appeared in the earlier *Flipper* movies and the TV series, in a cameo as a fisherman. In 1973's *Day of the Dolphin*, George C. Scott and wife Trish Van Devere taught dolphins how to speak rudimentary English ("Fa loves pa!"). Don Knotts played a meek bookkeeper who becomes an animated dolphin and joins the Navy in the charmless 1964 fantasy *The Incredible Mr. Limpet*. A deep sea diver jilted Rosanna Arquette for a pair of playful dolphins in 1988's *The Big Blue*. Zeus the dog befriended Roxanne the dolphin in the 1997 family film *Zeus and Roxanne*. See also **Fish; Sharks; Whales**.

Boy on a Dolphin (1957); *Flipper* (1963); *Flipper's New Adventure* (1964); *The Incredible Mr. Limpet* (1964); *Island of the Blue Dolphins* (1964); *Day of the Dolphin* (1973); *The Big Blue* (1988); *Splash Too* (1988 TVM); *Ace Ventura: Pet Detective* (1994); *Flipper* (1996); *Zeus and Roxanne* (1997)

Dracula

Although Bram Stoker's immortal vampire novel was published in 1897, a film version was not attempted until F.W. Murnau's *Nosferatu* appeared in 1922. To avoid royalty payments, Murnau never mentioned Dracula by name. Stoker's widow nevertheless sued on the grounds of copyright infringement and some of the prints were destroyed. In 1930, Universal and Tod Browning signed horror great Lon Chaney for the title role in a film version of John Balderston and Hamilton Deane's popular stage play. However, Chaney died unexpectedly and the role went to Bela Lugosi, a screen unknown who had played Count Dracula on stage. Lugosi's compelling presence and Browning's moody direction made *Dracula* a great success (it has dated rather poorly). Interestingly, a Spanish-language version was filmed concurrently on the same sets. It starred Carlos Villarias and ran 29 minutes longer. Although Universal followed Browning's *Dracula* with several popular horror films (*Frankenstein*, etc.), a sequel did not appear until 1936's *Dracula's Daughter*. An offbeat love story with some fine performances, this sequel attracted little attention and was Universal's last attempt at a first-class vampire film. Seven years later, Lon Chaney, Jr., turned up as Count Alucard (spell it backwards) in Robert Siodmak's lively programmer *Son of Dracula*. Despite Chaney's miscasting, this unusual entry had its share of memorable moments — notably Dracula's transformation into mist as his coffin floated toward the surface in a swamp. The Count's Universal career ended with bit parts in 1944's *House of Frankenstein*, 1945's *House of Dracula* (played by John Carradine in both), and 1948's *Abbott and Costello Meet Frankenstein* (in which Lugosi reprised his interpretation). Except for the 1953 Turkish film *Dracula Istanbulda*, Dracula lay dormant for almost a decade. Then, Hammer Films resurrected him with style with their 1958 classic *Horror of Dracula*. As embodied by tall, imposing Christopher Lee, Dracula was a vicious, powerful, handsome vampire whose cunning was matched only by his brilliant adversary Van Helsing (superbly played by Peter Cushing). The Hammer version was a smash, but Lee (and the Count himself) were oddly missing from the equally-memorable sequel *Brides of Dracula* (1960). Lee was back in 1966's *Dracula, Prince of Darkness*, but his role was brief and, amazingly, he had no dialogue. Except for the atmospheric *Dracula Has Risen from the Grave* (1968), the subsequent Hammer Dracula films were run-of-the-mill vampire features. Technically, the last was 1974's *Legend of the Seven Golden Vampires* (aka *The Seven Brothers Meet Dracula*), but Lee's absence and an emphasis on martial arts made this hardly seem like a Dracula picture. In between the Hammer entries, Lee also appeared as Dracula in Jesus Franco's *Count Dracula* (1971), a fairly literal adaptation of Stoker's book, and a French comedy *Dracula and Son* (1976). Although Lee and Lugosi were the screen's most famous Draculas, a host of other actors have essayed the role. The usually vicious Jack Palance emphasized the Count's sympathetic side in Dan Curtis' handsome 1973 TV movie. PBS's *Count Dracula* (1978) featured Louis Jourdan in an aristocratic, sensual interpretation. Klaus Kinski was disturbing (and quite "unsensual") in Werner Herzog's 1978 remake of *Nosferatu*, while Frank Langella was surprisingly forgettable recreating his Broadway performance in 1979's big-budgeted *Dracula*. In 1992, Francis Ford Coppola mounted the stylish *Bram Stoker's Dracula*, which restored much of the novel's plot, although the Dracula-Mina romance would have shocked Stoker. Mel Brooks crafted a funny, but belated spoof three years later with *Dracula: Dead and Loving It*. On television, Michael Nouri played the Count in the "The Curse of Dracula" segment of the NBC series *Cliffhangers* and Geordie Johnson played him in the syndicated *Dracula: The Series*. See also **Vampires**.

UNIVERSAL'S DRACULA FILMS: *Dracula* (1931) (Bela Lugosi); *Dracula's Daughter* (1936) (Gloria Holden as the daughter); *Son of Dracula* (1943) (Lon Chaney, Jr.); *House of Dracula* (1945) (John Carradine); *House of Frankenstein* (aka *Chamber of Horrors*) (1944) (Carradine); *Abbott and Costello Meet Frankenstein* (1948) (Lugosi)

HAMMER'S DRACULA FILMS: *Horror of Dracula* (aka *Dracula*) (1958) (Christopher Lee); *Brides of Dracula* (1960) (actually, the Count is never seen); *Dracula, Prince of Darkness* (1964) (Lee); *Dracula Has Risen from the Grave* (1968) (Lee); *Taste the Blood of Dracula* (1970) (Lee); *Scars of Dracula* (1970) (Lee); *Dracula A.D. 1972* (aka *Dracula Today*) (1972) (Lee); *The Satanic Rites of Dracula* (aka *Count Dracula and His Vampire Bride*; *Count Dracula Is Alive and Well and Living in London*) (1973) (Lee); *The Legend of the Seven Golden Vampires* (aka *The Seven Brothers Meet Dracula*) (1974) (John Forbes Robertson)

OTHER DRACULA FILMS: *Nosferatu* (1922) (Max Schreck); *Spanish Dracula* (1931) (Carlos Villarias); *Dracula Istanbulda* (1953) (Atif Kaptan); *Curse of Dracula* (aka *Return of Dracula*; *The Fantastic Disappearing Man*) (1958) (Francis Lederer); *Billy the Kid vs. Dracula* (1965) (Carradine); *Mad Monster Party?* (1967) (puppet); *Santo and Dracula's Treasure* (aka *Santo en el Tesoro de Drácula*; *El Vampiro y el Sexo*) (1968) (Aldo Monti); *The Man Who Came from Ummo* (aka *El Hombre Que Vino de Ummo*; *Assignment Terror*; *Los Monstruos Del Terror*; *Dracula vs. Frankenstein*) (1970) (Angel del Pozo); *Count Dracula* (1971) (Christopher Lee); *Dracula vs. Frankenstein* (aka *Blood of Frankenstein*; *The Revenge of Dracula*; *They're Coming to Get You*) (1971) (Zandor Vorkov); *Blacula* (1972) (Charles Macaulay); *Santo and Blue Demon vs. Dracula and the Wolf Man* (aka *Santo y Blue Demon Contra Dracula y el Hombre Lobo*) (1972) (Aldo Monti); *Dracula's Great Love* (aka *El Grande Amore del Conde Dracula*) (1972) (Paul Naschy); *Lake of Dracula* (aka *Choisu Me*) (1972) (Mori Kishida); *Dracula* (1973 TVM) (Jack Palance); *Lady Dracula* (aka *Legendary Curse of Lemora*; *Lemora, the Lady Dracula*) (1973) (Leslie Gilb); *Blood for Dracula* (aka *Andy Warhol's Dracula*) (1974) (Udo Kier); *Vampira* (aka *Old Dracula*) (1975) (David Niven); *Dracula and Son* (1976) (Lee); *Nocturna* (1978) (Carradine); *Nosferatu* (1978) (Klaus Kinski); *Count Dracula* (1978 TVM) (Louis Jourdan); *Dracula* (1979) (Frank Langella); *The True Life of Dracula* (1979) (Stefan Sileanu); *Dracula's Last Rites* (1980) (Gerald Fielding); *The Monster Club* (1987) (Duncan Regehr); *Waxwork* (1988) (Miles O'Keeffe); *Bram Stoker's Dracula* (1992) (Gary Oldham); *Nadja* (1994) (Peter Fonda); *Dracula: Dead and Loving It* (1995) (Leslie Nielsen); *The Creeps* (1997) (Phil Fondacaro)

Dragons

The dragon has made little impact as a cinematic monster, being relegated principally to supporting roles. A splendid animated dragon dominated the fiery climax of Disney's *Sleeping Beauty* (1959), but his screen time was all too short. The same can be said of *The Reluctant Dragon* (1941), a documentary about the Disney Studios which featured a short cartoon version of Kenneth Grahame's story. Special effects genius Ray Harryhausen devised very life-like dragons for 1958's *The Seventh Voyage of Sinbad* and 1963's *Jason and the Argonauts*. After Jason slew the seven-headed hydra in the latter film, its teeth turned into skeleton warriors which promptly attacked the mythological hero. A year earlier, fairy-tale protagonist Jack battled a sorcerer-turned-dragon in the Harryhausen-inspired fantasy *Jack the Giant Killer*. Only three films have given dragons what could be called leading roles. *Dragonheart* (1996) featured a lonely dragon (voiced by Sean Connery) who partners with an out-of-work knight (Dennis Quaid)

on a dragon-slaying scam. The film's Oscar-nominated special effects provided Draco the dragon with an impressive emotional range. *Pete's Dragon*, a 1977 live action/animation film, also starred a friendly dragon (animated) who helps a young boy (live action) find a loving home. The dragon Elliott, a rather plump creature with tiny wings, could make himself invisible—a rare trait for his species. In contrast to likable Elliott, Disney's *Dragonslayer* (1981) featured a hideous, fire-breathing dragon appeased only by human sacrifice. The special effects, also Oscar-nominated, compare favorably with *Dragonheart* and are enhanced by imaginative set design (especially the dragon's lair) and a grim fairy tale atomosphere. In terms of sheer opulence, *Dragonslayer* rates as the dragon's finest hour. As for contemporary dragons, there really are none. One could argue that *Q the Winged Serpent* (1982) had many dragon-like qualities, but technically he was the ancient bird-god Quetzalcoatl. Likewise, the Japanese monster Ghidrah (q.v.) boasted three heads, breathed fire, and flew. But whether he or any of his Japanese monster companions were dragons or unidentified dinosaurs remains a source of debate. The Philo Vance (q.v.) murder mystery *The Dragon Murder Case* (1934) revolved around a "dragon" pool where a swimmer mysteriously disappeared. Despite the presence of unusual claw prints and much talk about dragons, Vance exposed a human murderer. The medieval dragon in 1986's *Star Knight* turned out to be an alien spaceship. See also **Dinosaurs**; **Sea Serpents**.

The Niebelungen (1924); *The Reluctant Dragon* (1941); *The Sword and the Dragon* (aka *Ilya Mourometz*) (1956); *The Seventh Voyage of Sinbad* (1958); *Sleeping Beauty* (1959); *Goliath and the Dragon* (1960); *Jack the Giant Killer* (1962); *The Magic Sword* (1962); *The Wonderful World of the Brothers Grimm* (1962); *Captain Sinbad* (1963); *Jason and the Argonauts* (1963); *Ghidrah the Three-Headed Monster* (aka *The Greatest Battle on Earth*; *Sandai Kaiju Chikyu Saidai No Kessen*) (1965); *Pete's Dragon* (1977); *Jabberwocky* (1977); *Dragonslayer* (1981); *The NeverEnding Story* (aka *Die Unendliche Geschichte*) (1984); *Star Knight* (aka *The Knight of the Dragon*) (1986); *Erik the Viking* (1989); *The Pagemaster* (1994); *Dragonworld* (1994); *Dragonheart* (1996); *Merlin* (1998 TVM); *Mulan* (1998); *Arabian Nights* (2000 TVM)

Dreams

Nightmares, daydreams, dreams that come true—filmmakers have used dreams in a variety of ways in musicals, comedies, thrillers, and horror films. Musical dream sequences range from the ballet number in Michael Powell and Emeric Pressburger's *The Tales of Hoffman* (1951) to the Jeanette McDonald–Nelson Eddy duets in *I Married an Angel* (1942). Comedy films tend to favor daydream sequences as evidenced by *Sherlock, Jr.* (1924), *The Secret Life of Walter Mitty* (1947), *Dream Girl* (1948), and *A Christmas Story* (1983). The Alfred Hitchcock suspense film *Spellbound* (1945) contains a bizarre dream sequence that was partially designed by artist Salvador Dali. Other thrillers with memorable dream scenes include the Peter Lorre mystery *Stranger on the Third Floor* (1939), *Fear in the Night* (1947), and *In Dreams* (1999). In the latter film, Annette Bening played a woman whose dreams come true—a problem that also plagued dreamers in *Dead of Night* (1945), *Invaders from Mars* (1953), *The Night My Number Came Up* (1955), and *The Lathe of Heaven* (1980). Sleeping people have had their dreams inhabited by unwanted guests in *Dreamscape* (1984), *Dream Demon* (1988), and the *Nightmare on Elm Street* movies.

In the one-of-a-kind French fantasy *The City of Lost Children* (1995), an evil scientist who cannot dream tries to "steal" the dreams of children. Finally, movies that consist almost entirely of one extended dream sequence include *The Wizard of Oz* (1939), *The Woman in the Window* (1944), *The Horn Blows at Midnight* (1945), *Dead of Night* (1945), *Invaders from Mars* (1953), and *The 5,000 Fingers of Dr. T* (1953). Of course, sometimes it can be difficult to tell where the dream ends and reality begins, a question posed in intriguing films such as *The Deadly Dream* (1971), *Phantasm* (1979) and *The Company of Wolves* (1985). See also **Nightmare on Elm Street Series**.

Sherlock, Jr. (1924); *Delicious* (1931); *Bulldog Drummond's Secret Police* (1939); *The Wizard of Oz* (1939); *Stranger on the Third Floor* (1940); *I Married an Angel* (1942); *The Crime Doctor's Strangest Case* (1943); *Two Girls and a Sailor* (1944); *The Woman in the Window* (1944); *The Horn Blows at Midnight* (1945); *Spellbound* (1945); *Dead of Night* (1945); *Fear in the Night* (1947); *The Secret Life of Walter Mitty* (1947); *Dream Girl* (1948); *The Young and the Damned* (aka *Los Olvidados*) (1950); *Tales of Hoffman* (1951); *Glen or Glenda?* (aka *I Changed My Sex; I Led Two Lives; He or She?*) (1953); *Invaders from Mars* (1953); *The 5,000 Fingers of Dr. T* (1953); *Oklahoma!* (1955); *Artists and Models* (1955); *The Night My Number Came Up* (1955); *Freud* (1962); *Shock Corridor* (1963); *The Night Walker* (1964); *Nightmare* (1964); *Finnegans Wake* (1965); *The Projectionist* (1971); *The Deadly Dream* (1971 TVM); *Phantasm* (1979); *The Lathe of Heaven* (1980 TVM); *The Sender* (1982); *Echoes* (1983); *A Christmas Story* (1983); *Dreamscape* (1984); *Nightmare on Elm Street* (1984); *The Company of Wolves* (1985); *Dream Lover* (1986); *Dream Demon* (1988); *Paperhouse* (1989); *Little Nemo: Adventures of Slumberland* (1992); *Dream Lover* (1994); *The City of Lost Children* (1995); *Tall Tale* (1995); *In Dreams* (1999)

Drew, Nancy

Teenage sleuth Nancy Drew has appeared in countless books by "Carolyn Keene" (a pseudonym for numerous authors who worked for supervising writers Edward Stratemeyer and daughter Harriet Adams). Yet, her screen career was a surprisingly brief one, with Bonita Granville playing her in four formula B-films. Pamela Sue Martin starred in the 1977-78 TV series *The Nancy Drew Mysteries* and Janet Louise Johnson took over the role when that show merged into *The Hardy Boys Mysteries* during the 1978-79 season.

Nancy Drew, Detective (1938); *Nancy Drew and the Hidden Staircase* (1939); *Nancy Drew-Reporter* (1939); *Nancy Drew-Troubleshooter* (1939)

Drug Addiction

The United States' efforts to curb its drug addiction problems in the late 1980s brought the subject unprecedented attention in the cinema. No fewer than six major 1987-88 films portrayed the dangers of cocaine, crack, and other narcotics. Comedian Michael Keaton turned serious as a successful businessman forced to enter a clinic for treatment in *Clean and Sober* (1988). James Woods tackled a similar role, with his typical intensity, in the same year's *The Boost*. Even Michael J. Fox played against type as a nice guy turned druggie in *Bright Lights, Big City* (1988). Yet, despite the presence of these big-name stars, all three films crashed at the box-office, as did *Less Than Zero* (1987) and *Bird* (1988). Faced with grim nightly newscasts of drug-related crimes, it's likely that American moviegoers preferred to avoid seeing their screen fa-

vorites as manipulated addicts. Not surprisingly, the track record of earlier drug addiction pictures has been riddled with similar failures. *The Cocaine Fiends* (1936) was ignored upon its initial release and promoted as camp in the early 1970s along with *Reefer Madness* (1936). Yet, *Cocaine Fiends* contained little material that was even unintentionally funny, being a bleak tale of a young girl whose boyfriend hooks her, and eventually her brother too, on dope. Almost two decades later, producer-director Otto Preminger tumbled censorship barriers with his powerful, highly successful *The Man with the Golden Arm* (1955). Frank Sinatra, in his finest performance, played Frankie Machine, a drummer who turns to drugs to escape pressure. A scene of Sinatra "shooting up" was deleted when the film was originally shown in Maryland (a court ruling eventually restored it). In the wake of *Golden Arm*, smaller anti-drug films were released, but with little impact. Cameron Mitchell played boxer-turned-addict Barney Ross in *Monkey on My Back* (1957). Teen heartthrob James Darren fell in with the wrong crowd south of the border in *The Tijuana Story* (1957). And Peter Graves battled narcotics use among truckers in *Death in Small Doses* (1957). Another wave of addiction movies began in the early 1970s, following the gradual decline of drug culture hits like Roger Corman's *The Trip* (1967). The most effective was probably *The Panic in Needle Park* (1971) which starred a pre-*Godfather* Al Pacino as a heroin addict. Although drug addiction would seem to have little appeal as a comedy subject, cult director Larry Cohen broached the subject in *The Stuff* (1985), an uncomfortable satire about an addictive food. Stand-up comic Richard Pryor discussed his near-death after freebasing in his 1982 concert film *Richard Pryor Live on the Sunset Strip*. A fictionalized version of the incident also came into play in Pryor's semi-autobiographical *Jo Jo Dancer, Your Life Is Calling* (1986). See also **Alcoholism**.

The Cocaine Fiends (1936); *Reefer Madness* (aka *Tell Your Children; The Burning Question; The Dope Addict; Doped Youth; Love Madness*) (1936); *The Man with the Golden Arm* (1955); *A Hatful of Rain* (1957); *Death in Small Doses* (1957); *Monkey on My Back* (1957); *The Tijuana Story* (1957); *The Gene Krupa Story* (1959); *Corridors of Blood* (aka *The Doctor from Seven Dials*) (1958); *Believe in Me* (1971); *Dusty and Sweets McGee* (1971); *The Panic in Needle Park* (1971); *Born to Win* (1971); *Go Ask Alice* (1973 TVM); *The Death of Richie* (aka *Richie*) (1977 TVM); *A Hero Ain't Nothing but a Sandwich* (1978); *A Cry for Love* (1980 TVM); *Angel Dusted* (1981 TVM); *I'm Dancing as Fast as I Can* (1982); *Desperate Lives* (1982 TVM); *Scarface* (1983); *Cocaine: One Man's Seduction* (1983 TVM); *Torchlight* (1984); *The Stuff* (1985); *Jo Jo Dancer, Your Life Is Calling* (1986); *Cracked Up* (1987 TVM); *Less Than Zero* (1987); *The Boost* (1988); *Clean and Sober* (1988); *Bright Lights, Big City* (1988); *Bird* (1988); *Drugstore Cowboy* (1989); *Jumpin' at the Boneyard* (1991); *Seeds of Tragedy* (1991 TVM); *Rush* (1991); *Naked Lunch* (1991); *Light Sleeper* (1992); *Darkness Before Dawn* (1993 TVM); *Blind Spot* (1993 TVM); *Sweet Nothing* (1995); *Chasing the Dragon* (1996 TVM); *Her Last Chance* (1996 TVM); *Trainspotting* (1996); *Normal Life* (1996); *A Brother's Kiss* (1997); *Playing God* (1997); *Dream with the Fishes* (1997); *Gridlock'd* (1997); *Permanent Midnight* (1998)

Drummond, Bulldog

Although not a detective by trade, Captain Hugh "Bulldog" Drummond was always more than willing to crack a mystery, particularly if a young attractive woman was involved. The novels (and a play) were written by H.C. (Sapper) McNeile in the 1920s. Carlyle Blackwell and Jack Buchanan portrayed Drummond in the first screen adaptations in 1922 and 1925, respectively. But the ideal Drummond proved to be Ronald Colman, who played the gentleman detective in 1929's *Bulldog Drummond* (adapted from the play) and 1934's *Bulldog Drummond Strikes Back*. The impeccable Colman brought flair and a sense of fun to the part, and was ably assisted by Claud Allister or Charles Butterworth as Drummond's chum Algy. Other notable actors (e.g., Ray Milland and Ralph Richardson) played Drummond on their way to stardom, but an official series did not get underway until 1937. During the next three years, American John Howard made seven fast-moving, but undistinguished series entries with Reginald Denny as Algy and E. E. Clive as his butler. The first three Howard films also featured John Barrymore, whose career was floundering, as a Scotland Yard inspector who specialized in disguises. The Howard series ended with Hugh's marriage to his longtime fiancée Phyllis in *Bulldog Drummond's Bride*. Still, Drummond showed up as a bachelor eight years later in pictures starring Ron Randell and Tom Conway (both detective movie veterans). Walter Pidgeon played a middle-aged Drummond with a prized pig in 1951's *Calling Bulldog Drummond*. And in 1967, dashing Richard Johnson updated the character in the Bondian adventure *Deadlier Than the Male*. Johnson's Drummond bore little resemblance to McNeile's original but the movie did well enough to warrant a 1971 sequel *Some Girls Do*. It performed poorly at the box-office and killed off the series. However, *Bullshot*, an unexpected British spoof, surfaced in 1982. Its hero, Captain Hugh "Bullshot" Crummond, was played by Alan Shearman, who co-adapted his own stage play.

Bulldog Drummond (1929) (Ronald Colman); *Temple Tower* (1930) (Kenneth McKenna); *Bulldog Drummond Strikes Back* (1934) (Colman); *The Return of Bulldog Drummond* (1934) (Ralph Richardson); *Bulldog Jack* (aka *Alias Bulldog Drummond*) (1935) (Atholl Fleming); *Bulldog Drummond at Bay* (1937) (John Lodge); *Bulldog Drummond Escapes* (1937) (Ray Milland); *Bulldog Drummond Comes Back* (1937) (John Howard); *Bulldog Drummond's Revenge* (1937) (Howard); *Arrest Bulldog Drummond* (1938) (Howard); *Bulldog Drummond in Africa* (1938) (Howard); *Bulldog Drummond's Peril* (1938) (Howard); *Bulldog Drummond's Bride* (1939) (Howard); *Bulldog Drummond's Secret Police* (1939) (Howard); *Bulldog Drummond Strikes Back* (1947) (Ron Randell); *Bulldog Drummond at Bay* (1947) (Randell); *The Challenge* (1948) (Tom Conway); *Thirteen Lead Solders* (1948) (Conway); *Calling Bulldog Drummond* (1951) (Walter Pidgeon); *Deadlier Than the Male* (1967) (Richard Johnson); *Some Girls Do* (1971) (Johnson); *Bullshot* (1982) (Alan Shearman)

Dupree, Paula (The Ape Woman)

After the Wolf Man's debut in 1941, Universal had gone two years without introducing a new addition to its gallery of monsters which included Dracula, the Frankenstein Monster and the Invisible Man (all q.v.). Thus, the studio was anxious to come up with a creature of equal popularity. Perhaps inspired by the success of Val Lewton's *The Cat People* (1942), Universal opted for a female monster — an ape woman. So, in 1943's *Captive Wild Woman*, that formidable mad scientist John Carradine employed gland transplants to change Cheela the orangutan into sultry Paula Dupree (Acquanetta). The operation was quite a success until

Paula became jealous when Milburn Stone (Doc on *Gunsmoke*) failed to return her affections. That's when she turned into a murderous half-ape/half-woman (again, the plotline owes much to *Cat People* and even the earlier *Island of Lost Souls*). Paula gets gunned down during a circus stampede, but she nevertheless appeared in two sequels, played by Acquanetta again in *Jungle Woman* (1944) and by Vicky Lane in *Jungle Captive* (1945). Neither matched the tone of the original, one of Edward Dmytryk's last B-films before he made his mark with 1944's *Murder, My Sweet*. Sadly, Universal never paired Paula Dupree with the Wolf Man — they would have made an interesting couple. See also **Apes and Monkeys; Humanimals**.

Captive Wild Woman (1943); *Jungle Woman* (1944); *Jungle Captive* (1945)

Durango Kid

Charles Startlett portrayed this mysterious masked rider in a long-running "B" Western series for Columbia. Often described as a Robin Hood of the West, the Durango Kid used his guns more often than his guitar — thus distinguishing himself from his contemporaries, singing cowboys like Gene Autry, Roy Rogers, and Tex Ritter. Prior to acting, Startlett played football at Dartmouth, where he appeared as an extra in the 1926 Richard Dix film *The Quarterback*. The Durango Kid series ended when Startlett retired in 1953.

The Durango Kid (1940); *Return of the Durango Kid* (1945); *Both Barrels Blazing* (1945); *Rustlers of the Badlands* (1945); *Blazing the Western Trail* (1945); *Outlaws of the Rockies* (1945); *Lawless Empire* (1945); *Frontier Gun Law* (1946); *Roaring Rangers* (1946); *Gunning for Vengeance* (1946); *Galloping Thunder* (1946); *Two-Fisted Stranger* (1946); *The Desert Horseman* (1946); *Heading West* (1946); *Landrush* (1946); *Terror Trail* (1946); *The Fighting Frontiersman* (1946); *South of the Chisholm Trail* (1947); *The Lone Hand Texan* (1947); *West of Dodge City* (1947); *Law of the Canyon* (1947); *Prairie Raiders* (1947); *The Stranger from Ponca City* (1947); *Riders of the Lone Star* (1947); *Buckaroo from Powder River* (1947); *Last Days of Boot Hill* (1947); *Six Gun Law* (1948); *Phantom Valley* (1948); *West of Sonora* (1948); *Whirlwind Raiders* (1948); *Blazing Across the Pecos* (1948); *Trail to Laredo* (1948); *El Dorado Pass* (1948); *Quick on the Trigger* (1948); *Challenge of the Range* (1949); *Laramie* (1949); *The Blazing Trail* (1949); *South of Death Valley* (1949); *Bandits of Eldorado* (1949); *Desert Vigilante* (1949); *Horsemen of the Sierras* (1949); *Renegades of the Sage* (1949); *Trail of the Rustlers* (1950); *Outcast of Black Mesa* (1950); *Texas Dynamo* (1950); *Streets of Ghost Town* (1950); *Across the Badlands* (1950); *Raiders of Tomahawk Creek* (1950); *Lightning Guns* (1950); *Frontier Outpost* (1950); *Prairie Roundup* (1951); *Ridin' the Outlaw Trail* (1951); *Fort Savage Raiders* (1951); *Snake River Desperadoes* (1951); *Bonanza Town* (1951); *Cyclone Fury* (1951); *The Kid from Amarillo* (1951); *Pecos River* (1951); *Smoky Canyon* (1952); *The Hawk of Wild River* (1952); *Laramie Mountains* (1952); *The Rough Tough West* (1952); *Junction City* (1952); *The Kid from Broken Gun* (1952)

Earthquakes

The climactic crumble experienced by Spencer Tracy and Clark Gable in 1936's *San Francisco* ranks highest on the cinematic scale for impact. However, the California quake in 1974's all-star *Earthquake* was significantly louder, since it was accompanied by a rumbling sound system dubbed "Sensurround." The most stunning footage probably belongs the 1990 TV movie *After the Shock*, since it includes actual news film from the 1989 San Francisco–Oakland earthquake. Aerial photographers Jackie Cooper and Cleavon Little could not convince townsfolk that an earthquake was on the way in 1974's *The Day the Earth Moved*. Dana Andrews could not figure out how to stop the monstrous quake he initiated with missile tests in *Crack in the World* (1965). And scientists could not figure out what to do with the giant insect released by an Arctic earthquake in *The Deadly Mantis* (1957). Fortunately, Superman knew how to stop an earthquake from dropping California into the Pacific and did so quite effectively in 1978's *Superman*. See also **Disaster Movies**.

San Francisco (1936); *The Sisters* (1938); *The Rains Came* (1939); *Flame of the Barbary Coast* (1945); *Green Dolphin Street* (1947); *The Rains of Ranchipur* (1955); *The Deadly Mantis* (1957); *In Search of the Castaways* (1962); *The Night the World Exploded* (1964); *Crack in the World* (1965); *Short Walk to Daylight* (1972 TVM); *The Neptune Factor* (1973); *Earthquake* (1974); *The Day the Earth Moved* (1974 TVM); *Bug* (1975); *Superman* (1978); *Prisoners of the Lost Universe* (1983 TVM); *After the Shock* (1990 TVM); *The Big One: The Los Angeles Earthquake* (1990 TVM); *Life on the Edge* (1992); *Miracle on I-880* (1993 TVM); *Savage* (1996); *Aftershock: Earthquake in New York* (1999 TVM)

Earth's Core

Science fiction filmmakers have tended to ignore the fact that the earth's core actually consists of molten lava. In 1951's *Unknown World*, a group of scientists used a submarine-tank (called a cyclotram) to burrow their way 1,600 miles beneath the earth's surface. Their goal was to find a safe haven from atomic bomb warfare, but instead they found a world where the human race could not reproduce. On their *Journey to the Center of the Earth* (1959), James Mason and friends uncovered a forest of mushrooms, a crystal cavern, a salt vortex, prehistoric monsters, an underground sea, and a lost city. It was a marvelous showcase for the Jules Verne story, especially compared to the cut-rate 1978 Spanish version *Where Time Began*. Peter Cushing played another scientist with a drilling machine in 1976's *At the Earth's Core*, adapted from an Edgar Rice Burroughs fantasy. *Battle Beneath the Earth* (1967) did not take place at the earth's core, but it was nevertheless set far below the surface. Its imaginative premise concerned a Chinese plot to burrow tunnels from Hawaii to underneath the continental U.S. for the purpose of planting atomic bombs. *The Mole People* (1956) also featured extensive underground footage, but did not involve the earth's core. Dana Andrews set off an atomic bomb near the earth's core, causing *Crack in the World* (1965). *The Bunker Palace Hotel* (1989) was a concrete and marble political hideaway located at the core. See also **Tunnels**.

Unknown World (1951); *Journey to the Center of the Earth* (1959); *Adventure at the Center of the Earth* (1964); *Crack in the World* (1965); *Battle Beneath the Earth* (1967); *At the Earth's Core* (1976); *Where Time Began* (aka *Trip to the Centre of the Earth*) (1978); *Bunker Palace Hotel* (1989); *Journey to the Center of the Earth* (1993 TVM); *Journey to the Center of the Earth* (1999 TVM)

East Side Kids *see* The Bowery Boys

Elephants

Elephants have been steadily employed bit players, having stampeded through dozens of jungle pictures and pranced around numerous three-ring circuses. Starring roles have been relatively scarce, but almost always memorable. Elephants sporting tutus participated in an animated ballet in the "Dance of the Hours" segment in Disney's *Fantasia* (1940). The following year, Disney introduced the world's first flying elephant in the children's classic *Dumbo*. Bill Murray inherited an elephant and took it on an interesting road trip in *Larger Than Life* (1996). In his only starring role without Stan Laurel, Oliver Hardy played a doctor who treated—and then couldn't get rid of—a chummy elephant in *Zenobia* (1939). Two elephants appeared in the 1942 Lupe Velez vehicle *Mexican Spitfire's Elephant* (see also **Mexican Spitfire**). The first was a toy elephant stuffed with valuable jewels, while the second was a live pink one with green polka dots. Unfortunately, the movie was filmed in black and white. The Italian comedy *Hello, Elephant* (1952) was about a schoolteacher who receives an elephant as a gift from an Indian prince. Few viewers found it funny, although the film's alternate title—*Pardon My Trunk*—still has its admirers. Sabu, who played the Indian prince, starred 15 years earlier as the *Elephant Boy*. Other children-and-elephant movies include *The Bashful Elephant*, *Taffy and the Jungle Hunter*, and *Maya* with Jay ("Dennis the Menace") North. On the serious side, Trevor Howard embarked on a crusade to save African elephants from greedy ivory hunters in John Huston's *The Roots of Heaven* (1958). A smashing elephant stampede played a critical part in reuniting estranged couple Peter Finch and Elizabeth Taylor in 1954's *Elephant Walk*. Burt Reynolds and Sally Field transported a pregnant elephant cross-country in the feeble 1980 comedy *Smokey and the Bandit II*. Jean de Brunhoff's beloved children's character Babar, the King of the Elephants, made his big-screen debut in animated form in 1989's *Babar: The Movie*.

Chang (1927); *Elephant Boy* (1937); *Zenobia* (1939); *Fantasia* (1940); *Dumbo* (1941); *Mexican Spitfire's Elephant* (1942); *Elephant Stampede* (aka *Bomba and the Elephant Stampede*) (1951); *Hello, Elephant* (aka *Pardon My Trunk*) (1952); *Elephant Walk* (1954); *Jupiter's Darling* (1955); *The Roots of Heaven* (1958); *Elephant Gun* (1959); *Hannibal* (1960); *The Bashful Elephant* (1962); *Billy Rose's Jumbo* (aka *Jumbo*) (1962); *Taffy and the Jungle Hunter* (1965); *Maya* (1966); *Hannibal Brooks* (1969); *An Elephant Called Slowly* (1970); *The African Elephant* (aka *King of the Elephants*) (1972); *Journey Back to Oz* (1974); *Smokey and the Bandit II* (1980); *Babar: The Movie* (1989); *The Last Elephant* (aka *Ivory Hunters*) (1990 TVM); *White Hunter, Black Heart* (1990); *Madhouse* (1990); *Ava's Magical Adventure* (1994); *Operation Dumbo Drop* (aka *The Dumbo Drop*) (1995); *The Great Elephant Escape* (1995); *Jumanji* (1995); *Larger Than Life* (1996); *George of the Jungle* (1997)

Elevators (or Lifts)

"Take the stairs! Take the stairs! For God's sake, take the stairs!" proclaimed the ad line to 1984's *The Lift*. In general, that's advice that should be heeded by most film characters. Angie Dickinson played a housewife that was brutally murdered in an elevator in Brian De Palma's *Dressed to Kill* (1980). In another psychological thriller, the inferior *Scissors* (1991), Sharon Stone survived an elevator attack. The killer in *The List of Adrian Messenger* (1963) successfully booby trapped an elevator before the opening credits even rolled. In *The Lift*, an elevator with a mind of its own (well, courtesy of an experimental computer chip), bumped off apartment dwellers in imaginative, gory ways. Even Steve Martin's wacky comedy *The Man with Two Brains* (1983) featured a mysterious villain known as the Elevator Killer. Malfunctioning elevators have stranded their passengers between floors in films such as Ingmar Bergman's *Secrets of Women* (1952), *The Elevator* (1974), *Out of Order* (1984), and *Downtime* (1997). Olivia de Havilland played a wealthy invalid trapped in her home elevator and threatened by psychotic teens in *Lady in a Cage* (1964). Another psycho, played by Dennis Hopper, threatened to blow up passengers stuck in a high-rise elevator at the beginning of *Speed* (1994). Michael Rennie was the only passenger that plunged to his death aboard a malfunctioning elevator in *Hotel* (1967). Rennie fared far better as the alien Klaatu in *The Day the Earth Stood Still* (1951). When an elevator abruptly stops between floors, he explains to a frightened Patricia Neal why he has "neutralized" the Earth's electricity. In more fantastical films, elevators have been used to travel between planets (*Dream One*), travel through time (*Time at the Top*), and fly through the air (the "Wonkavator" in *Willy Wonka and the Chocolate Factory*). Many film characters, such as Bruce Willis' police detective in *Die Hard* (1988), have used elevator shafts as shortcuts in large buildings. Johnny Depp spent a lot of time traveling in glass elevators in *Nick of Time* (1995) and Sean Connery as James Bond looked very stylish standing atop an exterior, moving elevator in *Diamonds Are Forever* (1970). A woman had a child resulting from an elevator encounter in *Between Heaven and Earth* (1992), while a nude woman unexpectedly exited from a lift in Allen Funt's *What Do You Say to a Naked Lady?* (1970). Elevator operators have been relegated to supporting roles in most films, although they played significant roles in *Jimmy Boy* (1935), *Don't Bother to Knock* (1952), *Confessions of Felix Krull* (1957), and *Living Out Loud* (1998). See also **Apartments**; **Hotels**; **Stairs**.

Jimmy Boy (1935); *The Day the Earth Stood Still* (1951); *Secrets of Women* (aka *Waiting Women*) (1952); *Don't Bother to Knock* (1952); *Confessions of Felix Krull* (1957); *The List of Adrian Messenger* (1963); *Lady in a Cage* (1964); *Hotel* (1967); *What Do You Say to a Naked Lady?* (1970); *Willy Wonka and the Chocolate Factory* (1971); *The Elevator* (1974 TVM); *Deep Red* (aka *Profondo Rosso*; *Dripping Deep Red*) (1975); *Dressed to Kill* (1980); *The Man with Two Brains* (1983); *Dream One* (aka *Nemo*) (1984); *The Lift* (1984); *Out of Order* (aka *Abwärts*) (1984); *Die Hard* (1988); *Scissors* (1991); *Between Heaven and Earth* (1992); *Speed* (1994); *Downtime* (1997); *Living Out Loud* (1998); *Time at the Top* (1999)

Emmanuelle

One of the few softcore features to attract a mainstream audience, 1974's French import *Emmanuelle* cast Sylvia Kristel as the bored wife of an embassy official stationed in Thailand. The young bride is initially shocked when her free-thinking husband encourages her to explore her sexuality with other men and women. But she quickly proves willing to try anything once. This softfocus adaptation of Emmanuelle Arsan's scandalous 1957 novel lacked sizzle — its success probably a product of its lush look and clever marketing campaign ("X was never like this," proclaimed the ad). Kristel reprised the lead role in *Emmanuelle — The Joys of a Woman* and *Goodbye Emmanuelle*. She appears briefly in 1984's *Emmanuelle 4* before her character undergoes plastic surgery and emerges with a different face and body (Mia Nygren). Centerfold Monique Gabrielle, a veteran of the *Deathstalker* (q.v.) series, starred in 1987's *Emmanuelle 5*, but then gave way to Nathalie Uher in the following year's *Emmanuelle 6*. These six films comprise the "official" *Emmanuelle* series, but there have been many similarly-titled imitations. In fact, Laura Gemser starred in so many rip-offs that these films could be treated as another series. The Gemser titles include: *Emmanuelle the Queen* (1975), *Emmanuelle in the Country* (1978), *Emmanuelle's Daughter* (1979), and many others. The British *Carry On* (q.v.) gang spoofed the *Emmanuelle* pictures with 1978's raunchy *Carry On Emmanuelle*.

Emmanuelle (1974); *Emmanuelle — The Joys of a Woman* (1976); *Goodbye Emmanuelle* (1979); *Emmanuelle 4* (1984); *Emmanuelle 5* (1987); *Emmanuelle 6* (1988)

End of the World/Post-Apocalypse

Pessimism sells few movie tickets, thus making the total destruction of the Earth an unpopular film subject. Nevertheless, planet Earth was wiped out by a streaking star in 1951's *When Worlds Collide*, with only a few survivors escaping to a sister planet to continue the human race. An atomic bomb blew the Earth into dust particles in 1970's *Beneath the Planet of the Apes*. Although no one escaped during that film's climax, the crafty sequel, 1971's *Escape from the Planet of the Apes*, revealed that a trio of intelligent apes had hijacked a rocket and avoided the explosion. The world's fate was left up in the air in the final scene of *The Day the Earth Caught Fire* (1962). Two newspapers awaited a final verdict before distribution, one with a headline reading "World Saved: H-bomb Blasts Succeed," the other declaring "World Doomed: H-bomb Blasts Fail." Several films such as *On the Beach* (1959) and *Testament* (1983) have ended with the human race facing ultimate extinction as a result of radioactive fallout. In contrast, the "post-apocalypse" genre consists of films in which a handful of humans have survived a near-catastrophic event and built a new world. Former radio writer Arch Oboler pioneered this type of film with 1951's *Five*, a talky tale of conflict among the last five people on Earth. Seen today, it's hard to gauge the film's impact, but at the time of its release, *Variety* called it "intriguing...but depressing in its assumption." *The World, the Flesh, and the Devil* (1959) added gloss to the same theme, but is chiefly remembered for turning Manhattan into a ghost town. Similar post-apocalypse character dramas include Roger Corman's *The Day the World Ended* (1956), the underrated vampire-plague film *The Last Man on Earth* (1964), and the TV movie *Where Have All the People Gone?* (1974). Later low-budget films such as *A Boy and His Dog* and *The Ultimate Warrior* (both 1975) injected heavy action elements into their post-apocalypse plotlines. These led to the runaway success of 1982's *The Road Warrior* (aka *Mad Max 2*), which resulted in a slew of repetitive action films set in the barren wastelands of the future. More original views of the post-apocalypse are featured in *The War Game* (1967) and *The Bed Sitting Room* (1969). A bleak favorite at antinuke film showings, *The War Game* employs a vivid documentary style to show the devastating aftereffects of an atomic blast on London. On the other hand, *The Bed Sitting Room* makes its point with satire by showing nuclear survivors turning into furniture and pet birds. Many science fiction films have shown the Earth surviving a brush with total apocalypse, although, in a Biblical sense, none can match the close call detailed in 1988's *The Seventh Sign*. See also **Mad Max**.

When Worlds Collide (1951); *Five* (1951); *The Day the World Ended* (1956); *The World, the Flesh, and the Devil* (1959); *On the*

Beach (1959); *The Day the Earth Caught Fire* (1962); *Creation of the Humanoids* (1962); *The Last Man on Earth* (1964); *The End of August at the Hotel Ozone* (aka *The End of the World at the Hotel Ozone*) (1965); *The War Game* (1967); *The Bed Sitting Room* (1969); *Beneath the Planet of the Apes* (1970); *Glen and Randa* (1971); *Doomsday Machine* (1973); *Where Have All the People Gone?* (1974 TVM); *Last Days of Planet Earth* (aka *Catastrophe 1999: The Prophecies of Nostradamus*) (1974); *A Boy and His Dog* (1975); *The Ultimate Warrior* (1975); *Damnation Alley* (1977); *Wizards* (1977); *Mad Max* (1979); *Quintet* (1979); *Virus* (1980); *Testament* (1983); *The Day After* (1983 TVM); *Warlords of the 21st Century* (aka *Battletruck*) (1983); *Warriors of the Wasteland* (1983); *Stryker* (1983); *Threads* (1984 TVM); *The Final Combat* (aka *Le Dernier Combat*) (1984); *Def-Con 4* (1985); *The Quiet Earth* (1985); *Warriors of the Apocalypse* (1985); *Wired to Kill* (1986); *Radioactive Dreams* (1986); *Survivor* (1987); *Steel Dawn* (1987); *Warlords* (1988); *World Gone Wild* (1988); *Badlands 2000* (1988 TVM); *Cherry 2000* (1988); *Miracle Mile* (1989); *Cyborg* (1989); *Hardware* (1990); *The Blood of Heroes* (aka *Salute of the Jugger*) (1990); *The Rapture* (1991); *Dune Warriors* (1991); *Omega Doom* (1997); *Last Night* (1998); *Dogma* (1999); *End of Days* (1999); *On the Beach* (2000 TVM)

Episode Films *see* Anthologies

Ernest

"Know what I mean, Vern?" asked Ernest P. Worrell in hundreds of television commercials in the 1980s. The character with the bulging eyes, gaping mouth, and baseball cap was created by Nashville advertising executive John R. Cherry III for a series of dairy commercials. But much of the character's success belongs to Jim Varney, a rubber-faced television comedian who brought Ernest to life in regional commercials that made the obnoxious know-it-all a household name. Cherry directed and cowrote 1987's *Ernest Goes to Camp*, a juvenile comedy which gave Varney a chance to make Ernest more sympathetic than his commercial incarnation—but just as klutzy. Disney's Touchstone banner picked up the independently-produced film and walked away with a sleeper summer hit. The resulting series featured Ernest helping Santa Claus on Christmas Eve (*Ernest Saves Christmas*), going to prison in place of an evil lookalike (q.v.) (*Ernest Goes to Jail*), battling a pesky troll on Halloween night (*Ernest Scared Stupid*), and getting involved in other lowbrow hijinks.

Ernest Goes to Camp (1987); *Ernest Saves Christmas* (1988); *Ernest Goes to Jail* (1990); *Ernest Scared Stupid* (1991); *Ernest Rides Again* (1993); *Ernest Goes to School* (1994); *Slam Dunk Ernest* (1995); *Ernest Goes to Africa* (1997); *Ernest in the Army* (1998); *Ernest the Pirate* (1999)

Eternal Youth/Rejuvenation

The search for eternal youth has sparked movie explorations into fantastic lands as well as medically-questionable scientific experiments. In 1937's *Lost Horizon*, Ronald Colman and his fellow plane crash survivors found Shangri-La, James Hilton's utopia of eternal youth, quite by accident. H. Rider Haggard's oft-filmed *She* concerned an ageless queen obsessed with exposing her reincarnated lover to the Flame of Eternal Life. Unfortunately, when she re-entered the flame with him, her age caught up with her in a hurry. Oscar Wilde's aristocratic protagonist Dorian Gray sold his soul so that his portrait could age—while he retained his youth—in *The Picture of Dorian Gray* (1945). In the offbeat *Angel*

on the Amazon (1948), an elderly woman took on the appearance of a 25-year-old after a frightening encounter with a panther. Industrious individuals have sought everlasting youth through medical means in *The Man in Half-Moon Street* (1944), its remake *The Man Who Could Cheat Death* (1959), *The Leech Woman* (1960), *The Wasp Woman* (1960), and *The Night Strangler* (1972). Alas, the rejuvenation methods employed in these films required their users to obtain fluids, glands, or body parts from living humans. Ingrid Pitt experienced a similar problem as *Countess Dracula* (1972), who retained her youth by bathing in the blood of virgins. This gruesome tale was actually based on the life of murderess Elisabeth Bathory. On a lighter note, children flew to Never-Never Land to avoid adulthood in *Peter Pan* (1953), while a group of old-timers went to another planet to elude death in *Cocoon* (1985). Ponce de Leon never found the Fountain of Youth, but Tarzan did in 1949's *Tarzan's Magic Fountain*. It rejuvenated Cheetah into a baby chimp. Another chimpanzee caused mix-ups in *Monkey Business* (1952) when he poured Cary Grant's experimental rejuvenation formula into a water cooler. Nathaniel Hawthorne's classic Fountain of Youth short story "Dr. Heideggar's Experiment" reached the screen in 1963 as a segment of *Twice Told Tales*.

The Elixir of Life (1911); *She* (1935); *Lost Horizon* (1937); *The Corpse Vanishes* (1942); *The Man in Half-Moon Street* (1944); *The Picture of Dorian Gray* (1945); *Angel on the Amazon* (aka *Drums Along the Amazon*) (1948); *Tarzan's Magic Fountain* (1949); *Hurricane Island* (1951); *Monkey Business* (1952); *Peter Pan* (1953); *Jungle Moon Men* (1955); *The Man Who Could Cheat Death* (1959); *The Wasp Woman* (1960); *The Leech Woman* (1960); *Atom Age Vampire* (1961); *Twice Told Tales* (1963); *The Fat Spy* (1965); *She* (1965); *The Immortal* (1969 TVM); *Satanik* (1969); *Flesh Feast* (1970); *The Night Strangler* (1972 TVM); *Baron Blood* (aka *The Torture Chamber of Baron Blood*) (1972); *Countess Dracula* (1972); *Lost Horizon* (1973); *The Thirsty Dead* (1975); *Tuck Everlasting* (1980); *Cocoon* (1985); *Evil Spawn* (1987); *The Rejuvenator* (aka *Rejuvenatrix*) (1988); *Cocoon: The Return* (1988); *Metamorphosis* (1989); *The Spring* (1990); *Hook* (1991); *Death Becomes Her* (1992); *Orlando* (1992); *Jonny's Golden Quest* (1993 TVM); *Star Trek: Insurrection* (1998); *Code Name: Phoenix* (2000 TVM)

The Evil Dead Series

Sam Raimi was a 19-year-old amateur filmmaker when he and two friends decided to enter the movie industry by making a low-budget horror picture in Michigan. In 1979, they shot *Within the Woods*, a Super 8mm chiller which thrust some stupid teens into an isolated cabin where they unleash vengeful demons. Raimi and company, armed with this sample product, convinced doctors and lawyers to invest $90,000 in an expanded version of the Super 8mm movie. The resulting feature film, 1983's *The Evil Dead*, became an instant drive-in classic. It also earned a cult reputation in Great Britain, where copies of the videotape were seized and destroyed (although it played without censorship problems at the London Film Festival). Plotwise, *The Evil Dead* offers a highly derivative tale in which the aforementioned teens discover the Book of Dead and then play an audio tape containing incantations which summon the demons. The lone survivor, Ash (Bruce Campbell), becomes the hero by default. Raimi's stylish direction and a surprisingly humorous undertone elevated *The Evil Dead* from other low-budget horror pictures. However, the 1987 sequel

Evil Dead 2 proved to be a superior outing, a delirious blend of suspense and Three Stooges slapstick. It sends Ash into the woods again — where he naturally encounters more demons. When his hand becomes possessed (an absurdly funny scene), he severs it and connects a chainsaw (q.v.) to his arm. He winds up in a time warp at the film's climax and lands in the medieval ages. *Army of Darkness* (1993) picks up with Ash's capture by a band of bewildered knights. The plot evolves into a campy, fairly entertaining mixture of *A Connecticut Yankee in King Arthur's Court* and *Night of the Living Dead* (q.v.). The original ending, shown at the 1992 Sitges Film Festival, had our hero warp into the 21st century where he finds the planet in ruins. However, for its U.S. release, the ending was re-shot with Ash working in a hardware store — where he has another showdown with the Evil Dead! See also **Chainsaws**; **Time Travel**.

The Evil Dead (1983); *Evil Dead 2: Dead by Dawn* (aka *Evil Dead 2*) (1987); *Army of Darkness* (aka *Army of Darkness: Evil Dead 3*) (1993)

The Exorcist Series

Although divergent in their approach to horror, *Rosemary's Baby* and *The Exorcist* reign jointly as the most important horror films of the 1960s and 1970s. *The Exorcist* drew huge audiences to a well-mounted exercise in intense, unsubtle, and sometimes purely visual horror. It spawned countless imitations, with the most successful being the 1974 rip-off *Beyond the Door* and the chilling 1976 box-office hit *The Omen* (q.v.). Adapted by William Peter Blatty from his best seller, *The Exorcist* pits two priests — one who questions his faith — against the Devil in an all-out war over a young girl's soul. It's a straightforward story (a point overlooked by its sequels) and benefits from a fine cast: Max Von Sydow as the exorcist Father Merrin, playwright Jason Miller as his guilt-suffering assistant Father Karras, Linda Blair as 12-year-old Regan, and Mercedes McCambridge as the voice of the Devil within Regan. However, the true stars are William Friedkin's gripping direction and the special makeup effects by Dick Smith and Rick Baker. Blatty won an Oscar for his screenplay. Naturally, *The Exorcist* begot a sequel, 1977's *Exorcist II: The Heretic*, which unexpectedly crashed at the box-office — dead on arrival. It has acquired an undeserved reputation as a laughable turkey. Although certainly not a good film, it tries to maneuver the story into a different interesting direction. The plot picks up four years after the original exorcism, with the "cured" Regan (Blair) still undergoing psychiatric treatment. Regan's newly-acquired healing powers bring her to the attention of Father Lamont (Richard Burton), a priest investigating Father Merrin's death. Lamont discovers that the "Locust God" (not the Devil) still wants control of the girl. In the confusing climax, Regan splits into two people and a horde of locusts attack Lamont and her. They survive in the original ending, but, in a hastily re-shot alternate ending, Father Lamont dies. Most available prints include director John Boorman's first, more optimistic, ending. The "series" probably would have died if author Blatty had not written a fairly-successful sequel novel. He wrote the screenplay and directed 1990's *Exorcist III*, an interesting, but overly complex, possession tale. George C. Scott stars as Kinderman, a wily detective investigating a series of murders bearing the trademark of a killer executed 15 years earlier at the exact same time in which Father Karras (Miller again)

died. Despite respectable box-office earnings, *Exorcist III* apparently closed the door on additional series entries. See also **The Devil**.

The Exorcist (1973); *Exorcist II: The Heretic* (1977); *Exorcist III* (aka *Exorcist III: Legion*) (1990)

Eye of the Eagle Series

The three *Eye of the Eagle* films contain few similarities: a Vietnam (q.v.) setting, low budgets, and a common supporting actor in two of the three entries. The 1987 original involves a female newshound (Cec Verrell) who hooks up with a hunky soldier (Bret Clark) to investigate stories about a vigilante-like "lost command" made up of POWs and MIAs. It's a far more interesting plot than the revenge tale featured in *Eye of the Eagle II: Inside the Enemy*. William Field stars as the only soldier to survive an attack when his unit's commanding officer deserts his troops. Field later learns that the same officer is a black marketeer, drug pusher, and pimp — so naturally Field plots his vengeance. In both the first and second films, Mike Monty has a supporting role as Colonel Stark. The third film went for a big name star, but wound up with Steve Kanaly (Ray on TV's long-running *Dallas*). See also **Vietnam**.

Eye of the Eagle (1987); *Eye of the Eagle II: Inside the Enemy* (aka *Killed in Action; K.I.A.*) (1989); *Eye of the Eagle 3* (aka *Last Stand at Lang Mei*) (1992)

Fairs and Carnivals

Fairs on film have evoked a nostalgic atmosphere of Americana, as typified by the three film versions of *State Fair*. Will Rogers starred in the original 1933 film about a family's adventures at the Iowa State Fair, but the 1945 version, boasting Rodgers and Hammerstein's only film score, remains the best remembered. The turn-of-the-century musical *Meet Me in St. Louis* (1944) ended with the opening of the 1903 World's Fair and also provided Judy Garland with one of her biggest hits: "Have Yourself a Merry Little Christmas." Elvis Presley attended the Seattle World's Fair in 1963's *It Happened at the World's Fair*. A belly dancer caused quite a sensation at the 1890's Chicago Fair in *Little Egypt* (1951). Jean Simmons' brother mysteriously disappeared without a trace at the 1889 Paris Exposition in the intriguing mystery *So Long at the Fair* (1950). And *The World of Tomorrow* (1984) provided a retrospective look at the 1939 New York World's Fair. Fairs on a smaller scale provided the settings for comedy in *Ma and Pa Kettle at the Fair* (1952) and romance in the Dan Dailey musical *Meet Me at the Fair* (1953). In contrast to frivolous fairs, carnival films have tended to offer a darker view of life. Spencer Tracy played a ruthless carnival promoter who has visions of Hell in the 1935 curio *Dante's Inferno*. Tyrone Power, in a change-of-pace role, was a heartless carny hustler who hits the big time in the spiritualism racket in *Nightmare Alley* (1947). He gets his comeuppance, however, and eventually winds up as a sideshow freak. Linda Lawson played a sideshow mermaid (q.v.) who actually believed herself to be a descendant of the murderous Sea People in Curtis Harrington's minor cult favorite *Night Tide* (1961). A spooky carnival run by the mysterious Mr. Dark invaded a quiet, Midwestern town in the underrated 1983 adaptation of Ray Bradbury's chilling *Something Wicked This Way Comes*. Stupid teenagers got themselves killed one by one after hiding out in a funhouse filled with wackos in Tobe Hooper's dreary 1981 slasher picture *The Funhouse*. Less human monsters seem to prefer amusement parks over carnivals. *The Beast from 20,000 Fathoms* (1953) was toying with the Coney Island Cyclone rollercoaster when Lee Van Cleef shot him up with radioactive isotope. Godzilla (q.v.) battled his archnemesis Ghidrah (q.v.), along with several other creatures, in a children's amusement park in *Godzilla on Monster Island* (1971), one of Toho's sillier pictures. The amusement park in *Gorilla at Large* (1954) featured a murderous ape who turned out to be Anne Bancroft (!) in a gorilla suit. George Segal tracked a madman specializing in sabotaging rollercoasters throughout the nation in 1977's *Rollercoaster*. It was filmed in real amusement parks (e.g., King's Dominion in Virginia) and presented in "Sensurround," a sound system which simulated rumbling vibrations during key scenes. Alfred Hitchcock's 1951 classic *Strangers on a Train* featured several amusement park scenes, including the thrilling merry-go-round climax. Likewise, the famous hall of mirrors showdown in Orson Welles' *Lady from Shanghai* took place in an amusement park crazy house. The cinema's most famous amusement park is Coney Island, which provided the setting for *Sinner's Holiday* (1930), *Coney Island* (1943), its remake *Wabash Avenue* (1950), *Little Fugitive* (1953) and the aforementioned *Beast from 20,000 Fathoms* (1953). *The Third Man* featured a tense conversation between Joseph Cotten and Orson Welles atop a ferris wheel, while *Luv* opted for an awkward ferris wheel love scene. The rollercoaster rumbles in *Rollercoaster* may have been deafening, but the most stomach-churning rollercoaster footage still belongs to 1952's *This Is Cinerama* (see **Cinerama**), which projected its speeding dives and turns on a 165-degree curved movie screen. See also **Circuses**.

Sinner's Holiday (1930); *The Half Naked Truth* (1932); *Take a Chance* (1933); *State Fair* (1933); *Whirlpool* (1934); *Dante's Inferno* (1935); *Strike Me Pink* (1936); *Road Show* (1941); *Coney Island* (1943); *Meet Me in St. Louis* (1944); *State Fair* (aka *It Happened One Summer*) (1945); *Nightmare Alley* (1947); *Lady from Shanghai* (1948); *Are You with It?* (1948); *The Third Man* (1949); *Wabash Avenue* (1950); *So Long at the Fair* (1950); *Texas Carnival* (1951); *Strangers on a Train* (1951); *Little Egypt* (1951); *Ma and Pa Kettle at the Fair* (1952); *Lili* (1953); *Meet Me at the Fair* (1953); *The Beast from 20,000 Fathoms* (1953); *Little Fugitive* (1953); *Gorilla at Large* (1954); *The Glass Tomb* (aka *The Glass Cage*) (1955); *Dance with Me, Henry* (1956); *All at Sea* (1958); *Night Tide* (1961); *State Fair* (1962); *It Happened at the World's Fair* (1963); *Roustabout* (1964); *Luv* (1967); *She Freak* (aka *Alley of Nightmares*) (1967); *Godzilla on Monster Island* (aka *Godzilla vs. Gigan*; *Gojira tai Gaigan*) (1971); *Rollercoaster* (1977); *Kiss Meets the Phantom of the Park* (1978 TVM); *Carny* (1980); *The Funhouse* (1981); *Something Wicked This Way Comes* (1983); *The World of Tomorrow* (1984); *Slayground* (1984); *Breaking All the Rules* (1985); *Funland* (1986); *Ghoulies II* (1987); *Two-Moon Junction* (1988); *Kansas* (1989); *Howling VI: The Freaks* (1991); *Wild Hearts Can't Be Broken* (1991); *Beverly Hills Cop III* (1994); *Mighty Joe Young* (1998)

Faith Healers

Evangelists, ex-monks, and "dead" people have possessed — or thought they did — the ability to heal people with a touch of the hand. In *Leap of Faith* (1992), Steve Martin played a con man/evangelist who duped townspeople into believing he could cure the sick and crippled through faith. In the end, though, he winds up questioning himself when he apparently heals a crippled boy for real. Burt Lancaster's con man/evangelist had no such doubts in *Elmer Gantry* (1960), but his partner (played by Jean Simmons) came to believe that she possessed healing powers. In *Touch* (1997), adapted from an Elmore Leonard novel, a con man tries to exploit a former Franciscan monk who restores a woman's eyesight. Along similar lines, a gangster on the lam discovers a faith healer that can cure the crippled in both versions of *The Miracle Man* (1919 and 1932). Interestingly, the two most provocative films about faith healers were released in 1980. *Harlequin* starred Robert Powell as a mysterious modern-day Rasputin who heals the child of a powerful politician. In *Resurrection*, Ellen Burstyn received a Best Actress Oscar nomination for her portrayal of a woman who "returns" from a near-death experience with healing powers. The film focuses on her attempts to understand her newfound gift. Dana Delany played the same role in a 1999 TV movie remake. Young Bernadette Soubirous (Jennifer Jones) could not cure people in *The Song of Bernadette* (1943), but she did find the spring that produced the healing holy water. Madeleine Potter played the daughter of a faith healer in *The Bostonians* (1984), although her father's occupation had little to do with the love triangle involving Potter, Vanessa Redgrave, and Christopher Reeve. See also **Angels**; **Jesus**.

The Miracle Man (1919); *The Miracle Man* (1932); *Elmer Gantry* (1960); *Harlequin* (aka *Dark Forces*) (1980); *Resurrection* (1980); *The Bostonians* (1984); *Leap of Faith* (1992); *Touch* (1997); *Resurrection* (1999 TVM); *The Green Mile* (1999); *A Touch of Hope* (1999 TVM)

The Falcon

Rarely has a film series been spawned from so little and turned out so different. The Falcon's only appearance in literature was Michael Arlen's "Gay Falcon," a short story about Gay Lawrence, a hardboiled detective ("Lady, be calm…I don't want to get tough with you"). Yet, by the time the Falcon hit the screen in 1941 in the guise of George Sanders, he had become a charming, debonair rascal — very similar to the Saint (q.v.). The transformation was a practical one, since Sanders had just completed a series of five successful Saint features (ironically, RKO made both the Saint and Falcon series). Sometimes, it was difficult to tell if Sanders was supposed to be the Saint or the Falcon — in 1941, he made one of each (*The Saint in Palm Springs* and *The Gay Falcon*). Saint creator Leslie Charteris also took note of the Falcon/Saint similarities and threatened RKO with a lawsuit. But the series still continued with fairly enjoyable programmers like *The Falcon Takes Over*, which has the distinction of being the first screen version of Raymond Chandler's Philip Marlowe (q.v.) novel *Farewell, My Lovely*. Yet, after his third Falcon film, Sanders decided he'd had enough of the B-movie detective life. RKO was determined to save a profitable series, though, and chose to kill off Sanders' character and replace him with his brother. Such was the plot of 1942's *The Falcon's Brother*, in which Tom Conway — who really was Sanders' brother — played the title role. Conway slipped so smoothly into the role that the series never skipped a beat. Despite suave, British good looks and a Colmanesque voice, Conway never made the leap to stardom. Yet, he made a stalwart B-movie hero and his Falcon films were a notch above their competitors, with *The Falcon and the Co-eds* rating as a snappy mystery by any standard. Set in a girls' boarding school by a seaside cliff, it evoked a haunting atmosphere which was neatly balanced by low-key humor (pleasantly provided by three young girls instead of the typical wisecracking female reporter). Conway left the series in 1948 and was replaced by John Calvert in three additional entries. Meanwhile, Conway struggled with alcoholism in the 1950s and died of a liver ailment in 1964. Charles McGraw starred in the 1954 TV series *The Adventures of the Falcon*, which mysteriously changed the Falcon's name to Mike Waring.

The Gay Falcon (1941) (George Sanders); *A Date with the Falcon* (1941) (Sanders); *The Falcon Takes Over* (1942) (Sanders); *The Falcon's Brother* (1942) (George Sanders and Tom Conway); *The Falcon and the Co-eds* (1943) (Conway); *The Falcon in Danger* (1943) (Conway); *The Falcon Strikes Back* (1943) (Conway); *The Falcon in Hollywood* (1944) (Conway); *The Falcon in Mexico* (1944) (Conway); *The Falcon in San Francisco* (1945) (Conway); *The Falcon Out West* (1946) (Conway); *The Falcon's Adventure* (1946) (Conway); *The Falcon's Alibi* (1946) (Conway); *The Devil's Cargo* (1948) (John Calvert); *Appointment with Murder* (1948) (Calvert); *Search for Danger* (1949) (Calvert)

Family of Cops Series

Title tells all in this TV movie trilogy starring Charles Bronson as Inspector Paul Fein, the father of a detective, a patrol officer, a criminal lawyer, and — by the second film — a police academy trainee. Their cases ranged from a love triangle homicide involving one of their own to an encounter with the Russian mob in Milwaukee. Bronson, Sebastian Spence (as son Eddie), and Barbara Williams (as daughter Kate) appeared in all three films. During the same period, Williams also played Robert Urich's love interest, Susan Silverman, in the *Spenser* TV movies (q.v.).

Family of Cops (1995 TVM); *Breach of Faith: Family of Cops II* (1997 TVM); *Family of Cops III* (1999 TVM)

Fantômas

Pierre Souvestre and Marcel Allain created the super criminal Fantômas in 1911 for the French magazine *Arthème Fayard*. The duo wrote 32 novels over a two-year period, with Allain penning several more after Souvestre's death in 1914. Their creation is a master of disguises that runs a criminal organization specializing in chilling crimes, such as substituting sulfuric acid for perfume in a department store. Director Louis Feuillade first brought Fantômas to the screen with five popular serials produced between 1913 and 1914. A feature-length film starring Jean Galland appeared in 1931, but made little impression. The same can be said for two post–World War II efforts — *Fantômas* (1946) and *Fantômas Contre Fantômas* (1949) — although the former film featured Simone Signoret in one of her early roles. Between 1964 and 1966, Andre Hunebelle directed a trilogy of Fantômas films starring Jean Marsais as both the archvillain and Fandor, the journalist trying to help Inspector Juve capture Fantômas. These films featured a lighthearted tone and stylish sets, especially the elaborate volcano hideout in *Fantômas Strikes Back*. Finally, in 1979, Claude Chabrol and Juan Luis Buñuel (son of Luis) made a series of four 90-minute Fantômas TV movies starring Helmut Berger.

THE FEUILLADE SERIALS: *Fantômas* (1913) (René Navarre); *Juve versus Fantômas* (aka *Juve Contre Fantômas*) (1913) (Navarre); *The Murderous Corpse* (aka *Le Mort Qui Tue*) (1913) (Navarre); *Fantômas Contre Fantômas* (1914) (Navarre); *The False Judge* (aka *Le Faux Magistrat*) (1914) (Navarre)

FANTÔMAS FILMS: *Fantômas* (1931) (Jean Galland); *Fantômas* (1946) (Marcel Herrand); *Fantômas Contre Fantômas* (1949) (Maurice Teynac); *Fantômas* (1964) (Jean Marsais); *Fantômas Strikes Back* (aka *Fantômas se Déchaîne*) (1965) (Marsais); *Fantômas Against Scotland Yard* (aka *Fantômas Contre Scotland Yard*) (1966) (Marsais); *L'Echafaud magique* (1979 TVM) (Helmut Berger); *L'Etriente du diable* (1979 TVM) (Berger); *Le Mort Qui Tue* (1979 TVM) (Berger); *Le Tramway Fantôme* (1979 TVM) (Berger)

Fashion Models

Although models have fared better in the movies than centerfolds (q.v.), they still rank among the favorite targets of psychotic killers, leering males, and mutant aliens. Models were stalked by murderers in *Blood and Black Lace*, *Cover Girl Killer*, *She's Dressed to Kill*, *Lies of the Twins*, *Mind Over Murder*, and *Eyes of Laura Mars*. In *Mind Over Murder* (1979), model Deborah Raffin has premonitions about her would-be killer, while *Eyes of Laura Mars* (1978) features Faye Dunaway as a fashion photographer who "sees" through the eyes of a murderer. Plastic surgeon Albert Finney begins his own investigation when his model clients began dying rather suddenly in Michael Crichton's *Looker* (1981). The most tasteless model-killer film must surely be Ray Dennis Steckler's *Hollywood Strangler Meets the Skid Row Slasher* (1979), which was retitled for its video release as — quite aptly — *The Model Killer*. When not being stalked, models often find themselves exploited by men interested only in their outer beauty, as in cheesy drive-in movies such as *The Yum-Yum Girls* (1976) and *Game Show Models* (1977). In 1966's *Blood Beast from Outer Space*, a lecherous alien placed ads in *Bikini Girl* magazine to attract shapely models to populate his dying planet. Fortunately, some models have used their looks to their advantage. Julie Christie won a Best Actress Oscar as a model who becomes a lady of means in 1965's *Darling*. Fred Astaire transforms shy Audrey Hepburn into a glamourous model in 1957's *Funny Face*, and they fall in love along the way. Faye Dunaway, who photographed models in the aforementioned *Eyes of Laura Mars*, played one in the oddly-titled *Puzzle of a Downfall Child* (1970). Finally, Jon-Eric Hexum reversed stereotypical roles in the 1983 TV movie, *The Making of a Male Model*, which co-starred Joan Collins as his mentor and lover. Kurt Russell played a male model, too, in 1980's *Amber Waves*, but it was set in a Midwestern farming town as opposed to the fashion world. See also **Centerfolds**; **Photographers**.

Vogues (1937); *The Powers Girl* (aka *Hello Beautiful*) (1942); *The Girl from Manhattan* (1948); *A Life of Her Own* (1950); *The Model and the Marriage Broker* (1951); *Foxiest Girl in Paris* (1956); *Funny Face* (1957); *Cover Girl Killer* (1959); *Blood and Black Lace* (aka *Sei Donne per L'assassino*; *Fashion House of Death*; *Six Women for the Murderer*) (1964); *Darling* (1965); *Blood Beast from Outer Space*; (aka *The Night Caller*; *The Night Caller from Outer Space*) (1966); *Corruption* (1967); *The Model Shop* (1969); *Puzzle of a Downfall Child* (1970); *Love Hate Love* (1970 TVM); *Two People* (1973); *Cover Girl Models* (aka *The Models*) (1975); *The Yum-Yum Girls* (1976); *Lipstick* (1976); *Cover Girls* (1977 TVM); *The Sentinel* (1977); *Game Show Models* (1977); *Eyes of Laura Mars* (1978); *She's Dressed to Kill* (aka *Someone's Killing the World's Greatest Models*) (1979 TVM); *Mind Over Murder* (1979 TVM); *Hollywood Strangler Meets the Skid Row Slasher* (aka *The Model Killer*) (1979); *For the Love of It* (1980 TVM); *Amber Waves* (1980 TVM); *Looker* (1981); *Tattoo* (1981); *Paper Dolls* (1982 TVM); *Born Beautiful* (1982 TVM); *Exposed* (1983); *The Making of a Male Model* (1983 TVM); *Jungle Warriors* (1984); *Double Deal* (1984); *Covergirl* (1984); *Swim-*

suit (1989 TVM); *Lies of the Twins* (1991 TVM); *Bikini Island* (1991); *Hired to Kill* (1991); *A Perry Mason Mystery: The Case of the Wicked Wives* (1993 TVM); *Hexed* (1993); *The New Age* (1994); *Red* (1994); *French Silk* (1994 TVM); *Ready to Wear* (aka *Pret-a-Porter*) (1994); *Three Colors: Red* (1994); *Model By Day* (1994 TVM); *Private Obsession* (1995); *Unzipped* (1995); *The Truth About Cats and Dogs* (1996); *Gia* (1998 TVM); *Model Behavior* (2000 TVM)

Fassbinder's Women Trilogy

Between 1978 and 1982, director Rainer Werner Fassbinder made three films about women set in post–World War II Germany. Although sometimes referred to as a trilogy, the time period and the fact that each film focuses on a female character is all that connects the movies. In *The Marriage of Maria Braun* (1978), the title character rises from poverty to wealth while enduring separations from her husband. Although its plot sounds likes a Joan Crawford vehicle from the 1940s, the film evokes the atmosphere of a country in transition and its matter-of-fact ending is a shocker. *Lola* (1982) centers on the complex relationships between a prostitute, a corrupt small town businessman, and a naïve building commissioner. The third in the trilogy, *Veronika Voss* (1982) tells the story of a faded film actress addicted to morphine. Although considered essential Fassbinder viewing, it lacks the sterling reputation of *The Marriage of Maria Braun* and *Lola*. Fassbinder died the year that *Veronika Voss* was released; he was 36.

The Marriage of Eva Braun (aka *Die Ehe der Maria Braun*) (1978); *Lola* (1982); *Veronika Voss* (aka *Die Sehnsucht der Veronika Voss*) (1982)

FBI

The Federal Bureau of Investigation (FBI) has figured into the plotlines of dozens of movies. However, there have been relatively few films focusing specifically on the organization and its employees. Prior to the 1970s, filmmakers portrayed the FBI as an all-powerful, incorruptible, crimefighting machine. Some films, such as *I Was a Communist for the FBI* (1951), *Walk East on Beacon* (1952), and *The FBI Story* (1959), were produced in a documentary-like style which gave them an air of noble authenticity. This attitude carried over into television, where Efrem Zimbalist, Jr., played the never-ruffled Inspector Erskine in the popular 1965–74 TV series *The F.B.I.* However, by the late 1970s, films began to reflect a less whitewashed view of the Bureau. Larry Cohen's *The Private Files of J. Edgar Hoover* (1977) offered a very unflattering portrait of the former FBI director. *Johnnie Mae Gibson: FBI* (1986) was a fact-based account of the tribulations experienced by the Bureau's first black female agent. Sam Shepard played an FBI agent who tries to cover up a murder on an Indian reservation in 1992's *Thunderheart* (1992). Interestingly, *Thunderheart* director Michael Apted made a documentary, *Incident at Oglala*, about the event that inspired his fictional film. Other fact-based FBI films include: *Melvin Purvis: G-Man* (1974) and its sequel *The Kansas City Massacre* (1975), *Undercover with the KKK* (1979), and *In the Line of Duty: The FBI Murders* (1988). The TV movie *Attack on Terror: The FBI vs. the Ku Klux Klan* (1975) and the theatrical film *Mississippi Burning* (1988) were based on the same real-life case. In addition to the aforementioned *Johnnie Mae Gibson: FBI*, female agents took charge in *FBI Girl* (1951), *Feds* (1988), and *The Silence of the Lambs* (1991), in which Jodie

Foster won a Best Actress Oscar as special agent Clarice Starling. Still, the most famous female agent is Dana Scully (Gillian Anderson), who made the leap from television to the silver screen with partner (David Duchovny) in *The X-Files* (1998). Keanu Reeves played the screen's only surfing FBI agent in 1991's *Point Break*. See also **Gangsters (Real-Life)**; **In the Line of Duty Series**; **Persons in Hiding Series**.

"G" Men (1935); *Let 'Em Have It* (1935); *FBI 99* (1945); *I Was a Communist for the FBI* (1951); *FBI Girl* (1951); *Walk East on Beacon* (aka *The Crime of the Century*) (1952); *Down Three Dark Streets* (1954); *Security Risk* (1954); *Big House, U.S.A.* (1955); *The FBI Story* (1959); *Experiment in Terror* (1962); *That Darn Cat* (1965); *Who?* (1974); *The FBI Story—Alvin Karpis* (aka *The FBI Story—The FBI versus Alvin Karpis, Public Enemy Number One*) (1974 TVM); *Melvin Purvis: G-Man* (aka *The Legend of Machine Gun Kelly*) (1974 TVM); *The Kansas City Massacre* (1975 TVM); *Attack on Terror: The FBI vs. the Ku Klux Klan* (1975 TVM); *The Private Files of J. Edgar Hoover* (1977); *Undercover with the KKK* (aka *The Freedom Riders; My Undercover Years with the KKK*) (1979 TVM); *Johnnie Mae Gibson: FBI* (aka *Johnnie Gibson: F.B.I.*) (1986 TVM); *Manhunter* (1986); *The Wild Pair* (1987); *J. Edgar Hoover* (1987 TVM); *Hoover vs. the Kennedys: The Second Civil War* (1987 TVM); *The Hidden* (1987); *Feds* (1988); *Mississippi Burning* (1988); *Betrayed* (1988); *The House on Carroll Street* (1988); *In the Line of Duty: The FBI Murders* (1988 TVM); *Mr. Hoover and I* (1989); *My Blue Heaven* (1990); *Flashback* (1990); *The Silence of the Lambs* (1991); *Point Break* (1991); *Thunderheart* (1992); *Incident at Oglala* (1992); *Twins Peaks: Fire Walk with Me* (1993); *Golden Gate* (1994); *Betrayed By Love* (1994 TVM); *The Rock* (1996); *No Way Back* (1996); *Ruby Ridge: An American Tragedy* (1996 TVM); *Donnie Brasco* (1997); *Face/Off* (1997); *Dead Silence* (1997 TVM); *Clay Pigeons* (1998); *Mercury Rising* (1998); *The X-Files* (aka *The X-Files: Fight the Future*) (1998); *The Siege* (1998); *The Cell* (2000)

Feuds *see* Backwoods Feuds

Film and Theater Critics

With two notable exceptions, filmmakers have painted less than flattering portraits of critics in their films. Perhaps, it's a subtle case of unconscious revenge for bad film reviews. A Shakespearean actor skewered by drama critics attained his revenge by murdering them in the stylish *Theater of Blood* (1973). At least, he had the class to kill them by recreating murders from famous plays. William H. Macy played a cable TV film critic who almost got away with homicide in *A Slight Case of Murder* (1999). Alas, he made the fatal mistake of starting an affair with an investigating police detective's wife. *The McGuffin* (1985) featured Charles Dance as a film critic who thinks he's witnessed a murder. Obviously, the man had never seen Hitchcock's *Rear Window*. In *Critic's Choice* (1963), one of Bob Hope's weakest outings, he played a theater critic stuck in the unenviable position of reviewing his wife's play. Doris Day suspected her theater critic husband, David Niven, of having an affair in the comedy *Please Don't Eat the Daisies* (1960). To be fair, other critics have also fared poorly as film characters, as evidenced by the art critics bumped off in *House of Horrors* (1946). The notable exceptions to the mistreatment of critics are *Citizen Kane* (1941) and *All About Eve* (1950). In the latter film, George Sanders won a Best Supporting Actor Oscar for his delightful turn as acid-tongued theater critic Addison DeWitt. Joseph Cotton gave one of his finest performances as the drama critic for the *New York Enquirer* in *Citizen Kane*. His critic loses his job after writing a scathing (but honest) review of a dreadful operatic performance by Charles Foster Kane's wife.

Citizen Kane (1941); *All About Eve* (1950); *Please Don't Eat the Daisies* (1960); *Critic's Choice* (1963); *Theater of Blood* (1973); *The McGuffin* (1985); *A Slight Case of Murder* (1999 TVM)

Film Star Biographies

The cinema's relative youth is largely responsible for the scarcity of pre–1975 movie star screen biographies. Many of the performers that dominated the 1930s and 1940s were still making films in the 1950s and 1960s. Thus, early screen biographies focused on silent film greats like Rudolph Valentino, Will Rogers, Buster Keaton, Jeanne Eagels, and Lon Chaney (*Man of a Thousand Faces*). An interesting exception was 1955's *To Hell and Back*, in which then-current star Audie Murphy played himself. The film, though, ignored Murphy's Hollywood career in favor of his World War II adventures as the U.S. Army's most-decorated soldier. Diana Barrymore's screen career consisted of six mediocre films made in the early 1940s. But her life story warranted a 1958 big-screen treatment when her autobiography *Too Much Too Soon* shot up the best-seller charts. The film version dwelled on the sensationalistic aspects of Ms. Barrymore's book (e.g., her struggle with alcoholism) and, in many ways, set the pattern for the exploitative biographical tomes of the 1980s. There was little exploitative — or interesting — about the two 1965 films called *Harlow*, in which Jean Harlow was played by Carroll Baker and Carol Lynley. However, the 1975 TV movie *Valentino*, while strictly a fan magazine portrait, revived interest in the lives of movie stars. Over the next two years, three movie star biographies reached the theaters: *Gable and Lombard* (1976), *W.C. Fields and Me* (1976), and *Valentino* (1977). All three hit with a thud, chiefly due to miscasting in the principal roles (e.g., James Brolin as Gable, Rod Steiger as W.C. Fields). Concurrently, made-for-TV films continued to thrive, thanks to well-chosen subjects and some genuine craftsmanship. Horror film director John Carpenter and former child star Kurt Russell combined to produce a highly-rated biography of *Elvis!* (1979). Loni Anderson and Arnold Schwarzenegger certainly brought the right physical qualities to their roles of Jayne Mansfield and her husband Mickey Hargitay in 1980's *The Jayne Mansfield Story*. Garson Kanin's nostalgic book *Moviola* inspired biographies of Marilyn Monroe (*This Year's Blonde*) and Greta Garbo and John Gilbert (*The Silent Lovers*). The trend burned out quickly, however, and came to an end with *Mommie Dearest*, the 1981 theatrical version of Christina Crawford's shocking best-seller about her mother Joan, and two early 1980s films about Frances Farmer (*Will There Ever Be a Morning?* and *Frances*). Performers who have played themselves in film biographies include Audie Murphy, Sophia Loren (*Sophia Loren: Her Own Story*), Shirley MacLaine (*Out on a Limb*), Ann Jillian (*The Ann Jillian Story*), Patty Duke (*Call Me Anna*), Suzanne Somers (*Keeping Secrets*), and Joan and Melissa Rivers (*Tears and Laughter: The Joan and Melissa Rivers Story*). See also **Autobiographical Films; Movies About Movies.**

The Jolson Story (1946) (Al Jolson); *Valentino* (1951); *The Story of Will Rogers* (1952); *The Eddie Cantor Story* (1954); *To Hell and Back* (1955) (Audie Murphy); *The Buster Keaton Story* (1957); *Man of a Thousand Faces* (1957) (Lon Chaney); *Jeanne Eagels* (1957); *Too Much Too Soon* (1958) (Diana Barrymore); *The George Raft Story* (aka *Spin of a Coin*) (1961); *Harlow* (1965); *Harlow* (1965); *Funny Girl* (1968) (Fanny Brice); *The Legend of Valentino* (1975 TVM); *Funny Lady* (1975) (Brice); *Gable and Lombard* (1976); *W.C. Fields and Me* (1976); *Goodbye, Norma Jean* (1976) (Marilyn Monroe); *Valentino* (1977); *Bud and Lou* (1978 TVM) (Abbott and Costello); *Rainbow* (1978 TVM) (Judy Garland); *Elvis!* (1979 TVM) (Elvis Presley); *Bogie — The Last Hero* (aka *Bogie*) (1980 TVM) (Humphrey Bogart); *Haywire* (1980 TVM) (Margaret Sullavan and Leland Hayward); *The Jayne Mansfield Story* (1980 TVM); *Marilyn: The Untold Story* (1980 TVM) (Monroe); *Sophia Loren: Her Own Story* (1980 TVM); *The Silent Lovers* (1980 TVM) (Greta Garbo and John Gilbert); *This Year's Blonde* (aka *The Secret Love of Marilyn Monroe*) (1980 TVM); *The Patricia Neal Story* (1981 TVM); *Mommie Dearest* (1981) (Joan Crawford); *Mae West* (1982 TVM); *Frances* (1982) (Frances Farmer); *Grace Kelly* (1983 TVM); *Will There Ever Be a Morning?* (1983 TVM) (Farmer); *My Wicked, Wicked Ways…The Legend of Errol Flynn* (1985 TVM); *Out on a Limb* (1987 TVM) (Shirley MacLaine); *The Ann Jillian Story* (1988 TVM); *Rock Hudson* (1990 TVM); *Call Me Anna* (1990 TVM) (Patty Duke); *Lucy and Desi: Before the Laughter* (1991 TVM) (Lucille Ball and Desi Arnaz); *Reason for Living: The Jill Ireland Story* (1991 TVM); *White Hot: The Mysterious Murder of Thelma Todd* (1991 TVM); *Marilyn and Me* (1991 TVM) (Monroe); *Keeping Secrets* (1991 TVM) (Suzanne Somers); *Sinatra* (1992 TVM); *Chaplin* (1992); *Dragon: The Bruce Lee Story* (1993); *Marilyn and Bobby: Her Final Affair* (1993 TVM) (Monroe and Kennedy); *Roseanne & Tom: Behind the Scenes* (1994 TVM) (Roseanne and Tom Arnold); *Roseanne: An Unauthorized Biography* (1994 TVM); *Tears and Laughter: The Joan and Melissa Rivers Story* (1994 TVM); *A Dream Is a Wish Your Heart Makes: The Annette Funicello Story* (1995 TVM); *Flynn* (1996) (Errol Flynn); *The Rat Pack* (1998 TVM) (Frank Sinatra, Sammy Davis, Jr., Dean Martin, Peter Lawford, and Joey Bishop); *Michael Landon: The Father I Knew* (1999 TVM); *Introducing Dorothy Dandridge* (1999 TVM); *The Audrey Hepburn Story* (2000 TVM); *The Three Stooges* (2000 TVM)

Fires and Firefighters

Crackling flames of fate have provided a central premise, an initiating spark, or a climactic turn of events for dozens of films. Chronicles of historical fires have detailed the facts behind the 1666 Great Fire of London (*The Glorious Adventure*), the Great Chicago Fire (*In Old Chicago*), and the deadly turn-of-the-century New York City blaze which changed factory fire regulations forever (*The Triangle Factory Fire Scandal*). Producer Irwin Allen mounted a pair of large-scale fictional films built around out-of-control flames. *The Towering Inferno* (1974) merged the plots of two similar books (*The Tower* and *The Glass Inferno*) into a tense tale of a burning skyscraper occupied by an all-star cast led by Paul Newman and Steve McQueen. Allen transposed the plot to an outdoor setting for his TV movie *Fire!* (1977), leaving the character vignette structure intact. Another TV movie, 1974's *Terror on the 40th Floor*, duplicated *The Towering Inferno*'s fiery skyscraper plotline to less effect. Ravaging forest fires cut a path of smoldering destruction in *The Blazing Forest* and *Red Skies of Montana* (both 1952), while providing fiery climaxes to *Ring of Fire* and, most memorably, *Bambi*. An oil blaze required four men to drive two trucks of nitroglycerin over dangerous mountain roads in the classic 1952 French thriller *The Wages of Fear*. Less intense dramas focusing on oil firefighters include the John Wayne picture *Hellfighters* (1969) and the concisely-titled *Oil* (1977).

Firefighting of a more general variety has provided the background for slapstick farce (*Fireman Save My Child*), romantic comedy (*Roxanne*), family drama (*The Quinns* and *Backdraft*), a mediocre TV series pilot (*Firehouse*), and a fact-based biography (*Firefighter*, the story of the L.A.F.D.'s first female member). Oscar Werner played a futuristic fireman who burned books in François Truffaut's 1966 adaptation of Ray Bradbury's *Fahrenheit 451* (the best temperature for book-incinerating). Other firestarters have set plots ablaze in *Violent Playground* (1958), *She Played with Fire* (1957), *Pyro* (1964), and *Playing with Fire* (1985). Even Paul Newman played a character with a reputation for barn-burning in Martin Ritt's *The Long, Hot Summer* (1958). Drew Barrymore played the title role in Stephen King's *Firestarter* (1984), a fanciful thriller about a little girl who inherited the power to will fires to begin. Most movie dragons (q.v.) have possessed flame-inducing breath, with the most impressive scorcher being the creature Vertithrax from Disney's 1981 fantasy *Dragonslayer*. Large-scale fires have climaxed too many movies to mention and yet it's impossible to leave out the elaborately-staged burning of Atlanta in *Gone with the Wind* (1939). Likewise, the burning of Rome, best displayed in 1951's *Quo Vadis?*, deserves honorable mention. On the science fiction/fantasy front, 1958's *The Flame Barrier* introduced an alien protoplasm which could melt human flesh. *Quest for Fire* (1981) sent three cave people (q.v.) in search of replacement flames when a wolf attack extinguished their only campfire. Ursula Andress lost her eternal youth (q.v.) when she stepped into the cold Flame of Eternal Life for the second time in *She* (1965). The fate of the world was undecided at the conclusion of 1962's *The Day the Earth Caught Fire*, with our planet hurtling toward the sun for an incinerating destiny.

The Glorious Adventure (1921); *Soup to Nuts* (1930); *Fireman Save My Child* (1932); *She Loved a Fireman* (1937); *In Old Chicago* (1938); *The Shining Hour* (1938); *Gone with the Wind* (1939); *The Forest Rangers* (1942); *Fires Were Started* (aka *I Was a Fireman*) (1942); *The Blazing Forest* (1952); *Red Skies of Montana* (aka *Smoke Jumpers*) (1952); *The Wages of Fear* (1952); *Inferno* (1953); *Fireman Save My Child* (1954); *She Played with Fire* (aka *Fortune Is a Woman*) (1957); *The Flame Barrier* (1958); *Maracaibo* (1958); *Violent Playground* (1958); *The Long, Hot Summer* (1958); *Ring of Fire* (1961); *The Day the Earth Caught Fire* (1962); *Pyro* (1964); *Circus World* (aka *The Magnificent Showman*) (1964); *Harvey Middleman, Fireman* (1965); *Fahrenheit 451* (1966); *The Fireman's Ball* (1968); *Hellfighters* (1969); *The Firechasers* (1970); *Firehouse* (1972 TVM); *The Towering Inferno* (1974); *Terror on the 40th Floor* (1974 TVM); *Bug* (1975); *Fire!* (1977 TVM); *The Quinns* (1977 TVM); *Pine Canyon Is Burning* (1977 TVM); *The Storyteller* (1977 TVM); *Oil* (1977); *The Triangle Factory Fire Scandal* (1979 TVM); *City on Fire* (1979); *Don't Go in the House* (1980); *Quest for Fire* (1981); *Code Red* (1981 TVM); *Uncommon Valor* (1983 TVM); *Firestarter* (1984); *The Burning Bed* (1984 TVM); *The Long, Hot Summer* (1985 TVM); *Playing with Fire* (1985 TVM); *Firefighter* (1986 TVM); *On Fire* (1987 TVM); *Nice Girls Don't Explode* (1987); *Roxanne* (1987); *Always* (1989); *Spontaneous Combustion* (1990); *Backdraft* (1991); *Barton Fink* (1991); *Fire! Trapped on the 37th Floor* (1991 TVM); *Firestorm: 72 Hours in Oakland* (1993 TVM); *Torch Song* (1993 TVM); *Wilder Napalm* (1993); *Flashfire* (1994); *Backfire* (1995); *In the Line of Duty: Smoke Jumpers* (1996 TVM); *Firestorm* (1998); *Frequency* (2000)

Fish

The movies have been stocked with a small, but diverse, catch of fish — little ones with very sharp teeth, big ones capable of swallowing boats, and even a pair of prehistoric fish. It is one of these latter fish that proved particularly troublesome for college professor Arthur Franz in *Monster on the Campus* (1958). Any animal coming into contact with the dead fish's fluid reversed its evolution process — Franz's dog became a wolf-like creature and the professor turned to a homicidal Neanderthal man. A living, standard-issue prehistoric fish ate vacationers in the *Jaws*-inspired *Up from the Depths* (1979). No one questioned the age of the giant fish that swallowed Baron Munchausen and his mates in *The Adventures of Baron Munchausen* (1989). But judging from the contents of its "stomach," it must have been a pretty old fish. Oddly enough, the cinema's most celebrated horror movie fish is neither oversized nor prehistoric. In fact, the piranha looks rather wimpish, but its sharp teeth and carnivorous appetite have made him a popular villain's pet. Director Joe Dante made it a star with 1978's *Piranha*, a spoof strictly for horror film buffs and drive-in fanatics. The Italian-Brazilian coproduction *Killer Fish* featured a bizarre cast worthy of being fish food: Lee Majors, Karen Black, Margaux Hemingway, James Franciscus, and Marisa Berenson. Prior to hitting the big time with 1984's *The Terminator*, director James Cameron fashioned the 1981 in-name-only sequel *Piranha II: The Spawning*. Kevin Kline won a Best Supporting Actor Oscar as Otto, the inept thief and raw fish eater in the 1988 comedy hit *A Fish Called Wanda*. In Disney's *The Sword in the Stone*, magician Merlin turned himself and young King Arthur into fish. See also **Dolphins**; **Sharks**; **Whales**.

Maid's Night Out (1938); *Fantasia* (1940); *Monster on the Campus* (1958); *The Sword in the Stone* (1963); *The Day the Fish Came Out* (1967); *Barracuda* (aka *The Lucifer Project*) (1978); *Piranha* (1978); *Killer Fish* (aka *Deadly Treasure of the Piranha*) (1979); *Screamers* (aka *Isle of the Fishmen*; *Something Waits in the Dark*) (1979); *Up from the Depths* (1979); *Piranha II: The Spawning* (1981); *A Fish Called Wanda* (1988); *The Adventures of Baron Munchausen* (1989); *Next Stop Wonderland* (1998)

Five Little Peppers

The Peppers, another wholesome family in the Hardy Family (q.v.) mold, were the subject of a brief Columbia film series. *Five Little Peppers and How They Grew*, which opened in 1939 to promising reviews, set the flimsy premise: Mrs. Pepper worked at a factory while her oldest daughter Polly attended the other four little Peppers. Subsequent movies attracted little attention and the series came to an abrupt end after four entries. Dorothy Peterson starred as Mrs. Pepper and her five offspring were played by Edith Fellows (Polly), Charles Peck (Ben), Tommy Bond (Joey), Bobbie Larson (Dave) and Dorothy Ann Seese (Phronsie). Ronald Sinclair played the Pepper kids' rich friend Jasper with veteran character actor Clarence Kolb as his grandfather.

Five Little Peppers and How They Grew (1939); *Out West with the Peppers* (1940); *Five Little Peppers at Home* (1940); *Five Little Peppers in Trouble* (1940)

Flagg and Quirt

Brawling, patriotic Marines Captain Flagg and Sergeant Quirt first clashed with one another in 1926's *What Price Glory?* A silent screen adaptation of the Maxwell Anderson–Laurence Stallings play. Romantic lead Edmund Lowe played against type as the roughneck Quirt, with Victor McLaglen more than his match as

Flagg. Set in France during World War I, this deft mixture of raucous comedy and realistic adventure found the two Marines at odds over the charms of an irresistible girl named Charmaine. The chemistry between the stars and the nonstop action (expertly directed by Raoul Walsh) made the film immensely popular. McLaglen and Lowe returned as Flagg and Quirt in three lighthearted follow-ups, all directed by Walsh. Whether they were running liquor in South America (*Hot Pepper*) or soldiering in Sweden *(Women of All Nations)*, Flagg and Quirt were almost always quarreling over a woman. John Ford remade *What Price Glory?* in 1952 with James Cagney as Flagg and Dan Dailey as Quirt. The 1942 McLaglen-Lowe vehicle *Call Out the Marines* is sometimes erroneously listed as a Flagg and Quirt film. Actually, the two stars played characters named McGinnis and Curtis and the setting was World War II.

What Price Glory? (1926); *The Cockeyed World* (1929); *Women of All Nations* (1931); *Hot Pepper* (1933); *What Price Glory?* (1952)

Floods

Floods have appeared less frequently than other motion picture disasters (see **Earthquakes**; **Volcanoes**), despite the increased likelihood of their natural occurrence. The biggest flood, in terms of scope, was the biblical one that set *Noah's Ark* afloat in 1929. The potential love affair between Indian aristocrat Tyrone Power and English socialite Myrna Loy was disrupted by floods, earthquakes, and plague in 1939's *The Rains Came*. In *A Cry in the Wilderness* (1974), George Kennedy had himself locked inside a barn after being bit by a rabid skunk — and then learns a flood is on the way. Not all floods are caused by rain. The gravitational pull of another planet flooded metropolitan cities all over the world — including Manhattan — in *When Worlds Collide* (1951). Enterprising (and cheap) New World Pictures re-edited a 1973 Japanese film called *The Submersion of Japan* into the 1975 disaster-drama *Tidal Wave*. See also **Disaster Movies**.

Metropolis (1925); *The Johnstown Flood* (1926); *Noah's Ark* (1929); *Postal Inspector* (1936); *The Rains Came* (1939); *When Worlds Collide* (1951); *Heidi and Peter* (1955); *The Rains of Ranchipur* (1955); *Floods of Fear* (1958); *Wild River* (1960); *In Search of the Castaways* (1962); *Mister Moses* (1965); *The Little Ark* (1972); *A Cry in the Wilderness* (1974 TVM); *Irwin Allen's Flood!* (aka *Flood!*) (1976 TVM); *The River* (1984); *The Flood: Who Will Save Our Children?* (1993 TVM); *The Flood* (aka *Navodneniye*) (1994); *Jumanji* (1995); *Flood: A River's Rampage* (1997 TVM); *First-Time Felon* (1997 TVM); *Old Man* (1997 TVM); *Hard Rain* (aka *Flood*) (1998); *Terror in the Mall* (1998 TVM)

The Fly Series

Before *Shogun*, there was *The Fly*. Long before his novels made him a best-selling author, James Clavell penned this 1958 cult favorite about a scientist who transforms himself into a man/fly mutation. Al (David) Hedison played the inventor of an experimental device that broke matter into molecules, transported them from one terminal to another, and then reconstructed the original object. Hedison's obsession with his invention caused him to transport himself — unaware that a house fly had buzzed into the terminal with him. The device merged the human and fly molecules, the result being a man with a fly's head and "arm" (and a fly with the appropriate human parts). The rest of the film focused on the trauma experienced by Hedison's wife (Patricia Owens). Although consistently interesting, *The Fly* does

not work as a horror film because the "monster" elicits more sympathy than terror — and there's no villain. *The Return of the Fly* (1959) introduced some bad guys, but the basic plot remained the same except for an upbeat ending. The 1965 made-in-England *Curse of the Fly* dealt with a matter transmission device, but otherwise bore little resemblance to the first two films. In 1986, Canadian director David Cronenberg directed a stylish rethinking of *The Fly*, with Jeff Goldblum as a scientist who mutates himself and dreams of creating a new species. It was followed by *The Fly II*, a 1989 sequel which found son Eric Stolz experiencing mutation problems before discovering how to reverse the process. See also **Insects**; **Teleportation**.

The Fly (1958); *The Return of the Fly* (1959); *The Curse of the Fly* (1965); *The Fly* (1986); *The Fly II* (1989)

Flying People

Flying humans have become all but extinct in the cinema. *Superman*, and to a lesser extent *Supergirl*, were common air-bound sights in the late 1970s and early 1980s — but both of them were technically aliens since they hailed from the planet Krypton. Thus, the only major films in the past two decades to feature flying Earthlings have been *Condorman* (1981), *The Boy Who Could Fly* (1986), and *The Rocketeer* (1991). Michael Crawford, prior to becoming a Broadway sensation as *The Phantom of the Opera*, played a cartoonist-turned-superhero who attempted a winged flight over Paris in *Condorman*, a dismal Disney secret agent spoof produced during the studio's low point. Nick Castle's *The Boy Who Could Fly* was a tender fantasy about an apparently autistic teen who yearned to fly — and eventually soared into the clouds. Pre-1971 flights of fantasy have featured a unique brand of eccentricity. Bud Cort played a lad obsessed with donning his homemade wings and taking a flight around the Astrodome in Robert Altman's erratic satire *Brewster McCloud* (1970). The French fantasy *Fifi la Plume* (1964) concerned a thief who joined a circus as a "bird-man" and actually learned to fly. Comedian Soupy Sales starred as a "minuscule molecular particle surveillance monitor" (i.e., a janitor) who took to the air after becoming "ionized" in 1966's *Birds Do It*. A decade earlier, the Disney folks brought literature's most famous flying boy to the screen in the animated *Peter Pan* (1953). Schizophrenic Vietnam vet Matthew Modine longed to be a bird and take to the air in 1984's *Birdy*. A boy believed his long lost father could fly in 1995's *The Flying Dutchman*. Floating, not flying, people have also appeared in a handful of films like *Mary Poppins* (1964) and *The Fury* (1978). See also **Superman**.

Peter Pan (1953); *Fifi la Plume* (1964); *Birds Do It* (1966); *Brewster McCloud* (1970); *Superman* (1978); *Condorman* (1981); *Supergirl* (1984); *The Boy Who Could Fly* (1986); *The Rocketeer* (1991); *Hook* (1991)

Football

Baseball may be the national pastime, but football outranks it easily as the movies' favorite team sport. Yet, unlike baseball, football has enshrined few of its legends. Its movie hall of fame has covered the careers of players Jim Thorpe (*Jim Thorpe-All American*), Brian Piccolo (*Brian's Song*), Elroy "Crazylegs" Hirsch (*Crazylegs*), Rocky Bleier (*Fighting Back*) and others. To their credit, football-oriented filmmakers have shown equal respect for the men on the sidelines, with profiles of real-life collegiate coaching greats Knute Rockne (*Knute Rockne, All American*), Bear Bryant (*The Bear*), and Eddie Robinson (*Grambling's White Tiger*). On the fictional front, the movies have left no football field untouched. Tom Cruise, Anthony Michael Hall, and Gary Busey played high school gridiron stars in, respectively, *All the Right Moves, Johnny Be Good,* and *Blood Sport.* The replaying of a 20-year-old high school game was the subject of the Robin Williams comedy *The Best of Times* (1986). However, the majority of football pictures have dealt with the college game, often on a comic or musical level. Harold Lloyd starred as a clutzy student transformed into an unlikely football hero in his 1925 classic *The Freshman.* The Marx Brothers' hilarious *Horse Feathers* (1932) pitted their Huxley College team against archrival Darwin U. in one of the screen's more bizarre climactic games. Jack Oakie was the team's star and Bing Crosby a crooning college professor in the 1933 musical *College Humor.* Another gridiron musical, 1936's *Pigskin Parade,* co-starred Judy Garland (in her film debut) and Jack Haley three years before *The Wizard of Oz.* Fictional pro players have experienced more stressful careers. In 1974's *The Longest Yard,* former quarterback Burt Reynolds found himself in prison leading a bunch of fellow convicts against the warden's team. Charlton Heston was another quarterback, fighting to stay in the game despite his age, in 1969's *Number One.* A similar problem plagued injury-prone Nick Nolte in *North Dallas Forty* (1979), a perceptive seriocomedy that also addressed the business end of the sport. The most enjoyable film about the realities of professional football was probably *Paper Lion* (1968), based on writer George Plimpton's best-seller about his undercover stint as a rookie for the Detroit Lions. Unpleasant pro games were featured in *Black Sunday* (terrorists planted a bomb in the blimp*)*, *Two Minute Warning* (a sniper in the stadium), and *Superdome* (another killer on the loose). Two TV movies about the *Dallas Cowboy Cheerleaders* treated women with minimal respect. However, tough-minded ladies took to the football field in *The Oklahoma City Dolls* (1981), *Quarterback Princess* (1983), and *Backfield in Motion* (1991). The cinema's most unlikely gridiron stars include the quarterbacking chimp in *Bonzo Goes to College* (1952) and the field-goal kicking mule *Gus* (1976). See also **Cheerleaders**.

The Freshman (1925); Good News (1930); Horse Feathers (1932); Saturday's Millions (1933); College Coach (1933); College Humor (1933); Fighting Youth (1935); Pigskin Parade (1936); Hold 'Em Navy (1937); Navy Blue and Gold (1937); $1,000 a Touchdown (1939); Knute Rockne, All American (1940); Rise and Shine (1941); Pardon My Stripe (1942); The Iron Major (1943); Good News (1947); The Spirit of West Point (1947); Easy Living (1949); Father Was a Fullback (1949); Saturday's Hero (aka Idols in the Dust) (1951); The Guy Who Came Back (1951); Jim Thorpe—All American (aka Man of Bronze) (1951); The Rose Bowl Story (1952); Bonzo Goes to College (1952); The All-American (1953); Trouble Along the Way (1953); Crazylegs (aka Crazylegs, All American) (1953); Son of Flubber (1963); The Fortune Cookie (1966); Paper Lion (1968); Number One (1969); M*A*S*H (1970); Brian's Song (1970 TVM); Footsteps (aka Footsteps: Nice Guys Finish Last) (1972 TVM); A Fan's Notes (1972); Blood Sport (1973 TVM); The Longest Yard (1974); Gus (1976); Two Minute Warning (1976); Something for Joey (1977 TVM); Black Sunday (1977); Semi-Tough (1977); Heaven Can Wait (1978); Superdome (1978 TVM); North Dallas Forty (1979); H.O.T.S. (1979); Coach of the Year (1980 TVM); Fighting Back (1980 TVM); Gram-

bling's White Tiger (1981 TVM); The Oklahoma City Dolls (1982 TVM); All the Right Moves (1983); Quarterback Princess (1983 TVM); Off Sides (1984 TVM); The Bear (1984); The Best of Times (1986); Wildcats (1986); Everybody's All-American (1988); Johnny Be Good (1988); Glory Days (1988 TVM); Triumph of the Heart: The Ricky Bell Story (1991 TVM); Necessary Roughness (1991); Backfield in Motion (1991 TVM); School Ties (1992); The Program (1993); Rudy (1993); Forrest Gump (1994); Rise and Walk: The Dennis Byrd Story (1994 TVM); Little Giants (1994); Jerry Maguire (1996); Good Luck (1997); Angels in the Endzone (1997 TVM); The Waterboy (1998); The Garbage-Picking, Field-Goal Kicking, Philadelphia Phenomenon (1998 TVM); Varsity Blues (1999); Any Given Sunday (1999); The Replacements (2000)

Ford's Cavalry Trilogy

Director John Ford's sentimental homage to the U.S. Cavalry qualifies as a series only in the broadest sense. All three films share common themes, take place out West after the Civil War, and star John Wayne (and other Ford favorites such as Ward Bond and Victor McLaglen). However, Henry Fonda got the juicy role in *Fort Apache* (1948), which resembles Custer's final days, although it was based on James Warner Bellah's story "Massacre." Fonda plays Lieutenant Colonel Owen Thursday, a Civil War general who has been demoted and shipped to a desert command post. He is a harsh disciplinarian who fails to understand his daughter, his soldiers, and the Indians. When Thursday's blunders result in a Cavalry massacre — and his own death — patriotic Captain Kirby York (Wayne) covers up for his superior and paints a gallant portrait of the dead officer. It's an odd ending to an otherwise straightforward, albeit well-done, Western. Shirley Temple had one of her better adult roles as Fonda's daughter Philadelphia, and her then-husband John Agar played her love interest. Wayne dominates the second film, 1949's *She Wore a Yellow Ribbon*, which was based on two other Bellah stories: "War Party" and "Big Hunt." He plays Captain Nathan Brittles, a retiring Cavalryman preparing to pass his command to young Lieutenant Flint Cahill (John Agar again). But before Brittles can step down from his responsibilities, he must intercede to thwart a war with the Indians. Again, the plot takes a backseat to Ford's compassion for his characters and his breathtaking portrait of the Western frontier (as filmed by Oscar-winner Winston Hoch in Monument Valley). The trilogy's final chapter, 1950's *Rio Grande*, casts Wayne as a cavalry officer facing conflicts with a new recruit: the son he never knew. Maureen O'Hara and Victor McLaglen (who appeared in all three films) turn in fine supporting performances in the most underrated — and least shown — of the three films. Its songs were performed by the Sons of the Pioneers, which included future actor Ken Curtis, best known as Festus on the long-running TV series *Gunsmoke* (q.v.).

Fort Apache (1948); She Wore a Yellow Ribbon (1949); Rio Grande (1950)

Foreign Legion

P.C. Wren's 1925 adventure novel *Beau Geste* established a much-copied formula for desert tales of derring-do among soldiers in the French Foreign Legion. It was first filmed as a silent in 1926 with an all-star cast of Ronald Colman, Victor McLaglen, and William Powell. This exciting story of three honor-bound brothers and a ruthless sergeant struck box-office gold for Paramount, who released a hurried sequel two years later. *Beau Sabreur* was based on a Wren novel which took place within the framework of *Beau Geste*. Yet, despite the presence of William Powell and newcomer Gary Cooper, it failed to repeat its predecessor's success. Still, it fared better than another Wren-based sequel, 1931's *Beau Ideal*. Colman and McLaglen returned as Foreign Legion rivals in 1936's *Under Two Flags*, with aristocratic Rosalind Russell and commoner Claudette Colbert as the women vying for Colman's love. Its pre–*Geste* source novel had been filmed earlier in 1916 and 1922. Thirteen years after the release of Colman's 1926 *Beau Geste*, Paramount mounted a lavish scene-for-scene remake starring *Beau Sabreur* alumnus Gary Cooper, Ray Milland, and Robert Preston as the brothers. Brian Donlevy outshone the leads, however, earning an Oscar nomination for his sadistic sergeant. Telly Savalas played that role in Universal's best-forgotten 1966 *Beau Geste*, which trimmed the number of brothers to two (Guy Stockwell and Doug McClure) and tacked on a happy ending. For a change of pace, Dick Powell played a contemporary American agent who joins the Foreign Legion to track down Nazis in the World War II adventure *Rogue's Regiment* (1948). Foreign Legion films in general—and *Beau Geste* in particular—have been spoofed by Laurel and Hardy (*The Flying Deuces*), Abbott and Costello (*A&C in the Foreign Legion*), and the Carry On Gang (*Follow That Camel*). Marty Feldman's *The Last Remake of Beau Geste* (1977) was an uneven affair, basically a one-joke movie about unlikely twin brothers (!) Feldman and Michael York. That same year saw the release of *March or Die*, an awkward combination of traditional Foreign Legion adventure and 1970s-style violence. It died a swift box-office death. Jean-Claude Van Damme played a guy who deserted the Foreign Legion and became a streetfighter in *Lionheart* (1990). Then, in *Legionnaire* (1999), he played a boxer on the run who joined the Foreign Legion. Foreign Legion recruiters probably preferred the latter film.

Beau Geste (1926); *Beau Sabreur* (1928); *Morocco* (1930); *Renegades* (1930); *Beau Ideal* (1931); *Le Grand Jeu* (1934); *Under Two Flags* (1936); *Beau Geste* (1939); *The Flying Deuces* (aka *Flying Aces*) (1939); *Rogue's Regiment* (1948); *Outpost in Malaya* (1949); *Abbott and Costello in the Foreign Legion* (1950); *Ten Tall Men* (1951); *Flesh and the Woman* (1953); *Desert Legion* (1953); *Legion of the Doomed* (1958); *Desert Hell* (1958); *Beau Geste* (1966); *Follow That Camel* (aka *Carry On Follow That Camel*) (1967); *Man of Legend* (1971); *The Last Remake of Beau Geste* (1977); *March or Die* (1977); *Renegades* (1982 TVM); *Lionheart* (aka *A.W.O.L.*; *Wrong Bet*) (1990); *Savior* (1998); *Legionnaire* (1999)

Four Daughters Series

Fanny Hurst's story "Sister Act" reached the screen in 1938 as *Four Daughters*, a vehicle designed to spotlight the Lane Sisters. The movie was a popular and artistic smash, but the sensation turned out to be a young actor named John Garfield who played Priscilla Lane's erratic suitor and eventual husband. Unfortunately, Garfield's character committed suicide, so that he was limited to a flashback role in the 1939 follow-up *Four Wives*. Undaunted, Warner Bros. paired Garfield and Lane (along with Claude Rains who had played her father) in an unrelated but very similar picture called *Daughters Courageous* (1941). The studio then picked up with the original series, now Garfield-less and losing momentum, with 1941's *Four Mothers*. Priscilla, Rosemary, and Lola Lane, along with Gale Page, played the four Lemp sis-

ters in all three films. Claude Rains co-starred with them, while Eddie Albert appeared in the last two entries.

Four Daughters (1938); *Four Wives* (1939); *Four Mothers* (1941)

Francis, the Talking Mule

Chill Wills was the voice behind the mule and Donald O'Connor played the straight man in all but one entry in this popular Universal comedy series. The relationship between the bumbling, sincere human and the crafty (occasionally cruel) mule was established when they met in the Army in 1950's *Francis*. The running gag of the series—Francis would talk only to O'Connor, so that Donald always wound up looking crazy—naturally wore thin as the series progressed. But O'Connor, an underrated comedian, and Wills maintained a delightful rapport. The script writers gave them a fair share of decent material as well, with the funniest bit being when Francis psychoanalyzed an unmotivated race horse in *Francis Goes to the Races* (1951). The series began to show signs of wear when Wills showed up in a human supporting role in *Francis Joins the WACs* (1954) and O'Connor played a double role in *Francis in the Navy* (1955). The latter film turned out to be the final one for O'Connor and Wills. But Universal was not ready to end its last profitable series. Paul Frees spoke for Francis and Mickey Rooney played the mule's sidekick in 1956's best-forgotten *Francis in the Haunted House*. It ended the series on a down note. However, just five years later, veteran *Francis* director Arthur Lubin proved that talking animals could still be funny when he introduced television audiences to that famous talking horse—*Mr. Ed*. See also **Talking Animals**.

Francis (1950); *Francis Goes to the Races* (1951); *Francis Goes to West Point* (1952); *Francis Covers the Big Town* (1953); *Francis Joins the WACs* (1954); *Francis in the Navy* (1955); *Francis in the Haunted House* (1956)

Frankenstein/The Monster

The cinema's favorite mad scientist, Mary Shelley's Victor Frankenstein, has spent most of his film career in the shadow of his creation: the Frankenstein Monster. Indeed, when most people talk about Frankenstein, they are referring to the Monster—not the man. Yet, both the doctor and his creation rank as two of the movies' most enduring characters. Thomas Edison's film company produced the first version of Shelley's classic, 1910's *Frankenstein*, featuring contract player Charles Ogle as a shaggy, clawed monster. Two other silent versions followed, *Life Without a Soul* (1915) and an obscure Italian picture *The Monster of Frankenstein* (1920). A decade later, Universal Studios made Frankenstein a household name with the release of James Whale's 1931 horror classic. In Whale's version, Colin Clive played Henry Frankenstein as an intelligent, but definitely irrational, man of science (the name change—from Victor to Henry—has never been satisfactorily explained). Boris Karloff's man-made creature elicited both terror and sympathy, giving him a depth of character rare for a movie monster. Director Whale exploited these assets to even greater effect with his 1935 sequel *The Bride of Frankenstein*, considered by many critics as the finest of all Frankensteins. It also holds the distinction of being the only film in the Universal series in which the Monster spoke with his own voice. After *Bride*, Whale and Clive bowed out of the series.

Nevertheless, 1939's *Son of Frankenstein* remained a superior outing in which Henry's son Wolf (Basil Rathbone) revives the Monster (Karloff) much to the delight of the mad shepherd Ygor (Bela Lugosi). These first three entries were "A" pictures in every respect, but the series succumbed to the "B" level with 1942's *The Ghost of Frankenstein*. Bela Lugosi was still around as the disturbing Ygor, but Lon Chaney, Jr., made a mediocre monster and even reliable Cedric Hardwicke seemed uninspired as Henry's other son Ludwig. Universal subsequently paired the Monster with other creatures in its gallery, resulting in 1943's *Frankenstein Meets the Wolf Man* and the monster rallies *House of Frankenstein* (1944) and *House of Dracula* (1945). The Universal series ended with its self-spoof *Abbott and Costello Meet Frankenstein* (1948). However, Britain's Hammer Films revived the Frankenstein name in 1957 with its colorful, gory (for the time) adaptation *Curse of Frankenstein*. The Hammer series wisely shifted its focus from the Monster to the doctor. In a stroke of casting genius, Peter Cushing was chosen to play Victor Frankenstein and his crisp, energetic performance brought him well-deserved fame. As the series continued, Cushing developed his character, gradually becoming more ruthless, but always managing to evoke a measure of pity. The lone Hammer picture to star another actor was the ill-fated 1970 satire *Horror of Frankenstein*, which presented Ralph Bates as a younger, more sexually-active Victor. Although Hammer retired its series in 1974, the Frankenstein myth continued to thrive on film. Paul Morrissey directed a 1973 3-D version under the auspices of Andy Warhol called *Flesh for Frankenstein* (aka *Andy Warhol's Frankenstein*). The success of 1972's *Blacula* guaranteed the making of a "blaxploitation" Frankenstein. However, when *Blackenstein* appeared the following year, it lacked the style and polish of its vampire predecessor and vanished quietly. The most literate adaptations were probably the 1973 TV movie *Frankenstein: The True Story* and the overly stylish Kenneth Branagh version *Mary Shelley's Frankenstein* (1994). Both films featured human-looking monsters, with Robert De Niro projecting both sympathy and evil as the monster in the Branagh movie. *Frankenstein: The True Story* also featured a rare female monster (Jane Seymour), as did *Bride of Frankenstein* (Elsa Lanchester), *Frankenstein Created Woman* (Susan Denberg), and *The Bride* (Jennifer Beals). There was no real monster in 1973's *Spirit of the Beehive*, a Spanish film about a child deeply disturbed from watching Whale's original. David Carradine played a futuristic race car driver named Frankenstein in Paul Bartel's offbeat satire *Death Race 2000* (1975). *Gothic* (1986) and *Haunted Summer* (1988) dealt with the incidents surrounding Mary Shelley's writing of her novel. Ian McKellan portrayed James Whale in *Gods and Monsters*, a 1998 biography that cleverly mixed fact and fiction. It featured clips from *Bride of Frankenstein*, as well as fantasy sequences in which Whale turned up as both Dr. Frankenstein and his monster. In the following list, the doctor, or his replacement mad scientist, is listed prior to the monster in parentheses after the film's title:

UNIVERSAL SERIES: *Frankenstein* (1931) (Colin Clive/Boris Karloff); *Bride of Frankenstein* (1935) (Clive/Karloff and Elsa Lanchester); *Son of Frankenstein* (1939) (Basil Rathbone/Karloff); *The Ghost of Frankenstein* (1942) (Cedric Hardwicke/Lon Chaney, Jr.); *Frankenstein Meets the Wolf Man* (1943) (Patric Knowles/Bela Lugosi); *House of Frankenstein* (aka *Chamber of Horrors*) (1944)

(Karloff/Glenn Strange); *House of Dracula* (1945) (Onslow Stevens/Strange); *Abbott and Costello Meet Frankenstein* (1948) (Lugosi as Dracula/Strange)

HAMMER SERIES: *Curse of Frankenstein* (1957) (Peter Cushing/Christopher Lee); *Revenge of Frankenstein* (1958) (Cushing/Michael Gwynn); *Evil of Frankenstein* (1964) (Cushing/Kiwi Kingston); *Frankenstein Created Woman* (1967) (Cushing/Susan Denberg); *Frankenstein Must Be Destroyed* (1969) (Cushing/Freddie Jones); *Horror of Frankenstein* (1970) (Ralph Bates/Dave Prowse); *Frankenstein and the Monster from Hell* (1973) (Cushing/Prowse)

OTHER FRANKENSTEIN FILMS: *Frankenstein* (1910) (Augustus Phillips/Charles Ogle); *Life Without Soul* (1915) (William Cohill/Percy Standing); *The Monster of Frankenstein* (1920) (Luciano Albertini/Umberto Guarracino); *I Was a Teenage Frankenstein* (1957) (Whit Bissell/Gary Conway); *Frankenstein's Daughter* (1958) (Donald Murphy/Uncredited); *Frankenstein 1970* (1958) (Boris Karloff/Mike Lane); *How to Make a Monster* (1960) (Gary Conway as actor in Monster make-up); *Frankenstein Meets the Space Monster* (1964) (James Karen/Robert Reilly); *Jesse James Meets Frankenstein's Daughter* (1966) (Narda Onyx/Cal Bolder); *Frankenstein Conquers the World* (1966) (Koji Furuhata as the Monster); *Munster, Go Home!* (1966) (Fred Gwynne as Monster-lookalike Herman Munster); *Mad Monster Party?* (1967) (puppet); *Casino Royale* (1967) (Dave Prowse has a cameo as the Monster); *Santo and Blue Demon vs. the Monsters* (aka *Santo y Blue Demon Contra los Monstruós*) (1969) (Manuel Leal as the Monster); *Dr. Frankenstein on Campus* (aka *Flick*) (1970) (Robin Ward as doctor who was the Monster); *The Man Who Came from Ummo* (aka *El Hombre Que Vino de Ummo*; *Assignment Terror*; *Los Monstruos Del Terror*; *Dracula vs. Frankenstein*) (1970) (Paul Naschy); *Lady Frankenstein* (aka *La Figlia di Frankenstein*) (1971) (Joseph Cotten as Dr. Frankenstein); *Dracula vs. Frankenstein* (aka *Blood of Frankenstein*; *The Revenge of Dracula*; *They're Coming to Get You*) (1971) (J. Carrol Naish/John Bloom); *Frankenstein* (1973 TVM) (Robert Foxworth/Bo Svenson); *Blackenstein* (aka *Black Frankenstein*) (1973) (John Hart/Joe DiSue); *Flesh for Frankenstein* (aka *Andy Warhol's Frankenstein*) (1973) (Udo Kier/Srojan Zelenovic); *Spirit of the Beehive* (1973); *Frankenstein: The True Story* (1973 TVM) (Leonard Whiting/Michael Sarrazin); *Santo and Blue Demon vs. Dr. Frankenstein* (*Santo y Blue Demon Contra el Dr. Frankenstein*) (1973) (Jorge Russek as Dr. Irving Frankenstein); *Young Frankenstein* (1974) (Gene Wilder/Peter Boyle); *Death Race 2000* (1975); *Frankenstein-Italian Style* (1977) (Gianrico Tedeschi/Aldo Maccione); *Victor Frankenstein* (aka *Terror of Frankenstein*) (1977) (Leon Vitali/Pers Oscarsson); *Dr. Franken* (1980 TVM) (Robert Vaughn/Robert Perault); *The Bride* (1985) (Sting/Clancy Brown and Jennifer Beals); *Gothic* (1986); *The Vindicator* (aka *Frankenstein '88*) (1986) (Richard Cox/David McIllwraith); *The Monster Squad* (1987) (Tom Noonan as the Monster); *Haunted Summer* (1988); *Frankenhooker* (1990) (James Lorinz as Jeffrey Franken/Patty Mullen as Elizabeth, the Monster); *Frankenstein Unbound* (aka *Roger Corman's Frankenstein Unbound*) (1990) (Raul Julia/Nick Brimble); *Frankenstein: The College Years* (1991 TVM) (Vincent Hammond as the Monster); *Waxwork II: Lost in Time* (1991) (Martin Kemp/Stefanos Miltsakakis); *Frankenstein* (1993 TVM) (Patrick Bergin/Randy Quaid); *Mary Shelley's Frankenstein* (1994) (Kenneth Branagh/Robert De Niro); *Here Come the Munsters* (1995 TVM) (Edward Herrmann as Herman Munster); *Monster Mash: The Movie* (aka *Frankenstein Sings*) (1995) (Bobby Pickett as Dr. Frankenstein); *House of Frankenstein 1997* (1997 TVM) (Peter Crombie as the Monster); *The Creeps* (1997) (Thomas Wellington as the Monster); *Gods and Monsters* (1998)

Free Willy Series

Young viewers embraced *Free Willy*, making this story of a boy and his killer whale friend the sleeper hit of the summer of 1993.

Jason James Richter played Jesse, a former runaway who lives with foster parents, but who experiences difficulties with fitting into his new surroundings. He finds a needed friend in Willy, who performs at an amusement park. When the whale's safety becomes threatened, Jesse helps the orca escape. Michael Jackson had a hit with the film's theme song "Will You Be There?" Two less successful sequels followed, both starring Richter. In *Free Willy 2: The Adventure Home*, Jesse and his reunited younger brother help save whales from an oil spill. In *Free Willy 3: The Rescue*, Jesse and Willy encounter villains hunting endangered whales. The true star of all three films was Keiko, the killer whale (although many of his more dangerous tricks were "performed" by an animatronic double). Keiko's real-life story garnered a lot of attention throughout the mid–1990s. When the media revealed that Keiko lived in a small tank in Mexico, animal right activists became interested in his plight. The nonprofit Free Willy Keiko Foundation eventually bought the killer whale and temporarily relocated him to the Oregon Coast Aquarium. In 1998, the Foundation returned Keiko to his natural waters off the coast of Iceland, where the 9,000-pound whale could swim in a football field–sized floating pen. See also **Whales**.

Free Willy (1993); *Free Willy 2: The Adventure Home* (aka *Free Willy 2*) (1995); *Free Willy 3: The Rescue* (1997)

Friday the 13th Series

This modest 1980 *Halloween* (q.v.) clone has a lot to answer for — chiefly for inspiring the most successful film series of the 1980s. Who would have thought that watching teens get bumped off during summer camp would be so popular? Actually, the series' survival can be attributed to two clever ideas. It capitalized on 1982's 3-D craze with the gut-wrenching *Friday the 13th Part 3*. Then, after finally disposing of the indestructible killer Jason in *Friday the 13th — The Final Chapter*, it had another character assume Jason's identity. The series appeared to have run its course after the meager returns posted by 1989's eighth installment. However, New Line Cinema — the home of the Freddy Kreuger franchise — tried to revive the series with 1993's disappointing *Jason Goes to Hell: The Final Friday*. The popular syndicated TV series *Friday the 13th* ran from 1987 to 1990, but it bore no resemblance to the movies. It focused on the efforts of two teenaged cousins to recover cursed antiques (e.g., a doll, a quill pen, a teacup) sold by their uncle as part of a pact with the Devil. See also **Slasher Movies**; **Summer Camps**.

Friday the 13th (1980); *Friday the 13th Part 2* (1981); *Friday the 13th Part 3* (1982); *Friday the 13th — The Final Chapter* (1984); *Friday the 13th Part V: A New Beginning* (1985); *Friday the 13th Part VI: Jason Lives* (1986); *Friday the 13th Part VII — The New Blood* (1988); *Friday the 13th Part VIII: Jason Takes Manhattan* (1989); *Jason Goes to Hell: The Final Friday* (1993)

Frogs

As Kermit the Frog once sang: "It ain't easy being green." That goes double for the movie business where frogs and toads have been all but forgotten (as opposed to fairy tale literature where frogs get some respect). The only true frog star is Kermit, who has shared top billing with Miss Piggy in all the Muppet Movies (q.v.). Ben Kingsley voiced the title role in 1992's *Freddie as F.R.O.7*, an animated yarn about an amphibious secret agent.

Walt Disney brought Kenneth Grahame's classic *The Wind in the Willows* to the screen in animated form in the two-part feature *Ichabod and Mr. Toad* (1949). The wildly eccentric Mr. Toad came to life sharply as a result of superb animation and Eric Blore's marvelous comedic voice. (Oddly, the first half of Ichabod and Mr. Toad was an unrelated animated adaptation of "The Legend of Sleepy Hollow.") Although frogs and toads such as Kermit, Freddie, and Mr. Toad can be charming, these green amphibians also have a dark side. The environmentally-minded horror film *Frogs* (1972) carried this ominous ad line: "Millions of slimy bodies everywhere — millions of gaping mouths!" Actually, the frogs were not very frightening, though Ray Milland seemed to take offense to them. Additionally, the frogs made a strong political statement about how humans wreak havoc on the ecology. The "frog monster" in 1953's *The Maze* generated more sympathy than horror. He was actually a mutant human resembling a giant frog, who hid all day in a gloomy castle and hopped around at night in a giant maze. This bizarre film featured 3-D photography (q.v.) and delightfully weird sets designed by director William Cameron Menzies. A mutant tadpole surfaced briefly in *Prophechy* (1975), while the mutants in *Hell Comes to Frogtown* were unpleasant-looking, frog-like humanoids. See also **Frogtown Series**, **The Muppets**.

Ichabod and Mr. Toad (1949); *The Maze* (1953); *Frogs* (1972); *Prophecy* (1975); *The Muppet Movie* (1979); *Hell Comes to Frogtown* (1987); *The Frog Prince* (aka *Cannon Movie Tales: The Frog Prince*) (1988); *Freddie as F.R.O.7* (aka *Freddie the Frog*) (1992); *The Swan Princess* (1994); *The Wind in the Willows* (aka *Mr. Toad's Wild Ride*) (1996)

Frogtown Series

Set in the wake of a nuclear war, *Hell Comes to Frogtown* (1987) depicts a world where 68 percent of the male population has been killed and many of the survivors are sterile. A provisional government has established an agency, Medtech, dedicated to finding males with high sperm counts that can impregnate the female population. Medtech pardons criminal Sam Hell (Roddy Piper) when it learns of his sexual prowess and sends him into the "wastelands" to rescue fertile women held captive by frog-like mutants. Hell's journey leads him to Frogtown, a chilling industrial ghost town inhabited by "greeners" — humans who inexplicably became part frog as a result of the nuclear war. Herded into reservations, the greeners have established their own society ruled by Commander Toty (Brian Frank). Toty's soldiers promptly capture Hell and his female partner, forcing her to perform the amusing "Dance of the Three Snakes." With the help of a greener exotic dancer, Hell escapes and rescues the human women held captive in Toty's harem. Sadly, *Hell Comes to Frogtown* features some intriguing ideas that never get fully developed. Both societies use racial slurs against each other (the greeners refer to the "normal" humans as "flat lips"). The "normal" human society is portrayed as cruel and self-serving. After all, it forced the greeners to live in the equivalent of ghetto slums, instead of trying to help them. And Medtech takes its population mission to extremes — in one scene, a frightened girl is drugged so Hell can impregnate her. Though *A Boy and His Dog* explored the post-apocalypse infertility theme with much greater success, *Hell Comes to Frogtown* has built enough of a fan base to warrant two belated sequels:

Frogtown II (1993) and *Toad Warrior* (1996). Director Donald G. Jackson, who co-wrote the original story, helmed all three films. Former wrestler Roddy Piper skipped the sequels, but went on to score his biggest role in John Carpenter's sci-fi action film *They Live* (1989). See also **Frogs; Humanimals.**

Hell Comes to Frogtown (1987); *Frogtown II* (aka *Return to Frogtown*) (1993); *Toad Warrior* (aka *Frogtown III*) (1996)

Fu Manchu

Warner Oland, best known as Charlie Chan, portrayed Sax Rohmer's evil Oriental mastermind in three early talkies: *The Mysterious Fu Manchu, The Return of Fu Manchu,* and *Daughter of the Dragon* (as well as a cameo in the all-star revue *Paramount on Parade*). Boris Karloff took over in 1932's *Mask of Fu Manchu,* with Myrna Loy as his equally-dastardly daughter. Republic Pictures produced the 15-chapter serial *The Drums of Fu Machu* in 1940 with Henry Brandon in the title role. It was also edited into a 69-minute movie version released in 1943. Two decades later, producer Harry Alan Towers launched a new film series with *Face of Fu Manchu.* This entertaining debut entry starred Christopher Lee as Fu and Nigel Green as intrepid archnemesis Nayland Smith. Towers followed it with four additional entries with Lee. Unfortunately, these modest efforts were hampered by poor production values and increasingly dreadful scripts. Towers also made a movie version of Sax Rohmer's *The Million Eyes of Su-Muru* (1967) and a sequel *Rio 70.* Both films starred *Goldfinger* beauty Shirley Eaton as a female Fu called Su-muru. In 1978, Peter Sellers played both Fu and Nayland Smith in the dismal spoof *The Fiendish Plot of Dr. Fu Manchu.* Sadly, it turned out to be Sellers' swan song. A syndicated TV series, *The Adventures of Fu Manchu* starring Glen Gordon, ran briefly in the mid–1950s.

The Mysterious Fu Manchu (1929) (Warner Oland); *The Return of Fu Manchu* (1930) (Oland); *Paramount on Parade* (1930) (Oland appears in a skit); *Daughter of the Dragon* (1931) (Oland); *Mask of Fu Manchu* (1932) (Boris Karloff); *The Drums of Fu Manchu* (1943) (Henry Brandon); *Face of Fu Manchu* (1965) (Christopher Lee); *Bride of Fu Manchu* (1966) (Lee); *Blood of Fu Manchu* (aka *Kiss and Kill*) (1968) (Lee); *Castle of Fu Manchu* (aka *Assignment: Istanbul*) (1968) (Lee); *Vengeance of Fu Manchu* (1968) (Lee); *The Fiendish Plot of Dr. Fu Manchu* (1978) (Peter Sellers)

The Gambler Series

Country singer Kenny Rogers wisely banked on his easygoing charm to carry 1980's *The Gambler,* a TV movie western inspired by his hit song. The minimal plot starred Rogers as crafty gambler Brady Hawkes who teams up with a cowpoke (Bruce Boxleitner) on the road to lighthearted adventures. Linda Evans joined them for a 1983 sequel and Linda Gray signed on for a third film. The fourth entry featured TV Western heroes Wyatt Earp (Hugh O'Brien), Bat Masterson (Gene Barry), and the Rifleman (Chuck Connors). A final series entry, *The Gambler V: Playing for Keeps* (1994), found Brady looking for his teenage son and getting mixed up with Butch Cassidy and the Sundance Kid. All five *Gambler* films scored well in the TV ratings, as did another song-inspired Rogers hit *Coward of the County* (1981 TVM). However, moviegoers seemed less impressed with Rogers, brushing off his 1982 theatrical feature *Six Pack* and sending it to the flop pile.

The Gambler (aka *Kenny Rogers as The Gambler*) (1980 TVM); *The Gambler — The Adventure Continues* (aka *Kenny Rogers as The Gambler — The Adventure Continues*) (1983 TVM); *The Gambler III, the Legend Continues* (1987 TVM); *The Gambler IV: Luck of the Draw* (1991 TVM); *The Gambler V: Playing for Keeps* (1994 TVM)

Gambling

With the roll of a die or the flip of a card, gambling has made fortunes, wrecked relationships, shattered reputations, and led to cold-blooded murder. The most powerful films on the subject are those dealing with compulsive gamblers. Earnest writer Gregory Peck rescued Ava Gardner from the perils of gambling — only to catch the fever himself — in 1949's *The Great Sinner.* That same year's *The Lady Gambles* was described by one critic as "a kind of *Lost Weekend* of the gaming tables." Barbara Stanwyck played the woman who sacrificed everything, including husband Robert Preston, after falling under the spell of a roulette table. She nevertheless managed to pull off a happy ending. The gambling addicts of the 1970s were less fortunate. Robert Altman's *California Split* was a depressing comedy about a pair of hopeless losers played convincingly by George Segal and Elliott Gould (the film's title is slang for cutthroat high-low poker). *The Gambler* (1975) presented the same premise, less one character and minus the humor that made *California Split* tolerable. Ladies fared even worse in made-for-TV movies, with bored housewife Shirley Jones catching gambling fever in *Winner Take All* (1975) and lonely med student's wife Valerie Bertinelli following suit in *The Seduction of Gina* (1984). In contrast to compulsive players unable to control their fate, professional gamblers know when to quit — usually. Pro poker player Steve McQueen had "The Man" (Edward G. Robinson) on the ropes in the marathon stud poker game that climaxed 1965's *The Cincinnati Kid.* But The Kid played his cards wrong and wound up with nothing (except a $5,000 debt). Tony Curtis and Matt Dillon knew when to trash the cards and pocket the dice in *Mister Cory* (1957) and *The Big Town* (1987), respectively. However, neither of them hulled in winnings comparable to the loot accumulated by unlikely card shark/con artist Joanne Woodward in *Big Hand for the Little Lady* (1966). Dozens of other movies have featured professional gamblers, though their occupation has not always been of primary importance to the plot. Several films not exclusively about gambling have integrated it cleverly into their plots. A crooked card game and a subsequent lynching provoked a series of murders in the mystery/Western *Five Card Stud* (1968). Vacationing married couple Julie Haggerty and Albert Brooks stopped in Las Vegas long enough for Haggerty to lose their "nest egg" in the savagely funny *Lost in America* (1985). The scene in which the frantic Brooks tries to convince casino owner Garry Marshall to return the money is a delight. It's almost as funny as the gin rummy game between bubble-headed Judy Holliday and gruff gangster Broderick Crawford in *Born Yesterday* (1950).

Gambling Lady (1934); *The Man Who Broke the Bank at Monte Carlo* (1935); *Lady Luck* (1946); *The Lady Gambles* (1949); *The Great Sinner* (1949); *The Queen of Spades* (1949); *Gambling House* (1950); *The Lady Pays Off* (1951); *The Gambler and the Lady* (1952); *Mississippi Gambler* (1953); *Mister Cory* (1957); *Queen of Spades* (1960); *King of the Roaring 20's-The Story of Arnold Rothstein* (aka *The Big Bankroll*) (1961); *Who's Got the Action?* (1962); *Bay of Angels* (1962); *The Cincinnati Kid* (1965); *Big Hand for the Little*

Lady (aka *Big Deal at Dodge City*) (1966); *Five Card Stud* (1968); *The Gamblers* (1969); *California Split* (1974); *Thursday's Game* (1974 TVM); *The Gambler* (1975); *Winner Take All* (1975 TVM); *The Gambler* (aka *Kenny Rogers as The Gambler*) (1980 TVM); *Casino* (1980 TVM); *Lookin' to Get Out* (1982); *Stacy's Knights* (1983); *The Seduction of Gina* (1984 TVM); *Lost in America* (1985); *Fever Pitch* (1985); *The Big Town* (1987); *House of Games* (1987); *Let It Ride* (1989); *Family Prayers* (1993); *A Dreamscape: Gambling in America* (1994); *Maverick* (1994); *Hard Eight* (1997); *Rounders* (1998); *Croupier* (2000)

Game Shows

The quintessential game show movie remains 1950's *Champagne for Caesar*, a wry satire starring Ronald Colman as a genius who practically bankrupts quiz show sponsor Vincent Price. Art Linkletter, an ideal choice, played the show's ("Masquerade for Money") obnoxious host. Mary Steenburgen appeared on a quiz show in *Melvin and Howard*, while Diane Keaton competed on the "TV Tube of Knowledge" in *The Lemon Sisters*. Arnold Schwarzenegger was an unwilling contestant on a futuristic game show in *The Running Man* (a variation on the government-sponsored hunt in 1965's *The Tenth Victim*). *Shock Treatment* (1981), the seldom-seen sequel to *The Rocky Horror Picture Show*, was an appropriately bizarre satire on television quiz programs. Radio contests were the subject of *Christmas in July* (in which Dick Powell spends the money thinking he's won the cash), *The Jackpot* (contest winner James Stewart finds his life changing for the worse), and *Ma and Pa Kettle on Vacation*. And in Woody Allen's *Radio Days*, burglars emptying out a house answer a radio quiz show question and win the homeowners new furniture. See also **Television.**

Take It or Leave It (1944); *Blondie Hits the Jackpot* (1949); *Champagne for Caesar* (1950); *Game Show Models* (1977); *Three on a Date* (1978 TVM); *Melvin and Howard* (1980); *Shock Treatment* (1981); *For Love or Money* (1984 TVM); *National Lampoon's European Vacation* (1985); *The Running Man* (1987); *Death Row Game Show* (1987); *The Lemon Sisters* (1990); *Stay Tuned* (1992); *Quiz Show* (1994); *Reckless* (1995)

Gamera

Daiei Studios created this giant, flying, fanged, fire-breathing turtle to compete with rival Toho's Godzilla film series (q.v.). Like Godzilla, Gamera started his career as a bad guy, but turned good in later installments. He was also discovered in a similar fashion, when a plane containing an atomic bomb crashed in the Arctic. The giant turtle's initial appearance was not a total surprise, however, as a scientist in the dubbed version of 1965's *Gamera* confessed: "I heard there were giant turtles that lived on the Arctic continent." Gamera flew by withdrawing into his shell and rotating like a flying saucer. The original seven film series ended in 1971. An eighth installment, *Gamera, Super Monster*, appeared a decade later, but it was composed mostly of stock footage. Then, in 1995, following on the heels of the successful *Godzilla* (q.v.) revival, Gamera came out of retirement for *Gamera: The Guardian of the Universe* (1995). It earned surprisingly good reviews and launched a new series. Film critic Roger Ebert once noted: "Gamera ... has never attained the stardom of Godzilla, perhaps because of speciesism, which prejudices us to prefer dinosaurs to turtles." See also **Turtles.**

Gamera (aka *Gamera, the Invincible; Gammera; Daikaiju Gamera*) (1965); *Gamera vs. Barugon* (aka *War of the Monsters; Gamera tai Barugon*) (1966); *Gamera vs. Gyaos* (aka *Return of the Giant Monsters; Gamera tai Gyaos*) (1967); *Gamera vs. Outer-Space Monster Virus* (aka *Destroy All Planets; Gamera tai Viras*) (1968); *Gamera vs. Guiron* (aka *Attack of the Monsters; Gamera tai Guiron*) (1969); *Gamera vs. Jiger* (aka *Gamera vs. Monster X; Gamera tai Daimaju Jaiga*) (1970); *Gamera vs. Zigra* (aka *Gamera vs. the Deep Sea Monster Zigra; Gamera tai Shinkai Kaiju Jigura*) (1971); *Gamera, Super Monster* (aka *Uchu Kaijû Gamera; Space Monster Gamera; Super Monster Gamera* (1980); *Gamera: The Guardian of the Universe* (aka *Gamera: Giant Monster Midair Showdown; Gamera Daikaijû Kuchu Kessen*) (1995); *Gamera 2: Assault of the Legion* (aka *Gamera 2: Region Shurai*) (1996); *Gamera 3: The Awakening of Iris* (aka *Gamera 3: Iris Kakusei*) (1999)

Gangsters (Real Life)

Although gangsters have been a prominent screen fixture since the 1930s, the genre's early films focused almost exclusively on fictitious bad guys. The first major picture to borrow its plot from the nation's headlines was careful to change names and slightly alter the facts. Nevertheless, everyone — including the censors — recognized that Howard Hawks' *Scarface* (1932) was the story of Al Capone. In contrast, Paramount promoted the fact-based aspects of its *Persons in Hiding* series (q.v.), which was based on a best-seller written by J. Edgar Hoover. This series of four B-movies introduced to moviegoers the blood-splattered crime careers of Bonnie Parker and Clyde Barrow (1939's *Persons in Hiding*) and Ma Barker (1940's *Queen of the Mob*). Four years later, Twentieth Century–Fox produced *Roger Touhy, Gangster* starring Preston Foster as Capone's henchman. Fox hyped the fact that it was made in cooperation with the FBI and partially filmed at the Illinois State Penitentiary. The following year, poverty row studio Monogram mounted one of its finest films, *Dillinger*, a slick biography starring Lawrence Tierney as the 1930's most popular gangster. In a way, *Dillinger* established the gangster biopic formula for a wave of late 1950s films chronicling the careers of Machine Gun Kelly, Baby Face Nelson, Bonnie Parker, and Pretty Boy Floyd. Fact-based gangster movies declined in popularity in the mid–1960s, but shot back with a vengeance with Arthur Penn's 1967 blockbuster *Bonnie and Clyde*. The success of 1972's *The Godfather* further fueled interest in gangster films of any type. Subsequently, television jumped into the genre with a quartet of snappy pictures based on the careers of the 1930's most famous gangsters. Dale Robertson played FBI agent Melvin Purvis in two of these films, battling Machine Gun Kelly in *Melvin Purvis: G-Man* (1974) and then the Dillinger gang in *The Kansas City Massacre* (1975). The 1970s gangster film cycle ended with the theatrical box-office bomb *Capone* (1975). However, real-life gangster films were on the rise again in the late 1980s, thanks to the blockbuster hit *The Untouchables* (1987) and the publicity surrounding the opening of Al Capone's secret vault (alas, the contents turned out to be rather dull). The most popular real-life gangsters on films are: Al Capone (*Scarface, The Scarface Mob, The St. Valentine's Day Massacre, Capone, The Untouchables, The Revenge of Al Capone, The Lost Capone*); John Dillinger (*Dillinger, Young Dillinger, Dillinger, The Lady in Red*, the TV movie *Dillinger*); Pretty Boy Floyd (*Pretty Boy Floyd, A Bullet for Pretty Boy, The Story of Pretty Boy Floyd*); Ma Barker (*Queen of the Mob, Ma Barker's Killer Brood,*

Bloody Mama); and Bonnie Parker (*Persons in Hiding, The Bonnie Parker Story, Bonnie and Clyde, Bonnie and Clyde: The True Story*). See also **FBI; Persons in Hiding Series.**

Scarface (aka *Scarface, the Shame of a Nation*) (1932); *Persons in Hiding* (1939); *Queen of the Mob* (1940); *Roger Touhy, Gangster* (1944); *Dillinger* (1945); *Baby Face Nelson* (1957); *Machine Gun Kelly* (1958); *The Bonnie Parker Story* (1958); *The Scarface Mob* (1958); *The FBI Story* (1959); *Pretty Boy Floyd* (1960); *The Rise and Fall of Legs Diamond* (1960); *Ma Barker's Killer Brood* (1960); *Portrait of a Mobster* (1961); *Mad Dog Coll* (1961); *King of the Roaring 20's — The Story of Arnold Rothstein* (aka *The Big Bankroll*) (1961); *Young Dillinger* (1965); *Bonnie and Clyde* (1967); *The St. Valentine Day's Massacre* (1967); *Bloody Mama* (1970); *A Bullet for Pretty Boy* (1971); *The Valachi Papers* (1972); *Dillinger* (1973); *The FBI Story — Alvin Karpis* (aka *The FBI Story — The FBI versus Alvin Karpis, Public Enemy Number One*) (1974 TVM); *Melvin Purvis: G-Man* (aka *The Legend of Machine Gun Kelly*) (1974 TVM); *Crazy Joe* (1974); *The Virginia Hill Story* (1974 TVM) (Bugsy Siegel's moll); *The Story of Pretty Boy Floyd* (aka *Pretty Boy Floyd*) (1974 TVM); *Lepke* (1975); *The Kansas City Massacre* (1975 TVM); *Capone* (1975); *The Lady in Red* (1979); *The Untouchables* (1987); *Verne Miller* (1987); *Nitti* (1988 TVM); *The Revenge of Al Capone* (1989 TVM); *The Lost Capone* (1990 TVM); *Dillinger* (1991 TVM); *Mobsters* (1991) (Bugsy Siegel, Lucky Luciano, Meyer Lansky, and Richard Costello); *Billy Bathgate* (1991) (Dutch Schultz); *Bugsy* (1991); *Mad Dog Coll* (1992); *Hit the Dutchman* (1992) (Dutch Schultz); *Bonnie and Clyde: The True Story* (1992 TVM); *Hoodlum* (1997) (Ellsworth "Bumpy" Johnson); *The Newton Boys* (1998) (Willis, Joe, Jess, and Dock Newton); *The General* (1998) (Martin Cahill); *Witness to the Mob* (1998 TVM) (John Gotti); *Lanksy* (1999 TVM) (Meyer Lanksy, Bugsy Siegel, and Lucky Luciano)

Genies

Genies have been common fixtures in Arabian Nights fantasy-adventures, such as *Thief of Bagdad* (1940), *The Wonders of Aladdin* (1961), *A Thousand and One Nights* (1968), and *Aladdin* (1992). Rex Ingram still rates as the cinema's most intimidating genie for *Thief of Bagdad*. However, Robin Williams, who voiced the genie for Disney's *Aladdin* (q.v.), comes a close second in terms of resourcefulness and dependability. Surprisingly, genies and magic lamps have also found their way into contemporary-set films. In the 1945 musical *Where Do We Go from Here?* Army reject Fred MacMurray found a magic lamp and asked its bumbling genie (Gene Sheldon) to get him into the armed forces. The genie complied, but somehow kept putting Fred into the wrong army — in Valley Forge with Washington, on the Santa Maria with Columbus. Eric Blore was a grumpy genie in 1955's *Bowery to Bagdad*, but who wouldn't be with those overaged Bowery Boys Sach (Huntz Hall) and Slip (Leo Gorcey) around to cause trouble? Burl Ives donned the genie attire for 1964's *The Brass Bottle*, which co-starred Tony Randall and Barbara Eden. Eden went on to become the most famous of all genies in the 1965–70 TV sitcom *I Dream of Jeannie* and its 1985 made-for-TV reunion movie *I Dream of Jeannie: 15 Years Later*. Not all genies are nice — the evil one in 1987's *The Outing* was out to get some teens trapped in a museum overnight. The most interesting wish granted by a genie was in the 1963 "I Dream of Genie" episode of TV's *The Twilight Zone*, in which a man given only one wish wishes to become a genie. A bowling trophy housed a mischievous imp in the memorably-titled *Sorority Babes in the Slimeball Bowl-O-Rama* (1988). See also **Aladdin Series.**

Thief of Bagdad (1924); *Thief of Bagdad* (1940); *A Thousand and One Nights* (1945); *Where Do We Go from Here?* (1945); *Bowery to Bagdad* (1955); *The Seventh Voyage of Sinbad* (1958); *The Boy and the Pirates* (1960); *The Wizard of Baghdad* (1960); *The Wonders of Aladdin* (1961); *The Brass Bottle* (1964); *A Thousand and One Nights* (1968); *Aladdin* (1981); *I Dream of Jeannie: 15 Years Later* (1985 TVM); *The Outing* (1987); *Wildest Dreams* (1987); *Priceless Beauty* (1988); *Bernard and the Genie* (1991 TVM); *Aladdin* (1992); *Wish Me Luck* (1994); *Kazaam* (1996); *Wishmaster* (1997); *Wishmaster 2* (aka *Wishmaster 2: Evil Never Dies*) (1999); *Arabian Nights* (2000 TVM)

Ghidrah

A giant, winged dragon with three (count 'em) fire-breathing heads, Ghidrah was "hatched" when a meteorite exploded in *Ghidrah the Three-Headed Monster* (1965). He has been the most consistently vicious Japanese monster and a formidable opponent — his three heads can battle Godzilla, Rodan, and Mothra simultaneously. He earned his best reviews for *Godzilla vs. King Ghidrah*, one of the Godzilla (q.v.) revival films in the 1990s. It also featured Mecha-King Ghidrah, a robot version of the three-headed monster.

Ghidrah the Three-Headed Monster (aka *The Greatest Battle on Earth; Sandai Kaiju Chikyu Saidai No Kessen*) (1965); *Monster Zero* (aka *Invasion of the Astro-Monsters; Kaiju Daisenso*) (1965); *Destroy All Monsters* (aka *Operation Monsterland; Kaiju Soshingeki*) (1968); *Godzilla on Monster Island* (aka *Godzilla vs. Gigan; Gojira tai Gaigan*) (1971); *Godzilla vs. King Ghidrah* (aka *Godzilla vs. King Ghidorah; Gojira vs. Kingugidora*) (1992)

Ghosts

Although ghost films have never been in short supply, serious ghostly dramas have been few and far between. The ghost, unlike his supernatural peers the vampire (q.v.) and the werewolf (q.v.), became strongly associated with comedy early in his career. This resulted in a stigma that has been hard to erase. Nevertheless, several of those comedies have served the ghost well, resulting in semi-classics like *The Ghost Goes West* (1936), *Topper* (1937), and *The Ghost Breakers* (1940). Robert Donat played the title role in *The Ghost Goes West*, in which gravel-voiced Eugene Pallette purchased a castle and, unknowingly, the spirit doomed to haunt it. Cary Grant and Constance Bennett starred as the ghostly, fun-loving Kerby couple in 1937's *Topper* (q.v.). They became quite a headache for meek banker Cosmos Topper (Roland Young), who also grappled with ghosts in two sequels. A haunted house and voodoo trappings provided the atmospheric setting for *The Ghost Breakers*, a successful stage play transformed into one of Bob Hope's finest vehicles. Most comedy teams have encountered real or would-be ghosts, including Olsen and Johnson in *Ghost Catchers* (1944), Martin and Lewis in *Scared Stiff* (a 1953 remake of *The Ghost Breakers*), the Bowery Boys in *Ghost Chasers* (1951), and Abbott and Costello in *The Time of Their Lives* (1946). The latter film proved to be one of Abbott and Costello's best, with Lou and Marjorie Reynolds as a pair of frustrated Revolutionary ghosts and Bud as a mortal who tries to help them escape their earthly prison. The popularity of ghostly comedies has remained surprisingly steady over the years. In the 1980s, for example, box-office duds like *Kiss Me Goodbye* (1982) and *High Spirits* (1988) were counterbalanced and overshadowed by unexpected hits like

Ghostbusters (1984) and *Beetlejuice* (1988). Alas, serious ghost films have not fared nearly as well. *The Scoundrel* (1935) remains an obscure melodrama, despite the magnetic presence of Noel Coward as a cynical writer who returns to Earth after his death. (Its lack of success may have inspired Coward's sophisticated ghostly farce *Blithe Spirit*, which appeared first as a 1941 stage play and then a 1945 movie). In the 1940s, Hollywood made a rare excursion into ghostly horror with *The Uninvited* (1944). It featured Ray Milland, a creepy house overlooking rhythmic waves, a haunting theme by Victor Young, and a strange odor of mimosa. Oddly, it turned out to be an isolated success (there was nary a ghost in Paramount 1945's follow-up *The Unseen*). Sixteen years later, British director Jack Clayton ushered in the era of the intellectual ghost film with *The Innocents* (1961), a chilling adaptation of Henry James' *The Turn of the Screw*. This eerie tale of an unstable governess and her manipulative charges left its ghostly element up to the viewer's imagination. One could effectively argue that Deborah Kerr's governess was a little insane from the beginning or that she was driven to madness by a ghost. This same type of ambiguity could also be applied to Robert Wise's *The Haunting* and Stanley Kubrick's *The Shining* (1980). *The Legend of Hell House* (1973) was a more conventional horror film, but nevertheless a scary yarn about a nasty spirit harassing parapsychologists investigating a spooky house. *The Entity* (1983) claimed to be a fact-based story of a woman sexually assaulted repeatedly by a ghost. On a more pleasant note, mortal/ghost romances have been the subject of *The Ghost and Mrs. Muir*, *Sandcastles*, *Kiss Me Goodbye*, and the blockbuster hit *Ghost*. That master of gimmicks, William Castle, also produced a ghost movie. During the theatrical run of 1960's *13 Ghosts*, viewers were given cardboard glasses which allowed them to see "invisible" ghosts in the film. The ever-industrious Castle dubbed this gimmick "Illusion-O." Naturally, many ghost movies have settled for logical explanations in lieu of supernatural ones. *The Ghost of St. Michael's* (1941), for example, turned out to be a very mortal enemy agent. See also **Amityville Series**; **Casper**; **A Chinese Ghost Story Series**; **Mediums and Seances**; **Poltergeist Series**; **Witchboard Series**.

The Ghost Train (1927); *The Ghost Train* (1931); *The Scoundrel* (1935); *The Return of Peter Grimm* (1935); *The Ghost Goes West* (1936); *Topper* (1937); *A Christmas Carol* (1938); *Happy Landing* (1938); *The Ghost Breakers* (1940); *Earthbound* (1940); *The Ghost of St. Michael's* (1941); *Hold That Ghost* (1941); *The Ghost Train* (1941); *The Remarkable Andrew* (1942); *The Man in the Trunk* (1942); *A Guy Named Joe* (1943); *The Canterville Ghost* (1944); *Ghost Catchers* (1944); *The Uninvited* (1944); *A Place of One's Own* (1944); *Don't Take It to Heart* (1945); *Wonder Man* (1945); *Blithe Spirit* (1945); *The Time of Their Lives* (1946); *The Ghost and Mrs. Muir* (1947); *The Ghosts of Berkeley Square* (1947); *The Cockeyed Miracle* (1948); *Cardboard Cavalier* (1949); *A Christmas Carol* (aka *Scrooge*) (1951); *Ghost Chasers* (1951); *Ghost Ship* (1952); *Scared Stiff* (1953); *Brigadoon* (1954); *The Headless Ghost* (1958); *The Ghost of Dragstrip Hollow* (1959); *The Invisible Creature* (aka *The House on Marsh Road*) (1959); *Tormented* (1960); *The Innocents* (1961); *House of Mystery* (1961); *The Haunting* (1963); *The Ghost and Mr. Chicken* (1966); *The Ghost in the Invisible Bikini* (1966); *Blackbeard's Ghost* (1968); *Ghosts—Italian Style* (1969); *The Extraordinary Seaman* (1969); *Sole Survivor* (1970 TVM); *The Amazing Mr. Blunden* (1972); *Sandcastles* (1972 TVM); *The Legend of Hell House* (1973); *Madhouse Mansion* (aka *Ghost Story*) (1974); *Celine and Julie Go Boating* (1974); *Reflections of Murder* (1974 TVM); *The Haunting of Julia* (aka *Full Circle*) (1976); *Death at

Love House (1976 TVM); *Empire of Passion* (1978); *The Ghost of Flight 401* (1978 TVM); *Child of Glass* (1978 TVM); *Dominique* (aka *Dominique Is Dead*) (1978); *The Changeling* (1979); *An American Christmas Carol* (1979 TVM); *The Shining* (1980); *Beyond Evil* (1980); *Ghost Story* (1981); *Poltergeist* (1982); *Don't Go to Sleep* (1982 TVM); *O'Hara's Wife* (1982); *Kiss Me Goodbye* (1982); *The House Where Evil Dwells* (1982); *The Entity* (1983); *The Haunting Passion* (1983 TVM); *Somewhere Tomorrow* (1983); *Ghostbusters* (1984); *Haunted Honeyman* (1986); *A Chinese Ghost Story* (aka *Qian Nu Youhun*) (1987); *Ghost Fever* (1987); *Beetlejuice* (1988); *Lady in White* (1988); *Ghost Town* (1988); *High Spirits* (1988); *Field of Dreams* (1989); *Ghostbusters II* (1989); *She's Back* (1989); *Ghost* (1990); *Ghost Dad* (1990); *The Sleeping Car* (1990); *Heart Condition* (1990); *Ghosts Can't Do It* (1990); *Cello* (1990); *Escape* (1990); *Truly Madly Deeply* (1991); *And You Thought Your Parents Were Weird* (1991); *Grave Secrets: The Legacy of Hilltop Drive* (1992 TVM); *Love Can Be Murder* (1992 TVM); *Bedevil* (1993); *Cooperstown* (1993 TVM); *Ghost Mom* (1993 TVM); *Charlie's Ghost Story* (1994); *The Haunting of Seacliff Inn* (1994 TVM); *The Haunting of Helen* (1995 TVM); *Casper* (1995); *The Canterville Ghost* (1996 TVM); *Forest Warrior* (1996); *The Frighteners* (1996); *Fatally Yours* (1996); *Spirit Lost* (1997); *The Sixth Man* (1997); *Beloved* (1998); *Giving Up the Ghost* (1998); *The Haunting* (1999); *The Sixth Sense* (1999); *Stir of Echoes* (1999); *What Lies Beneath* (2000)

Ghoulies Series

Although considered a rip-off of *Gremlins* (1984), the original *Ghoulies* (1985) differs substantially in plot and tone — which does not necessarily make it original nor even interesting. It tells the story of Jonathan Graves (Peter Liapis), a college student who drops out to renovate his deceased parents' old mansion. Unbeknownst to Jonathan, his father practiced black magic and sacrificed Jonathan's mother. The teenager discovers his father's books and falls under the spell of their power — to the point that he summons the title characters (little slimy demons which admittedly resemble Gremlins). Jonathan unknowingly revives his father, who orders the ghoulies to kill most of Jonathan's friends and announces to his son that he wants to steal the boy's youth. The film is neither scary nor humorous; it's also fairly light on blood and gore, as evidenced by its PG-13 rating. The supporting cast features some interesting faces — such as Jack (*Eraserhead*) Nance, cult actress Bobbie Bresee, and Mariska Hargitay (Jayne Mansfield's daughter) — but they have little to do. The 1987 sequel, *Ghoulies II*, continued the first film's mediocrity despite a promising setting: a carnival house of horrors called Satan's Den, which is about to go out of business. The series' third entry, 1989's *Ghoulies III: Ghoulies Go to College*, added some recognizable talent: Kevin (*Invasion of the Body Snatchers*) McCarthy and Griffin O'Neal (Ryan's son). McCarthy plays crusty Professor Ragnor, who summons the ghoulies to teach the campus youth a lesson. *Ghoulies IV* (1994) picks up the original film's plot eight years later, with Jonathan Graves (Liapis again) as a cop battling the dark forces of magic. The ghoulies play a strictly supporting role.

Ghoulies (1985); *Ghoulies II* (1987); *Ghoulies III: Ghoulies Go to College* (aka *Ghoulies III*) (1989); *Ghoulies IV* (1994)

Ghouls

According to Muslim folklore, a ghoul is an evil spirit that robs graves and feasts upon dead flesh. Horror movies have modified that definition over the years and produced a loose variation of the term, defining a ghoul as a dead person who eats the flesh of the living. (For a discussion of noncarnivorous living dead, see **Zombies**.) Though less well-known than vampires and werewolves, ghouls have been around for awhile. Boris Karloff starred in the once-lost 1933 British film *The Ghoul*. Yet, while he rose from the dead to recover a stolen jewel, he was not technically a ghoul. Ten years later, *The Mad Ghoul* cast the delightful George Zucco as a mad scientist whose experiments with an ancient gas turn his nice assistant, David Bruce, into a creature who feeds on fresh human hearts. However, George Romero's 1968 cult shocker *Night of the Living Dead* (q.v.) set the gory standard by which most ghoul movies are judged. Shot near Pittsburgh for under $100,000, Romero's downbeat chiller centered around seven people trapped in a farmhouse surrounded by hungry resurrected dead people. It made little impact on its initial release, but by the early 1970s, it had emerged as a midnight movie staple and a critics' favorite. A trio of interesting ghoulish pictures appeared between 1972 and 1974, but only a few drive-in patrons saw them. Bob Clark (*A Christmas Story*) directed 1972's *Deathdream*, a reworking of "The Monkey's Paw" in which a dead Vietnam soldier returned home to eat his loved ones. The year after they produced *American Graffiti*, Gloria Katz and Willard Huyck made 1974's *Dead People*, which was reissued as *Return of the Living Dead* to capitalize on Romero's film. Italy's *Don't Open the Window* was an intriguing variation whereby a government device to kill insects transformed the dead into ghouls. By 1979, Romero had found the capital to make his long-awaited sequel *Dawn of the Dead*. This lengthy, gory, overly symbolic tale made a profit in the U.S. (where it was unrated), but performed exceptionally well overseas. Italian director Lucio Fulci subsequently made two Romero-inspired rip-offs: 1979's *Zombie* and 1980's *City of the Living Dead*. Meanwhile, *Night of the Living Dead* cowriter John Russo clashed with Romero on the rights to a *Living Dead* sequel. The two settled out of court, allowing Russo to make his 1985 ghoul satire *Return of the Living Dead*. Its surprise box-office success overshadowed Romero's *Day of the Dead* (1985), which, prior to its commercial and critical failure, was intended as the final chapter of Romero's ghoul trilogy. Romero has since produced a remake of the original and indicated another chapter might be on the drawing board. Bill Hinzman, who played the first ghoul in Romero's *Living Dead* original, made an amateurish 1989 tribute dubbed *Revenge of the Living Zombies*. See also **Cannibalism; Night of the Living Dead Series; Return of the Living Dead Series; Zombies**.

The Mad Ghoul (1943); *Night of the Living Dead* (1968); *Deathdream* (aka *The Night Walk; Dead of Night*) (1972); *Children Shouldn't Play with Dead Things* (1973); *Dead People* (aka *Return of the Living Dead; Messiah of Evil; Revenge of the Screaming Dead*) (1974); *Don't Open the Window* (aka *Breakfast at the Manchester Morgue*) (1974); *Dawn of the Dead* (aka *Zombie*) (1979); *Zombie* (aka *Zombie 2; Zombie Flesh-Eaters*) (1979); *Bloodeaters* (1980); *City of the Living Dead* (aka *Gates of Hell*) (1980); *Night of the Zombies* (1983); *City of the Walking Dead* (aka *Nightmare City*) (1983); *Return of the Living Dead* (1985); *Day of the Dead* (1985); *Return of the Living Dead II* (1988); *Zombie Brigade* (1988); *Redneck Zombies* (1989); *Revenge of the Living Zombies* (1989); *The Chilling* (1989); *Chopper Chicks in Zombietown* (1990); *Waxwork II: Lost in Time* (1991); *Braindead* (aka *Dead/Alive*) (1992); *Cemetery Man* (aka *Dellamorte Dellamore; Of Death and Love*) (1994); *I, Zombie* (aka *I, Zombie: The Chronicles of Pain*) (2000)

Giants

Bigger has not meant better for humans of gigantic proportions. In the science fiction genre, hardly anyone has grown big because they wanted to. *The Amazing Colossal Man* was a victim of a plutonium explosion, while an alien caused the *Attack of the 50-Foot Woman*. Neither of those title characters dealt with their newfound size very well and both eventually went crazy. A major problem that plagued them, along with *The 30 Foot Bride of Candy Rock* (1958), was their wardrobe. Embarrassingly, the Colossal Man wound up wearing big diapers, while the 30 Foot Bride made a nice-looking toga out of a parachute. Producer-director Bert I. Gordon, a major proponent of rear-screen projection, specialized in giant people movies. In addition to *The Amazing Colossal Man* (1957), he produced its sequel *War of the Colossal Beast* (1958), the very similar *Cyclops* (1957), and *Village of the Giants* (1965). The latter film, a very loose adaptation of H.G. Wells' *Food of the Gods*, starred little Ronnie Howard as a whiz kid who turns a bunch of teenagers into rowdy giants. Buddy Baer (whose nephew Max Jr. played Jethro on *The Beverly Hillbillies*) portrayed a gigantic conquistador in 1958's *Giant from the Unknown* and Abbott and Costello's oversized nemesis in 1952's *Jack and the Bean Stalk*. In Costello's only film sans Abbott, he turned his girlfriend Dorothy Provine into the aforementioned *30 Foot Bride of Candy Rock*. Richard Kiel—Jaws in the James Bond films—played the title role in *The Giant of Thunder Mountain* (1991), a wholesome family drama. But he and basketball player Gheorghe Muresan, who costarred in the Billy Crystal film *My Giant* (1998), just played *really* tall people. See also **Little People**.

Alice in Wonderland (1951); *Jack and the Bean Stalk* (1952); *Cyclops* (1957); *The Amazing Colossal Man* (1957); *War of the Colossal Beast* (1958); *Attack of the 50 Foot Woman* (1958); *Giant from the Unknown* (1958); *The 30 Foot Bride of Candy Rock* (1959); *Village of the Giants* (1965); *The Giant of Thunder Mountain* (1991); *Honey, I Blew Up the Kid* (1992); *Attack of the 50-Foot Woman* (1993 TVM); *The Pagemaster* (1994); *Attack of the 60 Foot Centerfold* (1995); *Gulliver's Travels* (1996 TVM); *My Giant* (1998)

Gidget

The original beach party teen was played by Sandra Dee in the 1959 eponymous opus. This first *Gidget* was semi-serious, with the teenager getting somewhat involved with an older man, a beachcomber played by Cliff Robertson. The follow-ups were more lighthearted, with the spunky teen being portrayed by five different actresses. However, the only one to capitalize on her Gidget exposure was Deborah Walley, who went on to star in several *Beach Party* movies. The films spawned two TV series: Sally Field's 1965-66 version and a syndicated series that cropped up in the mid–1980s. See also **Beach Party Series**.

Gidget (1959) (Sandra Dee); *Gidget Goes Hawaiian* (1961) (Deborah Walley); *Gidget Goes to Rome* (1963) (Cindy Carol); *Gidget Grows Up* (1969 TVM) (Karen Valentine); *Gidget Gets Married* (1972 TVM) (Monie Ellis); *Gidget's Summer Reunion* (1985 TVM) (Caryn Richman)

Gildersleeve, The Great

Portly, baritone-voiced comedian Harold Peary played Throckmorton P. Gildersleeve ("Gildy") in this short-lived RKO series inspired by a hit radio show. The character first appeared in the

1941 comedy *Look Who's Laughing*, which brought together radio favorites Bergen and McCarthy and Fibber McGee and Molly. After additional appearances as Gildy in *Here We Go Again* and *Seven Days Leave* (both 1942), Peary launched his own series with 1943's *The Great Gildersleeve*. He played the unlikely "custodian" of his teenage niece Margie (Nancy Gates) and enterprising nephew Leroy (Freddie Mercer). Jane Darwell, just three years after winning an Oscar as Ma Joad in 1939's *The Grapes of Wrath*, provided maternal support as Aunt Emma. The movies never rose above program filler and usually cast Gildy as an unlikely hero — clashing with gangsters, avoiding marriage-minded spinsters, and encountering ghostly ancestors. When Gildy got into a jam (e.g., zipped in a sleeping bag with a cat and dog), he typically responded with a bellowing "Oh, Leeeeroy!" When things were going well, though, one could count on hearing his trademark giggle.

Look Who's Laughing (1941); *Here We Go Again* (1942); *Seven Days Leave* (1942); *The Great Gildersleeve* (1943); *Gildersleeve's Bad Day* (1943); *Gildersleeve on Broadway* (1943); *Gildersleeve's Ghost* (1944)

Gilligan's Island Series

During its original 1964–66 telecasts, *Gilligan's Island* scored reasonably well in the ratings opposite *The Lawrence Welk Show* and then *The Donna Reed Show*. But the series' juvenile audience eventually spelled its doom on network television. Ironically, those same viewers turned the syndicated reruns of *Gilligan's Island* into a very profitable money-making machine. The series gradually built a large broad-based following which persuaded NBC to reunite the cast members for 1978's *Rescue from Gilligan's Island*. With the exception of Tina Louise as Ginger, all the original castaways returned. Time had not been kind to some of the performers, but the show's fans still enjoyed watching the *Minnow's* passengers finally get home — only to go on a reunion cruise and land back on the island. The movie performed very well in the ratings and there was talk of reviving the series. However, dwindling audiences for two additional films put that idea to rest. See also **Islands**; **Television Series Reunion Films**.

Rescue from Gilligan's Island (1978 TVM); *The Castaways on Gilligan's Island* (1979 TVM); *The Harlem Globetrotters on Gilligan's Island* (1981 TVM)

Gimmicks

When television entered American homes in the early 1950s, Hollywood panicked. Convinced that families would stay at home to watch the small screen, filmmakers sought innovative ideas to make theatrical films different. 3-D was revived (see separate entry), widescreen processes were introduced, and William Castle lured moviegoers with gimmicks that would make a carny barker jealous. A prolific B-movie director from 1943, Castle made his first horror feature in 1958. *Macabre* was a decent low-budget picture about a man trying to find his kidnapped daughter, who had been buried alive (q.v.). However, Castle turned it into a surprise money-maker by issuing viewers a $1,000 life insurance policy from Lloyds of London — in case anyone died of fright while watching the movie. Castle followed up with 1958's *House on Haunted Hill*, starring Vincent Price and a gimmick called "emergo." Not quite as clever as its name, "emergo" was

simply a skeleton on a wire which projectionists dropped over unsuspecting viewers during the film's big shock scene. *The Tingler* followed the same year and if there's a classic gimmick, this is it. Price stars again, this time as a doctor who discovers a crustacean-like creature that grows at the base of the spine during moments of intense fright. When one screams, the creature reduces in size and becomes harmless. However, if a person is too afraid to scream, the Tingler snaps the spine, causing instant death. At the highlight of the film, Price surgically removes a Tingler, which subsequently escapes to a movie theatre below him. The screen goes black and Price urges the real movie audience to: "Scream! Scream for your lives!" To heighten the effect, some patrons at selected movie theatres received mild electric shocks (yes, Castle had actually wired some of the seats!). Castle's next two gimmicks were far less elaborate. For *13 Ghosts* (1960), he provided viewers with filtered glasses which allowed them to see the movie's "invisible" ghosts (he called this "Illusion-O"). And in his 1961 psycho thriller *Homicidal*, he interrupted the film with a "fright break," which told viewers that "all those too timid to take the climax will be welcomed to the Coward's Corner." Director Joe Dante paid homage to Castle with *Matinee* (1993), a nostalgic tale of a horror film producer (John Goodman) who employs elaborately-named gimmicks like "Atomo-Vision." On a smaller scale, the 1991 horror-comedy *Popcorn* also spoofed Castle-type gimmicks. Although William Castle was the King of Gimmicks, others have resorted to similar tactics to draw audiences. See also **3-D**; **Cinerama**. Some of the more memorable gimmicks:

Scent of Mystery (1960) In selected theatres, over 30 aromas were piped in via plastic tubes. This was dubbed "Smell-O-Vision"; *Psycho* (1960) During first run, theaters refused to admit patrons once the film started; *Ten Little Indians* (1965) Featured a "murder minute" at the climax, informing viewers they had all the clues — and sixty seconds — to solve the mystery; *Chamber of Horrors* (1966) Sounded the "horror horn" and showed the "fear flasher" before every murder; *Wicked, Wicked* (1973) The entire movie was shown in a split-screen process the producers touted as "Duovision"; *Earthquake* (1974) First of the "Sensurround" movies, whereby the soundtrack was amplified in certain scenes to cause a rumbling sensation. It also caused headaches. Other "Sensurround" movies were *Midway* (1976) and *Rollercoaster* (1977); *The Beast Must Die* (1974) A "werewolf break" gave viewers time to guess the werewolf's identity; *Polyester* (1981) "Odorama" provided patrons with scratch-and-sniff cards with instructions on when to scratch during the flick; *Dead Men Don't Wear Plaid* (1982) Steve Martin "acted" with stars from Hollywood's golden days by intercutting footage from famous films; *Clue* (1985) Released with three endings, each one identifying a different character as the murderer; *Drowning by Numbers* (1987) The numerals 1–100 appear sequentially throughout the film, sometimes in expected places (e.g., clock faces) and sometimes in unexpected places (e.g., on a dead cow); *Million Dollar Mystery* (1987) Viewers could win a million dollars themselves by piecing together clues provided in the film; *Time Code* (2000) The frame was divided into four parts, each showing a different perspective of the story.

Ginger Series

Cheri Caffaro, who once won a Brigitte Bardot lookalike contest, played the lead role in this violent, sex-laden series about a blonde crimefighter. As Ginger McAllister, she broke up a vice ring in *Ginger*, freed cheerleaders from white slavery racketeers in *The Abductors*, and went undercover in the Virgin Islands in *Girls Are for Loving.* In addition to plenty of gratuitous nudity (both male and female), the *Ginger* films also featured lesbian love scenes, a castration-with-a-piano-wire scene, rapes, and bondage. William Granville played fellow crimefighter Jason Varone in all three series entries. Caffaro's husband Don Schain wrote and directed the films. Caffaro and Schain also teamed up for non–*Ginger* films such as *A Place Called Today* (1972) and *Too Hot to Handle* (1976), which featured Caffaro as a Ginger-like character called Samantha Fox.

Ginger (1971); *The Abductors* (1972); *Girls Are for Loving* (1973)

The Godfather Trilogy

Francis Ford Coppola and Mario Puzo's epic saga of the Corleone family spans three generations of Mafia gangsters from the turn-of-the-century to 1980. The first two films chalked up some impressive honors — each won Best Picture — but *The Godfather Part III* slipped into film history as little more than a postscript. *The Godfather* (1972), adapted from Puzo's best-seller and starring Marlon Brando in the title role, was a "film event" from the beginning. The principal action takes place between 1945 and 1955, during the final days of Don Vito's (Brando) reign as head of the powerful Corleone family. The Corleones struggle toward social and financial respectability, even as they destroy their rivals to ensure control of their "business." It's easy to guess which son will inherit his father's throne: college-educated Michael (Al Pacino), who wants no part of his inheritance; the violent, hot-tempered Sonny (James Caan); or the simple-minded Fredo (John Cazale). Yet, Michael's gradual transition into a strong-willed, ruthless-when-necessary gangster is the most engrossing plotline in the film. Coppola's sister Talia Shire (Adrienne in the *Rocky* films) plays Don Vito's only daughter Connie; Robert Duvall is the family's rational attorney Tom Hagen; and Diane Keaton plays Michael's eventual wife Kay Adams. *The Godfather Part II* (1974), also based on Puzo's novel, tells two parallel stories: Michael Corleone's attempt to take control of Las Vegas in the late 1950s and Vito Corleone's (Robert De Niro) immigration to America and his rise to Mafia power in 1917 New York. Although Pacino and other principals from the original film reprise their roles, De Niro dominates the screen in a star-making turn for which he won a Best Supporting Actor Oscar. Film critics disagreed sharply on the merits of *The Godfather Part II.* Some of them found the film's divergent structure intriguing, while others echoed the views of Vincent Canby of *The New York Times*: "I can't readily imagine what Mr. Coppola and Mr. Puzo were trying to do, except to turn their first film into a long parenthesis that would fit between the halves of the new movie." Coppola must have read that quote, because he did just that seven years later with *Godfather — The Complete Epic, 1902–1958,* a 386-minute chronological version of *The Godfather* and *The Godfather Part II* (with 15 minutes of "never-before-seen" footage). This special edition, which played on network television and videotape, appeared to be the end of the saga. However, after a string of disappointing films and financial troubles, Coppola returned to his biggest hit with 1990's *The Godfather Part III.* This stale rehash of the first two films brought back Pacino as Don Michael Corleone, but neglected to surround him with an interesting story. Diane Keaton and Talia Shire, also veterans of I and II, looked concerned and bored for most of the picture's lengthy 161 minutes. Only Andy Garcia, as Michael's cocky nephew (and obvious successor), brought a fresh intensity to his role. *The Godfather Part III* earned a Best Picture nomination and middling box-office results — both chiefly on the merits of the earlier films. In 1993, Coppola edited all three films together (and added still more "new footage") to create the epic videotape *The Godfather Trilogy: 1901–1980.*

The Godfather (1972); *The Godfather Part II* (1974); *The Godfather Part III* (1990)

Godzilla

Japan's biggest star, both literally (400 feet tall, 2 million tons) and in terms of popularity, Godzilla has starred in over 20 films since his 1954 debut. The first, and best, was *Godzilla, King of the Monsters,* in which H-bomb tests revive the prehistoric creature and equip him with radioactive breath. He leaves his native Oto island and topples most of Tokyo before an "oxygen destroyer" spells his doom. The film was a smash hit in Japan and fared very well when imported to the U.S. in 1956. It costarred Raymond Burr as a wheelchair-ridden reporter (shades of *Ironside*) named Steve Martin. Its sequel, *Godzilla Raids Again* (1955), has caused infinite nightmares for film historians. Besides sporting the alternate titles *Godzilla's Counterattack* and *The Return of Godzilla,* it was released in the U.S. as *Gigantis, the Fire Monster.* Confusingly, the title monster was not a Godzilla rival, but the Big G himself. After two more movies as a baddie, Godzilla turned good monster in 1965's *Ghidrah, the Three-Headed Monster.* He continued to soften as the series progressed: He was a single parent in *Son of Godzilla* and taught a human boy about courage in *Godzilla's Revenge.* By the early 1970s, he was a shadow of his ruthless self and the series appeared to end with *Terror of Godzilla* (aka *Terror of Mechagodzilla*). Toho Studios tried to revive Godzilla as a villain in *Godzilla 1985,* a semiremake of the original, but it was a tremendous flop in the U.S. However, four years later, the Big G mounted a successful comeback in his homeland with 1989's *Godzilla vs. Biollante,* which pitted him against a nice plant monster. After five follow-up films, Toho "retired" Godzilla again — until Roland Emmerich and Dean Devlin came calling. Fresh from their box-office smash *Independence Day* (1996), Emmerich and Devlin secured the rights to produce an epic scale *Godzilla* with digital special effects and a redesigned creature. The resulting film bore little resemblance to earlier Godzilla films; in one shocking twist, the Big Guy turned out to be capable of reproducing by himself! Although *Godzilla* earned over $100 million in the U.S. alone, most film industry insiders expected it to perform better and the media quickly dubbed the film a "disappointment." Still, Toho was impressed enough to start making their own Godzilla films again.

Godzilla, King of the Monster (aka *Godzilla*; *Gojira*) (1954); *Gigantis, the Fire Monster* (*The Return of Godzilla*; *Godzilla Raids Again*; *Godzilla's Counterattack*; *Gojira no Gyakushu*) (1955); *King Kong vs. Godzilla* (aka *Kingukongu tai Gojira*) (1963); *Godzilla vs. The Thing* (aka *Godzilla vs. Mothra*; *Godzilla tai Mothra*) (1964); *Ghidrah the Three-Headed Monster* (aka *The Greatest Battle on Earth*; *Sandai Kaiju Chikyu Saidai No Kessen*) (1965); *Monster Zero* (aka *Invasion of the Astro-Monsters*; *Kaiju Daisenso*) (1965); *Godzilla vs. the Sea Monster* (aka *Ebriah-Terror of the Deep*; *Nankai no Dai Ketto*) (1966); *Son of Godzilla* (aka *Gojira no Musuko*) (1967); *Destroy All Monsters* (aka *Operation Monsterland*; *Kaiju Soshingeki*)

(1968); *Godzilla's Revenge* (aka *Ord Kaiju Daishingeki*) (1969); *Godzilla on Monster Island* (aka *Godzilla vs. Gigan*; *Gojira tai Gaigan*) (1971); *Godzilla vs. the Smog Monster* (aka *Gojira tai Hedora*) (1971); *Godzilla vs. Megalon* (aka *Gojira tai Megaro*) (1973); *Godzilla vs. the Bionic Monster* (aka *Godzilla vs. the Cosmic Monster*; *Gojira tai Meka-Gojira*) (1974); *Terror of Godzilla* (aka *Terror of Mechagodzilla*; *Meka-Gojira no Gyakusyu*) (1975); *Godzilla 1985* (1985); *Godzilla vs. Biollante* (1989); *Waxwork II: Lost in Time* (1991) (cameo); *Godzilla vs. King Ghidrah* (aka *Godzilla vs. King Ghidorah*) (1992); *Godzilla vs. Mothra* (aja *Gojira vs. Mosura*; *Godzilla and Mothra: The Battle for Earth*) (1992); *Godzilla vs. Mechagodzilla* (aka *Gojira vs. Mekagojira*) (1993); *Godzilla vs. Space Godzilla* (aka *Gojira vs. Supesugojira*) (1994); *Gozdilla vs. Destroyer* (aka *Gojira vs. Desutoria*) (1995); *Godzilla* (1998); *Godzilla 2000* (aka *Godzilla 2000: Millenium*) (2000)

(Note: Godzilla's foot also appears in the memorable animated short *Bambi Meets Godzilla* and Bob Goldthwait dons a Godzilla suit and blunders through a miniature city in 1986's *One Crazy Summer*.)

Golf

Golf seldom ranks with its peers as a television sport — the ball being too small to follow and the game devoid of blue-collar suspense. That same handicap applies to its big screen career, resulting in but a handful of golf films. The 1967 *Banning* examined (somewhat superficially) the country club set obsessed with golfing. It starred Robert Wagner as a washed-up pro who regains his self-respect and teaches the snobs a lesson. In a similar vein, Kevin Costner played a has-been golfer who sets his sights on winning the U.S. Open in *Tin Cup* (1996). And Adam Sandler portrayed a hockey player who trades his stick for a club to become a professional golfer in *Happy Gilmore* (1996). One of the stories in *Dead of Night* (1945) concerned a pair of golfing buddies who make a wager — with one of them winding up a ghost. In 1964's *Goldfinger*, James Bond introduced himself to villain Auric Goldfinger by cheating in a golf game. The President was kidnapped on a golf course in the spy spoof *In Like Flint* (1967), while Shirley MacLaine portrayed a presidential widow who played golf in frigid temperatures in *Guarding Tess* (1994). Bing Crosby and Bob Hope engaged in their favorite pastime in a sketch for 1947's Paramount all-star extravaganza *Variety Girl*. The only real-life golfers to have their stories reach the screen were Ben Hogan in *Follow the Sun* (1951) and Tiger Woods in *The Tiger Woods Story* (1998).

The Cohens and Kellys in Scotland (1930); *You're Telling Me* (1934); *Carefree* (1938); *Going My Way* (1944); *Dead of Night* (1945); *My Favorite Brunette* (1947); *Variety Girl* (1947); *Follow the Sun* (1951); *Pat and Mike* (1952); *The Caddy* (1953); *Goldfinger* (1964); *Banning* (1967 TVM); *In Like Flint* (1967); *Once You Kiss a Stranger* (1969); *Enter the Dragon* (1973); *Caddyshack* (1980); *Caddyshack II* (1988); *Dead Solid Perfect* (1988 TVM); *Blades* (1989); *Coneheads* (1993); *Falling Down* (1993); *Guarding Tess* (1994); *Prehysteria 3* (1995); *Happy Gilmore* (1996); *Tin Cup* (1996); *The Tiger Woods Story* (1998 TVM); *Miracle on the 17th Green* (1999 TVM); *The Legend of Bagger Vance* (2000)

Gorgons

In Greek mythology, the gorgons were female creatures who had snakes for hair and eyes which could turn men into stone. There were three sisters: Stheno and Euryale, who were immortal, and Medusa, their well-known sibling, whose fame stems from her

death at the hands of Perseus (he used a reflecting shield and a decapitating sword). Hammer Studios, Britain's "House of Horror" (and never one to worry about tradition), added a fourth sister named Magaera in its 1964 chiller *The Gorgon*. Medusa, though, still reigns as cinema's most noteworthy gorgon. Ray Harryhausen brought her to life via stop-motion animation in 1981's *Clash of the Titans*. Tony Randall played Medusa, along with several other characters, in George Pal's juvenile fantasy *The Seven Faces of Dr. Lao* (1964). And she made a brief, and very fakey, appearance in the 1962 sand-and-sandal epic *Medusa vs. the Son of Hercules* (which had nothing to do with Hercules, since the hero was Perseus). The syndicated TV series *Swamp Thing* featured a contemporary gorgon in its "Heart of Stone" episode. See also **Cyclops**; **Unicorns**.

Medusa vs. the Son of Hercules (aka *Perseo l'invincibile*) (1962); *The Gorgon* (1964); *The Seven Faces of Dr. Lao* (1964); *Clash of the Titans* (1981)

Governesses and Nannies

Deborah Kerr heads an impressive group of actresses who have played governesses. She matched wits with the King of Siam (Yul Brynner) in *The King and I* (1956), fought would-be ghosts while losing her grip on sanity in *The Innocents* (1961), and "cured" troublesome teen Hayley Mills in *The Chalk Garden* (1964). However, references being what they are (and the *Innocents* episode being rather disturbing), one must recommend Julie Andrews over Ms. Kerr for employment as a governess. Andrews was a cheery, lyrical nanny who brought out the best in her charges in both *Mary Poppins* (1964) and *The Sound of Music* (1965). Bette Davis also proved capable in *All This and Heaven Too* (1940), but she was at her nastiest as *The Nanny* (1965). Other notable actresses to perform nanny duties include Ingrid Bergman (*Adam Had Four Sons*) and Katharine Hepburn (*Flame Over India*). Disney's animated *Peter Pan* (1953) featured the immortal Nana, the St. Bernard nanny. Wrestler Hulk Hogan played the title role in 1993's *Mr. Nanny*. Juliet Mills (Hayley's sister) portrayed a governess with a magic touch in the 1970-71 TV series *Nanny and the Professor*. See also **Babysitters**.

We Are Not Alone (1939); *All This and Heaven Too* (1940); *Adam Had Four Sons* (1941); *Jane Eyre* (1944); *The Unseen* (1945); *Anna and the King of Siam* (1946); *Blanche Fury* (1948); *Peter Pan* (1953); *The King and I* (1956); *Flame Over India* (aka *Northwest Frontier*) (1959); *The Innocents* (1961); *The Chalk Garden* (1964); *Mary Poppins* (1964); *The Sound of Music* (1965); *East of Sudan* (1964); *The Nanny* (1965); *Jane Eyre* (1970 TVM); *The Nightcomers* (1971); *Every Little Crook and Nanny* (1972); *Blue Blood* (1973); *Miss Mary* (1986); *The Haunting of Morella* (1990); *The Guardian* (1990); *The Hand That Rocks the Cradle* (1992); *Midnight's Child* (1992 TVM); *Mr. Nanny* (1993); *Mrs. Doubtfire* (1993); *Lily in Winter* (1994 TVM); *Martha & Ethel* (1994); *The Crazysitter* (1995); *Jack and Sarah* (1995); *Harriet the Spy* (1996); *Firelight* (1997); *The Governess* (1998); *Baby Monitor: The Sound of Fear* (1998 TVM); *Talk of Angels* (1998); *The King and I* (1999); *Au Pair* (1999 TVM); *Anna and the King* (1999); *Invisible Child* (1999)

Grave Robbers

The grisly real-life duo of William Burke and William Hare have been the subject of four films. These 19th-century Edinburgh grave robbers sold cadavers to medical students for purposes of dissection. When the supply of fresh corpses dried up, Burke and Hare turned to murder. Burke was accused of over a dozen murders and was hanged in 1829. Hare, who had testified against his partner, served a prison term and was later freed. On the screen, Burke was first portrayed by Boris Karloff (though the character was called Gray) in Val Lewton's 1945 adaptation of Robert Louis Stevenson's *The Body Snatcher*. Fifteen years later, Burke returned, with Hare this time, in *The Flesh and the Fiends*, a Hammer-style horror picture starring Peter Cushing. *Burke and Hare* (1971) elevated the gruesome twosome from supporting to principal characters, but lacked the style of Freddie Francis' handsome 1985 version *The Doctor and the Devils*. Other grave diggers have turned up frequently in horror films, most notably James Whale's original *Frankenstein*. Jacques Tourneur's 1964 horror spoof *A Comedy of Terrors* starred Vincent Price and Peter Lorre as budget-minded morticians who dug up graves to recover their coffins. In *Invisible Invaders*, creatures from outer space occupied the dead bodies of Earthlings and then dug themselves out of their graves.

Frankenstein (1931); *The Body Snatcher* (1945); *The Greed of William Hart* (1948); *The Abductors* (1957); *Invisible Invaders* (1959); *The Flesh and the Fiends* (aka *Mania*) (1960); *The Anatomist* (1961); *Mr. Sardonicus* (1961); *Corridors of Blood* (aka *The Doctor from Seven Dials*) (1962); *A Comedy of Terrors* (1964); *Burke and Hare* (1971); *Dr. Jekyll and Sister Hyde* (1972); *The Doctor and the Devils* (1985)

The Great Gildersleeve *see* Gildersleeve, The Great

Gunsmoke Series

Four made-for-television movies followed the demise of the 1955–1975 CBS TV series. *Gunsmoke: Return to Dodge* (1987) qualifies as an official TV series reunion movie (q.v.), with Marshal Matt Dillon (James Arness) and Miss Kitty Russell (Amanda Blake) meeting up in Dodge City 12 years later. Other series regulars on-hand included Buck Taylor as gunsmith Newly O'Brien and Fran Ryan as Miss Hannah, who ran the Longbranch Saloon after Miss Kitty left Dodge. This TV movie scored well in the ratings and prompted a 1990 sequel, *Gunsmoke: The Last Apache*, which bears a passing resemblance to John Ford's 1956 classic *The Searchers*. Matt receives a letter from an old flame (Michael Learned) whose daughter Amanda (Amy Stock-Poyton) has been kidnapped by Indians. Matt agrees to help and, in the process, learns that Amanda is his daughter, too. In 1992's *Gunsmoke: To the Last Man*, Matt, Amanda (Stock-Poyton), and her Eastern-born boyfriend fight some narrow-minded vigilantes. The remaining two entries focused more on Matt, although *Gunsmoke: The Long Ride* also featured Ali MacGraw as a reformed prostitute the marshal meets along the trail. Arness makes these latter films watchable (especially for *Gunsmoke* fans), but the script writers seem to have forgotten what made the TV series so successful: a large well-defined cast of supporting characters and the willingness to focus the stories on guest stars. In its later years, the TV series *Gunsmoke* rarely built stories solely around Matt. See also **Television Series Reunion Films.**

Gunsmoke: Return to Dodge (1987 TVM); *Gunsmoke: The Last Apache* (1990 TVM); *Gunsmoke: To the Last Man* (1992 TVM); *Gunsmoke: The Long Ride* (1993 TVM); *Gunsmoke: One Man's Justice* (1994 TVM)

Gypsies

The victims of movie stereotyping, gypsies have too often been portrayed as ominous fortunetellers or hot-blooded vagabonds. Maria Ouspenskaya created the most famous celluloid gypsy, as Maleva the fortuneteller who first informs Lon Chaney, Jr.: "Even a man who is pure in heart and says his prayers by night, can become a wolf when the wolfbane blooms and the autumn moon is bright." Alas, that's exactly what happened to Lon in 1941's *The Wolf Man*, following a bite from Maleva's gypsy-werewolf son (Bela Lugosi). Although father Claude Rains put his werewolf son out of his misery, both the Wolf Man and Maleva the gypsy returned two years later for *Frankenstein Meets the Wolf Man*. The talented Ouspenskaya lost her Russian nationality in gypsy guise, but other performers have looked downright out of place. The intentional miscasting was part of the fun in 1936's *The Bohemian Girl*, which featured Stan Laurel and Oliver Hardy as unlikely gypsies. However, Jane Russell made a silly gypsy temptress in *Hot Blood* (1955), while Marlene Dietrich chewed the scenery (in entertaining fashion) in *Golden Earrings* (1947). Frank Sinatra, in heavy makeup and sporting an earring, had a gypsy cameo in John Huston's gimmicky 1963 mystery *The List of Adrian Messenger*. Few films have focused on the plight of present-day gypsies. One that did was 1978's *King of the Gypsies*, an adaptation of Peter Maas' best seller about a dying gypsy ruler (Sterling Hayden) who passes the tribe's leadership to his grandson (Eric Roberts), ignoring the birth rights of his son (Judd Hirsch). Actor Robert Duvall directed *Angelo, My Love* (1983), a curious mixture of fact and fiction set in New York City and starring a former gypsy child (Angelo Evans). See **Hunchbacks** for the various versions of *The Hunchback of Notre Dame* featuring the gypsy Esmeralda.

Caravan (1934); *Vanessa, Her Love Story* (1935); *The Bohemian Girl* (1936); *Wings of the Morning* (1937); *The Hunchback of Notre Dame* (1939); *The Wolf Man* (1941); *Frankenstein Meets the Wolf Man* (1943); *Gypsy Wildcat* (1944); *Cry of the Werewolf* (1944); *House of Dracula* (1945); *Caravan* (1946); *Madonna of the Seven Moons* (1946); *Golden Earrings* (1947); *Jassy* (1947); *The Loves of Carmen* (1948); *Gypsy Fury* (1951); *Charge of the Lancers* (1954); *Hot Blood* (1955); *The Gypsy and the Gentleman* (1957); *Babes in Toyland* (1961); *Los Tarantos* (1962); *The List of Adrian Messenger* (1963); *From Russia with Love* (1963); *Gypsy Girl* (aka *Sky West and Crooked*) (1965); *The Virgin and the Gypsy* (1970); *The Art of Crime* (1975 TVM); *Alex and the Gypsy* (1976); *King of the Gypsies* (1978); *Angelo, My Love* (1983); *Time of the Gypsies* (1989); *Monkey Trouble* (1994); *The Whipping Boy* (1994 TVM); *Thinner* (1996); *Traveller* (1997)

Halloween Series

The most influential horror film of the late 1970s, this well-made psycho thriller inspired a rash of "slasher" movies (q.v.). Unfortunately, its imitators failed to realize that *Halloween* (1978) worked because of its suspense — not gore. The thin plot concerned a babysitter and her friends, who are terrorized by an emotionless psychopath on Halloween night in a small Illinois town. The film boasted effective performances, particularly Jamie Lee Curtis as teenage heroine Laurie Strode and Donald Pleasance as psycho-hunter Dr. Sam Loomis (a character not unlike Van Helsing in the *Dracula* films). But the true star of *Halloween* was John Carpenter, whose tour-de-force direction created some classic frights. Carpenter co-produced, but did not direct, 1981's pallid sequel *Halloween II*. Its plot picks up with the original film's closing scenes, with Laurie (Curtis again) being taken to a hospital where the killer — who didn't die after all — pursues her through many dark corridors until Dr. Loomis (Pleasance) comes to her rescue. This chapter's chief contribution to the series is the revelation that the killer is Laurie's brother Michael Myers. Neither Michael nor Laurie were in *Halloween III: Season of the Witch* (1983), an in name–only entry that ignored the plots of the earlier films and opted for a clever tale about a diabolical Halloween mask manufacturer. It bombed with critics and moviegoers. Five years later, the series resumed with *Halloween IV: The Return of Michael Myers* (1988), *Halloween V: The Revenge of Michael Myers* (1989), and *Halloween: The Curse of Michael Myers* (1995), non–Carpenter entries with Pleasance returning to confront the original killer. They ignored the second and third films and picked up where the original *Halloween* left off. Then, in 1998, Jamie Lee Curtis made an unexpected return to the series in *Halloween H20: Twenty Years Later*. Kevin Williamson, who had revived the teen horror genre two years earlier with *Scream*, masterminded this installment which ignored all series entries after *Halloween II*. Most of the action takes place at a California boarding school run by Laurie Strode, who has become a divorced, alcoholic, paranoid mother of a 17-year-old son. When brother Michael makes an unexpected visit on Halloween night, Laurie takes matters in her own hands and — in an attempt to end the bloodshed once and for all — decapitates her homicidal brother. One would think that even Michael Myers could not survive such a fate. But after several unexpected returns during the 20-year film series, who knows? See also **Slasher Movies**.

Halloween (1978); *Halloween II* (1981); *Halloween III: Season of the Witch* (1983); *Halloween IV: The Return of Michael Myers* (1988); *Halloween V: The Revenge of Michael Myers* (1989); *Halloween: The Curse of Michael Myers* (1995); *Halloween H20: Twenty Years Later* (aka *Halloween H20*) (1998)

Hammer, Mike

Mickey Spillane's rough and tough private eye has had a checkered screen career. Biff Elliott played the movies' first Hammer in the 1953 3-D flick *I, the Jury*, a pedestrian adaptation of Spillane's 1946 best seller. Ralph Meeker also missed the mark as Hammer in Robert Aldrich's *Kiss Me Deadly* (1955), but the picture nevertheless remains a stylish film noir with a loyal cult following. Spillane took a shot at the role himself in 1963's *The Girl Hunters*, but he quickly abandoned his acting career to return to writing. To date, the most successful Hammer has been Stacy Keach, who played the private eye in the 1983 TV movie *Murder Me, Murder You*, the TV series *Mickey Spillane's Mike Hammer* (later retitled *The New Mike Hammer*), and two follow-up films. Five years after Keach's last film, Rob Estes, a former regular on the sultry detective series *Silk Stalkings*, starred in another TV movie *Come Die with Me: A Mickey Spillane's Mike Hammer Mystery*. It also starred Pamela Anderson Lee as Hammer's voluptuous secretary Velma. In the earlier days of television, Darren McGavin starred in a 1957-58 syndicated TV series called *Mickey Spillane's Mike Hammer*.

I, the Jury (1953) (Biff Elliott); *Kiss Me Deadly* (1955) (Ralph Meeker); *My Gun Is Quick* (1957) (Robert Bray); *The Girl Hunters* (1963) (Mickey Spillane); *Mickey Spillane's Margin for Murder* (1981 TVM) (Kevin Dobson); *I, the Jury* (1982) (Armand Assante); *Murder Me, Murder You* (1983 TVM) (Stacy Keach); *The Return of Mickey Spillane's Mike Hammer* (1986 TVM) (Keach); *Murder Takes All* (1989 TVM) (Keach); *Come Die with Me: A Mickey Spillane's Mike Hammer Mystery* (1994 TVM) (Rob Estes)

Happy Hooker Series

Xaviera Hollander's best seller about her experiences as New York City's premiere madam served as the inspiration for three ill-conceived features. The original *The Happy Hooker* (1975) had pretensions of being a sly, naughty satire. But a leaden script and a miscast, red-headed Lynn Redgrave resulted in a major misfire. Blonde Joey Heatherton replaced Redgrave in *The Happy Hooker Goes to Washington* (1977), a sex-and-politics comedy that was sexually boring and politically unfunny. Brunette Martine Beswicke finished the series with *The Happy Hooker Goes Hollywood* (1980). The Brits proved that a funny movie could be made from the confessions of a real-life madam with 1987's *Personal Services*, an honest, sharply-etched portrait of Cynthia Payne (played by Julie Walters).

The Happy Hooker (1975); *The Happy Hooker Goes to Washington* (1977); *The Happy Hooker Goes to Hollywood* (1980)

Hardy, Andy

For a decade, the Hardys reigned as America's favorite family and Mickey Rooney, as Andy Hardy, captured the public's affection as had no other teenager. His growing pains were chronicled in 15 highly successful films released during 1937–1946. The MGM series made a modest debut with *A Family Affair*, Louis Mayer's attempt to duplicate the popularity of Eugene O'Neill's family comedy-drama *Ah, Wilderness*. Mayer even reunited three stars from the 1935 film version of O'Neill's play: Lionel Barrymore, Cecilia Parker, and 17-year-old Mickey Rooney. To MGM's surprise, *A Family Affair* was a solid hit, prompting an immediate sequel. In *You're Only Young Once*, Lewis Stone replaced Lionel Barrymore, with Rooney and Parker (as Andy's older sister Marian) remaining as the Hardy children. Other series regulars included British actress Fay Holden as Ma, Sara Haden as Aunt Millie, and Ann Rutherford as Andy's sometime girlfriend. The cast clicked immediately, especially the chemistry between stern, but understanding, Judge Hardy and his unpredictable son Andy. The popularity of Rooney's character became evident in the third film, 1938's *Judge Hardy's Children*, and the series shifted its focus to Andy. The plots typically centered on Andy's love life and this afforded MGM the opportunity to build up rising stars like Judy Garland, Donna Reed, Lana Turner, Esther Williams, and Kathryn Grayson. The series lost momentum during World War II, with its star in the Army, and never fully recovered. Mickey was growing up, too — he was 24 when college student Andy encountered a pair of vivacious twins in *Andy Hardy's Blonde Trouble*. The series apparently ended in style with 1946's *Love Laughs at Andy Hardy*. However, 12 years later, *Andy Hardy Comes Home* tried to turn Rooney into an understanding father figure. This one-time revival didn't work, due to the absence of Lewis Stone (he died in 1953) and the growing popularity of television family comedies. In 1998, Austrian filmmaker Martin Arnold made a 15-minute short film called *Alone — Life Wastes Andy Hardy*, in which Mickey Rooney and Judy Garland are cloned.

A Family Affair (1937); *You're Only Young Once* (1938); *Judge Hardy's Children* (1938); *Love Finds Andy Hardy* (1938); *Out West with the Hardys* (1938); *The Hardys Ride High* (1939); *Judge Hardy and Son* (1939); *Andy Hardy Gets Spring Fever* (1939); *Andy Hardy Meets Debutante* (1940); *Andy Hardy's Private Secretary* (1941); *Life Begins for Andy Hardy* (1941); *Andy Hardy's Double Life* (1942); *The Courtship of Andy Hardy* (1942); *Andy Hardy's Blonde Trouble* (1944); *Love Laughs at Andy Hardy* (1946); *Andy Hardy Comes Home* (1958)

Having Babies Series

Title tells all in this TV movie series about couples experiencing childbirth. The second film introduced Susan Sullivan as Dr. Julie Farr, who became the principal character in the third film. Sullivan subsequently starred in a 1978 TV series known both as *Having Babies* and *Julie Farr, M.D.* Less than three years after the show's demise, Ms. Sullivan showed up as Maggie on the long-running soap opera *Falcon Crest*. See also **Babies**.

Having Babies (aka *Giving Birth*) (1976 TVM); *Having Babies II* (1977 TVM); *Having Babies III* (1978 TVM)

Heaven

The cinema's view of heaven has tended to rely on soft focus and swirling mist. The most visually arresting conception along these lines is probably Michael Powell and Emeric Pressburger's *Stairway to Heaven* (1946), with its neverending staircase projecting itself from colorful Earth to black-and-white heaven. On the other hand, heaven looked very much like this world in *Made in Heaven*. In 1985's *The Heavenly Kid*, it was an ugly place filled with crowded trains and angels in frumpy clothes — no wonder the title character returned to Earth. *The Adding Machine* (1968) offered a bleak view of heaven with hellish overtones. It sent a clerk, who had murdered his boss after being replaced by a machine, to a heaven where he worked constantly with a similar machine. More humane heavenly activities have included celestial trials (*Stairway to Heaven, Defending Your Life,* and *The Story of Mankind*), plans for armageddon (*The Horn Blows at Midnight*), and preparation of children about to be born (*The Blue Bird* and *Made in Heaven*). Some of the most prominent heavenly authority figures include Rex Ingram's "de Lawd" in *The Green Pastures* (1936), Lionel Barrymore's "Heavenly General" in *A Guy Named Joe* (1943), and Abraham Sofaer as the judge in *Stairway to Heaven*. Peter Cook as the Devil went to heaven to tell God he had won the battle for souls in the irreverent comedy *Bedazzled* (1967). Actress Diane Keaton edited movie clips and interviews into her offbeat documentary *Heaven* (1987). Purgatory has been glimpsed in *Between Two Worlds* (1944), *Impure Thoughts* (1985), *In Between* (1992), *Purgatory* (1999), and, depending on one's interpretation, 1991's *The Rapture*. See also **Angels**.

Liliom (1930); *The Green Pastures* (1936); *The Blue Bird* (1940); *Here Comes Mr. Jordan* (1941); *A Guy Named Joe* (1943); *Heaven Can Wait* (1943); *The Horn Blows at Midnight* (1945); *That's the Spirit* (1945); *Down to Earth* (1947); *Ziegfeld Follies* (1946); *The Cockeyed Miracle* (aka *Mr. Griggs Returns*) (1946); *Stairway to Heaven* (aka *A Matter of Life and Death*) (1946); *The Bad Lord Byron* (1948); *You Never Can Tell* (1951); *Carousel* (1956); *The Story of Mankind* (1957); *The Flight That Disappeared* (1961); *Bedazzled* (1967); *The Adding Machine* (1968); *Heaven Can Wait* (1978); *Resurrection* (1980); *The Heavenly Kid* (1985); *Made in Heaven* (1987); *Heaven* (1987); *Defending Your Life* (1991); *Bill and*

Ted's Bogus Journey (1991); *A Life Less Ordinary* (1997); *What Dreams May Come* (1998); *After Life* (1999)

Heist/Caper Films

Jewelry stores, museums, banks, casinos, and trains have been the most frequent targets of elaborately-planned heists. Jules Dassin directed the two most famous jewel heist films: *Rififi* (1954) and *Topkapi* (1964). In *Rififi*, a violent ex-con recruits three specialists to stage the "perfect" heist of a jewelry store. The classic burglary sequence lasts almost thirty nail-biting minutes, with neither dialogue nor music. Dassin lightened the tone, but not the suspense, with *Topkapi*, in which the thieves set their sights on a jeweled dagger in an Istanbul museum. Although the heist sequence formed the film's centerpiece again, Peter Ustinov earned a Best Supporting Actor Oscar for his nervous performance. Though far less renowned, 1968's *Grand Slam* has its fans, who admire the $10 million diamond heist as well as Edward G. Robinson's charming performance as the professor who masterminds the intricate scheme. It's interesting to note that these three films, like many of their imitators, feature European settings and international casts. However, John Huston's seminal heist picture, 1950's *The Asphalt Jungle*, takes place in the American Midwest and includes a "perfect crime" which falls apart completely. It's been remade in various guises as the Western *The Badlanders* (1958), *Cairo* (1963), and *Cool Breeze* (1972). Other jewel heist films include *Caper of the Golden Bulls* (1967), the two versions of *Happy New Year* (1973 and 1987), *11 Harrowhouse* (1974), and *The Hot Rock* (1972) with Robert Redford. Although jewelry thefts represent the upper class side of the heist movie genre, carefully-plotted bank robberies have generated a proportionate amount of suspense. The legendary 1950 Brinks robbery served as the basis for *Six Bridges to Cross* (1955), *Brinks: The Great Robbery* (1976), and *The Brinks Job* (1978). Meek bank clerk Alec Guinness hatched a plan to rob a truck of gold bullion in the 1951 British comedy *The Lavender Hill Mob*. In another British picture, 1960's *The League of Gentlemen*, ex–army colonel Jack Hawkins recruits some of his former soldiers to execute a bank heist. Along similar lines, Peter Falk and two Korean War buddies scheme to stage a complex bank robbery in 1971's *A Step Out of Line*. George C. Scott and cohorts didn't rob the bank–they just stole the entire building in 1974's *Bank Shot* (a sequel to *The Hot Rock* with Scott playing Redford's character!). Jim Hutton, Milton Berle, and Joey Bishop broke into the U.S. mint in *Who's Minding the Mint* (1967), but their mission was to replace money which had been burned accidentally. And, as the title would indicate, the bank robbers in *The Doberman Gang* (1972), were strictly of the canine variety. In addition to banks, other attractive sources of large amounts of money include casino and trains. Casino robberies have been staged in *Bob Le Flambeur* (1955*)*, *5 Against the House* (1955), *Ocean's Eleven* (1960), and *They Came to Rob Las Vegas* (1968) and *Reindeer Games* (2000). The popularity of train robberies in films can be traced back to 1903's *The Great Train Robbery*. However, only a handful of these movies qualify as heist/caper films, such as *The Great British Train Robbery* (1967), *The Great Train Robbery* (1979), and *Buster* (1988). See **also Jewel Thieves**; **Trains**.

The Asphalt Jungle (1950); *The Lavender Hill Mob* (1951); *The Great Diamond Robbery* (1953); *Rififi* (1954); *Six Bridges to Cross* (1955); *Bob Le Flambeur* (1955); *5 Against the House* (1955); *The*

Killing (1956); *The Big Caper* (1957); *The Badlanders* (1958); *The League of Gentlemen* (1960); *Ocean's Eleven* (1960); *It Takes a Thief* (aka *The Challenge*) (1960); *Seven Thieves* (1960); *Rififi in Tokyo* (1963); *Cairo* (1963); *Topkapi* (1964); *Gambit* (1966); *Assault on a Queen* (1966); *How to Steal a Million* (1966); *Who's Minding the Mint?* (1967); *Robbery* (1967); *The Great British Train Robbery* (1967); *Caper of the Golden Bulls* (aka *Carnival of Thieves*) (1967); *Grand Slam* (1968); *Diamonds for Breakfast* (1968); *They Came to Rob Las Vegas* (1968); *The Thomas Crown Affair* (1968); *The Sicilian Clan* (1969); *The Italian Job* (1969); *Perfect Friday* (1970); *A Step Out of Line* (1971 TVM); *$ (Dollars)* (1971); *Cool Breeze* (1972); *The Doberman Gang* (1972); *The Hot Rock* (aka *How to Steal a Diamond in Four Uneasy Lessons*) (1972); *The Heist* (1972 TVM); *Snow Job* (1972); *Happy New Year* (aka *The Happy New Year Caper*) (1973); *Bank Shot* (1974); *11 Harrowhouse* (aka *Anything for Love; Fast Fortune*) (1974); *The Great Ice Rip-Off* (1974 TVM); *Thunderbolt and Lightfoot* (1974); *Live a Little, Steal a Lot* (aka *Murph the Surf; You Can't Steal Love*) (1975); *Diamonds* (1975); *Target Risk* (1975 TVM); *Brinks: The Great Robbery* (1976 TVM); *The Brinks Job* (1978); *The Great Train Robbery* (aka *The First Great Train Robbery*) (1979); *A Man, a Woman and a Bank* (aka *A Very Big Withdrawal*) (1979); *The Great Bank Hoax* (1979); *Happy New Year* (1987); *Bellman and True* (1988); *Buster* (1988); *Family Business* (1989); *Why Me?* (1990); *Sneakers* (1992); *The Diamond Fleece* (1992 TVM); *Reservoir Dogs* (1992); *The Real McCoy* (1993); *Dead Presidents* (1995); *Jackie Brown* (1997); *Out of Sight* (1998); *The Split* (1998); *The Thomas Crown Affair* (1999); *Entrapment* (1999); *Reindeer Games* (2000)

Helicopters

The cinema's love affair with airplanes (q.v.) has never extended to helicopters. Though the airplane features a stronger historical background, the helicopter's airborne maneuverability would seem to make it an ideal vehicle for visually exciting chase thrillers. Television filmmakers have exploited that genre with a quartet of fast-paced features: *Birds of Prey* (1972), *Sky Heist* (1975) *Deadly Encounter* (1982), and *The Chase* (1991). The helicopter hit the big time, in terms of budget, with the 1983 theatrical release *Blue Thunder*. Yet, despite a strong cast headed by Roy Scheider and Malcolm McDowell, this cartoonish tale of a super-helicopter never generated the thrills of its small screen counterparts (ironically, it later spawned a TV series). James Bond took to the air in helicopters built-for-one in *You Only Live Twice* (1967) and *For Your Eyes Only* (1981). Woody Allen invented a self-powered, single-seat helicopter in *A Midsummer Night's Sex Comedy* (1982), while Bruce Spence piloted another single-seater through a post-apocalyptic desert in 1981's *The Road Warrior* (aka *Mad Max 2*). See also **Airplanes**; **Balloons, Hot Air**; **Dirigibles**.

Up Goes Maisie (aka *She Goes Up*) (1945); *Battle Taxi* (1955); *Flight from Ashiya* (1964); *You Only Live Twice* (1967); *Birds of Prey* (1972 TVM); *Sky Heist* (1975 TVM); *For Your Eyes Only* (1981); *The Road Warrior* (aka *Mad Max 2*) (1981); *Deadly Encounter* (1982 TVM); *A Midsummer Night's Sex Comedy* (1982); *Blue Thunder* (1983); *Getting Even* (aka *Hostage: Dallas*) (1986); *Defense Play* (1988); *Fire Birds* (1990); *The Chase* (1991 TVM); *Cliffhanger* (1993); *Firehawk* (1993); *True Lies* (1994); *The Chase* (1994); *Pie in the Sky* (1995); *Courage Under Fire* (1996); *Mission: Impossible* (1996); *Escape from L.A.* (1996); *Gridlock* (1996 TVM)

Hell

No one wants to go to hell — and filmmakers have been no exception. Director Harry Lachman offered the most elaborate view, a striking 10-minute sequence of writhing souls in 1935's *Dante's Inferno*. Italian horror specialist Mario Bava created an atmospheric Hades for 1961's *Hercules in the Haunted World* (apparently, the producers decided against *Hercules in Hell*). Christopher Lee, as one of Pluto's disciples, kept the seas of lava flowing and the naked girls chained. Surprisingly, the 1972 TV movie *Haunts of the Very Rich* offered an interesting variation, whereby seven people trapped on a paradise island come to realize they are in hell. See also **The Devil**.

Dante's Inferno (1935); *Heaven Can Wait* (1943); *Angel on My Shoulder* (1946); *Huis Clos* (1954); *Hercules in the Haunted World* (aka *Hercules vs. the Vampires; Hercules at the Center of the Earth; Ercole al Centro Delle Terra*) (1961); *Haunts of the Very Rich* (1972 TVM); *The Sentinel* (1977); *Invitation to Hell* (1984 TVM); *The Gate* (1987); *Hellbound: Hellraiser II* (1988); *Bill and Ted's Bogus Journey* (1991); *Highway to Hell* (1992); *Stay Tuned* (1992); *Hercules* (1997); *What Dreams May Come* (1998); *South Park: Bigger, Longer & Uncut* (1999)

Hellraiser Series

Clive Barker's novella "The Hellbound Heart" provided the basis for 1987's *Hellraiser*, a grisly horror tale described by its author as a perverse love story. In the opening reel, Frank Cotton (Sean Chapman) unlocks the secret to a mysterious, Rubik Cube–like puzzle box called the Lamont Configuration. With its solution revealed, the box summons forth the Cenobites, a race of vile-looking, hellish creatures that torture Frank to death. However, the dead Frank, now hideously disfigured, shows up at his brother Larry's house. He convinces his former mistress, Larry's wife Julia (Clare Higgins), to obtain human flesh for his dinner so that he can regain his human form. This blatant exercise in visual horror is distinguished by a subtle thematic twist: A woman — not a man — lures and mutilates the victims (however, unlike her typical male counterparts, Julia kills out of love). The two sequels dispensed with such thematic concerns and raised the gore quotient to appeal to hardcore horror aficionados. *Variety* called 1988's *Hellbound: Hellraiser II* a "maggotty carnival of mayhem, mutation, and dismemberment." The plot follows Larry's daughter Kristy (Ashley Laurence) as she journeys to Hell to save her father from the Cenobites and Leviathan, Lord of Hell's Labyrinth. Her clever, albeit grisly, escape gives new meaning to the phrase "putting on another face." As with the first two films, *Hellraiser III* (1992) also features a female protagonist, a TV news reporter named Jody (Terry Farrell). In her dreams, Jody encounters the ghost of a British military officer, whose experiments first unleashed the Cenobites. Concurrently, a heinous nightclub owner buys a sculpture that introduces him to Pinhead, the leader of the Cenobites. Predictably, the finale pits Jody against Pinhead. A fourth film, *Hellraiser: Bloodline*, alternates confusingly between a 21th century space station (with Pinhead aboard) and flashbacks to the 18th century that show the Lamont Configuration's origin. The film's director Kevin Yagher, who helmed the original *Hellraiser*, had his named removed from the credits. In terms of originality, the series seems to have run its course — although that has never hampered other long-running horror series like *Friday the 13th*, *The Howling*, and *Nightmare on Elm Street* (qq.v.).

Hellraiser (1987); *Hellbound: Hellraiser II* (1988); *Hellraiser III: Hell on Earth* (1992); *Hellraiser: Bloodline* (aka *Hellraiser IV*) (1996)

Helm, Matt

In Donald Hamilton's books, secret agent Matt Helm "worked" as a freelance writer/photographer and drove an old pickup truck. In the movies, though, Dean Martin played him as a third-rate James Bond. Martin fumbled his way through four Helm pictures, all made between 1966–69 and co-starring Stella Stevens, Ann-Margaret, Senta Berger, and Elke Sommer. Tony Franciosa reprised the role for the 1975 TV movie *Matt Helm* and a short-lived series. Franciosa's Helm was a private eye, though, instead of a secret agent.

The Silencers (1966); *Murderer's Row* (1967); *The Ambushers* (1968); *The Wrecking Crew* (1969); *Matt Helm* (1975 TVM)

Henry Series

Character actor Raymond Walburn played Henry Latham, a rascally cheapskate with good intentions, in this minor Monogram series. The plots frequently hinged on Henry's outraged reactions to rising prices. In *Father Makes Good*, he bought a cow to avoid a milk tax. He refused to pay the butcher and took up hunting in *Father's Wild Game*. In other series entries, Henry bumbled routine jobs (e.g., accidentally burned up a toll bridge), but somehow managed to straighten things out in the end. Walter Catlett was Henry's pal Mayor Colton.

Henry the Rainmaker (1949); *Leave It to Henry* (1949); *Father Makes Good* (1950); *Father's Wild Game* (1951); *Father Takes the Air* (1951)

Herbie, the Love Bug

Disney's longest-running film series starred a lovable Volkswagen Beetle with a mind of its own. *The Love Bug* and *Herbie Rides Again* did brisk business, but the later *Herbie* movies were released when Disney Productions was struggling to recapture its youthful audience. Dean Jones played Herbie's human sidekick in the first and third films and revived his role for the hour-long(!) CBS television series *Herbie, the Love Bug*. It lasted just one month before being cancelled. In 1997, Disney produced a TV movie remake of *The Love Bug* starring Bruce Campbell of *The Evil Dead* series (q.v.). The plot pitted Herbie against a mean Volkswagen Beetle called Horace. Dean Jones had a cameo as Jim Douglas, his character from the original *Love Bug* film. See also **Auto Racing**.

The Love Bug (1969); *Herbie Rides Again* (1974); *Herbie Goes to Monte Carlo* (1977); *Herbie Goes Bananas* (1980); *The Love Bug* (1997 TVM)

Hercules

Super distributor Joseph E. Levine transformed *Hercules*, a modest Italian sword-and-sandal epic, into one of the biggest international hits of 1957. Steve Reeves, a former Mr. World and Mr. Universe, starred as the mythical muscle man who undertakes a series of perilous quests to win the hand of a beautiful princess (the worthy Sylva Koscina). Reeves repeated the role in the sequel *Hercules Unchained*, but bowed out after that. Since then, a succession of muscular hunks have essayed the role: Reg Park, Mark Forest, Alan Steel (real name Sergio Ciani), Gordon Scott, Arnold Schwarzenegger, and Lou (*Incredible Hulk*) Ferrigno. Even muscle builder Mickey Hargitay played Herc in *The Loves of Her-cules*—with wife Jayne Mansfield in support in a double role! None of these cheap programmers were particularly distinguished, although horror director Mario Bava's *Hercules in the Haunted World* presented an atmospheric view of Hell. In 1994, five Hercules TV movies were shown as part of a syndication package called the Universal Action Pack. The films were very tongue-in-cheek and Kevin Sorbo played a different kind of Hercules—good-looking, athletic, but minus the typical mounds of muscles. These TV movies spawned a highly successul weekly TV series, also starring Sorbo, called *Hercules: The Legendary Journeys*. At the peak of Sorbo's popularity, Disney released an animated musical version of *Hercules* (1997) that took a tongue-in-cheek approach, too. Although Hercules is the most famous mythical strong man, his film success, particularly in the 1960s, inspired a number of muscle man clones. Maciste (q.v.) and Goliath both had their own series, though it was often difficult to tell who was who. *Maciste e la Regina di Samar* wound up as *Hercules Against the Moonmen* when shown on American TV. Of course, it can often be dangerous to judge a film by its title. The 1993 Australian comedy *Hercules Returns* was about theater owners forced to provide their own dubbing when a Hercules film arrives with no English dialogue. The 1974 United Artists release *Hercules vs. Kung Fu* (aka *Mr. Hercules Against Karate*) had nothing to do with Hercules, being just another Kung Fu school "chop socky" picture. See also **Maciste**.

Hercules (aka *The Labors of Hercules*; *Le Fatiche di Ercole*) (1959) (Steve Reeves); *Hercules Unchained* (aka *Ercole e la Regina di Lidia*) (1960) (Reeves); *The Loves of Hercules* (aka *Hercules and the Hydra*) (1960) (Mickey Hargitay); *Ulysses Against Hercules* (aka *Hercules vs. Ulysses*; *Ulysses Against the Son of Hercules*; *Ulisse contro Ercole*) (1961) (Georges Marchal); *Hercules in the Haunted World* (aka *Hercules vs. the Vampires*; *Hercules at the Center of the Earth*; *Ercole al Centro Delle Terra*) (1961) (Reg Park); *Alakazam the Great* (1961) (animated); *The Fury of Hercules* (aka *La Furia di Ercole*) (1961) (Brad Harris); *Hercules in the Vale of Woe* (aka *Maciste Against Hercules in the Vale of Woe*; *Maciste Contro Ercole Nella Valle Dei Guai*) (1962) (Kirk Morris); *The Three Stooges Meet Hercules* (1962) (Samson Burke); *Hercules and the Captive Women* (aka *Hercules and the Haunted Women*; *Ercole alla Conquista della Atlantide*) (1963) (Park); *Hercules, the Invincible* (aka *Ercole l'Invincibile*) (1963) (Dan Vadis); *Jason and the Argonauts* (1963) (Nigel Green); *Conquest of Mycene* (aka *Hercules Attacks*; *Hercules vs. Moloch*; *Ercole contro Moloch*) (1963) (Gordon Scott); *Hercules vs. the Giant Warriors* (aka *Triumph of Hercules*; *Hercules and the Ten Avengers*; *Il Trionfoldi Ercole*) (1964) (Vadis); *Hercules Against Rome* (aka *Ercole contro Roma*) (1964) (Alan Steel); *Samson and the Mighty Challenge* (aka *Hercules, Maciste, Samson, and Urus vs. the Universe*; *Ercole, Sansone, Maciste, Ursus gli Invincili*) (1964) (Steel); *Hercules Against the Sons of the Sun* (*Ercole contro i Figli del Sole*) (1964) (Mark Forest); *Hercules and the Tyrants of Babylon* (aka *Ercole contro i Tiranni di Babilonia*) (1964) (Rock Stevens, also credited as Peter Lupus); *Hercules of the Desert* (aka *La Valle dell'Eco Tonante*) (1964) (Morris); *Hercules, Samson, and Ulysses* (aka *Ercole Sfida Sansone*) (1966) (Morris); *Hercules, Prisoner of Evil* (aka *Terror of the Kirghiz*) (1967) (Park); *Hercules in New York* (aka *Hercules: The Movie*; *Hercules Goes Bananas*) (1970) (Arnold Schwarzenegger); *Hercules* (1983) (Lou Ferrigno); *Hercules II* (aka *The Adventures of Hercules*) (1985) (Ferrigno); *Hercules and the Amazon Women* (1994 TVM) (Kevin Sorbo); *Hercules and the Circle of Fire* (1994 TVM) (Sorbo); *Hercules and the Lost Kingdom* (1994 TVM) (Sorbo); *Hercules in the Maze of the Minotaur* (1994 TVM) (Sorbo); *Hercules in the Underworld* (1994 TVM) (Sorbo); *Hercules*

(1997) (animated — voiced by Tate Donovan); *Young Hercules* (1998 TVM) (Ian Bohen); *Hercules and Xena — The Animated Movie: The Battle for Mount Olympus* (1998) (animated — voiced by Kevin Sorbo); *Jason and the Argonauts* (2000 TVM) (Brian Thompson)

Hickok, Wild Bill, Series

Frontier marshal James Butler Hickok, aka Wild Bill, has been portrayed by many actors, but only one was popular enough to borrow his nickname permanently. Gordon Elliott became Wild Bill Elliott after trail blazing his way to fame in Columbia's 1938 serial *The Great Adventures of Wild Bill Hickok*. Two years later, Columbia resurrected Wild Bill as Wild Bill and produced an eight film Hickok series. The series came to an end when Elliott signed with Republic in 1943 and went on to achieve his greatest success as Red Ryder (q.v.).

Prairie Schooner (aka *Through the Storm*) (1940); *Beyond the Sacramento* (aka *The Power of Justice*) (1941); *The Wildcats of Tucson* (aka *Promise Unfulfilled*) (1941); *Across the Sierras* (aka *Welcome Stranger*) (1941); *North from the Lone Star* (1941); *Hands Across the Rockies* (1941); *Lone Star Vigilantes* (aka *The Devil's Price*) (1942); *Bullets for Bandits* (1942)

The Higgins Family

With MGM's Hardy Family (q.v.) and Twenteith Century–Fox's Jones Family (q.v.) riding high in the late 1930s, it was inevitable that low-budget Republic Pictures would initiate its own family affair. Thus, the Higgins Family series was born. For the first seven films, it was indeed a family affair with James, Lucille, and son Russell Gleason portraying Joe, Lillian, and Sidney Higgins. The early entries centered on conflicts between Joe and Lillian. They wound up in divorce court in *The Higgins Family*, but a happy ending prevailed. However, they were at odds again in *Should Husbands Work?* with Lillian taking over Joe's job and leaving him the housework. The Gleasons, along with Harry Davenport as Grandpa, bowed out of the series after 1940's *Grandpa Goes to Town*. Roscoe Karns (Joe), Ruth Donnelly (Lil), George Ernest (Sidney), and Spencer Charters (Grandpa) took over the roles for the last two films. Interestingly, George Ernest and Russell Gleason both appeared in the Jones Family (q.v.) series. Ernest played young Roger Jones, while Gleason was Bonnie Jones's boyfriend and eventual husband Herbert Thompson. Russell Gleason's acting career ended suddenly when he fell from a hotel window in 1945. He was 37.

The Higgins Family (1938); *The Covered Trailer* (1939); *Money to Burn* (1939); *My Wife's Relations* (1939); *Should Husbands Work?* (1939); *Earl of Puddlestone* (1940); *Grandpa Goes to Town* (1940); *Meet the Missus* (1940); *Petticoat Politics* (1941)

The High Schoolers Series

The forerunner of AIP's *Beach Party* movies (q.v.), this Monogram series mixed energetic teens with popular music. Freddie Stewart and June Preisser played the main characters, bland high school lovers Freddie Trimball and Dodie Rogers. However, the series is best remembered for featuring supporting performers which TV would turn into familiar faces. Fellow student Noel Neill went on to become Lois Lane in the hit *Superman* TV series. College professor Frank Cady became Sam Drucker on *Green Acres*. And Alan Hale, Jr., the Marine-turned-student in 1947's *Sarge Goes to College*, wound up spending several years as the Skipper on *Gilligan's Island*. If the series' movies featured dull, stereotypical plots (a big football game, class elections, etc.), the music made up for it. In addition to boasting offbeat tunes like "Jungle Rhumba" and "Sherwood's Forest," the High Schoolers captured captivating performances by bands like the Gene Krupa Orchestra.

High School Hero (1946); *Junior Prom* (1946); *Sarge Goes to College* (1947); *Vacation Days* (1947); *Campus Sleuth* (1948); *Smart Politics* (1948)

Highlander

"There can only be one!" explains Connor MacLeod after lopping off the head of a man with a sword in a New York City parking garage. In the intriguing action fantasy *Highlander* (1986), viewers learn through flashbacks that MacLeod belongs to a race of immortal warriors who must battle among themselves until one remains. The premise itself is a paradox — the immortals are not really immortal since they can kill each other. Logic aside, the film benefits from its flashback structure, alternating between MacLeod's modern-day life as an antique dealer who carries a concealed sword and his early life in Scotland where his mentor Ramirez trained him for combat. Christopher Lambert gives MacLeod an appropriately mysterious quality, but Sean Connery steals the film as the charismatic Ramirez. Clancy Brown plays Kurgan, a one-dimensional, but undeniably evil, villain. In the U.S., *Highlander* garnered lukewarm reviews and earned back only $5 million of its then-hefty $16 million budget. Still, it performed well overseas (where Lambert was a bankable star) and gradually earned cult status in the U.S. when released on video. Lambert, Connery, and director Russell Mulcahy reteamed for the 1991 sequel *Highlander II: The Quickening*. It's a confusing effort set in the future that features too little of Connery and — worst of all — changes the original premise by revealing that immortals like MacLeod come from a planet called Ziest. A director's cut subtitled "The Renegade Version" was released in the U.S. on laserdisc in 1997. It runs 19 minutes longer and deletes the planet Ziest storyline. The film series might have ended after *The Quickening* if not for the surprising success of *Highlander: The Series*, a weekly one-hour syndicated TV show. It starred Adrian Paul as Duncan MacLeod, one of Connor's clansmen and a fellow immortal. Christopher Lambert appeared as Connor MacLeod in the TV series episode "The Gathering." It was later combined with another episode and released to videotape as *Highlander: The Gathering* (1992). In 1994, the popularity of the TV series inspired a third theatrical film with Lambert called *Highlander: The Final Dimension*. It pitted Connor against an evil magician named Kane (Mario Van Peebles) who killed one of Connor's teachers 400 years earlier. The film posted a lackluster worldwide gross of $36 million. Meanwhile, *Highlander: The Series* continued to thrive until Adrian Paul decided to bow out in 1997. The show was revamped the following year as *Highlander: The Raven* and focused on Amanda (Elizabeth Gracen), a female immortal introduced in the Adrian Paul series. In 1999, Dimension Films announced plans to film *Highlander: Endgame*, a fourth theatrical film starring both Lambert and Paul.

Highlander (1986); *Highlander II: The Quickening* (1991); *Highlander: The Gathering* (1992); *Highlander: The Final Dimension* (aka *Highland III: The Sorcerer*) (1994)

Hitchhiking

Hitchhiking has come into play in dozens of "road" movies, such as 1985's *The Sure Thing* and, most memorably, 1934's *It Happened One Night*. The latter featured the now-classic scene in which Clark Gable, after trying futilely to attract a ride via the traditional thumb method, receives instruction from Claudette Colbert on how to use one's legs to better effect. The dangers of picking up hitchhikers have been explored in subtle thrillers like *Hitchhike!* and gory horror pictures like *The Hitcher*. The horror anthology *Creepshow 2* spawned the most memorable hitchhiking line, with a walking corpse following Lois Chiles around and moaning repeatedly: "Thanks for the ride, lady!" The 1972 *Thumb Tripping* rates the most hitchhiking scenes per movie with its plot about two hippies (Michael Burns and Meg Foster) hitching across the country. Many movies have revolved around characters picked up from the roadside, including *Detour* (1945), *Three into Two Won't Go* (1969), and *Ginger in the Morning* (1973).

It Happened One Night (1934); *The Devil Thumbs a Ride* (1947); *The Hitch-Hiker* (1953); *The Notorious Mr. Monks* (1958); *Knife in the Water* (1962); *Nightmare in the Sun* (1964); *Thumb Tripping* (1972); *Hitchhike!* (1974 TVM); *Nightmare in Badham County* (aka *Nightmare*) (1976 TVM); *Diary of a Hitchhiker* (1979 TVM); *Road Games* (1981); *Vagabond* (1985); *The Hitcher* (1986); *Creepshow 2* (1987); *The Drifter* (1988); *Alligator Eyes* (1990); *Dust Devil: The Final Cut* (1993); *Even Cowgirls Get the Blues* (1994); *Ruby Jean and Joe* (1996 TVM); *Freeway* (1996); *Western* (1997); *Welcome to Woop-Woop* (1997)

Hitler

The role of Adolf Hitler has frustrated more than one good actor. Alec Guinness gave one of his lesser performances as the Nazi dictator in *Hitler: The Last Ten Days* (1973). Anthony Hopkins overplayed the part (but nevertheless won an Emmy) in the 1981 TV movie *The Bunker*. Even reliable Richard Basehart could not overcome his basic miscasting in the low-key 1962 biography *Hitler*. Derek Jacobi probably gave the best star turn as Hitler in the epic two-part TV movie *Inside the Third Reich* (1982). In the 1940s, character actor Robert Watson specialized in playing Hitler. In addition to starring in 1944's *The Hitler Gang*, he did cameos as Hitler in *The Devil with Hitler* (1942), *The Miracle of Morgan's Creek* (1944), *The Story of Mankind* (1957), and many others. Plots to assassinate Hitler provided the premise for: *Man Hunt* (1941), its remake *Rogue Male* (1976), *Hitler—Dead or Alive* (1943), *The Strange Death of Adolf Hitler* (1943*)*, *The Plot to Assassinate Hitler* (1955), the fact-based *Jackboot Mutiny* (1955), *The Plot to Kill Hitler* (1990), and as a subplot in *The Night of the Generals* (1967). Luther Adler played an impersonator who did kill Hitler and take his place in 1951's fanciful *The Magic Face*. Veronica Lake played a mad scientist who dumps a swarm of maggots on Hitler's face in the obscure gorefest *Flesh Feast* (1970). Another deranged scientist managed to keep Hitler's head alive atop a table in 1963's dreadful *They Saved Hitler's Brain*. Ira Levin fashioned an ingenious plot about Hitler cloning in 1978's *The Boys from Brazil*. The same year's *The Lucifer Complex* found Robert Vaughn investigating another Hitler cloning plot. Charlie Chaplin treated Hitler comically in his topical farce *The Great Dictator* (1940). Comedian Gilbert Gottfried cameoed as Hitler in 1992's *Highway to Hell*. Indiana Jones got Hitler's autograph in *Indiana Jones and the Last Crusade* (1989), while Woody Allen's *Zelig* (1983) turned up in newsreel footage with the German dictator. Mel Brooks' *The Producers* (1968) featured a stage musical called *Springtime for Hitler*.

The Great Dictator (1940); *Man Hunt* (1941); *To Be or Not To Be* (1942); *Hitler—Dead or Alive* (1943); *The Strange Death of Adolf Hitler* (1943); *The Hitler Gang* (1944); *The Magic Face* (1951); *Canaris Master Spy* (1954); *The Plot to Assassinate Hitler* (1955); *Jackboot Mutiny* (1955); *The Last Ten Days* (aka *The Last Ten Days of Adolf Hitler*) (1956); *Hitler* (1962); *The Black Fox* (1962); *They Saved Hitler's Brain* (aka *Madmen of Mandoras*) (1963); *The Producers* (1968); *Flesh Feast* (1970); *Adolf Hitler: My Part in His Downfall* (1972); *Hitler: The Last Ten Days* (1973); *Undercovers Hero* (aka *Soft Beds and Hard Battles*; *Soft Beds, Hard Battles*) (1973); *Rogue Male* (1976 TVM); *The Boys from Brazil* (1978); *The Lucifer Complex* (1978); *Our Hitler, a Film from Germany* (1980); *The Bunker* (1981 TVM); *Inside the Third Reich* (1982 TVM); *To Be or Not to Be* (1983); *Zelig* (1983); *Hitler's S.S.: Portrait in Evil* (1985 TVM); *Dirty Dozen: The Next Mission* (1985 TVM); *Indiana Jones and the Last Crusade* (1989); *Elves* (1989); *The Plot to Kill Hitler* (1990 TVM); *Hitler's Daughter* (1990 TVM); *Highway to Hell* (1992)

Hockey

This game's reputation for violence would seem to make it ideal subject matter for a movie. But even during the bloody 1970s, when *The Longest Yard* (1974) and *Rollerball* (1975) glorified sports violence, hockey made little impact. Its big shot at stardom came with 1977's *Slap Shot*, which cast Paul Newman as the desperate coach of a bush-league hockey team. The film fared well at the box-office, but its returns failed to inspire even a B-movie rip-off. ABC capitalized on the game's temporary popularity following the USA team's stunning upset of the Russians in the 1980 Olympics by producing a movie version titled *Miracle on Ice*. Five years later, Michael Keaton and Rob Lowe took to the ice in *Touch and Go* and *Youngblood*, respectively. Keaton's film sat on the shelf for over a year and then barely got released. Lowe's picture fizzled as well, signalling either a lack of public interest in hockey or the game's inability to attract serious filmmakers. Hockey also played a minor role in *Love Story*—Oliver (Ryan O'Neal) had a passion for playing it. Mel Gibson chased some thugs across the ice during a Los Angeles Kings hockey game in 1992's *Lethal Weapon 3*. *Friday the 13th*'s popular killer Jason made hockey masks fashionable for psychopaths. See also **The Mighty Ducks**.

King of Hockey (1936); *It's a Pleasure* (1945); *Love Story* (1970); *Paperback Hero* (1973); *Gross Misconduct* (1973 TVM); *Slap Shot* (1977); *The Deadliest Season* (1977 TVM); *The Boy Who Drank Too Much* (1980 TVM); *Miracle on Ice* (1981 TVM); *Hockey Night* (1984); *Generation* (1985 TVM); *Touch and Go* (1986); *Youngblood* (1986); *The Running Man* (1987); *The Cutting Edge* (1992); *Lethal Weapon 3* (1992); *The Mighty Ducks* (1992); *Sudden Death* (1995); *Happy Gilmore* (1996); *Mystery, Alaska* (1999); *H-E Double Hockey Sticks* (1999 TVM)

Holmes, Sherlock

Literature's most renowned detective is certainly one of the screen's busiest. Only Charlie Chan rivals him in number of film appearances in the sound era and, even at that, the Baker Street sleuth has been played by more actors than any detective. The first recorded screen appearance of Arthur Conan Doyle's fictional mastermind was in a 1903 silent short (very short, about a minute) called *Sherlock Holmes Baffled*. The Conan Doyle mysteries made popular silent film subjects, but a definitive Holmes interpretation did not emerge until William Gillette made *Sherlock Holmes* in 1916. The screenplay was based on Gillette's own stage play, originally performed in 1899. Ellie Norwood was the most prolific silent Holmes, appearing in seven films between 1921 and 1923. British screen veteran Clive Brook introduced Holmes to the "talkies" in 1929's *The Return of Sherlock Holmes*, an updated mystery about a retired Holmes lured into detecting again by Watson's grown daughter (!). Four other actors played Conan Doyle's sleuth from 1931–1937, with Arthur Wontner garnering the most praise. Already in his mid-fifties, Wontner played an older Holmes, ably assisted by Ian Fleming (not the author) as Dr. Watson in all but one case (*The Sign of Four* with Ian Hunter). It's interesting to note that the five Wontner films were based on Conan Doyle works. Despite his success, Wontner's Holmes interpretation was eclipsed in 1939, when, in a stroke of casting genius, Basil Rathbone was signed to play Holmes in 20th Century–Fox's lavish *The Hound of the Baskervilles*. Rathbone's crisp, energetic performance was delightfully balanced by Nigel Bruce's bumbling, but endearing, Watson (who in no way resembled Conan Doyle's intelligent physician/companion). *The Hound* was a rousing success and Fox quickly followed it with *The Adventures of Sherlock Holmes*, pitting Holmes against archvillain Professor Moriarty (superbly played by the menacing George Zucco). It rates as the finest of all Holmes films. Unfortunately, Fox let the series die and when Rathbone and Bruce reappeared as Holmes and Watson, it was for budget-minded Universal. Consisting of 12 movies shot between 1942 and 1946, the Universal series boasted updated story lines and shorter running times. Holmes battled Nazis, spies, and famous murderers with sinister names like The Creeper. The series peaked with *The Scarlet Claw*, an eerie, atmospheric puzzler featuring a marsh phantom and a murderous master of disguises. Roy William Neill produced and directed most of the entries and series regulars included Dennis Hoey as a frustrated Inspector Lestrade and Mary Gordon as the kindly housekeeper Mrs. Hudson. When Rathbone put his violin case away for good in 1946, other actors were hesitant to take up the role. Then in 1959, Hammer Films — England's foremost horror film factory — starred Peter Cushing in a colorful adaptation of *The Hound of the Baskervilles*. It was more violent than its predecessors, but handsomely mounted and boasting an excellent Watson in Andre Morell. Hammer could not secure rights for future films, although Cushing went on to play Holmes again on British television. With the Rathbone barrier broken, Holmes became a popular screen fixture again. John Neville played a dashing Holmes who encountered Jack the Ripper in *A Study in Terror* (1965), a film produced in association with Conan Doyle's son Adrian. Robert Stephens offered a complex, offbeat portrait in Billy Wilder's sly satire *The Private Life of Sherlock Holmes* (1970). Jack the Ripper reappeared to match wits with Christopher Plummer's sleuth in *Murder by Decree* (1979). The 1988 *Without a Clue* proposed the novel twist that Watson (Ben Kingsley) was the brains behind the duo and that Holmes was just an actor hired to play a part. On television, many performers have essayed the role, including Jeremy Brett, whose long-running series appears on PBS's *Mystery!* Author A. Conan Doyle has also appeared as a character in movies such as *Fairy Tale: A True Story* (1997) and *Houdini* (1998 TVM).

RATHBONE/BRUCE: *The Hound of the Baskervilles* (1939); *The Adventures of Sherlock Holmes* (1939); *Sherlock Holmes and the Voice of Terror* (1942); *Sherlock Holmes and the Secret Weapon* (1942); *Sherlock Holmes in Washington* (1943); *Sherlock Holmes Faces Death* (1943); *Crazy House* (1943) (cameo appearance); *The Scarlet Claw* (1944); *Sherlock Holmes and the Spider Woman* (aka *Spider Woman*) (1944); *The House of Fear* (1945); *The Woman in Green* (1945); *Pursuit to Algiers* (1945); *Terror by Night* (1946); *Dressed to Kill* (aka *Sherlock Holmes and the Secret Code*) (1946)

OTHERS: *The Return of Sherlock Holmes* (1929) (Clive Brook); *Paramount on Parade* (1930) (Brook appears in a skit); *Sherlock Holmes' Fatal Hour* (aka *The Sleeping Cardinal*) (1931) (Arthur Wontner); *The Speckled Band* (1931) (Raymond Massey); *The Hound of the Baskervilles* (1931) (Robert Rendel); *The Missing Rembrandt* (1932) (Wontner); *The Sign of Four* (1932) (Wontner); *Sherlock Holmes* (1932) (Brook); *A Study in Scarlet* (1933) (Reginald Owen); *The Triumph of Sherlock Holmes* (1935) (Wontner); *Silver Blaze* (1937) (Wontner); *The Hound of the Baskervilles* (1959) (Peter Cushing); *Sherlock Holmes and the Deadly Necklace* (1962) (Christopher Lee); *A Study in Terror* (1965) (John Neville); *The Private Life of Sherlock Holmes* (1970) (Robert Stephens); *The Hound of the Baskervilles* (1972 TVM) (Stewart Granger); *The Adventures of Sherlock Holmes' Smarter* Brother (1975) (Douglas Wilmer, with Gene Wilder as the brother); *Sherlock Holmes in New York* (1976 TVM) (Roger Moore); *The Seven-Per-Cent Solution* (1976) (Nicol Williamson); *Murder by Decree* (1979) (Christopher Plummer); *The Sign of Four* (1983) (Ian Richardson); *The Hound of the Baskervilles* (1983) (Ian Richardson); *Sherlock Holmes and the Masks of Death* (aka *The Masks of Death*) (1984 TVM) (Peter Cushing); *Young Sherlock Holmes* (aka *Sherlock Holmes and the Pyramid of Fear*) (1985) (Nicholas Rowe); *The Return of Sherlock Holmes* (1987 TVM) (Michael Pennington); *Without a Clue* (1988) (Michael Caine as Reginald Kincaid as Holmes); *Hands of a Murderer* (aka *Sherlock Holmes and the Prince of Crime*) (1990 TVM) (Edward Woodward); *The Crucifer of Blood* (1991 TVM) (Charlton Heston); *Sherlock Holmes: Incident at Victoria Falls* (1991 TVM) (Christopher Lee); *Sherlock Holmes and the Leading Lady* (1991 TVM) (Lee); *Sherlock Holmes in Caracas* (1992) (Jean Manuel Montesinos); *1994 Baker Street: Sherlock Holmes Returns* (aka *Sherlock Holmes Returns*) (1993 TVM) (Anthony Higgins); *The Hound of London* (1993 TVM) (Patrick Macnee); (Note: George C. Scott portrayed a man who believed himself to be Sherlock Holmes in 1971's *They Might Be Giants*. His psychiatrist, played by Joanne Woodward, was naturally named Dr. Watson. The plot was reworked in a 1976 TV movie *The Return of the World's Greatest Detective*); *The Great Mouse Detective* (1986) featured an animated Holmes-inspired rodent.

Honey, I Shrunk the Kids Series

Rick Moranis starred as absent-minded scientist Wayne Szalinski in this three-film series from the Disney studios. The first and best entry, *Honey, I Shrunk the Kids*, earned a surprising $100 million at the U.S. box-office en route to becoming one of 1989's biggest hits. The simple plot has two of the Szalinski children and their friends accidentally activating Dad's experimental miniaturization ray. After being shrunk to microscopic size, the kids get dumped — with the trash — into the backyard. They spend the rest of the movie experiencing unexpected adventures (e.g., a delirious flight aboard a bumblebee) as they try to return to their house. At its best, *Honey, I Shrunk the Kids* harks back to classic

Disney live action comedies like *The Absent Minded Professor* (1961). It's hard to believe the story was cowritten by Stuart Gordon, the man responsible for the outrageous, gory horror-comedy *Re-Animator* (1985). Moranis and most of the original cast returned for the 1992 sequel *Honey, I Blew Up the Kid*. Despite a cute premise—Wayne accidentally enlarges his three-year-old son to gigantic proportions—the film lacked the charm of its predecessor. Its disappointing box-office returns contributed to Disney's decision to release the third installment, *Honey, We Shrunk Ourselves* (1997), directly to video. Moranis headlined this entry, too, as Wayne, his wife, and two friends get reduced in size. The same year, Disney launched a syndicated one-hour TV series called *Honey, I Shrunk the Kids: The TV Show* with Peter Scolari as Wayne Szalinski. There is also a 3-D attraction at Disneyland called *Honey, I Shrunk the Audience*, which features Moranis in a 23-minute short. See also **Giants; Little People**.

Honey, I Shrunk the Kids (1989); *Honey, I Blew Up the Kid* (1992); *Honey, We Shrunk Ourselves* (1997)

Hood, Robin

Although five silent films appeared between 1909 and 1913, this legendary outlaw did not become a hot movie property until Douglas Fairbanks portrayed him in 1922. Since then, Robin Hood has never gone a decade without being featured in at least one movie. Errol Flynn was the definitive Robin in the 1938 classic *The Adventures of Robin Hood*. Apparently to avoid comparison with Flynn, no other major actor essayed the role until Richard Todd in Disney's 1952 *The Story of Robin Hood*. In the meantime, John Derek, Cornel Wilde, and June Laverick played the outlaw's offspring in, respectively, *Rogues of Sherwood Forest*, *Bandits of Sherwood Forest*, and *Son of Robin Hood* (actually daughter). Richard Greene leapt from his successful 1955–58 *Adventures of Robin Hood* TV series into a big-screen version, 1960's *The Sword of Sherwood Forest*. A few years later, Disney offered an animated *Robin Hood*, depicting the characters as animals (Robin was a fox). Sean Connery appeared as an older, wearier outlaw opposite Audrey Hepburn's Maid Marian in the "realist" version *Robin and Marian*. *Robin Hood: Prince of Thieves* (1991) was part adventure, part camp—but a miscast Kevin Costner still attracted enough fans to make it a big hit. Frank Sinatra and Bing Crosby headed an all-star cast in a musical gangster variation called *Robin and the Seven Hoods* (1964). Robin has been parodied in *Time Bandits* (1981*), The Zany Adventures of Robin Hood* (1984), and in Mel Brooks' *Robin Hood: Men in Tights* (1993). The latter film was inspired by Brooks' short-lived 1975 TV series *When Things Were Rotten*.

Robin Hood (1922); *The Adventures of Robin Hood* (1938); *Bandits of Sherwood Forest* (1946); *The Prince of Thieves* (1948); *Rogues of Sherwood Forest* (1950); *Tales of Robin Hood* (1951); *The Story of Robin Hood* (1952); *Ivanhoe* (1952); *Men of Sherwood Forest* (1954); *Son of Robin Hood* (1959); *Sword of Sherwood Forest* (1960); *A Challenge for Robin Hood* (1968); *Robin Hood* (1973); *Robin and Marian* (1976); *Time Bandits* (1981); *The Zany Adventures of Robin Hood* (1984 TVM); *Robin Hood and the Sorcerer* (1984 TVM); *Robin Hood: Prince of Thieves* (1991); *Robin Hood* (1991 TVM); *Robin Hood: Men in Tights* (1993)

Hornleigh, Inspector

Gordon Harker and Alastair Sim played Inspector Hornleigh and Sergeant Bingham in a trio of lively British comedy-mysteries produced from 1938–1940. Hans Priwin originally created the detectives for his "Monday Night at Eight" radio series. Although rarely shown on television today, the Hornleigh mysteries hold up well, mixing humor and thrills with an almost Hitchcockian flair. That should come as no surprise since two of the three films were co-written by Frank Launder, who penned the screenplay to Hitch's *The Lady Vanishes* (1938) with Sidney Gilliat (who also worked on *Inspector Hornleigh On Holiday*). Like *The Lady Vanishes*, Launder's *Inspector Hornleigh Goes to It* (1940) climaxes on a train (q.v.). After three stints as Hornleigh's sidekick, Alastair Sim graduated to chief detective roles in the British classics *Green for Danger* (1946), co-written and directed by Gilliat, and *An Inspector Calls* (1954).

Inspector Hornleigh (1938); *Inspector Hornleigh on Holiday* (1939); *Inspector Hornleigh Goes to It* (aka *Mail Train*) (1940)

Horse Racing/Equitation

Mickey Rooney is the undisputed champ of horse racing sagas with a track career spanning half a century. He played the son of a disgraced jockey in *Down the Stretch* (1936), Wallace Beery's jockey protégé in *Stablemates* (1938), a young jockey involved with crooks (and teamed with Judy Garland for the first time) in *Thoroughbreds Don't Cry* (1937), Elizabeth Taylor's young mentor in *National Velvet* (1944), the trainer of *The Black Stallion* (1979), and a horse owner in *Lightning, the White Stallion* (1986). Surprisingly, Rooney never made a race track comedy. However, horse racing hijinks seem to be a requirement for most comedians. The Marx Brothers produced the most memorable, 1937's *A Day at the Races*, which featured Groucho at his best as horse doctor Hugo Z. Hackenbush. Abbott and Costello raced a steed named Tea Biscuit in *It Ain't Hay* (1943). It was called *Money for Jam* in Great Britain, which one shouldn't confuse with *Money from Home* (1953), another stateside horse race comedy with Dean Martin and Jerry Lewis. Hope and Crosby never raced horses in the *Road* movies, but Bob gambled on them in *Sorrowful Jones* (1949) and *The Lemon Drop Kid* (1951), while Bing backed one in Frank Capra's *Riding High* (1950). Donald O'Connor and his talking mule sidekick Francis could have made a fortune in *Francis Goes to the Races* (1951), since the race horses told Francis that they always determined the winner before the race even began. A little boy's ability to predict horse race results with amazing accuracy ended in tragedy in *The Rocking Horse Winner*, a 1949 adaptation of the D.H. Lawrence short story. Filmmakers have deemed few real-life horse racing champions worthy of film biographies. The exceptions include the exceptional horses in *The Story of Seabiscuit* (1949), *The Great Dan Patch* (1949), and *Phar Lap* (1983), the latter being Australia's most famous racing champ. Although most horse races are of the thoroughbred variety, a handful have explored other horse racing events: Elizabeth Taylor entered "The Pie" in the Grand National Steeplechase in *National Velvet*; father and daughter Charles Coburn and Peggy Cummins raced trotting horses in *The Green Grass of Wyoming* (1948); Tatum O'Neal and Melissa Gilbert set their sights on equestrian championships in, respectively, *International Velvet* (1978) and *Sylvester* (1985); and Gene Hackman and James Coburn were two of the riders in the grueling cross-country horse race in *Bite the Bullet* (1975). Non–horse racing films with memorable sequences include *My Fair Lady* (1964) and the carousel horse race in *Mary Poppins* (1964). Film critics have pondered for years whether the title of *Million Dollar Legs* (1939) refers to the film's race horse or its star Betty Grable. See also **Horses**.

Sporting Blood (1931); *Broadway Bill* (aka *Strictly Confidential*) (1934); *Little Miss Marker* (aka *The Girl in Pawn*) (1934); *Down the Stretch* (1936); *Three Men on a Horse* (1936); *Charlie Chan at the Race Track* (1936); *A Day at the Races* (1937); *Thoroughbreds Don't Cry* (1937); *Racing Lady* (1937); *Saratoga* (1937); *Sing You Sinners* (1938); *Stablemates* (1938); *Come on George* (1939); *Million Dollar Legs* (1939); *The Lady's from Kentucky* (1939); *It Ain't Hay* (aka *Money for Jam*) (1943); *National Velvet* (1944); *Home in Indiana* (1944); *The Great Mike* (1944); *She Went to the Races* (1945); *My Brother Talks to Horses* (1946); *The Homestretch* (1947); *Black Gold* (1947); *The Green Grass of Wyoming* (1948); *The Story of Seabiscuit* (aka *Pride of Kentucky*) (1949); *The Great Dan Patch* (1949); *Sorrowful Jones* (1949); *Under My Skin* (1949); *The Rocking Horse Winner* (1949); *Boy from Indiana* (1950); *The Pride of Maryland* (1950); *Blue Grass of Kentucky* (1950); *Riding High* (1950); *Francis Goes to the Races* (1951); *Blue Blood* (1951); *The Galloping Major* (1951); *The Lemon Drop Kid* (1951); *The Rainbow Jacket* (1951); *Boots Malone* (1952); *Four Against Fate* (aka *Derby Day*) (1952); *A Girl in Every Port* (1952); *Money from Home* (1953); *Fast Company* (1953); *Pride of the Blue Grass* (1954); *The Fighting Chance* (1955); *Dry Rot* (1956); *Glory* (1956); *The Killing* (1956); *Photo Finish* (1957); *Just My Luck* (1957); *The Sad Horse* (1959); *Mary Poppins* (1964); *My Fair Lady* (1964); *The Reivers* (aka *The Yellow Winton Flyer*) (1969); *Bite the Bullet* (1975); *International Velvet* (1978); *Casey's Shadow* (1978); *Run for the Roses* (aka *Thoroughbred*) (1978); *My Old Man* (1979 TVM); *The Black Stallion* (1979); *Little Miss Marker* (1980); *On the Right Track* (1981); *Phar Lap* (1983); *Sylvester* (1985); *The Longshot* (1986); *Lightning, the White Stallion* (1986); *Hot to Trot* (1988); *Let It Ride* (1989)

Horses

The horse has been a favorite film subject since Eadweard Muybridge used photography to study a horse in motion (allegedly to settle a $5,000 bet) in 1872. Early horse roles were principally supporting ones, though Tom Mix's horse Tony attracted enough admirers to star in his own film, 1922's *Just Tony*. However, most early talkies either relegated horses to a mere means of transportation for cowboys or revolved around horse racing (see separate entry for a detailed discussion and list). *Kentucky* (1938) strayed from the race track long enough to offer a story of rival horse-breeding families. Yet, it lacked the horse appeal inherent in *My Friend Flicka* (1943), a heartwarming tale of the love between a young boy (Roddy McDowall) and a mare with madness in her bloodline ("flicka" is the Swedish word for girl). McDowall and cast returned two years later with *Thunderhead, Son of Flicka*, a picturesque sequel in which McDowall set his horse free at the end. The following year, the same studio, 20th–Century Fox also released *Smoky*, Will James' classic horse story about the friendship between a wild stallion and a drifting cowboy (Fred MacMurray). *Smoky* and *Flicka* turned out to be highly influential films, establishing the pattern for other non-racing, person-loves-horse plots. Even John Steinbeck's *The Red Pony* (1949) offered only a minor variation, giving equal time to a purely human subplot about a boy confused over love for his father and affection for a hired hand. Two superior children-and-horse films, *Misty* (1961) and *The Black Stallion* (1979), were set partially on islands and adapted from popular juvenile novels (by Marguerite Henry and Walter Farley, respectively). The touching 1994 adaptation of

Anna Sewell's children's classic *Black Beauty* was told from the horse's perspective. *The Appaloosa* (1966) was a horse film for adults, with brooding Marlon Brando stalking the bandits that stole his steed. The only horse in *The Horse Without a Head* (1963) was a toy one hiding stolen loot. The most colorful nag was the famous Horse of a Different Color that pranced around the Emerald City in 1939's *The Wizard of Oz*. Pegasus, the mythological winged horse, took to the air with Harry Hamlin aboard in the 1981 fantasy *Clash of the Titans*. Special effects artist Ray Harryhausen created the cinema's tiniest horse in 1969's *Valley of Gwangi*. Finally, for the record, the most famous cowboy horses were: Trigger (Roy Rogers), Buttermilk (Dale Evans), Champion (Gene Autry), Topper (Hopalong Cassidy), White Flash (Tex Ritter), Fritz (William S. Hart), Tarzan (Ken Maynard), and Blackjack (Allan Lane). Lane, in his post-cowboy days, provided the voice for TV's famous talking horse *Mr. Ed* (1961–65). See also **Horse Racing/Equitation**; **Unicorns**.

Just Tony (1922); *Kentucky* (1938); *Sergeant Murphy* (1938); *Konga, the Wild Stallion* (1939); *The Wizard of Oz* (1939); *Florian* (1940); *My Friend Flicka* (1943); *Thunderhead—Son of Flicka* (1945); *Smoky* (1946); *Black Beauty* (1946); *The Red Stallion* (1947); *King of the Wild Horses* (1947); *Stallion Road* (1947); *The Red Pony* (1949); *You Never Can Tell* (1951); *Flame of Araby* (1951); *The Lion and the Horse* (1952); *Gypsy Colt* (1954); *Black Horse Canyon* (1954); *The Courage of Black Beauty* (1957); *Tonka* (aka *A Horse Named Comanche*) (1958); *King of the Wild Stallions* (1959); *The Misfits* (1961); *Misty* (1961); *The Horse Without a Head* (1963); *The Miracle of the White Stallions* (1963); *Mary Poppins* (1964); *Indian Paint* (1964); *The Appaloosa* (aka *Southwest to Sonora*) (1966); *Smoky* (1966); *The Horse in the Gray Flannel Suit* (1968); *Valley of Gwangi* (1969); *Run Wild, Run Free* (aka *Philip*) (1969); *Black Beauty* (1971); *The Red Pony* (1973 TVM); *Running Wild* (1973); *Mustang Country* (1976); *The Littlest Horse Thieves* (aka *Escape from the Dark*) (1976); *Equus* (1977); *The Black Stallion* (1979); *Eagle's Wing* (1979); *The Electric Horseman* (1979); *Wild Horse Hank* (1979); *Clash of the Titans* (1981); *A Rare Breed* (1981); *The Man from Snowy River* (1982); *Danger Down Under* (1988 TVM); *Wild Hearts Can't Be Broken* (1991); *The Girl Who Came Late* (1991); *Dark Horse* (1992); *Into the West* (1993); *Black Beauty* (1994); *A Horse for Danny* (1995 TVM); *Tall Tale* (1995); *Two-Bits and Pepper* (1996); *The Horse Whisperer* (1998); *Running Free* (2000)

Hospitals

Film series about the medical profession, particularly the *Dr. Kildare* (q.v.) movies and the British *Doctor* (q.v.) comedies, have made extensive use of hospital settings. Non-series hospital dramas reached their peak during the 1960s, their production fueled by the success of popular TV programs like *Dr. Kildare* and *Ben Casey*. However, by the early 1970s, filmmakers had begun to view hospitals with increasing cynicism. Peter Sellers played a money-minded hospital administrator in the smutty comedy *Where Does It Hurt?* (1972). It lacked the bite of Paddy Chayefsky's *The Hospital*, a black comedy about a metropolitan medical establishment run by incompetents and housing a killer. Still, either of those was easier to digest than Frederick Wiseman's potent documentary *Hospital* (1970). A decade later, director Linday Anderson ripped into the British medical community with his irreverent hit-and-miss satire *Britannia Hospital* (1982). Other hospital-set comedies have been less ambitious, preferring to generate medical gags instead of social commentary. Nevertheless, the sight of the *Carry On* (q.v.) Gang carousing through a hospital is almost as frightening as it is funny. The hospital, as a setting for fright films, has been employed in *Halloween II* (1982), *Visiting Hours* (1982), and *Terminal Choice* (1985). The hospital in *Halloween II* rates as the creepiest—a cheap administrator's dream come true, where the staff is virtually nonexistent and the lights are turned off at every opportunity. In 1958's *Revenge of Frankenstein*, Dr. Frankenstein ran a clinic for the poor (which allowed him to amass spare body parts). Genevieve Bujold discovered a scheme in which patients were killed and their body parts sold in Michael Crichton's hospital thriller *Coma* (1978). Alastair Sim, as the witty, droll Inspector Cockrill, investigated multiple murders in a World War II hospital in the delightful 1946 mystery *Green for Danger*. See also **Doctor in the House Series**; **Nurses Series**.

Green for Danger (1946); *The Sleeping City* (1950); *White Corridors* (1951); *Emergency Hospital* (1956); *Behind the Mask* (1958); *Carry On Nurse* (1960); *The Young Doctors* (1961); *The Interns* (1962); *A Stitch in Time* (1963); *The New Interns* (1964); *U.M.C.* (aka *Operation Heartbeat*) (1969 TVM); *Hospital* (1970); *The Hospital* (1971); *The Carey Treatment* (1972); *Where Does It Hurt?* (1972); *The Young Nurses* (aka *Emergency Nurses*) (1973); *The Healers* (1974 TVM); *Medical Story* (1975); *One of Our Own* (1975); *Coma* (1978); *Doctors' Private Lives* (1978); *House Calls* (1978); *Halloween II* (1982); *Visiting Hours* (1982); *Young Doctors in Love* (1982); *Britannia Hospital* (1982); *Hospital Massacre* (1982); *Emergency Room* (1983 TVM); *Terminal Choice* (1985); *Critical Condition* (1987); *Paper Mask* (1990); *Deliver Them from Evil: The Taking of Alta View* (1992 TVM); *Article 99* (1992); *State of Emergency* (1994 TVM); *Mortal Fear* (aka *Robin Cook's Mortal Fear*) (1994 TVM); *Nothing Lasts Forever* (1995 TVM); *Terminal* (1996 TVM); *Extreme Measures* (1996); *Cosi* (1997); *Desperate Measures* (1998)

Hotels

The hotel setting has registered as a favorite among filmmakers ever since *Grand Hotel*'s impressive guest roster made multicharacter dramas fashionable. This 1932 Best Picture, set in a Berlin hotel, featured Greta Garbo as a lonely ballerina, John Barrymore as a down-on-his-luck thief, Wallace Beery as a cold-hearted businessman, Lionel Barrymore as a dying man, and Joan Crawford as an ambitious secretary. It was officially remade with an American setting as 1945's *Weekend at the Waldorf*, but dozens of unofficial copies have borrowed the format. *Hotel Berlin* (1945), based on a novel by *Grand Hotel* author Vicki Baum, was a thinly-disguised reworking bolstered by an all-star Warner Bros. cast. *Separate Tables* (1958) was set at a seaside resort and earned Oscars for Best Actor David Niven and Best Supporting Actress Wendy Hiller. The 1933 *International House* brought an eclectic group of comedians (W.C. Fields, Burns and Allen, etc.) together at an Oriental hotel in a wild plot about early television. Other all-star hotel pictures have included Arthur Hailey's *Hotel* (1967) and the Neil Simon comedies *Plaza Suite* (1971) and *California Suite* (1978). Deserts seem like unsuitable locations for hotels, but Field Marshal Rommel (Erich Von Stroheim) visited one in Billy Wilder's *Five Graves to Cairo* (1943) and Yvonne DeCarlo operated one in *Hotel Sahara* (1951). Despite the scorching sun, those hotels boasted great life-saving offers that you just can't find at cheaper, horrific places like the Bates Motel of *Psycho* fame. While the Bates has a corner on the terror motel market, it has received some competition from the Overlook Hotel in *The Shining* (1980), *Horror Hotel* (1960), and *Motel Hell* (1980). Jean Simmons' brother—and his hotel room—mysteriously disappeared in 1950's *So Long at the Fair*. Jean's frustration increased significantly when the hotel staff refused to acknowledge existence of the room or her brother. More pleasant hotels have provided the settings for musicals and comedies. Bing Crosby's *Holiday Inn* (1942) opened only on holidays, but still attracted quite a crowd due to Bing's crooning, Fred Astaire's dancing, and Irving Berlin's catchy tunes. Bing and Danny Kaye put on a big show to save their old Army general's hotel in 1954's *White Christmas*. Groucho played a desk clerk who had to deal with rowdy guests like Chico and Harpo in the 1929 Marx Brothers comedy *The Cocoanuts*. Nine years later, *Room Service* found Groucho and the boys sidestepping eviction from their hotel suite, while desperately trying to salvage a stage play. See also **Apartments**; **Restaurants**; **Simon's Suites Series**.

The Cocoanuts (1929); *Grand Hotel* (1932); *International House* (1933); *Hollywood Hotel* (1937); *Hotel Haywire* (1937); *Room Service* (1938); *Hotel for Women* (aka *Elsa Maxwell's Hotel for Women*) (1939); *Holiday Inn* (1942); *Five Graves to Cairo* (1943); *Hotel Reserve* (1944); *Step Lively* (1944); *Escape in the Desert* (1945); *Hotel Berlin* (1945); *Weekend at the Waldorf* (1945); *So Long at the Fair* (1950); *Hotel Sahara* (1951); *White Christmas* (1954); *The Girl Rush* (1955); *The Green Man* (1957); *Separate Tables* (1958); *The Bellboy* (1960); *Psycho* (1960); *Horror Hotel* (aka *The City of the Dead*) (1960); *Wake Me When It's Over* (1960); *Man at the Carlton Tower* (1961); *The Inn on the River* (1962); *Tiara Tahiti* (1962); *Honeymoon Hotel* (1964); *The Moon-Spinners* (1964); *The End of August at the Hotel Ozone* (aka *The End of the World at the Hotel Ozone*) (1965); *Hotel* (1967); *Nightmare Hotel* (1970); *Plaza Suite* (1971); *Snowball Express* (1972); *Private Parts* (1972); *Inn of the Damned* (1974); *Motel Hell* (1980); *The Shining* (1980); *Somewhere in Time* (1980); *Experience Preferred...But Not Essential* (1983 TVM); *Pink Motel* (1983); *The Hotel New Hampshire* (1984); *The Rosebud Beach Hotel* (aka *The Big Lobby*) (1984); *Private Resort* (1985); *Bates Motel* (1987 TVM); *Puppet Master* (1989); *Mystery Train* (1989); *The Witches* (1990); *Blame It on the Bellboy* (1991); *Desire and Hell at Sunset Motel* (1992); *Dragon Inn* (1992); *Bed and Breakfast* (1992); *Hotel Room* (1993 TVM); *For Love or Money* (1993); *King of the Hill* (1993); *Bank Robber* (1993); *Mario and the Magician* (1994); *The Haunting of Seacliff Inn* (1994 TVM); *Nick of Time* (1995); *Daisies in December* (1995 TVM); *Four Rooms* (1995); *Dunston Checks In* (1996); *Hotel de Love* (1996); *I Still Know What You Did Last Summer* (1998); *Psycho* (1998); *The Big Kahuna* (2000)

House Party Series

Rap duo Kid 'n Play (Christopher Reid and Christopher Martin) made their film debut in *House Party*, a winning 1990 teen comedy that Roger Ebert described as "silly and high-spirited...and that is just as it should be." The story takes place during a single night as Kid, who has been grounded by his stern father (Robin Harris), tries to figure out how to get to Play's big party ("a super def throwdown"). Before the evening ends, Kid has created a dance step, escaped from a vicious gang, found a girlfriend, and landed in jail. Writer-director Reginald Hudlin, who based *House Party* on a short film made at Harvard, peppers his script with warm humor and clever in-jokes. For example, Kid—who sports a high, cone-shaped hairdo—gets harassed by cops who call him Eraserhead. Neither Reginald Hudlin nor his producer-brother Warrington were involved with *House Party 2*, an agreeable sequel in which Kid loses the $10,000 raised by his church's congregation to send him to college. Several original cast members returned, including Martin Lawrence as Kid and Play's friend Bilal. Unfortunately, Robin Harris, who had earned strong notices as Pops in the original, died prior to filming *House Party 2*. A belated third entry, *House Party 3*, revolved around Kid's engagement and bachelor party. Neither fans nor critics received it favorably and any plans for future installments were scrapped. Christopher Reid and Christopher Martin played essentially the same roles in 1990 children's animated TV series *Kid 'n Play*.

House Party (1990); *House Party 2* (1991); *House Party 3* (1994)

House Series

This quirky series, saddled with an incongruent third entry, has juggled horror and humor with very uneven results. The original *House* (1986) starred William Katt as a depressed horror writer who moves into the title abode after his aunt vacates it via suicide. He is soon assailed by a variety of nightmarish apparitions as well as nosy neighbor George Wendt (Norm on TV's *Cheers*). *House II: The Second Story* (1987) substituted Arye Gross as the new owner, but otherwise followed a similar structure. It even featured John Ratzenberger (Cliff on *Cheers*) in a memorable cameo as an electrician/adventurer. As indicated by the presence of the *Cheers* regulars, neither *House* nor *House II* harbored any pretensions as straight horror films. However, the third entry, *The Horror Show* (1989) went straight for the jugular with a slasher film plot devoid of humor. It was written by the infamous Alan Smithee (q.v.) and released outside the U.S. as *House III*. The humor was still missing in *House IV* (1992), a direct-to-videotape release. William Katt appeared briefly as a character with the same name as the one he played in *House*. However, it does not appear to be the same character. At any rate, he is killed in the opening reel, leaving his wife (Terri Treas) the task of battling supernatural creatures as well as dastardly human bad guys. See also **Amityville Series**; **Ghosts**.

House (1986); *House II: The Second Story* (1987); *The Horror Show* (aka *House III*) (1989); *House IV* (1992)

The Howling Series

This loosely-connected werewolf series continued the 1980s trend of milking a decent horror film for as many sequels as possible (see also **Halloween Series, Friday the 13th Series,** and **Nightmare on Elm Street Series**). Joe (*Gremlins*) Dante directed 1981's *The Howling*, an affectionate mixture of gruesome horror and dark humor (peppered with inside jokes). Dee Wallace played the television newscaster who encounters a werewolf, suffers trauma, and goes to a retreat to recover. Alas, the place turns out to be crawling with bloodthirsty werewolves and Wallace unwillingly joins the pack. The Wallace character (played by another actress) appeared fleetingly in 1984's *The Howling II: Your Sister Is a Werewolf*, a U.S.-European coproduction. This cheap-looking sequel featured a tasteless werewolf lovemaking session and excessive footage of Sybil Danning's cleavage. Wit, style, and adequate werewolf makeup were conspicuously missing. The remaining films in the series bore even less resemblance to the original. The best of the bunch was Philippe Mora's *The Howling III*, which shifted the locale to Down Under and introduced two tribes of Aussie "werewolves" (who carry their offspring in

pouches). The tongue-in-cheek premise strove to prove that werewolves are people, too. It even featured a defected Russian ballerina who transforms into a werewolf while on stage. *Howling IV* (1988), lensed on a shoestring budget in South Africa, rehashed the first film by sending an emotionally unstable novelist to a retreat once again populated by werewolves. *Howling V: The Rebirth* (1989) resembled Agatha Christie's *Ten Little Indians*, only with a werewolf for a murderer. *Howling VI: The Freaks* (1991) found a lyncanthrope working in a carnival sideshow run by a vampire. In the last series entry, *The Howling: New Moon Rising* (1994), residents of a small town suspected an Australian drifter of being a werewolf when a series of murders begins. See also **Werewolves**.

The Howling (1981); *The Howling II: Your Sister Is a Werewolf* (1984); *The Howling III: The Marsupials* (1987); *Howling IV... The Original Nightmare* (1988); *Howling V: The Rebirth* (1989); *Howling VI: The Freaks* (1991); *The Howling: New Moon Rising* (1994)

Huggetts Family

Described by film critic Leslie Halliwell as "Britain's answer to the Hardys," the Huggetts appeared in four features for Gainsborough. They were not even top-billed in their debut film, 1947's *Holiday Camp* (Jack Warner as Mr. Huggett was listed third in the cast). This charming comedy-drama, set at a highly-regimented holiday resort, interwove the story of several characters. But British moviegoers favored the Huggetts and they were given their own vehicle with 1948's *Here Come the Huggetts*. The next year, they became involved in politics and then concluded the series with a trip to Africa and an encounter with smugglers. Jack Warner and Kathleen Harrison, who played parents Joe and Ethel Huggett, continued to make films together (e.g., 1951's *A Christmas Carol*). Hazel Court played their widowed daughter Joan in *Holiday Camp*. Other Huggett children included Susan Shaw as Susan and 15-year-old Petula Clark as Pet. Diana Dors and David Tomlinson, who both became familiar faces to British film fans, also appeared in supporting roles.

Holiday Camp (1947); *Here Come the Huggetts* (1948); *Vote for Huggett* (1948); *The Huggetts Abroad* (1949)

Hulot, Monsieur

Writer-director Jacques Tati introduced his alter-ego in 1953's *Monsieur Hulot's Holiday*, a highly visual comedy about a middle-aged bachelor with a knack for unintentionally causing disruptions at a summer resort. The film featured minimal dialogue, inviting critics to compare Hulot to Chaplin's Tramp. Tati's later films expanded on his theme of man trapped in a technology-heavy, time-conscious world. A combination of financial problems and Tati's pursuit of perfection has severely limited his output. In addition to the four Hulot movies, he has produced only one other feature-length film, 1949's *Jour de Fête*. Tati did a cameo as Mr. Hulot in François Truffaut's *Bed and Board* (1970).

Monsieur Hulot's Holiday (1953); *Mon Oncle* (1958); *Playtime* (1967); *Traffic* (aka *Trafic*) (1971)

Humanimals

Not quite human, not quite animal, and not just a werewolf—that's an apt description of a humanimal. The phrase was coined in the 1951 comedy-fantasy *You Never Can Tell* to describe animals reincarnated as humans (Dick Powell played ex-dog Rex Shepard). More loosely defined, "humanimal" includes all creatures that are animal-turned-human, human-turned-animal, or a combination of species (see **Werewolves** entry for lycanthropes and were-cats). In *Island of Lost Souls* (1933), the first adaptation of H.G. Wells' *Island of Dr. Moreau*, Charles Laughton played a mad scientist who medically transformed animals into men. It was obviously not a pleasant process, as the animal-men referred to the operating room as the House of Pain. Another mad scientist (John Carradine) turned a female ape into a beautiful woman in 1943's *Captive Wild Woman* (see **Dupree, Paula**), while George Zucco tried a monkey-to-man experiment in 1942's *Dr. Renault's Secret*. Malcolm McDowell accidentally discovered a pig-man in an experimental hospital in the 1973 satire *O Lucky Man!* Similar medical experiments yielded disappointing results in bottom-of-the-barrel horror pictures like *Terror Is a Man* and *Twilight People*. Not all humanimals were produced by science or reincarnation. Puppet boy *Pinocchio* fell in with a crowd of naughty kids on Pleasure Island and they were all transformed into donkeys in Disney's version of the famous fairy tale. John Sayles' charming *The Secret of Roan Inish* (1994) recounts the legend of "selkies," seals who can transform into humans. Two children had the power to transform themselves into bears at night in the offbeat fable *The Two Little Bears* (1961). See also **Dupree, Paula; Frogtown Series; The Shaggy Dog Series; Werewolves**.

A Blind Bargain (1922); *Island of Lost Souls* (1933); *Pinocchio* (1940); *Dr. Renault's Secret* (1942); *The Mad Monster* (1942); *Captive Wild Woman* (1943); *You Never Can Tell* (1951); *Terror Is a Man* (aka *Blood Creature*) (1959); *The Two Little Bears* (1961); *Atlantis, the Lost Continent* (1961); *The Incredible Mr. Limpet* (1964); *The Reptile* (1966); *The Vulture* (1967); *Twilight People* (1972); *O Lucky Man!* (1973); *The Island of Dr. Moreau* (1977); *Oh, Heavenly Dog!* (1980); *Ladyhawke* (1985); *Kiss of the Beast* (aka *Meridian*) (1989); *Nightbreed* (1990); *The Secret of Roan Inish* (1994); *Fluke* (1995); *Whiskers* (1996 TVM); *The Island of Dr. Moreau* (1996)

Hunchbacks

The most famous, of course, is that charismatic bellringer Quasimodo, created by Victor Hugo in his classic *The Hunchback of Notre Dame* and portrayed on the screen by a bevy of fine actors, most notably: Lon Chaney, Sr. (1923), Charles Laughton (1939), Anthony Quinn (1957), Anthony Hopkins (1981), and Mandy Patinkin (1997). Quasimodo's only rival for film popularity has been Ygor, the hunchbacked once-hanged shepherd immortalized by Bela Lugosi in *Son of Frankenstein* (1939) and *The Ghost of Frankenstein* (1942) and parodied by Marty Feldman in *Young Frankenstein* (1974). John Mills won a Best Supporting Actor Oscar as the hunchbacked village idiot in David Lean's epic romance *Ryan's Daughter* (1970). Gérard Depardieu gave one of his finest performance as the struggling hunchbacked farmer in *Jean de Florette* (1986).

The Hunchback of Notre Dame (1923); *Son of Frankenstein* (1939); *The Hunchback of Notre Dame* (1939); *The Ghost of Frankenstein* (1942); *House of Frankenstein* (aka *Chamber of Horrors*) (1944); *House of Dracula* (1945); *The Secret Garden* (1949); *Phantom from Space* (1953); *Richard III* (1956); *The Hunchback of Notre Dame* (1957); *Revenge of Frankenstein* (1958); *The Hunchback of Rome* (aka *Il Gobbo*) (1960); *Mad Monster Party?* (1967); *Candy* (1968); *Ryan's Daughter* (1970); *The Hunchback of the Morgue*

(1972); *Terror in the Wax Museum* (1973); *Captain Kronos: Vampire Hunter* (aka *Kronos*) (1974); *Young Frankenstein* (1974); *Mr. Quilp* (aka *The Old Curiosity Shop*) (1975); *The Rocky Horror Picture Show* (1975); *The Hunchback of Notre Dame* (1981 TVM); *Alsino and the Condor* (1982); *Jean de Florette* (1986); *The Name of the Rose* (1986); *The Secret Garden* (1987 TVM); *Big Man on Campus* (1990); *The Ballad of the Sad Café* (1991); *The Secret Garden* (1993); *The Hunchback of Notre Dame* (1996); *The Hunchback* (1997 TVM)

Hunting Parties

A favorite pastime of the movies' idle rich, hunting parties served as social allegories in *The Shooting Party* (1984) and Jean Renoir's *The Rules of the Game* (1939). In Renoir's masterpiece, a rabbit hunt involving wealthy guests at a French chateau forms the center of the movie's structure. The hunters wait patiently, rifles in hand, for servants to beat the brush and scare rabbits from their hiding place. Then, they take part in a cruel, vivid massacre of dozens of rabbits. The death of these innocent animals — by a society they cannot comprehend — is mirrored later in the film by the accidental murder of a naive romantic. The death of a young boy during a fox hunt in 1988's *A Handful of Dust* signals the disintegration of his affluent parents' marriage. Bored European aristocrats Brigitte Bardot and Stephen Boyd visited the American West to mount a hunting expedition in Louis L'Amour's *Shalako* (1969). They found little game, but a lot of restless Apaches and an unlikely cowboy hero in Sean Connery. Errol Flynn saved an Indian chieftain during a tiger hunt in *The Charge of the Light Brigade* (1936) and lived to regret it. John Huston's gimmicky mystery *The List of Adrian Messenger* (1963) opened and closed with a fox hunt. The film's murderer, a master of disguises, plots a young boy's death, but meets his own demise in the heat of the climactic hunt. Hunting parties of a different kind, led by men obsessed, comprised the plots to *Moby Dick* (1930, 1956), *The White Buffalo* (1977, and *The Perfect Storm* (2000).

Moby Dick (1930); *The Charge of the Light Brigade* (1936); *The Rules of the Game* (1939); *Moby Dick* (1956); *The List of Adrian Messenger* (1963); *The Hunt* (1966); *Shalako* (1969); *The White Buffalo* (1977); *Moonraker* (1979); *The Shooting Party* (1984); *A Handful of Dust* (1988); *Shoot to Kill* (1988); *The Perfect Storm* (2000)

Hurricanes and Tornadoes

Tornadoes have reigned over hurricanes as the cinema's wind storm of choice and it's easy to see why. The tornado's dark, ominous funnel provides a strong visual presence and its sudden fury adds an explosive dramatic element. The most famous tornado — the twister in the 1939 *Wizard of Oz* — made a rather brief appearance. But it made a lasting impression (e.g., the sight of Miss Gulch morphing into the Wicked Witch inside the funnel) and provided Dorothy with transportation to Oz. However, in terms of big budget special effects, *Twister* (1996) rates as the tornado's finest hour. Although its melodramatic story of two feuding tornado chasers lacked interest, most moviegoers cherished its visual spectacles — such as a cow flying in the wind currents. In the wake of *Twister*, the 1996 TV movies *Tornado!* and *Night of the Twister* tried to stage similar visual treats, but lacked the necessary budgets. Though Pecos Bill was not an official tornado chaser, he proved adept at lassoing them in *Tall Tale* (1995). One of the weapons sported by the superheroes in *Mystery Men* (1999) was a "tornado in a can." Aim the can, pop the top, and watch your adversary get swept up in a funnel cloud! While tornadoes have appeared in a variety of films, hurricanes have been limited mostly to island romances and seafaring adventures. Granted, it's not an intentional slight by filmmakers since hurricanes *are* restricted to oceanic settings. The Charles Nordhoff–James Norman Hall novel *Hurricane* reached the silver screen in 1937 and 1979, with film buffs favoring the early version with Dorothy Lamour and Jon Hall as South Pacific lovers. The destructive power of hurricanes, even on land, was displayed in the TV movies *The Death of Ocean View Park* (1979) and *Condominium* (1980). The former film blended footage from an actual hurricane that hit an amusement park in Norfolk, Virginia. The fact-based TV movie *Triumph Over Disaster: The Hurricane Andrew Story* (1993) chronicled the devastating storm that caused over two dozen deaths and $25 billion worth of damage along the southern coast of the U.S. See also **Disaster Movies; Lightning.**

Compromise (1925); *Steamboat Bill, Jr.* (1928); *Last of the Pagans* (1936); *The Hurricane* (1937); *The Wizard of Oz* (1939); *Tornado* (1943); *Slattery's Hurricane* (1949); *Hurricane Island* (1959); *The Killer Shrews* (1959); *The Passionate Summer* (1959); *S.O.S. Pacific* (1960); *Hurricane* (aka *Hurricane Hunters*) (1974 TVM); *The Death of Ocean View Park* (1979 TVM); *Hurricane* (aka *Forbidden Paradise*) (1979); *Condominium* (1980 TVM); *Something Wicked This Way Comes* (1983); *Tai-Pan* (1986); *Twister* (1988); *Shipwrecked* (1990); *Tall Tale* (1995); *Night of the Twisters* (1996 TVM); *Tornado!* (1996 TVM); *Twister* (1996); *Commandments* (1997); *Gone Fishin'* (1997); *Gummo* (1997) (set in town that never recovered from tornado); *The Meeting Place* (1998); *Storm Chasers: Revenge of the Twister* (1998 TVM); *The Gingerbread Man* (1998); *Storm* (1999 TVM); *Mystery Men* (1999); *Where the Heart Is* (2000); *The Perfect Storm* (2000)

Hypnotists

The hypnotist's unnerving stare, his piercing eyes aglow with flaming intensity, has been a trademark shot in almost all movies involving hypnosis. In 1909, film pioneer D.W. Griffith made *The Criminal Hypnotist*, one of the first movies in which hypnosis played a key role. A decade later, German director Robert Wiene made the highly expressionistic *The Cabinet of Dr. Caligari*, a macabre tale about a hypnotist who sends a somnambulist to commit murders. Two years later, fellow countryman Fritz Lang introduced *Dr. Mabuse* (q.v.), a criminal mastermind and hypnotist extraordinaire. The Mabuse character appeared in eight additional films, making him the screen's most enduring hypnotist. His fame has been equalled only by George du Maurier's *Svengali*, a mad Russian hypnotist whose mind-controlling eyes turned the beautiful, but untalented, Trilby into a singing sensation. Du Maurier's story has been filmed at least six times, with the 1931 version starring John Barrymore generally considered the finest. Jose Ferrer used hypnosis to manipulate Gene Tierney and implicate her in murder in Otto Preminger's *Whirlpool* (1949). A mesmerist employed it to control the Frankenstein Monster in *The Evil of Frankenstein* (1964). In 1953's *Invasion U.S.A.*, a man induced mass hypnosis on the patrons of a neighborhood bar so they could experience the effects of a Communist invasion. Count Dracula (q.v.) used a hypnotic look to great advantage in many of his films, although much of the effect could be attributed to his vampire charms. Hypnotism has played a major role in several reincarnation (q.v.) films, most notably *The Search for Bridey*

Murphy (1956), *Spell of the Hypnotist* (1956) and the Barbra Streisand musical *On a Clear Day You Can See Forever* (1970). See also **Brainwashing; Mabuse, Dr.**

The Criminal Hypnotist (1909); *The Cabinet of Dr. Caligari* (1919); *Dr. Mabuse, the Gambler* (aka *The Great Gambler-Image of a Generation*) (1921); *Dr. Mabuse, King of Crime* (aka *Inferno-People of a Generation*) (1922); *Running Wild* (1927); *Svengali* (1931); *Hypnotized* (1933); *The Garden Murder Case* (1936); *Night Monster* (aka *House of Mystery*) (1942); *Calling Dr. Death* (1943); *Shadows in the Night* (1944); *The Frozen Ghost* (1945); *The Woman in Green* (1945); *Bewitched* (1945); *The Seventh Veil* (1945); *The Mask of Dijon* (1946); *Mr. Hex* (1946); *Fear in the Night* (1947); *Road to Rio* (1947); *Whirlpool* (1949); *Invasion U.S.A.* (1953); *Svengali* (1954); *The Hypnotist* (1956); *Nightmare* (1956); *The Search for Bridey Murphy* (1956); *Spell of the Hypnotist* (aka *Fright*) (1956); *The She Creature* (1957); *Hold That Hypnotist* (1957); *I Was a Teenage Werewolf* (1957); *Blood of Dracula* (1957); *Curse of the Demon* (aka *Night of the Demon*) (1958); *The Hypnotic Eye* (1960); *Hypnosis* (aka *Dummy of Death*) (1963); *The Evil of Frankenstein* (1964); *The Misadventures of Merlin Jones* (1964); *Creature of Destruction* (1968); *On a Clear Day You Can See Forever* (1970); *The Hot Rock* (aka *How to Steal a Diamond in Four Uneasy Lessons*) (1972); *Let's Do It Again* (1975); *Svengali* (1983 TVM); *The Element of Crime* (1984); *Two Evil Eyes* (aka *Due Occhi Diabolic*) (1990); *The Shadow* (1994); *Jack Be Nimble* (1994); *Murder or Memory: A Moment of Truth Movie* (1994 TVM); *Stir of Echoes* (1999)

I Love a Mystery Series

Columbia Pictures produced this belated entry into the detective series sweepstakes of the 1940s. Based on Carleton E. Morse's hit radio show, the *I Love a Mystery* trilogy starred Jim Bannon as investigator Jack Packard and Barton Yarborough as his crony Doc Long. Their 1946 debut film was also their best, a strange little mystery about a secret Oriental society intent on securing a businessman's head because he resembles their dead founder. The story had been previously produced on the radio program as "The Head of Jonathan Monk." Despite offbeat plotlines, the film series failed to catch on and ended in 1945. Universal Pictures tried to revive the series with the made-for-TV film *I Love a Mystery*, which featured Les Crane as Packard and David Hartman as Long. A campy spoof of the radio series, it sat on the studio's shelf for six years before being televised in 1973.

I Love a Mystery (1945); *The Devil's Mask* (1946); *The Unknown* (1946); *I Love a Mystery* (1973 TVM)

Ice Cream

Ice cream has figured prominently in a handful of films ranging from comedy to action to horror. In Bill Forsyth's engaging Scottish comedy *Comfort and Joy* (1984), a lonely disc jockey becomes a negotiator between two rival ice cream companies, Mr. Bunny and Mr. McCool. The experience changes his life, for as he explains to a friend: "My life was the wrong flavor. I was raspberry when I should have been vanilla." Ice cream fell from the sky courtesy of a magical lamp in the animated *Duck Tales: The Movie-Treasure of the Lost Lamp* (1990). The Eddie Cantor musical comedy *Kid Millions* (1934) included a scene in an ice cream factory. In *Cheech and Chong's Nice Dreams* (1981), the comics sold marijuana from their ice cream truck. Jack Carson played the title character in *The Good Humor Man*, a 1950 film that mixed comedy (a lot) and murder (a little). Killing was more commonplace in *Chill Factor*, a 1999 action film in which Skeet Ulrich hijacked Cuba Gooding, Jr.'s, ice cream truck. His reason was a good one: He needed to transport a deadly chemical compound that detonated once it reached 50 degrees Fahrenheit. A supposedly dead killer dwarf was stored in an ice cream truck in the cult horror film *Phantasm* (1979). Homicidal sellers of ice cream gave the business a bad name in *Ice Cream Man* (1995) and *Mr. Ice Cream Man* (1996). Soda jerks who dish out ice cream treats have been played by many performers such as James Stewart (*It's a Wonderful Life*), Jackie Gleason (*Larceny, Inc.*), and Jeff Daniels (*Pleasantville*). In Larry Cohen's horror satire *The Stuff* (1985), ice cream company executives hired an industrial spy to uncover the secret ingredients of an addictive (literally) new dessert. In Ray Bradbury's 1998 fantasy *The Wonderful Ice Cream Suit*, the title garment's name was derived from its vanilla color.

Kid Millions (1934); *It's a Wonderful Life* (1948); *The Good Humor Man* (1950); *Phantasm* (1979); *Cheech and Chong's Nice Dreams* (1981); *Comfort and Joy* (1984); *Duck Tales: The Movie-Treasure of the Lost Lamp* (1990); *Ice Cream Man* (1995); *Mr. Ice Cream Man* (1996); *Pleasantville* (1998); *Chill Factor* (1999); *Ghost Dog: The Way of the Samurai* (2000)

Ice Skating

Ice skating movies fall into two categories: those starring Sonja Henie and all others. Henie won the world figure skating championship as a 15-year-old Norweigan. At 26, after three successful Olympics, she began her 20th Century–Fox film career opposite Don Ameche and the Ritz Brothers in 1936's *One in a Million*. Henie enjoyed a decade of popularity, skating in films such as *Thin Ice* (1938), *Second Fiddle* (1939), *Sun Valley Serenade* (1941), and *Wintertime* (1943). Other ice skating champions have ventured into films as well, although none can compare to Henie. Spunky Lynn-Holly Johnson gave a credible performance as a promising ice skater who goes blind in the sappy, but effective, *Ice Castles* (1979). She skated briefly in the James Bond adventure *For Your Eyes Only* (1981), but abandoned her blades to deal with unseen forces in *The Watcher in the Woods* (1980). British ice skating star Belita (real name Gladys Jepson Turner) starred in a handful of Hollywood films, such as *Ice Capades* (1941), *Silver Skates* (1943), and *Suspense* (1946). Champion skater Carol Heiss's career fared less well, her lone screen appearance being opposite Moe, Larry, and Joe in 1961's *Snow White and the Three Stooges*. Katarina Witt had a small role as (what else?) an ice skater in *Ronin* (1998). Olympian Tai Babilonia never made a movie, but her life and career with partner Randy Garner formed the basis for the 1990 TV movie *On Thin Ice: The Tai Babilonia Story*. Made-for-TV films have also been made about Olympic figure skating champion Oksana Baiul (*A Promise Kept: The Oksana Baiul Story*), speed skater Dan Jansen (*A Brother's Promise: The Dan Jansen Story*), and Nancy Kerrigan and Tonya Harding (*Tonya and Nancy: The Inside Story*). Fictitious skaters have overcome drastic odds—and often found romance—in features such as *Champions: A Love Story* (1979 TVM), *Skate!* (1987), *Blades of Courage* (1988), and *The Cutting Edge* (1992). Angel Cary Grant taught Loretta Young and cabbie Paul Gleason to ice skate in the 1947 fantasy *The Bishop's Wife*. Finally, Abbott and Costello set all-time low marks for figure skating in 1943's *Hit the Ice*. See also **Roller Skating**.

One in a Million (1936); *Thin Ice* (1938); *My Lucky Star* (1938); *Second Fiddle* (1939); *Ice Follies* (aka *Ice Follies of 1939*) (1939); *Sun Valley Serenade* (1941); *Ice Capades* (1941); *The People vs. Dr. Kildare* (aka *My Life Is Yours*) (1941); *Ice Capades Revue* (1942); *Iceland* (1942); *Wintertime* (1943); *Silver Skates* (1943); *Hit the Ice* (1943); *Lake Placid Serenade* (1944); *It's a Pleasure* (1945); *Suspense* (1946); *The Bishop's Wife* (1947); *Snow White and the Three Stooges* (1961); *Ice Castles* (1979); *Champions: A Love Story* (1979 TVM); *For Your Eyes Only* (1981); *Skate!* (1987); *Blades of Courage* (1988); *On Thin Ice: The Tai Babilonia Story* (1990 TVM); *The Cutting Edge* (1992); *Tonya and Nancy: The Inside Story* (1994 TVM); *A Promise Kept: The Oksana Baiul Story* (1994 TVM); *A Brother's Promise: The Dan Jansen Story* (1996 TVM); *Ronin* (1998)

If... Series

If... (1968), *O Lucky Man!* (1973), and *Britannia Hospital* (1982) comprise director Lindsay Anderson's loosely-connected, savagely satirical trilogy about rebellions against society. In *If...*, the most critically acclaimed of the trilogy, three boys revolt against their highly-structured, often cruel, British public school. Yet, unlike Jean Vigo's 1933 classic *Zero for Conduct*, this rebellion goes to the extreme, complete with Malcolm McDowell and his fellow revolters gunning down authority figures in attendance at Speech Day. The film's surrealistic tones — is it real or fantasy? — is heightened by Anderson's alternating use of color and black & white (an economical necessity according to him). *O Lucky Man!* narrowed the focus to one individual, an ambitious young coffee salesman (McDowell again), trying to fit into society — to be wealthy, successful, and powerful. But he is manipulated by his own ambition and by those he aspires to be like. His wealthy employer frames him for a crime, he goes to prison, gets re-educated and released, tries to "help" others as he was, gets mugged by ungrateful tramps, and finally does something because he *wants* to do it. This, too, becomes an act of rebellion against a society of manipulators. The third film, *Britannia Hospital*, opted for a broader view and a more obvious target in one of society's standard institutions. McDowell and other alumni from the first two films appeared in brief roles, but *Britannia Hospital*'s heavily-episodic structure made it very hit-or-miss. It has failed to achieve the faithful followings of *If...* and *O Lucky Man!*

If... (1968); *O Lucky Man!* (1973); *Britannia Hospital* (1982)

Ilsa, She Wolf of the SS

Dyanne Thorpe starred in this trash trilogy which acquired a notorious reputation for its S&M content in the mid–1970s. In *Ilsa, She Wolf of the SS*, the title character is a Nazi medical camp warden who tortures and kills female prisoners with glee. She forces the male prisoners to make love to her, then kills them brutally when none can satisfy her sexual desires. The basic premise bears a passing resemblance to 1974's *The Night Porter*, in which Dirk Bogarde and Charlotte Rampling portrayed, respectively, a former Nazi torturer and his victim, who resume their S&M relationship years later. That film may have had some social value. *Ilsa, She Wolf of the SS* is a reprehensible picture, which would have faded into obscurity if critics had not rebuked it so openly. Instead, the producers promptly mounted two dreadful sequels with Thorpe returning as Ilsa. The Thorpe film *Wanda, the Wicked Warden* (1977) was later retitled as both *Ilsa, the Wicked*

Warden and *Ilsa—Absolute Power*. Despite obvious similarities, it's not a part of the *Ilsa* series.

Ilsa, She Wolf of the SS (1974); *Ilsa, Harem Keeper of the Oil Sheiks* (1976); *Ilsa, Tigress of Siberia* (1976)

In Search of... Series

Budget-minded film company Sunn Classics pioneered the pseudo-documentary with this brief 1970s series. Its first release was its best, a faithful adaptation of Erich Von Daniken's bestseller *Chariots of the Gods?* (1974). Actually, the film had been made in Germany in 1969 and excerpts had been aired on American TV as the one-hour TV special *In Search of Ancient Astronauts*. Sunn picked the film up in 1974 and marketed it using a system called "four walling." This consisted of saturating the market with TV previews, renting theaters for limited runs (one or two weeks), and then keeping all box-office receipts. The system worked amazingly well, with Sunn receiving large returns on minimal investments. Subsequently, it produced "documentaries" about Noah's Ark, the Shroud of Turin, mysterious "monsters" like the Yeti and Nessie, and life and death. "Real" footage was frequently intercut with fictional reenactments. And one could always count on the narrator to add some sensationalism ("Would you like to see what it's like to enter that region between life and death?"). *In Search of Dracula* (1971) was produced by another company, though it was very much in the Sunn-style. Leonard Nimoy hosted a syndicated television program along the same lines. Dubbed *In Search of...*, it consisted of 144 episodes broadcast during 1976–82.

Chariots of the Gods? (1974); *In Search of Noah's Ark* (1976); *The Mysterious Monsters* (1976); *Beyond and Back* (1978); *In Search of Historic Jesus* (1979)

In the Line of Duty Series

NBC initiated this series of fact-based films about law enforcement officers after scoring big ratings with 1988's *In the Line of Duty: The FBI Murders*. Former TV nice guys Michael Gross (*Family Ties*) and David Soul (*Starsky and Hutch*) played against type as a pair of vicious murderers tracked down by special agent David Sheehan. Their ultimate confrontation in Miami in 1986 resulted in the bloodiest shootout in FBI history (and one of the most violent in TV movie annals). The "sequels," beginning with 1989's *In the Line of Duty: Howard Beach, Making a Case for Murder* bore no resemblance to the original or each other in terms of plot or characters. However, they all maintained the same gritty focus and behind-the-scenes attention to detail. In *A Cop for the Killing*, Stephen Weber becomes an unstable cop after his partner is murdered. Michael Gross, an FBI agent this time, goes after white supremacist/murderer Gordon Rahl (Rod Steiger) in 1991's *Manhunt in the Dakotas*. Dennis Franz and Ed Begley, Jr., headlined the next installment, *Siege at Marion* (1992), which dealt with an FBI confrontation with a group of armed religious fanatics. *In the Line of Duty: Street War* (1992) shifted the focus back to the cop on the beat. Mario Van Peebles (*New Jack City*) starred as a New York City Housing Authority policeman who seeks revenge when his partner is killed while patrolling their drug-ridden childhood neighborhood. It was originally scheduled to be broadcast in May 1992, but was delayed until the following fall

due to the Los Angeles riots. *In the Line of Duty: Ambush at Waco* (1993) covered ground similar to *Siege at Marion*, only this time the subject was religious cult leader David Koresh. NBC rushed the film into production—it appeared within months of the bloody shootout (but it did not cover the subsequent compound explosion and death of Koresh). Although variable in quality, the *In the Line of Duty* films provided a sharp realistic contrast to escapist TV detective shows of the same period, such as *Murder, She Wrote* and *Matlock*. However, one suspects that NBC decided an occasional jolt of realism was enough—thus, its decision to go with a film series as opposed to a weekly TV series. See also **FBI**.

In the Line of Duty: The FBI Murders (1988 TVM); *In the Line of Duty: Howard Beach, Making a Case for Murder* (1989 TVM); *In the Line of Duty: A Cop for the Killing* (1990 TVM); *In the Line of Duty: Manhunt in the Dakotas* (1991 TVM); *In the Line of Duty: Siege at Marion* (1992 TVM); *In the Line of Duty: Street War* (1992 TVM); *In the Line of Duty: Ambush at Waco* (1993 TVM); *In the Line of Duty: Price of Vengeance* (1994 TVM); *In the Line of Duty: Hunt for Justice* (1995 TVM); *In the Line of Duty: Kidnapped* (1995 TVM); *In the Line of Duty: Smoke Jumpers* (1996 TVM); *In the Line of Duty: Blaze of Glory* (1997 TVM)

The Incident Series

Walter Matthau made his TV movie debut as easygoing lawyer Harmon Cobb in 1990's Emmy-winning *The Incident*. Set in Colorado during World War II, the story focused on Cobb's attempts to defend a German prisoner of war accused of murder. His courtroom adversary, Judge Stoddard Bell (Harry Morgan), became his law partner when Cobb and his widowed daughter-in-law moved to Maryland in 1992's *Against Her Will: An Incident in Baltimore*. This unexceptional sequel found Cobb and Stoddard involved in a 1947 court case to release an immigrant girl wrongly imprisoned in a mental institution. It lacked the personal drama that distinguished its predecessor. That oversight was corrected in the third installment, 1994's *Incident in a Small Town*. It picked up six years later, with Cobb and Bell trekking to Plainfield, Illinois, where Bell's estranged daughter (Stephanie Zimbalist) eventually wound up accused of murdering her illegitimate 13-year-old son's father. The film benefited from a flavorful 1950s atmosphere and affecting performances (including Nick Stahl who turned in a memorable performance as the teenaged protagonist in 1993's *The Man Without a Face*). However, the identity of the true murderer was never in doubt. Viewers did not seem to care, though, for *Incident in a Small Town* garnered strong ratings. The series might have continued, except that Matthau and Morgan appeared content to leave it as a trilogy.

The Incident (1990 TVM); *Against Her Will: An Incident in Baltimore* (1992 TVM); *Incident in a Small Town* (1994 TVM)

The Incredible Hulk

Comic book legend Stan Lee created the Incredible Hulk, an interesting Jekyll and Hyde (q.v.) variant, in 1962. Lee's protagonist was Dr. Bruce Banner, a scientist accidentally altered by a massive dosage of radiation. The outcome was that, when overcome with anger, the normally reserved Banner transformed into a greenish, super-strong Hulk with the dimensions of a Mr. Universe. Eventually, the Hulk would change back to Banner, who would remember nothing about his alter ego's activities. CBS brought the comic book character to TV in 1977 first in a couple of pilot movies and then as a *Fugitive*-styled series with a clever casting twist. Mild mannered Bill Bixby played Banner, with bodybuilder Lou Ferrigno replacing him as the Hulk. The show enjoyed a modest four-year run on the basis of its juvenile audience. There have been three revival movies, the first one pairing the Hulk with Thor, another comic book superhero. See also **Comic Book Characters; Television Series Reunion Films**.

The Incredible Hulk (1977 TVM); *The Return of the Incredible Hulk* (aka *The Return of the Hulk*) (1977 TVM); *The Incredible Hulk Returns* (1988 TVM); *The Trial of the Incredible Hulk* (1989 TVM); *The Death of the Incredible Hulk* (1990 TVM)

Inner Sanctum Series

Lon Chaney, Jr., starred in this generally undistinguished low-budget mystery film series, which occasionally hinted at horror. The highlights were 1944's *Weird Woman*, the first film version of Fritz Leiber's *Conjure Wife* (later remade as the superior *Burn, Witch, Burn*) and an intriguing little puzzler titled *Calling Dr. Death*. In the latter film, Chaney plays a neurologist who uses hypnotism to determine if he unconsciously murdered his unfaithful wife. Inspired by a hit radio series, each movie was preceded by a warped head in a crystal ball who welcomed viewers to the Inner Sanctum (a mild version of *The Twilight Zone*). *Strange Confession* (1945) is frequently confused with Julien Duvivier's 1944 film of the same name, which is known as *The Impostor*. Oddly enough, the 1948 feature *Inner Sanctum* was not part of this series. In 1992, Victoria Principal starred in *Seduction: Three Tales from the Inner Sanctum*, a 1992 TV movie anthology based on the radio series.

Calling Dr. Death (1943); *Dead Man's Eyes* (1944); *Weird Woman* (1944); *The Frozen Ghost* (1945); *Pillow of Death* (1945); *Strange Confession* (1945); *Seduction: Three Tales from the Inner Sanctum* (1992 TVM)

Insects

Be they little specks or large enough to crush a man, insects have long been a big screen pest. A plague of locusts stripped the wheat fields in the climax to *The Good Earth* (an effect achieved by superimposing coffee grounds over oil-covered wheat). An army of soldier ants destroyed a South American plantation in 1954's *The Naked Jungle*, although the crisis served to mend Charlton Heston and Eleanor Parker's shaky marriage. That same year introduced a colony of 12-foot-high ants in *Them!*, the finest giant insect picture ever made. It was also the first to imply that nature was rebelling against man's misuse of radiation. Imitations quickly followed, featuring giant grasshoppers (*The Beginning of the End*) and a preying mantis (*The Deadly Mantis*). A single, regular-sized fly proved the culprit in 1958's *The Fly* (q.v.) when it interrupted an experiment and merged atomic particles with an affable scientist. Nine years later, *The Deadly Bees* started an insect film subgenre with its lively shock scenes of swarming bees stinging nice people to death. The number of bee films increased over the next decade, amid real-life reports of killer bees flying up from South America. A popular TV movie, *The Savage Bees*, was followed by *The Bees*, Irwin Allen's big-budget bust *The Swarm*, and *Terror Out of the Sky*. While bees have been portrayed as dangerous killers, filmmakers have taken a more lenient view of ants.

Certainly, the destructive side of ants was displayed in *The Naked Jungle, It Happened at Lakewood Manor,* and *Legion of Fire: Killer Ants.* But there have also been cute computer-animated ants (*A Bug's Life* and *Antz*) and intelligent ants seeking to breed humans to create a new super race in *Phase IV*. In other notable insect-related features: The Devil (Peter Cook) turned Dudley Moore into a fly in one of the episodes of *Bedazzled*; the Academy Award–winning pseudodocumentary *The Hellstrom Chronicle* explored the premise that insects will inherit the Earth one day; a government device designed to kill insects raised dead humans in *Don't Open the Window* and turned them into flesh-eating ghouls; the moon's inhabitants were discovered to be the insect-like Selenites in *First Men in the Moon*; and a nice wholesome family turned out to be roaches in disguise in *Meet The Applegates*. Burgess Meredith provided the voice for a talking horsefly in *Hot to Trot* (1988). The best six-legged singing insect was undoubtedly Jiminy Cricket of *Pinocchio* fame. See also **The Fly Series**.

The Good Earth (1937); *Pinocchio* (1940); *Hoppity Goes to Town* (aka *Mr. Bug Goes to Town*) (1941); *Once Upon a Time* (1944); *Them!* (1954); *The Naked Jungle* (1954); *The Deadly Mantis* (1957); *The Cosmic Monster* (aka *The Strange World of Planet X*) (1957); *Secrets of Life* (1957); *The Beginning of the End* (1957); *The Fly* (1958); *The Wasp Woman* (1960); *Mysterious Island* (1961); *First Men in the Moon* (1964); *The Deadly Bees* (1967); *Bedazzled* (1967); *The Hellstrom Chronicle* (1971); *The Abominable Dr. Phibes* (1971); *Invasion of the Bee Girls* (1973); *Phase IV* (1974); *Don't Open the Window* (aka *Breakfast at the Manchester Morgue*) (1974); *Killer Bees* (1974 TVM); *Locusts* (1974 TVM); *Bug* (1975); *The Savage Bees* (1976 TVM); *Empire of the Ants* (1977); *Damnation Alley* (1977); *Sinbad and the Eye of the Tiger* (1977); *It Happened at Lakewood Manor* (aka *Panic at Lakewood Manor; Ants*) (1977 TVM); *The Exorcist II: The Heretic* (1977); *Terror Out of the Sky* (1978 TVM); *The Bees* (1978); *The Swarm* (1978); *The Beast Within* (1982); *Creepshow* (1982); *Creepers* (1985); *The Nest* (1988); *Hot to Trot* (1988); *Honey, I Shrunk the Kids* (1989); *Meet The Applegates* (aka *The Applegates*) (1990); *Whispers* (1990); *Popcorn* (1991) (the movie-within-a-movie "Mosquito"); *Naked Lunch* (1991); *Matinee* (1993) (the movie-within-a-movie "Mant!"); *Skeeter* (1994); *Ticks* (1994); *Jumanji* (1995); *Jonny Quest vs. the Cyber Insects* (1995 TVM); *Angels and Insects* (1996); *James and the Giant Peach* (1996); *Microcosmos* (1996); *Joe's Apartment* (1996); *Ulee's Gold* (1997); *Mimic* (1997); *Starship Troopers* (1997); *Legion of Fire: Killer Ants* (1998 TVM); *Antz* (1998); *A Bug's Life* (1998); *The Mummy* (1999); *The 4th Floor* (2000); *They Nest* (2000 TVM)

Insurance Investigators

The cinema has shown little respect for insurance investigators, typically portraying them as private eyes without steady work, or as crafty con artists. Certainly, the investigators in *Mystery in Mexico, Banacek,* and *Coopersmith* could have passed for private eyes if we hadn't been told they were insurance men. At least, they were on the right side of the law. The insurance investigators in *Roadblock* (1951) and *She Played with Fire* (1957) — as well as insurance agent Fred MacMurray in *Double Indemnity* (1944) — turned crooked due to the influences of money-hungry women. George Kennedy played a family-oriented investigator scheming to defraud the insurance company to provide money for his loved ones in *Zigzag*. Laurence Harvey tried to swindle an insurance company, too, by faking his death in 1963's *The Running Man*, but he did not fool insurance man Alan Bates. The TV movie *Longstreet* (1970) served as a pilot for a TV show, as did the aforementioned *Coopersmith* (1992) and *Banacek* (1972). Two of the three produced regular TV series, with George Peppard as a freelance insurance investigator in *Banacek* (1972–74) and James Franciscus as a blind investigator in *Longstreet* (1971–72).

The Amazing Mr. Forrest (aka *The Gang's All Here*) (1939); *Double Indemnity* (1944); *Mystery in Mexico* (1948); *Pitfall* (1948); *Roadblock* (1951); *Duel in the Jungle* (1954); *Timetable* (1956); *She Played with Fire* (aka *Fortune Is a Woman*) (1957); *Backfire* (1961); *The Running Man* (1963); *The Thomas Crown Affair* (1968); *Zigzag* (1970); *Longstreet* (1970 TVM); *The Movie Murderer* (1970 TVM); *The Firechasers* (1970); *Banacek* (aka *Detour to Nowhere*) (1972 TVM); *Lady Ice* (1973); *Sunburn* (1979); *The Pursuit of D.B. Cooper* (1981); *Coopersmith* (1992 TVM); *Frauds* (1993); *Bitter Vengeance* (1994 TVM); *In the Mouth of Madness* (1995); *Fatal Pursuit* (1998); *Entrapment* (1999); *The Thomas Crown Affair* (1999)

Invasions/Takeovers of the U.S.

The cinema has rarely dealt with the end of U.S. democracy, viewing it as a sobering premise with limited commercial appeal. Arch Oboler's *Strange Holiday* was about a businessman (Claude Rains) who returns from an isolated vacation spot to discover that American Nazis have gained control of the country. The film was originally produced in 1940 for General Motors employees. GM shelved it, however, and later sold it to MGM. The film sat in MGM's vaults until Rains and Oboler bought it back and released it in 1945 through a small independent company. After *Strange Holiday*'s fate, it's easy to see why the enemy invasion in 1953's *Invasion U.S.A.* was framed by a plot device explaining its events as being induced by mass hypnosis. Still, the film's opening scene is undeniably powerful, with a television broadcaster reporting that an enemy task force has taken over Alaska and set off atomic bombs in Washington state. Rod Serling's *Seven Days in May* (1964) internalized the takeover attempt, focusing on a military coup to oust the U.S. president. The Russians seized an Alasakan pipeline in retaliation for a U.S. grain embargo in the two-part TV movie *World War III* (1982). John Milius's *Red Dawn* (1984) was a pre-Glasnost adventure about a successful Communist invasion of the U.S. and a subsequent guerilla counterattack staged by patriotic teenagers. The 1987 television miniseries *Amerika* expanded the same premise into a week's worth of TV viewing. The villainous Kryptonians of *Superman II* (1981) humbled the president and thrashed the White House before receiving their comeuppance from the Man of Steel. Along similar lines, the aliens in *Independence Day* (1996) blew up the White House, although the president refused to surrender. On the lighter side, the accidental grounding of a Russian submarine in New England triggered invasion rumors in the 1966 cold-war comedy *The Russians Are Coming! The Russians Are Coming!*

Strange Holiday (1945); *Invasion U.S.A.* (1953); *Seven Days in May* (1964); *The Russians Are Coming! The Russians Are Coming!* (1966); *Superman II* (1981); *World War III* (1982 TVM); *Red Dawn* (1984); *The Enemy Within* (1994 TVM); *Independence Day* (1996)

Invisibility

The father of movie invisibility was John P. Fulton, a special effects photographer who engineered the ingenious optical tricks in Universal's *Invisible Man* series. The original 1933 film set a standard that was difficult even for Fulton to better. How can anyone forget the eerie scene in which Jack Griffin (Claude Rains)

unwraps the bandages covering his face — only to reveal an apparently headless man? Employing double exposure and masked negatives, Fulton displayed his superb invisibility effects in six other Universal films (denoted below with *). Although no one has surpassed Fulton's trickwork, invisibility has shown up in movies with regularity since the late 1950s. The otherwise forgettable *Phantom from Space* (1953) introduced an invisible alien, a premise explored with more imagination in *Fiend Without a Face* (1958) and *Invisible Invaders* (1959). The murderous creature in 1956's *Forbidden Planet* could not be seen with the naked eye either. However, its invisibility status remains in question, since it turned out to be a "mental force" generated by Walter Pidgeon. Invisible criminals proliferated in the 1960s with Edgar G. Ulmer's *The Amazing Transparent Man* (1960) and the German series entry *The Invisible Dr. Mabuse* (1961). But gradually, invisibility became nothing more than a comedy gimmick in films like Disney's *Now You See Him, Now You Don't* (1972), the 3-D *Man Who Wasn't There* (1983), and *The Invisible Kid* (1988). Two TV movies served as pilots for "serious" series. David McCallum played an invisible scientist on the run in 1975's *The Invisible Man* and its subsequent 1975-76 series. NBC cancelled the show after half a season, but still had faith in the concept. So, another pilot film *Gemini Man* was made with Ben Murphy as a government agent who could turn invisible for 15 minutes a day. The show debuted in September 1976 and went off in the air in one month. An earlier TV series of *The Invisible Man* ran on CBS during 1958–60. The actor playing the lead role was never revealed.

*The Invisible Man (1933); **The Invisible Man Returns* (1940); *The Body Disappears* (1941); **The Invisible Woman* (1941); **Invisible Agent* (1942); **The Invisible Man's Revenge* (1944); **Abbott and Costello Meet Frankenstein* (1948) (cameo); **Abbott & Costello Meet the Invisible Man* (1951); *Phantom from Space* (1953); *Forbidden Planet* (1956); *The Invisible Boy* (1957); *The New Invisible Man* (aka *H.G. Wells' Invisible Man*) (1957); *Fiend Without a Face* (1958); *The Invisible Avenger* (aka *Bourbon Street Shadows*) (1958); *Invisible Invaders* (1959); *The Amazing Transparent Man* (1960); *The Invisible Dr. Mabuse* (aka *Die Unsichtbaren Krallen des Dr. Mabuse*; *The Invisible Horror*) (1961); *The Wonderful World of the Brothers Grimm* (1962); *The Invisible Terror* (1963); *Mad Monster Party?* (1967); *Mr. Superinvisible* (aka *The Invincible Invisible Man*) (1967); *Now You See Him, Now You Don't* (1972); *The Invisible Man* (1975 TVM); *Invisible Strangler* (1976); *Gemini Man* (aka *Code Name: Minus One*) (1976 TVM); *The Invisible Woman* (1983 TVM); *The Man Who Wasn't There* (1983); *The Invisible Kid* (1988); *The Neverending Story II: The Next Chapter* (1990); *The Invisible Maniac* (1990); *Alice* (1990); *Memoirs of an Invisible Man* (1992); *Sleepwalkers* (1992); *Mandroid* (1993); *Invisible: The Chronicles of Benjamin Knight* (1994); *The Shadow* (1994); *Invisible Mom* (1995); *Invisible Dad* (1997); *The Avengers* (1998); *Hollow Man* (2000)

Iron Eagle Series

This modest action series has persevered solely on the strength of star Lou Gossett, Jr. The original *Iron Eagle* (1986) introduced Gossett as retired Air Force colonel Charles "Chappy" Sinclair. Chappy teams up with an 18-year-old hotshot pilot for a fighter jet rescue when the kid's dad is wrongly imprisoned in the Middle East. Critics found the film hokey, but it nevertheless appealed to the same moviegoers who made *Top Gun* a box-office smash the same year. In 1988's glasnost-oriented *Iron Eagle II*,

Chappy — now a general — leads U.S. and Soviet pilots on a joint mission to destroy a nuclear weapons base in a fictional Middle East country. The third entry, *Aces: Iron Eagle III* stole its plot from 1990's *Delta Force 2* (apparently, there is no honor among rival B-movie action series). Gossett, bodybuilder Rachel McLish, and *Magnificent Seven* (q.v.) alumnus Horst Buchholz lead a team of pilots flying vintage World War II planes on a mission to destroy a South American cocaine factory. In *Iron Eagle IV* (1995), a retired Chappy opens a flight school for juvenile delinquents. Writer Kevin Elder had a hand in the scripts of the first three *Iron Eagle* films. Interestingly, spy movie veteran Sidney J. Furie (*The Ipcress File*) directed the first, second, and fourth entries, while former James Bond (q.v.) director John Glen helmed the third one. See also **Airplanes**.

Iron Eagle (1986); *Iron Eagle II* (1988); *Aces: Iron Eagle III* (aka *Iron Eagle III*) (1992); *Iron Eagle IV* (1995)

Islands

Tropical islands have long been a favorite movie setting — and with good reason. Where else is one apt to find cannibals, wild jungle animals, pirates, buried treasure, and erupting volcanoes? Monsters, too. King Kong lived on Skull Island, Godzilla visited Monster Island, Japan's favorite giant caterpillar, Mothra, was hatched on Infant Island, and an oversized pink crab harassed hungry humans on *The Mysterious Island*. Human monsters have inhabited islands, too, with Count Zaroff hunting human prey in *The Most Dangerous Game* and Dr. Moreau creating disfigured humans out of innocent animals in *Island of Lost Souls*. On the other hand, islands have also brought unlikely lovers together, as in *The Blue Lagoon*, *Her Jungle Love*, *Return to Paradise*, *Mutiny on the Bounty* and *Six Days, Seven Nights*. Island politics, as established by shipwrecked victims, are usually pretty simple, as portrayed in *Swiss Family Robinson*, *Robinson Crusoe*, and *Tempest*. But they can also get wildly out of hand, as in *Lord of the Flies*, William Golding's political parable about young shipwrecked boys who create their own civilization. Some of the more unique uses of island settings occur in the following: *And Then There Were None* (1945), Agatha Christie's classic whodunit about nine guests trapped in an island mansion with a murderer; *The Challenge* (1970), which pits two men, each representing his country, against one another to fight World War III on an island; and Val Lewton's *Isle of the Dead* (1945), an eerie horror tale about passengers quarantined on a Greek island where a dead woman seems to be alive. One unique aspect to island-set films is that they can end without warning. You never know when a volcano (*Atlantis, the Lost Continent*) or a tropical storm (*Hurricane*) is going to wipe out the whole place. See also **Crusoe, Robinson; Gilligan's Island Series**.

The Most Dangerous Game (1932); *Island of Lost Souls* (1933); *King Kong* (1933); *We're Not Dressing* (1934); *Isle of Fury* (1936); *Hurricane* (1937); *Ebb Tide* (aka *Adventure Island*) (1937); *The Edge of the World* (1937); *Her Jungle Love* (1938); *Road to Singapore* (1940); *Aloma of the South Seas* (1941); *Song of the Islands* (1942); *The Tuttles of Tahiti* (1942); *Beyond the Blue Horizon* (1942); *I Walked with a Zombie* (1943); *Isle of the Dead* (1945); *And Then There Were None* (1945); *A Game of Death* (1946); *Adventure Island* (1947); *On an Island with You* (1948); *The Blue Lagoon* (1949); *Tight Little Island* (aka *Whiskey Galore*) (1949); *Hurricane Smith* (1952); *Return to Paradise* (1953); *The Girls of Pleasure Island* (1953); *The Beachcomber* (1954); *The Admirable Crichton* (aka *Paradise Lagoon*) (1957); *Heaven Knows, Mr. Allison* (1957); *Island in the Sun* (1957); *Attack of the Crab Monsters* (1957); *Enchanted Island* (1958); *South Pacific* (1958); *SOS Pacific* (1959); *Wake Me When It's Over* (1960); *Swiss Family Robinson* (1960); *Atlantis, the Lost Continent* (1961); *The Mysterious Island* (1961); *No Man Is an Island* (aka *Island Escape*) (1962); *The Island* (1962); *Donovan's Reef* (1963); *Lord of the Flies* (1963); *Island of the Blue Dolphins* (1964); *Father Goose* (1964); *Island of Terror* (1966); *Hawaii* (1966); *Island of the Burning Doomed* (aka *Island of the Burning Damned*) (1967); *The Challenge* (1970 TVM); *Godzilla on Monster Island* (aka *Godzilla vs. Gigan*; *Gojira tai Gaigan*) (1971); *Papillon* (1973); *Terminal Island* (1973); *Enter the Dragon* (1973); *The Wicker Man* (1973); *Conrack* (1974); *The Savage Is Loose* (1974); *Islands in the Stream* (1976); *The Island of Dr. Moreau* (1977); *Rescue from Gilligan's Island* (1978 TVM); *The Blue Lagoon* (1980); *The Island* (1980); *Tempest* (1982); *Club Paradise* (1986); *Pascali's Island* (1988); *Trouble in Paradise* (1989 TVM); *Bare Essentials* (1990 TVM); *Shipwrecked* (1990); *And the Sea Will Tell* (1991 TVM); *Return to the Blue Lagoon* (1991); *Danger Island* (1992 TVM); *Jurassic Park* (1993); *Rapa Nui* (1994); *Exile* (1994); *Exit to Eden* (1994); *No Escape* (1994); *The Pagemaster* (1994); *The Secret of Roan Inish* (1995); *Cutthroat Island* (1995); *Escape from L.A.* (1996); *Six Days, Seven Nights* (1998); *The Governess* (1998); *The New Swiss Family Robinson* (1999 TVM)

It's Alive Series

Larry Cohen's 1974 low-budget shocker about a killer baby has attracted a strong cult following, chiefly due to its dual-sided view of modern morals. When his wife gives birth to a murderous mutant baby, John Ryan embarks on a personal crusade to destroy the creature. His wife pleads for the life of their "child," but Ryan feels socially responsible for all the deaths caused by it. However, when he finally confronts his son, he realizes that "it" is an innocent. He watches helplessly as the police brutally murder it. In the 1978 sequel *It Lives Again*, Ryan's character has evolved into an obsessed man fighting against a closed society that's unwilling to accept anything it cannot understand (e.g., the mutant children). Ryan dies, but converted parent Frederic Forrest carries on the crusade. Cohen returned to the theme nine years later in the barely-released *It's Alive III: Island of the Alive*. A reworking of the second film, it once again portrayed the children as helpless victims of a cruel, prejudiced society. See also **Babies**.

It's Alive (1974); *It Lives Again* (aka *It's Alive II*) (1978); *It's Alive III: Island of the Alive* (1987)

Jack the Ripper

This unidentified murderer of at least five prostitutes in London's Whitechapel district in 1888, the Ripper has been a screen fixture since the 1920s. He appeared briefly in a nightmare sequence in *Waxworks* (1924), in which his wax figure comes to life. And in G.W. Pabst's *Pandora's Box*, he popped up at the film's climax to deal retribution to a sinner. However, the first movie to feature Jack in a starring role was Alfred Hitchcock's 1926 adaptation of Marie Belloc Lowndes's chilling novel *The Lodger*. Unfortunately, when matinee idol Ivor Novello was cast in the title role, the ending was altered so that the Lodger turned out not to be the Ripper after all. The film was remade twice, in 1932 with Novello repeating his role (this version aka *The Phantom Fiend*) and in 1944 with Laird Cregar. The latter film was a gripping, atmospheric yarn, faithful to the book, and sporting a fine, frenzied performance from Cregar. (In fact, its success resulted in Cregar playing a psychotic murderer again in 1945's *Hangover Square*.) Over the next decades, the Ripper continued to appear in B-films such as *The Curse of the Wraydons* (1946) and *Room to Let* (1950). However, the Terror of Whitechapel regained the spotlight with the release of 1959's *Jack the Ripper*. Scripted by horror veteran Jimmy Sangster (who also wrote *Room to Let*), this ordinary thriller offered no new variations. Yet, in the hands of super-producer Joseph E. Levine, it was exploited into a sensational worldwide hit that paved the way for more serious "psycho" films like *Peeping Tom* and *Psycho*. Six years later, Jack encountered Sherlock Holmes in the stylish pastiche *A Study in Terror*. It was based on the short story "Fog," which was written by Conan Doyle's son Adrian. A similar fictional confrontation occurred in 1979's *Time After Time*, in which the Ripper (memorably played by David Warner) steals H.G. Wells' time machine and escapes to present-day San Francisco, where his acts of violence fit right in. In 1988's underrated *Jack's Back*, a modern-day killer replicated the Ripper's crimes in honor of Jack's 100th anniversary. The original *Star Trek* TV series featured a memorable episode called "Wolf in the Fold" about the spirit of Jack the Ripper.

The Lodger (1926); *The Lodger* (aka *The Phantom Field*) (1932); *The Lodger* (1944); *The Curse of the Wraydons* (1946); *Room to Let* (1950); *Man in the Attic* (1953); *Jack the Ripper* (1958) (four-part anthology with one episode about the Ripper); *Jack the Ripper* (1959); *A Study in Terror* (1965); *Hands of the Ripper* (1972) (Jack's daughter); *The Ruling Class* (1972); *Knife for the Ladies* (1973) (a Western variation); *Black the Ripper* (1975); *Jack the Ripper* (1976); *Murder by Decree* (1979) (Jack meets Holmes again); *Time After Time* (1979); *Bridge Across Time* (aka *Arizona Ripper*) (1985 TVM); *The Ripper* (1985); *Jack's Back* (1988); *Jack the Ripper* (1988 TVM); *Edge of Sanity* (1989); *Waxwork II: Lost in Time* (1991)

Janek, Frank

William Bayer's mystery best seller *Switch* provided the basis for the 1985 TV movie *Doubletake*, a grisly two-part mystery that introduced Richard Crenna as middle-aged NYC detective Lieutenant Frank Janek. The plot, revolving around two decapitated murder victims whose heads are switched, served as a backdrop for a character study of a likable, divorced, occasionally lute-playing detective. After Janek finally commits to a relationship with younger woman Beverly D'Angelo, she observes: "You're so smart about everything else, Janek, why do you have this blind spot about women?" Indeed, Janek's love life does not fare well in this detective film series. Although he and Diahann Carroll obviously feel a strong attraction toward each other in *Murder in Black and White* (1990), Janek backs away — to avoid professional conflict — after a single kiss. When engrossed in a case, Janek works closely with dependable colleague and friend Aaron Greenberg (series regular Cliff Gorman). Novelist Bayer penned an original screenplay for 1988's *Internal Affairs*, which like *Doubletake*, was broadcast originally as a two-part four-hour movie. The other films filled typical two-hour time slots.

Doubletake (1985 TVM); *Internal Affairs* (1988 TVM); *Murder in Black and White* (1990 TVM); *Murder Times Seven* (1990 TVM); *Terror on Track 9* (aka *Janek: The Grand Central Murders*) (1992 TVM); *A Silent Betrayal* (1994 TVM); *The Forget-Me-Not Murders* (1994 TVM)

Jaws Series

Despite a hefty (at one time) $12 million price tag and production difficulties, 1975's *Jaws* was pegged for blockbuster status from the start. Audiences had been carefully primed by Peter Benchley's thrilling best seller and a publicity campaign that beached a Great White shark on the cover of *Time* magazine. The simple story of an East Coast resort transformed into a hunting ground for an insatiable shark went on to gross $133 million. Discounting ticket inflation, that made it the box-office champ of all time until *Star Wars* (and eventually many other films) displaced it. The inevitable sequel, *Jaws 2*, followed in 1978, with local police chief Roy Scheider, his wife Lorraine Gary, and mayor Murray Hamilton returning from the original. Journeyman director Jeannot Szwarc replaced Spielberg as helmer in what was basically a rehash of the original. The shark was a female this time (spouse of the first one), but she was scary enough to earn $82.5 million in domestic rentals. No one seemed interested in making a second sequel, though a National Lampoon–style spoof *Jaws 3 People 0* sat on the drawing boards for awhile. Finally, in 1983, at the height of the 3-D craze (q.v.), Universal released *Jaws 3-D*. A sequel in name only, it pitted Sea World staffers Dennis Quaid and Bess Armstrong against another human-devouring shark. The 3-D effects were excellent, but the profit figures were disappointing and apparently ended the series. Unfortunately, however, *Jaws: The Revenge* unexpectedly surfaced in 1987. Lorraine Gary returned as Roy Scheider's widow, who has become convinced that another shark (the son of the first one?) has a personal vendetta against her family. It was nonsense from start to finish with the entire cast, including Michael Caine, looking thoroughly embarrassed. No one went to see it, either, hopefully ending the series for good. See also **Sharks**.

Jaws (1975); *Jaws 2* (1978); *Jaws 3* (aka *Jaws 3-D*) (1983); *Jaws: The Revenge* (1987)

Jekyll, Dr. Henry, and Mr. Hyde

Robert Louis Stevenson's dual-sided doctor has been one of the most active characters in cinema. Undoubtedly, much of his popularity stems from the challenge the double role affords actors, allowing them to run the gamut from good Dr. Jekyll to vile Mr. Hyde. Prior to 1920, no fewer than 12 silent versions appeared, ranging from Gene Gauntier's 1908 film to the comedy *Dr. Jekyll and Mr. Hyde Done to a Frazzle* (1914) to the offbeat *Miss Jekyll and Madame Hyde* (1915). Sheldon Lewis received good reviews as Jekyll/Hyde in a 1920 version for Louis B. Mayer. However, that same year, he was eclipsed by John Barrymore, whose flamboyant performance would remain the standard for the next decade. Barrymore's interpretation took a back seat, though, to Frederic March's Oscar-winning portrayal in Rouben Mamoulian's *Dr. Jekyll and Mr. Hyde* (1932). This remains the definitive adaptation of Stevenson's work, with March still the only performer to win an Academy Award for a horror film. Spencer Tracy wore minimal makeup in MGM's lavish 1941 version, trying to emphasize Jekyll's emotional (as opposed to physical) transformation into Hyde. Tracy and the film received mixed reviews, inviting less-than-favorable comparisons to the March version. Subsequently, a major Jekyll/Hyde film was not made until Jean Renoir's French variation *The Testament of Dr. Cordelier* (1959).

Nevertheless, Jekyll remained a popular character in lesser films. Abbott and Costello met the good doctor (as played by Boris Karloff) in 1951. In the film's funniest scene, Lou drinks Jekyll's potion and is transformed into a giant talking mouse. Louis Hayward played Jekyll's son and Gloria Talbott his daughter in a pair of unexceptional B-horror films (although Talbott's movie confused matters by making Jekyll a werewolf!). Hammer Films remade Stevenson's tale as 1960's *House of Fright* (aka *The Two Faces of Dr. Jekyll*). Naturally, the British studio stressed the story's sexual elements, but it also included a refreshing twist, presenting Henry Jekyll as a dull wimp and Hyde as a dashing, handsome devil. Hammer also deserves credit for another interesting variation, 1972's *Dr. Jekyll and Sister Hyde*, in which Ralph Bates drinks the serum and turns into Martine Beswick. A female character also figures prominently in *Mary Reilly* (1996), since it's the Jekyll/Hyde story shown from Jekyll's housemaid's point of view. Kirk Douglas starred in a 1973 musical version for television, which predated the hit Broadway musical by 24 years. Dozens of movies have featured dual-personality themes or paid homage to Stevenson's story, such as 1942's *Before I Hang*, *The Nutty Professor*, Jean-Luc Godard's *Alphaville* (which featured two characters named Jekyll and Hyde), and Ken Russell's *Altered States* (1980). See also **Multiple Personalities**.

Dr. Jekyll and Mr. Hyde (1920) (Sheldon Lewis); *Dr. Jekyll and Mr. Hyde* (1920) (John Barrymore); *Dr. Pyckle and Mr. Pride* (1925) (parody with Stan Laurel); *Dr. Jekyll and Mr. Hyde* (1932) (Fredric March); *Dr. Jekyll and Mr. Hyde* (1941) (Spencer Tracy); *Son of Dr. Jekyll* (1951) (Louis Hayward as the son); *Abbott and Costello Meet Dr. Jekyll and Mr. Hyde* (1953) (Boris Karloff); *Daughter of Dr. Jekyll* (1957) (Gloria Talbott as the daughter); *The Testament of Dr. Cordelier* (aka *The Doctor's Horrible Experiment*) (1959) (Jean-Louis Barrault as Dr. Cordelier); *House of Fright* (aka *The Two Faces of Dr. Jekyll*) (1960) (Paul Massie); *Mad Monster Party?* (1967) (puppet); *Dr. Jekyll and Mr. Hyde* (aka *The Strange Case of Dr. Jekyll and Mr. Hyde*) (1968) (Jack Palance); *Dr. Jekyll and the Werewolf* (aka *Dr. Jekyll y el Hombre Lobo*) (1971) (Jack Taylor); *I, Monster* (1971) (Christopher Lee as Dr. Charles Marlowe); *Dr. Jekyll and Sister Hyde* (1972) (Ralph Bates as Dr. Jekyll and Martine Beswick as Sister Hyde); *Dr. Jekyll and Mr. Hyde* (1973 TVM) (Kirk Douglas); *Twisted Brain* (aka *Horror High*) (1974) (Pat Cardi as Vernon Potts); *Dr. Black, Mr. Hyde* (aka *The Watts Monster*; *Dr. Black and Mr. White*) (1976) (Bernie Casey as Dr. Henry Pride); *Dr. Heckyl and Mr. Hype* (1980) (Oliver Reed as Dr. Heckyl); *Jekyll and Hyde...Together Again* (1982) (Mark Blankfield); *Edge of Sanity* (1989) (Anthony Perkins); *Jekyll and Hyde* (1990 TVM) (Michael Caine); *Waxwork II: Lost in Time* (1991) (Michael Viela); *The Pagemaster* (1994) (animated, voiced by Leonard Nimoy); *Dr. Jekyll and Ms. Hyde* (1995) (Timothy Daly as Dr. Richard Jacks and Sean Young as Helen Hyde); *The Nutty Professor* (1996) (Eddie Murphy as Sherman Klump); *Mary Reilly* (1996) (John Malkovich)

Jesus

The film industry's concern for reverence and its aversion to controversy have severely limited screen portraits of Jesus. In many biblical films, Christ's hand is shown or his voice is heard (as in 1959's *Ben-Hur*), but full figure shots are carefully avoided. Cecil B. DeMille mounted a tasteful story of Jesus' life with 1927's *King of Kings*, starring H. B. Warner in the title role. Nicholas Ray remade it to less effect in 1961 with 36-year-old (but still youthful-looking) Jeffrey Hunter as Christ. Unkind critics promptly dubbed it *I Was a Teenage Jesus*. George Stevens recruited solemn Swedish actor Max Von Sydow to play Jesus in his excessively lavish production of *The Greatest Story Ever Told* (1965). Originally released at over four hours in length, it was cut to 141 minutes—but still flopped. However, it did receive Harvard Lampoon's Please-Don't-Put-Us-Through-DeMille-Again Award for being the movie "which best embodied the pretensions, extravagance and blundering ineffectiveness of the traditional screen spectacular." The following year, Marxist filmmaker Pier Paolo Pasolini received the praise of both film critics and Roman Catholic leaders for his low-key, amateur-cast *The Gospel According to St. Matthew*. Other straightforward, reverent versions of Christ's life include Franco Zeffirelli's two-part, 6½ hour TV movie *Jesus of Nazareth* (1977), the Israeli-made *Jesus* (1979), and another TV movie *The Day Christ Died* (1980). In 1973, the popular stage musicals *Jesus Christ, Superstar* and *Godspell* reached the screen, but neither found an eager audience. The 1979 *In Search of Historic Jesus* purported to be a documentary about the Shroud of Turin, but was less than enlightening. Two films of significantly greater interest surfaced in 1988. *The Seventh Sign* mixed elements of mystery and fantasy into its plot about Jesus' (Jurgen Prochnow) return to Earth to prepare the human race for the forthcoming Apocalypse. Despite an intriguing theme, it attracted little attention, especially when compared to the exaggerated controversy surrounding Martin Scorsese's *The Last Temptation of Christ*. Fundamentalist groups tried to stop—sight unseen—this adaptation of Nikos Kazantzakis' novel, chiefly due to a dream sequence where Jesus (Willem Dafoe) was tempted by desires of the flesh. Monty Python's *Life of Brian* (1979) incurred less wrath, despite presenting a satirical tale about a poor bloke who is mistaken for Jesus and crucified (it ends with a song-and-dance number on the cross). Christ's life has been told in allegorical terms in a number of films, such as *El Topo* (1971) and *Greaser's Palace* (1972). Peter O'Toole and Peter Boyle played lunatics who believed they were Christ in, respectively, *The Ruling Class* (1971) and *The Dream Team* (1989).

Intolerance (1916); *King of Kings* (1927); *Ben-Hur* (1959); *King of Kings* (1961); *Barabbas* (1962); *The Greatest Story Ever Told* (1965); *The Gospel According to St. Matthew* (1966); *The Milky Way* (1969); *Godspell* (1973); *The Gospel Road* (1973); *Jesus Christ, Superstar* (1973); *The Passover Plot* (1976); *Jesus of Nazareth* (1977 TVM); *In Search of Historic Jesus* (1979); *Jesus* (1979); *The Day Christ Died* (1980 TVM); *The Inquiry* (1987); *The Last Temptation of Christ* (1988); *The Seventh Sign* (1988); *Jesus of Montreal* (1989); *Child of Light, Child of Darkness* (1991 TVM); *The Return* (aka *Jesus Vender Tilbage*) (1992); *Mary, Mother of Jesus* (1999 TVM); *Jesus* (2000 TVM)

Jewel Thieves

The classiest of criminals, jewel thieves have long enjoyed a popularity rarely accorded to other lawbreakers. This cinematic leniency can be traced to two key points: (1) Most jewel thieves are suave, witty, and good-looking (as played by David Niven, Cary Grant, etc.); and (2) jewel thieves typically steal from rich people or museums, so that the lost property is certain to be insured by large corporations which already "steal" money from the middle class. The concept of the "gentleman thief" owes much to E. W. Horung's book *The Amateur Cracksman*, which has been filmed as *Raffles* in 1917 (with John Barrymore), 1925 (House

Peters), 1930 (Ronald Colman), and 1940 (David Niven). Barrymore played gentlemanly jewel thieves again in the 1932 films *Arsene Lupin* (q.v.) and *Grand Hotel*. Niven continued to display an affection for other people's diamonds in *The Pink Panther* (1964) and *Rough Cut* (1980). Warren Williams and several other actors played *The Lone Wolf* (q.v.), a jewel-thief-turned-detective in a film series spanning the 1930s and 1940s. George Hamilton hid his tan lines under a black turtleneck in 1967's *Jack of Diamonds*. However, the cinema's most charming gentleman thief has to be Cary Grant, who portrayed a retired cat burglar chasing a copycat criminal (and Grace Kelly) in Hitchcock's *To Catch a Thief*. Hitchcock also dealt with jewel thieves, though less effectively, in his earlier *Number Seventeen* (1932). Female jewel thieves proved themselves just as effective as their male counterparts in *I Was an Adventuress* (1940), the aforementioned *To Catch a Thief*, and Lubitsch's sophisticated comedy *Trouble in Paradise* (1932). A cat burglar called The Phantom stole the Pink Panther diamond—but also encountered the ever-bumbling Inspector Clouseau—in *The Pink Panther* (1964) and *The Return of the Pink Panther* (1975). Clever thieves implemented elaborate schemes to steal the crown jewels in *The Adventures of Sherlock Holmes* (1939), *Traitor's Gate* (1965), and *The Jokers* (1966). For a discussion of movies in which the heists form the central plot, see **Heist/Caper Films**. See also **The Lone Wolf**; **Lupin, Arsene**; **Lupin III (The Wolf)**; **The Pink Panther Series**.

Raffles (1930); *Jewel Robbery* (1932); *Trouble in Paradise* (1932); *Grand Hotel* (1932); *Number Seventeen* (1932); *Arsene Lupin* (1932); *Now and Forever* (1934); *The Mystery of Mr. X* (1934); *The Lone Wolf Returns* (1935); *I Am a Thief* (1935); *The Return of Sophie Lange* (1936); *This Man Is News* (1938); *Stolen Heaven* (1938); *The Amazing Mr. Forrest* (aka *The Gang's All Here*) (1939); *The Adventures of Sherlock Holmes* (1939); *Raffles* (1940); *Adventure in Diamonds* (1940); *I Was an Adventuress* (1940); *They Met in Bombay* (1941); *The Peterville Diamond* (1941); *A Gentleman After Dark* (1942); *The Great Jewel Robber* (1950); *To Catch a Thief* (1955); *The Man Inside* (1958); *The Greengage Summer* (aka *Loss of Innocence*) (1961); *The Pink Panther* (1964); *Traitor's Gate* (1965); *The Jokers* (1966); *That Riviera Touch* (1966); *Jack of Diamonds* (1967); *Deadfall* (1968); *The Thief Who Came to Dinner* (1973); *The Return of the Pink Panther* (1975); *Rough Cut* (1980); *The Great Muppet Caper* (1981); *Thief of Hearts* (1984); *Oddball Hall* (1990); *Hudson Hawk* (1991); *Ice* (1994); *Blood and Wine* (1997); *Absolute Power* (1997)

Jiggs and Maggie

George McManus created this comic strip in 1916 about a nouveau riche Irish couple with social aspirations. Comedian Johnny Ray played Jiggs in a series of silent two-reelers produced by Pathé Studios. The characters also appeared in a successful 1921 stage play called *Bringing Up Father*. That play served as the basis for a 1928 MGM film starring J. Farrell McDonald as the badgered Jiggs and Marie Dressler as society-minded Maggie. However, a series did not appear until budget-conscious Monogram reintroduced the characters in 1946 with another version of *Bringing Up Father*. Joe Yule (Mickey Rooney's father) and Renie Riano starred as Jiggs and Maggie in that film and four subsequent entries. Yule died in 1950, shortly after completing *Jiggs and Maggie Out West*. For sheer silliness, *Jiggs and Maggie in Society* rates as the series highlight, with Maggie taking dancing lessons from Arthur Murray and Jiggs learning etiquette from Dale Carnegie. Neil

O'Malley and Agnes Moorehead also played the couple on a 1941 radio program. See also **Comic Strip Characters**.

Bringing Up Father (1928); *Bringing Up Father* (1946); *Jiggs and Maggie in Court* (1948); *Jiggs and Maggie in Society* (1949); *Jiggs and Maggie in Jackpot Jitters* (aka *Jackpot Jitters*) (1949); *Jiggs and Maggie Out West* (1950)

Johnson, Coffin Ed *see* Coffin Ed Johnson and Grave Digger Jones

Jones, Grave Digger *see* Coffin Ed Johnson and Grave Digger Jones

The Jones Family

While the Hardys (q.v.) are still fondly remembered, the Jones' have been all but forgotten. Yet, 20th Century–Fox's *Jones Family* series actually came first and set the pattern for the wholesome family comedy/dramas of the late 1930s and 1940s. For the first film, 1936's *Every Saturday Night*, the family's last name was Evers. It switched to Jones that same year in *Educating Father*, the entry that set the tone for the rest of the series by putting Pa Jones in the spotlight. This emphasis on a none-too-perfect father figure is what distinguishes the Jones comedies from the Hardy pictures, which clearly belong to teenager Andy Hardy (Mickey Rooney). Veteran character actor Jed Prouty played bespectacled Pa Jones and Spring Byington, who made a career of maternal roles, was Ma. Florence Roberts provided additional adult supervision as Granny Jones. June Lang portrayed Bonnie, the oldest daughter in the first film, but was replaced by Shirley Deane. The rest of the Jones kids were played by Kenneth Howell (Jack), George Ernest (Roger), June Carlson (Lucy), and Billy Mahan (Bobby). Bonnie Jones married her boyfriend Herbert Thompson (Russell Gleason) and became a mother in 1938's *Love on a Budget*. But stagestruck little sister Lucy remains the best remembered of the children, stealing scenes with her impersonations of Katharine Hepburn and Greta Garbo. Typical plots involved Pa's candidacy for mayor (*Hot Water*), a family vacation in Yosemite (*Back to Nature*), and an oil swindle (*Big Business*). Despite its modest popularity, the *Jones Family* series ended in 1940, while the Hardys lasted well into the decade. Many of the cast members, though, continued in similar movies, with Russell Gleason even appearing in the rival *Higgins Family* series (q.v.). Veronica Lake, who was acting under the name of Constance Keane, had a small role in *As Young as You Feel*.

Every Saturday Night (1936); *Educating Father* (1936); *Back to Nature* (1936); *Off to the Races* (1937); *Big Business* (aka *The Jones Family in Big Business*) (1937); *Hot Water* (1937); *Borrowing Trouble* (1937); *Love on a Budget* (1938); *A Trip to Paris* (1938); *Safety in Numbers* (1938); *Down on the Farm* (1938); *Everybody's Baby* (1939); *The Jones Family in Hollywood* (1939); *Quick Millions* (aka *The Jones Family in Quick Millions*) (1939); *Too Busy to Work* (1939); *Young as You Feel* (1940); *On Their Own* (1940)

Jones, Indiana

Steven Spielberg on *Raiders of the Lost Ark*: "The film's like popcorn, it doesn't fill you and it's easy to digest and it melts in your mouth and it's the kind of thing you can just go and chow down over and over again." That's precisely what moviegoers did with

1981's blockbuster homage to the days of serial thrills. Director Spielberg and executive producer George Lucas (who cowrote the story) received most of the credit, with the witty screenplay by Lawrence Kasdan (pre–*Big Chill*) being largely ignored. Harrison Ford, playing a part not dissimilar from Han Solo in the *Star Wars* (q.v.) films, created the whip-carrying archaeologist/adventurer who battled Nazis for the Ark of the Covenant circa 1936. For some reason, the 1984 follow-up *Indiana Jones and the Temple of Doom*, turned out to be a prequel (q.v.) set three years before *Raiders*. The plot sent Indiana to India to fetch a magical jewel and rescue some enslaved children. The film made tons of money, but incurred a surprising amount of wrath. It was criticized for being racist toward Indians, anti-feminist, and overly violent for the young members of its audience. The last complaint contributed to the Motion Picture Association of America's creation of a PG-13 film rating. Spielberg and Lucas set the series on track with what they claimed would be the final entry, 1989's *Indiana Jones and the Last Crusade*. Although *Batman* eclipsed it as the year's top money-maker, the *Last Crusade* received an overwhelming thumbs up from both critics and the public. The teaming of Ford and Sean Connery as his father turned out to be pure magic, which set the rumor mill about a fourth film into motion. Ford also appeared in a 1993 episode of the *Young Indiana Jones Chronicles* TV series starring Sean Patrick Flanery as a 16-year-old Indy. Four made-for-television films, also with Flanery, followed the short-lived 1992-93 TV series.

Raiders of the Lost Ark (1981); *Indiana Jones and the Temple of Doom* (1984); *Indiana Jones and the Last Crusade* (1989); *Young Indiana Jones and the Hollywood Follies* (1994 TVM); *Young Indiana Jones and the Treasure of the Peacock's Eye* (1995 TVM); *Young Indiana Jones and the Attack of the Hawkmen* (1996 TVM); *Young Indiana Jones and Travels with Father* (1996 TVM)

Josser, Jimmy

British vaudeville comedian Ernie Lotinga played the "much put upon" Jimmy Josser on the stage and in a series of shorts before making the transition to feature-length films. *P.C. Josser* (1931), an adaptation of Lotinga's play *The Police Force*, was a minor comedy about Josser's attempts to regain his job as a policeman. It pretty much set the pattern for the rest of the series, which briefly enjoyed minor popularity in its native country.

P.C. Josser (1931); *Dr. Josser KC* (1931); *Josser Joins the Navy* (1932); *Josser on the River* (1932); *Josser in the Army* (1932); *Josser on the Farm* (1934)

Judges

While lawyers have garnered most of the courtroom limelight, judges have proven themselves to be more versatile outside the typical legal settings. In *The Life and Times of Judge Roy Bean* (1972), the legendary Western judge (Paul Newman) appointed himself to his post and heard cases in the local saloon. The judges in 1983's *The Star Chamber* moonlighted as vigilantes who executed criminals that avoided sentencing due to legal loopholes. Robert Van Gulick's Judge Dee, a seventh-century oriental detective, solved his only celluloid case in the engaging 1974 TV movie *Judge Dee and the Monastery Murders*. Female judges have been represented by Susan Hayward in *The Bachelor and the Bobby-Soxer* (1947) and Jill Clayburgh in *First Monday in Octo-*

ber (1981). The latter film, based on a play predating Sandra Day O'Connor's appointment, cast Clayburgh as the first woman on the Supreme Court. Arthur Hill may have played the screen's most courageous judge, as the real-life official who battled a racially-prejudiced town in *Judge Horton and the Scottsboro Boys* (1976), a vivid account of the trial of nine blacks accused of raping a white woman. As Judge Hardy in the *Andy Hardy* series (q.v.), stern but fair Lewis Stone played a judge more often than any other performer. See also **Courts-Martial**.

Ann Vickers (1933); *Judge Priest* (1934); *The Westerner* (1940); *Design for Scandal* (1941); *Steppin' in Society* (1945); *And Then There Were None* (1945); *Angel on My Shoulder* (1946); *Cass Timberlane* (1947); *The Bachelor and the Bobby-Soxer* (aka *Bachelor Knight*) (1947); *Behind Locked Doors* (1948); *The Man from Colorado* (1948); *An Act of Murder* (aka *Live for Tomorrow*) (1948); *The Judge Steps Out* (1949); *Judgment at Nuremberg* (1961); *The Chalk Garden* (1964); *The Judge and Jake Wyler* (1972 TVM); *The Life and Times of Judge Roy Bean* (1972); *Judge Dee and the Monastery Murders* (1974 TVM); *Jury of One* (aka *The Verdict*) (1974); *The Judge and the Assassin* (1975); *Judge Horton and the Scottsboro Boys* (1976 TVM); *All God's Children* (1980 TVM); *First Monday in October* (1981); *The Star Chamber* (1983); *Crime of Innocence* (1985 TVM); *Penalty Phase* (1986 TVM); *Suspect* (1987); *Double Standard* (1988 TVM); *Naked Lie* (1989 TVM); *Nothing But Trouble* (1991); *Hitz* (aka *Judgment*) (1992); *Crimebroker* (1993); *Judicial Consent* (1994); *The Pelican Brief* (1994); *Three Colors: Red* (1994); *Broken Trust* (1995 TVM); *Eye of the Stalker: A Moment of Truth Movie* (1995 TVM); *Head Above Water* (1996); *The Crucible* (1996); *Nightmare in Big Sky Country* (1998); *Swing Vote* (1999 TVM); *Strange Justice* (1999 TVM)

Jungle Jim

Johnny Weissmuller hung up his loincloth after 1948's *Tarzan and the Mermaids*, but he didn't stay out of the jungle for long. That same year, he moved from RKO to Columbia and kicked off a series of low-budget action pictures for producer Sam Katzman. Weissmuller's Jungle Jim, although based on a comic strip and radio program, was clearly inspired by Tarzan (q.v.). Sure, Jungle Jim wore clothes and spoke in complete sentences (most of the time), but the fast-paced plots (which got progressively sillier) were pure Burroughs. In the first film, Jim had a pet crow and a little dog. These "unjungle" denizens were later traded for a trusty chimp sidekick. The Jungle Jim films never rose above the level of backlot juvenile features, but the supporting cast sometimes included a surprising face or two, such as B-movie faves Buster Crabbe and Ray "Crash" Corrigan. The outrageousness of the plots deserves special mention, too. Jim battled "man monsters" (*Jungle Jim in the Forbidden Land*), pesky pygmies (*Jungle Moon Men*), and Nazis (*Voodoo Tiger*). In the last three films, Weissmuller dropped the Jungle Jim moniker and went by his real name. When the series ended in 1955, he moved to television and made the half-hour *Jungle Jim* syndicated series. It lasted for 26 episodes and co-starred Martin Huston. See also **Comic Strip Characters**.

Jungle Jim (1948); *The Lost Tribe* (1949); *Captive Girl* (1950); *Mark of the Gorilla* (1950); *Pygmy Island* (1950); *Fury of the Congo* (1951); *Jungle Manhunt* (1951); *Jungle Jim in the Forbidden Land* (1952); *Voodoo Tiger* (1952); *Killer Ape* (1953); *Savage Mutiny* (1953); *Valley of the Headhunters* (1953); *Jungle Maneaters* (1954); As Johnny Weissmuller (but still considered part of Jungle Jim series): *Cannibal Attack* (1954); *Devil Goddess* (1955); *Jungle Moon Men* (1955)

The Karate Kid

Critics dubbed it a junior-league *Rocky*, but the 1984 sleeper hit *The Karate Kid* had its own winning formula built around the friendship between a gawky teen (Ralph Macchio) and a janitor/philosopher/martial artist (Noriyuki "Pat" Morita). Okay, it *was* directed by *Rocky* veteran John Avildsen and *did* climax with a dramatic fight in the ring — but there were no characters named Adrienne, Mick, or Apollo. In 1986, *The Karate Kid Part II* took Morita and Macchio to the Orient with predictable results, being notable only for spawning Peter Cetera's number one song "The Glory of Love." Audiences snubbed a third installment, released in 1989, which basically rehashed the original. Still, in 1994, Columbia Pictures tried to breathe new life in the franchise by casting Hilary Swank as *The Next Karate Kid*. Despite another engaging performance by Morita as Mr. Miyagi, the film adhered too close to a tiresome formula and put an end to the series. For other martial arts films, see **American Ninja Series**, **Best of the Best Series**; **Bloodfist Series**; **Kickboxer Series**; and **No Retreat, No Surrender Series**.

The Karate Kid (1984); *The Karate Kid Part II* (1986); *The Karate Kid Part III* (1989); *The Next Karate Kid* (1994)

Karnstein Trilogy

Hammer Films, the "House of Horror" in the 1960s, saw its once-loyal audience dwindling rapidly in the early 1970s. To attract new horror fans, it updated its Christopher Lee *Dracula* (q.v.) films and introduced a new series about lesbian vampire Mircalla Karnstein. Based on Sheridan Le Fanu's novel *Carmilla*, 1970's *The Vampire Lovers* pitted veteran vampire hunter Peter Cushing against buxom Ingrid Pitt as Mircalla. In the end, she lost her head and was staked as well. She was resurrected in the form of Yutte Stensgaard for 1971's *Lust for a Vampire*, a lively sequel directed by horror veteran Jimmy Sangster. The series concluded with 1972's *Twins of Evil*, in which Mircalla (now played by Katya Keith) takes a back seat to a tale about twin village girls — one an innocent and one a vicious vampire. Again, Peter Cushing was around to provide the necessary heroics, although his character died in the process. Hammer was gasping for its dying breath, too. It produced its last theatrical film in 1974. See also **Vampires**.

The Vampire Lovers (1970); *Lust for a Vampire* (aka *To Love a Vampire*) (1971); *Twins of Evil* (1972)

Keate, Nurse Sarah [Sally Keating]

Mignon G. Eberhart's medically-minded detective never made a successful transition from page to screen in the 1930s. In Eberhart's novels, Sarah Keate was a middle-aged nurse who solved mysteries with the assistance of young police detective Lance O'Leary. Aline MacMahon played a thirtyish Nurse Keate in 1935's *While the Patient Slept*, a Warner Bros. adaptation of a popular Eberhart novel. Guy Kibbee, who was 53, portrayed Lance as a character altogether different from the one in Eberhart's books and stories. Warner Bros. subsequently used the Keate series as a training ground for promising actresses: Kay Linaker (*The Murder of Dr. Harrigan*), Marguerite Churchill (*Murder by an Aristocrat*), and Ann Sheridan (*The Patient in Room 18* and *Mystery House*). In the Linaker and Churchill movies, the heroine's name was changed to Sally Keating. Patric Knowles, another rising star, played Lance in *The Patient in Room 18*. Jane Darwell, a good choice for the spinsterish detective, played Nurse Keats (not Keate) in 20th Century–Fox's *The Great Hospital Mystery* (1937). Although Eberhart's Nurse Keate books resulted in strictly B-movies, she enjoyed a fine career as a mystery writer. The Mystery Writers of America gave her the prestigious Grand Master award in 1970. See also **Hospitals**.

While the Patient Slept (1935) (Aline MacMahon); *The Murder of Dr. Harrigan* (1936) (Kay Linaker as Sally Keating); *Murder by an Aristocrat* (1936) (Marguerite Churchill as Sally Keating); *The Great Hospital Mystery* (1937) (Jane Darwell as Nurse Keats); *The Patient in Room 18* (1938) (Ann Sheridan); *Mystery House* (1938) (Ann Sheridan)

Keating, Sally *see* Keates, Nurse Sarah

Kettle, Ma and Pa

Marjorie Main and Percy Kilbride made their debut as Ma and Pa Kettle in the 1947 Universal comedy *The Egg and I*. Adapted from Betty McDonald's bestseller, the picture featured Claudette Colbert as a Bostonian lass introduced to chicken farming by new hubby Fred MacMurray. The Kettles were merely supporting characters, but they were responsible for the film's funniest scenes. Universal reteamed Main and Kilbride the following year in the cornpone Donald O'Connor comedy *Feudin', Fussin' and A-Fightin'* and then turned them into stars with 1949's *Ma and Pa Kettle*. Produced for $200,000 to $400,000 each, the Kettle movies earned tidy profits for Universal through the mid–1950s. The simple series formula usually found lazy, laidback Pa getting into unintentional mischief, while Ma ruled the Kettle brood of 15 kids. Several entries derived humor by moving the Kettles (temporarily) to big cities. Thus, the Kettle clan visited New York (*Go to Town*), Paris (*Vacation*), and Hawaii (*Waikiki*). Richard Long played Tom, the Kettles' oldest son, and other children included Lori Nelson (Rosie) and Brett Halsey (Elwin). Pa's Indian cohort Crowbar was played by four actors: Vic Potel, Chief Yowlachie, Teddy Hart, and Zachary Charles. After seven films in as many years, Percy Kilbride quit the series. There was no Pa Kettle in 1956's *The Kettles in the Ozarks*, although Arthur Hunnicutt's Uncle Sedge was mighty similar. Pa was back, though, in the guise of character actor Parker Fennelly in 1957's *The Kettles on Old MacDonald's Farm*. It turned out not only to be the last Kettle film, but also Marjorie Main's final screen role. She retired from acting and died in 1975.

The Egg and I (1947); *Ma and Pa Kettle* (1949); *Ma and Pa Kettle Go to Town* (1950); *Ma and Pa Kettle Back on the Farm* (1951); *Ma and Pa Kettle at the Fair* (1952); *Ma and Pa Kettle on Vacation* (1953); *Ma and Pa Kettle at Home* (1954); *Ma and Pa Kettle at Waikiki* (1955); *The Kettles in the Ozarks* (1956); *The Kettles on Old MacDonald's Farm* (1957)

Kickboxer Series

Belgian martial artist Jean-Claude Van Damme clinched his niche in the 1990s action movie field with 1989's *Kickboxer*. The plot, instantly recognizable to any martial arts film enthusiast, has Van Damme swearing vengeance against a vicious Thai fighter who crippled his older brother, a world kickboxing champion. However, to beat his adversary, Van Damme must master Muay-Thai fighting, which he can learn only from the elusive Dennis Chan (Xian Chow). The outcome is never in doubt, of course, and *Kickboxer* fails to register the emotional uplift generated by *Rocky* or even *The Karate Kid*. Still, the film's popular success warranted a sequel — without the charismatic Van Damme, unfortunately. Sasha Mitchell, best-known as J.R. Ewing's illegitimate son on TV's *Dallas*, toplined 1990's *Kickboxer 2: The Road Back*. An odd choice, Mitchell did boast prior film fighting credentials, having played a boxer in the 1989 comedy-drama *Spike of Bensonhurst*. In *Kickboxer 2*, Mitchell plays Van Damme's younger brother, who attracts the attention of gangsters after getting behind on his gym's mortgage payments. Mitchell appeared in two more entries, *Kickboxer 3: The Art of War* and *Kickboxer 4: The Aggressor*. Mark Dacascos headlined *Kickboxer 5: The Redemption* (1996), an in-name only series entry. Xian Chow played martial arts master Dennis Chan in the first three films. For other martial arts films, see **American Ninja; Best of the Best Series; Bloodfist Series; The Karate Kid;** and **No Retreat, No Surrender Series** (in which an unknown Van Damme appears briefly).

Kickboxer (1989); *Kickboxer 2: The Road Back* (1990); *Kickboxer 3: The Art of War* (1992); *Kickboxer 4: The Aggressor* (1994); *Kickboxer 5: The Redemption* (1996)

Kildare, Dr. James

The year after Joel McCrea introduced Dr. James Kildare in Paramount's *Interns Can't Take Money* (1937), MGM launched an immensely popular *Kildare* film series starring Lew Ayres. The supporting cast at Blair General Hospital was a potent one, featuring wheelchair-bound Lionel Barrymore as Dr. Gillespie, Laraine Day as Mary Lamont, and Nell Craig as Nurse Parker. Ayres and company made nine movies, dealing efficiently with daily medical crises and topical subjects like insulin shock. Then, in 1941, the series stunned moviegoers with *Dr. Kildare's Wedding Day*, in which Day's character was killed off. That same year, Ayres elicited a wave of bad publicity by refusing to enter the army on the grounds he was a conscientious objector. MGM promptly dropped Ayres from the *Kildare* series, although the actor eventually enlisted and served in combat. Rather than casting a new Kildare, MGM shifted the series focus to Barrymore with 1942's *Calling Dr. Gillespie*. Later that year, Van Johnson was introduced as *Dr. Gillespie's New Assistant*, a role he continued in four of the final five Gillespie pictures. Throughout the Kildare/Gillespie series, MGM introduced up-and-coming stars like future *Marcus Welby* Robert Young, Donna Reed, and child star Margaret O'Brien. *Dr. Kildare* came to television in 1961 with Richard Chamberlain in the lead and Raymond Massey as Dr. Gillespie. It enjoyed high ratings and a five-year run. A half-hour syndicated program, *Young Dr. Kildare*, lasted for 24 episodes in 1972. See also **Hospitals.**

Interns Can't Take Money (aka *You Can't Take Money*) (1937) (Joel McCrea); *Young Dr. Kildare* (1938) (Lew Ayres); *Calling Dr. Kildare* (1939) (Ayres); *The Secret of Dr. Kildare* (1939) (Ayres); *Dr. Kildare Goes Home* (1940) (Ayres); *Dr. Kildare's Crisis* (1940) (Ayres); *Dr. Kildare's Strange Case* (1940) (Ayres); *The People vs. Dr. Kildare* (aka *My Life Is Yours*) (1941) (Ayres); *Dr. Kildare's Wedding Day* (aka *Mary Names the Day*) (1941) (Ayres); *Dr. Kildare's Victory* (1941) (aka *The Debutante and the Doctor*) (Ayres); *Calling Dr. Gillespie* (1942) (Lionel Barrymore); *Dr. Gillespie's New Assistant* (1942) (Barrymore); *Dr. Gillespie's Criminal Case* (aka *Crazy to Kill*) (1943) (Barrymore); *Between Two Women* (1944) (Barrymore); *Three Men in White* (1944) (Barrymore); *Dark Delusion* (aka *Cynthia's Secret*) (1947) (Barrymore)

Killer Tomatoes Series

Attack of the Killer Tomatoes (1979) established its reputation as one of the "worst films of all-time" in a remarkably short period. Indeed, that status may have been the filmmakers' aim when they produced this sophomoric ode to low-budget, sci-fi camp. It's not as bad as one would hope — the inane title song is downright funny and a Japanese character dubbed out-of-sync makes an amusing tribute to sci-fi imports. The 1988 sequel, *Return of the Killer Tomatoes*, starred Anthony Starke as a pizza delivery boy who develops a crush on scientist John Astin's daughter — only to discover that she's a tomato converted into a woman! Astin returned as Professor Gangreen in the next two films. A Saturday morning animated series followed on the Fox TV network. See also **Plants.**

Attack of the Killer Tomatoes (1979); *Return of the Killer Tomatoes* (1988); *Killer Tomatoes Strike Back* (1990); *Killer Tomatoes Eat France!* (1991)

King Kong

"The Eighth Wonder of the World," as showman Carl Denham proclaimed Kong in the 1933 original, was actually a three-foot model brought to life by master stop-motion animator Willis O'Brien. The marvelous O'Brien had previously performed his camera trickery on the dinosaurs (q.v.) in 1925's *The Lost World*. His post–Kong work included some excellent effects in the seldom-shown 1933 sequel *Son of Kong* and another giant friendly ape opus, 1949's *Mighty Joe Young*. But O'Brien's contribution accounts for just part — albeit a crucial one — of *King Kong*'s enduring success. The other critical ingredients are the film's simplistic beauty-and-the-beast theme and its capability to make Kong a character audiences can identify with. Subsequent Kong films have floundered drastically on both counts. Japan monster moviemaker Inoshira Honda revived Kong after a 29-year hiatus for "the colossal clash of all time," 1963's *King Kong vs. Godzilla*. Featuring a man in an ape suit as Kong, it was a dull affair, of interest only in that Kong won the fight in U.S. prints and Godzilla won in the Japanese version. Honda mounted a sequel of sorts with 1968's *King Kong Escapes*, which pitted the giant ape against a robotic replica called Mechani-Kong. At least, Honda did not dare compare it to the original *Kong*. Unfortunately, Dino De Laurentiis did just that with his $24 million man-in-ape-suit 1976 remake. *Variety* dubbed it "a brilliant remake," but most critics drubbed it and plans for an immediate sequel were temporarily scrapped. However, that sequel finally reached the screen in 1986 as *King Kong Lives*. Kong, it turns out, had survived his fall from the World Trade Center, but required a blood transfusion. Enter Mrs. Kong. This ludicrous picture turned the giant ape into a giant turkey at the box-office. Nevertheless, it introduced star Linda Hamilton to the beauty and the beast angle — excellent training for her 1987 TV series *Beauty and the Beast*. See also **Apes and Monkeys.**

King Kong (1933); *Son of Kong* (1933); *King Kong vs. Godzilla* (aka *Kingukongu tai Gojira*) (1963); *King Kong Escapes* (aka *Kingukongu No Gyakushu*) (1968); *King Kong* (1976); *King Kong Lives* (1986)

Kojak, Theo

1973's fact-based *The Marcus-Nelson Murders* introduced bald, lollipop-licking police lieutenant Theo Kojak to TV audiences. The film was adapted from Selwyn Rabb's book *Justice in the Back Room*, an account of the 1963 Wylie-Hoffert murders which played a major role in the Supreme Court's *Miranda* decision. Savalas's Emmy-nominated portrayal resulted in the popular 1973–78 *Kojak* TV series. After a vacation from the role, Savalas revived Kojak in two TV movies before returning on a regular basis as a revolving character in 1989 on *The ABC Saturday Mystery*. See also **Television Series Reunion Films.**

The Marcus-Nelson Murders (aka *Kojak and the Marcus-Nelson Murders*) (1973 TVM); *Kojak: The Belarus Files* (1985 TVM); *Kojak: The Price of Justice* (1987 TVM)

Korean War

If not for the escapades of TV's Hawkeye Pierce and the rest of the *M*A*S*H* unit, the Korean War might have slipped into relative obscurity. And yet, during the days when American forces fought in Korea, the war was a popular film subject. Significantly, these war films of the 1950s differed in tone from their World War II counterparts of the 1940s. While escapist entertainment and glossy romances still drew crowds, many of these new pictures were grim, realistic adventures uninterested in glorifying war. Cult movie favorite Samuel Fuller produced two violent, powerful Korean War adventures in 1951: *The Steel Helmet* and *Fixed Bayonets*. The first film dealt with the war's brutal ironies, beginning with a sergeant whose unit is wiped out, while he alone survives because of his helmet. The horror of war dominated *Fixed Bayonets*, as evidenced by a chilling scene where soldiers put their feet together to avoid frostbite — and one foot, already without feeling, is left out. Similar tough-minded films like *Retreat, Hell!* (1952) and *Men in War* (1957) substituted sturdy stars (e.g., Frank Lovejoy, Robert Ryan) for big-name draws. Nevertheless, Hollywood favorites like Humphrey Bogart (*Battle Circus*) and Robert Mitchum (*One Minute to Zero*) donned fatigues long enough to fight a skirmish or two. William Holden starred as a jet pilot in love with Grace Kelly in the popular hit *Bridges at Toko-Ri* (1954) and then romanced Jennifer Jones in Hong Kong during the war in *Love Is a Many Splendored Thing* (1955). Lower-budgeted Korean War pictures provided roles for an impressive crop of rising young stars, such as Lee Marvin (*The Glory Brigade*), Charles Bronson (*Target Zero*), Robert Redford (*War Hunt*), and Michael Caine and Robert Shaw (both in *Hell in Korea*). Future best-selling author Tom Tryon (*Harvest Home*) played a soldier on shore leave from Korea in *Marines, Let's Go!* (1961). Veteran Western character actor L.Q. Jones and Alvy Moore (Mr. Kimble on *Green Acres*) had supporting roles in, respectively, *Target Zero* and *The Glory Brigade*. Two decades later, these two would team to produce and direct the science fiction cult hit *A Boy and His Dog* (1975). The effects of the Korean War back home in the states was a rare film subject, although 1951's *I Want You* dealt with it sensitively. On the other hand, 1953's *Take the High Ground* was a routine boot camp picture about soldiers undergoing intensive training prior to being shipped to Korea. The horror of war lasted beyond the battlefield for the soldiers tried for treason in gripping court-martial dramas like *The Rack* (1956), *Time Limit* (1957), and

Sergeant Ryker (1968). With exceptions like the latter film, Korean War pictures became increasingly scarce after Gregory Peck closed out the 1950s with the frightening, realistic *Pork Chop Hill*. The 1963 Kirk Douglas picture *The Hook* was a brutally effective portrait of combat. John Frankenheimer's political thriller *The Manchurian Candidate* (1962) turned a Korean vet into a brainwashed assassin. Robert Altman's film version of *M*A*S*H* (1970) showed battlefield physicians acting crazy in order to maintain their sanity in face of war's atrocities. It made a successful transition to television in 1972, where it enjoyed an 11-year run.

Fixed Bayonets (1951); *I Want You* (1951); *The Steel Helmet* (1951); *A Yank in Korea* (1951); *Battle Circus* (1952); *Battle Zone* (1952); *One Minute to Zero* (1952); *Retreat, Hell!* (1952); *Mission Over Korea* (1953); *Combat Squad* (1953); *The Glory Brigade* (1953); *Sabre Jet* (1953); *Torpedo Alley* (1953); *Take the High Ground* (1953); *Bridges at Toko-Ri* (1954); *Dragonfly Squadron* (1954); *Flight Nurse* (1954); *Men of the Fighting Lady* (1954); *Prisoner of War* (1954); *Battle Taxi* (1955); *Hell's Horizon* (1955); *Love Is a Many Splendored Thing* (1955); *Target Zero* (1955); *Hell in Korea* (aka *A Hill in Korea*) (1956); *Hold Back the Night* (1956); *The Rack* (1956); *Strange Intruder* (1956); *Men in War* (1957); *Time Limit* (1957); *The Hunters* (1958); *Jet Attack* (1958); *Pork Chop Hill* (1959); *Battle Flame* (1959); *All the Young Men* (1960); *Marines, Let's Go!* (1961); *Sniper's Ridge* (1961); *War Hunt* (1961); *The Manchurian Candidate* (1962); *The Nun and the Sergeant* (1962); *War Is Hell* (1963); *The Hook* (1963); *Sergeant Ryker* (1968); *M*A*S*H* (1970); *The Reluctant Heroes* (1971 TVM); *Collision Course* (1975 TVM); *Inchon* (1982)

Ku Klux Klan and Other White Supremacists

Controversy has stalked the KKK from its inception and has naturally overflowed into its sporadic film appearances. D.W. Griffith's landmark 1915 film *Birth of a Nation* continues to incur the wrath of racial rights groups for its glorification of the KKK. Based on Thomas Dixon, Jr.'s *The Clansmen*, Griffith's film ends with a Southern family being rescued from marauding black men by heroic members of the KKK. The National Association for the Advancement of Colored People (NAACP) mounted an effective boycott of the film on its initial release. That inspired Griffith to write a defense of his film, a pamphlet entitled "The Rise and Fall of Free Speech in America." The 1936 *Black Legion* never referred to the KKK, but the racist organization which recruited Humphrey Bogart was obviously patterned after the Ku Klux Klan. *The Texans* (1938), a post–Civil War Western, featured a subplot involving the KKK. It was not until 1950's *Storm Warning* that another film dealt exclusively — and frankly — with the Ku Klux Klan. Ginger Rogers starred as a woman who sought help from liberal D.A. Ronald Reagan after learning that her sister (Doris Day) has married a racist, and possibly murderous, Klansman. It was far superior to the 1974 fiasco *The Klansman*, an unlikely all-star mishmash starring Richard Burton, Lee Marvin, O.J. Simpson, and Linda Evans. The 1979 TV movie *Attack on Terror: The FBI vs. the Ku Klux Klan* was an engrossing fact-based drama about the murder of three civil rights workers in Mississippi in 1964. The same case provided the basis for another fine film, 1988's Oscar-nominated picture *Mississippi Burning*. Other fact-based films about white supremist groups include: *In the Line of Fire: Manhunt in the Dakotas* (1991), *Ghosts of Mississippi* (1996), and *Rosewood* (1997). *Fried Green Tomatoes* (1992) and *Sommersby* (1993) featured subplots involving the KKK.

Birth of a Nation (1915); *Black Legion* (1936); *The Texans* (1938); *Storm Warning* (1950); *The FBI Story* (1959); *The Black Klansman* (1966); *The Klansman* (1974); *Attack on Terror: The FBI vs. the Ku Klux Klan* (1975 TVM); *Brotherhood of Death* (1976); *Undercover with the KKK* (aka *The Freedom Riders; My Undercover Years with the KKK*) (1979 TVM); *In the Homeland* (1987 TVM); *Betrayed* (1988); *Mississippi Burning* (1988); *Unconquered* (1989 TVM); *Dead-Bang* (1989); *Cross of Fire* (1989 TVM); *Murder in Mississippi* (1990 TVM); *Line of Fire: The Morris Dees Story* (1991 TVM); *In the Line of Fire: Manhunt in the Dakotas* (1991 TVM); *Fried Green Tomatoes* (1992); *Romper Stomper* (1992); *Sommersby* (1993); *Highway of Heartache* (1994); *Sophie & the Moonhanger* (1995); *A Time to Kill* (1996); *The Chamber* (1996); *Ghosts of Mississippi* (1996); *Divided by Hate* (1997 TVM); *Rosewood* (1997); *Ambushed* (1998); *American History X* (1998)

Labor Unions and Strikes

The sight of defiant workers and waving picket signs can form powerful images capable of transcending the themes of even mediocre films. In the hands of a Sergei Eisenstein, the result can be chilling, as was the case with *Strike* (1924), the famed director's gripping account of a 1912 revolt against working conditions in Czarist Russia. Equally compelling was John Sayles' *Matewan* (1987), the fact-based story of a West Virginia coal mine labor dispute circa 1920 which erupted into violence and bloodletting. British films, such as 1944's *The Agitator* and 1960's *The Angry Silence*, have best explored the roles played by powerful individuals on both sides of the picket fence. The latter film concerned a worker ostracized by his peers for refusing to join the walkout. The British even satirized its labor problems with 1960's cunning farce *I'm All Right, Jack*. It was much more adroitly handled than 1958's *Never Steal Anything Small*, an uncomfortable American musical starring James Cagney as a crooked labor leader. In 1992, Jack Nicholson and James Woods starred in, respectively, the union leader biographies *Hoffa* and *Teamster Boss: The Jackie Presser Story*.

Strike (1924); *Metropolis* (1925); *The Guns of Loos* (1927); *The Revolt of the Fishermen* (1934); *Black Fury* (1935); *The Agitator* (1944); *The Whistle at Eaton Falls* (aka *Richer than the Earth*) (1951); *Salt of the Earth* (1953); *Inside Detroit* (1955); *The Garment Jungle* (1957); *The Pajama Game* (1957); *Chicago Confidential* (1957); *Never Steal Anything Small* (1958); *The Big Operator* (aka *Anatomy of a Syndicate*) (1959); *The Angry Silence* (1960); *I'm All Right, Jack* (1960); *Men of Brazil* (1960); *Flame in the Streets* (1961); *Jessica* (1962); *Adalen 31* (1969); *Ramparts of Clay* (1971); *Harlan County, U.S.A.* (1977); *Sleeping Dogs* (1977); *Blue Collar* (1978); *F.I.S.T.* (1978); *Norma Rae* (1979); *Keeping On* (1981); *Power* (1980 TVM); *The River* (1984); *A Matter of Sex* (1984 TVM); *The Killing Floor* (1984 TVM); *Matewan* (1987); *Last Exit to Brooklyn* (1989); *American Dream* (1989); *Teamster Boss: The Jackie Presser Story* (1992 TVM); *Hoffa* (1992); *The Replacements* (2000)

The Land Before Time Series

During the 1980s, Don Bluth challenged the Disney studios as the leading producer of quality theatrical animated films. While Disney struggled temporarily with less-than-stellar efforts like *The Black Cauldron* and *Oliver & Company*, Bluth scored three critical and popular hits. Bluth's *The Secret of NIMH* (1982) and *An American Tail* (1986) offered charming tales of mice families, while *The Land Before Time* (1988) tackled a far bigger subject with its adorable dinosaurs. The film boasted a strong pedigree

(Steven Spielberg and George Lucas were executive producers) and its release was perfectly timed to benefit from a "dinosaur craze" among U.S. youngsters. The premise owes a lot to *Bambi*—the film opens with the death of a young brontosaurus' mother. Littlefoot, the little dino, goes in search of the Great Valley, a land of peace described by his mother. Along the way, he befriends other young dinosaurs who join his quest: Cera, a triceratops; Ducky, an anatosaurus; Petrie, a pterodactyl; and Spike, a stegosaurus. This simple tale scored big at the box-office, although its success was eclipsed a year later when Disney revived its fortunes with *The Little Mermaid*. Bluth continued to make animated films throughout the 1990s, but he never again mounted a serious challenge against Disney. In 1994, MCA Home Entertainment released *The Land Before Time II: The Great Valley Adventure* directly to videotape. It did well enough to warrant additional series entries, though none of these videotapes captured the rich color and detail of the original film. See also **Animated Films (Feature Length)**; **Dinosaurs**.

The Land Before Time (1988); *The Land Before Time II: The Great Valley Adventure* (1994); *The Land Before Time III: The Time of the Great Giving* (1995); *The Land Before Time IV: The Journey Through the Mists* (1996); *The Land Before Time V: The Mysterious Island* (1997); *The Land Before Time VI: The Secret of Saurus Rock* (1998)

Lassie

The caring collie made her debut in 1943's *Lassie, Come Home*, one of the finest of all dog (q.v.) movies. Eric Knight wrote the original novel about a family forced to part with its cherished collie, which manages to overcome all obstacles and return to them. The MGM cast was an exceptional one: established child star Roddy McDowell, promising 11-year-old Elizabeth Taylor, plus adults Donald Crisp, Nigel Bruce, and Elsa Lanchester. Pal, a male collie, played Lassie. Donald Crisp, Nigel Bruce, and Pal returned in the 1945 follow-up *Son of Lassie*, with Peter Lawford and June Lockhart (shades of foreshadowing) playing adult versions of McDowell and Taylor. Elizabeth Taylor was back, however, for the following year's *Courage of Lassie*, a confusing entry in which the dog (played by Pal again) was actually called Bill, not Lassie. Fortunately, Lassie was Lassie in 1948's *The Hills of Home*, a colorful entry that reunited Crisp and the collie and featured the always enjoyable Edmund Gwenn and a young Janet Leigh. MGM's last three *Lassie* entries were unremarkable programmers, although 1949's *The Sun Comes Up* was notable as Jeanette MacDonald's final film appearance. In 1954, Lassie embarked on a long-running, immensely popular TV series. During the original 1954–71 *Lassie* run, the collie was paired with an assortment of owners, including Jeff (Tommy Rettig), Timmy and his Mom (Jon Provost and June Lockhart), and Corey the forest ranger (Robert Bray). Several TV series episodes were edited together for a theatrical feature called *Lassie's Great Adventure* (1963). *The Magic of Lassie* (1978) and *Lassie* (1994) attempted to revive the courageous collie's career. But despite good casts, including James Stewart and Richard Farnsworth, these modest family films attracted little interest. See also **Dogs**.

Lassie, Come Home (1943); *Son of Lassie* (1945); *Courage of Lassie* (1946); *The Hills of Home* (1948); *Challenge for Lassie* (1949); *The Sun Comes Up* (1949); *The Painted Hills* (1951); *Lassie's Great Adventure* (1963); *The Magic of Lassie* (1978); *Lassie* (1994)

Lemon Popsicle Series

Former Cannon Films moguls Menahem Golan and Yorum Globus produced this Israeli series of nostalgic teen sex comedies. The films proved to be immensely popular in Europe, inspiring Cannon to produce an Americanized version in 1981, appropriately titled *The Last American Virgin*. Boaz Davidson directed this variation as well as the first four *Popsicle* films.

Lemon Popsicle (aka *Eskimo Limon*) (1978); *Lemon Popsicle II* (aka *Yotz im Kavua*; *Greasy Kids Stuff*; *Going Steady*) (1979); *Lemon Popsicle III: Let's Go to Paris* (aka *Shifshuf Naim*; *Hot Bubblegum*) (1980); *The Last American Virgin* (1981); *Lemon Popsicle IV* (aka *Sapihes*; *Private Popsicle*) (1982); *Lemon Popsicle V* (aka *Roman Za'ir*; *Baby Love*) (1983); *Lemon Popsicle VI* (aka *Ha-Rimu Ogen*; *Up Your Anchor*) (1984); *Lemon Popsicle VII* (aka *Ahava Tzeira*; *Young Love*) (1987)

Leprechaun Series

Writer-director Mark Jones deserves credit for a novel idea, if nothing else. In 1993's *Leprechaun*, he transformed one of the Irish pranksters into a wise-cracking killer from the Freddy Krueger school of slasher movie villains. Warwick Davis headlined as a 600-year-old leprechaun who travels to North Dakota in a suitcase in search of his stolen gold coins. He kills several people in supposedly humorous ways (e.g., after dispatching a coin collector with a pogo stick, the leprechaun quips: "He'll bounce back in no time"). He meets his end when a young boy shoots a four-leaf clover wrapped around a piece of gum in the leprechaun's mouth. Apparently, moviegoers found the idea of a nasty leprechaun amusing, for *Leprechaun* turned into a sleeper hit. It also introduced viewers to Jennifer Aniston, who would find far greater fame a year later on the TV series *Friends*. The remaining films in the *Leprechaun* series neither boasted famous alumni nor qualified as sleeper hits. Instead, they followed the first film's formula, with the leprechaun either seeking a bride or trying to recover his gold. As with the *Nightmare on Elm Street* series (q.v.), the emphasis on humor increased with each entry—in *Leprechaun 3*, the Irish prankster even encounters an unlucky Elvis impersonator. The three-feet, four-inch Davis played the title character in all four films. Davis is probably best-known for his role as Willow Ufgood in Ron Howard's 1988 fantasy *Willow*. See also **Little People**.

Leprechaun (1993); *Leprechaun 2* (aka *One Wedding and a Lot of Funerals*) (1994); *Leprechaun 3* (1995); *Leprechaun 4 in Space* (aka *Leprechaun 4*) (1997); *A Very Unlucky Leprechaun* (1998); *Leprechaun in the Hood* (2000)

L.E.T.H.A.L. Ladies *see* Malibu Express

Lethal Weapon Series

The continuing popularity of a film series almost always hinges on its ability to evolve over time. Even the Bond films modified their popular formula by emphasizing gadgetry and humor significantly more as the series progressed. On a smaller scale, the four *Lethal Weapons* films have evolved from their original intent. That may explain why they have thrived at the box-office, while a *48 HRS.* sequel received a series-killing, lukewarm reception. In the first *Lethal Weapon* (1987), detective Roger Murtaugh (Danny Glover), a stable, black family man, gets a new partner in the white, single, and dangerously short-fused Martin Riggs (Mel Gibson). As they bicker their way through the inevitable shoot-outs and explosions, Murtaugh and Riggs acquire mutual respect for one another. It's a classic buddy action film (q.v.) premise. The formula was altered for 1989's *Lethal Weapon 2*, which stressed character development and humor, while still maintaining enough fist fights and gunplay to please action fans. Joe Pesci provided most of the laughs, with a hyperactive turn as Leo Getz, a money-laundering bank accountant requiring witness protection from the detective odd couple. Pesci popped up again in *Lethal Weapon 3* (1992), which introduced Rene Russo as a karate-kicking internal affairs investigator who catches Riggs' eye. Their unusual romance, Glover's easygoing charm, and Pesci's comic outbursts generated $80 million in North American box-office rentals. The whole gang—Gibson, Glover, Pesci, and Russo—returned six years later for *Lethal Weapon 4*. Despite the addition of sharp-tongued comedian Chris Rock and martial artist Jet Li, this formulaic entry lacked the box-office sizzle of its predecessors. The *Lethal Weapon* films were spoofed, with mediocre results, in 1993's *National Lampoon's Loaded Weapon 1*. See also **Buddy Action Films**.

Lethal Weapon (1987); *Lethal Weapon 2* (1989); *Lethal Weapon 3* (1992); *Lethal Weapon 4* (1998)

Letters

Letters have brought lovers together, torn marriages apart, incriminated the innocent, blackmailed the guilty, and caused endless misunderstandings. Pen pals James Stewart and Margaret Sullavan fell in love through their letters, not realizing they were coworkers in *The Shop Around the Corner* (1940). A little girl sent her mother's photo to her lonely soldier pen pal in *Never Say Goodbye* (1946), never suspecting that he would come visiting. Similar pen pal deceptions occurred in 1945's *A Letter for Evie* and the 1947 hit comedy *Dear Ruth* (q.v.). One cannot always be certain of the identity of a letter's author. Cyrano de Bergerac (Jose Ferrer) wrote poignant love letters to the beautiful Roxanne, but signed the name of his hapless friend Christian in the 1950 adaptation of Edmund Rostand's celebrated play. Jennifer Jones suffered amnesia in *Love Letters* (1945) after learning that her wartime love letters were not written by her fiancé. The deceiving letters penned by the devious Marquise de Merteuil (Glenn Close) in *Dangerous Liaisons* (1988) eventually led to the death of her lover (John Malkovich). Celeste Holm provided the voice of the authoress of *A Letter to Three Wives* (1949), in which three ladies learn that one of their husbands has run off with Holm's character. Paul Lukas played a converted Nazi incriminated by false letters sent by a former friend in *Address Unknown* (1944). Loretta Young tried to retrieve another incriminating letter, one framing her for murder, in 1951's *Cause for Alarm*. Pat Boone was similarly panic-stricken over a hard-to-retrieve letter in the British comedy *Never Put It in Writing* (1964). An unsigned love note dropped into a high school locker revealed numerous hidden feelings in the pleasant 1985 comedy *Secret Admirer*. Misdirected letters reaching their destination after a year-long delay provided the premise for the three-part TV movie *The Letters* and its sequel *Letters from Three Lovers* (both 1973). *84 Charing Cross Road* (1987) traced the charming 20-year letter-writing relationship between a New York book lover (Anne Bancroft) and a British book dealer (Anthony Hopkins). See also **Dear Ruth Series**; **Postal Workers**.

The Strong Man (1926); *Poison Pen* (1939); *The Shop Around the Corner* (1940); *The Letter* (1940); *Le Corbeau* (aka *The Raven*) (1943); *Address Unknown* (1944); *Love Letters* (1945); *A Letter for Evie* (1945); *Never Say Goodbye* (1946); *The Captive Heart* (1946); *Dear Ruth* (1947); *The Lost Moment* (1947); *Letter from an Unknown Woman* (1948); *A Letter to Three Wives* (1949); *Cyrano de Bergerac* (1950); *Cause for Alarm* (1951); *The 13th Letter* (1951); *Demoniaque* (1958); *Fate Takes a Hand* (1961); *Never Put It in Writing* (1964); *Dear Brigitte* (1965); *The Go-Between* (1971); *The Letters* (1973 TVM); *Letters from Three Lovers* (1973 TVM); *No Sex Please, We're British* (1973); *Dirty Tricks* (1980); *Touched by Love* (aka *To Elvis, with Love*) (1980); *The Letter* (1982 TVM); *Love Letters* (aka *My Love Letters*) (1983); *A Letter to Three Wives* (1985 TVM); *Secret Admirer* (1985); *84 Charing Cross Road* (1987); *Dear America: Letters Home from Vietnam* (1987 TVM); *Dangerous Liaisons* (1988); *The Anonymous Letter* (aka *El Anonimo*) (1990); *The Love She Sought* (1990 TVM); *Dear God* (1996); *The Daytrippers* (1996); *Central Station* (1998); *The Love Letter* (1998 TVM); *Message in a Bottle* (1999); *Love Letters* (1999 TVM); *The Love Letter* (1999); *Sealed with a Kiss* (1999 TVM); *Mermaid* (2000 TVM); *Reindeer Games* (2000)

Levinson's Baltimore Series

Writer-director Barry Levinson has made four films set in his hometown of Baltimore, Maryland, during the 1950s and 1960s. Although connected only by their shared setting and time period, the quartet of films are often referred to as a series. *Diner* (1982), which marked Levinson's debut as a writer-director, focused on the lives of five young men contemplating life and a Baltimore Colts football championship during the final week of December 1959. The title characters in *Tin Men* (1987) were two rival aluminum siding salesmen (Danny DeVito and Richard Dreyfuss) who sold their products in Baltimore in 1963. The semiautobiographical *Avalon* (1990) spanned several decades of a family's life in Baltimore, although much of it took place during the 1950s and revolved around a family business that capitalized on the growing sales of television sets. Finally, *Liberty Heights* (1999) focused on a Jewish family in Baltimore in 1954 that dealt with race and religious issues.

Diner (1984); *Tin Men* (1987); *Avalon* (1990); *Liberty Heights* (1999)

Librarians

It's been difficult for movie librarians to move away from their stereotyped image as shy, conservative bookworms. Despite their star power, Greer Garson (*Adventure*), June Allyson (*Good News*), Shirley Jones (*The Music Man*), and Barbara Eden (*The Seven Faces of Dr. Lao*) did little to alter the stereotyping. In contrast, Bette Davis portrayed a fiery librarian fired for her refusal to censor a book on communism in 1956's *Storm Center*. Jewish college dropout–turned–librarian Richard Benjamin ignored social conventions in his pursuit of country club heiress Ali MacGraw in the film version of Philip Roth's frank best-seller *Goodbye, Columbus* (1969). Meek librarian Jason Robards, Jr., turned out to be the only person in town with enough courage and will power to confront the mysterious Mr. Dark in Ray Bradbury's chilling, turn-of-the-century fantasy *Something Wicked This Way Comes* (1983). In the 1974 oddity *Mr. Sycamore*, Robards played a mail-

man with a crush on librarian Jean Simmons and a bizarre desire to become a tree.

Scandal Street (1938); *Adventure* (1945); *Good News* (1947); *Katie Did It* (1951); *Elephant Walk* (1954); *Storm Center* (1956); *Desk Set* (aka *His Other Woman*) (1957); *The Music Man* (1962); *Only Two Can Play* (1962); *The Seven Faces of Dr. Lao* (1964); *Goodbye, Columbus* (1969); *Mr. Sycamore* (1974); *Celine and Julie Go Boating* (1974); *Something Wicked This Way Comes* (1983); *Off Beat* (1986); *The Gun in Betty Lou's Handbag* (1992); *Tale of a Vampire* (1993); *The Pagemaster* (1994); *Daisies in December* (1995 TVM); *The Sphinx* (aka *Le Sphinx*) (1995); *Necronomicon: Book of the Dead* (1996); *The Mummy* (1999); *Where the Heart Is* (2000)

Lighthouses

Not surprisingly, horror and fantasy films have made the best use of lighthouse settings. The Rhedosaurus in *The Beast from 20,000 Fathoms* (1953) attacked a lighthouse in a sequence adapted from Ray Bradbury's short story "The Foghorn." Adrienne Barbeau operated a lighthouse radio station in John Carpenter's *The Fog* (1980)—at least until pirate ghosts with grappling hooks forced her to abandon the broadcast booth and seek refuge on the top of the cylindrical structure. People-eating plants harassed lighthouse resident Janette Scott in 1963's *Day of the Triffids*. She discovered that, like most plants, triffids don't care for salt water. In fantasy films, a lighthouse played a prominent role during the climactic storm in *Portrait of Jennie* (1948) and Michael Redgrave's life changed for the better after experiencing ghostly visions in his lighthouse home in *Thunder Rock* (1942). The dull side of lighthouse living was displayed in *The Light at the Edge of the World* (1971), in which lighthouse keeper Kirk Douglas fights boring pirates (led by Yul Brynner) for the affections of boring Samantha Eggar. The sweet side found Shirley Temple brightening up lighthouse-keeper Guy Kibbee's life in *Captain January* (1936).

Lighthouse by the Sea (1925); *Captain January* (1936); *Sh! The Octopus* (1938); *Thunder Rock* (1942); *Seven Miles from Alcatraz* (1942); *A Stolen Life* (1946); *Portrait of Jennie* (1948); *The Beast from 20,000 Fathoms* (1953); *The Monster of Piedras Blancas* (1958); *A Summer Place* (1959); *Tormented* (1960); *Day of the Triffids* (1963); *Sandy the Seal* (1969); *The Light at the Edge of the World* (1971); *Pete's Dragon* (1977); *The Fog* (1980); *Eye of the Needle* (1981); *Final Analysis* (1992); *Dead of Night* (aka *Lighthouse*) (1999)

Lightning

The most common uses of lightning in the cinema have been to restore life and destroy life. In the former category, James Whales' *Frankenstein* (1931) serves as the best example of a film where a mad scientist used lightning to create a "monster." *The Ghost of Frankenstein* (1942), a routine entry in the same Frankenstein series (q.v.), warrants mention for a truly bizarre scene of the monster enjoying himself as lightning strikes his electrodes repeatedly. Lightning restored life to an evil Spanish conquistador in *Giant from the Unknown* (1958), a friendly caveman in *Dinosaurus!* (1960), and even that famous hockey-masked killer in *Friday the 13th, Part VI: Jason Lives* (1986). It also struck a nice little robot and brought it to life in *Short Circuit* (1986). Lightning even played a key role in somehow transferring a serial killer's soul into a mainframe computer in *Ghost in the Machine* (1993). In contrast, several films have used lightning for lethal purposes. In *Scars of Dracula* (1970), the vampire count (Christopher Lee) is struck by lightning (and set ablaze) when he pulls a poorly-thrown iron stake from his stomach. A sudden bolt provides quite a jolt at the climax of *The Bad Seed* (1956). A young man with mysterious powers loses his mother to a stroke of lightning and becomes a human lightning rod himself in *Powder* (1995). Lightning hit the cockpit of a Boeing 747 in *Panic in the Skies* (1996) and an airborne dirigible in Cecil B. DeMille's *Madame Satan* (1930). Of course, lightning has not always been used for life and death purposes. In *Just Imagine* (1930), a man is struck by lighting in 1930 and awakens to find himself in 1980. In contrast, a lightning bolt sends Tyrone Power into the past in the romantic *I'll Never Forget You* (1951). Christopher Lambert played the Lightning God, Lord Rayden, in the film version of the video game *Mortal Kombat* (1995). Roy Hobbs (Robert Redford) cut his "Wonderboy" bat from a tree struck by lightning in the baseball parable *The Natural* (1984). Aidan Quinn played a man who was hit by lightning after questioning God in *Commandments* (1997). Several traveling salesmen have sold lightning rods in movies such as *The Rainmaker* (1956) and *Something Wicked This Way Comes* (1983). Peter Greenaway's 25-minute documentary *Act of God* (1980) was about people struck by lightning. See also **Hurricanes and Tornadoes**.

Madame Satan (1930); *Just Imagine* (1930); *Frankenstein* (1931); *The Ghost of Frankenstein* (1942); *I'll Never Forget You* (aka *The House in the Square*) (1951); *The Bad Seed* (1956); *Giant from the Unknown* (1958); *Dinosaurus!* (1960); *Scars of Dracula* (1970); *The Natural* (1984); *Friday the 13th, Part VI: Jason Lives* (1986); *Short Circuit* (1986); *Lightning Field* (aka *The Lightning Incident*) (1991 TVM); *Ghost in the Machine* (1993); *Mortal Kombat* (1995); *Powder* (1995); *Panic in the Skies* (1996 TVM); *Commandments* (1997)

Lions and Tigers

The big cats have alternated effectively between roles as cuddly, playful felines and vicious, merciless maneaters. In the former category, one must begin with Bert Lahr's lovable Cowardly Lion from *The Wizard of Oz* (1939), who was too afraid to be ferocious ("I'm just a dandy lion"). In the wonderful screwball comedy *Bringing Up Baby* (1938), Katharine Hepburn "lost" Baby, her pet leopard. This required Cary Grant and her to roam through the woods singing the big cat's favorite tune: "I can't give you anything but love, Baby." *Fluffy* and *Clarence, the Cross-Eyed Lion* (both 1965) were harmless pets, too, though their tendency to frighten strangers provided much of the films' humor. Clarence was even popular enough to warrant his own 1966–69 TV series, *Daktari*. However, as its title suggests, the series devoted more time to Clarence's veterinarian (q.v.) owner Marshall Thompson. Lions have been the frequent subjects of both live-action and animated Disney films, to include: *The Jungle Book* (1967), *Charlie, the Lonesome Cougar* (1968), *Napoleon and Samantha* (1972), and its 1993 blockbuster *The Lion King*. Real-life lions probably peaked in popularity with the release of 1966's family hit *Born Free*, the engrossing true story of a husband and wife's efforts to train their domesticated lioness to fend for herself in the wilds of Africa. A belated sequel, *Living Free*, followed in 1972, accompanied two years later by a short-lived *Born Free* TV series. In contrast to these friendly lions, other features, such as 1981's *Savage Harvest*, have portrayed big cats as powerful, silent killers

stalking their prey. Escaped animals in urban settings have proven to be a continuing problem ever since a black leopard slipped away from Jean Brooks during a publicity stunt in 1943's *The Leopard Man*. Films employing a similar premise include 1964's *A Tiger Walks* and two 1978 TV movies, *Maneaters are Loose!* and *The Beasts are on the Streets*. The 1953 jungle adventure *Bwana Devil* introduced the cinema's first 3-D cat and promised to "put a lion in your lap." Stop-action animator Ray Harryhausen created a saber-toothed tiger for his colorful fantasy *Sinbad and the Eye of the Tiger* (1977). No discussion of big cats would be complete without mentioning the animated pencil-thin panther with the pink skin that hams his way through the opening credits of Blake Edwards' *Pink Panther* (q.v.) films. See also **Cats**.

The Extra Girl (1923); *Sequoia* (aka *Malibu*) (1934); *East of Java* (1935); *Bringing Up Baby* (1938); *The Wizard of Oz* (1939); *The Jungle Book* (1942); *The Leopard Man* (1943); *Maneater of Kumaon* (1948); *Samson and Delilah* (1949); *Androcles and the Lion* (1952); *Fearless Fagan* (1952); *The Lion and the Horse* (1952); *Track of the Cat* (1954); *The African Lion* (1955); *Cat Girl* (1957); *The Flute and the Arrow* (1957); *Harry Black and the Tiger* (aka *Harry Black*) (1958); *Jungle Cat* (1960); *Ursus in the Valley of Lions* (1961); *The Lion* (1962); *Rampage* (1963); *A Tiger Walks* (1964); *Fluffy* (1965); *Clarence, the Cross-Eyed Lion* (1965); *Born Free* (1966); *The Cat* (aka *Cat!*) (1966); *The Jungle Book* (1967); *Charlie, the Lonesome Cougar* (1968); *Living Free* (1972); *Napoleon and Samantha* (1972); *Maneater* (1973 TVM); *When the North Wind Blows* (1974); *Christian the Lion* (1976); *Sinbad and the Eye of the Tiger* (1977); *Maneaters are Loose!* (1978 TVM); *The Beasts are on the Streets* (1978 TVM); *Night Creature* (aka *Out of the Darkness*) (1978); *Savage Harvest* (1981); *The White Lions* (1981); *Cheetah and Friends* (aka *Cheetah*) (1989); *Running Wild* (1992); *The Lion King* (1994); *Jumanji* (1995); *The Ghost and the Darkness* (1996); *The Leopard Son* (1996); *Fast, Cheap & Out of Control* (1997); *The Lion King: Simba's Pride* (1998)

Little House on the Prairie Series

Michael Landon executive produced and starred in the 1974 TV movie *Little House on the Prairie*, a wholesome drama about a pioneer family based on the writings of Laura Ingalls Wilder. The telefilm spawned a very successful 1974–83 TV series which featured Landon as Charles Ingalls, Karen Grassle as his wife Caroline, and Melissa Gilbert and Melissa Sue Anderson as daughters Laura and Mary. Twins Lindsay and Sidney Greenbush alternated as the youngest child Carrie. The show's characters evolved significantly over the years (e.g., Mary went blind; daughter Grace was born) and Landon left the series in 1982 (the title changing to *Little House: A New Beginning*). Without Landon, the series folded — only to be revived in the form of three TV movie "specials." Landon directed and appeared in the first and third postseries pictures. The town of Walnut Grove was blown up in *The Last Farewell*, leaving Landon free to play an angel in his *Highway to Heaven* series. See also **Television Series Reunion Films**.

Little House on the Prairie (1974 TVM); *Little House on the Prairie: Look Back to Yesterday* (1983 TVM); *Little House: Bless All the Dear Children* (1984 TVM); *Little House: The Last Farewell* (1984 TVM)

Little People

They come in all sizes — they may be as minute as an atom or as tall as four feet. So, in that aspect, little people is a pretty big category. The tiniest person was probably *The Incredible Shrinking Man*. At the conclusion of Richard Matheson's philosophical 1957 sci-fi film, the hero continues to shrink until he can literally see atomic particles. In both *Fantastic Voyage* and *Innerspace*, people are reduced in size until they can be injected into the bloodstreams of normal-sized folks. Considerably bigger, say around three or four inches in height, are the scientists in *Dr. Cyclops*, the Lilliputians in film adaptations of *Gulliver's Travels*, and the title character in *tom thumb*. *Dr. Cyclops* has evolved into something of a cult classic, being the first picture in which little people are harassed by a cat, a chicken, raindrops, and the like. Finally, there are the "little people" of folklore: leprechauns, gnomes, and mischievous dwarfs. They have appeared in numerous movies, typically in charming, playful roles. Of course, not all movies involving little people are fantastic in nature. In *The Tin Drum*, a child injures himself (becoming a dwarf) so that he can never grow up. Dwarf-sized killers figure prominently in Nicholas Roeg's *Don't Look Now* and David Cronenberg's bizarre chiller *The Brood*. See also **The Alilenas**; **Giants**; **Honey, I Shrunk the Kids Series**; **Leprechaun Series**; **Phantasm Series**.

MICROSCOPIC PEOPLE: *Fantastic Voyage* (1966); *Innerspace* (1987)

UNDER TWELVE INCHES: *The Devil Doll* (1936); *Gulliver's Travels* (1939); *Dr. Cyclops* (1940); *Peter Pan* (1953); *Girl in His Pocket* (1957); *The Incredible Shrinking Man* (1957); *Attack of the Puppet People* (1958); *The Seventh Voyage of Sinbad* (1958); *tom thumb* (1958); *The Three Worlds of Gulliver* (1960); *Babes in Toyland* (1961); *Mothra* (aka *Mosura*) (1962); *Ghidrah the Three-Headed Monster* (aka *The Greatest Battle on Earth*; *Sandai Kaiju Chikyu Saidai No Kessen*) (1965); *Help!* (1965); *The Borrowers* (1973 TVM); *Don't Be Afraid of the Dark* (1973 TVM); *Gulliver's Travels* (1977); *The Incredible Shrinking Woman* (1981); *Here Come the Littles* (1985); *Honey, I Shrunk the Kids* (1989); *Dollman* (1991); *FernGully...The Last Rainforest* (aka *FernGully*) (1992); *The Pagemaster* (1994); *Hans Christian Andersen's Thumbelina* (1994); *Gulliver's Travels* (1996 TVM); *Fairy Tale: A True Story* (1997); LEPRECHAUNS AND GNOMES: *The Luck of the Irish* (1948); *Darby O'Gill and the Little People* (1959); *Jack the Giant Killer* (1962); *The Gnomemobile* (1967); *Even Dwarfs Started Small* (1968); *Finian's Rainbow* (1968); *Getting Lucky* (1990); *Leprechaun* (1993); *A Gnome Named Gnorm* (1994); *Leapin' Leprechauns!* (1995); *Spellbreaker: Secret of the Leprechauns* (1996); DWARFS AND MIDGETS; *The Unholy Three* (1925); *The Unholy Three* (1930); *Freaks* (1932); *Snow White and the Seven Dwarfs* (1937); *The Terror of Tiny Town* (1938); *It's a Small World* (1950); *Ship of Fools* (1965); *Don't Look Now* (1973); *Little Cigars* (1973); *The Brood* (1979); *The Tin Drum* (1979); *Phantasm* (1979); *Under the Rainbow* (1981); *Time Bandits* (1981); *Dance of the Dwarfs* (aka *Jungle Heat*) (1983); *The Sign of Four* (1983); *Rumpelstiltskin* (aka *Cannon Movie Tales: Rumpelstiltskin*) (1987); *Snow White* (aka *Cannon Movie Tales: Snow White*) (1987); *Willow* (1988); *I Don't Want to Talk About It* (1994); *Frankie Starlight* (1995); *Austin Powers: The Spy Who Shagged Me* (1999)

The Little Tough Guys *see* The Bowery Boys

The Living Dead *see* Ghouls; Night of the Living Dead Series

The Lone Rider

After years of playing Stony in *The Three Mesquiteers* movies (q.v.), veteran cowboy actor Robert Livingston got his own series

courtesy of Producers Releasing Corporation (PRC). Livingston played Rocky Cameron, also known as The Lone Rider — an odd *nom de plume* since he was always accompanied by Al St. John as his sidekick Fuzzy. Rocky and Fuzzy battled Nazi agents (*Wild Horse Rustlers*), a crooked sheriff (*Law of the Saddle*), and various outlaws during this brief B-western series.

Overland Stagecoach (1942); *Wolves of the Range* (1943); *Wild Horse Rustlers* (1943); *Raiders of Red Gap* (1944); *Law of the Saddle* (1944); *Death Rides the Plains* (1944)

The Lone Wolf

Michael Lanyard, better known as The Lone Wolf, was a jewel thief–turned-detective created by Louis Joseph Vance in 1914. The character led a lively screen life, being played by eight actors over a span of 29 years. Bert Lytell (a one-time Boston Blackie) starred as Lanyard in five silent films, starting with 1917's *The Lone Wolf*. Other actors followed in his footsteps, including Jack Holt and Henry B. Walthall. However, it was Lytell who returned to the role one last time for the first Lone Wolf "talkie," 1930's *Last of the Lone Wolf*. Five years later, Melvyn Douglas made a promising debut as Lanyard in Columbia's *The Lone Wolf Returns*. With Douglas too much in demand for other roles, Czech import Francis Lederer took over for 1938's *The Lone Wolf in Paris*. He was replaced the following year by Warren William in *The Lone Wolf Spy Hunt*. William, a veteran "gentleman detective," had previously played both Philo Vance (q.v.) and Perry Mason (q.v.). He was an actor in search of a role to call his own — and he found it with Michael Lanyard. William made nine *Lone Wolf* films, with Eric Blore providing reliable comedy relief as his valet/sidekick. The series was a showcase for promising Columbia starlets and William's leading ladies included Rita Hayworth and Ida Lupino. William retired from the series after 1943's *Passport to Suez*. Gerald Mohr played Lanyard in three films during 1946–47 and ex–Bulldog Drummond (q.v.) Ron Randell starred in the series finale, 1949's *The Lone Wolf and His Lady*. Like most B-movie detectives, the Lone Wolf found a home on television, where Louis Hayward played him in a 39-episode 1953 series known as both *The Lone Wolf* and *Streets of Danger*. See also **Jewel Thieves**.

The Lone Wolf (1917) (Bert Lytell); *False Faces* (1919) (Lytell); *The Lone Wolf Returns* (1926) (Lytell); *Alias the Lone Wolf* (1927) (Lytell); *The Lone Wolf's Daughter* (1929) (Lytell); *Last of the Lone Wolf* (1930) (Lytell); *Cheaters at Play* (1932) (Thomas Meighan); *The Lone Wolf Returns* (1935) (Melvin Douglas); *The Lone Wolf in Paris* (1938) (Francis Lederer); *The Lone Wolf's Spy Hunt* (1939) (Warren William); *The Lone Wolf Meets a Lady* (1940) (William); *The Lone Wolf Strikes* (1940) (William); *The Lone Wolf Keeps a Date* (1941) (William); *The Lone Wolf Takes a Chance* (1941) (William); *Secrets of the Lone Wolf* (1941) (William); *Counter-Espionage* (1942) (William); *One Dangerous Night* (1943) (William); *Passport to Suez* (1943) (William); *The Notorious Lone Wolf* (1946) (Gerald Mohr); *The Lone Wolf in London* (1947) (Mohr); *The Lone Wolf in Mexico* (1947) (Mohr); *The Lone Wolf and His Lady* (1949) (Ron Randell)

Lone Wolf and Cub

A samurai-for-hire that pushes around his son in a baby cart rigged with hidden weapons? That's the premise of this acclaimed Japanese film series, based on the popular manga (Japanese comic books) written by Kazuo Koike and illustrated by Goseki Kojima in the 1970s. The first film *Sword of Vengeance* introduces Tomisaburo Wakayama as Ogami Itto, the official executioner of the Tokugawa Shogunate. Unfortunately, the evil Yagyu Clan covets Ogami's position as second-in-command to the Shogun. The Yagyu frame the samurai as a traitor and kill his family — except for infant son Daigoro. Ogami becomes a "ronin," a samurai without a master, willing to kill anyone for 500 pieces of gold. He also seeks vengeance against the Yagyu as he journeys throughout Japan, pushing his son in a booby-trapped baby cart. *Sword of Vengeance* is a stylish, very bloody samurai epic that provides the foundation for the rest of the series, particularly in a key father-son scene where Ogami has Daigoro choose between a ball and a sword. If the boy selects the ball, then he dies — joining his mother in the "Void." If he selects the sword, then he joins his father in a life of killing. Fans of the Lone Wolf and Cub series generally consider the second film, *Baby Cart at the River Styx*, to be the best. It pits Ogami against a clan of lethal female ninja and three martial arts masters known as the Gods of Death (some fans believe these latter villains provided the inspiration for the Three Storms in John Carpenter's *Big Trouble in Little China*). For their U.S. release in the early 1980s, the six Lone Wolf and Cub films were edited into two dubbed features: *Shogun Assassin* and *Lightning Swords of Death*. The films featured narration by little Daigoro to cover plot holes created by the editing process. The six original films were finally released in the U.S. on videotape in 1997. See also **Comic Book Characters**.

Lone Wolf and Cub: Sword of Vengeance (aka *Kozure Ôkami: Kowokashi udekashi tsukamatsuru*; *Sword of Vengeance*) (1972); *Lone Wolf and Cub: Baby Cart at the River Styx* (aka *Kozure Ôkami: Sanzu no kawa no ubaguruma*; *Sword of Vengeance II*) (1972); *Lone Wolf and Cub: Baby Cart to Hades* (aka *Kozure Ôkami: Shinikazeni mukau ubaguruma*; *Baby Cart to Hades*; *Sword of Vengeance III*) (1972); *Lone Wolf and Cub: In Peril* (aka *Kozure Ôkami: Oya no kokoro ko no kokoro*; *Baby Cart in Peril*; *Sword of Vengeance IV*) (1972); *Lone Wolf and Cub: Baby Cart in the Land of Demons* (aka *Kozure Ôkami: Meifumando*; *Baby Cart in the Land of Demons*; *Sword of Vengeance V*) (1973); *Lone Wolf and Cub: White Heaven in Hell* (aka *Kozure Ôkami: Jigoku e ikuzo! Daigoro*; *Baby Cart 6: Go to Hell, Daigoro!*; *Sword of Vengeance VI*) (1974)

Long Running Times

United States–released theatrical features with running times longer than three hours have been rare, especially prior to the 1950s. Erich Von Stroheim's original, unreleased version of his 1924 silent classic *Greed* fitted onto 42 reels (approximately nine hours worth of film). MGM production head Irving Thalberg insisted on cuts and Von Stroheim and friend Rex Ingram deleted six reels of footage. Still not satisfied, Thalberg hired June Mathis to cut eight more reels. By the time it was released, *Greed* boasted a scant 150 minutes. Existing prints run even shorter at 110 minutes. Amazingly, just four years later, Von Stroheim made *The Wedding March*, which clocked in at 196 minutes. It was released in two parts and failed miserably at the box-office. Leni Riefenstahl's *Olympia*, an epic documentary of the 1936 Olympic Games in Berlin, was also released in two parts (118 minutes and 107 minutes). However, MGM released all 179 minutes of 1936's *The Great Ziegfeld* in one lump sum. This biopic of legendary showman Flo Ziegfeld ranked as Hollywood's longest talkie film until *Gone with the Wind* (yet another MGM release) topped it by 41

minutes in 1939. Despite *GWTW's* success, Hollywood refrained from overwhelming wartime audiences with lengthy films. Short features cost less and made tidy profits. The studios' perspective changed, though, in the 1950s when television was seen as a growing threat to theatrical movies. Gimmicks such as 3-D (q.v.) and Cinemascope came into vogue, and so did lengthy theatrical epics. In 1956 alone, *The Ten Commandants*, *Giant*, and *War and Peace* were released. If a viewer watched them on a triple feature (thankfully they were never billed together), he'd be watching movies for over ten hours! This trend of long running times continued through the mid–1960s, with an average of two or three epic films being released yearly. No one genre dominated the releases, though Biblical pictures like *The Ten Commandments*, *Ben-Hur*, and *The Greatest Story Ever Told* seemed to hold an edge. Still, there were long war films *(The Longest Day)*, long comedies *(It's a Mad, Mad, Mad, Mad World)*, and long musicals *(Star!)*. The number of lengthy releases gradually decreased through the 1970s and 1980s, as budget-minded theater owners realized longer movies meant fewer showings and therefore less profit. Television's ability to broadcast multiple-part movies on successive nights also made it a desirable viewer alternative to sitting in a movie theatre for over three hours. Thus, as the miniseries thrived, the long movies faded. A final note: Many long films were trimmed after preview showings or their original releases and thus now exist in multiple versions. Various cuts of 1970's *Ryan's Daughter* run 206 minutes, 192 minutes, and 176 minutes. Only the original running times are listed below:

Greed (1924) 570m (approximately); *Napoleon* (1927) 235m; *The Wedding March* (1928) 196m; *Olympia* (aka *Olympische Spiele*) (1936) 225m; *The Great Ziegfeld* (1936) 179m; *Gone with the Wind* (1939) 220m; *Children of Paradise* (1944) 195m; *Aan* (aka *Savage Princess*) (1952) 190m; *The Seven Samurai* (1954) 200m; *A Star Is Born* (1954) 181m; *The Ten Commandments* (1956) 220m; *Giant* (1956) 201m; *War and Peace* (1956) 208m; *Raintree County* (1957) 187m; *Les Miserables* (1957) 210m; *Ben-Hur* (1959) 212m; *The Big Fisherman* (1959) 180m; *The Alamo* (1960) 192m; *Knights of the Teutonic Order* (1960) 180m; *Exodus* (1960) 213m; *Pepe* (1960) 195m; *Rocco and His Brothers* (1960) 180m; *Spartacus* (1960) 196m; *El Cid* (1961) 184m; *Judgment at Nuremberg* (1961) 190m; *The Longest Day* (1962) 180m; *Mutiny on the Bounty* (1962) 185m; *Cleopatra* (1962) 243m; *Lawrence of Arabia* (1962) 222m; *It's a Mad, Mad, Mad, Mad World* (1963) 192m; *The Leopard* (1963) 195m; *The Fall of the Roman Empire* (1964) 187m; *The Greatest Story Ever Told* (1965) 225m; *Dr. Zhivago* (1965) 180m; *Hawaii* (1966) 189m; *The Sand Pebbles* (1966) 193m; *Camelot* (1967) 180m; *Star!* (1968) 194m; *War and Peace* (1968) 373m; *Ryan's Daughter* (1970) 206m; *Nicholas and Alexander* (1971) 183m; *Fiddler on the Roof* (1971) 181m; *Ludwig* (1972) 246m; *The Iceman Cometh* (1973) 239m; *The Godfather Part II* (1974) 200m; *Barry Lyndon* (1975) 183m; *The Memory of Justice* (1976) 278m; *The Sorrow and the Pity* (1976) 260m; *1900* (1977) 243m (restored to 311m in 1991); *Mohammed, Messenger of God* (aka *The Message*) (1977) 180m; *Renaldo and Clara* (1978) 232m; *The Deer Hunter* (1978) 183m; *Heaven's Gate* (1980) 225m; *Reds* (1981) 199m; *Gandhi* (1982) 188m; *Fanny and Alexander* (1983) 197m; *The Right Stuff* (1983) 193m; *Once Upon a Time in America* (1984) 227m; *Shoah* (1985) 570m; *Little Dorrit* (1988) 360m *(Nobody's Fault* 182m/*Little Dorrit's Story* 178m); *Dances with Wolves* (1990) (183m); *At Play in the Fields of the Lord* (1991) 187m; *JFK* (1991) (188m); *Idiot* (1992) (185m); *Gettysburg* (1993) 254m; *Short Cuts* (1993) 189m; *Schindler's List* (1993) 185m; *Wyatt Earp* (1994) 189m; *My Sex Life…(Or How I Got into an Argument)* (aka *Comment Je Me Suis Dispute…Ma Vie*

Sexuelle) (1996) 178m; *Hamlet* (1996) 238m; *The Postman* (1997) 178m; *Titanic* (1997) 194m; *Meet Joe Black* (1998) 180m; *The Last Emperor* (1998 director's cut of 1987 original release) 219m; *The Green Mile* (1999) (187 m)

Long Titles

Long movie titles (ten words or more) have posed nightmarish problems to film publicists and theater owners. Imagine trying to get the complete 24-word title to Peter Brooks's *Marat/Sade* on a marquee at a multiscreen complex! To solve this obvious dilemma, most long-titled films have been given shorter alternate names. Thus, Lina Wertmuller's *Swept Away...by an unusual destiny in the blue sea of August* (1975) is more commonly referred to as simply *Swept Away*. Indeed, Wertmuller fans may be the only ones who know the film's full title. Not surprisingly, the reasons behind most long titles remain an ambiguous mystery. However, schlockmeister Roger Corman offers a simple explanation for the first 16-word American film title, 1957's *The Saga of the Viking Women and Their Voyage to the Waters of the Great Sea Serpent*. He claims that he came up with "the longest title in the history of motion pictures" because he was unable to think up a one or two word title to describe his film's plot. Corman's attitude toward the title was very tongue-in-cheek. He opened his film with a shot of a book's front page reading "The Saga of the Viking Women, etc." If Corman pioneered the long title, Stanley Kubrick made it fashionable by subtitling 1964's *Dr. Strangelove* as *Or, How I Learned to Stop Worrying and Love the Bomb*. Subsequently, alternate titles appeared on major studio pictures like Roman Polanski's *The Fearless Vampire Killers* (1967) and *Those Magnificent Men in Their Flying Machines* (1969). The banner year for long titles was 1967, with three lengthy ones averaging out to 17.7 words each. Long titles have been scarce since Lina Wertmuller turned more conventional in the late 1970s.

The Saga of the Viking Women and Their Voyage to the Waters of the Great Sea Serpent (aka *The Viking Women and the Sea Serpent*) (1957); *The Incredibly Strange Creatures Who Stopped Living and Became Mixed Up Zombies* (aka *The Teenage Psycho Meets Bloody Mary*) (1963); *Dr. Strangelove; or, How I Learned to Stop Worrying and Love the Bomb* (1964); *A Funny Thing Happened on the Way to the Forum* (1966); *The Fearless Vampire Killers; or Pardon Me, But Your Teeth Are in My Neck* (1967); *Oh Dad, Poor Dad, Mama's Hung You in the Closet and I'm Feeling So Sad* (1967); *The Persecution and Assassination of Jean-Paul Marat as Performed by the Inmates of the Asylum of Charenton Under the Direction of the Marquis de Sade* (aka *Marat/Sade*) (1967); *Those Magnificent Men in Their Flying Machines, or How I Flew from London to Paris in 25 Hours 11 Minutes* (aka *Those Magnificent Men in Their Flying Machines*) (1969); *Why Would Anyone Want to Kill a Nice Girl Like You?* (1969); *Can Hieronymus Merkin Ever Forget Mercy Humpe and Find True Happiness?* (1969); *Gas-s-s-s* (aka *Gas-s-s-s...Or, It May be Necessary to Destroy the World in Order to Save It*) (1970); *Who Is Harry Kellerman and Why Is He Saying Those Terrible Things About Me?* (1971); *You've Got to Walk It Like You Talk It or You'll Lose the Beat* (1971); *Everything You Always Wanted to Know About Sex* (*But Were Afraid to Ask*) (1972); *The Effect of Gamma Rays on Man-in-the-Moon Marigolds* (1972); *I Could Never Have Sex with Anyone Who Has So Little Respect for My Husband* (1973); *Swept Away...by an unusual destiny in the blue sea of August* (aka *Swept Away*) (1975); *Buffalo Bill and the Indians, or Sitting Bull's History Lesson* (1976); *The End of the World in Our Usual Bed in a Night Full of Rain* (aka *A Night Full of Rain*) (1978); *Come Back to the 5 &*

Dime, Jimmy Dean, Jimmy Dean (1982); *A Joke of Destiny in Wait Around the Corner Like a Bandit* (aka *A Joke of Destiny*) (1983); *Summer Night with Greek Profile, Almond Eyes, and Scent of Basil* (aka *Summer Night*) (1987); *The Return of the Six Million Dollar Man and the Bionic Woman* (1987 TVM); *The Decline of Western Civilization Part II: The Metal Years* (1988); *The Search for Signs of Intelligent Life in the Universe* (1991); *I Can Make You Love Me: The Stalking of Laura Black* (1993 TVM); *Don't Be a Menace to South Central While Drinking Juice in the Hood* (1995); *A Dream Is a Wish Your Heart Makes: The Annette Funicello Story* (1995 TVM); *Young Indiana Jones and the Treasure of the Peacock's Eye* (1995 TVM)

Longstocking, Pippi

Swedish children's author Astrid Lindgren introduced Pippi Longstocking, a rather unconventional nine-year-old orphan, in a 1945 novel. In all, she wrote three books about the pig-tailed, red-headed Pippi, who possesses superhuman strength, defies adults, and tells tall tales which may or may not be true (her father supposedly lives on an island as a "cannibal king"). Swedish director Olle Hellbron brought Pippi to the screen in the early 1970s in a four-film series starring Inger Nilsson. These movies rank as the most irritating and obnoxious children's films in cinema history. However, if viewed from the perspective of a pseudointellectual film critic, the *Pippi* pictures can be at least be appreciated as political statements on the advantages of anarchy. The Hellbron-Nilsson films were shot in 1969, but released over several years. A new, bigger-budgeted version appeared in 1988, complete with a publicized talent hunt for a new Pippi (Tami Erin). Despite energetic musical numbers and some familiar performers (e.g., Eileen Brennan), the new *Pippi* was not much of an improvement over the old Pippi. An animated version with Pippi voiced by Melissa Altro attracted little interest when released in 1997.

Pippi Longstocking (1969); *Pippi in the South Seas* (1970); *Pippi on the Run* (1970); *Pippi Goes on Board* (1971); *The New Adventures of Pippi Longstocking* (1988); *Pippi Longstocking* (1997)

Look Who's Talking Series

Between *Grease* (1978) and *Pulp Fiction* (1994), John Travolta experienced his share of box-office failures. One notable exception was 1989's *Look Who's Talking*, a one-joke movie in which the audience—but not the characters—could hear the thoughts of a cute, smart-alecky baby. Actually, the gimmick distracted slightly from the sweet romance between Kirstie Alley's single mom and John Travolta's good-natured cabbie. Still, Baby Mikey's quips as voiced by Bruce Willis were sometimes amusing. Surprisingly, the basic premise—a baby talking as an adult—was explored 29 years earlier in the British comedy *Bobbikins*. Travolta, Alley, and Willis returned for *Look Who's Talking Too* (1990), a redundant sequel that introduces Mikey's new sister Julie (voiced by Roseanne Barr). Despite poor reviews, a third entry, *Look Who's Talking Now* (1993), added "talking" dogs (voiced by Danny DeVito and Diane Keaton) to Travolta and Alley's family. It was Travolta's last film before his comeback in *Pulp Fiction*. In 1991, ABC tried to adapt *Look Who's Talking* into a sitcom called *Baby Talk*. The series was revamped almost as soon as it hit the air, with Julia Duffy replacing Mary Page Keller as Mikey's mother. Tony Danza provided the voice of Mikey. The TV series also featured George Clooney long before his fame on *ER*. See also **Babies**.

Look Who's Talking (1989); *Look Who's Talking Too* (1991); *Look Who's Talking Now* (1993)

Lookalikes

Although very similar to twins (q.v.), this category addresses movies with characters that look alike, but remain distinctly unrelated. The two most famous sets of movie lookalikes were adapted from Anthony Hope's *The Prisoner of Zenda* and Mark Twain's *The Prince and the Pauper*. In the oft-filmed *Prisoner of Zenda*, a gallant gentleman — a dead ringer for a recently kidnapped king — impersonates the monarch in order to save Ruritania. The 1988 *Moon Over Parador* borrowed the plot and updated it to contemporary Latin America. Twain's tale of a young prince who playfully trades places with a lookalike pauper has been filmed many times. The best adaptation was the rousing 1937 Errol Flynn version, but Disney fashioned an adequate remake and an all-star rendition appeared in 1978 under the deceiving title of *Crossed Swords*. In other films, lookalikes have been played for laughs or as part of devious espionage plots. Danny Kaye played lookalikes in both *On the Double* and *On the Riviera*, while Bob Hope was the spitting image of a clever secret agent in *My Favorite Spy*. Yul Brynner had dual roles in the overly-complicated thriller *The Double Man*, playing an East German mole who underwent plastic surgery (q.v.) and special grooming to replace a CIA agent. Sometimes, the government convinces actors (or ordinary lookalikes) to double for VIPs. Thus, the real Winston Churchill was not assassinated in *The Eagle Has Landed* and an actor was persuaded to pose as General Montgomery for diversion purposes in the World War II action picture *I Was Monty's Double*. That's also how space officials tried to cover up the death of an astronaut in the 1972 TV Movie *The Astronaut*. An interesting variation on the lookalike premise is the doppelgänger. Literally translated from the German as "double-goer," a doppelgänger is often a ghostly double of a living person. In the "William Wilson" segment of 1968's *Spirits of the Dead*, the protagonist murders the mysterious stranger who has been following him — only to find out it was himself. In the 1969 science fiction puzzler, *Journey to the Far Side of the Sun*, Roy Thinnes played an an astronaut who landed on a parallel Earth and thereby exchanged places with an exact duplicate of himself (see also **Parallel Worlds**). Timothy Hutton and Bruce Campbell "split" into two people in, respectively, *The Dark Half* and *Army of Darkness* (both 1993). While doppelgängers may be lookalikes who are the same person, clones are lookalikes derived from the same genes but nonetheless separate entities. Laurence Olivier tracked down little Hitler clones in Ira Levin's ingenious *The Boys from Brazil*. Robert Forster cloned himself and ran into all kinds of trouble in *The Darker Side of Terror*. Additional clones turned up in *The Clone Master* (1978), *Anna to the Infinite Power* (1983), and *Mr. Murder* (1999). Kim Novak played a lookalike in Hitchcock's *Vertigo* who turned out not to be a lookalike after all. Contrary to its title, *The Lookalike* (1990) was actually a twin and therefore does not belong in this category. See also **Twins**.

The Phantom President (1932); *All the King's Horses* (1934); *The Whole Town's Talking* (1935); *Honolulu* (1937); *The Prince and the Pauper* (1937); *The Prisoner of Zenda* (1937); *So You Won't Talk* (1940); *The Saint's Double Trouble* (1940); *Berlin Correspondent* (1942); *Assignment in Brittany* (1943); *The Bullfighters* (1945); *Pardon My Past* (1945); *Hollow Triumph* (aka *The Scar*) (1948); *The Forbidden Street* (aka *Britannia Mews*) (1948); *Callaway Went Thataway* (1951); *My Favorite Spy* (1951); *The Man with My Face* (1951); *On the Riviera* (1951); *The Prisoner of Zenda* (1952); *The Brigand* (1952); *Stolen Face* (1952); *The Four-Sided Triangle* (1953); *Flesh and the Woman* (1953); *The Most Wanted Man in the World* (aka *The Most Wanted Man*) (1953); *Mad About Men* (1954); *Francis in the Navy* (1955); *Invasion of the Body Snatchers* (1956); *I Was Monty's Double* (1958); *The Square Peg* (1958); *The Scapegoat* (1959); *On the Double* (1961); *A Coming-Out Party* (aka *Very Important Person*) (1961); *The Double Man* (1967); *Spirits of the Dead* (the segment "William Wilson") (1968); *It's Your Move* (1968); *Journey to the Far Side of the Sun* (aka *Doppelgänger*) (1969); *The Man Who Haunted Himself* (1970); *Diamonds Are Forever* (1971); *The Astronaut* (1972 TVM); *The Stranger* (1973 TVM); *Royal Flash* (1975); *Obsession* (1976); *Casanova and Co.* (1976); *The Eagle Has Landed* (1977); *End of the World* (1977); *Crossed Swords* (1978); *The Boys from Brazil* (1978); *Parts: The Clonus Horror* (1978); *The Clone Master* (1978 TVM); *The Darker Side of Terror* (1979); *The Wild, Wild West Revisited* (1979 TVM); *The Prisoner of Zenda* (1979); *Anna to the Infinite Power* (1983); *Dark Mansions* (1986 TVM); *Double Switch* (1987 TVM); *Julia and Julia* (1987); *Moon Over Parador* (1988); *Bullseye!* (1989); *Ernest Goes to Jail* (1990); *The Lookalike* (1990 TVM); *The Double Life of Veronique* (1991); *Double Edge* (1992 TVM); *Army of Darkness* (aka *Army of Darkness: Evil Dead 3*) (1993); *Dave* (1993); *The Dark Half* (1993); *Doppelgänger* (1993); *Dark Side of Genius* (1994); *It Takes Two* (1995); *Multiplicity* (1996); *The Assignment* (1997); *Cloned* (1997 TVM); *The Avengers* (1998); *Mr. Murder* (1999 TVM)

Lottery

Lottery tickets have brought lovers together, torn friends apart, and led to contemplations of murder. Strangers Ronald Colman and Ginger Rogers purchased a ticket together in 1940's *Lucky Partners* and, after a court dispute, wound up confessing their love to each other. David Niven played a film star who agreed to be a lottery prize in 1953's *The Love Lottery* (1953), as did Jeanette MacDonald in 1930's *The Lottery Bride*. Misplaced or stolen lottery tickets caused frantic confusion of the comedy kind in *Uptown Saturday Night* (1974) and Rene Clair's *Le Million* (1931). In *Babette's Feast* (1987), cook extraordinaire Stephane Audran used lottery winnings to show her gratitude to her employers for giving her a home. She spent all the money on a lavish feast, which also provided her with a final chance to practice her culinary art. In the 1966 black comedy *The Wrong Box*, John Mills and family sought to murder Ralph Richardson, thereby winning a tontine, a form of lottery in which the surviving player receives all the money. A whole town tries to swindle lottery officials when a town resident wins the jackpot and then promptly dies in the Irish comedy *Waking Ned Divine* (1998). Michael Keaton uncovered a crooked lottery run by John Davidson in the 1987 flop *The Squeeze*. *29th Street* (1991) told the true story of actor Frank Pesce, who won the first New York State Lottery in 1976. Chloe Webb played a mentally retarded young woman who wins a lottery in 1991's *Lucky Day*. *Deep Impact* (1998) featured a lottery in which the winner received something more valuable than money — a chance to survive a comet hurtling toward Earth.

The Lottery Bride (1930); *Le Million* (1931); *La Belle Equipe* (1936); *Love from a Stranger* (aka *A Night of Terror*) (1937); *Lucky Partners* (1940); *Three Strangers* (1945); *Dual Alibi* (1947); *The Love Lottery* (1953); *The Wrong Box* (1966); *Uptown Saturday Night* (1974);

Fox and His Friends (aka *Fist Right of Freedom*) (1975); *Dragonslayer* (1981); *Lots of Luck* (1985 TVM); *Babette's Feast* (1987); *The Squeeze* (1987); *29th Street* (1991); *Lucky Day* (1991 TVM); *Loser* (1991); *Yankee Zulu* (1993); *It Could Happen to You* (1994); *The Lottery* (aka *Wariko, Le Gros Lot*) (1994); *Just Your Luck* (aka *Whiskey Down*) (1996); *The Lottery* (1996 TVM); *The Ticket* (1997 TVM); *Deep Impact* (1998); *Waking Ned Devine* (1998)

Lumberjacks

With the trademark crack of falling trees and shouts of "timber!" films about the rugged men who run lumber camps have tended toward sprawling outdoor melodrama. Howard Hawks and William Wyler fashioned a reliable formula with 1936's *Come and Get It*, Edna Ferber's tale of conflict between lumber tycoon Edward Arnold, his son Joel McCrea, and the woman they both loved (Frances Farmer). The 1938 *Valley of the Giants* offered the now-familiar tale about a ruthless lumber man attempting to strip California of its redwood forests. The same story was previously filmed in 1919 and 1927 and remade as the 1952 Kirk Douglas vehicle *The Big Trees*. Wayne Morris, the man who thwarted Charles Bickford in *Valley of the Giants*, fought to save a lumber camp in 1950's *The Tougher They Come*. Paul Newman's *Sometimes a Great Notion* focused on the hardships endured by a family of lumberjacks after they defied a local strike. *Fire in the Sky* (1993) recounted real-life lumberjack Travis Walton's claims that he was "probed" by aliens.

Come and Get It (aka *Roaring Timber*) (1936); *God's Country and the Woman* (1936); *Valley of the Giants* (1938); *Moon Over Burma* (1940); *Lumberjack* (1944); *The Tougher They Come* (1950); *The Blazing Forest* (1952); *The Big Trees* (1952); *Timberjack* (1955); *Spoilers of the Forest* (1957); *Girl in the Woods* (1958); *Guns of the Timberland* (aka *Stampeded*) (1960); *Freckles* (1960); *Sometimes a Great Notion* (aka *Never Give an Inch*) (1971); *And Now For Something Completely Different* (1972); *Trouble in High Timber Country* (1980 TVM); *The Journey of Natty Gann* (1985); *Fire in the Sky* (1993)

Lupin, Arsene

In Maurice Leblanc's short stories, this French jewel thief (q.v.) was a product of the Parisian streets. However, he became quite a polished gentleman on the screen, especially as portrayed by John Barrymore in 1932's *Arsene Lupin*. Brother Lionel Barrymore starred as Lupin's detective nemesis and Karen Mortley turned up naked in Lupin's bed (pre–Hays Code) as an undercover police agent. Melvyn Douglas played Lupin in the belated MGM sequel, 1938's entertaining *Arsene Lupin Returns*. Interestingly, both Douglas and co-star Warren William also played thief-turned-detective The Lone Wolf (q.v.). Although a Lupin film series never materialized, a French television program did appear in the 1970s. See also **Jewel Thieves**; **Lupin III** (aka **The Wolf**).

Arsene Lupin (1932); *Arsene Lupin Returns* (1938); *Enter Arsene Lupin* (1944); *The Adventures of Arsene Lupin* (1957)

Lupin III (The Wolf)

Under the pseudonym "Monkey Punch," Katou Kazuhiko introduced Arsene Lupin III in 1967 in *Manga Action Weekly*, a Japanese comic book. The grandson of the famous French gentleman thief Arsene Lupin (q.v.), Lupin III carried on the family trade with aplomb. He was assisted in his larcenous exploits by Jigen Daisuke, a hitman, and Ishigawa Goemon, a modern day samurai. Mine Fujiko, a voluptuous rival thief, frequently crossed paths

with Lupin III. And Zenigata Keibu, a dedicated police officer, pursued the Lupin Gang with little success. The comic book adventures of these colorful characters eventually inspired three animated TV series, a live action theatrical film, six animated theatrical films, and a continuing series of made-for-TV movies. The first TV series ran from 1971 to 1972 and consisted of only 23 episodes. However, Lupin III fans consider it the closest in spirit to the original Monkey Punch stories. The second TV series, *The New Lupin III* (1977–80), lightened the tone and earned a faithful following among Japanese animation (or *anime*) fans. A third TV series lasted for 50 episodes in 1984. On the big screen, a now-obscure live action film, *Lupin III: Strange Psycho-kinetic Strategy*, made little impact in 1974. However, four years later, *Lupin III: The Mystery of Mamo* initiated a successful series of anime films featuring imaginative plots. In the most popular entry, *Castle of Cagliostro* (1979), Lupin robs a casino only to discover his loot is counterfeit. He traces the fake bills to the principality of Cagliostro, where he falls in love with the evil Count of Cagliostro's bride-to-be. With high-speed car chases, lethal lasers, and a castle fortress, *Castle of Cagliostro* comes off as a cross between an Indiana Jones movie and a James Bond film. The made-for-TV films, starting with *Lupin III: Bye Bye Liberty — Begin Emergency* (1989), represented a drop in quality although some of the plots remained intriguing (e.g., the Statue of Liberty is stolen). Interestingly, the Lupin III character is often referred to as Rupin or The Wolf because of copyright problems. When Katou Kazuhiko first created his thief-hero, he did not secure permission from the copyright owners of the original Arsene Lupin. To avoid potential legal action, the name was changed to Rupin in the films — although fans still referred to their idol as Lupin III. See also **Comic Book Characters**; **Jewel Thieves**; **Lupin, Arsene**.

Lupin III: Strange Psycho-kinetic Strategy (aka *Rupan Sansei: Nenriki Chin Sakusen*) (1974); *Lupin III: The Mystery of Mamo* (aka *Rupan Sansei: Mamo Karen Chousen*; *Mamo's 1st Copy*) (1978); *Lupin III: Castle of Cagliostro* (aka *Rupan Sansei: Kariosutoro No Shiro*) (1979); *Lupin III: The Golden Legend of Babylon* (aka *Rupan Sansei: Babiron No Ogon Densetsu*; *Legend of the Gold of Babylon*) (1985); *Lupin III: The Fuma Conspiracy* (aka *Rupan Sansei: Fûma Ichizoku No Inbô*; *Plot of the Fuma Clan*) (1987); *Lupin III: Bye Bye Liberty — Begin Emergency* (aka *Bye Bye Liberty — Kiki Ippatsu*) (1989 TVM); *Lupin III: The Hemingway Papers* (aka *Hemingway Paper no Nazo*) (1990 TVM); *Lupin III: Napoleon's Dictionary* (aka *Napolean no Jishou o Ubae*; *Lupin III: The Theft of Napoleon's Dictionary*) (1991 TVM); *Lupin III: From Russia with Love* (aka *Russia Yori Ai o Komete*) (1992 TVM); *Lupin III: Orders to Assassinate Lupin* (aka *Rupan Sansei: Rupan Ansatsu Shirei*; *Dark Order of Assassination*) (1993 TVM); *Lupin III: The Mighty Sword That Can Cut Steel* (aka *Moe-yo Zantetsuken*; *Lupin III: Zantetsu Sword is Burning*) (1994 TVM); *Lupin III: The Hunt for Harimao's Treasure* (aka *Harimao no Zaiho o oe!*) (1995 TVM); *Lupin III: Die! Nostradamus* (aka *Rupan Sansei: Kutabare! Nostradamus*; *To Hell with Nostradamas*) (1995); *Lupin III: Dead or Alive* (1996); *Lupin III: The Secret of Twilight Gemini* (aka *Twilight Jemini no Himitu*) (1996 TVM); *Lupin III: Walther P38* (1997) (aka *Rupan Sansei: Walther P38*) (1997 TVM); *Lupin III: Tokyo Crisis* (aka *Rupan Sansei: Honô No Kioku Tokyo Crisis*) (1998 TVM)

Lynching

Fritz Lang's *Fury* (1936) rattled Depression Era moviegoers with its powerful depiction of contemporary mob violence. Spencer Tracy portrayed the innocent stranger locked up in a small jail after being charged with kidnapping a young girl. When an incensed mob's lynching effort fails, it burns the jail. However, Tracy's character escapes unseen and lives to administer his own justice/revenge. William Wellman's *The Ox-Bow Incident* (1943), based on Walter Van Tilburg Clark's Western novel, shifted the emphasis from the victim to the lynchers. Again, a mob (in this case, a posse) passes judgment based on weak circumstantial evidence. However, those who oppose the lynching, like drifters Henry Fonda and Harry Morgan, are too passive to make their arguments convincing. Despite these fine films, the most powerful statement against mob violence remains 1950's underrated *The Sound of Fury*. Based on Joe Pagano's novel *The Condemned*, it followed the first half of *Fury's* plotline before developing into a chilling morality tale. In this case, the accused — Frank Lovejoy and Lloyd Bridges — really are guilty. In fact, Bridge's character murdered a boy in cold blood. But after whipping the townspeople into a frenzy, even journalist Richard Carlson is shocked to see the two criminals hanged in the town square. Other films about lynching lack the conviction of these three, although *The Hanging Tree* (1959) effectively proposes that greed can quench even the bloodthirstiest mob. Of course, not all lynchings result in deaths, as evidenced by Clint Eastwood surviving his own hanging and setting out on a path of revenge in the 1968 Western *Hang 'Em High*.

Fury (1936); *Young Mr. Lincoln* (1939); *The Ox-Bow Incident* (1943); *Intruder in the Dust* (1949); *The Sound of Fury* (aka *Try and Get Me*) (1950); *The Woman They Almost Lynched* (1953); *A Man Alone* (1955); *The Young Land* (1957); *The Hanging Tree* (1959); *Johnny Reno* (1966); *The Violent Ones* (1967); *Five Card Stud* (1968); *Hang 'Em High* (1968); *Border Shootout* (1990); *Grim Prairie Tales* (1990)

Mabuse, Dr.

Norbert Jacques' criminal mastermind was the subject of three motion picture classics and an offbeat, low-budget film series. Famed director Fritz Lang and his screenwriter wife Thea Von Harbou introduced Mabuse to German audiences in 1921 with *Dr. Mabuse, the Gambler*. Rudolf Klein-Rogge, Von Harbou's ex-husband, starred as the crazed genius and master hypnotist bent on world domination. The same team completed a "second part," titled *Dr. Mabuse, King of Crime*, the following year. The two parts were intended to be shown on consecutive evenings and are frequently listed as one film. For their 1927 U.S. release, the films were heavily cut and edited into a single feature, *The Fatal Passions*. Lang and Von Harbou resurrected Mabuse for 1932's *The Testament of Dr. Mabuse*, which was banned for its anti–Hitler statements. Lang subsequently left Germany, while Von Harbou stayed behind. Following a successful career in the U.S., Lang returned to Germany (West Germany) in 1960 to make *The Thousand Eyes of Dr. Mabuse*, his directorial swan song, for producer Artur Brauner. Even without Lang, Brauner continued the series for five more films starring Wolfgang Preiss as Mabuse. In 1990, director Claude Chabrol made *Dr. M*, whose villain Dr. Marsfelt (Alan Bates) and plot were "inspired by Norbert Jacques' novel *Mabuse der Spieler*." The Mabusian storyline has Dr. M causing Berlin residents to commit suicide by sending out subliminal messages on TV.

Dr. Mabuse, the Gambler (aka *The Great Gambler-Image of a Generation; Dr. Mabuse, der Spieler*) (1921); *Dr. Mabuse, King of Crime* (aka *Inferno-People of a Generation; Inferno-Menschen der Zeit*) (1922); *The Testament of Dr. Mabuse* (aka *The Last Will of Dr. Mabuse; The Crimes of Dr. Mabuse; Das Testament des Dr. Mabuse*) (1932); *The Thousand Eyes of Dr. Mabuse* (aka *Eyes of Evil; Die Tausend Augen des Dr. Mabuse*) (1960); *The Invisible Dr. Mabuse* (aka *Die Unsichtbaren Krallen des Dr. Mabuse; The Invisible Horror*) (1961); *The Return of Dr. Mabuse* (aka *Phantom Fiend; Im Stahlnetz des Dr. Mabuse*) (1961); *The Testament of Dr. Mabuse* (aka *The Terror of Dr. Mabuse; Das Testament des Dr. Mabuse*) (1962); *Dr. Mabuse vs. Scotland Yard* (aka *Scotland Yard Hunts Dr. Mabuse; Scotland Yard Jagt Dr. Mabuse*) (1963); *The Secret of Dr. Mabuse* (aka *Dr. Mabuse's Ray of Death; Die Todesstrahlen des Dr. Mabuse; The Diabolical Dr. Mabuse*) (1964); *Dr. M* (aka *Club Extinction*) (1990)

Maciste

A muscular Italian hero in the Hercules (q.v.) mold, Maciste remains anonymous in this country although over a dozen films about him have received U.S. release. The culprits behind this unintentional conspiracy have been American distributors, which changed the original Maciste titles (and subsequently dubbed the dialogue) to misrepresent the films' hero as more widely-known musclemen like Hercules, Goliath, or Samson. Thus, *Maciste alla Corte del Genghis Khan* became *Samson and the Seven Miracles of the World*, while *Maciste e la Regina di Samar* became *Hercules Against the Moon Men*. One of the few imports to retain Maciste in its title was 1964's sand-and-sandal spoof *Maciste Against Hercules in the Vale of Woe*. Not suprisingly, that film was later retitled *Hercules in the Vale of Woe*, thus dropping Maciste into anonymity again. Just to confuse matters even further, brawny actors Mark Forest, Reg Park, Kirk Morris, and Alan Steel (aka Sergio Ciani) all played Hercules as well as Maciste.

Maciste in Hell (aka *Maciste all'Inferno*) (1926) (Umberto Guarracino); *Son of Samson* (aka *Maciste the Mighty; Maciste nella Valle dei Re*) (1960) (Mark Forest); *The Witch's Curse* (aka *Maciste all'Inferno*) (1960) (Kirk Morris); *Molemen vs. the Son of Hercules* (aka *The Strongest Man in the World; Maciste l'Uomo Piu Forte del Mondo*) (1961) (Forest); *Atlas Against the Cyclops* (aka *Monster from the Unknown World; Maciste nella Terror dei Ciclopi*) (1961) (Mitchell Gordon); *Colossus and the Headhunters* (aka *Maciste Contro i Cacciatori de Teste*) (1962) (Morris); *Death in the Arena* (aka *Colossus of the Arena; Maciste il Gladiatore Pi — Forte del Mondo*) (1962) (Forest); *Fire Monsters Against the Son of Hercules* (aka *Colossus of the Stone Age; Maciste Contro i Monstri*) (1962) (Reg Park); *Triumph of the Sons of Hercules* (aka *El Trionfo di Maciste*) (1962) (Morris); *Goliath and the Sins of Babylon* (aka *Maciste l'Eroe Pi — Grande del Mondo*) (1963) (Forest); *Samson and the Slave Queen* (aka *Zorro Contro Maciste*) (1963) (Alan Steel); *Samson vs. the Giant King* (aka *Giant of the Lost Tomb; Maciste alla Corte dello Zar*) (1963) (Morris); *Samson and the Seven Miracles of the World* (aka *Maciste alla Corte del Gran Khan*) (1963) (Gordon Scott); *Goliath and the Vampires* (aka *The Vampires; Maciste Contro il Vampiro*) (1964) (Scott); *Hercules in the Vale of Woe* (aka *Maciste Against Hercules in the Vale of Woe; Maciste Contro Ercole Nella Valle Dei Guai*) (1964); *Maciste, Spartan Gladiator* (aka *Maciste, Gladiatore di Sparta*) (1964) (Forest); *Hercules of the Desert* (aka *La Valle dell'Eco Tonante*) (1964) (Morris); *Samson and the Mighty Challenge* (aka *Hercules, Maciste, Samson, and Ursus Against the Universe; Ercole, Sansone, Maciste, Ursus: gli Invincibli*) (1964); *Samson in King Solomon's Mines* (aka *Maciste nelle Miniere de Re Salomone*) (1964) (Park); *Hercules Against the Moon Men* (aka *Maciste Contro gli Uomini Della Luna; Maciste e la Regina di Samar*) (1964) (Steel); *Hercules Against the Barbarians* (aka *Maciste nell'Inferno di Genghis Khan*) (1964) (Forest)

Mad Max

The Australian-imported *Mad Max* movies not only made a star of Mel Gibson, but they also managed to make the near-impossible transition from drive-in cult status into mainstream major hits. The 1979 *Mad Max* starred Gibson as the title character, a futuristic cop who patrols a post-apocalyptic world populated with motorcycle gangs and other riff-raff. When his partner and family are murdered, Max becomes a one-man vigilante force and wipes out the "Glory Riders." From the beginning, director/co-writer George Miller's film found favor with science fiction and action fans, but it attracted little critical attention. Undoubtedly, the release of some dubbed prints (in which even Gibson spoke with someone else's voice) limited its appeal. That all changed with the superior sequel, 1981's *The Road Warrior* in which Gibson and Miller transformed Max into a mythic warrior. Critics jumped on the bandwagon ("Apocalypse Pow!" proclaimed *Time*) and Gibson's career began to ascend rapidly. He was an established star when he returned to his homeland for 1985's *Mad Max Beyond Thunderdome*. This slick rehash of *Road Warrior*, bolstered by the presence of rock queen Tina Turner, racked up impressive box-office figures — but nevertheless lacked the enduring popularity of *Road Warrior*. In 1999, Miller announced plans to shoot a fourth *Mad Max* film, with a younger actor replacing Gibson (whose escalating salary probably affected the decision to go with a lesser-known performer). See also **End of the World/Post-Apocalypse**.

Mad Max (1979); *The Road Warrior* (aka *Mad Max 2*) (1981); *Mad Max Beyond Thunderdome* (1985)

Magicians

Even though its running time was a scant two minutes, 1896's *Conjuring a Lady at the Robert-Houdin's* holds a unique double distinction among magician films. In addition to containing one of the first filmed magic tricks, it spotlighted the moviemaking talents of former conjuror and cinema pioneer Georges Méliès. Unlike this landmark work, other magician movies have often forgotten that the cinema is a magical medium. They have been largely content to pass off the magician as a devious trickster or bland do-gooder. In 1946's *The Strange Mr. Gregory*, Edmund Lowe played a magician/hypnotist who pretended to be dead to win the affections of Jean Rogers. Vincent Price was a 19th century illusionist who went mad in the well-titled *The Mad Magician* (1954). He sought revenge on his cheating wife (Eva Gabor) and other magicians by murdering them with his famous tricks (the imaginative murder angle was repeated in later Price films like *The Abominable Dr. Phibes* and *Theatre of Blood*). Satanic cult leader Niall MacGinnis performed Halloween magic shows for the kiddies in the classic *Curse of the Demon* (1958) and then explained to Dana Andrews the critical distinctions between black and white magic. On the other hand, heroic magicians have been far less interesting. *Chandu the Magician*, culled from a 1932 serial, sent Edmund Lowe (again) against Bela Lugosi's evil Roxor (oddly, Bela showed up as Chandu two years later in another serial). In TV movies, Christopher George's escape artist in *Escape* (1970) and Bill Bixby's illusionist in *The Magician* (1973) both helped people in trouble — that's TV talk for detective work. Bixby's film served as the pilot for a shortlived 1973-74 TV series. Neither Laurel and Hardy nor Jerry Lewis could mix magic and comedy to much effect in, respectively, *A-Haunting We Will Will Go* (1942) and *The Geisha Boy* (1958). However, Tommy Smothers had some amusing scenes in *Get to Know Your Rabbit* (1972) and Woody Allen lost his mother at a magic show in his *New York Stories* segment (1989). The famous magician/escape artist Harry Houdini has been played by Tony Curtis (*Houdini*), Paul Michael Glaser (*The Great Houdinis*), and Johnathon Schaech (*Houdini*). Ingmar Bergman explored the mystical side of magic in *The Magician* (1958), a haunting tale about an illusionist detained by villagers unconvinced by his magical powers.

Conjuring a Lady at the Robert Houdin's (aka *The Vanishing Lady*) (1896); *The Phantom of Paris* (1931); *Chandu, the Magician* (1932); *Lady in Distress* (aka *A Window in London*) (1939); *Eternally Yours* (1939); *A-Haunting We Will Go* (1942); *Having Wonderful Crime* (1945); *The Great Mystic* (1945); *The Strange Mr. Gregory* (1946); *Houdini* (1953); *The Mad Magician* (1954); *Curse of the Demon* (aka *Night of the Demon*) (1958); *The Geisha Boy* (1958); *The Magician* (1958); *Two on a Guillotine* (1965); *The Mysterious Magician* (1965); *The Magus* (1968); *Escape* (1970 TVM); *Get to Know Your Rabbit* (1972); *The Magician* (1973 TVM); *The Golden Voyage of Sinbad* (1974); *Celine and Julie Go Boating* (1974); *The Great Houdinis* (1976 TVM); *The Magician of Lublin* (1979); *Mandrake* (1979 TVM); *The Escape Artist* (1982); *Bagdad Cafe* (1988); *New York Stories* (1989); *Waiting for the Light* (1990); *Cthulhu Mansion* (aka *Black Magic Mansion*) (1991); *Shadows and Fog* (1992); *Mario and the Magician* (1994); *Lord of Illusions* (1995); *Leprechaun 3* (1995); *Rough Magic* (1995); *Fairy Tale: A True Story* (1997); *Houdini* (1998 TVM)

The Magnificent Seven

John Sturges' 1960 remake of the Japanese classic *Seven Samurai* has grown in popularity over the years, becoming — according to *TV Guide* — one of the most frequently shown movies on television. The original seven gunfighters hired to protect a Mexican village were (and this is a great "list" question in its own right): Yul Brynner, Steve McQueen, James Coburn, Robert Vaughn, Charles Bronson, Brad Dexter, and Horst Buchholz. Only Yul returned for the first sequel *Return of the Seven* (1966). But Elmer Bernstein's great music score (best known as the Marlboro theme) was used in all four *Seven* films. The original plot has been recycled extensively and transplanted to contemporary Arizona (the 1985 TVM *Command 5*), the Middle East (1968's *The Invincible Six*), outer space (1980's *Battle Beyond the Stars*) and an ant colony (1998's *A Bug's Life*). *The Adventures of the Magnificent 6½* (1988) was a children's variation. A *Magnificent Seven* television series, with Michael Biehn as the group's leader, surfaced on CBS in 1998.

The Magnificent Seven (1960); *Return of the Seven* (1966); *Guns of the Magnificent Seven* (1969); *The Magnificent Seven Ride* (1972)

Maids and Housekeepers

Although they typically form the backbone of celluloid domestic staffs, maids and housekeepers have labored in the shadow of butlers. For example, while the 1930s featured prime butler roles in *Ruggles of Red Gap* (1935) and *My Man Godfrey* (1936), maids and housekeepers were relegated to minor — albeit essential — roles in the 1939 releases *Rules of the Game*, *The Cat and the Canary*, and *Gone with the Wind*. Of course, Hattie McDaniel won a Best Supporting Actress Oscar for her role as Mammy in

GWTW (an honor not bestowed on a performer playing a butler until John Gielgud's Best Supporting Actor award for 1981's *Arthur*). Gale Sondergaard created the prototype for sinister domestics in *The Cat and the Canary*. However, Judith Anderson refined the evil housekeeper role with her chilling portrayal of Mrs. Danvers in Alfred Hitchcock's *Rebecca* (1940). Anderson received a well-deserved Oscar nomination, but lost to Jane Darwell's good-natured Ma in *The Grapes of Wrath*. Loretta Young won a Best Actress Oscar for 1947's *The Farmer's Daughter*, in which she played a Swedish maid who falls in love with her employer and then runs against him in Congress. Other maids who married, or had affairs with, their employers were featured in *Common Clay* (1930), *Jassy* (1947), and *Houseboat* (1958). In the latter film, Sophia Loren was a socialite posing as a housekeeper for Cary Grant. Likewise, Ally Sheedy was a spoiled rich girl working as a domestic in 1987's *Maid to Order*. In contrast, *That Funny Feeling* (1965) cast Sandra Dee as a maid intent on hiding her occupation from her new boyfriend. She moves into her employer's swank apartment — not realizing that her boyfriend is her employer. Men have taken their turns as maids, although not too successfully, in movies such as 1982's *Maid in America* (with Alex Karras) and 1990's *The Maid* (with Martin Sheen). Maids have fared extremely well on television in the series *Hazel* (1961–66), *Grindl* (1963–64), *The Good Life* (1971–72), and, most memorably, *Upstairs, Downstairs* (1971–75). Although there was never a film series about a maid, Maisie (q.v.) worked as one in *Maisie Was a Lady* (1940) and Mary Gordon cleaned up after Sherlock Holmes (q.v.) in the Rathbone/Bruce film series. See also **Butlers**; **Chauffeurs**.

Common Clay (1930); *Downstairs* (1932); *Servants' Entrance* (1934); *If You Could Only Cook* (1935); *Private Number* (1936); *Maid's Night Out* (1938); *Rules of the Game* (1939); *The Cat and the Canary* (1939); *Gone with the Wind* (1939); *Rebecca* (1940); *Maisie Was a Lady* (1940); *His Butler's Sister* (1943); *Standing Room Only* (1944); *Mrs. Parkington* (1944); *Diary of a Chambermaid* (1946); *The Farmer's Daughter* (1947); *Jassy* (1947); *Footsteps in the Fog* (1955); *Papa, Mama, the Maid and I* (1956); *Houseboat* (1958); *Upstairs and Downstairs* (1959); *13 Ghosts* (1960); *Diary of a Chambermaid* (1964); *That Funny Feeling* (1965); *For Love of Ivy* (1968); *Whatever Happened to Aunt Alice?* (1969); *The Maids* (1975); *A Matter of Time* (1976); *That Obscure Object of Desire* (1977); *Heartland* (1980); *Private Lessons* (1981); *Maid in America* (1982 TVM); *In the White City* (1983); *Loyalties* (1986); *A Judgment in Stone* (aka *The Housekeeper*) (1986); *Maid to Order* (1987); *The Maid* (1990); *Maid for Each Other* (1992 TVM); *The Remains of the Day* (1993); *Corrina, Corrina* (1994); *Dolores Claiborne* (1995); *La Cérémonie* (aka *A Judgment in Stone*) (1995); *Mary Reilly* (1996); *Gods and Monsters* (1998)

Mail Order Brides

Unlikely romances set in the American West have comprised the majority of films about mail order brides. Robert Taylor led a wagon train of mail order brides to meet their husbands in *Westward the Women* (1951). Likewise, in the Spaghetti Western *Blindman* (1972), blind gunslinger Tony Anthony escorted a group of future wives — fifty, in fact — until his partner doublecrossed him and sold the women to a bandit. Lawman Buddy Ebsen played matchmaker for Keir Dullea and mail order bride Lois Nettleton in the unimaginatively-titled *Mail Order Bride* (1964). Blacksmith Dan Blocker thought Nanette Fabray was a mail order

spouse — but she wasn't — in *The Cockeyed Cowboys of Calico County* (1970). And in *Zandy's Bride* (1974), rancher Gene Hackman and mail order bride Liv Ullman started out hating each other and wound up as loving spouses and parents. In contrast to Westerns, contemporary movies about mail order brides have dealt with diverse topics such as airplane disasters (*The High and the Mighty*), investigative reporting (*I Was a Mail Order Bride*), and cultural differences between the spouses (*90 Days*). Several movies, while not about *mail order* brides, certainly warrant a mention. Women answered newspaper ads to become wives in *Mississippi Mermaid* (1969) and *Sarah, Plain and Tall* (1991). Charlton Heston and Eleanor Parker were married by proxy in *The Naked Jungle* (1954). Brides were bought in *East Is West* (1930) and *Paint Your Wagon* (1969). Finally, young Japanese girls were contracted to marry Japanese men working in Hawaii in the critically-acclaimed *Picture Bride* (1995). See also **Marriage Brokers and Dating Services**; **Personal Ads**; **Sarah, Plain and Tall Series**.

The Peace of Roaring River (1919); *A Lady to Love* (1930); *The Purchase Price* (1932); *The Harvey Girls* (1946); *Westward the Women* (1951); *The High and the Mighty* (1954); *Mail Order Bride* (aka *West of Montana*) (1964); *The Cockeyed Cowboys of Calico County* (aka *A Woman for Charley*) (1970); *Blindman* (1972); *Zandy's Bride* (aka *For Better, For Worse*) (1974); *I Was a Mail Order Bride* (1982 TVM); *Mail Order Bride* (1984); *90 Days* (1986); *Kissing Miranda* (1995)

Maisie

The year 1939 was a banner year for MGM, featuring the releases of *Gone with the Wind*, *The Wizard of Oz*, and *Goodbye, Mr. Chips*. So it's no wonder that no one remembers it as the year Ann Sothern made her debut as Maisie, a tough, spunky girl with a heart of gold. At age 30, Sothern was already a B-movie veteran, having played similar roles for both Columbia and RKO. Robert Young (as a ranch hand!) co-starred with her in the first series entry, *Maisie*. A few months later, Sothern was back in *Congo Maisie*, a revamped version of the Clark Gable–Jean Harlow sizzler *Red Dust*. Eight more *Maisie* adventures appeared between 1940 and 1947, making the title character the busiest single woman in the movies. She was a maid in *Maisie was a Lady*, a police detective in *Undercover Maisie*, and an aircraft factory worker in *Swing Shift Maisie*. Sothern's film career slacked off during the 1950s and she turned to television, experiencing modest success with *Private Secretary* and *The Ann Sothern Show*.

Maisie (1939); *Congo Maise* (1939); *Gold Rush Maisie* (1940); *Maisie Was a Lady* (1940); *Ringside Maisie* (aka *Cash and Carry*) (1941); *Maisie Gets Her Man* (aka *She Got Her Man*) (1942); *Swingshift Maisie* (aka *The Girl in Overalls*) (1943); *Maisie Goes to Reno* (aka *You Can't Do That to Me*) (1944); *Up Goes Maisie* (aka *Up She Goes*) (1945); *Undercover Maisie* (1947)

Majin

A stone statue comes to life to battle an evil Japanese warlord in *Majin, Monster of Terror* (1966), a minor cult classic set in the 18th century. The film's first half resembles samurai epics like *The Seven Samurai* in which peaceful villagers seek protection from oppression. When the warlord Samanosuke (Yutaro Gomi) enslaves villagers to build a fortress, they pray to the stone idol Majin for freedom. To squelch any remaining morale, the warlord kills the local priestess and dispatches his henchmen to drive a spike into the statue's head. However, they flee in terror when the spike draws blood from the stone idol! Majin the stone warrior promptly comes to life and wreaks havoc on the bad guys — stomping them into the ground, destroying Samanosuke's castle, and pinning the warlord to a wall with the aforementioned spike. Majin then decides to annihilate the village, too. Fortunately, the tears of a girl cause him to disintegrate (temporarily, as evidenced by the sequels). The story bears a strong resemblance to *The Golem* films, which were based on a Jewish myth about a giant man of clay who protects persecuted Jews. As in *Majin*, a young girl destroys the Golem (by removing the Star of David from the statue's chest). The two *Majin* sequels followed the same formula as the first film, although *The Return of Majin* features a remarkable scene where the stone idol — which has been blown to bits — emerges from the sea to punish evil again. The three films are sometimes known as the Daimajin Trilogy. See also **Statues Come to Life**.

Majin, Monster of Terror (aka *Majin, the Hideous Monster; Daimajin; The Devil Got Angry*) (1966); *The Return of Majin* (aka *The Return of Giant Majin; Daimajin Ikaru*) (1966); *Majin Strikes Again* (aka *Daimajin Gyakushu*) (1968)

Major League Series

In the wake of *Bull Durham* (1988), Paramount released *Major League*, a formulaic comedy about a bunch of baseball misfits who somehow transform themselves into a winning Cleveland Indians team. Like the *Police Academy* (q.v.) movies, *Major League* gets most of its laughs by focusing on an ensemble of colorful characters: a has-been catcher (Tom Berenger); an erratic fastball pitcher nicknamed Wild Thing (Charlie Sheen); a voodoo practicing slugger (Dennis Haysbert); a third baseman more interested in his stock portfolio than baseball (Corbin Bernsen); a base stealer named Willie Mays Hayes (Wesley Snipes); and an owner (Margaret Whitton) who tries to ruin the team so attendance will drop and she can move it to the livelier city of Miami. Written and directed by David S. Ward, *Major League* performed solidly at the box-office, but paled in comparison to *Bull Durham* (though both featured over-the-hill catchers and wild pitchers). Ward directed a sequel in 1994 that reassembled most of the original cast: Berenger, Sheen, Bernsen, and Haysbert. It also rehashed the original plot by having the Indians play poorly at first so they could evolve into a good team by the end. The film was retitled *Wild Thing II* for some overseas markets to capitalize on the popularity of Charlie Sheen in the Far East. Sheen, Berenger, and Ward were missing from *Major League: Back to the Minors*, a third entry focusing on a Minnesota Twins farm team consisting of — surprise! — a bunch of misfits. The film flopped quickly, likely ending the series. Bernsen, Haysbert, and Bob Uecker starred in all three films. See also **Baseball**.

Major League (1989); *Major League II* (aka *Wild Thing II*) (1994); *Major League: Back to the Minors* (aka *Major League III*) (1998)

Malibu Express Series

Husband-and-wife team Andy and Arlene Sidaris masterminded this B-movie series, an R-rated variation of *Charlie's Angels* featuring one less female lead, but much more flesh. Hunky Darby Hinton starred as Texan troubleshooter Cody Abilene in the se-

ries' first installment, 1985's *Malibu Express* (the title being the name of Cody's yacht). Set in Hawaii, it offset poor thesping with some lively action footage staged by Andy, a former Emmy-winning director for *ABC's Wide World of Sports*. Ronn Moss took over as cousin Rowdy Abilene in the 1987 follow-up *Hard Ticket to Hawaii* and former soap star Steve Bond played enforcement agent Travis Abilene in *Picasso Trigger* (1988). Although they both made bland leads, former *Playboy* Playmates Dona Speir and Hope Marie Carlton attracted attention as Donna and Taryn, a pair of freelance flyers. Their supporting characters received a hefty amount of screen time and went on to headline 1989's *Savage Beach*, which featured a meatier story and less gratuitous nudity. Carlton bowed out after this installment. Thus, Speir sported a new partner, Roberta Vasquez as Nicole, in 1990's *Guns*, which had the distinction of casting Erik Estrada as a baddie. Speir, Vasquez, and Estrada returned for 1991's *Do or Die*, although Estrada played a different character (a good guy). *The Karate Kid's* former mentor, Pat Morita, took over as villain. The principal villains in 1992's *Hard Hunted* were played by movie star offspring R.J. Moore (Roger's son) and Tony Peck (Gregory's son). Speir and Vasquez made their final appearances as Donna and Nicole in 1993's *Fit to Kill*. Suzi Simpson took over the lead female role as Becky Midnite in *Enemy Gold* (1994), but she generated far less interest than former *Penthouse* Pet Julie Strain in a supporting henchman role. Strain earned star billing in the next series entry, *The Dallas Connection*, which introduced her as heroine Willow Black, head of L.E.T.H.A.L. (Legion to Ensure Total Harmony and Law). Her cohorts in espionage included a bevy of former centerfolds: Shae Marks as Tiger; Julie K. Smith as Cobra; and Tammy Parks as Scorpion. Wrestler Marcus Bagwell played the title villain in 1996's *Day of the Warrior*, only to reform and join the L.E.T.H.A.L. team in *Return to Savage Beach* (1998) — a smart choice given the obvious fringe benefits.

Malibu Express (1985); *Hard Ticket to Hawaii* (1987); *Picasso Trigger* (1988); *Savage Beach* (1989); *Guns* (1990); *Do or Die* (1991); *Hard Hunted* (1992); *Fit to Kill* (1993); *Enemy Gold* (1994); *The Dallas Connection* (1994); *Day of the Warrior* (aka *L.E.T.H.A.L. Ladies: Day of the Warrior*) (1996); *Return to Savage Beach* (1998)

A Man Called Horse Series

Richard Harris starred in this offbeat Western about an English aristocrat captured by Sioux Indians in 1825. He suffers torture, learns to live with his captors, grows to understand them, and becomes their leader. It was based on Dorothy M. Johnson's 1950 *Collier's* story and featured the harrowing Sun Vow ritual, which required Indian males to be suspended by clamps inserted in their pectoral muscles. Although Harris' character returned to civilization at the film's end, he came back to help his Indian friends in 1976's *The Return of a Man Called Horse*. This sequel lacked the box-office zip of its predecessor, but that did not deter the belated release of a third film, 1983's *Triumphs of a Man Called Horse*, which starred Harris and Michael Beck as his son.

A Man Called Horse (1970); *The Return of a Man Called Horse* (1976); *Triumphs of a Man Called Horse* (1983)

The Man from U.N.C.L.E.

NBC introduced the lighthearted spy TV series *The Man from U.N.C.L.E.* in 1964, shortly after the third James Bond thriller,

Goldfinger, struck the mother lode at the national box-office. U.N.C.L.E. stood for United Network Command for Law and Enforcement and was run by gruff, fatherly Mr. Waverly (Leo G. Carroll). The agency's top two agents were American Napoleon Solo (Robert Vaughn) and Russian Illya Kuryakin (David Mc-Callum). (The fact that Americans and Russians were fighting together for world peace makes *The Man from U.N.C.L.E.* the first glasnost TV series.) The show was an immediate hit, especially with the younger set, and inspired MGM to release a big-screen feature, *To Trap a Spy*, in 1965. Actually, it had been originally shown as a 1964 TV episode called "The Vulcan Affair," but fans didn't seem to mind that they had seen it before. Seven additional movies were released between 1965 and 1968. Meanwhile, the television edition spun off the short-lived series *The Girl from U.N.C.L.E.* (starring Stefanie Powers) and dropped in the ratings after peaking at No. 13 for the year in the 1965-66 season. The series was cancelled in January 1968 and replaced by *Rowan and Martin's Laugh-in*. A reunion TV movie, *The Return of the Man from U.N.C.L.E.*, surfaced in 1983. See also **Television Series Reunion Films**.

   To Trap a Spy (1965); *One of Our Spies Is Missing* (1966); *One Spy Too Many* (1966); *The Spy with My Face* (1966); *The Karate Killers* (1967); *The Spy in the Green Hat* (1967); *The Helicopter Spies* (1968); *How to Steal the World* (1968); *The Return of the Man from U.N.C.L.E.* (1983 TVM)

The Man with No Name

Clint Eastwood first portrayed this laconic gunslinger in 1964's *A Fistful of Dollars*, Sergio Leone's spaghetti Western version of Akira Kurosawa's samurai epic *Yojimbo*. Although it's not actually specified, Eastwood apparently played the same character in Leone's follow-ups *For a Few Dollars More* and *The Good, the Bad, and the Ugly* (Clint was the Good, Lee Van Cleef the Bad, and Eli Wallach the Ugly). Clint may have played the role in other Westerns, too (e.g., *High Plains Drifter*, *Pale Rider*). Given his subtle acting style, it's sometimes hard to tell.

   A Fistful of Dollars (1964); *For a Few Dollars More* (1965); *The Good, the Bad, and the Ugly* (1967)

Maniac Cop Series

"You have the right to remain silent...forever!" proclaimed the ad for *Maniac Cop* (1988), an exploitation thriller from B-movie veterans Larry Cohen and William Lustig. Producer/screenwriter Cohen, the low-budget auteur responsible for the *It's Alive* films, fashioned a clever premise in which a series of gruesome New York City murders appear to be the work of a policeman. It's chilling when a potential victim expresses relief at the appearance of a police officer — only to discover that he's the killer! Unfortunately, director Lustig (*Maniac*) lacked the style and budget to embellish the film with sufficient atmosphere and tension. The cast is a "who's who" of B-movies: Richard Roundtree as the mayor; Bruce Campbell as a falsely accused cop; Tom Atkins as a puzzled detective; and William Smith and Sheree North. *Evil Dead* director Sam Raimi and ex-boxer Jake LaMotta show up in cameos. Cohen and Lustig reteamed for both of the unexceptional sequels. In *Maniac Cop 2* (1991), killer cop Matt Cordell (Robert Z'Dar) rises from the dead and pairs up with another murderer to make the streets of NYC unsafe again. The plot-

heavy *Maniac Cop 3: Badge of Silence* has a Santeria priest revive Cordell who tries to make a brain-dead cop his "bride." The film shows signs of tampering with producer Joel Soisson being credited with "additional scenes." Ted Raimi, Sam's brother, makes a brief appearance as a TV reporter.

   Maniac Cop (1988); *Maniac Cop 2* (1991); *Maniac Cop 3: Badge of Silence* (1993)

Marlowe, Philip

The screen exploits of Raymond Chandler's tough, cynical private eye make for fascinating trivia. The first adaptation of a Marlowe mystery (*Farewell, My Lovely*) was tailored for George Sanders as 1942's *The Falcon Takes Over*, an entry in the long-running *Falcon* (q.v.) film series. That same year, the Philip Marlowe novel *The High Window* was adapted for detective Michael Shayne (q.v.) as *Time to Kill*. Two years later, Marlowe finally reached the screen in the guise of Dick Powell, who made the switch from crooner to tough guy in *Murder, My Sweet*, another version of *Farewell, My Lovely*. Powell was terrific as Marlowe, setting a standard that even Bogart couldn't surpass in 1946's *The Big Sleep*. Later that year, actor-director Robert Montgomery filmed *The Lady in the Lake* in first-person, showing audiences everything as Marlowe saw it. It was a novel experiment (e.g., kisses filled the screen, the camera rocked back after a punch to Marlowe's face), but ultimately it was more irritating than interesting. George Montgomery (no relation to Robert) played Marlowe in 1947's *The Brasher Doubloon*, the second version of Chandler's *The High Window*. There were no Marlowe films in the 1950s, but James Garner played the part in 1969's *Marlowe* (which featured Bruce Lee as a minor villain). Elliott Gould played an unrecognizable Marlowe in Robert Altman's 1973 *The Long Goodbye*. And in the late 1970s, a weary-looking Robert Mitchum played the detective in *Farewell, My Lovely* (set in the '40s) and *The Big Sleep* (updated to the present). James Caan played an older Marlowe in the made-for-cable *Poodle Springs* (1998). It was adapted from an unfinished Chandler novel completed by mystery writer Robert Parker. Ironically, the only Marlowe novel never filmed was *Playback*, which was originally an unsold Chandler screenplay.

   Murder, My Sweet (1944); *The Big Sleep* (1946); *The Lady in the Lake* (1946); *The Brasher Doubloon* (1947); *Marlowe* (1969); *The Long Goodbye* (1973); *Farewell, My Lovely* (1975); *The Big Sleep* (1978); *Poodle Springs* (1998 TVM)

Marple, Miss Jane

Agatha Christie introduced Miss Jane Marple, a 70-year-old amateur detective, in the 1930 novel *The Murder at the Vicarage*. Living in the small town of St. Mary Mead, the inquisitive spinster divided her time between her passions of gardening and solving murders. Miss Marple enjoyed modest success in the 1960s when Margaret Rutherford's *Murder, She Said* sparked a four-film series. Rutherford also made a cameo appearance as Miss Marple opposite Tony Randall's Hercule Poirot (q.v.) in 1966's *The Alphabet Murders*. Despite the popularity of the Rutherford films, Agatha Christie readers complained that the actress was miscast and that her films downplayed the mysteries in favor of light comedy. Angela Lansbury (pre–*Murder, She Wrote*) fared much better in *The Mirror Crack'd* (1980), but sadly did not return for an encore. That made it possible for Helen Hayes to star as Miss Marple in a pair of entertaining, if easily forgotten, made-for-TV mysteries. However, most critics and Christie readers agree that Joan Hickson did the best job of recreating Jane Marple for a British TV series that first aired in the U.S. in the 1980s on *Mystery!* Ironically, Hickson had a small role opposite Margaret Rutherford in *Murder, She Said.*

Murder, She Said (1962) (Margaret Rutherford); *Murder at the Gallop* (1963) (Rutherford); *Murder Ahoy!* (1964) (Rutherford); *Murder Most Foul* (1965) (Rutherford); *The Mirror Crack'd* (1980) (Angela Lansbury); *A Caribbean Mystery* (1983 TVM) (Helen Hayes); *Murder with Mirrors* (1985 TVM) (Hayes)

Marriage Brokers and Dating Services

The arrangement of marriages is a dangerous profession that requires an understanding of love and compatibility to ensure success. As a result, it's a rare occupation both in real life and in film. Still, the cinema has featured a handful of marriage brokers, such as Thelma Ritter who played Cupid for X-ray technician Scott Brady and model Jeanne Crain in *The Model and the Marriage Broker.* Shirley Booth and Barbra Streisand each played the grand dame of marriage brokers—Miss Dolly Levi—in, respectively, *The Matchmaker* and its musical remake *Hello Dolly!* Charles Boyer proved that men could be matchmakers (though not successful ones, apparently) in 1963's *Love Is a Ball.* His attempts to use Glenn Ford to push Hope Lange into Ricardo Montalban's arms resulted in a Ford-Lange romance. Michael Callan and Paula Prentiss played marriage brokers who discover they have unknowingly arranged a series of illegal marriages in the 1969 TV movie comedy *In Name Only.* Dating services, not marriage brokers, paired unlikely couples in *Promise Him Anything* (1974), *The Love Tapes* (1980), *Lonely Hearts* (1983) and *The Whole Truth* (1992). See also **Mail Order Brides.**

The Model and the Marriage Broker (1951); *The Matchmaker* (1958); *Love Is a Ball* (aka *All This and Money Too*) (1963); *Hello, Dolly!* (1969); *In Name Only* (1969 TVM); *Fiddler on the Roof* (1971); *Promise Him Anything* (1974 TVM); *The Love Tapes* (1980 TVM); *Lonely Hearts* (1983); *Crossing Delancey* (1988); *The Whole Truth* (1992); *Ladykiller* (1992 TVM); *Emma* (1996); *The Matchmaker* (1997)

The Marseilles Trilogy

The characters of Marcel Pagnol's French trilogy of *Marius, Fanny,* and *Cesar* have maintained universal appeal ever since their first appearances. Thus, in addition to the trilogy, they have appeared (sometimes under different names) in German, Italian, and American features based on Pagnol's works. Pagnol was a rising French playwright when Paramount expressed interest in filming his 1929 hit play *Marius.* The movie version, with Alexander Korda directing from a Pagnol screenplay, was released in 1931. Pierre Fresnay played Marius, who dreams of a life at sea although he has fallen in love with Fanny (Orane Demazis). Fanny tries to make Marius jealous by flirting with the rich, middle-aged Panisse, a friend of Marius' father Cesar (Raimu). Eventually, she and Marius make love, but even that cannot cure Marius' wanderlust. Fanny sacrifices her own happiness and Marius leaves for the sea. Marc Allegret directed the second chapter, 1932's *Fanny,* which Pagnol again adapted from his play. Fanny, who has become pregnant with Marius' child, agrees to marry Panisse. Cesar becomes

upset with this arrangement, but eventually agrees to be the child's godfather. After two years at sea, Marius returns and wants Fanny and the child. Panisse won't give the child up and Fanny, although she still loves Marius, again sacrifices her own happiness—this time for her son. Pagnol wrote an original screenplay and directed the final installment, 1936's *Cesar.* Set 17 years later, it opens with the death of Panisse. Fanny tells her 18-year-old son Cesariot that Marius, not Panisse, was his father. With Cesar's help, Cesariot seeks out his father and eventually reunites Fanny, Marius, and Cesar. While film critics preferred the first and last films, *Fanny* attained the greatest popularity at the time of its release. It was remade in Italy in 1933, in Germany in 1934 (with Emil Jannings), and in the U.S. in 1938 as *Port of Seven Seas.* The latter film made little impression despite a solid cast of Wallace Beery, Frank Morgan, and Maureen O'Sullivan. In 1961, producer Joshua Logan condensed the trilogy into *Fanny,* a colorful, but overlong reworking. It reunited *Gigi* stars Leslie Caron (as Fanny) and Maurice Chevalier (as Panisse) and added Charles Boyer (Cesar) and Horst Buchholz (Marius). Unfortunately, Logan's ownership of the rights to *Fanny* prevented Pagnol's trilogy from being shown outside France for several years. Jacques Demy's charming musical *The Umbrellas of Cherbourg* (1964) borrowed and updated Fanny's plot.

Marius (1931); *Fanny* (1932); *Fanny* (1933) (Italian remake); *Fanny* (1934) (German remake); *Cesar* (1936); *Port of Seven Seas* (1938); *Fanny* (1961)

Marsh, Abel

Lane Slate wrote a theatrical film and two made-for-TV movies featuring contemporary small-town sheriff Abel Marsh. James Garner played Marsh on the big screen in 1972's *They Only Kill Their Masters,* a sly mystery about a Doberman with apparently murderous tendencies. The film emphasized offbeat humor and Garner's laidback charm over action or suspense. It made little impact at the box-office. However, five years later, Slate resurrected Abel Marsh in the form of Andy Griffith, who played the plaid-shirted detective in two TV movies: *The Girl in the Empty Grave* (1977) and *Deadly Game* (1977). The purpose of these films was to launch an Abel Marsh TV series for Griffith, but further Marsh mysteries never materialized. Interestingly, Griffith starred in an earlier TV movie, 1974's *Winter Kill,* which was "inspired" by *They Only Kill Their Masters.* Although not written by Slate, *Winter Kill* featured Griffith as a ski resort sheriff (named Sam McNeill) investigating mysterious murders. It was also a failed pilot for a TV series. Griffith, of course, finally turned in his sheriff's badge and found TV series success in 1986 as a lawyer in *Matlock.*

They Only Kill Their Masters (1972); *The Girl in the Empty Grave* (1977 TVM); *Deadly Game* (1977 TVM)

Mason, Perry

Raymond Burr will always be Perry Mason for millions of mystery fans, but Erle Stanley Gardner's lawyer/detective hit the big screen twenty years before the long-running TV series. Warren William was a sharp-witted, gourmet-minded Mason in four Warner Bros. films, beginning with 1934's *The Case of the Howling Dog.* William seemed a natural for the part, having already played that urbane sleuth Philo Vance (q.v.) and destined to play the Lone Wolf (q.v.), a jewel thief and detective. In fact, William's

Mason did so much detection that it was easy to forget he was a lawyer and some entries were devoid of courtroom scenes. Two of William's films are of special interest. *The Case of the Curious Bride* featured superstar-to-be Errol Flynn as a murder victim and Donald Woods, a future Perry Mason, in another supporting role. *The Case of the Velvet Claws* found Mason and secretary Della Street (Claire Dodd) married and trying to take a honeymoon! Comic actor Allen Jenkins played Perry's detective assistant Spudsy (not Paul) Drake. In 1936, former Sam Spade Ricardo Cortez replaced Williams in *The Case of the Black Cat* and Donald Woods finished the Warner series with 1937's *The Case of the Stuttering Bishop*. The *Perry Mason* TV series debuted in 1957 and enjoyed a nine-year run on CBS. Burr played the lead, of course, with Barbara Hale as Della Street, William Hopper as detective Paul Drake, William Talman as prosecuting attorney Hamilton Burger, and Ray Collins as police Lieutenant Arthur Tragg (Collins died prior to the 1965-66 season). In 1973, CBS revived the show as *The New Adventures of Perry Mason* starring Monte Markham, but it folded after half a season. Then, in 1985, NBC brought back Burr in the TV movie *Perry Mason Returns*, reuniting him with Hale and introducing William Katt (Hale's real-life son) as Paul Drake's son. The film's ratings went through the roof and a series of equally high-rated made-for-TV movies quickly evolved. NBC broadcast two to four Mason films annually for the next eight years. William Katt bowed out after the 1988 season, with William R. Moses coming aboard as new private eye Ken Malansky. Following Burr's death from kidney cancer in 1993, NBC produced four *Perry Mason Mysteries* that starred either Paul Sorvino or Hal Holbrook as Mason-like lawyers. Barbara Hale and William R. Moses continued as series regulars. With a total of 29 films, the NBC *Perry Mason* films reign as the longest TV movie series in broadcast history. See also **Television Series Reunion Films**.

THEATRICAL FILMS: *The Case of the Howling Dog* (1934) (Warren William); *The Case of the Curious Bride* (1935) (William); *The Case of the Lucky Legs* (1935) (William); *The Case of the Velvet Claws* (1936) (William); *The Case of the Black Cat* (1936) (Ricardo Cortez); *The Case of the Stuttering Bishop* (1937) (Donald Woods)

RAYMOND BURR TV MOVIES: *Perry Mason Returns* (1985 TVM); *Perry Mason: The Case of the Notorious Nun* (1986 TVM); *Perry Mason: The Case of the Shooting Star* (1986 TVM); *Perry Mason and the Case of the Sinister Spirit* (1987 TVM); *Perry Mason: The Case of the Lost Love* (1987 TVM); *Perry Mason: The Case of the Murdered Madam* (1987 TVM); *Perry Mason: The Case of the Scandalous Scoundrel* (1987 TVM); *Perry Mason: The Case of the Avenging Ace* (1988 TVM); *Perry Mason: The Case of the Lady in the Lake* (1988 TVM); *Perry Mason: The Case of the All-Star Assassin* (1989 TVM); *Perry Mason: The Case of the Lethal Lesson* (1989 TVM); *Perry Mason: The Case of the Musical Murder* (1989 TVM); *Perry Mason: The Case of the Poison Pen* (1990 TVM); *Perry Mason: The Case of the Silenced Singer* (1990 TVM); *Perry Mason: The Case of the Desperate Deception* (1990 TVM); *Perry Mason: The Case of the Defiant Daughter* (1990 TVM); *Perry Mason: The Case of the Ruthless Reporter* (1991 TVM); *Perry Mason: The Case of the Maligned Mobster* (1991 TVM); *Perry Mason: The Case of the Glass Coffin* (1991 TVM); *Perry Mason: The Case of the Fatal Fashion* (1991 TVM); *Perry Mason: The Case of the Fatal Framing* (1992 TVM); *Perry Mason: The Case of the Reckless Romeo* (1992 TVM); *Perry Mason: The Case of the Heartbroken Bride* (1992 TVM); *Perry Mason: The Case of Skin Deep Scandal* (1993 TVM); *Perry Mason:*

The Case of the Tell-Tale Talk Show Host (1993 TVM); *A Perry Mason Mystery: The Case of the Wicked Wives* (1993 TVM) (Paul Sorvino as Anthony Caruso); *A Perry Mason Mystery: The Case of the Lethal Lifestyle* (1994 TVM) (Hal Holbrook as "Wild Bill" McKenzie); *A Perry Mason Mystery: The Case of the Grimacing Governor* (1995 TVM) (Holbrook); *A Perry Mason Mystery: The Case of the Jealous Jokester* (1995 TVM) (Holbrook)

Matadors/Bullfights

Blood and Sand reigns as the best-remembered bullfight film, chiefly because the 1922 and 1941 versions provided screen favorites Rudolph Valentino and Tyrone Power with one of their best roles. Vicente Blanco Ibáñez wrote the original story in 1908 and Tom Cushing adapted it for the stage in 1921. The following year, Valentino starred as the young matador who rises from poverty to stardom in the bullring, only to fall victim to the charms of an irresistible temptress (Nita Naldi). The matador died in the Ibáñez story, but the Valentino version was altered so that his faithful wife nursed him to recovery from near-death. The Tyrone Power remake followed the original closely (with Rita Hayworth as the seducer), but restored the climactic death scene in the bullring. Ex-matador Budd Boetticher, a technical advisor on the Power film, subsequently became a director and made three films about the perils of the bullring and the lifestyles of those who enter it. His semiautobiographical *The Bullfighter and the Lady* (1951) starred Robert Stack as an American (like Boetticher) in Mexico who convinces a famous matador (Gilbert Roland) to help him become a bullfighter. Boetticher followed it with 1955's *The Magnificent Matador*, which cast Anthony Quinn as an aging matador who trains his illegitimate son for the ring despite premonitions of death. Boetticher left Hollywood in 1960 to make a documentary in Mexico about the legendary bullfighter Carlos Arruza. The venture proved disastrous, with the producer-director facing endless personal and production problems. The film was finally completed in 1967 and released in 1972 as *Arruza*. Not surprisingly, bullfighting has been played for laughs in a number of films. In the 1945 comedy *The Bullfighters*, bumbling detectives Laurel and Hardy discover that Stan resembles a famous matador. Naturally, he winds up facing an unpleasant-looking bull in the ring. A similar fate befell Lou Costello in the 1948 Abbott and Costello comedy *Mexican Hayride*. In 1956's *Around the World in Eighty Days*, Cantiflas entered the bullring so he and David Niven could borrow Gilbert Roland's yacht. In one of the livelier scenes in 1957's *The Sun Also Rises*, Errol Flynn and Eddie Albert played rompish drunks who posed the dangerous question: "Bully, bully, where's the bull?" Tony Franciosa tried to interrogate Raquel Welch about a stolen jewel as an angry bull chased her around the bullring in *Fathom* (1967). Esther Williams (!) played an unlikely-looking female matador in the 1947 musical *Fiesta*. Still, she looked at ease with the role compared to the Volkswagen-turned-matador in *Herbie Goes Bananas*.

Blood and Sand (1922); *The Kid from Spain* (1932); *The Trumpet Blows* (1934); *Blood and Sand* (1941); *The Bullfighters* (1945); *Masquerade in Mexico* (1945); *Fiesta* (1947); *Mexican Hayride* (1948); *The Bullfighter and the Lady* (1951); *The Brave Bulls* (1951); *The Magnificent Matador* (aka *The Brave and the Beautiful*) (1955); *Around the World in Eighty Days* (1956); *The Sun Also Rises* (1957);

Alakazam the Great (1961); *Fun in Acapulco* (1963); *The Bobo* (1967); *Fathom* (1967); *Arruza* (1972); *Herbie Goes Bananas* (1980); *Bolero* (1984); *Matador* (1986); *Blood and Sand* (aka *Sangre y Arena*) (1989); *Jamon Jamon* (1993); *Only the Brave* (aka *Romance de Valentía*) (1994)

Matchmakers *see* Marriage Brokers/Dating Services

Meatballs Series

Five years before 1984's *Ghostbusters* lined their pockets with gold, comedian Bill Murray and director Ivan Reitman made this Canadian sleeper about life in a summer camp. Despite an abundance of teen comedy stereotypes, it was raunchy, occasionally schmaltzy, and pretty funny when Murray was around. Wisely, Murray went on to bigger roles and avoided further association with Camp Sasquatch in *Meatballs II*, *Meatballs III*, and *Meatballs 4*. John Laroquette, Sally Kellerman, Patrick Dempsey, and Corey Feldman were not as selective. See also **Summer Camps**.

Meatballs (1979); *Meatball II* (1983); *Meatballs III* (1987); *Meatballs 4* (1992)

Mediums and Seances

The movies have treated mediums with both respect and disdain. Sadly, in movies where they get the most footage, mediums are typically portrayed as charlatans. In 1947's *Nightmare Alley*, Tyrone Power gave one of his best performances as a sideshow hustler who becomes a financially successful spiritualist through trickery and deceit. He is eventually exposed as a fraud and winds up back in the carnival as "the geek." Along similar lines, Turhan Bey played *The Amazing Mr. X* (1948), a fake spiritualist who plots with a "dead man" to dupe the man's wife. And in *Seance on a Wet Afternoon* (1964), an unbalanced medium (Kim Stanley) hatches a plot to kidnap a child and then hold a seance which will reveal the child's whereabouts. Real-life magician (q.v.) Harry Houdini spent the latter portion of his life exposing fake spiritualists, a pastime explored briefly in 1953's *Houdini*. In the 1990 box-office smash *Ghost*, Whoopi Goldberg won a Best Supporting Actress Oscar as a fake medium who becomes a real one when Patrick Swayze's spirit returns to protect his wife Demi Moore. Margaret Rutherford played an eccentric—but legitimate—medium in *Blithe Spirit* (1945), as did spunky Zelda Rubinstein in 1982's *Poltergeist* (q.v.). Claire Bloom was a psychic and Julie Harris a lonely spinster in 1963's eerie classic *The Haunting*, but one (or both?) of them seemed to attract (or cause?) supernatural happenings in an old mansion. Seances have played minor parts in many ghost (q.v.) movies, with some of the most memorable ones appearing in *The Uninvited*, *Curse of the Demon*, and Abbott and Costello's *The Time of Their Lives*. See also **Clairvoyants and Fortunetellers**; **Ghosts**.

Palmy Days (1932); *Miracles for Sale* (1939); *The Spell of Amy Nugent* (aka *Spellbound*; *Passing Clouds*) (1940); *The Uninvited* (1944); *Blithe Spirit* (1945); *The Time of Their Lives* (1946); *Nightmare Alley* (1947); *The Amazing Mr. X* (aka *The Spiritualist*) (1948); *The Medium* (1951); *Houdini* (1953); *Curse of the Demon* (aka *Night of the Demon*) (1958); *13 Ghosts* (1960); *The Haunting* (1963); *Seance on a Wet Afternoon* (1964); *The Legend of Hell House* (1973); *Family Plot* (1976); *The Manitou* (1978); *Poltergeist* (1982); *Grave Secrets* (1989); *Ghost* (1990); *The Haunting* (1999)

Mermaids

Mermaid movies seem to come in waves, with 1947's *Miranda* sparking the first volley. It starred Glynis Johns as a comely mermaid who rescues a drowning physician on a Cornwall holiday. To show his gratitude, the doctor takes the mermaid back to London, where she moves in with him and his wife and decides that she prefers the sophisticated land-life. This light comedic concoction inspired a 1954 sequel, *Mad About Men*, in which mermaid Johns trades places with a lookalike (q.v.) human. In the meantime, producer-writer Nunnally Johnson mounted an American imitation of Miranda with 1948's *Mr. Peabody and the Mermaid*. William Powell played a man in the midst of a midlife crisis who hooks mermaid Ann Blyth while on a fishing trip. Complications ensue when he takes her back and deposits her into a fish pond near his beach house. A gap of five years separated *Mad About Men* from the next group of mermaid movies. *Mermaids and Sea Robbers* (1959), a Japanese import, and *The Mermaids of Tiburon* (1962) were low-grade fantasies with no redeeming traits. Curtis Harrington's *Night Tide* (1961) was an atmospheric yarn about a sailor (Dennis Hopper) who meets an odd girl (Linda Lawson) who plays a mermaid in a carnival sideshow. She claims to be a descendant of the "sea people," who must kill during a full moon. Far less compelling was 1965's *Beach Blanket Bingo*, which featured a subplot involving a mermaid played by Marta Kristen (the oldest daughter in TV's *Lost in Space*). Almost 20 years later, a mermaid subplot in Bill Forsyth's charming Scottish fantasy *Local Hero* (1983) initiated another round of mermaid movies. The following year's *Splash* was a solid sleeper hit about a young man (Tom Hanks) reunited with the fetching mermaid (Daryl Hannah) who rescued him from drowning as a boy. Ariel the mermaid also fell in love with the human prince she rescued in Disney's 1989 animated version of *The Little Mermaid*. Cher donned flippers to attend a costume party in 1990's *Mermaids*.

Miranda (1947); *Mr. Peabody and the Mermaid* (1948); *Hans Christian Andersen* (the "Little Mermaid" sequence) (1952); *Peter Pan* (1953); *Mad About Men* (1954); *Mermaids and Sea Robbers* (1959); *Don't Give Up the Ship* (1959); *Night Tide* (1961); *The Mermaids of Tiburon* (aka *The Aqua Sex*) (1962); *Beach Blanket Bingo* (1965); *Local Hero* (1983); *Splash* (1984); *Splash Too* (1988 TVM); *The Little Mermaid* (1989); *Hook* (1991)

Meteors *see* Asteriods, Comets, and Meteors

Mexican Spitfire

By the time she was 30, spicy Latin American actress Lupe Velez had experienced a flirtation with stardom (opposite Douglas Fairbanks in 1927's *The Gaucho*), a scandalous romance with Gary Cooper, and an unhappy marriage to Johnny Weissmuller. Her career was in a slow tailspin when she made a lightweight 1939 comedy called *The Girl from Mexico*. Donald Woods starred as a young advertising executive who falls for a fiery Latin entertainer (Velez), while dealing with his own devious Uncle Matt (Leon Errol). To everyone's surprise, the movie's success spawned a *Mexican Spitfire* series. Although Velez was the star, Errol stole the show at every turn-playing both Uncle Matt and a delightful drunken Englishman named Lord Epping. Sometimes, the antics got a wee silly—one entry featured a live pink elephant with green polka dots. Sadly, the series ended abruptly in 1944 with Velez's elaborately staged sleeping-pill suicide.

The Girl from Mexico (1939); *Mexican Spitfire* (1939); *Mexican Spitfire Out West* (1940); *Mexican Spitfire at Sea* (1941); *Mexican Spitfire's Baby* (1941); *Mexican Spitfire Sees a Ghost* (1942); *Mexican Spitfire's Elephant* (1942); *Mexican Spitfire's Blessed Event* (1943)

(Note: Although both Velez and Errol appeared in 1941's *Six Lessons from Madame La Zonga*, it was not a *Spitfire* entry.)

Mice *see* Rodents

The Mighty Ducks

This uninspired hockey variation of *The Bad News Bears* (q.v.) proved that a good formula could yield box-office gold regardless of its ingredients. Emilio Estevez starred as Gordon Bombay, a yuppie lawyer arrested for a DUI and sentenced to community service. He winds up coaching a Pee Wee hockey team of misfits called the Mighty Ducks. Building upon every cliché imaginable, Gordon falls in love with the mother of a troubled player, turns the Ducks into a championship-caliber team, and earns self-respect by facing the hockey coach who ridiculed Gordon when he played as a boy. In *D2: The Mighty Ducks*, Bombay (Estevez) returns to coach Team USA, comprised of several former Ducks, for the Junior Goodwill Games (a plot similar to *The Bad News Bears Go to Japan*). Estevez makes a brief appearance in *D3: The Mighty Ducks*, which sends several Duck players to snobby Eden Hall on hockey scholarships. Joshua Jackson, who played Duck player Charlie Conway in all three films, became a teen heartthrob as Pacey in the 1997 TV series *Dawson's Creek*. An animated series appeared in 1996, with the hockey players fighting criminals in their spare time. When the Disney studios acquired a National Hockey League franchise in Anaheim, California, in 1993, it dubbed the team the Mighty Ducks. See also **Ice Hockey**.

The Mighty Ducks (1992); *D2: The Mighty Ducks* (1994); *D3: The Mighty Ducks* (1996)

Military Academies

As one would expect, the United States Military Academy — better known as West Point — has provided the bulk of military school settings. West Point stories have ranged from inspirational sport sagas (*The Spirit of West Point*) to musical revues (*West Point Story*) to true-life dramas (*The Silence* and *Dress Gray*). Ask any cadet about his favorite West Point film and he will probably answer *The Long Gray Line*, a sentimental tale about an athletic trainer (Tyrone Power) and his wife (Maureen O'Hara) who become an institution at the school. West Point comedies have been rare, though Francis the Talking Mule tutored Donald O'Connor in 1952's *Francis Goes to West Point* and females invaded the academy in the 1979 TV movie *Women of West Point*. An "illegal" woman caused Eddie Albert quite a bit of trouble at the Virginia Military Institute in the 1940 comedy *Brother Rat*. The woman turned out to be his pregnant wife (Jane Bryan) — a fact he had hidden from school officials who did not accept married cadets. It was remade as the musical *About Face* with Eddie Bracken in 1952. Not surprisingly, controversial dramas have taken place in fictitious military schools. Ben Gazarra played a sadistic cadet with a dominating hold over classmates in 1957's *The Strange One*, adapted from Calder Willingham's novel *End*

as a Man. (Ironically, *Sorority Girl*, a female version of the same novel, was also released in 1957.) In 1981's *Taps*, Timothy Hutton led a group of fellow cadets, including Sean Penn and Tom Cruise, in a revolt against school officials trying to turn their beloved academy into a condominium. David Keith battled modern-day prejudice at a Southern military academy in 1983's *The Lords of Discipline*. The most unlikely military school is the one run by an order of nuns in the Charlton Heston picture *The Private War of Major Benson*. See also **Boarding Schools**.

Tom Brown of Culver (1932); *Flirtation Walk* (1934); *Dinky* (1935); *Navy Blue and Gold* (1937); *The Duke of West Point* (1938); *Lord Jeff* (1938); *Spirit of Culver* (1939); *Brother Rat* (1940); *They Died with Their Boots On* (1941); *Ten Gentlemen from West Point* (1942); *Best Foot Forward* (1943); *The Spirit of West Point* (1947); *Beyond Glory* (1948); *West Point Story* (aka *Fine and Dandy*) (1950); *About Face* (1952); *Francis Goes to West Point* (1952); *The Long Gray Line* (1955); *The Private War of Major Benson* (1955); *The Strange One* (aka *End as a Man*) (1957); *The Silence* (1975 TVM); *Women of West Point* (1979 TVM); *Up the Academy* (1980); *Taps* (1981); *Evilspeak* (1982); *The Lords of Discipline* (1983); *Hard Knox* (1984 TVM); *Dress Gray* (1986 TVM); *Combat High* (1986 TVM); *Child's Play 3* (1991)

Mirrors

Employed principally in fantasy films, mirrors have also been used effectively in comic sequences and climactic confrontations. An imaginary mirror was the gimmick in *Duck Soup*, in which Harpo Marx posed as Groucho's reflection, mimicking perfectly his brother's every movement. Errol Flynn and Donald Woods, both attired in Santa suits, repeated the "no mirror" trick in 1946's *Never Say Goodbye* (as did Lucille Ball and Harpo Marx in TV's *I Love Lucy*). A man's reflection stepped out of a mirror to offer advice to his owner in the 1936 comedy *The Man in the Mirror*. And a magician's trick mirror saved Woody Allen from the strangler in 1992's *Shadows and Fog*. Orson Welles confronted murderess Rita Hayworth in a carnival hall of mirrors in the gripping climax of Welles' *Lady from Shanghai* (1948). In a similar fashion, Bruce Lee outdueled villain Shih Kien in a chamber of mirrors in the 1973 martial arts classic *Enter the Dragon*. However, fantasy films have used mirrors most imaginatively, beginning with the Wicked Witch's magic mirror in Disney's *Snow White and the Seven Dwarfs* (1937). In 1945's *Dead of Night*, an antique mirror haunted a happy husband by reflecting the room of its previous owner: a jealous gent who strangled his wife. Another old mirror allowed Bradford Dillman to return from the dead to visit fiancée Linda Day George in the 1969 TV Movie *Fear No Evil*. On a more intellectual scale, a mirror provided the door between Earth and the Zone (a sort of Heaven/Hell) in Jean Cocteau's eerie classic *Orpheus* (1949). For the most bizarre use of mirrors, it's hard to beat *The Boogeyman*, a 1980 sleeper about a shard of a broken mirror which turned people into killers. Finally, mirrors have exposed quite a few vampires, for those smart enough to know that the bloodsuckers cast no reflection.

Duck Soup (1933); *The Man in the Mirror* (1936); *Snow White and the Seven Dwarfs* (1937); *Kitty Foyle* (1940); *Dead of Night* (1945); *Beauty and the Beast* (1946); *Never Say Goodbye* (1946); *Fear in the Night* (1947); *Lady from Shanghai* (1948); *Orpheus* (1949); *Nightmare* (1956); *The Witch's Mirror* (1960); *The Devil's Bride* (aka *The Devil Rides Out*) (1968); *Fear No Evil* (1969 TVM); *Vampire Circus* (1971); *Enter the Dragon* (1973); *The Boogeyman* (aka *The*

Boogey Man) (1980); *The Mirror Crack'd* (1980); *Come Back to the 5 & Dime, Jimmy Dean, Jimmy Dean* (1982); *Something Wicked This Way Comes* (1983); *Big Business* (1988); *Fright Night 2* (1989); *Curse of the Blue Lights* (1989); *Mirror, Mirror* (1990); *Shadows and Fog* (1992); *Candyman* (1992); *Amityville: A New Generation* (1993); *Mirror Mirror 2: Raven Dance* (aka *Mirror Mirror*) (1994)

Missing in Action Series

This 1984 Chuck Norris action picture cashed in on the public's "new patriotism" and shot to the top of the box-office charts. In many ways, it paved the way for 1985's *Rambo: First Blood Part II*, with a plot that sent Colonel Norris back into Vietnam to rescue some buddies imprisoned in a P.O.W. camp. It was followed by a prequel and then a sequel. *Missing in Action 2: The Beginning* (1985), which was actually filmed before the earlier film, focused on Norris' P.O.W. escape. *Braddock: Missing in Action III* (1988) had Norris returning to Vietnam again, this time to save his own son. Neither of these two films matched the popularity of the original. See also **Prisoners of War**; **Vietnam**.

Missing in Action (1984); *Missing in Action 2: The Beginning* (1985); *Braddock: Missing in Action III* (1988)

Mr. Vampire Series

Hopping vampires? They abound in this Asian comedy-horror series starring Lam Ching Ying as a Taoist vampire killer. A popular explanation for the "hopping" mode of travel is that rigor mortis prevents the vampires from walking normally. They still manage to get around nicely and kill people, although — unlike Western vampires — they don't suck blood. In the original *Mr. Vampire* (1985), Lam Ching Ying's "one eyebrow priest" (so named because his eyesbrows meet) teams with his two bumbling assistants to fight a vampire outbreak caused when a corpse is reburied. One assistant (Ricky Hui) gets bitten by a vampire and begins to transform into one of the undead. The other assistant (Chin Siu-Ho) falls in love with a beautiful ghost. The film earned a host of nominations, including best picture, at the Fifth Annual Hong King Film Awards and turned a big profit at the box-office. It also made an Asian superstar of Lam Ching Ying, who starred in all the entries except *New Mr. Vampire* (1986) and *Mr. Vampire 4* (1990). Lam Ching Ying, who died in 1997, had a long, prosperous film career, working with major Asian stars such as Bruce Lee, Sammo Hung, and Michelle Yeoh. Sammo Hung's 1981 *Close Encounters of the Spooky Kind* pioneered the Hong Kong comedy-horror formula and heavily influenced the *Mr. Vampire* films. For the record, *Magic Cop*, a 1989 Lam Ching Ying film also called *Mr. Vampire 5*, is not part of the *Mr. Vampire* series. See also **Vampires**.

Mr. Vampire (aka *Geung Si Sin Sang*) (1985); *Mr. Vampire 2* (aka *Geung Si Sin Sang Juk Jaap*) (1986); *New Mr. Vampire* (aka *Geung Si Faan Sang*; *Kung Fu Vampire Buster*) (1986); *Mr. Vampire 3* (aka *Ling Waan Sin Sang*) (1987); *New Mr. Vampire 2* (aka *One Eyebrow Priest*) (1989); *Mr. Vampire 4* (aka *Geung Si Suk Suk*; *Mr. Vampire Saga*) (1990); *Mr. Vampire 1992* (aka *San Geung Si Sin Sang*; *Mr. Vampire 5*; *Vampire vs. Vampire*) (1991)

Mobile Homes

Not many movie residents have lived in mobile home parks. Dick Powell and Rhonda Fleming called the Clover Trailer Park home in *Cry Danger*, but their place of residence had little to do with the plot. The same can be said of mobile home dwellers Jamie Lee Curtis (*Grandview, U.S.A.*), John Travolta and Debra Winger (*Urban Cowboy*), Bette Midler (*Jinxed*), and Holly Hunter and Nicolas Cage (*Raising Arizona*). The first half of 1984's delightful *The Last Starfighter* took place in an atmospheric trailer park where an ugly alien tried to liquidate a teen video game expert. Two memorable comedies have dealt with couples who have taken their trailers on the road. In *The Long, Long Trailer* (1954), Lucille Ball and Desi Arnaz went on their honeymoon in a particularly troublesome trailer. Yuppies Albert Brooks and Julie Haggerty gave up the "rat race" for an enlightening life on the road in *Lost in America* (1985). However, they didn't count on Haggerty losing their nest egg on their first stop — at a casino in Las Vegas.

Cry Danger (1951); *The Long, Long Trailer* (1954); *Anatomy of a Murder* (1959); *Pretty Poison* (1968); *Pink Flamingos* (1972); *Urban Cowboy* (1980); *Jinxed!* (1982); *Grandview, U.S.A.* (1984); *The Last Starfighter* (1984); *Lost in America* (1985); *Raising Arizona* (1987); *Pals* (1987 TVM); *Little Vegas* (1990); *Gas, Food, Lodging* (1992); *Wilder Napalm* (1993); *Hold Me, Thrill Me, Kiss Me* (1993); *Showgirls* (1995); *Touch* (1997); *Wild Things* (1998); *Ringmaster* (1998)

Models *see* Fashion Models

Moment of Truth Series

When NBC launched this long-running series of made-for-TV films in 1993, its goal was simple: capture an audience composed of female viewers aged 18–49, a cherished demographic for television networks. The films featured no recurring characters, but were similar in that they usually featured strong female characters and focused on family issues such as child custody (*A Child Too Many*), adoption (*The Other Mother*), and teenage eating disorders (*A Secret Between Friends*). Still, a couple of the films did not seem to fit the formula, such as *Caught in the Crossfire*, which starred Dennis Franz as a reporter accused of extortion. NBC ended the film series' five-year run in 1999. By then, the network had replaced its Monday night movies with sitcoms and had shifted its focus to a more general audience with its Sunday night movies. With its 21 entries, the *Moment of Truth* films ranks as the second longest TV movie series. Top honors belong to Raymond Burr's *Perry Mason* TV films (q.v.), which also aired on NBC.

Moment of Truth: A Child Too Many (1993 TVM); *Moment of Truth: Stalking Back* (1993 TVM); *Moment of Truth: Why My Daughter?* (1993 TVM); *Moment of Truth: A Mother's Deception* (1994 TVM); *Moment of Truth: Broken Pledges* (1994 TVM); *Moment of Truth: Caught in the Crossfire* (1994 TVM); *Moment of Truth: Cradle of Conspiracy* (1994 TVM); *Moment of Truth: To Walk Again* (1994 TVM); *Murder or Memory: A Moment of Truth Movie* (1995 TVM); *Eye of the Stalker: A Moment of Truth Movie* (1995 TVM); *The Other Mother: A Moment of Truth Movie* (1995 TVM); *A Secret Between Friends: A Moment of Truth Movie* (1996 TVM); *Justice for Annie: A Moment of Truth Movie* (1996 TVM); *Abduction of Innocence: A Moment of Truth Movie* (1996 TVM); *Stand Against Fear: A Moment of Truth Movie* (1996 TVM); *The Accident: A Moment of Truth Movie* (1997 TVM); *Into the Arms of Danger: A Moment of Truth Movie* (1997 TVM); *Playing to Win: A Moment of Truth Movie* (1998 TVM); *Someone to Love Me: A*

Moment of Truth Movie (1998 TVM); *Race Against Fear: A Moment of Truth Movie* (1998 TVM); *A Champion's Fight: A Moment of Truth Movie* (1998 TVM)

Monks

In comparison to priests and nuns, monks have been poorly represented in films. The only ones to achieve celebrity status have been Friar Tuck of Robin Hood (q.v.) fame and Rasputin, the Russian monk whose alleged healing powers gained him influence over the Imperial family. This colorful character has attracted many performers, most notably Christopher Lee (*Rasputin—the Mad Monk*), Tom Baker (*Nicholas and Alexandra*), Edmund Purdom (*Nights of Rasputin*), Alan Rickman (*Rasputin*), and, in the definitive performance, Lionel Barrymore (*Rasputin and the Empress*). The portly frame of Friar Tuck has been inhabited by even more actors, though Eugene Pallette's portrayal in 1938's *The Adventures of Robin Hood* outshines all others. With the exception of Rasputin, other film biographies of monks have been of the saintly variety. Both Franco Zeffirelli's *Brother Sun, Sister Moon* (1973) and the earlier *Francis of Assisi* (1961) told how St. Francis of Assisi founded the Franciscan order of monks. The 1974 *Luther* was a straightforward adaptation of John Osborne's play about the leader of Protestant Reformation. In fictional films, Harrison Ford and Sean Connery encountered an ancient monk who guarded the Holy Grail in the 1989 blockbuster *Indiana Jones and the Last Crusade*. Three years earlier, Connery solved devious murders in a 13th century Italian monastery in *The Name of the Rose*. It was not, however, the first monastery mystery. That distinction belongs to the offbeat 1974 TV movie *Judge Dee and the Monastery Murders*, which was set in seventh century China. Another Chinese monastery appeared briefly in another TV movie, 1972's *Kung Fu*, the pilot for the 1972–75 series about a fugitive Buddhist monk in the American West. The most unusual monks have been played by Charles Boyer (opposite Marlene Dietrich in *The Garden of Allah*), Marty Feldman (*In God We Trust*), and Edward G. Robinson (as a gangster who reforms in *Brother Orchid*). Contrary to its title, the 1969 TV movie *The Monk* had nothing to do with monks. George Maharis played a private eye named Gus Monk. See also **Nuns; Popes and Cardinals.**

Rasputin and the Empress (1932); *The Garden of Allah* (1936); *The Adventures of Robin Hood* (1938); *Brother Orchid* (1940); *Letters from My Windmill* (1954); *Nights of Rasputin* (1960); *Francis of Assisi* (1961); *Rasputin-the Mad Monk* (1966); *I Killed Rasputin* (1967); *Nicholas and Alexandra* (1971); *Kung Fu* (1972 TVM); *Brother Sun, Sister Moon* (1973); *Luther* (1974); *Judge Dee and the Monastery Murders* (1974 TVM); *In God We Trust* (1980); *The Name of the Rose* (1986); *Indiana Jones and the Last Crusade* (1989); *Little Buddha* (1993); *Temptation of a Monk* (aka *You Seng*) (1994); *Rasputin* (1996 TVM); *Anastasia* (1997)

Mothra

Toho Studios, the home of Godzilla, introduced this giant female caterpillar (and occasional moth) in 1962. Her debut film marked a turning point in the studio's Japanese monster series: It was the first movie to be shot in color and feature a sympathetic creature. Of course, Mothra wreaked plenty of havoc, just like her predecessors Godzilla (q.v.) and Rodan (q.v.). However, the carnage was a justified response to the kidnapping of two fairies from Mothra's home island. Mothra's next appearance was in 1964's *Godzilla vs. the Thing*, in which the radioactive "King of Monsters" destroyed the giant caterpillar. However, an egg hatched to unleash two baby giant caterpillars which wove a web of silk around Godzilla and rendered him helpless. Thus, the Mothras that appear in subsequent films are either children or grandchildren of the original Mothra—it's never made clear. The giant caterpillar's film appearances decreased after Godzilla made the switch from bad guy to good in 1965's *Ghidrah, the Three-Headed Monster*. However, she staged a comeback along with Godzilla in the 1990s. See also **The Alilenas.**

Mothra (aka *Mosura*) (1962); *Godzilla vs. the Thing* (aka *Godzilla vs. Mothra; Gojira tai Mothra*) (1964); *Ghidrah the Three-Headed Monster* (aka *The Greatest Battle on Earth; Sandai Kaiju Chikyu Saidai No Kessen*) (1965); *Godzilla vs. the Sea Monster* (aka *Ebriah-Terror of the Deep; Nankai no Dai Ketto*) (1966); *Destroy All Monsters* (aka *Operation Monsterland; Kaiju Soshingeki*) (1968); *Godzilla's Revenge* (aka *Ord Kaiju Daishingeki*) (1969); *Godzilla vs. Mothra* (aka *Gojira vs. Mothra*) (1992); *Mothra* (aka *Mosura*)(1996); *Mothra 2* (aka *Mosura 2—Kaitei No Daikessen; Mothra 2—Showdown Beneath the Sea*) (1997)

Moto, Mr.

J.P. Marquand's Japanese sleuth was a brilliant thinker, a master of disguises, and a martial arts expert. That description does not exactly bring Peter Lorre to mind, but he nevertheless made a fine movie Moto. He made eight films in a two-year period, beginning with 1937's *Think Fast, Mr. Moto*. The series ended abruptly in 1939, its demise usually attributed to the U.S.'s growing disenchantment with Japan's World War II activities. In 1965, an unexpected update, *The Return of Mr. Moto*, appeared with movie heavy Henry Silva as Moto. This new Moto bore little resemblance to Marquand's detective and the movie died at the box-office. The only other "actor" to play Mr. Moto was Porky Pig in the 1939 cartoon "Porky's Movie Mystery."

Think Fast, Mr. Moto (1937); *Mr. Moto's Gamble* (1938); *Mr. Moto Takes a Chance* (1938); *The Mysterious Mr. Moto* (1938); *Thank You, Mr. Moto* (1938); *Mr. Moto on Danger Island* (1939); *Mr. Moto's Last Warning* (1939); *Mr. Moto Takes a Vacation* (1939); *The Return of Mr. Moto* (1965)

Motorcycle Gangs

Sheriff's daughter to motorcycle gang leader Marlon Brando: "What are you rebelling against?" Brando: "What ya got?" That simple line of dialogue from 1953's *The Wild One* summarizes the attitude of pointless rebellion that would eventually spark the motorcycle gang films of the late 1960s and early 1970s. Considering the popularity of Brando's film with youth audiences of the 1950s, it's amazing that the genre was not born earlier. In all likelihood, however, audiences were not yet prepared to accept antiestablishment criminals as their idols. Thus, the teen bikers in 1957's *Motorcycle Gang* were presented as a "bad crowd" to be avoided by nice teens. Likewise, Oliver Reed and his fellow "Teddy Boys" had no redeeming features in Joseph Losey's science fiction cult film *These Are the Damned* (1962). Harvey Lembeck brought a little humanity—and a disarming ridiculousness—to his role of gang leader Eric Von Zipper in 1963's *Beach Party* (q.v.) and its subsequent sequels. Three years later, the biker antihero roared onto the screen in the guise of leather-clad, joint-smoking, Hell's Angel leader Peter Fonda in Roger Corman's *The*

Wild Angels about which Hollis Alpert of *The Saturday Review* wrote: It "strings together such incidents as the invasion of a hospital and the rape of a Negro nurse, a gang fight, and an orgy in a church…the film is faulty, and in a sense, irresponsible." Still, many mid–1960s teenagers identified with the angry, ultimately pessimistic attitudes of Fonda's Heavenly Blues and Bruce Dern's Loser. Cheaper, cruder biker films filled drive-in screens in the wake of *Wild Angels'* success. At their best, these exploitation films provided steady work for rising talents like Jack Nicholson (*Hell's Angels on Wheels*, *Rebel Rousers*), Harry Dean Stanton (*The Miniskirt Mob*), Tyne Daly (*Angel Unchained*), Bruce Dern (*The Cycle Savages*, *Rebel Rousers*), and disc jockey Casey Kasem (*Wild Wheels*). The worst films were the ones that capitalized on returning Vietnam veterans, such as *Angels from Hell* and *The Angry Breed*. An interesting exception was 1967's *Born Losers*, which introduced a peace-loving, former Green Beret named Billy Jack (Tom Laughlin). Four years later, Laughlin revived the character for the influential, nonbiker sleeper hit *Billy Jack* (q.v.). Still, few motorcycle gang films strayed from the *Wild Angels'* violence-drugs-orgy formula, although female bikers took charge effectively in *The Miniskirt Mob*, *She-Devils on Wheels*, and *Angels' Wild Women*, and supernatural twists livened up *Werewolves on Wheels* and *Psychomania* (the latter concerning bikers revived from the dead). In 1973, the motorcycle gang movie craze gave way to other blossoming, low-budget genres like the martial arts imports and blaxploitation (q.v.) pictures. Ironically, the most influential biker film of the 1966–72 period turned out to be Dennis Hopper and Peter Fonda's 1967 sleeper smash *Easy Rider*— and it was not about motorcycle gangs. Post-1972 film appearances by biker gangs have been rare. A hapless gang incurred the wrath of Clint Eastwood in his comedy hit *Every Which Way But Loose*. Don Murray reunited his old gang to get rid of some contemporary punks in the 1981 TV movie *Return of the Rebels*. Ed Harris played King Arthur to a travelling group of jousting bikers in George Romero's heavyhanded parable *Knightriders* (1981). On television, *Monty Python's Flying Circus* presented a hilarious skit about a gang of vicious, motorcycle-riding grannies. Motorcycles — without the gangs — are featured in movies such as *Evel Knievel* (1972), *I Bought a Vampire Motorcycle* (1990), and *Murdercycle* (1999).

The Wild One (1953); *Motorcycle Gang* (1957); *These Are the Damned* (aka *The Damned*) (1962); *Beach Party* (1963); *Motor Psycho* (1965); *The Wild Angels* (1966); *Born Losers* (1967); *Hell's Angels on Wheels* (1967); *Rebel Rousers* (1967); *The Glory Stompers* (1967); *Angels from Hell* (1968); *Girl on a Motorcycle* (aka *Naked Under Leather*) (1968); *The Miniskirt Mob* (1968); *She-Devils on Wheels* (1968); *The Savage Seven* (1968); *The Angry Breed* (1969); *The Cycle Savages* (1969); *Wild Wheels* (1969); *Angels Die Hard* (1970); *Hell's Bloody Angels* (aka *The Fakers*; *Smashing the Crime Syndicate*) (1970); *Angel Unchained* (1970); *The Black Angels* (1970); *C.C. and Company* (1971); *Chrome and Hot Leather* (1971); *Psychomania* (1971); *The Hard Ride* (1971); *The Peace Killers* (1971); *The Jesus Trip* (1971); *Werewolves on Wheels* (1971); *Angels' Wild Women* (1972); *The Dirt Gang* (1972); *Hex* (1973); *The Northville Cemetery Massacre* (1976); *Every Which Way But Loose* (1978); *Dawn of the Dead* (aka *Zombie*) (1979); *Hog Wild* (1980); *Return of the Rebels* (1981 TVM); *The Loveless* (1981); *Knightriders* (1981); *Hear No Evil* (1982 TVM); *Hell's Angels Forever* (1983); *Mask* (1985); *Eye of the Tiger* (1986); *Nam Angels* (1989); *Easy Wheels* (1989); *Chopper Chicks in Zombietown* (1990); *Masters of Menace* (1990); *The Last*

Riders (1990); *Beyond the Law* (1992); *Iron Horsemen* (1994); *Motorcycle Gang* (1994 TVM)

Mountain Climbing

No fictional film has been able to match 1953's *Conquest of Everest* in terms of portraying the awesome beauty and never-ending danger of mountain climbing. Sadly, this gripping chronicle of Edmund Hillary's Everest expedition lost the Best Documentary Oscar to Disney's *The Living Desert*. On the dramatic front, Glenn Ford led a group of climbers intent on scaling the Swiss Alps in *The White Tower* (1950). In *Cliffhanger* (1993), Sylvester Stallone flexed his muscles as a Rocky Mountain Rescue pro who grapples with a gang of money-hungry villains. James MacArthur played a young man intent on conquering a peak called the Citadel (actually the Matterhorn) in the 1958 Disney adventure *Third Man on the Mountain*. *Five Days One Summer* and *The Mountain* ended with mountain climbing tragedies. In the latter film, Spencer Tracy followed greedy brother Robert Wagner up the slopes to prevent the looting of plane wreckage. *The Ascent* (1994), based on a true story, had Italian POWs challenging their British captors to a race to the top of Mount Kenya. *Everest* (1998), a 44-minute documentary, presented the wonders of the world's highest peak on a huge 1.44:1 aspect ratio IMAX screen. Numerous films have boasted extensive mountain climbing footage, ranging from the scaling of the German fortress in *The Guns of Navarone* to the Clint Eastwood spy adventure *The Eiger Sanction* to the James Bond picture *For Your Eyes Only*.

The White Tower (1950); *Conquest of Everest* (1953); *The Mountain* (1956); *The Abominable Snowman of the Himalayas* (aka *Abominable Snowman*) (1957); *Third Man on the Mountain* (1959); *The Guns of Navarone* (1961); *Climb an Angry Mountain* (1972 TVM); *The Eiger Sanction* (1975); *High Ice* (1980 TVM); *The Constant Factor* (1980); *For Your Eyes Only* (1981); *Five Days One Summer* (1982); *A Breed Apart* (1984); *Storm and Sorrow* (1990 TVM); *Dreams* (1990) ("The Blizzard" segment); *Scream of Stone* (1991); *K2* (1992); *Cliffhanger* (1993); *The Ascent* (1994); *Everest* (1998); *Mission: Impossible 2* (aka *Mission Impossible II*) (2000)

Mounties

Television has treated the Royal Canadian Mounted Police far more generously than the cinema. *Sergeant Preston of the Yukon* and *Dudley Doright* may have done little for Mountie prestige, but they still accounted for some brief popularity. On the big screen, Mountie musicals and a handful of modest adventures have attracted minimal attention. Cecil DeMille saluted the Royal Mounted with his lavish *Northwest Mounted Police* (1940), starring Gary Cooper and Robert Preston. Critic Otis Ferguson called it "two hours of colour, killing, kindness and magnificent country" (Oregon and Hollywood, not Canada). Despite racking up Paramount's biggest grosses of the year, DeMille's film inspired no imitations. Instead, Warner Bros. offered Errol Flynn as a contemporary Mountie tracking a Nazi across Canada in *Northern Pursuit* (1943). *Death Hunt* (1981) followed a similar plotline, with Mountie Lee Marvin hunting down trapper-murder suspect Charles Bronson. The gentle side of married Mountie life was covered in the 1949 Dick Powell–Evelyn Keyes vehicle *Mrs. Mike*. The only true Mountie musical remains *Rose Marie*, which was first filmed without the music as a 1928 silent picture. In 1936, Nelson Eddy and Jeanette MacDonald lent their voices to the operatic songs and enjoyed one of their biggest hits. Howard Keel and Ann Blyth remade *Rose Marie*, with less success, in 1954. Little Shirley Temple sang a bit as *Susannah of the Mounties* (1939) and B-movie series Mountie *Renfrew* (q.v.) could always be counted on for a song if the bad guys were behind bars. The 1994 TV movie *Due South*, about a contemporary Mountie in Chicago, served as the pilot for a 1994–97 TV series. The most offbeat casting for a Mountie belongs to Tom Smothers, who played one in the *Friday the 13th* spoof *Pandemonium* (1982). Jean-Claude Van Damme made an unlikely Mountie who goes undercover as a prison inmate in 1990's *Death Warrant*. See also **Renfrew of the Mounties**.

Rose Marie (1936); *King of the Royal Mounted* (1936); *O'Malley of the Mounted* (1936); *Renfrew of the Royal Mounted* (1937); *The Girl of the Golden West* (1938); *Susannah of the Mounties* (1939); *Northwest Mounted Police* (1940); *Northern Pursuit* (1943); *R.C.M.P. and the Treasure of Genghis Khan* (1948); *Mrs. Mike* (1949); *Pony Soldier* (aka *MacDonald of the Canadian Mounted*) (1952); *Fort Vengeance* (1953); *Missile Base at Taniak* (aka *Canadian Mounties vs. Atomic Invaders*) (1953); *Rose Marie* (1954); *Yukon Vengeance* (1954); *The Canadians* (1961); *Alien Thunder* (aka *Dan Candy's Law*) (1973); *Death Hunt* (1981); *Pandemonium* (1982); *Death Warrant* (1990); *Conspiracy of Silence* (1991 TVM); *Due South* (1994 TVM); *Dudley Do-Right* (1999)

Movie Theaters

Films about movie theaters fall into three general categories: cinemas, projectionists, and drive-ins. Cinemas have been the principal subject of only a handful of films. A young couple inherits, and subsequently manages, a run-down theater in the 1957 British comedy *The Smallest Show on Earth*. The 1989 Oscar winner *Cinema Paradiso* lovingly depicts a young boy's obsession with the only movie theater in his small Italian village. A projectionist and a concession girl try to save a closed theater by raising mushrooms in it and selling them in *Coming Up Roses* (1986). Movie characters come to life — and walk off the screen — in *The Purple Rose of Cairo* (1985) and *Last Action Hero* (1993). Woody Allen and Bette Midler made out in a movie theater showing the solemn *Salaam Bombay* in *Scenes from a Mall* (1991). *The Hard Way* (1991) features a climactic shootout in a theater showing one of star Michael J. Fox's movies. In Lamberto Bava's *Demons* (1985), a movie prop on display in the lobby unleashes a horde of nasty demons on a theater of unsuspecting patrons. Along similar lines, some mischievous gremlins invade a movie theater briefly in 1990's *Gremlins 2: The New Batch*. The men that show the movies have been the subject of *Merton of the Movies* (1947), *The Projectionist* (1971), *The Picture Show Man* (1977), and Buster Keaton's classic *Sherlock Jr.* (1924). In the latter film, Buster runs down the aisle in one scene and steps into the movie on the screen, obviously serving as the inspiration for Woody Allen's reverse trick in *Purple Rose*. Drive-in theaters served as the principal setting for two cult favorites: *Targets* (1968) and *Dead End Drive-In* (1986). The low-budget *Targets* starred Boris Karloff as a has-been horror star promoting his latest picture at a drive-in where a mentally unstable sniper begins randomly killing moviegoers. The Australian oddity *Dead End Drive-In* takes place at a futuristic drive-in where patrons are not allowed to leave once they enter. Their tires are stolen during the movies. In other films about drive-ins: A tornado annihilated an outdoor theater in *Twister*

(1996); drive-in owner Todd Tomorrow (Tab Hunter) specialized in showing esoteric triple-features in John Waters' campy *Polyester* (1981); and villain Will Patton showed *The Sound of Music* over and over to his soldiers at a make-shift outdoor theater in *The Postman* (1997). The following films are either about movie theaters or feature key scenes set in movie theaters:

Sherlock Jr. (1924); *The Good Fairy* (1935); *Sabotage* (aka *A Woman Alone*) (1936); *One Rainy Afternoon* (1936); *This Way Please* (1937); *Contraband* (aka *Blackout*) (1940); *Merton of the Movies* (1947); *White Heat* (1949); *Singin' in the Rain* (1952); *The Smallest Show on Earth* (aka *Big Time Operators*) (1957); *The Blob* (1958); *The Tingler* (1959); *Crime Does Not Pay* (aka *The Gentle Art of Murder*) (1962); *Targets* (1968); *The Last Picture Show* (1971); *The Projectionist* (1971); *Drive-in* (1976); *One Summer Love* (aka *Dragonfly*) (1976); *Drive-In Massacre* (1976); *Ruby* (1977); *The Picture Show Man* (1977); *Grease* (1978); *The Meateater* (1978); *Something Short of Paradise* (1979); *Polyester* (1981); *Night of the Comet* (1984); *Demons* (1985); *The Purple Rose of Cairo* (1985); *Desperately Seeking Susan* (1985); *Coming Up Roses* (1986); *Dead End Drive-In* (1986); *Anguish* (1987); *American Drive-in* (1987); *Who Framed Roger Rabbit* (1988); *Invasion Earth: The Aliens Are Here* (1988); *Cinema Paradiso* (1989); *Apartment Zero* (1989); *Gremlins 2: The New Batch* (1990); *Popcorn* (1991); *Scenes from a Mall* (1991); *The Hard Way* (1991); *Into the West* (1993); *Matinee* (1993); *Last Action Hero* (1993); *Movie Days* (1994); *Twister* (1996); *The Postman* (1997); *Scream 2* (1997); *Scary Movie* (2000)

Movies About Movies

The film industry's love affair with itself has been a long-term relationship, though frequently a stormy one. The inhabitants of Tinseltown have stereotypically portrayed themselves as ruthless producers, crazed directors, alcoholic actors, and ambitious starlets. Still, the best of these movies have provided an entertaining behind-the-scenes look at filmmaking and/or the gossip scene. An occasional film has actually delved into the psyche of moviemakers. The first talking picture to seriously tackle the subject was 1932's *What Price Hollywood?*, George Cukor's tragic tale of a director who transforms a waitress into a star while he slides into alcoholism. The same plot, with Fredric March as an established star and Janet Gaynor as a promising newcomer, surfaced in 1937 as the now-classic *A Star Is Born*. Joel McCrea played a film director who felt he had lost touch with his audience, so he set out to learn about them in Preston Sturges' seriocomic *Sullivan's Travels* (1941). World War II kept the movies about movies light-hearted, leaving it to the 1950s to introduce a bitter view of Hollywood. Gloria Swanson was overpowering as a faded star desperate for public adoration in Billy Wilder's wry *Sunset Boulevard* (1950). Kirk Douglas portrayed an ambitious producer with a bad habit of stepping on people in Vincente Minnelli's hugely entertaining *The Bad and the Beautiful* (1952). Still, even Hollywood insiders liked the film, honoring it with five Oscars, including Best Supporting Actress for Gloria Grahame. The 1954 remake of *A Star Is Born* was even more effective than the original, thanks to James Mason's searing performance as a washed-up star. *The Goddess*, a downbeat, thinly-disguised 1958 biography of Marilyn Monroe, signalled the continuation of "realistic" films about Hollywood, a trend which blossomed in the 1960s. That decade produced a line of trashy, but often enjoyable, fare about filmmaking: *Two Weeks in Another Town* (1962) with Kirk Douglas again, *The Carpetbaggers* (1964), *The Oscar* (1966), and

The Movie-Maker (1967 TVM). "Serious" movies about the industry decreased over the next two decades, though even satiric features like *The Stunt Man* (1980) and *S.O.B.* (1981) offered darkly cynical views of Hollywood. More mainstream comedies have poked gentle fun at the people behind the movies. A host of deft comedians have employed film studio settings, including: Buster Keaton in *Movie Crazy* (1932), Olsen and Johnson in *Hellzapoppin* (1941), Red Skelton in *Merton of the Movies* (1947), Bud and Lou in *Abbott and Costello Meet the Keystone Kops* (1955), and Jerry Lewis in *The Errand Boy*. Woody Allen's *The Purple Rose of Cairo* (1985) was about a movie character who stepped off the screen and caused all kinds of complications. The early days of filmmaking were remembered fondly in *Singin' in the Rain* (1952) and *Nickelodeon* (1976). On the other side of the Atlantic, England produced *The Magic Box* (1951), an all-star biography of film pioneer William Friese-Greene. Joseph Losey's *Finger of Guilt* (1956) offered a rare look inside a British film studio. French New Wave directors Jean-Luc Godard and François Truffaut paid homage to their craft with *Contempt* (1963) and *Day for Night* (1973). Federico Fellini's semi-autobiographical *8½* (1963) explored the mind of fantasy-ridden director Marcello Mastroianni. The title was a reference to the number of movies Fellini had previously made. See also **Film Star Biographies; Stunt People.**

The Studio Murder Mystery (1929); *Movie Crazy* (1932); *What Price Hollywood?* (1932); *Once in a Lifetime* (1932); *Bombshell* (aka *Blonde Bombshell*) (1933); *The Death Kiss* (1933); *A Star Is Born* (1937); *Stand-In* (1937); *Hollywood Cavalcade* (1939); *The Bank Dick* (aka *The Bank Detective*) (1940); *Sullivan's Travels* (1941); *Hellzapoppin* (1941); *The Reluctant Dragon* (1941); *World Premiere* (1941); *Crazy House* (1943); *The Falcon in Hollywood* (1944); *Merton of the Movies* (1947); *It's a Great Feeling* (1949); *You're My Everything* (1949); *Sunset Boulevard* (1950); *The Magic Box* (1951); *Hollywood Story* (1951); *The Bad and the Beautiful* (1952); *Singin' in the Rain* (1952); *The Star* (1952); *A Star Is Born* (1954); *Susan Slept Here* (1954); *Abbott and Costello Meet the Keystone Kops* (1955); *Finger of Guilt* (aka *The Intimate Stranger*) (1956); *The Goddess* (1958); *Paradise Alley* (aka *Stars in the Back Yard*) (1961); *The Errand Boy* (1961); *Two Weeks in Another Town* (1962); *Contempt* (1963); *8½* (1963); *The Carpetbaggers* (1964); *Inside Daisy Clover* (1965); *The Oscar* (1966); *After the Fox* (1966); *The Movie Maker* (1967 TVM); *Everything for Sale* (1968); *The Legend of Lylah Clare* (1968); *David Holzman's Diary* (1968); *Alex in Wonderland* (1970); *Bombay Talkie* (1970); *The Movie Murderer* (1970 TVM); *The Last Movie* (aka *Chinchero*) (1971); *Day for Night* (1973); *The Sex Symbol* (1974 TVM); *Day of the Locust* (1975); *Hollywood Boulevard* (1976); *The Last Tycoon* (1976); *Nickelodeon* (1976); *The World's Great Lover* (1977); *Evening in Byzantium* (1978 TVM); *The Users* (1978); *An Almost Perfect Affair* (1979); *The Stunt Man* (1980); *The Dream Merchants* (1980 TVM); *Loose Shoes* (aka *Coming Attractions*) (1980); *S.O.B.* (1981); *Burden of Dreams* (1982); *Passion* (1982); *Strangers Kiss* (1983); *Love Scenes* (1984); *Special Effects* (1984); *The Last Horror Film* (1984); *The Purple Rose of Cairo* (1985); *Means and Ends* (1985); *Malice in Wonderland* (1985 TVM); *I Hate Actors* (1986); *Overnight* (1986); *Smart Alec* (aka *The Movie Maker*) (1986); *Sweet Liberty* (1986); *Good Morning, Babylon* (1987); *The Big Picture* (1989); *Sexbomb* (1989); *Stardumb* (1990); *Twisted Obsession* (1990); *Postcards from the Edge* (1990); *Barton Fink* (1991); *The Inner Circle* (1991); *The Player* (1992); *Mistress* (1992); *Double Threat* (1992); *A Woman, Her Men and Her Futon* (1992); *Matinee* (1993); *Torch Song* (1993 TVM); *Last Action Hero* (1993); *My Life's in Turnaround* (1993); *The Pickle* (1993); *Visions of Light* (1993); *Ed Wood* (1994); *Midnight Movie* (1994); *The Film Thief* (aka *Ladri di Cinema*) (1994); *I'll Do Anything* (1994); *The Buddy Factor* (1994);

Playmaker (1994); *Paint Cans* (1994); *Dangerous Game* (1994); *Living in Oblivion* (1995); *Boogie Nights* (1997); *Gods and Monsters* (1998); *Bowfinger* (1999); *The Blair Witch Project* (1999); *American Movie* (1999); *Scream 3* (1999); *RKO 281* (1999 TVM); *Catch a Falling Star* (2000 TVM); *Best Actress* (2000 TVM); *Cecil B. Demented* (2000); *Shadow of the Vampire* (2000)

Movies Without Dialogue

Since the advent of "talkies," movies without dialogue have been screen oddities. Charlie Chaplin, who felt uncomfortable with dialogue, resisted making a talking picture until 1940's *The Great Dictator*. Thus, his two classic comedies of the 1930s, *City Lights* and *Modern Times*, were both sans dialogue, their soundtracks consisting solely of sounds and music. Given Chaplin's success as a silent filmmaker, these "nontalkies" were taken in stride. That was not the case with 1952's *The Thief*, an unusual mainstream experiment devised by producer Clarence Greene and director Russell Rouse. This dialogueless film cast Ray Milland as an enemy spy pursued by the FBI. Initially intriguing, *The Thief's* gimmick grows tiresome and becomes a forced irritation. A similar fate befell Gene Kelly's *Invitation to the Dance* (1957), an ambitious attempt to tell three stories completely in dance. Obviously, the movie puzzled MGM's head brass, who delayed its release for five years. A handful of foreign films have bypassed all language barriers by telling their plots completely in visuals. French director-writer-star Jacques Tati's *Mr. Hulot's Holiday* (1953) continues to charm international audiences with its winning visual humor. Poetic visual splendor replaced dialogue in Kaneto Shindo's *The Island* (1962), the low-key story of a solitary family inhabiting a tiny isle. *Le Bal* (1982) told the story of a ballroom through fifty years of dancing. Back in the U.S., Mel Brooks spoofed Hollywood of the 1920s in his wacky 1976 comedy *Silent Movie* (in which mime Marcel Marceau had the film's single line of dialogue). Eleanor Antin directed *The Last Night of Rasputin* (1989) and *The Man Without a World* (1992), which both look like vintage black and white silent films. Many movies have employed minimal dialogue to great effect, such as Cornel Wilde's thrilling adventure film *The Naked Prey* (1966).

City Lights (1931); *Modern Times* (1936); *The Thief* (1952); *Mr. Hulot's Holiday* (aka *Monsieur Hulot's Holiday*) (1953); *Invitation to the Dance* (1957); *The Island* (aka *Hadaka no Shima*) (1962); *Silent Movie* (1976); *Le Bal* (1982); *The Final Combat* (aka *Le Dernier Combat*) (1984); *Sidewalk Stories* (1987); *Missing Link* (1989); *The Last Night of Rasputin* (1989); *The Man Without a World* (1992)

Multiple Personalities

Schizophrenia resulting in multiple personalities has enabled several fine performers to display their acting versatility. Ronald Colman won his only Oscar as a psychologically unstable Shakespearean actor who begins to play Othello for real in 1947's *A Double Life*. Joanne Woodward also won an Oscar for her career-breakthrough performance as a woman with three personalities in 1957's *The Three Faces of Eve*. Almost two decades later, Woodward played the psychiatrist to Sally Field's *Sybil* in the fact-based story of a young woman plagued by 17 distinct personalities. The film also provided Field with her acting breakthrough, proving her TV days as *The Flying Nun* were behind her. Hitchcock's *Psycho* (1960) ended with the once-shocking revelation that

Norman Bates was also his mother. In the seldom-shown 1945 thriller *Bewitched*, Phyllis Thaxter murdered a man as one personality, but remembered nothing about it as her other self. And in *Three Nuts in Search of a Bolt* (1964), three neurotics hired an unemployed actor to visit a psychiatrist for them. When he acts out all their neuroses, the psychiatrist diagnoses him as a victim of multiple personalities! See also **Jekyll, Dr., and Mr. Hyde**; **Psychiatrists**.

Bewitched (1945); *A Double Life* (1947); *Half Angel* (1951); *Lizzie* (1957); *The Three Faces of Eve* (1957); *Psycho* (1960); *Three Nuts in Search of a Bolt* (1964); *The Boston Strangler* (1968); *Sybil* (1976 TVM); *The Strange Possession of Mrs. Oliver* (1977 TVM); *The Five of Me* (1981 TVM); *Loose Cannons* (1990); *Voices Within: The Lives of Truddie Chase* (1990 TVM); *Femme Fatale* (1991); *Raising Cain* (1992); *Voices from Within* (1994 TVM); *Fight Club* (1999); *Me, Myself and Irene* (2000)

Multiple Roles

The challenge of playing three or more roles in the same film has appealed to very few performers. It is also likely that the profession's more serious actors have viewed the ploy as mere gimmickry. For whichever reason, it has been a rare screen occurrence. Peter Sellers has played at least three roles in each of three movies. He first performed the trick for the 1959 comedy sleeper *The Mouse That Roared*, appearing as the picture's hero, a count, and the Grand Duchess of Fenwick. Five years later, he landed his most famous triple role as U.S. President Muffey, Captain Mandrake, and Nazi scientist Dr. Strangelove in Stanley Kubrick's cold war satire *Dr. Strangelove, or How I Learned to Stop Worrying and Love the Bomb* (1964). In the twilight of his career, Sellers took on six roles in the barely-released comedy *Undercovers Hero* (1975). Second to Sellers is America's own Jerry Lewis, who must have decided he was ready for bigger numbers after his double role in *The Nutty Professor* (1963). Lewis played five roles in 1966's *Three on a Couch* and seven roles in 1965's *The Family Jewels*. The latter film was obviously patterned after the droll British classic *Kind Hearts and Coronets* (1949), which featured marvelous Alec Guinness as eight murder victims. Except for Malcolm McDowell, the principal cast of the sparkling British satire *O Lucky Man!* (1973) appeared in multiple roles. In a similar vein, the members of the Monty Python comedy troupe have essayed a variety of roles in their pictures, particularly *Monty Python and the Holy Grail* (1975) and *The Life of Brian* (1979).

Mexican Spitfire Sees a Ghost (1942) (Leon Errol); *Kind Hearts and Coronets* (1949) (Alec Guinness); *Watch the Birdie* (1950) (Red Skelton); *The Mouse That Roared* (1959) (Peter Sellers); *Dr. Strangelove, or How I Learned to Stop Worrying and Love the Bomb* (1964) (Peter Sellers); *The Seven Faces of Dr. Lao* (1964) (Tony Randall); *The Family Jewels* (1965) (Jerry Lewis); *Three on a Couch* (1966) (Jerry Lewis); *Press for Time* (1966) (Norman Wisdom); *Arabella* (1969) (Terry-Thomas); *O Lucky Man!* (1973); *Blazing Saddles* (1974) (Mel Brooks); *Monty Python and the Holy Grail* (1975); *Undercovers Hero* (aka *Soft Beds and Hard Battles*; *Soft Beds, Hard Battles*) (1975) (Peter Sellers); *Which Way Is Up?* (1977) (Richard Pryor); *Circle of Iron* (aka *The Silent Flute*) (1978) (David Carradine); *Hot Lead and Cold Feet* (1978) (Jim Dale); *The Man in the Santa Claus Suit* (1979 TVM) (Fred Astaire); *The Life of Brian* (1979) (Monty Python Troupe); *Cracking Up* (aka *Smorgasbord*) (1983) (Jerry Lewis); *Cheech and Chong's Corsican Brothers* (1984) (Cheech Marin and Tommy Chong); *Coming to America* (1988) (Eddie Murphy and Arsenio Hall); *Joe vs. the Volcano* (1990) (Meg Ryan); *Seduction: Three Tales from the Inner Sanctum* (1992 TVM) (Victoria Principal and John Terry); *Being Human* (1994) (Robin Williams); *From Dusk Till Dawn* (1996) (Cheech Marin); *The Nutty Professor* (1996) (Eddie Murphy); *Austin Powers: The Spy Who Shagged Me* (1999) (Mike Myers); *Nutty Professor II: The Klumps* (2000) (Eddie Murphy); *Sunshine* (2000) (Ralph Fiennes)

The Mummy

With facial features swathed in bandages (or wrinkles) and a vocabulary limited to growls, the Mummy lacked the personality of his cinematic peers: Dracula, the Frankenstein Monster, and the Wolf Man (qq.v.). For most of his career, he has been used as a slow-moving killing machine. He did not start out that way, though. Karl Freund's *The Mummy* (1932) was a haunting film about reincarnation and eternal love. As the mummified priest Imhotep, Boris Karloff appeared only briefly in Jack Pierce's famous Mummy makeup. He spent most of the film in his reincarnated form, playing a menacing Egyptian archaeologist. In a fitting climax, he was reduced to dust when the heroine calls upon the ancient god Isis. Oddly, the Mummy was not revived until 1940, when former cowboy star Tom Tyler replaced Karloff in *The Mummy's Hand*, the first of a low-budget series. Lon Chaney, Jr., took over the role (the Mummy having undergone a name change, from Imhotep to Kharis) for three additional installments. None of these films rose above the routine, although *The Mummy's Curse* offered a different setting (the Louisiana Bayou) and the heroine actually turned into a mummy in *The Mummy's Ghost*. The official Universal series ended in 1944, although the studio brought back the Gauzed One (played by Eddie Powell) for one final fling in 1955's *Abbott and Costello Meet the Mummy*, one of the comedy duo's last efforts. After laying dormant for a couple years, the Mummy turned up in Mexico and Britain almost simultaneously. Like most Mexican horror films of the late 1950s, Rafael Portillo's *The Aztec Mummy* (1957) boasted fine black-and-white photography and, despite an absurd plot, recalled the eerie atmosphere of Universal's 1940s features. The title mummy, named Popoca, did well enough to inspire a series of Aztec Mummy movies, which still crop up on television today. Meanwhile, fresh on the heels of its Dracula success, Britain's Hammer Studios produced a colorful remake of *The Mummy* (1959). Transplanting the story to England in 1895, this version profited from Peter Cushing's steady performance as an intrepid archaeologist and Christopher Lee's imposing presence as the movies' quickest-footed Mummy. Despite good notices, Hammer waited five years before continuing the series. It was hardly worth the effort, since two of the three sequels were cheap programmers. The other, however, was 1972's *Blood from the Mummy's Tomb*, an adaptation of Bram Stoker's story "Jewel of the Seven Stars" and a welcome return to the literate approach of Freund's original film. The same story served as the basis for *The Awakening* (1980), with Charlton Heston and Stephanie Zimbalist, and *The Legend of the Mummy* (1997) starring Louis Gossett, Jr. Two years after the former film, Universal released *The Mummy*, a loose, *Indiana Jones*–style remake of the Karloff film with Arnold Vosloo as Imhotep. Vosloo spent little time hidden under bandages, which was ironic considering that he twice played Darkman (q.v.). Spanish horror star Paul Naschy, who has played more monsters than anybody, took his turn in the bandages for *The Mummy's Revenge* (1973). And in 1982's ridiculous *Timewalker*, a nasty mummy is revealed to be a misunderstood alien who just wanted to go home — shades of *E.T.* See also **Reincarnation**.

UNIVERSAL'S MUMMY: *The Mummy* (1932); *The Mummy's Hand* (1940); *The Mummy's Tomb* (1942); *The Mummy's Curse* (1944); *The Mummy's Ghost* (1944); *Abbott and Costello Meet the Mummy* (1955)

THE AZTEC MUMMY: *The Aztec Mummy* (aka *La Momia; La Momia Azteca*) (1957); *Robot vs. the Aztec Mummy* (aka *La Momia Azteca Contra el Robot Humano*) (1959); *Curse of the Aztec Mummy* (aka *La Maldicion de la Momia Azteca*) (1959); *Wrestling Women vs. the Aztec Mummy* (aka *La Luchadoras Contra la Momia*) (1964)

HAMMER'S MUMMY: *The Mummy* (1959); *Curse of the Mummy's Tomb* (1964); *The Mummy's Shroud* (1967); *Blood from the Mummy's Tomb* (1972)

OTHERS: *The Egyptian Mummy* (1914); *Eyes of the Mummy* (1918); *The Pharaoh's Curse* (1956); *Curse of the Faceless Man* (1958) (very Mummy-like); *Attack of the Mayan Mummy* (1963); *Mad Monster Party?* (1967); *Santo and Blue Demon vs. the Monsters* (aka *Santo y Blue Demon Contra los Monstruos*) (1969); *The Man Who Came from Ummo* (aka *El Hombre Que Vino de Ummo; Assignment Terror; Dracula vs. Frankenstein*) (1970); *Santo in the Mummy's Revenge* (aka *Santo en la Venganza de la Momia*) (1970); *The Mummies of Guanajuato* (aka *Las Momias de Guanajuato*) (1970); *The Mummy's Revenge* (1973); *The Awakening* (1980); *Dawn of the Mummy* (1981); *Timewalker* (1982); *The Monster Squad* (1987); *Waxwork* (1988); *Tales from the Darkside: The Movie* (1990); *Legend of the Mummy* (aka *Bram Stoker's The Mummy*) (1997); *The Creeps* (1997); *Talos the Mummy* (aka *Russell Mulcahy's Talos the Mummy*) (1998); *The Mummy* (1999)

The Muppets

Kermit the Frog and Miss Piggy were established television stars and pop icons when they and their furry friends made the leap to the big screen in 1979's *The Muppet Movie*. Film industry watchers expected a guaranteed audience of loyal children, but the film's widespread success surprised even them. The 1981 sequel *The Great Muppet Caper* pitted the gang against jewel thieves (q.v.) who had stolen the Fabulous Baseball Diamond. It performed even better than its predecessor at the domestic box-office. Muppet creator Jim Henson interrupted the series in 1982 to produce *The Dark Crystal*, a more conventional "quest fantasy" with puppets. He returned to the Muppets with 1984's *The Muppets Take Manhattan*, in which Kermit took his college musical to the Great White Way. Its box-office receipts were disappointing and another theatrical feature did not appear until 1992's *The Muppet Christmas Carol*. In interim, Jim Henson had died and his son Brian had taken over as producer. *Muppet Treasure Island* (1996) featured Tim Curry as Long John Silver, and *Muppets from Space* (1999) revealed that Gonzo is an alien. Jim Henson coined the phrase "muppet" in the 1950s to describe a combination of "marionette" and "puppet." See also **Puppets**.

The Muppet Movie (1979); *The Great Muppet Caper* (1981); *The Muppets Take Manhattan* (1984); *The Muppet Christmas Carol* (1992); *Muppet Treasure Island* (1996); *Muppets from Space* (1999)

My Favorite... Series

Bob Hope made the three *My Favorite...* films during the peak of his Paramount career. Technically, he played a different character in each film, but that seems irrelevant considering that Hope acted pretty much the same in all his movies (although there were exceptions such as 1957's *Beau James*). The series' premise has Bob encountering mysterious women who get him involved in murder mysteries and spy intrigue. In *My Favorite Blonde*, he meets Madeleine Carroll (already a spy movie veteran after 1935's *The 39 Steps*) on a train and winds up helping her elude Nazi agents. *My Favorite Brunette* turned out to be Bob's *Road* movie (q.v.) co-star Dorothy Lamour. She lures him into a hilarious mystery spoof revolving around a photo taken by Bob's "keyhole camera." The supporting cast includes an amusing Peter Lorre and a cameo by Bing Crosby as a prison executioner. This entry also features one of Hope's funniest scenes, in which the villains administer truth serum to him. The final series entry was 1951's *My Favorite Spy*, which paired him with the gorgeous Hedy Lamarr in a spy spoof casting Bob as a comedian posing as a tough secret agent. The *My Favorite...* films hold up very well despite numerous in-jokes certain to be lost on many contemporary viewers.

My Favorite Blonde (1942); *My Favorite Brunette* (1947); *My Favorite Spy* (1951)

The Naked Gun Series

Riding the success of their box-office hit *Airplane* (1980), Jerry Zucker, Jim Abrahams, and David Zucker created *Police Squad!* a 1982 TV series featuring the same kind of nonstop joke-a-minute humor. The show starred Leslie Nielsen as the bumbling, incompetent detective Lieutenant Frank Drebin with Alan North as his superior Captain Ed Hocken and Peter Lupus as slow-witted Officer Nordberg. Despite good press, ABC Television cancelled *Police Squad!* after just six episodes. Although the TV series attracted a cult following over the next six years, it still came as a surprise when Zucker, Abrahams, and Zucker mounted a theatrical version called *The Naked Gun: From the Files of Police Squad!* (1988). Nielsen returned as Frank Drebin, but — in an effort to add some familiar faces to the nonstar cast — George Kennedy took over as Captain Hocken and O.J. Simpson played Nordberg. This time, the wacky humor clicked with audiences and critics, prompting even Roger Ebert to observe: "*The Naked Gun* is an utterly goofy movie and a lot of fun, and don't let anyone tell you all the jokes before you go." Sample gag: When the villain falls to his death in a baseball stadium, his body is crushed by a bus, flattened by a steamroller, and then trampled on by a marching band. The plots in the *Naked Gun* movies naturally take a backseat to the sight gags, puns, and slapstick, but they provide an amusing framework for the comedy. In the first film, Frank protects Queen Elizabeth from being assassinated by a brainwashed baseball player (shades of *The Manchurian Candidate*). *The Naked Gun 2½: The Smell of Fear* (1991) pits Frank against evil industrialists who kidnap a scientist to block publication of an ecology report. Frank comes out of retirement in *The Naked Gun 33⅓: The Final Insult* (1994) to battle a terrorist — and winds up disrupting the Academy Awards. In addition to Kennedy and Simpson, other series regulars included Priscilla Presley as Frank's love interest Jane Spencer and Ed Williams as scientist Ted Olsen (a role he also played on the TV series). See also **Theatrical Films Based on TV Series**.

The Naked Gun: From the Files of Police Squad! (1988); *The Naked Gun 2½: The Smell of Fear* (1991); *The Naked Gun 33⅓: The Final Insult* (1994)

National Lampoon's Vacation Series

The leisure-time exploits of the Griswold Family have formed the basis for three *Vacation* films cowritten by prolific producer-writer John Hughes (*Home Alone*). Hughes based the first film (loosely, one hopes) on his magazine article "Vacation '56," a satirical remembrance of a family trip. The plot sends the Griswolds on a wild, sometimes wacky, odyssey across the U.S. in search of the theme park Wally World. The family consists of parents Clark (Chevy Chase) and Ellen (Beverly D'Angelo), son Rusty (Anthony Michael Hall), and daughter Audrey (Dana Barron). They meet other relatives, including uncouth cousin Eddie (Randy Quaid), along the way. Capitalizing on Chase's silly *Saturday Night Live* persona, *National Lampoon's Vacation* signalled Hughes' arrival as a producer with a midas touch (he followed up this hit with *Sixteen Candles* and *The Breakfast Club*). However, critics and moviegoers were unkind to the dreadful 1985 sequel, *National Lampoon's European Vacation*, which had the Griswolds — dressed as pigs — winning a transcontinental vacation on the TV quiz show *Pig in a Poke*. Chase and D'Angelo returned as the parents, but Jason Lively took over as Rusty and Dana Hill as Audrey. The Griswolds fared much better by staying home for the holidays in 1989's *National Lampoon's Christmas Vacation*. This second sequel mixed a little sentiment with the irreverent humor — most of which was supplied by the unexpected arrival of cousin Eddie (Quaid again). Chase and D'Angelo returned again, with their children being played by Johnny Galecki and Juliette Lewis (two years away from her Oscar-nominated performance in *Cape Fear*). Although *Christmas Vacation* was the most successful series entry, a follow-up did not appear for eight years. *National Lampoon's Vegas Vacation* was released quietly in 1997 and died softly at the box-office. It featured Chase, D'Angelo, and Quaid once more, with the Griswold children played by Ethan Embry and Marisol Nichols.

National Lampoon's Vacation (1983); *National Lampoon's European Vacation* (1985); *National Lampoon's Christmas Vacation* (1989); *National Lampoon's Vegas Vacation* (1997)

Nemesis Series

This highly derivative sci-fi series combined elements of *Blade Runner* (1982), *Robocop* (1987), and *Escape from New York* (1981) with mediocre results. The initial installment, 1993's *Nemesis*, starred French martial artist Olivier Gruner as cyborg Alex Rain, who works for the L.A.P.D. in the year 2027. An interesting political scenario — a merger between the U.S. and Japan — serves merely as a backdrop to a battle between bad cyborgs that want to eliminate the human race and good cyborgs that want to protect mankind. Alex, who starts out as 86.5 percent human, spends most of the film trying to figure out if a group of "terrorists" called the Red Army Hammerheads are behind the cyborg conspiracy. He doesn't have much time once the baddies insert a time bomb in his chest. Gruner takes off his shirt a lot, Deborah Shelton has a topless scene, and there are lots of shootouts (the cyborgs are very bad shots). The film ends with Alex pledging to destroy all the evil cyborgs. The 1995 sequel, *Nemesis 2: Nebula*, is a *Terminator* rip-off set 73 years later. The cyborgs rule the world and the humans' only hope is a DNA strain that could destroy the evil cyborgs. A woman injected with the DNA strain escapes from the cyborgs by traveling back in time to 1980. She dies, but her daughter Alex (Sue Price) survives. Twenty years later, a cyborg named Nebula arrives to destroy Alex. The last two entries trace the further exploits of Alex, with Sue Price reprising the role. Albert Pyum, best known for Jean-Claude Van Damme's *Cyborg* (1989) directed all four films. Tim Thomerson from the *Trancers* (q.v.) movies played the cyborg villain Farnsworth in the first and third films. See also **Androids and Cyborgs**.

Nemesis (1993); *Nemesis 2: Nebula* (aka *Nemesis 2*) (1995); *Nemesis 3: Time Lapse* (aka *Nemesis 3: Prey Harder*) (1996); *Nemesis 4: Death Angel* (aka *Nemesis 4*) (1996)

Neutron

Neutron was one of three Mexican wrestler superheroes to enjoy South-of-the-Border popularity in the 1960s. The silver-masked Santo (q.v.) was the undisputed king, but Neutron held his own against latecomer rival The Blue Demon (q.v.). Mexico's America Studios shot the first three Neutron films in 1960, starting with *Neutron, the Black Masked*. This introductory effort pitted the wrestler against evil Dr. Caronte and his neutron bomb. Caronte returned in both *Neutron vs. the Amazing Dr. Caronte* and *Neutron Against the Robots*. In the U.S., the films were released out of order and sometimes shown as serials. This latter oddity occurred because the films were originally made in three parts and edited together later. This was a necessity for the filmmakers, since Mexican labor agreements allowed America Studios to produce short features only. See also **Blue Demon**; **Santo**; **Wrestling**.

Neutron, the Black Masked (aka *Neutron el Enmascarado Negro*) (1960); *Neutron vs. the Amazing Dr. Caronte* (aka *Neutron Contra el Doctor Caronte*) (1960); *Neutron Against the Death Robots* (aka *Los Automatas de la Muerte*) (1961); *Neutron Battles the Karate Assassins* (1962); *Neutron vs. the Maniac* (aka *Neutron and the Cosmic Bomb*) (1962); *Neutron Traps the Invisible Killers* (1963)

The NeverEnding Story Series

After directing the acclaimed World War II submarine drama *Das Boot* (1981), Wolfgang Petersen changed course completely by choosing a children's fantasy for his next film. Adapted from Michael Ende's popular 1979 German novel, *The NeverEnding Story* focuses on a lonely 10-year-old named Bastion who escapes his dreary life by reading a magical book. He reads about the exploits of Atreyu, a young warrior who must save the kingdom of Fantasia from the Nothingness. As Bastion becomes more involved with the story, he realizes he is becoming a character in it — and that he must take action to save Fantasia. Although author Ende disowned it, *The NeverEnding Story* became a hit in Europe and a more modest success in the U.S. Its popularity received a boost by the film's title track, sung by Limhal, which became a #17 hit in 1985 on the *Billboard* Top 40 chart. Petersen and youth stars Barret Oliver (Bastion) and Noah Hathaway (Atreyu) steered clear of the two inferior sequels released in 1990 and 1994. In *The NeverEnding Story II: The Next Chapter*, Bastion (Jonathan Brandis) returns to Fantasia to save it from an evil sorceress. In *The NeverEnding Story III*, Bastion (*Free Willy* star Jason James Richter) becomes trapped in Fanastia after the magical book is stolen by school bullies. *Variety* dubbed it "Bastian Goes to High School." An animated series followed in 1996 and a videotape was released containing three episodes from that series.

The NeverEnding Story (aka *Die Unendliche Geschichte*) (1984); *The NeverEnding Story II: The Next Chapter* (aka *Die Unendliche Geschichte 2*) (1990); *The NeverEnding Story III* (aka *The NeverEnding Story III: Escape from Fantasia; Die Unendliche Geschichte III — Rettung aus Phantasien*) (1994)

Night Eyes Series

The most popular direct-to-video genre of the 1990s was the "erotic thriller," a term used loosely to define a film that combined crimes of passion, obvious plot twists, and softcore sex. The movie that pioneered this genre was *Night Eyes* (1990), a mediocre mystery cowritten by Andrew Stevens. He also starred as Will Griffith, a security surveillance expert who becomes involved with a wealthy *femme fatale* (Tanya Roberts) and ends up killing her husband. The film would have attracted little attention if not for the sex scenes between the two stars. The tape was released in R-rated and "unrated" versions, the latter showing tantalizing footage that approached softcore territory. The film's surprising success resulted in an immediate sequel and a slew of imitators, often starring Stevens (*Victim of Desire, Body Chemistry III*) or Roberts (*Inner Sanctum, Sins of Desire*). Stevens wrote the story for *Night Eyes 2* and reprised his role of Will Griffith. In this second outing, Will gets involved with another *femme fatale* (former *Playboy* Playmate Shannon Tweed) with similar results. Both Stevens and Tweed returned for *Night Eyes 3*, with Stevens adding director to his credits and Tracy Tweed joining her sister. Stevens produced *Night Eyes 4*, but his character spent most of the film in a coma after being shot. That left protégé Steve Caldwell (Jeff Trachta) to romance shapely psychologist Angela Cross (played by O.J. Simpson's one-time girlfriend Paula Barbieri). By the fourth installment, though, the series had long run out of steam (and steamy sex scenes) — the result of repetitive plotting and more risqué erotic thrillers. See also **Animal Instincts Series; Body Chemistry Series;** and **Secret Games Series.**

Night Eyes (aka *Hidden View; Hidden Vision*) (1990); *Night Eyes 2* (1991); *Night Eyes 3* (1993); *Night Eyes 4* (aka *Night Eyes...Fatal Passion*) (1995)

Night of the Demons Series

This low-budget, three-film series bears no relation to the 1958 British classic *Night of the Demon* (aka *Curse of the Demon*). Instead, it borrows heavily from Sam Raimi's *Evil Dead* series (q.v.) and that's not necessarily bad. The first film takes place on Halloween night with teenaged Angela (Mimi Kinkade) throwing a party for her friends at Hull House, an abandoned funeral home. What the kids don't know is that Hull House was the scene of a family massacre many years earlier. Angela becomes possessed by the demonic spirit of the killer and proceeds to uninvite — permanently — her party guests. In *Night of the Demons 2* (1994), Angela's sister Mouse (Merle Kennedy) and some of her friends unexpectedly wind up in Hull House on Halloween night — which is unfortunate because an occult buff has raised Angela's spirit. Like *Evil Dead 2*, the second *Night of the Demons* emphasized humor more than its predecessor (e.g. holy water is shot out of super-soaker water cannons). Most critics considered it an improvement on the original. Sadly, the final installment, *Night of the Demons 3*, converted to formula with a gang of young criminals choosing the wrong place, Hull House, as a hideout.

Kinkade played Angela in all three entries, although she was billed as Amelia Kinkade in the latter two installments.

Night of the Demons (aka *Halloween Party*) (1987); *Night of the Demons 2* (1994); *Night of the Demons 3* (aka *Demon House*) (1997)

Night of the Living Dead Series

On commenting on the scenes of "ghouls" devouring human flesh in 1968's *Night of the Living Dead*, director George Romero once wrote: "I was delighted when one of our investors, who happened to be in the meat packing business, turned up on the set one day with a sackful of animal innards which made the sequences seem so real." The film was shot outside of Pittsburgh over a span of nine months for the rock-bottom price of $118,000. *Night* was panned by the few critics who saw it during its original 1968 release. However, Romero and the film gained some recognition after a glowing *Village Voice* review in 1969 and a 1970 screening at the Museum of Modern Art. Theaters began showing it as a midnight feature in 1971 and its status as a cult classic grew quickly. Romero's subsequent films made little money and he experienced difficulty in financing a sequel. However, with the help of Italian horror filmmaker Dario Argento, he produced 1979's *Dawn of the Dead*. Not surprisingly, the film was hailed by some critics as a brilliant analogy of our times and condemned by others as a violent, pretentious time waster. Both *Night* and *Dawn* dealt with the resurrection of dead people who feed upon the flesh of the living. The former film confined the action to seven people trapped in an isolated farmhouse. They all die. *Dawn* began in an urban setting before moving its four central characters to an abandoned shopping mall (the scene of many obvious analogies). Although *Dawn of the Dead* was released without a rating (Romero feared it would be given an "X"), it performed well both in the U.S. and abroad (interestingly, as part of their deal, Argento re-cut the film for its European release). Romero's long-awaited final installment, *Day of the Dead*, appeared in 1985 and was greeted with much disappointment. Rather than concluding the trilogy (either plotwise or thematically), it opted for a 1950s-style story of understanding scientists trying to prevent the military from killing all the ghouls. It naturally left plenty of room for a fourth *Dead* picture. Meanwhile, Romero produced a 1990 color remake of the original *Night of the Living Dead*, with makeup expert Tom Savini handling the directing chores. See also **Ghouls; Return of the Living Dead Series.**

Night of the Living Dead (1968); *Dawn of the Dead* (aka *Zombie*) (1979); *Day of the Dead* (1985); *Night of the Living Dead* (1990)

Nightmare on Elm Street Series

With a black felt hat, a red-and-green striped sweater, and a right-hand glove with steel "finger knives," Freddy Kreuger can hardly be considered a stylish dresser. Still, that has not deterred him from overtaking Jason (see *Friday the 13th*) as the 1980s most popular killer of teens. The 1984 *Nightmare on Elm Street* introduced Mr. Kreuger (Robert Englund), a janitor at Springwood High with a special interest in kidnapping and murdering teens. The law finally caught up with him, but a court freed him on a technicality. This inspired some vigilante parents to track him down and fry him in a boiler room. In revenge, he invades the dreams of the parents' children and dispenses with them in ghastly fashion. In a *Time* interview, director Wes Craven offered his explanation for the film's unexpected popularity among teens: "Freddy is the most ruthless primal father. The adult who wants to slash down the next generation." The films' flippant humor may have also contributed to "Freddymania." In one scene, Freddy bashes an aspiring teen actress's head into a TV set and then quips: "This is it, Jennifer, your big break in TV." Englund has been the only performer to appear in all seven entries, though Heather Langenkamp played the heroine in the first, third, and seventh films. The sixth entry, 1991's *Freddy's Dead: The Final Nightmare*, boasted a ten-minute finale shown in 3-D (q.v.). The last entry, *Wes Craven's New Nightmare* (1994), was a heady mix of reality and fantasy devised by Craven. He and Langenkamp play themselves in a wild plot in which they must make a new *Nightmare* film to defeat the demonic force manifested into the fictional Freddy Kreuger. A syndicated hour-long TV anthology dubbed *Freddy's Nightmares* ran for a few seasons in the late 1980s. Englund introduced the stories and occasionally appeared in them (including the first, a prequel to the original film, directed by Tobe Hooper). Finally, Freddy's hand made a cameo appearance at the climax of 1993's *Jason Goes to Hell: The Final Friday*. See also **Dreams**; **Slasher Movies**.

Nightmare on Elm Street (1984); *Nightmare on Elm Street II: Freddy's Revenge* (1986); *Nightmare on Elm Street III: The Dream Warriors* (1987); *Nightmare on Elm Street IV: The Dream Master* (1988); *Nightmare on Elm Street V: The Dream Child* (1989); *Freddy's Dead: The Final Nightmare* (1991); *Wes Craven's New Nightmare* (1994)

9½ Weeks Series

The value of a brand name — no matter how bad the product — is the only logical explanation for the existence of this series. The original *9½ Weeks* (1986) was neither a critical hit nor a popular success. But it did garner a lot of attention with its allegedly provocative depiction of Mickey Rourke and Kim Basinger engaging in kinky sexual situations. Despite the hoopla, moviegoers found nothing steamy (or even interesting) about Mickey Rourke's uses for whipped cream. Director Adrian Lyne claimed the censors destroyed a serious film, but a subsequent unrated version on videotape did not support his contention. Four years later, Rourke made the similar *Wild Orchid* (1990), in which he and costar Carrie Otis allegedly had intercourse during one of the film's sex scenes. Given Rourke's track record, a *9½ Weeks* sequel was inevitable and the first one appeared in 1997. In *Another 9½ Weeks*, Rourke reprised his role of financier John Gray, who has become obsessed with finding Elizabeth (Basinger's character from the first film). Elizabeth turns out to be dead, but Gray starts a sexual affair with her friend Lea (Angie Everhart). He eventually becomes bored with kinky perversions and he leaves Lea in the end. The next installment was an in name-only sequel, *The First 9½ Weeks* (1998), starring Paul Mercurio, who fared far better in the Australian comedy *Strictly Ballroom*.

9½ Weeks (1986); *Another 9½ Weeks* (aka *Another Nine and a Half Weeks*) (1997); *The First 9½ Weeks* (1998)

1918 Trilogy

Playwright Horton Foote (*Tender Mercies*, *The Trip to Bountiful*) wrote these three understated films, in which the storylines unfold in reverse chronological order. That is, each succeeding film goes further back in time to reveal incidents in the characters' pasts. The first installment, *1918*, introduces Horace Robedaux (William Converse-Roberts), his wife Elizabeth (Hallie Foote), and their baby, who live in the little town of Harrison, Texas, where Horace runs a dry-cleaning store. The plot consists of several touching vignettes, which climax with a subplot about an epidemic which brings tragedy to the townspeople. The second film, *On Valentine's Day*, takes place in 1917, a year after Horace and Elizabeth's elopement — an event which results in the silent treatment from her parents. The final entry, *Convicts*, takes place on a sugar plantation in 1902, with a young Horace (Lukas Haas) befriending the chain gang laborers. All three movies were produced in association with PBS' *American Playhouse*. In fact, *1918* and *On Valentine's Day* were broadcast together as *Story of a Marriage*. The three movies were based on Foote's autobiographical nine-play cycle *An Orphan's Home*. Hallie Foote is Horton's daughter. Matthew Broderick played her rakish brother, strictly in a supporting role, in the first two films.

1918 (1984); *On Valentine's Day* (1986); *Convicts* (1991)

No Retreat, No Surrender Series

Frequently described as a *Karate Kid*/*Rocky IV* hybrid rip-off, 1985's *No Retreat, No Surrender* stars Kurt McKinney as Jason, a young Seattle lad who must battle a ruthless Russian in a martial arts showdown. Our hero is bright enough to know he needs a good coach to prepare him for the big fight, but, sadly, Pat Morita (the *Karate Kid*'s mentor) is nowhere to be found. Luckily, Bruce Lee's ghost has the time to give the kid some pointers. In front of a meager crowd (in what appears to be a school gym), Kurt outkicks and punches his Russian opponent, who turns out to be future martial arts star Jean-Claude Van Damme. Understandably, the belated 1989 sequel dispensed with Jason altogether and shifted the action to Bangkok. This time, Loren Avedon plays the lead character, a nice guy named Scott who gets really mad when his Vietnamese girlfriend is kidnapped by some of her father's enemies. Scott recruits a couple of friends (including the then–Queen of Kung Fu Cynthia Rothrock) and mounts a rescue in which he winds up challenging Russian killer Matthias Hues (this "Soviet bad guy" angle is apparently the thematic link to the original film). Avedon returned for 1990's *No Retreat, No Surrender III: Blood Brothers*, in which he and his bickering brother (Keith Vitali) go their separate ways as they avenge their father's death at the hands of terrorists. Although the two latter films are slightly better than the first, this subpar action series will best be remembered for introducing Van Damme to American audiences. For other martial arts films, see **American Ninja Series**; **Best of the Best Series**; **Bloodfist Series**; **The Karate Kid**; and **Kickboxer Series**.

No Retreat, No Surrender (1985); *No Retreat, No Surrender II* (1989); *No Retreat, No Surrender III: Blood Brothers* (1990)

North Pole/South Pole

The North Pole may be best known as Santa's home, but, in movies, it's been home to a variety of unpleasant creatures. An atomic explosion in the Arctic awoke *The Beast from 20,000 Fathoms*. Both *Frankenstein: The True Story* and the Swedish *Victor*

Frankenstein (aka *Terror of Frankenstein*) restored the original ending of Mary Shelley's novel, in which the Monster was stranded in the frozen wastelands. And in Howard Hawks' 1951 sci-fi classic *The Thing (from Another World)*, an unfriendly alien tried to devour a group of scientists at an Arctic research station. On the plus side, the North Pole was also where Superman built his personal fortress (and "honeymooned" with Lois Lane) in *Superman II*. The South Pole, despite having a continental advantage in terms of mass, has been the setting for fewer movies. *Scott of the Antarctic* chronicled the exploits of real-life explorer Robert Scott. George Maharis and Bobby Morse explored ways to get women to their isolated residence in *Quick Before It Melts*. John Carpenter transplanted his 1982 remake of *The Thing* from the North Pole to the South Pole. Only two scientists survived in this version, with the fate of the alien (he may be one of the survivors) heavily in doubt.

NORTH: *S.O.S. Iceberg* (1933); *She* (1935); *The Thing (from Another World)* (1951); *The Beast from 20,000 Fathoms* (1953); *The Perfect Furlough* (aka *Strictly for Pleasure*) (1958); *The Atomic Submarine* (1959); *Voyage to the Bottom of the Sea* (1961); *Ice Station Zebra* (1968); *Frankenstein: The True Story* (1973 TVM); *Island at the Top of the World* (1974); *Victor Frankenstein* (aka *Terror of Frankenstein*) (1977); *Superman II* (1981); *Cook and Peary: The Race to the Pole* (1983 TVM); *Santa Claus, the Movie* (1985); *Ordeal in the Arctic* (1993 TVM)

SOUTH: *The Secret Land* (1948); *Scott of the Antarctic* (1948); *The Land Unknown* (1957); *Quick Before It Melts* (1964); *Cry of the Penguins* (aka *Mr. Forbush and the Penguins*) (1971); *The Thing* (1982); *Antarctica* (1983); *The X-Files* (aka *The X-Files: Fight the Future*) (1998); *Sometimes They Come Back...For More* (aka *Frozen*; *Ice Station Erebus*) (1999)

Nostradamus

Mexican horror movie veteran German Robles played a descendant of the prophet Nostradamus (now a vampire) in a ten-part South-of-the-Border serial. In the U.S., it was edited into four feature films, dubbed in English, and released directly to television. The prophecies of the original Nostradamus reached the screen in exploitative splendor with the 1974 Japanese import *The Last Days of Planet Earth* (aka *Prophecies of Nostradamus: Catastrophe 1999*).

Blood of Nostradamus (aka *La Sangre de Nostradamus*) (1960); *Curse of Nostradamus* (aka *La Maldición de Nostradamus*) (1960); *The Monster Demolisher* (aka *Nostradamus y el Destructor de Monstruos*) (1960); *The Genii of Darkness* (aka *Nostradamus, el Genio de las Tinieblas*) (1960)

Nuns

The call of the convent and life within its walls have provided filmmakers with a wealth of varied plotlines. Young would-be nuns have been frequently forced to choose between the convent and the man they love, a problem confronted by Helen Hayes in *The White Sister* (1933), Julie Andrews in *The Sound of Music* (1965), and Mary Tyler Moore in *Change of Habit* (1969). Deborah Kerr and her fellow nuns faced a crisis of faith at a remote Himalayan mission in Powell and Pressburger's hypnotic *Black Narcissus* (1946). Vanessa Redgrave's deranged nun in Ken Russell's *The Devils* (1971) provided the testimony necessary to burn outspoken priest Oliver Reed for practicing witchcraft. More conventional nuns have dealt with more humane problems: Rosalind Russell played the real-life nurse who initiated treatment for polio in *Sister Kenny* (1946); Celeste Holm and Loretta Young earned Oscar nominations as French nuns trying to build a children's hospital in *Come to the Stable* (1949); and Bonnie Franklin founded a home for women prison parolees in *Sister Margaret and the Saturday Night Ladies* (1987). Movie nuns have been often paired with unruly types, whom they typically reform. These unlikely pairings include nun Deborah Kerr and soldier Robert Mitchum in *Heaven Knows, Mr. Allison* (1957), Robert Webber and Anna Sten in *The Nun and the Sergeant* (1962), detective David Janssen and Susannah York in *The Golden Gate Murders* (1979), and gunfighter Clint Eastwood and Shirley MacLaine in *Two Mules for Sister Sara* (1970). In the latter film, however, MacLaine turned out to be a prostitute disguised as a nun. Although not disguised, Dudley Moore wound up in a nun's habit in the fiendishly funny Faust spoof *Bedazzled* (1967). Tricked by the Devil (Peter Cook), Moore was transformed into a sister in the Order of the Leaping Nuns. The serious side of being a nun has been examined vividly by Fred Zinnemann in *The Nun's Story* (1959) and French director Alain Cavalier in *Therese* (1986). The most troubled nun was the one played by Meg Tilly in *Agnes of God* (1985), the story of a young nun accused of killing a child she claims was immaculately conceived. See also **Monks; Popes and Cardinals**.

The White Sister (1933); *Song of Bernadette* (1943); *Till We Meet Again* (1944); *The Bells of St. Mary's* (1945); *Black Narcissus* (1946); *Sister Kenny* (1946); *Come to the Stable* (1949); *Thunder on the Hill* (aka *Bonaventure*) (1951); *Appointment with Danger* (1951); *Anna* (1951); *Heaven Knows, Mr. Allison* (1957); *Sea Wife* (1957); *The Miracle* (1959); *The Nun's Story* (1959); *Conspiracy of Hearts* (1960); *The Devil and the Nun* (aka *Mother Joan of the Angels*) (1960); *Viridiana* (1961); *The Nun and the Sergeant* (1962); *Lilies of the Field* (1963); *The Little Nuns* (1965); *The Nun* (1965); *The Sound of Music* (1965); *The Singing Nun* (1966); *The Trouble with Angels* (1966); *Bedazzled* (1967); *Where Angels Go, Trouble Follows* (1968); *Change of Habit* (1969); *Two Mules for Sister Sara* (1970); *Weekend of Terror* (1970 TVM); *Madron* (1970); *The Lady of Monza* (aka *The Nun of Monza*) (1970); *The Devils* (1971); *The Weekend Nun* (aka *Matter of the Heart*) (1972 TVM); *Airport 1975* (1974); *In This House of Brede* (1975 TVM); *Nasty Habits* (1976); *Changing Habits* (1997); *The Golden Gate Murders* (aka *Specter on the Bridge*) (1979 TVM); *The Runner Stumbles* (1979); *Dixie: Changing Habits* (1983 TVM); *Choices of the Heart* (aka *In December the Roses Will Bloom Again*) (1983 TVM); *Dark Habits* (1983); *September Gun* (1983 TVM); *Shattered Vows* (1984 TVM); *Agnes of God* (1985); *Sacred Hearts* (1985); *Therese* (1986); *Sister Margaret and the Saturday Night Ladies* (1987 TVM); *Angel in Green* (1987); *Nuns on the Run* (1990); *Child of Light, Child of Darkness* (1991 TVM); *Hudson Hawk* (1991); *Freejack* (1992); *Sister Act* (1992); *The Nun and the Bandit* (1992); *Walls and Bridges* (1992); *Quam Mirabilis* (1994); *Night of the Demons 2* (1994); *Knocks at My Door* (aka *Golpes en Mi Puerta*) (1994); *Dead Man Walking* (1995); *Sins of Silence* (1996 TVM); *Entertaining Angels: The Dorothy Day Story* (1996); *The Staircase* (1998 TVM); *All About My Mothers* (1999)

Nurses Series

B-movie mogul Roger Corman developed this "R"-rated, loosely-connected film series for the drive-in crowd. After leaving American International Pictures in the late 1960s, Corman started his own production/distribution company, New World

Pictures. He served as executive producer on New World's first movie, 1970's *The Student Nurses*. Directed by drive-in cult favorite Stephanie Rothman, this surprisingly unexploitative picture featured strong female characters and even some topical issues (e.g., abortion). One of its stars, Elaine Giftos, used it as a stepping stone for the 1970-71 TV series *The Interns*. Neither Corman nor Rothman had a hand in the other series films, which dealt with nothing more topical than waterbeds. The casts changed from film to film, although Corman movie veteran Dick Miller appeared in the last three entries. Future Oscar nominee Sally (*Anna*) Kirkland starred in *The Young Nurses*. See also **Hospitals**.

The Student Nurses (1970); *Private Duty Nurses* (1972); *Night Call Nurses* (1972); *The Young Nurses* (aka *Emergency Nurses*) (1973); *Candy Stripe Nurses* (1974)

Octopuses and Squids

The first octopus film of note, 1938's *Sh! The Octopus*, was ironically an adaptation of the stage play *The Gorilla*. That typifies the lack of respect shown to these homely creatures throughout most of their screen careers. A giant squid made a memorable splash in Cecil B. DeMille's *Reap the Wild Wind* (1942). Twelve years later, an even bigger squid attacked the submarine *Nautilus* during an intense storm sequence in Disney's *20,000 Leagues Under the Sea*. This was the squid's finest hour, its memorable death coming at the hands of Kirk Douglas (who harpooned it in the eye). Deep sea diver Bob Hope wrestled an oversized squid for laughs in *The Road to Bali* (1952). Special effects wizard Ray Harryhausen created a giant "octopus" for *It Came from Beneath the Sea*. Due to budget constraints, Harryhausen trimmed off two tentacles and subsequently dubbed his creation a "sexopus." The submarine *Seaview* electrocuted another giant octopus in *Voyage to the Bottom of the Sea*. Killer whales rescued a seaside resort from a similar menace in 1976's low-budget, *Jaws*-inspired rip-off *Tentacles*. Lovely Maud Adams kept a venomous octopus for a pet in the 1983 James Bond adventure *Octopussy*, while Esther Williams swam an underwater ballet with an animated octopus in 1953's *Dangerous When Wet*. Ghosts brought a cardboard squid to life in a hotel in 1988's *High Spirits*, while a fake octopus caused problems for the inept filmmakers in *Ed Wood* (1994). The human-devouring, tentacled creature in *Deep Rising* (1998) was neither octopus nor squid, but it must have been a close relation.

Sh! The Octopus (1938); *Reap the Wild Wind* (1942); *The Road to Bali* (1952); *The Magic Voyage of Sinbad* (aka *Sadlow*) (1952); *Beneath the Twelve Mile Reef* (1953); *Dangerous When Wet* (1953); *20,000 Leagues Under the Sea* (1954); *Monster from the Ocean Floor* (1954); *It Came from Beneath the Sea* (1955); *The Bride of the Monster* (1956); *The Fabulous World of Jules Verne* (1958); *Don't Give Up the Ship* (1959); *Mysterious Island* (1961); *Voyage to the Bottom of the Sea* (1961); *King Kong vs. Godzilla* (aka *Kingukongu tai Gojira*) (1963); *Octaman* (1971); *Tentacles* (1976); *Warlords of Atlantis* (1978); *Octopussy* (1983); *The Little Mermaid* (1989); *High Spirits* (1988); *Ed Wood* (1994); *The Pagemaster* (1994); *The Beast* (1996 TVM); *Deep Rising* (1998); *Sphere* (1998)

Oh, God Series

It took George Burns 81 years to find the role he will best be remembered for, but it was a heavenly part as the unlikely incarnation (complete with trademark cigar) of the Deity in *Oh, God!* (1977). This gentle, uplifting fantasy blossomed into a substantial hit and ultimately begot two sequels. *Oh, God! Book II* (1980) rehashed the original film and added a little girl and globs of sentiment. The 1984 *Oh God! You Devil* was a contemporary version of Faust with Ted Wass as a singer who sells his soul and Burns in a dual role as God and the Devil (q.v.).

Oh, God! (1977); *Oh, God! Book II* (1980); *Oh God! You Devil* (aka *Oh, God! Book III*) (1984)

Oil Wells

The sight of thick, black fluid gushing forth from the ground was a familiar one on the theater screens of the 1950s. How can anyone forget the classic scene where ecstatic, oil-soaked James Dean strikes black gold in 1956's *Giant*? Yet, even before *Giant*, viewers in the 1950s had the option of pulling for nice guy James Stewart to strike oil off the Louisiana Coast (*Thunder Bay*), hooting against oily villains like Gene Barry (*The Houston Story*), or simply pondering what former elephant-boy Sabu was even doing on an oil field (*Jaguar*). Pre-1950s fare offered more typical wildcatter heroes in the guise of Spencer Tracy, Clark Gable (both in *Boom Town*) and Richard Arlen (*Wildcat*). A notable exception was 1937's *High, Wide, and Handsome*, a nostalgic Hammerstein-Kern musical with Randolph Scott as an oil driller. Oil women have been scarce, though Faye Dunaway (with a little help from George C. Scott) proved more than tough enough to handle nasty Jack Palance in 1973's *Oklahoma Crude*. John Wayne fought oil fires for a living in *The Hellfighters* (1969), as did Cornel Wilde in *Maracaibo* (1958). A blazing oil fire sends four drifters on a deadly journey over mountainous roads in trucks carrying nitroglycerine in Henri Clouzot's *The Wages of Fear* (1952) and its remake *Sorcerer* (1977). An oil drilling team headed by Bruce Willis saved the world from a collision with an asteroid in *Armageddon* (1998).

Flaming Gold (1933); *Oil for the Lamps of China* (1935); *High, Wide, and Handsome* (1937); *Boom Town* (1940); *Flowing Gold* (1940); *Wildcat* (1942); *Black Gold* (1947); *Tulsa* (1949); *The Big Gusher* (1951); *Superman and the Mole Men* (1951); *The Wages of Fear* (1952); *Thunder Bay* (1953); *Blowing Wild* (1953); *Lucy Gallant* (1955); *The Houston Story* (1956); *Giant* (1956); *Jaguar* (1956); *The Magnificent Roughnecks* (1956); *Joe Dakota* (1957); *Maracaibo* (1958); *Black Gold* (1963); *The Hellfighters* (1969); *Five Easy Pieces* (1970); *Oklahoma Crude* (1973); *Oceans of Fire* (1976 TVM); *Oil* (1977); *Sorcerer* (1977); *Roughnecks* (1980 TVM); *The Intruder Within* (1981 TVM); *Dallas: The Early Years* (1986); *On Deadly Ground* (1994); *Armageddon* (1998)

Olympics

Documentaries, fact-based dramas, and fictitious tales of inspiring athletic feats have revolved around the greatest event in international sports. Leni Riefenstahl's *Olympia* (1936), a vivid record of the 1936 Berlin games, remains an unparalleled tribute to the athletes and the spirit of the games — all this despite an underlying theme praising Nazism. Kon Ichikawa's mesmerizing *Tokyo Olympiad* (1966) was trimmed from 170 minutes to 93 for its U.S. release, though the shortened version still included the dynamic volleyball match between the women of Japan and the Soviet Union. *Visions of Eight* (1973) featured segments by eight international directors (including Ichikawa again). Most critics found it disappointing, except for John Schlesinger's dramatic feature on the grueling marathon. Film biographies of inspirational Olympic athletes have been devoted to athletes such as: decathlete Bob Mathias (*The Bob Mathias Story*); track star Wilma Rudolph (*Wilma*); the 1980 U.S. hockey team (*Miracle on Ice*); gymnast Nadia Comaneci (*Nadia*); ice skater Oksana Baiul (*A Promise Kept: The Oksana Baiul Story*); and runners Billy Mills (*Running Brave*), Jesse Owens (*The Jesse Owens Story*), and Gail Devers (*Run for the Dream: The Gail Devers Story*). The 1976 TV movie *21 Hours at Munich* recreated the tragic terrorist killings that cast a dark cloud over the 1972 Olympics. Another TV movie, *The First Olympics—Athens 1896* (1984), chronicled the events that led up to the first modern-day games. *It Happened in Athens* (1962) offered a fictitious view of the same events, placing special emphasis on Jayne Mansfield as an actress who agrees to marry the winner of the marathon. Earl Derr Bigger's proverb-quoting detective Charlie Chan (q.v.) uncovered a murder plot at the Berlin Games in 1937's *Charlie Chan at the Olympics.* Charlie's No. 1 son (Keye Luke) was even a member of the U.S. swimming team. Jim Hutton played an Olympic walker in the 1966 romantic comedy *Walk, Don't Run*, which found him in overcrowded Tokyo sharing an apartment with Samantha Eggar and matchmaker Cary Grant. A 90-pound weakling sent off for a weight-lifting program and grew up to be a muscular Olympic hammer-thrower in 1956's charming British film *Wee Geordie.* *The Golden Moment: An Olympic Love Story* (1980) found an American decathlete (David Keith) falling in love with a Russian gymnast (Stephanie Zimbalist) at the 1980 Moscow Games — which the U.S. boycotted after this TV movie was made. The 1978 *Special Olympics* was a heartwarming story of a mentally retarded youngster who finds fulfillment playing sports and enters the Special Olympics.

Million Dollar Legs (1932); *Olympia* (aka *Olympische Spiele*) (1936); *One in a Million* (1936); *Charlie Chan at the Olympics* (1937); *Jim Thorpe-All American* (aka *Man of Bronze*) (1951); *The Bob Mathias Story* (aka *The Flaming Torch*) (1954); *Wee Geordie* (aka *Geordie*) (1956); *It Happened in Athens* (1962); *Tokyo Olympiad* (1966); *Walk, Don't Run* (1966); *Downhill Racer* (1969); *The Games* (1970); *Visions of Eight* (1973); *21 Hours at Munich* (1976 TVM); *The Loneliest Runner* (1976 TVM); *Wilma* (1977 TVM); *Special Olympics* (aka *A Special Kind of Love*) (1978 TVM); *Animalympics* (1979); *The Top of the Hill* (1980 TVM); *Swan Song* (1980 TVM); *The Golden Moment: An Olympic Love Story* (1980); *Miracle on Ice* (1981 TVM); *Personal Best* (1982); *Running Brave* (1983); *Nadia* (1984 TVM); *The Jesse Owens Story* (1984 TVM); *The First Olympics-Athens 1896* (1984 TVM); *Going for the Gold: The Bill Johnson Story* (1985 TVM); *16 Days of Glory* (1986); *On Thin Ice: The Tai Babilonia Story* (1990 TVM); *Reach for the Sky* (1991); *Alex* (1993); *A Promise Kept: The Oksana Baiul Story* (1994 TVM); *A Brother's Promise: The Dan Jansen Story* (1996 TVM); *Run for the Dream: The Gail Devers Story* (1996 TVM); *Prefontaine* (1997); *Without Limits* (1998)

The Omen Series

This 1976 movie about the coming of the "antichrist" was a slick, well-done chiller, bolstered by crisp performances by Gregory Peck and David Warner. Yet, despite its merits and box-office popularity, it hardly warranted a series — even a short-lived one. *Damien — Omen II* was a predictable follow-up, showing Damien coping with teen problems by killing people. The series apparently ended with *The Final Conflict*, which had Damien dabbling

in politics. However, ten years later, the TV movie *Omen IV: The Awakening* introduced the hellish adopted daughter of a politician. See also **The Devil**.

The Omen (1976); *Damien—Omen II* (1978); *The Final Conflict* (1981); *Omen IV: The Awakening* (1991 TVM)

Once Upon a Time in China Series

Tsui Hark produced this colorful, exciting series that chronicles the exploits of Chinese folk hero Wong Fei-hung. The opening installment, set in Canton in 1875, introduces Master Wong Fei-hung (Jet Li) as a martial artist/physician faced with the challenges of his country's changing political landscape. Hark portrays the once powerful Qing Dynasty as a government in decline (the dynasty would end in 1912). The influence of Western Civilization and the effect of internal uprisings play prominent roles throughout the series. The first film packs a lot of plot — and elaborate martial arts fights — into its 134-minute running time: Wong Fei-hung's clinic gets burned down; an American "businessman" lures Chinese men into slave labor; British soldiers mistakenly kill a Chinese "lion dancer"; and Master Wong finds himself attracted to Aunt Yee (Rosamund Kwan), a young woman whose overseas experiences have "Westernized" her. *Once Upon a Time in China* was a huge success in Asia, where it established the already-popular Jet Li as a box-office superstar and earned Hark the best director nod at the Hong Kong Film Awards. Many fans of the series, however, prefer the 1992 sequel *Once Upon a Time in China 2.* Set 20 years later, it pits Wong Fei-hung against the White Lotus cult, a radical group that wants to end British influence through violent means. The climactic fight sequences may rank as the series' most impressive martial arts display, with Master Wong killing one adversary with a bamboo splinter. After the third installment, director Hark and star Li went their separate ways. Hark continued the series by casting Chiu Man-Cheuk (aka Lao Wen Zhiou) in the lead role for the fourth and fifth films. Meanwhile, Jet Li portrayed Wong Fei-hung in a rival studio's *Last Hero in China*. Neither Hark's nor Li's films could compete against *another* Wong Fei-hung film: Jackie Chan's popular 1994 kung fu comedy *Drunken Master II*. So they resolved their differences and teamed again for *Once Upon a Time in China and America* (1997), a decidedly offbeat attempt to transplant Master Wong into the American Wild West. Despite mixed reviews, it scored at the Hong Kong box-office, placing second only to another Jackie Chan film (*Mr. Nice Guy*) during its opening week. Hark produced all the *Once Upon a Time in China* films. He directed the first three entries and the sixth, as well as contributing to the screenplays. Rosamund Kwan played Aunt Yee in all the entries except the fourth, in which she was replaced by Jean Wang. The real life Master Wong Fei-hung (aka Huang Fei-Hong) died in 1924. He has been the subject of many Asian films, though few can rival the pageantry of Hark's series.

Once Upon a Time in China (aka *Wong Fei-hung*) (1991); *Once Upon a Time in China 2* (aka *Wong Fei-hung ji yi: Naam yi dong ji keung*; *Wong Fei-hung 2: Man Should Be Self Sufficient*) (1992); *Once Upon a Time in China 3* (aka *Wong Fei-hung tsi sam: Siwong tsangba*; *Wong Fei-hung 3: Lion King Struggle for Supremacy*) (1993); *Once Upon a Time in China IV* (aka *Wong Fei-hung zhi sei: Wang zhe zhi feng*) (1993); *Once Upon a Time in China V* (aka *Wong Fei-hung zhi wu: Long cheng jian ba*; *Wong Fei-hung 5: Dragon City's*

Exterminator Tyrant) (1994); *Once Upon a Time in China and America* (aka *Wong Fei-hung chi saiwik hung si*; *Once Upon a Time in China VI*; *Wong Fei-hung: West Territory Mighty Lion*) (1997)

Outlaws (Real-Life Western)

Jesse James and Billy the Kid easily outdistance their peers as the most oft-filmed outlaws in American cinema. In James' case, his celluloid fame is deserved, since his legendary exploits are backed up with the famous ill-fated Northfield, Minnesota, bank robbery. Billy the Kid, however, was a minor bandit gunned down in an ambush at the age of 21. His real name was Henry McCarty, though he was also known as William H. Bonney. On the screen, Billy has been portrayed as a wronged hero, a psychopath, and a vampire killer. Western veteran Johnny Mack Brown starred as the talkies' first Kid in 1930's *Billy the Kid*, a lavish MGM production originally shown in 70mm. It was remade a decade later in Technicolor with Robert Taylor, dumping his romantic image, in the title role. In contrast to these big-budget efforts, Billy was also the subject of a minor 1939 Roy Rogers picture (*Billy the Kid Returns*) and 1940's *Billy the Kid Outlawed*, the first of a PRC series starring Bob Steele and later Buster Crabbe. Jane Russell's cleavage overshadowed Billy's story in Howard Hughes' much-publicized, long-delayed *The Outlaw* (1943). It was the Kid's last prestigious picture until Paul Newman played him in Arthur Penn's psychological Western *The Left-Handed Gun* (1958), based on a TV play by Gore Vidal (which was remade for cable TV in 1989). Billy the Kid's subsequent film appearances have ranged from ambitious to awful. Sam Peckinpah's *Pat Garrett and Billy the Kid* (1973) promised to examine the relationship between lawman Garrett and ex-crony Billy. However, miscasting (Kris Kristofferson as Billy) and an overemphasis on violence spelled box-office failure and critical doom. Billy discovered his girlfriend's uncle (John Carradine) was a vampire in *Billy the Kid vs. Dracula* (1966), a movie not as dreadful as its title — but close. Emilio Estevez made Billy a romantic antihero in the 1988 "brat pack" Western *Young Guns*, which drew audiences despite an abundance of critical pans. Yet, despite these frequent appearances, Billy still rates second to Jesse James in number of films. James' career first received the lavish treatment with 20th Century–Fox's colorful *Jesse James* (1939), starring Tyrone Power as Jesse and Henry Fonda as brother Frank. Fonda reprised his role in Fritz Lang's superior 1940 sequel *The Return of Frank James*, one of the finest outlaw pictures. Jesse was a common fixture in the programmer Westerns of the 1950s. He was portrayed by Dale Robertson (*Fighting Man of the Plains*), Audie Murphy (*Kansas Raiders*), Willard Parker (*The Great Jesse James Raid*), Robert Wagner (*The True Story of Jesse James*), Ray Stricklyn (*Young Jesse James*), and others. Even Bob Hope was mistaken for the famous outlaw in *Alias Jesse James* (1959), one of his funniest comedies. In 1966, while Billy fought Dracula on one half of a double bill, Jesse saw a pal turned into a bald monster in *Jesse James Meets Frankenstein's Daughter*. Writer-director Philip Kaufman stressed factual detail over interesting narrative in 1972's *The Great Northfield, Minnesota Raid*, which featured Robert Duvall as Jesse and Cliff Robertson as Cole Younger. Both characters also appeared in Walter Hill's stylish outlaw saga *The Long Riders* (1980), a family affair starring: Stacy and James Keach as Jesse and Frank James; David, Keith, and Robert Carradine as the Younger Brothers; and Dennis and Randy Quaid as the lesser-known Mills Brothers. The Younger Brothers were paired

with the James' in other pictures as well, such as *The Great Missouri Raid* (1950) and *The Intruders* (1970). It's interesting to note that Audie Murphy is the only actor to have played both Billy the Kid and Jesse James and he did it in the same year, starring in 1950's *The Kid from Texas* and *Kansas Raiders*. Belle Starr, the only female outlaw to achieve notoriety, has been portrayed by Gene Tierney (*Belle Starr*, 1941), Jane Russell (*Montana Belle*), and Elizabeth Montgomery (*Belle Starr*, 1980). Paul Newman and Robert Redford brought fame to a couple of minor outlaws with their 1969 smash *Butch Cassidy and the Sundance Kid*. William Katt and Tom Berenger starred in a 1979 prequel *Butch and Sundance: The Early Days*. In made-for-TV movies, the Sundance Kid's woman was played by Elizabeth Montgomery in 1974's *Mrs. Sundance* and Katharine Ross (recreating her role from the Newman-Redford picture) in 1976's *Wanted: The Sundance Woman*. Other outlaw gangs appearing in multiple features include the Clantons (*Law and Order, Gunfight at the OK Corral, Hour of the Gun*) and the Daltons (*The Last Day, The Last Ride of the Dalton Gang*). On the small screen, Clu Gulager played Billy the Kid opposite Barry Sullivan's Pat Garrett in the 1960–62 series *The Tall Man*, while Christopher Jones starred in 1965–66's *The Legend of Jesse James*. In the following, the outlaw's name is listed in parentheses unless specified in the title. See also **Billy the Kid/Billy Carson**.

Billy the Kid (aka *The Highwayman Rides*) (1930); *Law and Order* (1932) (Clantons); *Jesse James* (1939); *Billy the Kid Returns* (1939); *Billy the Kid* (1940); *Billy the Kid Outlawed* (1940); *When the Daltons Rode* (1940); *The Return of Frank James* (1940); *Belle Starr* (1941); *The Outlaw* (1943) (Billy the Kid); *My Darling Clementine* (1946) (Clantons); *Belle Starr's Daughter* (1947); *Fighting Man of the Plains* (1949) (Jesse James); *The Younger Brothers* (1949); *I Shot Jesse James* (1949); *The Kid from Texas* (1950) (Billy the Kid); *Kansas Raiders* (1950) (Jesse James); *The Great Missouri Raid* (1950) (James and Younger Brothers); *Best of the Badmen* (1951) (Jeff Clanton); *Montana Belle* (1952) (Belle Starr); *The Great Jesse James Raid* (1953); *Jesse James vs. the Daltons* (1954); *Jesse James' Women* (1954); *The Law vs. Billy the Kid* (1954); *The Parson and the Outlaw* (1955) (Billy the Kid); *The True Story of Jesse James* (1956); *Hell's Crossroad* (1957) (Jesse James); *Gunfight at the OK Corral* (1957) (Clantons); *The Dalton Girls* (1957); *Badman's Country* (1958) (Butch Cassidy); *The Left-Handed Gun* (1958) (Billy the Kid); *Alias Jesse James* (1959); *Young Jesse James* (1960); *Billy the Kid vs. Dracula* (1966); *Jesse James Meets Frankenstein's Daughter* (1966); *Hour of the Gun* (1967) (Clantons); *Butch Cassidy and the Sundance Kid* (1969); *The Intruders* (1970 TVM) (James and Youngers); *Chisum* (1970) (Billy the Kid); *Doc* (1971) (Clantons); *Dirty Little Billy* (1972); *The Great Northfield, Minnesota Raid* (1972) (James and Youngers); *Pat Garrett and Billy the Kid* (1973); *Mrs. Sundance* (1974 TVM); *The Last Day* (1975 TVM) (Daltons); *Wanted: The Sundance Woman* (aka *Mrs. Sundance Rides Again*) (1976 TVM); *Go West, Young Girl* (1978 TVM) (Billy the Kid); *Butch and Sundance: The Early Days* (1979); *The Last Ride of the Dalton Gang* (1979 TVM); *Cattle Annie and Little Britches* (1980) (Daltons); *The Long Riders* (1980) (James and Youngers); *Belle Starr* (1980 TVM); *The Grey Fox* (1982) (Bill Miner); *The Last Days of Frank and Jesse James* (1986 TVM); *Young Guns* (1988) (Billy the Kid); *Billy the Kid* (aka *Gore Vidal's Billy the Kid*) (1989 TVM); *Young Guns II* (1990) (Billy the Kid); *Tombstone* (1993) (The Clanton Gang); *Wyatt Earp* (1994) (The Clanton Gang)

Painted People

Covering one's body with paint is not exactly a healthy thing to do. In fact, it resulted in the death of one of the asylum inmates in *Bedlam* (1946), though the institution's vicious director (Boris Karloff) seemed rather undisturbed. Bond villain Auric Goldfinger killed 007's girlfriend (Shirley Eaton) by covering her in his trademark gold in 1964's *Goldfinger*. In contrast, partially painted people have led healthier lives. Marlene Dietrich sported a pair of painted legs for her famous dance scene in *Kismet* (1944). On the kinkier side, Britt Ekland exposed her painted breasts in *Scandal* (1989), while jungle natives dipped Bo Derek in an ugly shade of off-white in *Tarzan, the Ape Man* (1981). See also **Tattoos**.

Kismet (aka *Oriental Dream*) (1944); *Bedlam* (1946); *Mondo Cane* (1963); *Goldfinger* (1964); *The Swinger* (1966); *Slave of the Cannibal God* (1977); *Tarzan, the Ape Man* (1981); *Scandal* (1989)

Painters

The post–Impressionists of the late 19th century dominate film biographies of painters, primarily due to the influences of Vincent Van Gogh and Paul Gaugin. The 1956 *Lust for Life*, based on an Irving Stone book, was a colorful portrait of Van Gogh's tormented life. Kirk Douglas played the Dutch painter, with Anthony Quinn earning a Best Supporting Actor Oscar as his friend Gaugin. The unusual 1987 Australian tribute, *Vincent*, consisted mostly of Van Gogh's paintings accompanied by John Hurt's affective readings of his letters. Gaugin's life provided Somerset Maugham with the basis for his novel *The Moon and Sixpence*, which was filmed in 1942. George Sanders played the stockbroker who left his family to pursue painting and wound up dying of leprosy on a South Seas island. The Hays Office, the film industry's censorship watchdog, required that some of the film's nude paintings be toned down by adding leaves or flowers to cover appropriate body parts. Two Gaugin biographies surfaced in the 1980s. The 1980 TV movie *Gaugin, the Savage* boasted fine production values, including on-location footage of France and Tahiti, but a miscast David Carradine doomed the venture. Donald Sutherland made an appropriately passionate Gaugin in 1987's *Wolf at the Door*, a slow-moving account of Gaugin's brief return from Tahiti. Aside from Gaugin and Van Gogh, biographies of painters have been scarce and sporadic. Alexander Korda produced 1936's *Rembrandt*, an opulent version of the Dutch painter's life featuring a classic Charles Laughton performance. John Huston's *Moulin Rouge* (1953) fictionalized the life of dwarfish French painter Toulouse-Lautrec (Jose Ferrer). Yet, the film remains fondly remembered for its atmospheric 19th century Montmartre setting and an elaborate can-can sequence. Anthony Hopkins played Pablo Picasso in 1996's *Surviving Picasso*, although the Cubist painter inspired earlier films. Picasso created a canvas on screen for French director Henri-Georges Clouzot in the 1955 documentary *The Mystery of Picasso*. *The Picasso Summer* in 1969 starred Albert Finney and Yvette Mimieux as a vacationing couple who set off in search of the famous artist. It sat on the studio shelf for some time before debuting in the U.S. as a late-night network movie. In addition to providing biographical material for filmmakers, painters have contributed to the behind-the-scenes art of cinema. Spanish artist Salvador Dali designed a haunting, surrealistic dream sequence for Alfred Hitchcock's *Spellbound* (1945). The special effects crew of 1947's *The Private Affairs of Bel Ami* claimed that Van Gogh's canvas *The Garden of the Vicarage at Nuenen* gave them the idea of using plastic to create "dry rain." See also **Paintings**.

Rembrandt (1936); *The Moon and Sixpence* (1942) (Paul Gaugin); *Kitty* (1945) (Cecil Kellaway as Gainsborough in bit role); *Moulin Rouge* (1953) (Toulouse-Lautrec); *The Mystery of Picasso* (1955); *Lust for Life* (1956) (Van Gogh and Gaugin); *The Lovers of Montparnasse* (aka *Montparnasse 19*) (1957) (Modigliani); *The Naked Maja* (1959) (Francisco Goya); *The Agony and the Ecstasy* (1965) (Michaelangelo); *El Greco* (1966); *The Picasso Summer* (1969); *Savage Messiah* (1972) (Henri Gautier); *The Adventures of Picasso* (1978); *Gaugin the Savage* (1980 TVM); *The Rothko Conspiracy* (1983 TVM) (Mark Rothko); *Carravaggio* (1986); *Wolf at the Door* (1987) (Paul Gauguin); *Vincent— The Life and Death of Vincent Van Gogh* (aka *Vincent*) (1987); *Vincent* (1988); *My Left Foot* (1989) (Christy Brown); *Vincent and Theo* (1990 TVM) (Van Gogh); *Dreams* (1990) ("Crows" segment; features Vincent Van Gogh); *A Season of Giants* (1991 TVM) (Raphael, Michaelangelo, Da Vinci); *Van Gogh* (1991); *The Van Gogh Wake* (aka *La Passion Van Gogh*) (1993); *Zorn* (1994) (Anders Zorn); *Carrington* (1995); *Basquiat* (1996); *I Shot Andy Warhol* (1996); *Surviving Picasso* (1996); *Artemisia* (1997) (Gentileschi); *Ever After* (1998) (Da Vinci)

Paintings

Canvases have figured prominently in an odd assortment of horror films, fantasies, mysteries, and comedies. At least three films have been based on Oscar Wilde's wickedly clever *The Picture of Dorian Gray*, the story of a vile Victorian rake whose portrait ages while he retains his youth. The 1945 version remains the best-remembered, with the portrait appearing in color in an otherwise black-and-white film. Joseph Cotten played a struggling artist who paints a masterpiece after falling in love with a ghost in the marvelous 1948 fantasy *Portrait of Jennie*. Again, the film reverted to color for the closing shot of Cotten's painting. Dana Andrews fell in love with the portrait of Gene Tierney hanging over her mantle in Otto Preminger's stylish 1944 mystery *Laura*. That perceptive sleuth Sherlock Holmes cracked the case of *The Hound of the Baskervilles* by examining a painting of Sir Hugo Baskerville and deducing that an unlikely suspect was actually a murderous relative. A theft of a painting provided the excuse for the 1930 Marx Brothers romp *Animal Crackers*. In the 1942 British comedy *Much Too Shy*, George Formby played an unfortunate handyman whose paintings of his clients wound up at an advertising agency — with nude bodies added to them. A demonic portrait hanging in a museum required New York City to call for Bill Murray, Dan Aykroyd, and Harold Ramis in 1989's blockbuster comedy *Ghostbusters II*. See also **Painters**.

Animal Crackers (1930); *The Hound of the Baskervilles* (1939) (see **Sherlock Holmes** for other versions); *Much Too Shy* (1942); *Laura* (1944); *The Picture of Dorian Gray* (1945); *Portrait of Jennie* (1948); *The Golden Madonna* (1949); *The Fake* (1958); *Vertigo* (1958); *Color Me Blood Red* (1965); *Now You See It, Now You Don't* (1967 TVM); *Night Gallery* (1969 TVM); *The Picture of Dorian Gray* (1973 TVM); *Hullabaloo Over Georgie and Bonnie's Pictures* (1979 TVM); *The Sins of Dorian Gray* (1983 TVM); *A Month in the Country* (1987); *Hot Paint* (1988 TVM); *Ghostbusters II* (1989); *The Portrait* (1973 TVM); *Two If by Sea* (1996); *What Dreams May Come* (1998); *The Haunting* (1999); *The Thomas Crown Affair* (1999); *Mickey Blue Eyes* (1999)

Palmer, Harry

Michael Caine played Len Deighton's Cockney thief-turned-disenchanted spy five times, beginning with 1965's *The Ipcress File*. While other spy movies strove to imitate the Bond films (q.v.), the Palmer series played up its differences. Harry wore thick glasses, enjoyed cooking, and complained about his dirty profession. However, like 007, he had a weak spot for the ladies. Guy Doleman played Palmer's blackmailing superior, while Oscar Homolka was memorable as a Russian officer in the second and third films. *The Ipcress File* and *Funeral in Berlin* (1966) were exceptional spy films, but *Billion Dollar Brain* (1967) — directed by maverick director Ken Russell — was an overblown, jumbled affair. The series appeared to end with this installment, only to return after a 20-year hiatus in the form of two 1997 made-for-cable features. Palmer comes out of retirement to recover a stolen virus called the Red Death in *Bullet to Beijing* and tries to stop a nuclear war in *Midnight in St. Petersburg*. Neither film made much of an impression, although Caine was still convincing as the droll and world-weary Palmer. Interestingly, Len Deighton's character remained nameless in the novels.

The Ipcress File (1965); *Funeral in Berlin* (1966); *Billion Dollar Brain* (1967); *Bullet to Beijing* (1997 TVM); *Midnight in St. Petersburg* (1997 TVM)

Parallel Worlds

Few filmmakers have been attracted to the complex concept of a character floating back and forth between two mirrored worlds. Astronaut Roy Thinnes discovered a twin Earth on his *Journey to the Far Side of the Sun* (1969). It took him awhile to figure out that he had exchanged places with his exact duplicate. The 1973 TV movie *The Stranger* was an unofficial remake with Glenn Corbett as the baffled astronaut. Kathleen Turner's trips between two parallel worlds left her so confused that she murdered the wrong man in 1987's *Julia and Julia*. Gwyneth Paltrow fared much better in *Sliding Doors* (1998), finding romance after she missed a train in one reality and caught it in another. Tom Bell's journey into another dimension, courtesy of an explosion, enabled him to save a dying girl's life in *Quest for Love* (1971). A more common variation on the parallel world theme incorporates time travel, as when Lindsay Wagner transported herself into another age whenever she put on an old dress in 1979's *The Two Worlds of Jennie Logan*. See also **Lookalikes**; **Time Travel**.

Journey to the Far Side of the Sun (aka *Doppelganger*) (1969); *Quest for Love* (1971); *The Stranger* (1973 TVM); *The Two Worlds of Jennie Logan* (1979 TVM); *Julia and Julia* (1987); *Paperhouse* (1988); *Cool World* (1992); *Super Mario Bros.* (1993); *Sliding Doors* (1998); *Shattered Image* (1998); *Twice Upon a Time* (1998 TVM)

The Parent Trap Series

This 1961 adaptation of Erich Kästner's novel *Das Doppelte Lottchen* proved to be one of Disney's most successful live-action films. It was tailor-made for 15-year-old Hayley Mills, whose popularity had soared after the previous year's *Pollyanna*. In *The Parent Trap*, Mills plays twins Sharon and Susan, who are unaware of each other's existence until they meet at a summer camp. The twins figure out that when their parents divorced, they were divided up with the rest of the property. Naturally, Sharon and Susan plot to reunite their parents by switching places. Mills does a fine job portraying both the cultured, Boston-bred Sharon and the more liberated California-raised Susan. She also gets great support from Maureen O'Hara and Brian Keith as the perplexed parents. The film even spawned a hit song called "Let's Get To-

gether," which peaked at #8 in *Billboard* in 1961. Since Susan and Sharon sang the song as a duet in the movie, the single lists the performers as Hayley Mills and Hayley Mills. Surprisingly, Disney waited 25 years to make a sequel — and even then, it was a made-for-cable feature. In *Parent Trap II*, Hayley Mills reprises her roles as Sharon, now a single mother, and Susan. The plot centers on Sharon's daughter Nikki, who (with help from Aunt Susan) tries to play matchmaker for her mother. Mills also starred in two additional TV movies: *Parent Trap III* (in which Susan marries a single father with triplets!) and *Parent Trap: Hawaiian Honeymoon*. In 1998, Disney produced a pleasant remake with Lindsay Lohan as the twins (now named Hallie and Annie). It featured some clever references to the Disney original: Lohan sings a bit of "Let's Get Together" in one scene and Joanna Barnes plays the mother of the scheming fiancée she played in the 1961 version. In addition to *The Parent Trap* movies, Kästner's children's novel has been filmed as *Das Doppelte Lottchen* (1950), *Twice Upon a Time* (1953), and *Charlie & Louise — Das Doppelte Lottchen* (1993). Not surprisingly, none of the films dwell on the cruel, selfish aspects of the parents' actions — it seems pretty inhumane to keep twins in the dark about each other's existence. See also **Twins**.

The Parent Trap (1961); *Parent Trap II* (1986 TVM); *Parent Trap III* (1989 TVM); *Parent Trap: Hawaiian Honeymoon* (1989 TVM); *The Parent Trap* (1998)

Pasolini's Trilogy of Life

Italian filmmaker Pier Paolo Pasolini's three medieval-set anthology films are considered to be his most cheerful and most accessible works. Like most of the Pasolini oeuvre, the most prevalent themes intermingle religion and sex. *The Decameron* (1970), adapted from Giovanni Boccaccio's 14th-century book, contains eight raunchy tales linked by the director in a framing story. The most representative tale involves nuns eager to have sex with a deaf mute who can tell no one of their sins. The irony is that the man can actually hear and speak — he is taking advantage of the nuns. *The Decameron* was an artistic and commercial triumph for Pasolini, who quite logically turned to Geoffrey Chaucer for his follow-up. *The Canterbury Tales* (1971) starred Pasolini as Chaucer, who introduces several tales focusing on sex, brutality, and human waste. Despite winning the prestigious Golden Bear at Berlin Film Festival, *The Canterbury Tales* did not duplicate the critical success of *The Decameron*. The trilogy's third film, *Arabian Nights* (1974), ended the series on a high note. Ines Pellegrini starred as the slave girl who disguises herself as man, takes a wife, and becomes a king. Her story serves as a frame for other erotic tales taking place in exotic locations like India and Nepal. It won the Grand Jury Prize at the Cannes Film Festival and became a popular arthouse picture. Pasolini was murdered after completing his next and final film *Salo* (1975).

The Decameron (aka *Il Decameron*) (1970); *The Canterbury Tales* (aka *I Racconi di Canterbury*) (1971); *Arabian Nights* (aka *Il Fiore elle mille e una notte*; *A Thousand and One Nights*) (1974)

Peanuts Series

Charles Schulz's lovable *Peanuts* characters leapt from the comic pages to theater screens with 1969's *A Boy Named Charlie Brown*, a full-length animated feature with songs by Rod McKuen. After three more films, Charlie, Snoopy, Lucy, Linus, and the rest of the gang gave up their screen careers and concentrated on their long-running, apparently neverending series of TV specials. See also **Animated Movies (Feature-Length)**; **Comic Strip Characters**.

A Boy Named Charlie Brown (1969); *Snoopy, Come Home* (1972); *Race for Your Life, Charlie Brown* (1977); *Bon Voyage, Charlie Brown* (*and Don't Come Back*) (1980)

Penitentiary Series

The 1979 film *Penitentiary* was the first installment in the saga of Too Sweet, an unjustly imprisoned black convict reformed by boxing. Written, produced, and directed by Jamaa Fanaka, the film earned a reputation as a minor league *Rocky* (q.v.), although its gritty approach was praised. Fanaka and star Leon Isaac Kennedy continued with two disappointing sequels, *Penitentiary 2* (1982) and *Penitentiary 3* (1987). The *Rocky* similarities became blatant in these films, right down to the presence of *Rocky III* alumnus Mr. T in *Penitentiary 2*. Kennedy and his then-wife, sportscaster/model Jayne Kennedy, also made a 1981 remake of the 1947 boxing classic *Body and Soul*. See also **Boxing**; **Prisons**.

Penitentiary (1979); *Penitentiary 2* (1982); *Penitentiary 3* (1987)

Penrod

Booth Tarkington wrote three books about Penrod Schofield, "The Worst Boy in Town," who consistently stirred up trouble in a quiet, Midwestern town circa 1914. Gordon Griffith appeared in a 1922 version and Ben Alexander took over as Penrod in the following year's *Penrod and Sam*. The latter film was remade by Warner Bros. in 1931 with Leon Janney in the lead and Dorothy Peterson (later Mrs. Pepper in the *Five Little Peppers*) as his mother. However, Warner's official *Penrod* series began in 1937 with the third version of *Penrod and Sam*, with Bobby Mauch as a much nicer boy. This movie also updated the setting, making Penrod the head of a Junior G-Men Club (which met in a barn just like Our Gang). Bobby's twin brother, Billy, joined the cast for the last two films: *Penrod and His Twin Brother* and *Penrod's Double Trouble* (both 1938). The Mauch Twins, who had their greatest success in Errol Flynn's *The Prince and the Pauper* (1937), virtually disappeared from films in the 1940s. However, Penrod showed up again — in diluted form — in two Doris Day musicals: *Moonlight Bay* (1951) and *By the Light of the Silvery Moon* (1953). These films restored the earlier setting, but relegated Penrod to a supporting character and changed his name to Wesley. He was played by Billy Gray, best known as Bud on TV's *Father Knows Best*.

Penrod (1922); *Penrod and Sam* (1923); *Penrod and Sam* (1931); *Penrod and Sam* (1937); *Penrod and His Twin Brother* (1938); *Penrod's Double Trouble* (1938); *Moonlight Bay* (1951); *By the Light of the Silvery Moon* (1953)

People Hunters/Human Prey

The premise of hunting human prey for sport was explored vividly in Richard Connell's famous short story "The Most Dangerous Game." Connell's story about ruthless hunter Count Zaroff has been filmed "officially" as *The Most Dangerous Game* (1932), *A Game of Death* (1946), *Run for the Sun* (1956), and *Blood Lust* (1966). The 1932 version is best remembered, chiefly for Leslie Banks' campy, despicable villain. Future nice guy Alan Alda

played a mad, crippled Vietnam veteran who tracked down a harmless couple trapped on his island in *To Kill a Clown*. In the 1973 TV movie *Maneater*, Richard Basehart portrayed a deranged animal trainer who unleashed two hungry tigers on four visitors. One of the more interesting variations on Connell's plot has people stalking each other as part of a socially acceptable pastime, a twist featured in *The Tenth Victim* (1965) and Stephen King's *The Running Man* (1987). Perhaps the finest film about people hunters was Cornel Wilde's gripping 1966 adventure *The Naked Prey*. Director Wilde played a safari guide, the only survivor of a native ambush, who is freed by his captors and then methodically tracked down. No other film matches this one for showing how self-survival can force a man to evolve into a killer as brutal as his pursuers.

The Most Dangerous Game (1932); *A Game of Death* (1946); *Johnny Allegro* (1949); *Run for the Sun* (1956); *The Tenth Victim* (1965); *The Naked Prey* (1966); *Blood Lust* (1966); *Woman Hunt* (1972); *To Kill a Clown* (1972); *Maneater* (1973 TVM); *Open Season* (1974); *Savages* (1974 TVM); *Escape 2000* (aka *Turkey Shoot*) (1981); *The Running Man* (1987); *Predator* (1987); *Lethal Woman* (1989); *High Desert Kill* (1989 TVM); *Deadly Game* (1991 TVM); *Do or Die* (1991); *Hard Target* (1993); *Final Round* (1993); *Surviving the Game* (1994); *Dominion* (1995); *The Hunted* (1998 TVM)

Personal Ads

Filmmakers have typically used personal ad columns to bring unlikely lovers together. After reading the personals and suffering amnesia, bored yuppie housewife Rosanna Arquette wound up with practical projectionist Aidan Quinn in *Desperately Seeking Susan* (1985). Recently-divorced Bill Schuppert thought he had found the perfect companion in 1981's *The Personals* — until she turned out to be married. In 1981's *I Sent a Letter to My Love*, a lonely woman discovered romance by taking up correspondence with a man listed in the personals. In a bittersweet twist, he turns out to be her paralyzed brother. A serial murderer used the personals to attract victims in the 1989 thriller *Sea of Love*.

Snares (aka *Personal Column; Plèges*) (1939); *The Personals* (1981); *I Sent a Letter to My Love* (1981); *Desperately Seeking Susan* (1985); *The Perfect Match* (1987); *Classified Love* (1987 TVM); *Sea of Love* (1989); *Personals* (1990 TVM); *Single White Female* (1992); *Dying to Love You* (1993 TVM); *Wacko* (aka *Parano*) (1994); *Sweethearts* (1996); *Unmade Beds* (1997); *Kiss Me, Guido* (1997); *Next Stop Wonderland* (1998); *The Personals* (aka *Zhenghun Qishi*) (1999)

Persons in Hiding Series

J. Edgar Hoover's nonfiction best-seller *Persons in Hiding* provided the basis for this modest Paramount four-film gangster series. Actually, Courtney Riley Cooper ghostwrote the book, but the FBI director's name sold the copies and gave the series what marquee value it possessed. The best entries were the first and last, tight thrillers featuring a potent combination of rising and veteran stars (e.g., Richard Denning, William Frawley, J. Carrol Naish, Robert Ryan, Ralph Bellamy, Jack Carson, and Hedda Hopper). The 1939 *Persons in Hiding* traced the exploits of Bonnie Parker (later of *Bonnie and Clyde* fame), while 1940's *Queen of the Mob* was based on the career of Ma Barker. See also **Gangsters (Real Life)**.

Persons in Hiding (1939); *Undercover Doctor* (1939); *Parole Fixer* (1940); *Queen of the Mob* (1940)

Peyton Place Series

Grace Metalious's cynical small town exposé made quite an impact when released in 1957. Its 1961 sequel, *Return to Peyton Place*, was a more conventional soap opera, but it did well enough to inspire a television series. The show premiered in 1964 and became an immediate runaway hit. It ran two or three times weekly for five years, thanks largely to an all-star cast featuring Dorothy Malone, Mia Farrow, Ryan O'Neal, and Ruth Warrick (pre–*All My Children*). *Murder in Peyton Place*, a 1977 made-for-TV movie, killed off Allison MacKenzie and Rodney Harrington (Farrow and O'Neal), but reunited regulars Malone and Ed Nelson. *Peyton Place: The Next Generation* (1985), another TV movie, was a feeble attempt to drum up interest for a new series.

Peyton Place (1957); *Return to Peyton Place* (1961); *Murder in Peyton Place* (1977 TVM); *Peyton Place: The Next Generation* (1985 TVM)

Phantasm Series

Lethal flying spheres. Killer dwarfs that bleed yellow ooze. A dismembered living finger that turns into an insect-like creature. It's no wonder that viewers of Don Coscarelli's 1979 cult classic *Phantasm* nod their heads when one of the film's characters muses aloud: "I can't figure this thing out." If one ignores the dream vs. reality ending, the plot has something to do with a Tall Man (Angus Scrimm) who turns dead people into dwarfs, stores them in barrels, and then tosses them through a portal to another planet to be used as slave labor. The fate of the world rests in the hands of an apparently unemployed musician named Jody (Bill Thornbury), his teenage brother Michael (Michael Baldwin), and their friend Reggie (Reggie Bannister), who drives an ice cream truck. Though silly at times and burdened with uneven acting, *Phantasm* is a surreal, genuinely creepy film filled with haunting images. To stretch his miniscule budget, the 21-year-old Coscarelli wrote, directed, photographed, and edited *Phantasm*. Over the next nine years, Coscarelli made one movie, *The Beastmaster* (q.v), and worked on the Stephen King werewolf picture *Silver Bullet*. When he finally decided to make *Phastasm II*, Universal Pictures gave him a $3 million budget and guidance to produce a more traditionally structured film. The latter decision hurts *Phantasm II*, which is far less hypnotic and interesting than the original. The story picks up with Michael (now played by James LeGros) leaving a mental hospital after admitting that the events of the first film were not real. Michael still believes they happened, however, and he teams up again with Reggie to fight the Tall Man. The series improved with the next two installments, *Phantasm III: Lord of the Dead* (1994) and *Phantasm: Oblivion* (1998). The third picture finds the original film's heroic trio in dire straits: The dead Jody (Thornbury) is a spirit that resides in one of the flying spheres; Michael (Baldwin) gets kidnapped by the Tall Man; and Reggie (Bannister) must contend with hoodlums that have nothing to do with killer dwarfs and yellow ooze. Finally, in *Phantasm: Oblivion*, Jody's spirit becomes evil, Michael gets the bad end of an encounter with the Tall Man, and Reggie has to save the day. Coscarelli wrote and directed all the sequels. In 1999, *Entertainment Weekly* listed the first *Phantasm* as the seventeenth scariest film in cinema history.

Phantasm (1979); *Phantasm II* (1988); *Phantasm III: Lord of the Dead* (aka *Phantasm III*) (1994); *Phantasm: Oblivion* (aka *Phantasm IV: Oblivion*; *Phantasm: OblIVion*) (1998)

Photographers

News photographers, army photographers, fashion photographers, amateur shutterbugs — photography is a wide field that has interested filmmakers on a regular basis. Photo journalists in volatile environments played key supporting roles in the 1983 films *Under Fire* and *The Year of Living Dangerously*. The latter film featured Linda Hunt in a Best Supporting Oscar performance as a philosophizing *male* photographer in 1965 Indonesia. Nick Nolte played a photojournalist in contemporary Nicaragua in *Under Fire*, while 1986's *Salvador* starred James Woods as a cynical freelance photographer unable to distance himself from his subjects. The title of *84 Charlie Mopic* is the Army job classification for a motion picture cameramen. This 1989 film showed viewers the Vietnam War through the soldier's — or rather, his camera. The photographer is glimpsed only when he hands his camera to someone else to engage in a little horseplay. Most female camera clickers in the movies have been fashion photographers, such as Faye Dunaway in *Eyes of Laura Mars* and Pam Grier in *Friday Foster*. Photographer Claudette Colbert unexpectedly fell in love with subway digger Fred MacMurray in the 1943 comedy *No Time for Love*. In other comic escapades, Buster Keaton starred in the classic 1928 comedy *The Cameraman*. It was remade, much less effectively, with Red Skelton as 1950's *Watch the Birdie*. Allegedly, an uncredited Keaton supervised many of the gags. Bob Hope played a photographer-turned-detective in *My Favorite Brunette* (which was Dorothy Lamour, of course). The source of Bob's trouble was not Dorothy, but a valuable picture taken with his "keyhole camera." Photographers have not fared well in horror films. David Warner was one of the first to realize that little Damien was not an angelic child in 1976's *The Omen*. Unfortunately, that knowledge lost him his head in the film's goriest sequence. In Michael Powell's cult classic *Peeping Tom* (1960), Carl Boehm played a deranged photographer obsessed with capturing his murder victims on film at the precise moment of their deaths. Scientist Robert Stephens invented a camera that could capture one's spirit as it leaves the body in 1972's intriguing *The Asphyx*. Michelangelo Antonioni's *Blow-Up* (1966) remains the most overrated movie about a photographer. It took a promising premise (David Hemmings unintentionally photographs what may be a murder) and burdened it with heavy-handed symbolism. See also **Centerfolds**; **Fashion Models**.

The Cameraman (1928); *Picture Snatcher* (1933); *Murder in Greenwich Village* (1937); *Dust Be My Destiny* (1939); *China Girl* (1942); *Escape from Crime* (1942); *Hit the Ice* (1943); *No Time for Love* (1943); *Double Exposure* (1944); *Lover Come Back* (aka *When Lovers Meet*) (1946); *My Favorite Brunette* (1947); *Watch the Birdie* (1950); *I Love Melvin* (1953); *Rear Window* (1954); *Joe Butterfly* (1957); *Funny Face* (1957); *Peeping Tom* (1960); *A Girl Named Tamiko* (1962); *If a Man Answers* (1962); *Blow-Up* (1966); *Negatives* (1968); *Live a Little, Love a Little* (1968); *La Prisonniere* (1969); *Little Murders* (1971); *Private Parts* (1972); *The Asphyx* (1972); *Friday Foster* (1975); *The Omen* (1976); *Eyes of Laura Mars* (1978); *Girlfriends* (1978); *Georgia, Georgia* (1982); *Under Fire* (1983); *The Year of Living Dangerously* (1983); *No Small Affair* (1984); *Salvador* (1986); *The Fantasist* (1986); *The Girl in the Picture* (1986); *Double Exposure* (1989); *84 Charlie Mopic* (1989); *Margaret Bourke-White* (1989 TVM); *Somebody Has to Shoot the Picture* (1990 TVM); *Curiosity Kills* (1990 TVM); *Two Evil Eyes* (aka *Due Occhi Diabolic*) (1990); *In the Cold of the Night* (1990); *Drop Dead*

Gorgeous (1991 TVM); *The Public Eye* (1992); *Proof* (1992); *Lethal Exposure* (1993 TVM); *Calendar* (1993); *Seduce Me* (aka *The Pamela Principle 2*) (1994); *At Risk* (1994); *Of Love and Shadows* (1994); *Dazzle* (1995 TVM); *Beyond Rangoon* (1995); *The Bridges of Madison County* (1995); *Temptress* (1995); *Out There* (1995); *Addicted to Love* (1997); *Wild America* (1997); *Fools Rush In* (1997); *The Edge* (1997); *Billy's Hollywood Screen Kiss* (1998); *Stepmom* (1998); *Pecker* (1998); *The Deep End of the Ocean* (1999); *Guinevere* (1999); *Striking Poses* (1999)

Pianists

While movie violinists (q.v.) have been limited to classical settings and trumpet players (q.v.) to jazz scenes, movie pianists have crossed all musical boundaries. The film appearances of a divergent group of real-life musicians confirms this point: Ignace Jan Paderewski and Liberace played the classics in, respectively, *Moonlight Sonata* (1937) and *Sincerely Yours* (1955); Ray Charles opted for the blues in *Blues for Lovers* (1964); and contemporary singer/pianist Charles Aznavour mixed jazz and popular music in *Shoot the Piano Player* (1960), as did Barry Manilow in *Copacabana* (1985). A wide variety of physical impairments and emotional problems have plagued pianists. Liberace went deaf in *Sincerely Yours*, while blind piano players were the subject of *Night Song* (1947), *Torch Song* (1953), and Charles' *Blues for Lovers*. Geoffrey Rush won a Best Actor Oscar for playing emotionally fragile concert piantist David Helfgott in *Shine* (1996). Jack Nicholson abandoned a promising career as a concert pianist to become an aimless drifter in *Five Easy Pieces* (1970). The pianists in *Shoot the Piano Player* and *Fingers*— the first a washed-up concert performer, the second a promising star — both became involved with gangsters. A dying concert pianist tried to possess Alan Alda's body in the Satanic thriller *The Mephisto Waltz* (1971). That was a mild problem, however, compared to Peter Lorre's struggles with the severed hand of a piano player in *The Beast with Five Fingers* (1946). Still, the incredibly weird Dr. Seuss fantasy *The 5,000 Fingers of Dr. T* (1953) rates as the most terrifying pianist film. Little Tommy Rettig starred as a boy who dreams that his vicious piano teacher has imprisoned him and 499 other boys in a castle where they play a giant piano all day long. In comparison, the troubled young piano players of *Madame Sousatzka* and *Running on Empty* (both 1988) had it easy. Richard Dreyfuss and Amy Irving played young adults going for the same career-making prize, while falling in love in *The Competition* (1980). Two teenage groupies stalked pianist Peter Sellers wherever he went in *The World of Henry Orient* (1964). No discussion of piano players would be complete without at least mentioning Dooley Wilson as Sam in *Casablanca* (1942). Although they were not pianists, Tom Hanks and Robert Loggia danced out a catchy rendition of "Chopsticks" on a giant piano in *Big* (1988). See also **Trumpet Players; Violinists.**

Mad Love (1935); *Moonlight Sonata* (1937); *Stolen Heaven* (1938); *When Tomorrow Comes* (1939); *The Great Lie* (1941); *That Uncertain Feeling* (1941); *Dangerous Moonlight* (aka *Suicide Squadron*) (1941); *Casablanca* (1942); *The Constant Nymph* (1943); *Love Story* (aka *A Lady Surrenders*) (1944); *A Voice in the Wind* (1944); *The Seventh Veil* (1945); *Detour* (1945); *Deception* (1946); *The Beast with Five Fingers* (1946); *Carnegie Hall* (1947); *Night Song* (1947); *Letter from an Unknown Woman* (1948); *A Kiss in the Dark* (1949); *Quartet* (1949) ("The Alien Corn" segment); *Too Young to Kiss* (1951); *Strange Fascination* (1952); *The 5,000 Fingers of Dr. T* (1953); *Torch Song* (1953); *Rhapsody* (1954); *Sincerely Yours* (1955); *The Eddy Duchin Story* (1956); *Julie* (1956); *Shoot the Piano Player* (aka *Shoot the Pianist*) (1960); *Tormented* (1960); *The Hands of Orlac* (aka *Hands of the Strangler*) (1960); *The World of Henry Orient* (1964); *Blues for Lovers* (aka *Ballad in Blue*) (1964); *The Battle of the Villa Fiorita* (aka *Affair at the Villa Fiorita*) (1964); *30 Is a Dangerous Age, Cynthia* (1968); *The Story of a Woman* (1969); *Five Easy Pieces* (1970); *The Mephisto Waltz* (1971); *The Abominable Dr. Phibes* (1971) (an organist actually); *Deep Red* (aka *Profondo Rosso*; *Dripping Deep Red*) (1975); *Autumn Sonata* (1978); *Fingers* (1978); *Practice Makes Perfect* (1978); *The Competition* (1980); *Copacabana* (1985 TVM); *Ghost of a Chance* (1987 TVM); *Madame Sousatzka* (1988); *Running on Empty* (1988); *Liberace* (1988 TVM); *Great Balls of Fire!* (1989); *Matters of the Heart* (1990 TVM); *The Fabulous Baker Boys* (1990); *The Winter in Lisbon* (1990); *The Pianist* (1991); *The Accompanist* (aka *L'Accompagnatrice*) (1992); *The Piano* (1993); *Twenty-two Short Films About Glenn Gould* (1994); *Shine* (1996); *Love Walked In* (1998); *A Song from the Heart* (1999 TVM)

Pickpockets

The colorful pickpockets of Charles Dickens' *Oliver Twist* have reached the screen in five official adaptations, with David Lean's 1948 version and Carol Reed's 1968 musical attracting the most admirers. George C. Scott played Fagin in the 1982 TV movie. Coincidentally, Scott's one-time wife Trish Van Devere played one of master pickpocket James Coburn's new recruits in 1973's *Harry in Your Pocket*. Ginger Rogers played another lady pickpocket in the 1946 comedy *Heartbeat*, while *Thick as Thieves* (1991) featured a brother-and-sister pickpocket team who unwisely select an undercover cop as their target. A movie extra disrupts pickpocket Ben Gazzara's plans in the Italian-made comedy *The Passionate Thief* (1960). Pickpocket Richard Widmark inadvertently thwarts enemy spies by stealing valuable microfilm in Samuel Fuller's *Pickup on South Street* (1953). Martial artist Jean-Claude Van Damme made an unlikely NYC pickpocket in *The Quest* (1996). Finally, French director Robert Bresson produced the cinema's most philosophical essay on the subject with 1959's *Pickpocket*.

Oliver Twist (1922); *Oliver Twist* (1933); *Main Street After Dark* (1944); *Heartbeat* (1946); *Oliver Twist* (1948); *Pickup on South Street* (1953); *Pickpocket* (1959); *The Passionate Thief* (1960); *Oliver!* (1968); *The Daughters of Joshua Cabe* (1972 TVM); *Harry in Your Pocket* (1973); *Oliver Twist* (1982 TVM); *Thick as Thieves* (1991); *Life with Mikey* (1993); *Pigalle* (1994); *The City of Lost Children* (1995); *The Quest* (1996); *On the 2nd Day of Christmas* (1997 TVM)

Pigs

Leading roles for pigs have been few and far between. Dick King-Smith's children's novel *The Sheep-Pig* provided the basis for *Babe* (1995), the cinema's most famous oinker. The principal characters in the 1955 British adaptation of George Orwell's satire *Animal Farm* were two pigs named Napoleon and Snowball. E.B. White's children's classic *Charlotte's Web* (1973) focused on a friendship between a matronly spider and a shy pig. A little porker in *Gordy* (1995) tries to save his family from being turned into bacon. In supporting roles, real-life pigs have stolen their fair share of scenes. A frolicking contraband porker upstaged Maggie Smith and Michael Palin in the deft food-rationing comedy *A Private Function* (1985). Michael J. Fox acquired a pet pig named Jasmine in 1991's *Doc Hollywood*. A talking pig popped up opposite

Pee Wee Herman in 1988's *Big Top Pee Wee*. In the horror genre, a giant killer pig stalked the Australian countryside in 1984's *Razorback*, while an ad for 1982's *Pigs* proclaimed: "They'll eat anything so she had the perfect method to dispose of her victims." The daffy and dangerous Annie Wilks (Kathy Bates) named her pet pig after her favorite romance novel heroine in Stephen King's *Misery* (1990). Bizarre man/pig love relationships were explored in *Futz* and Pier Paolo Pasolini's *Pigsty* (both 1969). People were transformed into pigs in *Ulysses* (1955), *O Lucky Man!* (1973), and *Elvira—Mistress of the Dark* (1988). Hugh "Bulldog" Drummond (Walter Pidgeon) retired from sleuthing to raise pigs in 1951's *Calling Bulldog Drummond*. Animated shorts have featured Pooh's friend Piglet and that world-famous stuttering pig Porky. There's a 1911 silent short boasting the interesting title *The Electrified Pig*. Television introduced Miss Piggy and Arnold Ziffel of *Green Acres* fame. See also **The Muppets**.

Calling Bulldog Drummond (1951); *Animal Farm* (1955); *Ulysses* (1955); *Pigsty* (aka *Pig Pen; Porcile*) (1969); *Futz* (1969); *Charlotte's Web* (1973); *O Lucky Man!* (1973); *The Muppet Movie* (1979); *Pigs* (1982); *Evilspeak* (1982); *Razorback* (1984); *A Private Function* (1985); *Elvira-Mistress of the Dark* (1988); *The Milagro Beanfield War* (1988); *Big Top Pee Wee* (1988); *Return to Green Acres* (1990 TVM); *Misery* (1990); *Doc Hollywood* (1991); *Leon the Pig Farmer* (1992); *The Advocate* (aka *Hour of the Pig*) (1993); *Babe* (1995); *Gordy* (1995); *Babe: Pig in the City* (1998); *Animal Farm* (1999 TVM)

Pinball/Video Games

Brooke Shields as a pinball player? The movie was 1978's *Tilt* and Shields, age 13, played a wandering pinball wizard who mounted a challenge against champ Charles Durning. The "tension-filled" pinball matches bore no resemblance to Paul Newman's pool scenes in *The Hustler* or Steve McQueen's poker games in *The Cincinnati Kid*. Three years prior to *Tilt*, flamboyant director Ken Russell brought The Who's rock opera *Tommy* to the screen. The rock group's lead singer Roger Daltry recreated his stage role as "the deaf, dumb, and blind kid who sure plays a mean pinball." Elton John appeared as his opponent, the Pinball Wizard. The ultimate video game movie was Disney's *Tron* (1982), a visually marvelous, but dramatically empty, hi-tech adventure. Jeff Bridges starred as a computer genius sucked into a computer and forced to play a "real" video game for his survival. Cocky video gamemaster Emilio Estevez also wound up inside a video game in one of the segments of the 1983 horror anthology *Nightmares*. In 1984's *The Last Starfighter*, aliens used an Earth-bound video game to test fighter-pilot skills to assist in recruiting warriors to save their dying planet. Jennifer Jason Leigh played a game designer who creates a virutal reality game that can be "plugged into" the human body in David Cronenberg's *eXistenZ* (1999). See also **Theatrical Films Based on Video Games**.

Sensations (aka *Sensations of 1945*) (1944); *Tommy* (1975); *Tilt* (1978); *Pick-up Summer* (aka *Pinball Summer; Pinball Pick-up*) (1981); *Tron* (1982); *Nightmares* (1983); *Joysticks* (aka *Video Madness*) (1983); *Never Say Never Again* (1983); *The Last Starfighter* (1984); *The Wizard* (1989); *Brainscan* (1994); *Arcade* (1994); *eXistenZ* (1999)

The Pink Panther Series

Blake Edwards' 1964 comedy *The Pink Panther* was a mildly amusing all-star farce about a jewel thief called the Phantom try-

ing to steal the famous Pink Panther diamond. It starred David Niven, Claudia Cardinale, Robert Wagner, and introduced Peter Sellers as that classic bumbling detective Inspector Clouseau. Thanks to Sellers' hilarious performance, the movie was a hit and he and Edwards reteamed for the 1964 sequel *A Shot in the Dark*. It's the best of all Clouseau movies and marked the debuts of eventual series regulars Herbert Lom (as Clouseau's boss/nemesis) and Burt Kwouk (as the kung fu–minded valet Kato). Surprisingly, another Sellers/Clouseau comedy did not appear for a decade. In the meantime, Alan Arkin starred in *Inspector Clouseau*, a 1968 flop not directed by Edwards. Fortunately for Clouseau fans, Sellers and Edwards revived both their careers with *The Return of the Pink Panther*, the surprise hit of summer 1975. After two more popular entries, Sellers died in 1980. Nevertheless, outtakes of him were edited into the shoddily-constructed *Trail of the Pink Panther*. It was a well-deserved box-office disaster, as was *Curse of the Pink Panther* with Ted Wass following in Sellers' footsteps. The persistent Edwards tried to resurrect the series a decade later with 1993's *Son of the Pink Panther*, which starred Italian comedian Roberto Benigni as Clouseau's bumbling, illegitimate son. See also **Jewel Thieves**.

The Pink Panther (1964); *A Shot in the Dark* (1964); *The Return of the Pink Panther* (1975); *The Pink Panthers Strikes Again* (1976); *The Revenge of the Pink Panther* (1978); *The Trail of the Pink Panther* (1982); *The Curse of the Pink Panther* (1983); *Son of the Pink Panther* (1993)

Pirates

The jolly roger has been a screen fixture since before Douglas Fairbanks, Sr., took to the high seas in 1926's colorful *The Black Pirate*. In fact, Robert Louis Stevenson's immortal pirate Long John Silver appeared in an adaptation of *Treasure Island* six years earlier. In the talking film era, Errol Flynn probably logged the most appearances as a pirate. He played Rafael Sabatini's gentlemanly buccaneer in 1935's *Captain Blood*—the role that made him an overnight star. Flynn also played a queen's privateer in *The Sea Hawk*, a British spy among pirates in *Against All Flags*, and a Scottish nobleman–turned–temporary pirate in *The Master of Ballantrae*. Long John Silver easily outdistances his closest rival, Sabatini's Peter Blood, as the screen's busiest pirate. He has been portrayed most memorably by Wallace Beery (1934), Robert Newton (1950 and 1954), and Orson Welles (1972). Female pirates have been scarce, but Maureen O'Hara proved a fiery match for Flynn in *Against All Flags*. Other lady pirate captains were featured in *Anne of the Indies*, *The Pirate Queen*, *Queen of the Pirates*, and *Cutthroat Island*. Pirate musicals have proven to be dismal box-office failures, despite the presence of some heavyweight talent. RKO's *Dancing Pirate* (1936) was an early Technicolor film (as was the aforementioned *Black Pirate*) featuring a music score by Rodgers and Hart. The 1948 Gene Kelly–Judy Garland musical *The Pirate* is fondly remembered for its fancy footwork (courtesy of Kelly and the Nicholas Brothers) and catchy tunes like "Be a Clown." *The Pirate Movie* (1982) was an inept rip-off of Gilbert and Sullivan's operetta *The Pirates of Penzance*, which reached the screen itself the following year. To the astonishment of music lovers, it fared little better financially than its predecessor. Pirate comedies have included the obvious (*Abbott and Costello Meet Captain Kidd*), the offbeat (*Blackbeard's Ghost*) and the inane

(*Yellowbeard*). Modern-day pirates harassed Michael Caine in *The Island* and futuristic pirates sought water, not treasure, in *Ice Pirates*.

The Black Pirate (1926); *Old Ironsides* (1926); *Treasure Island* (1934); *Captain Blood* (1935); *The Dancing Pirate* (1936); *The Buccaneer* (1938); *The Sea Hawk* (1940); *The Black Swan* (1942); *The Princess and the Pirate* (1944); *Captain Kidd* (1945); *The Spanish Main* (1945); *Pirates of Monterey* (1947); *The Pirate* (1948); *Old Mother Riley's Jungle Treasure* (1949); *Buccaneer's Girl* (1950); *Fortunes of Captain Blood* (1950); *Last of the Buccaneers* (1950); *Treasure Island* (1950); *Anne of the Indies* (1951); *Double Crossbones* (1951); *The Pirate Queen* (1951); *Abbott and Costello Meet Captain Kidd* (1952); *Against All Flags* (1952); *Blackbeard the Pirate* (1952); *Captain Pirate* (1952); *Caribbean* (*Caribbean Gold*) (1952); *The Crimson Pirate* (1952); *Yankee Buccaneer* (1952); *Peter Pan* (1953); *The Master of Ballantrae* (1953); *Prince of Pirates* (1953); *Raiders of the Seven Seas* (1953); *Yankee Pasha* (1954); *His Majesty O'Keefe* (1954); *Long John Silver* (1954); *Pirates of Tripoli* (1955); *The Buccaneer* (1958); *Queen of the Pirates* (1960); *The Boy and the Pirates* (1960); *Morgan the Pirate* (1961); *The Pirate and Slave Girl* (1961); *Pirates of Tortuga* (1961); *The Son of Captain Blood* (1962); *Tiger of the Seven Seas* (1962); *Pirates of Blood River* (1962); *Hero's Island* (1962); *Fury at Smugglers Bay* (1963); *Devil-Ship Pirates* (1964); *A High Wind in Jamaica* (1965); *The King's Pirate* (1967); *The Rover* (1967); *Blackbeard's Ghost* (1968); *When Eight Bells Toll* (1971); *Treasure Island* (1972); *Ghost in the Noonday Sun* (1973); *Scalawag* (1973); *Swashbuckler* (aka *The Scarlet Buccaneer*) (1976); *The Island* (1980); *The Pirate Movie* (1982); *Pirates of Penzance* (1983); *Yellowbeard* (1983); *Ice Pirates* (1984); *Pirates* (1986); *The Princess Bride* (1987); *Shipwrecked* (1990); *Treasure Island* (1990 TVM); *Hook* (1991); *George's Island* (1991); *Captain Ron* (1992); *The Pirate* (1994); *Cutthroat Island* (1995); *Muppet Treasure Island* (1996); *Ernest the Pirate* (1999)

Planet of the Apes Series

In its 1968 review, *Variety* called *Planet of the Apes* an "intriguing blend of chilling satire, a sometimes ludicrous juxtaposition of human and ape mores, optimism and pessimism." It's a fitting description for an unusual series that featured both brilliant plot twists and incredibly dull science fiction. Rod Serling wrote the original film, adapting Pierre (*Bridge Over the River Kwai*) Boulle's satirical novel. Charlton Heston starred as an astronaut hurled into a time warp and landing on a planet where intelligent apes are masters over men. In the film's climactic closing scene, Heston finds the remains of the Statue of Liberty and realizes that he has seen man's future on planet Earth. Critics raved over Serling's witty screenplay, but most of the publicity centered on John Chambers' brilliant ape makeup (which won a special Oscar). Two years later, a dull sequel, *Beneath the Planet of the Apes*, ended with the detonation of an atomic bomb which destroyed the world — and apparently the series. However, when it scored at the box-office, producer Arthur P. Jacobs and screenwriter Paul Dehn revived the series with a crafty twist. *Escape from the Planet of the Apes* revealed that two nice apes (Roddy McDowall and Kim Hunter) escaped from the exploding Earth in a spaceship and entered into the same time warp that Heston encountered. They land on Earth circa 1971 and run afoul of human prejudice. However, before they are murdered, they smuggle their infant son to safety. He grows up and, in the fourth film *Conquest of the Planet of the Apes*, leads an ape revolt. In the final series entry, 1973's mediocre *Battle for the Planet of the Apes*, the timeline comes full

circle and ends where *Planet of the Apes* began. A year later, an hour-long TV series was launched, with McDowall repeating his original role. It bombed in the ratings and became a midseason casualty, although the pilot episode, *Back to the Planet of the Apes*, was later released as a TV movie. A Saturday morning cartoon version also surfaced during the 1975-76 TV season. See also **Apes and Monkeys**.

Planet of the Apes (1968); *Beneath the Planet of the Apes* (1970); *Escape from the Planet of the Apes* (1971); *Conquest of the Planet of the Apes* (1972); *Battle for the Planet of the Apes* (1973); *Back to the Planet of the Apes* (1974 TVM); *Forgotten City of the Planet of the Apes* (1974 TVM culled from series episodes); *Farewell to the Planet of the Apes* (1974 TVM culled from series episodes)

Plants

Perhaps because of their decorative and unthinking nature, plants have been greatly ignored by filmmakers. In fact, prior to the 1950s, they were restricted to bit roles–nothing they could really sink their roots into. A rare flower, which bloomed only in the moonlight, was featured prominently in 1935's *Werewolf of London*. Called the marifesa, it could cure lycanthropy, but ironically Henry Hull was bitten by a werewolf while searching for the flower. In the 1940s, Egyptian high priests used a brew made from tana leaves to periodically revive the Mummy (q.v.). But the first abnormal plants of note appeared in *The Wizard of Oz* (1939), in which Dorothy and the Scarecrow encountered a grove of apple trees who didn't like their fruit to be picked. Later in the film, they experienced the effects of sleep-inducing poppies. Arguably, the most renowned plant movie is 1951's *The Thing from Another World* (subsequently shortened to *The Thing*). It starred an alien frequently described (even in the movie) as a giant carrot (actually, his shape seemed inspired by the Frankenstein Monster). He was electrocuted — one could say "cooked" — at the film's climax. Alien pods invaded a small California community and systematically replaced its residents with lookalikes (q.v.) in Don Siegel's *Invasion of the Body Snatchers* (1956). Less memorable vegetation movies of the 1950s included *From Hell It Came*, in which radiation created a silly-looking tree monster, and *Voodoo Island*, which featured a "woman-eating cobra plant." B-movie mogul Roger Corman gave the screen its most charismatic plant with his campy cult classic *The Little Shop of Horrors* (1960). It was a about a nerd named Seymour Krelboined who nurtured a mysterious plant that grows to human size and periodically craves people for dinner, screaming: "Feed me! Feed me! I'm hungry!" It spawned an Off-Broadway musical in 1982 and a big-budget remake in 1986. The plants in John Wyndham's *The Day of the Triffids* couldn't talk, but they could communicate via shrill sounds. In many ways, *Triffids* is the ultimate plant movie. At a height of 10 feet, the poisonous, people-eating Triffids were a menacing crop, indeed. And unlike in other plant pictures, there wasn't just one monster in *Triffids*— it was a large-scale invasion. Talking trees appeared in *Babes in Toyland* (1961) and *Monty Python and the Holy Grail* (1975). A meteorite caused Stephen King to turn into a plant in 1982's *Creepshow*. And a mad scientist crossbred humans and plants to create *The Mutations* (1973). See also **Killer Tomatoes**.

The Werewolf of London (1935); *The Wizard of Oz* (1939); *The Thing* (1951); *Fury of the Congo* (1951); *Invasion of the Body Snatchers*

(1956); *From Hell It Came* (1957); *Voodoo Island* (1957); *The Woman Eater* (1959); *The Little Shop of Horrors* (1960); *Babes in Toyland* (1961); *The Day of the Triffids* (1963); *Dr. Terror's House of Horrors* (1965); *Maneater of Hydra* (aka *Island of the Doomed*) (1966); *Navy vs. the Night Monsters* (1966); *Please Don't Eat My Mother* (1972); *The Mutations* (1973); *Mr. Sycamore* (1974); *Monty Python and the Holy Grail* (1975); *The Kirlian Witness* (aka *The Plants Are Watching*) (1978); *Nick Carter in Prague* (aka *Dinner for Adele; Adele Hasn't Had Her Supper Yet*) (1978); *Invasion of the Body Snatchers* (1978); *Attack of the Killer Tomatoes* (1978); *Creepshow* (1982); *The Little Shop of Horrors* (1986); *Godzilla vs. Biollante* (1989); *The Guardian* (1990); *Dreams* (1990) ("The Peach Orchard" segment); *Jumanji* (1995) (man-eating plants); *The Balloon Farm* (1999 TVM)

Plastic Surgery

Movie surgeons have wasted little time on routine facelifts and nose jobs (though Steve Martin pleaded for a nose alteration in 1987's *Roxanne*). Instead, they have concentrated far more on extensive plastic surgery, frequently resulting in horror movie plots. In 1935's *The Raven*, Bela Lugosi played a Poe-reciting surgeon who turned gangster Boris Karloff's face into a hideous mass of scar tissue. Karloff exacted his revenge by escorting Lugosi to the torture chamber in the film's climax. However, the most common plastic surgery plot involves the scientist who murders innocent bystanders in order to rebuild the facial features of a loved one. Georges Franju's chilling *The Horror Chamber of Dr. Faustus* is considered the classic example of this type. Rock Hudson probably underwent the most elaborate makeover in John Frankenheimer's *Seconds*. He played an elderly millionaire who emerged from high-tech surgery as a new, younger man — only to find out later that the price was too steep. *The Girl Most Likely to...* uncovered a vein of dark humor in its story of a mistreated ugly duckling (Stockard Channing) transformed into a revenge-minded beauty. A car accident, plastic surgery, and a mean mother kept lovers Kathleen Quinlan and Stephen Collins apart in *The Promise*, a rare change-of-face romance.

The Raven (1935); *A Woman's Face* (1941); *Black Dragons* (1942); *First Yank into Tokyo* (1945); *Dark Passage* (1948); *The Second Face* (1950); *A Stolen Face* (1952); *Jail Bait* (1954); *The Mirror Has Two Faces* (aka *Le Miroir a Deux Faces*) (1958); *The Face of Terror* (1959); *Circus of Horrors* (1960); *The Awful Dr. Orloff* (1961); *The Horror Chamber of Dr. Faustus* (aka *Eyes Without a Face*) (1962); *Seconds* (1966); *Corruption* (1968); *The Groundstar Conspiracy* (1972); *The Girl Most Likely to...* (1973 TVM); *Ash Wednesday* (1973); *Who?* (1974); *Scalpel* (aka *False Face*) (1976); *Rabid* (1977); *The Promise* (1978); *Mirror, Mirror* (1979 TVM); *The Man with Bogart's Face* (aka *Sam Marlowe, Private Eye*) (1980); *Looker* (1981); *The Jigsaw Man* (1984); *Why Me* (1984 TVM); *Emmanuelle 4* (1984); *Batman* (1989); *Johnny Handsome* (1989); *Doc Hollywood* (1991); *Shattered* (1991); *Death Becomes Her* (1992); *Face/Off* (1997)

Poe, Edgar Allan *see* Corman's Poe Series

Poirot, Hercule

Agatha Christie's Belgian sleuth was brought to the screen in the guise of British actor Austin Trevor in the early 1930s in mysteries like *Alibi* and *Lord Edgware Dies*. Decades later, Tony Randall (*The Alphabet Murders*) and Albert Finney (*Murder on the Orient Express*) took shots at playing Poirot. However, Christie fans quibbled with those interpretations and an acceptable Poirot

was not discovered until Peter Ustinov made the role his own, beginning with 1978's *Death on the Nile*. Sadly, the quality of the Ustinov/Poirot films declined gradually after his second film *Evil Under the Sun* (1982). But Ustinov remained entertaining in spite of the progressively worse conditions. Hercule Poirot was also among the many detectives spoofed in Neil Simon's *Murder by Death* (1976). On television, David Suchet played Poirot in a popular series that first aired in the U.S. on *Mystery!* in 1989.

Alibi (1931) (Austin Trevor); *Black Coffee* (1931) (Trevor); *Lord Edgware Dies* (1934) (Trevor); *The Alphabet Murders* (aka *The ABC Murders*) (1966) (Tony Randall); *Murder on the Orient Express* (1974) (Albert Finney); *Death on the Nile* (1978) (Peter Ustinov); *Evil Under the Sun* (1982) (Ustinov); *Thirteen at Dinner* (1985 TVM) (Ustinov); *Dead Man's Folly* (1986 TVM) (Ustinov); *Murder in Three Acts* (1986 TVM) (Ustinov); *Appointment with Death* (1988) (Ustinov)

Poison Ivy Series

Drew Barrymore gave one of her best teenage performances as a psychotic vamp in 1992's *Poison Ivy*. She brought the right amount of sex appeal, danger, and subtle vulnerability to the role of Ivy, a mysterious teen intent on insinuating herself into the Cooper family. She befriends Sylvie Cooper (Sara Gilbert), seduces Sylvie's father (Tom Skerritt), and causes Mrs. Cooper (Cheryl Ladd) to fall from a window to her death. It soon becomes apparent that Ivy's goal is to assume the sister/mother role in the family at all costs. The film enjoyed a modest theatrical run, but performed well as a videotape rental, inspiring two minor followups. Former TV child star Alyssa Milano (*Who's the Boss?*) assumed the lead role for *Poison Ivy 2: Lily*. Its only connection to the first film is Ivy's diary, which the sexually-repressed Lily finds and uses as a basis for a minor makeover (i.e., she dresses more provocatively and finally makes love to her boyfriend). Compared to the original Ivy, Lily's character comes across as very tame — and also boring. *Poison Ivy: The Seduction* returned the series to its roots, with Ivy's sister Violet (Jaime Pressly) seducing her best friend's father *and* her boyfriend. Despite the plot's similarities to the first film, its emphasis on nudity and sex owes more to "erotic thrillers" like *Secret Games* and *Body Chemistry* (both q.v.).

Poison Ivy (1992); *Poison Ivy 2: Lily* (1996); *Poison Ivy: The Seduction* (1997)

Police Academy Series

An unexpected commercial success, the *Police Academy* series proved to be the 1980s answer to Britain's *Carry On* comedies (q.v.) of the 1960s. Both series manufactured low-brow humor which moviegoers thrived on and critics found distasteful. The 1984 *Police Academy* naturally set the tone for the rest, focusing on a class of unlikely police recruits led by smart guy Steve Guttenberg, former football player Bubba Smith, and human noise machine Michael Winslow. Unpredictable stand-up comic Bobcat Goldthwait joined the series for the third and fourth entries. After the fourth film, Guttenberg graduated to bigger roles (1987's monster hit *Three Men and a Baby*) and Smith bowed out temporarily. Only Winslow remained for all seven entries. The *Police Academy* movies spawned a 1988 Saturday morning cartoon series and an hour-long 1997 live-action sitcom called *Police Academy: The Series* starring Winslow and Matt Borlenghi.

Police Academy (1984); *Police Academy 2* (1985); *Police Academy 3: Back in Training* (1986); *Police Academy 4: Citizens on Patrol* (1987); *Police Academy 5: Assignment Miami Beach* (1988); *Police Academy 6: City Under Siege* (1989); *Policy Academy: Mission to Moscow* (1994)

Police Story Series

The four *Police Story* films, featuring martial arts stylist Jackie Chan, bear no relation to the 1973–77 U.S. television anthology series (nor the TV movies based on it). Instead, the Chan films are fast-paced action pictures, emphasizing their star's athletic prowess, comic touch, and incredible stunts. Chan once said: "The audience comes in the theater to see Jackie Chan — not the double. That's why I do my own stunts." His daredevil antics are legendary. In one sequence in *Police Story II*, Chan jumps off a building onto a fast-moving truck, leaps over to a passing bus, and then dives into a second-story window. No insurance company will issue him a policy, especially after a fall in *Armor of God* resulted in a cracked skull requiring extensive surgery. In addition to acting and choreographing the action scenes, Chan directed the first two *Police Story* films. Tony Kwei Lai (aka Stanley Tong) took over for the third entry, which paired Chan with a no-nonsense female partner played by Michelle Yeoh (who would make an international splash opposite James Bond in 1997's *Tomorrow Never Dies*). Despite superb action scenes and clever bits of humor, Chan's films never scored with American audiences until *Rumble in the Bronx* was released in the U.S. in 1996.

Police Story (aka *Jackie Chan's Police Story; Police Force; Ging Chaat Goo Si*) (1985); *Police Story II* (aka *Ging Chaat Goo Si Juk Jaap*) (1988); *Police Story III: Supercop* (aka *Jing Cha Gu Shi III: Chao Ji Jing Cha; Supercop*) (1992); *First Strike* (aka *Jing Cha Gu Shi IV: Jian Dan Ren Wu; Police Story 4; Jackie Chan's First Strike*) (1996)

Pool

Paul Newman's second tour through the world of smoke-filled pool halls finally resulted in his first Academy Award, as Best Actor for 1986's *The Color of Money*. Newman played Eddie Felson, a smooth veteran pool shark he introduced as an ambitious youth fifteen years earlier in *The Hustler*. Eddie's match against the legendary Minnesota Fats (Jackie Gleason) in the 1961 picture easily ranks as pool's finest moment in the movies. But other actors have also taken their shot at the eight ball: James Coburn in *The Baltimore Bullet*, Whoopi Goldberg in *Kiss Shot*, and Johnny Cash in *The Baron and the Kid*, a TV movie inspired by his country hit "The Baron." W.C. Fields played pool in movies such as *Six of a Kind* and *Follow the Boys*. But Timothy Carey played the most bizarre pool player, South Dakota Slim, in the Beach Party (q.v.) movies. The creepy Slim, who called everyone "booby," tried to saw Linda Evans in half in *Beach Blanket Bingo* (1965).

Six of a Kind (1934); *Follow the Boys* (1944); *The Hustler* (1961); *The Baltimore Bullet* (1980); *The Baron and the Kid* (1984 TVM); *The Color of Money* (1986); *Kiss Shot* (1989 TVM)

Pop, Rock, and Country Singer Biographies

The life stories of pop and rock singers of the 1950s and 1960s have dominated musical biographies. Even in the early days of rock 'n' roll, singers such as British teen idol Tommy Steele and Bill Haley were popular enough to warrant film biographies in which they played themselves. However, the first significant rock singer biography did not appear until *The Buddy Holly Story* in 1978. Gary Busey's Oscar-nominated performance as Holly and a carefully crafted feel-good ending turned the film into a sleeper hit. The following year, Bette Midler also earned an Oscar nomination for *The Rose*, the depressing story of a Janis Joplin–like singer. After a dry spell in the early 1980s, the unexpected success of 1987's *La Bamba* renewed interest in rock 'n' roll biographies. Lou Diamond Phillips's earnest performance breathed life into the story of Ritchie Valens, who had only two Top 40 hits in the late 1950s before dying in the same plane crash that killed Buddy Holly. Ironically, the movie accomplished what Valens never did — its soundtrack featured a cover version of "La Bamba" by Los Lobos that reached No. 1 on the *Billboard* music chart. Spurred by the success of *La Bamba*, the next ten years saw the release of film biographies on Jerry Lee Lewis, the Doors, Tina Turner, and Latin singer Selena. Even the Beatles were not immune to the biographical treatment as *Backbeat* (1993) told the story of Stuart Sutcliffe, the "fifth Beatle." In the 1990s, television turned to rock 'n' roll and made TV movies based on the lives of Sonny and Cher, the Temptations, and Ricky Nelson. The latter film, *Ricky Nelson: Teen Idol*, was produced by the cable network VH1 as part of a continuing series of made-for-TV rock biographies. Compared to rock stars, country singers have been virtually ignored, although *Coal Miner's Daughter* — the story of Loretta Lynn — accomplished something no rock bio has ever done: It earned a Best Actress Oscar for leading lady Sissy Spacek. The lives of country legend Hank Williams and his son Hank, Jr., were profiled in, respectively, *Your Cheatin' Heart* (1964) and *Living Proof: The Hank Williams Jr., Story* (1983). And Annette O'Toole played Tammy Wynette in the 1981 TV movie *Stand By Your Man*. On the pop music front, Larry Parks played Al Jolson in both *The Jolson Story* (1946) and its sequel *Jolson Sings Again* (1949). Although Ann Blyth played the lead role in *The Helen Morgan Story* (1959), Gogi Grant dubbed her voice when it came to performing the 1920s torch singer's hits. Doris Day provided her own vocals as 1930s torch singer Ruth Etting in *Love Me or Leave Me* (1955), but it was James Cagney who earned an Oscar nomination as her mobster promoter. Diana Ross also received an Oscar nomination as Billie Holiday in *Lady Sings the Blues* (1972). Barbra Streisand won an Academy Award for her performance as Fanny Brice in *Funny Girl* (1968), a role she later repeated for the less successful *Funny Lady* (1975). Finally, the life of Frank Sinatra has been explored in the TV movies *Sinatra* (1992) and *The Rat Pack* (1999). Several fictional films are considered to be thinly-veiled biographies. *The Idolmaker* (1980) appears to be based on the life of rock producer Bob Marcucci and his "discovery" Fabian and *The Five Heartbeats* (1991) strongly resemble the rhythm and blues group the Dells. See also **Composers (Popular)**; **Concert Movies**; **Presley, Elvis**.

The Jolson Story (1946) (Al Jolson); *Jolson Sings Again* (1949) (Jolson); *With a Song in My Heart* (1952) (loosely based on the life of Jane Froman); *Love Me or Leave Me* (1955) (Ruth Etting); *Rock Around the Clock* (1956) (Bill Haley and the Comets); *Rock Around the World* (aka *The Tommy Steele Story*) (1957); *The Helen Morgan Story* (1959); *Your Cheatin' Heart* (1964) (Hank Williams); *The Sound of Music* (1965) (The Von Trapp Family); *Funny Girl* (1968)

(Fanny Brice); *Lady Sings the Blues* (1972) (Billie Holiday); *Piaf* (1974) (Edith Piaf); *Funny Lady* (1975) (Brice); *Bound for Glory* (1976) (Woody Guthrie); *Leadbelly* (1976) (Huddie Ledbetter); *The Buddy Holly Story* (1978); *Rainbow* (1978 TVM) (Judy Garland); *The Rose* (1979) (loosely based on the life of Janis Joplin); *Coal Miner's Daughter* (1980) (Loretta Lynn); *Stand by Your Man* (1981 TVM) (Tammy Wynette); *Side by Side: The True Story of the Osmond Family* (1982 TVM); *Living Proof: The Hank Williams Jr. Story* (1983 TVM); *John and Yoko: A Love Story* (1985) (John Lennon and Yoko Ono); *Sid and Nancy* (1986) (Sid Vicious and girlfriend Nancy Spungen); *La Bamba* (1987) (Ritchie Valens); *Great Balls of Fire!* (1989) (Jerry Lee Lewis); *The Doors* (1991); *The Jacksons: An American Dream* (1992 TVM); *Sinatra* (1992 TVM); *What's Love Got to Do with It* (1993) (Tina Turner); *Backbeat* (1993) (The Beatles); *Naomi and Wynonna: Love Can Build a Bridge* (1995 TVM) (The Judds); *Selena* (1997) (Selena Quintanilla); *The Rat Pack* (1998 TVM) (Frank Sinatra, Dean Martin, Sammy Davis, Jr., plus non-singers Joey Bishop and Peter Lawford); *The Temptations* (1998 TVM); *And the Beat Goes On: The Sonny and Cher Story* (1999 TVM); *Sweetwater: A True Rock Story* (1999 TVM); *Ricky Nelson: Original Teen Idol* (1999 TVM); *Come On Get Happy: The Partridge Family Story* (1999 TVM); *The Beach Boys: An American Family* (2000 TVM); *The David Cassidy Story* (2000 TVM); *Take Me Home: The John Denver Story* (2000 TVM); *Little Richard* (2000 TVM); *The Linda McCartney Story* (2000 TVM); *Daydream Believers: The Monkees Story* (2000); *Meat Loaf: To Hell and Back* (2000 TVM)

Popes and Cardinals

Cardinal Richelieu, who virtually ruled France from 1624 to 1642, has been the cinema's most prominent senior church figure. George Arliss portrayed him as an unscrupulous scoundrel in *Cardinal Richelieu* (1935), while others who have donned the red robe include Nigel du Brulier in *The Three Musketeers* (1935) and *The Man in the Iron Mask* (1939), Raymond Massey in *Under the Red Robe* (1937), Christopher Logue in *The Devils* (1971), and Charlton Heston in *The Three Musketeers* (1974) and *The Four Musketeers* (1975). *Guilty of Treason* (1949) was a fact-based account of the trial of Cardinal Mindszenty, while *The Cardinal* (1963) offered a fictitious tale of a young American's (Tom Tryon) rise to prominence within the church. Few actors have portrayed popes, although Albert Finney had the lead in the 1984 TV movie *Pope John Paul II* and Anthony Quinn ruled from the Vatican in *Shoes of a Fisherman* (1968). The 1964 documentary *A Man Named John* traced the accomplishments of Pope John XXIII. A plot to assassinate the Pope lurked behind the comedy bits in Chevy Chase's *Foul Play* (1978). Finally, Liv Ullmann disguised herself as a man to reach the papacy in 1972's *Pope Joan*. See also **Monks; Nuns.**

Cardinal Richelieu (1935); *The Three Musketeers* (1935); *Under the Red Robe* (1937); *The Man in the Iron Mask* (1939); *Guilty of Treason* (1949); *Never Take No for an Answer* (1951); *The Prisoner* (1955); *The Cardinal* (1963); *A Man Named John* (1964); *Becket* (1964); *The Agony and the Ecstasy* (1965); *And There Came a Man* (1965); *Shoes of a Fisherman* (1968); *The Devils* (1971); *Pope Joan* (aka *The Devil's Impostor*) (1972); *Brother Sun, Sister Moon* (1973); *The Abdication* (1974); *The Three Musketeers* (aka *The Three Musketeers: The Queen's Diamonds*) (1974); *The Four Musketeers* (aka *The Four Musketeers: The Revenge of Milady*) (1975); *Foul Play* (1978); *From a Far Country: Pope John Paul II* (1981 TVM); *Monsignor* (1982); *Pope John Paul II* (1984 TVM); *Saving Grace* (1986); *The Godfather Part III* (1990); *The Pope Must Die* (aka *The Pope Must Diet*) (1991); *Sister Act* (1992); *Stigmata* (1999); *Dogma* (1999)

Porky's Series

Shortly before he made the delightful family favorite *A Christmas Story*, director Bob Clark filmed this 1982 Canadian-made comedy smash about horny teens in Florida circa 1954. The majority of the action centered around the title establishment, a bar/brothel located just across the county line. Most critics called *Porky's* smutty and pointless, but a lot of teens saw it. Perhaps it was the timing, for the 1983 sequel, *Porky's II: The Next Day*, lacked the box-office fire despite reteaming teen leads Dan Monahan, Mark Herrier, and Wyatt Knight. The same trio showed up in a third installment which attracted little attention.

Porky's (1982); *Porky's II: The Next Day* (1983); *Porky's Revenge* (1985)

Postal Workers

Just as librarians (q.v.) have been stereotyped as drabbily-dressed spinsters, postal carriers have struggled with their cliched portrayals as mild-mannered unmarried men. However, in those rare films in which postal characters have been given major roles, they have proven themselves to be an eclectic lot — rarely mild-mannered and sometimes downright peculiar. The pleasant Mr. Potts turned out to be a devious murderer who almost outwitted Sherlock Holmes in 1944's *The Scarlet Claw*. Of course, Potts was actually an actor named Ramson who killed the real postman and assumed his identity (nonetheless, Ramson/Potts delivered the mail, making him a postal carrier). In another murder mystery, the British *Green for Danger*, a postman provided a critical clue in uncovering an operating room killer. Alan Ladd played a postal inspector in *Appointment with Danger* (1951), while Eli Wallach played a postman-turned-kidnapper in the 1967 satire *The Tiger Makes Out*. French comedian Jacques Tati, best known for his *Mr. Hulot* (q.v.) movies, played a mailman in 1949's delightful *Jour de Fete*. Kevin Costner posed as a mail carrier and then really become one in the post-acpocalytic epic *The Postman* (1997). In *EDtv* (1999), Jenna Elfman was not a postal carrier, but still delivered packages — for UPS. On a more bizarre level, postman Jason Robards, Jr., turned into a tree in 1974's *Mr. Sycamore!* A family of cannibals devoured the mailman in the offbeat horror-comedy *Spider Baby* (1964). Finally, no discussion of postal carriers would be complete without mentioning Cliff Clavin (John Ratzenberger), the bar-bound know-it-all on the 1982–93 TV series *Cheers*. See also **Letters.**

Postal Inspector (1936); *Joe and Ethel Turp Call on the President* (1939); *The Scarlet Claw* (1944); *Green for Danger* (1946); *Jour de Fete* (aka *The Big Day*) (1949); *Side Street* (1950); *The Barefoot Mailman* (1951); *Appointment with Danger* (1951); *Postman's Knock* (1961); *Spider Baby* (aka *Spider Baby, or the Maddest Story Ever Told; The Liver Eaters; Cannibal Orgy*) (1964); *Happiness* (1965); *The Tiger Makes Out* (1967); *Mr. Sycamore* (1974); *Queen of the Stardust Ballroom* (1975 TVM); *Harry's War* (1981); *Stepfather II* (aka *Stepfather II: Make Room for Daddy*) (1989); *The Tommyknockers* (1993 TVM); *Second Best* (1994); *Il Postino* (aka *The Postman*) (1994); *La Cérémonie* (aka *A Judgment in Stone*) (1995); *Dear God* (1996); *The Postman* (1997); *Dear Claudia* (1999); *EDtv* (1999); *The Minus Man* (1999)

Prehysteria Series

Charles Band, the 1990s equivalent of Roger Corman, produced and directed *Prehysteria* (1993), a low-budget, family-oriented comedy about five "pygmy dinosaurs." The film opens with a slimy antiques dealer stealing five dinosaur eggs from a South American temple. However, the stolen eggs soon fall into the hands of a widower and his family when their dog unknowingly picks up the wrong cooler. When the eggs hatch, they reveal mini-versions of a brachiosaur, a ceratops, a pterodactyl, a stegosaur, and tyrannosaurus rex (which the kids name Elvis). The plot — the bad guys naturally want the little dinos back — takes a back seat to David Allen's entertaining special effects. Allen performed similar work on earlier Band pictures, including the *Puppet Master* series (q.v.). *Prehysteria* performed well as a direct-to-video release, thanks largely to Allen's dinos and good timing: Star Austin O'Brien had landed the teen lead opposite Arnold Schwarzenegger in *Last Action Hero* (1993), and *Jurassic Park* (1993), with its big dinosuars, was a huge hit. Two *Prehysteria* sequels followed. The quintet of little dinosaurs brought a lonely boy and his father together in *Prehysteria 2* (1994). And in *Prehysteria 3* (1995), they played a pivotal role in the success of a miniature golf course! See also **Dinosaurs**.

Prehysteria (1993); *Prehysteria 2* (1994); *Prehysteria 3* (1995)

Prequels

A prequel is the opposite of a sequel, in that its narrative takes place earlier than the original film. For example, German filmmaker Paul Wegener destroyed the Golem, a stone statue brought to life, in 1914's *The Golem: Monster of Fate*. However, six years later, Wegener went back and told the story of the Golem's origin in *The Golem: How He Came to Be*. The 1926 Foreign Legion classic *Beau Geste* inspired two partial prequels, as the plots of *Beau Sabreur* (1928) and *Beau Ideal* (1931) took place in the same time frame as — instead of prior to — the original film. However, the first Hollywood prequel was 1948's *Another Part of the Forest*, which depicted the early days of the ruthless Hubbard family first introduced in 1941's *The Little Foxes*. Dan Duryea (as Leo Hubbard) was the only holdover from the original film's cast. Sporadic prequels (e.g., 1966's *Nevada Smith*) and "partial prequels" (e.g., 1950's *The Fortunes of Captain Blood*) appeared throughout the 1950s and 1960s. However, it was not until the sequel-crazy early 1980s that the prequel attracted much attention. Even then, however, prequels typically performed poorly at the box-office, as evidenced by flops such as *Butch and Sundance: The Early Days* (1979). A noteworthy exception, of course, was *Indiana Jones and the Temple of Doom* (1984), a blockbuster prequel to *Raiders of the Lost Ark* (1981). The longest gap between prequel and original is the 30 years that separated the 1990 TV movie *Psycho IV: The Beginning* from Alfred Hitchcock's 1960 original. Anthony Perkins played Norman Bates in both films and Joseph Stefano wrote the screenplays. Sometimes, the distinction between prequel and original becomes a bit confusing. The Chuck Norris action picture *Missing in Action 2: The Beginning* (1985) was actually filmed before *Missing in Action* (1984). It became a prequel only when the producers decided to release the second film first. (Note: The 1986 TV movie *Dallas: The Early Years* was similar to a prequel, in that it took place chronologically prior to the television series *Dallas*. And the 1992 theatrical feature *Twin Peaks: Fire Walk with Me* was a prequel to the 1990-91 TV series *Twin Peaks*.) In the following list, the prequel is listed first, followed by the original film.

The Golem: How He Came to Be (aka *Der Golem, Wie Er in die Welt Kam*) (1920) — *The Golem: Monster of Fate* (aka *Der Golem*) (1914); *Beau Sabreur* (1928) — *Beau Geste* (1926); *Beau Ideal* (1931) — *Beau Geste* (1926); *Another Part of the Forest* (1948) — *The Little Foxes* (1941); *The Fortunes of Captain Blood* (1950) — *Captain Blood* (1935); *Nevada Smith* (1966) — *The Carpetbaggers* (1964); *The Nightcomers* (1972) — *The Innocents* (1961); *Butch and Sundance: The Early Days* (1979) — *Butch Cassidy and the Sundance Kid* (1969); *Zulu Dawn* (1979) — *Zulu* (1964); *The Getting of Wisdom* (1977) — *Rhapsody* (1954); *Bálint Fábián's Encounter with God* (1980) — *Hungarians* (1979); *Amityville II: The Possession* (1982) — *The Amityville Horror* (1979); *Indiana Jones and the Temple of Doom* (1984) — *Raiders of the Lost Ark* (1981); *Missing in Action 2: The Beginning* (1985) — *Missing in Action* (1984); *On Valentine's Day* (1986) — *1918* (1984); *The Rainbow* (1989) — *Women in Love* (1970); *A Better Tomorrow III* (aka *Love and Death in Saigon*) (1989) — *A Better Tomorrow* (1986); *Psycho IV: The Beginning* (1990 TVM) — *Psycho* (1960); *Puppet Master III: Toulon's Revenge* (1991) — *Puppet Master* (1989); *Wide Sargasso Sea* (1993) — *Jane Eyre* (1944; 1971); *Rudyard Kipling's The Second Jungle Book: Mowgli and Baloo* (aka *Jungle Book Two*) (1997) — *The Jungle Book* (1994); *Bartok the Magnificent* (1999) — *Anastasia* (1997); *The Flintstones in Viva Rock Vegas* (2000) — *The Flintstones* (1994)

Presidents (U.S.)

The cinema has not treated all presidents equally, but then neither has American history. Abraham Lincoln, according to Guinness, has appeared as a character in over 150 films, far more than any other president. Actor Frank McGlynn specialized in portraying Lincoln for most of his career, beginning with 1915's *The Life of Abraham Lincoln* and continuing in bit roles in films like *The Littlest Rebel* (1935), *The Prisoner of Shark Island* (1936), and *The Plainsman* (1937). Most Lincoln biographies have been reverent sagas starring distinguished performers such as Walter Huston (1930's *Abraham Lincoln*), Henry Fonda (*Young Abe Lincoln*), and Raymond Massey (*Abe Lincoln in Illinois*). In 1951, *The Tall Target* offered a suspenseful change of pace, with Dick Powell as a detective (named John Kennedy!) trying to thwart an 1861 assassination attempt on Lincoln. In an even greater fictional elaboration, *The Lincoln Conspiracy* (1977) proposed that assassin John Wilkes Booth was conspiring with members of the U.S. Senate. Ronald Reagan ranks second to Lincoln in number of film appearances — but only because he really was an actor. More legitimate screen appearances have been logged by Andrew Jackson and John F. Kennedy, both of whom have been the subjects of several film biographies. Jackson's exploits in the War of 1812 played a major role in both versions of *The Buccaneer* (1938 and 1958). The scandal surrounding his alleged adulterous affair with future-wife Rachel Robards formed the basis for *The Gorgeous Hussy* (1936) and *The President's Lady* (1953). Interestingly, Charlton Heston played Jackson in both *The President's Lady* and *The Buccaneer* (1958). William Holden befriended Jackson's ghost in the unremarkable 1942 fantasy *The Remarkable Andrew*. Kennedy's pre-presidential adventures as a patrol torpedo boat commander were played for escapist entertainment in 1963's *PT 109*, with Cliff Robertson in the lead. The 1977 TV movie *Johnny, We Hardly Knew Ye* dealt with Kennedy's first try for public office, while 1984's *Prince Jack* was an inconsequential chronicle about the Kennedy clan. Other Kennedy-related pictures include the documentary *John F. Kennedy: Years of Lightning, Day of Drums*

(1966), the assassination thriller *Executive Action* (1973), *Jacqueline Bouvier Kennedy* (1982), *Hoover vs. the Kennedys: The Second Civil War* (1987), and Oliver Stone's conspiracy drama *JFK* (1991). In 1991's *Point Break*, bankrobbers calling themselves the President Gang wore rubber masks of Reagan, Carter, Nixon, and Johnson. Fictional presidents have been portrayed in many films, several of which have cast our nation's leader into intriguing situations. President Henry Fonda ordered the destruction of New York City in order to avoid a war with the Soviet Union in 1964's *Fail Safe*. That same year, military officer Burt Lancaster plotted a coup to overthrow President Fredric March in *Seven Days in May*. In 1971 TV movies, a top presidential advisor disappeared in *Vanished*, which more or less prepared viewers for *The President's Plane Is Missing*. The President has also been kidnapped by lethal ladies (*In Like Flint*), terrorists (*The Kidnapping of the President*), and futuristic New York City convicts (*Escape from New York*). If those films portrayed the president as a helpless victim, then *Independence Day* and *Air Force One* proved that the presidents could also be a man of action. Polly Bergen played the country's first female commander-in-chief in the 1964 comedy *Kisses for My President*. James Earl Jones portrayed a black senator thrust into the Oval Office when the president is killed in *The Man* (1972). The following list includes only films specifically about presidents or featuring them in prominent roles (for instance, although George Washington has been a minor character in over a dozen movies, those films are not listed). The president's name is shown in parentheses if it is not apparent from the title; some are about fictitious presidents.

Abraham Lincoln (1930); *The Phantom President* (1932); *Gabriel Over the White House* (1933); *The Gorgeous Hussy* (1936) (Jackson); *First Lady* (1937); *This Is My Affair* (aka *His Affair*) (1937) (McKinley); *The Buccaneer* (1938) (Jackson); *Joe and Ethel Turp Call on the President* (1939); *Young Mr. Lincoln* (1939); *Abe Lincoln in Illinois* (1940); *Tennessee Johnson* (aka *The Man on America's Conscience*) (1942) (Andrew Johnson); *The Remarkable Andrew* (1942) (Jackson); *Wilson* (1944); *Magnificent Doll* (1946) (Madison); *The Tall Target* (1951) (Lincoln); *The President's Lady* (1953) (Jackson); *Suddenly* (1954); *The Buccaneer* (1958) (Jackson); *Sunrise at Campobello* (1960) (Franklin Roosevelt); *Advise and Consent* (1962); *PT 109* (1963) (Kennedy); *The Best Man* (1964); *Kisses for My President* (1964); *Dr. Strangelove, Or How I Learned to Stop Worrying and Love the Bomb* (1964); *Seven Days in May* (1964); *Fail Safe* (1964); *The Eleanor Roosevelt Story* (1965); *John F. Kennedy: Years of Lightning, Day of Drums* (1966); *In Like Flint* (1967); *The President's Analyst* (1967); *The Virgin President* (1968) (Fillmore spoof); *The Great Man's Whiskers* (1971) (Lincoln); *Vanished* (1971 TVM); *The President's Plane Is Missing* (1971 TVM); *The Man* (1972); *Hail to the Chief* (aka *Hail, Washington, B.C.*) (1973); *Executive Action* (1973) (Kennedy); *Collision Course* (1975 TVM) (Truman); *Give 'Em Hell, Harry!* (1975) (Truman); *The Wind and the Lion* (1975) (Theodore Roosevelt); *Eleanor and Franklin* (1976 TVM) (Franklin Roosevelt); *The Lincoln Conspiracy* (1977); *Johnny, We Hardly Knew Ye* (1977 TVM) (Kennedy); *F.D.R. — The Last Year* (1980 TVM); *First Family* (1980); *The Kidnapping of the President* (1980); *Escape from New York* (1981); *Jacqueline Bouvier Kennedy* (1982 TVM); *World War III* (1982 TVM); *Eleanor Roosevelt, First Lady of the World* (1982 TVM); *The Indomitable Teddy Roosevelt* (1983); *Prince Jack* (1984) (Kennedy); *Secret Honor: The Last Testament of Richard M. Nixon* (1984 TVM); *The Betty Ford Story* (1987 TVM); *Assassination* (1987); *Hoover vs. the Kennedys: The Second Civil War* (1987 TVM); *LBJ: The Early Years* (1987 TVM); *Gore Vidal's Lincoln* (1988 TVM); *The Final Days* (1989 TVM) (Nixon); *The Perfect Tribute* (1991 TVM) (Lincoln); *JFK* (1991); *Running Mates* (1992 TVM); *Dave* (1993); *Fatal Deception: Mrs. Lee Harvey Oswald* (1993 TVM); *In the Line of Fire* (1993); *The War Room* (1993) (Clinton); *Clear and Present Danger* (1994); *Forrest Gump* (1994) (JFK, LBJ, Nixon); *The Pelican Brief* (1994); *Guarding Tess* (1994); *The American President* (1995); *Truman* (1995 TVM); *Jefferson in Paris* (1995); *Nixon* (1995); *My Fellow Americans* (1996); *Independence Day* (1996); *Mars Attacks!* (1996); *First Kid* (1996); *Elvis Meets Nixon* (1997 TVM); *Absolute Power* (1997); *Shadow Conspiracy* (1997); *Rough Riders* (1997 TVM) (Theodore Roosevelt); *Murder at 1600* (1997); *Air Force One* (1997); *Amistad* (1997) (John Quincy Adams); *Wag the Dog* (1997); *Deep Impact* (1998); *The Day Lincoln Was Shot* (1998 TVM); *Primary Colors* (1998) (Clinton, indirectly); *Dick* (1999) (Nixon); *First Daughter* (1999 TVM); *Deterrence* (1999); *Sally Hemings: An American Scandal* (2000 TVM) (Jefferson)

Presley, Elvis

It used to be that the cinema endured a waiting period before spinning off biographical films about deceased personalities. The FDR biography *Sunrise at Campobello* (1960) did not appear until fifteen years after the former president's death. Evidently, the film industry deemed Elvis Presley's life more marketable. Less than two years after Presley's death, ABC ushered in *Elvis*, the made-for-TV story of his life. Over the next ten years, five additional Presley-related films appeared amid rumors that the "King" still lived. None of these films surpassed ABC's *Elvis*, a solid picture directed by talented horror specialist John Carpenter and starring an effective Kurt Russell in the title role. North Carolina filmmaker Earl Owensby's *Living Legend* (1980) made no claims about being based on Elvis' life. But the plot similarities and the presence of Elvis' last girlfriend, Ginger Alden, left little doubt as to the picture's intent. The same year's *Touched by Love* was a fact-based story about the pen-pal relationship between a young girl with cerebral palsy and Presley. The made-for-cable "mockumentary" *Elvis Meets Nixon* (1997) was based on an actual 1970 Presley visit to the White House. Don Johnson made an unlikely Elvis in the 1981 TV movie *Elvis and the Beauty Queen*, the story of Presley's five-year relationship with Linda Thompson (Stephanie Zimbalist). Elvis' only wife, Priscilla Presley, executive-produced 1988's *Elvis and Me*, the TV version of her best-seller. David Keith was Elvis in 1989's box-office bomb *Heartbreak Hotel*, a light-hearted, fictionalized account of Presley's friendship with a teenaged boy. Presley also played himself in his final two screen appearances: the behind-the-scenes documentary *Elvis: That's the Way It Is* (1970) and the concert film *Elvis on Tour* (1972). Elvis was glimpsed briefly in *Great Balls of Fire* (1989) and *Forrest Gump* (1994). Finally, *Honeymoon in Vegas* (1992) featured a troupe of flashily-dressed skydivers called the Flying Elvises. See also **Pop, Rock, and Country Singer Biographies**.

Elvis: That's the Way It Is (1970); *Elvis on Tour* (1972); *Elvis* (1979 TVM); *Living Legend* (1980); *Touched by Love* (aka *To Elvis, with Love*) (1980); *Elvis and the Beauty Queen* (1981 TVM); *Elvis and Me* (1988 TVM); *Heartbreak Hotel* (1989); *Great Balls of Fire* (1989); *Honeymoon in Vegas* (1992); *Elvis and the Colonel: The Untold Story* (1993 TVM); *The Woman Who Loved Elvis* (1993 TVM); *Forrest Gump* (1994); *Elvis Meets Nixon* (1997 TVM)

Prisoners of War

POW films fall into three basic camps: German, Japanese, and Vietnamese. Each of these groups features an Oscar winner of some sort. William Holden won a Best Actor Oscar for his portrayal of a cynical prisoner wrongly tagged an informer in Billy Wilder's *Stalag 17* (1953). Although not among the first POW films, Wilder's movie combined humor, suspense, and an assortment of motley characters to create a much-imitated formula. *The Password Is Courage*, one of several mid–1960s POW pictures, was based on the real-life exploits of Sergeant-Major Charles Coward, who made a military career out of escaping from German camps. *Von Ryan's Express* (1965) opened in a POW camp, but expanded into a perilous train journey through Nazi-occupied territory. Allied prisoners escaped during a climactic soccer game with a Nazi team in *Victory* (1981), while less athletic prisoners built a glider in the 1971 TV movie *Birdmen*. *The Great Escape* (1963) made a star of Steve McQueen, while rolling up enough ticket receipts to make it the most profitable POW film of the last four decades. It was co-written by James (*Shogun*) Clavell, whose novel *King Rat* reached the screen in 1965. Set in a Japanese POW camp, it chronicled the rise and fall of a manipulating con artist (George Segal). However, the best-remembered Japanese-set POW film remains David Lean's *The Bridge on the River Kwai* (1957). It earned Oscars for Best Picture, Best Director, and Best Actor, the latter honoring Alec Guinness's portrayal of a stubborn, manipulated British officer. Other Japanese prison camp films include *The Purple Heart* (1944), *Escape to Mindinao* (1968), *Merry Christmas, Mr. Lawrence* (1983), and *Empire of the Sun* (1987). *The Deer Hunter*, the 1978 Oscar winner for Best Picture, was partially set in a Vietnamese POW camp where prisoners were subjected to a chilling game of Russian roulette. *When Hell Was in Session* (1979) was a grim account of a Navy officer held prisoner for seven years in North Vietnam. However, *Missing in Action 2* (1985), *P.O.W. The Escape* (1986), and *The Hanoi Hilton* (1987) used Vietnamese prison camps strictly for their topical exploitation value. A handful of films have dealt with female POW camps, most notably *Two Thousand Women* (1944), *Three Came Home* (1950), *A Town Like Alice* (1956), *Women of Valor* (1986), and *Paradise Road* (1997). Although most movie POWs seem to be American or British, there have been exceptions. Jean Renoir's anti-war classic *Grand Illusion* (1937) focused on French prisoners during World War I. *Until Hell Is Frozen* (1960) was set in a Russian camp and *The McKenzie Break* (1970) had captured Germans escaping from a Scottish POW camp! Television introduced the infamous POW camp sitcom *Hogan's Heroes* in 1965. It enjoyed a six-year network run and a profitable after-life in syndication. See also **Prisons**.

Everything Is Thunder (1936); *Grand Illusion* (aka *La Grande Illusion*) (1937); *The Cross of Lorraine* (1943); *Two Thousand Women* (1944); *The Purple Heart* (1944); *The Captive Heart* (1946); *Act of Violence* (1949); *The Wooden Soldier* (1950); *Three Came Home* (1950); *Stalag 17* (1953); *Break to Freedom* (aka *Albert RN*) (1953); *The Bamboo Prison* (1954); *Prisoner of War* (1954); *A Town Like Alice* (aka *Rape of Malaya*) (1956); *The Bridge on the River Kwai* (1957); *The Colditz Story* (1957); *The Camp on Blood Island* (1958); *Breakout* (aka *Danger Within*) (1958); *Until Hell Is Frozen* (1960); *A Coming-Out Party* (aka *A Very Important Person*) (1961); *The Manchurian Candidate* (1962); *The Great Escape* (1963); *The Password Is Courage* (1963); *Von Ryan's Express* (1965); *King Rat* (1965); *Escape to Mindinao* (1968); *The McKenzie Break* (1970); *Birdmen* (aka *Escape of the Birdmen*) (1971 TVM); *The Deer Hunter* (1978); *Escape to Athena* (1979); *When Hell Was in Session* (1979 TVM); *Victory* (1981); *Merry Christmas, Mr. Lawrence* (1983); *Missing in Action 2: The Beginning* (1985); *Women of Valor* (1986

TVM); *Opposing Force* (aka *Hellcamp*) (1986); *P.O.W. The Escape* (aka *Behind Enemy Lines*) (1986); *Empire of the Sun* (1987); *The Hanoi Hilton* (1987); *The Last P.O.W.?: The Bobby Garwood Story* (1993 TVM); *A Hero's Life* (aka *La Vie d'un Heros*) (1994); *The Ascent* (1994); *Paradise Road* (1997)

Prisons

The most engrossing accounts of life behind bars are those based on real-life exploits. Robert Stroud, a prisoner who became a leading ornithologist, was portrayed in Oscar-nominated fashion by Burt Lancaster in *Birdman of Alcatraz* (1962) and by Art Carney in *Alcatraz: The Whole Shocking Story* (1980). The appeals to prevent the execution of Caryl Chessman, a rapist/murderer known as the "Lover's Lane Bandit," were the subject of 1955's *Cell 2455, Death Row* and 1977's *Kill Me If You Can*. *Papillon* chronicled Henri Charrière's thrilling escape from Devil's Island. *Escape from Alcatraz* (1979) was inspired by a daring 1962 breakout engineered by convict Frank Norris (Clint Eastwood). As one might expect, Alcatraz rates as the cinema's busiest real-life prison. Other actual penitentiaries which have provided movie settings include Sing Sing (*20,000 Years in Sing Sing*, *Castle on the Hudson*), San Quentin (*Duffy of San Quentin*, *Women of San Quentin*), and Folsom (*Inside the Walls of Folsom Prison*). Foreign prisons have proven to be harrowing places, especially as depicted in *Midnight Express* (1978), *Kiss of the Spider Woman* (1985), *Jacobo Timerman: Prisoner Without a Name, Cell Without a Number* (1983), and *Dadah Is Death* (1988). Not all movie prisons have been surrounded by four walls. Futuristic New York City was envisioned as a prison in John Carpenter's *Escape from New York* (1981). A similar premise was explored earlier in 1973's *Terminal Island*, which was set in a futuristic coed penal colony off the coast of California. The prison in the 1993 Australian film *Fortress* was built 30 stories underground. An entire planet was used as a prison in 1985's *Space Rage*. *Caged* (1950) set the standard for women prison pictures, although its most disturbing scene (a prisoner gets her head shaved) seems tame by today's standards. Since Jonathan Demme's drive-in feature *Caged Heat* earned critical kudos in 1974, exploitative "women in prison" films have proliferated. Linda Blair was lusted after by both fellow female inmates and male guards in *Chained Heat* (1983) after being sexually assaulted with a broom handle in the 1974 made-for-TV film *Born Innocent*. Other women prison movies include *The Weak and the Wicked* (1953), *School for Unclaimed Girls* (1969), *The Concrete Jungle* (1982) and *Reform School Girls* (1986). Although most inmates have concentrated solely on escaping from prison, Peter Sellers was concerned with how to break out and then back into one in the 1960 comedy *Two Way Stretch*. Convict Noël Coward led a luxurious prison life — and even masterminded elaborate crimes — in 1969's *The Italian Job*. See also **Penitentiary Series; Prisoners of War**.

The Big House (1930); *Ladies of the Big House* (1931); *The Criminal Code* (1931); *The Last Mile* (1932); *Hold 'Em Jail* (1932); *20,000 Years in Sing-Sing* (1933); *Ladies They Talk About* (1933); *San Quentin* (1937); *Alcatraz Island* (1937); *King of Alcatraz* (1938); *Blackwell's Island* (1939); *The Big Guy* (1939); *Castle on the Hudson* (aka *Years Without Days*) (1940); *San Quentin* (1946); *Brute Force* (1947); *Prison Warden* (1949); *White Heat* (1949); *Caged* (1950); *Inside the Walls of Folsom Prison* (1951); *Hellgate* (1952); *The Weak and the Wicked* (1953); *Riot in Cell Block Eleven* (1954); *The Steel*

Cage (1954); *Duffy of San Quentin* (1954); *Betrayed Women* (1955); *Cell 2455, Death Row* (1955); *Women's Prison* (1955); *Gang Busters* (1955); *Hold Back Tomorrow* (1955); *Unchained* (1955); *Behind the High Wall* (1956); *Girls in Prison* (1956); *Jailhouse Rock* (1957); *Escape from San Quentin* (1957); *The Last Mile* (1958); *Two Way Stretch* (1960); *Birdman of Alcatraz* (1962); *The Concrete Jungle* (aka *The Criminal*) (1962); *Convicts Four* (aka *Reprieve*) (1962); *House of Women* (1962); *The Hill* (1965); *Cool Hand Luke* (1967); *99 Women* (1969); *School for Unclaimed Girls* (aka *The Smashing Birds I Used to Know; House of Unclaimed Women*) (1969); *Riot* (1969); *Breakout* (1970); *There Was a Crooked Man* (1970); *The Glass House* (aka *Truman Capote's The Glass House*) (1972 TVM); *The Hot Box* (1972); *Sweet Sugar* (aka *Chaingang Girls*) (1972); *Papillon* (1973); *Terminal Island* (1973); *Caged Heat* (aka *Renegade Girls*) (1974); *Breakout* (1975); *Short Eyes* (aka *Slammer*) (1977); *Kill Me If You Can* (1977 TVM); *Midnight Express* (1978); *Escape from Alcatraz* (1979); *Penitentiary* (1979); *Alcatraz: The Whole Shocking Story* (1980 TVM); *Attica* (1980 TVM); *Brubaker* (1980); *Stir Crazy* (1980); *Inmates: A Love Story* (1981 TVM); *Escape from New York* (1981); *The Concrete Jungle* (1982); *Love Child* (1982); *Dangerous Company* (1982 TVM); *Bad Boys* (1983); *Women of San Quentin* (1983 TVM); *Chained Heat* (1983); *Jacobo Timerman: Prisoner Without a Name, Cell Without a Number* (aka *Prisoner Without a Name, Cell Without a Number*) (1983 TVM); *Beyond the Walls* (1984); *Mrs. Soffel* (1984); *Kiss of the Spider Woman* (1985); *Space Rage* (1985); *Doin' Time* (1985); *Star Slammer: The Escape* (aka *Prison Ship*) (1986); *Vendetta* (1986); *The Naked Cage* (1986); *Reform School Girls* (1986); *Prison for Children* (1987 TVM); *Prison on Fire* (aka *Gaam Yuk Fung Wan*) (1987); *Weeds* (1987); *Prison* (1988); *Dadah Is Death* (1988 TVM); *Lock Up* (1989); *Caged Fury* (1989); *Prison Stories: Women on the Inside* (1990 TVM); *Ernest Goes to Jail* (1990); *Death Warrant* (1990); *Club Fed* (1990); *Prison on Fire II* (aka *Tao Fan*) (1991); *Bloodfist III: Forced to Fight* (1992); *Alien³* (1992); *American Me* (1992); *Fortress* (1993); *Last Light* (1993 TVM); *New Crime City: Los Angeles 2020* (1994); *Against Their Will: Women in Prison* (1994 TVM); *Everynight…Everynight* (1994); *Girls in Prison* (1994 TVM); *Reform School Girl* (1994 TVM); *The Shawshank Redemption* (1994); *Against the Wall* (1994 TVM); *No Escape* (1994); *Captives* (1994); *Convict Cowboy* (1995); *Dead Man Walking* (1995); *The Rock* (1996); *Last Dance* (1996); *Cellblock Sisters: Banished Behind Bars* (1996); *Killer: A Journal of Murder* (1996); *Prison of Secrets* (1997 TVM); *Slam* (1998); *Life* (1999); *The Green Mile* (1999)

Problem Child Series

Screenwriters Scott Alexander and Larry Karaszewski were bound to encounter some career bumps along the road from *Beyond Our Control*, a youth television show co-written by Larry, to the duo's critically acclaimed films *Ed Wood* and *The People vs. Larry Flynt* (1996). The irony is that one of those bumps — the sophomoric comedy *Problem Child*— made lots of money and inspired two sequels and an animated TV series. The premise, a comic twist on *The Bad Seed*, shows promise at the outset. But midway through *Problem Child*, it becomes apparent that seven-year-old orphan Junior isn't an incarnation of juvenile evil, but rather an extremely bratty child that needs to be loved. His fate then becomes obvious and the movie becomes nothing more than a collection of Junior's tasteless pranks (e.g., he puts firecrackers on a birthday cake). Michael Oliver starred as Junior, with John Ritter and Amy Yasbeck as his new parents. All three returned for the 1991 sequel, although Yasbeck played a different character. The new wrinkle in *Problem Child 2*, also written by Alexander and Karaszewski, is that Junior must cope with a little girl as devilish as himself.

The film grossed only half as much as its predecessor — which undoubtedly was one of the reasons *Problem Child 3* skipped theatrical release to premiere on television. William Katt replaced John Ritter, with Justin Chapman taking over as Junior. An animated TV series also appeared in 1993. Gilbert Gottfried, who played adoption agent Mr. Peabody in the first two films, provided the voice for his character.

Problem Child (1990); *Problem Child 2* (1991); *Problem Child 3* (aka *Problem Child 3: Junior in Love* (1993 TVM)

Project: Shadowchaser *see* Shadowchaser Series

Prom Night Series

The original entry in this slasher film series toplined the scream queen of the early 1980s: Jamie Lee Curtis. Like many slasher films, it featured a killer seeking revenge for an earlier crime (in this case, the death of Jamie Lee's little sister). Despite above-average acting for this genre, *Prom Night* hardly warranted a sequel. However, the popularity of horror videotapes toward the end of the decade sent low-budget producers clamoring for recognizable titles. *Hello Mary Lou: Prom Night II* (1987) lifted its plot shamelessly from Stephen King's *Carrie*. At her 1957 high school prom, senior class party girl Mary Lou gets mysteriously elected prom queen. Alas, a good time does not await her — she winds up burning in flames on the dance floor. Thirty years later, her vengeful spirit returns and the student body of Hamilton High quickly becomes less populous. A second sequel covers similar ground with Mary Lou popping up again to possess another teen. The fourth installment dropped Mary Lou in favor of a vengeful male spirit, making it a series entry in name only. See also **Slasher Movies**.

Prom Night (1980); *Hello Mary Lou: Prom Night II* (1987); *Prom Night: The Last Kiss* (1989); *Prom Night IV: Deliver Us from Evil* (1991)

Psychiatrists

Sympathetic, homicidal, crazy — psychiatrists and the occasional psychologist have run the gamut of screen characters. Michael Caine played a murderous shrink in desperate need of psychiatric help himself in *Dressed to Kill*. Surprisingly, women psychiatrists have proven even more adept at murder. Psychology professor Loretta Young accidentally killed a student and then covered up her crime in 1949's *The Accused*. Manipulated psychiatrist Lindsay Crouse went over the edge in the final scene of *House of Games* (1987) and unexpectedly shot Joe Mantegna. In Hitchcock's *Spellbound*, Gregory Peck played an amnesiac who thought he was a prominent psychiatrist. Dan Aykroyd was a patient masquerading as a radio talk show psychiatrist in *The Couch Trip*. The world's most famous psychiatrist, Sigmund Freud, had his life chronicled in 1962's *Freud* (with Montgomery Clift in the lead role). Alan Arkin played Freud to Nicol Williamson's Sherlock Holmes in the stylish 1976 adaptation of Nicholas Meyers' *The Seven-Per-Cent Solution*. And Alec Guinness took his turn as Freud, having imaginary conversations with contemporary psychiatrist Dudley Moore in *Lovesick*. Fred Astaire made a most unlikely psychiatrist in the Astaire-Rogers musical *Carefree*. Brian

Cox and Anthony Hopkins each played the cinema's creepiest psychologist, the cannibalistic Hannibal Lecter, in the movies *Manhunter* (1986) and *The Silence of the Lambs* (1991). James Coburn and Billy Crystal portrayed shrinks stuck with clients they didn't want—Coburn was *The President's Analyst*, while Crystal had gangster Robert De Niro for a patient (a premise also explored in the made-for-cable TV series *The Sopranos*). Robin Williams won a Best Supporting Actor Oscar for playing a sensitive psychiatrist in *Good Will Hunting* (1997). John Vernon had the best line as a psychiatrist in 1982's *Airplane II: The Sequel*. When a lawyer asked him to give his impression of the defendant, he replied: "I'm sorry, I don't do impressions. My expertise is in psychiatry." See also **Asylums**; **Hypnotists**; **Multiple Personalities**.

Carefree (1938); *The Cat People* (1942); *Lady in a Jam* (1942); *Spellbound* (1945); *She Wouldn't Say Yes* (1945); *Shock* (1946); *The Dark Past* (1948); *The Accused* (1949); *The Astonished Heart* (1950); *Tony Draws a Horse* (1950); *Bedtime for Bonzo* (1951); *Teresa* (1951); *Sleeping Tiger* (1954); *The Cobweb* (1955); *The Three Faces of Eve* (1957); *The Undead* (1957); *Oh Men! Oh Women!* (1957); *Psycho* (1960); *Stop Me Before I Kill!* (aka *The Full Treatment*) (1961); *Mix Me a Person* (1961); *The Couch* (1962); *Pressure Point* (1962); *Freud* (1962); *David and Lisa* (1962); *Tender Is the Night* (1962); *Captain Newman, M.D.* (1963); *Sex and the Single Girl* (1964); *Blindfold* (1965); *Three on a Couch* (1966); *The President's Analyst* (1967); *The Impossible Years* (1968); *Coming Apart* (1969); *Dial Hot Line* (1969 TVM); *The Psychiatrist: God Bless the Children* (aka *Children of the Lotus Eater*) (1970 TVM); *They Might Be Giants* (1971); *Klute* (1971); *Dark Places* (1972); *Diagnosis: Murder* (1975); *One Flew Over the Cuckoo's Nest* (1975); *The Seven-Per-Cent Solution* (1976); *Sybil* (1976 TVM); *Face to Face* (1976); *Equus* (1977); *High Anxiety* (1977); *Dressed to Kill* (1980); *Simon* (1980); *Ordinary People* (1980); *Phobia* (1980); *Still of the Night* (1982); *Zelig* (1983); *Lovesick* (1983); *Private Sessions* (1985 TVM); *Manhunter* (1986); *Beyond Therapy* (1987); *A Different Affair* (1987 TVM); *House of Games* (1987); *The Couch Trip* (1988); *Jack's Back* (1988); *The Dream Team* (1989); *The Last Best Year* (1990 TVM); *Disturbed* (1991); *The Silence of the Lambs* (1991); *Victim of Love* (1991 TVM); *What About Bob?* (1991); *Red Wind* (1991 TVM); *Love Kills* (1991 TVM); *The Prince of Tides* (1991); *Final Analysis* (1992); *Whispers in the Dark* (1992); *Raising Cain* (1992); *Loving Lulu* (1992); *Relentless: Mind of a Killer* (1993 TVM); *House of Cards* (1993); *Mr. Jones* (1993); *Betrayal of Trust* (1994); *Web of Deception* (1994 TVM); *Blindfold: Acts of Obsession* (1994 TVM); *Silent Fall* (1994); *Color of Night* (1994); *Batman Forever* (1995); *Never Talk to Strangers* (1995); *A Holiday to Remember* (1995 TVM); *Don Juan DeMarco* (1995); *Good Will Hunting* (1997); *The Ugly* (1997); *Analyze This* (1999); *The Sixth Sense* (1999); *The Cell* (2000)

Psycho Series

In François Truffaut's 1967 interview book *Hitchcock*, Hitch offered this explanation for making *Psycho*: "I think that the thing that appealed to me and made me decide to do the picture was the suddenness of the murder in the shower, coming, as it were, out of the blue. That was about all." Shot on a backlot with Hitchcock's TV series crew, *Psycho* was a clever shocker about meek hotel owner Norman Bates (Anthony Perkins), who periodically assumed his dead mother's identity and became a jealous murderess. This inexpensive picture made its famed director a wealthy man and eventually became Hitch's best-known film to a generation of baby boomers. Yet, even when his film career began to decline after failures like *Torn Curtain* (1966) and *Topaz*

(1969), Hitchcock resisted a *Psycho* sequel. Yet, just three years after Hitchcock's death, the inevitable *Psycho II* was released. In an attempt to out-twist its predecessor, this sequel revealed that, despite dual personalities, alleged murderer Norman Bates (Perkins) was not as mad as most people thought. Perkins directed and starred in the 1986 follow-up *Psycho III*, which proved to be an uneasy mixture of dark humor and studio-inserted gore. The 1987 TV movie *Bates Motel* strove for a lighter touch, but failed to find one. It starred Bud Cort (Harold in *Harold and Maude*) as a former mental patient who inherited the motel from fellow ex-inmate Norman Bates. A second TV Movie, 1990's *Psycho IV: The Beginning*, starred former *E.T.* youngster Henry Thomas as a young Norman. In 1998, director Gus Van Zant followed up his acclaimed hit *Good Will Hunting* with an unexpected remake of the original *Psycho*. Van Zant virtually recreated the original film scene by scene with the addition of color and, of course, a different cast (headed by Vince Vaughn as Norman). It found little favor with critics (who wondered what the point of such a faithful remake was) and flopped miserably at the box-office amid an onslaught of holiday releases. See also **Hotels**.

Psycho (1960); *Psycho II* (1983); *Psycho III* (1986); *Bates Motel* (1987 TVM); *Psycho IV: The Beginning* (1990 TVM); *Psycho* (1998)

Puppet Master Series

Following on the heels of 1987's *Dolls*, 1989's *Puppet Master* (1989) tried to generate terror by transforming harmless toys into murderous little monsters. The film's prologue opens in 1939 at the Bodega Bay Inn (an apparent reference to Hitchcock's *The Birds*). Elderly puppeteer Andre Toulon (William Hickey) has discovered an ancient secret for breathing life into inanimate objects. However, fearing that his discovery will be exploited for evil, Toulon hides his work and commits suicide. Fifty years later, four psychics journey to the now-isolated hotel to investigate the death of a colleague who had been obsessed with Toulon. Shortly thereafter, a quartet of homicidal puppets—with colorful names like Pinhead, Tunneler, and Ms. Leech—begin bumping off the psychics in gruesome fashion. Despite its predictability and overemphasis on gore, horror aficionados made *Puppet Master* a popular videotape rental. A 1990 sequel rehashed most of the original's elements, although it was enlivened by a mysterious stranger wrapped in gauze and sporting sunglasses à la Claude Rains in *The Invisible Man*. The series then took an unexpected turn by producing a cleverly-plotted prequel (q.v.). *Puppet Master III: Toulon's Revenge* (1991) essentially turns the killer-puppets into heroes by pitting them against the ruthless Nazis responsible for the murder of Andre Toulon's wife. As with the earlier films, the special effects are somewhat interesting. However, the puppets never really generate terror—they can be outmaneuvered and kicked out of the way too easily. The next two series entries, shot back to back, return to present day and continue to portray the puppets as good guys. In both films, Pinhead and his cohorts assist young inventor Rick Myers (Gordon Currie) in a battle against the demon lord Sutek, who has sent the Totems (doll-sized evil creatures) to retrieve the reanimating elixir stolen by Toulon. Although *Puppet Master 5* was subtitled *The Final Chapter*, the series resumed in 1998 with *Curse of the Puppet Master*, which pitted the puppets against Dr. Magrew, a mad scientist intent on creating a race of "puppet people." The 1994 movie *Robert Heinlein's The Puppet*

Masters is not part of this series, but is an adaptation of Heinlein's 1951 novel about alien parasites. See also **Puppets**.

Puppet Master (1989); *Puppet Master II* (1990); *Puppet Master III: Toulon's Revenge* (1991); *Puppet Master 4* (1993); *Puppet Master 5: The Final Chapter* (1994); *Curse of the Puppet Master* (aka *Curse of the Puppet Master: The Human Experiment; Puppet Master 6*) (1998); *Retro Puppet Master* (1999)

Puppets

Puppetry, as the sole means of telling a story, has garnered little interest in the cinema. Except for Jiri Trnka's *A Midsummer Night's Dream* (1958), most all-puppet features have been aimed strictly at juveniles. Early efforts, such as *Willy McBean and His Magic Machine* (1965) and *Mad Monster Party?* (1967), were viewed as low-cost alternatives to animation. The James Bond–style 1966 British TV puppet series *Thunderbirds* attracted a more sophisticated audience. It inspired two theatrical features, *Thunderbirds Are Go* (1966) and *Thunderbird 6* (1968). American puppeteer Jim Henson hit box-office gold in the early 1980s with movies using characters from his television series *The Muppet Show* (q.v.). However, his elaborate 1983 non–Muppet, puppet fantasy *The Dark Crystal* baffled Miss Piggy fans and was only modestly successful. Charming puppet sequences have graced a handful of films, most notably the Cary Grant–Katharine Hepburn romantic comedy *Holiday* (1938) and the family musicals *The Sound of Music* (1965) and *Lili* (1953). In the latter film, Leslie Caron sang "Hi Lili, Hi Lo" with a quartet of puppets and later danced a semi-ballet with life-size puppet replicas. In the 1931 Marx Brothers comedy *Monkey Business*, Harpo pretended to be a puppet. A good fairy transformed a puppet-boy into a real boy in Disney's classic *Pinocchio* (1940). The TV movie *Special People* (1984) told the true-life story of a puppet troupe composed of mentally handicapped young people. Master mime Marcel Marceau played a puppeteer who could revive the dead in the disturbing 1974 fantasy *Shanks*. Murderous puppeteers have appeared in *The Falcon Strikes Back* (1943) and *Bluebeard* (1944). A crazy scientist reduced humans to puppet size in schlockmeister Bert I. Gordon's *Attack of the Puppet People* (1958). See also **Dolls; The Muppets; Puppet Master Series**.

Monkey Business (1931); *Holiday* (1938); *Pinocchio* (1940); *The Falcon Strikes Back* (1943); *Bluebeard* (1944); *The Forbidden Street* (aka *Britannia Mews*) (1948); *Lili* (1953); *tom thumb* (1958); *A Midsummer Night's Dream* (1958); *The Sound of Music* (1965); *Willy McBean and His Magic Machine* (1965); *Thunderbirds Are Go* (1966); *Mad Monster Party?* (1967); *Thunderbird 6* (1968); *Shanks* (1974); *Side Show* (1981 TVM); *The Dark Crystal* (1983); *Special People* (1984 TVM); *Puppet Master* (1989); *The Adventures of Pinocchio* (1996); *Pinocchio's Revenge* (1996); *Still Breathing* (1998); *A Rat's Tale* (1998); *Being John Malkovich* (1999); *Geppetto* (2000 TVM)

Purple, Alvin

Australian playwright Alan Hopgood created Alvin Purple, a homely chap with inexplicable sex appeal — women simply cannot stay away from him. Graeme Blundell played Alvin in two popular 1970s feature film comedies and a 1976 TV series. He also reprised the role for *Melvin, Son of Alvin* (1984), which starred Gerry Sont as Alvin's 18-year-old son, who — like his dad — is a "babe magnet."

Alvin Purple (1973); *Alvin Rides Again* (1974); *Melvin, Son of Alvin* (1984)

Quatermass, Professor Bernard

The intrepid, brilliant, sometimes eccentric scientist Bernard Quatermass made his initial appearance on TV in Nigel Kneale's 1954 three-hour BBC serial *The Quatermass Experiment*. The program, about an astronaut who returns to Earth and evolves into a "vegetable monster," was phenomenally successful. A big-screen version was naturally in order and it came in 1955, courtesy of a struggling studio called Hammer Films. Hammer promptly replaced Reginald Tate, TV's Quatermass, with American Brian Donlevy — the biggest star it could afford — and dubbed the film *The Creeping Unknown* for its American showings. Despite Donlevy's lackluster performance, the movie was a hit and a sequel, *Enemy from Space* (aka *Quatermass II*), was released in 1957. It was also based on a Kneale TV serial and Donlevy again ousted the small-screen lead (John Robinson). A ten-year hiatus followed, then Hammer revived the series in grand fashion with 1967's *Five Million Years to Earth* (aka *Quatermass and the Pit*). A unique blend of science fiction and gothic horror, it boasted a fine lead performance by Scottish actor Andrew Keir and an ingenious premise ("As far as anybody is," concludes Quatermass emphatically, "we're the Martians."). Quatermass's next and final appearance was in the 1979 serial *Quatermass*. Distinguished actor John Mills took his turn as the heroic scientist, whose demise at the end of the film signalled an end to the series. This 200-minute TV miniseries was trimmed to 107 minutes and given a limited theatrical release as *The Quatermass Conclusion*.

The Creeping Unknown (aka *The Quatermass Experiment; The Quatermass Xperiment*) (1956); *Enemy from Space* (aka *Quatermass II*) (1957); *Five Million Years to Earth* (aka *Quatermass and the Pit*) (1967); *The Quatermass Conclusion* (aka *Quatermass*) (1979)

Queen, Ellery

A unique literary creation, Ellery Queen is famous as both a fictional detective and a best-selling "author" (as a pseudonym for cousins Frederic Dannay and Manfred B. Lee). His film career, however, has been an unequivocal disaster. Donald Cook made an uninspired Queen in 1935's *The Spanish Cape Mystery*. A year later, he was followed by comedian Eddie Quillan in *The Mandarin Mystery*. Columbia launched an official series in 1940 by casting Ralph Bellamy as *Ellery Queen, Master Detective*. Charley Grapewin played Ellery's police inspector father, Richard Queen. These movies relied heavily on comic relief, and Bellamy's clumsy detective resembled the literary Queen in name only. After four mysteries, sturdy William Gargan replaced Bellamy for three additional films. In the 1950s, four actors played Queen on television. Richard Hart was Ellery in 1950's *The Adventures of Ellery Queen*. He died in 1951 and was replaced by Lee Bowman until the series was cancelled in 1952. In 1954, Hugh Marlowe starred in a syndicated TV series also titled *The Adventures of Ellery Queen* (aka *Mystery Is My Business*). George Nader popped up as Queen in a 1958-59 series called *The Further Adventures of Ellery Queen* (aka *Ellery Queen*). Peter Lawford made the screen's worst Queen in the 1971 TV movie *Ellery Queen: Don't Look Behind You*, while Jim Hutton and David Wayne played Ellery and Inspector Queen, respectively, in another made-for-TV mystery, 1975's

Ellery Queen (aka *Too Many Suspects*). Hutton's film evolved into a fairly entertaining weekly series that lasted a year. Queen's story "Ten Days Wonder" (which did not feature Queen as the detective) was made into a 1972 film starring Orson Welles and Anthony Perkins.

The Spanish Cape Mystery (1935) (Donald Cook); *The Mandarin Mystery* (1936) (Eddie Quillan); *Ellery Queen, Master Detective* (1940) (Ralph Bellamy); *Ellery Queen and the Murder Ring* (1941) (Bellamy); *Ellery Queen and the Perfect Crime* (1941) (Bellamy); *Ellery Queen's Penthouse Mystery* (1941) (Bellamy); *A Close Call for Ellery Queen* (1942) (William Gargan); *Enemy Agents Meet Ellery Queen* (1942) (Gargan); *A Desperate Chance for Ellery Queen* (1942) (Gargan); *Ellery Queen: Don't Look Behind You* (1971 TVM) (Peter Lawford); *Ellery Queen* (aka *Too Many Suspects*) (1975 TVM) (Jim Hutton)

Rabbits

Despite their ability to reproduce in massive numbers, bunnies have been pretty scarce in the cinema. The Disney children's classic *Bambi* made a star out of Thumper the rabbit. Another animated feature, 1978's *Watership Down*, offered a literary fable about a warren of rabbits seeking a new home. Bugs Bunny, the cinema's only Oscar-winning rabbit, has a few theatrical cartoon compilations (q.v.) to his name. And, naturally, one must not forget James Stewart's six-foot, invisible rabbit chum in *Harvey*. A 1965 spy spoof called *The Nasty Rabbit* featured the unforgettable song "The Jackrabbit Shuffle." The picture's plot revolved around virus-carrying rabbits. Still, they were bunnies without malice, unlike the nasty ones — standing four feet tall and weighing 150 pounds — that terrorized Janet Leigh in 1972's *Night of the Lepus* (surely a movie she'd like to forget). In *The Lemon Sisters* (1990), Elliott Gould created "taffits" — taffy rabbits — but found few buyers. *Rabbit Run*, *The Rabbit Trap*, *Bunny Lake Is Missing*, and *Bunny O'Hare* were rabbit films in name only. Ditto for *A Bunny's Tale*, which was about Gloria Steinem's undercover stint as a *Playboy* bunny.

Alice in Wonderland (1933); *Rules of the Game* (1939); *Bambi* (1942); *Song of the South* (with Brer Rabbit) (1946); *Harvey* (1950); *Alice in Wonderland* (1951); *The Nasty Rabbit* (aka *Spies a Go Go*) (1965); *Get to Know Your Rabbit* (1972); *Night of the Lepus* (1972); *Coonskin* (aka *Streetfight*) (1975); *Monty Python and the Holy Grail* (1975); *Bugs Bunny, Superstar* (1975); *Watership Down* (1978); *The Bugs Bunny/Roadrunner Movie* (1979); *The Adventures of the American Rabbit* (1986); *Jean de Florette* (1986); *Who Framed Roger Rabbit* (1988); *Celia* (aka *Celia: Child of Terror*) (1989)

Racing *see* Auto Racing; Horse Racing

Radio

During the Great Depression, movies ranked as the second most popular form of entertainment—with radio firmly entrenched in the number one position. Surprisingly, the film industry promoted its rival, with dozens of films set behind the scenes of radio programs. Many of these films were built around the era's big radio singing stars, such as Dick Powell in *Twenty Million Sweethearts* (1934) and Bing Crosby in the series-inspiring *The Big Broadcast* (1932). On the dramatic side, *Two Against the World* (1936) starred Humphrey Bogart as a moralistic radio station manager. Mystery radio shows provided the background for real

murders in the Abbott and Costello comedy *Who Done It?* (1942) and the Claude Rains vehicle *The Unsuspected* (1947). Few films have been principally about radio stations. Paul Newman played a drifter-turned-DJ who gains fame broadcasting on the right-wing radio station *WUSA* (1970). A rock station's management rebelled against its uptight parent company in the 1978 satire *FM*, which laid the groundwork for the broader 1978–82 TV sitcom *WKRP in Cincinnati*. Disc jockeys have appeared as principal characters in the guise of Clint Eastwood (*Play Misty for Me*), Adrienne Barbeau (*The Fog*), Wolfman Jack (*American Graffiti*), and Bill Paterson (*Comfort and Joy*). Real life DJs have been played by Robin Williams (as Adrian Cronauer in *Good Morning, Vietnam*), Tim McIntire (as rock legend Alan Freed in *American Hot Wax*), and Howard Stern (as himself in *Private Parts*). Oliver Stone's *Talk Radio* (1988) was practically a one-man show about a controversial radio talk show host, but it was not the first film on the subject. Call-in radio programs were integral to the plots of Jack Nicholson's *The King of Marvin Gardens* (1972) and George Romero's vampire chiller *Martin* (1978). Of course, not all radio broadcasts have originated from Earth. *Orpheus* (1949) and *Christine* (1983) both featured cars equipped with radios that picked up otherworldly signals. Celestial broadcasts were the subject of *Red Planet Mars* (1952) and *The Next Voice You Hear* (1950), which co-starred Nancy Davis Reagan. Both these films conveyed optimistic religious messages, although their heavyhanded approach limited their showings. Radio's subtler influence on its listening audience was explored in *Music Hath Charms* (1935) and Woody Allen's *Radio Days* (1987). The former film showed how a dance band's music played different roles in the lives of those listening to it. In contrast, radio's ability to incite hysteria was powerfully displayed in 1975's *The Night That Panicked America*, a fact-based drama about Orson Welles' 1938 "War of the Worlds" broadcast.

The Big Broadcast (1932); *Death at Broadcasting House* (1934); *Music Hath Charms* (1935); *Two Against the World* (aka *One Fatal Hour; The Case of Mrs. Pembroke*) (1936); *Love Is on the Air* (1937); *The Great American Broadcast* (1940); *Wake Up and Live* (1942); *Who Done It?* (1942); *Appointment in Berlin* (1943); *I'll Tell the World* (1945); *The Falcon's Alibi* (1946); *The Hucksters* (1947); *Where There's Life* (1947); *The Unsuspected* (1947); *Orpheus* (1949); *The Next Voice You Hear* (1950); *Red Planet Mars* (1952); *WUSA* (1970); *Play Misty for Me* (1971); *The King of Marvin Gardens* (1972); *Slipstream* (1974); *The Night That Panicked America* (1975 TVM); *American Hot Wax* (1978); *FM* (1978); *Martin* (1978); *On the Air Live with Captain Midnight* (aka *Captain Midnight*) (1979); *Radio On* (1979); *The Fog* (1980); *Christine* (1983); *Comfort and Joy* (1984); *Radio Days* (1987); *Good Morning, Vietnam* (1987); *Talk Radio* (1988); *Pump Up the Volume* (1990); *Straight Talk* (1992); *Bad Channels* (1992); *Loose Screws* (aka *La Folie Douce*) (1994); *Airheads* (1994); *Radioland Murders* (1994); *The Truth About Cats and Dogs* (1996); *Power 98* (1996); *Grosse Point Blank* (1997); *Private Parts* (1997); *Lovesick on Nana Street* (1997); *Winchell* (1998 TVM); *Frequency* (2000)

Rambo

Rambo named after a poet? University of Iowa professor David Morrell, who created one-man army John Rambo in his novel *First Blood*, claims that he derived his hero's name from 19th century symbolist poet Arthur Rimbaud. But when Morrell sold the film rights to his book for $90,000, it's doubtful if he envisioned bare-chested, muscle-rippling Sylvester Stallone as his character. Stallone, though, was anxious to break away from his *Rocky* (q.v.) image when he was offered the chance to do *First Blood*. The 1982 film introduced Rambo as a misunderstood drifter, a former Green Beret, who runs afoul of a redneck sheriff in a small town. Despite substituting explosions for punches, *Rambo* and *Rocky* are very much alike — two underdogs fighting apparently insurmountable odds to make a point. The picture proved to be Stallone's first non–*Rocky* hit. His 1985 sequel, *Rambo: First Blood Part II*, sent its hunky hero into Camdodia in search of POWs. Stallone brilliantly capitalized on a new wave of patriotism and the sequel's grosses went through the roof. Again, the actor portrayed Rambo as a soldier betrayed at every turn and yet still patriotic to his country. That tone changed with 1988's *Rambo III*, which paired Rambo with his trusty ex-commander (Richard Crenna) and made him less of a loner fighting the establishment. The public noticed the difference. It made a lot of quick cash, but failed to follow the highly profitable path of its predecessors.

First Blood (1982); *Rambo: First Blood Part II* (1985); *Rambo III* (1988)

The Range Busters

Monogram Pictures launched this low-budget Western series in an effort to duplicate rival Republic's successful *Three Mesquiteers* (q.v.) films. John "Dusty" King joined former Mesquiteers Ray "Crash" Corrigan and Max Terhune to form Monogram's cowboy trio. Their adventures followed the Mesquiteers closely, even to the point of mixing Old West stories with contemporary adventures (e.g., the boys clashed with Nazis in 1943's *Cowboy Commandos* and the Japanese in *Texas to Bataan*). A more interesting series might have focused on the stars' varied backgrounds: Corrigan was a stunt daredevil, Terhune a former ventriloquist, and King a band vocalist.

The Range Busters (1940); *Trailing Double Trouble* (1940); *West of Pinto Basin* (1940); *Trail of the Silver Spurs* (1941); *The Kid's Last Ride* (1941); *Tumbledown Ranch in Arizona* (1941); *Wrangler's Roost* (1941); *Fugitive Valley* (1941); *Saddle Mountain Roundup* (1941); *Tonto Basin Outlaws* (1941); *Underground Rustlers* (1941); *Thunder River Feud* (1942); *Boot Hill Bandits* (1942); *Texas Trouble Shooters* (1942); *Texas to Bataan* (1942); *Trail Riders* (1942); *Two Fisted Justice* (1943); *The Haunted Ranch* (1943); *Land of Hunted Men* (1943); *Cowboy Commandos* (1943); *Black Market Business* (1943); *Bullets and Saddles* (1943)

Rats *see* Rodents

Rebel Highway Series

The Showtime cable network launched this TV movie series consisting of remakes of B-films produced by American-International Pictures in the 1950s. The filmmakers boasted impressive resumes, many of them moonlighting from their theatrical film careers. William Friedkin (*The Exorcist*) directed the cheerleader-hoodlum movie *Jailbreakers*. The juvenile crime drama *Girls in Prison* was directed by John McNaughton (*Wild Things*) and written by Sam Fuller and his wife Christa Lang. Animator Ralph Baskin (*Fritz the Cat*) wrote and directed *Cool and the Crazy*. And Robert Rodriguez (*From Dusk Till Dawn*) directed and co-wrote *Roadracers*. Some of the films spoofed the originals (like *Runaway*

Daughters), some were direct remakes (*Confessions of a Sorority Girl*), and others used the old titles only (*Dragstrip Girl*).

Confessions of a Sorority Girl (1993 TVM) (remake of *Sorority Girl*); *Cool and the Crazy* (1994 TVM); *Dragstrip Girl* (1994 TVM); *Girls in Prison* (1994 TVM); *Jailbreakers* (1994 TVM); *Motorcycle Gang* (1994 TVM); *Reform School Girl* (1994 TVM); *Roadracers* (1994 TVM); *Runaway Daughters* (1994 TVM); *Shake, Rattle, and Rock!* (1994 TVM)

Reincarnation

The definitive film on this intriguing subject has yet to be made. In the past, reincarnation has been chiefly employed in comedies and low-budget efforts that emphasized its sensationalistic values. The first of these latter films was 1956's *The Search for Bridey Murphy*, an adaptation of Morey Bernstein's allegedly fact-based best-seller about a housewife who reveals under hypnosis that she led another life 200 years earlier. This dreary, uninvolving tale captured the public's fancy and imitations followed in rapid succession. *Spell of the Hypnotist* (1956), Roger Corman's *The Undead* (1957), and the Bowery Boys' *Hold That Hypnotist* (1957) all concerned people who learned of previous existences through hypnotism. Corman's movie, shot in a refurbished supermarket, was the best of the bunch, mixing witch trials and time travel elements with its reincarnation plot. Hypnotism also played a prominent role in the only reincarnation musical comedy, Barbra Streisand's *On a Clear Day You Can See Forever*. Men were reincarnated as women in *Goodbye, Charlie* (1964), *Cleo/Leo* (1989), and *Switch* (1991). Finally, no discussion on celebrity reincarnation would be complete without mentioning Shirley MacLaine, who espoused her beliefs in *Out on a Limb*, a TV movie based on her autobiographical best-seller. In *Defending Your Life* (1991), Shirley introduced people to their past lives at the heavenly Past Lives Pavilion. See also **The Mummy**.

She (1935); *Corridor of Mirrors* (1948); *You Never Can Tell* (1951); *The Search for Bridey Murphy* (1956); *Spell of the Hypnotist* (aka *Fright*) (1956); *I've Lived Before* (1956); *Hold That Hypnotist* (1957); *The She Creature* (1957); *The Undead* (1957); *Curse of the Faceless Man* (1958); *Goodbye, Charlie* (1964); *She* (1965); *On a Clear Day You Can See Forever* (1970); *Night of Dark Shadows* (1971); *The Reincarnation of Peter Proud* (1975); *Audrey Rose* (1977); *Oh, Heavenly Dog!* (1980); *All of Me* (1984); *Déjà Vu* (1985); *Out on a Limb* (1987 TVM); *Chances Are* (1989); *Manika: The Girl Who Lived Twice* (1989); *Cleo/Leo* (1989); *Identity Crisis* (1990); *Switch* (1991); *Defending Your Life* (1991); *Hi Honey, I'm Dead* (1991 TVM); *Dead Again* (1991); *Dying to Remember* (1993 TVM); *Fatally Yours* (1996); *The Demolitionist* (1996); *Kundun* (1997); *I've Been Waiting for You* (1998 TVM)

Relentless Series

Leo Rossi played Los Angeles police detective Sam Dietz in four movies pitting him against homicidal psychopaths. His quarries included once-promising performers such as Judd Nelson as the "Sunset Killer" (*Relentless*) and Ray Sharkey as a murderous FBI agent (*Dead On: Relentless 2*). William Forsythe portrayed the killer in the third film, which most critics consider the best in the series. Rossi also produced *Relentless IV* (1994), a grisly final outing in which the murderer recreated different sacrifical rituals.

Relentless (1989); *Dead On: Relentless 2* (1991); *Relentless III* (1993); *Relentless IV: Ashes to Ashes* (1994)

Remakes of Foreign Films

The problems inherent in remaking foreign films into English-language pictures have both intrigued and frustrated filmmakers. No rule of thumb has met with steady success. John Sturges translated Akiro Kurosawa's classic *The Seven Samurai* (1954) into the enduringly popular American western *The Magnificent Seven* (1960). Likewise, Italian "spaghetti Western" king Sergio Leone also exploited the samurai/Western link and turned Kurosawa's *Yojimbo* (1961) into Clint Eastwood's breakthrough film, *A Fistful of Dollars* (1964). But Martin Ritt's *The Outrage* (1964), a philosophical Western remake of Kurosawa's *Rashomon* (1951), missed the tone of the Japanese original and bored audiences and critics equally. Although Kurosawa's films have been popular targets for remakes, American and British filmmakers have shown a special fondness for the French cinema. Julien Duvivier's *Pépé Le Moko* (1937) was remade as *Algiers* just a year after its release. The remake incorporated the same setting and plot and even cast a Frenchman in the lead — Charles Boyer as the charming gangster originally created by Jean Gabin. French thrillers from the 1940s and 1950s have been turned into little films (*Midnight Episode*) and costly bombs (*Sorcerer*). The popularity of French light comedies in the 1970s and 1980s inspired a slew of Americanized versions. Most of these stateside remakes compared poorly with their continental counterparts and fizzled at the box-office. Big name stars did not help either. Walter Matthau and Jack Lemmon looked out of place in *Buddy, Buddy* (1981), while Richard Pryor floundered in *The Toy* (1982). However, the surprise successes of 1986's *Down and Out in Beverly Hills*, 1987's *Three Men and a Baby* and, to a lesser degree, 1989's *Cousins*, have ensured that the French cinema will continue to be raided for remake properties. Occasionally, the original director has even helmed the English-language version, as did Francis Veber (*Les Fugitifs*; *Three Fugitives*), Roger Vadim (*And God Created Woman*), and George Sluizer (*The Vanishing*). Interestingly, not all remakes have gone the direct route of foreign film into English-language film. Bergman's *Smiles of a Summer Night* (1955) and Fellini's *Nights of Cabiria* (1957) stopped at Broadway long enough to be transformed into the hit musicals *A Little Night Music* and *Sweet Charity*. Thus, the film versions of these musicals are indirect remakes of the original movies. Along similar lines, one could argue that Fritz Lang's *Human Desire* (1954) was based solely on Emile Zola's novel *La Bête Humaine* and not on Jean Renoir's 1938 adaptation of Zola's book. Occasionally, this question of whether a film is or is not a remake becomes a matter of opinion. Many critics consider Curtis Harrington's *Games* (1967) a remake of Clouzot's *Les Diaboliques*, although the films differ substantially in setting and premise (perhaps, it's more a variation than a remake). Likewise, Claude Lelouch's *Another Man, Another Chance* (1977) is often listed as a western remake of his own contemporary romance *A Man and a Woman* (1966) since the plots of both films are about a widow and widower falling in love. That's a pretty common plot, allowing one to argue that 1968's *With Six You Get Eggroll* was an earlier remake of Lelouch's original. Occasionally, foreign countries have remade American films, as in the case of 1957's *The Burglar* and 1971's *La Casse* (aka *The Burglars*). In the following list, the remakes are listed chronologically first, followed by the original films.

Port of Seven Seas (1938)—*Fanny* (1932); *Algiers* (1938)—*Pépé Le Moko* (1937); *A Woman's Face* (1941)—*En Kvinnas Ansikte*

(1938); *Scarlet Street* (1945)—*La Chienne* (1931); *The Unfinished Dance* (1947)—*Ballerina* (1938); *The Long Night* (1947)—*Le Jour se Lève* (aka *Daybreak*) (1939); *Midnight Episode* (1951)—*Monsieur le Souris* (aka *Midnight in Paris*) (1947); *The Thirteenth Letter* (1951)—*Le Corbeau* (aka *The Raven*) (1948); *Human Desire* (1954)—*La Bête Humaine* (aka *The Human Beast*; *Judas Was a Woman*) (1938); *The Magnificent Seven* (1960)—*The Seven Samurai* (aka *Shichi-nin no Samurai*) (1954); *The Outrage* (1964)—*Rashomon* (1951); *A Fistful of Dollars* (1964)—*Yojimbo* (1961); *Games* (1967)—*Les Diaboliques* (aka *Diabolique*) (1955); *Cop-Out* (1968)—*Les Inconnus dans la Maison* (aka *Strangers in the House*) (1949); *Sweet Charity* (1969)—*Nights of Cabiria* (aka *Le Notti di Cabiria*) (1957); *Another Man, Another Chance* (1977)—*A Man and a Woman* (aka *Un Homme et une Femme*) (1966); *Sorcerer* (1977)—*The Wages of Fear* (aka *La Salaire de la Peur*) (1952); *Which Way Is Up?* (1977)—*The Seduction of Mimi* (aka *Mimi Metallurgico Ferito nell'Onore*) (1974); *A Little Night Music* (1978)—*Smiles of a Summer Night* (aka *Sommarnattens Leende*) (1955); *Dear Detective* (1979 TVM)—*Dear Detective* (aka *Tendre Poulet*; *Dear Inspector*) (1978); *Willie and Phil* (1980)—*Jules and Jim* (aka *Jules et Jim*) (1961); *Buddy, Buddy* (1981)—*A Pain in the A-* (aka *L'Emmerdeur*) (1974); *Kiss Me Goodbye* (1982)—*Dona Flor and Her Two Husbands* (aka *Dona Flor e Seurs Dois Maridos*) (1977); *The Toy* (1982)—*Le Jouet* (1976); *Breathless* (1983)—*À Bout de Souffle* (aka *Breathless*) (1960); *The Lost Honor of Kathryn Beck* (aka *Act of Passion*) (1984 TVM)—*The Lost Honor of Katharina Blum* (aka *Die Verlorene Ehre der Katharina Blum*) (1975); *Crackers* (1984)—*Big Deal on Madonna Street* (aka *I Soliti Ignoti*) (1958); *The Woman in Red* (1984)—*Pardon Mon Affaire* (aka *Un Elephant ca Troupe Enormement*) (1976); *Blame It on Rio* (1984)—*One Wild Moment* (1977); *The Man with One Red Shoe* (1985)—*The Tall Blond Man with One Black Shoe* (1972); *Down and Out in Beverly Hills* (1986)—*Boudu Saved from Drowning* (aka *Boudu Sauvé des Eaux*) (1932); *Happy New Year* (1987)—*Happy New Year* (aka *La Nonne Ann*; *The Happy New Year Caper*) (1973); *Three Men and a Baby* (1987)—*Three Men and a Cradle* (aka *Trois Hommes et un Couffin*) (1985); *Dangerous Liaisons* (1988)—*Les Liaisons Dangereueses* (aka *Dangerous Meetings*) (1959); *And God Created Woman* (1988)—*Et Dieu...Crea La Femme* (aka *And God Created Woman*) (1957); *Three Fugitives* (1989)—*Les Fugitifs* (1986); *Cousins* (1989)—*Cousin, Cousine* (1975); *Baby Cakes* (1989 TVM)—*Zuckerbaby* (aka *Sugarbaby*) (1985); *Men Don't Leave* (1990)—*Continue* (aka *Life Goes On*) (1981); *Paradise* (1991)—*The Big Road* (aka *Le Grand Chemin*; *The Grand Highway*) (1987); *Pure Luck* (1991)—*Le Chevre* (aka *The Goat*) (1981); *Scent of a Woman* (1992)—*Profumo di Donna* (1974); *Sommersby* (1993)—*The Return of Martin Guerre* (1982); *The Vanishing* (1993)—*The Vanishing* (1988); *Point of No Return* (1993)—*La Femme Nikita* (aka *Nikita*) (1991); *Intersection* (1994)—*Les Choses de la Vie* (1970); *My Father, the Hero* (1994)—*Mon Pere, Ce Heros* (1991); *Mixed Nuts* (1994)—*Le Pere Noel Est Une Ordure* (1992); *12 Monkeys* (1995)—*The Jetty* (aka *La Jette*; *The Pier*) (1963); *The Associate* (1996)—*L'Associe* (1979); *Diabolique* (1996)—*Diabolique* (1955); *The Birdcage* (1996)—*La Cage aux Folles* (1978); *War of the Buttons* (1996)—*La Guerre Des Boutons* (aka *War of the Buttons*) (1961); *Head Above Water* (1996)—*Pathfinder* (1987); *Last Man Standing* (1996)—*Yojimbo* (1961); *Father's Day* (1997)—*Les Compères* (1983); *Jungle 2 Jungle* (1997)—*Little Indian, Big City* (aka *Un Indien dans La Ville*) (1994); *City of Angels* (1998)—*Wings of Desire* (aka *Der Himmel über Berlin*) (1988); *Nightwatch* (1998)—*Nattevagten* (1995); *EDtv* (1999)—*Louis 19, Le Roi des Ondes* (1994); *The Talented Mr. Ripley* (1999)—*Plein Soleil* (aka *Purple Noon*) (1960)

Renfrew of the Royal Mounted

Renfrew the singing Mountie had already appeared in Laurie York Erskine's books and on the radio before Monogram gave him his own film series. James Newill, a singer on the Burns and Allen radio show, played Sergeant Renfrew and always found time to sing a sturdy tune or two like "Mounted Men." Lightning the Dog accompanied him on his first trek, but Dave O'Brien became Renfrew's regular sidekick Kelly beginning with 1939's *Crashing Thru*. The plots were naturally action-oriented and somewhat lacking in plausibility (in *Sky Bandits*, the bad guys hijacked a plane carrying an experimental death ray). Newill later became one of the *Texas Rangers* (q.v.), creating the role that Tex Ritter would later play. See also **Mounties**.

Renfrew of the Royal Mounted (1937); On the Great White Trail (aka Renfrew of the Royal Mounted on the Great White Trail; Renfrew on the Great White Trail) (1938); Crashing Thru (1939); Fighting Mad (1939); Danger Ahead (1940); Yukon Flight (1940); Murder on the Yukon (1940); The Sky Bandits (1940)

Restaurants

Dozens of films have revolved around eating establishments and their employees, although few movies have taken place predominantly within the confines of a restaurant. Among those that have taken maximum advantage of the restaurant setting are the talkative *My Dinner with Andre* (1981), the classic screen adaptation of Robert E. Sherwood's *The Petrified Forest* (1936), the hostage drama *When You Comin' Back, Red Ryder?* (1979), and the stylish, but unpleasant, *The Cook, the Thief, His Wife & Her Lover* (1989). In the latter film, each room in the restaurant is bathed in a single dominant color — even the characters' clothes change color when they enter a room. *The Cook, the Thief, His Wife & Her Lover* also features a grisly scene in which one of the restaurant's patrons is served as a dish to the gangster that killed him. Other eateries with people on the menu were the subject of *Cannibal Girls* (1973), *Eating Raoul* (1982), and *Eat the Rich* (1987). Connoisseurs of fine food would also be advised to avoid the roadside diner in *Dying Room Only* (Cloris Leachman's husband disappears mysteriously) and the Chinese restaurant in *Return of the Dragon* (it's harassed by gangsters until diner employee Bruce Lee beats them all up). In contrast to such violence, other celluloid restaurants have been used as a pleasant place for friends to "hang out" in movies such as *American Graffiti* (1973), *Diner* (1982), *Swingers* (1996), and even *Mystery Men* (1999). Restaurants have also provided the setting for stories of love and friendship in *Bagdad Café* (1988), *Frankie and Johnny* (1991), and *Untamed Heart* (1993). Michelle Pfeiffer, who was a waitress in *Frankie and Johnny*, played a restaurant owner in *Tequila Sunrise* (1988). Other restaurant owners have been played by Charles Laughton (*Ruggles of Red Gap*), Joan Crawford (*Mildred Pierce*), Danny Aiello (*Do the Right Thing*), Mary Stuart Masterton (*Fried Green Tomatoes*), David Finch (*Lost & Found*), Sarah Michelle Gellar (*Simply Irresistible*), and Tony Shalhoub and Stanley Tucci in *Big Night*. Sometimes, it's hard to differentiate between a restaurant and a nightclub that serves food — but, to be on the safe side, one ought to include establishment owners Al Pacino in *Carlito's Way* and Humphrey Bogart in *Casablanca* (his place is called Rick's Café Americain). Laurence Olivier managed a posh restaurant, but didn't own it, in *Carrie* (1952). On the non-management side, restaurant waitresses and waiters have been portrayed by numerous actors, with Ellen Burstyn (*Alice Doesn't Live Here Anymore*) and Helen Hunt (*As Good as It Gets*) earning Best Actress

Oscars for their performances. Judy Garland sang the Oscar-winning song "On the Atchison, Topeka and the Santa Fe" as a waitress in *The Harvey Girls*. Surprisingly, films about chefs often take place outside of restaurants as evidenced by: *Under Siege* (Steven Seagal cooks aboard a ship), *Mr. Nice Guy* (Jackie Chan as a TV chef), *Babette's Feast* (a former chef cooks and keeps house for two sisters in 19th century Denmark), and *Who Is Killing the Great Chefs of Europe?* Along similar lines, not all eating establishments fit the typical definition of restaurant, such as the mobile grill housed aboard *The Van* (1996) and dining cars in train movies like *The Lady Vanishes* (1938). Finally, several movies have featured notable scenes in restaurants, to include: Meg Ryan's fake orgasm in *When Harry Met Sally...* (1989); the "how to tip" discussion in *Reservoir Dogs* (1992); the assassination scenes in *La Femme Nikita* (1990) and its American remake *Point of No Return* (1993); the stylish shootout in John Woo's *Hard-Boiled* (1992); Samuel Jackson's "Kung Fu" speech in *Pulp Fiction* (1994); Jack Nicholson ordering toast in *Five Easy Pieces* (1970); and the obese man who ate one wafer-thin mint too many in *Monty Python's The Meaning of Life* (1983). See also **Hotels**.

Bordertown (1935); Ruggles of Red Gap (1935); The Petrified Forest (1936); The Lady Vanishes (1938); Hi'ya Chum (1943); Casablanca (1943); Mildred Pierce (1945); The Harvey Girls (1946); The Postman Always Rings Twice (1946); The Time of Your Life (1948); Carrie (1952); The Undertaker and His Pals (1966); Bedazzled (1967); Alice's Restaurant (1969); Five Easy Pieces (1970); Road to Salina (1971); American Graffiti (1973); Cannibal Girls (1973); Return of the Dragon (aka Way of the Dragon) (1973); Dying Room Only (1973 TVM); Alice Doesn't Live Here Anymore (1974); Six-Pack Annie (1975); When You Comin' Back, Red Ryder? (1979); Lunch Wagon (aka Lunch Wagon Girls) (1980); My Dinner with Andre (1981); Waitress (1981); Diner (1982); Eating Raoul (1982); Monty Python's The Meaning of Life (1983); Over the Brooklyn Bridge (1984); Tampopo (1986); Babette's Feast (1987); Eat the Rich (1987); Mystic Pizza (1988); Tequila Sunrise (1988); Bagdad Café (aka Out of Rosenheim) (1988); Do the Right Thing (1989); The Cook, the Thief, His Wife & Her Lover (1989); When Harry Met Sally... (1989); La Femme Nikita (1990); Perfectly Normal (1990); Fried Green Tomatoes (1991); The Linguini Incident (1991); Frankie and Johnny (1991); Under Siege (1992); Hard-Boiled (1992); Combination Platter (1993); Untamed Heart (1993); Carlito's Way (1993); Point of No Return (1993); Chungking Express (1994); Eat Drink Man Woman (1994); It Could Happen to You (1994); Pulp Fiction (1994); Grumpier Old Men (1995); Bikini Bistro (1995); The Spitfire Grill (1996); The Van (1996); Big Night (1996); American Strays (1996); Heavy (1996); As Good as It Gets (1997); Mr. Nice Guy (1997); My Best Friend's Wedding (1997) (Julia Roberts as a restaurant critic); Good Burger (1997); A Chef in Love (1997); Down in the Delta (1998); Lost & Found (1999); Simply Irresistible (1999); Notting Hill (1999); Deterrence (1999)

Return of the Living Dead Series

Although *Alien* screenwriter Dan O'Bannon wrote and directed *Return of the Living Dead* (1985), John Russo deserves credit for making the film a reality. Russo, who cowrote *Night of the Living Dead* (1968) with George Romero, shared rights to the original story. That work provided the premise for O'Bannon's script about people-eating ghouls. Most of the similarities between O'Bannon's film and Romero's *Dead* trilogy end there. In *Return of the Living Dead*, employees at Uneeda Medical Supply accidentally release a secret government chemical that revives the dead. When a cadaver comes to life, they take it to a nearby morgue and burn the body — releasing the mysterious gas into the atmosphere. When it rains, the gas condenses, soaks into the soil, and turns a bunch of buried corpses into flesh-eating zombies craving human brains. Gory and funny, *Return of the Living Dead* clicked at the box-office. Ironically, it stole much of the thunder from *Day of the Dead* (1985), Romero's highly anticipated (but disappointing) conclusion to his *Night of the Living Dead* trilogy (q.v.). *Return of the Living Dead Part II*, a 1988 sequel written and directed by Ken Wiederhorn, basically reprised the first film. Critics and fans preferred *Return of the Living Dead 3* (1993), a clever little picture in which a teenager uses the mysterious gas to resurrect his dead girlfriend out of love. Like the same year's *Body Snatchers*, the film makes excellent use of its military base setting, drawing subtle parallels between government officials and ghouls. The 1974 film *Return of the Living Dead* is not a part of this series nor Romero's *Dead* trilogy. It is an alternate title for *Dead People*, a horror film produced by *American Graffiti* writers Willard Huyck and Gloria Katz. See also **Ghouls**; **Night of the Living Dead Series**.

Return of the Living Dead (1985); *Return of the Living Dead Part II* (1988); *Return of the Living Dead 3* (1993)

Revenge of the Nerds Series

In a clever bit of role reversal, the *Nerd* films portray nerdism as cool and yuppiedom as bogus. Unfortunately, most of the series' good ideas can be found in the first film, a likable 1984 comedy about a nerd fraternity formed by friends Lewis (Robert Carradine), Gilbert (Anthony Edwards), and Booger (Curtis Armstrong). The 1987 sequel followed Lewis and Booger to Fort Lauderdale for some bland hijinks at a United Fraternity Conference. Edwards appeared briefly as Gilbert. A belated third installment, the made-for-TV *Revenge of the Nerds III: The Next Generation* (1992), squandered a promising premise. Set several years later, it reveals that Lewis has become a yuppie, right down to the BMW with the LEWSTER license plate. Fortunately, he reverts to his old self when his nerdish nephew Harold encounters yuppie trouble at Adams College. In a second TV movie, *Revenge of the Nerds IV: Nerds in Love*, Booger gets married — an event originally broadcast in 3-D as part of a ratings stunt. Carradine and Armstrong appeared in all four *Nerds* films.

Revenge of the Nerds (1984); *Revenge of the Nerds II: Nerds in Paradise* (1987); *Revenge of the Nerds III: The Next Generation* (1992 TVM); *Revenge of the Nerds IV: Nerds in Love* (1994 TVM)

Revere, Johnny

John Paul (Johnny) Revere was another sturdy Western hero in the typical Republic Pictures mold. Eddie Dew played him in the first two films, getting comic support from Gene Autry's usual sidekick Smiley Burnette. Robert Mitchum played a bit part in 1943's *Beyond the Last Frontier*, but Dew's second entry, *Raiders of Sunset Pass*, was much more interesting. A sort of feminist Western, it pitted a group of tough ladies (dubbed the Women's Army of the Plains, or WAPs) against some male rustlers during World War II. Western series veteran Bob Livingston (see **The Three Mesquiteers**) replaced Dew in the final two entries.

Beyond the Last Frontier (1943); *Raiders of Sunset Pass* (1943); *Pride of the Plains* (1944); *Beneath Western Skies* (1944)

Riley, Dexter

Kurt Russell played this energetic, quick-thinking college student in a trilogy of Disney comedies produced in the 1970s. In each film, the easygoing Dexter acquired some superhuman trait while enjoying campus life at Medfield College. An electrical accident gave him super intelligence in *The Computer Wore Tennis Shoes*. He accidentally discovered an invisibility potion in *Now You See Him, Now You Don't*. A lab experiment gave him incredible strength in *The Strongest Man in the World*. Other series regulars included: Joe Flynn as Dexter's nemesis Dean Higgins; Cesar Romero as gangster A. J. Arno (who wants to steal the inventions); and William Schallert as nice Professor Quigley. Interestingly, Dexter bears a strong resemblance to an earlier Disney campus hero, Merlin Jones (Tommy Kirk), who appeared in *The Misadventures of Merlin Jones* (1964) and *The Monkey's Uncle* (1965). Kirk Cameron played Dexter Riley in a 1995 TV movie remake of *The Computer Wore Tennis Shoes*.

The Computer Wore Tennis Shoes (1969); *Now You See Him, Now You Don't* (1972); *The Strongest Man in the World* (1975); *The Computer Wore Tennis Shoes* (1995 TVM)

Riley, Old Mother

Donning a gray wig, a frumpy dress, and a plaid-colored shaw, British comedian Arthur Lucan transformed himself into Old Mother Riley, a spunky Irish washerwoman, in 15 features between 1937 and 1952. Katie MacShane, Lucan's wife, played Old Mother Riley's daughter. The two had created the characters in a vaudeville sketch called "Bridget's Night Out." Despite their popularity in Britain, the movies never caught on in the U.S., although 1952's *My Son, the Vampire* (aka *Old Mother Riley Meets the Vampire*) finally showed up on American screens in 1963. By then, Lucan had been dead for nine years and co-star Bela Lugosi for seven.

Old Mother Riley (aka *The Original Old Mother Riley, The Return of Old Mother Riley*) (1937); *Old Mother Riley in Paris* (1938); *Old Mother Riley Joins Up* (1938); *Old Mother Riley MP* (1939); *Old Mother Riley in Business* (1940); *Old Mother Riley's Ghosts* (1940); *Old Mother Riley's Circus* (1941); *Old Mother Riley in Society* (1942); *Old Mother Riley Detective* (1943); *Old Mother Riley Overseas* (1943); *Old Mother Riley at Home* (1944); *Old Mother Riley Headmistress* (1945); *Old Mother Riley's New Venture* (aka *Old Mother Riley's New Look*) (1947); *Old Mother Riley's Jungle Treasure* (aka *Jungle Treasure*) (1949); *My Son, the Vampire* (aka *Old Mother Riley Meets the Vampire; Vampires Over London*) (1952)

Road Movies

The *Road to Singapore* was originally written for George Burns and Gracie Allen. When they turned it down, it was revamped as a "buddy comedy" for Fred MacMurray and Jack Oakie. But prior commitments kept MacMurray and Oakie tied up, so Paramount — in a stroke of casting magic — paired Bing Crosby and Bob Hope for their musical comedy debut. Their initial *Road* picture (*Singapore*) was a huge success, but, when seen today, it clearly lacks the wacky humor that made the series memorable. Everyone has their favorite *Road* picture, but it's hard to top the bizarre Alaskan outing, *Road to Utopia*–which featured animated fish, the Paramount mountain, and the only ending in which Bob got the girl (well, sort of). Dorothy Lamour co-starred in all but

Road to Hong Kong, in which she made only a cameo appearance, leaving the female lead to a young Joan Collins.

Road to Singapore (1940); *Road to Zanzibar* (1941); *Road to Morocco* (1942); *Road to Utopia* (1945); *Road to Rio* (1947); *Road to Bali* (1952); *Road to Hong Kong* (1962)

Robin Hood *see* Hood, Robin

RoboCop

Director Paul Verhoeven's slick, ultraviolent approach masks the emotional core that separates *RoboCop* (1987) from its sequels and imitators. The film's central premise is a man's search to regain his identity — a theme Verhoeven would explore again in *Total Recall* (1990). Set in Detroit in the near future, *RoboCop* presents an urban world where crime has taken a stronghold and a private corporation called Omni Consumer Products (OCP) runs the police force. When police officer Alex Murphy (Peter Weller) barely survives a brutal gangland execution, OCP "erases" his memory and converts him into a cyborg crimefighter dubbed RoboCop. OCP programs RoboCop with three prime directives: (1) Serve the public trust; (2) Protect the innocent; and (3) Uphold the law. A fourth classified directive plays a critical role in the film's climax. Although Verhoeven stages some amazing action scenes and hits the mark with some clever satire, the film never loses its grip on RoboCop's struggle to regain at least part of his identity. At one point, he explains to his partner (Nancy Allen) that he can *feel* his family, but cannot *remember* them. *RoboCop 2* (1990) dispenses with such weighty matters for a more conventional tale about violent crime, corporate corruption, and cyborg law enforcers that malfunction. The film earned the wrath of many critics for its inclusion of a young criminal who spews profanity, deals in large-scale drug distribution, and kills without remorse. Director Irvin Kershner fared far better with his *Star Wars* sequel *The Empire Strikes Back* (1981). Peter Weller bowed out of the series after #2, with Robert Burke replacing him in *RoboCop 3*. Filmed in 1990 but unreleased in the U.S. until 1993, its plot had RoboCop rebelling against OCP when the corporation tried to evict innocent homeowners. Despite the disappointing returns for the third film, the syndicated *RoboCop: The Series* appeared on television in 1994. Richard Eden played the cyborg hero in these less violent weekly outings. An animated series appeared the same year. See also **Androids and Cyborgs**.

RoboCop (1987); *RoboCop 2* (1990); *RoboCop 3* (1993)

Robots

For purposes of categorization, robots are defined as machines requiring guidance to function and which look distinctively different from humans. Human-like machines capable of independent thought are discussed under the **Androids and Cyborgs** entry. Although it is a difficult distinction to draw, there are obvious differences between *Forbidden Planet*'s Robbie the Robot and the androids played by Rutger Hauer and Daryl Hannah in *Blade Runner*. The robot's origin in film can be traced back to early silent films like *The Electric Servant* (1909). Yet, while the Golem thrived in the early 1920s and the Frankenstein Monster ruled in the 1930s, robots were restricted to sporadic appearances in serials such as *The Phantom Empire* and *The Undersea King-*

dom. The robot's relative anonymity finally ended with 1951's *The Day the Earth Stood Still*. This superior science fiction saga worked on many levels, but remains fondly remembered for introducing the first robot "star": Gort. Standing 12-feet tall with no facial features nor visible joints, Gort was a rather imposing "mechanical man," especially when he opened his visor and unleashed his disintegration ray on a helpless tank. Gort could not talk, however, and that certainly placed some constraints on his personality. MGM corrected that quirk with its contribution to the robotic race, the ever-helpful — and talking — Robby the Robot. After his popular debut in 1956's *Forbidden Planet*, Robby turned up again in a larger role in *The Invisible Boy* (1957), in which a computer temporarily converted him to evil. Except for guest appearances, Robby retired after *The Invisible Boy*, although a robot bearing an amazing resemblance to him later joined the cast of TV's 1965–68 *Lost in Space* series. No other robotic stars emerged until 1977, when George Lucas' *Star Wars* introduced that charismatic robotic pair: C3PO and R2D2. Their skyrocketing popularity, especially among the younger set, revitalized interest in robots and accounted for their major supporting roles in films like *The Black Hole* and *Buck Rogers in the 25th Century* (both 1979). In other robot films of interest: The robot "drones" Huey, Dewey, and Louie in 1971's *Silent Running* appear to be the conceptual forerunners to R2D2. Lightning struck a meek little robot, No. 5, and brought him "alive" in *Short Circuit* (1986). Both King Kong (q.v.) and Godzilla (q.v.) fought robot versions of themselves in, respectively, *King Kong Escapes* (1968) and *The Terror of Godzilla* (1975). *Tobor, the Great* (1954) had the catchiest robot name (spell it backwards). See also **Androids and Cyborgs**; **Computers**.

The Electric Servant (1909); *The Day the Earth Stood Still* (1951); *Robot Monster* (1953); *Gog* (1954); *Target Earth* (1954); *Tobor the Great* (1954); *Forbidden Planet* (1956); *The Invisible Boy* (1957); *Attack of the Robots* (aka *Cards on the Table*; *Cartes sur la Table*) (1962); *King Kong Escapes* (1968); *Silent Running* (1971); *Terror of Godzilla* (aka *Terror of Mechagodzilla*) (1975); *Star Wars* (1977); *Buck Rogers in the 25th Century* (1979); *The Black Hole* (1979); *C.H.O.M.P.S.* (1979); *Runaway* (1984); *Chopping Mall* (aka *Killbots*) (1986); *Short Circuit* (1986); *Space Camp* (1986); *Robot Holocaust* (1987); *Too Much* (1987); *Short Circuit 2* (1988); *Robot Jox* (1990); *And You Thought Your Parents Were Weird* (1991); *Steel Justice* (1992 TVM); *Apex* (1994); *W.E.I.R.D. World* (1995 TVM); *Robo Warriors* (1996); *Fast, Cheap & Out of Control* (1997); *Flubber* (1997); *Lost in Space* (1998); *The Iron Giant* (1999); *Bicentennial Man* (1999)

Rock Singer Biographies *see* Pop, Rock, and Country Singer Biographies

Rockford, Jim

By the time James Garner appeared in the TV movie pilot *The Rockford Files* in 1974, he had forged a modestly successful film career and starred in TV series that were hits (*Maverick*) and misses (*Nichols*). The expectations for *The Rockford Files* were modest, but the results — a top 15 show in its first year — were a pleasant surprise for NBC. The easy-going Garner seemed born to play Jim Rockford, a private detective who had served time in prison for a crime he didn't commit. Rockford's colorful supporting characters included his former cellmate Angel Martin

(Stuart Margolin) and his retired father Rocky (played by Robert Donley in the pilot and Noah Beery, Jr., in the TV series). The series ran from 1974 to 1980 and ended when Garner decided to call it quits. After a 14-year hiatus, Garner revived his detective for *The Rockford Files: I Still Love L.A.*, a TV movie costarring Margolin and Joanna Cassidy as Rockford's ex-wife. Its rating success led to a series of Rockford TV movies. See also **Television Series Reunion Films**.

The Rockford Files (1974 TVM); *The Rockford Files: I Still Love L.A.* (1994 TVM); *The Rockford Files: A Blessing in Disguise* (1995 TVM); *The Rockford Files: Crime and Punishment* (1996 TVM); *The Rockford Files: Friends and Foul Play* (1996 TVM); *The Rockford Files: Godfather Knows Best* (1996); *The Rockford Files: If the Frame Fits…* (1996 TVM); *The Rockford Files: Murder and Misdemeanors* (1997 TVM); *The Rockford Files: If It Bleeds…It Leads* (1999 TVM)

Rocky

In 1976, an unknown character actor named Sylvester Stallone wrote a script (in three-and-a-half days, reportedly) about a mediocre, small-time boxer who gets a shot at the world championship. Producers Irwin Winkler and Robert Chartoff offered Stallone $300,000 for the screenplay, but the actor held out for $75,000, a percentage of the profits, and the lead role. He got what he wanted — and the rest is history. A simple picture, *Rocky* boasted a memorable cast: Talia Shire as Rocky's shy girlfriend, Burt Young as her obnoxious, hustling brother, Burgess Meredith as Rocky's grizzled manager, and Carl Weathers as cocky heavyweight champion Apollo Creed. Rocky lost the title bout (in a split decision), but audiences loved the film's old-fashioned emotion. It went on to gross $55 million and win an Academy Award for Best Picture. Subsequently, Stallone tried his hand at other movies, but none approached the success of *Rocky*. Thus, the inevitable sequel, *Rocky II*, appeared in 1979. A rehash of the original, it had Rocky winning a rematch with Creed and almost losing his wife due to medical complications. Although it was a box-office smash, Stallone vowed it would be the last *Rocky* picture. Nevertheless, no one was surprised when *Rocky III* was released in 1982. Probably the cleverest film in the series, it traced Rocky's decline as a champion, capped by a humiliating defeat at the hands of ruthless Clubber Lang (Mr. T) and the death of faithful manager Meredith. Encouraged by former opponent and new-found friend Apollo Creed, Rocky recaptured that "eye of the tiger" and beat Clubber into a pulp. Again, Stallone insisted this was the last of the series, but the box-office receipts led him to a different decision. The dismal *Rocky IV* followed in 1985, with Rocky avenging Creed's death at the hands of a heartless Russian "fighting machine" (Dolph Lundgren). Critics panned it, but audiences made it another hit, thereby leaving the door open for *Rocky V* (1990). Even audiences avoided this fifth outing, which found a retired Rocky training a young boxer. In 1999, MGM and Sylvester Stallone briefly discussed making a *Rocky VI*. See also **Boxing**.

Rocky (1976); *Rocky II* (1979); *Rocky III* (1982); *Rocky IV* (1985); *Rocky V* (1990)

Rodan

This pterodactyl-like creature with supersonic wing speed made an illustrious debut in 1956's *Rodan*. However, he never achieved the popularity of Godzilla (q.v.) or even Mothra (q.v.) and was quickly relegated to a supporting player in the mid–1960s Japanese "monsteramas." One of the reasons for Rodan's lesser fame might have been his weapon arsenal. While Godzilla boasted fiery breath and Mothra a cocoon-producing fluid, Rodan dispensed with foes (and buildings) by simply flapping his gigantic wings.

Rodan (1956); *Monster Zero* (aka *Invasion of the Astro-Monsters; Kaiju Daisenso*) (1965); *Ghidrah the Three-Headed Monster* (aka *the Greatest Battle on Earth; Sandai Kaiju Chikyu Saidai No Kessen*) (1965); *Destroy All Monsters* (aka *Operation Monsterland; Kaiju Soshingeki*) (1968)

Rodents

Rats have had an image problem in the movies, typically being pictured as untrustworthy. There have been exceptions, of course, such as the lovable rat family in the animated feature *The Secret of NIMH* (1982). And technically, the people-killing rats in *Willard* (1971) and *Ben* (1972) did not dispose of anyone who didn't deserve it. In fact, *Ben* was basically a heartwarming story of the friendship between a boy and his rat (and, lest we forget, this film featured Michael Jackson's popular hit "Ben"). Giant rats have populated horror films such as *Food of the Gods* (1976) and *Deadly Eyes* (1982). Sondra Locke's *Ratboy* (1986) was a sympathetic film about a disfigured boy who resembled a rat, while the Russian import *The Redeemer* (1977) was about rat people disguising themselves in order to infiltrate the human race. Chuck Norris killed a rat with his teeth in *Missing in Action 2— The Beginning* (1985), while people have tramped through rat-infested chambers in *Inferno* (1978) and *Indiana Jones and Last Crusade* (1989). On the other hand, mice on film have been portrayed as cute, charming creatures, especially in animated form. Thoughtful mice helped Cinderella get ready for the ball in Disney's 1950 version of the fairy tale. Adventurous mice formed the Mouse Rescue Aid Society in *The Rescuers* (1977). A sleuthing mouse resembling Sherlock Holmes matched wits with a devious rat (Professor Ratigan) in 1986's *The Great Mouse Detective*. One of the biggest holiday hits of 1986, *An American Tail,* concerned the plight of two immigrant mice children in turn-of-the-century New York City. Finally, people have been turned into mice in *Abbott and Costello Meet Dr. Jekyll and Mr. Hyde* (1953) and Roald Dahl's delightful children's fantasy *The Witches* (1990).

Cinderella (1950); *Abbott and Costello Meet Dr. Jekyll and Mr. Hyde* (1953); *Lady and the Tramp* (1955); *The Pied Piper of Hamlin* (1957 TVM); *The Aristocats* (1970); *Willard* (1971); *The Abominable Dr. Phibes* (1971); *The Rats Are Coming, the Werewolves Are Here* (1972); *Ben* (1972); *The Pied Piper* (1972); *Charlotte's Web* (1973); *The Missing Are Deadly* (1974 TVM); *Food of the Gods* (1976); *The Mouse and His Child* (1977); *The Redeemer* (1977); *The Rescuers* (1977); *Inferno* (1978); *Rock 'n' Roll High School* (1979); *Deadly Eyes* (aka *The Rats*) (1982); *The Secret of NIMH* (1982); *Of Unknown Origin* (1983); *Nightmares* (1983); *El Norte* (1983); *Missing in Action 2: The Beginning* (1985); *An American Tail* (1986); *Ratboy* (1986); *The Great Mouse Detective* (aka *The Adventures of the Great Mouse Detective*) (1986); *Indiana Jones and the Last Crusade* (1989); *Gnaw: Food of the Gods II* (1989); *The Witches* (1990); *Teenage Mutant Ninja Turtles* (1990); *The Rescuers Down Under* (1990); *An American Tail: Fievel Goes West* (1991); *Babe* (1995); *Mouse Hunt* (1997); *The Wind in the Willows* (1997); *A Rat's Tale* (1998); *The Phantom of the Opera* (1998); *Stuart Little* (1999); *The Green Mile* (1999); *The Bone Collector* (1999); *Flowers for Algernon* (2000 TVM)

Rodeos

Few filmmakers seemed interested in the rodeo setting prior to the 1970s. A handful of B-films, including the 3-D effort *Arena*, emerged in the 1950s. However, the rodeo gained more exposure through a bit part in 1956's *Bus Stop*, in which Don Murray played a naive rodeo star visiting the big city for the first time and struggling to understand urban conventions. Thirteen years later, *The Wild Bunch*, and its theme of the aging cowboy as a symbol of social change, revived interest in the contemporary cowboy. Subsequently, four features about aging rodeo stars appeared in 1972, all starring veteran performers well into their forties or older: Richard Widmark (age 58 in *When the Legends Die*), Cliff Robertson (47 in *J.W. Coop*), James Coburn (44 in *The Honkers*), and Steve McQueen (42 in *Junior Bonner*). The latter film was made by *Wild Bunch* director Sam Peckinpah. The plight of the younger rodeo wrangler was explored in *Riding Tall*, yet another 1972 release. It starred Andrew Prine as a rodeo rider coping with conventional love problems. The 1980 TV movie *Rodeo Girl* was the true story of world champion rodeo star Sue Pirtle. Luke Perry played real-life bull riding champion Lane Frost in *8 Seconds* (1994), the title referring to the amount of time a rider must stay on the bull. Documentaries include *Colorado Cowboy: The Bruce Ford Story* (1995) and *The Great American Cowboy* (1974), the life of rodeo legend Larry Mahan. Scott Glenn, who rode a mechanical bull in *Urban Cowboy* (1981), encountered a mean rodeo bull named Thunderbolt in *My Heroes Have Always Been Cowboys* (1991).

The Cowboy and the Lady (1938); *A Lady Takes a Chance* (aka *The Cowboy and the Girl*) (1943); *Rodeo* (1952); *The Lusty Men* (1952); *Bronco Buster* (1952); *Arena* (1953); *Bus Stop* (aka *The Wrong Kind of Girl*) (1956); *Born Reckless* (1959); *Stay Away Joe* (1968); *Black Rodeo* (1971); *The Honkers* (1972); *Junior Bonner* (1972); *J.W. Coop* (1972); *When the Legends Die* (1972); *Riding Tall* (aka *Squares*) (1972); *Cotter* (1973); *The Great American Cowboy* (1974); *Mustang Country* (1976); *Goldenrod* (1977 TVM); *Rodeo Girl* (1980 TVM); *My Heroes Have Always Been Cowboys* (1991); *The Cowboy Way* (1994); *8 Seconds* (1994); *F.T.W.* (1994); *Colorado Cowboy: The Bruce Ford Story* (1995); *Convict Cowboy* (1995 TVM); *Ruby Jean & Joe* (1996)

Rohmer's Comedies and Proverbs

Eric Rohmer initiated this new series in 1980 after completing his "Six Moral Tales" (q.v.) and two nonseries excursions, *The Marquise of O* and *Perceval*. Although less thematically linked than the "Moral Tales," Rohmer's "Comedies and Proverbs" extended the filmmaker's views on love, loneliness, and irony. In *The Aviator's Wife* (1980), a man pining for the title character forgets her after falling for an attractive student — whom he later discovers in the arms of another man as well. In *The Perfect Marriage* (1982), a woman tries to persuade a man that she will make the perfect wife and he will make the perfect husband — only to find out the man has been engaged to another all along. As with his "Moral Tales" series, critics ignored the early entries, while heaping praise on later ones like the international hit *Pauline at the Beach* (1982), *Boyfriends and Girlfriends* (1988), and *Summer* (1986). The original title of the latter film *Le Rayon Vert* actually translates as *The Green Ray*, referring to a "flash of green" seen in rare sunsets in Southern climates. Keeping with the series' theme, it opened with

a proverb from Rimbaud: "Ah, let the season start/ When fancy takes the heart." See also **Rohmer's Moral Tales; Rohmer's Tales of the Four Seasons**.

The Aviator's Wife (aka *La Femme de l'Aviateur*) (1980); *The Perfect Marriage* (aka *Le Beau Marriage*) (1982); *Pauline at the Beach* (aka *Pauline à la Plage*) (1982); *Full Moon in Paris* (aka *Les Nuits de la Pleine Lune*) (1984); *Summer* (aka *Le Rayon Vert; The Green Ray*) (1986); *Boyfriends and Girlfriends* (aka *L'Ami de Mon Amie; My Girlfriend's Boyfriend*) (1988)

Rohmer's Moral Tales

Eric Rohmer was best known as a writer and editor for the prestigious cinema journal *Cahiers du Cinema* when he set out to make a series of films linked by a common theme. His initial effort, the 1962 short *La Boulangère de Monceau*, established the premise for what would eventually comprise a six-film series. A young man about to commit to one woman meets a second woman who causes him to question his original choice. Rohmer expanded on that premise in 1963's hour-long *Suzanne's Profession*, but the series attracted little attention until his fourth entry, 1969's *My Night at Maud's*, garnered international raves. Rohmer completed his "Six Moral Tales" in 1972 with *Chloe in the Afternoon*. In the 1980s, he embarked on his "Comedies and Proverbs" (also referred to as "Parables") series. See also **Rohmer's Comedies and Proverbs; Rohmer's Tales of the Four Seasons**.

La Boulangère de Monceau (1962); *Suzanne's Profession* (aka *La Carriere de Suzanne*) (1963); *La Collectioneuse* (1967); *My Night at Maud's* (aka *Ma Nuit chez Maud*) (1969); *Claire's Knee* (aka *Le Genou de Claire*) (1970); *Chloe in the Afternoon* (aka *L'Amour, l'apres-midi; Love in the Afternoon*) (1972)

Rohmer's Tales of the Four Seasons

Love and the choices we make in life are the central themes in Eric Rohmer's four-film series revolving around the four seasons. A young girl tries to play matchmaker for her father and a high school teacher in *A Tale of Springtime*. In *Autumn Tale*, a widow must contend with *two* matchmakers eager to pair her up with their ideas of Mr. Right. *A Summer's Tale* finds a young student torn between three women. The most bittersweet entry, *A Tale of Winter*, focuses on a young woman named Felicie who has a passionate affair with a cook, Charles, at a beach resort. When her vacation ends, she loses contact with her lover and therefore cannot tell him that she has become pregnant. Five years later, in wintertime Paris, Felicie is wooed by two suitors and haunted by the memory of Charles and the life they could have had together. See also **Rohmer's Comedies and Proverbs; Rohmer's Moral Tales**.

A Tale of Springtime (aka *Conte de Printemps*) (1989); *A Tale of Winter* (aka *Conte d'hive*) (1992); *A Summer's Tale* (aka *Conte d'été*) (1996); *Autumn Tale* (aka *Conte d'automn*) (1998)

Roller Blade Seven Series

Producer-director Donald G. Jackson (*Hell Comes to Frogtown*) and martial artist Scott Shaw teamed up for this would-be series. Actually, the third film, *The Legend of the Roller Blade Seven*, is an edited combination of the first two. Jackson shot *The Roller Blade Seven* and *Return of the Roller Blade* back-to-back in the early 1990s for a total budget of $100,000. Both features starred

Shaw as Hawk, a long-haired martial artist/swordsmen sent on a rescue mission by B-movie veteran William Smith. The cast also included Frank Stallone (Sly's brother), Karen Black, and cable TV late movie hostess Rhonda Shear. Jackson claims he and Shaw shot the films without a script — an improvisational technique he dubbed "Zen filmmaking." Jackson alleges that executive producer Tanya York re-edited the films without his consent. Jackson also made the earlier unrelated pictures *Roller Blade* (1985) and *Roller Blade Warriors: Taken By Force* (1989) and he was the man behind the *Frogtown* trilogy (q.v.). See also **Roller Skating/Skateboards**.

The Roller Blade Seven (1991); *The Legend of the Roller Blade Seven* (1992); *Return of the Roller Blade Seven* (1993)

Roller Skating/Skateboards

On the silver screen, roller skating has never enjoyed the popularity of ice skating, although trendy filmmakers have tried to capitalize on both roller derby and roller disco fads. At the height of the roller derby craze in the early 1970s, Raquel Welch donned knee pads and a helmet for her rough-and-tumble title role in *Kansas City Bomber* (1972), the saga of a derby queen. A more enlightening look at those roller skating ladies was provided in the previous year's documentary *Derby*. James Caan participated in a futuristic, and even more violent, variation of roller derby in *Rollerball* (1975). The most unlikely champion roller skater was probably Mickey Rooney, who strapped on skates for 1950's *The Fireball*. The most graceful skaters were Fred Astaire and Ginger Rogers, who performed a roller skate dance number to "Let's Call the Whole Thing Off" in 1937's *Shall We Dance*. Later dancers have naturally lacked their polish. Scott Baio and Dorothy Stratten took to the disco dance floor on roller skates in *Skatetown, U.S.A.*, as did Linda Blair in *Roller Boogie* (1979). Mercifully, both movies slid out of theaters in no time. More interesting uses of roller skates can be found in *Return to Oz* (1985) and *Solarbabies*. In the former film, a gang of skating humanoids called the Wheelers pestered Dorothy. The futuristic teens in *Solarbabies* (1986) used skates as their primary means of transportation. Movies featuring skateboards include *Skateboard*, *Thrashin'*, *Gleaming the Cube*, and even *Back to the Future*. Bill Murray's *Loose Shoes* included a trailer for the make-believe movie "Skateboarders from Hell." See also **Back to the Future Series; Ice Skating; Roller Blade Seven**.

Shall We Dance (1937); *The Fireball* (1950); *It's Always Fair Weather* (1955); *Derby* (1971); *Kansas City Bomber* (1972); *Unholy Rollers* (1972); *Roll, Freddy, Roll* (1974 TVM); *Rollerball* (1975); *Rollerbabies* (1976); *Skateboard* (1977); *Skatetown U.S.A.* (1977); *Roller Boogie* (1979); *Xanadu* (1980); *Loose Shoes* (aka *Coming Attractions*) (1980); *The Personals* (1981); *Return to Oz* (1985); *Back to the Future* (1985); *Roller Blade* (1986); *Solarbabies* (1986); *Thrashin'* (1986); *Madame Sousatzka* (1988); *Gleaming the Cube* (1989); *Roller Blade Warriors* (1989); *Hook* (1991); *Prayer of the Rollerboys* (1991); *Airborne* (1993); *Brink!* (1998 TVM); *Blade Squad* (1998 TVM); *Dogma* (1999); *Big Daddy* (1999)

Room at the Top Series

This dour 1958 drama is best remembered for its frank attitude toward sex, its depressing northern England setting, and Simone Signoret's Oscar-winning performance as an ambitious young man's mistress. Laurence Harvey played Joe Lampton, the working-class lad determined to get to the top at all costs — even the death of his lover. Harvey returned to the role in 1965's *Life at the Top*, his character's ambition now replaced by disillusion. Kenneth Haigh starred as Lampton in a popular 1971–73 British TV series called *Man at the Top*. It subsequently led to a third film, 1975's *Man at the Top*, the dramatics now transformed into big business soap opera. John Braine wrote the original novel.

Room at the Top (1958); *Life at the Top* (1965); *Man at the Top* (1975)

The Rough Riders

Despite its title, this Monogram series had nothing to do with the early days of Teddy Roosevelt. Instead, it was just another Western series starring veteran screen cowboy Buck Jones. Jones had been Universal's major Western hero in the 1930s, but he was fading when Monogram cast him with Tim McCoy and Raymond Hatton as the Rough Riders. The trio played U.S. marshals with a penchant for infiltrating outlaw gangs. The series ended abruptly in 1942 when Jones died in the Cocoanut Grove nightclub fire while on a U.S. Savings Bonds campaign. Jones had actually escaped from the building, but was overcome by the flames when he returned to help others.

Arizona Bound (1941); *The Man from Bodie* (1941); *Forbidden Trails* (1941); *Below the Border* (1942); *Ghost Town Law* (1942); *Down Texas Way* (1942); *Riders of the West* (1942); *West of the Law* (1942)

Running

The melodic strains of the *Chariots of Fire* theme automatically bring to mind the vision of barefoot runners gliding across a sandy beach. That, plus the fact it won the 1981 Best Picture Oscar, makes *Chariots* the most well-known running film, but other pictures have covered the sport with equal depth. The 1962 *Loneliness of the Long Distance Runner* made Tom Courtenay a star for his portrayal of a lonely lad who finds solace in pounding a cross-country course. *See How She Runs* (1978), *Running* (1979), and *On the Edge* (1985) were more conventional examinations of the runner's psyche, dealing with the obsession and motivation that make some athletes push themselves to the limit. Olympic runners have been profiled in documentaries such as *Visions of Eight* and in the following fact-based biographies: *Running Brave* (Billy Mills), *Babe* (Babe Didrikson), *The Jesse Owens Story*, *Run for the Dream: The Gail Devers Story*, *Prefontaine* (Steve Prefontaine), *Without Limits* (Prefontaine again), and *Endurance* (Haile Gebrsellasie). Fictional features about Olympic runners include *The Loneliest Runner*, *The Games*, *Goldengirl*, and *Personal Best*.

Loneliness of the Long Distance Runner (1962); *Billie* (1965); *The Games* (1970); *Visions of Eight* (1973); *Babe* (1975 TVM); *Marathon Man* (1976); *The Loneliest Runner* (1976 TVM); *See How She Runs* (1978 TVM); *Goldengirl* (1979); *Running* (1979); *The Jericho Mile* (1979 TVM); *Three Hundred Miles for Stephanie* (1980 TVM); *Chariots of Fire* (1981); *Personal Best* (1982); *Running Brave* (1983); *The Terry Fox Story* (1983 TVM); *Courage* (aka *Raw Courage*) (1984); *The Jesse Owens Story* (1984 TVM); *On the Edge* (1985); *China Run* (1987); *Forrest Gump* (1994); *Run for the Dream: The Gail Devers Story* (1996 TVM); *Prefontaine* (1997); *Without Limits* (1998); *Endurance* (1999)

Rusty

Rusty was Columbia's answer to canine rival Lassie in this affable boy-and-dog series of the late 1940s. Al Martin wrote the series opener, 1945's *Adventures of Rusty*, which introduced Ted Donaldson as young Danny Mitchell and Rusty as his faithful German Shepherd, a former police dog. John Litel, best known as Henry Aldrich's (q.v.) dad, played Danny's father in the first three films before being replaced by Tom Powers. Ann Doran was Danny's stepmother. The stories usually centered on Danny's personal problems (e.g., misunderstandings with Dad in *For the Love of Rusty*), but it was Rusty who consistently saved the day. See also **Dogs**.

Adventures of Rusty (1945); *The Return of Rusty* (1946); *Son of Rusty* (1947); *For the Love of Rusty* (1948); *My Dog Rusty* (1948); *Rusty Leads the Way* (1948); *Rusty Saves a Life* (1949); *Rusty's Birthday* (1950)

Ryan, Jack

In Tom Clancy's bestselling novels, former Marine Jack Ryan gradually progressed from a CIA analyst (*The Hunt for Red October*) to deputy director of the CIA (*The Sum of All Fears*) to vice-president (*Debt of Honor*) to president (*Executive Orders*). On the silver screen, Ryan's career has not yet progressed to the Oval Office, but he has still been the subject of three hugely successful films. Alec Baldwin, in his first lead role, brought a youthful professionalism to the role of Ryan in *The Hunt for Red October*. To bolster the film's star power, Sean Connery was cast as the Russian submarine commander who may be a defector. The film's box-office success convinced Paramount that it had a potential franchise of Bondian proportions. The studio tried to sign Baldwin for a series of Jack Ryan movies, but the actor chose art over money and headed to the Broadway stage. Flustered, Paramount opted to go with a proven star and cast Harrison Ford as Ryan in *Patriot Games*. Some of Clancy's readers claimed that Ford—19 years older than the Ryan character—was miscast. But the moviegoing public found him to be a convincing hero and made the picture a hit. Ford returned for *Clear and Present Danger*, which reteamed him with director Phillip Noyce and Anne Archer as Ryan's wife Catherine. Plans for a fourth film stalled until 1999 when Paramount announced plans to make *The Sum of All Fears* with Ford. The Harrison Ford movie *Air Force One* has been compared with the Ryan films, since Ford plays the U.S. president and Jack becomes president in the Clancy novels.

The Hunt for Red October (1990); *Patriot Games* (1992); *Clear and Present Danger* (1994)

Ryder, Red

Republic Pictures first brought Fred Harmon's comic strip Western hero to the screen in the 1940 serial *The Adventures of Red Ryder*. Star Don Barry took the nickname "Red" and kept it for the rest of his career—but he was not Republic's choice to headline a Red Ryder film series. That distinction went to Wild Bill Elliott, a veteran B-Western star Republic lured away from Columbia in 1943. Elliott had acquired his nickname "Wild Bill" while playing Wild Bill Hickock (q.v.) in an earlier serial and series. Gabby Hayes played Elliott's grizzled sidekick in the first two Ryder pictures: 1944's *Tucson Raiders* and *Marshal of Reno*. But he was eventually dropped, allowing young Bobby Blake (Robert Blake of TV's *Baretta*) to assume the sidekick role as the Indian boy Little Beaver. After 16 films, Republic promoted Elliott to bigger pictures and signed Allan "Rocky" Lane to play Red. Lane had been a contract player since 1929 at Fox, Warners, and RKO before joining Republic as a serial star in 1940. His transition into the Ryder films went smoothly, assisted by Blake who provided continuity as Little Beaver. Lane played Red seven times before the Ryder series moved to Eagle Lion in 1949. After his acting career ended in 1961, Lane provided the voice of TV's *Mr. Ed*. The Eagle Lion pictures starred Jim Bannon, best-known as detective Jack Packard in Columbia's short-lived *I Love a Mystery* (q.v.) series. Don Reynolds co-starred as Little Beaver. Plagued by legal problems involving rights to the source comic strip, the Eagle Lion Red Ryder series folded within a year. See also **Comic Strip Characters**.

Tucson Raiders (1944) (Bill Elliott); *Marshal of Reno* (1944) (Elliott); *Vigilantes of Dodge City* (1944) (Elliott); *Cheyenne Wildcat* (1944) (Elliott); *The San Antonio Kid* (1944) (Elliott); *Sheriff of Las Vegas* (1944) (Elliott); *Marshal of Laredo* (1945) (Elliott); *Lone Texas Ranger* (1945) (Elliott); *The Great Stagecoach Robbery* (1945) (Elliott); *Phantom of the Plains* (1945) (Elliott); *Colorado Pioneers* (1945) (Elliott); *Wagon Wheels Westward* (1945) (Elliott); *Sun Valley Cyclone* (1946) (Elliott); *Sheriff of Redwood Valley* (1946) (Elliott); *California Gold Rush* (1946) (Elliott); *Conquest of Cheyenne* (1946) (Elliott); *Santa Fe Uprising* (1946) (Allan Lane); *Stagecoach to Denver* (1946) (Lane); *Homesteaders of Paradise Valley* (1947) (Lane); *Rustlers of Devil's Canyon* (1947) (Lane); *Vigilantes of Boom Town* (1947) (Lane); *Marshal of Cripple Creek* (1947) (Lane); *Oregon Trail Scouts* (1947) (Lane); *The Fighting Redhead* (1949) (Jim Bannon); *The Cowboy and the Prizefighter* (1949) (Bannon); *Roll, Thunder, Roll* (1949) (Bannon); *Ride, Ryder, Ride* (1949) (Bannon)

Sabata

When Clint Eastwood abandoned the Italian "spaghetti Westerns" that made him an international star in the 1960s, Lee Van Cleef stepped right into his boots. Van Cleef had the necessary credentials—he had played opposite Eastwood in two of the three "Man with No Name" (q.v.) films: *For a Few Dollars More* (1965) and *The Good, the Bad, and the Ugly* (1967). Furthermore, Van Cleef made the perfect anti-hero and his well-groomed mustache and classy duds contrasted nicely with Eastwood's scruffy character. Thus, by all accounts, 1970's *Sabata* should have made Van Cleef a superstar. However, that never occurred, although *Sabata* enhanced Van Cleef's popularity among European moviegoers. His character—a friendly variation of his earlier bad guys—gambled freely, shot people without remorse, and broke the law if it suited his purpose. He also carried gimmicky guns (e.g., a derringer that fires an extra bullet from the handle). The year after *Sabata* was released, a film called *Adios, Sabata* appeared in theaters. At first glance, it looks like a sequel with Yul Brynner replacing Van Cleef in the title role. However, it's actually a completely different film also known as *Indigo Black*. Its producers redubbed the film, changing the name of Brynner's character from Black to Sabata. This is confusing, to say the least, since Yul wears a black outfit (including an unbuttoned shirt which would never be found in Sabata's wardrobe). Interestingly, Van Cleef and Eastwood pursued a character named Indio in *For a Few*

Dollars More. As for the real Sabata, Van Cleef came back to play him in 1972's *The Return of Sabata*. Gianfranco Parolini, a director with a fetish for quick zooms, helmed all three films, and Ignazio Spalla played supporting roles.

> *Sabata* (aka *Ehi Amico… C'è Sabata, Hai Chiuso!*) (1970); *Adios, Sabata* (aka *Indigo Black*; *Indio Black Sai Che to Dico: Sei Un Gran Giglio…*) (1971); *The Return of Sabata* (aka *È tornato Sabata… Hai Chiuso Un'altra V*olta) (1972)

The Saint

Leslie Charteris' dapper adventurer Simon Templar walked a thin line between crime and the law. His moniker, The Saint, was derived from his initials S.T. and his calling card featured a stick figure with a halo. The movies never alluded to the Saint's criminal tendencies—he was strictly a good guy with a mischievous streak. George Sanders was the screen's busiest Saint, although Louis Hayward and Hugh Sinclair each starred in two movies. Jean Marais played the class-conscious sleuth on the French screen. In the 1960s, Roger Moore made the role his own with a highly successful TV series, which even spawned a theatrical film (composed of two episodes). Although Moore's show ended in 1969, fellow Brit Ian Ogilvy starred in a short-lived revival series, *The Return of the Saint*, nine years later. In 1997, Paramount tried unsuccessfully to launch a new franchise with *The Saint* starring Val Kilmer as Simon Templar. Kilmer seemed like a good choice for Templar based on his easy-going charm as Bruce Wayne in *Batman Forever*. But *The Saint* saddled him with a glum character (not at all like the one Charteris created) and a tired plot about a formula for cold fusion.

> *The Saint in New York* (1938) (Louis Hayward); *The Saint in London* (1939) (George Sanders); *The Saint Strikes Back* (1939) (Sanders); *The Saint's Double Trouble* (1940) (Sanders); *The Saint Takes Over* (1940) (Sanders); *The Saint in Palm Springs* (1941) (Sanders); *The Saint Meets the Tiger* (1941) (Hugh Sinclair); *The Saint's Vacation* (1941) (Sinclair); *The Saint's Girl Friday* (aka *The Saint Returns*) (1953) (Hayward); *The Fiction-Makers* (1968 TVM) (Roger Moore); *The Saint and the Brave Goose* (1981 TVM) (Ian Ogilvy); *The Saint* (1997) (Val Kilmer)

St. Trinian's Series

An unruly girls' school where young ladies spent more time studying betting sheets than history, St. Trinian's provided the setting for a popular series of British farces spanning 26 years. The director-writing team of Frank Launder and Sidney Gilliat created the series, but it was droll comic genius Alastair Sim who made the first entries consistently entertaining. Actually, Launder, Gilliat, and Sim had teamed up earlier for 1950's *The Happiest Days of Your Life*, a riotous comedy about a girls' school (St. Swithin) which was accidentally "displaced" into a boys' school (Nutbourne). Sim and Margaret Rutherford played the respective heads of the schools, but they generously devoted screen time to their youthful, mischievous co-stars. *The Belles of St. Trinian's* (1954) initiated the series proper and introduced a swarm of rebellious girls which made St. Swithin's look like a charm school. Sim was doubly delightful as both the headmistress (in drag, of course) and her brother. Sim also appeared, albeit too briefly, in 1958's follow-up *Blue Murder at St. Trinian's*, in which a jewel thief on the lam wishes he had never stumbled into the "perfect hiding place." Launder and Gilliat produced two additional lackluster entries without Sim. The series apparently ended with 1966's *The Great St. Trinian's Train Robbery*. However, Launder returned to the school 14 years later for *The Wildcats of St. Trinian's*, a time-capsule comedy that failed to find an audience. Gilliat served as a production consultant, but did not have an active role in the writing chores. Launder and Gilliat broke into the movies as writers in the 1930s. They penned the screenplay for Hitchcock's classic *The Lady Vanishes* (1937) as well some of the Inspector Hornleigh (q.v.) films. See also **Boarding Schools**.

> *The Belles of St. Trinian's* (1954); *Blue Murder at St. Trinian's* (1958); *The Pure Hell of St. Trinian's* (1961); *The Great St. Trinian's Train Robbery* (1966); *The Wildcats of St. Trinian's* (1980)

Samurai Trilogy

Hiroshi Inagaki adapted Eiji Yoshikawa's acclaimed novel *Musashi* in 1941—only to return to the same literary source in 1954 with *Miyamoto Musashi*. This remake, the first part of an epic trilogy, eclipsed the original in presenting the legend of the 17th century Japanese samurai/philosopher. It won an honorary Academy Award as best foreign film of 1955 (the category for Best Foreign Language Film was created the following year). *Miyamoto Musashi* opens with the young man Takezo (Toshiro Mifune) and his best friend Matahachi (Rentaro Mikuni) leaving the village of Miyamoto with dreams of becoming great warriors. After surviving the bloody Battle of Sekigahara, they encounter Oku (Mitsuko Mito) and her daughter Akemi (Mariko Okada). When Matahachi becomes Oku's lover, Takezo returns to Miyamoto alone and explains what happened to his friend's family and betrothed, Otsu (Kaoru Yachigusa). Matahachi's angry parents refuse to believe their son would dishonor them and Otsu. When they demand that Takezo be arrested for treason, he seeks sanctuary in Priest Takuan's temple. In an unlikely turn of events, Takezo and Otsu fall in love. He studies to become a samurai and takes the name Musashi. At the film's conclusion, he leaves Otsu behind—temporarily one hopes—to seek enlightenment. *Miyamoto Musashi* is less a traditional samurai film than a character study and love story enhanced by Jun Yasumoto's stunning color photography. When released in the U.S., it included narration by William Holden, apparently to clarify story points for Western audiences. In the second part of the trilogy, *Duel at Ichijoji Temple* (1955), Musashi earns a reputation as a master swordsman—his accomplishments attracting the attention of a young samurai named Kojira Saski (Koji Tsuruta). Both Otsu and Akemi wait for Mushashi. However, when Mushashi declares his love for Otsu in a violent fashion, he dishonors her and leaves in disgrace. In the final installment, *Duel at Ganryu Island* (1956), Mushashi leaves behind his samurai days and becomes a farmer. When bandits threaten the village, though, he takes up his sword to protect its residents. He also declares his love for Otsu, who, along with Akemi, has followed him. The film ends with a spectacular sunset duel on the beach between Musashi and Kojira Saski. The second and third films, while always interesting, lack the emotional impact of the first, which devotes the most time to the Musashi-Otsu love story. Additionally, the subplot involving the village and the bandits in *Duel at Ganryu Island* seems lifted from *The Seven Samurai* (1954). Director Hiroshi Inagaki also made *Kojira* (1967), which naturally focused on the life of Musashi's

Ganryu Island opponent. The real-life Musashi wrote many books, including *The Book of Five Rings*, an essay on samurai strategy that business executives of the 20th century adopted as a guide on effective management techniques.

Samurai 1: Miyamoto Musashi (aka *Miyamoto Musashi*; *The Legend of Musashi*; *Master Swordsman*) (1954); *Samurai 2: Duel at Ichijoji Temple* (aka *Ichijoji No Ketto*; *Samurai 2: Ichijoji No Ketto*; *Zoku Miyamoto Musashi*) (1955); *Samurai 3: Duel at Ganryu Island* (aka *Ketto Ganryu Jima*; *Samurai 3: Ketto Ganryu Jima*; *Miyamoto Musashi Yori: Ketto Ganryu Jima*) (1956)

Sanders, Commissioner Harry

Prolific mystery writer Edgar Wallace created Commissioner Sanders, a stern administrator stationed in Africa, with 1911's *Sanders of the River*. However, in their lavish 1935 film version, Alexander and Zoltan Korda made Sanders a more mellow character and relegated him to a supporting role. Paul Robeson took top billing as Bosambo, a native chief loyal to the British and a friend of Sanders (Leslie Banks). The plot pitted Sanders against ruthless traders, while Bosambo confronts a rebellious rival chief. The film is remembered chiefly for its striking on-location photography and its unintentionally depressing view of British colonialism. Although the film did not spawn a sequel, Francis Gerard penned the novel *Return of Sanders of the River* in 1939. Three decades later, British actor Richard Todd starred as Sanders in two inexpensive B-pictures. The first Todd film, 1963's *Sanders of the River*, was a loose adaptation that found Sanders investigating a murder in an African hospital. The 1964 follow-up, *Coast of Skeletons*, found Sanders encountering a gang of diamond-seeking heavies in southwest Africa. Sanders' creator Edgar Wallace wrote over 170 novels during his career, many of which were adapted by German filmmakers in the 1950s. Wallace also wrote the original story for the 1933 classic *King Kong* (q.v.).

Sanders of the River (aka *Bosambo*) (1935); *Sanders of the River* (aka *Death Drums Along the River*) (1963); *Coast of Skeletons* (1964)

El Santo

Mexican wrestler El Santo, whose trademark silver mask covered his head, achieved fame in the ring long before he became a film star. The wrestler, whose real name was Rodolfo Guzman Huerta, had fought under other names, but fame eluded him until he created his El Santo (The Saint) persona in 1942. A year later, he won the first of several national Mexican titles, becoming famous for his "la de a caballo" (arm camel clutch) finishing move and for wearing the silver mask (which he never removed). El Santo was a national celebrity and comic book hero when he made the Cuban-produced wrestling movie *The Brain of Evil* (aka *El Cerebro del Mal*) (1958). He eventually signed with Mexican producer Alberto Lopez and starred in *Santo vs. the Zombies* (1961). This film laid the groundwork for other Santo films that portrayed the Silver Masked One as a wrestler-crimefighter. These wild, action-packed films peaked in popularity during the 1960s, a decade in which the silver-masked wrestler fought a plethora of vampires, zombies, witches, man-made monsters, and other wrestlers. Rival wrestlers the Blue Demon (q.v.) and Neutron (q.v.) were introduced in the mid–1960s. Neutron made little impact, but the Blue Demon eventually costarred with Santo in 1969's *Santo Against Blue Demon in Atlantis*. Its success led to additional wrestler pair-

ings, culminating in the Mexican monster extravaganza *Santo and Blue Demon vs. the Monsters*, which pitted the tag team against three vampires, a mummy, a cyclops, a Frankenstein monster, a mad doctor, and a robot double of the Blue Demon. Between 1963 and 1974, Santo often made several films a year while continuing to make live appearances in the ring. However, the popularity of wrestling movies in Mexico declined quickly in the mid–1970s. By the early 1980s, El Santo — who was now in his sixties — retired from acting and wrestling. One of his final film appearances was a cameo in 1981's *Chanoc y el Hijo del Santo vs. Los Vampiros Asesinos* (*Chanoc and The Son of Santo vs. the Killer Vampires*) in which he introduced his son El Hijo del Santo as his heir apparent. Three years later, Rodolfo Guzman Huerta, the man behind the silver mask, died of a heart attack. In 1992, El Hijo del Santo made *Santo: La Leyenda del Enmascarado de Plata* (*Santo: The Legend of the Silver-Masked One*), in which Daniel Garcia played the role of younger Santo's father. Interestingly, the Santo films remained relatively unknown in the U.S. until cable networks gave them new exposure in the 1980s. Even then, Santo faced an identity crisis since some dubbed prints referred to him as Samson. See also **Blue Demon**; **Neutron**; **Wrestling**. In the following list, the dates refer to when the films were produced, since release dates could not be confirmed.

The Brain of Evil (aka *El Cerebro del Mal*) (1958); *Santo vs. the Infernal Men* (aka *Santo Contra Hombres Infernales*) (1958); *Santo vs. the Zombies* (aka *Invasion of the Zombies*; *Santo Contra los Zombies*) (1961); *Santo vs. the King of Crime* (aka *Santo Contra el Rey de Crimen*) (1961); *Santo in the Hotel of the Dead* (aka *Santo en el Hotel de la Muerte*) (1961); *Santo Against the Diabolical Brain* (aka *Santo Contra el Cerebro Diabólico*) (1961); *Samson vs. the Vampire Women* (aka *Santo Contra las Mujeres Vampiras*) (1962); *Samson in the Wax Museum* (aka *Santo in the Wax Museum*; *Santo en el Museo de Cera*) (1963); *Santo vs. the Strangler* (aka *Santo Contra el Estrangulador*) (1963); *The Ghost of the Strangler* (aka *Espectro del Estrangulador*; *Santo Contra el Espectro*) (1963); *Santo Attacks the Witches* (aka *The Witches Attack*; *Santo Ataca a las Brujas*; *Atacan las Brujas*) (1964); *The Diabolical Hatchet* (aka *El Hacha Diabólica*) (1965); *Grave Robbers* (aka *Profanadores de Tumbas*) (1965); *Santo vs. Baron Brakola* (aka *Santro Contra el Barón Brakola*) (1965); *Santo vs. the Martian Invasion* (aka *Santo Contra Invasión de los Marcianos*) (1966); *Santo vs. The Villains of the Ring* (aka *Santo el Enmascarado de Plata vs. Los Villanos del Ring*) (1966); *Operation 67* (aka *Operación 67*) (1966); *The Treasure of Montezuma* (aka *El Tesoro de Montezuma*) (1966); *Santo and Dracula's Treasure* (aka *Santo en el Tesoro de Drácula*; *El Vampiro y el Sexo*) (1968); *Santo vs. Capulina* (1968); *Santo Against Blue Demon in Atlantis* (aka *Santo Contra Blue Demon en la Atlántida*) (1969); *Santo and Blue Demon vs. the Monsters* (aka *Santo y Blue Demon Contra los Monstruós*) (1969); *The World of the Dead* (aka *El Mundo de los Muertos*) (1969); *Santo vs. the Head Hunters* (aka *Santo Contra los Cazadores de Cabezas*) (1969); *Santo Faces Death* (aka *Santo Frente a la Muerte*) (1969); *Santo vs. the Riders of Terror* (aka *Santo Contra los Jinetes del Terror*) (1970); *Santo in the Revenge of the Vampire Women* (aka *Santo en la Venganza de las Mujeres Vampiras*) (1970); *Santo vs. the Vice Mafia* (aka *Santo Contra la Mafia del Vicio*) (1970); *Santo in the Mummy's Revenge* (aka *Santo en la Venganza de la Momia*) (1970); *The Mummies of Guanajuato* (aka *Las Momias de Guanajuato*) (1970); *Santo Against the Daughter of Frankenstein* (aka *The Daughter of Frankenstein*; *Santo Contra la Hija de Frankenstein*) (1971); *Suicide Mission* (aka *Misión Suicida*) (1971); *Murderers from Other Worlds* (aka *Asesinos de Otros Mundos*; *Killers from Other Worlds*) (1971); *The Royal Eagle* (aka *El Águila Real*; *Santo y la Tigresa en el Águila*) (1971);

Santo and Blue Demon vs. Dracula and the Wolf Man (aka *Santo y Blue Demon Contra Dracula y el Hombre Lobo*) (1972); *Santo versus the Kidnappers* (aka *Santo Contras Los Secuestradores*) (1972); *Santo Against the Black Magic* (aka *Santo Contra la Magia Negra*) (1972); *The Beasts of Terror* (aka *Las Bestias del Terror*) (1972); *Santo vs. the She Wolves* (aka *Santo vs. Las Lobas*) (1972); *Anonymous Death Threat* (aka *Anónimo Mortal*) (1972); *Santo and Blue Demon vs. Dr. Frankenstein* (aka *Santo y Blue Demon Contra el Dr. Frankenstein*) (1973); *Santo vs. the Dr. Death* (aka *Santo Contra el Dr. Muerte*; *Masked Man Strikes Again*) (1973); *Santo in the Mystery of the Black Pearl* (aka *Santo en el Misterio de la Perla Negra*) (1974); *Santo and Mantequilla in The Vengeance of the Crying Woman* (aka *Santa y Mantequilla en la Venganza de la Llorona*) (1974); *Santo in Black Gold* (aka *La Noche de San Juan*; *Santo en Oro Negro*; *Night of San Juan*) (1975); *Mystery in Bermuda* (aka *Misterio en las Bermudas*) (1977); *Santo on the Border of Terror* (aka *Santo en la Frontera del Terror*) (1979); *Santo vs. the TV Killer* (aka *Santo Contra el Asesino de la T.V.*) (1981); *Chanoc and the Son of Santo vs. the Killer Vampires* (aka *Chanoc y el Hijo del Santo vs. Los Vampiros Asesinos*) (1981); *The Fist of Death* (aka *El Puño de la Muerte*) (1982); *The Fury of the Karate Experts* (aka *La Furia de los Karatecas*) (1982); *Santo: The Legend of the Silver-Masked One* (aka *Santo: La Leyenda del Enmascarado de Plata*) (1992)

Sarah, Plain and Tall Series

Patricia MacLachlan's award-winning novel *Sarah, Plain and Tall* reached television in 1991 as a presentation of the Hallmark Hall of Fame. Set in the early 1900s, it starred Glenn Close as Sarah Wheaton, a Maine spinster who answers a newspaper ad placed by widower father Jacob Witting (Christopher Walken). Sarah, who describes herself as "plain and tall," journeys to the Witting's prairie home to see if she can "make a difference" during a 30-day trial period. Viewers responded warmly to the slow-building relationship between Sarah and Jacob, making *Sarah, Plain and Tall* one of the most successful TV movies of 1991. Television audiences also embraced *Skylark*, the 1993 sequel written by MacLachlan and again starring Close and Walken. It pitted the now-married couple against a severe drought that threatened their farm. Close earned Emmy nominations for Best Actress in a Special or Miniseries for both films. In a third installment, *Sarah, Plain and Tall: Winter's End* (1999), Jack Palance joined Close and Walken as Jacob's father who returns home to make peace with his son. See also **Mail Order Brides**.

Sarah, Plain and Tall (1991 TVM); *Skylark* (aka *Skylark: The Sequel to Sarah, Plain and Tall*) (1993 TVM); *Sarah, Plain and Tall: Winter's End* (1999 TVM)

Sartana

While most spaghetti Western gunfighters killed for revenge or profit, Sartana served a higher justice as an "Angel of Death." Sometimes, he pitted evil against evil, giving men of greed just enough rope to hang themselves. However, he typically rendered his final verdict with his deadly aim. John (Gianni) Garko played the Western vigilante in five films, with George Hilton taking over for a final entry. Spaghetti Western enthusiasts recognize the six Garko/Hilton films as the "official" series. However, there were many other Italian-made Westerns featuring a character named Sartana. To make matters more confusing, Garko played a different character named Sartana in the 1967 movie *One Thousand Dollars on the Black*. That film was released two years later

with a new title (*Sartana's Blood at Sundown*) and promoted as one of the Sartana films. Despite their popularity in Europe, the Sartana films never achieved the American success of the Sergio Leone–Clint Eastwood *Man with No Name* movies (q.v.) nor the later *Trinity* series (q.v.).

Sartana (aka *Se Incontri Sartana Prega per la Tua Morte*; *If You Meet Sartana…Pray for Your Death*; *Gunfighters Die Harder*) (1968) (John Garko); *I Am Sartana…Your Angel of Death* (aka *Sono Sartana, il Vostro Becchino*; *Sartana and the Gravedigger*) (1969) (Garko); *Sartana Kills Them All* (aka *Lo Irritarono…e Sartana Fece Piazza Pulita*) (1970) (Garko); *Light the Fuze…Sartana Is Coming* (aka *Una Nuvola di Porvere…un Grido di Morte Arriva Sartana*) (1971) (Garko); *Have a Good Funeral, My Friend…Sartana Will Pay* (aka *Buon Funerale, Amigos…Paga Sartana*) (1971) (Garko); *I Am Sartana…Trade Your Guns for a Coffin* (aka *Ce Sartana, Vendi la Pistola e Comprati la Bara*) (1972) (George Hilton)

Scanners Series

A marketing campaign emphasizing its eye-popping visual effects turned 1981's *Scanners* into a modest mainstream hit for Canadian cult director David Cronenberg. Thematically, this science fiction thriller differs little from Cronenberg's previous and subsequent works — all of which revolve around human metamorphosis (e.g., an operation turns a woman into a blood-seeking killer in 1977's *Rabid*, an experiment transforms a man into a mutant in 1986's *The Fly*). In *Scanners*, a drug has created a race of humans with telekinetic powers who roam as social outcasts through a city of the near-future. There are good scanners and bad ones, and two opposing brothers engage in a climactic telekinetic showdown that results in eyeballs spurting out of their sockets. Despite such occasional descents into visual gore, *Scanners* emerged as a stylish film with a sound following. Yet, as Cronenberg progressed to bigger-budgeted films, the likelihood of a *Scanners* sequel appeared to fade forever. However, in the early 1990s, executive producer Pierre David mounted a modest four-film series built around Cronenberg's original premise. *Scanners II: The New Order* (1991) sacrificed original storytelling for visual flair. Once again, a good scanner tracks down a bad one and saves other scanners from a power-hungry "normal" human. The only new element was a drug addiction theme (we learn that scanners can be controlled by an addictive drug that relieves their mental pain). *Scanners III: The Takeover* (1992) featured an evil female scanner who learns that she can "scan" normal humans via television. David produced, directed, and cowrote a fourth entry, *Scanner Cop* (1994), about an LAPD rookie (Daniel Quinn) who uses his scanning powers to thwart a mad scientist turning innocent people into cop killers. Quinn returned for the following year's *Scanner Cop 2*, which pitted his police hero against a scanner-killing scanner. See also **Telekinesis**.

Scanners (1981); *Scanners II: The New Order* (1991); *Scanners III: The Takeover* (1992); *Scanner Cop* (1994); *Scanner Cop 2* (aka *Scanner Cop 2: Volkin's Revenge*; *Scanners: The Showdown*) (1995)

The Scarlet Pimpernel

Emma Magdalena Rosalia Maria Josefa Barbara Orczy — better known as Baroness Orczy — created one of the cinema's most memorable swashbucklers in her 1905 novel *The Scarlet Pimpernel*. Set during the French Revolution, Orczy's tale centers on Sir Percy Blakeney, an English gentleman who leads a double life. In

England, he plays the part of a fop described as "the sleepiest, dullest, most British Britisher that had ever set a pretty woman yawning." In France, though, he assumes the guise of the gallant Scarlet Pimpernel, who stages daring rescues to spare aristocrats from the bloody blade of the guillotine. Orczy's novel, first published as a play, was a huge success and spawned a series of Pimpernel books. Its inevitable transition to the silver screen first occurred in 1917 with an obscure version produced by Fox. Three other silent films followed, all based on Orczy novels: Cecil Humphreys played the title role in *The Elusive Pimpernel* (1920); Holmes Herbert played the lead in *I Will Repay* (1923); and Matheson Lang was Sir Percy in *The Triumph of the Scarlet Pimpernel* (1928). In 1934, producer Alexander Korda mounted the most famous version of Orczy's novel, with Leslie Howard excelling as both the dandyish gentleman and the cavalier Pimpernel. Merle Oberon sparkled as Percy's puzzled wife Marguerite and Raymond Massey oozed venom as the villain Chauvelin. Still, the film belonged to Howard, who tossed off the classic movie line: "They seek him here, they seek him there / Those Frenchies seek him everywhere / Is he in Heaven? Is he in Hell? / That damned elusive Pimpernel!" Korda co-produced a less-successful 1938 sequel, *The Return of the Scarlet Pimpernel*, with Barry Barnes replacing the incomparable Howard. Three years later, Howard produced, directed, and starred in *Pimpernel Smith*, which updated the action to World War II and cast Howard as an apparently absent-minded professor who rescued refugees from the Nazis. The 1950 Swedish film *Pimpernel Svesson* featured a similar plot with Edvard Persson going behind the Iron Curtain. The 1945 film *Paris Underground* (aka *Madame Pimpernel*) also takes place during World War II, but it's a *Pimpernel* movie in name only. Constance Bennett and Gracie Fields starred in the fact-based story of two women who smuggle Allied aviators out of Nazi-occupied France. Korda returned to Orczy's novel in 1953 when he convinced Michael Powell and Emeric Pressberger to make *The Elusive Pimpernel* starring David Niven. Occasionally conceived as a musical, the film featured plenty of style (e.g., animated stars represent a sneeze), but oddly lacked charm — perhaps because Powell never wanted to make it. In the 1960s, the *Carry On* (q.v.) movies spoofed the Pimpernel with *Don't Lose Your Head* (1967). An unexpectedly lavish TV movie surfaced in 1982 with Anthony Andrews as a dashing Pimpernel, Jane Seymour as a beautiful and intelligent Marguerite, and brooding Ian McClellan as Chauvelin. In 1999, Richard E. Grant took his turn as Sir Percy in the A&E cable network's adaptation of *The Scarlet Pimpernel*. Sir Percy's first appearance on television was in the form of Marius Goring who starred in *The Scarlet Pimpernel*, a 1958 syndicated TV series. A Broadway musical of *The Scarlet Pimpernel*, written by Frank Wildhorn and Nan Knighton, opened in 1997. Though panned by many critics, it blossomed into a moderate hit, thanks to the popularity of star Douglas Sills.

The Scarlet Pimpernel (1917); *The Elusive Pimpernel* (1920); *I Will Repay* (1923); *The Triumph of the Scarlet Pimpernel* (1928); *The Scarlet Pimpernel* (1934); *Return of the Scarlet Pimpernel* (1938); *Pimpernel Smith* (aka *Mister V*; *The Fighting Pimpernel*) (1941); *Pimpernel Svensson* (1950); *The Elusive Pimpernel* (aka *The Fighting Pimpernel*) (1953); *Don't Lose Your Head* (aka *Carry On Don't Lose Your Head*; *Carry On Pimpernel*) (1967); *The Scarlet Pimpernel* (1982 TVM); *The Scarlet Pimpernel* (1999 TVM)

Scream Series

Kevin Williamson's smart screenplay and an energetic young cast propelled *Scream* into a huge sleeper hit in late 1996. Williamson deftly satirized slasher movie conventions while simultaneously delivering legitimate slasher movie thrills. For example, the opening scene in *Scream* pays subtle homage to *Psycho* while borrowing its set-up from *When a Stranger Calls*. Yet, its most chilling moment relies on the audience's knowledge of slasher pictures: A character dies because she thought Jason — not his mother — was the killer in the original *Friday the 13th*. The cast consisted of a "who's who" of young talent: Neve Campbell (as heroine Sidney Prescott), David Arquette (as Deputy Dewey Riley), Courtney Cox (as newshound Gale Weathers), plus Drew Barrymore, Jamie Kennedy, Liev Schreiber, Rose McGowan, and Skeet Ulrich. Campbell, Arquette, and Cox returned for two sequels. In *Scream 2* (1997), Sidney Prescott, having survived the brutal murders in the first film, enrolls in college — where the killings start all over again. Again, the film's opening is its cleverest set piece: A young woman is murdered in a movie theater while watching *Stab*, a movie based on the incidents detailed in the first *Scream*. The making of a *Stab* sequel provided the plot for *Scream 3* (1999), which transferred the setting and the killings to Hollywood. Written by Ehren Kruger, instead of Williamson, its movie-within-a-movie structure bears a slight resemblance to *Wes Craven's New Nightmare* (1997). That's not too surprising, considering that Wes Craven directed all three *Scream* movies. The 2000 comedy *Scary Movie* spoofed the slasher movie genre and the Scream Films in particular. See also **Slasher Movies**.

Scream (1996); *Scream 2* (1997); *Scream 3* (1999)

Sea Serpents

Judging from their reluctance to be photographed, one might assume that sea serpents are shy creatures. Filmmakers have certainly honored the creatures' privacy. *The Secret of the Loch*, a mild 1934 British comedy, and 1982's *The Loch Ness Horror* may be the only feature films exclusively about the Loch Ness Monster. Holmes encountered "Nessie" in *The Private Life of Sherlock Holmes* (1970), but he revealed "the serpent" to be a mechanical trick. Nessie was one of *The Mysterious Monsters* (1976) addressed in the exploitative Sunn Classics "documentary." And a tiny fish grew into Nessie in one of the magical moments in George Pal's 1964 fantasy *The Seven Faces of Dr. Lao*. Some of the suspects in *The Dragon Murder Case* (1934) pointed to murder evidence which suggested a sea serpent, but Philo Vance knew better and later identified a human culprit. Quests for sea serpents opened *20,000 Leagues Under the Sea* (1954), *The Viking Women and the Sea Serpent* (1957), and, quite naturally, *The Quest* (1986). Timothy Bottoms and Ray Milland found what they were looking for in *The Sea Serpent* (1986), a film they would surely like to forget. See also **Dragons**.

The Secret of the Loch (1934); *The Dragon Murder Case* (1934); *The Viking Women and the Sea Serpent* (1957); *The Seven Faces of Dr. Lao* (1964); *The Private Life of Sherlock Holmes* (1970); *The Mysterious Monsters* (1976); *The Loch Ness Horror* (1982); *The Sea Serpent* (1986); *The Quest* (1986); *Freddie as F.R.O.7* (1992)

Seals and Sea Lions

With their dog-like muzzles, charismatic flippers, and friendly barks, seals and sea lions have specialized in children's films such as: *Sammy the Way Out Seal* (1962), *Sandy the Seal* (1969), *Salty* (1974), *The Golden Seal* (1983); *Andre* (1994), and *Slappy and the Stinkers* (1998). The plots of these films often revolve around protecting the sea mammals from cruel poachers. In *The Sea Spoilers* (1936), John Wayne played a Coast Guard skipper who battles seal poachers. Suzanne Somers portrayed a lawyer trying to stop the slaughtering of baby seals in *Nothing Personal* (1980). In stark contrast, Gregory Peck and Anthony Quinn played seal hunters in the 1850s nautical adventure *The World in His Arms* (1952). The most memorable seal movie is undoubtedly John Sayles' mystical *The Secret of Roan Inish* (1995), which concerns the Irish legend of "selkies." These mysterious sea creatures could transform themselves from seals into humans. Finally, it must be pointed out that many seals are played by sea lions in movies. In *Andre*, the fact-based story of a grey harbor seal, the title character was actually played by a California sea lion.

The Sea Spoilers (1936); *The World in His Arms* (1952); *Sammy the Way Out Seal* (1962); *Sandy the Seal* (1969); *Salty* (1974); *Nothing Personal* (1980); *The Golden Seal* (1983); *Andre* (1994); *The Secret of Roan Inish* (1995); *Slappy and the Stinkers* (1998)

Secret Games Series

Luis Buñuel's classic *Belle de Jour* served as the apparent inspiration for this series of "erotic thrillers" about a bored housewife who becomes a prostitute. In lieu of Catherine Deneuve, *Secret Games* presents Michelle Brin as Julianne, who resents being neglected by her architect husband (Billy Drago) and joins a high-class brothel. She finds sexual liberation in the arms of Eric (Martin Hewitt), a mysterious client who becomes obsessed with Julianne. Good sex turns into a bad time when Eric tries to blackmail, and eventually murder, Julianne's husband. As erotic thrillers go, it's neither erotic nor thrilling. Still, there's plenty of nudity in the R-rated version and even more in the unrated one (which stops shy of showing explicit footage). The videotape's minor popularity resulted in two unrelated sequels. In *Secret Games 2: The Escort*, Martin Hewitt plays a cheating husband who gets involved with *two* other women. *Secret Games 3* is basically a remake of the first film with May Karasun as the neglected housewife. Gregory Hippolyte, who directed all three films, specialized in making erotic thrillers in the 1990s. See also **Animal Instincts Series**; **Body Chemistry Series**; and **Night Eyes Series**.

Secret Games (1992); *Secret Games 2: The Escort* (1993); *Secret Games 3* (1994)

Secret Service Series *see* Bancroft, Brass

Serials into Features

The practice of condensing movie serials into feature films was pioneered in the 1930s by a small company called Mascot Pictures. A major producer of early serials, Mascot discovered it could get twice the value out of its serials by also re-releasing highlights as feature films. Thus, the 1933 John Wayne Western serial *The Three Musketeers* was recut and released as *Desert Command*. A rival studio, Principal, squeezed two feature films out of its Bela Lugosi serial *The Return of Chandu* (1934). The first four chapters were condensed into the film *The Return of Chandu*, while the last eight chapters were edited into another feature called

Chandu on Magic Island. In a unique reversal, Burroughs–Tarzan Enterprises edited its 1935 feature film *The New Adventures of Tarzan* (aka *Tarzan and the Green Goddess*) into a 12-chapter serial in a desperate attempt to compete with MGM's Tarzan series (q.v.). The company reasoned that theater owners uninterested in showing the feature version might be induced to play the serial version. The ploy did not work. In 1936, Universal released its first Flash Gordon serial, an expensive ($350,000 according to most sources) space opera that earned a fervent following. Inspired by Orson Welles' famous *War of the Worlds* radio broadcast and the success of the serial sequel *Flash Gordon's Trip to Mars*, Universal released two Flash Gordon feature versions in 1938. *Trip to Mars* was condensed into *Mars Attacks the World*, while the original *Flash Gordon* became *Rocketship*. Confusingly, the footage from these serials, a third Flash Gordon entry, and a Buck Rogers serial have been re-edited into other feature versions as well. For example, *Trip to Mars* can be viewed as the 99-minute *Deadly Ray from Mars* in addition to the aforementioned 101-minute *Mars Attacks the World*. Although Universal encountered great success with its Flash Gordon serials, little Republic Pictures eventually became the most popular producer of serials. Throughout the 1940s and midway through the 1950s, Republic filled matinee screens with exciting chapters of *Spy Smasher* (1942), *Captain America* (1944), and *Panther Girl of the Kongo* (1955). The television series format contributed greatly to the death of theatrical serials in the mid–1950s. However, in 1965, Columbia revived interest in serials by mounting a limited release of its 1943 *Batman* serial. This, along with the 1966 *Batman* TV series, inspired Republic to condense 26 of its best serials and release them directly to television. In the following list, the serials are listed chronologically first, followed by the feature versions shown on the right.

The Three Musketeers (1933)—*Desert Command*
The Return of Chandu (1934)—*The Return of Chandu*
Chandu on Magic Island
The New Adventures of Tarzan (1935)—*The New Adventures of Tarzan*
Darkest Africa (1936)—*Batmen of Africa* (aka *King of Jungleland*)
Undersea Kingdom (1936)—*Sharad of Atlantis*
Robinson Crusoe of Clipper Island (1936)—*Robinson Crusoe of Mystery Island*
Flash Gordon (1936)—*Rocketship*
Spaceship to the Unknown
Space Soldiers
Atomic Rocketship
Zorro Rides Again (1937)—*Zorro Rides Again*
Fighting Devil Dogs (1938)—*Torpedo of Doom*
Flash Gordon's Trip to Mars (1938)—*Mars Attacks the World*
Deadly Ray from Mars
Hawk of the Wilderness (1938)—*Lost Island of Kioga*
Buck Rogers (1939)—*Planet Outlaws*
Destination Saturn
Flash Gordon Conquers the Universe (1940)—*Purple Death from Outer Space*
Perils from the Planet Mongo
Space Soldiers Conquer the Universe
The Mysterious Dr. Satan (1940)—*Dr. Satan's Robot*
Spy Smasher (1940)—*Spy Smasher Returns*
The Perils of Nyoka (1942)—*Nyoka and the Lost Secrets of Hippocrates*
G-Men vs. the Black Dragon (1943)—*Black Dragon of Manzanar*

The Masked Marvel (1943)—*Sakima and the Masked Marvel*
The Tiger Woman (1944)—*Jungle Gold*
Manhunt of Mystery Island (1945)—*Captain Mephisto and the Transformation Machine*
Federal Operator 99 (1945)—*FBI 99*
The Purple Monster Strikes (1945)—*D-Day on Mars*
The Crimson Ghost (1946)—*Cyclotrode "X"*
The Black Widow (1947)—*Sombra, the Spider Woman*
G-Men Never Forget (1948)—*Code 645*
Dangers of the Canadian Mounted (1948)—*R.C.M.P. and the Treasure of Genghis Khan*
Federal Agents vs. Underworld, Inc. (1948)—*Golden Hands of Kurigal*
King of the Rocket Men (1949)—*Lost Planet Airmen*
The Invisible Monster (1950)—*Slaves of the Invisible Monster*
Flying Disc Man from Mars (1951)—*Missile Monsters*
Radar Men from the Moon (1952)—*Retik, the Moon Menace*
Zombies of the Stratosphere (1952)—*Satan's Satellites*
Jungle Drums of Africa (1952)—*U-238 and the Witch*
Canadian Mounties vs. Atomic Invaders (1953)—*Missile Base at Taniak*
Trader Tom of the China Seas (1954)—*Target: Sea of China*
Panther Girl of the Kongo (1955)—*The Claw Monsters*

Sewers

Until olfactory films can be refined (see "Smellovision" under **Gimmicks**), sewer settings will be underappreciated. Still, the dark catacombs that lurk beneath urban areas have served the horror film well, providing an atmospheric retreat for people-shy monsters. *The Phantom of the Opera* played piano and plotted murder in his tastefully-decorated sewer lair. To his dismay, Christine, the unwilling object of his affections, found it a loathsome place. Rats are a common sight in sewers, so naturally 1972's *Ben*, a tale about a misunderstood rodent and his young human friend, featured extensive sewer footage. Other more horrific sewer residents include the giant ants in *Them!* (1954), the killer baby in *It's Alive!* (1974), and the title creatures in *Alligator* (1980) and the 1988 remake of *The Blob*. The 1984 *C.H.U.D.* (that's Cannibalistic Humanoid Underground Dwellers) was about a mutant race that lived in the sewers by day and sought surface victims at night. It was obviously inspired by the H.P. Lovecraft short story "Pickman's Model," which was adapted into a chilling segment on Rod Serling's 1970–73 TV series *Night Gallery*. *The Third Man* (1949) featured a memorable scene in which Harry Lime (Orson Welles) is chased through a Vienna sewer. Lex Luthor's sewer lair in *Superman* (1978) looked very posh, possibly setting a new standard for screen supervillains. And a band of Christians trekked through the Caesar Augustus Memorial Sewer in *Monty Python's Life of Brian* (1979).

Les Miserables (1935); *The Phantom of the Opera* (1943); *The Third Man* (1949); *Them!* (1954); *Kanal* (aka *They Loved Life; Sewer*) (1956); *Who's Minding the Mint?* (1967); *Ben* (1972); *It's Alive!* (1974); *99 and 44/100% Dead* (aka *Call Harry Crown*) (1974); *Superman* (1978); *Life of Brian* (1979); *Alligator* (1980); *The Blues Brothers* (1980); *C.H.U.D.* (1984); *Underworld* (aka *Transmutations*) (1985); *The Vindicator* (aka *Frankenstein '88*) (1986); *Wild Thing* (1987); *Something Is Out There* (1988 TVM); *The Blob* (1988); *Cyborg* (1989); *Ghostbusters II* (1989); *Teenage Mutant Ninja Turtles* (1990); *The Rainbow Thief* (1990); *It* (1990 TVM); *Jonny's Golden Quest* (1993 TVM); *Super Mario Bros.* (1993); *Judgment Night* (1993); *Demolition Man* (1993); *The Punisher* (1994); *Escape from L.A.* (1996); *Mimic* (1997)

Sex Change

Exploitation films have frequently tackled subjects considered taboo even by serious filmmakers. Thus, it is not surprising that the first films to address men undergoing surgical operations to become women (and vice versa) were drive-in second features. Edward D. Wood, Jr., director of the infamous *Plan 9 from Outer Space*, broached the subject back in 1953 with *Glen or Glenda?* A shoddily-constructed film (like most of Wood's), it told the stories of transvestite Glen and ex-marine Alan who becomes Ann. Although undoubtedly inept, the film was nevertheless ahead of its time in terms of subject matter. Seventeen years later, United Artists released the low-budget filler *The Christine Jorgensen Story* (1970), the alleged facts behind "the world's first sex change operation." That same year, Gore Vidal's satiric sex-change novel *Myra Breckinridge* reached the screen, with film critic Rex Reed as Myron who becomes surgically transformed into Raquel Welch as Myra! The film drowned in its own tastelessness despite a memorable cast and a decent budget. The obscure British picture *I Want What I Want* (1972) treated the subject with much greater respect. Both critics and audiences responded well to 1975's *Dog Day Afternoon*, the story of a man who stages a bank robbery to pay for his male lover's sex-change operation. Karen Black shocked her diner companions by revealing she was once a man in *Come Back to the 5 & Dime, Jimmy Dean, Jimmy Dean* (1982). The 1986 TV movie *Second Serve* was the biography of surgeon Richard Raskins who became tennis player Renee Richards (Vanessa Redgrave played both roles). Two other movies have dealt with non-surgical change of sexes. Young Dr. Jekyll (Ralph Bates) downed his formula and transformed into an evil woman (Martine Beswicke) in Hammer Films' sly 1972 variation *Dr. Jekyll and Sister Hyde*. A 14-year-old girl wished to become a boy—and did—in the 1986 fantasy *Something Special*.

Glen or Glenda? (aka *I Changed My Sex; I Led Two Lives; He or She?*) (1953); *Homicidal* (1961); *The Christine Jorgensen Story* (1970); *Myra Breckinridge* (1970); *I Want What I Want* (1972); *Dr. Jekyll and Sister Hyde* (1972); *Dog Day Afternoon* (1975); *Let Me Die a Woman* (1979); *The Woman Inside* (1981); *Come Back to the 5 & Dime, Jimmy Dean, Jimmy Dean* (1982); *The World According to Garp* (1982); *Shadey* (1985); *Second Serve* (1986 TVM); *Something Special* (aka *Willy/Milly; I Was a Teenage Boy*) (1986); *Night of the Living Babes* (1987); *Sleepaway Camp II: Unhappy Campers* (1988); *Cleo/Leo* (1989); *The Crew* (1994)

The Shadow

"Who knows what evil lurks in the hearts of men?" The Shadow knew, and this mysterious do-gooder dealt out his own brand of justice in a series of immensely popular pulp novels, a radio program, and a handful of films. Created by Maxwell Grant (real name Walter Gibson) in 1931, the Shadow sent his agents into the underworld to infiltrate the ganglords. When they got into trouble, the Shadow—revolvers blazing at his side—came out of the darkness to rescue them. Grant established in an early novel that the Shadow was not wealthy socialite Lamont Cranston. Nevertheless, both on radio and in the movies, Cranston and the Shadow were synonymous. Former silent film star Rod La Rocque brought the Shadow to the screen in 1937's *The Shadow Strikes* and 1938's *International Crime*. La Rocque retired from acting in the early 1940s and entered into a successful real estate career. Monogram Pictures revived the Shadow for a 1946 three-film series starring serial star Kane ("Spy Smasher") Richmond. Republic Pictures revived the Shadow in 1958 with *The Invisible Avenger*, a New Orleans–set mystery starring Richard Derr, which was re-released in 1962 as *Bourbon Street Shadows*. In 1994, director Russell (*Highlander*) Mulcahy directed *The Shadow*, an interesting box-office failure praised for its lavish sets and criticized for its trite story. Alec Baldwin played Lamont Cranston/The Shadow, with John Lone as archvillain Shiwan Khan (one of Genghis Khan's last ancestors).

The Shadow Strikes (1937) (Rod La Rocque); *International Crime* (1938) (La Rocque); *Behind the Mask* (1946) (Kane Richmond); *The Shadow Returns* (1946) (Richmond); *The Missing Lady* (1946) (Richmond); *The Invisible Avenger* (aka *Bourbon Street Shadows*) (1958) (Richard Derr); *The Shadow* (1994) (Alec Baldwin)

Shadowchaser Series

Villainous androids run rampant in this run-of-the-mill, derivative action series. *Project: Shadowchaser* (1992) combines elements of *Die Hard* and *The Terminator* with its plot of a sinister android who holds the president's daughter hostage in a high-rise hospital. The 1994 sequel, *Night Siege Project*, shifts the action to a nuclear research facility where more nasty androids plot to steal a $400 million bomb. *Project: Shadowchaser 3000* (1995), which cribs its plot from *Alien*, places a murderous android aboard an isolated spaceship. B-movie veteran Frank Zagarino played the muscular android lead in all three films; John Eyres directed all three entries. Zagarino also starred in *Alien Chaser* (1996), a film sometimes billed as *Project Shadowchaser 4*. However, Zagarino played an alien — not an android — so it's not included as part of the *Shadowchaser* series. See also **Androids and Cyborgs**.

Project: Shadowchaser (1992); *Night Siege Project: Shadowchaser 2* (aka *Shadowchaser* II; *Armed and Deadly*) (1994); *Project: Shadowchaser 3000* (1995)

Shaft, John

A slick, violent action picture about a supercool black private eye, 1971's *Shaft* ignited the "blaxploitation" craze while enjoying its own mainstream success. Ernest Tidyman's screenplay practically turned John Shaft into a black male stereotype (a tough dude described in the theme song as a "sex machine"). But Richard Roundtree's rugged performance and Gordon Park's gritty direction gave the film a new look much copied by other black filmmakers. Isaac Hayes' hit theme won an Oscar (despite having minimal words) and eventually landed him a starring role in the 1974 movie *Truck Turner*. Roundtree appeared in both *Shaft* sequels and then made the jump to television. His 90-minute *Shaft* TV series rotated with *The CBS Tuesday Night Movie* and a James Stewart lawyer show called *Hawkins*. The TV version whitewashed the Shaft character (less violence, no sex) and caught the cancellation axe after one season. Almost three decades after the original *Shaft*, Samuel Jackson headlined a big budget remake. However, instead of taking over Roundtree's signature role, Jackson played Shaft's nephew. Roundtree appeared briefly as Uncle John and Isaac Hayes reworked his classic song for the opening credits. See also **Blaxploitation Films**.

Shaft (1971); *Shaft's Big Score* (1972); *Shaft in Africa* (1973); *Shaft* (2000)

The Shaggy Dog Series

An ancient curse and a magical ring made Tommy Kirk his own best friend as the boy-turned-dog in 1959's *The Shaggy Dog*. This amusing variation on the werewolf theme established a juvenile formula that worked very well for Disney during the 1960s (e.g., *Son of Flubber*, *The Misadventures of Merlin Jones*). The film also provided major roles for future 1960s teen superstars Annette Funicello and Tommy Kirk, while co-starring Fred MacMurray and Tim Considine a year before *My Three Sons*. Dean Jones portrayed Kirk's character as an adult in 1976's *The Shaggy D.A.* The 1987 TV movie *The Return of the Shaggy Dog* ignored the second film, being a direct sequel to the 1959 original. Disney also aired a TV movie remake of the original film in 1994. See also **Dogs**; **Humanimals**.

The Shaggy Dog (1959); *The Shaggy D.A.* (1976); *The Return of the Shaggy Dog* (1987 TVM); *The Shaggy Dog* (1994 TVM)

Sharks

Except for bit parts, sharks had a hard time finding movie roles prior to 1975's *Jaws* (q.v.). *Killer Shark* (1950) put Roddy McDowell aboard a shark-hunting vessel, but offered little excitement. Victor Mature became concerned about the way sharks gobbled up Navy flyers in 1956's *The Sharkfighters*. He eventually devised a shark repellent, derived from octopus ink, that turned away even the hungriest underwater predator. *Blue Water, White Death* was a striking 1971 documentary about the Great White shark. It failed to find an audience until four years later, after the release of *Jaws*. Naturally, the phenomenal success of Steven Spielberg's blockbuster inspired a host of imitators. The 1982 *Great White* was so similar to *Jaws* that Universal Pictures went to court and acquired an injunction to remove the rip-off from circulation. Two films offering interesting variations on the *Jaws* story include *Deep Blue Sea* (1999), which introduced genetically-engineered, intelligent killer sharks, and *Mako: The Jaws of Death*, with Richard Jaeckel as a man trying to protect sharks from people who would exploit them. See also **Dolphins**; **Fish**; **Jaws Series**; **Whales**.

Killer Shark (1950); *The Sharkfighters* (1956); *Tiko and the Shark* (1965); *Let's Kill Uncle* (1966); *Shark!* (aka *Maneater*) (1969); *Blue Water, White Death* (1971); *Shark's Treasure* (1974); *Jaws* (1975); *Mako: The Jaws of Death* (aka *The Jaws of Death*) (1976); *Shark Kill* (1976 TVM); *Tintorera-Bloody Waters* (1977); *Great White* (1982); *Mission of the Shark* (1991 TVM); *Deep Blue Sea* (1999); *Shark Attack* (1999)

Shayne, Michael

Brett Halliday's two-fisted private eye made his film debut with 1941's *Michael Shayne, Detective*. Lloyd Nolan, a veteran tough guy, starred as Shayne in seven films in 1941 and 1942. Hugh Beaumont, best known as Ward Cleaver on TV's *Leave It to Beaver*, reprised Shayne for five additional features in 1946 and 1947. Although these fast-paced mysteries never rose above the programmer level, they paved the way for more serious private eye films, such as the 1944 Philip Marlowe vehicle *Murder, My Sweet*. Ironically, the Shayne movie *Time to Kill* was based on the

Marlowe novel *The High Window*. Richard Denning starred in the *Michael Shayne* TV series in 1960-61.

Michael Shayne, Detective (1941) (Lloyd Nolan); *Blue, White, and Perfect* (1941) (Nolan); *Dressed to Kill* (1941) (Nolan); *Sleepers West* (1941) (Nolan); *Just Off Broadway* (1942) (Nolan); *The Man Who Would Not Die* (1942) (Nolan); *Time to Kill* (1942) (Nolan); *Blonde for a Day* (1946) (Hugh Beaumont); *Larceny in Her Heart* (1946) (Beaumont); *Murder Is My Business* (1946) (Beaumont); *Three on a Ticket* (1947) (Beaumont); *Too Many Winners* (1947) (Beaumont)

Shoes

While clothing and most accessories have rarely been film subjects, shoes at least made a minor impression. Charlie Chaplin ate his shoes—the laces substituting for spaghetti—in the silent comedy classic *The Gold Rush* (1925). He also stabbed bread rolls with two forks and did an impressive table-top soft shoe with his food. Johnny Depp paid homage to the latter scene in a restaurant in 1993's *Benny & Joon*—but he didn't eat his shoes. However, men do just that in order to survive in the outrageous *Cannibal! The Musical* (1996). A surprising number of extraordinary shoes have graced the feet of film characters. Dorothy used her famous ruby slippers (they were silver in the book) to get back home in *The Wizard of Oz* (1939). Fred MacMurray and Robin Williams both attached "flubber" to the bottom of their shoes in, respectively, *Son of Flubber* (1963) and its remake *Flubber* (1998). The flubber soles enabled their college athletic teams to bound to amazing physical feats. Magical shoes transformed Ernest P. Worrell into an unlikely basketball star in *Slam Dunk Ernest* (1995). Secret agent Maxwell Smart used a shoe phone to communicate with his superiors in the *Get Smart!* TV series and the 1989 TV movie *Get Smart, Again!* Secret agent James Bond (Sean Connery) barely avoided the point of the knife blade protruding from Lotte Lenya's shoe in a memorable fight scene in *From Russia with Love* (1963). The classic ballet film *The Red Shoes* (1948) contains a dancing sequence based on Hans Christian Andersen's fairy tale about a girl with magical shoes that won't let her stop dancing. In another fairy tale, Cinderella left behind one of her glass slippers at the Prince's ball in films such as Disney's animated *Cinderella* (1950), *The Glass Slipper* (1955), and *Ever After* (1998). Shoes are used to identify people in other films as well. An ordinary citizen is selected as a spy decoy in the French film *The Tall Blond Man with One Black Shoe* (1972) and its American remake *The Man with One Red Shoe* (1985). Mia Farrow played a blind woman trapped with a killer—identified to the audience only by his boots—in the 1971 thriller *See No Evil*. In *Jason and the Argonauts* (1963), Pelias (Douglas Wilmer) is warned that a one-sandaled man will be his downfall. A murderer steals a pair of boots so a vicious dog can attack the right victim in the oft-filmed Sherlock Holmes mystery *The Hound of the Baskervilles*. Shoemakers have been played by actors such as Charles Laughton (*Hobson's Choice*) and Don Ameche (*Things Change*). Joan Crawford played the daughter of a shoe manufacturer in the silent comedy *Tramp, Tramp, Tramp* (1926). Shoe stores figured prominently in *Tight Shoes* (1941) and *I Don't Buy Kisses Anymore* (1992), while shoe shiners were integral to the plots of *On the Right Track* (1981), *Nick of Time* (1995), and *Mimic* (1998). Vittorio De Sica's haunting *Shoeshine* (1946) told the story of two boys who scratch out a living shin-

ing soldiers' boots in war-torn Rome. In the World War I classic *All Quiet on the Western Front* (1925), soldiers keep passing the same pair of boots around—whoever wears them gets killed. An inspirational scene in *Glory* (1989) occurs when the black Union soldiers are finally issued military boots.

The Gold Rush (1925); *Tramp, Tramp, Tramp* (1926); *All Quiet on the Western Front* (1930); *The Hound of the Baskervilles* (1939); *The Wizard of Oz* (1939); *Tight Shoes* (1941); *Shoeshine* (1946); *The Red Shoes* (1948); *Cinderella* (1950); *Hobson's Choice* (1954); *The Glass Slipper* (1955); *Son of Flubber* (1963); *From Russa with Love* (1963); *See No Evil* (aka *Blind Terror*) (1971); *The Tall Blond Man with One Black Shoe* (1972); *On the Right Track* (1981); *The Man with One Red Shoe* (1985); *Things Change* (1988); *Glory* (1989); *Get Smart, Again!* (1989 TVM); *London Kills Me* (1991); *I Don't Buy Kisses Anymore* (1992); *Johnny Suede* (1992); *Benny & Joon* (1993); *Nick of Time* (1995); *Slam Dunk Ernest* (1995); *Cannibal! The Musical* (1996); *Mimic* (1997); *Flubber* (1997); *The Shoe* (1998); *Ever After* (1998); *Children of Heaven* (aka *Bacheha-Ye aseman*) (1999)

Shopping Malls *see* Stores

Silent Night, Deadly Night Series

Film ads showing a murderous Santa Claus created a minor controversy when *Silent Night, Deadly Night* was released in 1984. Actually, this low-budget slasher picture did not depict Santa as a killer—the knife-wielding murderer turned out to be just a psycho dressed up like St. Nick. Still, the ploy generated plenty of free publicity for a film which otherwise would have sunk into obscurity. Instead, it spawned a series. The 1987 *Silent Night, Deadly Night Part II* recycled a large chunk of the original's footage before setting up the first killer's baby brother, Ricky, as another Santa-dressed slasher. Ricky emerges from a six-year coma in *Silent Night, Deadly Night III: You Better Watch Out!* (1989). It's considered the highlight of the series (though not necessarily a good film), chiefly due to the efforts of once-promising director Monte Hellman (*Two-Lane Blacktop*). The films *Silent Night, Bloody Night* (1972) and *Silent Night, Evil Night* (1974) are not a part of this series. See also **Slasher Movies**.

Silent Night, Deadly Night (1984); *Silent Night, Deadly Night Part II* (1987); *Silent Night, Deadly Night III: You Better Watch Out!* (1989); *Silent Night, Deadly Night IV: Initiation* (1990); *Silent Night, Deadly Night V: The Toymaker* (1991)

Simon's Suites Series

Neil Simon's successful 1968 Broadway comedy *Plaza Suite* consisted of three one-act plays set in the same suite at the famous New York City Plaza Hotel: "Visitors from Mamaroneck"; "Visitors from Hollywood"; and "Visitors from Forest Hills." Simon dropped a potential fourth segment, which he later developed into the Jack Lemmon–Sandy Dennis film *The Out-of-Towners* (1970). In the stage version of *Plaza Suite*, George C. Scott and Maureen Stapleton played all three couples. However, when Simon adapted his play for a 1971 film version, Walter Matthau replaced Scott and his three female leads were played by Stapleton, Barbara Harris, and Lee Grant. *California Suite* (1978), also adapted from a popular Simon play, shifted the locale to a West Coast hotel and featured four stories. The highlights are Matthau as a husband whose wife interrupts his rendezvous with a prostitute and Maggie Smith as a British actress who loses an Academy Award. In real life, Smith *won* a Best Supporting Actress Oscar for her incisive performance in *California Suite*. Simon concluded his stage trilogy with *London Suite*, an Off-Broadway play that lacked the acclaim of its predecessors. NBC produced a TV movie version in 1996 as a showcase for several of its sitcom stars (e.g. Kelsey Grammer, Julia Louis-Dreyfus, and Kristen Johnson). A TV movie version of *Plaza Suite* also appeared in 1987. It starred Carol Burnett and Dabney Coleman. See also **Hotels**.

Plaza Suite (1971); *California Suite* (1978); *Plaza Suite* (1987 TVM); *London Suite* (1996 TVM)

Sinbad the Sailor

This Arabian Nights adventurer owes his film fame to producer Charles Schneer and special effects creator Ray Harryhausen, who made Sinbad the subject of a colorful movie trilogy. The first of the three films, 1958's *The Seventh Voyage of Sinbad*, was a marvelous fantasy, though its plot must have confused Sinbad purists. It combined Sinbad's encounter with a two-headed roc (which actually occurred on the sailor's second voyage) with his climactic clash with a cyclops (the subject of his third voyage). Naturally, none of this bothered filmgoers enraptured with Harryhausen's spectacular special effect: a fire-breathing dragon, a four-armed siren, and a classic swordfight between Sinbad and a skeleton. Surprisingly, although *The Seventh Voyage* turned an impressive profit, Schneer and Harryhausen waited 16 years to mount a sequel. *The Golden Voyage of Sinbad* was a stylish rehash featuring a new Sinbad (John Phillip Law replacing Kerwin Matthews) and a bevy of eye-popping special effects. Although Harryhausen failed to top his earlier skeleton swordfight, he still wove visual magic with a six-armed statue come-to-life (q.v.) and a clash between a centaur and a griffin. *The Golden Voyage*'s warm reception resulted in 1977's *Sinbad and the Eye of the Tiger*, which was, in comparison to its predecessors, a disappointment. Patrick Wayne played a leaden Sinbad and Harryhausen's creatures were less fantastic (e.g., a saber-toothed tiger, a walrus, and a chess-playing baboon). It turned out to be Schneer and Harryhausen's last Sinbad voyage. There have been other celluloid Sinbads, of course, including Douglas Fairbanks, Jr.'s, entertaining *Sinbad the Sailor*, 1963's *Captain Sinbad* with Guy Williams (Disney's TV Zorro), and *Sinbad and the Seven Seas* with Lou Ferrigno (the green half of TV's *The Incredible Hulk*). Gene Kelly danced with Hanna-Barbera cartoon characters in the "Sinbad" segment of 1957's *Invitation to the Dance*. A tongue-in-cheek syndicated television series, *The Adventures of Sinbad*, aired in 1996.

Arabian Nights (1942); *Sinbad the Sailor* (1947); *Thief of Damascus* (1952); *Son of Sinbad* (1955); *Invitation to the Dance* (1957); *The Seventh Voyage of Sinbad* (1958); *Captain Sinbad* (1963); *The Golden Voyage of Sinbad* (1974); *Sinbad and the Eye of the Tiger* (1977); *Sinbad and the Seven Seas* (1990); *Sinbad: The Battle of the Dark Knights* (1998)

The Six Million Dollar Man Series

Martin Caidin's novel *Cyborg* inspired the 1973 TV movie and subsequent 1974–78 TV series *The Six Million Dollar Man*. Lee Majors starred as Steve Austin, a critically injured astronaut who had certain body parts replaced by "atomic-powered electro-

mechanical devices." The end result was a superhero — part human, part machine (but not nearly as interesting as *Robocop*). He acquired a bionic girlfriend in 1975, when tennis pro Jaime Sommers (Lindsay Wagner) met with a sky-diving accident. She proved too popular for just one man, so she got her own show, *The Bionic Woman*, in 1976. It went off the air in 1978, a few months after the final telecast of *The Six Million Dollar Man*. However, just to show you can't keep a bionic pair down for good — and in the wake of the hit movie *RoboCop* — Steve and Jaime were reunited for 1987's *The Return of the Six Million Dollar Man and the Bionic Woman*. It proved to be a ratings hit, thus inspiring two more post–TV series movies featuring the popular cyborgs. See also **Androids and Cyborgs**; **Television Series Reunion Films**.

The Six Million Dollar Man (1973 TVM); *The Return of the Six Million Dollar Man and the Bionic Woman* (1987 TVM); *Bionic Showdown: The Six Million Dollar Man and the Bionic Woman* (1989 TVM); *Bionic Ever After?* (1994 TVM)

Skiing

Fictional Olympic skiers have been portrayed in the movies as obsessive, self-centered types, as evidenced by Robert Redford's character in *Downhill Racer* (1969) and Wayne Rogers in *The Top of the Hill* (1980). Real-life Olympic skiers-turned-actors have chosen more likable roles, though that's done little to extend their brief film careers. Olympic great Jean-Claude Killy starred in the 1972 heist film *Snow Job*, earning high marks for his slalom skills and low ones for his thesping. Suzy ("Chapstick") Chaffee's role was strictly a supporting one in the 1978 TV movie *Ski Lift to Death*. Non-Olympic real-life skiers have appeared in the documentaries *Last of the Ski Bums* (1969) and *The Man Who Skied Down Everest* (1976). The latter film, which chronicled the exploits of Japanese skier Yuichiro Miura, won an Oscar for Best Documentary. *Ski Bums* was a less serious affair about the joys of skiing, produced by the makers of the classic surfing documentary *The Endless Summer*. The James Bond spy thrillers have exhibited a special flair for ski scenes. A lengthy, breathtaking ski sequence, among the finest chases in the entire series, forms the centerpiece of 1969's *On Her Majesty's Secret Service*. A shorter chase opened 1977's *The Spy Who Loved Me*, ending with Bond skiing off a cliff and releasing a parachute. Bond was back on the slopes in 1985's *A View to a Kill* and 1999's *The World Is Not Enough*. The fact-based drama *Going for the Gold: The Bill Johnson Story* (1985) chronicled the life of the 1984 Olympic downhill champion. A skiing accident proved to be the turning point in a weekend among friends in Alan Alda's 1981 comedy-drama *The Four Seasons*. A life-threatening accident ended the career of 1956 Olympic hopeful Jill Kilnmont in the fact-based *The Other Side of the Mountain* (1975). And a skiing accident turns out to be murder in Alfred Hitchcock's *Spellbound*. On a cheerier note, the Beatles frolicked on the slopes to the tune of "Ticket to Ride" in Richard Lester's hectic 1965 farce *Help!*

The Man Who Knew Too Much (1934); *I Met Him in Paris* (1937); *Everything Happens at Night* (1939); *Two-Faced Woman* (1941); *Sun Valley Serenade* (1941); *Spellbound* (1945); *The Duchess of Idaho* (1950); *Ski Troop Attack* (1960); *The Pink Panther* (1964); *Help!* (1965); *Ski Party* (1965); *Winter a Go Go* (1965); *Wild, Wild Winter* (1966); *Caprice* (1967); *The Double Man* (1967); *Ski on the*

Wild Side (1967); *Last of the Ski Bums* (1969); *On Her Majesty's Secret Service* (1969); *Ski Fever* (1969); *Downhill Racer* (1969); *The Ski Bum* (1971); *The Ski Raiders* (1972); *Snow Job* (1972); *Snowball Express* (1972); *The Other Side of the Mountain* (aka *A Window to the Sky*) (1975); *The Man Who Skied Down Everest* (1976); *The Spy Who Loved Me* (1977); *The Deadly Triangle* (aka *Crisis in Sun Valley*) (1977 TVM); *Ski Lift to Death* (1978 TVM); *Lost and Found* (1979); *The Top of the Hill* (1980 TVM); *Swan Song* (1980 TVM); *The Four Seasons* (1981); *Hot Dog...The Movie* (1984); *Just the Way You Are* (1984); *Better Off Dead* (1985); *A View to a Kill* (1985); *Going for the Gold: The Bill Johnson Story* (1985 TVM); *Fire and Ice* (1987); *Striker's Mountain* (1987); *Ski Patrol* (1990); *Ski School* (1990); *Born to Ski* (1991); *Ski School 2* (1994); *Fire on the Mountain* (1996); *Downhill Willie* (1997); *Silverwolf* (1999); *The World Is Not Enough* (1999)

Skydiving

By strict definition, skydiving is the sport of parachuting from airplanes and performing various body maneuvers before pulling the ripcord. Legitimate cinema skydivers include an odd assortment of performers, ranging from Raquel Welch to Burt Lancaster to Keanu Reeves to Frankie and Annette. In *Fathom*, skydiver Welch landed in the midst of a lighthearted spy caper. John Frankenheimer's *The Gypsy Moths* took a more serious view although it occasionally dipped into soap opera despite the presence of Burt Lancaster and Deborah Kerr. Unlikely FBI agent Keanu Reeves jumped from a plane on a dare from thrill-seeker/bank robber Patrick Swayze in *Point Break*. Even Frankie Avalon and Annette Funicello took the plunge in *Beach Blanket Bingo* (in the same film, Linda Evans took credit for someone else's jump). However, the most unlikely group of skydivers were probably the Flying Elvises — and non–Elvis Nicolas Cage — who landed just outside the Bally Casino in the climax to *Honeymoon in Vegas*. Technically, James Bond (Roger Moore) was not parachuting for the fun of it in *Moonraker's* pre-title sequence. However, his freefall fight with Jaws (Richard Kiel) certainly deserves an honorable mention. Likewise, parachuting (not skydiving) played a significant role in the Jerry Lewis–Dean Martin comedy *Jumping Jacks* and has been featured briefly in other military movies such as *Objective Burma*, *Where Eagles Dare*, and *Red Dawn*. Poor Eddie Albert spent most of *The Longest Day* hanging from a parachute stuck in a tree. See also **Airplanes**.

Jumping Jacks (1952); *Beach Blanket Bingo* (1965); *Fathom* (1967); *Thin Air* (aka *The Body Stealers; Invasion of the Body Stealers*) (1968); *The Gypsy Moths* (1969); *Moonraker* (1979); *Fandango* (1985); *Point Break* (1991); *Honeymoon in Vegas* (1992); *Drop Zone* (1994); *Terminal Velocity* (1994); *The Big Fall* (1997)

Slasher Movies

A subgenre of the psycho thriller, the slasher movie enjoyed tremendous popularity among young adults during the 1978–83 period. John Carpenter's *Halloween* (1978) is generally considered the prototype, introducing what would become the mandatory ingredients: sexually active teenage protagonists, a conspicuous absence of adults, gory murders (the higher the body count, the better), and a seemingly indestructible killer. Despite a low budget and frail storyline, Carpenter's incredibly tense direction brought *Halloween* (q.v.) critical acclaim as well as box-office millions. Amazingly, imitations were slow to follow (although the grisly-titled *Driller Killer* was released the next year). Then in

1980, Sean S. Cunningham exploited a routine thriller called *Friday the 13th* (q.v.) into a box-office smash. (Nine years earlier, Cunningham had produced the infamous shocker *Last House on the Left*.) Unlike Carpenter's movie, *Friday the 13th* garnered few favorable reviews, but its lucrative grosses did not go unnoticed by low-budget filmmakers. Slasher films flooded the nation's screens during 1981, exhibiting a special fondness for titles involving special occasions: *Graduation Day*, *Happy Birthday to Me*, *My Bloody Valentine*, and *New Year's Evil*. Yet, with the exception of the *Friday the 13th* series, slasher films began to fade temporarily by 1983, primarily a victim of their own lack of originality. The genre was practically dead in its grave when Wes Craven (who directed *Last House on the Left*) introduced a razor-fingered killer named Freddy Krueger in 1984's *Nightmare on Elm Street* (q.v.). The *Elm Street* and *Friday the 13th* series maintained their core audiences into the early 1990s, spawning television series and numerous imitations along the way. However, even those stalwart franchises were generating anemic box-office returns by 1994. Yet, two years later, Craven — with assistance from first-time screenwriter Kevin Williamson — revived the slasher genre again with *Scream*. Williamson's clever script paid homage to slasher film cliches while still generating legitimate chills. Its unexpected popularity started another slasher film cycle that included Williamson's more conventional *I Know What You Did Last Summer* (1997) and *Halloween H20: Twenty Years Later* (1998). See also **Friday the 13th Series; Halloween Series; Nightmare on Elm Street Series; Prom Night Series; Scream Series; Silent Night, Deadly Night Series; Sleepaway Camp Series; Slumber Party Massacre Series**.

Halloween (1978); *The Driller Killer* (1979); *Friday the 13th* (1980); *Mother's Day* (1980); *Prom Night* (1980); *Silent Scream* (1980); *Terror Train* (1980); *The Burning* (1981); *Final Exam* (1981); *The Final Terror* (1981); *Funhouse* (1981); *Graduation Day* (1981); *Happy Birthday to Me* (1981); *My Bloody Valentine* (1981); *New Year's Evil* (1981); *Night School* (1981); *Road Games* (1981); *Student Bodies* (1981); *Slumber Party Massacre* (1982); *Death Valley* (1982); *The House on Sorority Row* (1983); *Deadly Lessons* (1983 TVM); *Silent Night, Deadly Night* (1984); *Nightmare on Elm Street* (1984); *Splatter University* (1985); *Slaughter High* (1986); *April Fool's Day* (1986); *Cheerleader Camp* (aka *Bloody Pom Poms*) (1987); *Bad Dreams* (1988); *Shocker* (1989); *Cutting Class* (1989); *Darkroom* (1990); *There's Nothing Out There* (1991); *Scream* (1996); *I Know What You Did Last Summer* (1997); *Scary Movie* (2000)

Sleepaway Camp Series

In the wake of the *Friday the 13th* (q.v.) films, 1983's *Sleepaway Camp* emerged as a weak carbon copy about another bloody killer running amok among teenage campers. However, when its sequels appeared five years later, they shifted the emphasis from gore to black humor. Shot back to back, *Sleepaway Camp II: Unhappy Campers* (1988) and *Sleepaway Camp III: Teenage Wasteland* both starred Pamela Springsteen (Bruce's sister) as the murder-minded camp counselor. Just in case any viewers had actually seen the original — in which the stalker was a man — *Unhappy Campers* explained that the killer had undergone a sex change (q.v.) operation. The transformation gave the murderer a much-needed sense of humor, as she dispatched one-liners along with the inhabitants of Camp New Horizons. In addition to Springsteen, these sequels featured other interesting casting choices. Michael J.

Pollard, an Oscar nominee for *Bonnie and Clyde*, played the loony head counselor in *Unhappy Campers*. Tracy Griffith, Melanie's sister, turned up as a camper in that film, while Renee Estevez, Emilio's sister, had a supporting role in *Teenage Wasteland*. See also **Slasher Movies**; **Summer Camps**.

Sleepaway Camp (1983); *Sleepaway Camp II: Unhappy Campers* (1988); *Sleepaway Camp III: Teenage Wasteland* (1989)

Slumber Party Massacre Series

Feminist author Rita Mae Brown penned the script for 1982's *Slumber Party Massacre*, an unexceptional slasher film (q.v.) featuring a driller killer. Amy Jones, fresh from studying film at M.I.T., rescued Brown's screenplay (originally titled *Don't Open the Door*) from the file cabinets of Roger Corman's New World Pictures. Yet, despite its female author and director, *Slumber Party Massacre* exploited young girls in true stereotypical slasher film fashion. Nevertheless, it still managed to turn a nifty profit during the genre's low period. Five years later, on the heels of 1986's similar *Sorority House Massacre*, a *Slumber Party Massacre* sequel appeared, featuring Crystal Bernard of the TV series *Wings* in a major role. It found a niche in home video rentals and paved the way for a third installment starring Brittain Frye as Ken the killer and, in a minor role, former *Playboy* playmate Hope Marie Carlton of *Malibu Express* (q.v.) fame. See also **Slasher Movies**.

Slumber Party Massacre (1982); *Slumber Party Massacre II* (1987); *Slumber Party Massacre III* (1990)

Smithee, Allen/Alan

When a director or writer wishes his name to be withdrawn from a movie (for whatever reason), he must petition the Director's or Writer's Guild of America (providing he's a member, of course). If the Guild grants his request, his credit is assigned to a fictitious person named Allen (or Alan) Smithee. At least, this has been the standard practice since 1967, when Smithee "replaced" Robert Totten and Don Siegel as directors of *Death of a Gunfighter*. In that instance, both Totten and Siegel alleged that star Richard Widmark had interfered with their creative control of the picture. Prior to the "Smithee rule," George Cukor had his name removed from 1947's *Desire Me*. Its credits simply did not list a director.

Death of a Gunfighter (1967) (directors: Robert Totten and Don Siegel); *Fade-in* (1968) (director: Jud Taylor); *The Challenge* (1970 TVM) (director unknown); *City in Fear* (1980 TVM) (director: Jud Taylor); *Fun and Games* (1980 TVM) (director: Paul Bogart); *Student Bodies* (1981) (producer: Michael Ritchie); *Moonlight* (1982 TVM) (directors: Jackie Cooper and Rod Holcomb); *Dune*— TV version (1984) (director: David Lynch); *Stitches* (1985) (director: Rod Holcomb); *Appointment with Fear* (1985) (director: Ramzi Thomas); *Let's Get Harry* (1986) (director: Stuart Rosenberg); *Dalton: Code of Vengeance II* (1986 TVM) (director unknown); *I Love N.Y.* (1987) (director: Gioanni Bozzacchi); *Ghost Fever* (1987) (director unknown); *Morgan Stewart's Coming Home* (1987) (director: Paul Aaron); *Riviera* (1987 TVM) (director: John Frankenheimer); *The Horror Show* (aka *House III*) (1989) (writer unknown); *The Shrimp on the Barbie* (1990) (director: Michael Gottlieb); *Starfire* (aka *Solar Crisis*; *Crisis 2050*) (1990) (director: Richard Sarafian); *Bloodsucking Pharaohs in Pittsburgh* (1991) (director unknown); *Fatal Charm* (1992 TVM) (director: Fritz Kiersch); *Thunderheart*— TV version (1992) (director: Michael Apted); *Rudy*— TV version (1993) (director: David Anspaugh); *The Birds*

II: Land's End (1994 TVM) (director: Rick Rosenthal); *Gypsy Angels* (1994) (director unknown); *Heat*— TV version (1995) (director: Michael Mann); *Raging Angels* (1995) (director unknown); *Hellraiser: Bloodline* (1996) (director: Kevin Yagher); *An Alan Smithee Film: Burn, Hollywood, Burn* (1997) (director: Arthur Hiller); *Sub Down* (1997) (director: Gregg Champion)

Smokey and the Bandit

Burt Reynolds' star power peaked with this 1977 road comedy in which he, then-girlfriend Sally Field, and Jackie Gleason seem to be having more fun than the audience. Burt played a bootlegger who spends the entire film eluding redneck sheriff Gleason, while having a good ol' time with chum Jerry Reed and perky passenger Field. The humor was so tongue-in-cheek that Burt almost seemed to be winking at the audience after every line. The formula provided more of the same with 1980's *Smokey and the Bandit II*, only this time it tasted a little stale, despite the presence of a baby elephant. *Smokey and the Bandit III* (1983) was a misguided attempt to make a Burt Reynolds film without Burt. Initially, Jackie Gleason played a double role, as the pursued and the pursuer. When this confused preview audiences, it was reshot with sheriff Gleason chasing Jerry Reed. By that point, no one really cared either way. Brian Bloom played the Bandit in five 1994 syndicated TV movies, starting with *Bandit*. Hal Needham, who helmed the first two Reynolds entries, directed all of the television features.

Smokey and the Bandit (1977); *Smokey and the Bandit II* (1980); *Smokey and the Bandit III* (1983); *Bandit* (1994 TVM); *Bandit, Bandit* (1994 TVM); *Beauty and the Bandit* (1994 TVM); *Bandit's Silver Angel* (1994 TVM); *Bandit Goes Country* (1994 TVM)

Snails and Slugs

Snails and slugs, which are both classified as gastropods, have come in all shapes and sizes on the silver screen. According to the 1974 Japanese film *Last Days of Planet Earth*, Nostradamus prophesized that the first sign of the apocalypse would be the appearance of giant slugs. Alas, as soon as the movie introduces the slugs, the Japanese army destroys them with flame-throwers. Some critics have incorrectly identified *The Monster That Challenged the World* as a caterpillar. The title creature may look somewhat like a caterpillar, but it's clearly a gastropod — enlarged by radiation exposure — that secretes a sticky white substance. In terms of size, though, the biggest gastropod is the Pink Snail sought by Rex Harrison and friends in *Doctor Doolittle* (1967). Ironically, the nastiest gastropods are the normal-sized slugs transformed by toxic waste into flesh-eaters in the Spanish horror film *Slugs* (1987). On the gentler side, a scene in *Microcosmos* (1996) shows snails mating to the accompaniment of opera music. Other musically-minded gastropods appeared in *The Little Mermaid* (1989). In the lavish production number "Under the Sea," Sebastian the Crab sang about "two little slugs here, cutting a rug here" and "two little snails here, know how to wail here, under the sea." Although snails and slugs have a reputation for being slow, a little man rode a "racing snail" in *The NeverEnding Story* (1984).

The Monster That Challenged the World (1957); *Doctor Doolittle* (1967); *Last Days of Planet Earth* (aka *Catastrophe 1999: The Prophecies of Nostradamus*) (1974); *Slugs* (1987); *The NeverEnding Story* (1984); *The Little Mermaid* (1989); *Microcosmos* (1996)

SnakeEater Series

Jack "Soldier" Kelly (Lorenzo Lamas) was, according to a police detective crony, the "rebellious type, doesn't like authority figures." So naturally, this former Marine and undercover agent had trouble battling criminals within the confines of the law — especially when some crazed hillbillies murdered his parents and kidnapped his sister. The inaugural film in this Canadian-lensed series started out as a tongue-in-cheek action picture, but quickly degenerated into an uninteresting revenge tale. Lamas displayed his athletic talents, but not his acting ones. He did sport a catchy belt buckle depicting a snake (a SnakeEater, one character explains, is a special type of elite Marine). The 1991 sequel opened with Soldier in a mental hospital, where he was sent for examination following his violent vigilante acts. He soon escaped, however, and set out to combat a drug kingpin. As evidenced by his delight in demolishing a biker gang in *SnakeEater III*, Soldier Kelly still needs to find more sedate ways to express himself.

SnakeEater (1989); *SnakeEater II — The Drug Buster* (1991); *SnakeEater III…His Law* (1992)

Snakes

Snakes have led a charismatic screen existence, often stealing pictures on the basis of a scene or two. A wispy snake made a brief guest appearance in the 1931 Sherlock Holmes mystery *The Speckled Band*, but the picture nevertheless remained named after the viper. Likewise, the snake pit scene in *Raiders of the Lost Ark* (1981) made a lasting impression despite its brevity. A solitary snake, such as the Black Mambo in *Venom* (1982), has wreaked as much havoc as a slew of them slithering rampantly throughout a submarine, as in *Fer-de-Lance* (1974). A shy teenager conjured up giant snakes to kill her thoughtless classmates in 1978's *Jennifer*. The 40-foot slithering killer in *Anaconda* swallowed snake hunter Jon Voight whole and then regurgitated him. *Stanley* (1972) used his influence on regular-sized snakes, with just as much effect. A Mayan curse turned a Cornish lass into a snake-woman in 1966's *The Reptile*, while Strother Martin's experiments slowly transformed Dirk Benedict into a king cobra in 1973's *Sssssss* ("Don't say it, hiss it!" said the ads). Amanda Donohoe boasted some ugly-looking fangs in *Lair of the White Worm* (1988), but the film's real monster turned out to be the hideous snake god she worshiped. The only one of *The Seven Faces of Dr. Lao* (1964) not played by Tony Randall was the animated serpent. However, Bob Fosse did play a hissing snake in the 1974 fantasy *The Little Prince*.

The Speckled Band (1931); *The Lady Eve* (1941); *Cobra Woman* (1944); *The Shanghai Cobra* (1945); *Cult of the Cobra* (1955); *The Seven Faces of Dr. Lao* (1964); *The Reptile* (1966); *The Jungle Book* (1967); *Snake People* (aka *Isle of the Snake People*; *Cult of the Dead*) (1968); *Stanley* (1972); *Sssssss* (1973); *Night of the Cobra Woman* (1974); *The Little Prince* (1974); *Fer-de-Lance* (1974 TVM); *Jennifer* (aka *Jennifer, the Snake Goddess*) (1978); *Raiders of the Lost Ark* (1981); *Venom* (1982); *Jaws of Satan* (aka *King Cobra*) (1982); *Spasms* (1983); *Hard Ticket to Hawaii* (1987); *Lair of the White Worm* (1988); *Fair Game* (1989); *The Fifth Monkey* (1990); *Green Snake* (aka *Ching Se*) (1993); *Anaconda* (1997); *Rudyard Kipling's The Second Jungle Book: Mowgli and Baloo* (aka *Jungle Book Two*) (1997); *Soldier* (1998); *Silent Predators* (1999 TVM); *King Cobra* (aka *Seth*) (1999); *Road Trip* (2000)

Soap Operas

Daytime dramas, a potentially rich source for satire, have been underutilized by big screen scripters. Still, soap opera settings have provided two fine performers, Beryl Reid and Dustin Hoffman, with meaty parts. *The Killing of Sister George* (1968) cast Reid as an aging actress who suspects that her once-popular soap opera character is about to be dropped permanently from the series. The film, based on Frank Marcus' play, dealt frankly with the main character's lesbianism — it was rated "X" originally. It also provided American viewers with a rare glimpse behind the scenes of British television (where soaps such as *Coronation Street* thrived). Compared to *Sister George*, *Tootsie* (1982) generated far less controversy, although Hoffman's character spends most of the film disguised as a woman so he can act on a soap (which certainly provides an interesting subtext). The comedy misfire *Delirious* (1991) wasted a witty premise: Soap writer John Candy bumps his head and winds up in his own fictional daytime drama (complete with veteran soap actress Emma Samms). Peter Falk played a writer of radio daytime drama in 1990's *Tune in Tomorrow....* Mary McDonnell portrayed a soap star who becomes paralyzed in 1992's *Passion Fish*, while clairvoyant Demi Moore provided advice to a soap star in *The Butcher's Wife* (1991). Several real-life soap stars, including Demi Moore and Janine Turner of *General Hospital*, had cameos in the lame 1982 comedy *Young Doctors in Love*. On the flip side, *Peyton Place* (1961) (q.v.), a big screen all-star soap, spawned two television versions: the nighttime serial *Peyton Place* (1964–69) and the daytime drama *Return to Peyton Place* (1972–74). See also **Television**.

Phffft! (1954); *The Killing of Sister George* (1968); *Tootsie* (1982); *Tune in Tomorrow...* (1990); *The Butcher's Wife* (1991); *Delirious* (1991); *Soapdish* (1991); *Passion Fish* (1992); *Naked in New York* (1994); *Never Say Never: The Deidre Hall Story* (1995 TVM); *The Real Blonde* (1997); *54* (1998)

Soccer

Probably the most popular sport worldwide, soccer has only recently made strides in endearing itself to American athletes and fans. The shortage of English-language soccer films reflects the game's relative obscurity in the U.S. prior to the 1980s. Great Britain produced soccer films like *The Winning Goal* (1920) and *The Ball of Fortune* (1926) in the days of silent cinema. In 1942's *One of Our Aircraft Is Missing*, one of the bomber's crewmembers was a famous fictitious soccer player. A few other scattered British releases also surfaced in the 1930s and 1950s. However, in countries like Czechoslovakia and Brazil, where soccer reigns supreme, a flood of soccer films reached the public in the decades following World War II. None of these films received a major U.S. release. However, the game gained some American exposure when Sylvester Stallone headed an all-star cast, including former soccer great Pele, in the 1981 POW/soccer adventure *Victory*. That same year saw the release of Bill Forsyth's charming Scottish comedy *Gregory's Girl*, in which an incompetent goalie pursues a hot-shot female soccer teammate. An animated animal soccer game was played in the Disney 1971 fantasy *Bedknobs and Broomsticks*.

The Winning Goal (1920); *The Ball of Fortune* (1926); *The Great Arsenal Stadium Mystery* (1939); *One of Our Aircraft Is Missing* (1942); *Four Ways Out* (1951); *The Great Game* (1953); *Small Town Story* (1953); *Bloomfield* (1969); *The Goalie's Anxiety at the*

Penalty Kick (1971); *Bedknobs and Broomsticks* (1971); *The Hero* (1972); *Yesterday's Hero* (1979); *Victory* (aka *Escape to Victory*) (1981); *Gregory's Girl* (1981); *Hotshot* (1987); *Ladybugs* (1992); *The Golden Ball* (1994); *The Big Green* (1995); *Soccer Dog: The Movie* (1998); *Fever Pitch* (1999); *Switching Goals* (2000)

Sometimes They Come Back... Series

Stephen King's short story "Sometimes They Come Back," from his 1978 anthology *Night Shift*, provided the inspiration for this in-name-only film series. The 1991 TV movie *Sometimes They Come Back* at least resembled King's story with a plot about a school teacher (Tim Matheson) who returns to his town home — only to be haunted by the ghosts of teenage delinquents killed 30 years earlier. A 1996 direct-to-video follow-up was more of a remake than a sequel. Michael Gross played single father Jon Porter, who returns home and encounters an old nemesis named Tony Reno (Alexis Arquette). The problem is that Jon accidentally killed Tony several years earlier and now the back-from-the-dead Tony wants revenge. Another direct-to-video release, 1999's *Sometimes They Come Back...More Than Once* strayed even further from the original premise by moving the action to Antarctica. It was co-written by Adam Grossman, who wrote and directed the second film. None of the three films featured the same characters. Other short stories from King's *Night Shift* collection also reached the silver screen as *Children of the Corn* (1984), *The Lawnmower Man* (1992), and *The Mangler* (1995). See also **Children of the Corn Series**.

   Sometimes They Come Back (aka *Stephen King's Sometimes They Come Back*) (1991 TVM); *Sometimes They Come Back...Again* (1996); *Sometimes They Come Back...More Than Once* (aka *Frozen*; *Ice Station Erebus*) (1999)

Somewhere Series

War-weary British audiences of the 1940s found the *Somewhere* films agreeably silly in spite of their nonexistent plots and sloppy production values. The movies consisted mostly of old, loosely-connected vaudeville sketches performed by dancehall veterans like Frank Randle, Harry Korris, and Robbie Vincent. The low-brow humor frequently bordered on tasteless, making the *Somewhere* films the forerunners of the *Carry On* (q.v.) comedies of the late 1950s and 1960s. Ironically, Randle made a 1949 non–*Somewhere* film called *What a Carry On*.

   Somewhere in England (1940); *Somewhere in Camp* (1942); *Somewhere on Leave* (1942); *Somewhere in Civvies* (1943); *Somewhere in Politics* (1949)

South Pole *see* North Pole/South Pole

Spenser

Mystery writer Robert B. Parker introduced his Boston-based sleuth Spenser (first name unknown) in the 1973 novel *The Godwulf Manuscript*. Written in first-person, the books revealed only snippets about the private detective's past as a Vietnam soldier, boxer, and policeman. A modestly successful TV series, *Spenser: For Hire*, debuted on ABC in 1985. It starred Robert Urich as Spenser with Avery Brooks as his mysterious cohort Hawk. Barbara Stock played Spenser's love interest, Susan Silverman, a school guidance counselor. Urich's performance divided fans of the novels, despite Parker's presence as a consultant for the TV series. Although the series folded in 1988, ABC premiered a spin-off, *A Man Called Hawk*, the following year. Avery Brooks continued in his role as the literate, violent Hawk, who had moved from Boston to Washington — but the series lasted only half a season. Four years later, though, Brooks and Urich reteamed for a series of four made-for-TV *Spenser* films. Barbara Williams played Susan in the first two films, with Wendy Crewson replacing her for the last two. The A&E cable network tried to launch its own *Spenser* film series in 1999. Author Parker adapted his own novel for *Spenser: Small Vices* which starred Joe Mantegna as Spenser, Shiek Mahmud-Bey as Hawk, and Marcia Gay Harden as Susan. The source novel was Parker's 24th featuring Spenser. See also **Television Series Reunion Films**.

   Spenser: Ceremony (1993 TVM); *Spenser: Pale Kings and Princes* (1993 TVM); *Spenser: The Judas Goat* (1994 TVM); *Spenser: A Savage Place* (1995 TVM); *Spenser: Small Vices* (1999 TVM)

Spiders

Is it their shape? Their four pairs of eyes? The fact that some are deadly poisonous? It's hard to figure out why the movies have cast good-natured spiders as vile henchmen or oversized people-eaters. Nevertheless, silly-looking giant spiders appeared in *The Spider* (1958), *The Lost World* (1960), *Son of Godzilla* (1967), and *Giant Spider Invasion* (1975). Jungle Jim (q.v.) chased a big one which produced a valuable drug in 1951's *Fury of the Congo*. Raquel Welch ran in the opposite direction of another giant web-spinner, created with precision by special effects expert Ray Harryhausen in *One Million Years B.C.* (1966). Scientist Leo G. Carroll's artificial food was responsible for creating the most famous oversized spider in 1955's *Tarantula*. The spider killed by Grant Williams with a straight pin in *The Incredible Shrinking Man* runs a close second, even though it was not really giant (but certainly appeared that way to the incredibly small Williams). Man/fly David Hedison also encountered a little spider that probably looked big to him in 1958's *The Fly*. Unfortunately, he did not have access to a handy pin. Normal-sized spiders have been used for evil purposes by satanists (*The Devil's Bride*) and crafty murderers. Indeed, Gale Sondergaard employed spiders to make her murders look like suicides in 1944's *Spider Woman*. She might have escaped detection if not for the presence of that master sleuth Sherlock Holmes (Basil Rathbone). Interestingly, Sondergaard also starred in a 1946 film called *The Spider Woman Strikes Back*— but she played a different character and there were no spiders! Meanwhile, Holmes (Peter Cushing this time) saved Henry Baskerville from a deadly tarantula in 1959's *The Hound of the Baskervilles*. For the most part, though, a solitary little spider has posed little trouble. A thousand or more? That's a different story altogether, as evidenced by the invasions detailed in *Kingdom of the Spiders* (1977), *Tarantulas: The Deadly Cargo* (1977 TVM), and *Arachnophobia* (1990). Tom Selleck met up with a robot spider in the 1982 sci-fi thriller *Runaway* and Will Smith encountered an 80-foot steam-powered tarantula in *Wild Wild West* (1999). And — at last — nice spiders got starring roles in the adaptations of the children's classics *Charlotte's Web* and *James and the Giant Peach*. See also **The Fly Series; Insects**.

   Tarzan's Desert Mystery (1943); *Spider Woman* (aka *Sherlock Holmes and the Spider Woman*) (1944); *Sombra, the Spider Woman* (aka *The Black Widow*) (1947); *Fury of the Congo* (1951); *Tarantula*

(1955); *The Incredible Shrinking Man* (1957); *The Spider* (aka *Earth vs. the Spider*) (1958); *The Fly* (1958); *The Hound of the Baskervilles* (1959); *The Lost World* (1960); *One Million Years B.C.* (1966); *Son of Godzilla* (aka *Gojira no Musuko*) (1967); *The Devil's Bride* (aka *The Devil Rides Out*) (1968); *Charlotte's Web* (1973); *Giant Spider Invasion* (1975); *Kingdom of the Spiders* (1977); *Spider-Man* (1977 TVM); *Tarantulas: The Deadly Cargo* (1977 TVM); *Runaway* (1982); *Arachnophobia* (1990); *An American Tail: Fievel Goes West* (1991); *James and the Giant Peach* (1996); *A Bug's Life* (1998); *Wild Wild West* (1999)

Stairs

Alfred Hitchcock, the master of suspense, was also the master of memorable staircase sequences. James Stewart's inability to climb the stairs of a Spanish mission proved integral to the plot of *Vertigo* (1958). Cary Grant carried a glowing glass of milk *up* the stairs in *Suspicion* (1941), then carried an ailing Ingrid Bergman *down* the stairs in the tense climax to *Notorious* (1946). Martin Balsam encountered a knife-wielding killer at the top of the stairs in the Bates house in *Psycho* (1960). Ironically, Hitchcock's film version of *The 39 Steps* (1935) omitted the elaborate stairs to the beach described in John Buchan's spy novel. Despite Hitchcock's impressive use of stairs, none of his sequences has achieved the fame of Sergei Eisenstein's "Odessa Steps" scene in the classic Russian silent film *Potemkin* (1925). Considered by many critics as one of the famous sequences ever put on film, it starts with Czarist soldiers marching down a long flight of steps and firing on fleeing citizens. In the midst of this massive carnage, a mother is killed and the baby carriage containing her child tumbles down the many steps. Brian De Palma paid homage to the Odessa Steps sequence in the exciting train station shootout in *The Untouchables* (1987)—a scene that was spoofed seven years later in *Naked Gun 33⅓: The Final Insult*. Despite the impact of the Odessa Steps, the most visually stunning staircase was the moving one that transported souls from the Earthly world to the celestial one in the classic fantasy *Stairway to Heaven* (1946). Boxer Rocky Balboa (Sylvester Stallone) trained for his heavyweight championship bout in *Rocky* (1976) by running up and down the steep stairs of the Philadelphia Museum of Art. In a greater athletic endeavor, the tiny hero of *The Incredible Shrinking Man* (1957) tried to climb the stairs out of his basement using a thread and a straight pin as a rope and grappling hook. Several musical numbers have taken place on stairs, though few can compare to the classic routine performed by Shirley Temple and Bill "Bojangles" Robinson in *The Little Colonel* (1935). On the darker side, stairs have also been used for homicidal purposes. In *Kiss of Death* (1947), Richard Widmark's psychotic killer gleefully pushed a wheelchair-bound woman down a flight of stairs. Nasty cop Edmund O'Brien murdered a blind man in a similar manner in *Shield for Murder* (1954). Neither of those cold-blooded killers can compare with Gene Tierney's obsessive wife portrayal in *Leave Her to Heaven* (1946). Unwilling to share husband Cornel Wilde with *anyone*, she hurled herself down the stairs upon learning of her pregnancy. People have fallen or been pushed down staircases in many other films such as *Before Dawn* (1931), *Don't Be Afraid of the Dark* (1973), and *Deadly Friend* (1986). A homicidal psychopath met his fate when Ethel Barrymore, Dorothy McGuire, and George Brent converged on the title structure in the climax of *The Spiral Staircase* (1946). Chow Yun Fat proved adept at sliding down stairs

with both revolvers blazing in both *A Better Tomorrow II* (1988) and *Hard-Boiled* (1992). Al Pacino used an escalator for his shootout in *Carlito's Way* (1993). In Wes Craven's horror picture *The People Under the Stairs* (1991), the title characters were kidnapped boys who didn't fit into a "perfect family." On television's *The Munsters*, the family's pet dragon Spot lived under the stairs. Finally, in the fact-based 1998 TV movie *The Staircase*, William Petersen played a carpenter who built a one-of-a-kind church staircase for nun Barbara Hershey. See also **Elevators (or Lifts)**.

Potemkin (aka *Battleship Potemkin*) (1925); *Before Dawn* (1931); *The Little Colonel* (1935); *Nancy Drew and the Hidden Staircase* (1939); *Suspicion* (1941); *Leave Her to Heaven* (1945); *The Spiral Staircase* (1946); *Notorious* (1946); *Stairway to Heaven* (aka *A Matter of Life and Death*) (1946); *Kiss of Death* (1947); *Shield for Murder* (1954); *The Incredible Shrinking Man* (1957); *Vertigo* (1958); *Psycho* (1960); *Barefoot in the Park* (1967); *Staircase* (1969); *Don't Be Afraid of the Dark* (1973 TVM); *The Spiral Staircase* (1975); *Rocky* (1976); *High Anxiety* (1977); *Deadly Friend* (1986); *The Untouchables* (1987); *A Better Tomorrow II* (1988); *The People Under the Stairs* (1991); *Hard-Boiled* (1992); *Carlito's Way* (1993); *Naked Gun 33⅓: The Final Insult* (1994); *The Staircase* (1998 TVM)

Star Trek Series

The road from cancelled TV series to phenomenally-successful film series is a bizarre one travelled only by the starship *Enterprise*. Gene Roddenberry's science fiction TV series debuted on NBC in 1966. Sci-fi fans embraced it, but it was a consistent ratings loser opposite veteran series like *My Three Sons* and *Bewitched*. An enthusiastic write-in campaign saved it from cancellation after its second season, but the series was axed after its third year in 1969. Shortly thereafter, its 78 episodes went into syndication and began playing almost daily on local TV stations. By 1974, the show had developed a dizzying loyal cult following (dubbed "trekkies"), who honored stars William Shatner (Kirk) and Leonard Nimoy (Spock) at national conventions and urged Roddenberry to revive the series. Roddenberry tried just that. He had laid the groundwork for a "Star Trek" made-for-TV movie (and pilot for a new series) when George Lucas' *Star Wars* went through the box-office roof in 1977. Eager to duplicate *Star Wars*' receipts, Paramount decided to turn its Star Trek movie into a lavish theatrical space opera. The $40 million *Star Trek—The Motion Picture* was rushed into theaters just in time for Christmas 1979. Trekkies made it a hit, but the reviews were mixed, with critics and fans complaining of an overemphasis on special effects. However, best-selling writer-turned-director Nicholas Meyer set the film series on track with the 1982 sequel *Star Trek II: The Wrath of Khan*. Jack Soward's script resurrected super-villain Khan (Ricardo Montalban) from the TV episode "Space Seed" and climaxed with Spock's "death." Leonard Nimoy took over the directing reins for *Star Trek III: The Search for Spock* (1984) and *Star Trek IV: The Voyage Home* (1986), both of which were praised for capturing the flavor of the series. After helming the non–Trek smash *Three Men and a Baby* (1987), Nimoy handed over *Star Trek* directing chores to his co-star. William Shatner directed and co-wrote the story for 1989's *Star Trek V: The Final Frontier*, which opened strongly enough to temporarily oust *Indiana Jones and the Last Crusade* from number one on *Variety*'s box-office charts. Its popularity was short-lived however, as even faithful fans found it a plodding, unexciting trek with old friends.

The Enterprise crew returned two years later with the satisfying, though unremarkable, *Star Trek VI: The Undiscovered Country*. Its sentimental ending served as a farewell for most of the original cast. Back on the small screen, Roddenberry and producer Rick Berman launched *Star Trek: The Next Generation*, a syndicated TV series with a cast of newcomers, in 1987. Set 78 years after the original *Star Trek*, it introduced a whole new crew headed by Patrick Stewart as Captain Jean-Luc Picard and Brent Spiner as the android Data (the equivalent of Spock). Over the next seven years, *The Next Generation* built its own following, eventually becoming the top-rated non-network drama series on television. In 1994, Berman surprisingly halted production of the TV program so he could launch a film series with *The Next Generation* characters. *Star Trek: Generations* (1994) was an awkward attempt to transition from the old to the new, with Captain Pickard meeting up with Captain Kirk. However, *The Next Generation* crew found its own groove with the 1996 follow-up *Star Trek: First Contact*, which featured the popular Borgs from the TV series. See also **Theatrical Films Based on TV Series**; **Teleportation**.

Star Trek-The Motion Picture (1979); *Star Trek II: The Wrath of Khan* (1982); *Star Trek III: The Search for Spock* (1984); *Star Trek IV: The Voyage Home* (1986); *Star Trek V: The Final Frontier* (1989); *Star Trek VI: The Undiscovered Country* (1991); *Star Trek: Generations* (1994); *Star Trek: First Contact* (1996); *Star Trek: Insurrection* (1998)

Star Wars Series

George Lucas' tremendously popular space adventure series has developed its own mythos in an amazingly short period of time. When *Variety* predicted a "huge outlook" for *Star Wars* back in 1977, it turned out to be the venerable trade paper's grossest understatement. But the film's greatest impact was not in dollars, but in influencing the near-future of American cinema. Like another late 1970s hit, *Halloween* (q.v.), *Star Wars* fostered dozens of imitations, such as *Battle Beyond the Stars* (1980), *Spacehunter* (1983), *The Ice Pirates* (1984), and the Mel Brooks spoof *Spaceballs* (1986). However, whereas *Halloween* impacted on a specific genre, Lucas' mixture of adventure and morals carried over into non–science fiction films — most notably his and Steven Spielberg's Indiana Jones (q.v.) movies. Curiously, Lucas' interest in the *Star Wars* films seemed to diminish as the series progressed. He turned over the directing reins to Irvin Kershner on 1980's *The Empire Strikes Back* (arguably the best) and to Richard Marquand on 1983's *Return of the Jedi*. Despite insisting that the original trilogy was the middle three chapters of a longer series, Lucas initially showed little interest in making the framing films. However, he did give the furry little friendly Ewoks (introduced in *Return*) two TV movie adventures. Although oriented toward the juvenile audience, these small-screen sequels boasted the usual excellent production values and a reasonable amount of charm. The major theatrical stars — Harrison Ford, Mark Hamill, Carrie Fisher — were naturally missing. They *did* appear in the earlier *Star Wars Holiday Special*, a two-hour movie that aired on CBS in 1978. This rare TV movie about Chewbacca's efforts to get home to his family on Kashyyyk has never been rebroadcast nor released to video. Allegedly, Lucas, who had little to do with the project, disowned it. In 1997, Lucas and 20th Century–Fox released back-to-back "special editions" of the theatrical films that contained new footage (as well as improved technical elements like digitally re-mastered sound). These re-releases, *Stars Wars* in particular, performed exceptionally well at the box-office and whetted the public's appetite for the heavily-hyped *Star Wars Episode I: The Phantom Menace* (1999). This prequel, the first of three films leading up to *Star Wars*, was met with mixed critical reactions. An eager moviegoing public nevertheless made it an instant blockbuster.

Star Wars (1977); *The Star Wars Holiday Special* (1978 TVM); *The Empire Strikes Back* (1980); *Return of the Jedi* (1983); *The Ewok Adventure* (1984 TVM); *Ewoks: The Battle for Endor* (1985 TVM); *Star Wars Episode I: The Phantom Menace* (1999)

Statues Come to Life

German director/actor Paul Wegener gave the cinema its first living statue with his 1914 horror classic *The Golem: Monster of Fate* and its 1920 prequel *The Golem: How He Came to Be*. These films were based on a Jewish myth about a Rabbi who brought to life a giant man of clay to protect persecuted Jews. However, when the Rabbi lost control of his creation, a young girl destroyed it by removing the Star of David from its chest. The same story served as the basis for Julian Duvivier's *Golem* (1936), the French television film *Le Golem* (1966), and an updated British version called *It* (1966) starring Roddy McDowall. An interesting Japanese variation, *Majin, Monster of Terror* (1966) told the story of a giant stone god summoned to wreak vengeance on those who displaced a kingdom's rightful rulers. Bill Murray, Dan Aykroyd, and Harold Ramis used "positive slime" to bring the Statue of Liberty to life to battle evil in 1989's *Ghostbusters II*. Not all living statues have been of the giant variety nor have they been necessarily human-like. Ava Gardner played a storefront statue of Venus who became a living mortal in 1948's *One Touch of Venus*. Yet another Venus statue came to life in the form of game show hostess Vanna White in the 1988 TV movie *The Goddess of Love*. A contemporary witch sent a giant stone eagle to dispense with a college professor and his wife in the intelligent 1962 fantasy *Burn, Witch, Burn*. Statues turned into people and people into statues in Jean Cocteau's stylized *Blood of a Poet* (1930). See **Gorgons** for other movies where people have been transformed into statues. See also **Majin**.

The Golem: Monster of Fate (aka *Der Golem*) (1914); *The Golem: How He Came to Be* (aka *Der Golem, Wie Er in die Welt Kam*) (1920); *Blood of a Poet* (aka *Le Sang d'un Poete*) (1930); *One Touch of Venus* (1948); *The Miracle* (1959); *Burn, Witch, Burn* (aka *Night of the Eagle*) (1962); *Jason and the Argonauts* (1963); *It* (1966); *Majin, Monster of Terror* (aka *Majin, the Hideous Monster; Daimajin*) (1966); *The Golden Voyage of Sinbad* (1974); *Mannequin* (1987); *Creepshow 2* (1987); *The Goddess of Love* (1988 TVM); *Ghostbusters II* (1989); *Leprechaun 3* (1995); *The Haunting* (1999)

The Stepfather Series

One good movie does not make a good series. *The Stepfather* (1987) was an effective sleeper featuring an outstanding performance from Terry O'Quinn as a psychopath. The film starts with a family squabble which results in the father's massacre of the rest of the family. It seems that Dad (O'Quinn) wants a perfect family and will settle for nothing less. He departs calmly for another city where he romances a young mother and takes on a new family — complete with suspicious stepdaughter. The unnecessary 1989 sequel revealed that O'Quinn's character had survived the first film, only to be imprisoned in an asylum. He promptly escapes, sets up business as a marriage counselor (of all things!), and begins romancing another young widow. Wisely, O'Quinn bowed out of the series after this installment. Robert Wightman replaced him for the 1992 made-for-cable *Stepfather III*, in which the killer undergoes plastic surgery (thus explaining the new face) and pursues Priscilla Barnes. As with the second film, it offered no new deviations from the original idea. Unfortunately, that's not always a prerequisite for ending a film series as evidenced by the plethora of low-budget series such as *Sleepaway Camp* and *Silent Night, Deadly Night* (qq.v.). See also **Television Movie Sequels to Theatrical Films**.

The Stepfather (1987); *Stepfather II* (aka *Stepfather II: Make Room for Daddy*) (1989); *Stepfather III* (1992 TVM)

The Stepford Wives

A dark satire disguised as a horror film, 1975's *The Stepford Wives* took male chauvinism to outrageous extremes. Katharine Ross starred as a young wife who accompanies her husband to their new home in the quiet suburban town of Stepford, Connecticut. It's not long before Ross begins to notice something odd about her fellow females. Slowly, she discovers that the husbands of Stepford are "trading in" their human wives for obedient robotic replicas. Unlike another adaptation of an Ira Levin novel, *Rosemary's Baby* (1968), *The Stepford Wives* did not burn up the box-office. However, like *Rosemary's Baby*, it did spawn a made-for-TV sequel. In *Revenge of the Stepford Wives* (1980), Sharon Gless played a TV reporter who uncovers another dark suburban secret about Stepford. Apparently, no one listened to her, for Don Murray moved his family there in another TV movie sequel, 1987's *The Stepford Children*. In this slight variation, the Stepford men seek to replace their troublesome kids with well-behaved robots. It took nine years for the wives and children of Stepford to get the male population under control — but they did in *The Stepford Husbands*, another TV movie. Fortunately, the series ended before the Stepford pets could be replaced. See also **Androids and Cyborgs**; **Television Movie Sequels to Theatrical Films**.

The Stepford Wives (1975); *Revenge of the Stepford Wives* (1980 TVM); *The Stepford Children* (1987 TVM); *The Stepford Husbands* (1996 TVM)

Stevens, Cat

Not to be confused with the same-named singer, this double-crossing con artist and gunfighter appeared in a spaghetti Western trilogy directed by Giuseppe Colizzi. Terrence Hill (real name Mario Girotti) played Cat in all three entries, although he would later find far greater fame and fortune as the lead in the Trinity series (q.v.). The first Cat Stevens entry, 1966's *God Forgives, I Don't*, is notable for pairing the handsome Hill with gruff, burly Bud Spencer (real name Carlo Pedersoli). Hill and Spencer would go on to enjoy great success as an Italian odd couple, starring together in all three Cat Stevens entries, the two best Trinity films, and even contemporary action comedies such as *All the Way, Boys* (1973) and *Watch Out, We're Mad* (1974). See also **Trinity**.

God Forgives, I Don't (aka *Dio Perdona…Io No!*; *Blood River*) (1966); *Ace High* (*I Quattro dell'Ave Maria*; *Revenge at El Paso*; *Four Gunmen of Ave Maria*) (1967); *Boot Hill* (aka *La Collina degli Stivali*) (1969)

Stores

Where would you shop for a vicious dog, flesh-eating ghoul, or a mannequin-come-to-life? If you lived in a movie, you could walk down to the nearest department store and find these unusual items and more. Stores have provided colorful background settings for a number of films. Few movies, however, have confined themselves to a store setting for the bulk of their running times. In 1973's *Trapped*, James Brolin recovered from a mugging to find himself locked overnight in a department store — in the company of a nasty, people-eating security dog. Still, that sounds preferable to the shopping mall in 1979's *Dawn of the Dead*, which was populated by flesh-eating ghouls (q.v.) and a gang of crazy bikers. Other mall-bound movies feature similar horrific elements: killer security robots in *Chopping Mall* (1986) and inept dialogue between Woody Allen and Bette Midler in *Scenes from a Mall* (1991). Movies less confined to their store settings have induced an impressive list of Hollywood stars to step behind the counters: James Stewart and Margaret Sullavan (*The Shop Around the Corner*), Rod Steiger (*The Pawnbroker*), Ginger Rogers (*Bachelor Mother*), and Gene Hackman (*All Night Long*). The Marx Brothers and Jerry Lewis wreaked havoc on department stores in, respectively, *The Big Store* and *Who's Minding the Store?* Rock Hudson, in one of his first roles, played a store detective in 1950's *I Was a Shoplifter*. Bob Hoskins played a pet shop owner who moonlighted as a private detective in *Shattered* (1991). Talia Shire also worked in a pet store before she married Sylvester Stallone in *Rocky* (1976), while Rod Taylor and Tippi Hedren met in a pet shop at the beginning of *The Birds* (1963). However, the most famous specialty store probably remains Mr. Mushnik's flower shop, better known as *The Little Shop of Horrors* (1960). It gained fame as the home of the Audrey II, the world's most famous people-devouring plant.

It (1927); *Our Blushing Brides* (1930); *Shop Angel* (1932); *Sweepings* (1933); *Employees' Entrance* (1933); *Many Happy Returns* (1934); *The Nitwits* (1935); *Bachelor Mother* (1939); *The Shop Around the Corner* (1940); *The Big Store* (1941); *The Devil and Miss Jones* (1941); *Miracle on 34th Street* (aka *The Big Heart*) (1947); *One Touch of Venus* (1948); *I Was a Shoplifter* (1950); *Trouble in Store* (1953); *Bundle of Joy* (1956); *The Little Shop of Horrors* (1960); *Who's Minding the Store?* (1963); *The Shop on Main Street* (aka *The Shop on High Street*) (1965); *The Pawnbroker* (1965); *Trapped* (1973 TVM); *Fire Sale* (1977); *The Girls in the Office* (1979 TVM); *Dawn of the Dead* (aka *Zombie*) (1979); *All Night Long* (1981); *Come Back to the 5 & Dime, Jimmy Dean, Jimmy Dean* (1982); *Chopping Mall* (aka *Killbots*) (1986); *The Little Shop of Horrors* (1986); *Mannequin* (1987); *Lady Beware* (1987); *Big* (1988); *Scenes from a Mall* (1991); *Career Opportunities* (1991); *To Be the Best* (1992 TVM); *Clerks* (1994); *Miracle on 34th Street* (1994); *Mallrats* (1995); *Terror in the Mall* (1998 TVM); *You've Got Mail* (1998); *GO* (1999); *Where the Heart Is* (2000)

Strippers

Strippers have appeared in the background of many films, but have been the subject of few. Celebrated stripper/actress/author Gypsy Rose Lee had a hand in four films about strippers. Her mystery novel *The G-String Murders* was adapted for the screen as the 1943 Barbara Stanwyck vehicle *Lady of Burlesque*. This potentially grisly story about a backstage strangler wisely mixed in comedy elements. In Britain, it sported the more exploitative title *Striptease Lady*. Lee's play *Doll Face*, about a burlesque queen with Broadway ambitions, was turned into the same-titled 1945 film. Likewise, her autobiography *Gypsy* spawned a hit Broadway musical and a 1962 movie version. Finally, she appeared in a supporting role in 1963's *The Stripper*. Based on William Inge's play *A Loss of Roses*, it starred a miscast Joanne Woodward as a former stripper seeking a new life and becoming involved with a 19-year-old. Danish actress Britt Ekland played an Amish girl-turned-stripper in William Friedkin's fond homage to old-time burlesque *The Night They Raided Minsky's* (1968). Other actresses who have played strippers include Goldie Hawn (*CrissCross*), Melanie Griffith (*Fear City*), Demi Moore (*Striptease*), Sherilyn Fenn (*Ruby*), and Elizabeth Berkley (in the notorious flop *Showgirls*). The serious side of striptease was explored in 1986's *Stripper*, a surprisingly straightforward, non-exploitative documentary about three professional strippers entering a Las Vegas contest. Naturally, B-movie directors have exploited striptease for its cheese-cake value. Drive-in filler of this kind has ranged from disgusting tripe like 1987's *Stripped to Kill* to modestly amusing fodder like Stephanie Rothman's *The Working Girls*. The latter film, a pay-TV favorite, featured Cassandra Petersen (TV horror hostess Elvira) as a part-time stripper. Male strippers have not received equal time, although Christopher Atkins played one in 1983's best-forgotten *A Night in Heaven*. His leading lady was Lesley Ann Warren, an ecdysiast herself in 1982's *Portrait of a Stripper*. See also **Centerfolds**.

Lady of Burlesque (aka *Striptease Lady*) (1943); *Delightfully Dangerous* (1945); *Lady Godiva Rides Again* (1951); *Sex Kittens Go to College* (aka *The Beauty and the Robot*) (1960); *A Cold Wind in August* (1961); *Danger by My Side* (1962); *Gypsy* (1962); *The Stripper* (aka *Woman of Summer*) (1963); *Faster, Pussycat! Kill! Kill!* (1966); *The Night They Raided Minsky's* (1968); *The Working Girls* (1973); *Portrait of a Stripper* (1982 TVM); *A Night in Heaven* (1983); *Fear City* (1984); *Little Treasure* (1985); *Stripper* (1986); *Kandyland* (1987); *Stripped to Kill* (1987); *Ladykillers* (1988 TVM); *Dance of the Damned* (1988); *Stripped to Kill 2* (1989); *Blaze* (1989); *Criss-Cross* (1992); *Ruby* (1992); *Somebody's Daughter* (1992 TVM); *Candy the Stripper* (1993); *Twenty Bucks* (1993); *Carlito's Way* (1993); *Hold Me, Thrill Me, Kiss Me* (1993); *Gypsy Angels* (1994); *The Smile* (aka *Le Sourire*) (1994); *Exotica* (1994); *Showgirls* (1995); *The Sphinx* (aka *Le Sphinx*) (1995); *Independence Day* (1996); *Striptease* (1996); *Dangerous Ground* (1997); *The Full Monty* (1997); *The Players Club* (1998)

Stunt People

Films about stunt people naturally tend to emphasize action over intellect, as in 1978's *Hooper*, an easy-going Burt Reynolds vehicle about an aging stuntman contemplating one last death-defying feat. In both *Stunt Seven* (1979) and *Stunts Unlimited* (1980), the government sent stunt experts on top-secret rescue missions. No one bothered to question the logic behind substituting Hollywood union men for military-trained specialists. The engrossing real-life story of a deaf stuntwoman was the subject of *Silent Victory: The Kitty O'Neil Story* (1979). In 1980, *The Stunt Man* offered a thought-provoking yarn about a desperate fugitive (Steve Railsback) hired by a crazy film director (Peter O'Toole) to perform dangerously real stunts. Ty Hardin played a stunt man on

vacation—and romancing Connie Stevens—in 1963's *Palm Springs Weekend*. Two years later, the rock band the Dave Clark Five appeared as fun-loving stuntmen in *Having a Wild Weekend*. The casting of these rock 'n' rollers as stunt men is not as odd as it sounds—Dave Clark actually performed stunts in over forty films. On television, Lee Majors played a stuntman who tracked down bail jumpers on the side in *The Fall Guy*. See also **Movies About Movies**.

Lucky Devils (1932); *Miss Tatlock's Millions* (1948); *Palm Springs Weekend* (1963); *Having a Wild Weekend* (*Catch Us If You Can*) (1965); *Stuntman* (1968); *Night Moves* (1975); *Hollywood Boulevard* (1976); *Stunts* (aka *Who Is Killing the Stuntmen?*) (1977); *Hooper* (1978); *Texas Detour* (1978); *Silent Victory: The Kitty O'Neil Story* (1979 TVM); *Stunt Seven* (1979 TVM); *Stunts Unlimited* (1980 TVM); *The Stunt Man* (1980); *Safari 3000* (1982); *The End of Violence* (1997)

Submarines

Tense war melodramas and fanciful science fiction adventures have made the most effective use of submarine settings. The 1938 *Submarine Patrol* was a routine World War I actioner that unknowingly paved the way for later World War II star-studded efforts. In 1943 alone: Cary Grant navigated a submarine into Japanese waters in *Destination Tokyo*; Humphrey Bogart took on the Germans in *Action in the North Atlantic*; John Mills helmed a British sub in *We Dive at Dawn*; and Tyrone Power clashed with Dana Andrews in *Crash Dive*. The popularity of sub war dramas decreased in the 1950s, but big name stars still kept them afloat at the box-office. Sub officers Clark Gable and Burt Lancaster engaged in a bitter conflict in 1958's *Run Silent, Run Deep*. That same year, Glenn Ford was given a mission to destroy a Japanese ship carrying his family in *Torpedo Run*. The only World War II films to survive into the 1960s were epic-scale features like *The Longest Day* (1962) and *Battle of the Bulge* (1965). The submarine war film disappeared into obscurity until the German-made *Das Boot* (*The Boat*) unexpectedly surfaced to wow art-house audiences in 1981. An incredibly tense, claustrophobic thriller, it traced the final days of a doomed German submarine during World War II. In contrast to the realism of war, futuristic submarines have appeared principally in escapist entertainment. Two Jules Verne novels have provided the basis for the best-known submarine fantasies. Disney's 1954 adaptation of *20,000 Leagues Under the Sea* remains a splendid spectacle for children of all ages, highlighted by a thrilling attack by a giant squid. Verne's sequel *Mysterious Island* has been filmed twice, first as a loose adaptation in 1929 and later as a compact 1961 adventure (which actually contained little footage of the famous submarine *Nautilus*). Irwin Allen, in his pre–disaster movie days, produced 1961's *Voyage to the Bottom of Sea*, which starred Walter Pidgeon as commander of the submarine *Seaview*. The wild plot pitted the *Seaview* against a giant octopus, on-board saboteurs, and a radiation belt threatening to burn the Earth to a crisp. The *Seaview*, with Richard Basehart replacing Pidgeon, made the move to television in the 1964–68 series *Voyage to the Bottom of the Sea*. The most elaborate submarine was probably the supership featured in the 1963 Japanese fantasy *Atragon*—it could travel underwater, on land, or in the air! Animated Beatles sailed aboard 1968's *Yellow Submarine* (which is where they all lived). In 1966's *Batman*, the

Penguin, the Riddler, the Joker, and the Cat Woman plotted mischief from within a penguin-shaped submarine. James Bond used a minisub in *Thunderball* (1965), while a full-size submarine was stolen in the 1977 Bond adventure *The Spy Who Loved Me*. Herpephobes should try to avoid *Fer-de-Lance*, a 1974 TV movie about snakes slithering rampantly about a damaged submarine.

Mysterious Island (1929); *The Devil and the Deep* (1932); *Hell Below* (1933); *Submarine D-1* (1937); *Submarine Patrol* (1938); *Escape to Glory* (aka *Submarine Zone*) (1940); *Crash Dive* (1943); *Destination Tokyo* (1943); *We Dive at Dawn* (1943); *Action in the North Atlantic* (1943); *The Damned* (1947); *Operation Disaster* (aka *Morning Departure*) (1950); *Hell and High Water* (1954); *20,000 Leagues Under the Sea* (1954); *Above Us the Waves* (1956); *The Deep Six* (1958); *Run Silent, Run Deep* (1958); *The Silent Enemy* (1958); *Torpedo Run* (1958); *Atomic Submarine* (1959); *On the Beach* (1959); *Operation Petticoat* (1959); *Up Periscope* (1959); *Atlantis, the Lost Continent* (1961); *Mysterious Island* (1961); *Voyage to the Bottom of the Sea* (1961); *Mystery Submarine* (aka *Decoy*) (1962); *Atragon* (1963); *The Bedford Incident* (1965); *Around the World Under the Sea* (1966); *The Russians are Coming! The Russians are Coming!* (1966); *Batman* (1966); *Assault on the Wayne* (1966 TVM); *Yellow Submarine* (1968); *Submarine X-1* (1968); *Nobody's Perfect* (1968); *Ice Station Zebra* (1968); *Latitude Zero* (1969); *The Land That Time Forgot* (1974); *Fer-de-Lance* (1974 TVM); *The Spy Who Loved Me* (1977); *Gray Lady Down* (1978); *Das Boot* (aka *The Boat*) (1981); *The Fifth Missile* (1986); *The Abyss* (1989); *The Hunt for Red October* (1990); *Full Fathom Five* (1990); *Endless Descent* (1991); *Crimson Tide* (1995); *Down Periscope* (1996); *Escape from L.A.* (1996); *Up Periscope* (1996); *Crash Dive* (1997); *Hostile Waters* (1997); *Sub Down* (1997); *The Hunley* (1999 TVM); *The World Is Not Enough* (1999); *Phantom, the Submarine* (1999); *U-571* (2000).

Subspecies Series

Full Moon Pictures produced this direct-to-video vampire series that stretched its modest budget by making excellent use of its Romanian locations. Anders Hove and Michael Watson, who both appeared in the TV soap opera *General Hospital*, play the sons of vampire ruler Vlad. The evil Radu (Hove) kills his father and steals the Bloodstone, a relic that oozes the blood of saints. The good Stefan (Watson), who has fallen in love with a pretty tourist named Michelle (Laura Tate), tries to destroy his brother. He eventually succeeds, but not before Michelle has become a vampire, too. Hove, decked out in long hair and grotesque makeup, overacts as the villainous bloodsucker. The brooding, intense Watson fares much better and keeps the film from straying into camp. Unfortunately, a resurrected Radu (Hove again) destroys Stefan at the beginning of *Bloodstone: Subspecies II* (1993). However, Michelle (Denise Duff) steals the Bloodstone, escapes from Radu, and contacts her sister Rebecca (Melanie Shatner, William Shatner's daughter). Both *Subspecies II* and *Bloodlust: Subspecies III* (1994) deal with Radu's plans to make Michelle his vampiric bride and Rebecca's attempts to save her sister. The fourth installment, *Subspecies IV: Bloodstorm* (1998), adds a few new twists. Michelle, still being pursued by Radu, meets a physician who claims he can cure her vampirism. Meanwhile, Radu must cope with a young ambitious vampire named Ash (Jonathan Morris). The vampire Ash was the subject of *Vampire Journals*, a 1997 Full Moon production also starring Morris. Ted Nicolaou directed all four *Subspecies* entries as well as *Vampire Journals*. He also wrote the latter film and the second and fourth *Subspecies* installments. See also **Vampires**.

Subspecies (1991); *Bloodstone: Subspecies II* (1993); *Bloodlust: Subspecies III* (1994); *Subspecies IV: Bloodstorm* (1998)

Subways

Underground trains have been underutilized as film settings, principally because their frequent stops and passenger turnover prohibit the development of an involved plot. Nevertheless, French director Luc Besson fashioned a stylish tale about contemporary underground denizens in 1985's *Subway*. The underrated horror film *Raw Meat* was about the trapped survivors of a London subway disaster and their descendants — who evolved into cannibals. Vicious Robert Shaw and cronies hijacked an NYC subway and held the passengers for ransom in the 1974 thriller *The Taking of Pelham One Two Three*. Exciting subway chase sequences appeared in *Predator 2, Highlander 2: The Quickening, Eve of Destruction, Lethal Weapon 3,* and *Speed*. The difficulties of getting a seat on the morning subway were explored in the 1950 comedy *Pretty Baby*. Youth gangs harassed subway passengers in *The Warriors* (1979) and *We're Fighting Back* (1981). Subway workers figured prominently in the plots of *No Time for Love* (1943) and *Sugarbaby* (1985). The remains of an alien spaceship were unearthed during a subway station excavation in the clever sci-fi fantasy *Five Million Years to Earth* (1967). See also **Trains**.

No Time for Love (1943); *Pretty Baby* (1950); *Dutchman* (1966); *Five Million Years to Earth* (aka *Quatermass and the Pit*) (1967); *The Incident* (1967); *Short Walk to Daylight* (1972 TVM); *Raw Meat* (aka *Deathline*) (1973); *The Taking of Pelham One Two Three* (1974); *The Warriors* (1979); *We're Fighting Back* (1981); *Subway* (1985); *Sugar Baby* (1985); *Predator 2* (1990); *Highlander 2: The Quickening* (1991); *Eve of Destruction* (1991); *Lethal Weapon 3* (1992); *Speed* (1994); *Angel Dust* (aka *Tenshi No Kuzu*) (1994); *Money Train* (1995); *While You Were Sleeping* (1995); *Extreme Measures* (1996); *Mimic* (1997); *The Taking of Pelham One Two Three* (1998 TVM); *The Bone Collector* (1999)

Suicide

Although suicide has played an integral role in dozens of features, films expressly about it fall into two general categories. The first includes movies in which someone attempts to thwart a potential suicide. In 1951's *Fourteen Hours*, Richard Basehart spent the better part of a day on a skyscraper's ledge as likable policeman Paul Douglas and others (including Grace Kelly) tried to talk him out of taking the plunge. While Basehart's character fell into a net and lived, Sissy Spacek succeeded in killing herself in 1986's *'Night, Mother*, despite desperate pleas from parent Anne Bancroft. An angel named Clarence dissuaded James Stewart from suicide in Frank Capra's perennial holiday offering *It's a Wonderful Life* (1946). Paralyzed Richard Dreyfuss fought a hospital staff for his right to die in the powerful *Whose Life Is It Anyway?* (1981). The second category of suicide films revolves around how a loved one's suicide affects the living. Families and friends dealt with devastating teenage suicides in *Silence of the Heart* (1984), *Surviving* (1985), and *Permanent Record* (1988). Angie Dickinson played a woman trying to rebuild her life after her husband took his in *The Suicide's Wife* (1979). On the lighter side, suicide has been played for laughs in a handful of offbeat comedies. After tightening a noose around his neck in *Reuben, Reuben*, poet Tom Conti changed his mind — only to have a dog burst into the room and knock his chair out from under him. Bud Cort delighted in staging elaborate fake suicides in the cult classic *Harold and Maude* (1971). In 1978's *The End*, a dying man unable to commit suicide decides he needs professional help with his death. Would-be suicide victims met and fell in love in *Paris in Spring* (1935) and *Tulips* (1981). And four middle-aged men decided to commit group suicide by eating themselves to death in the French farce *La Grande Bouffe* (1973). Several films have climaxed in shocking suicides. *Guyana Tragedy: The Story of Jim Jones* (1980) ended with the bizarre mass suicide staged in the late 1970s by the Rev. Jones and his cult followers. A murderess (Jean Simmons) rejected by her lover (Robert Mitchum) backed their car off a cliff in Otto Preminger's *Angel Face* (1953). In 1948's *The Red Shoes*, a ballerina confronted with choosing between art and love plunges to her death. Ship steward Edmund Gwenn explained the ultimate fate of suicide victims to the dead passengers aboard his ship in *Between Two Worlds* (1944).

Dangerous Corner (1934); *Paris in Spring* (aka *Paris Love Song*) (1935); *Between Two Worlds* (1944); *It's a Wonderful Life* (1946); *The Red Shoes* (1948); *Fourteen Hours* (1951); *Angel Face* (1953); *The Slender Thread* (1965); *The Art of Love* (1965); *Harold and Maude* (1971); *La Grande Bouffe* (1973); *The End* (1978); *Leap into the Void* (1979); *The Suicide's Wife* (aka *A New Life*) (1979 TVM); *Guyana Tragedy: The Story of Jim Jones* (1980 TVM); *Tulips* (1981); *Whose Life Is It Anyway?* (1981); *The Eyes, the Mouth* (1982); *Reuben, Reuben* (1983); *Right of Way* (1983 TVM); *Silence of the Heart* (1984 TVM); *A Reason to Live* (1985 TVM); *Mishima* (1985); *Surviving* (1985 TVM); *'Night Mother* (1986); *Permanent Record* (1988); *Retribution* (1988); *Last Wish* (1992 TVM); *Woman on the Ledge* (1993 TVM); *After Jimmy* (1996 TVM); *One True Thing* (1998); *Soft Toilet Seats* (1999); *The Virgin Suicides* (2000)

Summer Camps

Summer camp settings seem to foster rivalries, love affairs, and pranks among their teen residents. Rivals Kristy McNichol and Tatum O'Neal wagered each other on who would lose her virginity first at the summer camp in *Little Darlings* (1980). On a broader scale, the boys and girls of Camp Sasquatch challenged the rich kids' camp across the river to an absurd athletic contest in *Meatballs* (q.v.) (1979). And the Peanuts Gang (q.v.) got involved in a river race in *Race for Your Life, Charlie Brown* (1977). Michael J. Fox and Nancy McKeon found summer camp love in the 1975 TV movie comedy *Poison Ivy*. A more honest relationship, between a disfigured teenage boy and a blind girl, took place at the summer camp in *Mask* (1985). The 1987 *Ernest Goes to Camp* dispensed with any pretensions of plot and focused on the antics of a bumbling counselor and his practical joke-prone charges. Hayley Mills played a pair of twins who meet accidentally at a summer camp and wind up reuniting their divorced parents in *The Parent Trap* (1961). *The Acorn People* (1981) was a heartwarming story about a camp for severely handicapped youngsters. Murders galore took place at the isolated summer camps in the *Friday the 13th* films (q.v.), *The Burning* (1981), and *Summer Camp Nightmare* (1987). See also **Friday the 13th Series**; **Sleepaway Camp**.

Make a Wish (1937); *The Under-Pup* (1939); *There's Magic in Music* (1941); *Summer Love* (1958); *Beware of Children* (1961); *The Parent Trap* (1961); *Please Sir* (1971); *Poison Ivy* (1975 TVM); *Race for Your Life, Charlie Brown* (1977); *Piranha* (1978); *Meatballs* (1979); *Friday the 13th* (1980); *Little Darlings* (1980); *G.O.R.P.* (1980); *The Burning* (1981); *The Acorn People* (1981 TVM); *Oddballs* (1983); *Sleepaway Camp* (1983); *Mask* (1985); *Party Camp* (1986); *Ernest Goes to Camp* (1987); *Summer Camp Nightmare* (aka *The Butterfly Revolution*) (1987); *Camp Cucamonga* (1990 TVM); *Princes in Exile* (1991 TVM); *Indian Summer* (1993); *The Flood: Who Will Save Our Children?* (1993 TVM); *Camp Nowhere* (1994); *Camp Stories* (1997); *The Parent Trap* (1998); *Down Will Come Baby* (1999 TVM)

Superfly

One of the most successful blaxploitation (q.v.) films of the early 1970s, *Superfly* remains a morally ambiguous tale about a black drug dealer who doublecrosses his cronies, goes "straight," and jets off to Italy. Youngblood Priest (Ron O'Neal) dresses sharply and always acts cool. He's a charming drug lord, especially compared to the scum surrounding him (this apparently justifies his actions). Despite its questionable social values, the film clicked at the box-office and with critics who admired its hip style. Composer Curtis Mayfield scored two top ten singles with "Freddie's Dead" and "Superfly." O'Neal took the directorial reins for the inevitable sequel, 1973's *Superfly T.N.T.* This meandering follow-up found a disenchanted Priest getting involved with running guns to help an oppressed African country. It faded quickly at theaters and relegated O'Neal to supporting roles. A third entry, *The Return of Superfly*, unexpectedly surfaced in 1990. Nathan Purdee took over as Priest, who returns from exile in Paris to get even with his old gang. Mayfield completed the music score shortly before his death. See also **Blaxploitation Films**.

Superfly (1972); *Superfly T.N.T.* (1973); *The Return of Superfly* (1990)

Superman

"You'll believe a man can fly!" proclaimed the ads when *Superman* was released in 1978. Millions of moviegoers did just that, making the Man of Steel's celebrated screen return the first of a profitable series. Actually, Superman made his first feature-length movie appearance in 1951 in the guise of stocky George Reeves. *Superman and the Mole Men* (1951) was a low-budget independent feature aimed at the juvenile trade. It would have likely remained a B-movie oddity, except that its minor success resulted in a phenomenal, syndicated TV series *The Adventures of Superman*. In all, 104 half-hour episodes were broadcast originally between 1952 and 1957. Reeves starred as Clark Kent/Superman, with Phyllis Coates and later Noel Neill as Lois Lane, Jack Larson as Jimmy Olsen, and John Hamilton as Perry White. Despite obvious budget limitations, the series made the most of its special effects. Later episodes were even filmed in color, a television rarity in the 1950s. Sadly, Reeves became typecast by the role and had difficulty finding work, a fact that may have attributed to his alleged 1959 suicide. The Superman character, created by writer Jerry Siegel and artist Joe Shuster, first appeared in comic book form in 1939. Bud Collyer provided the voice of Superman for a 1940–51 radio series. Kirk Allyn also played the Man of Steel in 1948 and 1950 serials. He can be glimpsed as Lois Lane's father in the TV-expanded version of 1978's *Superman*. That box-office smash starred Christopher Reeve, who made the superman role his own for a generation of comic book lovers. Much of the 1981 sequel *Superman II* was filmed simultaneously with the first film, partially accounting for the original's $55 million price tag. Whereas *Superman* dealt with the Man of Steel's origin and introduced the supporting characters, *Superman II* promptly pitted our hero against three vicious outlaws from his own planet. The romance between Lois Lane (Margot Kidder) and Clark Kent/Superman was also developed, to the extent that they consummated their relationship. The series took an inexplicable turn for the worse with 1983's *Superman III*, which boasted the additional marquee value of Richard Pryor. Margot Kidder made a brief appearance as Lois Lane, but Superman's love interest was old flame Lana Lang (Annette O'Toole). Reeve balked at starring in a fourth film, so executive producers Ilya and Alexander Salkind brought *Supergirl* to the screen in 1984. Casting an unknown (as they did with Reeve), the Salkinds failed to create another star in girl-next-door Helen Slater. The silly plot and Faye Dunaway's hammy villainess were a far cry from *Superman II*. The only cast holdover from the Superman films was Marc McClure as Jimmy Olsen. The failure of *Supergirl* apparently ended the series. However, Cannon Films acquired distribution rights from Warner Bros. and lured Reeve back into the fold. The actor wrote the story and directed some scenes in 1987's *Superman IV: The Quest for Peace*. Despite the presence of Gene Hackman (returning as Lex Luthor) and a token appearance by Kidder, *Superman IV* was a victim of shoddy special effects and a pretentious plot. The franchise lay dormant for almost nine years, although the character enjoyed modest success with the 1993–97 TV series *Lois & Clark: The New Adventures of Superman*. Then, in 1998, Warner Bros. announced plans to film *Superman Lives* with Nicolas Cage as the Man of Steel. Tim Burton (*Batman*) signed on as director, but script and scheduling problems kept the project from getting off the ground. Meanwhile, the popular *Superman* animated TV series resulted in the made-for-TV feature *The Batman/Superman Movie*. See also **Comic Book Characters**.

Superman and the Mole Men (1951); *Superman* (1978); *Superman II* (1981); *Superman III* (1983); *Supergirl* (1984); *Superman IV: The Quest for Peace* (1987); *The Batman/Superman Movie* (1998 TVM)

Surfing

The quest for the Big Wave was a constant teenage concern in the lightweight *Gidget* (q.v.) and *Beach Party* (q.v.) movies of the 1960s. However, serious surfers had little opportunity to promote their sport prior to Bruce Brown's 1966 documentary *The Endless Summer*. This lyrical homage to the beauties and dangers of surfing earned critical raves and a loyal cult following. Dramatic films have been far less interesting. The 1978 *Big Wednesday* traced the lives of surfing buddies Jan-Michael Vincent, William Katt, and Gary Busey from the mid–1960s to the late 1970s. *Shimmering Light* (1978) sent Beau Bridges to Australia in search of the Big Wave. *North Shore* (1987) starred Matt Adler as a cocky surfer eager to challenge the famed Oahu waves in Hawaii. David Dukes played a man permanently paralyzed by a surfing accident in the 1979 TV movie *Some Kind of Miracle*. The 1987 *Beach Party* reunion film *Back to the Beach* featured Frankie Avalon staging a surfing duel against a wonderfully tacky rear-screen wave. Australian filmmaker-star Yahoo Serious had Albert

Einstein inventing the first surfboard and riding a few waves in the offbeat 1989 comedy *Young Einstein*.

Ride the Wild Surf (1964); *The Endless Summer* (1966); *Pacific Vibrations* (1971); *Big Wednesday* (aka *Summer of Innocence*) (1978); *Shimmering Light* (1978 TVM); *California Dreaming* (1979); *Some Kind of Miracle* (1979 TVM); *North Shore* (1987); *Back to the Beach* (1987); *Surf Nazis Must Die* (1987); *Aloha Summer* (1988); *Under the Boardwalk* (1988); *Young Einstein* (1989); *Red Surf* (1990); *Point Break* (1990); *The Endless Summer 2* (1994); *Blue Juice* (1995); *Escape from L.A.* (1996); *In God's Hands* (1998)

Surrogate Motherhood

Television movies have frequently borrowed their stories from the headlines, with no better example than the four films about surrogate motherhood broadcast between 1979 and 1988. The celebrated case of *Baby M* garnered the most attention, but earlier efforts explored the same territory with less fanfare. In fact, *The Seeding of Sarah Burns* (1979) was a fictional drama with remarkable similarities to *Baby M*. Kay Lenz played the woman who undergoes an embryo transplant and then has second thoughts about giving up the baby. Two 1982 TV movies covered the same ground, with Susan Dey and Stephanie Zimbalist as the surrogate mothers in *The Gift of Life* and *Tomorrow's Child*. The 1984 theatrical release *The Surrogate* dispensed with emotional crises in favor of a whodunit plot. *Private Practices: The Story of a Sex Surrogate* (1986) was a detailed documentary on the subject. Along similar lines, a sterile wife and her spouse hired a young woman to conceive a child with the husband in 1970's *The Baby Maker*. See also **Babies**.

The Baby Maker (1970); *The Seeding of Sarah Burns* (1979 TVM); *Paternity* (1981); *Tomorrow's Child* (aka *Genesis*) (1982 TVM); *The Gift of Life* (1982 TVM); *The Surrogate* (1984); *Private Practices: The Story of a Sex Surrogate* (1986); *Baby M* (1988 TVM); *Waiting* (1990); *The Handmaid's Tale* (1990); *Moment of Truth: A Child Too Many* (1993 TVM); *The Surrogate* (1995 TVM)

Suspended Animation

If one is to believe science fiction cinema, the most popular method for inducing suspended animation is to freeze living cells. The Frankenstein Monster was discovered frozen in ice, and subsequently revived to full strength, in both *House of Frankenstein* (1944) and *The Evil of Frankenstein* (1964). Likewise, a Neanderthal Man encased in ice was thawed in Fred Schepisi's heavyhanded social parable *Iceman* (1984). Warped scientist Dana Andrews tried to bring back frozen Nazis in 1967's *The Frozen Dead*. And a man frozen through cryogenic means returned to life as a killer in Wes Craven's offbeat 1985 TV movie *Chiller*. *Star Trek* creator Gene Roddenberry produced three TV pilot films about a 20th century man awakened from suspended animation to find himself in the future. Alex Cord starred in *Genesis II* (1973), with John Saxon playing the lead in both *Planet Earth* (1974) and *Strange New World* (1975). None of these TV movies resulted in a weekly series. Actually, the 1939 *Buck Rogers* serial was probably the first "film" to use suspended animation as a means of placing contemporary man into the future. It was re-edited into two feature films (1953's *Planet Outlaws* and 1965's *Destination Saturn*) and later remade as 1979's *Buck Rogers in the 25th Century*. Woody Allen borrowed the basic premise for comedic purposes in 1973's *Sleeper*. Other interesting uses of suspended animation have appeared in *This Island Earth* (1954) and *In Like Flint* (1967). The aliens in the former film were among the first to use suspended animation as a method for enabling living beings to endure unbearably long space voyages. The villains in *Flint* suspended a golf game long enough to replace the real president with a lookalike substitute. On television, the 1967-68 sitcom *The Second Hundred Years* was about a 33-year-old man who was frozen in a glacier in 1900, only to thaw out 67 years later and encounter his now elderly son. See also **Coma**.

The Man with Nine Lives (1940); *House of Frankenstein* (aka *Chamber of Horrors*) (1944); *This Island Earth* (1954); *Dinosaurus* (1960); *Frozen Alive* (1964); *The Evil of Frankenstein* (1964); *Kiss the Girls and Make Them Die* (1966); *In Like Flint* (1967); *The Frozen Dead* (1967); *Sleeper* (1973); *Genesis II* (1973 TVM); *Planet Earth* (1974 TVM); *Live Again, Die Again* (1974 TVM); *Strange New World* (1975 TVM); *Buck Rogers in the 25th Century* (1979); *Iceman* (1984); *Chiller* (1985 TVM); *Aliens* (1986); *The Chilling* (1989); *Late for Dinner* (1991); *Critters 4* (aka *Critters 4: They're Invading Your Space*) (1992); *Forever Young* (1992); *1994 Baker Street: Sherlock Holmes Returns* (aka *Sherlock Holmes Returns*) (1993 TVM) (Anthony Higgins); *Austin Powers: International Man of Mystery* (1997)

Swamps

Sun-baked bodies trudging slowly through murky waters. Bloodsucking leeches clinging to human flesh. The crisp snap of an alligator's jaws. These are familiar sights and sounds in movie swamps, which have been used chiefly as convenient hideouts, treacherous shortcuts, and unlikely long-term residences. In Jean Renoir's *Swamp Water* (1941), Dana Andrews chased his dog into a Georgia swamp and discovered the secret hiding place of an alleged murderer (Walter Brennan). He also discovered Brennan's lonely daughter Ann Baxter and, eventually, the real murderers (who met their fate in a pit of quicksand). Brennan repeated his role for the 1952 remake *Lure of the Wilderness*. Richard Gere and Kim Basinger took a short-cut through the Louisiana swamps to elude pursuers in 1986's *No Mercy*. In contrast, Michael Beck and hostage Lee Remick took a Carolina swamp route to avoid the law in the 1984 TV movie *Rearview Mirror*. Barbara Hershey won a Cannes Best Actress Award in 1987's *Shy People* as a Bayou widow whose life is disrupted by an unexpected visit from city relative Jill Clayburgh. Hershey's swampy residence reflected her character's internal strength and emotional isolation. No hidden meanings were behind the swamp setting in *Gator Bait*, a drive-in quickie about a Cajun girl (former Playmate Claudia Jennings) navigating a zippy launch to avoid lusty Bayou males. Nine National Guardsmen wound up fighting unfriendly Cajuns in the *Deliverance*-inspired *Southern Comfort* (1981). The Mouse Rescue Aid Society ventured into a threatening swamp to find a helpless child mouse in Disney's 1977 animated feature *The Rescuers*. The 1982 *Swamp Thing*, based on a cult comic book, was about a good scientist transformed into a half-man, half-plant monstrosity. He ventured out of the marshy waters to periodically rescue girlfriend Adrienne Barbeau from the clutches of evil scientist Louis Jourdan. The plot was essentially repeated in the 1989 sequel *Return of the Swamp Thing*, with Jourdan returning as the villain and Heather Locklear replacing Barbeau.

Swamp Water (aka *The Man Who Came Back*) (1941); *Strangler of the Swamp* (1946); *Swamp Fire* (1946); *Lure of the Wilderness* (1952); *Cry of the Hunted* (1953); *Swamp Women* (aka *Swamp Diamonds; Cruel Swamp*) (1955); *Lure of the Swamp* (1957); *Attack of the Giant Leeches* (aka *The Giant Leeches*) (1959); *Curse of the Swamp Creature* (1966); *Frogs* (1972); *Live and Let Die* (1973); *Gator Bait* (1976); *The Rescuers* (1977); *Southern Comfort* (1981); *Swamp Thing* (1982); *Rearview Mirror* (1984 TVM); *No Mercy* (1986); *Down by Law* (1986); *Shy People* (1987); *Return of the Swamp Thing* (1989); *Ridicule* (1996); *Old Man* (1997 TVM)

The Swan Princess Series

Richard Rich, who helmed Disney's *The Fox and the Hound* (1981) and *The Black Cauldron* (1985), co-wrote and directed this colorful non–Disney animated musical. Partially inspired by the *Swan Lake* ballet, *The Swan Princess* (1994) recounts the tale of Princess Odette, who has been turned into a swan by the evil Rothbart and becomes a young woman again only when the moon casts its rays upon the lake. Although lacking the lyrical quality of *Beauty and the Beast* (1991), *The Swan Princess* nevertheless captures the essence of Disney's 1990s formula: a spunky female heroine, charming supporting characters, and Broadway-style musical numbers including the Golden Globe–nominated "Far Longer Than Forever." Unfortunately, despite good reviews, *The Swan Princess* failed to attract an audience during its theatrical release. It performed significantly better as a videotape release, inspiring two belated sequels courtesy of Rich and his co-writer Brian Nissen. Despite repeating the same formula, these second and third entries faded quickly into obscurity. See also **Animated Movies (Feature-Length)**.

The Swan Princess (1994); *The Swan Princess: Escape from Castle Mountain* (aka *The Swan Princess: The Secret of the Castle*) (1997); *The Swan Princess III: The Mystery of the Enchanted Treasure* (1998)

Sword and Sorcery

Although its literary basis dates back to the 1930s, the sword and sorcery genre of the 1980s probably owes its cinematic inspiration to George Lucas' *Star Wars* (1977) and *The Empire Strikes Back* (1980). Han Solo and Luke Skywalker, while lacking the physical attributes of muscular heroes, together form the basic mold of an ironic adventurer sent forth on a preordained quest. However, the genre proper—complete with muscle-bulging hunks and heavy swords—began with 1982's *Conan the Barbarian*. Robert E. Howard wrote 17 Conan stories, which appeared in *Weird Tales* pulp magazine between 1932–36 (four others were published posthumously). John Milius' film version offered little more than a straightforward telling of Conan's beginnings, but it made a star of Arnold Schwarzenegger and inspired a sequel as well as a rash of imitators. One rip-off, *The Sword and the Sorcerer*, starring TV stars-to-be Lee Horsley (*Matt Houston*) and Kathleen Beller (*Dynasty*), actually beat *Conan* to the theaters. More typical imitations included an ineptly-made Italian series starring former *Tarzan* Miles O'Keefe as a silly beefcake hero named *Ator* (q.v.). Despite attempts to infuse the genre with good-natured camp (Don Coscarelli's *Beastmaster*) or elaborate production design (Peter Yate's *Krull*), the sword and sorcery craze died softly in 1985 with *Red Sonja*, a box-office failure despite the potentially potent pairing of Arnold Schwarzenegger and Brigitte Nielsen. See also **Ator; Beastmaster; Deathstalker**.

Hawk the Slayer (1980); *The Sword and the Sorcerer* (1982); *Conan the Barbarian* (1982); *Sorceress* (1982); *Beastmaster* (1982);

Krull (1983); *Yor-the Hunter from the Future* (1983); *Ator the Fighting Eagle* (1983); *Conan the Destroyer* (1984); *Red Sonja* (1985); *Amazons* (1986); *Iron Warrior* (1987); *The Barbarians* (1987); *Wizard of the Lost Kingdom II* (1989); *Wizards of the Demon Sword* (1991); *October 32nd* (1992)

Talking Animals

Talking animals have been a screen oddity, with the exceptions of Francis the Talking Mule (q.v.) and various animated critters. Bing Crosby and Bob Hope's wacky *Road* comedies featured a talking fish and bear in *Road to Utopia* and a pair of conversing camels in *Road to Morocco*. Another talking camel made a cameo in the adventure spoof *Slave Girl* (1947). Walter Abel had a talking dog in *The Fabulous Joe* (1947), Mickey Rooney a conversant duck in *Everything's Ducky* (1961), and Pee Wee Herman a prose-producing pig in *Big Top Pee Wee* (1988). Bob Goldthwait conversed with a horse in 1988's *Hot to Trot* (which also featured a chattering horsefly), while another talking horse named Renaldo had a brief scene in *High Spirits* (1988). But the most famous talking animal is probably the sheep-pig in *Babe* (1995), although the film is a controversial choice for this category. Unlike the aforementioned talking animal movies, the critters and the humans in *Babe* do not understand each other. Don Johnson understood his dog Blood, although the two could only communicate telepathically in Harlan Ellison's science fiction satire *A Boy and His Dog* (1975). No discussion of talking animals would be complete without mentioning TV's famous talking horse *Mr. Ed*. See also **Francis the Talking Mule**; **Humanimals**.

Road to Morocco (1942); *Road to Utopia* (1945); *Slave Girl* (1947); *The Faboulous Joe* (1947); *Francis* (1949); *Everything's Ducky* (1961); *A Boy and His Dog* (1975); *Hot to Trot* (1988); *Big Top Pee Wee* (1988); *High Spirits* (1988); *Naked Lunch* (1991); *Babe* (1995); *Gordy* (1995); *Two-Bits and Pepper* (1996); *Aaron's Magic Village* (1997); *Paulie* (1998); *Doctor Doolittle* (1998); *Babe: Pig in the City* (1998)

Tammy

A wholesome backwoods teenager, Tammy managed to charm the socks off of everyone she met. Her adventures were mild, to say the least, but nevertheless influential. They set the stage for similar fodder such as *Gidget* (q.v.) and thus proved there was a lucrative market for teen-oriented, nonhorror pictures (a fact exploited by AIP's *Beach Party* series). Twenty-five-year-old Debbie Reynolds, already an established star, created the role in 1957's *Tammy and the Bachelor*. She also sang the memorable title tune, which hit #1 on *Billboard*'s pop chart in July 1957. Sandra Dee, after introducing Gidget two years earlier, played Tammy in two sequels, with John Gavin and Peter Fonda as her love interests. A half-hour sitcom starring Debbie Watson debuted in September 1965 and lasted a single season. Four of its episodes were edited into an 87-minute movie and released theatrically as *Tammy and the Millionaire*.

Tammy and the Bachelor (aka *Tammy*) (1957) (Debbie Reynolds); *Tammy Tell Me True* (1961) (Sandra Dee); *Tammy and the Doctor* (1963) (Dee); *Tammy and the Millionaire* (1967) (Debbie Watson)

Tarzan

Edgar Rice Burroughs' muscular jungle hero has shown remarkable endurance since his film debut in 1918. He has survived ill-conceived character changes, gross miscastings, and cheap-looking backlot jungles. Elmo Lincoln, a D.W. Griffith player who had appeared in *Birth of a Nation*, was the first actor to don the loincloth in 1918's *Tarzan of the Apes*. From the beginning, Burroughs stressed that he wanted the film to be a faithful adaptation. Yet, despite his presence during filming, the plot strayed slightly from the book—a problem that would plague Burroughs on a much larger scale in future *Tarzan* pictures. The movie performed well at the box-office and a less successful sequel, *Romance of Tarzan*, came out later that year. Burroughs reaped little profit off these films and sold the rights to subsequent novels to other producers. During the silent era: Goldwyn distributed *The Revenge of Tarzan* (1920); National Film Corporation turned the novel *Son of Tarzan* into a 1921 serial; Elmo Lincoln reprised the role for another serial *The Adventures of Tarzan* (1921); and Film Booking Offices (later RKO Radio) released *Tarzan and the Golden Lion* (1927). The star of the latter picture, Jim Pierce, married Burroughs' daughter Joan and they later played Tarzan and Jane in a radio series. Following two more Tarzan serials in the early 1930s, Irving Thalberg acquired series rights for MGM. *Tarzan, the Ape Man* (1932) was a lavish jungle epic. It made a film star of former Olympic swimming champion Johnny Weissmuller, but also unfortunately dispensed with Burroughs' conception of Tarzan as an educated man. Weissmuller's Tarzan spoke in broken English ("Tarzan—Jane") and strayed from his beloved jungle only once in the MGM series. Still, audiences loved the wild animal thrills and the romance between primitive Tarzan and civilized Jane (Maureen O'Sullivan). MGM mounted an even more impressive sequel in 1934's *Tarzan and His Mate*, which most critics consider Weissmuller's finest Tarzan epic. MGM produced four more *Tarzan* entries, introducing Johnny Sheffield as Boy in 1939's *Tarzan Finds a Son* and concluding the series with 1942's *Tarzan's New York Adventure*. Although the MGM Tarzan films dominated the 1930s, other independent efforts competed against them. Sol Lesser, who had acquired an option from Burroughs through a third party, signed Buster Crabbe for *Tarzan the Fearless* (1933). It was edited into two different versions, so theater owners could show it as a 71-minute feature or as a serial. The same fate befell 1935's *The New Adventures of Tarzan*. This historic oddity was produced by Burroughs' own company, thus ensuring that Tarzan acted like an educated man. Herman Brix, later known as Bruce Bennett, played the lead. Initially available as a feature or serial, the film was recut again in 1938 and released with a new title *Tarzan and the Green Goddess*. A third non–MGM effort, 1938's *Tarzan's Revenge*, offered minimal backlot thrills and a lackluster hero as played by Glenn Morris. MGM may have felt these low-budget rivals weakened the box-office attraction of their films. However, RKO did not hesitate to grab Weissmuller and launch its own *Tarzan* series in 1943. Johnny Sheffield accompanied Weissmuller to RKO, but Maureen O'Sullivan bowed out as Jane. There was no Jane—but lots of Nazis—in RKO's first entry *Tarzan Triumphs*. The film marked Sol Lesser's return as a Tarzan producer and he eventually installed Brenda Joyce as the series' new Jane. Although relying heavily on stock footage, the RKO films drew steady business. Johnny Sheffield, who had outgrown his role as Boy, left the series after 1947's *Tarzan and the Huntress*. Monogram subsequently signed him to play Bomba, the Jungle Boy (q.v.). Weissmuller turned in his loincloth the following year, after Lesser refused to give him a percentage of the profits. Producer Sam Katzman grabbed Weissmuller for the lead in his Jungle Jim (q.v.) series. Bland Lex Barker replaced Weissmuller for the five remaining RKO pictures, beginning with 1949's *Tarzan's Magic Fountain*. When Barker balked at signing a multi-picture contract, Lesser dropped him in favor of muscular Gordon Scott, a former lifeguard with no acting experience. Scott's first Tarzan picture, *Tarzan's Hidden Jungle* (1955) was RKO's last. Unperturbed, industrious producer Lesser took Scott and the series to MGM and unleashed the first Technicolor Tarzan adventure with 1957's *Tarzan and the Lost Safari*. Lesser and Scott also did *Tarzan's Fight for Life* (1958) for MGM and then made three TV pilots which were edited into *Tarzan and the Trappers* (1958). The latter films fared poorly and Lesser sold his film and TV series rights to Sy Weintraub in 1959. Weintraub produced four superior Tarzan films, the first two starring Scott and the last two introducing stunt man and veteran actor Jock Mahoney. The Mahoney films featured exotic locales, vibrant colors, and a literate interpretation by the star. Unfortunately, Mahoney stepped aside after his second film and the Weintraub series took a turn for the worse. Mahoney's replacement, former Rams linebacker Mike Henry, had the right physique, but his performance doomed 1966's *Tarzan and the Valley of Gold* and two sequels. Henry turned down Weintraub's TV series, allowing Ron Ely to became the small screen's first Tarzan. The series debuted in 1966 and enjoyed a two-year run. In 1970, unsuspecting moviegoers were lured to the theaters to see *Tarzan's Jungle Rebellion* and *Tarzan's Deadly Silence*, two features compiled from TV series episodes. Except for an "R"-rated cartoon spoof *Shame of the Jungle* (1975), the 1970s was a quiet decade for Tarzan. In 1981, John and Bo Derek produced the unintentionally funny *Tarzan, the Ape Man*, devoting more screen time to Bo's frequently nude Jane than to Miles O'-Keefe's hunky Tarzan. In contrast, 1984's *Greystoke: The Legend of Tarzan, Lord of the Apes* made a legitimate stab at transferring Burroughs' novel to the screen intact. Tarzan's childhood in the jungle was depicted splendidly, but his eventual trip to England brought the picture to a standstill. Christopher Lambert made a fine Tarzan, while Andie McDowell's voice as Jane was dubbed by actress Glenn Close. Five years later, Tarzan unexpectedly reappeared in *Tarzan in Manhattan*, an ill-conceived TV movie with Jane as a taxi driver. It starred Joe Lara, who played the ape man again seven years later in the TV movie *Tarzan Returns*, which served as the pilot for the syndicated television series *Tarzan: The Epic Adventures*. After fighting bug-like aliens in *Starship Troopers* (1997), Casper Van Dien put on a loincloth for the quickly-forgotten *Tarzan and the Lost City* (1998). The following year, Disney produced a lavish animated *Tarzan* with songs by Phil Collins. Jimmy Durante spoofed Tarzan (and Johnny Weissmuller in particular) by playing "Schnarzan" in the 1934 musical comedy *Hollywood Party*. See also **Children Raised by Animals**.

Tarzan of the Apes (1918) (Elmo Lincoln); *Romance of Tarzan* (1918) (Lincoln); *The Revenge of Tarzan* (1920) (Gene Pollar); *Tarzan and the Golden Lion* (1927) (Jim Pierce); *Tarzan, the Ape Man* (1932) (Johnny Weissmuller); *Tarzan the Fearless* (1933) (Buster Crabbe); *Tarzan and His Mate* (1934) (Weissmuller); *The New Adventures of Tarzan* (aka *Tarzan's New Adventure;* re-edited in 1938 as *Tarzan and the Green Goddess*) (1935) (Herman Brix, aka Bruce Bennett); *Tarzan Escapes* (1936) (Weissmuller); *Tarzan's Revenge* (1938) (Glenn Morris); *Tarzan Finds a Son!* (1939) (Weiss-

muller); *Tarzan's Secret Treasure* (1941) (Weissmuller); *Tarzan's New York Adventure* (1942) (Weissmuller); *Tarzan Triumphs* (1943) (Weissmuller); *Tarzan's Desert Mystery* (1943) (Weissmuller); *Tarzan and the Amazons* (1945) (Weissmuller); *Tarzan and the Leopard Woman* (1946) (Weissmuller); *Tarzan and the Huntress* (1947) (Weissmuller); *Tarzan and the Mermaids* (1948) (Weissmuller); *Tarzan's Magic Fountain* (1949) (Lex Barker); *Tarzan and the Slave Girl* (1950) (Barker); *Tarzan's Peril* (aka *Tarzan and the Jungle Queen*) (1951) (Barker); *Tarzan's Savage Fury* (1952) (Barker); *Tarzan and the She-Devil* (1953) (Barker); *Tarzan's Hidden Jungle* (1955) (Gordon Scott); *Tarzan and the Lost Safari* (1957) (Scott); *Tarzan's Fight for Life* (1958) (Scott); *Tarzan and the Trappers* (1958) (Scott); *Tarzan's Greatest Adventure* (1959) (Scott); *Tarzan, the Ape Man* (1959) (Denny Miller); *Tarzan the Magnificent* (1960) (Scott); *Tarzan Goes to India* (1962) (Jock Mahoney); *Tarzan's Three Challenges* (1963) (Mahoney); *Tarzan and the Valley of Gold* (1966) (Mike Henry); *Tarzan and the Great River* (1967) (Henry); *Tarzan and the Jungle Boy* (1968) (Henry); *Tarzan's Jungle Rebellion* (1970) (Ron Ely); *Tarzan's Deadly Silence* (1970) (Ely); *Shame of the Jungle* (1975) (voiced by Johnny Weissmuller, Jr.); *Tarzan, the Ape Man* (1981) (Miles O'Keefe); *Greystoke: The Legend of Tarzan, Lord of the Apes* (1984) (Christopher Lambert); *Tarzan in Manhattan* (1989 TVM) (Joe Lara); *Tarzan Returns* (1996 TVM) (Lara); *Tarzan and the Lost City* (1998) (Casper Van Dien); *Tarzan* (1999) (voiced by Tony Goldwyn)

Tattoos

The most tattooed characters in cinema history are probably *The Illustrated Man* (1969) and Queequeg of *Moby Dick* (1956) fame. As to which of these has the most tattoos, well, that's difficult to determine, although Queequeg may get the edge on the basis of his tattooed face. Still, one could make an argument in favor of the Illustrated Man. His face may have been unmarked, but his tattoos did move and tell stories. In other films: Burt Lancaster sported *The Rose Tattoo* (1955) on his chest, symbolizing his "sexual prowess" and also reminding widow Anna Magnani of her deceased husband. Bruce Dern played a wacko artist in 1981's *Tattoo* who kidnaps Maud Adams so he can tattoo her entire body. It was written by Joyce Buñuel, Luis' daughter. Tattoos have been used less dramatically for concealing treasure maps, as in *The Stranger and the Gunfighter* (1976). See also **Painted People**.

The Rose Tattoo (1955); *Moby Dick* (1956); *The Illustrated Man* (1969); *The Golden Voyage of Sinbad* (1974); *Get Charlie Tully* (1976); *The Stranger and the Gunfighter* (1976); *Tattoo* (1981); *Octopussy* (1983); *Lust in the Dust* (1985); *Double Exposure* (1989); *Cape Fear* (1991); *The Piano* (1993); *The Son-in-Law* (1993); *Skin Art* (1994); *Teresa's Tattoo* (1994); *Love and a .45* (1994); *Blue Tiger* (1994); *Snapdragon* (1994); *Cyber Bandits* (1995); *The Pillow Book* (1997)

Taxi Drivers

Colorful cabbies have appeared as memorable supporting characters in dozens of movies and have been played by an impressive group of veteran character actors. James Gleason drove Loretta Young and angel Cary Grant to a frozen lake in *The Bishop's Wife* (1947) and wound up ice skating with them. Streetwise cabbie Ernest Borgnine navigated Kurt Russell through the hazardous ruins of futuristic Manhattan in the sci-fi adventure *Escape from New York* (1981). Yaphet Kotto played the unfortunate cab driver stuck with taking self-confessed murderer David Janssen to Mexico in the suspense-drama *Night Chase* (1970).

Ricardo Cortez was one of the first actors to play a taxi driver in a leading role, starring opposite Barbara Stanwyck in 1931's *Ten Cents a Dance* (a rare directorial effort by Lionel Barrymore). Other star performers who have played cabbies include George Raft (*Pick-up*), Red Skelton (*The Yellow Cab Man*), Fred Astaire (*The Purple Taxi*), Bruce Willis (*The Fifth Element*), Whoopi Goldberg (*Eddie*), and Mel Gibson (*Conspiracy Theory*). In the respective box-office bombs *Rhinestone* (1984) and *Die Laughing* (1980), Sylvester Stallone and Robby Benson proved that taxi drivers can't sing professionally. Stallone played a cabbie again in *Daylight* (1996), although this disaster drama focused more on his previous job as an Emergency Medical Services chief. Lady cabbies have been represented on-screen by Beulah Bondi in *She's a Soldier Too* (1944) and Sophia Loren in *Aurora* (1984). In the 1989 TV movie *Tarzan in Manhattan*, Jane turned out to be a cab driver! Britain's long-running *Carry On* comedy film series (q.v.) featured the appropriately-titled entry *Carry On Cabby* (1963). The 1981 animated feature *Heavy Metal* included a segment about a futuristic NYC cab driver. *Total Recall* (1990) featured both a murderous mutant cab driver and a robotic "Johnnycab." *D.C. Cab* (1983) was an episodic comedy about a cab company, obviously inspired by the 1978–83 *Taxi* TV series. The best-remembered cabbie performance remains Robert De Niro's splendid portrait of unbalanced Vietnam vet Travis Bickle in Martin Scorsese's *Taxi Driver* (1976). See also **Automobiles**; **Chauffeurs**.

Taxi (1932); *Pick-up* (1933); *The Big City* (aka *Skyscraper Wilderness*) (1937); *She's a Soldier Too* (1944); *Two O'Clock Courage* (1945); *Two Guys from Milwaukee* (1946); *The Bishop's Wife* (1947); *The Yellow Cab Man* (1950); *Taxi* (1953); *99 River Street* (1953); *The Catered Affair* (aka *Wedding Breakfast*) (1956); *Carry On Cabby* (1963); *Night Chase* (aka *The Man in the Back Seat*) (1970); *Pigeons* (aka *The Sidelong Glances of a Pigeon Kicker*) (1971); *Law and Disorder* (1974); *For Pete's Sake* (1974); *Taxi Driver* (1976); *Adventures of a Taxi Driver* (1976); *The Purple Taxi* (1977); *Love in a Taxi* (1980); *Die Laughing* (1980); *The Princess and the Cabbie* (1981 TVM); *Escape from New York* (1981); *Heavy Metal* (1981); *Chan Is Missing* (1982); *Hit and Run* (aka *Revenge Squad*) (1982); *D.C. Cab* (1983); *Signal 7* (1983); *Rhinestone* (1984); *Aurora* (1984 TVM); *Walls of Glass* (1985); *I-Man* (1986 TVM); *Graveyard Shift* (1987); *Ernest Saves Christmas* (1988); *Tarzan in Manhattan* (1989 TVM); *Wired* (1989); *Look Who's Talking* (1989); *Total Recall* (1990); *Breathing Under Water* (1991); *Baby on Board* (1991); *The Tune* (1992); *Night on Earth* (1992); *My Life's in Turnaround* (1993); *Night Taxi* (1993); *The Abadamis* (aka *Abadani-Ha*) (1994); *Illusions* (1994); *Daylight* (1996); *Eddie* (1996); *The Fifth Element* (1997); *Conspiracy Theory* (1997); *Chicago Cab* (aka *Hellcab*) (1998); *My Son the Fanatic* (1998); *The Bone Collector* (1999)

Teen Apocalypse Trilogy

Entertainment Weekly described writer-director Gregg Araki's trilogy as three films about "lost Los Angeles young people with too much time, money, and consumer product on their hands." *Totally F***ed Up* focused on a group of gay friends who talk extensively about sex, music, and astrology. More than one critic described it as a gay, darker version of John Hughes' high school talkfest *The Breakfast Club*. The second film, *The Doom Generation*, boasted the accurate ad line: "Sex. Mayhem. Whatever." It painted an unflattering portrait of two troubled teens (James Duval and Rose McGowan) who team up with a violent drifter (Johnathon Schaech) for a blood-soaked cross-country odyssey.

The final film in the trilogy, *Nowhere* (1997), returned to the teen alienation theme explored in the first film. This time, amidst the sex, drugs, and lengthy dialogues, Araki injected some offbeat humor by having some of the alienated youths abducted by aliens. Lead actor Duval appeared in all three films.

Totally F***ed Up (1993); *The Doom Generation* (1995); *Nowhere* (1997)

Teenage Mutant Ninja Turtles

This quartet of karate-chopping, pizza-eating, turtle do-gooders first appeared in Peter Laird and Kevin Eastman's underground comic books (q.v.) in 1984. They were media stars and popular toy characters long before their film debut in 1990. However, few film industry analysts predicted that their self-titled film opus would earn over $100 million in the U.S. alone. The origin of the turtles goes like this: They were flushed down the toilet and discovered in the sewer (q.v.) by an exiled ninja master named Splinter. When a toxic slime seeps into the sewer system, the turtles mutate into "half-teens" and Splinter becomes a rat. He teaches them martial arts (they learn to devour pizza and ice cream on their own) so they can battle the evil Foot Clan. The turtles are named after Renaissance artists Raphael, Leonardo, Michaelangelo, and Donatello. Although an animated film was planned at one time, the turtles' screen debut was a live-action film in which Jim Henson's Creature Shop designed the costumes. Judith Hoag co-starred as TV reporter April O'Neil, who befriends the turtles (but proves that humans are boring compared to turtle teens). Paige Turco replaced Hoag for the 1991 sequel, which also featured David Warner as the scientist who created the ooze. Turco and the Turtle Quartet traveled back in time to feudal Japan in 1993's *Teenage Mutant Ninja Turtles III*. Mark Caso, as Leonardo, is the only actor to play a Turtle in all three films. The Turtles made a cameo appearance in the 1993 buddy cop spoof *National Lampoon's Loaded Weapon 1*. See also **Comic Book Characters**; **Turtles**.

Teenage Mutant Ninja Turtles (1990); *Teenage Mutant Ninja Turtles II: The Secret of the Ooze* (1991); *Teenage Mutant Ninja Turtles III* (aka *Teenage Mutant Ninja Turtles III: The Turtles Are Back...In Time*) (1993)

Telekinesis [Psychokinesis, or PK]

Movie teenagers have displayed a special knack for acquiring telekinesis, the power to move objects with the mind. Sissy Spacek showed just how much havoc a mistreated, revenge-minded, telekinetic teen could wreak in the 1976 adaptation of Stephen King's *Carrie*. She veered cars off course, sent knives flying through the air, and demolished a high school gym with a fire hose. Imitations were bound to follow and Brian De Palma produced an interesting one with 1978's *The Fury*, which offered two telekinetic teens — one good (Amy Irving) and one gone bad (Andrew Stevens). In contrast, the telekinetic teen comedy *Zapped!* (1982) offered a trite plot about a horny guy (Willie Aames) who takes a perverse interest in friend Scott Baio's newly-acquired talent. A young boy and a teenage girl used their telekinetic powers to battle a demon and the hockey-masked Jason, respectively, in the 1988 films *Cameron's Closet* and *Friday the 13th Part VII — The New Blood*. And in Roald Dahl's children's fantasy *Matilda* (1996), a young girl (Mara

Wilson) used telekinesis to save her classmates from a cruel principal. As for adults, some playful gods endowed meek Roland Young with temporary telekinetic powers in the H.G. Wells fantasy *The Man Who Could Work Miracles*. In George Pal's underrated 1968 thriller *The Power*, scientist George Hamilton tracked down a mysterious telekinetic killer capable of changing his appearance by controlling people's minds (which made him devilishly difficult to find). Chevy Chase explored the frivolous side of telekinesis as an air traffic controller in the mild 1981 comedy *Modern Problems*. Richard Burton played the most destructive — and lazy — telekinetic villain by causing all sorts of disasters from his hospital bed in *The Medusa Touch* (1978). See also **Scanners Series**.

The Man Who Could Work Miracles (1936); The Power (1968); Carrie (1976); The Man with the Power (1977 TVM); The Fury (1978); The Medusa Touch (1978); Patrick (1979); Modern Problems (1981); Scanners (1981); Zapped! (1982); Firestarter (1984); Cameron's Closet (1988); Friday the 13th Part VII- The New Blood (1988); Firehead (1991); The Lawnmower Man (1992); Matilda (1996); Phenomenon (1996); Yesterday's Target (1996 TVM); Sphere (1998); Dark City (1998); The Rage: Carrie 2 (1999); X-Men (2000)

Telephones

Although telephones have played bit parts in thousands of movies, a few particularly memorable roles are called to mind. A foreign agent used the telephone (and a Robert Frost poem) to activate brainwashed killers in *Telefon*. A party line brought Doris Day and Rock Hudson together in *Pillow Talk*. Judy Holliday ran a telephone answering service called Susanswerphone in the otherwise forgettable musical comedy *Bells Are Ringing*. Barbara Stanwyck inadvertently learned of her own proposed murder via the phone in *Sorry, Wrong Number*. Jennifer Jason Leigh and Theresa Randle played phone-sex operators in, respectively, *Short Cuts* and *Girl 6*. Telephone numbers have been played for drama in the fact-based *Call Northside 777* and for strained chuckles in the goofy *Transylvania 6-5000*. Telephones were employed as spur-of-the-moment murder weapons in *The Naked Kiss* and *The Stepfather*. Clever premeditated murderers found ingenious uses for phones in *The Invisible Killer* and *Murder by Phone*. Devious Vincent Price bumped off a victim with a spiked telephone receiver in *Dr. Phibes Rises Again*. Finally, phone booths have played prominent roles in several movies: James Coburn was almost killed in one in *The Carey Treatment*; somebody did die in a phone booth in a funny scene from *Waking Ned Devine*; Tippi Hedren sought safety from a bird attack in a booth in *The Birds*; and Christopher Reeve used them for dressing rooms in the *Superman* movies.

Ladies Should Listen (1934); Party Wire (1935); The Invisible Killer (1940); Detour (1945); Call Northside 777 (aka Calling Northside 777) (1948); For the Love of Mary (1948); Sorry, Wrong Number (1948); Southside 1-1000 (1950); Chicago Calling (1951); Dial M for Murder (1954); Pillow Talk (1959); Bells Are Ringing (1960); The Birds (1963); The Naked Kiss (1964); I Saw What You Did (1965); The Slender Thread (1965); Boy, Did I Get a Wrong Number! (1966); Dial Hot Line (1969 TVM); The Day the Hot Line Got Hot (1969); Dr. Phibes Rises Again (1972); When Michael Calls (1972 TVM); The Secret Night Caller (1975 TVM); Telefon (1977); When a Stranger Calls (1979); Don't Answer the Phone (1980); Murder by Phone (aka Bells) (1980); Dial M for Murder (1981 TVM); E.T. the Extra-Terrestrial (1982); Hotline (1982 TVM); Transylvania 6-5000 (1985); The Stepfather (1987); Call Me (1988); The Telephone (1988); Out of the Dark (1988); I Saw What You Did (1988 TVM); 976-EVIL (1989); Party Line (1989); Dial: Help (1989); Bill and Ted's Excellent Adventure (1989); Murder on Line One (aka Helpline) (1990); Lisa (1990); Julia Has Two Lovers (1991); Intimate Stranger (1991); The Phone Call (1991); Danzón (1991); Short Cuts (1993); Mixed Nuts (1994); Erotique (1995); Girl 6 (1996); Waking Ned Devine (1998); Happiness (1998)

Teleportation

Science fiction buffs have defined teleportation as the process of almost instantaneously transmitting matter from one place to another. This is usually accomplished by breaking down an animal or object into its molecules, transporting the molecules through space, and then reassembling them. Edward Page Mitchell may have been the first writer to describe the process in his 1877 short story "The Man Without a Body." In the *Star Trek* (q.v.) TV series and films, the crew of the starship *Enterprise* used a teleporter as a routine mode of travel. The Delambre and Brundle families had a terrible time with teleportation experiments in *The Fly* (q.v.) movies. Andre Delambre initiated the problems by unknowingly allowing a fly to sneak into the teleportation booth with him. Their molecules merged, resulting in a disgusting combination of man/fly (and also fly/man). Bryant Halliday encountered a slightly different problem in 1966's *The Projected Man*. His "projection device" transported him successfully, but it also charred half his face and endowed him with a deadly electric touch. Alien Tommy Kirk had no trouble teleporting between Mars and the Earthly beach occupied by Annette Funicello in *Pajama Party* (1964). See also **The Fly Series; Star Trek Series**.

The Fly (1958); Pajama Party (1964); The Projected Man (1966); Willy Wonka and the Chocolate Factory (1971); Star Trek- The Motion Picture (1979); Galaxy Quest (1999)

Television

Even before television's success threatened the popularity of theatrical movies, the big screen all but ignored the little screen. The 1933 comedy *International House* used an early television experiment as the premise for jamming an all-star cast into a Chinese hotel. The stars included W.C. Fields, George Burns and Gracie Allen, Bela Lugosi, and — appearing in a TV broadcast — Rudy Vallee and Cab Calloway. On a smaller scale, comedians operated a pirate TV station out of a castle in 1939's *Band Waggon*, which was inspired by a hit British radio series. Amazingly, this lighthearted comedy was considerably ahead of its time, for pirate TV broadcasts were not further explored until 1983's *Videodrome* and 1986's *Riders of the Storm*. During the 1950s, the early days of network TV provided the setting for fluffy comedies like *Two Gals and a Guy* and *Simon and Laura*. A noteworthy exception was 1956's *The Great Man*, a scathing look at a much-loved TV personality revealed by Jose Ferrer to have been an unscrupulous, egotistical heel. The decade also produced Arch Obler's *The Twonky* (1953), a bizarre satire that remains an oddity after several decades. The title creature was a futuristic robot which begins running Hans Conried's life after becoming accidentally trapped inside the man's TV set. The sarcastic *Variety* review commented that the "thought is posed that *Twonky* can reduce mankind to automatons" — a charge television is still facing today.

Indeed, by the mid–1970s, television was ingrained as an integral part of American society, prompting renewed interest in movies about TV. *The Groove Tube* (1974) was the first of several movies consisting of loosely-connected comedy sketches built around television. *The Front* (1976) and *My Favorite Year* (1982) evoked nostalgia toward the early days of television. The former film skillfully covered a dark period in TV history: the blacklisting of writers accused of Communist activities. Ethics in the television industry have been addressed principally in films about network TV news. News broadcasts were packaged as entertainment in 1976's *Network*, while news reporter William Hurt faked an emotional tear for the camera in 1987's *Broadcast News*. The 1983 TV movie *Special Bulletin* looked just like a news broadcast, with anchors Ed Flanders and Kathryn Walker keeping viewers informed about a terrorist group threatening to destroy Charleston, S.C., with a nuclear bomb. The film simulated the feel of a real broadcast so well that the final outcome carried a shattering, terrifying jolt. Horror filmmakers have used television to temporarily house transient ghosts, demons, and extraterrestrials in *Poltergeist*, *Demons 2*, and *Terrorvision*, respectively. None of those was nearly as frightening as David Cronenburg's powerful horror/satire *Videodrome*, which cast James Woods as a broadcast executive metamorphosed into a television/man (at one point, he slips a videotape into a newly-formed slot in his stomach). This overly complex film (was it all a hallucination?) disgusted many moviegoers and died quickly at the box-office. The 1985 *Explorers*, while not a movie about television, featured aliens who learned everything they knew about humans from watching Earth TV — a frightening premise when one thinks about it. The 1985 comedy-drama *Static* was about a young man who claimed to have invented a television capable of tuning in Heaven. *The Truman Show* (1998) was about a man whose life was secretly filmed and then broadcast as a TV series to everyone else. A similar premise was explored earlier in Paul Bartel's 1969 short film *Secret Cinema*. In *EDtv* (1999), Matthew McConaughey played a video store clerk who willingly agreed to have his life filmed for television. Two teenagers found themselves magically transported into a 1950s black and white family sitcom in *Pleasantville* (1998). See also **Game Shows**; **Soap Operas**.

International House (1933); *Murder by Television* (1935); *Band Waggon* (1939); *Two Gals and a Guy* (1951); *The Twonky* (1953); *Meet Mr. Lucifer* (1953); *The Glass Web* (1953); *Simon and Laura* (1955); *The Great Man* (1956); *A Face in the Crowd* (1957); *The Gazebo* (1959); *The Thrill of It All* (1963); *Panic Button* (1964); *The Barefoot Executive* (1971); *The Love Machine* (1971); *The Groove Tube* (1974); *The Front* (1976); *Network* (1976); *Tunnelvision* (1976); *Telethon* (1977 TVM); *KGOD* (aka *Pray TV*) (1980); *Deathwatch* (1980); *Agency* (aka *Mind Games*) (1980); *Shock Treatment* (1981); *My Favorite Year* (1982); *This is…Kate Bennett* (1982 TVM); *Wrong Is Right* (1982); *Poltergeist* (1982); *Videodrome* (1983); *Special Bulletin* (1983 TVM); *The Record* (1984); *The Ratings Game* (1984 TVM); *Static* (1985); *Reckless Disregard* (1985 TVM); *Ginger and Fred* (1985); *America* (1986); *News at Eleven* (1986 TVM); *Terrorvision* (1986); *Riders of the Storm* (aka *The American Way*) (1986); *Broadcast News* (1987); *Pass the Ammo* (1988); *Switching Channels* (1988); *Demons 2* (1988); *The Brain* (1988); *UHF* (1989); *Shocker* (1989); *Instant Karma* (1990); *Avalon* (1990); *Soapdish* (1991); *Wayne's World* (1992); *Secrets* (1992 TVM); *Stay Tuned* (1992); *Exclusive* (1992 TVM); *Kika* (1993); *I'll Do Anything* (1994); *Witness to the Execution* (1994); *Without Warning*

(1994 TVM); *Natural Born Killers* (1994); *Quiz Show* (1994); *Reality Bites* (1994); *The Barefoot Executive* (1995 TVM); *The Cable Guy* (1996); *Open Season* (1996); *Up Close and Personal* (1996); *Meet Wally Sparks* (1997); *The Truman Show* (1998); *Pleasantville* (1998); *Holy Man* (1998); *Ringmaster* (1998); *EDtv* (1999); *The Insider* (1999); *Galaxy Quest* (1999)

Television-Expanded Films

Television has long practiced the "art" of dicing up theatrical films to fit a specified time period or to delete material its censors deemed unacceptable. However, the equally offensive practice of expanding theatrical films for television showings did not gain widespread popularity with the networks until the mid–1970s. That's when network executives realized that it was cheaper to add leftover footage to an existing film than to pay for new programming. Thus, instead of one night of *Superman*, they could add enough footage to stretch its impressive ratings over two nights. In the case of *Superman*, the new scenes did allow film buffs to glimpse Kirk Allyn (Superman in the movie serials) and Noel Neill (Lois in the TV series) as Lois Lane's parents. However, other TV expansions have been less thoughtful. The James Bond adventure *On Her Majesty's Secret Service* was expanded by simply tacking the climactic ski chase onto the front of the film, adding a voiceover, and repeating the same scene (in its proper sequence) later in the broadcast. Director Gene Palmer shot almost an hour of new footage, complete with new cast, for the network TV broadcast of the already-inflated *Two Minute Warning*. Alas, one cannot blame the networks alone. Director David Lynch had his name removed from the credits of *Dune* when the movie was lengthened for its syndicated showing. On the other hand, Francis Ford Coppola played a central role in altering his *Godfather* films for a special television broadcast. He intercut scenes from the 175-minute *The Godfather* (1972) and 200-minute *The Godfather Part II* (1974), added footage from the cutting room floor, and produced the mammoth 475-minute *The Godfather Saga*. In addition to expanding movies for television, distributors have begun to release alternate versions of the same film in limited theatrical releases and on videotape/laserdisc/DVD. This practice is nothing new — Steven Spielberg's *Close Encounters of the Third Kind — The Special Edition* followed his original 1977 version three years later. Recent alternate versions include *Blade Runner*, *JFK*, *The Abyss* and *Basic Instinct*.

Requiem for a Heavyweight (1962); *Secret Ceremony* (1968); *The Evil of Frankenstein* (1964); *On Her Majesty's Secret Service* (1969); *They Might Be Giants* (1971); *Jeremy* (1973); *Earthquake* (1974); *Two Minute Warning* (1976); *The Godfather Saga* (1977); *The Deep* (1977); *The Concorde: Airport '77* (*Airport '77*) (1977); *Superman* (1978); *When Time Ran Out…* (aka *Earth's Final Fury*) (1980); *Dune* (1984); *Cry Freedom* (1987); *Born in East L.A.* (1987); *Sea of Love* (1989); *Dances with Wolves* (1990); *Far and Away* (1992); *Needful Things* (1993) (expanded version shown as *More Needful Things*); *Waterworld* (1995); *Phenomenon* (1996)

Television Movie Sequels to Theatrical Films

ABC-TV pioneered the concept of the television movie sequel with 1974's *Mrs. Sundance*, a small-screen continuation of 1969's *Butch Cassidy and the Sundance Kid*. Elizabeth Montgomery replaced Katharine Ross in the role of Etta Place, the Sundance Kid's widow and the new quarry of ruthless bounty hunters. Although produced by 20th Century–Fox, who made the original, *Mrs. Sundance* caused no confusion in regard to its origin—it looked and played like a made-for-TV movie, right down to the perfectly-timed commercial breaks. Interestingly, just two years later, 20th Century–Fox convinced Katharine Ross to recreate the role for *Wanted: The Sundance Woman*, another TV sequel. This version ignored *Mrs. Sundance* (which no doubt confused some meticulous viewers) and involved Etta with Mexican rebel Pancho Villa. Ross is one of a handful of performers to play the same role in both a theatrical film and its TV movie sequel. George C. Scott repeated his Oscar-winning 1970 portrayal of General George Patton for the 1986 TV film *The Last Days of Patton*. Lee Marvin returned as the leader of *The Dirty Dozen* in *The Dirty Dozen: The Next Mission*. Carol Kane and Robert Carradine repeated their theatrical roles in, respectively, *When a Stranger Calls Back* (1993) and *Revenge of the Nerds III: The Next Generation* (1992). And Barry Newman played lawyer Tony Petrocelli on the big screen in *The Lawyer* (1970) and on the small screen in *Night Games* (1974). The latter served as a pilot for Newman's short-lived TV series *Petrocelli*. Other TV movie sequels have also doubled as pilots for prospective series, such as *Matt Helm*, *Nevada Smith*, *True Grit*, and *Our Man Flint: Dead on Target*. In some of these features, the only connection with the original feature was the name of the main character. Dean Martin's Matt Helm was a boozing super secret agent, while Tony Franciosa's TV incarnation was a wisecracking private eye with a steady girlfriend. The longest gap between a theatrical film and its made-for-TV sequel is 44 years-from 1946's *It's a Wonderful Life* to 1990's *Clarence*. *The Dirty Dozen* has spawned the most TV sequels: three and still counting. See also **The Dirty Dozen**; **The Stepford Wives**. In the following list, the TV movies are listed chronologically first followed by theatrical film (if a theatrical series, the last series entry is shown):

Mrs. Sundance (1974 TVM)—*Butch Cassidy and the Sundance Kid* (1969); *Sidekicks* (1974 TVM)—*Skin Game* (1971); *Night Games* (1974 TVM)—*The Lawyer* (1970); *Nick and Nora* (1975 TVM)—*Song of the Thin Man* (1947); *Matt Helm* (1975 TVM)—*The Wrecking Crew* (1969); *Nevada Smith* (1975 TVM)—*Nevada Smith* (1966); *Look What's Happened to Rosemary's Baby* (aka *Rosemary's Baby II*) (1976 TVM)—*Rosemary's Baby* (1968); *Wanted: The Sundance Woman* (aka *Mrs. Sundance Rides Again*) (1976 TVM)—*Butch Cassidy and the Sundance Kid* (1969); *Our Man Flint: Dead on Target* (1976 TVM)—*Our Man Flint* (1966); *Serpico: The Deadly Game* (1976 TVM)—*Serpico* (1973); *A Matter of Wife...and Death* (1976 TVM)—*Shamus* (1973); *The Girl in the Empty Grave* (1977 TVM)—*They Only Kill Their Masters* (1972); *Murder in Peyton Place* (1977 TVM)—*Return to Peyton Place* (1961); *True Grit* (1978 TVM)—*True Grit* (1969); *A Real American Hero* (1978 TVM)—*Final Chapter-Walking Tall* (1977); *Christmas Lilies of the Field* (1979 TVM)—*Lilies of the Field* (1963); *High Noon II: The Return of Will Kane* (1980 TVM)—*High Noon* (1952); *Revenge of the Stepford Wives* (1980 TVM)—*The Stepford Wives* (1975); *Trackdown: Finding the Goodbar Killer* (1983 TVM)—*Looking for Mr. Goodbar* (1977); *The Jerk Too* (1984 TVM)—*The Jerk* (1979); *The Dirty Dozen: The Next Mission* (1985 TVM)—*The Dirty Dozen* (1967); *Popeye Doyle* (1986 TVM)—*The French Connection II* (1975); *The Parent Trap II* (1986 TVM)—*The Parent Trap* (1961); *The Last Days of Patton* (1986 TVM)—*Patton* (1970); *Bates Motel* (1987 TVM)—*Psycho III* (1986); *If It's Tuesday, It Still Must Be Belgium* (1987 TVM)—*If It's Tuesday, It Must Be Belgium* (1969); *The Return of the Shaggy Dog* (1987 TVM)—*The Shaggy Dog* (1959); *The Great Escape II: The Untold Story* (1988 TVM)—*The Great Escape* (1963); *Amityville: The Evil Escapes* (1989 TVM)—*Amityville 3-D* (aka *Amityville: The Demon*) (1983); *Clarence* (1990 TVM)—*It's a Wonderful Life* (1946); *Omen IV: The Awakening* (1991 TVM)—*The Final Conflict* (1981); *Revenge of the Nerds III: The Next Generation* (1992 TVM)—*Revenge of the Nerds II: Nerds in Paradise* (1987); *When a Stranger Calls Back* (1993 TVM)—*When a Stranger Calls* (1979); *Bandit* (1994 TVM)—*Smokey and the Bandit II* (1980); *Midnight Runaround* (1994 TVM)—*Midnight Run* (1988); *The Birds II: Land's End* (1994 TVM)—*The Birds* (1963); *Annie: A Royal Adventure* (1995 TVM)—*Annie* (1982); *Problem Child 3* (aka *Problem Child 3: Junior in Love*) (1995 TVM)—*Problem Child 2* (1991); *Encino Woman* (1996 TVM)—*Encino Man* (1992); *To Sir with Love II* (1996 TVM)—*To Sir with Love* (1967); *Angels in the Endzone* (1997 TVM)—*Angels in the Outfield* (1994); *Bullet to Beijing* (1997 TVM)—*Billion Dollar Brain* (1967); *Universal Soldier II: Brothers in Arms* (1998 TVM)—*Universal Soldier* (1992); *The Day After the Miracle* (1998 TVM)—*The Miracle Worker* (1962)

Note: The 1989 TV movie *Get Smart, Again!* was obviously intended as a television series reunion movie (q.v.) and thus is not listed as a sequel to 1980's *The Nude Bomb* (aka *The Return of Maxwell Smart*).

Television Series Reunion Films

A wave of nostalgia washed over television viewers of the 1980s, making small screen movies based on old television series the most significant TV movie trend of the decade. The nostalgia went beyond mere revival of a TV show's premise, for, in almost all cases, the made-for-TV movies reunited some of the series's original cast members. The 1969 *Dragnet* could lay claim to being the first TV series reunion film. It was based on the then-running 1967–70 *Dragnet* series which was an updated revival of the original 1952–59 *Dragnet*. Jack Webb starred as police sergeant Joe Friday in the movie and both runs of the series. *The New Maverick* (1978) reunited James Garner and Jack Kelly as free-wheeling brothers Bret and Bart Maverick, roles they originated in the popular 1957–62 Western series. However, the purpose of the 1978 TV movie was to launch a new show starring Charles Frank as their nephew Ben (the series *Young Maverick* ran very briefly in 1979). On the other hand, 1977's *Father Knows Best Reunion* and 1978's *Rescue from Gilligan's Island* offered nothing new, just pure nostalgia with the original cast members returning (except for Tina Louise as Ginger Grant in the latter film). Their successful ratings (*Gilligan* resulted in two sequels) initiated a steady growth in the number of TV series reunion films. Interestingly, the *Gilligan's Island* TV series was only a modest hit during its 1964–67 run, cracking the top twenty shows only once. The series gained tremendous popularity, especially among young viewers, through syndicated repeats running on local stations. Subsequently, syndication success became a criteria for determining if a series had potential as a reunion film, thus accounting for TV movies based on *The Brady Bunch*, *The Munsters*, and *I Dream of Jeannie*. Indeed, hit series have not always resulted in hit movies. *The Return of the Beverly Hillbillies* (1981) was a painful reunion highlighted by the absence of series regulars Irene Ryan (Granny), Max Baer, Jr. (Jethro), and Raymond Bailey (Mr. Drysdale). Without the 1960s spy movie genre to spoof, 1983's *The Return of the Man from U.N.C.L.E.* came across as dry and dated, despite the presence of stars Robert Vaughn and David McCallum. In contrast, Raymond Burr's triumphant *Perry Mason Returns* (1985) was a well-conceived update that inaugurated a series of highly-rated *Perry Mason* (q.v.) TV movies. The longest gap between a series' last year and its reunion film is the 28 years separating the 1959–63 series *The Untouchables* from 1991's *The Return of Eliot Ness*. Twenty-seven years separated the series *Peter Gunn* from the 1989 TV movie—however, the TV movie *Peter Gunn* was a reunion only in that Blake Edwards produced and directed both movie and show. Peter Strauss and an all new cast replaced Craig Stevens and the other series regulars. Michael Landon, Jr., was the only link between his father's *Bonanza* series and 1988's *Bonanza: The Next Generation*. The 1987 *Police Story: The Freeway Killing* was an oddity—a revival of an anthology TV show. In the following list, only the first reunion film is shown (e.g., see **Gilligan's Island** for a list of other movies based on the series). See also **Columbo, Lieutenant; Gunsmoke Series; The Incredible Hulk; Kojak, Theo; Little House on the Prairie Series; The Man from U.N.C.L.E.; Mason, Perry; Rockford, Jim; The Six Million Dollar Man Series; Spenser; Theatrical Films Based on Television Series; The Waltons; Welby, Marcus.**

Dragnet (1969 TVM); *Father Knows Best Reunion* (1977 TVM); *The New Maverick* (1978 TVM); *Rescue from Gilligan's Island* (1978 TVM); *The Return of the Mod Squad* (1979 TVM); *The Wild, Wild West Revisited* (1979 TVM); *The Return of Frank Cannon* (1980 TVM); *The Brady Girls Get Married* (1981 TVM); *The Munsters' Revenge* (1981 TVM); *The Return of the Beverly Hillbillies* (1981 TVM); *A Wedding on Walton's Mountain* (1982 TVM); *The Return of the Man from U.N.C.L.E.* (1983 TVM); *Still the Beaver* (1983 TVM); *The Return of Marcus Welby, M.D.* (1984 TVM); *I Dream of Jeannie: 15 Years Later* (1985 TVM); *Kojack: The Belarus File* (1985 TVM); *Perry Mason Returns* (1985 TVM); *Kung Fu: The Movie* (1986 TVM); *Return to Mayberry* (1986 TVM); *Eight Is Enough: A Family Reunion* (1987 TVM); *Gunsmoke: Return to Dodge* (1987 TVM); *The Return of the Six Million Dollar Man and the Bionic Woman* (1987 TVM); *Police Story: The Freeway Killing* (1987 TVM); *Still Crazy Like a Fox* (1987 TVM); *Bonanza: The Next Generation* (1988 TVM); *Bring Me the Head of Dobie Gillis* (1988 TVM); *The Incredible Hulk Returns* (1988 TVM); *The Return of Ben Casey* (1988 TVM); *Get Smart, Again!* (1989 TVM); *Peter Gunn* (1989 TVM); *The Return of Sam McCloud* (1989 TVM); *The Love Boat: A Valentine Voyage* (1990 TVM); *Return to Green Acres* (1990 TVM); *Knight Rider 2000* (1991 TVM); *The Return of Eliot Ness* (1991 TVM); *Dynasty: The Reunion* (1991 TVM); *I Still Dream of Jeannie* (1991 TVM); *Back on the Streets of San Francisco* (1992 TVM); *Jonny's Golden Quest* (1993 TVM); *The Return of Ironside* (1993 TVM); *Spenser: Ceremony* (1993 TVM); *Hart to Hart Returns* (1993 TVM); *Bonanza: The Return* (1993 TVM); *Wyatt Earp: Return to Tombstone* (1994 TVM); *Young Indiana Jones and the Hollywood Follies* (1994 TVM); *Alien Nation: Dark Horizon* (1994 TVM); *Simon & Simon: In Trouble Again* (1994 TVM); *MacGyver: Lost Treasure of Atlantis* (1994 TVM); *Saved by the Bell: Wedding in Las Vegas* (1994 TVM); *I Spy Returns* (1994 TVM); *The Rockford Files: I Still Love L.A.* (1994 TVM); *Cagney & Lacey: The Return* (1994 TVM); *Alien Nation: Millenium* (1995 TVM); *Here Come the Munsters* (1995 TVM); *The Invaders* (1995 TVM); *Project: ALF* (1996 TVM); *CHiPs '99* (1998 TVM); *The Patti Duke Show: Still Rockin' in Brooklyn Heights* (1999 TVM); *Dr. Quinn, Medicine Woman: The Movie* (1999 TVM); *The Dukes of Hazzard: Hazzard in Hollywood* (2000 TVM); *Homicide: The Movie* (2000 TVM); *Mary & Rhoda* (2000 TVM)

Tennis

Tennis and golf (q.v.) have failed to interest many filmmakers, perhaps because the two sports were once viewed as leisure activities reserved for the country club set. Director Ida Lupino lent a feminist slant to 1951's *Hard, Fast and Beautiful*, an overwrought drama about a domineering mother who pushed her daughter toward tennis stardom. The 1978 TV biography *Little Mo* told the story of teen Grand Slam champion Maureen Connelly, who died after a long struggle with cancer. Two theatrical tennis movies were released the following year and both flopped badly. *Racquet* starred Bert Convey as a tennis pro who used sex to get what he wanted, while *Players* featured Dean Paul Martin as a promising player forced to choose between the game and a woman (Ali MacGraw). Real-life tennis stars Pancho Gonzalez (*Players*) and Bobby Riggs (*Racquet*) lent the movies a touch of credibility. 1983's *Spring Fever* (1983) simply recruited a real player to play the lead role, but teenaged Carling Bassett showed no promise as an actress (of course, neither did the rest of the cast, which included Susan Anton as the girl's mother). The 1986 *Second Serve* examined the fascinating real-life saga of Richard Raskins, the male surgeon who underwent a sex-change operation and became tennis player Renee Richards. Tennis games have served as memorable set pieces in several movies. Monsieur Hulot (q.v.) experienced a great deal of trouble with the game in one of the funniest scenes in *Monsieur Hulot's Holiday*. A troupe of mimics played an imaginary game of tennis in the symbolic denouement of *Blow-Up*. And in Alfred Hitchcock's *Strangers on a Train*, tennis player Farley Granger rushes through a big match so he can thwart psychopath Robert Walker from framing him for murder.

You Can't Cheat an Honest Man (1939) (table tennis); *Come to the Stable* (1949); *Quartet* (1949) ("The Facts of Life" segment); *Hard, Fast and Beautiful* (1951); *Strangers on a Train* (1951); *Monsieur Hulot's Holiday* (1953); *Dial M for Murder* (1954); *The Chalk Garden* (1964); *Blow-Up* (1966); *The High Commissioner* (aka *Nobody Runs Forever*) (1968); *The Christian Licorice Store* (1971); *Little Mo* (1978 TVM); *Racquet* (1979); *Players* (1979); *Spring Fever* (1983); *Second Serve* (1986 TVM); *Jocks* (aka *Road Trip*) (1987); *Nobody's Perfect* (1990); *The Smile* (aka *Le Sourire*) (1994); *Ever After* (1998)

The Texas Chainsaw Massacre Series

This gruesome 1974 shocker was loosely based on the case of real-life Wisconsin mass murderer Ed Gein, whose exploits also provided the basis for *Psycho* (1960) and *Deranged* (1974). Shot on a tight budget in Texas, the film traces the plight of a group of young people stranded near an isolated farmhouse run by three crazy cannibalistic brothers and their all-but-dead grandfather. As directed by Tobe Hooper, *Chainsaw Massacre* turned into a derivative exercise in shock, recalling Herschell Gordon Lewis' *Two Thousand Maniacs* (1964) and George Romero's *Night of the Living Dead* (1968). Still, the film attracted a faithful cult following and eventually provided Hooper with a ticket to mainstream Hollywood (e.g., 1982's *Poltergeist*). After flirting with the big time, Hooper returned belatedly to his Texan roots for 1986's *Texas Chainsaw Massacre II*. Jim Siedow reprised his role as one of the crazy Sawyer brothers, but Bill Moseley replaced fan favorite Gunnar Hansen as the chainsaw-wielding brother Leatherface. As if to compensate, Dennis Hopper joined the cast as Lefty Enright, a Texas Ranger who carries a chainsaw in his holster. Despite its attempts at black humor, the film found little favor with horror fans. Nevertheless, New Line Cinema rolled out a third installment, *Leatherface: Texas Chainsaw Massacre III*, four years later. Jeff Burr replaced Hooper as director and R. A. Mihailoff played the title role. It too faded quickly at the box-office. Kim Henkel, who penned the original film, wrote and directed a fourth installment, *The Return of the Texas Chainsaw Massacre* in 1993. Distribution problems plagued the film, which was reedited and retitled *The Texas Chainsaw Massacre: The Next Generation*. By the time it was released with little fanfare in 1997, its unknown stars, Renée Zellweger and Matthew McConaughey, had become familiar faces courtesy of *Jerry Maguire* (1996) and *A Time to Kill* (1996), respectively. See also **Cannibalism**; **Chainsaws**.

The Texas Chainsaw Massacre (1974); *The Texas Chainsaw Massacre II* (1986); *Leatherface: Texas Chainsaw Massacre III* (1990); *The Return of the Texas Chainsaw Massacre* (aka *The Texas Chainsaw Massacre: The Next Generation*) (1997)

The Texas Rangers

This was another routine Western series (once again built around three lawmen) until Tex Ritter joined the cast in 1944. The original lineup consisted of Dave O'Brien, Guy Wilkerson, and James Newill, best known as the singing Mountie of the Renfrew series (q.v.). Ritter replaced Newill after *Brand of the Devil* and distinguished the films with his familiar voice. Ironically, Ritter's biggest hit song occurred in a Western in which he did not star—1952's *High Noon*. Eagle Lion reissued the Texas Ranger pictures, with different titles, in the late 1940s.

Rangers Take Over (1943); *Bad Men of Thunder Gap* (aka *Thundergap Outlaws*) (1943); *West of Texas* (aka *Shootin' Irons*) (1943); *Border Buckaroos* (1943); *Fighting Valley* (1943); *Trail of Terror* (1944); *The Return of the Rangers* (1944); *Boss of the Rawhide* (1944); *Gunsmoke Mesa* (1944); *Outlaw Roundup* (1944); *Guns of the Law* (1944); *The Pinto Bandit* (1944); *Spook Town* (1944); *Brand of the Devil* (1944); *Gangsters of the Frontier* (1944); *Dead or Alive* (1944); *The Whispering Skull* (1944); *Marked for Murder* (1945); *Enemy of the Law* (1945); *Three in the Saddle* (1945); *Frontier Fugitives* (1945); *Flaming Bullets* (1945)

That's Entertainment Series

Jack Haley, Jr., provided the driving force behind the highly-successful *That's Entertainment!* (1976), a compilation film featuring clips from MGM's best musicals. The film showcased such gems as: Gene Kelly's energetic dance in the rain in *Singin' in the Rain*; Fred Astaire dancing on the walls and ceilings in *Royal Wedding*; and the barn-raising musical number from *Seven Brides for Seven Brothers*. It also featured classic scenes from many other favorites like *The Wizard Oz*, *Meet Me in St. Louis*, and *An American in Paris*. MGM's 1976 follow-up *That's Entertainment Part 2* added clips from nonmusical films such as *A Tale of Two Cities*, *Adam's Rib*, and *Boom Town*. Fred Astaire and Gene Kelly, who co-hosted the first *That's Entertainment*, introduced the new clips—and also danced together as well. Nine years later, Haley compiled an impressive collection of dance scenes for *That's Dancing*, a celebration of fancy footwork on celluloid. The highlight was probably the never-before-seen extended version of Ray Bolger's acrobatic "If I Only Had a Brain" routine from *The Wizard of Oz*. A fourth

compilation film, *That's Entertainment! III* (1994), garnered good reviews, though it attracted little attention. Critics and film buffs were less kind to the direct-to-video *That's More Entertainment!* (1995), a collection of less-than-stellar footage. See also **Compilation Films (Fictional)**.

That's Entertainment! (1974); *That's Entertainment Part 2* (1976); *That's Dancing* (1985); *That's Entertainment! III* (1994); *That's More Entertainment!* (1995)

Theatrical Films Based on TV Series

The reasons why some TV series have been developed into theatrical films, while others have not, defies logic. Surprisingly, television ratings have rarely been used as criteria. The 1964–66 sitcom *The Munsters* was hardly a ratings hit, but that did not deter Universal from releasing a 1966 theatrical version dubbed *Munster, Go Home*. Likewise, the Saturday morning kiddie show *H.R. Pufnstuf* seemed an odd choice for a big-screen musical when 1970's *Pufnstuf* appeared in theaters. Ironically, both the *Pufnstuf* and *Munsters* TV series were cancelled almost simultaneously with the release of their feature film versions. Cult television shows have fared far better as theatrical films. The gothic soap opera *Dark Shadows* had a built-in audience of loyal fans when the movie *House of Dark Shadows* premiered in 1967. It did well enough to inspire a second picture, 1971's *Night of Dark Shadows*. The classic TV series *Star Trek* performed dismally in the ratings (ranking 52 in its best season) during its original 1966–69 run. However, by the time an expensive big-screen version was mounted in 1979, the show had turned into a national phenomenon thanks to syndicated showings on local TV stations. The *Star Trek* (q.v.) film series initiated by *Star Trek— The Motion Picture* easily outdistances all other TV series–inspired films in terms of both box-office and popularity. Its closest competition comes from Jim Henson's Muppets (q.v.), which used the syndicated *Muppet Show* as a springboard for several theatrical features beginning with 1979's *The Muppet Movie*. The *Star Trek* and Muppet movies exemplify the principal reason for making a film based on a TV series: Loyal fans will follow their shows from the little screen to the big screen. Although this rationale works in most cases, there are some puzzling exceptions. It's doubtful that many teens who watched Steve Martin in the 1996 theatrical version of *Sgt. Bilko* had even heard of the 1955–59 *Phil Silvers Show* that inspired it. Likewise, one suspects the *Wild Wild West* (1999) was not made with the TV series fans in mind—Will Smith's Jim West bore little resemblance to Robert Conrad's portrayal. Surprisingly, the sketch comedy series *Saturday Night Live* has inspired the most theatrical films, to include: *The Blues Brothers* (1980), *Wayne's World* (1992), *Coneheads* (1993), *It's Pat* (1994), *Stuart Saves His Family* (1995), and *A Night at the Roxbury* (1998). The longest span between a series' last season and its theatrical version was the 37 years that separated the aforementioned *Sgt. Bilko* from *The Phil Silvers Show*. The most successful movie based on a television flop was 1988's *The Naked Gun*, which evolved from the very short-lived comedy series *Police Squad* (1982). The *Man from U.N.C.L.E.* movies (q.v.) were not "new" theatrical films, but merely episodes of the TV series edited together. See also **Dark Shadows Series**; **The Man from U.N.C.L.E.**; **The Muppets**; **The Naked Gun Series**; **Star Trek Series**.

Here Come the Nelsons (1952); *Our Miss Brooks* (1956); *Foreign Intrigue* (1956); *The Lone Ranger* (1956); *The Creeping Unknown* (aka *The Quatermass Experiment; The Quatermass Xperiment*) (1956); *The Lineup* (1958) (based on the TV series *San Francisco Beat*); *McHale's Navy* (1964); *Munster, Go Home* (1966); *A Man Called Flintstone* (1966); *Batman* (1966); *Gunn* (1967); *House of Dark Shadows* (1967); *Pufnstuf* (1970); *On the Buses* (1971) (from a British series); *Dad's Army* (1971) (from a British series); *Doomwatch* (1972) (from a British series); *Callan* (1974) (from a British series); *Sweeney!* (1976) (from a British series); *Wombling Free* (1977) (from a British TV series); *Doing Time* (1979) (from a British series); *Star Trek—The Motion Picture* (1979); *The Muppet Movie* (1979); *The Blues Brothers* (1980) (from the TV series *Saturday Night Live*); *The Gong Show Movie* (1980); *The Nude Bomb* (aka *The Return of Maxwell Smart*) (1980); *Twilight Zone—The Movie* (1983); *Smurfs and the Magic Flute* (1984); *Sesame Street Presents Follow That Bird* (1985); *Dragnet* (1987); *Masters of the Universe* (1987); *The Naked Gun* (1988); *Tales from the Dark Side: The Movie* (1990); *Jetsons: The Movie* (1990); *Duck Tales: The Movie-Treasure of the Lost Lamp* (1990); *The Addams Family* (1991); *Wayne's World* (1992) (from the TV series *Saturday Night Live*); *Twin Peaks: Fire Walk with Me* (1992); *Coneheads* (1993) (from the TV series *Saturday Night Live*); *The Fugitive* (1993); *Batman: Mask of the Phantasm* (1993); *Maverick* (1994); *The Flintstones* (1994); *Police Rescue* (1994) (from an Australian TV series); *It's Pat* (1994) (from the TV series *Saturday Night Live*); *Car 54, Where Are You?* (1994); *The Brady Bunch Movie* (1995); *Stuart Saves His Family* (1995) (from the TV series *Saturday Night Live*); *Mighty Morphin Power Rangers: The Movie* (1995); *Tales from the Crypt Presents Demon Knight* (1995); *Mission: Impossible* (1996); *Beavis and Butthead Do America* (1996); *Mystery Science Theater 3000: The Movie* (1996); *Sgt. Bilko* (1996); *Tales from the Crypt: Bordello of Blood* (1996); *McHale's Navy* (1997); *George of the Jungle* (1997); *Leave It to Beaver* (1997); *Bean* (1997); *Barney's Great Adventure: The Movie* (1998); *The X Files* (aka *The X Files: Fight the Future*) (1998); *Lost in Space* (1998); *The Avengers* (1998); *The Rugrats Movie* (1998); *A Night at the Roxbury* (1998) (from the TV series *Saturday Night Live*); *My Favorite Martian* (1999); *Inspector Gadget* (1999); *Doug's 1st Movie* (1999); *The Mod Squad* (1999); *South Park: Bigger, Longer & Uncut* (1999); *Wild Wild West* (1999); *Dudley Do-Right* (1999); *Superstar* (1999) (from the TV series *Saturday Night Live*); *The Adventures of Elmo in Grouchland* (1999); *The Adventures of Rocky and Bullwinkle* (2000)

Theatrical Films Based on Video Games

Despite their built-in appeal, especially for teenaged males, films based on popular video games have often fared poorly. The success stories are *Street Fighter* (a modest hit), *Mortal Kombat* (which grossed over $70 million in the U.S.), and the Japanese-made *Pokémon* (1998). In contrast, *Super Mario Bros.* (1993) boasted plenty of special effects, but lacked the charm of its source video game. *Double Dragon* (1994) was barely released and generated a puny $2.4 million at the U.S. box-office. And *Wing Commander* (1999) failed to capitalize on the popularity of Freddie Prinze, Jr., whose previous films included hits like *She's All That* (1998) and *I Know What You Did Last Summer* (1997). Still, the popularity of the lively martial arts/special effects extravaganza *Mortal Kombat* and its 1997 sequel prove that the genre has potential. See also **Pinball/Video Games**.

Super Mario Bros. (1993); *Double Dragon* (1994); *Street Fighter* (1994); *Mortal Kombat* (1995); *Mortal Kombat: Annihilation* (aka *Mortal Kombat 2*) (1997); *Pokémon: The First Movie* (1998); *Wing Commander* (1999); *Pokémon: The Movie 2000* (1999)

The Thin Man Series

In the 1930s and 1940s, one detective film series stood above all the others. With two big stars in the leads and plenty of MGM gloss, the six Thin Man mysteries clearly separated themselves from their B-movie competitors. These were "A" efforts and marketed as such, with new entries released only at two or three-year intervals. The first film, based on Dashiell Hammett's novel, cast William Powell and Myrna Loy as wealthy, amateur detectives Nick and Nora Charles. Powell already had extensive detective film experience, having played Philo Vance (q.v.) in four films for Paramount and Warner Bros. But unlike the urbane Vance, Nick Charles afforded Powell the opportunity to display his gift for light comedy. Myrna Loy provided the perfect foil, becoming a role model for spunky film heroines. The third family member was Asta, Nick and Nora's faithful, and mischievous, fox terrier. Nick Jr. made his series debut in the third entry, *Another Thin Man* (actually the title made little sense since the "thin man" was a murder victim played by Edward Ellis in the first film). The quality of the mysteries declined as the series progressed, but the films remained popular due to the Charles' sophisticated relationship, a natural blend of good-natured insults and honest affection. As with the Hardy series (q.v.), MGM used the *Thin Man* films as a training ground for its brightest acting prospects: James Stewart (playing against type) in *After the Thin Man*, Donna Reed in *Shadow of the Thin Man*, and Gloria Grahame and Dean Stockwell (as Nick Jr.) in *Song of the Thin Man*. Peter Lawford and Phyllis Kirk played Nick and Nora on television, enjoying a modest two-year run with their 1957 series *The Thin Man*. Craig Stevens (TV's *Peter Gunn*) and Jo Ann Pflug tried to update the characters in the charmless 1975 TV movie *Nick and Nora*. The Charleses were among the detectives spoofed in Neil Simon's *Murder by Death* (1976).

The Thin Man (1934); *After the Thin Man* (1936); *Another Thin Man* (1939); *Shadow of the Thin Man* (1941); *The Thin Man Goes Home* (1944); *Song of the Thin Man* (1947); *Nick and Nora* (1975 TVM)

Three Colors Trilogy (Liberty, Equality, Fraternity)

Polish filmmaker Krzysztof Kieslowski directed this acclaimed three-film series about life in contemporary Europe. The titles — *Blue*, *White*, and *Red*— represent the colors of the French flag and each film uses as its theme part of the French national motto "liberty, equality, and fraternity." The films also take place in three different European countries: France (*Blue*), Poland (*White*), and Switzerland (*Red*). In *Three Colors: Blue* (1993), a young woman (Juliette Binoche) travels a long road to emotional recovery after losing her husband and five-year-old daughter in a car accident. The "liberty" she seeks is freedom from humanity and her painful memories (at one point, she attempts suicide). *Three Colors: White* (1994) addresses the "equality," or lack thereof, between husband and wife. Karl (Zbigniew Zamachowski) loves his wife Dominique (Julie Delpy) passionately, but she divorces him because he cannot consummate their marriage. But that's just the beginning of a series of unusual events — Karl stalks Dominique, she burns down his hair salon, he travels to Poland in a trunk. Eventually, Karl becomes a wealthy businessman and tries to win back his ex-wife. The concluding film in the trilogy, *Three Colors: Red* (1994), deals with "fraternity" in the form of a relationship that blossoms between a melancholy fashion model (Irene Jacobs) and an older, cynical retired judge (Jean-Louis Trintignant). Its unexpected ending brings closure to the trilogy by featuring brief appearances of characters from *Blue* (Binoche) and *White* (Zamachowski and Delpy). After completing *Red*, Kieslowski announced it was his final film; he died two years later of a heart attack.

Three Colors: Blue (aka *Trois couleurs: Bleu*; *Trzy kolory: Niebieski*) (1993); *Three Colors: White* (aka *Trois couleurs: Blanc*; *Trzy kolory: Bialy*) (1994); *Three Colors: Red* (aka *Trois couleurs: Rouge*; *Trzy kolory: Czerwony*) (1994)

3-D

Three-dimensional, or stereoscopic, films create an illusion of depth by separating each eye's field of view. This is usually accomplished by requiring viewers to wear cardboard glasses with clear polarized lenses or lenses tinted red and blue-green (the latter process is called anaglyphic 3-D). Although experimental 3-D films date back to 1915, the depth process was largely ignored until the early 1950s. Faced with the growing popularity of television, movie moguls felt that something new was needed to lure patrons back to the theaters. The astonishing success of Arch Obler's low-budget, three-dimensional jungle adventure *Bwana Devil* ("A lion in your lap!" proclaimed the poster) convinced Hollywood that 3-D was the answer to its problems. Over 30 stereoscopic films were released between 1953 and 1954. Arguably, the finest was 1953's *House of Wax*, which launched Vincent Price's horror career by casting him as a mad sculptor who makes wax figures from his murder victims. Unfortunately, quality efforts like *House of Wax* and *It Came from Outer Space* were quickly overshadowed by technically inept, let's-make-a-buck features like *Robot Monster* and *Cat Women of the Moon*. By 1955, the 3-D craze had ended, brought to an early death by the popularity of less expensive wide-screen processes like Cinemascope (which also offered something TV couldn't). Attempts to revive 3-D proved fruitless for almost two decades. Then, in 1969, the unexpected success of *The Stewardesses*, a low-budget sex picture, inspired a fleeting interest in 3-D again. However, as in the 1950s, poor quality 3-D movies flooded the market and snuffed out the chances of a big comeback. But just to prove you can't keep a good idea down, 3-D surfaced once more in the early 1980s with the release of a ludicrous Italian Western dubbed *Comin' at Ya*. This time, the major studios jumped on the bandwagon and produced big-budget features like *Jaws 3* and *Metalstorm*. Despite a few legitimate hits (e.g., *Friday the 13th Part 3*), 3-D never really captured the public's fancy and 3-D faded within a year. Nevertheless, the 1980s craze did produce the first 3-D feature-length cartoon, 1985's *Starchaser: The Legend of Orin*. The climax to 1991's *Freddy's Dead: The Final Nightmare* was shown in Freddyvision — a catchy term for 3-D. The 40-minute IMAX feature *Encounters in the Third Dimension* (1999) was a 3-D movie about 3-D. See also **Cinerama**; **Gimmicks**.

Bwana Devil (1952); *Arena* (1953); *The Charge at Feather River* (1953); *Devil's Canyon* (1953); *Fatal Desire* (1953); *Money from Home* (1953); *The Moonlighter* (1953); *Fort Ti* (1953); *Flight to Tangier* (1953); *Hondo* (1953); *House of Wax* (1953); *I, the Jury* (1953); *It Came from Outer Space* (1953); *Invaders from Mars* (1953); *Inferno* (1953); *Kiss Me Kate* (1953); *Man in the Dark* (1953); *Miss Sadie Thompson* (1953); *The Maze* (1953); *Outlaw Territory* (aka *Hannah Lee*) (1953); *Robot Monster* (1953); *Sangaree* (1953); *Wings of the Hawk* (1953); *Second Chance* (1953); *The Stranger Wore a Gun* (1953); *Cat Women of the Moon* (aka *Rocket to the Moon*) (1954); *Creature from the Black Lagoon* (1954); *Dial M for Murder* (1954); *Drums of Tahiti* (1954); *The French Line* (1954); *Gog* (1954); *Gorilla at Large* (1954); *The Mad Magician* (1954); *Phantom of the Rue Morgue* (1954); *Taza, Son of Cochise* (1954); *Son of Sinbad* (1955); *Eyes of Hell* (aka *The Mask*) (1961); *The Bubble* (aka *Fantastic Invasion of Planet Earth*) (1966); *The Mark of the Werewolf* (aka *Frankenstein's Bloody Terror*) (1968); *The Stewardesses* (1969); *Three Dimensions of Greta* (1972); *The Flesh and Blood Show* (aka *Asylum of the Insane*) (1972); *Andy Warhol's Frankenstein* (aka *Flesh for Frankenstein*) (1973); *The Playmates* (1973); *A*P*E* (1976); *The Surfer Girls* (1980); *Comin' at Ya!* (1981); *Rottweiler* (aka *Dogs of Hell*) (1981); *Friday the 13th Part 3* (1982); *Treasure of the Four Crowns* (1982); *Parasite* (1982); *Jaws 3* (aka *Jaws 3-D*) (1983); *The Man Who Wasn't There* (1983); *Metalstorm: The Destruction of Jared-Syn* (1983); *Spacehunter: Adventures in the Forbidden Zone* (1983); *Tales of the Third Dimension* (1984); *Silent Madness* (aka *Omega Factor*; *Night Killer*) (1984); *Hit the Road Running* (1984); *Starchaser: The Legend of Orin* (1985); *Blonde Emmanuelle in 3-D* (1990); *Freddy's Dead: The Final Nightmare* (1991); *Revenge of the Nerds IV: Nerds in Love* (1994 TVM) (the wedding climax only); *Encounters in the Third Dimension* (1999)

The Three Mesquiteers

Popular Western novelist William Colt MacDonald created these three Dumas-inspired do-gooders: Stony Brooke, the trio's hot-tempered leader; Tucson Smith, his more rational friend and frequent romantic rival; and Lullaby Joslin, the easy-going comedian of the group. *Law of the 45's* (1935) was the first Mesquiteer novel to reach the screen, but it did not feature all *three* Mesquiteers. That distinction belongs to RKO's *Powdersmoke Range* (1935), which starred Harry Carey, Hoot Gibson, and Big Boy Williams as, respectively, Tucson, Stony, and Lullaby. The following year, little Republic Pictures snatched up the property and launched the *official* Three Mesquiteers series. Republic's original Mesquiteer line-up featured Ray "Crash" Corrigan as Tucson, Robert Livingston as Stony, and Syd Saylor as Lullaby. Max Terhune replaced Saylor in the second film and it's this cast — Corrigan, Livingston, and Terhune — that's best remembered. Other performers, though, also spent time in the saddle. Ralph Temp temporarily replaced Livingston and an upcoming actor named John Wayne played Stony for awhile. A cowboy singer named Dick Weston had a musical number in 1937's *Wild Horse Rodeo*. Weston later became a Western star in his own right — after changing his name to Roy Rogers. Duncan Renaldo, best known as the Cisco Kid (q.v.), joined the cast in 1939 for a brief stint as a new character named Rico. Meanwhile, Corrigan, Livingston, and Terhune moved to other studios and launched new series. Corrigan and Terhune joined John "Dusty" King to form the Range Busters (q.v.) for Monogram. Livingston teamed up with Al "Fuzzy" St. John in PRC's Lone Rider movies (q.v.). These series and many similar ones owe much to the "Western trio" premise fostered by the first Mesquiteer pictures.

Law of the 45's (1935); *Powdersmoke Range* (1935); *The Three Mesquiteers* (1936); *Ghost Town Gold* (1936); *Roarin' Lead* (1936); *Riders of the Whistling Skull* (1937); *Hit the Saddle* (1937); *Gunsmoke Ranch* (1937); *Come on, Cowboys* (1937); *Range Defenders* (1937); *Heart of the Rockies* (1937); *The Trigger Trio* (1937); *Wild Horse Rodeo* (1937); *The Purple Vigilantes* (1938); *Call the*

Mesquiteers (1938); *Outlaws of Sonora* (1938); *Riders of the Black Hills* (1938); *Heroes of the Hills* (1938); *Pals of the Saddle* (1938); *Overland Stage Raiders* (1938); *Santa Fe Stampede* (1938); *Red River Range* (1938); *The Night Riders* (1939); *Three Texas Steers* (1939); *Wyoming Outlaws* (1939); *New Frontier* (1939); *The Kansas Terrors* (1939); *Cowboys from Texas* (1939); *Heroes of the Saddle* (1940); *Pioneers of the West* (1940); *Covered Wagon Days* (1940); *Rocky Mountain Rangers* (1940); *Oklahoma Renegades* (1940); *Under Texas Skies* (1940); *The Trail Blazers* (1940); *Lone Star Raiders* (1940); *Prairie Pioneers* (1941); *Saddlemates* (1941); *Gangs of Sonora* (1941); *Outlaws of the Cherokee Trail* (1941); *Gauchos of El Dorado* (1941); *West of Cimarron* (1941); *Code of the Outlaw* (1942); *Raiders of the Range* (1942); *Westward Ho* (1942); *The Phantom Plainsmen* (1942); *Shadows on the Sage* (1942); *Valley of Hunted Men* (1942); *Thundering Trails* (1943); *The Blocked Trail* (1943); *Santa Fe Scouts* (1943); *Riders of the Rio Grande* (1943)

The Three Musketeers

Alexandre Dumas' novels *The Three Musketeers*, *Twenty Years After*, and *The Man in the Iron Mask* have provided rich sources for cinematic swashbucklers. Silent versions of *The Three Musketeers* appeared in 1911, 1913, 1914, and 1921. The latter adaptation starred Douglas Fairbanks, Sr., in one of his most memorable roles as D'Artagnan. It was so successful that Fairbanks took another turn as D'Artagnan in 1929's *The Iron Mask*. Other actors have donned the hot-headed Gascon's sword, but none have made a lasting impression. Character actor Walter Abel was miscast in 1935's *The Three Musketeers*. Don Ameche's 1939 version was played for laughs, with the Ritz Brothers as the trio of Athos, Porthos, and Aramis. Gene Kelly gave an energetic performance in the lavish 1948 adaptation, but he lacked the necessary charisma. Warren William and Michael York may be the best post–Fairbanks D'Artagnans due to their different interpretations. In 1939's *The Man in the Iron Mask*, William portrayed D'Artagnan as a middle-aged swordsman, while York made him an awkward youth anxious to be a musketeer in Richard Lester's *The Three Musketeers* (1974). Interestingly, a number of coincidences surround the directors and performers in the Musketeer movies. There's a Frankenstein connection between James Whale's *The Man in the Iron Mask* (1939) and Rowland V. Lee's *The Three Musketeers* (1935). Whale directed Boris Karloff in *Frankenstein* and *The Bride of Frankenstein*, while Lee directed Karloff's last appearance as the Monster in *Son of Frankenstein*. Louis Hayward played the lead role in the 1939 *Man in the Iron Mask*, but switched to the part of D'Artagnan for *Lady in the Iron Mask* (1952). Eugene Pallette, who played the musketeer Aramis in the 1921 *Three Musketeers*, is best remembered as Friar Tuck in Errol Flynn's *The Adventures of Robin Hood*. One of his co-stars in that film was Alan Hale, Sr. (as Little John), who played the musketeer Porthos in Whale's *The Three Musketeers*. His son, Alan Hale, Jr., played Porthos in *Lady in the Iron Mask* and *The Fifth Musketeer* and the son of Porthos in *At Sword's Point*. That same film featured Cornel Wilde as D'Artagnan's son, Dan O'Herlihy as Aramis' son, and Maureen O'Hara as Athos' daughter. Richard Lester filmed his *The Three Musketeers* and *The Four Musketeers* in 1973, but they were released in 1974 and 1975 respectively. The same cast reunited 15 years later for 1989's *Return of the Musketeers*. It played theatrically in Europe, but debuted in the U.S. on a cable network two years later. In 1993, Disney cast its version of *The Three Musketeers* with young performers like Kiefer

Sutherland, Charlie Sheen, and Oliver Platt—trade papers dubbed it "Young Guns in Tights." Five years later, Leonardo DiCaprio's post–*Titanic* popularity made a hit out of a mediocre version of *The Man in the Iron Mask*.

The Three Musketeers (1921); *The Iron Mask* (1929); *The Three Musketeers* (1935); *The Three Musketeers* (1939); *The Man in the Iron Mask* (1939); *The Three Musketeers* (1948); *Lady in the Iron Mask* (1952); *At Sword's Point* (1952); *Sword of D'Artagnan* (1952); *The Three Musketeers* (aka *Les Trois Mousquetaires*) (1953); *Count of Bragelonne* (aka *The Last Musketeer*; *Le Vicomte de Bragelonne*) (1954); *The Three Musketeers* (1961); *The Secret Mark of D'Artagnan* (1962); *The Three Musketeers* (aka *The Three Musketeers: The Queen's Diamonds*) (1974); *The Four Musketeers* (aka *The Four Musketeers: The Revenge of Milady*) (1975); *The Man in the Iron Mask* (1977 TVM); *The Fifth Musketeer* (1979); *The Return of the Musketeers* (1989); *The Three Musketeers* (1993); *Ring of the Musketeers* (1993); *The Daughter of D'Artagnan* (aka *La Fille de D'Artagnan*; *Revenge of the Musketeers*) (1994); *The Man in the Iron Mask* (1998)

3 Ninjas Series

In industry slang, *3 Ninjas* was a Disney "pick up," a movie produced by another company and released to fill in the gap between major releases. Undoubtedly, Disney's low expectations were pleasantly exceeded when *3 Ninjas* blossomed into a modest 1992 hit. Its success should have been more obvious, given its ingredients: three cute brothers, wholesome family values, and some lively martial arts action. The formulaic plot pits the ninja-trained brothers Tum Tum (Chad Power), Colt (Max Elliott Slade), and Rocky (Michael Treanor), ages 7–12, against a crime czar being pursued by their FBI agent father. There's never any doubt that the boys will triumph over their adversaries, especially with the help of ninja master Grandpa Mori (Victor Wong). Tri-Star released the less-successful sequels out of order, creating some confusing cast changes. For example, *3 Ninjas Kick Back* (1994) featured Sean Fox and Evan Bonifant as Rocky and Tum Tum, respectively. However, the original cast members were back a year later for *3 Ninjas Knuckle Up*. In *3 Ninjas: High Noon at Mega Mountain* (1998), the chop-socky trio were played by all new actors: Matthew Botuchis (Rocky), Michael O'Laskey (Colt) and John Paul Roeske (Tum Tum). Victor Wong provided continuity in the series, his Grandpa Mori role coming across as a sillier version of Mr. Miyagi from *The Karate Kid* (q.v.) films.

3 Ninjas (1992); *3 Ninjas Kick Back* (1994); *3 Ninjas Knuckle Up* (1995); *3 Ninjas: High Noon at Mega Mountain* (1998)

Three Smart Girls Series

Teen star Deanna Durbin made her feature film debut in 1936's *Three Smart Girls*, a sentimental comedy about the efforts of three sisters to reunite their separated parents. Nan Grey and Barbara Read played the other two sisters. Helen Parrish replaced Read in the 1939 follow-up *Three Smart Girls Grow Up*, which focused on Deanna's plans to marry off her older sisters. This fluffy sequel gave the 18-year-old Durbin one of her biggest recording hits with "Because." She reprised the Penelope Craig character one more time, as an adult, in the more serious World War II romance *Hers to Hold* (1943).

Three Smart Girls (1936); *Three Smart Girls Grow Up* (1939); *Hers to Hold* (1943)

Tibbs, Virgil

An urbane black detective from Philadelphia, Tibbs first appeared as a fish out of water in the 1967 Best Picture *In the Heat of the Night*, a mystery set in a racially prejudiced Southern town. Rod Steiger won a Best Actor Oscar as the town's sheriff, but it was Tibbs, as portrayed by Sidney Poitier, who came back for a sequel. *They Call Me MISTER Tibbs* (1970) sent Tibbs to San Francisco to solve a homicide. He was still there in 1971, working with a vigilante group to crack a drug ring in *The Organization*. That was the last Tibbs film, except for a 1988 TV version (and series pilot) of *In the Heat of the Night* starring Howard Rollins as Virgil Tibbs.

In the Heat of the Night (1967); *They Call Me MISTER Tibbs* (1970); *The Organization* (1971); *In the Heat of the Night* (1988 TVM)

Time Travel

The subject of time has long fascinated filmmakers, as evidenced by 1910's *The Times Are Out of Joint*, an obscure sci-fi feature about a clock that manipulates time by accelerating motion. Generally, however, movies about time travel fall into three categories: traveling into the past, traveling into the future, and traveling from the future back to present day. The first category is by far the most common, dating back to Mark Twain's *A Connecticut Yankee in King Arthur's Court*. Twain's novel alone has been filmed numerous times, to include a silent version, a Will Rogers comedy, a Bing Crosby musical, and a Disney feature (mysteriously titled *Unidentified Flying Oddball*). Leslie Howard traveled back to 18th century England in *Berkeley Square*, as did Tyrone Power in the remake *I'll Never Forget You*, while Christopher Reeve willed himself back to turn-of-the-century America in *Somewhere in Time*. All three fell in love with beautiful ladies, lost them temporarily, and then were reunited in one way or another. Spacecrafts accidentally stumbled through time warps in *World Without End* (1956) and *Planet of the Apes* (1968). In 1986's *Star Trek IV: The Voyage Home*, the Enterprise used warp speed to go back in time to save some whales. Curious scientists have naturally preferred to travel to the future, as in *The Time Travelers* (1964) and George Pal's 1960 adaptation of H.G. Wells' *The Time Machine*. A cornered Jack the Ripper used Wells' time machine to make a quick escape to modern-day San Francisco in Nicholas Meyer's stylish thriller *Time After Time* (1979). Finally, inhabitants of the future have sought to change their course of events by traveling back to present day in *Cyborg 2087* (1966), its partial remake *The Terminator* (1984), and *Trancers* (1985). *Cyborg 2087*, an underrated cheapie, cast Michael Rennie as a cyborg assigned to stop the creation of his own "race." Other time-related movies of interest include: *It Happened Tomorrow* (1944), in which a reporter acquires tomorrow's newspaper today (a premise that inspired the 1996–99 TV series *Early Edition*); in *Repeat Performance* (1947) and its 1989 TV movie remake *Turn Back the Clock*, two people live a year over again; a scientist in 1956's *The Atomic Man* could move 7.5 seconds ahead of everyone else; and in *The Jetty* (1963) and its semi-remake *12 Monkeys* (1995), a man remembers his own future death. See also **Back to the Future Series; Clocks and Watches; Trancers Series.**

A Connecticut Yankee in King Arthur's Court (1921); *A Connecticut Yankee in King Arthur's Court* (1931); *Berkeley Square* (1933); *Time Flies* (1944); *Fiddlers Three* (1944); *Where Do We Go from Here?* (1945); *Repeat Performance* (1947); *A Connecticut Yankee in King Arthur's Court* (1949); *I'll Never Forget You* (aka *The House in the Square*) (1951); *The Atomic Man* (aka *Timeslip*) (1956); *World Without End* (1956); *The 30 Foot Bride of Candy Rock* (1959); *Beyond the Time Barrier* (1960); *The Time Machine* (1960); *The Jetty* (aka *La Jetée; The Pier*) (1963); *The Time Travelers* (1964); *Dr. Who and the Daleks* (1965); *Willy McBean and His Magic Machine* (1965); *Cyborg 2087* (1966); *Daleks-Invasion Earth 2150 A.D.* (aka *Invasion Earth 2150 A.D.*) (1966); *Journey to the Center of Time* (1967); *The Planet of the Apes* (1968); *A Witch Without a Broom* (1968); *Hu-Man* (1975); *Time Travelers* (1976); *The Time Machine* (1978 TVM); *Jubilee* (1978); *Time After Time* (1979); *Unidentified Flying Oddball* (aka *A Spaceman in King Arthur's Court*) (1979); *The Day Time Ended* (aka *Time Warp*) (1980); *The Final Countdown* (1980); *Somewhere in Time* (1980); *Time Bandits* (1981); *Through the Magic Pyramid* (1981 TVM); *Timerider* (1983); *The Philadelphia Experiment* (1984); *The Terminator* (1984); *The Cold Room* (aka *The Prisoner*) (1984 TVM); *Arthur the King* (1985 TVM); *The Blue Yonder* (aka *Time Flyer*) (1985 TVM); *Trancers* (aka *Future Cop*) (1985); *My Science Project* (1985); *Back to the Future* (1985); *Biggles: Adventures in Time* (aka *Biggles*) (1986); *Peggy Sue Got Married* (1986); *Star Trek IV: The Voyage Home* (1986); *The Time Guardian* (1987); *Timestalkers* (1987 TVM); *Out of Time* (1988 TVM); *Light Years* (1988); *Earth*Star Voyager* (1988 TVM); *The Navigator: A Medieval Odyssey* (aka *The Navigator*) (1988); *Bill and Ted's Excellent Adventure* (1989); *Quantum Leap* (1989 TVM); *Time Trackers* (1989); *Millennium* (1989); *Turn Back the Clock* (1989 TVM); *Frankenstein Unbound* (aka *Roger Corman's Frankenstein Unbound*) (1990); *Running Against Time* (1990 TVM); *Spirit of '76* (1991); *Warlock* (1991); *Beastmaster 2: Through the Portal of Time* (1991); *Waxwork II: Lost in Time* (1991); *The Visitors* (1993); *Timecop* (1994); *A.P.E.X.* (1994); *12 Monkeys* (1995); *Nemesis 2: Nebula* (aka *Nemesis 2*) (1995); *W.E.I.R.D. World* (1995 TVM); *Doctor Who* (1996 TVM); *Star Trek: First Contact* (1996); *Yesterday's Target* (1996 TVM); *When Time Expires* (1997); *Lost in Space* (1998); *The Corridors of Time: The Visitors II* (1998); *A Knight in Camelot* (1998 TVM); *Phantasm: Oblivion* (aka *Phantasm IV: Oblivion; Phantasm: oblIVion*) (1998); *Retroactive* (1998); *Clockmaker* (1998); *Time at the Top* (1999); *Austin Powers: The Spy Who Shagged Me* (1999); *The TimeShifters* (1999 TVM)

Titanic

The 1912 luxury liner disaster was a popular film subject long before James Cameron's Oscar-winning 1999 epic shattered box-office records. Twentieth Century–Fox's 1953 version boasted that it was "Titanic in emotion…in spectacle…in climax…in cast!" Indeed, the cast was impressive — with Clifton Webb, Barbara Stanwyck, Robert Wagner, and Thelma Ritter — but the film was strictly stolid Hollywood gloss. The 1958 adaptation of Walter Lord's book *A Night to Remember* took a semi-documentary approach and earned kudos for its authenticity and emotional drama. Debbie Reynolds played one of *Titanic*'s survivors in the glossy musical *The Unsinkable Molly Brown* (1964). On a smaller scale, *S.O.S. Titanic* (1979) was a made-for-TV rehash, while *Raise the Titanic!* (1980) was a dull adaptation of Clive Cussler's best seller about salvaging the sunken ship. The *Titanic* returned as a ghost ship, complete with spooky passengers, in 1989's *Ghostbusters II*. Peter Gallagher starred in the 1996 two-part television movie *Titanic*. It was quickly eclipsed a year later by Cameron's *Titanic*, which featured a 775-foot long, nearly full-size exterior set of the ship. Still, Cameron's mammoth spectacle is better remembered for its fictitious romance between fateful lovers Jack (Leonard DiCaprio) and Rose (Kate Winslet).

Titanic (1953); *A Night to Remember* (1958); *The Unsinkable Molly Brown* (1964); *S.O.S. Titanic* (1979 TVM); *Raise the Titanic!* (1980); *Ghostbusters II* (1989); *Titanic* (1996 TVM); *No Greater Love* (1996); *Titanic* (1997)

TNT Bible Stories

Turner Network Television (TNT) launched its ambitious series of Old Testament biblical epics in 1994 with *Abraham*. This first made-for-television film established the formula for all other entries: veteran big screen performers (Richard Harris and Barbara Hershey); on-location filming in exotic locales like Morocco; and long running times. *Joseph* (1995), which starred Ben Kingsley (*Gandhi*) in the title role, won an Emmy for Best Miniseries. However, in terms of epic scope, *David* (1997) towers above the rest of the series, with an elaborate battle scene involving 600 extras. German and Italian companies co-produced the films with TNT, with the network retaining exclusive broadcast rights in the U.S.

Abraham (aka *Abraham: A TNT Bible Story*) (1994 TVM); *Jacob* (aka *Jacob: A TNT Bible Story*) (1994 TVM); *Joseph* (aka *Joseph: A TNT Bible Story*) (1995 TVM); *Moses* (aka *Moses: A TNT Bible Story*) (1996 TVM); *Samson and Delilah* (aka *Samson and Delilah: A TNT Bible Story*) (1996 TVM); *David* (aka *David: A TNT Bible Story*) (1997 TVM)

Topper

George and Marion Kerby were a fun-loving couple until a car crash put a premature end to their earthly existence. Required to perform a good deed to earn admittance into Heaven, the ghostly Kerbys turned their attention to meek banker Cosmo Topper. Cosmo's subsequent problems with George and Marion generated most of the laughs in 1937's *Topper*. The film was a guaranteed success, with Cary Grant, Constance Bennett, and Roland Young in the principal roles. Bennett and Young returned for the 1939 sequel *Topper Takes a Trip*, which found Marion badgering Cosmo on his Riviera vacation. Only Young (and Billie Burke as Mrs. Topper) remained for 1941's *Topper Returns*. It drew poor comparisons with the first two films, but has since come to be regarded as a first-rate haunted house comedy. It also gave Burke a chance to shine with some wacky dialogue: "My, my, it's strange how it's always cold in the winter and warm in the summer, isn't it?" Leo G. Carroll played Cosmo in the 1953–56 TV series *Topper*, with Robert Sterling and Anne Jeffreys as the Kerbys. Kate Jackson and then-husband Andrew Stevens produced and starred (as the Kerbys) in a lackluster 1979 TV movie, co-starring Jack Warden as Cosmo Topper. In 1983's *Somewhere Tomorrow*, a lonely teenage girl watched Topper, bumped her head, and then met a boy ghost. See also **Ghosts**.

Topper (1937); *Topper Takes a Trip* (1939); *Topper Returns* (1941); *Topper* (1979 TVM)

Tora-san

The most popular film series in Japan remains virtually unknown to English-language moviegoers. Yet, the Tora-san films have appealed to their faithful Japanese fans for over 20 years and 45 episodes. Amazingly, the title character has always been played by the same actor, Kiyoshi Atsumi, and almost all the entries were

directed by Yoji Yamada. The popularity of the films can be traced to the lovable title character, Tora-san (a colloquial reference to Torajiro Kuruma), whom *Variety* once described as "a none-too-bright, bumbling but streetwise peddler who most often fouls up the plot and lets the woman get away." A middle-aged bachelor, Tora-san travels throughout Japan when not living with his aunt and uncle. He also spends time with his sister's family, especially nephew Mitsuo (Hidetaka Yoshioka). As a teenager, Mitsuo's relationship with Tora-san became a focal point of later series entries—a development credited with introducing the films to a wider, more youthful audience in the late 1980s. Star Kiyoshi Atsumi was 42 when the series' debut entry, *Tora-san, Our Lovable Tramp* (*Otoko wa tsurai yo*), was released in 1969. He appeared in an average of two Tora-san films annually from 1969 to 1987, before the production pace decreased to one per year. According to some sources, he outranked the Emperor as the most recognizable face in Japan. The Tora-san series ended when Atsumi died of lung cancer in 1996 at the age of 68. The Associated Press reported that 21,000 people attended Atsumi's memorial service. At one time, the *Guinness Book* listed the Tora-san entries as the world's longest-running film series with the same star.

Tora-san, Our Lovable Tramp (aka *Otoko wa tsurai yo*) (1969); *Tora-san's Cherished Mother* (aka *Zoku otoko wa tsurai yo*) (1969); *Tora-san: His Tender Love* (aka *Otoko wa tsurai yo: Fuuten no Tora*) (1970); *Tora-san's Grand Scheme* (aka *Shin otoko wa tsurai yo*) (1970); *Tora-san's Runaway* (aka *Otoko wa tsurai yo: Boukyou hen*) (1970); *Tora-san's Shattered Romance* (aka *Otoko wa tsurai yo: Junjo hen*) (1971); *Tora-san, the Good Samaritan* (aka *Otoko wa tsurai yo: Funto hen*) (1971); *Tora-san's Love Call* (aka *Otoko wa tsurai yo: Torajiro koiuta*) (1971); *Tora-san's Dear Old Home* (aka *Otoko wa tsurai yo: Shibamata bojo*) (1972); *Tora-san's Dream-Come-True* (aka *Otoko wa tsurai yo: Torajiro yumemakura*) (1972); *Tora-san's Forget-Me-Not* (aka *Otoko wa tsurai yo: Torajiro wasurenagusa*) (1973); *Tora-san Loves an Artist* (aka *Otoko wa tsurai yo: Watashi no tora-san*) (1973); *Tora-san's Lovesick* (aka *Otoko wa tsurai yo: Torajiro koiyatsure*) (1974); *Tora-san's Lullaby* (aka *Otoko wa tsurai yo: Torajiro komoriuta*) (1974); *Tora-san's Rise and Fall* (aka *Otoko wa tsurai yo: Torajiro aiaigasa*) (1975); *Tora-san, the Intellectual* (aka *Otoko wa tsurai yo: Katsushika risshihen*) (1975); *Tora-san's Sunrise and Sunset* (aka *Otoko wa tsurai yo: Torajiro yuuyake koyake*) (1976); *Tora-san's Pure Love* (aka *Otoko wa tsurai yo: Torajiro junjoshishu*) (1976); *Tora-san Meets His Lordship* (aka *Otoko wa tsurai yo: Torajiro to tonosama*) (1977); *Tora-san Plays Cupid* (aka *Otoko wa tsurai yo: Torajiro gambare!*) (1977); *Stage-Struck Tora-san* (aka *Otoko wa tsurai yo: Torajiro wagamichi wo yuku*) (1978); *Talk-of-the-Town Tora-san* (aka *Otoko wa tsurai yo: Torajiro wagamichi wo yuku*) (1978); *Tora-san, the Matchmaker* (aka *Otoko wa tsurai yo: Tonderu torajiro*) (1979); *Tora-san's Dream of Spring* (aka *Otoko wa tsurai yo: Torajiro haru no yume*) (1979); *Tora-san's Tropical Fever* (aka *Otoko wa tsurai yo: Torajiro haibisukasu no hana*) (1980); *Foster Daddy, Tora-san* (aka *Otoko wa tsurai yo: Torajiro kamome uta*) (1980); *Tora-san's Love in Osaka* (aka *Tora-san's Many-Splintered Love*; *Otoko wa tsurai yo: Naniwa no koino torajiro*) (1981); *Tora-san's Promise* (aka *Otoko wa tsurai yo: Torajiro kamifusen*) (1981); *Hearts and Flowers for Tora-san* (aka *Otoko wa tsurai yo: Torajiro ajisai no koi*) (1982); *Tora-san, the Expert* (aka *Otoko wa tsurai yo: Hana mo arashi mo Torajiro*) (1982); *Tora-san's Song of Love* (aka *Otoko wa tsurai yo: Tabi to onna to Torajiro*) (1983); *Tora-san Goes Religious* (aka *Otoko wa tsurai yo: Kuchibue wo fuku Torajiro*) (1983); *Marriage Counselor Tora-san* (aka *Otoko wa tsurai yo: Yogiri ni musebu torajiro*) (1984); *Tora-san's Forbidden Love* (aka *Otoko wa tsurai yo: Torajiro shinjitsu ichiro*) (1984); *Tora-san, the Go-Between* (aka *Otoko wa tsurai yo: Torajiro renaijuku*) (1985); *Tora-san's Island*

Encounter (aka *Otoko wa tsurai yo: Shibamata yori ai wo komete*) (1985); *Tora-san's Bluebird Fantasy* (aka *Otoko wa tsurai yo: Shiawase no aoi tori*) (1986); *Tora-san Goes North* (aka *Otoko wa tsurai yo: Shiretoko bojo*) (1987); *Tora-san Plays Daddy* (aka *Otoko wa tsurai yo: Torajiro monogatari*) (1987); *Tora-san's Salad Date Memorial* (aka *Otoko wa tsurai yo: Torajiro sarada kinenbi*) (1988); *Tora-san Goes to Vienna* (aka *Otoko wa tsurai yo: Torajiro kokoro no tabiji*) (1989); *Tora-san, My Uncle* (aka *Otoko wa tsurai yo: Boku no ojisan*) (1989); *Tora-san Takes a Vacation* (aka *Otoko wa tsurai yo: Torajiro no kyuujitsu*) (1990); *Tora-san Confesses* (aka *Otoko wa tsurai yo: Torajiro no kokuhaku*) (1991); *Tora-san Makes Excuses* (aka *Otoko wa tsurai yo: Torajiro no seishun*) (1992); *Otoko wa tsurai yo: Torajiro no endan* (1993); *Otoko wa tsurai yo: Haikei, Kuruma Torajiro sama* (1994); *Otoko wa tsurai yo: Torajiro kurenai no hana* (1995)

Tornadoes *see* Hurricanes and Tornadoes

The Toxic Avenger

Melvin Ferd, Tromaville's town "nerd," worked as a janitor at the local health club. He regularly incurred the ridicule of the club's snobbish clientele and, after a particularly degrading experience he jumped out a second-story window and landed in a vat of chemical toxins. This accident transformed meek Melvin into a muscular, green, disfigured superhero (resembling *Swamp Thing*). All this happened in the first twenty minutes of 1985's *The Toxic Avenger*, a hopeless comedy that found a video audience and evolved into a campy, low-budget series. The rest of the first picture found the Toxic Avenger, janitor's mop in hand, beating up bad guys and falling in love with a blind blonde named Sara. Mark Torgi played Melvin, while Mitchell Cohen took over as Toxie (with Kenneth Kessler providing the voice). The Troma Team (yes, the studio named the film's town after itself), waited four years to produce *The Toxic Avenger Part II*. The gap between installments must have confused the Troma staff, for in *Part II*, Melvin's last name had changed to Junko and Sara (still blonde and blind) had become Claire. The plot sent Toxie to Tokyo to find his father, while the evil Apocalypse, Inc. took over Tromaville. Ron Fazio and John Altamura teamed up as Toxie. They also headlined the same year's *The Toxic Avenger Part III: The Last Temptation of Toxie*, an effort described by *Variety* as a "toxic stew that, in no particular order, mixes lots of entrails, half-naked women and sound effects plucked from the Three Stooges."

The Toxic Avenger (1985); *The Toxic Avenger Part II* (1989); *The Toxic Avenger Part III: The Last Temptation of Toxie* (1989)

Tracy, Dick

Chester Gould's comic strip police detective had been the subject of four 1937–41 Republic serials before RKO decided he had potential as a B-film series hero. Former tough guy Morgan Conway brought Tracy alive in 1946's *Dick Tracy* and 1947's *Dick Tracy vs. Cueball*, a pair of lively action pictures balanced nicely by a sense of humor. The scripts stayed close to the comic strip characters, with Anne Jeffreys as Tess Truehart, Esther Howard as Filthy Flora of the Dripping Dagger Inn, and Ian Keith as Vitamin Flintheart. Ralph Byrd, who had played the detective for Republic, took over the role in the last two films in the series. Since they appeared when film series were declining in popularity, the Tracy films are all but forgotten today. That's a shame, for they featured some very col-

orful villains: Mike Mazurki's Spitface (*Dick Tracy*), Dick Wessel's Cueball, Jack Lambert's The Claw (*Dick Tracy's Dilemma*), and Boris Karloff's Gruesome. In 1990, Warren Beatty mounted a colorful screen adaptation, but — despite Madonna as a femme fatale and some catchy Stephen Sondheim songs — it was a rather dull affair. See also **Comic Strip Characters**.

Dick Tracy (aka *Spitface*) (1946); *Dick Tracy vs. Cueball* (1947); *Dick Tracy's Dilemma* (aka *Mark of the Claw*) (1947); *Dick Tracy Meets Gruesome* (aka *Dick Tracy's Amazing Adventure*) (1947); *Dick Tracy* (1990)

The Trail Blazers

Monogram Pictures was the home of the B-Western in the 1940s. The budget-minded studio was already producing the Rough Riders (q.v.) and the Range Busters (q.v.) films when it introduced the Trail Blazers series in 1943. Monogram signed the three biggest names available (at budget price) and wound up with cowboy greats Hoot Gibson, Ken Maynard, and Bob Steele. Gibson and Maynard had retired in the 1930s, but Monogram lured them back to the screen even though they were 51 and 48, respectively. After just seven pictures, the series came to an end and Gibson and Maynard closed out their film careers except for occasional appearances.

Blazing Guns (1943); *The Law Rides Again* (1943); *Wild Horse Stampede* (1943); *Arizona Whirlwind* (1944); *Death Valley Rangers* (1944); *Outlaw Trail* (1944); *Westward Bound* (1944)

Trailers *see* Mobile Homes

Trains

Trains have long been a favorite setting for tense dramas and mysteries, primarily since the close confines force character interaction by restricting movement beyond a limited area. Mysteries that take place almost entirely on trains include the Basil Rathbone Sherlock Holmes entry *Terror by Night* and the 1974 all-star adaptation of Agatha Christie's *Murder on the Orient Express*. Two of Alfred Hitchcock's most famous works are set aboard trains: A little old lady who's really a spy (Dame May Whitty) gets kidnapped in *The Lady Vanishes*, while Robert Walker thinks he and Farley Granger swap murders in a chilling scene in *Strangers on a Train*. Trains are hijacked and used as getaway vehicles in *Runaway Train* (Jon Voight and Eric Roberts as convicts) and *Von Ryan's Express* (with Frank Sinatra and fellow escaped POWs speeding through Germany to freedom). A thawed-out primeval monster and a demented Cossack (Telly Savalas) wreaked havoc aboard the *Horror Express* — thank heavens, sturdy hero Peter Cushing was a passenger! However, that's nothing compared to the deadly virus threatening Sophia Loren and Burt Lancaster as they raced through Europe in *The Cassandra Crossing*. Other potentially deadly trains include the ones used to transport atomic bombs in *Detonator*, *Broken Arrow*, and *Atomic Train*. It's enough to make one revel in fluffier (and far more entertaining) outings like the Gene Wilder–Richard Pryor action-comedy *The Silver Streak*. See also **Subways**. The following movies either take place on trains or feature memorable train scenes:

The Iron Horse (1924); *Number Seventeen* (1932); *The Phantom Express* (1932); *Shanghai Express* (1932); *Rome Express* (1932); *Union*

Depot (1932); *The Silver Streak* (1934); *Twentieth Century* (1934); *Streamline Express* (1935); *Florida Special* (1936); *Night Mail* (1936); *California Straight Ahead* (1937); *La Bête Humaine* (*The Human Beast*) (1938); *The Lady Vanishes* (1938); *Union Pacific* (1939); *Night Train to Munich* (aka *Night Train*) (1940); *Inspector Hornleigh Goes to It* (aka *Mail Train*) (1940); *Broadway Limited* (1941); *Lady on a Train* (1945); *One Way to Love* (1945); *Terror by Night* (1946); *Sleeping Car to Trieste* (1948); *Berlin Express* (1948); *Train of Events* (1949); *Peking Express* (1951); *Strangers on a Train* (1951); *Diplomatic Courier* (1952); *The Narrow Margin* (1952); *Terror on a Train* (aka *Time Bomb*) (1952); *The Titfield Thunderbolt* (1953); *The Paris Express* (aka *The Man Who Watched the Trains Go By*) (1953); *Human Desire* (1954); *The Great Locomotive Chase* (aka *Andrews' Raiders*) (1956); *Flame Over India* (aka *Northwest Frontier*) (1959); *North by Northwest* (1959); *Night Train* (1959); *Train Robbery Confidential* (1962); *From Russia with Love* (the most memorable of several James Bond train scenes) (1963); *Stop Train 349* (1964); *Dr. Terror's House of Horrors* (1965); *The Sleeping Car Murders* (1965); *The Train* (1965); *Von Ryan's Express* (1965); *Trans-Europe Express* (1966); *Closely Watched Trains* (1966); *The Great St. Trinian's Train Robbery* (1966); *The Great British Train Robbery* (1967); *Istanbul Express* (1968); *The French Connection* (1971); *Boxcar Bertha* (1972); *Horror Express* (aka *Panic on the Trans-Siberian Express*) (1972); *Emperor of the North* (aka *Emperor of the North Pole*) (1973); *The Train Robbers* (1973); *Hijack* (1973 TVM); *Runaway!* (aka *The Runaway Train*) (1973 TVM); *Murder on the Orient Express* (1974); *Breakheart Pass* (1976); *The Silver Streak* (1976); *The Cassandra Crossing* (1977); *The Stationmaster's Wife* (1977); *Julia* (1977); *The Great Train Robbery* (aka *The First Great Train Robbery*) (1979); *The Lady Vanishes* (1979); *Avalanche Express* (1979); *Disaster on the Coastliner* (1979 TVM); *Hanging by a Thread* (1979 TVM); *Cafe Express* (1980); *Terror Train* (1980); *Chattanooga Choo Choo* (1984); *Romance on the Orient Express* (1985 TVM); *Runaway Train* (1985); *Stand by Me* (1986); *Planes, Trains, and Automobiles* (1987); *Throw Momma from the Train* (1987); *The Sleeping Car* (1990); *Back to the Future III* (1990); *Narrow Margin* (1990); *The Railway Station Man* (1992 TVM); *Death Train* (aka *Detonator*) (1993 TVM); *Weird Tales* (aka *Strane Storie*) (1994); *Desire in Motion* (1994); *Tall Tale* (1995); *Under Siege 2: Dark Territory* (1995); *Night Watch* (aka *Detonator 2: Night Watch*) (1995 TVM); *Before Sunrise* (1995); *Broken Arrow* (1996); *Riding the Rails* (1997); *Train of Life* (1998); *Atomic Train* (1999 TVM); *Wild Wild West* (1999); *Final Run* (1999 TVM); *Thomas and the Magic Railroad* (2000)

Trancers Series

The law of diminishing returns applies to this low-budget series which got off to a promising — if derivative — beginning. *Trancers* (1985) starred Tim Thomerson as Jack Deth, a 24th-century hardboiled cop (shades of Harrison Ford in *Blade Runner*) who chases a villain back through time to prevent him from killing the father of a future government leader (shades of the previous year's *Terminator*). Deth's task is complicated by the title creatures, zombie-like humans with extraordinary strength and the ability to withstand a handful of bullets at close range (usually four or five shots can down a trancer). The film has its admirers, chiefly due to its light touch and quick pace. Director Charles Band tried to mount a follow-up as a segment in the three-part feature *Pulse Pounders*, but the project was never completed. Instead, Thomerson encored as Deth in 1991's *Trancers II*, an unsurprising sequel featuring perennial bad guy Richard Lynch as the brother of the original film's villain. The film's saving grace is Deth's attempts to deal with two wives — one from the present (Helen Hunt) and

one from the future (Megan Ward). The third installment, 1992's *Trancers III* (1992), explained how trancers were first created (by a drug invented by Colonel "Daddy" Muthuh). It also ended Deth's marriage with his present-day wife. However, its primary purpose was to set up further entries in the series. In its closing scene, the high council appointed Deth "peace-keeping emissary of time and space" — a job he kept for the final two entries of the *Trancer* series. See also **Time Travel**.

Trancers (aka *Future Cop*) (1985); *Trancers II* (aka *Trancers II: The Return of Jack Deth*) (1991); *Trancers III* (aka *Trancers III: Deth Lives*) (1992); *Trancers 4: Jack of Swords* (1993); *Trancers 5: Sudden Deth* (1994)

Traveling Salespersons

The exploits of those who earn their living selling door-to-door have been played mostly for laughs. Lady vendors have proven to be far more adept than their male counterparts at peddling products: Joan Blondell sold booze-flavored toothpaste in *The Traveling Saleslady* (1935); Joan Davis tried to convince Westerners they needed soap in *The Traveling Saleswoman* (1950); Ginger Rogers marketed girdles in *The First Travelling Saleslady* (1956); Phyllis Diller pushed pianolas in *Did You Hear the One About the Traveling Saleslady?* (1968); and Lucille Ball specialized in cosmetics as *The Fuller Brush Girl* (1950). Red Skelton had one of his best roles as *The Fuller Brush Man* (1948), the hit which inspired Ball's similarly-titled sequel. Lou Costello played an incompetent vacuum cleaner salesman in 1946's *Little Giant*, as did Jimmy Durante and Phil Silvers in *You're in the Army Now* (1941). Both comedies featured the patented scene in which dirt is dumped on a clean carpet for an unsuccessful vacuum demonstration. Serious films about traveling salesmen include the 1951 and 1985 adaptations of Arthur Miller's searing stage play *Death of a Salesman*. The 1960 *Never Let Go* was about a salesman victimized by car thieves. Steve Martin played a Depression-era sheet-music salesman in the offbeat dramatic musical *Pennies from Heaven* (1981).

The Traveling Saleslady (1935); *You're in the Army Now* (1941); *The Boogie Man Will Get You* (1942); *Little Giant* (aka *On the Carpet*) (1946); *The Emperor Waltz* (1948); *The Fuller Brush Man* (aka *That Mad Mr. Jones*) (1948); *The Traveling Saleswoman* (1950); *The Fuller Brush Girl* (aka *The Affairs of Sally*) (1950); *Death of a Salesman* (1951); *The Bigamist* (1953); *The First Traveling Saleslady* (1956); *Never Let Go* (1960); *The Dark at the Top of the Stairs* (1960); *Dear Heart* (1964); *Salesman* (1969); *Did You Hear the One about the Traveling Saleslady?* (1968); *The Strange Vengeance of Rosalie* (1972); *O Lucky Man!* (1973); *Paper Moon* (1973); *Naughty Wives* (1974); *Pennies from Heaven* (1981); *Death of a Salesman* (1985 TVM); *Tin Men* (1987); *Traveling Man* (1989 TVM); *Three Lives and Only One Death* (1996); *Western* (1997)

Trinity

Terrence Hill (aka Mario Girotti) had established himself as a rising Italian star by the late 1960s. After promising supporting roles in quality dramas like Visconti's *The Leopard* (1963), Hill switched to leading roles in spaghetti Westerns such as the Cat Stevens (q.v.) films, which paired him with Bud Spencer (aka Carlo Pedersoli). The blonde, handsome Hill and dark-haired, burly Spencer quickly became the Odd Couple of spaghetti Westerns. Their reputations were sealed with the international success of 1970's *They Call Me Trinity*, a spirited romp featuring Hill as a lazy, quick-drawing rascal named Trinity and Spencer as his surly, cattle-thief-turned-sheriff brother Bambino. The 1972 sequel, *Trinity Is Still My Name*, was funnier and also bigger at the box-office, especially in Italy where it was a huge hit. Oddly, these were the only Trinity pictures featuring the Hill-Spencer team, although they made several other movies together. Without Spencer, Hill made 1971's *Trinity Sees Red*, but it was a humorless Western which bore no resemblance to the other Trinity movies. In the final "official" series entry, *Trinity Plus the Clown and a Guitar*, George Hilton replaced Hill in the lead role. There are several other spaghetti Westerns with heroes named Trinity, but they do not appear to be *the* Trinity. Hill played a Trinity-like character in the 1974 Henry Fonda Western *My Name Is Nobody*. He remains a popular star in his homeland. In 1991, Hill directed and starred in *Lucky Luke*, a Western comedy along the same lines as the Trinity films. Enzo Barboni, who directed the first two *Trinity* films, tried to revive the series in 1995 with the TV movie *Trinity and Bambino: The Legend Lives On*. It starred Heath Kizzier and Keith Neubert as, respectively, Trinity Jr. and Bambino Jr. See also **Stevens, Cat.**

They Call Me Trinity (aka *Lo Chiamavano Trinita*) (1970) (Terrence Hill); *Trinity Sees Red* (aka *La Collera del Vento*; *Trinita Voit Rouge*) (1971) (Hill); *Trinity Is Still My Name* (aka *Continuavano a Chiamarlo Trinita*) (1972) (Hill); *Trinity Plus the Clown and a Guitar* (aka *Prima Ti Suono e Poi Ti Sparo*; *First I Play You...Then I Shoot You*) (1975) (George Hilton); *Trinity & Bambino: The Legend Lives On* (aka *Son of Trinity*) (1995 TVM) (Heath Kizzier as Trinity, Jr.)

Truck Drivers

Truckers have been stereotyped as macho men of action, particularly during the 1970s. Typical roles featured country singer Jerry Reed playing a good ole boy trucker in *High-Ballin'* (1978), Claude Akins and Frank Converse as no-nonsense truck drivers in *In Tandem* (1974), and Kris Kristofferson as the leader in charge of a *Convoy* (1978). Lady truckers have been virtually ignored, although a few females have nevertheless proven themselves as tough as their male counterparts. Kim Darby and Annie Potts played spunky women truckers in *Flatbed Annie and Sweetiepie: Lady Truckers* (1979), as did Deborah Raffin in *Willa* (1979) and Helen Shaver in *High-Ballin'*. Few big-name stars have been attracted to truck-driving roles, although Humphrey Bogart was behind a rig's wheel in *They Drive by Night* (1940). James Cagney, while still on the road to stardom, drove a truck as the *St. Louis Kid* (1934). Patrick Swayze played an ex-con trucker tricked into transporting assault weapons in *Black Dog* (1998). Sylvester Stallone drove a truck in *Over the Top* (1987), but he was more concerned with arm wrestling. And Kurt Russell tried to outsmart bad truckers who kidnapped his wife in *Breakdown* (1997). The most existential truckers were the ones driving nitroglycerin over dangerous mountain roads in 1952's *The Wages of Fear* and its 1977 remake *Sorcerer*. The most mysterious one was the unseen rig driver who tried to run Dennis Weaver off the road in Steven Spielberg's 1971 TV movie *Duel*. The TV series *Movin' On* and *B.J. and the Bear* both evolved from made-for-TV movies. In the latter series, the "Bear" was a mischievous truck-ridin' chimpanzee. See also **Automobiles.**

Quick Millions (1931); *St. Louis Kid* (1934); *California Straight Ahead* (1937); *They Drive by Night* (aka *The Road to Frisco*) (1940); *Desperate* (1947); *Speed to Spare* (1948); *Thieves' Highway* (1949); *The Wages of Fear* (1952); *The Rose Tattoo* (1955); *Death in Small Doses* (1957); *Hell Drivers* (aka *Hard Drivers*) (1957); *The Long Haul* (1957); *The Big Gamble* (1960); *Moonfire* (1970); *Duel* (1971 TVM); *Deadhead Miles* (1972); *In Tandem* (aka *Movin' On*) (1974 TVM); *White Line Fever* (1975); *The Great Smokey Roadblock* (aka *The Last of the Cowboys*) (1976); *Breaker! Breaker!* (1977); *Handle with Care* (aka *Citizen's Band*) (1977); *Sorcerer* (1977); *F.I.S.T.* (1978); *High-Ballin'* (1978); *Steel Cowboy* (1978 TVM); *Convoy* (1978); *B.J. and the Bear* (1978 TVM); *Every Which Way But Loose* (1978); *Flatbed Annie and Sweetiepie: Lady Truckers* (aka *Flatbed Annie*) (1979 TVM); *Willa* (1979); *Coast to Coast* (1980); *Road Games* (1981); *Brothers-in-Law* (1985 TVM); *Big Trouble in Little China* (1986); *Killing Machine* (1986); *Maximum Overdrive* (1986); *Tampopo* (1986); *Rolling Vengeance* (1987); *Over the Top* (1987); *Driving Force* (1989); *Think Big* (1990); *Close to Eden* (aka *Urga*) (1991); *Unhook the Stars* (1996); *...first do no harm* (1997 TVM); *Breakdown* (1997); *Trucks* (1997); *Black Dog* (1998); *Chill Factor* (1999)

Trumpet Players

Young trumpet players have been portrayed as brash, compulsive musicians by Kirk Douglas in *Young Man with a Horn* (1950) and Steve McQueen in *Love with the Proper Stranger* (1953). Burt Young was a down-on-his-luck trumpeteer who befriended a terminally-ill youth in the maudlin *Uncle Joe Shannon* (1978). Carole Lombarde rescued Fred MacMurray from the skids in 1937's *Swing High, Swing Low*. Danny Kaye played real-life band-leader/trumpet player Red Nichols in *The Five Pennies*. He even played a duet with Louis Armstrong, whose story reached the TV screen in 1976's *Louis Armstrong—Chicago Style*. Ben Vereen starred as "Satchmo." See also **Pianists; Violinists.**

Swing High, Swing Low (1937); *Syncopation* (1942); *Orchestra Wives* (1942); *Young Man with a Horn* (1950); *The Five Pennies* (1959); *Love with the Proper Stranger* (1963); *Dr. Terror's House of Horrors* (1965); *A Man Called Adam* (1966); *Louis Armstrong—Chicago Style* (1976 TVM); *Uncle Joe Shannon* (1978); *Mo' Better Blues* (1990); *Dingo* (1991); *The Mambo Kings* (1992); *Giant Steps* (1992); *Lush Life* (1994 TVM); *Brassed Off* (1997)

Tunnels

Tunnels have been a common fixture in P.O.W. (q.v.) sagas like *The Wooden Horse* (1950) and, of course, *The Great Escape* (1963). The Germans built secret tunnels, too, though a British spy thwarted their efforts in *The W Plan* (1930). John Garfield masterminded a tunnel through a cemetery to assassinate a Cuban official in 1949's *We Were Strangers*. On a considerably larger scale, the 1933 German film *The Tunnel* was about the construction of a tunnel connecting Europe and the U.S. It was remade in Britain in 1935's *Transatlantic Tunnel*. A Chinese army tried to "burrow" its way into the U.S. to mount an invasion in *Battle Beneath the Earth* (1967). In 1988's *The Navigator*, some medieval villagers enter a tunnel to escape from the Black Plague—and wind up in 20th-century New Zealand! Several films have featured "tunnels of love," while TV even offered a 1966-67 *Time Tunnel* series.

The W Plan (1930); *The Tunnel* (aka *Der Tunnel*) (1933); *Transatlantic Tunnel* (aka *The Tunnel*) (1935); *Tycoon* (1947); *We Were Strangers* (1949); *The Wooden Horse* (1950); *The Hole* (1959); *Escape from East Berlin* (aka *Tunnel 28*) (1962); *The Great Escape*

(1963); *Battle Beneath the Earth* (1967); *Prophecy* (1979); *Berlin Tunnel 21* (1981 TVM); *El Norte* (1983); *The Navigator: A Medieval Odyssey* (aka *The Navigator*) (1988); *Criminal Act* (1989); *Tunnel Child* (aka *Tunnelkind*) (1990); *Lurking Fear* (1994); *Daylight* (1996); *Chill Factor* (1999)

Turtles

Lewis Carroll, Peter Laird, and Kevin Eastman are responsible for creating the cinema's most famous turtles. Carroll, of course, introduced the Mock Turtle in *Alice in Wonderland*, which has been filmed many times (though the 1933 and 1951 versions remain best known). Laird and Eastum created the underground comic book superheroes, the Teenage Mutant Ninja Turtles, in 1984. They went mainstream in the late 1980s, eventually launching a film series with 1990's *Teenage Mutant Ninja Turtles* (1990). The title character in *Gamera* (1965) could also qualify as a mutant turtle, though he was big, had fangs, and could fly. Other giant turtles harassed humans in *The Lost Continent* (1968) and *Where Time Began* (1978). A young boy who refused to speak befriended a giant albino turtle in the mystical New Zealand film *The Silent One* (1984). The French film *Totor* (1994) also revolved around the friendship between a boy and a turtle. Glenda Jackson and Ben Kingsley played two lonely people who freed sea turtles from a London aquarium in *Turtle Diary* (1985). Rocky Balboa (Sylvester Stallone) owned two turtles he named Cuff and Link in *Rocky* (1976). And, just to show the turtle's versatility, a tortoise hosted the animal Olympics in the appropriately-titled *Animalympics* (1979). See also **Gamera**; **Teenage Mutant Ninja Turtle Series**.

Alice in Wonderland (1933); *Alice in Wonderland* (1951); *Gamera* (aka *Gamera, the Invincible*; *Gammera*; *Daikaiju Gamera*) (1965); *The Lost Continent* (1968); *Rocky* (1976); *Where Time Began* (aka *Trip to the Centre of the Earth*) (1978); *Animalympics* (1979); *The Silent One* (1984); *Turtle Diary* (1985); *Teenage Mutant Ninja Turtles* (1990); *Totor* (1994)

Twins

The most frequent use of twins has been to portray good and evil, as in *Dead Ringer* and *The Dark Mirror* (featuring Bette Davis and Olivia de Havilland, respectively, in double roles). But comedies of mistaken identities have been popular, too. Hayley Mills swapped places with her sister (Hayley Mills, too) and reunited their divorced parents in *The Parent Trap* (q.v.). In a neat technical trick, the two Hayleys even sang a duet. Two sets of twins separated at birth caused all kinds of confusion in *Start the Revolution Without Me* and *Big Business*. Horror movies such as Brian De Palma's *Sisters* and cult favorite *Basket Case* have featured Siamese twins in murderous roles. In *Whispers* (1990), twins are made to believe they are one person. In contrast, *Seduction: Three Tales from the Inner Sanctum* (1992) has Victoria Principal acting like twins as part of a sexual fantasy game. Finally, in *The Miracle of Morgan's Creek*, Betty Hutton gave birth to sextuplets, which certainly seems to fit this category in spirit. See also **Basket Case Series**; **Lookalikes**; **The Parent Trap Series**.

Freaks (aka *Nature's Mistakes*) (1932); *Strangers in Love* (1932); *The Sphinx* (1933); *The Black Room* (1935); *Our Relations* (1936); *Man of Affairs* (aka *His Lordship*) (1936); *A Stolen Life* (1938); *The Man in the Iron Mask* (1939); *The Boys from Syracuse* (1940); *Among the Living* (1941); *Two-Faced Woman* (1941); *Keep 'Em Flying* (1941); *The Corsican Brothers* (1941); *The Dark Mirror* (1942); *The Palm Beach Story* (1942); *Nazi Agent* (1942); *Dead Men Walk* (1943); *Cobra Woman* (1944); *Here Come the Waves* (1944); *Miracle of Morgan's Creek* (1944); *Wonder Man* (1945); *A Stolen Life* (1946); *The Guilty* (1947); *Dual Alibi* (1947); *Campus Honeymoon* (1948); *Chained for Life* (1950); *I Cover the Underworld* (1955); *House of Numbers* (1957); *The Girl in the Kremlin* (1957); *Duel of the Titans* (1961); *The Parent Trap* (1961); *Dead Ringer* (aka *Dead Image*) (1964); *Open the Door and See All the People* (1964); *Cat Ballou* (1965); *Start the Revolution Without Me* (1970); *Twins of Evil* (vampires, to be exact) (1972); *The Other* (1972); *Sisters* (1973); *Twin Detectives* (1976 TVM); *The Man in the Iron Mask* (1977 TVM); *Zorro, the Gay Blade* (1981); *Basket Case* (1982); *The Dark Mirror* (1984 TVM); *Slapstick* (*Of Another Kind*) (1984); *Cheech and Chong's The Corsican Brothers* (1984); *Brotherly Love* (1985 TVM); *Deceptions* (1985 TVM); *The Covenant* (1985 TVM); *Killer in the Mirror* (1986 TVM); *Double Agent* (1987 TVM); *Nightmare at Shadow Woods* (1987); *Big Business* (1988); *Dead Ringers* (1988); *Dominick and Eugene* (1988); *Take Two* (1988); *Jack's Back* (1988); *Twins* (1988); *The Krays* (1990); *Whispers* (1990); *The Lookalike* (1990 TVM); *Life Is Sweet* (1990); *A Kiss Before Dying* (1991); *Lies of the Twins* (1991 TVM); *Double Impact* (1991); *Double Trouble* (1991); *Twin Dragons* (1992); *Twogether* (1994); *A Change of Place* (1994); *Separated by Murder* (1994 TVM); *Nadja* (1994); *It Takes Two* (1995); *Steal Big, Steal Little* (1995); *Hotel de Love* (1996); *Maximum Risk* (1996); *Ripe* (1997); *The House of Yes* (1997); *Love! Valour! Compassion!* (1997); *The Parent Trap* (1998); *Pleasantville* (1998); *The Rugrats Movie* (1998); *The Man in the Iron Mask* (1998); *Meet the Deedles* (1998); *The Patti Duke Show: Still Rockin' in Brooklyn Heights* (1999 TVM); *Half a Dozen Babies* (1999 TVM); *Take My Advice: The Ann and Abby Story* (1999 TVM); *Twin Falls Idaho* (1999)

Two-Headed Creatures

The old adage that two heads are better than one has never held true for the movies. The first two-headed monster movie of note, 1959's U.S./Japanese co-production *The Manster* (aka *The Split*), concerned a reporter who grew a second head after a mad scientist injected him with an experimental serum. Eventually, the man/beast split apart totally and the parts fought each other. Bruce Dern transplanted a head onto a new body in the aptly-titled *The Incredible Two-Headed Transplant* (1971). That film was quickly eclipsed by the following year's *The Thing with Two Heads*, the heads belonging to Ray Milland and Rosey Grier. The theme of two men — one white, one black — connected to each other was better explored in the Tony Curtis–Sidney Poitier chase drama *The Defiant Ones*. But, on strictly visual terms, the sight of Milland and Grier jammed together in one big suit remains a whole lot more fun to watch. An ad man working on a pimple cream campaign grew an obnoxious second head in Bruce Robinson's black comedy *How to Get Ahead in Advertising* (1989). Finally, *Ghidrah, the Three-Headed Monster* (q.v.) deserves special mention since he sported the minimum requirement of two heads.

The Seventh Voyage of Sinbad (1958); *The Manster* (1959); *The Magic Sword* (1962); *Jack the Giant Killer* (1962); *The Incredible Two-Headed Transplant* (1971); *The Thing with Two Heads* (1972); *Monty Python and the Holy Grail* (1975); *Willow* (1988); *How to Get Ahead in Advertising* (1989)

U.N.C.L.E. *see* **The Man from U.N.C.L.E.**

Unicorns

Unicorns have appeared rarely in the cinema, but they have turned up in a Three Stooges comedy, a Tom Cruise fantasy, and two 1980s animated films. When Moe, Larry, and Curly Joe traveled to Venus in *Have Rocket, Will Travel* (1959), they discovered a talking unicorn. Ridley Scott's visually splendid *Legend* (1985) starred Tom Cruise as a forest denizen who caused all kinds of havoc when he took his beloved Princess Lili to see the unicorns. Christopher Lee provided the voice for evil King Haggard, who wanted to destroy all the unicorns in the animated 1983 feature *The Last Unicorn*. The following year, a little unicorn appeared in another animated kiddie feature, *The Fantastic Adventures of Unico*. There were no unicorns in Carol Reed's touching *A Kid for Two Farthings* (1955). Instead, a poor London lad searched for a magical unicorn, only to find a sick goat with a single horn. In a key scene in Tennessee Williams' oft-filmed play *The Glass Menagerie*, the horn on a glass unicorn is broken off— making him just like all the other horse figurines. In *The Abominable Dr. Phibes* (1971), the revenge-seeking doctor (Vincent Price) catapults a brass unicorn head into the chest of one his victims. The unicorn's horn pins the corpse against the wall, so that it has to be un-screwed by Scotland Yard's finest. Finally, in *Doctor Doolittle* (1967), the good doctor's parrot Polynesia professed to speaking over two thousand languages — including unicorn. See also **Cyclops**; **Gorgons**; **Horses**.

The Glass Menagerie (1950); *A Kid for Two Farthings* (1955); *Have Rocket, Will Travel* (1959); *The Abominable Dr. Phibes* (1971); *The Glass Menagerie* (1973); *Blade Runner* (1982) (a dream sequence in the director's cut); *The Last Unicorn* (1983); *The Fantastic Adventures of Unico* (1984); *Legend* (1985); *The Glass Menagerie* (1987); *Heavenly Creatures* (1994) (a fantasy sequence)

Universal Soldier Series

Jean-Claude Van Damme, the "Muscles from Brussels," seemed on the verge of breaking out of B-action movies when he starred in 1992's *Universal Soldier*. But while the makers of *Universal Soldier* hit the big time four years later with *Independence Day*, Van Damme quickly returned to run-of-the-mill action pictures like *Timecop* (1994) and *Legionnaire* (1999). In *Universal Soldier*, Van Damme played Luc Deveraux, a soldier killed in Vietnam only to be "revived" as a cyborg "UniSol" 25 years later. Although scientists were supposed to erase his memory, Luc and another UniSol named Scott (Dolph Lundgren) experience flashbacks from their combat days when Scott tried to kill Luc. In no time at all, Scott takes up where he left off in Vietnam and seeks to destroy Luc, along with a reporter (Ally Walker) trying to expose the truth about the malfunctioning UniSols. Thematically, *Universal Soldier* pales in comparison to *RoboCop* (1987), which also dealt with past memories experienced by a man transformed into a cyborg. However, as an upscale action film, *Universal Soldier* satisfied audiences and earned respectable reviews. Surprisingly, a sequel did not appear until 1998 when the Showtime cable network aired *Universal Soldier II: Brothers in Arms* and *Universal Soldier III: Unfinished Business*. Both movies starred Matt Battaglia as Luc and Chandra West as Veronica, the news reporter from the original film. Gary Busey and Burt Reynolds, both a long way from their days as Oscar nominees, played the bad guys chasing after Luc and Veronica. The following year, Van Damme tried to make a comeback with *Universal Soldier: The Return*, a theatrical release that ignored the made-for-cable movies. It reintroduces Luc as a widower with a cute kid! However, it's not long before Luc takes on a computer called SETH (Self-Evolving Thought Helix) that has assumed control of a research facility with UniSols. Released at the end of the 1999 summer movie season with no press screenings, *Universal Soldier: The Return* died quickly at the boxoffice. See also **Androids and Cyborgs**.

Universal Soldier (1992); *Universal Soldier II: Brothers in Arms* (1998 TVM); *Universal Soldier III: Unfinished Business* (1998 TVM); *Universal Soldier: The Return* (1999)

Uptown Saturday Night Series

Sidney Poitier directed Bill Cosby and himself in this silly 1974 comedy about two friends, a stolen lottery ticket, and a *Godfather*-like gangster (Harry Belafonte). In the 1985 follow-up *Let's Do It Again*, they used hypnosis to turn Jimmie Walker (from TV's *Good Times*) into an unlikely boxer. The final installment, 1977's *A Piece of the Action*, balanced the laughs with a more serious plot about ghetto kids. Technically, Poitier and Cosby played different characters in each film, but audiences did not seem to notice.

Uptown Saturday Night (1974); *Let's Do It Again* (1975); *A Piece of the Action* (1977)

Vampires

With his sexuality, air of mystery, and aristocratic manners, the vampire has long been a favorite subject of filmmakers. Count Dracula and his descendants dominated the 1930s and 1940s (see **Dracula** entry for details). However, there were some notable exceptions, such as 1932's *Vampyr* (aka *The Strange Adventure of David Gray*) and 1943's *Return of the Vampire*. Directed by Carl Dreyer, *Vampyr* is a wonderfully atmospheric, but slow moving, classic, while *Return* is of interest solely because it features Bela Lugosi as a very Dracula-like character stalking victims in World War II England. The vampire was generally ignored through the mid–1950s, although *Old Mother Riley Meets the Vampire* (aka *My Son, the Vampire*) sadly marked Lugosi's last appearance as one of the undead. However, vampire movies made a resounding comeback in 1957-58. Herman Cohen, the man responsible for *I Was a Teenage Frankenstein*, made 1957's teen-oriented *Blood of Dracula* (in which a young girl is made to believe she's a vampire). That same year, German Robles made his debut as Count Lavud in the Mexican movie *The Vampire* and John Beals took pills to grow fangs in *Mark of the Vampire* (not to be confused with Lugosi's 1935 film of the same title). In 1958, Jimmy Sangster wrote two vampire films: the competent *Blood of the Vampire* and Hammer Films' landmark *Horror of Dracula* (aka *Dracula*), arguably the most influential of all vampire movies. The Hammer approach, with its blatant emphasis on Dracula's sexual attraction, put vampirism in a new light. Hammer continued that trend with 1960's *Brides of Dracula*, another fine effort in which Baron Meinster (not the Count) preys upon a girls' boarding school. French director Roger Vadim offered *Blood and Roses* in 1960, a less subtle variation of the sexuality theme featuring a lesbian vampire. Naturally, other countries tried to cash in on the vampire's new-found popularity. The U.S. contributed a vampire Western *Curse of the Undead* (1959); Italy produced *The Vampire and the Ballerina* (1960); and Mexico added *World of Vampires* (1960). Hammer returned to its favorite subject in 1963 with *Kiss of the Vampire*, a well-acted, though unsurprising, bloodsucking tale. A year later, Vincent Price fought a world infected by a vampire plague in Italy's *The Last Man on Earth*, an underrated adaptation of Richard Matheson's chilling novel *I Am Legend*. Yet, despite these lively efforts, the vampire was becoming anemic at the box-office by the late 1960s. Hence, some new twists were introduced to draw back the dwindling audience. Hammer Studios resurrected lesbian vampires with its 1970–72 Karnstein trilogy (q.v.) *The Vampire Lovers*, *Lust for a Vampire*, and *Twins of Evil*. Robert Quarry played a contemporary vampire confronted by hippies in 1971's *Count Yorga*. And in another contemporary-set tale, William Marshall played a Black African prince who is bit by Dracula and becomes *Blacula*. Despite modest success, these films failed to ignite a major revival and the vampire sank quietly into his grave, except for occasional trips to the blood bank (e.g., Dan Curtis' high-rated 1971 TV movie *The Night Stalker* and the 1979 spoof *Love at First Bite*). By the early 1980s, the vampire was lost amid the slasher films made in the wake of *Halloween* and *Friday the 13th*. But, just to show you can't keep a good bloodsucker down, he was revived yet again in a rash of youth-oriented pictures like *Fright Night* (1985), *The Lost Boys*, and *Near Dark* (both 1987). These movies proved that there would always be an audience for well-done vampire pictures, especially ones with something new to offer. For example, Wesley Snipes played a half-vampire that hunted other bloodsuckers with a vengeance in the box-office hit *Blade* (1998). The villainous ladies in *Lair of the White Worm* and *The Kiss* (both 1988), while technically not vampires, exhibited similar neck-biting traits. People believed they were vampires in *Vampire's Kiss* (1989) and *A Vampire in Paradise* (1991). *Variety* noted that the title vehicle in 1990's *I Bought a Vampire Motorcycle* "runs on blood, doesn't function in daylight, recoils from crucifixes, and consumes humans and animals." See also **Bats**; **Dracula**; **Karnstein Trilogy**; **Mr. Vampire Series**; **Subspecies Series**.

Vampyr (aka *The Strange Adventure of David Gray*) (1932); *The Return of the Vampire* (1943); *The Vampire's Ghost* (1943); *Dead Men Walk* (1943); *My Son, the Vampire* (aka *Old Mother Riley Meets the Vampire*; *Vampires Over London*) (1952); *Mark of the Vampire* (aka *The Vampire*) (1957); *Blood of Dracula* (1957); *The Vampire* (aka *El Vampiro*) (1957); *The Vampire's Coffin* (aka *El Ataud del Coffin*) (1958); *Blood of the Vampire* (1958); *Uncle Was a Vampire* (1959); *Curse of the Undead* (1959); *The World of Vampires* (aka *El Mundo de los Vampiros*) (1960); *Blood and Roses* (1960); *The Vampire and the Ballerina* (1960); *Slaughter of the Vampires* (aka *Curse of the Blood Ghouls*) (1961); *Samson vs. the Vampire Women* (aka *Santo Contra las Mujeres Vampiras*) (1962); *Kiss of the Vampire* (aka *Kiss of Evil*) (1963); *The Last Man on Earth* (1964); *Goliath and the Vampires* (aka *The Vampires*) (1964); *Planet of the Vampires* (aka *The Demon Planet*) (1965); *Munster, Go Home!* (1966); *Planet of Blood* (aka *Queen of Blood*) (1966); *Track of the Vampire* (aka *Blood Bath*) (1966); *The Fearless Vampire Killers; or Pardon Me, But Your Teeth Are in My Neck* (1967); *Santo and Blue Demon vs. the Monsters* (aka *Santo y Blue Demon Contra los Monstruós*) (1969); *House of Dark Shadows* (1970); *Vampire Men of the Lost Planet* (1970); *The House That Dripped Blood* (1970); *Santo in the Revenge of the Vampire Women* (aka *Santo en la Venganza de las Mujeres Vampiras*) (1970); *Count Yorga, Vampire* (1971); *The Velvet*

Vampire (aka *Cemetery Girls*) (1971); *The Return of Count Yorga* (1971); *The Bloodsuckers* (aka *Incense for the Damned*) (1971); *The Night Stalker* (1971 TVM); *Daughters of Darkness* (1971); *Vampire Circus* (1971); *Blacula* (1972); *The Bloody Vampire* (1972); *The Deathmaster* (1972); *Scream, Blacula, Scream* (1973); *Captain Kronos: Vampire Hunter* (aka *Kronos*) (1974); *Spermula* (1975); *Martin* (1978); *Vampire Hookers* (aka *Sensuous Vampires*) (1979); *Love at First Bite* (1979); *Vampire* (1979 TVM); *Thirst* (1979); *Last Rites* (aka *Dracula's Last Rites*) (1980); *I, Desire* (1982 TVM); *The Hunger* (1983); *Fright Night* (1985); *Lifeforce* (1985) (an energy vampire); *Vampire Hunter D* (1985); *Vampires in Havana* (1985); *Mr. Vampire* (aka *Geung Si Sin Sang*) (1985); *Once Bitten* (1985); *Vamp* (1986); *Near Dark* (1987); *The Lost Boys* (1987); *Graveyard Shift* (1987); *My Best Friend Is a Vampire* (1988); *Dance of the Damned* (1988); *The Vampire at Midnight* (1988); *The Understudy: Graveyard Shift II* (1988); *Fright Night Part 2* (1989); *Nightlife* (1989 TVM); *Beverly Hills Vamp* (1989); *Dracula's Widow* (1989); *Vampire's Kiss* (1989); *Transylvania Twist* (1989); *To Die For* (1989); *Daughter of Darkness* (1990 TVM); *I Bought a Vampire Motorcycle* (1990); *Sundown: The Vampire in Retreat* (aka *Sundown*) (1990); *Subspecies* (1990); *The Reflecting Skin* (1990); *Pale Blood* (1990); *Son of Darkness: To Die For II* (1991); *Blood Ties* (1991 TVM); *Howling VI: The Freaks* (1991); *Buffy, the Vampire Slayer* (1992); *Innocent Blood* (1992); *Children of the Night* (1992); *A Vampire in Paradise* (aka *Un Vampire au Paradis*) (1992); *To Sleep with a Vampire* (1992); *Tale of a Vampire* (1993); *The Vampyr* (1993); *Dracula Rising* (1993); *Interview with the Vampire* (1994); *Nadja* (1994); *Darkness* (1994); *Embrace of the Vampire* (1995); *Here Come the Munsters* (1995 TVM); *Vampire in Brooklyn* (1995); *The Addiction* (1995); *From Dusk Till Dawn* (1996); *Tales from the Crypt: Bordello of Blood* (1996); *Vampire Journals* (1997); *Blade* (1998); *Razor Blade Smile* (1998); *Vampires* (aka *John Carpenter's Vampires*) (1998)

Vance, Philo

S.S. Van Dine's dapper, erudite sleuth never made much of a hit on the screen. William Powell first played the part, enjoying modest success in four mysteries. Ironically, although Powell looked the part, he lacked the briskness of manner that made Vance such a memorable literary character, and his portrayal is somewhat overrated. In his pre–Holmes days, Basil Rathbone made a more effective Vance in the slowly-paced, but cleverly-plotted *Bishop Murder Case* (the murderer wrote nursery rhymes containing clues about the identity of his next victim). Perhaps, the best Vance was Warren William, whose white gloves-and-cane portrayal sparkled in 1934's *The Dragon Murder Case*. Based on a Van Dine novel, this underrated puzzler found Vance investigating a young man's apparent drowning in a mysterious pool (haunted by a sea serpent?). William reprised the role in 1939's *The Gracie Allen Murder Case*, a comedy-mystery written for Allen by Van Dine. Other actors played the part, but none could make it their own. Later Vance films like *Philo Vance's Secret Mission* and *Philo Vance's Gamble* were Vance films in name only — their detectives were clearly closer to Philip Marlowe.

The Canary Murder Case (1929) (William Powell); *The Greene Murder Case* (1929) (Powell); *The Benson Murder Case* (1930) (Powell); *Paramount on Parade* (1930) (Powell appears in a skit); *The Bishop Murder Case* (1930) (Basil Rathbone); *The Kennel Murder Case* (1933) (Powell); *The Dragon Murder Case* (1934) (Warren William); *The Casino Murder Case* (1935) (Paul Lukas); *The Scarab Murder Case* (1936) (Wilfred Hyde-White); *The Garden Murder Case* (1936) (Edmund Lowe); *Night of Mystery* (1937) (Grant

Richards); *The Gracie Allen Murder Case* (1939) (William); *Calling Philo Vance* (1940) (James Stephenson); *Philo Vance Returns* (1947) (William Wright); *Philo Vance's Gamble* (1947) (Alan Curtis); *Philo Vance's Secret Mission* (1947) (Curtis)

Ventriloquists

The difficulties inherent in injecting a distinct personality into a wooden dummy have caused identity problems for a number of movie ventriloquists. In the most chilling story in the classic anthology *Dead of Night* (1945), ventriloquist Michael Redgrave went insane after becoming convinced that his foul-mouthed dummy Hugo was looking for a new partner. Anthony Hopkins gave a tour-de-force performance in 1978's *Magic* as another mentally-unstable ventriloquist taking murderous advice from a dummy with an apparent mind of its own. Another dummy named Hugo (an obvious reference to *Dead of Night*) really did have a soul in the underrated 1964 fantasy *Devil Doll*. Bryant Halliday starred as Hugo's "partner," a ventriloquist who has transferred the soul of his assistant into his dummy. Aside from horror films, the most famous film ventriloquist remains Edgar Bergen. He enjoyed a prosperous career during the late 1930s accompanied by dummies Charlie McCarthy or Mortimer Snerd in comedies like *A Letter of Introduction* (1938), *Charlie McCarthy, Detective*, (1939) and the W.C. Fields vehicle *You Can't Cheat an Honest Man* (1939). He earned a special Academy Award in 1937 for his creation of Charlie McCarthy. Major stars who have played ventriloquists include Erich von Stroheim in *The Great Gabbo* (1929), Danny Kaye in *Knock on Wood* (1954), and Lon Chaney in both the silent and talkie versions of *The Unholy Three* (1925 and 1930). In 1984's *Broadway Danny Rose*, theater agent Woody Allen had a hard time finding employment for a stuttering ventriloquist. See also **Dolls**.

The Unholy Three (1925); *The Great Gabbo* (1929); *The Unholy Three* (1930); *A Letter of Introduction* (1938); *You Can't Cheat an Honest Man* (1939); *Charlie McCarthy, Detective* (1939); *Dead of Night* (1945); *Knock on Wood* (1954); *Stop! Look! And Laugh!* (1960); *Hypnosis* (aka *Dummy of Death*) (1963); *Devil Doll* (1964); *Magic* (1978); *Broadway Danny Rose* (1984); *When a Stranger Calls Back* (1993 TVM)

Veterinarians

The cinema has typically portrayed veterinarians as gentle, charming animal-lovers blessed with understated strength. James Stewart played a German vet who falls in love with Margaret Sullavan and plots to escape from the Nazis in 1940's *The Mortal Storm*. James Herriot's autobiographical novels about life as a Yorkshire veterinarian served as the basis for *All Creatures Great and Small* (1974) and *All Things Bright and Beautiful* (1979). In supporting roles, veterinarians provided the love interests in *Another Man, Another Place* (James Caan), *Baby Boom* (Sam Shepard), and *Turner and Hooch* (Mare Winningham). Vet William Shatner battled a host of hungry tarantulas in the 1977 sci-fi thriller *Kingdom of the Spiders*. In contrast, *Billy: Portrait of a Street Kid* (1979) offered a realistic portrayal of a ghetto youth (LeVar Burton) given a chance to become a veterinarian's assistant. Patrick McGoohan played an atypical heartless veterinarian, unable to comprehend his daughter's love for her cat, in Disney's *The Three Lives of*

Thomasina (1964). The most suspicious vet was probably Hal Holbrook in the 1972 murder mystery *They Only Kill Their Masters*.

A Day at the Races (1937); *The Mortal Storm* (1940); *Stallion Road* (1947); *The Three Lives of Thomasina* (1964); *Clarence, the Cross-Eyed Lion* (1965); *They Only Kill Their Masters* (1972); *All Creatures Great and Small* (1974 TVM); *Another Man, Another Chance* (1977); *Kingdom of the Spiders* (1977); *The Beasts Are on the Streets* (1978 TVM); *Billy: Portrait of a Street Kid* (1979 TVM); *All Things Bright and Beautiful* (aka *It Shouldn't Happen to a Vet*) (1979); *Baby Boom* (1987); *Turner and Hooch* (1989); *Bird on a Wire* (1990); *Watch It* (1993); *The Getaway* (1994); *Go Fish* (1994) (a vet assistant); *The Truth About Cats and Dogs* (1996); *Best Laid Plans* (1999) (a vet assistant)

Vice Academy Series

A successful film series — no matter how inept — will invariably spawn imitations. Nevertheless, it's hard to conceive that the *Police Academy* films (q.v.) could actually serve as a role model for another lowbrow comedy series such as *Vice Academy*. The first *Vice Academy* premiered in 1988, the same year as the fast-fading *Police Academy 5: Assignment Miami Beach*. It sparked the interest of B-movie viewers chiefly due to its two stars: former porn queen Ginger Lynn Allen and cult movie favorite Linnea Quigley. They played against type as two innocent undercover cops (Holly and Didi, respectively). Although by no means a good movie, *Vice Academy* was an improvement over an earlier *Police Academy* rip-off, the 1985 Linda Blair vehicle *Night Patrol*. In 1989, Allen and Quigley reprised their roles for a sequel co-starring bodybuilder Teagan Clive as the cyborg Bimbocop. Its plot dealt with a villain named Spanish Fly who schemes to contaminate the city water supply with an aphrodisiac. Allen also headlined 1991's *Vice Academy III*, with Elizabeth Kaitan playing her new partner Candy.

Vice Academy (1988); *Vice Academy II* (1989); *Vice Academy III* (1991)

Videotaped Films

Prior to the "digital revolution" in the late 1990s, American television movie producers maintained that film's sharp, vibrant image compensated for its added expense when compared to videotape. As a result, very few U.S. made-for-TV movies have been shot on tape. The romantic ghost story *Sandcastles* (1972) was the first to employ a single videotape camera system, but even it was later transferred to film. *Special Bulletin* (1983) was shot on videotape to simulate the "look" of a television newscast. Oddly, there have also been a handful of theatrical features shot originally on videotape and then transferred to film. The 1965 videotape drama *Harlow*, starring Carol Lynley, was converted to film to compete theatrically with a rival biography of the blonde comedienne (confusingly, this second film was also called *Harlow* and starred Carroll Baker). Industrious producers dubbed this tape-to-film process "electronovision." The advent of high-definition videotape in the 1980s renewed interest in "filming" with videotape. However, *Julia and Julia* (1987), the first major movie shot on high-definition tape, turned into a box-office disaster. Shortly after its U.S. theatrical release, it showed up — ironically — on videotape.

Harlow (1965); *Two Hundred Motels* (1971); *Sandcastles* (1972 TVM); *The Catcher* (1972 TVM); *Numero Deux* (1975); *Give 'Em Hell, Harry!* (1975); *Norman...Is That You?* (1976); *Victory at Entebbe* (1976 TVM) (later transferred to film); *Monty Python Live at the Hollywood Bowl* (1982); *Special Bulletin* (1983 TVM); *Desperate Intruder* (1983 TVM); *Emergency Room* (1983 TVM); *The Invisible Woman* (1983 TVM); *Rocket to the Moon* (1986 TVM); *Julia and Julia* (1987); *The Little Victims* (1989 TVM)

Vietnam

The United States' "longest war" was ignored in movies for most of its duration. The 1964 *A Yank in Vietnam*, a low-budget action picture, was the first to deal with U.S. involvement. The 1968 propaganda adventure *The Green Berets* glorified the fighting, while the searing 1974 documentary *Hearts and Minds* criticized it. Surprisingly, TV movies dealt effectively with returning vets long before their theatrical counterparts. In 1969's *The Ballad of Andy Crocker*, Lee Majors returned home to find himself a stranger to those he loved. It seemed upbeat compared to the brutal frankness of Joseph Papp's production of the TV special *Sticks and Bones*, which several CBS affiliates refused to air. In the late 1970s, mainstream Hollywood finally addressed Vietnam in a roundabout fashion — *Coming Home* dealt with returning veterans, while Francis Coppola's *Apocalypse Now* portrayed the violence of war in a poetic manner. It was not until 1986's Academy Award winner *Platoon* and Stanley Kubrick's *Full Metal Jacket* that the major studios backed brutal, realistic portrayals of the Vietnam War. Those successes have been followed by low-budget clones (e.g., *Hamburger Hill* and *Platoon Leader*), big-budget clones (*Casualties of War*), and one or two films of genuine originality (*84 Charlie Mopic*). See also **Eye of the Eagle Series; Missing in Action Series.**

A Yank in Vietnam (aka *Year of the Tiger*) (1964); *The Anderson Platoon* (1967); *The Benefit of the Doubt* (aka *US*) (1967); *The Green Berets* (1968); *The Ballad of Andy Crocker* (1969 TVM); *Hearts and Minds* (1974); *Rolling Thunder* (1977); *The Boys in Company C* (1978); *Coming Home* (1978); *The Deer Hunter* (1978); *Go Tell the Spartans* (1978); *Apocalypse Now* (1979); *The Odd Angry Shot* (1979); *A Rumor of War* (1980 TVM); *The Children of An Lac* (1980 TVM); *Don't Cry, It's Only Thunder* (1982); *Boat People* (1982); *Uncommon Valor* (1983); *Missing in Action* (1984); *Purple Hearts* (1984); *Platoon* (1986); *P.O.W. The Escape* (aka *Behind Enemy Lines*) (1986); *Full Metal Jacket* (1987); *Gardens of Stone* (1987); *Good Morning, Vietnam* (1987); *In Love and War* (1987 TVM); *Hamburger Hill* (1987); *The Hanoi Hilton* (1987); *Dear America: Letters Home from Viet Nam* (1987 TVM); *Bat 21* (1988); *The Iron Triangle* (1988); *84 Charlie Mopic* (1989); *Platoon Leader* (1989); *Casualties of War* (1989); *Born on the Fourth of July* (1989); *Air America* (1990); *Jacob's Ladder* (1990); *Fatal Mission* (1990); *Flight of the Intruder* (1991); *Beyond the Call of Duty* (1991); *Firehawk* (1993); *Heaven and Earth* (1993); *Forrest Gump* (1994); *Dead Presidents* (1995); *Operation Dumbo Drop* (aka *The Dumbo Drop*) (1995); *A Bright Shining Lie* (1998 TVM); *Three Seasons* (1999)

Vigilantes

Although contemporary vigilante films appeared prior to 1974, the genre began officially with 1974's *Death Wish* (q.v.), a highly manipulative revenge tale in which an average guy turns cold vigilante after punks kill his wife and rape his daughter. Charles Bronson clicked in the lead role and the film scored big at the box-office. In its wake, exploitative producers rushed out cheap imitations, like *Vigilante* and *Vigilante Force*. The most financially successful of these rip-offs was 1980's *The Exterminator*, which starred Robert Ginty as a Vietnam vet who used a flame-thrower to avenge a buddy's mugging. Abel Ferrera's feminist variation, 1981's *Ms. 45* (aka *Angel of Vengeance*), garnered some good reviews and has since earned minor cult status. *The Star Chamber*, *The Death Squad*, and the Dirty Harry picture *Magnum Force* showed vigilantism used by law enforcers to "correct" loopholes in our legal system, a plotline derived loosely from 1942's *The Strange Case of Dr. Rx*. See also **Death Wish Series.**

The Mad Executioners (1963); *Magnum Force* (1973); *Death Wish* (1974); *The Death Squad* (1974 TVM); *Law and Disorder* (1974); *Rape Squad* (aka *Act of Vengeance*) (1974); *Vigilante* (aka *Street Gang*) (1976); *Vigilante Force* (1976); *Dirty Knight's Work* (aka *Trial by Combat; Choice of Weapons*) (1976); *Siege* (1978 TVM); *One Man Jury* (aka *Dead on Arrival*) (1978); *The Exterminator* (1980); *Ms. 45* (aka *Angel of Vengeance*) (1981); *Fighting Back* (1982); *Victims* (1982 TVM); *Young Warriors* (1983); *The Star Chamber* (1983); *Exterminator II* (1984); *The Executioner, Part II* (1984; there was no part I); *Sudden Death* (1985); *Streets of Justice* (1985 TVM); *The Annihilators* (1985); *Brotherhood of Justice* (1986 TVM); *Band of the Hand* (1986); *Shadows Run Black* (1986); *Street Soldiers* (1990); *Shoot First: A Cop's Vengeance* (1991 TVM); *Keeper of the City* (1992 TVM); *Guilty as Charged* (1992); *Jimmy Hollywood* (1994); *Scarred City* (1998)

Vikings

These Scandinavian pirates plundered the European coasts from the ninth to the eleventh centuries. They would appear to be ripe subjects for fact-based adventure films. Instead, filmmakers have shown an intense interest in fictionalizing Viking history. Producer-director Roger Corman proposed that there were statuesque Viking women who were just as tough as their men in the memorably-titled *Saga of the Viking Women and Their Voyage to the Waters of the Great Sea Serpent* (1957). Hammer Films confirmed this hypothesis with its costume drama *The Viking Queen* (1967). It mixed time periods joyously with a plot in which a Roman soldier (Don Murray) falls in love with a Viking queen (Carita) battling the Druids. The Disney folks revealed that a Viking settlement survived into the twentieth century in the 1974 adventure-fantasy *The Island at the Top of the World*. And Terry Jones, of *Monty Python* fame, spoofed the Norsemen with 1989's *Erik the Viking*, in which the title character goes in search of a life more meaningful than killing and pillaging. Naturally, there have been some serious Viking films, such as 1958's *The Vikings*, which ranks as a fine costume epic by any standard. Kirk Douglas and Tony Curtis starred as Norse brothers (although they didn't know it) vying for the affections of fetching Janet Leigh amid the rousing swordplay. *The Norseman* (1978) was intended as a serious film, but somehow Lee Majors as a Viking warrior strikes a humorous chord. The expensive Norwegian epic *The White Viking* (1991) played only to arthouse audiences in the U.S. Antonio Banderas played an Arab ambassador who teams up with Vikings to fight cannibals in *The 13th Warrior* (1999), an adaptation of Michael Crichton's novel *Eaters of the Dead*. Finally, there were no living Vikings in *Curse of the Viking Grave*, a 1991 Canadian TV movie intended for youngsters.

Prince Valiant (1954); *The Saga of the Viking Women and Their Voyage to the Waters of the Great Sea Serpent* (aka *The Viking Women and the Sea Serpent*) (1957); *The Vikings* (1958); *The Last of the Vikings* (1960); *Erik the Conqueror* (aka *The Invaders*) (1963); *The Long Ships* (1964); *The Viking Queen* (1967); *The Island at the Top of the World* (1974); *The Norseman* (1978); *Berserker* (1987); *Erik the Viking* (1989); *Curse of the Viking Grave* (1991 TVM); *The White Viking* (aka *Den Hvite Viking*) (1991); *Kilian's Chronicle* (1994); *The 13th Warrior* (1999)

Violinists

Violinists (and other string musicians) have been faced with a variety of hard decisions. Young William Holden had to choose between a distinguished career as a violinist and a lucrative one as a prizefighter in *Golden Boy* (1939). That same year, Swedish violinist Leslie Howard had to decide whether to stay with his loyal wife (Edna Best) or run off with beautiful protégée Ingrid Bergman in *Intermezzo*. And in 1946's *Humoresque*, John Garfield played a moody musician torn briefly between wealthy patron Joan Crawford and his love of music. Real-life violin virtuoso Paganini was the subject of 1947's *The Magic Bow*, while *Hilary and Jackie* (1998) told the fact-based story of concert cellist Jacqueline Du Pré and her sister Hilary. See also **Pianists**; **Trumpet Players**.

The Smiling Lieutenant (1931); *Intermezzo* (1936); *Dreaming Lips* (1937); *They Shall Have Music* (1939); *Golden Boy* (1939); *Intermezzo* (aka *Escape to Happiness; Intermezzo, A Love Story*) (1939); *My Love Came Back* (1940); *Melody for Three* (1941); *The Phantom of the Opera* (1944); *The Magic Bow* (1947); *Humoresque* (1946); *Rhapsody* (1954); *All These Women* (aka *Now About All These Women*) (1964); *Shame* (1968); *Jeremy* (1973); *Basileus Quartet* (1982); *The Man with One Red Shoe* (1985); *Duet for One* (1986); *The Living Daylights* (1987); *Cello* (1990); *Two Evil Eyes* (aka *Due Occhi Diabolici*) (1990); *Camilla* (1994); *The Violin Player* (aka *Le Jouer de Violon*) (1994); *Hilary & Jackie* (1999); *The Red Violin* (1999); *Music of the Heart* (1999); *A Song from the Heart* (1999 TVM)

Viral Epidemics

The threat of viral annihilation has been the subject of several movies. Quarantined scientists raced against the clock to combat an inexplicable, self-reproducing virus in *The Andromeda Strain* (1971). George Maharis tracked down a lunatic who stole a deadly experimental virus in 1965's *The Satan Bug*, a plot more or less borrowed from *Panic in the Streets* (1950) and *No Place to Hide* (1956). And Count Dracula revealed his plan to initiate viral warfare in the decidedly offbeat horror tale *The Satanic Rites of Dracula* (1973). In other horror films, Vincent Price met disease incarnate in 1964's *The Masque of the Red Death* and then battled a plague of vampirism in the underrated low-budget gem *The Last Man on Earth* (1964). A 1924 silent film also called *The Last Man on Earth* portrayed a world where a plague had wiped out most of the male population. A parasite, not a disease, was the culprit in David Cronenberg's 1975 cult thriller *They Came from Within*. In Lloyd C. Douglas's *Green Light* (1937), Errol Flynn discovered a cure for a more typical disease, Rocky Mountain spotted fever. The threat of epidemics aboard moving vehicles was the subject of *The Cassandra Crossing* (1977), *Killer on Board* (1977), and *Pandora's Clock* (1996).

The Last Man on Earth (1924); *Yellow Jack* (1938); *Isle of the Dead* (1945); *Panic in the Streets* (1950); *The Killer That Stalked New York* (aka *Frightened City*) (1950); *The Command* (1954); *No Place to Hide* (1956); *The Seventh Sin* (1957); *The Risk* (1960);

80,000 Suspects (1963); *The Last Man on Earth* (1964); *The Masque of the Red Death* (1964); *Spies a Go Go* (aka *The Nasty Rabbit*) (1964); *The Satan Bug* (1965); *What's So Bad About Feeling Good?* (1968); *Project X* (1968); *On Her Majesty's Secret Service* (1969); *Quarantined* (1970 TVM); *No Blade of Grass* (1970); *The Andromeda Strain* (1971); *Killer By Night* (1971 TVM); *The Satanic Rites of Dracula* (aka *Count Dracula and His Vampire Bride; Dracula Is Alive and Well and Living in London*) (1973); *The Crazies* (aka *Code Name: Trixie*) (1973); *Where Have All the People Gone?* (1974 TVM); *The Missing Are Deadly* (1974 TVM); *The Specialists* (1975 TVM); *The Cassandra Crossing* (1977); *Panic in Echo Park* (1977 TVM); *Killer on Board* (1977 TVM); *Plague* (aka *M3: The Gemini Strain*) (1978); *Virus* (1980); *The Plague Dogs* (1982); *1918* (1984); *City Limits* (1985); *Warning Sign* (1985); *Wired to Kill* (1986); *Quiet Killer* (1992 TVM); *The Plague* (1992); *Condition: Critical* (1992 TVM); *12 Monkeys* (1995); *Outbreak* (1995); *Terminal Virus* (1995); *Virus* (aka *Robin Cook's Virus*) (1995 TVM); *Bullet to Beijing* (1995 TVM); *Deadly Outbreak* (1996); *Pandora's Clock* (1996 TVM); *Contagious* (1997 TVM); *Body Armor* (1997); *Mimic* (1997); *Airborne* (1998)

Volcanoes

Mountainous rumbles and spurting lava have brought an end to numerous South Seas sagas, displaying a particular affection for Dorothy Lamour vehicles like *The Jungle Princess* (1936) and *Aloma of the South Seas* (1941). Historical pictures, such as *Krakatoa, East of Java* (1969) and *St. Helens* (1981), have tended to build plodding stories around their spectacular volcanic eruptions. *The Last Days of Pompeii* (1935) was an exception, thanks mostly to a fine performance by Basil Rathbone as Pontius Pilate. Yet, despite Rathbone and the thrilling Mount Vesuvius finale, the film lost almost $250,000 at the box-office. James Mason and crew entered an extinct volcano at the beginning of their *Journey to the Center of the Earth* (1959) and then were blown out the top of Mount Etna at the film's climax (they managed to survive unharmed, though). The worldly Baron Munchausen and his followers duplicated the same feat in 1989's *The Adventures of Baron Munchausen*. Actually, the Baron and friends had been enjoying the hospitality of Vulcan inside his volcano home until Venus (aka Mrs. Vulcan) began displaying affection for the distinguished Baron. In *Superman IV: The Quest for Peace* (1987), the Man of Steel capped an erupting volcano with another mountain top and blow-dried the lava. Movie villains Fantômas and Ernst Blofeld have used extinct volcanoes for elaborate hideouts in *Fantômas Strikes Back* (1965) and the James Bond picture *You Only Live Twice* (1967), respectively. In the movie industry, 1997 was known as the "Year of the Volcano" since it featured the releases of three rival 1997 lava-spewing pictures: *Dante's Peak*, *Volcano*, and the TV movie *Volcano: Fire on the Mountain*. See also **Disaster Movies**.

East of Borneo (1931); *The Last Days of Pompeii* (1935); *The Jungle Princess* (1936); *One Million B.C.* (aka *Man and His Mate; The Cave Dwellers*) (1940); *Aloma of the South Seas* (1941); *The Lost Volcano* (1950); *Stromboli* (1950); *Fair Wind to Java* (1953); *Secrets of Life* (1957); *Journey to the Center of the Earth* (1959); *The Last Days of Pompeii* (1960); *Atlantis, the Lost Continent* (1961); *The Devil at Four O'Clock* (1961); *Mysterious Island* (1961); *Fantômas Strikes Back* (1965); *One Million Years B.C.* (1966); *You Only Live Twice* (1967); *Krakatoa, East of Java* (aka *Volcano*) (1969); *Creatures the World Forgot* (1971); *Up Pompeii* (1971); *Island at the Top of the World* (1974); *The Land That Time Forgot* (1974); *When Time Ran*

Out... (aka *Earth's Final Fury*) (1980); *St. Helens* (1981); *Warrior Queen* (1987); *Superman IV: The Quest for Peace* (1987); *The Adventures of Baron Munchausen* (1989); *Joe vs. the Volcano* (1990); *Journey to the Center of the Earth* (1993 TVM); *Dante's Peak* (1997); *Volcano: Fire on the Mountain* (1997 TVM); *Volcano* (1997); *Eruption* (aka *Volcano Run*) (1998)

Walking Tall Series

The real-life story of modern-day Tennessee sheriff Buford Pusser unexpectedly snowballed into a major hit in 1973. The film drew its biggest audiences in the Southeastern U.S., the region where *Billy Jack* (q.v.), a similar man-against-corruption tale, encountered sleeper success in 1971. Screen heavy Joe Don Baker brought conviction — and a huge baseball bat — to the role of Pusser. Elizabeth Hartman played his quiet, supportive wife. When Baker showed no interest in a sequel, Bing Crosby Productions signed imposing Bo Svenson for the lead role. He played Pusser in two sequels and a very brief 1981 TV series. Brian Dennehy also played Pusser in the 1978 TV movie *A Real American Hero*. The real Sheriff Pusser was supposed to have played himself in another theatrical sequel before he died in an automobile crash — under mysterious circumstances, according to some sources.

Walking Tall (1973); *Part 2: Walking Tall* (aka *Legend of the Lawman*) (1976); *Final Chapter-Walking Tall* (aka *Walking Tall-The Final Chapter*) (1977); *A Real American Hero* (1978 TVM)

The Waltons

Wholesome families have a way of lingering around — even when their TV series are cancelled. The Waltons, just like the Ingalls in *Little House on the Prairie* (q.v.), appeared in a series of telefilms after the demise of the long-running TV program. However, unlike the Ingalls, the Waltons originated in a theatrical film. *Spencer's Mountain* (1963), written by *Waltons* creator Earl Hamner, Jr., introduced the family that would evolve — with several changes — into the Waltons. Henry Fonda and Maureen O'Hara played the parents, with James McArthur in the eventual John-Boy role. Hamner first brought the Waltons to television in the 1971 telefilm *The Homecoming—A Christmas Story*, with Patricia Neal as Olivia Walton and future series regulars Richard Thomas (John-Boy), Ellen Corby (Grandma), Judy Norton (Mary Ellen), and David W. Harper (Jim-Bob). The series debuted in 1972 and enjoyed a successful nine-year run. Many changes occurred over the years, with even Olivia leaving Waltons Mountain after contracting tuberculosis. Shortly after CBS cancelled the series in 1981, the Waltons resurfaced in three made-for-TV movies on NBC. Erin (Mary Beth McDonough) married Paul Northridge (Morgan Stevens) in 1982's *A Wedding on Waltons Mountain*. That same year found Olivia (Michael Learned) returning from a sanitarium in *Mother's Day on Waltons Mountain* and the family reuniting for Thanksgiving in *A Day for Thanks on Waltons Mountain*. Richard Thomas did not appear in any of these post-series films. However, he did appear later as John-Boy in three TV movies broadcast in the 1990s. See also **Television Series Reunion Films.**

Spencer's Mountain (1963); *The Homecoming—A Christmas Story* (aka *The Homecoming*) (1971 TVM); *A Wedding on Waltons Mountain* (1982 TVM); *Mother's Day on Waltons Mountain* (1982 TVM); *A Day for Thanks on Waltons Mountain* (1982 TVM); *A*

Walton Thanksgiving Reunion (1993 TVM); *A Walton Wedding* (1995 TVM); *A Walton Easter* (1997 TVM)

Warsaw Trilogy

Andrzej Wajda's powerful trilogy of life in Poland during World War II made him a major force in Eastern European cinema. *A Generation* (1954), the first important post–World War II film to emerge from Poland, dealt with the "lost generation" of Warsaw youth who became involved with the Resistance. *Kanal* (1956) followed a group of resisters ordered to escape crumbling Warsaw through the city's intricate network of sewers. Quickly lost in the darkness, they become stalked by the Nazis above them. The 1958 *Ashes and Diamonds* shifted to the end of the war and focused on a youth forced to choose between love and carrying out an assassination. The title was derived from a gravestone inscription which appears in the film and summarizes Wajda's themes: "Here nothing but ashes will remain, the storm in an instant to oblivion will sweep them; from the ashes perhaps a diamond will emerge, shining victoriously for centuries, it will have blossomed for you."

A Generation (aka *Pokolenie; Generation*) (1954); *Kanal* (aka *They Loved Life; Sewer*) (1956); *Ashes and Diamonds* (aka *Popiol i Diament*) (1958)

Watchers Series

When asked about the first three *Watchers* films in a TV interview on TNT, Dean Koontz replied: "I sometimes question whether anybody involved in any of those movies ever read the book on which any of those movies were based." Indeed, the films jettisoned most of Koontz's plot, retaining only the basic premise: Two telepathically-linked creatures escape from a government research facility — a friendly super-intelligent dog named Einstein and a homicidal monster called The Outsider. The first, second, and fourth movies are all slight variations of one another, the chief difference being that the dog befriends a teenage boy (Corey Haim) in *Watchers*, a Marine (Marc Singer) in *Watchers 2*, and a homicide detective (Mark Hamill) in *Watchers Reborn*. The heroes in *Watchers 2* and *Watchers 3* have the same name, but appear to be different characters and are played by different actors (with Wings Hauser replacing Singer). The plot for the third installment resembles *Predator* as much as Koontz's novel. Hauser plays a Delta Force veteran sent to a Central American jungle to investigate the massacre of a military camp. Once there, he discovers his mission is part of a military experiment involving The Outsider and Einstein. Koontz, who resented the day he sold rights to Roger Corman's New Horizons film studio, sued to have his name removed from all advertising associated with the *Watchers* films. For the record, the term "watchers" in the novel does not refer to The Outsider, but to Einstein and his eventual family — they *watch* over each other. See also **Dogs.**

Watchers (1988); *Watchers 2* (1990); *Watchers 3* (1994); *Watchers Reborn* (1998)

Wax Museums

There are two basic types of wax museum movies. First, there's the one about the resident insane sculptor who molds figures by pouring hot wax over his murder victims. Lionel Atwill made this practice popular in 1933's *Mystery of the Wax Museum*, one of the first color horror films. Twenty years later, Vincent Price recreated the role in another technically historic horror film, the 3-D classic *House of Wax*. As the demented sculptors, Atwill and Price were splendid — no one has approached their level of depravity. Bad movie favorite Cameron Mitchell gave it a half-hearted shot in 1969's *Nightmare in Wax*, in which he injected folks with a drug that made them look (and act) like wax figures. The second type of wax museum film is the one where figures come to life. Although a popular television plot, it has been used sparingly on the big screen. In 1924's *Waxworks*, there was a nightmare sequence in which the wax figure of Jack the Ripper comes to life. Several decades later, another story called "Waxworks" was included in the anthology film *The House That Dripped Blood*. It starred Peter Cushing as a gentleman who becomes obsessed with an attractive, very life-like figure.

Waxworks (1924); *Mystery of the Wax Museum* (1933); *Steamboat 'Round the Bend* (1935); *Charlie Chan at the Wax Museum* (1940); *The Frozen Ghost* (1945); *House of Wax* (1953); *Samson in the Wax Museum* (aka *Santo in the Wax Museum*; *Santo en el Museo de Cera*) (1963); *Chamber of Horrors* (1966); *Nightmare in Wax* (aka *Crimes in the Wax Museum*) (1969); *The House That Dripped Blood* (1970); *Terror in the Wax Museum* (1973); *Lisa and the Devil* (aka *The House of Exorcism*) (1975); *Waxwork* (1988); *Dracula's Widow* (1989); *Seduction: Three Tales from the Inner Sanctum* (1992 TVM) (the "Sacrifice" segment)

Welby, Marcus

Seven years after "retiring" from the long-running TV series *Father Knows Best*, Robert Young took up medical practice as the title character in the 1969 TV movie *Marcus Welby, M.D.* The telefilm paired veteran general practitioner Welby with young, brash Dr. Steven Kiley (James Brolin). Naturally, the two doctors clashed initially before gaining respect for one another and becoming close friends. As intended, this shrewd drama appealed to a broad range of viewers, and a *Marcus Welby, M.D.* TV series debuted on ABC the following fall. Young and Brolin repeated their roles in the TV series, as did Anne Baxter as Welby's love interest Myra Sherwood (she left the series after the first year). Penny Santon, who played Nurse Consuelo Lopez in the pilot film, was replaced by Elena Verdugo. The *Welby* series enjoyed a seven-year run on ABC, becoming the nation's highest-rated TV show in 1970-71. In 1984, Young reprised his role in *The Return of Marcus Welby, M.D.*, a novel attempt to revive the series (Elena Verdugo was back as Consuelo, but the Kiley character was not). The plot picked up several years after the original series with Welby working at a hospital where he's being forced into retirement. Although a new Welby series never materialized, this second TV movie performed well enough to warrant another sequel four years later. *Marcus Welby, M.D.: A Holiday Affair* found the good doctor in France romancing divorcee Alexis Smith. It had little to do with the TV series, but even non–Welby fans had to admit that the hard-working physician deserved a vacation after all those years. See also **Television Series Reunion Movies**.

Marcus Welby, M.D. (aka *A Matter of Humanities*) (1969 TVM); *The Return of Marcus Welby, M.D.* (1984 TVM); *Marcus Welby, M.D.: A Holiday Affair* (1988 TVM)

Wenders' Road Movie Trilogy

"All my films have as their underlying current the Americanization of Germany," once noted German director Wim Wenders. That theme runs throughout the three films known as Wenders' "Road Movie" trilogy, each of which focuses on a journey taken by its characters. In *Alice in the Cities* (1974), a German journalist (Rüdiger Vogler) traveling in the U.S. unexpectedly finds a young girl left in his custody. *Wrong Move* (1974) focuses on a German writer (Vogler) who meets three people on a train ride and eventually learns that one of them once ran a Nazi concentration camp. The final film in the trilogy, *Kings of the Road*, is generally considered the best. After wrecking his car, Robert (film critic Hanns Zischler) hitches a ride with movie projector repairman Bruno (Vogler). As the two travel Bruno's rural repair route, Wenders offers commentary on friendship, the cinema, the division between East and West Germany, and the U.S. influence on Europe. The film's title comes from the Roger Miller hit song "King of the Road."

Alice in the Cities (aka *Alice in den Städten*) (1974); *Wrong Move* (aka *Falsche Bewegung*; *The Wrong Movement*) (1974); *Kings of the Road* (aka *Im Lauf der Zeit*) (1976)

Werewolves

The subject of silent films like *The Werewolf* (1913) and *The White Wolf* (1914), the werewolf made little impact until Universal Studios introduced it at the end of its first horror movie cycle with 1935's *Werewolf of London*. Featuring not one but two lycanthropes, it abandoned familiar werewolf lore in favor of a more novel approach (dealing with a rare flower that cures lycanthropy). For Universal's next furry film, *The Wolf Man* (q.v.), it returned to the basics, integrating a gypsy fortune-teller and a silver-handled cane into a contemporary terror tale. The film made Lon Chaney, Jr., a horror star and he repeated the role in four more movies. Hoping to capitalize on Universal's success, other studios also tried their hands at werewolf pictures. But sometimes, things weren't always what they seemed to be. A plotting housekeeper convinced James Mason he was a werewolf in *The Night Has Eyes*— but he wasn't. June Lockhart suffered from the same delusion in *She-Wolf of London*. As the 1940s ended and science fiction films gained momentum, the popularity of the werewolf declined sharply. Fresh ideas were needed and they came unexpectedly in the late 1950s in the form of two low-budget drive-in features. *The Werewolf* (1956) presented a creature created by a scientist, a theme aimed to please both science fiction and horror fans. Far more successful was the following year's *I Was a Teenage Werewolf*, a trend-setting mixture of teen problems, rock'n'roll, and an adolescent werewolf (Michael Landon). In 1961, Britain's Hammer Films tried to revive the European legends with *Curse of the Werewolf*, a brooding, literary picture that was a box-office disappointment. Except for a brief appearance in the anthology *Dr. Terror's House of Horrors*, the werewolf was silent through most of the 1960s. However, he rebounded strongly at the end of the decade in the guise of Spanish horror star Paul Naschy. His 1968 film *Mark of the Werewolf* (aka *Frankenstein's Bloody Terror*) was a European sensation and spawned eight sequels with colorful translated titles like *The Werewolf vs. the Vampire Woman* and *The Werewolf and the Yeti* (see *Daninsky, Waldemar*). Still, the werewolf did not regain his popularity in the U.S. until the 1980s, when *The Howling* (q.v.) and *An American Werewolf in London* combined humor and horror for big box-office bucks. One of the most original variations on the standard werewolf premise was the spellbinding 1984 British fantasy *The Company of Wolves*, a fanciful adult reworking of "Little Red Riding Hood" with a wolfman in lieu of a wolf. In addition to the werewolf, there have been a handful of "werecat" movies, such as *The Cat People*, its 1982 remake, *Cat-Man of Paris*, and *The Cat Girl*. And in 1933's *Island of Lost Souls*, a panther is surgically transformed into a beautiful girl. But that's not really lycanthropy. See also **Daninsky, Waldemar; The Howling Series; Humanimals; The Wolf Man**.

The Werewolf (1913); *The White Wolf* (1914); *Werewolf of London* (1935); *The Wolf Man* (1941); *The Undying Monster* (1942); *The Night Has Eyes* (aka *Terror House*) (1942); *Return of the Vampire* (1943); *Cry of the Werewolf* (1944); *She-Wolf of London* (1946); *The Werewolf* (1956); *I Was a Teenage Werewolf* (1957); *Daughter of Dr. Jekyll* (a mixed-up movie claiming Jekyll was a werewolf) (1957); *How to Make a Monster* (an actor in makeup is the killer) (1958); *Curse of the Werewolf* (1961); *Werewolf in a Girls' Dormitory* (1961); *Dr. Terror's House of Horrors* (1965); *Mad Monster Party?* (1967); *The Maltese Bippy* (1969); *Santo and Blue Demon vs. the Monsters* (aka *Santo y Blue Demon Contra los Monstruos*) (1969); *Werewolves on Wheels* (1971); *Santo and Blue Demon vs. Dracula and the Wolf Man* (aka *Santo y Blue Demon Contra Dracula y el Hombre Lobo*) (1972); *Santo vs. the She Wolves* (aka *Santo vs. Las Lobas*) (1972); *Moon of the Wolf* (1972 TVM); *Blood* (1973); *The Boy Who Cried Werewolf* (1973); *The Werewolf of Washington* (1973); *The Beast Must Die* (1974); *Legend of the Werewolf* (1975); *Wolfman!* (1979); *An American Werewolf in London* (1981); *Full Moon High* (1981); *The Howling* (1981); *The Company of Wolves* (1984); *Silver Bullet* (1985); *Teen Wolf* (1985); *The Monster Squad* (1987); *Teen Wolf Too* (1987); *Waxwork* (1988); *My Mom's a Werewolf* (1989); *Full Eclipse* (1993 TVM); *Wolf* (1994); *Here Come the Munsters* (1995 TVM); *Bad Moon* (1996); *The Creeps* (1997); *House of Frankenstein 1997* (1997 TVM); *An American Werewolf in Paris* (1997)

Whales

Whales on film have been portrayed as sympathetic creatures — with the notable exceptions of Herman Melville's immortal white whale *Moby Dick* and the people-eating Monstro in *Pinocchio*. Although Monstro was a true terror, it's hard to classify Moby as a villain, for Captain Ahab's crew perished solely because of its captain's obsession to kill the symbolic whale. The single-minded Ahab has been played by John Barrymore in both *The Sea Beast* (1926) and *Moby Dick* (1930), Gregory Peck in John Huston's 1956 adaptation, and Patrick Stewart in a made-for-cable film. The killer whale *Orca* (1977) devoured quite a few humans, including Bo Derek, but his actions were in retaliation for the murder of his spouse (killer whales mate for life, we are told). Humans were also portrayed as thoughtless whale killers in *The White Dawn* (1974) and *A Whale for the Killing* (1981). A mistreated killer whale befriends a lonely boy and escapes from an amusement park in the 1993 sleeper *Free Willy*. Whales were glimpsed from a distance in the opening of *The Whales of August* (1987), but, again, they played a symbolic part in the tender story of two elderly sisters. The crew of the *Enterprise* went back in time to save some important humpback whales in *Star Trek IV: The Voyage Home* (1986). The cartoon compilation *Make Mine Music* (1946) featured a segment on Willie, the Singing Whale. See also **Dolphins; Fish; Free Willy Series; Sharks**.

The Sea Beast (1926); *Moby Dick* (1930); *Pinocchio* (1940); *Make Mine Music* (1946); *Moby Dick* (1956); *Namu, the Killer Whale* (1966); *Island at the Top of the World* (1974); *The White Dawn* (1974); *Orca* (aka *Orca, the Killer Whale*) (1977); *A Whale for the Killing* (1981 TVM); *Star Trek IV: The Voyage Home* (1986); *The Whales of August* (1987); *When the Whales Came* (1989); *Free Willy* (1993); *Shadow of the Wolf* (1993); *Moby Dick* (1998 TVM); *Fantasia 2000* (1999)

The Whistler

In the mid–1940s, when most detective series were coming to an end, Columbia launched this offbeat mystery anthology series. The films were inspired by a popular radio program, in which a mysterious narrator introduced each story with the ominous opening: "I am the Whistler — and I know many things." Only one film, 1948's *Return of the Whistler*, followed the radio format. The others were linked solely by their twisty plots and the presence of star Richard Dix. A former Oscar-nominated actor (for 1931's *Cimarron*) Dix was in the twilight of his career. The Whistler films allowed him to show his versatility, playing the hero in some pictures, the villain in others. In 1944's *The Whistler*, he played a husband so depressed over his wife's death that he hires a killer to murder him — only to discover his wife is alive. In 1945's *The Power of the Whistler*, Dix was a murderer suffering from amnesia. William Castle, best known for his gimmicky 1950s thrillers (e.g., *The Tingler*), produced and directed some of the entries. Following Dix's death in 1947, one more picture was made and then the series died. Columbia revived it for television in 1954, producing 39 half-hour episodes.

The Whistler (1944); *The Mark of the Whistler* (1944); *The Power of the Whistler* (1945); *The Voice of the Whistler* (1946); *Mysterious Intruder* (1947); *The Secret of the Whistler* (1947); *The 13th Hour* (1947); *Return of the Whistler* (1948)

Whistling in the Dark Series

Edward Childs Carpenter and Laurence Cross's hit Broadway comedy *Whistling in the Dark* was about a mystery writer forced to devise the perfect murder. MGM first filmed it in 1932 with Ernest Truex as the hero and Edward Arnold the villain. That version made a nifty profit, but was eclipsed by the 1941 remake starring Red Skelton as a radio sleuth called "The Fox," Ann Rutherford as his girlfriend, and Conrad Veidt as the heavy. The film's surprise success resulted in MGM reuniting Skelton and Rutherford for two sequels. Their Southern honeymoon plans go astray when murder gets in the way in *Whistling in Dixie* (1942). Baseball and mystery provided the mixture for the last film *Whistling in Brooklyn* (1943). George Haight produced and S. Sylvan Simon directed all three skeleton films.

Whistling in the Dark (1932); *Whistling in the Dark* (1941); *Whistling in Dixie* (1942); *Whistling in Brooklyn* (1943)

Who, Doctor

Doctor Who, the time-traveling hero of the long-running British TV series, has appeared in just three movies. Peter Cushing portrayed the nomadic Time Lord in *Dr. Who and the Daleks* (1965) and *Daleks—Invasion Earth 2150 A.D.* Both features pitted Dr. Who and his comrades against the fearsome Daleks from the planet Skaro. Encased in pot-shaped time machines armed with mounted guns, the Daleks sought to turn all life forms into their slaves. In 1996, Paul McGann took over the title role for *Doctor Who*, a TV movie in which a malfunctioning time machine landed both Who and The Master, an evil Time Lord, in San Francisco in 1999. None of the Who films duplicated the appeal of the TV series. In the series, Dr. Who would periodically regenerate himself, which conveniently allowed different actors to assume the role. Each performer gave Dr. Who a different personality, which contributed substantially to the enduring popularity of the show. On television, Dr. Who has been played by: William Hartnell (1963–66); Patrick Troughton (1966–69); Jon Pertwee (1969–73); Tom Baker (1974–80); Peter Davison (1980–84); Colin Baker (1984–86); and Sylvester McCoy (1986–96). See also **Time Travel**.

 Dr. Who and the Daleks (1965); *Daleks—Invasion Earth 2150 A.D.* (aka *Invasion Earth 2150 A.D.*) (1966); *Doctor Who* (1996)

Windmills

No movie has been able to top the splendid climax of 1960's *Brides of Dracula* for imaginative use of a windmill. In Terence Fisher's lively vampire film, an athletic Van Helsing (Peter Cushing) dives onto a revolving windmill, his weight pulling the arms into the shape of a cross. The light of a full moon behind him casts the shadow of the cross onto the ground, thus destroying a hissing vampire caught in its path. The Frankenstein Monster was burned in a windmill at the end of 1931's *Frankenstein*, only to escape from the flames in the beginning of 1935's *Bride of Frankenstein*. Windmills were used to signal enemy planes in Hitchcock's *Foreign Correspondent* (1940). In the underrated 1986 fantasy *Highlander*, Christopher Lambert and Clancy Brown staged an elaborate swordfight throughout Lambert's windmill home. Michael Caine played a spy whose kidnapped son was being held hostage in *The Black Windmill* (1974). No discussion of windmills would be complete without mentioning *Don Quixote*, the gallant Spanish gentleman who imagined them to be dragons. Of related interest, Joanne Woodward's river mill home provided an atmospheric setting for the 1964 mystery-thriller *Signpost to Murder*.

 Frankenstein (1931); *Bride of Frankenstein* (1935); *Foreign Correspondent* (1940); *Brides of Dracula* (1960); *The Aristocats* (1970); *Don Quixote* (1973); *The Black Windmill* (1974); *Highlander* (1986); *Army of Darkness* (aka *Army of Darkness: Evil Dead 3*) (1993); *Madame L'eau* (aka *Madam Water*) (1993); *Don Quixote* (2000 TVM)

Witchboard Series

The "witchboard" is a Ouija board that allows mortals to communicate with spirits — both good and bad — in this competent horror film series. In *Witchboard* (1987), a young woman named Linda (Tawny Kitaen) uses the board to "talk" to the friendly ghost of a ten-year-old. Unfortunately, one day the spirit of a murderer makes a visit through the Ouija board and Linda begins displaying symptoms of "progressive entrapment" (i.e., unknowingly allowing oneself to be possessed by a ghost). The sequel, *Witchboard 2: The Devil's Doorway* (1993), finds another

young woman (Ami Dolenz) moving into an apartment where she finds a Ouija board left by the deceased previous tenant. Before you can spell "possession," a spirit — who may be good or may be evil — inhabits the young woman's body. Both the original film and its first sequel were written and directed by Kevin S. Tenney, a UCLA film school graduate who was also responsible for the *Night of the Demons* series (q.v.). Tenney cowrote the screenplay, but had less to do with the third installment, *Witchboard III: The Possession* (1995). This final outing featured a young stockbroker named Brian (David Nerman) who inherits a Ouija board after his landlord commits suicide and develops a *Faust*-like relationship with a soul-hungry demon. See also **Ghosts**.

 Witchboard (1987); *Witchboard 2: The Devil's Doorway* (aka *Witchboard 2*) (1993); *Witchboard III: The Possession* (aka *Witchboard: The Possession*) (1995)

Witchcraft Series

The twelve *Witchcraft* films undermine a smart premise with weak plotting and poor thesping. The first film, 1989's *Witchcraft*, recalls *Rosemary's Baby* with its tale about a pregnant woman who discovers that her baby is a warlock — along with her husband and witch of a mother-in-law. Thematically, it functions as a prologue, for the series' premise is introduced in 1990's *Witchcraft Part II: The Temptress*. The warlock baby has grown into a 17-year-old named Will (Charles Solomon). However, instead of practicing black magic for his own ends, Will denies his dark side. He even dates a minister's daughter (Mia Ruiz), until a voluptuous witch (Delia Sheppard) almost lures him back into the fold of witchery (and a marriage of evil). Will fights off such temptations, however, and becomes a lawyer in *Witchcraft III: The Kiss of Death*. This third installment pits the heroic warlock against a vampire-like creature which sucks the life out of its victims (shades of *Lifeforce*). In 1992's *Witchcraft IV: Virgin Heart*, Will gets mixed up with a stripper/singer/witch, a warlock disc jockey, and a girl so suspiciously good that she must be bad. The script borrows shamelessly from David Lynch's *Blue Velvet* and Walter Hill's *Crossroads* (both 1986). Charles Solomon, who played Will in the middle three entries, lacked screen charisma and failed to bring out the potential complexities of his character's internal good/evil battle. David Byrne took over as Will Spanner in later entries like *Witchcraft 7: Judgment Hour* (1995) and *Witchcraft IX: Bitter Flesh* (1996). However, by that point, the *Witchcraft* films had become mired in a repetitive sex-and-sorcery formula. See also **Witches**.

 Witchcraft (1989); *Witchcraft II: The Temptress* (aka *Witchcraft Part II: The Temptress*) (1990); *Witchcraft III: The Kiss of Death* (1991); *Witchcraft IV: Virgin Heart* (1992); *Witchcraft V: Dance with the Devil* (1993); *Witchcraft 6: The Devil's Mistress* (aka *Witchcraft VI*) (1994); *Witchcraft 7: Judgment Hour* (1995); *Witchcraft 8: Salem's Ghost* (aka *Witchcraft: Salem's Ghost*) (1996); *Witchcraft IX: Bitter Flesh* (1996); *Witchcraft X: Mistress of the Craft* (1998); *Witchcraft XI: Weird Sisters* (1999); *Witchcraft XII: Sisters in Blood* (2000)

Witches

Not surprisingly, witches show up in all kinds of movies: children's fantasies, comedies, horror flicks, and literary adaptations. Margaret Hamilton played the most famous of them all: the

Wicked Witch of the West in *The Wizard of Oz* (which also boasts Billie Burke as Glinda the Good Witch). Other children's films featuring notable witches include *Snow White and the Seven Dwarfs*, *Sleeping Beauty*, and *Bedknobs and Broomsticks*. Bewitching comedies have garnered laughs by casting against stereotype. Hence, instead of featuring witches with green skin and warts, both *I Married a Witch* and *Bell, Book, and Candle* offer curvaceous, blonde-haired witches (Veronica Lake and Kim Novak, respectively). The best horror film about witches is probably *Burn, Witch, Burn* (aka *Night of the Eagle*), in which Janet Blair resorts to witchcraft, first to further her husband's career and then to save his life. Barbara Steele was a revenge-minded witch in Mario Bava's eerie *Black Sunday* and Mia Farrow discovers her neighbors belong to a witches' coven in *Rosemary's Baby*. On the literary side, prophesying witches open up all film versions of *Macbeth*, and Arthur Miller's *The Crucible* remains a potent condemnation of the infamous Salem witch trials. Roald Dahl's charming children's book *The Witches* reached the screen in 1990, with Angelica Huston making a marvelous Grand High Witch. The 1999 sleeper *The Blair Witch Project* was a "fictional documentary" about a three young people who disappear while making a movie about a legendary witch. See also **Witchcraft Series**.

Witchcraft Through the Ages (aka *Haxan*) (1922); *Maid of Salem* (1937); *Snow White and the Seven Dwarfs* (1937); *I Married a Witch* (1942); *Day of Wrath* (1943); *Weird Woman* (1944); *The Woman Who Came Back* (1945); *Macbeth* (1948); *The Undead* (1957); *The Crucible* (*Witches of Salem*) (1957); *Bell, Book, and Candle* (1958); *The Day the Earth Froze* (1959); *Sleeping Beauty* (1959); *Black Sunday* (1960); *Horror Hotel* (aka *The City of the Dead*) (1960); *The Witches' Curse* (1960); *The Witches Mirror* (1960); *Snow White and the Three Stooges* (1961); *Burn, Witch, Burn* (aka *Night of the Eagle*) (1962); *The Magic Sword* (1962); *Terror in the Crypt* (aka *Crypt of Horror*) (1963); *Witchcraft* (1964); *The Devil's Own* (aka *The Witches*) (1966); *The She-Beast* (1966); *The Witch* (1966); *A Witch Without a Broom* (1968); *The Conqueror Worm* (aka *Witchfinder General*) (1968); *Crowhaven Farm* (1970 TVM); *Cry of the Banshee* (1970); *Night of the Witches* (1970); *Pufnstuf* (1970); *The Witches' Mountain* (1970); *Bedknobs and Broomsticks* (1971); *The Blood on Satan's Claw* (aka *Satan's Skin*; *Satan's Claw*) (1971); *Macbeth* (1971); *Night of Dark Shadows* (1971); *Brotherhood of Satan* (1971); *Simon, King of Witches* (1971); *Touch of Melissa* (aka *Touch of Satan*; *Night of the Demon*) (1971); *Daughters of Satan* (1972); *Necromancy* (aka *The Witching*) (1972); *Race with the Devil* (1975); *Deathmoon* (1978 TVM); *A Stranger in the House* (1978 TVM); *Witches Brew* (1980); *Midnight Offerings* (1981 TVM); *The Worst Witch* (1986); *Bay Coven* (1987 TVM); *Love at Stake* (1987); *Hansel and Gretel* (aka *Cannon Movie Tales: Hansel and Gretel*) (1987); *The Witches of Eastwick* (1987); *Spellbinder* (1988); *Teen Witch* (1989); *Witchery* (aka *Witchcraft*) (1989); *The Witches* (1990); *The Haunting of Morella* (1990); *To Save a Child* (1991 TVM); *Ernest Scared Stupid* (1991); *Warlock* (1991); *Hocus Pocus* (1993); *Sorceress* (1994); *Witch Hunt* (1994 TVM); *Four Rooms* (1995) ("Strange Brew" segment); *Here Come the Munsters* (1995 TVM); *The Craft* (1996); *The Crucible* (1996); *A Simple Wish* (1997); *Lady of the Lake* (1998); *I've Been Waiting for You* (1998 TVM); *The Blair Witch Project* (1999); (Despite their titles, the Disney kiddie adventures *Escape to Witch Mountain* and *Return to Witch Mountain* have nothing to do with witches — only alien children.)

Withers, Hildegarde

Edna May Oliver first brought Stuart Palmer's umbrella-toting schoolteacher sleuth to the screen in 1932's *The Penguin Pool Mur-*

der. It was a lively yarn, with a dramatic courtroom climax, but the film's highlight was the rapport between Oliver and co-star James Gleason as Inspector Oscar Piper. The gruff, wisecracking Piper masked his respect for Hildegarde, calling her a "nosy old dame" but later conceding: "That old battleaxe is the best friend I have in the world." The pair teamed for two more RKO series entries, then Oliver bowed out due to poor health. Helen Broderick replaced her for one film and then a miscast Zasu Pitts made the last two RKO Hildegarde Withers mysteries. James Gleason remained as Inspector Piper for all these films. In 1971, Eve Arden revived Hildegarde Withers for a TV pilot movie called *A Very Missing Person*, but a regular series never materialized.

The Penguin Pool Murder (aka *The Penguin Pool Mystery*) (1932) (Edna May Oliver); *Murder on the Blackboard* (1934) (Oliver); *Murder on a Honeymoon* (1935) (Oliver); *Murder on a Bridle Path* (1936) (Helen Broderick); *The Plot Thickens* (aka *The Swinging Pearl Mystery*) (1936) (Zasu Pitts); *Forty Naughty Girls* (1937) (Pitts); *A Very Missing Person* (1971 TVM) (Eve Arden)

The Wizard of Oz

Published in 1900, L. Frank Baum's immortal children's novel was filmed twice in the silent era, first as a 1910 two-reeler starring Bebe Daniels (later a femme fatale) and then in 1925, with Dorothy Dwan as Dorothy and Oliver Hardy as the Tin Woodman. The screenplay for the latter version was written by L. Frank Baum, Jr. Of course, the most famous adaptation is MGM's classic 1939 musical *The Wizard of Oz*, which annually ranks among the most-watched films on television. Amazingly, it was not a commercial success when originally released. Budgeted at a hefty $2.8 million, it took *The Wizard of Oz* twenty years to recoup its cost. The cast, one of the finest ever assembled, was formed almost by accident. Shirley Temple, a huge box-office star in 1938, was the first choice to play Dorothy. However, 20th Century–Fox, which owned her contract, refused to cooperate with MGM. (To atone for its poor decision, Fox cast Shirley in 1940's *The Blue Bird*, a similar fantasy — and a financial flop.) The rest of the original cast included Ray Bolger as the Tin Man, Buddy Ebsen (later Jed on *The Beverly Hillbillies*) as the Scarecrow, and Bert Lahr as the Cowardly Lion. However, Bolger, a Broadway dancer, lobbied for the role of the Scarecrow and he and Ebsen switched parts. Then, Ebsen developed an allergic reaction to the metallic paint used on his face and was replaced by Jack Haley, who gave his most memorable performance as the Tin Man. More liberal adaptations of Baum's book include 1976's *Oz*, an Australian rock musical, and *The Wiz* (1978), a film version of the hit Broadway play starring Diana Ross as an older Dorothy, Michael Jackson as the Scarecrow, and Richard Pryor as the Wiz. Although Baum wrote 13 additional books (and others have added to that total), few of those have made it to the screen. In 1914, he adapted his own novel *The Patchwork Girl of Oz* and then wrote and directed *His Majesty, the Scarecrow of Oz* (aka *The New Wizard of Oz*). An obscure musical version of *The Wonderful Land of Oz* appeared in 1969. Five years later, Liza Minnelli (Judy Garland's daughter) and Margaret Hamilton provided voices for the animated *Journey Back to Oz*. In 1985, Disney released a costly, non-musical called *Return to Oz*, which was based on Baum's novels *The Land of Oz* and *Ozma of Oz*. Despite impressive technical wizardry, it received scathing reviews and died at the box-office. Foreign language interpretations of Baum's works include *Aysecik and the Bewitched Dwarfs in Dreamland*, a Turkish version of *The Wizard of Oz*, and *Mago de Oz Cuento de Frank Baum*, a film of a Mexican stage production. John Ritter played Baum in the 1990 TV movie biography *The Dreamer of Oz*. The same year, cult director David Lynch offered a warped Ozian analogy — complete with violence, sex, and Elvis Presley songs — in *Wild at Heart*. Finally, Baum's original book played a major role in John Boorman's futuristic fantasy *Zardoz* (1974), which derived its title from The WiZARD of OZ.

The Wizard of Oz (1910); *The Patchwork Girl of Oz* (1914); *His Majesty, the Scarecrow of Oz* (aka *The New Wizard of Oz*) (1914); *The Wizard of Oz* (1925); *The Wizard of Oz* (1939); *The Wonderful Land of Oz* (1969); *Aysecik and the Bewitched Dwarfs in Dreamland* (aka *Aysecik ve Sihirli Cüceler Rüyalar Ülkesinde*) (1971); *Journey Back to Oz* (1974); *Oz* (aka *Twentieth Century Oz*) (1976); *The Wiz* (1978); *Under the Rainbow* (1981); *Mago de Oz Cuento de Frank Baum* (aka *El Mago de Oz*) (1985 TVM); *Return to Oz* (1985); *The Dreamer of Oz* (1990 TVM)

The Wolf Man

The Wolf Man appeared in five Universal films in the 1940s and yet it's difficult to classify these movies as a series. That's because he was the featured monster only once — in his 1941 debut *The Wolf Man*. This simply-plotted picture reaped benefits from a splendidly foggy atmosphere and a fine cast of Claude Rains, Ralph Bellamy, Warren William, Bela Lugosi, Maria Ouspenskaya, and Lon Chaney, Jr., as the sympathetic werewolf Larry Talbot. Despite a warm box-office reception, Universal decided that Chaney needed some horrific support, so he was paired with the Frankenstein Monster (Lugosi) in 1943's *Frankenstein Meets the Wolf Man*. The two monsters' climactic confrontation lacked excitement and was cut short by a torrent of water released by the local villagers. But the film inspired Universal to package the Wolf Man, Dracula, the Frankenstein Monster, and a couple of mad scientists in *House of Frankenstein* (1944) and *House of Dracula* (1945). Thankfully, Chaney/Talbot/Wolf Man was cured in this last entry. He did, however, turn up in fur again in 1948's *Abbott and Costello Meet Frankenstein*. Lon Chaney, Jr., was the only actor to play Larry Talbot/the Wolf Man. North Carolina filmmaker Earl Owensby's *Wolfman!* had nothing to do with Talbot. See also **Werewolves**.

The Wolf Man (1941); *Frankenstein Meets the Wolf Man* (1943); *House of Frankenstein* (aka *Chamber of Horrors*) (1944); *House of Dracula* (1945); *Abbott and Costello Meet Frankenstein* (1948)

Wolfe, Nero

Rex Stout's heavyweight detective genius has been restricted to a handful of screen appearances. Edward Arnold made a delightfully self-indulgent Wolfe in 1936's *Meet Nero Wolfe*, an adaptation of Stout's classic mystery *Fer-de-Lance*. Arnold seemed well-cast and the critics were kind, but a series failed to materialize. The following year, Walter Connolly took over the role in *League of Frightened Men* (aka *League of Missing Men*). Lionel Stander played Wolfe's legman Archie Goodwin in both films. Over forty years later, Stander was still playing in mysteries, as the Harts' chauffeur Max in the 1979–84 TV series *Hart to Hart*. Nero made his own television debut in the 1977 TV movie *Nero Wolfe*, starring David Thayer and Tom Mason as Archie. The movie was a

pilot for a series that was postponed when Thayer died unexpectedly. However, the hour-long TV series *Nero Wolfe* finally aired in 1981 with William Conrad in the lead and Lee (*Matt Houston*) Horsley as faithful Archie.

Meet Nero Wolfe (1936); *League of Frightened Men* (aka *League of Missing Men*) (1937); *Nero Wolfe* (1977 TVM)

Wong, Mr. James Lee

Monogram initiated this low-budget film series in 1938, hoping to duplicate the success of the *Charlie Chan* and *Mr. Moto* mysteries. Hugh Wiley's Chinatown detective proved nowhere nearly as popular as either of his contemporaries and the films are pretty obscure today. Boris Karloff, who was eager to break from horror movie typecasting, played Mr. Wong in all but the last entry. In 1940's *Phantom of Chinatown*, Keye Luke, Charlie Chan's former #1 son, played Wong, but he didn't prove to be right for the part.

Mr. Wong, Detective (1938); *Mr. Wong in Chinatown* (1939); *Mystery of Mr. Wong* (1939); *Doomed to Die* (1940); *The Fatal Hour* (1940); *Phantom of Chinatown* (1940)

Worrell, Ernest P. *see* Ernest

Wrestling

Championship wrestling broadened its appeal — and its outrageousness — in the late 1970s and suddenly became a hot movie property. Subsequently, recent films have tended to focus on the sport's sillier side. In contrast, John Ford's *Flesh* (1932) was a gloomy tale about a German immigrant wrestler (Wallace Beery) involved with shady characters. Richard Widmark was a loser trying to break into the London wrestling racket — and running afoul of kingpin Herbert Lom — in Jules Dassin's moody *Night and the City* (1950). Early wrestling comedies include *Swing Your Lady* (1937), with Humphrey Bogart as a promoter who sets up a male/female wrestling match and 1945's *Here Come the Co-eds*, which sent Lou Costello into the ring for one of his better vignettes. In Mexico in the 1960s, movie wrestlers turned into superheroes in highly-popular series such as *Santo*, *Blue Demon*, and *Neutron* (qq.v.). These films typically pitted the masked wrestlers against armies of vampires, werewolves, and mummies. Probably, the most interesting films for American audiences were those starring the Wrestling Women. These rough-and-tumble senoritas never achieved the popularity of Santo, but they more than held their own against the baddies in wonderfully-titled pictures like *The Wrestling Women vs. the Aztec Mummy* (1964). In the dubbed English version, the Wrestling Women were known as Loretta and Ruby. In the early 1980s, stateside lady wrestlers were the subjects of *Below the Belt* (1980), *All the Marbles* (1981), and *Mugsy's Girls* (1985). Henry Winkler donned a blonde wig in the ring as a flamboyant wrestler trying to attract attention in 1978's *The One and Only*. Two 1985 movies, *Vision Quest* and *Hadley's Rebellion*, explored the world of high school wrestling. Sylvester Stallone took leave from the Rocky series (q.v.) long enough to make *Paradise Alley*, a nostalgic wrestling picture about three ambitious brothers. *Grunt! The Wrestling Movie* (1985) was a documentary-style satire (along the lines of *This Is Spinal Tap*) about an outrageous wrestler called Mad Dog Joe De Curso. Some real-life wrestlers made cameo appearances in the 1986 comedy *Bad Guys*, while wrestling superstar Hulk Hogan starred in his own feature, 1989's *No Holds Barred*. Nils Allen Stewart played the title role in *The Jesse Ventura Story* (1999), a hastily-assembled TV movie biography of the wrestler-turned-governor of Minnesota. Paul Le Mat and Sylvester Stallone played arm wrestlers in, respectively, *P.K. and the Kid* (1982) and *Over the Top* (1987). See also **Blue Demon**; **Neutron**; **Santo**.

Flesh (1932); *Swing Your Lady* (1937); *Here Come the Co-eds* (1945); *Alias the Champ* (1949); *Bodyhold* (1949); *Night and the City* (1950); *Mr. Universe* (1951); *Doctor of Doom* (1962); *The Wrestling Women vs. the Aztec Mummy* (1965); *Babe* (1975 TVM); *Mad Bull* (1977 TVM); *The One and Only* (1978); *Take Down* (1978); *Blood and Guts* (1978); *Paradise Alley* (1978); *Below the Belt* (1980); *All the Marbles* (1981); *Tough Enough* (1983); *Hadley's Rebellion* (1985); *Mugsy's Girls* (aka *Delta Pi*) (1985); *Vision Quest* (1985); *Grunt! The Wrestling Movie* (1985); *Bad Guys* (1986); *Spooner* (1989 TVM); *No Holds Barred* (1989); *The American Angels: Baptism of Blood* (1990); *Knockouts* (1992); *Mr. Nanny* (1993); *The Jesse Ventura Story* (1999 TVM); *Beyond the Mat* (2000); *Ready to Rumble* (2000)

Year in Title

Sweeping sagas with year-oriented titles include Bernardo Bertolucci's six-hour Italian epic *1900*, Horton Foote's nostalgic family drama *1918*, and Stanley Kubrick's science fiction classic *2001: A Space Odyssey*. George Orwell's bleak view of the future, *1984*, has been filmed twice, in 1956 and (appropriately enough) 1984.

One Million B.C. (1940); *1984* (1956); *Terror from the Year 5000* (1958); *Panic in the Year Zero* (1962); *Daleks — Invasion Earth 2150 A.D.* (aka *Invasion Earth — 2150 A.D.*) (1966); *One Million Years B.C.* (1966); *2001: A Space Odyssey* (1968); *Summer of '42* (1971); *Dracula A.D. 1972* (aka *Dracula Today*) (1972); *Class of '44* (1973); *Class of '63* (1973 TVM); *Death Race 2000* (1975); *1900* (1977); *September 30, 1955* (aka *9/30/55*; *24 Hours of the Rebel*) (1978); *1941* (1979); *Class of 1984* (1982); *1990: The Bronx Warriors* (1983); *Nineteen Eighty-Four* (1984); *1918* (1984); *2010* (1984); *1919* (1986); *'68* (1988); *Cherry 2000* (1988); *Class of 1999* (1990); *1871* (1990); *The Spirit of '76* (1991)

Zombies

Commonly confused with ghouls, zombies are dead folks brought back to life, usually by means of voodoo. Ghouls (q.v.) are dead, too, but unlike zombies they must feed upon the flesh of the living for their sustenance. With their slow movements and blank stares (apparently indicating a lack of wit), zombies rank among the screen's duller, less menacing monsters. Still, there is something bothersome about being chased by a dead person. And zombies often display great strength, which comes in handy for murder. There have been only two zombie classics: The Halperin Brothers' *White Zombie* (1932) and Val Lewton's *I Walked with a Zombie* (1943). In the primitive, but eerily effective *White Zombie*, Bela Lugosi plays a zombie master named Murder Legendre. The film's most famous sequence shows a zombie falling silently to his "death" in a sugar mill, while his zombie coworkers continue to grind sugar emotionlessly. *I Walked with a Zombie* is a more literate movie, sort of *Jane Eyre* set in the West Indies. Darby Jones's brief, powerful appearance during a climactic walk through the sugar fields is startling — one of the cinema's finest moments of quiet terror. In addition to *White Zombie*, Lugosi appeared in

two other zombie movies: *Voodoo Man* (1944), a Monogram programmer co-starring George Zucco and John Carradine, and the classically inept *Zombies on Broadway* (1945). In the latter film, gangsters import some real zombies (including Darby Jones again) as a novelty act for their night club. It was the only zombie foray into show business. A more common use of the undead was for soldiers, as in *Revolt of the Zombies* (1936), *King of the Zombies* (1941), and *Revenge of the Zombies* (1943). Cesare the somnambulist from the German classic *The Cabinet of Dr. Caligari* (1919) exhibited many zombie traits, although he was merely asleep, not dead. See also **Ghouls**.

White Zombie (1932); *Revolt of the Zombies* (1936); *The Ghost Breakers* (1940); *King of the Zombies* (1941); *I Walked with a Zombie* (1943); *Revenge of the Zombies* (1943); *Voodoo Man* (1944); *Zombies on Broadway* (1945); *Scared Stiff* (1953); *Creature with the Atom Brain* (1955); *Voodoo Island* (1957); *Zombies of Mora Tau* (1957); *The Dead One* (1961); *Plague of the Zombies* (1964); *Zombies* (aka *Zombie*; *I Eat Your Skin*; *Voodoo Blood*) (1964); *War of the Zombies* (aka *Night Star-Goddess of Electra*) (1965); *Terror Creatures from the Grave* (1965); *Sugar Hill* (aka *The Zombies of Sugar Hill*) (1974); *The Dead Don't Die* (1975 TVM); *Shock Waves* (aka *Death Corps*) (1977); *Revenge of the Zombies* (aka *Black Magic II*) (1981); *Zombie Island Massacre* (1984); *I Was a Teenage Zombie* (1987); *Zombie High* (1987); *Dead Heat* (1988); *Zombie Brigade* (1988); *Hardrock Zombies* (1988); *The Serpent and the Rainbow* (1988); *Voodoo Dawn* (1989); *Cast a Deadly Spell* (1991 TVM); *My Boyfriend's Back* (1993)

Zoos

While circuses (q.v.) have proven to be popular film settings, zoos have attracted the interest of few filmmakers. This favoritism toward circuses could be a result of the human-to-wild-animal ratio. In other words, circuses emphasize human performers over the animals, while zoos focus almost totally on the animals. At any rate, there have been very few films set principally in zoos. Loretta Young played a homeless girl who lived in one in the 1933 romantic-comedy *Zoo in Budapest*. Michael Gough ran a bizarre private zoo — he employed the lions to dispose of his enemies — in *The Black Zoo* (1963). John Cleese and Jamie Lee Curtis struggled to keep a marginally-profitable zoo open in the lightweight comedy *Fierce Creatures* (1997). And acclaimed documentary filmmaker Frederick Wiseman took his cameras inside Miami's MetroZoo for 1993's *Zoo*. Several films, set primarily outside zoos, have featured notable scenes behind the concrete walls. Both Simone Simon and Nastassia Kinski were attracted to the leopards in, respectively, the 1942 and 1982 versions of *The Cat People*. The ever-growing Venusian monster in Ray Harryhausen's *20 Million Miles to Earth* (1957) escaped from a Rome zoo and wreaked havoc before being destroyed. Ben Kingsley and Glenda Jackson "rescued" turtles from a zoo in 1985's *Turtle Diary*, while Clint Eastwood smuggled his orangutan into a zoo for a simian rendezvous in 1978's *Every Which Way But Loose*. In Disney's *Lady and the Tramp*, the canine couple visited a zoo where a beaver helped Lady remove a confining muzzle. The Mel Gibson–Goldie Hawn comedy *Bird on a Wire* (1990) and the offbeat French-Canadian *Night Zoo* (1987) featured climaxes in zoos. Although technically not zoos, the wildlife park in *The Beasts Are on the Streets* (1978 TVM) and the Sea World setting in *Jaws 3* (1983) deserve honorable mention. Likewise, *Jurassic Park* (1993) would have been a zoo for dinosaurs had it ever opened officially. See also **Circuses**.

Zoo in Budapest (1933); *Murders in the Zoo* (1933); *The Cat People* (1942); *The Reformer and the Redhead* (1950); *Lady and the Tramp* (1955); *20 Million Miles to Earth* (1957); *The Black Zoo* (1963); *Zebra in the Kitchen* (1965); *Legend of the Werewolf* (1975); *Every Which Way But Loose* (1978); *The Cat People* (1982); *Wild Beasts* (1983); *Turtle Diary* (1985); *Night Zoo* (1987); *Bird on a Wire* (1990); *Zoo* (1993); *Baby's Day Out* (1994); *Eraser* (1996); *Fierce Creatures* (1997); *Mighty Joe Young* (1998)

Zorro

Johnston McCulley created the masked hero Zorro in "The Curse of Capistrano," which was published in 1919 in the pulp magazine *All-Story Weekly*. But it was Douglas Fairbanks, Sr., who immortalized the character a year later in the swashbuckling classic *The Mark of Zorro*. Fairbanks gave one of his best performances as Don Diego Vega — the son of a Spanish aristocrat in Old California — who transforms himself into Zorro to fight a wicked, greedy governor. It's this film version, and not McCulley's novel, that originated Zorro's calling card of a large "Z" etched with the tip of his sword. The story owes much to the Robin Hood legends and to Baroness Orczy's *The Scarlet Pimpernel* (like Sir Percy, Don Diego plays the part of a lazy, self-centered gent to throw suspicion off himself). In 1925, Fairbanks made a sequel, *Don Q, Son of Zorro*, an adaptation of the novel *Don Q's Love Story* by Kate and Hesketh Prichard. It afforded him the opportunity to play both son Don Cesar and father Don Diego. Over the next 15 years, the Zorro character appeared in the B-movie *The Bold Caballero* (played by cowboy veteran Bob Livingston) and in two Republic serials. The masked hero made a spectacular comeback in 1940 with *The Mark of Zorro*, a remake that improved on the original Fairbanks film. Tyrone Power gave a strong performance as both the more-foppish-than-ever Don Diego and as the dashing, mischievous Zorro. He displayed his charming side in a scene in which he poses as a priest to listen to beautiful Linda Darnell's confessions of love. He showed off his man-of-action side in one of the cinema's most famous fencing duels (opposite the villainous Basil Rathbone). The Power film remains Zorro's finest hour. Throughout the rest of the 1940s and 1950s, Zorro appeared periodically in serials (Linda Stirling was a female Zorro in *Zorro's Black Whip*) and in a couple of European films. The character generated renewed interest with the premiere of the Disney TV series *Zorro* in 1957. Although the audition for TV's Zorro drew well-known performers such as Hugh O'Brien, Dennis Weaver, and David Janssen, the part went to former bit-player Guy Williams (now best remembered as John Robinson on TV's *Lost in Space*). The series scored good ratings, but was canceled following a legal dispute about ownership between Disney and ABC. Disney edited several episodes into *The Sign of Zorro* (1960), which was released theatrically to mild results. Another film derived from TV episodes, *Zorro, the Avenger* (1960), was released overseas only and made its U.S. debut decades later on the Disney cable channel. In 1959, in the wake of the Disney series, Republic released edited movie versions of its earlier serials *Zorro Rides Again* and *Ghost of Zorro* (Clayton Moore had since achieved fame as TV's *The Lone Ranger*). In the 1960s, Zorro's popularity sky-rocketed in Europe, where the character appeared in numerous Spanish and Italian films. Some of these films showed no re-

gard for Zorro's origins — pairing him with the Three Musketeers and with the mythic muscleman Maciste (qq.v.). Sean Flynn, Errol Flynn's son, unexpectedly showed up as the masked hero in 1963's *Il Segno di Zorro*. French star Alain Delon earned good notices for *Zorro* (1974), which transplanted the action to South America. That same year, Frank Langella starred in a respectable TV movie remake of *The Mark of Zorro*. On the heels of his successful vampire spoof *Love at First Bite*, George Hamilton made *Zorro, the Gay Blade* (1981), an uneven comedy with Hamilton playing Zorro and his twin gay brother Bunny Wigglesworth. Not surprisingly, it was the last significant Zorro until the character was revived with style in 1998's *The Mask of Zorro*. It starred Anthony Hopkins as an aging Don Diego de la Vega who grooms the young, revenge-minded Alejandro Murrieta (Antonio Banderas) to take his place as Zorro. Despite an over-the-top climax, this big-budgeted Zorro tale captured the spirit of McCulley's stories en route to becoming one of 1998's biggest hits. In addition to his many film appearances, the Zorro character has been featured in at least three live-action TV series: the aforementioned Disney series; *Zorro and Son* (1983) with Henry Darrow and Paul Regina; and *Zorro* (1990–93) with Duncan Regehr. Zorro has also been the subject of a stage musical, animated TV series, comic books, and a comic strip. By the way, the word "zorro" is Spanish for fox.

The Mark of Zorro (1920) (Douglas Fairbanks, Sr.); *Don Q, Son of Zorro* (1925) (Douglas Fairbanks Sr.); *The Bold Caballero* (1936) (Robert Livingstone); *The Mark of Zorro* (1940) (Tyrone Power); *Il Sogno di Zorro* (1952) (Walter Chiari); *El Zorro Escarlata* (1957) (Luis Aguilar); *The Sign of Zorro* (1960) (Williams); *Zorro, the Avenger* (1960) (Guy Williams); *La Venganza del Zorro* (aka *The Shadow of Zorro*; *Zorro the Avenger*) (1962) (Frank Latimore); *Zorro Alla Corte di Espagni* (1962) (Giorgio Ardisson); *Zorro and the Three Musketeers* (aka *Zorro e i Tre Moschiettieri*) (1963) (Gordon Scott); *The Three Swords of Zorro* (aka *La Tre Spade di Zorro*) (1963) (Guy Stockwell); *Il Segno di Zorro* (aka *Duel at the Rio Grande*) (1963) (Sean Flynn); *L'Ombra di Zorro* (aka *Cabalgando Hacia la Muerte El Zorro*) (1963) (Frank Latimore); *Samson and the Slave Queen* (aka *Zorro Contro Maciste*) (1963) (Pierre Brice); *El Zorro Cabalga Otra Vez* (aka *Il Giuramento di Zorro*) (1965) (Tony Russel); *Zorro il Ribelle* (1966) (Howard Ross, also billed as Renato Rossini); *I Nippoti di Zorro* (1968) (Dean Reed); *El Zorro la Volpe* (aka *El Zorro*) (1968) (Giorgio Ardisson); *El Zorro de Monterrey* (aka *Zorro, the Invincible*; *Zorro il Dominatore*; *Zorro, La Maschera Della Vendetta*) (1969) (Carlos Quiney, also billed as Charles Quiney); *Zorro Alla Corte D'Inghilterra* (1969) (Spyros Focas); *El Zorro Justiciero* (1969) (Martin Moore); *Zorro Marchese di Navarro* (1969) (Nino Vingelli); *The Erotic Adventures of Zorro* (1972) (Douglas Frey); *Les Aventures Galantes de Zorro* (aka *Zorro dans Ses Aventures Galantes*) (1972) (Jean-Michel Dhermay); *Il Figlio di Zorro* (aka *El Hijo del Zorro*) (1973) (Alberto Dell'Acqua, also billed as Robert Widmark); *El Zorro* (1974) (Julio Aldama); *Zorro* (aka *El Zorro la belva del Colorado*) (1974) (Alain Delon); *The Mark of Zorro* (1974 TVM) (Frank Langella); *Il Sogno di Zorro* (1975) (Franco Franchi); *Zorro, the Gay Blade* (1981) (George Hamilton); *The Mask of Zorro* (1998) (Anthony Hopkins and Antonio Banderas)

THE REPUBLIC ZORRO SERIALS: *Zorro Rides Again* (1937) (John Carroll); *Zorro's Fighting Legion* (1939) (Reed Hadley); *Zorro's Black Whip* (1944) (Linda Sterling as a female Zorro); *Son of Zorro* (1947) (George Turner); *Ghost of Zorro* (1949) (Clayton Moore)